CW00524721

1 MONTH OF
FREE
READING

at

www.ForgottenBooks.com

By purchasing this book you are eligible for one month membership to ForgottenBooks.com, giving you unlimited access to our entire collection of over 1,000,000 titles via our web site and mobile apps.

To claim your free month visit:

www.forgottenbooks.com/free1242801

* Offer is valid for 45 days from date of purchase. Terms and conditions apply.

ISBN 978-0-428-54197-2
PIBN 11242801

This book is a reproduction of an important historical work. Forgotten Books uses
state-of-the-art technology to digitally reconstruct the work, preserving the original format
whilst repairing imperfections present in the aged copy. In rare cases, an imperfection in
the original, such as a blemish or missing page, may be replicated in our edition. We do,
however, repair the vast majority of imperfections successfully; any imperfections that
remain are intentionally left to preserve the state of such historical works.

Forgotten Books is a registered trademark of FB &c Ltd.
Copyright © 2018 FB &c Ltd.
FB &c Ltd, Dalton House, 60 Windsor Avenue, London, SW19 2RR.
Company number 08720141. Registered in England and Wales.

For support please visit www.forgottenbooks.com

CORNELL UNIVERSITY
MAR 22 1929
LAW LIBRARY

TO HIS EXCELLENCY

EDWARD JOHN EYRE, ESQ.,

GOVERNOR OF THE ISLAND OF JAMAICA, &c., &c.,

THIS WORK IS RESPECTFULLY DEDICATED BY

his EXCELLENCY's

MOST OBEDIENT HUMBLE SERVANT,

JAMES MINOT.

PREFACE.

THIS compilation is the result of many years' labour, but without the aid of a Legislative Grant, and the hope of further assistance from the same source, the publication would not have been hazarded.

It has been the endeavor of the compiler to furnish, within the compass of a portable volume, a copious Digest of the Laws of this Island, now practically in force, with abstracts of, or references to other existing enactments not abridged, and to supersede the necessity of reference to the ponderous quartos in which they lie scattered.

With this object, it will be found that the several Acts, affecting Public, Military, Naval, and Parochial property, the Division of the Island into Parishes, and the Police Regulations of the several Towns, are, with few exceptions, only briefly abstracted. They have, however, been all collected and arranged under appropriate heads, in case it should be deemed advisable to amend, simplify and consolidate them, and to bring the laws relating to the Police Regulations of the several Towns into harmony with each other, and with recent legislation; and thereby to remove from our Statute Book about 140 Acts.

The clauses of the several Acts in operation which establish or incorporate public companies are digested only so far as they concern the community. In other respects they are private Acts. They are all but such as relate to abandoned undertaking referred to under appropriate heads.

The only Acts in force which are altogether unnoticed, are those relating to Insolvent Debtors, the Police, the Post Office and the Registrar in Chancery, which are all on the point of expiry and must be subjects for legislation in the present Session. If the Legislature consider the continuance of this work deserving the encouragement of a small annual grant, the present Acts, unless superseded, will be introduced into a Supplemental Digest of the Laws of the Session, along with the Acts continuing them in force.

The Chronological Table of Acts, will afford, at a glance, ready and complete information respecting the existing state of our Laws, and of the Acts or clauses no longer in operation or not requiring abridgment. It dispenses with the necessity of noticing elsewhere merely repealing Acts or clauses.

Kingston, Jamaica, November, 1865.

CONTENTS.

xii.   CONTENTS.

Chronological Table of Acts

EXPIRED, DISALLOWED, REPEALED AND IN FORCE, OR NOT EXPRESS-
LY AND SPECIFICALLY REPEALED, SHEWING THE PORTIONS IN THE
DIGEST, AND THE HEADS UNDER WHICH THEY ARE ARRANGED.

CHRONOLOGICAL TABLE OF ACTS

EXPIRED, DISALLOWED, REPEALED AND IN FORCE, OR NOT EXPRESSLY AND SPECIFICALLY REPEALED, SHEWING THE PORTIONS IN THE DIGEST, AND THE HEADS UNDER WHICH THEY ARE ARRANGED.

Year of Reign	Expired or Disallowed	Repealed	Repealing Act.	In Force, &c. — In Digest.	In Force, &c. — Not in Digest.	Under Head of—
33, C. 2		2	6 V., c. 35	1		Assembly.
		3	....	5, s. 2 pt. 3—5	5, s. 1, 2 pt.	Blasphemy, 2; Gaming, 3, 5; Rum and Spirits, 4.
		4	....			
		6	....	12, s. 1, 3 pt. 4, 7	12, s. 5	Deeds, 1, 3, pt.; Mortgages, 4; Patents, 7.
		7	....	15		Charitable grants.
		8	....	16 pt.		Broad Seal.
		9	....	17, s. 2, 4, 7	17, s. 5, 6	Fire, 2; Harbours, 4; Seamen, 7.
		10	} 7 W. 4, c. 36, s. 1	18, s. 12.		Parishes.
		11	27 V.. S. 1, c. 34, s. 66	22, s. 2, 3, 4		Escheats, 2. 4; Husband and Wife conveyances, 3.
		12, s. 2, 6, 9	6 V., c. 35			
		s. 3 pt.	27 V., S. 1, c. 17, s. 11			
		s. 8	2 W. 4. c. 16, s. 1			
		13	6 V., c. 35	23, s. 1 pt. 3, 4, 5, 6 pt. 7—9, 10 pt. 16, 20	23, s. 1 pt. 2, 10 pt. 16 pt.	Court, Supreme, 1, pt. 4, 5, 7, 10. Amendments, 5; Attachment, Foreign, 8, 9; Attorneys-at-Law, 4; Barristers, 4; Judges, 3, 20; Venditioni, 16; Waste, 6.
		14	19 V., c. 29, s. 1			
		16 pt.	6 V., c. 35			
		17, s. 1, 3	} 15 V., c. 34, s. 1 } 21 V., c. 44, s. 15			
		18, s. 1	9 V., c. 33, s. 1	24, s. 1 pt.		Laws of the Island.
		s. 2—11	22 V., c. 23, s. 65			
		19	6 V., c. 35			
		20	....			
		21	....			
		22, s. 1	5 V., c. 26, s. 12			
		23, s. 1	19 V., c. 46, s. 3.			
		s. 6 pt.				
		s. 11, 12, 13, } pt. 14, 15, } 17—19	6 V., c. 35			
		24, s. 1 pt. 2, 3	....			

CHRONOLOGICAL TABLE OF ACTS, &c.

Year of Reign.	Expired or Disallowed.	Repealed.	Repealing Act.	In Force, &c. In Digest.	In Force, &c. Not in Digest.	Under Head of—
35 C. 2	8 Disallowed 13	1 2 3, s. 3 4, s. 1, 5—8—10 5 6 7, s. 2—11 9 10 11 14 15 16	5 V., c. 15, s. 1 6 V., c. 35 .... 3 V., c. 18, s. 13 6 V., c. 35	3, s. 1, 2 4, s. 6, 7 7, s. 1 12		Aliens. Seamen, 6; Justices, 7. Vestry. Patents, 1; Port-Royal, 2.
5 W. and M.	7, 8	2 4, s. 2 pt. 3—8 5 6	.... 9 V. c. 38, s. 12	1 3, s. 1	3, s. 2, 3 4, s. 1 pt. 2 pt.	Fnsts. Assembly—Kingston. Port-Royal.
7 W. 3	2, 3	1 2	6 V., c. 35	1		St. Andrew's Free School.
8 W. 3		1	.....			
10 W. 3		1				
11 W. 3		1 2 3 4, s. 2, 3, 4	.... 23 V., c. 6, s. 8 6 V., c. 35	4, s. 1, 5, 6		Port-Royal
1 Ann	2	1	.....			
2 Ann	2, 3,	1, s. 2	.....	1, s. 1		St. Elizabeth, Westmoreland.

Year						Subject
2 Ann	5, 6, 7, s. 5—14, 16, 17, s. 15		6 V., c. 35	7, s. 1—4	4	Revenue. Patents, 1—3—Boundaries, 4.
3 Ann	1	2, s. 1—4, 6	27 V., c. 17, s. 11	2, s. 5		Port-Royal
4 Ann	2	1, 3	6 V., c. 35		4	Kingston Courts—Gunpowder.
5 Ann	1, 2, 3		9 V., c. 33, s. 1; 22 V., c. 23, s. 65; 6 V., c. 35			
6 Ann	1, 2			8, s. 6, 8	8, s. 4	Harbours. Port-Royal.
8 Ann	3, 4, 5, 6, 7; Disallowed 1, 2	8, s. 1—3, 5; 10			9	
9 Ann	1, 2, 3, 4					
10 Ann	1, 2, 3, 7, 8, 9, 11, 13, 14, 15; Disallowed 5, 6, 10, 17	4, s. 1, 2 pt. 3 pt.; 4 pt.; 7; 16; 26; 30; s. 1, 2 pt. 3, pt. 5, 14, 15, 18, 21, 23, 27—29, 31, 33, 35, 38	56 G. 3, c. 19, s. 18; 56 G. 3, c. 23, s. 14; 19 V., c. 10, s. 53; 21 V., c. 31; 18 V., c. 18, s 17; 23 V., c. 12, s. 20; 9 V., c. 38, s. 12	4, s. 2, pt. 3, pt. 4, 6, 8, 17, 20, 22, 24, 25, 32, 34 pt.	4, s. 4, pt. 9—13, 19, 34, pt. 36, 37	Deeds, 2; Laws, Island, 3; Cryers of Courts, 4; Provost-Marshal, 6, 8, 34; Constables, 17; Broad Seal, 20; Governor, 20, 22; Court of Chancery, 8, 24; Attorney-General, 25; Clerk of the warrants, 32. Deeds.
		12, s. 1, 2; 16; 18, s. 2	6 V., c. 35; 2 W. 4, c. 16, s. 1	12, s. 3; 18, s. 1		Executors.
11 Ann	1	2, 3, 4, s. 1—4, 6	6 V., c. 35	4, s. 5, 7		Records, Public

CHRONOLOGICAL TABLE OF ACTS, &c.

Year of Reign.	Expired or Disallowed.	Repealed.	Repealing Act.	In Force, &c. In Digest.	In Force, &c. Not in Digest.	Under Head of—
12 Ann	1, 3 Disallowed 2, 4					
2 G. 1	Disallowed 3	2	6 V. c. 35		1	Constables.
3 G. 1	1, 7 Disallowed 2, 3, 4, 5, 6, 8					
4 G. 1	1, 2, 3, 4, 5, 6, 8	1 3 4	....			
5 G. 1	1	2	..			
6 G. 1	1, 2, 3, 6	4 5	..			
7 G. 1	1, 2, 3	4	...			
8 G. 1	6, 7, 8, 9	1 2 3 4 5 pt.	8 V., c. 16, s. 9 8 V., c. 28, s. 22	5		Partition.
9 G. 1	2, 3, 4, 5, 9 Disallowed 10, 11, 12	6 7 8, s. 1—5, 8—12	6 V., c. 35	1 8, s. 6, 7		Fasts Portland.
10 G. 1	1, 2, 3, 4, 6, 10	5, s. 2 7	.	5, s. 1 8, s. 4—6	8, s. 5	Westmoreland and Hanover. Portland.

10 G. 1	8, s. 1—3; 7—13 9		6 V., c. 35 …			
11 G. 1	1, 4, 5, 6, 7	3 3 8	8 V., c. 16, s. 9 6 V., c. 35 …			
12 G. 1	1, 2, 3, 5, 7, 8, 9, 12 Disallowed 4	6 10, s. 1, 2, 4—6	… …	10, s. 3 11 pt.	11 pt.	Portland. Customs.
13 G. 1	1					
1 G. 2	2, 3, 4, 5, 6, 7, 8, 9, 10, 12	1 11 13	8 V., c. 16, s. 9 6 V., c. 35 …			
2 G. 2	1, 3	2				
3 G. 2	3, 4, 5, 7, 8, 9, 10, 14, 15, 16, 17, 18 Disallowed 6	2 11 12 13	5 W. 4, c. 29, s. 1 23 V., c. 5, s. 19 6 V., c. 35 …	1		Portland.
4 G. 2	1, 3, 7, 8, 9, 10, 11, 12 Disallowed 6	2 4, s. 3, 6, 8 5, s. 1, 4, 9—11	… …	4, s. 1, 2, 7 pt. 5, s. 2, 3—5, 8	4 s. 7 pt.	Possessory Title, 1; Boundaries, 2; Patents, 7. Evidence, 2, 3; Deeds, 5—8.
5 G. 2	1, 3, 4	2	{ 7 V., c. 53, s. 1 { 8 V., c. 39, s. 1 { 18 V., c. 61, s. 1			
6 G. 2	1, 3, 4, 6, 8, 11, 14, 15, 16, 17, 18, 19	2 5 7, s. 1, 4, 7—14 9 12	{ 15 V., c 34, s. 1 { 22 V., c. 5, s. 37 6 V., c. 35 … …	7 s. 5, 6 10 s. 5, 6, 9,	10, s. 1—4, 7, 8, 10 20	Escheats. Military defences. Manumission.

b

CHRONOLOGICAL TABLE OF ACTS, &c.

Year of Reign.	Expired or Disallowed.	Repealed.	Repealing Act.	In Force, &c. — In Digest.	In Force, &c. — Not in Digest.	Under Head of—
6 G. 2		13	{ 7 W. 4, c. 36, s. 1 { 27 V., S. 1, c 34, s. 66			
7 G. 2	1, 2, 3, 5, 6, 7, 8, 9			4		Naval service.
8 G. 2	1, 2, 3, 4, 7, 8, 9	5, s. 9, 11, 13, 15 6	6 V., c. 35	5, s. 1—5, 7, 8, 10. 12, 14, 16, 17	5, s. 6	Provost-Marshal, 1—3, 10, 12, 17. Venditioni, 4, 5, 7, 8, 10, 12, 14; Court, Supreme, 16. Free Schools—Woolmer's.
9 G. 2	1, 2, 3, 7, 8	4 5 6 s, 1 pt. s. 4 9 10 11	{ 7 W. 4, c. 36, s. 1 { 27 V., S. 1, c. 34, s. 66 15 G. 3, c. 14, s. 1 6 V., c. 35 ---- 19 V., c. 15, s. 1	6, s. 1 pt. 2, 3, 5—9		
10 G. 2	1, 2, 3, 5	4	....	6		Military defences.
11 G. 2	1, 2, 3, 6, 8, 10, 11	4, s. 1, 2, 3 5, s. 1—13, 15 7 9, s. 4	6 V., c. 35 .... 9 G. 3, c. 4, s. 1 6 V., c. 35	4, s. 4, 5 5, s. 14 9, s. 2, 3, 5—9		Secretary, Island. Portland. Free Schools, Mannings.
12 G. 2	1, 2, 4, 7, 8	3, s. 1 5 9 10	{ 5 V., c. 40, s. 1 { 19 V., c. 25, s. 5 6 V., c. 35	3 s. 2 6		Bills and Notes. Vere.
13 G. 2	1, 2, 3, 4, 5, 12, 13	6 7	....	9, s. 1—4 11	9, s. 5	Accounts, Produce, &c. Naval service.

Session	Chapters	Repealing Acts			Subject
13 G. 2	8 10	5 V., c. 49, s. 1 19 V., c. 35, s. 5 18 V., c. 54, s. 32	2? 3		Naval service. Commissioner's Affidavits.
14 G. 2	1, 4, 8, 9, 10, 11 Disallowed 5 6 7	6 V., c. 35 5 V., c. 49, s. 1 19 V., c. 35, s. 5			
15 G. 2	1, 2, 4, 5, 6 3				Deeds.
16 G. 2	1, 2, 3, 4, 6, 7, 8, 9	4 V., c. 46, s. 1	5		
17 G. 2	1, 2, 3, 4, 5, 6, 8, 13, 14, 16 9, s. 2, 3, 5—8 7 10 11 15 17	30 G. 3, c. 7, s. 1 6 V., c. 35 27 V., S. 1, c. 19, s. 1 6 V., c. 35	9, s. 1, 4, 9		Public Buildings.
18 G. 2	1, 2, 3, 4, 5, 6, 7, 9, 10 8 11	9 V., c. 33, s. 1 22 V., c. 33, s. 65 6 V., c. 35			
19 G. 2	1, 2, 3, 4, 5, 6, 8, 9, 10, 12 Disallowed 7 11 13				
20 G. 2	1, 2, 3, 4, 5, 6, 7, 8, 11, 10, s. 3 12, 13, 17 9 14 15	— — —	10, s. 1, 2, 4—6	10, s. 7 16	St. Catherine. Assay. Gold and Silver.
21 G. 2	1, 2, 3, 4, 5 6 7	9 V., c. 33, s. 1 22 V., c. 23, s. 65 6 V., c. 35	8 s. 3 pt	8, s. 1, 2, 3, pt 4—6	St. Catherine.
22 G. 2	1, 2, 4, 5, 7, 8 3, 11, 15, 10 9, 17, 20, 21 12	31 G. 3, c. 2, c. 19, s. 6 6 V., c. 35	6, s. 2 19, s. 1	6, s. 1—3	St. Catherine. Military Defences.

CHRONOLOGICAL TABLE OF ACTS, &c.

Year of Reign	Expired or Disallowed	Repealed	Repealing Act	In Force, &c. — In Digest	In Force, &c. — Not in Digest	Under Head of—
22 G. 2		13 14 16 18 19, s. 2 22	23 V., c. 6, s. 9 6 V., c. 35 15 V., c. 31, s. 1 6 V., c. 35 --- ---			
23 G. 2	1, 2, 3, 4, 7, 9, 10, 11, 13, 14, 15	5 6 8 16, s. 1—3, 7, 8 s. 4, 5, 7	7 V., c. 50, s. 1 --- ---		12 16, s. 6	Transcripts, Chancery. River-Road.
24 G. 2	1, 2, 3, 4, 6, 7, 8, 11, 12, 18 Disallowed 5, 10, 13, 14, 20	9 15 17 19, s. 10 21	27 V., S.1, c.17, s.11 6 V., c. 35 --- ---	16 19, s. 1—9, 12	10, s. 11	Venditioni. Costs, 1—3; Extent, 4—6; Accounts, Produce, 7; Commissions, 8; Coin, 9; Interest, 12.
25 G. 2	1, 2, 3, 4, 6, 7, 8, 9, 10, 12 Disallowed 11, 13	5 14, s. 1 8, 2, 3 15	18 V., c. 48, s. 1 6 V., c. 35 ---			
26 G. 2	1, 3, 5, 8, 9, 10	2 pt. 4 6 7	8 V., c. 48, s. 2 6 V., c. 35 ---	2 pt.		Arrest.
27 G. 2	1 2		--- ---			
28 G. 2	6, 10, 11, 12, 13	2, s. 2, 3 3	--- ---	2, s. 1	8	Bills and Notes. Assay. Gold and Silver.

					Naval Service. Foreign Produce.	Counties, 1; Parishes, 1, Court, Suppreme, 5, 13; Provost-Marshal, 21. Assize Courts. Escheats. Ports of Entry and Clearance.	Prisons.
28 G. 2	Disallowed 1, 4, 5, 9	7		6 V., a. 35	18	4	
29 G. 2	1, 2, 7, 8, 10, 11, 12, 13, 15, 16, 17, 20, 21, 22, 23, 24 Disallowed 9 19	3 / 4 pt. / 5 / 6 / 14	24 V., c. 13 / 6 V., c. 35 / .... /				
30 G. 2	1, 2, 3, 4, 5, 7, 8, 9, 11 Disallowed 6	10	....				
31 G. 2	1, 2, 3, 6, 7, 12, 14, 15 Disallowed 16	4 s. 1 pt. / 5 pt. / s. 7–11, 16–19 / s. 2—4, 5 pt. / 6, 12, 13 pt. / 14, 15, 20, / 24—27 / 22, 23	56 G. 3, c. 20, s. 1 / 22 V., c. 39, s. 4. / 3 V., c. 65, s. 54 / 19 V., c. 10, s. 53 / .... /	4 s. 1 pt. 5 pt. / 13 pt. 21	18	8	19 s. 1—6
		5 / 9 / 10 / 13 / 17	20 V., c. 22, s. 41 / 6 V., c. 35 / 5 V., c. 49, s. 1 / 19 V., c. 25, s. 5 / 6 V., c. 35				
		19 pt. / s. 7 / 20				
32 G. 2	4, 5, 6, 7, 8, 9, 13, 14, 15, 16 Disallowed 10	1 / 2 / 3, s. 2 / 11 / 12	5 V., c. 14, s. 4 / 18 V., c. 18, s. 18 / 23 V., c. 12, s. 20 / 23 V., c. 5, s. 19 / 6 V., c. 35	3, s. 1			

CHRONOLOGICAL TABLE OF ACTS, &c.

Year of Reign.	Expired or Disallowed.	Repealed.	Repealing Act.	In Force, &c.		Under Head of—
				In Digest.	Not in Digest.	
32 G. 2	17 18		27 V.. S. 1 c. 19; s. 1 6 V., c. 35			
1 G. 3	1, 2, 3, 4, 6, 7, 8, 10, 11, 12, 14, 15, 16, 17, 24, 26, 27, 28 Disallowed 19 25, 30,	9 13 pt. s. 6 18 19 20 22 23 29	{ 5 V., c. 47, s. 12 21 V., c. 23, s 13 20 V., c. 23, s. 40, 6 V., c. 35	13 pt. s. 1—5, 7—11 21	5	St. Elizabeth parsonage, Fines, &c. Costs.
2 G. 3	1, 2, 3, 4, 5, 6, 9, 11, 13, 14, 15, 16, 17, 18, 20, 21, 22, 23, 24, 25	7 8 10 12 19				
3 G. 3	1, 2, 4, 5, 6, 7, 8, 9, 10, 11	12		3		Port-Royal.
4 G. 3	1, 3, 4, 5, 6, 7, 9, 10, 11, 12, 14	2 13		8 s. 4	8, s. 1—3	Attorneys-at-Law.
5 G. 3	1, 2, 3, 4, 7	5 6 8 9				
6 G. 3	3, 5, 6, 7, 8, 9,	2		4 pt.	4 pt.	St. Catherine.

Clarendon.

Free Schools, Manning's, 2 pt.;
Westmoreland, 5, 7—9
Quit Rents.

Transcript Chancery Plat Books.

Mutual Debts set off.
Kingston.

St. Catherine.
Coroners.
Judgments.

Military defences.

6 G. 3	11, 12, 14, 4 pt. 15, 16, 17, 13 19, Disallowed 18 1, 10	11 G. 3, c. 14, s. 11 2 G. 3, c. 13 6 V., c. 35	
7 G. 3	1, 2, 3		
8 G. 3	1, 2, 3, 4, 5, 6, 8 7, 10, 9 11 13 14 15	6 V., c. 35	12
9 G. 3	4, 2, 3, 5, 7, 8, 4 s. 2 pt. 10, 11, 14, 6 16, 18, 19, 9, s. 2 pt. 12, 14 20, 21, 12, 13, 15	28 V., c. 6, s. 3 18 V., c. 54, s. 32 6 V., c. 35	4, s. 2 pt. 5, 7—9	4, s. 1, 3, 4, 6 9, s. 1, 2 pt. 3—11, 13 17
10 G. 3	2, 3, 4, 6, 7, 5 8, 9, 10, 12, 11, s. 1—6, 10 13, 14, 15 16, 17	5 V., c. 49, s. 1 19 V., c. 25, s. 5 9 V., c. 38, s. 12	4	11 s. 7—9, 11
11 G. 3	1, 2, 4, 5, 6, 3 7, 8, 9, 10, 11 13, 21, 22, 12 23, 14, s. 4—8 Disallowed 8, s. 1—7 17, 16 18 19	6 V., c. 35 9 V., c. 38, s. 12 9 V., c. 33, s. 1 22 V., c. 23, s. 65 6 V., c. 35	14, s. 11 15 pt. 20, s. 2	14, s. 9, 10 15 pt. 20, s. 1
12 G. 3	1, 2, 3, 4, 5, 6, 7 8, 9, 10, 11, 15 13, 14, 16 17		12	

CHRONOLOGICAL TABLE OF ACTS, &c.

Year of Reign.	Expired or Disallowed.	Repealed.	Repealing Act.	In Force, &c. — In Digest.	In Force, &c. — Not in Digest.	Under Head of—
13 G. 3	1, 2, 3, 4, 5, 6, 7, 8, 9, 10, 12, 13, 14, 17, 15, 21, 18, 20		9 V., c. 20, s. 6 18 V., c. 54, s. 32 6 V., c. 35	16 19, s. 1—3, 5—7	11 19, s. 4	Taxes, public. Mortgages. Gaming, Lotteries, &c.
14 G. 3	1, 2, 4, 7, 8, 9, 10, 12, 14, 15, 11, 20, 21, 23, 13, 26, 27, 29, 16, 30	18, s. 1 pt. 4 pt. 5—7, 10 19 22 24 28 s. 7, 8, 16 pt. s. 9—11, 18 s. 14 31, s. 2, 3, 6 s. 5	18 G. 3, c. 18, s. 1 22 V., c. 27, s. 7 9 V., c. 33, s. 1 22 V., c. 23, s. 65 6 V., c. 35 19 V., c. 29, s. 1 6 V., c. 35 …. 20 V., c. 22, s. 40 6 V., c. 35 27 V., S. 1, c. 27, s. 1 6 V., c. 35 9 V., c. 33, s. 1 22 V., c. 23, s. 65	3 s. 1—5, 7, 9 5 6 s. 1 pt. 17 18, s. 1, pt. 2, 3, 4, pt. 9 25 28, s. 2—6, 12, 13, 15 16, 19 31, s. 1.	3, s. 6, 8 6, s. 1, pt. 2—4 18, s. 8 28, s. 1, 17 31, s. 4	Attorneys-at-Law. Possessory Title, 1; boundaries, 2. Prisons. Forcible entry, &c. Coin. Port Royal; St. Andrew. Bonds, 2—5, 12; Judgments, 6—15, 16, 19; Interest, 13. St. James; Trelawny.
45 G. 3	1, 2, 3, 5, 15, 16, 17, 19, 20 7 pt. 8 Disallowed 12	6 8 10 11 13 18 22 23 24 25	3 V., c. 65, s. 54 56 G. 3, c. 19, s. 18 15 V., c. 34, s. 1 7 V. S. 1, c. 33, s. 104 6 V., c. 35 …. 6 V., c. 58, s. 1 6 V., c. 35 ….	4 7 pt. 14, s. 2—8 21	9 14, s. 1	Executive Committee. Provost-Marshal. Collecting Constables Free Schools—Woolmer's. Bills and Notes.

d

CHRONOLOGICAL TABLE OF ACTS, &c.

Year of Reign.	Expired or Disallowed.	Repealed.	Repealing Act.	In Force, &c. In Digest.	In Force, &c. Not in Digest.	Under, Head of—
21 G. 3	19, 20, 21, 24, 26, 27			13 22 s. 1, 2 23, s. 2—7	18 22, s. 3 23 s. 1	St. Catherine. Westmoreland Transcripts. Portland Provost Marshal, 2, 3, 7; Vendi-tioni 4, 7; Deeds 5; Secretary Island 5, 6. Judges
22 G. 3	1, 2, 3, 4, 5, 6, 7, 9, 10, 11, 12, 13, 14, 15, 16, 17, 18, 20, 21, 22, 23, 24, 25, 26, 27	8 19	6 V., c. 35 7 V., c. 53, s. 1 8 V., c. 39, s. 1 18 V., c. 61, s. 1	25		
23 G. 3	1, 2, 3, 4, 5, 6, 7, 11, 12, 18, 19, 20, 22, 24, 25, 28, 29	8, s. 1—16 17—26	25 V., c. 18, s. 66 23 V., c. 5, s. 19 6 V., c. 35 … … … … 23 V., c. 5, s. 19 ….	8, s. 27—29 9 14 15		St. Elizabeth. Military Defences. Mortgages. Port Royal, St. David.
24 G. 3	1, 2, 3, 4, 5, 6, 7, 8, 9, 10, 14, 15, 16	11	8 V., c. 16, s. 9			
25 G. 3	2, 4, 6, 12, 13, 15, 18	3 5	5 W. 4, c. 29, s. 1 7 V., c. 57, s. 1	1 7, s. 1	7, s. 2, 3, 4	Emblements. Landlord and Tenant.

Session	Subject			
55 G. 3	Arrests. Mortgages, 1, 2; Accounts Produce, &c. 3	9, s. 1 / 10	6 V., c. 35 / 15 V., c. 22, s. 3 / 6 V., c. 35 / 23 V., c. 5, s. 19 / 6 V., c. 35	19, 20, 22, 23, 24, 25, 26, 27, 28, 29 / 8 / 9, s. 2 / 11 / 16 / 17 / 31
56 G. 3	Free School, Titchfield. Transient Traders,	13 / 7, s. 1 pt. 2—8	19 V., c. 40, s. 1	1, 2, 3, 4, 5, 6, 7, 8, 9, 10, 11, 12, 14, 15, 16 / 7, s. 1 pt.
57 G. 3	Kingston.	5	6 V., c. 35	1, 4, 6, 7, 8, 9, 10, 11, 12, 13, 14 / 2 / 3
58 G. 3			19 V., c. 23, s. 1 / 5 W. 4, c. 39, s. 1 / 6 V., c. 35 / 15 V., c. 34, s. 1 / 6 V., c. 35	2, 3, 4, 7, 8, 9, 10, 12, 13, 14, 18, 19, 20, 21, 22, 23, 24, 25, 26 / 1 / 5 / 6 / 11 / 15 / 16 / 17
59 G. 3	Interest, 1; Costs, 2; Executors, 3; Dormant Obligations, 4. Transient Traders. Hanover, Westmoreland.	16 / 13 / 29	6 V., c. 35 / 8 V., c. 16, s. 9 / 5 W. 4, c. 39, s. 1 / 6 V., c. 35	2, 3, 5, 6, 7, 8, 9, 10, 11, 17, 21, 24, 25 / 1 / 4 / 12 / 14 / 15 / 18 / 19 / 20 / 23
60 G. 3	Replevin. Troops. Laws of Island.	20, s. 4 / 2 / 9 / 20, s. 1—3	35 G. 3, c. 31, s. 1 / 22 V., c. 5, s. 37 / 6 V., c. 35 / 9 V., c. 33, s. 1 / 22 V., c. 23, s. 65 / 8 V., c. 16, s. 9	4, 5, 6, 7, 8, 11, 12, 16, 17, 18, 19, 22, 23 / 1 / 3 / 10 / 13 / 14

CHRONOLOGICAL TABLE OF ACTS, &c.

Year of Reign.	Expired or Disallowed.	Repealed.	Repealing Act.	In Force, &c. In Digest.	In Force, &c. Not in Digest.	Under Head of—
30 G. 3						
31 G. 3	1, 2, 5, 7, 8, 9, 10, 12, 13, 14, 16, 17, 15, 20, 23, 25, 26	3 & 13 pt. Sch., 11, 15, 18, 19, 21, 22, 24	6 V., c. 35, ----, ----, 8 V., c. 16, s. 9, 7 W., 4, c. 40, s. 1, 27 V. S.1, c. 33, s. 104, 5 W., 4, c. 29, s. 1, 6 V., c. 35, ----	8, s. 2–12, 13, pt. 14–163, s. 1, 4	6	Droghers. Assembly. Transient Traders.
32 G. 3	1, 2, 3, 5, 6, 8, 9, 10, 14, 15, 16, 17, 18, 19, 20, 13, 21, 23, 24, 33, 34, 36	4, 7, 11, 13, 25, s. 6—8, 26, 28, 30, 33, 35	5 V., c. 49, s. 1, 19 V., c. 25, s. 5, 6 V., c. 35, 3 V., c. 18, s. 13, 6 V., c. 35, ----, ----, 6 V., c. 58, s. 1, 6 V., c. 35	35, s. 1—5, 27, 29, s. 1—3, 31	12, 25, s. 9, 29, s. 4, 5	Martial Law. Military Defences. Naval Stores. Laws of Island. Military Defences.
33 G. 3	1, 2, 3, 4, 5, 6, 13, 7, 8, 9, 10, 18, 11, 12, 15, 19, s. 2, 16, 17, 20, 22		----, ----, ----	14, 19, s. 1; 3—9, 21, s. 1, 23	21, s. 2	Gregory's Charity. Milk River Bath. Accounts Produce, &c. St. James.
34 G. 3	1, 2, 3, 4, 5, 11, s. 1, 6, 7, 8, 9, 12		27 V., c. 17, s. 11, 35 G. 3, c. 31, s. 1, 22 V., c. 5, s. 37	11, s. 2	13	Evidence. Assembly.

34 G. 3	10, 14, 15, 18 16, 17 19 21 22 23 24 25, s. 2		9 V., c. 38, s. 12 6 V., c. 35 22 V., c. 40, s. 1 6 V., c. 35	20 25, s. 1	Military Defences. Milk River Bath.
35 G. 3	1, 2, 3, 4, 5, 7, 8, 10, 11, 12, 13, 14, 18 15, 16, 17, 19 32, 33, 38, 23 41, 43 25 27 28, s. 3, 4 29 30 31 34 s. 17 pt. 35, s. 12, 24—28, 38 s. 44, 45 s. 46—48 36 37 39 40		6 V., c. 35 8 V., c. 16, s. 9 18 V., c. 61, s. 1 6 V., c. 58, s. 1 6 V., c. 35 6 W. 4, c. 32, s. 15 6 V., c. 35 .... 22 V., c. 5, s. 37 40 G. 3, c. 22, s. 1 6 V., c. 35 23 V., c. 5, s. 19 60 G. 3, c. 16, s. 1 1 V., c. 27, s. 1 6 V., c. 35	34, s. 1—16, 17 p. 18—54 35, s. 1—11, 13—23, 20—37, 39—43, 49—53 24 26 28, s. 1, 2, 5—8 35, s. 1—11, 13—23, 20—37, 39—43, 49—53 42	Boundaries. Milk River Bath. Trelawney. Montego-Bay, Close Harbour. St. James. Military Defences.
36 G. 3	2, 3, 4, 5, 6, 1 7, 8, 9, 11, 10 12, 13, 14, 15 16, 17, 18, 22 19, 20, 21, 23 25, 26, 27, 32 28, 29, 30, 33, s. 4—6 31 34 35, s. 15—18 20, 21 36 37		9 V., c. 38, s. 12 6 V., c. 35 .... 9 V., c. 38, s. 12 6 V., c. 35	24 33, s. 1, 3 pt. 35, s. 1—14, 19, 22—29 33 s. 2, 3 pt.	Kingston Aqueduct. Maroons. St. James.

CHRONOLOGICAL TABLE OF ACTS, &c.

Year of Reign.	Expired or Disallowed.	Repealed.	Repealing Act.	In Force, &c. In Digest.	In Force, &c. Not in Digest.	Under Head of—
37 G. 3	1, 2, 3, 4, 5, 6, 7, 8, 10, 12, 13, 14, 17, 18, 19, 20, 22, 23, 27	11 15 16 21 24 25 26, s. 1, 2 s. 3	} 7 V., c. 46, s. 1 19 V., c. 26 6 V., c. 35 ... ... 19 V., c. 10, s. 39	9		Governor.
38 G. 3	1, 2, 3, 4, 5, 6, 7, 8, 9, 11, 14, 15, 16, 17, 18, 19, 22, 25, 26, 31, 32, 33	12 13 21, s. 3 23, s. 1 s. 3, 10 s. 5 s. 6, 7 24 27 28 29 30	6 V., c. 35 4b G. 3, c. 28, s. 4 6 V., c. 35 3 V., c. 65, s. 54 6 V., c. 35 20 V., c. 22, s. 40 20 V., c. 22, s. 41 9 V., c. 33, s. 1 } 22 V., c. 27, s. 65 6 V., c. 35	20 21 s. 1, 2 23, s. 4	10 23, s. 2, 8, 9	Accounts, Produce, &c Military Defences. Public buildings. Commissioners de bone yse, 4.
39 G. 3	1, 2, 3, 4, 5, 6, 8, 9, 14, 15, 16, 17, 18, 19, 20, 21, 23, 26, 27, 28, 30, 31	11 12 13 22, s. 1—3 s. 4, 6—9, 15 24 29 32 33	1 V., c. 27, s. 1 } 1 V., c. 27, s. 1 19 V., c. 26 15 V., c 11, s. 1 15 V., c. 34, s. 1 54 G. 3, c. 15, s. 1 7 V., c. 57, s. 1 6 V., c. 35	7, s. 2—17 10 22, s. 22—24 25 34, s. 1, 2—6	7 s. 1 22, s. 5, 10—14, 16 21, 23, 25 28	Gaming, 2, 4, 10—17 ; Billiard Tables, 5—9, 12, 13. Naval service. Vestries. Kingston. Kingston, St. Andrew.

39 G. 3	34, s. 3—5				
	35				
	36				
40 G. 3	1, 2, 3, 4, 5, 6, 14	6 V., c. 35		92	Montego-Bay, close Harbour.
	7, 8, 9, 10, 16	7 V., c. 57, s. 1		26	Purchase of land for Troops.
	11, 12, 13, 18	6 V., c. 58. s. 1	29, s. 14, 17—27	29, s. 1—13, 15, 16, 28—30	Falmouth Water Company.
	15, 17, 19,				
	20, 24, 25, 30,	6 V., c. 35	33		Free Schools, Woolmer's
	27, 28,	7 V., c. 53, s. 1	35		Military Defences.
	31, 32	8 V., c. 39, s. 1	36		
	33, s. 2, 5, 6	18 V., c. 61, s. 1			
	34	6 V., c. 35			
41 G. 3	1, 2, 3, 4, 5, 6, 10	14 V., c. 53, s. 1	13, s. 2—4	13, s. 1, 5	Coroners.
	7, 8, 9, 11, 14	21 V., c. 4, s. 32	18		Assembly.
	12, 15, 20, 16	5 W., c. 29, s. 1	22		St. George.
	24, 25, 26, 17	4 V., c. 32, s. 1	23, s. 1, 3, 4, 7—9		Hanover,
	19	6 V., c. 35	30		Port Royal
	21	6 V., c. 53, s. 1			
	23, s. 2, 5, 6, 27	6 V., c. 35			
	27	9 V., c. 33, s. 1			
	28	22 V., c. 23, s. 65			
	29	6 V., c. 35			
	31	8 V., c. 39, s. 1			
		18 V., c. 61, s. 1			
		7 W., 4, c. 36, s. 1			
		27 V., S. 1, c. 34, s. 66			
42 G. 3	1, 2, 3, 4, 5, 12	7 W., 4, c. 40, s. 1	24	19	Chief Justice.
	6, 7, 8, 9,	27 V. S.1, c.33, s.104	26, s. 1—3, 4 pt. 5	23	Portland.
	10, 11, 14, 13	9 V., c. 33, s. 1	27		St. James.
	15, 16, 17,	22 V., c. 23, s. 65			Commissioners' Affidavits.
	20, 22, 25, 18	7 W., 4, c. 41, s. 1			Military Defences.
	29	27 V. S.1, c.32, s.64			
	21	6 V., c. 35			
		20 V., c. 22, s. 41			
42 G. 3	26, s. 4 pt.	27 V., S. 1, c. 17, s. 11			
	s. 6, 7	6 V., c. 35			
	28				

CHRONOLOGICAL TABLE OF ACTS, &c.

Year of Reign	Expired or Disallowed	Repealed	Repealing Act	In Digest	Not in Digest	Under Head of—
43 G. 3	2, 3, 4, 5, 6, 7, 9, 10, 11, 12, 13, 14, 15, 16, 17, 18, 19, 26, 27 Disallowed 30	8, 20 s. 8 pt., 21, 22, 24, 25 s. 1, pt. 2, 31, 32, s. 2, 10, 11, 34, 35	54 G. 3, c. 10, s. 1 / 20 V., c. 22, s. 40, 41 / 5 W. 4, c. 39, s. 1 / 6 V., c. 58, s. 1 / 7 V., c. 46, s. 19 / 19 V., c. 26 / 19 V., c. 10, s. 47 / 56 G. 3, c. 22 / 6 V., c. 35 / 7 V., c. 46, s. 19 / 19 V., c. 26 / 7 V., c. 46, s. 19 / 19 V., c. 26	20, s. 1—7, 8 pt 9, 10 / 23 / 28 / 29 / 32	1 / 25 s. 1 pt. / 33	Collecting Constables. Provost-Marshal. Hanover. Judges. Juries warned on Writs. Bills and Promissory Notes. Free Schools, Jamaica. Montego-Bay, Close Harbour.
44 G. 3	1, 2, 3, 4, 5, 6, 7, 8, 9, 11, 12, 13, 14, 16	15, 18, 20, 22, s. 2, 23, 24, 26, 27, 28, 30, 31, 32	7 V., c. 57, s. 1 / 46 G. 3, c. 28, s. 4 / 23 V., c. 5, s. 19 / 3 V., c. 65, s. 54 / 7 V., c. 57, s. 1 / ---- / 6 V., c. 35 / ---- / 9 V., c. 35, s. 1 / 20 V., c. 11 s. 3 / 7 V., c. 57, s. 1	10 / 19 / 21 / 22, s. 1 / 25 / 29	17	Customs' Prize Goods. Transient Traders. Fishing and Fowling. Public Buildings. Court Supreme. Military Defences. Milk River Bath.
45 G. 3	1, 2, 3, 4, 5, 6, 7, 8, 9, 11, 18, 12, 13, 14, 15, 16, 19, 20, 21, 22	17, 23, 24, 25, 26	47 G. 3, c. 13, s. 1 / 6 V., c. 35 / 9 V., c. 33, s. 1 / 22 V., c. 23, s. 65 / 5 V., c. 15, s. 1 / 7 V., c. 57, s. 1 / ----	10 s. 2—8	s. ?	Troops.

				Arrests, Common Pleas. Military Defences. St. Ann.

46 G. 3

27, 28, 29, 30, 31, 32   1, 2, 3, 4, 5, 6, 7, 8, 9, 10, 16   11, 12, 13, 17   15, 20, 21, 19   22, 23

26, s. 20, 27   23—28

{ 8 V., c. 39, s. 1
{ 18 V., c. 61, s. 1
7 V., c. 57, s. 1
6 V., c. 35
....
23 V., c. 20, s. 9

18

Arrests, Common Pleas.
Military Defences.
St. Ann.

47 G. 3

25   26, s. 20, 27   23—28   29   1, 2, 3, 4, 5, 6, 7, 8, 9, 14, 11, 12, 14, 15, 16, 19, 22   20, 21, 24

6 V., c. 35
23 V., c. 5, s. 19
5 W. 4, c. 29, s. 1
5 V., c. 49, s. 1
19 V., c. 25, s. 5
6 V., c. 35

9 V., c. 38, s. 12
19 V., c. 15, s. 1

24
26, s. 1—19, 21, 22, 26
28—35
27, s. 1—10
28 s. ½, 3

18
27 s. 1½
28, s. 2, 4
17
18
23
13, s. 1, 4

Free Schools, St. James.
Public Hospital, Tonnage Dues.
Chief Justice.
Military Defences.
Laws of the Island.
Military Defences.

48 G. 3

13 s. 2   8. 3   17 s. 4 pb.   25, 26, 27, 28, 29, 30   1, 2, 5, 6, 7, 8, 9, 10, 11, 12, 13, 15, 16, 18, 31   Disallowed   17, 20

{ 20 V., c. 22, s. 41
{ 19 V., c. 10, s. 47
19 V., c. 10, s. 53
3 V., c. 41
6 V., c. 35
48 G. 3, c. 14
23 V., c. 6, s. 9
9 V., c. 35, s. 1
{ 50 G. 3, c. 20, s. 1
6 V., c. 35
....
23 V., c. 5, s. 19
6 V., c. 35

14
22
23, s. 1—7, 9, 1½
25, s. 1—9, 11, 14, 15

19
24
25, s. 10, 12, 13, 16

St. Ann.
Public Taxes.
Military Defences.
St. Ann.
Pilots.
Free Schools, Jamaica.

49 G. 3

23, s. 8   26, 27, 28, 29, 30   1, 2, 3, 4, 5, 6, 14, 7, 8, 9, 10,

....
23 V., c. 5, s. 19
6 V., c. 35
....
21 V., c. 32, s. 2
26 V., c. 2, s. 8

} {
26

Falmouth Water Company.

CHRONOLOGICAL TABLE OF ACTS, &c.

Year of Reign.	Expired or Disallowed.	Repealed.	Repealing Act.	In Force, &c. In Digest.	In Force, &c. Not in Digest.	Under Head of—
49 G. 3	11, 12, 13, 17, 15, 16, 17, 20, 18, 19, 20, 25, 21, 23, 29	22, 24, 25, 27, 28, s. 2, 3, 30	5 V., c. 49, s. 1; 19 V., c. 25, s. 5; 7 V., c. 57, s. 1; 1 V., c. 27, s. 1; 23 V., c. 5, s. 19; 8 V., c. 39, s. 1; 18 V., c. 61, s. 1; 6 V., c. 35	28 s. 1 pt,		Kingston Corporation.
50 G. 3	1, 2, 3, 4, 5, 6, 7, 8, 9, 10, 11, 12, 13, 18, 19	14, 16, 17, 21	6 V., c. 35; 9 V., c. 35, s. 1; 6 V., c. 35	15	20	Parishes, Robertson's Maps. Produce, Protection.
51 G. 3	1, 2, 4, 6, 7, 8, 9, 11, 13, 15, 20, 21, 23, 24, 31, 32	3, 10, 12, 14, 16, 17, 26, 27, 29, 30	5 W. 4, c. 29, s. 1; 6 V., c. 35; 7 V., c. 57, s. 1; 21 V., c. 32, s. 2; 26 V., S. 2, c. 8; 6 V., c. 58, s. 1; 5 V., c. 15, s. 4; 18 V., c. 18, s. 18; 23 V., c. 12, s. 20; 7 V., c. 57, s. 1; 3 V., c. 65, s. 54; 6 V., c. 35	5, 19, 22, 28	18, 25	Interest. St. Elizabeth; Black River bridge St. Thomas in the East. Vere. Free Schools Manning's. Arrest.
52 G. 3	1, 2, 3, 4, 5, 6, 7, 8, 9, 10, 11, 12, 13, 14, 15, 16, 17	18, 19	· · · ; · · ·			

Assembly.
Trelawny.
Westmorieand Tonnage Dues.
Salvage.
Emblements.

Parish Taxes.
Jamaica Sya.

Servants
Manchester.

Manning's Estates.
Secretary, Island.
St. James, 1; Prisons, 3.
St. Catherine.
Clerk Supreme Court.
Escheats.
Naval Service.

Judges.
St. Mary.
Military Defences.
St. Thomas in the Vale.

---

53 G. 3

1, 2, 3, 4, 5, 6,
7, 8, 10, 11,
12, 13, 14,
15, 16, 21,
27, 29

17
18
19, s. 4, 11
s. 6 pt.
20
23
24
25, s. 9—12
28

23 V., c. 20, s. 9
7 W. 4, c. 41, s. 1
27 V., S. 1, c. 32, s. 64
6 V., c. 35
6 V., c. 38, s. 12
6 V., c. 35
9 V., c. 35, s. 1
6 V., c. 35
27 V., S. 1, c. 33, s. 104
6 V., c. 35

9
19, s. 1, 3, 5—14
23, s. 1, 6, 7 pt. 8, 14, 25, s. 7 pt. 13
15

---

54 G. 3

1, 2, 3, 4, 5,
6, 7, 8, 9,
10, 11, 12,
13, 14, 20,
22, 23

15, s. 4, 5, 12—15
16
17
19
21

5 W. 4, c. 29, s. 1
6 V., c. 35
....
....
....

18 s. 2, 3

15, s. 1, 3, 6, 11, 16
—31
18, s. 1

Parish Taxes.
Jamaica Sya.

---

55 G. 3

1, 2, 3, 4, 5, 6,
7, 8, 9, 10,
11, 12, 13, 23,
14, 15, 16, 25,
17, 18, 22,
24, 26, 27,
28

20
21

6 V., c. 35
....
7 V., c. 57, s. 1

19, s. 1—4
23, s. 1, 2, 4—12

19 s. 5

Servants
Manchester.

---

56 B. 3

1, 2, 3, 4, 5, 6,
7, 8, 9, 10,
11, 12, 13, 23,
15, 16, 17, 26,
28

18
21
s. 1, 2, 11—13
27

6 V., c. 35
20 V., c. 22, s. 40, 41
6 V., c. 35
15 V., c. 34, s. 1
22 V., c. 5, s. 37

19, s. 1—17
20, s. 1, pt. 3
22
24
25

14
19, s. 18
20, s. 1, pt. 2
23, s. 3—10, 14, 16

---

57 G. 3

1, 2, 3, 4, 5,
6, 7, 8, 9,
11, 12, 13,
14, 19, 21,
22, 29, 30,
32

10
15
16
18
20, s. 4, 6, 8
24

6 V., c. 35
....
....
....
9 V., c. 33, s. 1
22 V., c. 23, s. 65

17
20 s. 1—3, 5, 7, 9—15
23
26

Judges.
St. Mary.
Military Defences.
St. Thomas in the Vale.

CHRONOLOGICAL TABLE OF ACTS, &c.

Year of Reign.	Expired or Disallowed.	Repealed.	Repealing Act.	In Force, &c. In Digest.	In Force, &c. Not in Digest.	Under Head of—
57 G. 3		25, 27, 28, 31	6 V., c. 35; 19 V., c. 15, s. 1; 6 V., c. 35			
58 G. 3	1, 2, 3, 4, 5, 6, 7, 8, 9, 10, 11, 12, 13, 15, 16, 20, 21, 22, 28, 30, 31	17, 18, 19, 24, 25, 27; a. 5, 8, 9	19 V., c. 10, s. 53; 6 V., c. 35; 4 V., c. 32, s. 1; 15 V., c. 11, s. 1	17, s. 1—3, 6, 10; 23, s. 1—3, 8, 9; 26	14; 17, s. 4, 7; 23, s. 4—7, 10; 29	Sale of Escheated Property. Public Buildings. Coroners. Public Buildings. St. George.
59 G. 3	1, 2, 3, 4, 5, 6, 7, 8, 9, 10, 11, 12, 13, 16, 17, 23, 25	15, 18, 19, 20, 21, 22	23 V., c. 5, s. 19; 9 V., c. 33, s. 1; 22 V., c. 23, s. 65; 7 W. 4, c. 41, s. 1; 27 V. S. 1, c 32, s. 64; 6 V., c. 35	14; 24		Naval service. Laws of the Island
60 G. 3	1, 2, 3, 4, 5, 6, 7, 8, 9, 10, 11, 12, 13, 14, 17, 22, 24; Disallowed 18, 19	15; 21 s. 12—14	23 V., c. 5, s. 19; 4 G. 4, c. 21, s. 1	16; 23, s. 1, 3—6	20; 21, s. 1—11, 15; 23, s. 2	St. James, Tonnage Dues, 4. Montego-Bay Barracks. Registrar in Chancery. Secretary, Island
1 G. 4	2, 3, 4, 6, 7, 8, 9, 10, 11, 12, 13, 14, 15, 17, 24, 25	5, 18, 19, 21, 22, 23	6 V., c. 35; 9 V., c. 35, s. 1; 9 V., c. 33, s. 1; 22 V., c. 23, s. 65; 3 V., c. 65, s. 54; 6 V., c. 35	16; 19; 20	1	Repeals a Repealed Act, partly. St. Mary's Tonnage Dues, 2. St. James. Metcalfe.

Troops.		21	6 V., c. 35	1, 2, 3, 4, 5, 6, 7, 8, 9, 10, 11, 12, 13, 14, 23	15 16 17 18 19 20 22
2 G. 4			· · ·		
			· · ·		
			18 V., c. 54, s. 32		
			6 V., c. 35		
Sale of Escheated Property.	10		· · ·	13, s. 1 pt. 2 pt.	
Governor's Secretary.	22	13 pt.	{ 18 V., c. 30; 19 V., c. 20 }	1, 2, 3, 4, 5, 8, 9,	15
Produce Protection.			6 V., c. 35	6, 7, 8, 9,	17
3 G. 4				11, 12, 14,	18
				16, 20	19
				Disallowed	
				21	
Provost Marshal, Secretary Island.	13, s. 1, pt. 2, 1½	12	{ 9 V., c. 33, s. 1; 22 V., c. 23, s. 65 }	1, 2, 3, 4, 5, 6, 7,	13, s. 10
Treasonable Meetings, &c. 13—5, 7, 11, 12.; Commissions for trial of Offences, 6. Chancery Deposits, 2.		13, s. 1 pt. 3—7, 11, 12	21 V., c. 14, s. 16	8, 9, 10, 11, 12, 14,	15
4 G. 4			6 V., c. 35	13, 16,	16
			18 V., c. 33, s. 10	8—9, 14, 21, s. 2 pt.	21, s. 2 pt.
		21 s. 2 pt	6 V., c. 35	17, 18, 19,	23
	21, s. 1, 3—5		4 V., c. 32, s. 1	20	
Provost Marshal	20 s. 20	13	6 V., c. 35	1, 2, 3, 4, 5, 6,	17
Free School, Manchester,		20, s. 1—19	· · ·	7, 8, 9, 10,	19
5 G. 4			· · ·	11, 12, 14,	21
			· · ·	15, 16, 18,	22
				24	23
Troops		15	23 V., c. 6, s 9	1, 2, 3, 4, 5,	9
St. Catherine.		16	9 V., c. 35, s. 1	6, 7, 10, 11,	14
6 G. 4	★		6 V., c. 35	12, 13, 17,	19
				18, 20, 21	
				Disallowed	
				8	
Manning's Estate.	13	15, s. 1—4, 8—10, 12, 14—19	6 V., c. 35	1, 2, 3, 4, 5,	14
Hanover. Paupers, 1—7; Apprentices, Parish, 8—20.	13, s. 21	26, s. 1—20	· · ·	6, 7, 8, 9, 15, s. 5—7, 11, 13	15, s. 5—7, 11, 13
7 G. 4			· · ·	10, 11, 12, 17	17
				16, 18, 19,	
				20, 21, 22,	
				24, 25	

CHRONOLOGICAL TABLE OF ACTS, &c.

Year of Reign.	Expired or Disallowed.	Repealed.	Repealing Act.	In Force, &c. — In Digest.	In Force, &c. — Not in Digest.	Under Head of—
7 G. 4	Disallowed 23, 27					
8 G. 4	1, 2, 3, 4, 5, 6, 7, 8, 9, 10, 11, 12, 13, 15, 16, 17, 18, 19,	20 21 22, s. 1—3	9 V., c. 35, s. 1 6 V., c. 35 13 V., c. 24, s. 23	14, s. 1—3, 4 pt. 22, s. 4—7, 9, 8	14, s. 4 pt. 22, s. 9	Fishing and Fowling. Coroners, 4, 5; Indictments, 6, 7, 9.
9 G. 4	1, 2, 3, 4, 5, 7, 8, 9, 13, 14, 16, 18, 21, 22 Disallowed 15 17	10 11 12 15 19, s. 9 24, s. 1 s. 2, 3 25	6 V., c. 35 9 V., c. 35, s. 1 5 W. 4, c. 29, s. 1 15 V., c. 11, s. 1 4 V., c. 46, s. 1 19 V., c. 10, s. 53 3 V., c. 65, s. 54 6 V., c. 58, s. 1	6 19, s. 1—3 5—8, 10 20, s. 1—7 23, s. 1—3 24, s. 4	s. 4 20, s. 8 23, s. 4	Assembly. Indictment, 1, 2, 8; Benefit of Clergy, 3; Criminal Punishment, 5—7; Oaths, &c., 10. Written Acknowledgments, 1, 3, 5—7; Abatement, 4 Jews, 1; Aliens, 2, 3 Foreign Attachments,
10 G. 4	1, 2, 3, 4, 5, 6, 7, 8, 9, 10, 11, 16, 17, 18, 19, 20, 21, 22	14, s. 3—5	6 V., c. 35 21 V., c. 14, s. 16	12 13 15	14, s. 1, 2	Roman Catholics. Naval Officer. Transportation. Produce Protection.
11 G. 4	1, 2, 6, 8, 14, 15 Disallowed 11 10 13	3 7 9	20 V., c. 11, s. 3 1 W. 4, c. 17, s. 1 7 V., c. 46, s. 19 19 V., c. 26 6 V., c. 35 1 W. 4, c. 2, s. 1 16 V., c. 39, s. 2.	4, s. 2 5 12, s. 1—4 16, s. 2, 3	4, s. 1, 3 12, s. 5 16, s. 1	Free School, St. James. Clarendon. Secretary, Island. Jews.

	Speaker's Salary.	Complexional Disabilities.	Chief Justice.	Jews.	Variances.	Manchester.	Leases, &c.	Indemnity Act.	Crop Accounts.	Loan Rebellion Debts.	Public Officers Securities.	Seamen.	Transportation.	Public Taxes.	Masters in Chancery.	Capt. and Mr. Finlayson's Annuities.	Militia.	Intercolonial Mail Boats.	United States Ships' Registers.	Taxes.
	2	17, s.1	1				16, s.1	25	26	27	37	38	41	41					46	18
	17, s. 2		2	10	11	16, s. 2, 3					31	32							47	

1 W. 4

```
7 W. 4, c. 41, s. 1
27 V. S.1, c. 32, s. 64
19 V., c. 46, s. 19
19 V., c. 26, s. 19

7 W. 4, c. 40, s. 1
27 V. S.1, c. 33, s. 104
19 V., c. 46, s. 19
19 V., c. 26
6 V., c. 35

7 V., c. 46, s. 19
19 V., c. 26
6 V., c. 35
```

8   9   11   12
16   19   24   27   30   31

1, 3, 4, 5, 6,
7, 10, 13,
14, 15, 18,
20, 21, 22,
23, 25, 26,
28, 29

2 W. 4

```
7 W. 4, c. 41, s. 1
27 V., S.1, c. 32, s. 64
6 V., c. 35

9 V., c. 35, s. 1
5 V., c. 49, s. 1
19 V., c. 25, s. 5
6 V., c. 35
5 W. 4, c. 29, s. 1
18 V., c. 38, s. 10
6 V., c. 35
```

12   15   23   28   30   34   35   39   40   41 s. 3 pt.   45

3, 4, 5, 6, 7,
8, 9, 13, 14,
17, 18, 19,
20, 21, 22,
24, 28, 29,
36, 42, 48,
49
Disallowed
33, 43

3 W. 4

16, s. 1   25   26   27
37   38   41   41   46   18

1, 2, 3, 4, 5,
6, 7, 8, 9,
10, 11, 12,
13, 14, 15,
16
Disallowed
17, 19

CHRONOLOGICAL TABLE OF ACTS, &c.

Year of Reign.	Expired or Disallowed.	Repealed.	Repealing Act.	In Force, &c. In Digest.	In Force, &c. Not in Digest.	Under Head of—
4 W. 4, S. 1	3, 5, 8, 11, 13, 17, 14, 16, 17, 20, 21, 22, 23, 24, 26, 27, 28, 31, 32, 39, 40	4 pt.	20 V., c. 22, s. 41	2	1	Martial Law Accounts. Loan, Government. Sir J. Rowe's Salary.
		6	7 W. 4, c. 41, s. 1 / 27 V. S1, c. 32, s. 64		4 pt	
		7	6 V., c. 35			
	Disallowed	9	....	19	12	Annuities Rebellion. Seamen.
	36	10		29		Constables, Special.
		15	9 V., c. 35, s. 1	33		Trustees.
		18	6 V., c. 35			Constables.
		25	7 W. 4, c. 40, s. 1 / 27 V. S.1, c. 33, s.104			Religious Worship, Dissenters, 70; Slavery, Abolition.
		30	6 V., c. 35		37	
		34	7 W. 4, c. 36, s. 1 / 27 V. S.1, c. 34, s.66 / 27 V. S.1, c. 33, s.104	41, s. 70	41, s. 1—69, 71	
		35	7 W., 4, c. 40, s. 1			
		37	24 V., c. 11, s. 64			
		38	9 V., c. 35, s. 1			
4 W. 4, S. 2	1, 4, 5	2	6 V., c. 35		3	Assize Courts.
5 W. 4	2, 4, 6, 7, 8, 9, 10, 11, 12, 13, 15, 16, 17, 20, 22, 26, 27, 19, 28, 30, 31, 32, 33, 34, 21, 36, 37, 41, 23, 45	1	6 V., c. 28, s. 1	18	14	Clerk Court and Provost Marshal Commissions for Trials. St. Catherine; St. Thomas in the Vale.
		3	6 W. 4, c. 32, s. 15	24		
		5	5 V., c. 15, s. 4 / 18 V., c. 18, s. 18 / 23 V., c. 12, s. 20			
		19	6 V., c. 35			
		29, s. 52—54, 69	6 V., c. 28, s. 1	38, s. 1—37, 39, 40	29, s. 1—51, 55—68	Highways.
			19 V., c. 15, s. 1	39, s. 1—30, 34—52		
	Disallowed 44	35	6 W. 4, c. 13, s. 1			
		38, s. 38	6 V., c. 35 / 1 V., c. 9, s. 1			Sligo Water Works. St. Catherine.
		39, s. 31—33	9 V., c. 38, s. 12			

					Subjects
5 W. 4	40, 12, 43				Highways.
6 W. 4	1, 2, 3, 4, 5, 6, 7, 8, 9, 10, 11, 12, 14, 15, 16, 17, 18, 19, 23, 24, 27, 28, 30, 31; Disallowed 21	20, 25, 26, 3; s. 2—4, s. 6, s. 7, s. 9, s. 10	15 V., c. 34, s. 1; 7 V., c. 22, s. 1; 6 V., c. 58, s. 1; 18 V., c. 66, s. 1; 15 V., c. 12, s. 1; 6 V., c. 35; 27 V., s.1, c. 33, s.104; 27 V., s. c. 34, s. 66; 7 V., c. 14, s. 33; 15 V., c. 11, s. 1; 24 V., c. 11, s. 64	23	Port-Royal.
				13; 33, s. 1, 5, 8, 11—15	Protection, Constables, &c.
7 W. 4	1, 3, 4, 5, 6, 7, 8, 9, 16, 19, 21, 22, 23, 24, 25, 26, 28, 29, 32, 34, 38; Disallowed 10, 11, 31, 32, 37	2, 13, 14, 15, 18, 19, 22, 36, 37, 39, 40, 41; s. 3	13 V., c. 35, s. 32; 21 V., c. 14, s. 16; 6 V., c. 35; 1 V., c. 16; 10 V., c. 18, s. 1; 24 V., c. 10, s. 1; 27 V., s.1, c. 34, s. 66; 9 V., c. 35, s. 1; 7 V., c. 22, s. 1; 27 V., s.1, c. 33, s.104; 27 V., s.1, c. 32, s. 64	27; 18	Treasonable Meetings, &c.
					Saving's Banks.
			12 s. 1, 2; 14 s. 1—14, 16, 17, 20, 21, 23, 24	15	Expired Patent.
					St. Elizabeth.
					Banks.
				20	Expired Patent.
					Westmoreland.
			30, s. 1—8; 35	30, s. 9	Free Schools, Jamaica.
				33	Taxes.
					Governor.
1 V.	1, 2, 3, 4, 5, 6, 7, 8, 11, 12, 13, 14, 15, 17, 18, 19, 23, 24, 25, 26, 32, 33, 39; Disallowed 18, 20, 23, 31, 37	10, 12, 13, 17; 21, s. 1 pt.; 27, s. 41—44, 47, 60—69; 28, s. 1, s. 4, pt. 12, 15, s. 8, s. 10—13, s. 18, s. 19 pt, 20 pt.	7 V., c. 22, s. 1; 6 V., c. 35; 25 V., c. 17, s. 5; 7 V., c. 51; 9 V., c. 38, s. 12; 7 V., c. 46, s. 19; 19 V., c. 26; 16 V., c. 15, s. 10; 4 V., c. 47, s. 1; 21 V., c. 14, s. 16; 20 V., c. 11, s. 3; 20 V., c. 13, s. 1; 10 V., c. 42, s. 1	9, s. 3	Sligo Water Company.
				16	Repealing Act.
				21	British Silver Coin.
			22, s. 2, 3	22, s. 1	Troops.
			25		Distresses, Rent and Taxes.
			26; 27, s. 1—40, 45, 46, 48—59, 70—74		Landlord and Tenant.
					Trelawney.
			28, s. 2—5, 7, 19—20	28, s. 9, 14, 16, 17, 21	Insane Prisoners, 2, 3; Criminal Punishment, 4, 5; Prisons, 7; Witnesses, &c. expenses, 19, 20. C. R. Scott, Attorney-at-Law.
				30	

CHRONOLOGICAL TABLE OF ACTS, &c.

Year of Reign.	Expired or Disallowed.	Repealed.	Repealing Act.	In Force, &c. — In Digest.	In Force, &c. — Not in Digest.	Under Head of:—
1 V.		29	6 V., c. 35	34	35	Parishes,
		36	13 V., c. 35, s. 32	38		Maumee Bridge Turnpike,
		42	6 V., c. 35		40	Porters and Carriers.
		43	...		41	Assize Courts.
		44	...		45	Ferry Road.
						Taxes, Discounts
3 V.	1, 2, 3, 4, 5,	13	25 V., c. 10, s. 1	18, s. 1 pt. 3—5, 7—12	7	Insolvent Debtors.
	6, 8, 9, 10,	14	19 V., c. 37, s. 1		11	A. Rodgers, Attorney-at-Law.
	12, 15, 16,	18 s. 1 pt.	28 V., c. 5, s. 1	18, s. 6, 13		Rogues and Vagabonds.
	17, 19, 20,	s. 2	4 V., c. 42, s. 1		21	Common Pleas.
	22, 23, 24,	27	17 V., c. 29, s. 43		26	Parochial Loans.
	25, 28, 40,	29	14 V., c. 53, s. 1	30		Combinations.
	44, 45, 47,		21 V., c. 4, s. 32		31	Capital Felonies.
	52, 53, 59,	33	25 V., c. 46, s. 1	34		Inheritance.
	60, 63	35	19 V., c. 15, s. 1	36		Harbours.
	Disallowed	37	15 V., c. 11, s. 1	39, s. 1—3, 8, 10 pt. 11, 12	39, s. 4—7, 9	Currency Assimilation, 1—3, 8, 11, 12, Coin, 10.
	32, 57	38	4 V., c. 11, s. 1			Droghers.
		39 s. 10 pt.	5 V., c. 28 / 7 V., c. 51	41		Gunpowder, 10—12; Trespasses, 13, 14.
		42	20 V., c. 22, s. 40	43, s. 10—14	43, s. 1—9, 15	Servants.
		46	7 V., c. 47, s. 1	48		Hanover.
		49	18 V., c. 66, s. 1	50, s. 1—48, 53—68	51, s. 2	Wills.
		50, s. 49—52	9 V., c. 38, s. 12	51, s. 1, 3—29	54	Imports.
		55	27 V., s. 1, c. 34, s. 66		58	Tonnage Duties, &c.
		56	6 V., c. 35		61	Stamps.
		66, s. 1—5, 7—11,	19 V., c. 10, s. 53	65, s. 6, 12, 18, 21—23,	62	Law, Commission.
		13—17, 26—37,	21 V., c. 32, s. 57	25, 46	64	Insurance Company,
		44, 45, 47—52	4 V., c. 44, s. 1		65, s. 19, 20, 24, 40	Court of Chancery, 6; Court Supreme, 12, 21—23, 25; Judgments, 18; Clerk of the Peace, 46.
		38, 39			—43, 53, 54	
		67		66, s. 1—15	66, s. 16	Light House, Morant Point.

CHRONOLOGICAL TABLE OF ACTS, &c.

Year of Reign.	Expired or Disallowed.	Repealed.	Repealing Act.	In Force, &c. In Digest.	In Force, &c. Not in Digest.	Under Head of—
5 V.	47 49 55 57	55, s. 2	21 V., c. 23, s. 13 19 V., c. 25, s. 5 17 V., c. 29, s. 43 15 V., c. 34, s. 1			
6 V.	1, 2, 3, 4, 5, 6, 7, 8, 9, 10, 11, 12, 15, 16, 17, 18, 19, 20, 21, 23, 25, 26, 36, 37, 42, 43, 44, 45, 47, 48, 51, 54	14 27, s. 38 28, s. 10, pt. 11, 13 pt. 33 38 39, s. 3 41 46 49 50 52, s. 4—6, 8—10 53 57 58, s. 4, 6, 9, 15, 24 59, s. 30, 31	27 V. S1, c.32, s. 64 7 V., c. 12 10 V., c. 46, s. 1 23 V., S.2, c.1, s. 9 24 V., c. 12, s. 1 27 V. S-1, c. 33, s.104 19 V., c. 15, s. 1 17 V., c. 29, s. 43 9 V., c. 39, s. 1 8 V., c. 38, s. 1 20 V., c. 11, s. 3 ---- 9 V., c. 35, s. 1 11 V., c. 31, s. 1 9 V., c. 38, s. 12	22, s. 2 24, s. 1—10 27, s. 1—37, 39—41 28, s. 2—24 30 31 34 39, s. 1, 2, 4—6 40 52, s. 1—3, 7 55 56 59, s. 2—29, 32—60 60	13 22, s. 1—3 24, s. 11 28, s. 1, 25—27 29 32 35 58, s. 1—3, 5, 7, 8, 10—14, 16—23 25—50 61	St. Domingo. Royal Mail Steam Packet Comy. Oaths, &c. Friendly Societies. Weights and Measures. Assize Courts. Hawkers and Pedlars Judgment as in case of Nonsuit Petty Debts. Military Defences. General Repealing Act. Fishing and Fowling. Coin, Copper. Prisons. Court of Ordinary, 1—3, 5; Executors, 4. Court of Chancery. Ferry Road. Port-Royal. St. James. Penitentiary.
7 V.	1, 2, 3, 4, 7, 8, 9, 10, 13, 16, 17, 18, 20, 26, 27, 28, 29, 36,	11 pt. 31 31, s. 1 pt. 33	11 V., c. 33, s. 3 20 V., c. 11, s. 3 22 V., c. 16, s. 1 {14 V., c. 53, s. 1 {21 V., c. 4, s. 32	5 11 pt. 14, s. 1—28, 30—32 34	6 12 14, s. 29—38, 35	Evidence. Indemnity Act. Lunatic Asylum. Friendly Societies Repeal. Towns, &c. 1—11, 15—20, 23 —28, 30—39, 34; Gaming, 12 —14; Sunday, 21, 22.

Session	Subject				
7 V.	Loan, £200,000 Extension.	38, 39, 44, 34	19 V., c. 35, s. 5		15
	Attorney Genl. (O'Reilly) Salary.	45, 58, 61, 41	25 V., c. 10, s. 1		19
	Emigrant Townships Sale.	46	19 V., c. 26		22
	Fishing and Fowling.	s. 1, 2, 4			
	Kingston Loan.	53	18 V., c. 39, s. 1 / 18 V., c. 61, s. 1		24
	Jamaica Railway.	54		33	
	Census.	57, Sch. pt.	18 V., c. 29	35	30
	Evidence.	62	27 V., s. 1, c. 21		
	Interpleader, 1—7; Mandamus, 8.	63	19 V., c. 10, s. 53	31, s. 1, pt. 2	
	Sunday, &c.	64	20 V., c. 11, s. 3	32	
	Public Hospital.	65	9 V., c. 35, s. 1	35	37
	Annotto Bay Improvement Com.	66	8 V., c. 38, s. 2		40
	Extents.		22 V., c. 36, s. 84	42	
	Venditioni.			43	
	Banks.			47, s. 12—16	47, s. 1—11, 17
	Stamps.				48
	United Royal Agricultural &c. Societies.			49	
	River Road Turnpike.				50
	Coin.			51	
	Bills and Notes.			52	
	Common Pleas.			56	55
	Westmoreland, Hanover.			57, s. 2—19	
	Wharves, Public.				57, s. 1
	Laws Commission.				59
	Highways.				60
	Clergy.			61, s. 3	61, s. 5
8 V.	St. David, St. Thos. in the East.	1, 2, 3, 4, 5, 6, 7, 10, 11, Sch.	18 V., c. 47	8	9
	Lazaretto.	14, 15, 21, s. 5, 6, Sch.	21 V., c. 34, s. 7	12	
	Jamaica Railway.	13, s. 18	17 V., c. 29, s. 35		13, s. 19
	Jamaica Mutual Life Assurance Society.	16, s. 3—6	14 V., c. 46, s. 1	13, s. 1—17	
	Land Tax, 1, 2; Laws of England, 7.	22, 23, 24, 18	19 V., c. 37, s. 1	16, s. 1, 2, 7	16, s. 8—10
	Taxes.	25, 26, 27, 20, 29, 49, 31	22 V., c. 12		17
	Deeds, 2, 5, 9; Leases, 3, 10; Contingent &c. Interests, 4, 6; Mortgages, 7, 8; Trustees, 8;	38, s. 12, 13, 14 pt., 39, 44, 45, 47, 48, s. 3—7, 16 pt.	15 V., c. 20, s. 3 / 18 V., c. 61, s. 1 / 17 V., c. 29, s. 43 / 18 V., c. 29 / 21 V., c. 13, s. 14 / 20 V., c. 22, s. 9	19, s. 2—10	19, s. 1, 11

CHRONOLOGICAL TABLE OF ACTS, &c.

Year of Reign.	Expired or Disallowed.	Repealed.	Repealing Act.	In Force, &c. In Digest.	In Force, &c. Not in Digest.	Under Head of—
8 V.				28		Executors, 1, 7, 14; Abatement, 2—5; Initials, &c· 6; Court Supreme, 8, 20, 24; Evidence, 9, 24; Payment into Court, 10; Variances, 11, 12; Special Cases, 13; Distresses for Rent, 15, 16 : Arbitration, 17—19; Costs, 21, 22; Commissions de bone esse and Foreign, 23.
						Holidays.
					32	St. Catherine Loan.
					33	St. Jane's Loan.
					34	Clarendon Loan.
					35	St. Andrew Loan.
					36	St. Dorothy Loan.
				30	37	Ferry Road.
				38, s. 1, 3—8, 10, 11, 14 pt, 15—20	38, s. 2, 9, 21	Island Curates' Fund.
				40	41	Education.
				42, s. 1	42, s. 2	Vestries.
				43		Evidence.
				46		Troops.
				48, s. 1, 2, 8—17, 19	48, s. 18	Jamaica Gazette.
						Arrest, 1, 2; Extents, 8, 17; Vendition, 9; Judgments, 10—17, 19.
9 V.	1, 2, 3, 4, 5, 11		22 V., c. 36, s. 84	18, s. 4, 7	18, s. 1—3, 5, 6, 8, 9	Public Hospital.
	6, 7, 8, 9, 17		11 V., c. 29, s. 1			
	10, 12, 13, 19		17 V., c. 29, s. 43			
	14, 15, 16, 27		19 V., c. 25, s. 5	20, s. 1—5	20, s. 6	Lumber Measurers.
	24, 33, 36, 32, s. 62		10 V., c. 17, s. 1		21	Public & Parochial Assessments.
	37, 40, 41, 33		22 V., c. 23, s. 65	22, s. 1—19	22, s. 20—24	Railways; Mails.
	42, 43, 45 34 pt.		10 V., c. 19, s. 1	23, s. 1—5	23, s. 6—10	Railways; Troops, &c.
	35, s. 7 pt.	35, s. 8—11, 13,	13 V., c. 31, s. 1		25	Parochial Taxes.
			22 V., c. 43, s. 23		26	St. Elizabeth Loan.

Vol.					Subject
9 V.	,			28	St. Mary's Loan.
				29	South Midland Railway.
				30	Jamaica Railway Extension.
		15 V., c. 27		31	Great Interior Railway.
				32, s. 1—61, 63—75	Price's Tramway.
		18 V., c. 19, s. 1	35, s. 2—6, 7 pt. 18, 23 —30, 35—40, 42 —67 71—83, 85—89, 91 pt., 92—97, 98 pt., 99—117	34 pt. 35, s. 1, 14, 17, 98 pt.	Smith's Agricultural Society.
	15, 16, 19—22, 31—34, 41, 68—70, 90, s. 12, 84, 91 pt.	39, s. 7, 8 pt.			Militia.
			38, s. 1—11	38, s. 12, 13	Markets.
			39, s. 2—6, 8 pt., 9—17	39, s. 1, 18	Rectors' Fund.
			44		Parishes.
10 V.	1, 2, 3, 4, 5, 8, 11 9, 10, 12, s. 26 1, 13, 14, 33 15, 21, 24, 37 25, 27, 28, 44 31, 32, 35, 40, 41, 47 Disallowed 16, 38	27 V., s. 1, c. 21, s. 2 22 V., c. 36, s. 84 11 V., c. 33, s. 3 21 V., c. 22, s. 57 27 V. s. 1. c. 16, s. 15	6, s. 1—5 7 12, s. 2 18, s. 2, 3 29, s. 1—26 30 34, s. 1 45, s. 1, 2 46	6, s. 6, 7 12, s. 3 17 18, s. 1 19 20 22 23 29, s. 27—29 34, s. 2 36 39 42 45, s. 3 48 49	Deaths by Neglect, &c. Deodands. Coroners. Price's Tramway. Savings' Banks. Smith's Agricultural Society. South Midland Railway. Customs Differential Duties. Taxes. Hackney Carriages. Markets. Vestries. &c. Westmoreland Loan. Official Assignee. Quarter Sessions. Parochial Loans. St. Catherine. Weights and Measures. North Jamaica Railway. Jamaica Central Factory Com.
11 V.	13, s. 3 14, s. 2 19, s. 3, 4, 5 1, 2, 3, 5, 6, 8, 9, 10, 12, 18, 22, 23,	18 V., c. 33, s. 10 18 V., c. 46, s. 1 18 V., c. 51, s. 1		4 7 11	Arms and Ammunition. Martial Law. Banks.

CHRONOLOGICAL TABLE OF ACTS, &c.

Year of Reign.	Expired or Disallowed.	Repealed.	Repealing Act.	In Force. In Digest.	In Force. Not in Digest.	Under Head of—
11 V.	26, 27, 39, 40	20 21 24 25 31, s. 3, 5, 6 32 33, s. 4 35	27 V., S. 1, c. 7, s. 52 21 V., c. 14, s. 16 21 V., c. 22, s. 57 19 V., c. 37, s. 1 12 V., c. 8, s. 1 22 V., c. 66, s. 84 19 V., c. 5, s. 3 20 V., c. 11, s. 3	13, s. 1, 2, 4 14, s. 1, 3—5 16 17 19, s. 1, 6 pt.	15 19, s. 2, 6, pt. 7—9 28 29 30	Trustees. Towns, &c. 1, 3, 5; Sunday, 4. Vere loan. Island Curates' Fund. Trelawney. Kingston Town Dues. Insolvent Debtors. Immigrants Back Passages. Manning's Hill Turnpike.
				33, s. 1, 2 34 36 37	31, s. 1, 2, 4, 7 33, s. 3, 5—20 38	Ferry Road. Lunatic Asylum. Court of Chancery. Pawnbrokers. Trelawney. Parochial Officers' Salaries.
12 V. S. 1	1, 2, 3, 4, 5, 6, 7, 10, 11	9	19 V., c. 37, s. 1		8 12	Ferry Road. Parochial Officers' Salaries.
12 V. S. 2	1, 2					
13 V.	1, 2, 3, 8, 9, 10, 11, 12, 13, 14, 16, 18 17, 19, 20, 23, 28, 29, 30, 34, 36	5 6 25 26 27 31, s. 1—3, 6, 7 32 35, s. 27 30	14 V., c. 56, s. 1. 22 V., c. 36, s. 84 14 V., c. 56, s. 1 { 14 V., c. 1, s. 1 { 17 V., c. 29, s. 43 14 V., c. 55, s. 1 22 V., c. 43, s. 23 19 V., c. 25, s. 5 21 V., c. 22, s. 57 18 V., c. 57, s. 3	7, s. 1, 2, 4 15 21 22, s. 1—6 24, s. 1—21 35, s. 1—26, 28, 29, 31 38	4 7. s. 3 22, s. 7 24, s. 22—24 31, s. 4, 5, 8 33 35, s. 32—35 37	Parochial Taxes. Accessories, 1, 2; Variances, 4. Justices Actions. Medical Practitioners. Leases. Justices, Indictable Offences. Militia. Cornwall Insolvent Court. Justices, Convictions. Arson. Executors, &c.
14 V. S. 1	3	1 2	17 V., c. 29, s. 43	4, s. 1	4, s. 2, 3	Jamaica Gazette.

14 V. s. 2	14 V. s. 3		17 V., c. 14, s. 2			Subject
1	1, s. 5, 6				1	Cholera Funds.
			15 V., c. 37, s. 1		17	Island Checks.
			21 V., c. 23, s. 13		22	Collecting Constables.
			17 V., c. 21		25	Cholera Deaths Registers.
	35 pt.		15 V., c. 20, s. 3		30	Cholera Funds.
			27 V., S.1, c. 33, s. 104	34, s. 1—8	34, s. 9	Defamation.
			21 V., c. 22, s. 57	35 pt.		Island Curates' Fund.
			19 V., c. 19, s. 1	40		Aliens.
			27 V., S.1, c. 33, s. 104		43	Salaries, Prospective Reduction.
			16 V., c. 15, s. 19	46, s. 2—13	46, s. 1, 14	Trespasses.
			20 V., c. 11, s. 3		47	Insolvent Debtors.
			21 V., c. 4, s. 32		49	Courts Common Pleas.
			18 V., c. 18, s. 1			Court of Chancery.
			23 V., c. 12, s. 20			
				52	55	Tolls.
				56, s. 2—4	56, s. 1	Tonnage Dues, 2, 3 : Customs, 4.
					63	Cholera Funds.
					64	Stamps.
4	18, s. 2, 3, 7 pt.		20 V., c. 2, s. 10	7		Arsenic.
5	12, 13, 15		22 V., c. 21, s. 1	9, s. 3	11, s. 1	Juries.
6			27 V., S.1, c. 32, s. 8	64	11, s. 2—25	Pounds; Dividing Fences, 24, 25.
9, s. 1, 2			19 V., c. 23, s. 1	16	17, s. 16	Court of Chancery.
12			21 V., c. 8, s. 8	17, s. 1—15	18, s. 4, 5, 7 16—24	Light Houses, Plumb Point.
			22 V., c. 77, s. 1	18, s. 1, 6, 7 pt. 8—11, 14, 25	26, 27	Executive Committee.
			17 V., c. 29, s. 26	20	22, s. 3	Island Curates' Fund.
21			16 V., c. 42, s. 1	22, s. 1, 2	28, s. 1, 3, 4	Dividing Fences.
26			19 V., c. 15, s. 1	27	29	Militia.
28, s. 2			17 V., c. 14, s. 2			Cholera Funds.
34			22 V., c. 5, s. 37	30	37	Metcalfe Loan.
38			22 V., c. 1, s. 85	32		Rectors' Fund.
39, s. 2 pt.			16 V., c. 20			Trelawney.
16—21			22 V., c. 1, s. 85	39, s. 1—15	42	Cholera.
40			.....			Loans guaranteed by Government; Immigration.
41					13	Insolvent Debtors.
12	15, s. 11, 13—18		21 V., c. 30, s. 40	15, s. 1—3, 5—9, 12, 20—30	15, s. 4, 10, 19, 31, 32	Vestries.
			27 V., S.1, c. 33, s. 104			Indictment 1—3, 6, 7, 9, 12, 24—27, 30.

14 V. S. 3: 2, 3, 4, 5, 6, 7, 8, 9, 10, 11, 12, 13, 14, 15, 16, 18, 19, 20, 21, 24, 26, 27, 28, 29, 31, 32, 35, 36, 41, 54, 58, 59, 60, 61, 62, 65 — 23, 33, 44, 48, 50, 51, 53, 57

15 V.: 1, 2, 3, 13, 14, 19, 23, 25, 35, 36, 10, 15, 24, 31, 33, 43

16 V.: 1, 2, 3, 4, 5, 6, 7, 8, 9, 10

CHRONOLOGICAL TABLE OF ACTS, &c.

Year of Reign	Expired or Disallowed	Repealed	Repealing Act	In Force, &c.		Under Head of—
				In Digest	Not in Digest	
16 V.	11, 14, 17, 16, 24, 26, 28, 18, 31, 35, 36, 19, 37, 38, 39, 29, 40, 30, 41, 42, 45		17 V., c. 21 22 V., c. 1, s. 85 23 V., c. 5, s. 19 22 V., c. 1, s. 85 20 V., ...c. 11, s. 3 27 V. S.1, c.33, s.104 19 V., c. 37, s. 1	20 23, s. 1 25 27 32 33 34 43 44	22 28, s. 2—7	Forgery, 5, 8 ; Perjury, 20—22; Evidence, 23 ; Autre fois acquit or convict, 28 ; Criminal Punishment, 29. Loans guaranteed by Government; Immigration. Partnerships Limited. Returns of Taxable Property. Prisons. Loans Guaranteed by Government; Immigration. Tonnage Dues. Patents for Improvements. Ditto Ditto. Ditto Ditto. Vestries. Titles of Congregations, &c.
17 V.	1, 3, 5, 17, 8, 9, 10, 11, 6, 12, 13, 17, 15, 19, 22, 24, 16, 26, 27, 37, 29, 40	s. 36 pt. 40 pt. Sch. E pt. 60 pt. 30, s. 8, 9 32, s. 2, 4, 9 pt. 52 pt. 53 pt. Sch. H K 33, s. 3, 19, 21, 22, 24 31	22 V., c. 5, s. 37 22 V., c. 1, s. 85 19 V., c. 37, s. 1 27 V. S.1, c.32, s. 64 21 V., c. 34, s. 7 24 V., c. 13 19 V., c. 5, s. 1 18 V., c. 64 18 V., c. 42, s. 1 20 V., c. 5, s. 1 23 V., c. 10, s. 3	2, s. 1—44 23 (29), s. 1—25, 27—31, 34, 36—42, 45—50, 52, 53	i2, s. 45 14 18 20 21 25 28 29, s. 26, 32, 33, 35, 43, 44, 51, 54	Customs. Cholera & Small Pox Expenses. Highways. Trelawney Loan. Repealing Act, Orphan Asylum. Coroners. Tax Collection. Tolls Exemption ; Police. Legislative Council, 1—11, 34, 52, 53; Assembly, 1, 23, 34, 49; Privy Council, 12—14; Executive Committee, 15—25, 27—31 ; Permanent Revenue, 36—42, 45—48, 50, 53 ; Loans £500,000, 38, 40—42, 46—50.

Subject			19/22 V.	17 V.	18 V.
Public liabilities to January, 1854.				35, s. 4 pt.	
Legislative Council.	30, s. 1—7, 10—11		19 V., c. 5, s. 1	36	
Mining Companies.		31	22 V., c. 1, s. 85		
Customs.		32, s. 1—48, 49 pt. 50, 51, 52 pt. 53 pt. 54—65			
Jamaica Railway, extension.	34	33. s. 1, 2, 4—18, 20, 23, 25—30, 32—35			
Loans guaranteed by Government, £500,000.					
Coroners.		35			
Infants.		38			
		39			
Parochial Officers' Salaries Arrears.	2		22 V., c. 5, s. 37		1, 3, 4, 5, 6, 7
Governor.		17	22 V., c. 1, s. 85		8, 9, 10, 11, 21
Rector's Fund.		19	20 V., c. 6, s. 11		12, 13, 14, 25, s. 63, 66 pt.
Island Curates' Fund.		20	19 V., c. 5, s. 4		15, 16, 18, 33, s. 6, 7
Prisons.	22, s. 10	22, s. 1—9	23 V., c. 18, s. 9		26, except s. 8 pt 27, 45
Ditto.	23, s. 5	23, s. 1—4	19 V., c. 37, s 1		35
Harbours.		24	22 V., c. 1, s. 85		36, 37, 38, 52
Tax Collection.	25, s. 1—62, 64, 65, 66 pt. 67—75		22 V., c. 13, s. 74		39, 40, 41, 55, s. 1, 49, s. 1, 50, 62, 63
Rum Licenses.		26, s. 8 pt.			
Stamps.					
Registrations, Births and Burials, repeal.	28	30			
Governor's Secretary.	29	31			
Laws of the Island, Time, 6.		32			
Mining Lease.					
Chancery Deposits.	33, s. 10	33, s. 1—5, 8, 9			
Court of Ordinary.		34			
Mining Companies.		42			
Tolls Commutation.					
Defamation.	43	44			
Gaming.		46, s. 2—6, 8, 9			
Repealing Act; Jamaica Mutual Assurance Company.	46, s. 1, 7				
	47				
Interest.		48			
Public Hospital.	49, s. 2, 3				
Kingston Town dues.	51, s. 1, 4	51, s. 2, 3			

CHRONOLOGICAL TABLE OF ACTS, &c.

Year of Reign.	Expired or Disallowed.	Repealed.	Repealing Act.	In Force, &c. In Digest.	In Force, &c. Not in Digest.	Under Head of—
18 V.				53, s. 1—40	53, s. 41—43	Free Schools, Munro and Dickenson.
				54, s. 1—26	54, s. 27—33	Free Schools, Vere district.
				55, s. 2		Rum and Spirits.
					56	Jamaica Railway extension.
				57, s. 1, 2, 4—11	57, s. 3	Justices Convictions.
				58		Infants, s. 1; Court Chancery, 2—5.
				59	60	Mines and Minerals. Cholera Funds.
				61, s. 2, 3, 5—20, 22—23	61, s. 1, 4, 21, 34—39	Kingston Corporation. Repealing Act; Specie Payments. Tax Collection.
					64 65 66	Kingston and Annotto-Bay Road.
19 V.	1, 2, 4, 9, 12, 18, 21, 24, 28, 33, 43, 47, 48, 49	4	26 V., S. 1, c. 4, s. 39	3		Legislative Printing.
		6, s. 2	25 V., c. 36, s. 1	5, s. 1—3, 5, 6	5, s. 4	Chancery Deposits. Clergy.
		10, s. 22, 25, Sch A pt. s. 46 s. 57	22 V., c. 39, s. 1 / 28 V., c. 34, s. 3 / 20 V., c. 22, s. 40	6, s. 1, 3, 4	7 8	Tax Collection. Ditto.
		14, s. 14 pt. 22 23, s. 10 12—15 34 37, s. 39, Sch. pt.	27 V. S. 1, c. 17, s. 11 / 28 V., c. 10, s. 14 / 20 V., c. 3, s. 20 / 21 V., c. 25, s. 1 / 20 V., c. 14, s. 1 / 27 V. S1, c. 30, s. 43 / 20 V., S1, c. 20, s. 1 / 23 V. c. 35, s. 4	10, s. 1—21, 23, 24, 26—37, 39—43, 45, 49—51, 54, 55, 59	10, s. 38, 44, 47, 52, 53, 56, 59	Judges, 1—5, 13—16, 49—51, 54, 58. Court of Chancery, 2, 9, 14. Court Supreme, 6—8, 20, 24, 32, 35. Court Ordinary, 10, 14. Circuit Courts, 11, 12, 14, 17—19, 21, 23, 26—31, 33, 34, 45, 48. Courts Common Pleas and Quarter Sessions, 17. Clerk Peace, 28—32. Criers of Courts, 33. Costs, 36, 37. Venditioni, 39—42.

			19 V.	20 V.
	11			
13	14, s. 1—15, 17—21			
14, s. 16	15, s. 2—40			
15, s. 1	16			
	17			
19				
	20			
23, s. 1, 22, 24	23, s. 2—9, 11, 16—21, 23			
26	25			
27				
	29			
	30			
	31			
	32			
35				
36				
37, s. 30, 34, 40	37, s. 1—29, 31—33, 35—38, 41—58			
38, s. 4	38, s. 1—3			
39, s. 4, 29	39, s. 1—3, 5—28			
40, s. 12	40, s. 1—11, 13			
42	41			
	44			
	45			
46, s. 1, 2,	46, s. 3			
		27 V. S. 1, c. 34, s. 66		
2	3, s. 1—17, 19	22 V., c. 20, s. 1		
3, s. 20, 21		23 V., c. 10, s. 3		
4, s. 1, 3		21 V., c. 21, s. 1		
5, s. 1	5, s. 2—7, 9—26			

19 V.	20 V.
	3, s. 18
	4, s. 2
	5, s. 8
1, 10, 17, 18,	
21, 24, 25,	
26, 27	7

CHRONOLOGICAL TABLE OF ACTS, &c.

Year of Reign.	Expired or Disallowed.	Repealed.	Repealing Act.	In Force, &c. In Digest.	In Force, &c. Not in Digest.	Under Head of—
20 V.		8	22 V., c. 1, s. 85	9	6	Tax Arrears Collection.
		11, Sch. B. 29	21 V., c. 16, s. 2	11, s. 1, 2, 4–43, 45–70	11, s. 3, 44	Coroners.
		20, s. 7 pt	23 V., c. 35, s. 4	12		Prisons.
		23, s. 2	22 V., c. 30, s. 1	13, s. 2–4	13, s. 1	Court, Supreme.
				14, s. 2–12	14, s. 1	Witnesses Expenses
					15	Juries, Special
				16		St. Thomas ye Vale Circuit Court, January, 1857.
				19		Executive Committee.
				20, s. 1–4, 6, 7	20, s. 5	Evidence, Arbitration, 11.
				22, s. 1–10, 12, 14–34, 36–39	22, s. 11, 13, 35, 40–42	Petty Debts.
						Clerk Supreme Court and Crown.
						Circuit Court, 18. Judgments, 28, 31. Fines, 30, 39.
					23, s. 1, 3–6	Stamps.
21 V.	18, 19, 21, 29, 35, 37, 38, 40, 43, 45, 46	2	21 V., c. 21, s. 1	1, s. 1–13, 17, 19, 20	1, s. 14–16, 18	Audit of Public Accounts.
		8	22 V., c. 17, s. 1*	3		Board of Works.
		10	25 V., c. 46, s. 1	4, s. 1–30, 33	4, s. 31, 32	Receiver-General.
		11, s. 5	27 V., S.1, c. 34, s. 6b		7	Insolvent Debtor's Court
		15	27 V., S.1, c. 33, s. 104	9		Justices
	Disallowed 5, 6	25, s. 3	28 V., c. 33 s. 9	11, s. 1–4, 6–13		Riots
		26, s. 3	28 V., c. 1	12		Markets
		32, s. 36, 56	22 V., c. 23, s. 65	13, s. 1–13, 15	13, s. 14	Arrests
		33	27 V., S.1, c. 36, s. 12	14, s. 1–15, 17, 18	14, s. 16	Penal Servitude
		34, s. 6	25 V., c. 12, s. 45	16		Prisons
		8, 9, 19	27 V., S 1, c. 25, s. 1	17, s. 1–4	17, s. 2, 3	Private bills, &c., Assembly s. 4; Legislative Council, s. 4
		22	28 V., c. 28, s. 3	20		Martial Law
		41, s. 21	28 V., S 2, c. 21, s. 1	22, s. 1–56, 58, 59	22, s. 57	Appeals
			23 V., c. 24, s. 2	23, s. 1–12, 14	23, s. 13	Fines
				24		Obeah and Myalism
				25, s. 8 2, 6, 7	25, s. 1, 4, 5	Juries
				26, s. 1, 2		Private bills, &c.
				27, s. 1–6, 8	27, s. 7	Kingston Police Magistrate

	21 V.				22 V.	
Patents for Inventions				15, 22, 25, 31, 35, 49, 50		
Justices	30, s. 40	30, s.1—39—41				
Main Roads		31				
Main Road Fund, 1, 2, 36, 41; Loan; 3—5; Land Tax, 7—21, 23—35, 37—40; permanent revenue, 38		32, s.1—35, 37—55, 57—64		1, s. 8 pt. 11, 12, 59—63		
	34, s. 10—18, 20, 39	34, s. 1—5, 7, 21, 23—38, 40, 41	24 V., c. 16, s. 28	Forms 9—11		
Tax Collection				48, pt.		
Receiver General's Moneys Transfer	36	39		3, s. 2 pt. 7		
Industrial Schools			27 V., S.2, c. 5, s. 19	8		
Insolvent Debtors			24 V., c. 15, s. 11, 13			
Loans, Parochial Debts, 1—14; Parishes 15	42	41, s. 1—20, 22—24	25 V., c. 35, s. 6	5 s. 23		
		44	24 V., s. 8, s. 1	6		
Immigrants			27 V., S 1, c. 30, s. 43	10, s. 9, 12—50		
..... Chinese Private Exps.	1, s. 85	1 s.1—10, 3—58, 64—84, 86	25 V. c. 44, s. 1	14, s. 3 pt		
Loans, Immigration	2, s. 2	2, s.1, 3—6	28 V., c. 27, s. 18	18 pt.		
Immigrants, Liberated Africans	; s. 6	3, s. 12 pt. 3—6, 9	28 V., c. 2, s. 5	19		
Assembly	3, s. 35, 37	4, s.1—5, 7	25 V., c. 12, s. 45	23, s. 14		
Naval Service		5, s.1—23, 24—34, 37	28 V., c. 43, s. 4	4, s. 58 pt.		
Immigrants, Education.		7	25 V., c. 21, s. 4	29		
Clergy.		8	23 V., c. 20, s. 9	38		
Loans; Tramroads.		9	25 V., c. 40, s. 22			
Mining Companies.		10, s.1—8, 10, 11	28 V., c. 33, s. 6	39, Sch. pt.		
Repealing Act, Trespasses.	12	11	{ 28 V., c. 2—5			
Rum Duty Collection.	13, s. 1, 24, 74, 75	13, s. 2—23, 25—73, 76	28 V., c. 34, s. 2			
Rum Warehouses.		14	25 V., c. 27, s. 3	40, s. 13		
Evidence.	16, s. 1	16, s. 2—5	24 V., c. 10 s. 1	41, s. 9, 10		
Hogs, Dogs, Goats.	17, s. 1	17, s. 2—10	26 V. S.1, c. 4, s. 39	44		
Assembly.		18	27 V. S.1, c. 7, s. 52	47		
Police.	20	21, s. 2—10, 12, 13				
Copyright.	21, s. 1, 11	23, s. 1—13, 15—64				
Clergy.	23, s. 65	66—68				
Loans, Parochial Debts.	26	24	23 V., c. 11, s. 1	48, s. 1		
Highways.	27, s. 7	27, s. 1—6				
Admiral's Pen.		28				
Costs.	30	32				
Stamps.						
Industrial Schools.						

CHRONOLOGICAL TABLE OF ACTS, &c.

Year of Reign	Expired or Disallowed.	Repealed.	Repealing Act.	In Force, &c. — In Digest.	In Force, &c. — Not in Digest.	Under Head of—
22 V.				33		Executive Committee.
					34	License, &c. Duty.
					35	Elections, 1859.
				36, s. 1—83	36, s. 84, 85	Kingston, &c. Water Company.
					37	Jamaica South Coast Railway.
				39, s. 2—4	39, s. 1	Circuit Courts, 2 ; Court Supreme, 3, 4.
				40, s. 2—12, 14—34	40, s. 1	Surveyors.
				41, s. 1—8, 11—15		Saving's Banks.
					42	Tax Collection.
				43, s. 1—20, 22, 24	43, s. 21, 23	Militia.
					45	Insolvent Debtors.
					46	Judicial Amendment.
				48, s. 2—7		United States Mail.
23 V., s. 1	1, 2, 8, 13, 22, 23, 25, 27, 28, 32, 33, 39	6 s. 1 pt. 14 17, s. 12, 13, 20 26 29, s. 9 34	24 V., c. 23 27 V. s. 1, c. 33, s. 104 23 V., s. 2, c. , s. 1 26 V., s. 2, c. 6, s. 1 24 V., c. 16, s. 4 25 V., c. 40, s. 22	4, s. 1—19, 21—38, 40	3, s. 20, 39	Special Commission, Cornwall.
				5, s. 1—18, 20, 21	5, s. 19	Rum Licenses.
				6, s. 1—6	6, s. 7—9	Harbours.
				7		Bath, St. Thomas the Apostle.
				9		Naval Service.
				10, s. 1, 2	10, s. 3	Clergy.
				11, s. 2—5	11, s. 1, 6	Customs.
				12, s. 1—19, 22	12, s. 20, 21	United States Mail.
				15, s. 1—5	15, s. 6	Customs, 1—9, 18, 19, 22; Tonnage Duties, 10—17.
					16	Commission for trial of Offences.
				17, s. 1—11, 14—19, 21—26		Police.
				18, s. 1—8, 10—13	18, s. 9	Medical Practitioners.
				19		Clerks Peace, &c.
				20, s. 1—8	20, s. 9	Coroners; Criers of Courts; Vestries; Weights and Measures; Trelawney; Tonnage Duties, 4 ; Kingston ; St. Andrew's.
				21		

Industrial Schools.	24, s. 2	24, s. 1	
Immigrants, Chinese.	29, s. 4	29, s. 1—3, 5—8, 10—12	
Loans, Immigration.		30	
Immigrants.		31	
Petty Debts.		35	
Highways.			
Public and Parochial Buildings, Repairs.	36		
License and Registration Duties Amendment.	38	37	
Medical Practitioners.	1, s. 1, 9	1, s. 2—8	
Census.	1		
Fire.			
Tonnage Duties.	3, s. 1	2, s. 2—8	
West Indian Incumbered Estates.	4, s. 8	3, s. 2—7	
Judges.		4, s. 2—7	
Hospital Commission.	6	5	
Receiver General's Moneys Transfer.		7	
Assembly.		8	
Free Schools, Manchester District.	10, s. 1	9	
Savings Banks.	11	10, s. 2—4	
Police.	12, s. 1, 2		
Tradesmen Breaches of Trust.	13	12, s. 3—12	
Repealing Act, Molasses.		13	
Immigrants, 1—3, 5—8, 10, 19, 22, 27, 28, 31; Chinese, 4, 21; Further Fund, 16, 18, 21, 22, 24, 25; Education, 30; Loan, 5, 14—18, 22, 25, 26.	16, s. 9, 11, 13, 20, 29	16, s. 1—8, 10, 14—19, 21, 22, 24—28, 30, 31	
Prisons		19	
Insane Prisoners		22	
Bath, St. Thomas the Apostle.		23	
Executors.		24	
Vendryes, Henry		25	
Loan Main Roads, 1, 2, 4; Land Tax 5.		26, s. 1, 2, 4, 5	

25 V., c. 1, s. 1
25 V., c. 35, s. 6, 7
27 V., S. 1, c. 11, s. 6
27 V., S. 2, c. 25, s. 1
26 V., S. 2, c. 21, s. 1

14, 15, 20, 21, 4, s. 1
28, 29, 30, 16, s. 12, 23
31, 32, 33, 17
Disallowed 26, s. 3
18 26, s. 6
1

23 V., S. 1

23 V., S. 2

23 V., S. 3

24 V.

CHRONOLOGICAL TABLE OF ACTS, &c.

Year of Reign.	Expired or Disallowed.	Repealed.	Repealing Act.	In Force, &c. — In Digest.	In Force, &c. — Not in Digest.	Under Head of—
24 V.				27		Loan Public Liabilities.
25 V.	5, 8, 13, 14, 15, 33, 39, 41, 42, 43, 45, 47 Disallowed 24	3 7 9, s. 9 pt. 12, s. 10 pt. 19 pt. 24, 25, 29	26 V., S. 2, c. 6, s. 1 27 V., S. 1, c.32, s. 64 26 V., S. 1, c. 4 s. 19 27 V., S.1.c. 36 s.4,12	1 s. 2	1, s. 1	West Indian Incumbered Estates.
				2		Industrial Schools.
				4		Forts and Barracks, Executive Committee.
				6		Education.
				9, s. 1—11, 13—28	9, s. 12, 29	Lunatic Asylum.
				10		Cruelty to Animals.
				11		Towns and Communities.
				12, s. 1—23, 26—28 30 —44, 46, 47, 49, 50	12, s. 45, 48	Main Roads, Highways, 33.
				16		Public and Parochial Buildings Repairs.
				17		Ditto ditto Highways not Main Roads.
				18, s. 2—44, 46—67, 88—95	18, s. 1, 4, 5, 68 87	Immigrants, Liberated Africans.
				19		Immigrant Settlements.
				20		Clergy.
				21, s. 2, 3	21, s. 1, 4	Free Schools, Munro and Dickenson's.
				22		Arms and Ammunition.
				23		Cayman Island.
				25		Wills.
				26		Surveyors.
				27		Collectors of Dues.
				28		Servants.
				29		Fire.
				30		Prisons.
				31		People's Railway.
				34	32	Island Curates & Rectors Funds.
				35, s. 1, 3—8	35, s. 2, 9	Immigrants, 1, 3—5; Further Funds, 5; Chinese, 8; Loan, 5-7.

Session	Subject				
25 V.	Clergy.	36, s. 1	36, s. 2—4		
	Executive Committee.		37		
	Ditto Ditto.		38		
	Kingston Floating Dock.	40			
	Tramroads Loan, 2, 37.	44, s. 1	44, s. 2—56		
	Ejectments.		46		
26 V. S. 1	Arms and Ammunition.		1		
	Naval Service.	4, s. 39	2		
	Horses and Cattle.		3		
	Public Hospital.		4, s. 1—38	22 V., c. 38, s. 77	Disallowed 5
	Attorney-General.				
	Post Office.	7	6		
26 V. S. 2	Loan Government.		1		
	Military Defences.		2		
	Oaths.		3		
	Loans, Mainroads.		5		
	Perpetual Annuity Repeal.	6			
	Highways, Mainroads.		8		4, 7, 13, 14, 16, 24
	Light Houses, Plumb Point.		9		
	Secretary Island, Dissenter's Marriages, 12.		10		
	Horses and Cattle.		11		
	Assembly.		12		
	Costs.	15, s. 4	15, s. 1—3		
	Falmouth Water Co.	17, s. 6, 7	17, s. 1—5		
	Prisons.		18		
	Traction Engines.		19		
	Public and Parochial Buildings Repairs 1—6, 14 : Loans 7—13		20		
	Land Tax.	21, s. 1	21 s. 2		
	Tonnage Duties.		22		
	Medical Practitioners.	23, s. 3	23 s. 1, 2, 4		
27 V. S. 1	United States Mail.	1, s. 3	1 s. 1, 2	28 V., c. 28, s. 40	31 s. 21—31
	Rum Mephylated.		2	28 V., c. 4, s. 1	33 s. 23, 24
	Still License Repeal.	3			6
	Clerk Supreme Court, &c.		4 s. 1—3		
	Rum Duties.	4 s. 2	5		
	Vestries.	7 V., s. 52	7, s. 1—51, 53, 54		
	Circuit Courts.	8			

CHRONOLOGICAL TABLE OF ACTS, &c.

Year of Reign.	Expired or Disallowed.	Repealed.	Repealing Act.	In Force, &c.		Under Head of—
				In Digest.	Not in Digest.	
27, V. S. 1				9		Assembly.
				10, s. 1—8	10, s. 9	Markets.
				11, s. 1—5	11, s. 6	Customs.
				12		Tramroad Kingston.
				13		Larceny, &c. summarily punishable.
				14		Amendments.
				15		Appeals.
				16, s. 1—14	16, s. 15	Administrations, Petty 1—7, 10—14; Executors, &c, 8, 9.
				17, s. 1—10	17, s. 11	Deeds Probate.
				18		Merchant Shipping.
				19, s. 2—13	19, s. 1	Free Schools, St. Jago de la Vega.
				20		Governor's Aide-de-Camp.
				21, s. 1	21, s. 2	Wharfage.
				22		United Royal Agricultural Society, &c.
				23		Board of Works.
				24		Loans, Main Roads.
				25, s. 2—4	25, s. 1	Ditto ditto.
				26		Highways.
				27, s. 2, 3	27, s. 1, 4	Judgments.
				28		Replevin.
				29		Ditto.
				30, s. 1—42	30, s. 43	Constabulary Force.
				31, s. 1—20, 32—47	31, s. 48	Collectors of Dues.
				32, s. 1—63	22, s. 64	Offences against the Person, 1—62; Attainder, 63.
				33, s. 1—22, 25—103	33, s. 104	Larceny, &c.
				34, s. 1—65	34, s. 66	Malicious Injuries.
				35		European Assurance Society.
				36, s. 1—3, 5—11, 13	36, s. 4, 12	Main Roads; Highways.
				37		Public and Parochial Buildings.

CHRONOLOGICAL TABLE OF ACTS, &c.

Year of Reign.	Expired or Disallowed	Repealed.	Repealing Act.	In Force, &c.		Under Head of—
				In Digest.	Not in Digest.	
28 V.				27, s. 1—20	27, s. 21	Rum Duty Collection, 1—17, 20, Warehousing, 18—90.
				28, s. 1—51	28, s. 52	Licence and Registration Duties; Collector of Dues, 30, 34, 50.
				29		Free Schools, Vere District
				30		Main Roads.
				31		Audit of Public Accounts.
				33		Circuit Courts, 1, 3—7 ; Juries, 2, 8.
				34		Circuit Court's.
				35		Costs.
				36		Court of Chancery, 1—7, 12—14; Masters in Chancery, 8—12.
				37		Court Supreme, Pleadings.
				38, s. 1—76, 78	38, s. 77	Militia, 76, Volunteers 1—75, 78.
				39		Kingst. Ship Dock 1, 3—5, 8—18, 20.
				40		Loan 2, 5—8, 19 Tonnage Duties, 20
				41		Kingston Gas Works.
				42		Vaccination.
				43, s. 1—3	43, s. 4	Companies Winding up.
				44		Clergy.
						Leases.

DIGEST OF THE LAWS OF JAMAICA.

PRINTED BY
M. DE CORDOVA, & CO.,
GLEANER OFFICE, KINGSTON, JAMAICA.

DIGEST OF THE LAWS OF JAMAICA.

Abatement, Pleas in.

If a defendant plead in abatement, that any other ought to be jointly sued, and issue be joined, and it appears at the trial that the Action could not be maintained by reason of 21 James 1, chap. 16 (Statute of Limitations) be maintained against the others, or any of them, the issue shall be found against the party pleading 10 G. 4, c. 20, s. 2. *To be found for plaintiff if claim barred by Statute of Limitations.*

No plea for non-joinder of a co-defendant shall be allowed, unless it is stated that the person is resident within the jurisdiction and the place of residence stated with convenient certainty in an Affidavit verifying the plea 8 V., c. 28, s. 2. *Requisites of plea of non-joinder of a defendant's Affidavit.*

To a plea of non-joinder, the plaintiff may reply that the person has been discharged under an Act for the relief of Insolvent Debtors 8 V., c. 28, s. 3. *Replication Discharge of Insolvent.*

If after such plea the plaintiff commences another Action against the defendant in the Action in which the plea in Abatement was pleaded, and the persons named in such plea as joint contractors, and it appears by the pleadings or on the evidence, that all the original defendants are liable, but one or more of those named in such or some subsequent plea in Abatement are not liable, the Plaintiff shall be entitled to judgment, or to a verdict and judgment against the other defendants who appear liable, and every defendant not liable shall have judgment, and his costs against the plaintiff to be allowed as costs in the cause against such as pleaded the non joinder. Any defendant who so pleaded may, on the trial adduce evidence of the liability of the defendant named in his plea in Abatement 8 V., c. 28, s. 4. *Costs where party named is not liable Evidence of liability.*

No plea of Misnomer shall be allowed, but the defendant may cause the declaration to be amended at the costs of the plaintiff, by inserting the right name upon a Judge's order founded on an Affidavit of the right name. If the order is discharged, the costs shall be paid by the party applying if the Judge think fit, 8th V., c. 28, s. 5. *No plea of Misnomer. Amendment and costs.*

Accessories.

Any Accessory before the fact to any Felony, whether at common Law or by Statute, may be indicted, tried, convicted, and punished, as if he were a principal felon 13 V., c. 7, s. 1. *Before the fact. Indictment, &c.*

Any Accessory after the fact, may be indicted and convicted, either as an Accessory after the fact, together with, or after the conviction of the principal felon, or of a substantive felony, whether the principal has or has not been previously convicted, or be or be not amenable to justice, and punished as if convicted as an accessory, and his offence, howsoever indicted, may be tried and punished by any Court which has jurisdiction to try the principal felon as if the act by reason of which he became an accessory, had been committed at the same place as the principal felony. No person once duly tried, whether as an accessory after the fact, or as for a substantive felony, shall be again indicted for the same offence 13 V., c. 7, s. 2. *After the fact. ditto.* *No more than one trial for the same offence.*

Any number of Accessories may be charged with substantive felonies in the same indictment, notwithstanding the principal is not included, or is not in custody or amenable to justice 16 V., c. 15, s. 15. *Any number may be included in same indictment.*

Accounts Produce, and Accounts Current.

To be annually recorded on oath Attornies and Agents of Absentees, Trustees, Guardians, Executors, or Administrators, acting for minors or others, Mortgagees, their heirs Executors, Administrators, or Assigns in possession, Sequestrators appointed by the Court of Chancery, having the management or receipt of the Rents and Profits of any Real Estate shall annually, before 25th March, record in the Secretary's Office, an account upon their or Overseer's, or principal Managing Servant's oath, of all the rents, profits, produce, and proceeds, made the preceding year ending 31st Dec., 13 Geo. 2, c. 9, s. 1.

Penalty. Penalty £100 (£60 sterling) half to the person who sues, and loss of Commission, 13 G. 2, c. 9, s. 2.

Form of Memorandum False swearing to be recorded Form of Memorandum of oath to be signed by the persons administering and taking same. False Swearing Perjury. 13 G. 2, c. 9, s. 3.

The Secretary of the Island shall enrol accounts 13 G. 2 c. 9   .

Act revived and made perpetual 24 G. 2. c. 19 s. 7.

Mortgagees in possession shall record upon oath the whole accounts giving credit for the net proceeds of every crop within 18 months after they have recorded the crops, as well of the sales of the annual crop as of the account current respecting the same and shall state how much is applicable and has been applied to their mortgages under penalty of £500 (£300 stg.) recoverable by action of debt &c. one moiety to informer 25 G. 3 c. 10 s. 3.

As also trustees and guardians in possession (except under order of the Court of Chancery to account) within the same period under like penalty one moiety to the party aggrieved and forfeiture of commission 33 G. 3 c. 21.

Memorandum of oath, 13 G. 2, c. 9, s. 3. Memorandum this   day of   18   personally appeared before me   one of the Judges &c.
A.B. of   Attorney for   (or whatever capacity, such person shall act) and upon the Holy Evangelists made oath (or being of the people called Quakers solemnly affirmed) that the account above written or annexed is a true and just account of all rents, profits, produce and proceeds of the plantation and premises (or whatever real estate it may be) of   under his care and direction or which he is in possession of, and that in such account is particularly set forth the quantity of Sugar, Rum, Molasses, Cotton, Ginger, Coffee, Cocoa, Pimento or other produce produced and made in the year   and ending the thirty-first day of December last past, of from or upon the said

Since the abolition of the Courts of Common Pleas, crop accounts and accounts current, in strictness can only be sworn before a Judge of the Supreme Court.

Account, Action of.

Auditors may be appointed by Circuit Court. The Judge of [Circuit Courts 19 V. c. 10 s. 19] in actions of account brought down for trial before them immediately upon verdicts, that the defendants are accountable, shall name and appoint auditors, receive their returns and give final Judgment as the Judges of the Supreme Court did, 17 G. 3 c. 13, s. 1.

And the writ made returnable to that Court, if plaintiff desires. And the writs directed to the Auditors shall be made returnable immediate before the [Judge of the Circuit Court], where Judgment is obtained if the plaintiff so desire, 17 G. 3, c. 13, s. 2.

Administrations, Petty.

Proceedings and affidavit to obtain (property not exceeding £50.) Any party desiring to obtain administration on the personal property not exceeding £50 of any person who has died intestate shall give notice to the next of kin or widow, if either is known and make affidavit of the name and time of the death of the deceased, the nature and amount of the personal property he died possessed of, and the character in which administration is claimed, and if as a creditor, the nature and amount of the debt due to him which he shall deliver to and leave with the Clerk of the Peace of the Parish in which the property of the deceased is 27 V. S. 1, c. 16, s. 1.

The Clerk of the Peace shall file the affidavit in his office, enter an abstract. (Form A.) in a book kept for the purpose, exhibit a copy for public inspection and publish another copy in the "Jamaica Gazette by Authority" for 3 weeks successively 27 V. S. 1., c. 16, s. 2.

To be filed with Clerk of the Peace, and published.

If at the expiration of that period there be no opposition, and the party produces to the Clerk of the Peace an affidavit sworn before a Justice that he will well and truly administer the estate of the deceased, according to law and enters into bond (Form B), with one or more sureties to be approved of by the Clerk of the Peace, conditioned that he will within 30 days after date, return into the Clerk of the Peace's Office, an inventory and appraisement of the personal property of the deceased, and cause an account of all his transactions with the estate to be lodged in his office, within three months' from the date of such bond, and will continue to lodge accounts of his transactions once every 3 months, until the affairs of the estate are finally closed, and the personal property which came to his hands is fully accounted for, the Clerk of the Peace shall deliver to the applicant a certificate (Form C,) 27 V., S. 1, c. 16, s. 3.

Further proceedings, if claim is unopposed

Affidavit

Bond

Certificate

I do swear that I will well and truly administer the Estate of late of the Parish of   and will cause true accounts thereof to be lodged in the Office of the Clerk of the Peace, according to the provisions of the Petty Administrations Act. So help me God.

The applicant on receipt of certificate shall be authorized to take upon himself the administration of the estate of the deceased and perform the duties of an administrator thereon, 27 V., S. 1, c. 16, s. 4.

Powers conferred thereby

Where there is more than one application for administration, the Clerk of the Peace within 15 days of the meeting, of the first Circuit Court, after they have been lodged, shall summon each of the claimants. (Form D,) to appear at such Court. The Judge on proof of service of the summons and upon the affidavit being laid before him, shall decide upon the claims, determine to whom administration shall be granted, and deliver a certificate (Form E,) to the party obtaining administration, who upon leaving it with the affidavit and bond before provided for with the Clerk of the Peace, shall receive from him the certificate, (Form C,) and proceed to administer the estate as the administrator thereon, 27 V., S. 1, c. 16, s. 5.

Proceedings where claim is opposed

The Clerks of the Peace shall carefully file and keep in their offices the affidavits, bonds, inventories and account required to be lodged, and permit reference to and copies or extracts to be made by parties applying for permission, and on 31st March, 30th June, 30th September, and 31st December, or within 30 days thereafter, forward to the Island Secretary's Office, a list of the grants of administration. (Form A,) Penalty not exceeding £5. 27 V., S. 1, c. 16, s. 6.

Duties of Clerk of the Peace.

Lists of grants to be forwarded to Island Secretary.

The Secretary shall cause the names in such lists to be alphabetically arranged and indices made in a book for the purpose, and to be paid at the rate of 1s. 6d. per legal sheet, 27 V., S. 1, c. 16, s. 7.

To be alphabetically arranged, and indexed.

Not to prevent the Ordinary from granting administration in any case as heretofore, Letters so granted shall supersede administrations under this Act. Any person acting thereunder after having had notice, that the letters had been so superseded shall be responsible as an executor "'de son tort,'" 27 V., S. 1, c. 16, s. 10.

Superseded by letters of administration by ordinary.

Fees of the Clerk of the Peace. (Schedule F), Knowingly and wilfully demanding or receiving any larger sum for any such services or neglect of duty punishable as a misdemeanor at Common Law, 27 V., S. 1, c. 16, s. 11.

Fees of Clerk of the Peace.

Penalties to be recovered before 2 Justices, and appropriable to the credit of the General Revenue, 27 V., S. 1, c. 16, s. 12.

Penalties.

"Affidavit" shall include a declaration in writing, and any person making a false declaration shall be liable to the penalties of perjury, 27 V., S. 1, c. 16, s. 13.

"Declaration," false declaration.

The Petty Administrations Act, 27 V., S. 1, c. 16, s. 14.

Short title.

FORMS.

APPLICATIONS FOR ADMINISTRATIONS.—CLERK OF THE
PEACE'S OFFICE, PARISH OF

Name of Deceased Person.	Name of Party applying for Administration.	Nature of Claim.	Amount of Personally.	When claim was Lodged.	Period for grant of Administration.	Whether opposed or not.

Bond B s. 3

Know all men by these presents, that we   are held
and firmly bound unto our Sovereign Lady Victoria. Queen of the United
Kingdom, in the sum of   pounds, lawful money of Jamaica, to be paid
to our said Sovereign Lady, her heirs, and successors, to which payment well,
and truly to be made, we bind ourselves, our heirs, executors, and administrators, jointly and severally by these presents.

Sealed with our seals, and dated the   day of
A. D. 186

The condition of this obligation is, that if the above bound
do make a true and perfect inventory and appraisement of all and singular
the goods and chattels, rights, and credits of   , deceased, which
have or shall come to his hands, possession or knowledge, or into the hands or
possession or knowledge of any other person or persons for him, and the
same do return into the office of the Clerk of the Peace for the parish of
    , within thirty days from the date of this bond, and also do
cause a just and true account of this his administration, to be lodged in the
office of the said Clerk of the Peace, within three months from the date of
this bond; and further do cause a just and true account of this his administration, to be lodged in the office of the Clerk of the Peace aforesaid every
three months, until the whole of the personal property which came unto his
hands has been fully accounted for, then this obligation to be void, else to
remain in full force.

Sealed and delivered in the presence of

On the estate of A. B. late of the parish of   deceased.

Certificate C s. 3

I do hereby certify that C. D. of the parish of   , made application for a grant of administration of the estate of A. B., late of the parish of
     deceased, of which public notice has been given, according
to the provisions of an Act, entitled the Petty Administration Act, and that no
opposition has been made thereto; and the said C. D. has been sworn to administer the said estate according to law, and has entered into bond to return an inventory and appraisement of the personal property of the deceased
into my office within 30 days, and lodge an account of such his or her administration within three months from the date hereof, and continue

to lodge such accounts every three months until the affairs of the estate are finally closed. And I further certify, that the said C. D. is entitled to the administration of the personal estate of the said A. B., and is hereby authorized to take possession of, and to administer the same, accordingly.

Given under my hand, this   day of   18

Clerk of the Parish of

JAMAICA. ss.   } On the estate of A. B., late of the parish of   Summons D, s. 5
Insert Parish. }   deceased.

To C. D. et al.

These are to require you personally to be, and appear before the Judge of the Circuit Court, of this district, on   the   day of   next, between the hours of   and   in the forenoon; and in case there shall not be a court held on that day, then to appear at the next ensuing court that shall be held, to shew cause why administration of all and singular the goods and chattels, rights and credits of A. B., late of the Parish of   , deceased, should not be granted to E. F. of the Parish of   , and thereof you are to take due notice.

Given under my hand, this   day of   18

Clerk of the Peace of the parish of

JAMAICA, ss.   } On the estate of A. B., late of the parish of   Judge's Certificate
Parish   }   deceased.   E s. 5

I do hereby certify, that C. D. and E. F., both of them claimants for the administration of the personal estate of A. B., late of the Parish of   , deceased, appeared before me, and that having examined into their claims, and referred to their respective affidavits, I am of opinion that C. D. is entitled to the and administration; and upon taking the oath and entering into the Bond required by the "Petty Administration Act." should obtain the certificate of the Clerk of the Peace to enter upon the said administration-

Given under my hand, this   day of   18

For filing application of persons seeking administration, making abstract thereof for public inspection, and transmitting same for publication -- -- --	£0	1	0	Clerk of the Peace Fees F s. 11
For each certificate .. .. -- -- --	0	0	6	
For each copy recorded by the Clerk of the Peace.	0	0	3	
For recording each account at the rate of sixpence per legal sheet				
For each summons -- .. .. .. --	0	0	9	
For each copy, if required to be made -- -- --	0	0	3	
For filing each summons, and affidavit of service	0	0	3	
For attending before the Judge of the Circuit Court on a disputed application for administration -- --	0	2	0	

And for the performance of any duty, not herein particularly mentioned, at and after the rates fixed in the schedule.

Admirals Pen, St. Andrew.

Vested in the Crown, as a depot for immigrants, landed in Kingston, or to be rented, leased, or sold by the Executive Committee, 22 VIC. c. 27.

Aliens.

The Governor may by instrument, under the Broad Seal, make any   Naturalization alien, or foreigner coming to settle and plant in the island, having first taken the oath of allegiance, to be completely naturalized, and the persons named in the Letters Patent shall enjoy to them and their heirs the same immunities and rights to the laws of this island, as natural born subjects, 35 C., 23 s. c. 1.

'eos]

Governor's fee on Letters Patent, £5 (£3 sterling) his clerk 10s. (6s. sterling). No more to be paid to any other person 35, C. 2 c. 3, s. 2.

Stat. 13, G. 2, c. 7 Foreign Protestants

Statute 13 G. 2 c. 7, for naturalizing foreign protestants and others settling in the Colonies in America, shall be in full force and operation, 9, G. 4, c. 23, s 2.

But no person who becomes a natural born subject, under this Act, shall be a member of the Council or Assembly, 9, G. 4, c. 23, s. 3.

Exemption from stamps

No Stamp Duties shall be levied upon any document necessary for the naturalization of any person intending to settle, 19 V. c. 20.

Children of natural born mothers

All persons now, or to be born out of Her Majesty's Dominions of a mother a natural born subject of the United Kingdom, may take by devise, or purchase, inheritance or succession any estate, real or personal, 14, V. c. 40 s. 1.

Alien subjects of States in amity may hold personal property not chattels, real

Aliens the subjects of a State in amity with the United Kingdom, may take and hold by purchase, gift, bequest, representation, or otherwise, every species of personal property, except chattels, real, as fully as natural born subjects, 14 V. c. 40, s. 2.

Or lands, &c. for purposes of business, &c., but not to vote at elections of Assembly, or be a member of the Council or Assembly

And may by grant, lease, demise, assignment, bequest, representation, or otherwise, take and hold any lands, &c. for the purpose of residence, or of occupation by him, or his servants, or of business, trade, or manufacture, for not exceeding 21 years, and with the same rights, &c. except to vote at elections for Members of Assembly, or to be a Member of the Council or Assembly, as if they were natural born subjects, 14, Vic., c. 40, s. 3.

Not to affect pre-existing rights to 23 May, 1861

Act not to prejudice any rights or interests in law, or equity, whether vested or contingent under any will, deed, or settlement, executed by any natural born subject before it passed, or under any descent or representation from, or under any such natural born subjects, who have died before it passed, 14 V., c. 40, s. 4.

Nor to take away or diminish any right heretofore lawfully possessed by, or belonging to aliens residing so far as relates to the possession or enjoyment of any real or personal property, but they shall continue to be enjoyed as amply as before, 14, V. c. 40, s. 5.

Wives of natural born or naturalized subjects

Any woman married to a natural born subject, or person naturalized in this island, shall be deemed to be herself naturalized, and have all the rights and privileges of a natural born subject, 14 V. c. 40, s. 6.

Amendments.

Powers to order amendment of pleadings before trial by adding or striking out plaintiffs.

The Court or a Judge may at any time before trial order any person not joined as plaintiff to be so joined, or any person originally joined to be struck out, if it appear that injustice will not be done by the amendment, and the person to be added, consent in person or by writing under his hand, or if the person to be struck out was originally introduced without his consent or he consents as aforesaid to be struck out, the amendment to be made upon such terms as to amendment of pleadings, postponement of trial, and otherwise as the court or Judge thinks proper, and when made, the liability of the person added subject to any terms imposed, shall be the same as if he had been originally joined, 27, V., S. 1, c. 14, s.1.

Amendment at the trial in case of misjoinder or non-joinder or plaintiffs

If it appears at the trial that there has been a misjoinder of plaintiffs, or some person not joined ought to have been so, and the defendant at or before pleading did not give notice in writing that he objects to the non-joinder, specifying the name of the person, such misjoinder, or non-joinder, may be amended as a variance at the trial in like manner as to the mode of amendment and proceedings consequent thereon, or as near as circumstances will admit, as in cases of amendments of variances under 8 Vic. c. 28: if it appear to the Court, Judge, or Presiding Officer that the misjoinder or non-joinder was not to obtain an undue advantage, and injustice will not be done and the person to be added consent in person or by writing under his hand to be joined, or that the person to be struck out was originally introduced without his consent, or consents as aforesaid to be struck out, the amendment to be made upon such terms as the Court, &c. think proper, and when made the liability of any person added subject to any terms imposed, shall be the same as if he had been originally joined, 27 V. S. 1; c. 14, s. 2.

Amendments by plaintiff without order

If notice be given or any plea in abatement of non-joinder, of a person as co-plaintiff where such plea in abatement may be pleaded, the plaintiff may without any order amend the declaration and other proceedings be' fore plea, by adding the name of the person named in such notice or plea in abatement and proceed without any further appearance on payment of the costs of, and occasioned by such amendment only, and the defendant may plead denovo, 27 V. S. 1, c. 14, s. 3.

The Court or a Judge in case of the joinder of too many defendants, in any action on contract before trial, may order the names of one or more to be struck out if it appear injustice will not be done upon such terms as the Court, &c. thinks proper. If it appear at the trial there has been a misjoinder of defendants, it may be amended as a variance in like manner as misjoinder of plaintiffs and upon such terms as the Court, &c. think proper, 27 V. S. 1, c. 14, s. 4.

In any action or contract where the non-joinder, as co-defendant is pleaded in abatement, the plaintiff may without order amend the declaration by adding the names of the persons named in the plea of abatement as joint contractors, and serve the amended declaration upon the persons so named, and proceed against the original defendant, and such persons the date of such amendment as between him and the plaintiff, to be considered for all purposes as the commencement of the action, 27 V. S. 1, c. 1. s. 14 s. 5.

After such plea in abatement and amendment, if it appear upon the trial that the person named therein was jointly liable with the original defendant, the latter shall be entitled as against the plaintiff to the costs of the plea and amendment, but if it appear that the original defendant or any of the original defendants is or are liable, but one or more of the persons named in the plea in abatement is, or are not liable as contracting parties, the plaintiff shall be entitled to judgment against the others who appear to be liable; and every defendant not liable, shall have judgment and be entitled to costs as against the plaintiff who shall be allowed the same with the costs of the plea in abatement and amendment as costs in the cause against the original defendants who pleaded the non-joinder. Any defendant who so pleaded may on the trial produce evidence of the liability of the defendants named in his plea, 27 V. S. 1, c. 14, s. 6.

In any action by a man and his wife for an injury to the wife in respect of which she is necessarily joined as a co-plaintiff, the husband may add claims on his own right and separate actions in respect of such claims, may be consolidated, if the Court or a Judge think fit. In case of the death of either plaintiff the suit so far as relates to the causes of action if any which do not survive shall abate, 27 V. S. 1, c. 14, s. 7.

The joinder of too many plaintiffs shall not be fatal, but every action may be brought in the name of all the persons in whom the legal right is supposed to exist and judgment given in favor of the plaintiffs or one or more of them, or in case of any question of non-joinder being raised, then in favor of such one or more as shall be adjudged by the Court, entitled to recover. But the defendant though unsuccessful shall be entitled to his costs, occasioned by joining any persons in whose favor judgment is not given, unless otherwise ordered by the Court or a Judge, 27 V. S. 1, c. 14, s. 8.

Upon the trial a defendant who has pleaded a set off, may obtain the benefit of his set off, by proving either that all the parties named as plaintiffs are indebted to him, notwithstanding one or more were improperly joined, or that those who establish their right to maintain the cause are indebted to him, 27 V. S. 1, c. 14, s. 9.

No other action shall be brought against the defendant by any person so joined as plaintiff in respect of the same cause of Action, 27 V., S. 1, c. 14, s. 10.

The Supreme Court and every Judge and any Judge at nisi prius, or any Circuit Court, or other presiding officer may at all times amend all defects and errors in any proceeding in civil causes, whether there is anything in writing to amend by or not, and whether the defect or error he that of the party applying to amend or not, such amendment to be with or without costs and upon such terms as may seem fit, and all such amendments as may be necessary for the purpose of determining, on the existing suit, the real question in controversy between the parties, shall be made if duty applied for 27 V., S. 1, c. 14, s. 11.

The Judges shall at all times on motion in Court, order amendments, and shall not upon arrest of Judgment or writ of error for matter of form only, reverse any Judgment whatever, 33 C. 2, c. 23 s. 5.

Marginal notes:

Powers in case of misjoinder or non-joinder of defendant before trial.

Or at trial

Amendment by plaintiff where non-joinder of a co-defendant is pleaded in abatement to action on contract

Date of amendment, commencement of action

Judgment & costs

Evidence of liability

Action by husband and wife

Joinder of too many plaintiffs

Benefit set off

No other action by any person joined

Power to amend all defects and errors in civil causes

No judgment to be reversed for matter of form only

Appeals.

Appeal Courts.   The Judges within their Circuits shall exercise the jurisdiction in matters of Appeal, before exercised by the Chairman of Quarter Sessions, 19 V. c. 10, s. 19.

Short title.   " The Appeal Regulation Act 1857," 21 V., c. 22, s. 1.

Interpretation.   " Appellant" shall mean the party to any proceeding who gives notice of Appeal, requires a case to be stated for the opinion of the Supreme Court or a Judge. " Respondent" the opposite party. " Judgment," any conviction, judgment, order or other affirmative adjudication or any dismissal of or refusal to hear or adjudicate on any complaint, information or summons in a matter of summary jurisdiction, 21 V. c. 22, s. 2.

Who may appeal.   Any person aggrieved or affected by any judgment of any Justice exercising summary jurisdiction or by the decision or report of any other officer or body taking any proceeding or acting under any law, now or to be in force, whereby the right of appeal is allowed, may appeal to the Court of Appeal, of the Parish or precinct in which Judgment is pronounced or to the Supreme Court, or a Judge, as after provided, 21 V., c. 22, s. 3.

Right extended to future acts.   The right of appeal shall extend to all Acts already or to be passed giving summary jurisdiction to Justices or any other officer or body, unless where otherwise expressly provided, 21 V. c. 22, s. 4.

Parties to be informed of their right of appeal and furnished with notice and recognizance on payment of fees.   The Justice or other officer or body, when the person adjudicated against, appears ignorant thereof, shall instruct him of his right of appeal, and the Clerk, when required, and his fees are paid or tendered shall furnish to any appellant, the necessary notice and recognizance of appeal, 21 V. c. 22, s. 5.

Time within which to appeal—verbal or written notices, Grounds of appeal. Service on the Clerk, sufficient, 27 V. S. 1, c. 15, s. 7. Where the grounds are not apparent, 27 V. S. 1, c. 15, s. 1.   The appellant shall either during the sitting of the Court, or tribunal at which judgment is pronounced, give verbal notice of appeal, or within 14 days after judgment delivered, give a written notice of appeal, to the adjudicating Justices &c. and respondent, also within the 14 days, deliver to the Clerk of the Magistrates or other proper officer and to the respondent the grounds in writing of his appeal. The time shall not commence to run in the case of an affirmative judgment, until the copy of the conviction, order or adjudication has been drawn up and is ready for delivery to the appellant, 21 V., c. 22, s. 6.

Service of notice.   When verbal notice is given, the Clerk &c., shall make a minute thereof, which shall operate as a notice of appeal to the Justices &c., and to the respondent if present in person or by attorney or agent, if not notice of appeal shall be served in writing as provided in other cases within the 14 days after judgment, 21 V. c. 22, s. 7.

On Attorney or Agent, where sufficient. In other cases.   Where the respondent has appeared by attorney or agent, it shall be sufficient to serve them with notice and grounds of appeal. In other cases service may be made personally on the respondent, or at his place of residence or business, 21 V., c. 22, s. 8.

In case of death or absence from the island of respondent   In case of the respondent's death or absence from this island, service shall be made on his representative in the manner, and within the time directed to be made on the respondent, and in case of the respondent or his representative being out of the jurisdiction of the Court of Appeal, or of the respondent being absent or dead, and there being no representative, copies of the notice and grounds, shall be posted on the door of the Court House, of the parish, where the decision was made, and within the time limited for service. The destruction obliteration or taking down of any such posted copy, by any other than the appellant or his agent, or any person acting with his privity or assent, shall not prejudice, the appellant, 21 V. c. 22, s. 9.

Signature &c.   Not necessary to state in any written notice, that the appellant is aggrieved by the decision. Every notice shall be sufficiently signed, if signed by or on behalf of the appellant, with his name or mark, or the name of his Attorney, but if signed with his mark, the signature shall be attested by a subscribing witness, 21 V. c. 22, s. 10.

Recognizance to prosecute &c.   To entitle any person aggrieved or affected to appeal, the appellant shall within the 14 days provided for giving notice, enter into recognizance, with one or more sureties, in a sum sufficient in the case of a judgment, inflicting a penalty or awarding a sum of money, or costs to cover the penalty, or sum awarded and costs, and £3, for the costs of appeal if adjudged, and in case of judgment of dismissal or refusal so adjudicated in a sum to cover the costs of dismissal if awarded, and £3, for the costs of appeal in case they shall be adjudged and conditioned for the due prosecution of the appeal, and that the appellant perform and obey the judgment, orders and determinations of the appellate Court or Judge in the matter, and in case the judgment be affirmed that he will pay the penalty or sum adjudged, with all costs as well of the judgment, as of the Court of Appeal at such time as the Court or Judge shall direct, and where the appellant has been adjudged to imprisonment, in the first instance, the condition shall be that the appellant surrender himself into custody forthwith, to undergo the term of imprisonment adjudged, and that he pay all costs to be adjudged by the appellate Court or Judge in case the judgment is affirmed, 21 V. c. 22, s. 11.

Where an appellant is under legal disability, the recognizance of his surety shall be sufficient, 21 V. c. 22, s. 12. *Appellant under legal disability*

Any justice of the parish in which the judgment &c., is made or in which the appellant or his surety resides, may take the recognizance, 21 V. c. 22, s. 13. *By whom recognizance taken.*

The appellant shall give to the respondent notice of the names of his intended sureties, and of the time and place of entering into recognizance, and the justice taking it shall determine any objection raised by the respondent to the sufficiency of any surety, and require, if satisfied of his insufficiency, that another be tendered and shall require every surety to justify on oath, which he shall administer (Form A.) such oath to be written upon the recognizance, and no surety shall be accepted, who refuses or declines to justify. Surety taking false oath, guilty of perjury and punishable accordingly, 21 V. c. 22, s. 14. *Notice and justification of sureties* *False oath*

When notice has been given and served and recognizance entered into, execution or further proceedings shall be stayed, and the appellant if in custody, liberated until the judgment on appeal is given, or the appeal is withdrawn or not proceeded with on production of a certificate from the Clerk of the Court of Appeal, that the notice and recognizance have been entered into. In case of affirmation any imprisonment undergone before liberation to be reckoned as part of the imprisonment under such judgment, 21 V. c. 22, s. 15. *Stay of proceedings* *Imprisonment before liberation.*

If the appellant fail to serve notice and grounds of appeal and enter into recognizance, his right to appeal shall cease, and the party in whose favor judgment &c. was made, may forthwith enforce it, and any Justice, &c., may issue all necessary process for enforcing it, 21 V. c. 22, s. 16. *Appeal determined, on failure to give and serve notices and enter into recognizance. As to necessity of grounds, see 21 V. S. 1, c 15, s. 2.*

The Clerks of the Magistrates or proper officer (their legal fees being first paid or tendered) shall under penalty of £20, to be recovered before two Justices, supply every party applying, a certified copy of the evidence, proceedings and decision, 21 V. c. 22, s. 17. *Copies of evidence &c., to be supplied to parties applying on payment of fees*

Also under a like penalty, shall make up and certify and deliver to the Clerk of the Court of Appeal, the originals or copies of all original documents, and a copy of the evidence, proceedings and decision in every matter of Appeal, for the use of the Judge, not later than 14 days after the delivery of the judgment &c., 21 V. c. 22, s. 18. *As also for the appellate Judge To be paid by appellant & part of the costs, if allowed, 27 V, S. 1, c. 15, s. 6.*

The Clerk of the Court, on the first day of the sitting of the Circuit Court, shall make out a list of all Appeals, for hearing at such Court and deliver to the Judge such list with the certified documents or copies and copies of evidence, proceedings and decision, and grounds of appeal, furnished to him, 21 V. c. 22, s. 19. *To be delivered to him, by the Clerk of the Court, on the first day of Court.*

Either party to the proceedings may obtain from the Clerk of the Court, who shall have authority to sign summonses for witnesses with or without a clause requiring the production of books and documents in their possession and control in which any number of names may be inserted, and any person on whom any summons or copy although containing his name only shall be served and to whom at the same time, payment or a tender of his expences is made on the scale established with regard to witnesses, subpœnsed to attend any Circuit Court, and who refuses, or neglects without sufficient cause to appear, or if appearing to give evidence, or to produce any books or documents and also every person present in Court, required to give evidence and refusing to be sworn or to give evidence, or wilfully prevaricating shall be liable to be committed to Jail by the Appeal Court or Judge, for not exceeding 7 days, 21 V. c. 22, s. 20. *Summons for witness at appeal Court Failure to appear, &c.*

The Circuit Court shall be the Court of Appeal, for matters arising in every parish or precinct, 21 V. c. 22, s. 21. *Circuit Court, the Court of appeal.*

Every appeal shall be heard at the next succeeding Court, if it meet within one month after the perfection of the judgment, but if a longer interval occur, the appellant or respondent may require, and the Magistrates' Clerk transmit a transcript of the information, summons, evidence, conviction, *when appeal to be heard at succeeding Court of appeal. when before a Judge in chambers* order or judgment, and submit the same for adjudication before any Judge in Chambers, who shall thereupon, if he conceive the proceedings to be questionable, issue his summons to the opposite party to attend to show cause before him or any other Supreme Court Judge, why the judgment should not be quashed, but if the judgment on application of the appellant, appear to be valid, the Judge shall endorse his confirmation on the proceedings and return them into the office of the Clerk of the Magistrates, and upon the appearance, or default of appearance on any such summons by a Judge, he shall examine into the matter of appeal, and determine it finally, 21 V. c. 22, s. 22.

Conditions on which appeal to be heard. See now, 27 V. S. 1. c. 15, s. 22. No appeal shall be heard unless the appellant has served the notice and grounds of appeal, and entered into recognizance within the period limited, 21 V. c. 22, s. 23.

Practice in Court The following general rules of practice shall prevail in the Courts of Appeal :—

1. None but Barristers or Attorneys or Appellants and respondents, in person, shall be entitled to address the Court.

See 27 V. s. 1, c. 15, s. 12.
2. The appellant shall begin by proving that he has served the notice and grounds of appeal, and entered into recognizance as required.

The party asserting the affirmative shall begin, 27 V. S. 1, c. 15, s. 7.
3. The respondent if matters of fact are in issue, shall then produce his witnesses or evidence after which the appellant shall call witnesses or produce evidence in reply, which evidence or witnesses on both sides, shall be the same as were examined, and produced at the proceeding appealed from.

where necessary 27 V. S. 1, c. 15, s. 1.
4. If no matters of fact are in issue, but a question of law only is raised, the appellant will state his objections after proving his notice and grounds of appeal, and the recognizance, and the respondent will be heard in reply, 21 V. c. 22, s. 24.

Proof of service, of notice &c. Proof of service of the notice and grounds, may be made by affidavit sworn before the Judge, a commissioner for taking affidavits or master extraordinary of the Court of Chancery or Justice. Wilfully false statements in any such affidavit to be punished as perjury. The Judge if not satisfied with any affidavit, may require the service to be proved "viva voce" on oath. Any written admission of service of notice by the Justices shall be sufficient as far as they are concerned, 21 V. c. 22, s. 25.

See 27 V. c. 15, s 4

Amendments at hearing. The Court or Judge on the hearing, may amend any defect in form, in any proceedings, or the record, and if any variance appear between any matter in writing or in print, produced in evidence and the recital or setting forth in any proceeding, or the record, may cause the same to be amended, and the case shall proceed, and the proceedings be attended with the like effects with regard to the liabilities of parties, or of witnesses to be indicted for perjury, or otherwise as if no amendment had been made. The Court may direct any amendment to be made only upon terms, 21 V. c. 22, s. 26.

See s. 59.

No proceedings to be set aside for form. Every information, summons, order, conviction, warrant of distress, commitment or other proceeding, shall be valid and sufficient, in which the offence or claim is set forth in the words of the act, creating the offence or giving jurisdiction, or which follows the form given by any act, relating to the offence or claim, or the general form given by 13 V. c. 35, or any other Act, for the like purpose, and no proceeding shall be set aside for form merely, where it appears that the party was duly summoned and had notice of the offence charged or claim made against him, 21 V. c. 22, s. 27.

Amendment of recognizance, &c. See 27 V.S. 1 c. 15, s 5 Where any recognizance has been entered into, within the time required, but appears to have been informally entered into or drawn up or signed or stamped or to be otherwise defective or invalid, the Court or Judge may permit a new and sufficient recognizance to be entered into, but the trial shall not be delayed unless the appellate Judge, on application postpone it to the next Court, and no longer, and he may impose terms as to payment of costs to the respondent or otherwise. and the substituted recognizance shall be as valid as if it had been duly entered into at any earlier time as required, 21 V. c. 22, s. 28.

Evidence on appeal, see 27 V. c. 15, s. 5. The evidence taken and certified by the Magistrates' Clerk, at the hearing, shall be read and received, as the evidence in the case, unless the appellant and respondent, or either within 14 days after perfection of the judgment, signify to the Clerk of the Magistrates' his dissatisfaction therewith, in which case they or he may examine "viva voce" before the appellate Judge, and come prepared with the witnesses examined by the adjudicating

Justices, or any he requires, and no other than such as were examined or tendered and refused by the Justices, shall be called as witnesses on the appeal, nor other documentary evidence than was admitted or tendered and refused before such Justices, 21 V. c. 22, s. 29.

The Judge may administer oaths or take solemn affirmation where it may by law be taken instead of an oath. Wilful, false evidence shall be punished as perjury, and any party or witness, who appears to give false evidence, wilfully and corruptly may be committed and detained for examination on such charge of perjury, by any Justice of the parish, wherein the charge is made, and be dealt with as in other cases of perjury, 21 V. c. 22, s. 30. *Judge to administer oath. False evidence, perjury.*

The Judge may award costs not exceeding £3, in any case either heard before him or in which the notice of appeal and recognizance having been given the appeal is withdrawn or not prosecuted, 21 V. c. 22, s. 31. *Costs of appeal, 27 V. s. 1 c. 15, s. 3, 6*

The Court or Judge may respite or adjourn the appeal as often as Justice requires, 21 V. c. 22, s. 32. *Adjournment.*

If the decision is affirmed, the Judge shall endorse thereon "judgment affirmed" with his signature, if the appeal is not withdrawn or not proceeded with or prosecuted, he shall endorse, "appeal withdrawn" or "not proceeded with or "not prosecuted" and the amount of costs (if any) given by the Court of Appeal and thereupon any Justice of the parish wherein the proceeding took place, shall immediately on application by the party entitled, add the costs so given to any penalty or sum of money and costs if any ordered to be paid on the proceedings and issue all necessary warrants for the recovery of the whole by distress and sale or commitment or otherwise according to the forms given by the particular Act, or by any general Act, for enforcing summary orders or convictions, 21 V. c. 22, s. 33. *Judges endorsement of disposal of appeal, enforcement thereof, see s. 58.*

If the decision be affirmed and the principal make default in satisfying the judgment forthwith, any Justice of the parish wherein the decision was made, may issue process (Form B.) on the recognizance of the sureties for the recovery of the penalty or sum of money and costs, on the original proceedings, and on the appeal, if any which the appellant is liable to pay, as also 3s, for costs, on such process against any or every surety, 21 V. c. 22, s. 34. *Proceedings against sureties on recognizance.*

Payment by the appellant or any surety of the whole amount, which the appellant is liable to pay and of the costs for issuing process on the recognizance, shall be full satisfaction and discharge of all liability of the appellant and his sureties, 21, V. c. 22, s. 35. *Satisfaction of recognizance &c.*

The imprisonment of the sureties, shall not extend beyond the time to which the appellant is liable to be imprisoned by the act, under which he is convicted or ordered to pay the money and costs, or be otherwise committed, 21 V. c. 22, s. 36. *Limit of surety's imprisonment.*

If the decision be reversed the Judge shall endorse thereon "judgment reversed" with his signature and the amount of costs, if any are given, and the Judge or any Justice of the parish, may issue a warrant of distress for the costs against the goods of the respondent, and if no distress or insufficient distress is found then to commit the respondent to the nearest Jail or house of correction, without hard labor, not exceeding three calendar months, unless sooner paid. Any such warrant may be in the form provided by 13 V. c. 35 or any act for enforcing summary proceedings, 21 V. c. 22, s. 37. *Enforcement of decision, reversing judgment with costs.*

If the appellant from any cause, as from not having served or proved the service of the notice or grounds of appeal or from having given a defective recognizance or otherwise is not in a condition to carry on his appeal, and the decision is bad on its face, the Court may simply dismiss the appeal without affirming the decision. The Court or Judge may make such amendments, in matters of form only, as are authorized in other cases, and after amendment give the proper judgment, 21 V. c. 22, s. 38. *Dismissal of appeal from appellants not being in a condition to carry it on where the decision is bad on its face.*

If any person, wilfully insult the Judge or any officer of the Court, during its sitting, or attendance in Court, or in going to or returning from the Court, or wilfully interrupt its proceedings, or otherwise misbehave in Court or in the neighbourhood thereof, any police officer or constable, with or without the assistance of any other person or any constable, sworn specially for the purpose, may by the order of the Judge, take the offender into custody, and detain him until the rising of the Court, and the Judge may by warrant under his hand, commit the offender to prison, not exceeding seven days, 21 V. c. 22, s. 39. *Contempt of Court.*

No appeal from judgment admitted or conviction on a plea of guilty.

No party shall be entitled to appeal from a Judgment, order of dismissal, decision, report or determination, admitted or assented to by him, or his duly authorized Attorney or agent, or from a conviction entered upon a plea of guilty, 21 V. c. 22, s. 40.

Nor from a judgment by default except on special grounds on oath.

Nor from any judgment &c., which has gone by default, for want of appearance or otherwise unless he make affidavit in writting, setting forth his grounds of appeal and the reasons why he did not appear at the hearing or trial, and that such appeal is not made for delay, but to obtain substantial justice in the matter, to be filed along with a written notice of appeal, and a recognizance within the like period of 14 days, as limited in other cases, 21 V. c. 22, s. 41.

Case for opinion of the Supreme Court, may be submitted by the Judge or Justices on matters of law proceedings thereon.

The Judge or Justices or other body or officer, before whom any proceedings may be brought from which an appeal may be given, may transmit a case for the opinion of the Supreme Court, in matter of law or upon the construction of any act. And the Supreme Court after notice to the parties, and after hearing them, if they appear, shall certify its opinion thereon, under the seal of the Court, to the Court of Appeal Justices &c., and judgment shall thereupon be pronounced in accordance with the certificate, and carried into execution as a judgment of the Court of Appeal or Justices, &c., 21 V. c. 22, s. 42.

Power of parties to apply to Supreme Court for an Order on Justices to state a case for their opinion

After the hearing and determination or order of dismissal, or refusal to adjudicate, either party may if dissatisfied with the judgment as being erroneous in point of law, apply in writing within three days after to the Justice, to state and sign a case setting forth the facts and the grounds of such judgment or order for the opinion of the Supreme Court, and the appellant shall within fourteen days after receiving the case transmit it to the Clerk of the Supreme Court, first giving notice in writing of the appeal, with a copy of the case to the respondent, 21 V. c. 22 s. 43.

Appellant to enter into recognizance,

The app llant at the time of making application and before a case is stated and delivered to him by the Justices, shall in every instance enter into a recognizance before a Justice, with surety in such sum as to the Justice seems meet and subject to all the p s in respects to other recognizauces, and at the same time and before the case is delivered pay to the Clerk of the Magistrates or other officer his fees for the case and recognizance and any other fees he is entitled to, which fees except such as already provided for by law shall be according to schedule C., and the appellant if then in custody shall be liberated, 2 V. c. 22, s. 44.

Refusal of case by Justices.

If the Justice be of opinion that the application is merely frivolous but not otherwise, he may refuse to state a case and shall on the request of the appellant sign and deliver to him a certificate of refusal. The Justices shall not refuse to state a case where application is made to them by or under the direction of the Attorney-General, 21 V. c. 22 s. 45.

Proceedings thereon to compel case.

Where the Justices refuse to state a case the appellant may apply to the Supreme Court upon an affidavit of the facts for a rule calling upon them and respondent to show cause why such case should not be stated, and the Court may make the rule absolute, or discharge it with or without costs, and the Justices upon being served with the rule absolute shall state a case accordingly upon the appellant entering into recognizance as before provided, 21 V. c. 22, s. 46.

Powers of Supreme Court to determine on case.

The Supreme Court shall hear and determine the questions of law arising on any case transmitted at the instance of the Justices or other body or officer, or Judge of the Appeal Court or of any party and thereupon reverse, affirm, or amend the judgment, &c. or remit the matter to the Judge, &c. with the opinion of the Court thereon, or make such other order and such orders as to costs as may seem fit which shall be conclusive on all parties. No Justice. &c. who states and delivers a case shall be liable to any costs in respect of such appeal, 21 V., c. 22, s. 47.

To send it back for amendment

The Supreme Court may cause any case to be sent back for amendment and judgment shall be delivered after it has been amended, 21 V. c. 22, s. 48.

Judge in Chambers may exercise jurisdiction, but not appellate judge who stated case

The authority and jurisdiction of the Supreme Court for the opinion of which any case is stated may (subject to any rules of such Court in relation thereto) be exercised by a Judge in Chambers, and as well in vacation, as in term time—where the case is stated at the instance of any Judge of a Court of Appeal, he shall not exercise the authority and jurisdiction given by this section, 21 V., c. 22, s. 49,

After the decision in relation to any case the Judge, Justices, &c. in relation to whose judgment, &c. or at whose instance the case has been stated, or any other Justice exercising the same jurisdiction may enforce any conviction or order, and no action or proceeding shall be commenced or had against any Justice, &c. for enforcing such judgment, &c. by reason of any defect, 21 V. c. 22, s. 50.

Enforcement of decision on case

No writ of certiorari or other writ shall be required for the removal of any judgment, &c. in relation to which any case is stated for the judgment of the Supreme Court, 21 V. c. 22 s. 51.

No writ of certiorari

Where the conditions in the last mentioned recognizance have not been complied with the like proceedings shall be taken to enforce same as provided with respect to forfeited recognizances for the prosecution of appeals 21 V. c. 22, s. 52.

Enforcement of recognizance on case

Any person who appeals by requiring a case to be stated, shall be taken to have abandoned his right of appeal finally, and conclusively, 21 V. c. 22, s. 53.

Application for case. Abandonment of appeal

On any appeal from a dismissal or refusal to adjudicate, the Appellate Judge shall hear and determine the matter, and for that purpose exercise all the powers given to the Justices before whom the matter was originally brought for adjudication, and thereupon issue the necessary process and execution for enforcing such judgment, 21 V. c. 22, s. 54.

Appellate judge may enforce decision on appeal from a dismissal or a refusal to adjudicate

Penalties, the mode of recovering which is not prescribed, may be recovered before two Justices, and enforced by any Justice by the like proceedings as are provided by 13th V. c. 35, or any Act, for enforcing summary proceedings ; and the penalties, the appropriation whereof is not otherwise directed, shall be paid to the Receiver-General, to the credit of the General Revenue, 21 V. c. 22, s. 55.

Enforcement of penalties

The Supreme Court may make, and alter rules and orders to regulate the practice and proceedings in reference to all cases of appeal, 21 V. c. 22, s. 56

Rules of practice, &c.

The distringas and capias under s. 33, shall run into, and may be executed in any parish wherein any surety shall be found. If he be in any other parish than that, as of which he is described, or from which the process issues, the same shall on demand by the Constable charged with its execution, be endorsed by any Justice of the parish wherein he is found 21 V. c. 22, s. 58.

Execution of distringas and capias against surety out of parish.

The Appellate Judge or Court shall have independently of the powers before conferred the same powers in all respects to cause any judgment, &c. appealed from, and all proceedings connected therewith, amended, in like manner as the Courts of Assize, &c. may be, by any law now or to be in force, empowered to do, 21 V. c. 22, s. 59.

Power of appellate judge to order amendments. See amendments s. 7 V 8 1 C 14 s 11

It shall not be necessary for the appellant to serve any grounds of appeal with respect to objections apparent on the face of the proceedings, or of the evidence ; and the provisions of, 21 V. c. 22, are only obligatory when the grounds of appeal are not so apparent, 27 V. S. 1, c. 15, s. 1.

Grounds of appeal apparent on proceedings or evidence need not be served

21 V. c. 22 shall be construed liberally in favor of the right of appeal, and in case any formalities prescribed by the Act have been inadvertently or from ignorance, or necessity, omitted to be observed, the Appellate Judge, if the Justice of the case so require, may upon terms admit the appellant to impeach the judgment, &c. appealed from, 27 V. S. 1. c. 15, s. 2.

21 V 22, c to be construed liberally. Formalities

When notice of appeal is given, and the respondent is induced to incur any expense, and the appellant does not afterwards perfect or prosecute his appeal, the Court may award costs against him, 27 V. S. 1. c. 15, s. 3.

Costs on not perfected appeal

Service of notice of appeal upon the Clerk of the Justices shall be sufficient notice to those who adjudicated, 27 V. S. 1, c. 15, s. 4.

Service of notices for Justices on Clerk.

The Appellate Judge may refer the case back to the Justices for further investigation or further evidence, on any point on which he deems the evidence defective, and the Justices who tried the case, or any other two Justices on the application of the appellant or respondent, shall summon witnesses and take all evidence tendered which may bear on the case generally, or on the specific points referred to their investigation, 27 V. S. 1, c. 15, s. 5,

Reference back of case for further investigation

Certified copies under 21 V c 22 s 18.to be paid for ·by appellant and form part of costs

Notwithstanding 21 V. c. 22, s. 18, the certified copies of proceedings and evidence for the use of the Judge, shall be charged to, and paid by the appellant, and form part of the costs of appeal, if allowed, 27 V. S. I, c. 15, s. 6.

Practice on hearing

21 V. c. 22, s. 24 ch. 3, amended by requiring the party asserting the affirmative of the issue of fact, to begin, and the other to reply, 27 V. S. 1, c. 15, S. 7.

Clerk of appeal court not to practice therein

No Clerk of any Court of Appeal, Clerk of the Magistrates, or other officer, whose duty it is to receive or file any of the proceedings, shall practice in the Court, of which he is clerk or officer, or be concerned directly or indirectly, on behalf of any party appellant or respondent, in initiating, prosecuting to final judgment, or carrying out any appeal, 27 V. S. 1, c., 15, s. 8.

FORMS—21 V. c. 22.

A.

Justification s. 14

I. E. F., of the parish of 　　　　　, one of the sureties in the (above within, or annexed) recognizance, do solemnly and sincerely swear, that I believe I am worth over and above, all my just debts and liabilities, the sum of 　　　, of lawful money of Jamaica, in which I propose to be a surety of A. B. of &c. the appellant above (or within, &c.,) named.

　　　　Sworn before me, this 　　　　　day of 　　　　18

　　C. D., Justice of the Peace for

B.

Distringas and Capias 21 V c 22 s 34

Victoria, by the grace of God, of the United Kingdom of Great Britain and Ireland, Queen, and of Jamaica, Lady defender of the faith, &c.

To any lawful constable of the parish of 　　　　, greeting. You are hereby required and commanded, to levy the sum of pounds for the penalty and 3s for costs, upon the goods and chattels of 　　　, in the parish of 　　　, and immediately pay over the same money to 　　　of 　　　(here name and describe the respondent), and if you can find no sufficient goods or chattels to satisfy the same, then that you take the body of the said 　　　, and lodge him in the Gaol or prison of the said parish of 　　　,(or the Gaol or prison nearest to such parish), to be there detained, until discharged in due course of law, or unless the said sums be sooner paid; and hereof you are to make return at the first day of the Circuit Court, to be held in and for the said parish of 　　　, (or precinct of) on the 　　　day of 　　　, now next ensuing.

　　Given under my hand and seal, this 　　　　day of 　　　18

　　　　　　　　　　　　　　　　　　L. S.

C.

	s.	d
Clerk of the Magistrates' Fees, r. 44		
Taking note of Appeal	1	0
Notice of appeal when required to make out same	0	9
Each copy	0	3
Taking recognizance of appeal	1	0
Recognizance when required to prepare the same, exclusive of stamp	3	0
Taking justification and making out same	1	0
Certified copy of proceedings, for any party, 1s. per sheet, of 160 words		
For drawing case and copy, where the case does not exceed 6 legal sheets of 72 words each	10	0
Where case exceeds 6 legal sheets, for every additional folio	1	0
For certificate of refusal of case	2	0
Clerk of the Court of Appeals Fees.		
Filing recognizance	1	0
Entering appeal	1	0
Attending Court on argument and all other proceedings connected therewith	6	0
Entering up orders, each	1	0
For each copy	0	6
For signing each subpœna	0	9
Preparing subpœna when required	1	6
Each copy	0	6
Cost of distringas and capias	3	0

Apprenticeship of Minors.

Any householder carrying on or using any business, trade, handicraft, mystery or calling, may take persons under 16, with consent of their parent, guardian, or next friend, to be apprentices, and to be bound for 5 years at least, by indenture or other contract in writing, in original and duplicate, and executed by the parties to be bound, 4 V. c. 30, s. 1. *To whom apprentices may be bound, Conditions of indenture.*

Any master or mistress or his agent, may make complaint upon oath against any apprentice, before any Justice of the parish where he is employed for any misdemeanor, misconduct, ill-behaviour, negligence or absence, or if he has absconded, any Justice of the parish, where he is found or has been employed, upon complaint, on oath by the master &c., may issue his warrant for apprehending him, and any two Justices of such parish, may hear the complaint, and dismiss the same, or punish the offender by abating the whole or any part of his wages or allowances or otherwise by imprisonment, not exceeding 3 months, 4 V. c. 30, s. 2. *Complaints by masters to Justices.*

All complaints, differences and disputes between masters and apprentices concerning wages or allowance due to such apprentice, shall be heard by two Justices of the parish, where the apprentice is employed, who may examine any master, apprentice or witness and summon the master, and make order for payment of such wages or allowances to the apprentice as according to the terms of the indenture or contract, appear to be due and order the amount to be paid within such period as they think proper, and in case of refusal or non-payment shall issue their warrant, to levy the same by distress, and sale rendering the surplus if any to the owner, after payment of the sum awarded and charges of distress and sale, 4 V. c. 30, s. 3. *Complaints respecting wages,*
See as to costs, 13 V c 35, s 18, Justices.

Two Justices upon complaint on oath by or on behalf of any apprentice against his master of ill-usage (the master having been duly summoned to appear and answer, may impose upon conviction, a fine not exceeding £10 stg upon him as a punishment for such ill-usage, with costs if they think fit to be recovered as after directed, 4 V. c. 30, s. 4. *Complaints of ill-usage.*
See 13 V c 35 s 18,

The Justices who hear any complaint, may direct in addition to any other order the discharge of the apprentice, from his service, and the indenture or contract to be cancelled without fee, 4 V. c. 30, s. 5. *Justices may discharge apprentice.*

If any apprentice absent himself from the service of his master, before his apprenticeship expires without sufficient cause, he may at any time after when found, and apprehended, be compelled by order of two Justices of the parish, in which he contracted, or is found, to serve his master, for so long a time as he absented himself, unless he make satisfaction to his master, for the loss he sustained by such absence, and in case he refuses, the Justices making the order or any other Justices, may direct by warrant, that the apprentice be imprisoned not exceeding 6 months. No apprentice shall be compelled to do any service or make any compensation after 3 years, from the end of the term, nor for absenting himself, after attaining his majority, 4 V. c. 30, s. 6. *Absence from service.*

The Justices, if they direct any apprentice to be discharged, may take into consideration the circumstances, under which he is discharged, and make an order on the master, to refund all or any part of the premiums paid upon binding or placing him out, and if he neglect or refuse to refund the sums to the person directed in the order to receive them, may levy then by warrant of distress and sale, and if no sufficient goods whereon to levy, may commit the offender by warrant to the common Gaol, not exceeding 3 months, unless the sums ordered to be refunded, with costs and charges be sooner paid, 4 V. c. 30, s. 7. *Refund of premium on discharge,*

The Justices may examine any master, apprentice, or witness, and administer the necessary oaths, 4 V. c. 30 s. 8. *Power to examine master and apprentice,*

If any fine or penalty be not paid forthwith or at such time as the Justices direct, such or any two other Justices, may by warrant direct same and costs and charges to be levied by distress and sale, and in default of goods, may by warrant direct the offender to be imprisoned, not exceeding 3 months, unless sooner paid, 4 V. c. 30 s. 9. *Enforcement of penalties,*
One Justice, 13 V. c 35, s 29

Fines or penalties imposed, on any master, may at the discretion of the Justices be paid, to the use of the apprentice as compensation for the injury he has sustained, or to the treasurer of the parish, for the use of the poor. Those imposed on apprentices, to the master or to the use of the poor, of the *Application thereof.*

parish, notwithstanding the master may have given evidence, 4 V. c., 22, s. 10.

Hearing pro-
ceedings

When the Justices commencing proceedings, are prevented from attend-ing at the hearing or at any subsequent part of such proceedings , any other Justices may · hear the complaint or otherwise, and do all acts for enforcing orders, 4 V. 30, s. 11.

Protection from
suits.

No order or conviction shall be quashed for want of form nor any dis-tress, deemed unlawful, nor the party making it a trespasser, on account of any defect or want of form, in the summons, conviction, warrant of distress, or other proceedings, nor the party be deemed a trespasser, on account of any irregularity afterwards done by the party distraining, but the person ag-grieved, may recover satisfaction for the special damage, if any, in an action on the case, and no plaintiff shall recover for such irregularity if tender of sufficient amends, have been made by or on behalf of the party distraining before action, 4 V. c. 30, s. 13.

Appeal.

Any person aggrieved by any judgment &c., under 4 V. c. 30, may ap-peal, 5 V. c. 35, s. 2.

Apprentices, Parish.

How to be in-
dentured.

Members of the
corporation have
ceased to possess
the powers of Jus-
tices.

The Corporation of Kingston, and Justices and Vestry of other parishes, or such number of those bodies as may by law act, may by indenture under the hands and seals of two Justices, bind poor children apprentices, where and to whom they see convenient, till a male child attains 21, or a female that age, or marriage, which indenture, shall be as effectual, as if the child had been of full age, and by indenture of covenant, had bound himself or her self, and the Corporation and Justices and Vestry, may make such terms and agreements with the master or mistress, as may most effectually secure their care and maintainance, and instruction in useful trade and occupation, 7 G. 4, c. 26, s. 8.

Powers of Jus-
tices to hear com-
plaints.

Discharge ap-
prentice.

Any two of the Corporation or Justices upon complaint, or application by any apprentice, touching any mis-usage, refusal of necessary provision, cruelty, or other ill-treatment by his master, may summon the master to ap-pear before them, and examine into the complaint, and on proof upon oath to their satisfaction, whether the master be present or not, if service of the summons be also upon oath proved, may discharge the apprentice by war-rant or certificate, under their hands and seals, for which no fees shall be paid, 7 G. 4, c. 26, s. 9.

Punish offen-
ders.

And may also upon application or complaint upon oath, by any master against any apprentice touching any misdemeanor, mis-carriage or ill-behavi-our in his service (which oath they are empowered to administer) hear and ex-amine the same and punish the offender by commitment, to the house of cor-rection, to be held to hard labor, not exceeding one calendar month, or other-wise by discharging the apprentice, 7 G. 4, c. 26, s. 10.

Apprentice may
be punished for
misdemeanor

Where any parish apprentice is discharged, on account of any misde-meanor, mis-carriage or ill-behaviour, they may by warrant, punish the of-fender by commitment, to be kept to hard labor, for not exceeding three ca-lendar months, 7 G. 4, c. 26, s. 11.

Apprentice may
be compelled to
make satisfaction
for absence.

If any apprentice absent himself from the service of his master, before his apprenticeship expires, he shall at any time, when found be compelled to serve for so long a time as he has absented himself from service, unless he makes satisfaction to his master for the loss he has sustained by his absence, and so from time to time, as often as he shall without leave, absent himself from service before the term of his contract is fulfilled, and in case of refusal to serve or make satisfaction, the master may complain upon oath to any Justice of the parish where he resides, which the Justice is empowered to administer and issue a warrant for apprehending the apprentice and upon hearing the complaint, may determine what satisfaction shall be made, to the master, by such apprentice, and in case the apprentice shall not give security to make such satisfaction according to such determination, may commit him, not exceeding 3 months. No apprentice shall be compelled to serve for any time or term, or to make satisfaction to any master, after seven years after the end of the term, for which he has contracted to serve, 7 G. 4, c. 26, s. 12.

Any master may by endorsement on the indenture, or by other instrument in writing, with the consent of two of the Corporation or two Justices of the parish where the master dwells, testified under their hands, assign such apprentice to any person willing to take him for the residue of the term, provided such person at the same time, by endorsement upon the counterpart, or by writing under his hand, stating the indenture and the endorsment, and consent, declares his acceptance of the apprentice, and acknowledge himself bound by the agreements in the indenture on the part of the master, which may be in the form in schedule ; and in such case the apprentice shall be deemed to be the apprentice of the subsequent master, to whom the assignment is made ; and so from time to time, as often as it is necessary or convenient for any subsequent master to part with any apprentice, 7 G, 4, c. 26, s. 13. *Assignment of indenture by master.*

Any two of the Corporation or Justices, of the parish, where the master lives, on his application, requesting that the apprentice may be discharged, by reason that he is insolvent, or so reduced in his his circumstances as to be unable to maintain the apprentice, may enquire into the allegations, and discharge such apprentice, in case he find them to be true, 7 G. 14, c. 26, s. 14. *Discharge of apprentice on request of master*

If the master dies before the expiration of the term, the Corporation or Justices and Vestry, with the assent of two Justices, testified as aforesaid, may bind out the apprentice for the residue of the term. If any executor or administrator of the deceased master, desires to retain the apprentice for the residue of the term, and signifies his desire to the Corporation, or Justices, and Vestry, they may, with the assent of two Justices, testified as aforesaid, assign the indenture to the executor or administrator, for the residue of the term, 7, G. 4, c. 26, s. 15. *On death of master, to be bound for residue of term   Assignment to Executors*

The Clerk of the Common Council in Kingston, and Clerks of the Peace shall provide books at the expense of their parishes, and enter therein the name of every child, bound out by them as an apprentice, with the several other particulars required, according to schedule, such books to be kept in their respective offices, 7, G. 4, c. 26, s. 16. *Records of apprenticeship*

If they refuse, or neglect to provide and keep such books, or make such entry, or destroy, or permit to be destroyed any such books, or wilfully, and knowingly obliterate, deface, or alter any entry, so that it shall not be a true entry of the several particulars required, or wilfully and knowingly make a false entry, or permit, or cause the same to be done, or shall not produce, or lay such books before the Justices, or Corporation, for their signatures, or shall not deliver or tender, or cause, &c. such books to their successors in office, the offender shall on conviction before two Justices, on the oath of a credible witness, forfeit not exceeding £5 (£3 sterling), to be recovered by distress, and sale by warrant ; and in case sufficient distress cannot be found, or the penalties and forfeitures are not paid forthwith, the Justices shall by warrant commit him for not exceeding one calendar month, unless sooner paid, 7, G. 4, c. 26, s. 17. *Penalty for neglect*

Any person may at seasonable hours, inspect such books in their office, and take a copy of such entry, upon payment of 1s. 8d. (1s. sterling), and every such book shall be sufficient evidence of the existence of the indentures, and of the particulars specified in the register, 7, G. 4, c. 26, s. 18. *Inspection of books   Books evidence*

The Convictions shall be in the following form :— *Conviction.*

Be it remembered, that on the   ·day of   in the year of Our Lord   A. B. is convicted before us two of His Majesty's Justices of the Peace for the   (specifying the offence and the time and place when and where, committed as the case may be), contrary to an act made in the seventh year of the reign of King George the Fourth, entitled "An Act to enable the Justices and Vestrymen of the several parishes of this Island, by the acquisition and settlement of lands to furnish relief for paupers and promote habits of industry among them, to enable the Corporation of the City of Kingston, and the Justices and Vestrymen of the several parishes of this island, to bind out apprentices, and for other purposes."

Given under our hands and seals, the day and year above-mentioned, 7 G. 4 c. 26 s. 19.

When any apprentice is assigned or bound over to any other master, the Clerk of the Common Council or Clerk of the Peace, shall insert the name and residence of the master to whom the apprentice is assigned, with the other particulars in the books, to be provided and kept, and for non-performance, shall be liable to the penalties incurred in like manner, as if the apprentice had been originally bound to such master. Powers of appeal. No writ of certiorari shall issue to remove any proceedings into the Supreme Court, 7, G. 4, c. 26, s. 20. *Record of assignments   Appeal*

ARBITRATION.

SCHEDULE.

Form of Assign-
ment, s. 13

Parish of { Be it remembered that the within named   by
{ and with the consent and approbation of   and
two of Her Majesty's Justices of the Peace, for the said parish, whose
names are subscribed to the consent, hereunder written, doth hereby assign
            the apprentice within named unto   to
serve him (or her) during the residue of the term within mentioned, and
that he the said   doth hereby agree to accept and take
the said   , as an apprentice, for the residue of the said term,
and doth hereby acknowledge himself (or herself) to be bound by the agreements and covenants within mentioned on the part of the said
to be done and performed. In witness whereof, we the said (former and
new master) have hereunto set our hands, this   day of

We, two of Her Majesty's Justices of the Peace above mentioned, do
consent thereto, witness our hands, this   day of

FORM OF THE REGISTER.—S. 16.

No.	Date of Indenture.	Name of the Apprentice.	Sex.	Age.	His or her parents, or reputed parents name.	Their Residence.	Name of person to whom bound or assigned.	His or her Trade.	His or her Residence.	Term of the Apprenticeship or assignment.

Apprentices—Persons under 16 convicted of certain Larcenies.

Any two Justices exercising summary jurisdiction, may apprentice to any householder, carrying on business, or trade, handicraft, mystery, or calling, or to any proprietors of estates, pens, or plantations, as labourers, or to look after live stock, or to families as domestic servants, willing to take them for five years, any person under 16, convicted of stealing or of distroying, or damaging, with intent to steal any tree, plant, root, fruit, or other vegetable, production growing in any garden, orchard, provision ground; or cane, or coffee, or pimento field, whether inclosed or not, or of the larceny of other articles of produce, or small stock, the value whereof shall not exceed 10s., and who may be reported and proven to their satisfaction, to be leading an idle and vagrant life, not attending any school, or not being sufficiently under the control of their parents, such apprenticeship, so soon as entered into to be in lieu of any punishment or portion of punishment authorized by 27, V. c. 33, or any Act amending same, or in aid thereof, 28 V. c. 19 s. 1. *Powers of two Justices to apprentice persons under 16, convicted of certain offences*

In lieu of any or a portion of punishment under 27 V. c 33, &c

The Apprentices and their Masters or Mistresses shall be subject to the provisions of 7 G. 4. c. 26 s. 8—20, 4 V., c. 30, and 5 V., c. 35, except that it shall not be required, to obtain the consent of the parents to such apprenticeship, nor as by 4 V., c. 30, s. 5, to discharge such apprentice, and direct his other indenture to be cancelled; but on hearing and determining any complaint against any Master or Mistress, two Justices may transfer the indenture of the apprentice to any other parties who agree to take him for the unexpired time, and the transfer shall be under their hand and seal, 28 V. c. 19, s. 2. *Subject to provisions of 7 G, 4, c 26, 4 V, c 30, and 5 V, c 35, except as altered*

It shall also be required of the Master, &c. of the apprentice, to give him during a part of one day in each week, moral and religious instruction, or to appoint a competent person to do so, 28 V., c. 19, s. 3. *Religious instruction*

Arbitration.

The power of any Arbitrator or Umpire, appointed by, or in pursuance of any Rule of Court, or Judges order, or order of Court of Assize, in any Action, or by any submission to reference, containing an agreement that it may be made a Rule of the Court of Chancery or Supreme Court, shall not be revocable without the leave of the Court, or a Judge, and the Arbitrator or Umpire shall proceed with the reference, notwithstanding any revocation, and make such award, although the party making the revocation does not afterwards attend the reference; and the Court, or a Judge may, from time to time, enlarge the term for making the award, 8 V., c. 28, s. 17. *Under order of Court or Judge irrovocable*

Enlargement

When any reference is made by any Rule or order, or by submission, containing such agreement, the Court or a Judge may, by Rule or order, command the attendance and examination of any person to be named, or the production of any document to be therein mentioned, and disobedience shall be a contempt of Court; if in addition to the service, an appointment of the time and place of attendance, signed by one at least of the Arbitrators, or the Umpire before whom the attendance is required, is served either with, or after service of the Rule. The person whose attendance is required, shall be entitled to the like conduct money and payment of expences as for attendance at any trial. The application for the Rule shall set forth the parish where the witness is residing, at the time, or satisfy the Court or Judge, that he cannot be found. No person shall be compelled to produce any writing or document he would not be compelled to produce at a trial, or to attend at more than two consecutive days, to be named in such order, 8 V. c., 28, s. 18. *Enforcement of examination and production of documents*

Witnesses' expences

If it is ordered or agreed the witnesses shall be examined, on oath, the or Umpire, or any one Arbitrator, may administer an oath to them, or take Arbitrator their affirmation, where affirmation is allowed instead of oath. False evidence, perjury, 8 V. c. 28, s. 19. *Arbitrator may administer an oath,*

Any Arbitrator, having, by Law, or consent of parties, authority to hear, receive, and examine evidence, may administer an oath to all witnesses, 20 V. c. 19, s. 11. *As also where the arbitration is by consent*

Arms and Ammunition.

Prohibition of exportation

The Governor may issue a Royal Proclamation, prohibiting, for such time as appears to him necessary, and the exigency of things requires, the exportation of any description of Arms or Ammunition, without a license, under his hand, or unless such other regulations are complied with as are declared in the Proclamation, 11 V., c. 4, s. 1.

Harbour Master's to enforce Proclamation. (See 25, V. c, 23, s. 3, same powers to Customs' Officers)

The Harbour Masters shall go on board every vessel trading to, and from this island, or in any wise departing, or about to depart from any port, harbour, road, bay, creek, haven, or quay, contiguous to such port, and examine and see that it does not carry out at any time Arms or Ammunition prohibited; and all persons shall aid and assist them in making such examination; and in case the Master or any other person belonging to the ship, in any wise resist any such person in making such examination, he shall suffer three months' imprisonment in Gaol, on conviction before three Magistrates, 11 V., c. 4, s. 2.

Forfeiture and penalty

If any Arms or Ammunition are found on board any ship for the purpose of exportation contrary to Proclamation, the same shall be a forfeiture and confiscation thereof, and the Master shall be subject to a penalty of £120, one moiety to the Crown, and the other to the informer, and the Master shall suffer the further punishment of six months' imprisonment in Gaol, on conviction before three Magistrates, 11 V., c. 4, s. 3.

Recovery of penalties

Penalties shall be recovered before three Justices, who may commit the offender to Gaol, not exceeding twelve months, unless he sooner pay the same, 11 V., c. 4, s. 4.

Seizure and condemnation of Arms &c.

The Officers of the Customs, the Commanders of Forts, Harbour Masters, and Officers commanding ships of War, may stop and detain any ship having on board any description of Arms or Ammunition, with intent to be exported contrary to Proclamation, and seize them, and proceed to condemnation, in the Supreme (or Circuit Courts, 19 V. c. 10), 11 V., c. 4, s. 5.

Disposal of sale monies

One moiety of the monies to arise from the sale, shall be to the informer, and the other to the Crown, 11 V., c., 4, s. 6.

Duration of Act

Act in force until the 31st December, 1852, 11 V., c. 4, 7.

Further continuance

Further continued until 31st December, 1867, 26 V. S. 1, c. 1, s. 1.

Convertible articles

The Governor may by Proclamation in the "Jamaica Gazette," prohibit the exportation to any place beyond this island of any saltpetre, sulphate of potash, muriate of potash, (chloride of potassium) nitrate of soda, gunpowder, brimstone, percussion caps, tubes, lead, arms, or ammunition of war, 25 V., c. 23, s. 1;

Which articles shall be deemed ammunition within, 11 V., c. 4, 25 V., c. 23, s. 2

Powers of Customs' Officers

All powers possessed by the Harbour Masters of going on board and examining any ship for preventing the export of articles prohibited, are conferred on the officers of the Customs, 25 V., c. 23, s. 3.

Proclamation

The Governor may by subsequent Proclamation in the "Gazette", revoke any Proclamation under this Act, 25 V., c. 23, s. 4.

Convertible articles

Articles exported contrary to 25 V. c. 23, shall be deemed Ammunition within 11 V., c. 4, 26 V. S. 1, c. 1, s. 2.

Arrest.

Service

Warrants of Arrest may be served at any time, 33, C. 2, c., 23, s. 10 (see Court Supreme.)

Affidavit of debt

Endorsement on declaration.

No person shall be arrested or held to special bail unless on affidavit, or if a Quaker, a solemn affirmation is made of the cause of action before a Judge or Commissioner to take affidavits fee 1s. (9d. sterling), and the sum specified in the affidavit shall be endorsed on the back of the declaration, delivered with the writ of process to the Provost Marshal for which, and no more he shall take bail. If no affidavit and endorsement are made, the Provost Marshal shall not execute the writ, 26 G. 2, c. 2.

When it lies

No person shall be arrested upon mesne process in any civil action except as after provided, 8 V., 48, s. 1.

If a Plaintiff by the affidavit of himself, or of some other person shew to the satisfaction of a Judge that the plaintiff has a cause of action against the defendant to an amount exceeding £6, or has sustained damage to that amount, and that there is probable cause for believing the defendant is about to quit this island, unless forthwith apprehended, such Judge may by a special order endorsed on the affidavit, direct that the defendant be held to bail for such sum as he thinks fit, not exceeding the amount of the debt, or damages and costs, and thereupon the plaintiff may within the time expressed in the order, but not afterwards, sue out one or more writs of attachment into one or more parishes, as the case requires against any defendant so directed, to be held to bail in the form heretofore used in cases of arrest on mesne proces. Act to extend to all freeholders, 8 V. c. 48, s. 2. *(Affidavit to ground Sec 21, V, c 13 / Order thereon / Attachment / Extended to freeholders)*

Any person having cause of action for which a writ of attachment can now by Law issue (whether already, or intended to be instituted,) and unable to apply to a Judge for his fiat for the arrest of the debtor, or party liable, may apply to any Justice of the Peace, and upon affidavit, setting forth a cause of action as aforesaid, and the grounds of belief and probability that the debtor or party liable is about to quit the island before an application can be made to, and proceedings perfected before a Judge, the Justice may issue a writ of attachment, in the form heretofore in use, to hold the debtor or party liable to bail to appear to answer such action as has been or shall be filed against him in the Supreme Court, and the affidavit shall be entitled in the Supreme Court and in the cause if pending, and be sworn to either before a Commissioner, or the Justice issuing the same, and the writ shall be tested in the name of, and be signed by such Justice, and bear date the day of its issue, and it shall not be necessary to recite therein the facts and circumstances giving rise to the exercise of his substitutional jurisdiction, 21, V. c. 13 s. 1. *(Application to a Justice in the absence of a Judge)*

The Writ of Attachment whether originally or substitutionally issued by a Justice, may run into, and be executed in any parish other than that of the particular jurisdiction of the Justice signing it, 21 V. c. 13 s. 2. *(May be executed out of justices' jurisdiction)*

The party suing for the writ in either of the modes provided, may apply to the Court, or a Judge for liberty to issue an an alias writ or writs where the defendant is not taken on the first or subsequent writs; and in the event of any previously issued writ being in the hands of the Sheriff for execution, and the party chargable has evaded the same, and on being discovered or traced the writ already issued cannot be brought to bear upon him, any Judge or Justice, whether or not the original writ is issued by a Judge, may issue a further writ in aid for execution in the same or any other parish as often as occasion requires, such further writs in aid shall be grounded on affidavit sworn to before the Judge or Justice, to whom application is made or a Commissioner, stating the fact of the issue of the former writ, and the belief of their evasion and the probability of the party still further evading the same, and the authority for the issue of such writ in aid shall extend to, and be exercised by a Judge or Justice, interchangably in all cases whether originally issued by a Judge or a Justice. But resort shall only be had, substitutionally to a Justice, in the event of a Judge not being accessible, and such fact shall appear on the affidavit by which the Justice is sought to be set in motion, and such writs in aid shall simply recite the issue of the former writ and its apprehended evasion, and shall be otherwise in the form heretofore in use, and be directed to the Provost Marshal, but may be delivered in the absence of any deputy, to any constable or peace officer, and shall authorize the capture and delivery by him of the party named therein, to the custody of the Provost Marshal, under the original writ, 21 V., c. 13, s 3 *(Writs in aid / Grounded on affidavit / Caption by a constable)*

Upon every Writ of Attachment shall be endorsed the sum of the debt or claim for which bail shall be directed to be taken, as also the amount of costs of the attachment and action as fixed by the Judge or Justice, 21 V. c. 13, s. 4. *(Debt and costs to be endorsed on writ)*

The Provost Marshal or his Deputy, or other Officer charged with the execution of the writ, shall arrest the party indicated, and detain him in custody until he has paid the debt or claim and costs endorsed on the writ, and the fees of the arrest, or has given a bail bond with good and sufficient security to the Provost Marshal or other Officer, in a sum sufficient to cover the amount of principal, interest, costs, and charges, and conditioned for his appearance to the action already, or to be filed, and that the defendant shall at the time of appearance enter into fresh or further bail to the action above, if *(Arrest and detention of defendant until payment or bail / Bail bond)* the surety below is excepted to and deemed insufficient, and in that case will then and there surrender himself into custody under the writ; but if unexcepted to that, the surety below will be answerable for such amount of damages and costs as shall be recovered in the action, and for all fees incurred on the arrest, or that the defendant will render himself in execution and satisfaction of the judgment, and the plaintiff shall have fourteen days after appearance of the defendant to except to the bail, 21 V., c. 13, s. 5.

Time for exception to bail

In lieu of a bail bond the defendant may deposit with the officer arresting, the amount for which he is directed to be held to bail, and the money so received as a deposit by the Provost Marshal or other Officer under a Supreme Court writ, shall be forthwith returned into the Provost Marshal's Office, and be thereupon deposited by him in the Public Treasury to the credit of an account to be opened by the Receiver-General, to be called "The Common Law Suitors' Fund"; the moneys so invested only to be paid out under an order of the Court or a Judge, 21 V. c. 13, s. 6.

Deposit of damages and costs

If the defendant pays the amount of the claim and costs in satisfaction and not as a deposit, the costs shall be forthwith taxed, and the amount of the debt or claim and costs as taxed paid forthwith to the party suing out the writ, and the surplus if any after satisfaction of the fees for arrest paid to the defendant, 21 V., c. 13, s. 7.

Payment in satisfaction

A Writ of Attachment may be issued after verdict and before execution, and in such case shall direct the defendant to be held to bail to answer the debt or damages awarded or assessed, and the costs if taxed; but if not then taxed, such sum as they shall be sworn to amount to with such further sum as shall also be sworn to as likely to be incurred for the costs and fees of the arrest. and it shall not be necessary to file an action against the principal debtor on the original cause of action or on the judgment to be entered on such verdict; but the surety in the bail bond to be taken on such arrest, shall be bound on the perfection of the judgment to satisfy the debt, damages, and costs of judgment, as well as the costs of arrest which shall be included in, and form costs of the judgment, or to surrender the principal in execution and satisfaction of the same, and the bail bond shall be conditioned to such effect, 21 V., c. 13, s. 8.

Attachment between verdict and execution

Condition of bail bond thereunder

If there be no cause pending in Court at the time of the issue of a writ of attachment, and the same directs the party to be held to bail to answer an action to be filed it shall unnecessary to issue such action for service on the defendant, but the filing of the same and leaving a copy for the defendant with the Clerk of the Court on, or before the day fixed for the defendant's appearance shall be sufficient service on him, and unless appeared to, shall be marked default, and the appearance of a defendant to any such action to be filed, shall be entered in the Supreme Court, within fourteen days, after the execution of the writ; but if there are not so many days between the execution of the writ and the meeting of the Court, as of which the action dates, or the writ is returnable, then the appearance shall be entered on the first day of such succeeding Court, without regard to the date of the arrest, 21 V. c. 13 s. 9.

Service of action unnecessary— appearance

On the issue by a Judge of a writ, away from Spanish Town, or in the absence of the Clerk of the Court, the writ shall be signed by the Judge, and handed directly to the Provost Marshal, or other Officer for execution, without the necessity of filing the affidavit or writ in the first instance, in the office of the Clerk; but the proceedings shall, nevertheless, be forthwith thereafter returned into Court and filed with the proper Officer, 21 V., c. 13, s. 10.

Issue of writ before proceedings filed

The person arrested may apply at any time to the Supreme Court or a Judge for a rule to shew cause why he should not be discharged, and the Court or Judge shall determine such rule, and direct the costs of the application to be paid by either party, or make such other order as may seem meet. Any order of a Judge may be discharged or varied by the Court, 21 V. c. 13, s. 11.

Application for discharge

The Provost Marshal executing a writ by himself or his Deputy shall be entitled to a poundage fee or every capture thereunder of 5 per cent. on the amount for which the party is arrested, to be paid in the first instance by the plaintiff, but to be recovered from the defendant as part of his costs in the event of his success, 21 V. c. 13, s. 12.

Poundage

The Provost Marshal shall be entitled in addition to the following fees, to be paid and recovered as before mentioned —

On the execution of the writ ..   ..   5s.

Further fees

For mile money from the office of the Provost Marshal in Spanish Town to the Parochial Town of the Deputy, to whom the precept may be directed, 1d. per mile, if the writ be issued through the Clerk of the Court's Office.

For mile money for the first mile, and for each additional mile from the Parochial Town of each parish to the place to which the officer may have to travel for the apprehension of the debtor, ... 1s.

For mile money in the City of Kingston, 3s., 21 V., c. 12, s. 13.

The Mesne Process Act 1857, 21 V., c. 13, s. 15.

Short title

Where any defendant is taken or charged in custody and imprisoned, or detained in custody for want of sureties for appearance, and the prisoner does not appear and plead to the action on, or before the usual plea day, the plaintiff shall have default entered on the action and be at liberty to proceed therein as is usual upon other actions whereon defaults are entered. If the plaintiff do not proceed to final judgment within two Courts after default entered, the defendant shall be discharged out of custody, 51 G. 3, c. 28.

Where the Provost Marshal takes bail, and the bond is forfeited he shall assign it to the plaintiff, at whose suit the arrest issued, by subscribing his name in the presence of one witness to an assignment endorsed upon the bond in Form, as follows :—

I do hereby assign the within bond unto   , according to an Act of the Lieutenant-Governor, Council, and Assembly of this island, in such case made and provided.

And the Assignee, his Executors, or Administrators may bring actions against the bail, in their own names, and having obtained judgment mark on Writs of Venditioni Exponas, to be thereupon issued such levy as they may be entitled to mark on writs to be issued on the judgment in the original action, and also a further levy for the costs of the action upon the bail bond. If the defendant in the original action, at any time, before judgment obtained on the bail bond, appears and gives bail by manucaption to answer the condemnation with costs in case of judgment upon the original action, the bail bond shall be void, and the action, if any, discontinued upon payment of costs. No Writ of Venditioni shall be issued upon a judgment on a bail bond until judgment has been previously had in the original action, 25 G. 3, c. 9, s. 1.

Arsenic, Sales of

Every person who sells Arsenic, shall forthwith, and before delivery to the purchaser, enter or cause &c., in a fair and regular manner, in a book to be kept by him for the purpose. (Form Schedule, or to the effect) a statement of the sale, quantity and the purpose for which it is required or stated to be required, and the day of the month and year, and the name, place of abode, and condition or occupation of the purchaser, into all which circumstances, he shall enquire of the purchaser, before delivery of the Arsenic, such entries to be signed by the person making them, and by the purchaser unless he profess to be unable to write (in which case the person making the entry, shall add to the particulars " cannot write") and where a witness is required to the sale, shall also be signed by him, with his place of abode, 15 V. c. 7, s. 1.

No person shall sell Arsenic, to any person unknown to him, unless in the presence of a witness, known to the person selling, and to whom the purchaser is known, and who signs his name, and place of abode, to such entries before delivery. No person shall sell arsenic to any other than a person of full age, 15 V. c. 7, s. 2.

Nor unless it be before sale, mixed with soot or indigo in the proportion of one ounce of soot or half an ounce of indigo, at least, to one pound of the Arsenic. Where the Arsenic is stated to be required, not for use in agriculture, but for some other purpose, for which such admixture would according to the purchaser's representation, render it unfit, it may be sold without admixture in a quantity of not less than 10 lbs. at any one time, 15 V. c. 7, s. 3.

Default on actions where defendant in custody does not appear and plead

Final judgment within 2 Courts

Assignment of forfeited bond

Proceedings thereon

Venditioni.

Entry of sale

Sales to persons unknown to seller.

Only to persons of full age

To be mixed with soot, or indigo, or sold in quantity not less than 10 lbs

Penalties

If any person sells any Arsenic, save as authorized, or on sale, delivers it without having made and signed the entries or obtained, the signatures required or if any purchaser gives false information to the person selling in relation to the particulars, he is authorized to enquire into, or if any person sign his name as a witness to a sale to a person unknown to him, the offender shall on summary conviction, before two Justices, be liable to a penalty, not exceeding £5, 15 V. c. 7, s. 4.

Medical prescriptions, sales by wholesale

Not to extend to the sale of Arsenic, when it forms part of the ingredients of any Medicine, required to be made up or compounded according to the prescription of a legally qualified Medical Practitioner, or a member of the medical profession, or to the sale of Arsenic, by wholesale, to retail dealers, upon orders in writing in the ordinary course of wholesale dealing, 15 V. c. 7, s. 5.

Interpretation

" Arsenic" to include " Arsenious Acid" and the Arsenites Arsenic Acid and the Arseniates, and all other colorless, poisonous preparations of Arsenic, 15 V. c. 7, s. 6.

SCHEDULE.—S. 1.

Date of Sale.	Name and Surname of Purchaser.	Purchasers' Place of Abode.	Condition or Occupation.	Quantity of Arsenic Sold.	Purpose for which Required.

Purchaser's signature, if purchaser cannot write, Seller to put here the words " cannot write."

Witness.

Seller's signature.

Assembly.

In every Assembly, there shall be chosen three representatives for St. Catherine, the like number for Port Royal, and two for each other of the parishes, that now are or shall be in this island, and the Provost Marshal or his deputy, shall give to every person elected within 10 days after his election, notice that he is so elected. Every person elected, shall be a freeholder, 33 C. 2, c. 1.

Representatives

See 22 V. c. 18, s. 1, 3.

There shall be chosen three representatives for Kingston, 5 W. & M. c. 3, s. 1.

Kingston

No Assembly shall continue longer than seven years, at the furthest, from the day on which by the writ of summons, it is appointed to meet 20 G. 3, c. 3, s. 1.

Duration

Not to impeach any power the Governor has of dissolving any Assembly sooner, if he thinks fit, 20 G. 3, c. 3, s. 2.

Previous dissolution

The Act 2, (vulgo 1) Jas. 1, c. 13. relative to persons delivered out of execution, by privilege of parliament, declared to be in force and to comprehend and apply to attachment or other process of the Court of Chancery, or any other Court against the person. After the privilege of Assembly ceases, the party at whose suit the writ of Venditioni Attachment, or other process was pursued, his attorney, executors or administrators may sue forth and execute new writs, as if no former writ had been taken forth or served, 31 G. 3, c. 4.

Privilege from execution

No Member of the Council or Assembly, who has qualified or acted as executor, administrator, receiver, trustee or guardian, shall be exempted from attachments out of Chancery, on refusing or neglecting to obey any decree or order to account for monies come into his possession as executor &c., or to deliver possession to a receiver appointed by the Court, of the estate so coming into his possession as executor &c. Notice of such attachment to be served personally on such Member. Not to deprive him of his personal liberty during the sittings of the Council or Assembly, or 14 days immediately following the prorogation of a Session in which the Council and Assembly have met for the despatch of business, 9 G. 4, c. 6.

Attachments Chancery

Whenever a petition complaining of an undue election or return of a Member to serve in Assembly is presented, a day and hour shall be by the House appointed for taking it into consideration, and notice forthwith given by the Speaker to the petitioners and sitting members or their agents, with an order to them to attend the House, at the time appointed, by themselves, their counsel or agents. The House may alter the day and hour, and appoint some subsequent day and hour, giving to the parties the like notice of alteration, and order to attend on such subsequent day and hour, 41 G. 3, c. 18, s. 1.

Controverted elections

Appointments to consider petition against undue return.

See as to previous notice of scrutiny lists of objections &c. 22 V c. 5, s 20 to 27, 24 V c. 8.

If several parties on distinct interests or grounds of complaint present separate petitions, the like notice and orders shall be given to all or their agents. No petition shall be taken into consideration within 7 days after it is presented, but every petition shall be presented within 14 days after the return, to which it relates, is brought into the House, 41 G. 3, c. 18, s. 2.

Several petitions petition not to be considered within 7 days after presentation, to be presented within 14 days after return

On the day appointed, the House shall not proceed to any other business, except the swearing of members, previous to the reading of the order of the day, for that purpose, and at the time appointed, and previous to reading the order of the day, the Sergeant-at-Arms shall be directed to go to the places adjacent, and require the immediate attendance of members, and after his return, the House shall be counted, and if there be less than 25 members present, the order shall be immediately adjourned to a particular hour on the following day (Sunday and Christmas day excepted) and the House shall adjourn to that day, and the proceedings of all committees, subsequent to the notice from the Sergeant-at-Arms shall be void On the following day, the House shall proceed in the same manner, and so from day to day, until there is an attendance of 25 members, at the reading of the order of the day, 41 G. 3, c. 18, s. 3.

Proceedings on and after the day appointed, until 25 members attend

If after summoning members and counting the House, 25 members are present, the petitioners by themselves, their counsel or agents, and the counselor agents, for the sitting members, shall be ordered to attend at the bar, and then the door of the House be locked and no member suffered to enter into or depart from the House, until the petitioners, their counsel or agents, and those for the sitting members are ordered to withdraw. When the door is locked, the order of the day shall be read, and the names of all the mem-

Ballot for committee

bers, written or printed on distinct pieces of parchment or paper, all as near as may be of equal size and rolled up in the same manner, shall be put in equal numbers into two boxes or glasses to be placed on the table, and there shaken together, and the Clerk shall publicly draw out of the two boxes or glasses alternately, the pieces of parchment or paper, and deliver them to the Speaker, to be read to the House, and shall so continue to do until 19 names of members then present are drawn. If the name of any member, who gave his vote at the election or against whose return a petition is depending, or whose return has not been brought in 14 days, is drawn, his name shall

Setting aside and excusing members be set aside, with the names of those who are absent. If the name of any member, who has served upon such select committee, during the same Session, be drawn, he shall, if he requires, be excused from serving again, unless the House has resolved that the number of members, who have not served on such select committee, in the same Session, is insufficient to fulfill the purposes of this act, respecting the choice of such select committee, but no member, who after having been appointed to serve on any such select committee, is on account of inability or accident excused, from attending the same throughout, shall be deemed to have served, 41 G. 3, c. 18, s. 4.

Excuses on Oath If any member offer and verify upon oath, any excuses, the substance of the allegations shall be taken down by the Clerk, to be entered on the Journals, and the opinion of the House taken thereon, and if the House resolve the member is unable to serve or cannot without great detriment serve, he shall be excused, and the names of others shall be drawn, who may be in like manner excused, until the whole number of 19 members,

Nominees not liable to be set aside, or excused, is complete. And the petitioners or their agents, shall name one, and the sitting members or their agents, and other member present, whose names have not been drawn, to be added to those chosen by lot, either of whom may be set aside for any of the same causes as those chosen by lot, or if he requires it may be excused, and the party who nominated him, shall nominate another, and so continue to do until his nominee is admitted, 41 G. 3, c. 18, s. 5.

Striking Committee As soon as the 19 members, have been chosen by lot, and the two to be added nominated, the door shall be opened and the House, may proceed upon other business, and lists of the 19 members chosen by lot, shall be given to the petitioners, their counsel or agents, and the counsel or agents for the sitting members, who shall immediately withdraw, with the Clerk appointed to attend such select committee, and the petitioners and sitting members, their counsel or agents, beginning on the part of the petitioners, shall alternately strike off one of the 19 members, until the number be reduced to 11. And the

swearing them Clerk shall within one hour at furthest, from the time of withdrawing, deliver to the House, the names of the 11 members remaining, and they, together with the two members nominated, shall be sworn at the table, well and truly to try the matter of the petition, referred to them and a true judgment to give ac

Meeting cording to the evidence, and shall be a select committee to try and determine the merits of the return or election appointed to be that day taken into consideration, and the House shall order the select committee, to meet at a time to be fixed within 24 hours of their appointment, unless a Sunday or Christmas day intervene, and the place of their meeting and sitting, shall be some convenient room or place adjacent to the House, properly prepared, 41 G. 3, c. 18, s. 6.

Setting aside the name of an intended nominee. If upon drawing out the name of any member by lot, the petitioners or sitting members or their agents declare that such member is intended to be one of the two nominees, and the member consents, his name shall be set aside, and unless objected to he shall serve as nominee, and the name of another member drawn to supply his place to complete the number of nineteen.

When nominees to be supplied by lot If the petitioners or sitting members or their agents, shall not respectively nominate a member then present, who shall be admitted, the want of nomination shall be supplied by drawing out the name of one or two members, as the case requires, who shall be drawn by lot in like manner, and subject to the like objections and excuses, as the other 19, and be added to the lists and liable to be struck off in the same manner, leaving always the number of 13 members, and no more as a select committee, 41 G. 3, c. 18, s. 7.

Names of members to be previously prepared & fastened up The names of all the members so written and rolled up, shall previous to the day for taking any petition into consideration, be prepared by the Clerk and put into a box or parcel in the presence of the Speaker, with an attestation signed by the Clerk, that the names of all the members were by him put therein the   day of   in the year which the Speaker, shall seal with his own seal, and to the outside annex an

attestation signed by himself, that it was on the   day of
in the year   made up in his presence in the manner directed by the   *t* Undrawn names may be drawn and read
Act.   And as soon as the parties are withdrawn, and before the House enters
on any other   business, any member may require the names of all members
which remain undrawn, to be drawn and read aloud by the Clerk,   41G. 3,
c. 18, s. 8.

The select committee on meeting, shall elect a Chairman from among   Chairman
the members chosen by lot, and if there is an equal number of voices, the member whose name was first drawn in the house, shall have a casting voice, so
likewise in case there is an occasion for electing a new chairman, on the death
or necessary absence of the chairman first elected, 41 G. 3, c. 18, s. 9.

The select committee may send for persons, papers and records, and exa-   Powers of Com-mittee
mine witnesses on oath, and try the merits of the return or election or both, and
determine by a majority of voices, whether the petitioner or the sitting member,
or either, be duly returned or elected, or whether the election be void, which   Their determina-tion, final and to be carried out
determination shall be final, and the house on being informed thereof, by the
chairman, shall order it to be entered on the Journals, and give the necessary
directions for confirming or altering the return or the issuing of a new writ or   Witnesses, see 22 V, c. 5, s. 24.
for carrying the determination into execution, as the case requires, 41 G. 3, c.
18, s. 10.

They shall sit every day, Sunday and Christmas day only excepted, and   Adjournments
shall never adjourn for longer than 24 hours, unless a Sunday or Christmas
day, intervene without leave from the house, upon motion and special caus assigned for a longer adjournment, and if the house is sitting at the time to which
it is adjourned, the business of the house shall be stayed, and a motion made
for a further adjournment, for any time to be fixed by the House, not exceeding 24 hours, unless Sunday &c., intervene, 41 G. 3, c. 18, s. 11.

Where the time for meeting, sitting or adjournment by the intervention of   When sunday or christmas day in-tervenes
a Sunday &c., exceeds 24 hours, such meeting &c., shall be within 24 hours
from the time of appointing or fixing the same exclusive of Sunday &c. 41
G. 3, c. 18, s. 12.

No member of the select committee, shall absent himself without leave   Absentees
of, or an excuse allowed by the House, at its next sitting, upon special cause
verified upon oath, and the select committee shall never sit until all the members to whom leave has not been granted nor excuse allowed are met, and in
case they shall not all meet within one hour after the time, to which they
were adjourned a further adjournment shall be made as before directed and
reported with the cause to the House, 41 G. 3, c. 18, s. 13.

The Chairman shall at the next meeting of the House, always report the   To be reported by chairman
names of members who have been absent without leave or excuse, and the
members shall be directed to attend the House, at the next sitting, and shall
then be ordered to be taken into the custody of the Sergeant-at-Arms, for such
neglect of duty, and otherwise punished or censured at the discretion of the
House, unless it appear to them by facts specially stated and verified upon
oath, that he was by a sudden accident or necessity prevented from attending,   41 G. 3, c. 18, s. 14.

If more than 2 members of the select committee, are on any account ab-   Where   m o r e than two Mem-bers absent
sent, they shall adjourn, as before directed, and so from time to time, until
11 members are assembled, 41 G. 3, c. 18, s. 15.

In case the number of members able to attend, are by death or other-   If reduced be-low 11, the com-mittee to be dis-solved and an-other chosen
wise unavoidably reduced to less than 11, and so continues for 3 sitting
days, the select committee shall be dissolved and another chosen to try and
determine the matter of such petition, and the proceedings of that committee
shall be void, 41 G. 3, c. 18, s. 16.

If the committee come to any resolution other than the determination   Committee may report resolutions for the decision of the House
aforesaid, they may report the same to the House, at the time the chairman
informs the House of such determination, and the House may confirm or disagree with such resolution, and make orders thereon as to them seem proper.
If any person summoned by the committee, disobey, or any witness prevari-
cate or otherwise misbehave in giving or refusing to give evidence, the chairman, by their direction, may at any time during the course of their proceed-
ings, report the same to the House, for the interposition of their authority or   I f House a d-journed   w h e n committee apply, they shall adjourn to same day
censure. If the committee have occasion to apply or report to the House, in re-
lation to their adjournment, the absence of members, or the non-attendance or
misbehaviour of witnesses, summoned or appearing before them, and the
House is then adjourned to any a   a day, they may also adjourn to the
day appointed for the meeting of the House, 41 G. 3, c. 18, s. 17.

Committee may clear room

Whenever the committee think it necessary to deliberate upon any question, which arises in the course of the trial, or upon its determination, or upon any resolution, as soon as they have heard the evidence and counsel on both sides the room or place wherein they sit, shall be cleared if they think proper while they consider thereof, and all such questions as well as such determination, and all other resolutions shall be by a majority of voices, and if the voices are equal, the Chairman shall have the casting voice. But not unless 11 members are present, and no member shall have a vote on such determination, or an any other question or resolution, who has not attended during every sitting, 41 G. 3, c. 18, s. 18.

To decide by majority.

Of members who have attended every sitting

Oaths by whom to be administered.

Perjury.

The oaths to be taken in the House, shall be administered by the Clerk, in the same manner as those of allegiance and supremacy; those to be taken before the committee, by the Clerk attending them. Persons guilty of perjury in any evidence, they give before the House, or committee shall incur the like penalties to which any other person convicted of perjury is liable, 41 G. 3, c. 18, s. 19.

Prorogation, effect of

When the Assembly is prorogued, while a select committee is sitting, and before they have reported their determination, the committee shall not be dissolved, but shall be thereby adjourned to 12 o'clock, on the day immediately following that on which the Assembly meets again for the dispatch of business (Sunday &c. excepted) and all former proceedings shall continue of the same force as if the Assembly had not been prorogued, and the committee shall meet on the day and hour to which it shall be adjourned and thenceforth continue to sit from day to day, in the manner provided, until they have reported their determination, on the merits of the petition, 41 G. 3, c. 18, s. 20.

Any Assembly existing at the time of the death or demise of His Majesty, or of any of his heirs or successors, or at the time such death or demise is made known by authority, in this island, shall not determine or be dissolved, but shall continue and if convened and sitting at the time, may proceed and act notwithstanding for 6 calendar months after such death or demise and no longer unless sooner prorogued or dissolved by legal authority, and if the Assembly be then under prorogation the Governor may further prorogue or call and convene them in the usual manner, and they shall meet and sit on the day to which it was prorogued or called and convened and continue to act for the residue of the time, unless sooner prorogued or dissolved. Act not to alter or abridge the power of the Crown or Governor to convene prorogue or dissolve the Assembly, 53 G. 3, c. 9, s. 1.

Continuance of the Assembly, after the demise of the Crown.

Laws made after the demise of any former King, before it was known in this island, declared in force, 53 G. 3, c. 9, s. 2.

Acceptance of offices of emolument under the Crown.

If any person being chosen a member of Assembly, accepts of any office of emolument from the Crown, or under the provisions of any Act, during the time he is a member, his seat shall be vacated and a writ shall issue for a new election, as if he had resigned his seat. But he shall be capable of being again elected. Not to extend to any member being an officer of the Army or Navy, who receives any new or other Commission in the Army or Navy, 4 V., c. 19, s. 1.

Judges, Stipendiary Police Justices, ineligible.
See also as to Judges, 19 V. c 10, s. 11.

No person who holds any office of emolument under any act of the United Kingdom or of this island, either as a Judge or Stipendiary Police Justice shall be capable of being elected, or of sitting or voting as a member of Assembly, 4 V., c. 19, s. 2.

Returns of persons incapacitated void.

If nevertheless elected and returned as a member, the election and return shall be void, 4 V., c. 19, s. 3.

Executive Committee.

Exception in the case of the Executive Committee, 17 V., c. 29, s. 17.

Powers and privileges of the House

There shall be two Legislative Chambers or Houses. A Legislative Council and an Elective Legislative Assembly, as at present constituted, which shall continue to exercise and enjoy the like powers, privileges, rights and immunities as heretofore, which of legal right appertain to them except in so far as by this act abandoned, limited, extended or defined, 17 V., c. 29, s. 1.

The right now existing in every member to propose a vote of money, shall after the appointment of the Executive Committee, and during such period as their functions as organs of communication between the Governor and Assembly exist and are exercised, but not further or otherwise, cease, and during such period, the House of Assembly shall not originate or pass any vote, resolution or bill, for the imposition or appropriation of any tax or impost (not being in the nature of a fine or penalty) for any purpose, not first recommended by a message of the Governor to the House, or by the Executive Committee, during the Session, and the sole and exclusive power of proposing or originating any vote of money, shall vest in and be exercised by the Governor by message or through the Executive Committee, as organs of Government, or by one of them, under the authority and direction, and upon the sole responsibility of the Government, 17 V., c. 29, s. 23. *Limitation of powers to grant monies*

Accounts in detail of the expenditure and appropriation of all Revenue and other monies, under the control or direction of the Governor, or of any body in conjunction with him or acting under his authority, or within his control, shall be laid before the Legislative Council and Assembly, within 14 days after the beginning of the Session, after such expenditure and appropriation was made, 17 V. c. 29, s. 34. *Revenue accounts to be laid before the Legislative Council and Assembly.*

If any member become Bankrupt or be declared Insolvent, or take the benefit of any law relating to Insolvent Debtors, or become a public default or, or be convicted of felony, or of any infamous crime, his seat shall thereby become vacant, and any person convicted as aforesaid, shall be ineligible, 17 V. c. 29, s. 49. *Bankruptcy. Insolvency, or becoming a public defaulter to vacate seat, conviction of felony or infamous crime to render ineligible as well.*

Clerks' of the Vestry, ineligible, 16 V. c. 43, s. 46.

Auditors' General, 21 V. c. 1, s. 17.

Receiver-General or Bookkeeper, 21 V. c. 4, s. 19.

Inspector of Revenue, 28 V. c. 21, s. 10.

If a member dying during the recess, or is appointed a member of the Legislative Council, the Governor shall forthwith direct a writ to be issued by the Clerk of the patents, for the election of another, to fill up the vacancy, directed and delivered to the Provost Marshal for execution, as writs issued during the sitting of the Assembly, 22 V. c. 5, s. 1. *Vacancies during recess.*

When an Assembly is summoned, there shall be 40 days between the teste and return of the writs of summons, and the Provost Marshal shall with all convenient speed, transmit a warrant to the Custos or a Justice residing in each parish, addressed to the Inspector of Police, to warn the voters to appear at the election of members to represent the same, and the Custos or Justice, shall sign and cause it to be delivered to the Police, 22 V. c. 5, s. 2. *40 days between teste and return of Summons. Proceedings to warn voters.*

The Inspector shall warn the voters, by causing a notice in writing of the time and place of election to be fixed on or near the doors of the Court Houses of the Churches and Chapels for 5 days at least previous, to be computed from its date, the day of date being included, 22 V. c. 5, s. 3. *Notice.*

When a member resigns his seat during the sitting, and a writ issues for an election in his room, the warrant shall be transmitted, and the notice of the time and place of election given as before directed, 22 V. c. 5, s. 4. *Vacancies during Session.*

A separate day shall be appointed in each writ for the election in each parish, and no two parishes shall elect on the same day. If the writ is not executed on the day appointed (there being no interruption of proceedings at the elections as after provided) no new writ shall issue until after the meeting of the Assembly, 22 V. c. 5, s. 5. *Separate days of Election for each parish.*

The Provost Marshal shall be the returning officer, at elections for Members and Coroners, and shall appoint persons to assist in taking the poll, whenever necessary to open it at more than one place, 22 V. c. 5, s. 6. *Returning officer.*

The Custos of each parish (Kingston excepted) shall appoint one or more polling places at all elections, and persons to keep the poll at elections for Vestrymen and Churchwardens, whenever it is determined to open the poll at more than one place, 22 V. c. 5, s. 7. *Polling places.*

The Provost Marshal shall be paid £3, for each election at which one Member or a Coroner is returned and £5 at each election, at which two or more members are returned whether contested or not, 22 V. c. 5, s. 8. *Provost Marshal's fee.*

The Provost Marshal shall not employ as his assessor or professional assistant or adviser, any person retained or employed as the agent or professional adviser of any candidate, 22 V. c. 5, s. 9. *Assessor.*

Polling hours, declaring Election. Elections shall commence between 9 and 10 o'clock, a.m. and be closed at 4 p.m. of the same day. When the votes are taken at more than one place, the list shall be at each place, sealed up at 4 p.m. in the presence of 6 Electors, to be testified by their signatures to the Provost Marshal, who shall at the usual place of doing public business between 8 and 12 of the following day in the presence of 6 electors, who shall testify the fact by their signatures open such lists, cast up the votes, and declare who are duly elected. In case of an election on Saturday, the votes shall be cast up on the Monday following. 22 V. c. 5, s. 10.

Adjournment Riot. When the proceedings are interrupted by riot or open violence, the Provost Marshal shall adjourn until the following day, and if a Sunday or public holiday until the day after, and if necessary from day to day, until the interruption has ceased, upon which he shall proceed with the election at the same place or places, and where the poll has been taken at several places, and there is not time to ascertain before 4 o'clock, who has been duly elected, the poll shall be sealed up and the fact testified as before directed, and the Provost Marshal shall at the usual place of public business between 8 and 12 of the following day, open the lists cast up the votes in the presence of 6 electors, and declare who is duly elected. 22 V. c. 5, s. 11.

Closing poll no opposition. Where there is no opposition to the candidate or candidates proposed, the Provost Marshal shall close the poll, 2 hours after it was opened, 22 V. c. 5, s. 12.

Questions at poll (or poll keepers s 34 36) No enquiry shall be made at any election at the time of polling as to the right of any person to vote except by the Provost Marshal, who shall if required on behalf of any candidate put to the voter, at the time of tendering his vote and not afterwards the following questions, or any of them and no other and record in writing the answers.

How or in what capacity do you vote ?

* Have you now the same qualification for which your name was originally inserted in the Register of Voters now in force for this parish, and do you conscientiously believe that you are legally entitled to vote upon it at this election ? 22 V. c. 5, s. 13.

Oath to voter. The Provost Marshal shall if required on behalf of any candidate at the time aforesaid, administer an oath (or in case of a Quaker or Moravian an affirmation) to any voter in the following form:

You A. B. do swear (or being a Quaker or Moravian do affirm) that you are the same person whose name appears as A. B. on the Register of Voters now in force for this parish, that you have not before voted here or elsewhere at the present election, that you still and do now possess the qualification upon which you claim to be Registered as a Voter, and that you have done nothing to deprive you of your right to Vote at this election. So help you God. 22 V. c. 5, s. 14.

No other oath to be taken nor voter excluded who answers the questions and takes the oath. No person shall be required to take any other oath, nor be excluded from voting, unless it appears to the Provost Marshal, from the answers received to any of the questions put that he is not the same person, whose name appears in the Register or that he has previously voted or has not the same qualification for which his name was originally inserted in such Register, or unless he refuses to take the oath or make the affirmation or take or make any other oath or affirmation required by law, and no scrutiny shall be allowed at any election of any vote given or tendered, 22 V. c. 5, s. 15.

See Roman Catholics 10 G. 4, c. 12, s. 3.

Jurat to be written opposite the names of sworn voters. The Provost Marshal shall write jurat opposite the name of every voter, who takes the oath, 22 V. c. 5, s. 16.

False answers &c. Making false answer to any of the questions or swearing, or affirming falsely, punishable as perjury, and indictable at the public expense, 22 V. c. 5, s. 17.

Protection from civil process Every person whose name appears upon the Register, shall be protected in his person and usual personal equipage against all mesne and judicial process in civil causes on the day of election for the parish, 22 V. c. 5, s. 18.

No regiment of Militia or company or Troop of Horse, of any Parish, or precinct, where an election is to be held, shall be in arms on that day, and no voter shall be sent or forced out on any party or other military duty, till the election is over, except in case of invasion, actual insurrection or rebellion under penalty of £50 on the offender, to be recovered in the Supreme Court, one moiety to the person who sues, 22 V. c. 5, s. 19.

Militia not to bo called out.

When the return of any member is objected to at an election, and notice given to the Provost Marshal, previous to or upon the closing of the poll, that it is the intention of a candidate or voter, to petition the House for a scrutiny the Provost Marshal shall within 10 days after, transmit the poll to the office of enrolments to be enrolled and open to inspection, having first made affidavit before a Justice, under or on the back of the same, that it is really and bona fide the true and genuine poll, taken at such election, without any alteration, 22 V. c. 5, s. 20.

Proceedings in case of notice of petition for Scrutiny.
Enrolment of poll

The Provost Marshal, shall previously make a copy, which sworn to by him as true and correct, shall be received and enrolled in lieu of the original in case it is lost or rendered useless, 22 V. c. 5, s. 21.

Sworn copy.

If he wilfully neglect to take the poll, at any election, or where notice of a scrutiny is given, omits or neglects to return the poll as directed, he shall be liable to imprisonment not exceeding one year, and to a fine not exceeding £200. 22 V. c. 5, s. 22.

Penalties on Provost Marshal.

Whenever the return of a member is objected to and notice of scrutiny given, the candidate or voter shall by himself or his agent, within 21 days after the election, deliver to the person elected, a list of the Voters objected to either by personal service or by leaving the list at his usual place of residence, or in his absence from the island, by personal service upon the procuration attorney if known, or person who appeared as his agent, at the election, or at the usual place of residence of such attorney or agent, and shall assign opposite each name, upon the list a short and clear specification of the objections intended to be relied upon before the committee to try the election, 24 V. c. 8, s. 1.

Lists of Voters objected to be served by person objecting to return.

The person elected to entitle himself to object to the votes opposed to him shall within 21 days after service of the objection on him deliver in like manner a list of his objections with a like specification of the objections to be urged against each vote and on failure of such objection to any voter within the time he shall be deemed unobjected to 24 V. c. 8, s. 2.

List to be served by the person objecting to the return

No Summons to a witness shall issue from the committee, to try an election, except by order made on consideration of any objection or answer, or where it is deemed necessary by the committee to obtain further evidence as to any allegation made on one side, and disputed on the other 22 V. c. 5, s. 24.

Summons from Election Committee

Where any person has voted for the sitting member and petitioner, the notice of objection on behalf of one, shall operate to the full benefit of the other, 22 V. c. 5, s. 25.

Objection to voters for both parties by one.

On petition complaining of an undue election, the petitioner and person defending the election may impeach the correctness of the Register in force, by proving that the name of any person who voted was improperly inserted or retained, or the name of any person who tendered his vote, was improperly omitted, and the committee shall alter the poll according to the truth of the case, and report their determination to the House, by whom it shall be carried into effect, 22 V. c. 5, s. 26.

Impeachment of Register on Scrutiny.

If any candidate or voter after objecting to and serving notice of his intention to petition against the return of any person, omit or neglect to do so he shall be liable to pay all costs and expenses incurred by such person, to be recovered by action of debt in the Supreme Court, but if the voter or candidate objecting within 10 days after the election, give notice to the person whose return he objected to, that it is not his intention to proceed to try the validity of the election, he shall not be liable, 22 V. c. 5, s. 27.

Costs of Scrutiny, liability for

No candidate shall by himself or agent, directly or indirectly, give public entertainment of provisions or liquor previous to or on the day of election, in public houses or in houses or booths hired, lent or erected for the purpose, 22 V. c. 5, s. 28.

Entertainments

If any is given the election as to the candidate, giving or causing it to be given, shall be void, and if he have a majority of votes on the poll, a new writ shall issue, and he shall be incapable of being chosen to the Assembly, during the Session next after, 22 V. c. 5, s. 29.

To avoid the election of the candidate giving it.

Bribery by candidate

If any candidate by himself or agent, bribe or attempt to bribe or give money or goods, for securing the vote of any voter, or inducing him to record his vote in his favor, or to influence or procure any votes to be recorded in his favor, on the day of election, such candidate shall be liable to be indicted in any Circuit Court, for a misdemeanor, and upon conviction to pay a fine not exceeding £100, and to be imprisoned in any prison not exceeding 6 month's, and be incapacitated from sitting in the Assembly, for six years after conviction, 22 V. c. 5, s. 30.

Taking bribe

Every voter or person who receives or takes any bribe, shall be guilty of a misdemeanor, and conviction in any Circuit Court, be liable to a penalty not exceeding £50, and imprisonment in any prison, for not exceeding 3 months, and, if a voter, be deprived of the right of voting at any election, for 6 years after conviction, 22 V. c. 5, s. 31.

Fraudulent conveyances to qualify voters.

Conveyances to any person in a fraudulent and collusive manner, to qualify him at any election, subject to conditions or agreements to defeat or determine the estate, or to reconvey the same, shall be taken to convey the estate, in fee simple, and all bonds, covenants, collateral, and other securities, for redeeming, revoking or defeating such estates, or for restoring or reconveying the same, or any part to any person who made or executed any such conveyance or any person in trust for him or any of them, shall be void, and any person who makes and executes such conveyance or being privy to the purpose devises or prepares it, and every person, who by color thereof, gives any vote at any election, shall for every conveyance or vote, so created or given forfeit £100, to any person who sues by action of debt, 22 V. c. 5, s. 32.

Penalties.

If any person wilfully contravene. or disobey any of the provisions of this Act, for which no penalty is provided, he shall be liable to be sued in an action of debt, for the penal sum of £100, with full costs, to the party who sues, but no action shall be brought except by an elector, candidate, or member actually returned or other party aggrieved, and the remedy shall not supercede any remedy or action the parties may have against such person, 22 V. c. 5, s. 33.

Act applicable to other Elections.

This Act where not inconsistent, shall be applicable to and regulate elections for members of the Common Council of Kingston or Vestrymen and Churchwardens, and the persons appointed to take the poll at such elections, shall have the powers given to the Provost Marshal, as returning officer and the candidates, voters, and other persons taking part in such elections, shall be liable to the penalties imposed by this Act, so far as they can be enforced for the offences mentioned herein committed by them 22 V. c. 5, s. 34.

Interpretation.]

"Provost Marshal" shall mean also the Deputy of and any person appointed to take or assist in taking the poll, at any election by the Provost Marshal, 22 V. c. 5, s. 36.

Qualification of members.
Sec 39 C. 2, c. 1.

No person elected a member of Assembly, shall sit or vote unless he was previous to his election, a freeholder in his own or his wife's right, and possessed besides of one of the following qualifications.

   1. A clear annual income, after payment of all just debts of £150, arising from lands, held by him in his own right, or in right of his wife.

   2. A clear annual income as aforesaid, arising partly from lands, held by him as aforesaid, and partly from income, the produce of any freehold office, or any business (after deducting all charges and expenses of such office or business) of £200.

   3. A clear annual income as aforesaid, arising from any freehold office, or any business (after deducting all charges and expenses of such office or business) of £300.

   4. The payment annually of land tax, or other tax on houses, tax on horses, mules, asses, neat cattle, breeding stock and spring carriages, and still and cart licences, export duty paid by the produce or any one or more of them, to the extent of £10, or upwards.

Statement on oath of qualification.

Nor until he has produced to and left with the Clerk of the Assembly, and in the case of a new House, and until a Clerk has been elected, the Clerk of the Privy Council, attending the House with the writs of election and returns, a statement in writing of his qualification, signed by him and sworn to before a Justice, as true and correct in every particular in which he shall set out in words fully, distinctly and at length, the nature of his qualification, the name of the town, district and parish in which the lands are situate, the date of his title, the name of the person from whom he derived it, the liber in which it is enrolled in the office of enrolments, and the folio. Form Schedule A, 22 V. c. 18, s. 1.

The Clerk of the Privy Council, shall carefully keep the statements left with him, and as soon as a Clerk to the Assembly has been elected, deliver them to him, 22 V. c. 18, s. 2.

The Clerk of the Assembly, shall safely keep in his office, all statements left with him as aforesaid, and by members, and not deliver any of them, to any person except by order from a Judge in due course of law, 22 V. c. 18, s. 3.

To be kept by the Clerk to the Assembly.

1. Freehold. Every male person of 21, and not affected by any legal incapacity or convicted of any felony, registered and entitled to vote on 1st November, 1859, in any of the capacities of freeholder in respect of lands held as owner, trustee, cestuiqui trust, mortgagor or mortgagee in possession of the clear annual value of £6, shall so long as he continues to possess the same qualification, be entitled to vote thereon, the person claiming to be registered as an elector after 1st November. 1859, being in the actual possession of lands, as owner &c., the clear annual value whereof shall be not less than £6, per annum.

   Qualifications of Voters.

2. Rent. The person claiming as above, being in the receipt, in his own right of a rent payable out of lands of the clear annual value of not less than £20.

3. Tenant. The person claiming as above, being in the occupation of a House, as tenant, the annual rental of which paid by him, is not less than £20.

4. Salary. The person claiming as above, being in the receipt of an annual Salary, from the public, a parish, a company, a firm or an individual, of not less than £50.

5. Payment of Taxes. The person claiming as above, paying annually land tax, registration or other tax on houses, tax on horses, mules, asses, neat cattle, spring carriages, and cart license, or any one or more of them, or any other direct tax, which may be imposed, a sum amounting to 20s. or upwards.

6. Money. The person claiming as above, and having deposited in a Saving or other Bank, or having invested in island securities, a sum not less than £100, and having a Bank deposit receipt, or island certificate, in his own name, and in his own right for the same, dated at least 12 month, prior to the day of election, 22 V. c. 18, s. 4.

Payment of Taxes.—Each taxpayer to the extent of 30s and upwards, who has paid taxes on or before 30th September, in each year, shall be entitled, ipso facto, to be registered as a voter, and to exercise the right of voting at any election, in the parish, in which the taxes are paid for the succeeding year, without preferring or tendering any claim under 22 V. c. 18. And each Collector of Dues, shall on 1st October, or within 5 days after, make out an alphabetical list in duplicate of all persons, who paid in his office, taxes to the extent aforesaid, up to the preceding 30th September, and subscribe and swear to the truth of such lists, and deliver one to the Clerk of the Vestry, who shall thereupon transfer to and insert in the register of voters of the parish, the name of every such taxpayer, and the other list shall be affixed to the outer door of the Court House, 28 V. c. 2, s. 1.

Taxpayers, 30s.

Collectors of Dues to furnish Clerk of the Vestry with lists of, to be registered.

And affixed to Court House

The claim to vote may be preferred by attorney or agent. in the absence from the island, of the voter, but the right of voting, shall only be exercised in person, and the forms prescribed by 22 V. c. 18, may be adapted to such case, 28 V. c. 2, s. 2.

Claims may be preferred by Attorney or Agent

The claim to be registered and right to vote, shall be exercised in the parish only, where the land or premises in which the right is claimed, is situate or where the other personal qualification of rent, tenancy, salary, taxes, or deposits of money, are respectively existing arising, payable or invested, 28 V. c. 2, s. 3.

The right to vote, to be exercised only in the parish where the qualification exists

E

On one qualification only

No person shall vote in respect of more than one qualification, in any parish, or at any election, 22 V. c. 18, s. 5.

Several claimants as freeholders or tenants.

Where several persons claim to be registered in respect of land as free-holders or tenants they shall not be placed on the list of voters, unless the clear annual value or the annual rent paid therefore respectively, shall when divided by the number of such persons give an annual value of not less than £6, or an annual rental of not less than £20 to each, 22 V., c. 18, s. 6.

Rector.

The Rector shall be placed on the Register without any claim, and vote without being questioned or required to take an oath respecting his qualification, 22 V. c. 18, s. 7.

Notice to register,

The Clerk of the Vestry shall on, or before the 30th August in each year, cause to be fixed on, or near the doors of the Court Houses and Churches and Chapels in his parish, a notice in writing (Form Schedule B.) requiring all persons entitled to vote to deliver to him on or before 1st November their claims to be registered as voters according to Form Schedule C. No. 1, 22 V. c. 18, s. 8.

Caims

Stamp on claim

The Clerk shall not receive any claim unless impressed with stamps of 10s., under penalty of £5 for each claim, 22 V. c. 18, s. 9.

Exemption from 10s stamp.

Except in the case of a freeholder, whose land is of the actual value of £6, and who, on or before the 30th September preceding the year for which he claims to vote, pays taxes to the extent of 20s. per annum, who is relieved from payment of the Stamp Duty on his claim 28 V., c. 2 s. 1.

As are also tax-payers to the extent of 30s. and upwards who are relieved of the necessity of preferring claims, 28 V., c. 2 s.1.

Adaptation of forms in 22 V. c. 18, Sch. C.

The forms in 22 V. c. 18 Sch. C. for claims to vote on freehold and payment of taxes shall be adapted for the purposes of this Act, in respect of exemption from the 10s. stamp on the claim to vote on freehold, 28 V., c, 2 s. 4.

Title to vote continuance on renewed claim

Every person whose name is registered shall continue entitled to vote as long as he retains the same qualification in respect of which he originally claimed, and on, or before the 1st November in each year, sends, or leaves with the Clerk of the Vestry a declaration (Form Schedule C., No. 2) that he is at the time of making such declaration in possession of the qualification upon which he originally claimed to vote which shall be impressed with 10s stamps, 22 V. c. 18, s. 10.

Exemptions, 28 V. c. 2 s 1

Sworn particulars of freehold

No person shall be entitled to be registered as a voter on a freehold, unless he at the time of lodging his claim has produced te, and left with the Clerk of the Vestry a memorandum in writing (Form Schedule C., No. 3), signed by him, and declared to on oath before a Justice or the Clerk of the Vestry, setting forth the manner in which his freehold was acquired whether by deed or will, the name of the party who conveyed or devised it, the date of the conveyance or will, and of the record, and the liber and folio, and each Clerk of the Vestry shall file and preserve such memorandum in his Office, 22 V. c. 18, s. 11.

Rent. Tenancy

Nor in the case of rent or tenancy, unless a memorandum is lodged with the claim (Form Schedule C., No. 4 for rent, No. 5, for tenant), setting forth the name of the person from whom he obtained the rent, or rented the house, the period during which he has been in the receipt of the rent, or occupancy of the house, the annual amount of rent received or paid, when last received or last paid by him, and up to which it was received or paid, which memorandum shall be filed and preserved, 22 V., c. 18, s. 12.

Salary, taxes, money invested

Nor where the qualification is salary, the payment of taxes, or money invested in a Bank or in Island Securities without a memorandum (Forms, Schedule C., Nos. 6, 7, 8.), setting forth the amount of his salary, taxes, or money invested, or situation he holds, and when employed by a Firm or Company, or individual, the name of the Firm or Company, and the prenomen and surname of the individual, the period he first obtained the situation or commenced to pay taxes, and the name of the town or district of a parish in which he is employed, which memorandum shall be filed and preserved, 22 V. c. 18, s. 13.

Alphabetical list

The Register of electors for 18

See as to tax-payers of 30s, 28 V c. 2 s 1

The Clerk of the Vestry shall on, or before the 30th November, in each year, make out an Alphabetical list of all persons whose names are then on the Register, and who have lodged a declaration, and of all persons who on, or before the 1st November, have claimed to be registered as Electors of the parish, to be called "The Register of Electors of the parish of for the year 18 ", (Form Schedule D.) 22 V. c. 18, s. 14.

No person's name shall be placed on the Register in any year as a freeholder, unless his title has been enrolled for three months at least before the day of giving-in his claim, nor as a voter on rent, unless he has been in receipt of such rent received for three months at least next previous to the day of giving-in his claim, nor as a tenant, unless he has been in the occupation of the house rented for three months at least previously to his claim, or on salary, unless he has been constantly employed, and has received such salary for twelve months at least next previously, or upon taxes unless he has paid such taxes during the financial year, terminating the 30th September previously, or the amount deposited in a Bank or invested in Island Securities has been so deposited or invested for twelve months previously to giving-in the claim 22 V. c. 18, s. 15. *Period for which the party must be possessed before giving in claim*

The Clerk of the Vestry must on, or before 5th December exhibit in some conspicuous and accessible place in his Office a correct copy of the Register, and cause a sufficient number of copies to be made at the expense of the parish, and affixed on, or near the doors of the Court Houses and Churches and Chapels on, or before the 10th December, and kept affixed thereto until the 30th of the same month, 22 V. c. 18, s. 16, *Copy of Register to be exhibited in office and affixed to Court House, &c, Also duplicate of Collector of Dues return of taxpayers, 28 V c 2, s 1*

In the event of the death of any Clerk of the Vestry preventing the publication of the list of voters, the Act 22 V. c. 18 shall be construed as directory, and a publication of the list after the date specified shall not invalidate the rights of claimants to vote, 27 V. S. 1, c. 9. *Publication afterwards*

Any person whose name has been omitted from such Register (his claim having been duly lodged) shall come in at any time previous to the 30th December, and show to the satisfaction of the Custos and the Clerk of the Vestry that his name has been improperly omitted, and thereupon the Clerk of the Vestry shall place his name on the Register, 21 V. c. 18, s. 17. *Names omitted from Register—Applications to restore*

Any e n who fails in satisfying the Custos and Clerk of the Vestry, may apply to the Judge of the Circuit Court, to be held next after 30th December (giving previous notice in writing of his intention to the Clerk of the Vestry) to direct his name to be placed on the Register, 22 V. c. 18, s. 18. *Appeal*

The Register so prepared and exhibited shall be the lawful Register of voters in each parish, shall take effect, and be of force from 1st January to 31st December, in the next year, and be the guide of the Provost Marshal at all elections without the production of any document by, or on the part of the voters whose names appear thereon, 22 V. c. 18, s. 19. *Register to be in force for the succeeding year*

If any person whose name appears upon the Register is not qualified any voter of the parish may give notice in writing (Form Schedule E) to the Clerk of the Vestry of his intention to object to the name of such person being retained, and also give to the person objected, or leave at his place of abode a notice in writing (Form Schedule F) 22 V. c. 18, s. 20. *Revision of Register. Notices of objection*

The Clerk of the Vestry shall at the opening of the Circuit Court, held after the receipt of any such notice, lay a list (Form Schedule G) of every such notice before the Presiding Judge, 22 V. c. 18, s. 21. *To be laid before a Judge of Circuit Court*

The Judge shall on proof, (which may be by affidavit) of the service of notice immediately after hearing appeals, or at the time fixed for appeals, if there are none, proceed to hear and determine every such application and objection, and may summon and bring before him any person who he has reason to believe can furnish information respecting the subject of enquiry, and order the production before him of any books or documents necessary to the decision, 22 V. c. 18, s. 22. *For decision. He may summon witnesses, &c*

He may adjourn the hearing of any application or objection, 22 V c. 18, s. 23. *May adjourn hearing*

The Judge before whom the adjourned hearing comes, or is fixed to come, shall have equal jurisdiction with, and the like powers as the Judge before whom the application or objection originally came, 22 V. c. 18, s. 24.

If upon examination of books or documents or of any person on oath, the Judge is satisfied that the name of the person applying ought to be placed on the Register or that the person whose name appears thereon was not at the time he claimed, possessed of the qualification, or has since ceased to be qualified, or was, or has become disqualified, he shall direct the name of the person applying to be placed on the Register, or declare the person objected to disqualified, and shall certify accordingly to the Clerk of the Vestry; who shall thereupon place the name on, or erase it from the Register, 22 V. c. 18, s. 25 *Certificate of adjudication where upon name to be inserted or erased from Register*

False evidence · False evidence on examination punishable as perjury, and indictable ai the public expense as a matter of public prosecution, 22 V. c. 18, s. 2o·

Refusing to give evidence Refusing or neglecting to attend, or attending, refusing to give evidence on the hearing, punishable as refusal to attend, or to give evidence in a Court of Justice, and the penalties to be enforced by the Presiding Judge, 22 V. c. 18, s. 27.

Names of persons not lodging stamped declarations on 1st November to be expunged from lists *See as to stamps 28 V c 1, s 12* The Clerk of the Vestry shall strike off the list of voters the name of each person who has failed on, or before the 1st November, in any year to deliver, or cause, &c. to him the stamped declaration before required 22 V. c. 18, s. 28.

Fees of Clerk of the Vestry Fees of Clerk of the Vestry, 6d for each claim to be paid by the Receiver-General on the Governor's Warrant, 22 V. c. 18, s. 29.

Receiver-General to supply stamped forms The Receiver-General shall supply annually to each Clerk of the Vestry printed forms of claims and declarations, impressed with the stamp required, for which they shall be accountable to him, 22 V. c., 48 s. 30.

Penalties If any Clerk of the Vestry, or other person wilfully contravene or disobey any provisions of this Act, he shall be liable to be sued in an action of debt for the penal sum of £100, to be paid with full costs to the party who sues, 22 V. c. 18, s. 31.

Interpretation "Lands" shall include tenements and hereditaments. "House", dwelling house, store, shop, wharf, office, penn, estate, plantation, and settlement, "Clerk of the Vestry", the Clerk of the Common Council of Kingston, "Election", Elections for Members of Assembly, Coroners, Members of the Common Council of Kingston, and Vestrymen, aud Churchwardens of any other parish, "writing", p n, and part print, and a writing, "Parish" "City and Parish", "Town, City", 22 V. c. 18, s. 32 rt

False declarations to claims, &c. Wilfully swearing or affirming falsely in any oath or affirmation, or making any false statement in any memorandum, or statement of qualification required, shall be deemed and be punishable as perjury, and indictable as before provided (s. 26) 22 V. c. 18, s. 33.

Salaries

Speaker's Salary	£600,	17 V. c, 29, Schedule A,	£100,	21 V. c. 17.	
Clerks'	" 600	"	"	180	"
Serjeant-at-Arms	300	'	"	20	"
Chaplain	50	"			
Librarian	100	"			

Library The Library Committee of the House may frame, alter, and amend rules and regulations as may be deemed necessary for the due care and preservation of their Library, 26 V. S. 2, c. 12, s. 1.

Which shall, from time to time, be laid before the House within ten days after the meeting of the Session, after they have been framed, altered, or amended for confirmation, 26 V. S., 2 c. 12, s. 2

And unless rescinded or altered by the House within ten days after they have been laid before them, shall be as valid and effectual as if enacted by the Legislature, 26 V. S. 2 c. 12, s. 3.

FORMS, 22 V. c. 18.

SCHEDULE A

Statement of Qualification of Members.

Statement of the qualification of , of the parish of as
Member of Assembly, for the parish of , made the day of
18 , agreeably to the 22nd Victoria, Chapter 18, section 1

1. FREEHOLD—A house No, , situate in street, in the
to wn of or a plantation. penn,, or settlement, called
situated in district of the parish of held
by me, in my own right (or in right of my wife) the title for which is
dated day of 18 from to
aud enrolled in the office of enrolments on the day of
18 liber folio *the income from which
after payment of all my just debts, is pounds per annum.

2. INCOME—The nett income from my office of   (name the office)
   is   pounds.

3. TAXES—The taxes paid by me annually amount to   pounds.

I do swear that the above is a true and correct statement in every particular of my qualification as a Member of Assembly, for the parish of

Sworn before me this   day of   18

'' Where there are more than one freehold, give the situation, &c. as before of each.

SCHEDULE B.
Notice to be Given by Clerks of Vestries.

day of   18   , I hereby give notice, that I shall on, or before the thirtieth day of November. in this year, make out a list of all persons entitled to vote in elections of Members of Assembly, and others for the parish of   , and all persons so entitled are hereby required to deliver or transmit to me on, or before the first day of November next, a claim, in writing, according to the form in schedule C No. 1, with the memorandum mentioned therein in the 22nd Victoria, Chapter 18   ; persons omiting to deliver or transmit such claim, will be excluded from the Register of voters of the said parish of

A. B. Clerk of the Vestry of the parish of

SCHEDULE. C
No. 1.
Notice of Claim to be given to Clerk of Vestry.

I hereby claim to be registered as entitled to vote in the election of members of Assembly and others, for the parish of   and give notice that my qualification is (state the qualification, whether freehold, rent, payment of rent, salary, payment of taxes, or money deposited or invested) as will appear by the memorandum herewith, and that I reside at in the parish of

Dated at   this   day of   18

(Signed)   A.B.

No. 2.

I (A.B.) of the parish of   do declare that I am, at the time of making this declaration, in possession of the same qualification, upon which I originally claimed to vote as   in this parish, and I hereby require that my name shall be continued on the list of voters for the said parish of   for the year 18
A.B., day of month, month, and year

Declared before me this
day of   18   } C.D.

J.P., or C.V.

No. 3.

Memorandum of the qualification of A.B., as a voter for the pa is of freehold (state whether a house in any town or plantation, pen, or settlement in any parish ; if a house, give the number thereof, and the name of the street in which situated ; if a plantation, &c. the name of it and district of the parish in which situated.)

Acquired by deed (or will) from
Deed, or will dated   recorded liber   folio
annual value of freehold   pounds

I (A.B.) do swear that the above is a true and correct statement of the qualification upon which I claim to be registered as a voter for the parish of
A.B.

Sworn before me this
day of   18   } C.D.

J.P. or C.V.

No. 4.

Memorandum of the qualification of (A.B.) as a voter for the parish of

RENT—Acquired by deed or will from
Deed or will dated	day of	18
Recorded	day of	18
Liber	folio	
Annual amount of same	pounds	
In receipt for	months or years	
Last received	day of	18
Received up to	day of	18

I (A.B.) do swear that the above is a true and correct statement of the qualification, upon which I claim to be registered as a voter for the parish of

A.B.

Sworn before me this
day of   18   } C.D.

J.P. or C.V.

No. 5.

Memorandum of the qualification of (A. B.) as a voter for the parish of

PAYMENT OF RENT—A house situated in the town or parish of
Rented from
In my occupancy for	months or years at the present time	
Annual rent paid	pounds	
Amount of rent last paid	pounds	
Rent paid to	day of	18

I (A.B.) do swear that the above is a true and correct statement of the qualification upon which I claim to be registered as a voter for the parish of

A.B.

Sworn before me this
day of   18   } C.D.

J.P. or C.V.

No. 6.

Memorandum of the qualification of (A. B.) as a voter for the parish of

SALARY—Annual amount of   pounds
Situation (state nature of)
Obtained day of	18

Town (or parish) in which employed
Name of employer

I (A.B.) do swear that the above is a true and correct statement of the qualification upon which I claim to be registered as a voter for the parish of

A.B.

Sworn before me this
day of   18   } C.D.

J.P., or C.V.

No. 7.

Memorandum of the qualification of (A. B.) as a voter for the parish of

PAYMENT OF TAXES—Amount of taxes paid during the financial year, terminating the 30th September, 18

Upon Houses ..	£
Wheels	£
Horses	£
Mules	£
Asses ..	£
Neat Cattle ..	£
For Cart Licenses ..	£
	£ _____

I (A.B.) do swear that the above is a true and correct statement of the qualification upon which I claim to be registered as a voter for the parish of

A.B.

Sworn before me this
day of   18   } C.D.

J.P., or C.V.

———

No. 8.

Memorandum of the qualification of (A. B.) as a voter for the parish of
I (A.B.) do swear that I have, in my own name, and in my own right, a sum not less than one hundred pounds, deposited in the savings bank for the parish of   , or in the   bank, or invested in island securities, which sum was deposited or invested on the
day of   18   , and I
do hereby claim to vote in such respect.

A. B.

Declared before me this
day of   18   } C.D.

J.P., or C.V.

———

SCHEDULE D.

Register of voters of the parish of   for the year 18
Register of persons who have claimed to vote in the election of members of Assembly, Coroners, and others, for the parish of   for the year 18 .

First name and surname of each voter, at full length.	Place of abode.	Nature of Qualification.	Street, Lane, or other place, where the property is Situated or name of Property.

0

ASSEMBLY.

SCHEDULE E

Notice of Objection to be given to the Clerk of the Vestry.

To the Clerk of the Vestry of the parish of
I hereby give you notice, that I object to the name of
being retained on the list of voters for the parish of
he not being qualified according to law.

Dated this   day of   18

A. B.

Householder residing at (place of abode to be stated.)
  in the parish of

SCHEDULE F,

Notice of Objection to Person Registered.

To Mr. C. D.

I hereby give you notice, that I object to your name being retained on the list of voters for the parish of   and that you will be required to prove your qualification as a freeholder or in respect of (state the qualification in respect of which the person is registered) at the Circuit Court, to be holden in and for the parish of   or the precinct of   next after service of this notice.

Dated the   day of   18

A. B.

Voter, residing at (place of abode to be stated) in the parish of

---

SCHEDULE G

List of Persons Objected to as not Qualified as Voters in the Parish of

The following persons have been objected to as not being entitled to have their names retained on the list of voters for the parish of

First name and surname of persons objected to.	Place of abode.	Nature of supposed qualification, in respect of which name was placed on the Register.	By whom objected against.	Date when notice of objection given to Clerk of Vestry.

Attainder.

No attainder by judgment of death or outlawry in any case of felony shall be adjudged to work any corruption of blood, 27 V. S. 1 c. 32 s. 63.

Attorney General.

His fees for each common patent where there is but one parcel of land 20s. (12s sterling) if more 30s (18s. ster.) For an escheat patent £5 (£3 sterling) for each flat 10s. (6s sterling); for a pardon £5 (£3 sterling) ; for all prosecutions at the Queen's suit and other process relating thereto as the Governor and Coun. cil direct, 10 Ann. c. 4 s. 25.

Permanent salary, £240, 17 V. c. 29, Schedule A.

Further Salary, £500, 26 V. S. 1 c 6, until 31st December, 1868.

Attornies at Law.

No attorney shall practice in any Court until he is admitted and has taken as well the oath of an attorney as the oaths of allegiance and supremacy under the penalty of £20 (£12 sterling), And whatsoever Attorney by negligence or ignorance mistakes his clients cause and imperfectly lays his action or ill draws the declaration whereby the client suffers a non suit shall be liable by rule of Court without any other process or course of law to pay to the party aggrieved full costs of suit, 33 C. 2, c. 23 s. 4.

Penalty on Attorneys endorsing writs of venditioni with intent to distress the defendant for a greater sum than is really due, £100 (£60 sterling) besides being further liable to be discharged from practising in any Court if the Judges before whom he is convicted from the circumstances of the case think proper, 24 G. 2, c 16 s. 1.

One moiety of the penalty to the party injured to be recovered by action of debt, &c., 24 G. 2 c. 16 s. 2.

No partnership shall be allowed between any Attornies or Solicitors unless they reduce their agreement into writing and sign seal and deliver the same, and record it in the Secretary's Office, and such Attornies and Solicitors shall sign and endorse the names of all the persons concerned in such partnership. on all writs, process, proceedings or other business in which they are concerned, 4 G. 3, c. 8, s. 4.

No person shall be admitted or allowed to practice as an Attorney, Solicitor or proctor in the Court of Chancery, Supreme Court, Court of Ordinary, or Admiralty, who has not been admitted as an Attorney, Solicitor, Proctor, or writer to the signet either in the Supreme Court, Courts of King's Bench, Common Pleas, Chancery, Exchequer, or some of the Courts of England, Scotland, or Ireland, and who cannot produce from the Court wherein he was admitted a certificate under its seal of admission, 14 G. 3, c. 3 s. 1.

No Attorney Solicitor or Proctor shall receive or take into his office as an articled Clerk any person under 16 and for a less time than 5 years, under the penalty of articles contrary to this act being utterly void, 14 G. 3, c. 5, s. 2.

Every Attorney, &c., entering into articles with any person as a Clerk to the intent he may be admitted to practise shall within 3 months after execution procure the articles to be proved and recorded in the office of the Clerk of the Supreme Court, under the penalty of their being utterly void, 14 G. 3, c. 3, s. 3.

No person shall be admitted an Attorney, &c., until he has been examined by the Chief Justice, in open Court, nor before the master with whom he served his time as an articled clerk, or some other person, has made affidavit in the Supreme Court, or before a Commissioner, that such person has really and truly served as a Clerk in the office of such Attorney, &c. for, and during the time comprised in his articles of clerking, according to the best of his knowledge. 14 G. 3, c. 3, s. 4.

No admitted Attorney, &c. shall suffer any person except his own Clerks to practise or solicit business in any of the Courts, in his name, under the penalty of £100 (£60 sterling) and being struck off the list of Attornies. 14 G. 3, c. 3, s. 5.

F

Assignment of articles

If any Attorney, &c. having entered into articles of Clerkship with any person, dies before the expiration of the term, the Clerk shall be entitled to the benefit of the term he has actually served with him, and shall be admitted an Attorney, at the expiration of the term in his articles. provided he p   himself, immediately upon the death of such Attorney, to be turned ruxarto some other Attorney, &c. to serve for the remainder of his term. 14 G. 3, c. 3, s. 7.

Penalties

Penalties shall be recovered in a summary manner, by any person in the Supreme Court, by motion in open Court, and when recovered shall be paid to the Receiver General, towards the support of the Government, 14 G. 3, c. 3, s. 9.

Appearance in Circt Courts

Not entitled to appear for any party, to any proceeding, in any Circuit Court, unless admitted to practice in the Supreme Court, 19 V. c. 10, s. 27.

Before Justices

May appear before Justices on behalf of persons charged with indictable offences, to cross examine witnesses, 13 V. c. 24, s 10.

Right to appear on summary convictions &c., 13 V. c. 35, s. 12.

On summary trials for larceny, 20 V. c. 3, s. 8.

In Petty Courts, 19 V. c. 37, s. 51.

Liable for Provost Marshals' fees

The Provost Marshal may demand and receive payment of his fees immediately after he has performed the duty whereon they arise, and if payment is refused or delayed on proof of demand made, he shall under an order of Court, in every such case to be made, recover his legal fees from the Attorney who issues the process with £6, per cent, per annum, surcharged thereon, from the day of the demand of payment, as a compensation for withholding same, with full costs out of purse to be taxed. But not to preclude him from from an election, to enforce payment of his legal fees, by any other remedy open to him, 43 G. 3, c. 20, s. 10.

Costs

Not entitled to costs beyond those recoverable in an inferior Court, by reason of any privilege as an attorney, 22 V. c. 28.

Audit of Public Accounts.

Executive Committee constituted a board of Audit

The Executive Committee shall be " The Board for the Audit of the Public Accounts of Jamaica" and shall from time to time direct the examination of the books and accounts of the Receiver General, the Customs department, the Collectors of Taxes, district Collectors of Taxes where there are no Collectors and Collectors of Arrears of Taxes, of the different parishes, the accounts and vouchers of the General Penitentiary and District Prisons for the pay and disbursements of the Police Force, the Public Hospital, and all other accounts and vouchers involving an expenditure of public money, 21 V. c. 1, s 1.

Auditor General 28 V. c. 31, s. 2

The Commissioner for examining the public accounts (or Auditor-General) shall undertake the superintendence of the investigation into such of the books, accounts, and vouchers, having relation to the public accounts, as are allotted to him under any minute of the Governor, from time to time, but subject to the rules and regulations of the Executive Committee, 21 V, c. 1, s. 2.

Audit Office Services of Customs' Clerk

The Executive Committee may appoint a convenient place for an office for the Commissioner's discharge of his duties and if need be may require the services of a Clerk in the Custom House department, to attend from time to time, at such office, in the discharge of the duties imposed by this Act, 21 V. c. 1, s. 3.

Control of the Executive Committee over Auditor General

They may by minute or warrant under their hands, define the duties of the Commissioner, and direct arrangements, and make regulations in respect to his conduct and business, as well for the superintendence and examination of such books, accounts and vouchers, as for the control to be exercised over any officer or clerk or person employed or by under him in the discharge of the duties required by this Act, 21 V. c. 1, s. 4.

The Commisioner shall examine every demand upon the Public Treasury, with the accompanying certificate, or document previous, to its being paid by the Receiver-General, and countersign the same if found correct, he shall also countersign all receipts for monies paid to the Receiver-General, on account of the Public, and no discharge or acknowledgment for money received into the Treasury, or paid on account of the Public shall be valid unless countersigned by him, 21 V. c. 1, s. 5.

Commissioner to examine and countersign demands upon the Treasury, and receipts for monies paid in,

And shall preserve in the Audit Office, duly labelled, and carefully put up for reference all accounts paid by the Receiver-General, with the vouchers, orders, warrants, and certificates which accompanied them, 21 V. c. 1 s 6.

And preserve all accounts paid by the Receiver-General and vouchers

In order to ascertain the correctness of any Public Books, or accounts, the Commissioner may send for, and have the custody of any books or papers, under the control of any Public or Parochial Officer, and call for any returns under such custody relating to the examination of such public or parochial accounts, which may be necessary for the purpose aforesaid, and keep them for such time as is required, and also send for, and examine upon oath (which he is empowered to administer) any person touching any matter relating to such books, &c., 21 V. c. 1, s. 7.

And may send for and examine books of Public or Parochial Officers

And examine persons upon oath

If any person summoned to appear, to whom such reasonable charges, as by the Supreme Court are considered sufficient in the case of a witness attending a Circuit Court, have been paid or tendered, neglects or refuses to appear before the Commissioner or to bring or produce any books, accounts or vouchers or papers touching any such accounts or books in his possession or that of any other person, for him or with his assent, or if having come before the Commissioner, he refuses to be sworn or to answer any question the Commissioner may lawfully require to be answered, concerning such books &c. or refuses to answer any question relating to the expenditure of any public money, or neglects or refuses to bring with him to reproduce any books, papers, vouchers or accounts, or papers relating to such accounts, or books, or to make any return he is required to make from accounts books or documents in his possession or under his control, touching or relating to the expenditure of any public or parochial money, he shall forfeit for any such refusal not exceeding £50, to be recovered by attachment under the hand and seal of a Judge of the Supreme Court, to the use of the Crown, for the support of the Government of this island, but before the attachment issues, it shall be shewn to the satisfaction of the Judge, if the person complained against, had refused to be sworn, or to answer any lawful question or to produce any books, or papers, or to make any return, the Commissioner might lawfully require, that such conduct was contumacious, or in case of non-attendance, that the person had been duly summoned, that his expenses had been tendered to him, and that he had no reasonable excuse for his non-attendance, 21 V. c. 1, s. 8.

Refusal to be examined and produce books, &c.

Judge to be satisfied

That the conduct was contumacious, the party had been summoned his expenses tendered and he had no reasonable excuse for non attendance

When a public officer is summoned relative to the examination of his own accounts, he shall not be entitled to any payment for his expences 21 V., c. 1, s. 9.

Public officers to be examined on their own accounts, not entitled to payment for expences

Any person so examined wilfully and corruptly giving false evidence, shall be guilty of perjury and punishable accordingly, and the prosecution shall be undertaken as a public prosecution, 21 V. c. 1, s. 10.

False evidence-punishable as perjury and prosecution public

The Executive Committee shall at times to be fixed upon by them, not less than twice in each half year, examine and inspect all the reports, query letters, books and documents made and submitted to them, by the Commisioner, for their approval or decision, 21 V. c. 1, s. 11.

Executive Committee to examine half yearly at least commissioners reports &c. submitted to them

The Executive Committee may call upon any person, by whom or by whose order or through whose means it appears any irregular or improper payment, or expenditure has been made, or by whom, or through whose neglect any money due to the public has not been collected or any money actually collected or received, has not been paid to the public treasury, or to the person by law entitled to receive the same on account of the public, for any explanation of the circumstances under which it was expended or not collected, or not paid over, and if of opinion, he ought nevertheless to be charged with such money or any part, they may require him forthwith to render an account thereof, and if he does not forthwith do so, and pay over the same he shall be deemed a public defaulter in respect thereof, in the same manner as if the amount had been actually issued to and received by him on account of the public, 21 V. c. 1, s. 12.

May call for explanation and charge persons with monies they ought to account for and pay over

And in default they shall be deemed public defaulters

Commissioners salary £600 per annum The Commissioner shall receive a salary at the same rate, and payable at the same times and from the same permanent revenue fund, as he is now entitled to receive, but subject to removal at the Governor's pleasure, 21 V. **Removable at pleasure** c. 1, s. 13.

Salary £600 per annum, 17 V. c. 29, sch. **A.**

To have been resident 5 years before appointment When a vacancy occurs by death, resignation or removal, the Governor may appoint under his hand and seal, a person who has been resident in this island, for 5 years before appointment, and who shall be entitled to £600 per annum, payable quarterly, but shall not be entitled to such salary, unless so qualified, 21 V. c. 1, s. 16.

Not to be a member of the Legislature He shall not during his continuance in office, be elected or appointed to sit as a member of either branch of the Legislature, 21 V. c. 1, s. 17.

Short title The Public Audit Act, 1857. 21 V. c. 1, s. 19.

Duration In force to 31st December, 1864, 21 V. c. 1, s. 20.

Continuance Continued to 31st March, 1865, 28 V. c. 7.

Further continued to 31st March, 1872, 28 V. c. 31, s. 1.

Additional salary £150 In addition to the salary now payable to the sole Commissioner for examining the public accounts or Auditor-General, he shall be paid on the Governors warrants a further sum at the rate of £150 per annum, by monthly or other payments as the Governor, with the advice of the Executive Committee, shall direct. 28 V. c. 31, s. 2.

Clerks There shall be paid as annual salary to the first clerk in the office, £225; to the second clerk £180, to the third clerk £120; and no greater sums on the Governors warrant by monthly or other payments, 28 V. c. 31, s. 3.

Inspector of Revenues The Governor may appoint under his hand and seal, an Inspector of Revenues, at a salary of £600 per annum, payable monthly on his warrant, **Salary £600** with an allowance of £200 per annum, for travelling expenses, payable in **Travelling expences £200** like manner, subject to removal for just cause by the Governor, 28 V. **Removable for cause** c. 21, s. 2.

His duties to investigate and report upon the accounts of the several Revenue departments He shall twice a year or as often as directed by the Governor and Executive Committee, personally attend at and examine and investigate into every department of the public and parochial revenue, and examine all books of account and accounts, vouchers and papers, having relation to the revenue of every department or source, and in the possession or under the control of every officer or person charged or having to deal with the collection of the revenues of the several departments throughout the island, and shall after every examination make a separate report as to each department of his proceedings in, and the results of such examination, together with his observations, remarks or suggestions on any matter coming under his cognizance, to the Governor in Executive Committee, and also make examination and report on any further occasions whenever required by the Governor, with the advice of the Executive Committee, 28 V. c. 21, s. 3.

Governor, &c. may make orders for his direction The Governor and Executive Committee may make orders and regulations for the direction of the Inspector, in the full and due discharge of his duties and for carrying out the purposes and policy of this Act, 28 V. c. 21, s 4.

Powers for the purpose of investigation He shall visit and enter into every place of business occupied by every Officer or person charged with, or engaged in collection of any revenue or monies belonging to, or to be accounted for to the public in any department of the Public or Parochial service, and send for, and have the custody of any books or papers under his control, and call for any returns from him relating to any such revenue or public moneys, and may keep such books or papers for such time as may be required, and may also send for and examine upon oath which he is authorized to administer any person touching any matter relating to any revenue, source of revenue, or public money, or the accounts thereof, 28 V. c. 21, s. 5.

Refusal to be examined and produce books, &c If any Revenue Officer or other person when required or sent for by the Inspector, neglects or refuses to appear before him, or to deliver, or produce any books, &c. touching any matter connected with any revenue or public moneys for which he is accountable, or if having come before the Inspector he refuses to be sworn or to answer any question the Inspector may lawfully require to have answered, or neglects or refuses to bring with him, or to produce any books, &c., or to make any return he may be required to make re. **Penalty and recovery** lating to any such revenue, source of revenue, or public moneys he shall forfeit not exceeding £100, to be recovered by attachment under the hand and seal of a Judge of the Supreme Court, to the use of the Crown for the government of the island ; but before attachment issues it must be shewn that the conduct of the person was contumacious, or in case of non-attendance that he had been duly required to attend, and had no reasonable excuse, 28 V. c. 21, s. 6. *Judge to be satisfied, his conduct was contumacious, &c.*

No such Officer or person shall be required to give attendance out of his official or accustomed place of business, except where the Inspector requires to be attended in some more private or convenient place, not further than one mile from such place of business, or unless under special direction by the Governor in Executive Committee, 28 V. c. 21, s. 7. *Place of attendance for examination.*

Wilfully and corruptly giving false evidence. or making a false statement when under examination punishable as perjury, and to be prosecuted as a public prosecution, 28 V. c. 21, s. 8 *False evidence, perjury.*

Any person obstructing, hindering, or impeding the Inspector in the execution of his duty, or in carrying out any order, or direction of the Governor, in Executive Committee, shall on conviction forfeit not exceeding £50, or in default of payment be imprisoned for sixty days, the proceedings to be according to the provisions of any Act in force regulating summary proceedings before Justices, 28 V. c. 21, s. 9. *Obstructing Inspector.*

No Inspector during his continuance in office shall be elected or appointed to sit as a member of either branch of the Legislature, 28 V. c. 21, s 10. *Inspector not to be a member of the Legislature*

Autrefois, Acquit or Convict.

In any plea of autrefois convict or acquit, it shall be sufficient for the defendant to state that he has been lawfully convicted or acquitted, as the case may be of the offence charged in the indictment without setting out the same in any formal manner, 16, V. c, 15 s. 28 . *Form of plea.*

Banks.

Every Corporation, Copartnership, or Individual carrying on the trade of Banking and issuing notes, payable to bearer on demand, shall keep weekly accounts of the average amount of Notes in circulation, and make up quarterly accounts and returns, on oath, of the average amount in circulation at the end of each quarter to the Commissioner of Stamps in Kingston—penalty £500, 7 V. c. 47, s. 12. *Weekly and quarterly averages on notes in circulation.*

And publish in a Kingston newspaper an annual account on, or before 1st April, shewing the whole amount of their debts and assets at the close of the past year ; also of the Notes in circulation during each month, with the amount of specie and other assests immediately available in every month for their discharge, and deliver a copy to the Commissioner of Stamps—penalties for every week's default, £500, for false return the Bank £500—person making out £100, and penalties for perjury, 7 V. c. 47, s. 13, 15. *Annual statements of debts assetts &c*

Also take up, and pay such Notes in coin on presentation at the place of issue. Holders of dishonored Notes (having protested them) shall be entitled to interest from the date of protest, and expense of protest, 7 V. c. 47, s. 14. *Notes to be paid in coin on presentation.*

Penalties to be sued for in the Supreme Court, 7 V. c. 47, s. 16.

No demand, any member may have for any share or any dividends, interest, profits, or proceeds shall be set off against a demand of the Copartnership, 11 V. c. 11, s. 4. *No set off between members and copartnership.*

Members who steal or embezzle property of, or commit any fraud, forgery, crime, or offence against, or with intent to injure or defraud the Copartnership may be indicted and convicted as if they were not members, 11 V. c. 11, s. 5. *Crimes by members*

The record in the Secretary's Office of the Colonial Bank Charter, and certified copies declared evidence, 7 W. 4, c. 18. *Colonial Bank charter*

The Bank of Jamaica the only Joint-Stock Bank, being in course of liquidation the remaining clauses of 7 V. c. 47 and 11 V. c. 11, are not abridged as future Banking Companies must register under the Incorporated Companies Act, 21 V. S. 2, c. 4, or obtain Special Acts.

Barristers.

Admission, liability to client

Must be admitted and take the oaths of allegiance and supremacy before being allowed to practice. By negligence or ignorance, mistaking their client's case and imperfectly laying his action, or ill-drawing the declaration whereby the client suffers a non-suit, liable by rule of Court, without other process, to pay to the party aggrieved full costs of suit, 33 C. 2, c. 23, s. 4.

Certificates of fees

If demanded to give certificate of fees received to be produced on taxation of costs under 24 G. 2. c. 19, s. 2.

Circuit courts

To practice in Circuit Courts, 19 V. c. 10, s. 29.

Signature to pleadings unnecessary in the supreme court

Their signature not necessary to any pleading in the Supreme Court, 28 V. c. 37, s. 36.

Bath, St. Thomas the Apostle.

Incorporation.

The Custos and Members for St. Thomas in the East, the Curate of Bath, and five other persons residing in (St. Thomas in the East, 24 V. c. 23) to be elected by the Justices in Special Session not less than five, and such other persons residing in the parish as shall be in like manner elected to fill any vacancy from death, resignation, departure from the island, or removal from the parish, in the number of five persons incorporated as "the

To hold lands

Directors of the Bath of St. Thomas the Apostle," to hold the lands belonging to the Bath, 23, V. c. 6, s. 1.

Sue and be sued demise lands

Common Seal

clerk

Servants

Rules

Meetings

With power to sue and be sued, demise, lease, or rent the lands not required for the purposes of the Bath for not exceeding twenty-one years, for the most money that can be got, to have a common seal, to appoint a Clerk, who shall reside in the town of Bath, or its immediate neighbourhood—salary £20, remove him and fill up vacancies, employ servants for the care of the Bath and Garden, make rules for the government of the Bath and Garden and the Physician, Clerk, Servants, and Patients resorting to the Bath for the use of its waters, under seal, which are to be printed and hung up in the premises of the Bath. To meet quarterly in the town of Bath on 31st March, 30th June, 30th September, and 31st December, or as soon after as practicable, inspect the premises, enquire into matters connected with the Bath and Garden, examine and pass accounts, and at other times giving two week's notice in the "Gazette", of the days on which each Special Meeting is to be held, and the purpose, Three Directors a quo-

Quorum

rum, 23 V. c. 6, s. 2.

Physician.

They may appoint a Physician to the Bath, salary £48, remove him, and fill up vacancies from death, dismissal, removal from the town or immediate neighbourhood of Bath or resignation, 23 V. c. 6, s. 3.

Physician's annual returns.

The Physician shall prepare and lay before the Directors at their first meeting after 30th September, a return of the persons who during the year visited the Bath for the purposes of the waters, their diseases, the number cured or relieved, the period during which each remained at the Bath, the number remaining on 30th September. Three copies signed by the Physician

To be laid before the Legislature

shall be forwarded by the Clerk to the Governor, one to be laid before the Council, and another before the Assembly, 23 V. c. 6, s. 4.

Clerks duties

Quarterly accounts

The Clerk shall prepare and lay before the directors at their quarterly meetings, a schedule of quarterly salaries and accounts against the Bath, and on their being examined and passed shall certify and transmit it to the Commissioner of the Board of Audit, and the amounts in the schedule on

Annual accounts

his report shall be paid by the Receiver-General, upon the Governor's Warrant ; also at the September meeting, or after an account of the annual receipts and expenditure, setting forth the purposes of expenditure, and upon

To be laid before the Legislature

its being examined and found correct shall forward three copies, certified by him to the Governor, one for the Council, and another for the Assembly 23 V. c. 6, s. 5.

Expenditure of monies

The rents and profits of the lands, and all other monies for the use of the Bath, shall be expended in the payment of salaries, wages of servants, repairs and enlargement and improvement of buildings, and accommodation of such person visiting, for the use of the waters, the maintenance of such as are poor and unable to maintain themselves, the repairs of the road, from the town to the mineral springs, and the care of the Garden, in the town of Bath, and for no other purpose, 23 V. c. 6, s. 6.

Benefit of Clergy.

Abolished, G. 4, c. 19, s. 3.

Billiard Tables, Public.

No person shall by himself or any person employed by him, or for his benefit (unless he has obtained a license from the Justices and Vestry, which shall not be granted, but upon certificate of two respectable freeholders of the parish, that he is sober and discreet, and duly qualified and fit to be trusted to) keep a public Billiard Table, nor shall such license be granted until after reading the certificate in Public Vestry, under penalty of £200 (£120 sterling). Such license to be annually renewed, penalty £200 (£120 sterling), 39 G. 3, c. 7, s. 5. *To be licensed annually*

No person shall have a license without first becoming bound to the Churchwardens, in a bond with one security (a freeholder of the parish) in £500 (£300 sterling) for the maintenance of good order and rule in the house in which the Billiard Table is to be kept and also becoming bound to them with one security (a freeholder) in the penalty of £100 (£60 sterling) to pay the sum of £25 (£15 sterling) in aid of the parochial taxes, and the Clerk of the Peace shall not record the license, until a certificate is produced (from the Collector of Dues), that it has been pa , 39 G. 3, c. 7, s. 6. *sureties*

No person keeping a public Billiard Table, shall permit any playing before 8, a.m. nor after 6 p.m., on common week days, and none on Sunday, penalties fine and imprisonment, as directed for unlawful gaming, 39 G. 3, c. 7, s. 7. *Keeping open* *See gaming, 39 G. 3, c 7, s 2*

Every Clerk of the Peace or his Deputy, under penalty of £50 (£30 sterling) shall keep a separate book, for entering and recording such certificates Bonds and Licenses, 39 G. 3, c. 7, s. 8. *Licenses to be recorded*

For every such license, the person receiving the same shall pay £2 10s (£1 10s sterling) to the Clerk of the Peace, for his trouble of making out and taking the Bond, recording the certificate, and making out and passing the license and recording the same including, every charge, under penalty of £10 (£6 sterling) 39 G. 3, c. 7, s. 9. *Fees*

One moiety of the penalties shall go the informer, to be recovered by action of debt &c., in the Supreme Court, 39 G. 3, c. 7, s. 12. *Penalties*

Prosecutions shall be commenced within 6 months after the offence, 39 G. 3, c. 7, s. 13. *Prosecutions to be within 6 months*

Bills of Exchange, Promissory Notes.

Upon Bills of Exchange protested and returned for non-payment, a re-exchange at the rate of £8 per cent, shall be allowed and recovered over and above the usual exchange, and interest, 12 G. 2, c. 3, s. 2. *Re-exchange on bills protested for non-payment*

But no action shall be brought on any foreign bill of exchanges for damages, or re-exchange, until it has been protested for non-payment, 15 G. 3, c. 21. *But not until then*

When damages are assessed in any action upon a foreign bill, drawn in this island, and returned protested the Court, shall give judgment, that the plaintiff recover of the defendant, the damages, costs and interest upon the principal sum for which the bill was given, from the first day of the Court on which judgment is obtained until actual payment, and the plaintiff, his assignee, attorney-at-law or attorney shall mark or endorse on the writ of venditioni, as well the stated sum assessed for principal, interest, re-exchange and costs, as also interest on the sums for which such bills are given, from the first day of the Court, on which judgment is obtained to the time of actual payment, and the same shall be levied and paid by the Provost Marshall with the stated sum assessed for damages by the Jury, 28 G. 2, c. 2, s. 1. *Interest on Judgment on foreign bills*

All notes and orders carrying interest sued, shall carry interest after judgment, upon the principal, at the same rate they bore before judgment until fully satisfied, 14 G. 3, c. 28, s. 13. *On Judgments on notes and orders*

No note passed or paid away, shall be valid to the person receiving the same, for more than is really and bona fide due, at the time, 14 G. 3, c. 28, s. 2. *Notes not to be passed for more than is due thereon*

20 days indulgence to drawees of inland bills

_The holder of any inland bill, may allow time to the drawer, for not exceeding 20 days after it is payable, without prejudice to any recourse against other parties, 43 G. 3, c. 29, s. 1.

Grantors of promissory notes

As may also holders of promissory notes, 43 G. 3, c. 29, s. 2.

Inland bills need not be protested

Not necessary to have an inland bill protested, in order to a remedy against the drawer or indorser, 43 G. 3, c. 29, s. 2.

Payable to bearer on demand under £1

No Bank or Banking Company, person, firm, Company or copartnership, shall issue or re-issue or cause &c., any bill or promissory note, payable to bearer on demand of a lower denomination or value than £1, on pain of forfeiting for each, a sum equal to double the amount, 7 V. c. 52, s. 1.

Penalty

Recovery

For which any person may sue, to his own use, 7 V. c. 52, s. 2.

Blasphemy.

Punishment

Whosoever by public and open profaneness or Blasphemy, dishonors Almighty God, and is thereof duly convicted in the Supreme Court (now Circuit Court, 9 V. c. 10) shall be fined £20 (£12 sterling) or more at the discretion of the Court, and such as are servants, or not worth so much, shall be liable to such corporal punishment, as the Judges think meet, loss of life and limb only excepted, 33 C. 2, c. 5, s. 2.

Not whipping, 4 V. c. 52, s. 7

Board of Works.

Their powers over expenditure of grants for public buildings

The Governor and any two members of the Executive Committee, shall expend under this Act, the monies from time to time granted for repairing and altering the buildings belonging to the public and to complete and finish those already commenced, or which may be directed to be commenced (except such prisons as may be excepted) and may make contracts with workmen and others for materials, workmanship and labor, hire laborers, and send for and cause to come before them, any person, and examine him, on oath (which they may administer) touching any such matters, and send for books, papers and writings, having relation thereto, which they think requisite, whenever they think fit, 21 V. c. 3, s. 1.

Contracts &c

Examine upon oath

Send for books, &c

Take earth or stones, making compensation

They may order the digging and carrying away earth or stones, for the use of the buildings, out of lands not in cultivation, and not enclosed as a garden or yard, on making reasonable satisfaction, as they and the parties entitled thereto, agree upon, and in case of disagreement, the amount shall be settled by two justices, to be selected by the Executive Committee, and the owner not in any way interested, 21 V. c. 3, s. 2.

No monies to be issued without their warrant

No money shall be issued or paid out of the funds granted for the public buildings, but by the warrant of the Governor and Executive Committee, 21 V. c. 3, s. 3.

Not to contract &c., to a greater amount than is granted

They shall not contract for, agree to, or order any work, to any public buildings or commence any new buildings to a greater amount, than is granted from time to time, by the Legislature, for the purposes, 21 V. c. 3, s. 4.

Work to be contracted for

On all occasions except as after excepted, they shall publicly advertise for proposals and estimates for the work to be done, to be furnished at some specified time under cover and sealed up, in order that the persons who will execute them on the most reasonable and advantageous terms may be employed, 21 V. c. 3, s. 5.

And security required

No proposals or estimates shall be received, nor contract made, unless security is given by the tradesman or contractor for its due performance, 21 V. c. 3, s. 6.

In case of fraud &c. they may refuse any subsequent tender from the party

When they have reason to believe that any person has been guilty of any fraud or misconduct in obtaining any contract or in the improper or negligent performance of any work, they may refuse to such person, the contract of any other public work, for which he offers, notwithstanding his tender is the lowest offered, 21 V. c. 3, s. 7.

Bonds to be proved and evidence

All bonds shall be proved before a Justice, as deeds are and delivered to the Secretary of the Executive Committee, and shall be good evidence, and received without producing the attesting witness, 21 V. c. 3, s. 8.

The Governor and Executive Committee, shall not order payment for any work, except it has been contracted for and performed agreeably to contract previously advertised for according to this Act, unless the estimate of expense or value does not exceed £10, nor unless the whole amount ordered during any one year, without any previous contract does not exceed £200, and no money shall be expended under this section, unless it is by reason of some emergency required to be so immediately undertaken, as to render it impracticable to delay the performance until contracts can be advertised for, 21 V. c. 3, s. 9 *(margin: Emergency when contracts may be dispensed with)*

The Governor may appoint a Civil Engineer and Architect (s. 11.) to be called Colonial Engineer and Architect, removable at his pleasure, whose duty it shall be to inspect the public works and buildings, to make reports, when required by the Governor and Executive, on the state and condition of all such public buildings, the alterations, improvements and repairs they require, and the progress of any public work commenced or in progress with estimates in detail of the expense of any alteration, improvement and repairs of existing buildings and of any new building, and specifications and working plans thereof, to personally inspect and examine all erections, repairs, alterations and improvements while in progress, and, as often as he thinks fit, object to the further progress if he thinks the materials unsound or improper or the workmanship unskilful, to certify to the Governor &c., on the completion of any buildings &c., the manner in which it has been performed and whether according to contract, or otherwise, and generally to do and perform all acts and obey all orders directed or given by the Governor &c., his Salary £400 per annum, payable quarterly, with such reasonable sums not exceeding 20s per day for travelling expenses as they think fit, 21 V. c. 3, s. 10. *(margin: Colonial Engineer and Architect / His duties / Salary)*

No appointment shall be valid unless the person produce evidence of his having been admitted and allowed to practice as a Civil Engineer and Architect by some Society or institution, established for the purpose in the United Kingdom or Continent of Europe, 21 V. c. 3, s. 11. *(margin: Qualification)*

The Governor may appoint not exceeding 4 duly qualified persons (the Surveyors of public works upon the appointment of Colonial Engineer and so long as they retain their respective office included) to be superintendents of public works, subject to removal at pleasure, and whose duty it shall be to see that the Colonial Engineer's specifications and directions are in all cases strictly adhered to, and carried out to personally and regularly superintend all works, alterations, improvements and repairs of a public nature, and to any public buildings, ordered or commenced under this Act, and inspect all materials intended to be used thereon, and report to the Colonial Engineer, any attempt made to use any unsound or improper materials by any contractor or persons engaged, and every case of unskilful workmanship on their part, and prohibit them from proceeding until the Colonial Engineer can attend, for the purpose of determining on such report, and generally to do all acts and obey such orders as may be directed to be done or be given by the Governor &c., or the Colonial Engineer. And each superintendent (not being one of the present Surveyors of public works) shall be entitled to receive on the warrant of the Governor &c., a salary of £100, payable quarterly, and not exceeding 8s per diem, for every day he is engaged in the superintendence of any public work, out of the town or place in which he usually resides, 21 V. c. 3, s. 12. *(margin: Superintendents of public works)*

The present surveyors continued in the office, subject to removal at the Governor's pleasure, 21 V. c. 3, s. 13. *(margin: Present Surveyors)*

At a salary of £200 each, 21 V. c. 3, s. 14. *(margin: Salary)*

The present Surveyor of Surry, shall permanently reside in Kingston or within 6 miles; that for Cornwall in Montego Bay or Falmouth or within 6 miles of either town. If any absent himself from his place of residence, for one month without leave of the Governor &c., unless it is occasioned by the performance of any of the duties required by this Act, he shall be considered to have resigned, 21 V. c. 3, s. 15. *(margin: Residence / Absence)*

The Governor &c., may order their attendance at any place for transacting conjointly any business they may be directed to attend to, and their reasonable travelling expenses shall be pa by the Receiver-General, on being certified by the Governor &c., 21 V. dd3, s. 16. *(margin: Their attendance may be ordered any where)*

G

Colonial Engineers oath

Within 20 days after his appointment, the Colonial Engineer shall attend before a Judge, and take the following oath, which being reduced into writing and signed by the Judge and deponent, shall be transmitted to the Secretary of the Executive Committee, and preserved, which shall be sufficient evidence of an oath having been taken and of its contents.

I,　　　　　　　　　　　duly appointed Colonial Engineer and Architect in and over this island, do swear that I will, well and truly and duly perform and discharge the office and duties of such Colonial Engineer, faithfully, according to law, without favor, affection, malice or ill will, that I will not at any time, take or receive any fee or reward, directly or indirectly, from any person whatsoever, and that while I continue to hold the said office, I will not either directly or indirectly engage or be interested in the performance of any public work, except such as I may be permitted by the Governor, and the said Members of the Executive Committee, to undertake. So help me God, 21 V. c. 3, s. 17.

False swearing

False swearing or declaring to any matter where an oath or declaration is required declared to be perjury, and punishable as such, and the prosecution a public one, 21 V. c. 3, s. 18.

Short title

Board of Works Act, 1857, 21 V. c. 3, s. 19.

Duration

In force until 31st December, 1864, 21 V. s. 3, s. 20.

Continued until 31st March, 1871, 27 V. s. 1, c. 23.

Bonds.

Not to be assigned for more than due

No bond passed or paid away shall be valid to the person receiving it for a larger sum than is really and bonafide due at the time, 14 G. 3, c. 28, s. 2.

Form of assignment

Every bond passed or paid away, shall have on the back of it, an assignment to the effect.

Be it remembered that I.A.B., have this　　　　day of　　　　in the year of Our Lord　　　　assigned the within Bond to C.D. his executors, administrators and assigns, and that the sum of　　　　is due thereon for principal and　　　　for interest and that no payment hath been made thereon, than is this day set forth and allowed.

Which assignment shall be under the hand of the obliger or his attorney or of one or more of his executors or administrators, and shall be as valid as if the assignee had been the obligee with all the rights and powers of the obligee to put the Bond in suit, to take a Judgment in his own name, and to issue write for recovery thereof, but the names of the obligees and the assignments shall be set forth in the declaration, 14 G. 3, c. 28, s. 3.

Further assignments

When any assignee, his attorney, executors or administrators, passes or pays away such bond before Judgment, they shall assign the same to any future assignee in manner prescribed for and obligee, and future assignees shall have the same rights and powers as the first, 14 G. 3, c. 28, s. 4.

Assigning for more than is due

If any obligee assign a bond for a larger sum than is actually and bona fide due, he shall be guilty of a misdemeanor, and on conviction shall suffer fine and imprisonment, as the Judges think necessary, and shall remain in Gaol till the fine is paid, and such sum, also as has been overcharged to the person defrauded, 14 G. 3, c. 28, s. 5.

Notwithstanding the verdict on a Bond proved, shall be for the penal sum, if any payments have been made, which appear on the back of any Bond, put in suit, the jury shall set forth the same in their verdict, with their dates, and they shall be allowed, 14 G. 3, c. 28, s. 12.

Botanic Garden, Bath.

Purchase of lands at or near Bath, directed to be made by certain persons named, and the lands when, purchased to be vested in them, and the survivors and heirs of the survivor for the purposes of a public Botanic Garden, 19 G. 3, c. 17.

Boundaries Disputed

If any dispute arise upon any survey, where the plat given into the patent office varies from the real run and marked lines, the Judges shall adjudge the real run and marked lines, proved before them, to be the bounds,
2 Ann, c. 7, s. 4.

*What to be ad-
judged*

In suits where boundaries are disputed, the Judges shall adjudge the
real run and marked lines proved before them, or those so taken for 10 years
to be the true boundaries, or where the original run lines cannot be proved,
by such as best answer the course and distance of the original plat or patent, if made by a sworn surveyor, and the plat and field work, attested by
him, and the record of such plat to be made and recorded in the Clerk of the
patents' office shall be conclusive to all parties and determine the right of
the possessor to all the lands within the lines of the re-survey plat, 4 G. 2,
c. 4, s. 2.

*Ascertainment
of*

Where the lands of several proprietors bind upon each other, and a reputed boundary has been acquiesced in for 7 years, it shall be adjudged the
true boundary, and may be given in evidence upon the general issue, but not
to extend to minors, women under coverture or person of unsound mind,
who dispute the same within 5 years after the removal of their disability,
14 G. 3, c. 5, s. 2.

*7 Years acquies-
ced in*

In ejectments where it is made to appear to the Court upon affidavit,
that the matter to be tried and determined in the cause is really a question of
boundary between proprietors or persons in possession of adjoining lands,
the Court shall make an order, that the cause be tried as a question of boundary, and neither party shall be held upon the trial to prove title otherwise
than by possession, but the matter of boundary except as aforesaid shall only
be enquired of and tried. Either party may give in evidence upon the
question of boundary any deed or matter of record, 35 G. 3, c. 24.

*Trial of eject-
ments, respecting*

Broad Seal.

Falsifying, forging or counterfeiting Her Majesty's Broad Seal of
this Island, High Treason, and the offenders their Counsellor, aiders, abettors and concealers being convicted by the oaths of 2 witnesses upon trial
or otherwise to be adjudged traitors, 33 C. 2, c. 16.

Forgery of

Punishment, Penal Servitude for life, 19 V. c. 29, s. 1. 21 V. c. 14,
s. 3, 6.

Punishment

The fees of the Great Seal shall be for every 100 acres of lands patented 10s (6s sterling) and so in proportion for a greater or lesser quantity for
foot land 5s (3s sterling) not exceeding 50 feet square, adding 2 sides together, and 10s. (6s sterling) for every 100 feet, or any other number above 50,
for every order for taking up land, 2s 6d (1s 6d sterling) per 100, and no
more, and so in proportion for a greater or lesser number of acres, for sealing
a writ of execution of a decree, subpœna, or other process, 7½ (4½d sterling) 10 Ann, c. 4, s. 20.

*Fees of
On resurveys,
see 2 Ann, c. 7,
s. 3. Patents*

Building Societies.

Any number of persons may form themselves into Societies, for raising
a stock or funds for enabling any member, subject to the rules, to receive
out of the funds, money by way of loan, to be expended in purchasing,
erecting or repairing dwelling houses, and their appurtenances, and other
buildings, or the purchase of land or real estate, such loans to be secured
with interest as required by the rules, and for enabling the Society to purchase freeholds and erect thereon dwelling or other houses and appurtenances, to be sold or rented and to sell or rent them, or let them out on
terms of lease and sale, to persons willing to become purchasers or tenants
or any such purposes, to be called " Building Societies" or " Benefit Building Societies," 28 V. c. 17, s. 1.

*Building Socie-
ties, objects*

Also to raise its capital by shares, not exceeding an estimated, ultimate
value of £50 each, and provide for payment, by the shareholders in full, or
from time to time, on account, or by monthly or other pe   ca payments,
and every person making a payment, shall be deemed and entered as a
shareholder, and bound by the rules, 28 V. c. 17, s. 2.

*Shares and notes
of payment*

Admission of fresh shareholders   Subject to the rules for the time of each Society, fresh shareholders may be admitted and enrolled, 28 V. c. 17, s. 3.

Limited liability   No shareholder shall be liable to pay more towards the funds or liabilities than is payable in respect of his shares taken or agreed to be taken under the rules at time he became so. **Liability for fines &c., and for loans, interest and expenses** Any shareholder offending against any rule shall be liable to the fines and penalties for his offence, and those securing a loan shall be liable to repay same with expenses and interest, at the times and in manner provided, when the loan is granted or agreed for, 28 V. c. 17, s. 4.

Rules   Shareholders may assemble together and by majorities of those present, make rules for their government, as to the major part assembled seems meet, not repugnant to this act or law, and may inflict reasonable fines and **Fines** penalties upon offending shareholders to be paid for the benefit of the general funds, and may amend, rescind and make new rules, 28 V. c. 17, s. 5.

Rules to declare the purposes of the Society, the application of the funds   Every Society shall by its rules, declare the purposes for which it is established, and direct the uses and purposes to which the monies subscribed, paid or given, or to arise therefrom or belong to the Society, shall be appropriated or applied, and in what shares and proportions, and under what cir- **And how members become entitled to the benefits** cumstances any member may become entitled to the benefits thereof, 28 V. c. 17, s. 6.

Annual statements of funds &c   Also that the trustees, directors or principal officer, shall once a year, at least, prepare or cause &c., a general statement of the funds and effects of the Society, specifying in whose custody or possession they then are, with an account of all the various sums received, lent and expended by or on account of the Society, since the publication of the preceding periodical state- **To be attested by auditors, countersigned by secretary and every member to receive a copy** ment to be attested by two auditors, appointed for the purpose, and counter-signed by the Secretary or Clerk, and every member shall receive a copy, 28 V. c. 17, s. 7.

Appointments &c, of affairs   Also to provide for the appointment, removal and dismissal of such president, trustees, directors, committees, secretaries, treasurers, builders, surveyors, solicitors, auditors, clerks and other officers, deemed necessary or advisable for the working of the Society in such manner, on such terms, with such powers and by such majorities as may by the rules be provided, and, **Members may fill offices** they may be appointed, removed or dismissed accordingly. Any such offices, may be filled by members, notwithstanding their position as members, 28 V. c. 17, s. 8.

Rules to specify the trusts of mortgages and the powers &c. of trustees to be referred to   Each Society may by its rules, or schedules thereto, to be certified, confirmed, and filed as herein mentioned, specify the trusts on which mortgages accepted by them shall be taken and held, the powers and privileges which in all such mortgages shall be held by the Trustees, and which shall be therein referred to by apt words; and such trusts, powers, and privileges shall thereupon be as absolutely vested in, and devolve upon the Trustees, as if fully set out, and may also in like manner provide, or set out **Forms** forms in which mortgages, conveyances, surrenders, and releases on mortgage terms, and all conveyances may be taken in cases where it is practicable to adopt such forms, 28 V c. 17, s. 9.

Arbitration   Also for referring to arbitration, disputes between officers and members, or persons claiming under them, concerning the rules their meaning, or application or the affairs of the Society, or claims by, or against the Trustees **Without appeal** or officers, and their award, or that of the major part, according to the true purport of the rules, shall be conclusive and final without appeal, and not **Enforcement of award** removable or restrainable by injunction. In case the parties refuse or neglect to conform to the decision, any Justice residing in the parish where the Society holds its meetings, upon proof of the award, and the refusal or neglect to comply therewith by warrant under his hand and seal may cause the sum awarded, and costs not exceeding 10s, and the cost of warrant and distress to be levied by distress and sale of the moneys, goods, securities, and effects of the party in default with the further costs of distress and sale, returning any surplus, 28 V., c. 17, s. 10.

Two transcripts of the rules and regulations, and of all alterations, amendments, and rescissions shall be signed by three Directors and countersigned by the Clerk, and submitted within one month from meeting to the Barrister appointed to certify the rules of Savings' Banks, to advise and certify that they are calculated to carry into effect the intention and purposes for which the Society was formed, and also are in conformity to law, and to the provisions of this Act, and advising and certifying in what parts they are repugnant, which when certified shall be returned to the Society, one to be kept, and the other transmitted to the Clerk of the Supreme Court and Crown, to be laid before a Judge in Chambers, to allow and confirm same, and to be filed as a record without fee. If there be no Barrister appointed for the purpose, or he declines, or neglects to certify, the Chief Justice on the application of the Society or an officer may appoint a Barrister to certify, whose certificates shall thereupon be valid, 28 V. c. 17, s. 11.

2 Transcripts of the rules, &c

To be submitted to the savings banks' Barrister

To be certified

And returned

One to be kept and the other for confirmation of a Judge, and filed

If no savings' bank Barrister the Chief Justice may appoint

If the Barrister refuses to certify or certifies any rules to be repugnant, or desires the opinion of a Judge for his guidance on any point, the Society or an officer may submit the rules, alterations, &c., or any of them to a Judge in Chambers, with the reasons assigned by the Barrister, in writing for any such refusal, difficulty, or disapproval, and the Judge may confirm them, notwithstanding, or give such directions in reference to the certificate to be granted as he deems right, 28 V., c. 17, s. 12.

Application to a Judge to revise Barristers' certificates

The Barristers' Fee shall be 63s, and no more, and no fee shall be allowed in respect of any alterations, amendments, or rescissions of any rules upon which one fee has been already paid to him within three years, 28 V. c. 17, s. 13.

Barristers' fee

No Society shall be deemed a "Building Society" or "Benefit Building Society", within this Act, until its rules, particularly those required by sections, 6 and 7 have been certified, confirmed, and filed, and the rules, alterations, and additions shall be the rules from the dates of their confirmation until the rescission, &c., be certified and confirmed, and except in so far as rescinded, &c., and the rules for the time being so certified and confirmed, shall be binding on the members, officers, contributors, and subscribers, and their representatives, all of whom shall be taken to have full notice, thereof, 28 V. c. 17, s. 14.

No society to be within this Act, unless certified, &c:

Rules to be deemed in force

And binding

No rule after confirmation shall be altered nor new rule adopted, unless upon the requisition in writing of ten members holding, in all, not less than fifty shares, specifying the rules sought to be altered, &c., or adopted, and all alterations proposed to be made therein, which requisition shall be publicly exhibited at the rooms or office, at least one month before any meeting to consider same is called, nor unless a general meeting is thereupon duly convened to consider same, nor unless upon a vote of at least three-fourths the number of the shareholders present, and also upon the votes of shareholders, holding three-fourths of the number of shares held by the shareholders so present; 28 V., c. 17, s. 15.

How rules may be altered, &c.

All rules and alterations shall be entered in a book, to be kept by an officer appointed for the purpose, to which all members shall be entitled to access when the office is open for business, 28 V., c. 17, s. 16.

Rules to be entered in a book open to members

The General Business shall be carried on for the purposes in the manner and by the persons appointed under the rules, and the funds whil not required or used for the purposes thereof, shall be lodged in a Bank of the Island, in the manner and in the names of such persons as the rule direct require, or permit, and all interests therefrom applied to increase the general funds, 28 V., c. 17, s. 17.

General business to be carried on under the rules

Lodgment in banks

Interest

General Meetings shall be held at such times and places, and such manner, and notified as and for such times as required by the rule or if there be none on the subject, the time and place shall be notified by Public Advertisement, signed by two Directors, in two newspapers for at least two weeks previously, 28 V., c. 17, s. 18.

General meetings

All Committees to be appointed under the rules, or by a General Meeting, shall be appointed only at General Meetings convened under a resolution, specifying the purposes for which the Committee is appointed, and the powers delegated to them, and shall, in all things delegated, committed, or entrusted to them, act for the Society, and their acts and orders during the time they are appointed, or hold office, shall be binding on the whole members, their transactions shall be entered into a book of the Society, and liable to inspection by members, and subject to the review, allowance, disal.

Committees

Appointment

Powers

Transactions to be entered in a book, subject to review

lowance, and control of the Society or Directors, as provided by the rules, 28 V., c. 17, s. 19.

Donations
Application

Any Society may receive donations and bequests applicable to the general purposes of the Society, or the special purpose for which given in like manner as contributions of members, and in no other manner—28 V., c. 17, s. 20.

Bonus and interest

Any Society may receive from any members any money, by way of bonus on shares for the privilege of receiving same in advance prior to being realized, and also any interest for the shares received, or any part, 28 V·, c. 17, s. 21.

Securities to be given to, or by two, or more Trustees
Exempted from Stamps
And vest in the Trustees for the time being.
Without assignment
And enforceable by them
Investment in bank, &c,
Certificates of appointment of Trustees to be recorded in Secretary's Office
Extended to existing Societies coming under this Act

All mortgages, conveyances, bonds, and other securities to, or by any Society shall be made and given to two or more, Trustees and not chargeable with any Stamp Duty until this clause is specially repealed, 28 V., c. 17. s, 22.

And be made or given to, or by the Trustees for the time being, and on each change in such Trusteeship, the legal estate and interest shall immediately vest in the Trustees for the time, without assignment, conveyance, or other deed, and may be recovered and enforced by them in any Court of Law, or Equity, as if the securities, real or personal property, had been originally executed in favor of, or conveyed to them ; and all investments of moneys, and securities in any Bank, Savings' Bank, or Public Treasury, shall be forthwith transferred to the names of the Trustees for the time, upon the request in writing of any two Directors. Every appointment of Trustees shall be certified under the hand of three Directors to the Island Secretary to be recorded among the records of deeds. The advantages of this clause shall apply to all deeds. &c. of Societies already established, which become a " Building Society" or " Benefit Building Society", under this Act—28 V., c. 17, s. 23.

All property of the society vested in the Trustees for the time
Without assignment
Except securities in the Public, Treasury, Banks &c.
Civil and criminal proceedings in respect thereof
With consent of a meeting of the Directors
Action, &c. not to abate by death
Costs

All real estate, titles, securities for money, and other obligatory instruments, and evidences, and muniments of title, and other effects, rights, and claims of the Society shall be vested in the Trustees for the time being for the use of the Society and members, their Executors, and Administrators, according to their respective interests ; and after the death or removal of any Trustee shall vest in the succeeding or surviving Trustees for 'the same interest, and subject to the same trusts, without conveyance or assignment, except the transfer of stocks and securities in the Public Treasury or any Savings' Banks, or other Bank or place of deposit, or investment, and for all purposes of action or suit as well criminal as civil at law or in Equity shall be deemed the property of the Trustees for the time, in their proper names without further description, and they may bring or defend, or cause, &c. actions, suits, and prosecutions, criminal as well as civil in law or in Equity, touching the property, rights, or claims of the Society having been thereunto authorized by the consent of the majority of members present at a meeting of the Society or committee, or by a meeting of Directors, and may sue and be sued, &c; in their proper names as Trustees of the Society without other description ; and no suit, &c. shall be discontinued or abate by death or removal, but shall be proceeded in by the succeeding Trustees in the names of the persons commencing the same, and succeeding Trustees shall pay and receive costs as if the action or suit had been commenced in their names for the benefit of, or to be reimbursed. from the funds of. the Society—18 V., c. 17, s. 24.

Sufficient to record memorandum of mortgage until it is advisable to enforce same
Access to be allowed to mortgage
Secretary's fees

Not necessary to record any mortgage to the Society or the Trustees until it is advisable to enforce it ; but it shall be sufficient notice of the existence of such a charge if a memorandum, (Form, Schedule,) signed by the parties giving such mortgage is recorded in the Secretary's Office within three months after the mortgage, and every mortgage of which a memorandum is recorded shall have the same, and no other effect than if the deed had been fully recorded, and free access shall be had by every person interested in the original mortgage in the Society's possession. Secretary's fee to record memorandum 2s, and no more, but on recording any mortgage deed the usual fees shall be paid, 18 V., c. 17, s. 25.

Enforcement of subscriptions, fines, &c.

Arrears of subscriptions, fines, penalties, and forfeitures due to any Society under its rules shall be enforceable by petty debt summons, or action according to the amount to be sued in the names of the Trustees for the time, and by proceedings thereon to judgment and execution in form upon an account stated by the defendant with the plaintiff, 18 V.. c. 17, s. 26.

Members accepting any office or employment under the rules, or in any way indebted or liable to the Society, or having claims against it, may sue, and be sued by the Trustees, and be answerable civilly and criminally in respect to their actions, transactions and omissions in like manner as if they were not members or partners, and that fact shall not be set up or delay or defeat any civil or criminal proceeding or process in any Court,—28 V. c. 17, s. 27.

Members may sue, and be sued, and be criminally answerable

Every officer who shall have or receive any part of the monies, effects or funds of any Society, or shall be entrusted with the disposal, management or custody thereof, or of any securities' books, papers or property of the Society, his Executors, or Administrators shall, on demand made, or notice in writing given, or left at the officers' last, or usual place of residence in pursuance of an order of the Society, or of two Directors, or of a committee to be appointed for the purpose, within seven days after demand or notice, give in his account in writing at the next usual meeting of the Society, or to the Directors or committee, to be examined and allowed, or disallowed by them, and on the like demand or notice pay over all monies in his hands, and assign, transfer, and deliver all securities and effects, books, papers, and property taken or standing in his name, or in his hands or custody, to the Secretary or Directors, or to such persons as the Society or any committee appoint; and in case of neglect or refusal the Society in the name of the Trustee, as the case may be, may exhibit a petition to the Chancellor or Vice-Chancellor, who shall proceed summarily and make such order thereon in Chambers or in open Court as seems just, and all assignments, sales, and transfers in pursuance of such order shall be good, 28 V., c. 17, s. 28.

Proceedings against officers their executors, &c, to enforce account, transfer and delivery of property, books, &c., and payment of monies

If any p   appointed to any office established or recognized under this Act, and being entrusted with the keeping of the accounts, or having in his hands or possession, by virtue of his office or employment, any monies or effects of the Society, or any deeds or securities relating to the same dies or becomes Bankrupt or Insolvent, or has any extent, execution or attachment, or other process issued against his lands, goods, chattels or effects or property, or estate, real or personal, or makes any assignment, disposition or other conveyance thereof, for the benefit of his creditors, his heirs, executors, administrators or assigns, or other persons, having legal right, or the sheriff or other officer executing the process as the case may be, shall, within 40 days after demand in writing, by order of the Society, or any two Directors, or Committee, deliver and pay over all monies and other things belonging to the Society, to such persons as the Society, directors or Committee appoint, and pay out of the estates, assets, or any effects real or personal of such person, all sums remaining due, which he received by virtue of his office &c., before any other of his debts, and before the money directed to be levied is paid over to the party issuing such process and all such assets &c., shall be bound to the payment and discharge, 28 V. c. 17, s. 29.

Prior lien of the Society upon the property of its officers indebted to them or having property of theirs

Notice of claim to the persons in possession of the Society's property or of assets

The trustees or any other officer, shall not be liable to make good any deficiency in the funds of the Society, but shall be personally responsible and liable for all monies actually received by them on account, or for the use of the Society, 28 V. c. 17, s. 30.

Limitation of trustees or officers liabilities

For preventing fraud and imposition upon the funds of the Society, by any officer, member or other person, being or representing himself to be a member or the nominee, executor, administrator of any member, or any other person, who by any false representation or imposition, fraudulently obtains possession of any monies of the Society, or having in his hands any monies of theirs fraudulently withholds the same for which offence no special provision is made in the rules, any Justice of the parish, where the Society holds its meetings on complaint on oath, or affirmation by an officer appointed for the purpose, may summon the person complained of, and upon his appearance or in default thereof, upon due proof of the service, any two Justices residing in such parish, may hear the complaint according to the confirmed rules of the Society, and upon due proof convict the party and award double the amount of the money fraudulently obtained, or withheld to be paid to the trustees, to be applied to the purposes of the Society, with such costs as shall be awarded and if not paid to the person and at the time specified in the order, they shall by warrant under their hands and seals, cause the same to be levied by distress and sale, with the costs to be awarded, and those attending such distress and sale, or other legal proceedings, returning any surplus to the owner, and in default of distress being found, they shall commit the offend-

Summary proceedings before Justices in cases of fraudulent obtaining or withholding money

Not to prevent proceedings by indictment.
Unless a conviction has been obtained. Right of appeal.
er. to the Gaol, or house of correction, to be kept to hard labor, for not exceeding 3 calendar months, but not to prevent the Society from proceeding by indictment or complaint unless a previous conviction has been obtained under this Act. The right of appeal not taken away, 28 V. c. 17, s. 31.

Minors may be members with consent of parents &c.
A minor may become a member, execute instruments, give acquittances, and enjoy of the privileges, and be liable to all the responsibilities of members of matured age, if admitted with the consent of parents, masters or guardians, 28 V. c. 17, s. 32.

Payment of shares not exceeding £30, of deceased members
If any member dies entitled to not exceeding £30, the trustees and directors if satisfied that no will was made and left by the deceased, and that no letters of administration will be taken out, may pay the same at any time after, according to the rules, or if there are no rules in that behalf, the trustees or treasurer, may pay and divide the same among the persons entitled as next of kin, without letters testamentary or of administration, 28 V. c. 17, s. 33.

Such payment to be valid against the funds, but may be recovered against the person received it
Which payments shall be valid with respect to any demand of any other person as next of kin, or lawful representative of the deceased, against the funds of the Society, or the trustees, but such next of kin or representative shall have remedy against the persons who received it, as for money had and received to his use, 28 V. c. 17, s. 34.

Conditions of dissolution
No Society shall by any rule at any general meeting or otherwise, dissolve or determine so long as the declared instances and purposes or any of them remain to be carried into effect, without the votes of consent of five-sixths in number and value of the then existing members, nor unless the intended appropriation or division of their funds or other property be fairly and distinctly stated in the proposed plan of dissolution prior to such consent being given, and the plan is certified by such barrister as aforesaid (s. 11)

Liabilities in case of their violation
to be fair and equitable and in the event of such division of the property or misappropriation of the funds without the consent and certificate declared to be requisite, the trustees and their officers and persons aiding and abetting thereon, shall be liable to the penalties provided for in cases of fraud (s. 31) and also to the general members for the funds, so misappropriated, 28 V. c. 17, s. 35.

Societies already established
Any Society already formed, may lay its rules before such barrister (s. 11) and upon their being certified and confirmed, shall be deemed a " Building Society" or " Benefit Building Society" within this Act, and entitled to the rights, powers and privileges hereby granted to such Societies, 28 V. c. 17, s. 36.

Short title
The Benefit Building Society Act, 1865, 28 V. c. 17, s. 37.

FORM OF MEMORANDUM.

Date of Deed.
Names of parties.
Substance of recitals.
Description of p m .
Full abstract of provisions of deed.
Signatures of parties executing.
Signature of witness.
Date of probate and before whom taken.

Jamaica, s.s.—I swear that the above is a true extract of the mortgage, deed, to the trustees of the   Building Society.

Secretary of the Company.

Sworn before me, at Kingston, this   day of   186

J.P. Kingston.

Cayman Islands.

Magistrate.
After the appointment of a Resident Magistrate, in and for these Islands, the Governor may, by his warrant, direct payment to him of the amount of dues from time to time collected on droghers of or belonging to the Cayman Islands, or persons resident therein, 25 V., c. 25.

Chancery Deposits.

Monies ordered to be paid into the Court of Chancery to the credit of any cause, to await its further order, shall be paid to the Receiver General to the credit of the cause, and not be demandable without an order of Court in the cause—Receiver General to give a receipt therefor, his fee, 5s. (3s. sterling) beyond the stamp, and on paying out money 5s. (3s. sterling) for perusing the order [for the use of the public 21 V. c. 4, s. 5.] 4 G. 4., c. 21. s. 2. To be paid to Receiver General. His fees.

The debts and liabilities of the public in Schedule F (including Chancery deposits, £19,798 10s 4d, Insolvent Act deposits, £5,583 4s 9d, and monies mentioned in 19 V. c., 5 schedule) directed to be paid out of the £500,000 loan, 17 V. c. 29, s. 50. To be Paid out of £500,000 loan.

The Chancery Deposit Act, 1855, 18 V. c. 33, s. 1. Short Title.

All principal sums in the Receiver General's books under 4 G. 4, c. 21., 2 W. 4, c. 41, and 11 V. c. 13. (Title Trustees) required by 17 V. c. 29, to be discharged out of the loan, shall be invested jointly in the names of the Receiver General and Registrar in Chancery, in the British Funds, or Guaranteed Loan under 17 V. c. 29, in one entire sum or parcels, under order of the Court of Chancery. Or the Court may direct that any of such moneys remain in the Receiver General's hands without interest, from the time a sufficient sum is raised out of the loan 18 V. c. 33, s. 2. And invested in British funds or Guaranteed Loan.

The Insolvent deposits, £5,583 4s 9d, were directed to be applied towards making good the deficiency in the sum of £19,798 10s 4d, to discharge the Chancery deposits with interest, and to be invested accordingly, 19 V. c. 5, s. 1. Application of Insolvents deposits.

From the time of investment, interest was directed to cease to be payable by the island. 18 V. c. 33, s. 3. Island interest to cease.

In case of a vacancy in the office of the Receiver General or Registrar, the person causing it or his personal representatives, shall, within three months after the vacancy is filled, upon request, join with the surviving or continuing officer to execute the necessary instruments for the transfer of the funds, into the names of the person continuing in office jointly with the person appointed to fill the vacancy—penalty £100, 18 V. c. 33, s. 3. Transfers on vacancy in Receiver General's or Registrar's Office.

The Receiver General with the sanction of the Executive Committee, may authorize a cashier of the Bank of England or Island Agent, to receive and re-invest dividends, and as received, shall place the same to the credit of the cause; or if several principal sums have been invested in one entire sum, the proportional parts due to each at the cost of the fund invested, and the Court may, by order, vary the securities, 18 V. c. 33, s. 4.

Similar investments shall be made of all principal monies in office under any order of Court, for payment of which, provision was not made out of the loan, and thereupon interest shall cease to be payable by the Island, as also under an order of the court of all monies thereafter directed to be paid into the Receiver General's office, 18 V. c. 33, s. 5. Investment of further deposits.

When invested monies are directed to be paid out, the party, his solicitor, or agent, must attend the Receiver General with an office copy or certificate of the Registrar of the decree or order, as well as any report to which it refers, as specifying the money to be paid; and the Receiver General shall, at the cost of the person, or fund, cause the same, and all accruing interest, or so much as is directed to be paid, to be transferred or sold and paid to or for the benefit of such person as he shall in writing appoint—the entire cost of charges and advertisements being paid from the sum invested, and no order of the Court for payment shall be made in favor of any claimant, nor shall he receive the same until provision has been made for the full amount of such costs and charges, 18 V. c. 33, s. 8. Transfers or payments to persons entitled. Costs of

Receiver General's fee [for his own use, 21 V. c. 4, s. 5.] £2½ per cent, on the principal monies lodged and invested, for his trouble in keeping the accounts, 18 V. c. 33, s. 9. Receiver General's fees.

H

Further Invest-
ments.
The sums mentioned in schedule, and all sums which have been or may be deposited under 11 V. c. 33 and 35 (for lands taken for the Penitentiary and Lunatic Asylum) shall be invested under orders of the Court of Chancery, and interest shall cease thereon after investment, 19 V. c. 5, s. 2. 3.

Forfeited Depo-
sits.
After monies paid and deposited subject to any order of the Court of Chancery, have remained so deposited for 20 years, without application for payment, the Executive Committee (on certificate of the Register that the money has been deposited for that period, and no application or claim for payment made during such time) shall give notice by advertisement in the " London Gazette," and some other paper of large circulation in Great Britain, and in the " Jamaica Gazette by authority" for one year, from the date of the first publication in each, that the money was so paid and has remained unclaimed, and if not claimed or the right to the money substantiated within 2 years from the date of the first publication in Great Britain, it will become the absolute property of the public, 19 V. c. 5, s. 5.

After which time without any claim having been substantiated to the satisfaction of the Court of Chancery, the same, and all interest thereon shall become forfeited, and the absolute property of the island, 19 V. c. 5, s. 6.

SCHEDULE.

Trustees of Marriage Settlement of the Duke and Duchess of Buckingham, 11 V. c. 35	560	0	0	
Ditto ditto	180	16	8	
Ditto c. 33	80	5	0	821 1 8
Heir at Law of Stephen Denton, trustee under will of John Tait, and others 11 V. c. 35				70 0 9
Heir at Law of John Eardly Wilmot, 11 V. c. 35				203 6 8

Charitable Grants.

Confirmation of
gifts, &c., within
twenty years.
For 20 years next, all gifts, grants, conveyances, and devises of any lands, rents, goods, or chattels, to any good, pious, charitable or public uses, as for the maintenance of lawful ministers, erecting or maintaining of churches, chapels, schools, universities, colleges, or other places for education of youth, or maintenance of men of learning, or any alms houses, or hospitals, or any other uses theretofore made and to be made confirmed, the statute of mortmain or any other statute, &c., notwithstanding 33 C. 2. c. 15, s. 1.

But not of gifts-
&c., for superstiti-
ous uses, or Minis-
ters not of the
Church of England.
No gifts, grants, or devise to any persons for any superstitious use, or for maintenance of any minister or teacher, other than such as are lawfully ordained, and allowed of by the Church of England, be hereby confirmed and made good, 33 C. 2. c. 15, s. 2.

Charities (Perpetual Annuities).

Annual sums
payable for
The Receiver-General shall pay in every year, under the Governor's Warrants, out of the General Revenue, by way of perpetual annuities to the credit of the several Charities and Institutions, and to be applied by the Trustees thereof, according to the Trusts under which the annual incomes or funds are to be applied, the sums stated in the column " Interest or Annuities" in schedule opposite to the several Charities and Institutions amounting to £5,466 7s 10d, 28 V. c. 23, s. 1.

In full of princi-
pal and interest
In full and final settlement and discharge of all principal at any time, and interest to accrue on account of such Charities and Institutions, and the principal monies shall be excluded from the statement or account of debts due by the Public, 28 V., c. 23, s. 2.

Not to affect rights
to arrears of inter-
est
Not to affect the rights of the Trustees to the sums brought forward in the Receiver-General's Books as due to the respective Charities and Institutions at 30th September (1864) under the head of " Interests," 28 V., c. 23, s. 3.

The Governor and Executive Committee may allow any further sums already paid or invested in any Island Loan Fund, or accept any money hereafter offered for any such investment or payment otherwise to the account of the Public from or on behalf of any Charity or Institution, or Trust to be appropriated to the use of the Government, upon the understanding and agreement that it shall not be re-paid, withdrawn, or claimed in consideration of the payment by way of perpetual annuity of an amount to be calculated at, and made equal to £6 per cent. per annum thereon ; such annual payment to be made as directed in respect to the accounts in the schedule in settlement and discharge of the principal and interest monies which might otherwise be claimed, and shall not be stated as part of the Island Debt, 28 V. c. 23, s. 4. *Further investments at £6 per cent by way of perpetual annuity*

An account in detail of the expenditure of the yearly sum of £5,466 7s. 10d and other sums to be paid, shall be laid before the Assembly within the first two weeks after each meeting, 28 V., c. 23, s. 5. *Accounts of expenditure to be laid before the Assembly*

SCHEDULE.

STATUTE OR OTHERWISE.	CHARITIES AND INSTITUTIONS.	PRINCIPAL.	INTEREST OR ANNUITIES.
9 G 2, c. 6 40, G, 3 c 23.	Woolmer's	12,000 0 0	1,044 0 0
17 G. 2, c. 10 } Repled. by 32 G. 2, c. 17 } 27 V. c.19	St. Jago de la Vega	600 0 0	60 0 0
18 G. 3, c. 18	Rusea's	2,700 0 0	270 0 0
33 G. 3, c. 14	Gregory's	2,400 0 0	144 0 0
38 G. 3, c. 27 43 G. 3, c. 32 48 G. 3, c. 25	Jamaica Free School	12,451 0 0	996 0 0
51 G. 3, c. 25	Manning's	7,852 14 8	471 3 3
Resolutions of Assembly 7th Dec., 1822.	Presbyterian Institution.	2,262 12 0	181 0 0
Under Will of Testator, 1821, and Resolutions of Assembly, 22nd March, 1838	Merrick's	1,200 0 0	72 0 0
Under Will of Testator, and Resolutions of Assembly, 22nd March, 1838.	Smith's	1,800 0 0	108 0 0
18 V. c. 53	Munro & Dickenson's	23,337 4 3	1,400 4 7
18 V. c. 54	Vere	6,256 0 0	500 9 7
19 V. c. 38 19 V. c. 39	Manchester	2.744 0 0	219 10 5
		£64,803 10 11	£5,466 7 10

And any other Charity Institution or Trust as provided under the foregoing.

Circuit Courts.

The Island divided into 4 Circuits :— *Circuits*

1. The Home Circuit comprising the precincts of Kingston and St. Catherine,
2. The Cornwall Circuit, St. Elizabeth, Westmoreland, Hanover, St. James, and Trelawny.
3. The Surry Circuit, St. David, [now united to Kingston Precinct 28 V., c. 34, s. 2,] St. Thomas in the East, Portland, St. George, and Metcalfe ; and
4. The Middlesex Circuit, St. Mary, St. Ann, St. Thomas in the Vale, Vere, Clarendon, and Manchester, 19 V. c. 10, s. 11.

The Parishes of Kingston, Port Royal, and St. Andrew [to which St. David is now added, 28 V. c. 34, s. 2], shall form the Precinct of Kingston, St. Catherine, St. John, and St. Dorothy that of St. Catherine, 19 V. c. 12, s. 12. *Precincts*

From 1st April, 1865 the St. David's Court was abolished, thereafter to be deemed parcel of the Court of the precinct of Kingston, as if originally included in that Court, 28 V., c, 33, s. 6.

Presiding Judges

The Chief Justice shall preside in the Home Circuit Courts, and the three Assistant Judges shall preside each in the Courts of one of the other Circuits, 19 V. c. 10, s. 14.

The Assistant Judge for Surry to assist in criminal matters in the Kingston Court And sit in a separate Court

The Assistant Judge whose turn it is to preside in the Surry Circuit shall assist the Chief Justice to deliver the Gaols and hear and determine indictments ready for trial in the precinct of Kingston, and for such purpose shall sit in a separate Court from him, in the City of Kingston, and from day to day, according to the practice of the Court, and for so much of the period fixed by law for the sitting of the Court, as may be necessary, and shall act in the precinct as now established as a Judge of Assize, Oyer and Terminer and Gaol Delivery, fully and effectually in such precinct for the assistance of   C i f Justice in the discharge of such criminal business,—28 V, c. 36 s. 1. h e

Separate sets of Jurors to be drawn from the panel for the two Courts.

At the opening of the Court for the precinct of Kingston, or at such other time, if need be during such Court, as the Chief Justice shall fix, the Clerk of the Court or his Deputy shall put the names of the Jurors on the panel, written on separate pieces of cards or paper, into a box and separately draw therefrom the names of the Jurors, the first half of whom

But not to disqualify them from sitting in either Court if called on

shall be directed to sit as Jurors in the Court wherein the Chief Justice presides, and the other half in the Court wherein the Assistant Judge sits, but it shall not disqualify the Jurors from sitting in either of the Courts, if called on, and directed so to do, 28 V., c. 33, s. 3.

Alteration of time place and duration of Courts

The Governor may by writing under his hand and seal, alter the times and places for holding any Circuit Courts, and direct any such Courts shall be held at such other places within the parish and precinct, and at such other time, and to be of such duration as in his discretion appears best adapted for the convenience of suitors, and best to answer the ends of justice, the alteration to be made, at least, four weeks before the holding of the Circuit Court, the Sessions whereof are to be affected and to be previously published in the " Jamaica Gazette" for three weeks, 19 V., c. 10, s. 17.

Proceedings of certain Circuit Courts, the time of holding and duration of which had been altered, confirmed

In consequence of the non-publication of the Governor's orders of 26th May, 1862 and 19th January, 1863, altering the time and duration of several Circuit Courts in " The Jamaica Gazette, by Authority", for three weeks previously to the holding of the Courts, all Judges, Jurors, and Officers authorizing or parties to any proceedings already had in such Courts shall be held harmless, and indemnified against all consequences of irregularity in such proceedings by reason of such insufficient advertisements, and all their acts shall be of the like effects and validity, as if the advertisements of the several notices of change of time in the holding such Courts had been previously published in " The Jamaica Gazette by Authority," for 3 weeks, 28 V. c. 34, s. 1.

Meeting and duration of Kingston Circuit Courts

In the Home Circuit, the precinct Court of Kingston, Port Royal, and St. Andrew, and any other parish to be amalgamated therewith [St. David, 28 V. c- 33, s. 6.] shall meet on the 8th Monday after the rising of the Supreme Court, in each of the terms of February and June, and after the October term on the first Monday in January, thereafter, and shall sit as heretofore, in the City of Kingston, and endure for three weeks each time, if necessary, 28 V. c. 34, s. 2.

Cornwall Circuit Courts

The Schedule A in the Judicial Amendment Act, 1855. [19 V. c. 10, s. 22.] prescribing the times of holding, and the duration of the Courts in the Cornwall Circuit, shall continue to regulate the holding and duration of those Courts, 28 V. c. 34, s. 3.

St. George and Metcalfe

The District Court of St. George, in the Surry Circuit shall be held at Buff Bay, and meet on the Monday after the termination of the Portland Court, and sit for two days each time, if necessary. The District Court of Metcalfe in the Surry Circuit shall be held at Annotto Bay, and meet on the first Wednesday after the termination of the St George's Circuit Court, and sit for four days each time, if necessary, 28 V. c. 34, s. 4.

The District Court for St. Thomas in the Vale in the Middlesex Circuit *St Thomas in the Vale*
shall be held at Rodney Hall, and meet on the first Tuesday instead of the
first Thursday after the termination of the sittings of each Supreme Court and
sit for five days if necessary, the first of such altered sittings to commence
after the termination of the ensuing sittings of the Supreme Court for June
Term, 1865, 28 V. c, 34; s. 5.

The Courts for the precincts of St. James and Trelawny shall sit de die *Duration of Corn-*
in diem for a fortnight, if the business require it, but no longer, 19 V. c. *wall Courts*
10, s. 22.*

In case of non-attendance of the presiding Judge, the Clerk of the Court *Adjournment, in*
shall adjourn the Court from day to day until the lapse of the period limited *absence of Judge*
for the session, or the Judge's arrival, 19 V. c. 19, s. 18.

The Chief and Assistant Judges shall act in their circuits in all respects, *Jurisdiction and powers*
as the Judges of Assize, heretofore, and shall each within the jurisdiction
of the Court over which they preside, and at the times at which they are
required to be held, enquire by the oaths of good and lawful men of the
parish or precinct in or for which the Court is held of all treasons, mispri-
sions of treason, felonies, and misdemeanours, and accessories to the same,
and hear and determine the same and each within his circuit, and at the
times the Courts are required to be held, shall deliver the gaols, preside
and take verdicts upon issues and assessments of damages, dispose of and
determine matters of insolvency heretofore subject to the adjudication of
the Insolvent Debtors' Court, and exercise jurisdiction in matters of appeal
before exercised by the Chairman of Quarter Sessions, 19 V. c. 10, s. 19.

Upon application of an Insolvent Debtor or opposing creditor, the Judge *Insolvent.*
of a Circuit Court may refer the adjudication to the Supreme Court, 19
V. c. 10, s. 21.

The course of practice shall be to dispose of all applications to be *Course of prac-*
made in open Court, then to deliver the gaol and determine all indictments *tice*
ready for trial, then to proceed to the trial of civil issues, in the order they
stand, and the assessment of damages upon such issues or in cases of Judgments by default, and after that to dispose of Insolvent Debtors' cases and
appeals, and until the whole business is disposed, the Court shall sit de die in
diem, unless the Judge is unable to preside from ill-health or other un- *Judges ill-health*
avoidable cause, when he may direct an adjournment, until he can attend; *&c*
but the Session shall not extend with such adjournments, beyond the time
limited, for holding it. In case of continued indisposition, the Governor
may appoint a substitute to be remunerated out of the Judges Salary, but the
appointment to be exempt from any Stamp or other duty, 19 V. c. 10, s. 23.

The authority to try and determine issues civil or criminal joined in the *Venue*
Supreme Court, except where the venue is changed, shall be limited to the
Court for the parish or precinct within which the cause of action or offence
is stated to have arisen or been committed. Any Circuit Judge may change *Change of Venue*
the venue in any indictment for felony or misdemeanor proclaimed before
him to any other parish or precinct in the same Circuit, the order for such
change of venue to be attached to the original indictment. Not to affect the
existing powers of the Supreme Court to change the venue, 19 V. c. 10, s. 26.

The Judges of the Supreme Court, on application of the Crown, or the *Supreme Court*
accused, and on good cause shewn, may change the venue, and remove the *may change venue*
trial from any one Court to any other, 22 V. c. 39, s. 3.

Barristers and Attornies admitted in the Supreme Court only, shall be *Barristers and*
entitled to appear for parties to proceedings, but any party may appear in *Attornies*
person to advocate his own cause, 19 V. c. 16, s. 27.

---

*This section was repealed wholly by 22 V. c. 39, s. 1, but is revived by
28 V. c. 34, s. 3. The 23 V. c. 15, s. 6, also repealed so much of the 22 V. c.
39, as limited the duration of these Circuit Courts to nine days, and enacts,
that after February term, 1860, the Circuit Court for St. James, shall sit for
two weeks, if necessary, and that for Trelawny should be held on the first
Monday after the termination of the two weeks allowed for the St James
Circuit Court and sit for two weeks, if necessary. The table of the sittings
of the Circuit Courts infra gives full informations, as to place and time of
commencement and duration, if necessary, of all the Circuit Courts with references to the enactments in force.

Clerks of Circuit Courts The Clerks of the Peace, shall be Clerks of the Circuit Court of the parish, those of St. Andrew, Kingston and Port Royal, shall conduct the prosecutions of offences committed in their parishes, and the Clerk of the Peace of Kingston, shall be Clerk of the Circuit Court, in all matters of civil jurisdiction, 19 V. c. 10, s. 28.

Clerk of the Peace for St. David to conduct prosecutions from that parish The Clerk of the Peace of St. David, shall conduct in the Court of the precinct of Kingston, the prosecution of offences charged to have been committed in St. David, in the same manner, as such business is now conducted by the Clerks of the Peace, for Kingston, Port Royal and St. Andrew, 28 V. c. 33, s. 7.

Their duties The Clerk of the Peace shall attend the Court, call the Jurors and make known their defaults and excuses, in criminal cases call the parties required to appear under recognizance, prepare bills of indictment and present and receive them from the Grand Jury, arraign prisoners for trial, and receive and record verdicts in criminal trials, administer oaths, make entries of proceedings, and in the absence of the Attorney General or his Deputy, conduct the prosecution in all cases of felony and misdemeanor. In civil cases he shall discharge all the duties of the Clerk of the Assize Court, 19 V. c. 10, s. 29.

Bills of Indictment. But he shall not prepare and send before the Grand Jury, any bill of indictment, otherwise than in cases of private prosecution for misdemeanor, unless the information has been p f before a Justice, in the usual manner, or the prosecution directed by sworiJustices, or the accused committed or held to bail for the offence charged or the prosecution has been directed or assented to in writing by the Attorney General, 19 V. c. 10, s. 30.

May practise They may a as Attorney at law, in their Courts, in all civil actions, 19 V. c. 10prs.ctice

Cryers The presiding Judge shall appoint and remove cryers, their salary, **See title** 19 V. c. 10 s. 33

Trial by Jury, may be dispensed with In civil actions where the Crown is not a party, if all the parties consent in open Court, trial by Jury may be dispensed with, and the Judge substituted to hear and decide upon the evidence subject to the same proceedings for reversal or alteration as on a verdict, 19 V. c. 10, s. 34.

Records to be transmitted to the Clerk of the Supreme Court All civil and criminal records tried at the Circuit Courts, within 14 days after the termination of the Court, shall be transmitted to the Clerk of the Supreme Court and Crown, by the Clerks of the Peace, they keeping **The Clerks of the Peace, keeping dockets** dockets of all verdicts assessments, damages and indictments in their respective offices as records thereof, 20 V. c. 22, s. 18.

Affidavits Affidavits made before a Commissioner, may be used in the Circuit Courts, 19 V. c. 10, s. 45.

Fees Fees of Clerks of Circuit Courts, Schedule C, 19 V. c. 10, s. 48.

Lists of prisoners The Gaoler shall deliver to the Judge, Attorney General and Clerk of the Court on the first day of each Court, a list of prisoners in the County Gaol or Prison, of the Court, 19 V. c. 31, s. 3.

SITTINGS OF CIRCUIT COURTS.
HOME CIRCUIT.

Precinct of St. Catherine. St. Catherine, St. John, St. Dorothy.	To be held at St. Jago de la Vega.	2nd. Monday after the Supreme Court, and sit for two weeks, if necessary, 22 V. c. 39.
Precinct of Kingston, Kingston, Port Royal, St. Andrew and St. David,	Kingston,	8th Monday after the rising of the Supreme Court in each of the terms of February and June, and after the October term, on the 1st. Monday in January, and endure for three weeks if necessary, 28 V. c. 34, s. 2.

SURRY CIRCUIT.

St. Thomas in the East,	Bath and Morant Bay, alternately,	1st. Thursday after Supreme Court, 1 week, if &c., 22 V. c. 39.
Portland,	Port Antonio,	2nd Thursday after Supreme Court, 3 days if &c., 22 V. c. 39.
St. George,	Buff Bay,	Monday after Portland Court, 2 days, if &c., 28 V. c. 34, s. 4.
Metcalfe,	Anhotto Bay,	1st. Wednesday after St Georges Court, 4 days. if &c., 28 V. c. 34, s. 4.

MIDDLESEX CIRCUIT.

St. Thomas in the Vale,	Rodney Hall,	1st. Tuesday after Supreme Court, 5 days if necessary, 28 V. c. 34, s. 5.
St. Mary,	Port Maria,	1st. Tuesday after St. Catherine's Circuit Court, 5 days, if necessary, 22 V. c. 39.
St. Ann,	St. Ann's Bay,	1st. Mond. after Kingston Court, 1 week, if necessary, 22 V. c. 39.
Vere,	Alley,	1st. Tuesday after St. Ann's Court, 2 days, if necessary, 22 V. c. 39.
Clarendon,	Chapelton,	1st. Thursday after Vere Court, 3 days, if necessary, 22 V. c. 39.
Manchester,	Mandeville,	1st. Tuesday after Clarendon Court, 5 days if necessary, 22 V. c. 39.

CORNWALL CIRCUIT.

St. Elizabeth,	Black River,	2nd. Mond. after the Kingston Court, 1 week, if the business require it, 19 V. c. 10, s. 22, Sch. A, 28 V., c. 34, s. 3.
Westmoreland,	Savanna-la-Mar,	1st. Monday after St. Elizabeth Court, 1 week, if necessary, 19 V. c. 10, 28 V. c. 34, s. 3.
Hanover,	Lucea,	1st. Monday after Westmoreland Court, 1 week, if necessary, 19 V. c. 10, 28 V. c. 34, s. 3.
St. James,	Montego Bay,	1st. Monday after Hanover Court, 2 weeks, if necessary, 19 V. c 10, 28 V. c. 34, s. 3.
Trelawny,	Falmouth,	1st. Monday after St. James Court, 2 weeks, if necessary, 19 V. c 10, 28 V. c. 34, s. 3.

Adjournment of Insolvent and appeal Courts, Home Circuit

If either of the precinct Courts of St. Catherine or Kingston, is likely to extend over the time allotted for holding such Courts, for the disposal of business, the Chief Justice may order the adjournment of the Insolvent Debtors' and Appeal Courts to such time as he deems fit, giving public notice thereof, and such adjourned Courts shall be lawfully held, and the business discharged as if held under the provisions of the acts in force. If the business criminal or civil is likely to extend over the period now allotted, it shall be proceeded with on the additional days fixed for holding Insolvent and Appeal Courts, 28 V. c. 33, s. 4.

Notices of new trial &c. January Kingston Court

Notices for applications for new trial to enter or set aside a non suit, enter a verdict for defendant, or to arrest the Judgment in causes tried at the January Kingston precinct Court, may be given at any time before three days previous to the next Supreme Court, 28 V. c. 33, s. 5.

SCHEDULE C.—19 V. c. 10, s. 48.

Clerk of the Circuit Court's Fees

		s.	d.
Recording docket in the Court in which cause tried	..	1	6
For a habeas corpus, by order of the Court ..	..	1	6
For receiving and marking every verdict ..	..	0	3
For a non suit recorded, each	..	0	6
For a recognizance or deposition taken in Court ..	..	0	9
Filing common Affidavits and other proceedings ..	..	0	6

Clergy.

Retired Rectors allowances

The Receiver General shall pay to the order of every Rector who retired under 3 V. c. 60, s. 40, or his representatives, £330 per annum, instead of the retiring pension thereunder, by Quarterly payments, on 5th January, April, July, and October, with a proportional part to the day of his death, 7 V. c. 61, s. 3.

Moneague Chapel and burial ground, St. Ann. See 23 V., c. 23, s. 10.

The Trustees of the Jamaica Free School were empowered to convey two acres of land, belonging to the school part of Walton Pen, to the Bishop of Jamaica, and the Rector and Churchwardens of St. Ann for a chapel and burial ground for the use of the inhabitants of Moneague district, 5 V., c. 25, s. 2.

Maroon Lands, see 23 V. c. 23, s. 10. Moore Town Island Curate.

The Executive Committee were empowered to convey to the Bishop and his successors or trustees for the use and accommodation of the Incumbent of the Island Curacy of Moore Town, and to be attached to that Island Curacy, the house and ten acres of land, formerly reserved for the Superintendent as also four acres in that, and in each of the other townships for the site of a chapel, school house, and burial ground, 19 V. c. 35, s. 4.

Salaries of present Rectors and Curates, from 1st January, 1856, to 31st December, 1869.

Rectors and Curates holding preferment, who should not by 31st December, 1855, signify to the Executive Committee their dissent in writing to receive the reduced salaries provided, and those to be appointed whether by original appointment, or translation or removal, shall be paid out of the Treasury, the annual sums in the third column of figures in Schedule until 31st December, 1869, by Quarterly payments on 31st March, 30th June, 30th September and 31st December. Rectors and Curates absent from the island were allowed until 31st March, 1856, to signify their dissent, 19 V. c. 6, s. 1.

Of Register and Apparitor.

Similar provisions in respect of the salaries of the register and apparitor, 19 V. c. 6, s. 3.

After appointed Rectors and Curates.

Persons not having previously held a rectory or curacy shall be paid the salary in the third column of figures, 19 V. c. 6, s. 4.

SCHEDULE.

Salaries under 9 V. c. 33, and 14 V. c. 43, (expired as to the Clergy) and the further reduc.ions under 19 V. c. 6.

	Salaries payable under 9 Vic., c. 33.			Salaries payable under 14 Vic., c. 43.			Salaries to Rectors, &c. not dissenting to immediate reduction.			Salaries to Rectors, &c., dissenting to reduction (repealed 25 Vic, c. 36, s. 1).		
Rector of Kingston	720	0	0	650	0	0	600	0	0	525	0	0
St. Catherine	600	0	0	540	0	0	500	0	0	437	10	0
St. James	600	0	0	540	0	0	500	0	0	437	10	0
Trelawny	600	0	0	540	0	0	500	0	0	437	10	0
St. Andrew	540	0	0	490	0	0	450	0	0	393	15	0
Rectors of the other 17 Parishes, each	480	0	0	432	0	0	400	0	0	350	0	0
50 Curates, each	390	0	0	350	0	0	340	0	0	297	10	0
Register of the Diocese	120	0	0	80	0	0	76	0	0	66	10	0
Apparitor	30	0	0	15	0	0	14	0	0	12	5	0

The Rectors and Curates who dissented from 19 V. c. 6, alive, shall have written up to their credit in the Receiver General's books, the differences between the salaries they received since 1st January, 1860, and those they would have been entitled to had they not dissented, and thereafter until 31st December, 1869, shall be paid after the rate in the third column of 19 V. c. 6, 25 V. c. 36, s. 2. Salaries of dissentient Clergy from 1st January, 1860, to 31st December, 1869.

Each dissentient shall repay to the Treasury, the amount he received between 1st January, 1856, and 1st January, 1860, in excess of what would have been paid had he assented to 19 V. c. 6., 25 V. c. 36, s. 3. Repayment of excess of salaries received.

Such repayment to be made by deducting from the aggregate amount due the sums to be written up to their credit, and thereafter by deducting until the amount is satisfied, as the salaries are payable proportions of the balance to be repaid as near as can be calculated equal to the amounts, dates, and order of payment of the excess received, 25 V. c. 36, s. 4. By deductions from the sums to be written to their credit and the present salaries.

The Bishop shall, as occasion requires, summon Ecclesiastical Courts, (Form A) for the trial of Clerks in Holy Orders, charged with offences punishable by this Act, 22 V. c. 9, s. 1 Ecclesiastical Courts. How summoned.

Such Courts to be constituted and held by the Archdeacon or Commissary of the district or parish to which the offending clergyman belongs, or in which the offence was committed, who shall ex officio be President, and the Rector, and Island Curate whose church or chapel is nearest to the place where the Court is to be held, shall act with the President as members, 22 V. c. 9, s. 2. How constituted.

When illness, absence from the island, or other special circumstances, in the judgment of the Bishop, incapacitate the Archdeacon, or nearest Rector or Island Curate from acting, the Bishop, shall appoint another Archdeacon or Commissary, or summon the next nearest Rector or Island Curate to act, 22 V. c. 9, s. 3. In case of incapacity.

I

Challenging Rector or Curate.

If the accused challenges the nearest Rector and Curate, or either, he may, within one week after receiving notice that an Ecclesiastical Court has been summoned, object to them or either of them, and the Bishop shall summon the next nearest Rector or Island Curate to supply the place of that objected to, but no further challenge shall be allowed, 22 V. c. 9, s. 4.

Lay Assessor.

When it is represented by the Bishop that a Court is required to be held, the Governor may appoint a member of the Established Church being a Barrister, or Solicitor, of not less than eight years standing, who (by virtue of such appointment, and on the same being notified in "The Gazette by Authority," without being named in the Bishop's summons A) shall sit as Lay Assessor and advise the members of the Court on questions of law and evidence, but shall not vote, 22 V. c. 9, s. 5.

His remuneration.

He shall receive five guineas, for every day the court sits, from the Receiver General, under the Governor's warrant, on a certificate from the President, stating the number of days the Court was held. 22 V. c 9, s. 6.

Sittings and powers of the Court.

See 23 V. c. 43, s. 2

The Court shall be held in the parish or precinct in which the offending clergyman resides, or the offence was committed, and shall sit in the open Court House, have power to summon and examine on oath, witnesses, exercise all necessary jurisdiction for the trial of offences cognizable by this Act, return a finding of "Guilty," or "Not Guilty," on each charge, by a majority, and also award the sentence or punishment to be inflicted, with power to adjourn the sittings from day to day or for longer or shorter periods not exceeding one week at a time until the business is finally disposed of, 22 V. c. 9, s. 7.

Previous commission of enquiry when to issue

Complaints by Churchwardens. C. 22 V. c. 23, s. 33

If any person deliver a declaration in writing to the Bishop, signed in the presence of a credible witness, setting forth his belief, that any Clergyman has been guilty of any offence or neglect of duty punishable by this act, the Bishop may, or if any Clergyman, to his knowledge or belief, be charged and accused by common report, with any offence or neglect of duty, he shall issue a commission of enquiry, and no Court shall be summoned until the commissioners have made return in writing under their hands, setting forth their belief that there are sufficient grounds for prosecuting the charge, and have drawn up a presentment in writing, setting forth with reasonable precision the particular offences for which the Clergyman ought to be put upon his trial, 22 V. c. 9, s. 8.

Commissioners, their powers and duties

The commission shall be in form A, and directed to two beneficed Clergymen, Priests of 7 years standing, to be chosen by the Bishop, and three laymen, members of the Church and Magistrates or Churchwardens of the parish to which the accused belongs or wherein the offence was committed, to be appointed by the Governor, and they or any three shall have full power to enquire into the charges, to cite the Clergyman before them, to summon and examine all necessary witnesses on oath, and to adjourn from day to day, or longer, not exceeding one week at time, until their enquiry is concluded, and if the accused, being duly cited, shall not attend or refuses to answer before the Commissioners, they may suspend their further enquiry, and report that there is sufficient cause for proceeding to a trial, and draw up a presentment in accordance with such finding, 22 V., c. 9, s. 9.

Citation

The Citation or Summons shall be signed by three Commissioners, and set forth :

1. The name of the party preferring the charge—the time when, and the place where the offence is alleged to have been committed—the nature of each offence with reasonable certainty, and the names and places of abode of the witnesses, if known, intended to be examined.

2. The names and abode of the Commissioners, and the time and place appointed for the sitting of the Commission, 22 V., c. 9, s. 10.

Service

A copy of the Citation shall be served personally on the accused, or at his usual place of abode ten clear days at least before the time appointed for the enquiry, and in default of service, all proceedings shall be void, unless the accused voluntarily appear, 22 V. c. 9, s. 11.

Examination may be private

All examinations and enquiries before them may be conducted in private if desired by the accused, 23 V., c. 43, s. 2

No oath shall be taken by the Commissioners before entering upon the enquiry, but after it has been concluded, a return in writing shall be drawn up, and signed by them, or a majority, setting forth tha substance of the evidence taken, the names of the witnesses examined, and the titles of the written documents if any produced, and also the result of the enquiry, and whether in their opinion there is, or not, sufficient cause for prosecuting the offences complained of, 22 V., c, 9, s, 12. *Commissioners not to be sworn, their report*

If they report there are no sufficient grounds for proceeding further, their finding shall prevent any further proceedings, and shall be forthwith published by the Registrar in the "Gazette by Authority", 22 V., c, 9, s. 13 *Proceedings on report, if no grounds for proceeding to trial*

If they report, there is sufficient ground for proceeding further, they shall also draw up and sign a presentment setting forth with reasonable certainty, the offences for which the accused ought to be tried and forthwith transmit the same along with their return or finding to the Bishop, and deliver a copy of the presentment to the accused, 22 V. c. 9, s. 14. *Upon report recommending further proceeding*

Upon receipt whereof the Bishop shall forthwith intimate to the Governor, that a Court is required to be held, and proceed to summon a Court for the trial, and until trial may at his discretion suspend the accused without loss of stipend and shall issue his summons for a Court, within two months from the date of the presentment, 22 V. c. 9, s, 15. *The Bishop to summon a Court and may suspend accused*

Each member of any Court or Commission summoned, who refuses or fails to attend without sufficient cause shewn to the members who attend, or withdraws without excuse before the termination of the proceeding, shall for every day of absence or refusal to act and vote forfeit £10, 22 V c. 9, s. 16. *Penalty on members of court or commission not attending*

When any Rector or Stipendiary or other Curate licensed by the Bishop, or Island Curate, is guilty of any immorality not criminally punishable by the existing Courts of Law, or other act or conduct unbecoming the character of a Christian Minister, and not so punishable or of gross or habitual neglect of ministerial duty, he shall on conviction be punished by suspension or deprivation, or both according to the nature of the offence, or may be censured and admonished by the Bishop, in pursuance of the spiritual powers belonging to him, but no Clergyman shall be liable to imprisonment by any sentence of the Ecclesiastical Courts, 22 V. c. 9, s. 17.

Immediately after the Lay Assessor has been appointed, and the Bishop has issued his summons to the other members, fixing the time and place for holding thereof, the Bishop shall cause a notice, in writing to be served personally, or at the residence of the accused, twenty-one clear days, at least, before the Court, setting forth the time and place appointed, and the names of the members, and the time and place of holding the Court shall also be published in the "Gazette, by Authority", at least one week previous to the time of meeting, and if the accused does not appear, or refuses to take his trial, the Court may proceed in his absence and record a verdict and sentence against, or an acquittal of him, 22 V., c. 9, s. 18. *Notice of court to accused*

The Bishop shall, with the notice, cause a copy of the presentment to be served upon the accused, and a copy furnished to each member of the Court, the presentment shall alone be the subject of trial, and the accused shall not be called upon to answer for any charge or offence not included or set forth with reasonable certainty and no witnesses examined before the Commissioners, nor any documentary evidence produced at the time of their enquiry, shall be withdrawn or dispensed with at the trial, unless by permission of the Court on sufficient cause, 22 V,, c. 9, s. 19. *Enquiry to be confined to the charges, and all witnesses, &c. to be produced on trial*

No oath or declaration shall be made by the Lay Assessor, but he shall on formation of the Court administer the following declaration in open Court to the Ecclesiastical Members. *Declaration to be administered to Ecclesiastical members.*

I, A. B, do solemnly, and sincerely declare that I will well and truly try the charge or charges (describing the same as set forth in the presentment), and a true verdict return according to the evidence, 22 V., c. 9, s. 20.

Clerk of the Peace to act as clerk of the court Course of procedure.

The Court shall appoint the Clerk of the Peace to act as Clerk during their sitting. who shall receive three guineas for each day of its sitting from the Receiver-General, under the Governor's Warrant on certificate from the President. stating the number of days occupied by the sitting. In case of the non-attendance of a sufficient number of members to form a Court on any day, or adjourned day, the President or Lay Assessor, or in their absence, one of the Clerical Assessors may adjourn the Court from day to day until the arrival of a sufficient number of members. On their assembling, the presentment shall be read by the President, and the accused required to plead, and if he refuse, a plea of "Not guilty" shall be entered on his behalf. Any Clergyman proceeded against may have the aid of any Advocate

Professional, &c. assistance

or Solicitor, or presbyter. Prosecutors may appear by Counsel or Solicitors qualified to practise in the Courts of the Island, witnesses shall be sworn in open Court, and their testimony, both on direct and cross-examination, reduced to writing by the Clerk, and on the closing of the testimony and arguments (if such shall be had), the Court shall be cleared for deliberation on the verdict, the verdict of guilty or not guilty decided by the majority of the members, and pronounced in open Court by the President and endorsed on one of the copies of the presentment used at the trial, and signed by the members or a majority determining the verdict—the members shall then by a majority award the punishment, and reduce the award to writing, and sign it. A copy of the verdict, and award shall be given to the accused, and

Copies of award to be given to the accused and Bishop

another copy, with the evidence taken, forthwith transmitted to the Bishop by the President, and the Bishop shall thereupon have full power to inflict the penalty or sentence awarded, or remit any portion according to his dis-

Who may mitigate the penalty

cretion—the proceedings of the Courts with respect to the arguments and

Proceedings regulated by those of the supreme and circuit courts

addresses of Counsel or Attorney, and the examination of witnesses and production of evidence, shall be regulated by the prevailing practice of the Supreme and Circuit Courts, 22 V., c. 9, s. 21.

Final sentence To be recorded

The final sentence of the Bishop shall be pronounced within one month after he is informed of the award, and forthwith recorded in the Registry Office, 22 V., c. 2, s. 22.

And Gazetted

And published in the "Jamaica Gazette, by Authority," within fourteen days after its taking effect, 22 V., c. 9. s. 23.

Appropriation of stipend and parsonage house on suspension

In case sentence of suspension is pronounced, the Receiver-General shall hold the stipend of the Clergyman (after deducting the allowances for the Clergy Fund) applicable in the first place to the payment of a Curate or substitute to be appointed by the Bishop to perform his duties during suspension, and pay the remainder to the Clergyman himself, the sum assigned to the substitute, in no case, to be less than one-half, nor more than two-thirds of the stipend after the deduction, and the Rectory or Parsonage House, if belonging to the Incumbency, shall also be assigned to the substitute, if ordered as part of the sentence of the Court, but not otherwise, 22 V., c. 9., s. 24.

Sentence of deprivation

In case of sentence of deprivation, the Bishop may declare the Rectory, or Curacy vacant, and it may thereupon be filled up, 22 V., c. 9, s. 25.

Officiating during suspension, or after deprivation— disturbing successor, withholding Rectory registers or Church property

Any Clergyman attempting to officiate during the period of his suspension or after deprivation or in any way obstructing the Curate, substitute or successor, or refusing to give possession of the Rectory or Parsonage House or of the Registry books or any Church property in his custody, shall be guilty of a misdemeanor, and may be indicted and punished by fine

Governor may pardon

or imprisonment or both in the discretion of the Court, 22 V. c. 9, s. 26.

After sentence of suspension has been promulgated or put in force, the Governor, if he thinks fit, upon the written request of the Bishop, with reasons assigned, may remit the whole or any portion of the unexpired sentence, by way of pardon to the offending Clergyman, who shall thereupon be eligible to any benefice or Ecclesiastical appointment, 22 V. c. 9, s. 27.

Appeal

If any Clergyman think himself aggrieved, he may on notice to the Bishop, within 30 days after the sentence has been pronounced and promulgated, appeal to a Court composed of the Governor and Privy Council, being members of the Church of England, who shall have power to affirm or reverse the finding verdict or sentence, 22 V. c. 9, s. 28, 23 V. c. 9, s. 2.

Rules of Court of Appeal

The Governor and Privy Council were empowered before 1st June 1860, to frame and publish rules for the holding and course of proceedings at such Courts of Appeal. and from time to time to add to, alter, or amend the same, 23 V. c. 9. s. 29, 23 V. c. 9, s. 1.

Time further extended to 30th June 1865, and the rules may be at any time after, altered, added to or amended, 28 V. c. 43, s. 3,

Clergyman not deprived of any right of Appeal open to him by the laws of Great Britain and Ireland, applicable to this island, but no such right of appeal shall prevent the Receiver General, or other parties concerned, from carrying into immediate effect the Judgments and penalties imposed, nor shall they incur any liability for so doing, 22 V. c. 9, s. 30. *Appeal to England not to suspend sentence*

If any Clergyman, upon being informed, that a complaint has been made against him, either before a commission of enquiry issues, confesses to the Bishop his guilt, and makes a statement, in writing, of his willingness to submit himself to the decision of the Bishop, without trial, he may inflict such punishment or other correction as might have been awarded in case of a conviction, and the sentence shall be passed upon, in the presence of three Presbyters at least, and recorded in the Registry Office, 22 V. c. 9, s. 31. *Confession and submission to the Bishop's decision without trial*

No charge shall be brought or entertained unless complaint is made, and the commission of inquiry, actually issued within 12 months from the day the offence is said to have been committed, and no proceedings to be quashed or objected to before any Court or tribunal for want of form or on any technical ground, and no proceeding commission or document subject to any Stamp Duty, 22 V. c. 9, s. 32. *Proceedings to be within 12 months. No formal objections thereto. Exempted from Stamps*

In case sentence of deprivation is passed against any Rector or Island Curate, he, or any person on his behalf, may sustain the interest of his wife and children in the Rector's or Island Curates' Fund, or both, by paying to the Receiver General at the usual periods, the annual sum pa a le by him towards the fund at the ime of his deprivation, 22 V. c. 9, s. 33. y b *Interest in Clergy Fund, of deprived Clergyman's Family.*

If any deprived Clergyman or any person on his behalf has not continued to pay the annual sums, his family shall on his decease be entitled to such a proportion of the benefits of the fund, as shall be represented by a fraction which the numerator shall be the amount of his actual payments at his death, and the denominator, the sum to which his payments would have amounted had he, or any person on his behalf, paid on to the day of his death, 22 V. c. 9, s. 34.

Fines and penalties shall be recovered summarily under the Act, 13 V. c. 35, or any other act relating to summary convictions and orders, and paid over to the Receiver General, to be applied in reduction of the expenses of trials, 22 V. c. 9, s. 35. *Recovery and application of penalties*

The Inspectors of Police shall cause service to be effected of all process and notices, on being required so to do by the Bishop, Ecclesiastical Courts or Commissioners, 22 V. c. 9, s. 36. *Process to be served by the police*

The Co-adjutor Bishop, and, in case of his death or absence from the island or inability to act, the Bishop's, or any Special Commissaries in the absence of the Bishop from the island, or in case of a vacancy in the see, may exercise the powers vested in him, and shall be chargeable with the duties imposed on him, and their acts shall have the same force as if performed by the Bishop in person, 22 V. c. 9, s. 37. *Co-adjutor Bishops and commissaries' power*

The Judges of the Supreme and Circuit Court, shall aid the Ecclesiastical Courts in enforcing and carrying out all lawful orders, sentences and decrees, and any Judge shall, upon application. order, in writing, the attendance of any witness required before any Court or Commission of enquiry, and in case of non-attendance or refusal to be sworn, or to give evidence when sworn, or of any other contempt or disobedience to the lawful order of such Court or Commission, such Judge may cause the witness to be brought before him in chambers, by attachment, and then and there deal with him, as the Judges of the Supreme Court in like cases. False swearing before the Court or a Commission, perjury, 22 V. c. 9, s. 39. *Orders to be enforced by the Judges of the Supreme court* *Perjury*

No attachment shall issue unless the Judge is satisfied the witness was duly summoned, and, in case of a witness summoned on the part of any accused Clergyman, that his expences had been paid or tendered to him on a scale equal to that on which the expenses of any other person in the like condition of life, would have been paid or tendered on a subpœna in a Circuit Court, 22 V. c. 9, s. 39. *Attachment. Witnesses expences*

In case of a witness summoned to give evidence in support of any proceedings, the chairman of the Commissioners on any preliminary investigation, and the president of the Court, on any trial, shall when they see proper order payment of his expences by the Receiver General, on the warrant of the Governor, 22 V. c. 9, s. 40, *Witnesses expences for prosecution*

" The Clergy Discipline Act, 1858, 22 V. c. 9, s. 41. *short title*

SCHEDULE

A.

To A.B. Archdeacon of   or Commissary of the Bishop,
(as the case may be) and to C.D. Rector of   and E.F.
Island Curate of

REVEREND SIRS,

By virtue of the authority conferred, and in discharge of the duty imposed on me, by " The Clergy Discipline Act, 1858," I hereby summon you and each of you to attend, as designated Ministers thereof, a Court to be held in the Court House, in   on the   next for the trial of the Reverend A.B. of   &c., under the provisions of the above named Act, dated this   day of   18

Bishop of Jamaica, or
Co-adjutor Bishop, or
Commissary of Bishop.

B.

To the Reverend A.B., C.B.   and to A.B.
of   esquire, and C.D of   esquire, and E.F. of
esquire.

By virtue of the authority conferred, and in discharge of the duty imposed on me by the Clergy Discipline Act, 185J, I do hereby nominate and appoint you and every of you Commissioners to enquire into certain charges preferred by A.B. of   (or commonly or openly alleged) against the Reverend C.D. of   to the following effect viz. (state the nature of the charge) and to make a true return to me, pursuant to the said Act, of the result of your enquires into the said charges, and I hereby appoint that your first meeting in execution of the authority, hereby conferred, shall be holden at (name of the place of meeting) on the   day of

Given under my hand, and sealed with the Episcopal seal of Jamaica, this   day of   18

Ecclesiastical laws in force

All laws, ordinances and canons, Ecclesiastical, now used and in force in England, so far as they relate to the due ordering and Ecclesiastical regimen of, and jurisdiction over the Clergy, and so far as they do not derogate from, or interfere with this or any other Act of this island, and all rules of proceeding for carrying the same into effect, shall be in force in this island, in respect of the Clergy resident here, and all the processes and proceedings, orders, sentences, jurisdictions and decrees of the Right Reverend Father in God, Aubrey Bishop of Jamaica, and of the persons to be deputed in his stead, in respect of the Clergy, shall have the same authority, and be enforced and carried into execution in the same manner as those of the Ecclesiastical Courts in England, towards and against the Clergy there, but shall not give any judicial authority or coercion, spiritual or temporal, over the lay inhabitants, except over the parish Clerks, Beadles and Sextons as after enacted, or control abridge or alter the Jurisdiction of the Governor or ordinary in any suit or instance for the probate of wills and granting letters testamentary, and of administration or the repeal or revocation of any of them or in any other manner or with respect to the presentation to the several Churches, Chapels or parishes, or any other power or authority, judicial or otherwise, usually exercised by the Governor, 22 V. c. 23, s. 1.

The Judges of the Supreme Court to enforce proceedings

The Judges of the Supreme Court shall, if they see fit, aid and assist in enforcing and carrying into execution such processes and proceedings, orders, sentences, adjudications, and decrees, at any time, to be issued or made with respect to the Clergy, in the same manner as the Courts of Common Law in England are authorized or required to aid and assist the Ecclesiastical Courts there, in enforcing their processes, &c,, 22 V., c. 23, s. 2.

Powers of the Bishop how to be exercised in his absence, &c.

In case of the demise, disability, or absence of the Bishop, and, in case of his demise, until the appointment and arrival of his successor, all the Ecclesiastical jurisdiction, powers, and authorities which he could exercise, if personally present, shall be used and exercised by the Bishop of Kingston, or any Coadjutor or Suffragan Bishop of the Bishop of Jamaica, and (except those of Ordination and Confirmation) by the Commissaries appointed by the Bishop or Coadjutor Bishop, in the absence of an appointment by the Bishop; during the absence of the Coadjutor Bishop. And in case there be no Commissary, by any two Clergymen of the Church of England, whom the Governor shall appoint to act as Commissaries, as fully as if appointed by the Bishop of Jamaica. And the Bishop of Kingston or other Coadjutor or Suffragan Bishop shall act as Trustee, or otherwise, during the absence of the Bishop of Jamaica, in like manner as he is authorized to act under any other acts, 22 V., c. 23, s. 3. Trusts.

No license now, or to be granted by the Bishop shall be affected by the death, resignation, or absence of such Bishop, but shall remain in full force, 22 V., c. 23, s. 4.

The Bishop, with the consent of the Governor, may license or conse-crate as a place of Worship any district or other Church which he is satisfied is in a proper condition and situation to be licensed, and nominate and license a Minister to such Church, 22 V., c. 23, s. 5. Licenses not affected by his death

During, and previous to the completion of any district or other Church in course of erection the Bishop, with the consent of the Governor, may licence as a place of Worship any temporary building erected or rented for the pur-pose, and license and appoint a Minister thereto, 22 V., c. 23, s. 6. Licences of places of worship

Such temporary place of Worship and Minister shall not be subject to the authority of the Rector, but to the Ecclesiastical jurisdiction of the Bishop, 22 V. c. 23, s. 7. Temporary licenses

No Clergyman shall open any house or building as a place of Public Worship, other than such as have been provided and appointed for him by competent authority, without the consent of the Bishop, applied for, and obtained, 22 V., c. 23, s. 8. Jurisdiction over temporary places &c.

No nomination or appointment of a Minister to any district or other Church shall be made, unless it is capable of seating not less than 200 per-sons, 22 V., c. 23, s 9. None other to be used without Bishop's consent

Every Church, and the land and site whereon it is built, with the Ce-metry, if any, shall be vested in the Churchwardens, as a body corporate, to the use and intent that such Church with the Cemetery shall be forever set apart as a place of Divine Worship according to the liturgy and usages of the United Church, and be subject to the Bishop of the Diocese, as such, 22 V. c. 23, s. 10. No Minister to be appointed unless church can seat 200 persons
Estate in the church and ce-metry.

The Justices and Vestry shall, when necessary, include in their annual estimates of expenditure a sum sufficient for purchasing a burial ground, and for repairing all Churches, Parsonage houses, Fences of glebe lands and burial grounds, 22 V. c. 23, s. 11. Repairs, &c.

Any person may under regulations to be framed by the officiating Cler-gyman and Churchwardens, erect at his own expense in any Church, a pew stall or sitting, and be entitled to the use thereof so long as he continues a member of the congregation, attending such Church, to be from to time evinced by the certificate of the officiating Clergyman and Churchwardens, who shall have power to vary and regulate the positions and places of such pews, stalls or sittings. To entitle any person to the use of such pews, &c. a memo of the erection at the cost of such person, attested by the officiating Clergyman and Churchwardens, shall be recorded in the Vestry Books, of the parish. In no case shall any greater number of sittings than 5, be by the authority of this clause allotted to any one person or family, and in every Church at least one half of the entire sittings, or space for sittings, shall be served free for the general congregation, 22 V. c. 23, s. 12. Pews

The number of Island Curates for the several parishes, shall not exceed 50 in the whole ; and no clerk in holy orders shall be appointed to an Island Curacy, until a Church has been provided and approved of by the Bishop, in which he may perform Divine worship, 22 V. c. 23, s. 13. Island Curates.

* The Governor with the advice of the Executive Committee, may by his warrant direct payment out of the Treasury of not exceeding the rate of £150 per annum as part payment of the Stipend of any Stipendiary Cu-rate, provided not less than £1,100 per annum shall be appropriated out of funds at the Bishop's disposal in aid of the stipends as follows: Stipendiary Curates.

To 4 of such Curates, as the Governor and Bishop decide, at the rate of £150 per annum		£600	0 0
To 4 ditto ditto ditto, at the rate of £100		400	0 0
To 1 ditto ditto ditto,		75	0 0
To 1 ditto ditto ditto		25	0 0

and that the number be always kept up to 10, and that they be removable from place, to place at the discretion of the Governor and Bishop, 28 V. c. 43, s. 1.

Vacancies to be filled up as in case of Rectors &c

In case of any vacancy occurring in the number of the Stipendiary Curates to be paid, the appointment of a successor shall be made according to the rule observed with respect to the appointment of Rectors and Island Curates, 22 V. c. 23, s. 15.

To be subject to Ecclesiastical Discipline

Every Stipendiary Curate, paid as herein provided, shall be subject to this Act, and any other now or to be in force, relating to the Clergy or Ecclesiastical Discipline, 22 V. c. 23, s. 16.

Nomination to Island curacies

The nomination to an Island Curacy, by the Governor, shall be in form following:

JAMAICA, s.s.

Victoria, by the Grace of God of the United Kingdom of Great Britain and Ireland, and of Jamaica Lady defender of the faith.
To the Honorable and Right Reverend Father in God   by Divine permission (Lord) Bishop of Kingston (or Jamaica).

Whereas the Island Curacy of   in the parish of in the County of   and Diocese of Jamaica, is now void and doth of right belong to our nomination, these are to certify to you(r Lordship) that we do nominate the Reverend   Clerk to the Island Curacy aforesaid, requesting you(r Lordship) to grant him your license for serving the said cure, and moreover we believe him, in our conscience, to be a person worthy to be admitted to the cure of Souls. In witness whereof we have caused the Great Seal of Our Island of Jamaica to be hereunto affixed.

Witness His Excellency   Captain General and Governor-in-Chief, in and over our said Island of Jamaica and other the territories thereon depending in America, Chancellor and Vice Admiral of the same, at Saint Jago de la Vega, the   day of in the   year of our reign, A.D.,   22 V., c. 23, s. 17.

Removal

No Island or other Curate, shall be liable to be removed without his consent, except by due course of Ecclesiastical Law, and except in the case of Stipendiary Curates, 22 V. c. 23, s. 18.

Island Curate not to be burthened with the duties of the Stipendiary

In parishes where an Island and a Stipendiary Curate are employed, the Bishop or Rector shall not impose upon the Island Curate any duties which properly belong to, and ought to be performed by the Stipendiary, 22 V. c. 23, s. 19.

Curates in Deacons orders to take Priests orders within two years

If any person in Deacons Orders, who is appointed Curate, fails to be admitted into Priests Orders, for 2 years after the date of his appointment, it shall cease, 22 V. c. 23, s. 20.

Duties of clergy

Each Clergyman shall at all times, when not prevented by sickness or accidental circumstances, perform Divine Service, and preach and teach, or procure some other Clergyman to do so on his behalf, in his Church, or some other place, and as often on every Lords day, as the Bishop shall direct, and shall in all cases solemnize the rites and offices of the Church of England, according to the book of common prayer, and on each Lord's day, and once in every week or oftener if required by the Bishop (the day and hours to be by him appointed) attend for a reasonable time, in his Church, and catechise and instruct all persons who attend for the purpose, 22 V. c. 23, s. 21.

Banns and solemnization of Marriages

Banns of marriage shall be published in an audible manner in any Church of the parish in which the persons to be married or one of them dwell, according to the form of words prescribed by the rubric prefixed to the office of matrimony, in the book of common prayer, upon three Sundays preceding the solemnization of marriage, during morning service, 22 V. c. 23, s. 22.

Banns valid for six months only after Complete publication

Banns so published, shall be valid and authorize the performance of the marriage ceremony, by any Clergyman, for 6 calendar months, after their complete publication, but not longer, 22 V. c. 23, s. 23.

Penalty for Marrying without banns or license but marriage valid

No Clergyman shall marry any person whose banns have not been duly published, or having been published for more than six months, have not been republished at the like times and manner as prescribed for the publication, or who has not obtained a license, from the Governor, authorizing the marriage, under the penalty of £60. Any marriage solemnized without the publication of banns, or a license, shall nevertheless be valid, 22 V. c. 23, s. 24.

If any Clergyman suffer any corpse to be interred or buried in any Church or Chancel, he shall incur a penalty of £300, 22 V. c. 23, s. 25. — **No burial in a Church**

Each Clergyman shall at all times, actually and bona fide reside in the parish or district in which the Church to which he has been appointed is situate, unless otherwise permitted by the Bishop on sufficient cause shewn, 22 V; c. 23, s. 26. — **Residence**

The Governor may grant leave of absence, under the regulations to which officers in Her Majesty's civil service are subject, or other special regulation of Her Majesty, for that purpose, to any Clergyman upon receiving a certificate under the hand of the Bishop, stating that it had been shewn to his satisfaction that leave of absence was necessary, and ought to be granted, 22 V, c. 23, s. 27. — **Leave of absence**

Where leave of absence is granted to a Clergyman, the substitute shall be approved of by the Bishop, 22 V. c. 23, s. 28. — **Substitute**

If any Clergyman absent himself from his parish or ecclesiastical duties for one month, at any one time, without the consent in writing of the Bishop, and without appointing some other Clergyman to perform his duties, he shall be guilty of neglect of duty, and liable to be proceeded against under the Clergy Discipline Act, 1858, (22 V. c. 9,) accidental cases and inevitable preventions excepted, 22 V. c. 23, s. 29. — **Absence without leave**

If any Clergyman is absent, except through unavoidable circumstances, from his parish, longer than the period for which he has obtained leave or extended leave of absence, he shall be taken to have resigned his living or Curacy, and the Bishop shall declare it vacant, and recommend the Governor to, and he shall appoint any Clergyman in his room, as in the case of a death vacancy, 22 V. c. 23, s. 30. — **Absence beyond leave**

Nothing herein relating to residence and parochial duties, shall extend to the domestic chaplain of the Governor, or to the chaplains to the Legislative Council and Assembly, so long as they are actually engaged in the performance of their duties, as such, 22 V. c. 23, s. 31. — **Chaplains to the Governor, Council, or Assembly**

No Clergyman shall act as the procuration attorney of any absentee in the management of any estate or plantation, or be appointed or act as receiver, for any estate or plantation, except for his own or any estate in which he or any member of his family is interested, 22 V. c. 23, s. 32. — **Procuration Attornies**

When the Churchwardens complain to the Bishop of the neglect, or inattention to any of his duties, by any Rector or Curate, it shall be his duty to proceed under the Clergy Discipline Act, 1858, (22 V. c. 9) against such Rector or Curate, 22 V. c. 23, s. 33. — **complaints of churchwardens**

If any Clergyman is convicted of any offence against the common or Statute Law of Great Britain, or of this Island, the Governor, on the report of the Bishop, may suspend or dismiss him, and during suspension he shall only be entitled to one moiety of his stipend. In case of dismissal the living or Curacy shall be vacated, 22 V. c. 23, s. 34. — **convictions of offences against the common or statute Law**

The power of appointment of Clerks and Beadles shall be exclusively exercised by the Clergymen in their Churches, annually on the 1st July, or as soon after as practicable, and in case of death, or resignaton, or removal, as often as the offices become vacant, 22 V. c. 23, s. 35. — **Appointment of Clerks and Beadles**

The Bishop upon complaint by the Clergyman of misconduct or neglect of duty on the part of any Beadle, or Clerk, or Sexton, of his Church, may suspend him until he can enquire into the matter, and remove or dismiss him, if he thinks proper, 22 V., c, 23, s. 36. — **Removal of Clerks, Beadles or sextons**

The Clergyman appointed to every Church, shall keep a book to be furnished at the cost of the parish, and their property, in which shall be entered the duties performed each week, and the names of the officiating Clergyman on each occasion (Form Schedule E.) such book to be open to the inspection of any Clergyman, Justice, Vestryman, or Churchwarden, or person appointed by the Bishop, and transcripts forwarded to the Bishop at such times as he shall appoint, 22 V., c. 23, s. 37. — **Duty book**

Registers of Baptisms, Marriages, and Burials, solemnized according to the rites of the Established Church, shall be made and kept by the Rector or Minister officiating for him, in well bound books, to be provided out of the parochial funds, in which such Rector or Minister officiating for him shall as soon as possible after the solemnization of every baptism, marriage or burial, record and enter in a fair and legible hand the particulars in Schedules A, B and C., and sign the same, and in no case, unless prevented by sickness or other unavoidable impediment, later than within 14 days after the ceremony, 22 V., c. 23, s. 38, — **Registers of baptisms, marriages, and burials**

K

Burials not by parish clergyman

When the ceremony of the burial is performed by any other than the Clergyman of the parish in which the burial took place, the person performing it shall on the same or next day transmit to the Rector a certificate of such burial (Form Schedule D), signed by him, and the Rector shall thereupon enter it according to the certificate in the book, and add to the entry "according to the certificate transmitted to me by   on the   day of 18   ", and sign the same, 22 V., c. 23, s. 39.

Property in, and custody of Registers

The Registry book shall belong to the parish, and be kept by, and remain in the power and custody of the Rector or Minister officiating for him, and safely and securely kept, and shall not be taken or removed from the power or custody of the Rector, &c. at any time, or for any cause, except for the inspection of persons desirous to make search, or to obtain copies, or to be produced as evidence in some Court of Law or Equity, or to be inspected as to the state and condition, by the Churchwardens, quarterly, or by the proper Ecclesiastical Authorities, 22 V., c. 23, s. 40.

Quarterly returns to Rector by clergymen of the parish to be registered

Every Clergyman other than the Rector of each parish shall within seven days after the end of every three months render a return duly certified under his hand to the Rector, of all baptisms, marriages, and burials performed by him during the three preceding months, and containing as far as possible all the particulars in Schedule, A B C, under a penalty (payable to the Rector) of £12, to be recovered before a Justice, and payment enforced (by warrant of distress and sale), and the Rector shall enter in the Register Books such baptisms, marriages, or burials according to such returns, and add to the entry "according to the certificate of the Reverend A B., Island Curate (or as the case may be) transmitted to me on the   day of 18,   " and sign the same, 22 V., c. 23, s. 41.

Quarterly returns to the Registrar

The Rector, or Minister officiating for him shall transmit to the Registrar of the Diocese, a certified return of all registers of baptisms, marriages, and burials, within 20 days after the 1st January, April, July, and October in each year, under a penalty of £30 in form following :—

I, A B, Rector (or Minister officiating for the Rector), of the parish of   , in the County of   , do hereby certify that the writings hereunto annexed, purporting to be copies of the several entries contained in the several baptisms, marriages, and burials in the parish of   , from the   day of   to the   day of   18   , are true copies of all the several entries in the said Register books, respectively from the said   day of   , to the said   day of and that no other entry during such period is contained in any such book, to the best of my knowledge and belief.

A. B., Rector) or Minister officiating for the Rector), 22 V., c. 23, s. 42.

Extracts evidence

An extract or copy from the Register books, certified under the hand of the Rector, &c., or of any return made from the record thereof in the Bishop's Office of Registry, and certified under the hand of the Registrar, or by the oath of a witness, who had compared the extract or copy with the entry in the Register book or the record in the Bishop's Office, shall be admitted as legal evidence, to the extent the original would go, but not to its exclusion— 22 V., c. 23, s. 43.

False entries

Knowingly and wilfully inserting, or causing or permitting, &c., in any Register book, or in any copy to be transmitted to the Registrar, any false entry of a false statement in any writing or instrument, purporting to be an extract from any matter relating to any baptism, marriage, or burial, or falsely making, altering, forging, or counterfeiting, or causing or procuring, or wilfully permitting to be falsely made, &c., any part of any register, or any copy of, or any writing or instrument, purporting to be an extract from any such register, or wilfully destroying, defacing, or injuring, or causing or procuring, or permitting, &c., any Register book, or any part, or knowingly, or wilfully signing, or certifying any copy of, or extract from, any such register required to be transmitted, which shall be false in any part, knowing the same to be false, felony, 22 V., c. 23, s. 44.

No Rector, &c. who discovers any error in the form or substance of the entry in the Register book of any baptism, marriage or burial, shall be liable to any penalty, if he within one calendar month after the discovery, in the presence of the parents of the child whose baptism has been entered, or of the parties married, or of two persons who attended at any burial, or, in case of the death or absence of such respective parties, then in the presence of the Churchwardens, (who shall respectively attest the same) alter and correct the entry found erroneous, according to the truth, by entry in the margin of the book without any alteration or obliteration of the original entry and shall sign each entry in the margin, and add to such signature, the day month, and year when the correction was made, 22 V. c. 23, s. 45. *Correction of errors.*

The superscription upon letters and packets containing the copies of parish registers, to be transmitted by the post to the Office of the Registrar, shall be endorsed and signed by one of the Churchwardens. Form, Schedule F. 22 V. c. 23, s. 46. *Transmission of copies of Registers.*

The Registrar of the Diocese, in the event of any failure in the transmission of copies of registers by the Rectors, shall report the default specially to the Bishop, and within three months after he has received such quarterly returns or copies fully record the same in the books provided by him for that purpose, and shall also cause alphabetical lists or indexes to be made, in books suitable to the purpose, of the names of all persons and parishes mentioned in such copies of Registers, which indexes, and books and copies, shall be open to public search, at all times, during which the Island Secretary's Office is required to be open, 22 V. c. 23, s. 47 *Registrar's duties. Records, Indexes, searches.*

The Registrar shall cause all records in his office, as well as all copies, of Registers forwarded to him to be recorded, to be safely and securely deposited and p   from damage or destruction by fire, or otherwise, and to be carefully rearranged for the p r   of being resorted to as occasion may require. Penalty, £60, 22 V c. 23 s. 48. *Preservation of Records, &c.*

The fees of the Registrar in respect of records, or register of burials, baptisms, and marriages, and dockets, abstracts and searches shall be paid on the like scale as the fees of the Island Secretary, and he shall be entitled for duties performed in his office according to the scale of fees, G., but shall not ta   greater fees. Penalty, £60, one half to the informer, 22 V. c. 23, s. 49ke *Registrar's fees.*

The Registrar shall be paid by the public for recording copies of registers at the rate the Secretary is entitled to charge for deeds, and by persons requiring copies or extracts at the same rate, 22 V. c 23, s. 50.

Rectors may demise and lease to any person willing to become a lessee, all or any part of the lands annexed to their rectories called Glebe lands, for a number of years certain, not exceeding 21 years, subject to such covenants and agreements as shall be concluded between the respective parties, but no lease shall be valid unless it, or a counter part of it, is recorded in the Secretary's Office, within 90 days after execution, 22 V. c. 23, s. 51. *Leases of Glebe lands, and parsonage houses.*

The best improved rent that can be got shall be reserved in every lease for the benefit of the Rector and his successors, subject to the deduction after mentioned, 22 V. c. 23, s. 52. *Best improved rent.*

No Rector shall take or receive or suffer, &c., by any person, for his use or benefit, any fine, fee, reward, sum of money, or consideration for granting such lease other than the rent reserved therein, under the penalty of treble the value of such fine, &c., and the further sum of £100 to any person who shall sue for the same, 22 V, c. 23, s. 53. *Consequences of taking any other consideration.*

Any lease granted for, or by reason, or on account of any fine, &c., other than the rent reserved shall be ipso facto void, and the land so corruptly leased shall be vested in the Justices and Vestry, to be by them rented or otherwise disposed of, for the benefit of the poor of the parish during the lifetime of the Rector taking such fee or reward other than the rent reserved, who shall be for ever after disabled from granting any lease of the land or any part, and any lease granted by such Rector after such offence shall be void, 22 V. c. 23, s. 54.

No l c n s e to be
granted during any
existing lease.

No Rector shall grant any lease of any part of such land until the existing lease has expired, been surrendered, or otherwise determined, otherwise the same shall be void, 22 V. c. 23, s. 55.

Lease of parson-
age, house, &c. to
be with consent of
Justices and Ves-
try

The Rector shall not be empowered to lease the parsonage house, or any part of the Glebe lands of his parish requisite for the necessary uses and comfortable accommodation of the Incumbent and his family, unless with the consent of the Justices and Vestry, in which case he may lease or rent for not exceeding 21 years, 22 V. c. 23, s. 56.

One-tenth of rent
to be paid to the
Receiver General to
meet repairs.

When the parsonage house and lands, or either of them are leased or rented as aforesaid, a portion, not less than one tenth of the whole rent, shall be annually lodged by the Rector in the hands of the Receiver General, and held applicable to the repairs of such parsonage house and fences to such lands, whenever such repairs are required, 22 V. c. 23, s. 57.

Compensation in
lieu of Glebe and
fees.

The Rectors shall, during their respective incumbency, in addition to their stipends as Rectors, be entitled to receive under warrant of the Governor the sums set opposite the name of each parish in Schedule H., by quarterly or monthly payments, as the Governor shall direct, in full annual compensation for Glebe or parsonage house, servants, and all fees, except as after mentioned, 22 V, c. 23, s. 58.

The Reverend Charles Tuthill May, the present Rector of St. George, shall be paid during his incumbency, £140 per annum, and £73 and £18 shall be paid to each succeeding Rector of St. George, in full of all claims and allowances for Glebe, rectory house and servants, and for burials and otherwise, as provided by such schedule, 25 V. c. 21, s. 23.

Immediately after the decease, resignation, or removal of the Rector of St. Thomas in the East or Vere, the allowance to them for servants shall cease, and their successors shall not be entitled to any such allowance, 22 V. c. 23, s. 59.

Rector's fees.

The Rectors shall be entitled to the following fees :—

For each tablet, or cenotaph erected in the parish church or any chapel	£2	0	0
For a tomb, whether built of brick work or otherwise, over a grave in the churchyard	0	10	0
For a vault in the Churchyard, whether built of bricks, or otherwise, and whether enclosed with iron railing or not	2	0	0
For comparing and attesting, or preparing and attesting an extract from the parish register, of births, deaths, or marriages, 22 V. c. 23, s. 60.	0	1	0

No Rector or Minister officiating for him shall demand any fee for the performance of any clerical duty, 22 V. c. 23, s. 61,

Exemptions from
stamps.

All certificates for leave of absence, returns, and proceedings made necessary by this Act, shall be exempt from stamp duty, 22 V. c. 23, s. 62.

Penalties.

Penalties not declared how recoverable and applied, shall be recovered by action of debt. One moiety to the person who sues, 22 V. c. 23, s. 63.

Jurisdiction of
Supreme court.

Act not to alter, restrict, or affect the jurisdiction of the Supreme Court, touching the Bishop or any body, or person, or matter mentioned therein, 22 V. c. 23, s. 64.

Short Title. "The Clergy Act, 1858," 22 V. c. 23, s. 66.

Interpretation.

"Church," shall include chapels, and other places belonging to the Established Church in which Divine Worship shall by license of the Bishop be performed—"Clergyman," shall include Rector, Curate, or other Minister, of the Established Church duly licensed by the Bishop, and appointed to officiate in some Church, 22 V. c. 23, s. 67.

Duration

Act to determine 31st December, 1869, 22 V. c. 23, 68,

SCHEDULE A.—22 V., C. 23, S. 38.

BAPTISMS solemnized in the Parish of . in the County of . in the year 18

No.	When Baptized.	Child's Name, and when Born.	PARENT'S NAME.		Abode.	Quality, Trade, or Profession.	By whom the Ceremony was performed.
			Christian.	Surname.			
1	1832, October 10.	John, born 5th September, 1831.	William and Elizabeth	D—— his Wife	East Street.	Carpenter	A. B. Rector.
2	1832, October 20.	James Innes, born 4th April, 1830.			Duke Street		C. D., Curate

SCHEDULE B.—22 V. C. 23, S. 38-41.

BURIALS in the Parish of　　in the County of　　in the Year 18

No.	Name and Description.	Age.	Abode.	When Buried.	Where Buried.	By whom the Ceremony was Performed.
1.	James Thompson, Wheelwright.	45 Years.	King-Street.	July 5th, 1832.	New Burying Ground.	A. B., Rector.
2.	T. B., a Lieut. — Regt.	30 Years.	Kingston Barracks.	July 6th, 1832.	Church Yard.	C. D., Officiating Minister.

SCHEDULE C.—22 V. C. 23, S. 38-41.

MARRIAGES solemnized in the Parish of　　in the County of　　in the Year 18

No. 1.	A. B. of the Parish of　　the　　of　　and C. D. of this Parish, were married by　　in the year 18　　by me	E. F., Rector.

SCHEDULE D.—22 V. C. 23, S. 39.

I,   aged

A. B., of

To the Rector or Officiating Minister of

do certify that on the   day of

was buried at (the place of burial), and that the ceremony of burial was performed by me.

A. B.

SCHEDULE E.—22 V. C. 23, S. 31.

Date.	Duties Performed, including Number of Baptisms, Marriages, &c.	Signature of the Officiating Minister.
Morning		
Evening,		

F
Superscription of
returns, s. 46

To the Registrar of the Diocese of Jamaica

A.B. Rector (or officiating Minister), of   Spanish-Town.
C.D. Churchwarden.

G
Registers fees, s.
s. 49

	£	s.	d
For letters of orders, Deacon's or Priest's, according to the act of Ordination, and administering the Oaths	1	12	0
For a Clergyman's Licence, recording the same, and administering the Oaths	I	12	0
For schoolmaster, lay reader. or catechist licence, recording the same, and drawing out declaration paper	0	16	0
For licence of place of worship, and recording the same	3	4	0
Appointment of an apparitor, and recording the same	0	16	0
Appointment of a Chaplain, and recording the same	3	0	0
Appointment of a rural-dean or commissary, and recording same	6	0	0
Letters of institution to living, administering oaths, and recording memorandum thereof....	6	0	0
Mandate of induction, and instruction for reading in	3	0	0
Drawing up and filing a sentence of consecration, and preparing petition	3	0	0
Drawing up, recording, and attesting an act of consecration	1	12	0
Drawing up faculties or other ecclesiastical documents, not specified above, at the rate of one shilling and six pence per legal sheet			
Recording faculties appointments, or other ecclesiastical documents, not specified above, at one shilling and sixpence per legal sheet			

H
Allowances to Rectors, s. 58

Parishes.	In lieu of Glebe &c.	In lieu of Servants.	In lieu of Fees, 9 V. c. 32, s. 27.	Total allowances.
Kingston	£96	£..	£66	£162
Port Royal	60	..	18	78
St. David	72	..	18	90
St. Thomas ye East	63	50	30	143
Portland	50	..	12	62
St. George	73		18	91
Metcalfe	80		18	98
St. Mary	..		18	18
St. Ann		..	30	30
St. James		..	30	30
St. Elizabeth		..	30	30
Manchester			18	18
St. Dorothy	..		12	12
St. John	..		18	18
Trelawny	72		18	90
Hanover	30		30	60
Westmoreland	90	..	36	126
Clarendon	90	..	18	108
Vere	84	62	18	164
St. Catherine	84	..	42	126
St. Thomas ye Vale	122		18	140
St. Andrew	100	..	30	130

Clerks of the Peace and Magistrates.

To be admitted Attorneys No person shall be appointed Clerk of the Peace unless previously admitted to practise as an Attorney of the Supreme Court, 3 V., 65, s. 46.

Clerks of Circuit Courts . To be Clerks of Circuit Courts, 19 V., c. 10, s. 28-32, (See Circuit Courts.)

The powers and authorities heretofore vested in the Courts of Quarter Sessions, by any law of this island or of England, over Clerks of the Peace, are vested in the Judges of the Supreme Court, in respect of their suspension, or discharge from office, or otherwise, 19 V., c. 10, s. 32. *Amenable to the Supreme Courts*

The Clerks of the Peace and Magistrates' Clerks shall be paid monthly or quarterly, in full compensation for all proceedings for felonies, petty larcenies and aggravated misdemeanors indictable at the Assize or Circuit Courts, or triable at Petty Sessions, and for all other duties at the Assize or Circuit Courts and Special and Petty Sessions, relating to offences or matters of public nature or directed by two Justices, and all duties performed by them in furtherance of the general criminal justice, and in assisting the magistrates in public matters before them, the salaries in Schedule A— 23 V., c. 18, s. 1. *Salaries and duties therefore*

In respect of other matters, the Clerks of the Peace shall be entitled to the fees in Schedule B, and Magistrates' Clerks to those in Schedule C.— Whenever the duties of Magistrates' Clerks are performed by a Clerk of the Peace, he shall be entitled to the fees payable to the Magistrates' Clerk, in addition to those payable to him as Clerk of the Peace, 23 V., c. 18, s. 2. *Fees*

Such fees to be paid by the person requiring their services, unless the proceedings are directed by two Justices, 23 V., c. 18, s. 3.

Each Clerk of the Peace and Magistrates' Clerk shall, under penalty of £30, to be recovered by action of debt in the Circuit Courts, for the use of the parish or precinct, affix in a conspicuous part of the room in which the Justices hold their usual sittings in Petty Sessions, a fair and legible list or scale of all fees herein provided, so that the public may at all times have access thereto, 23 V., c. 18, s. 4. *Lists of fees to be exhibited*

Every Clerk of the Peace and Magistrates' Clerk shall, when required by the Governor, transmit to his Secretary a return of all trials in the Circuit or Petty Sessions, or other courts for which he is Clerk of the Peace or Magistrates' Clerk for such court or period as the Governor directs, and furnish such information in respect of any such trials as he requires as is in their power to afford. Penalty £30, to be recovered and appropriated as any other penalty under this Act, 23 V., c. 18, s. 5. *Returns to Governor*

Every Clerk of the Peace and Magistrates' Clerk shall have his permanent residence within the parish or precinct for which he holds his appointment, and no Clerk of the Magistrates shall be absent from the parish or precinct longer than seven days, nor any Clerk of the Peace than 30 days at one time, except by the consent in writing of the Custos and of not less than two Justices, but those for Kingston and Port Royal may, at their option, reside in Kingston, Port Royal, or St. Andrew, 23 V., c. 18, s. 6. *Residence*

In the event of a vacancy in the office of Clerk of the Peace for Kingston the salary shall be at the rate of £600 per annum, 23 V. c. 18, s. 7. *Salary of future Clerk of the Peace of Kingston, the new rate*

When the Custos is absent from the island, or there is a vacancy in the office of Custos for any parish in which there is a vacancy in the office of Clerk of the Peace, and there is a Magistrates' Clerk, an admitted Attorney, to discharge the duties, he shall do so until a permanent appointment is made, and receive the emoluments, fees, and perquisites while he acts, and be bound to discharge the duties appertaining, and be liable to the penalties attaching to the office; but if there is no Magistrates' Clerk qualified, the Chief Justice shall appoint a duly qualified Attorney-at-Law to fill the vacant office during the absence of the Custos, or until a Custos is appointed, 23 V., c. 18, s. 8. *Vacancies in office of Clerk of the Peace*

Upon any vacancy occurring in the office of Magistrates' Clerk, the Clerk of the Peace shall enter upon and perform the duties of the office, without increased remuneration, by way of salary, but shall be entitled to the fees payable to the Clerk of the Magistrates' in addition to those payable to him as Clerk of the Peace, and where the office of the Clerk to the Magistrates was held by the last Clerk of the Peace, the Clerk of the Peace to be appointed shall also enter upon, and perform the duties appertaining to the office of Clerk to the Magistrates,' and receive the salary and fees of the Clerk of the Peace, and also the fees, but not the salary, of the Magistrates Clerk, and whenever it becomes vacant, the office of Clerk to the Magistrates shall be abolished, and the salary shall determine. Every Clerk of the Peace who neglects, omits, or refuses to perform the duties of the office of Magistrates' Clerk, shall be deemed to have resigned his original appointment of Clerk of the Peace, 23 V. c. 18, s. 10. *Of Magistrates' Clerk*

L

They and their deputies to be attorneys at law. No person not being an admitted Attorney at Law shall be appointed to discharge any of the duties required under this Act, nor shall any deputy be permitted to perform the duties of any officer, unless he be an admitted Attorney at Law, duly qualified, 23 V. c. 18, s. 11—3 V. c. 65, s, 46.

Deputies not to act against the crown in their principal parishes. No deputy, or assistant of any Clerk of the Peace or Clerk of the Magistrates, shall act against the crown or prosecutor on any prosecution, for any offence charged or committed within the precinct or parish for which his principal is appointed, 23 V. c. 18, s. 12.

Duration. Act in force until 31st December, 1866, 23 V. c. 18, s. 13.

SCHEDULE, 23 V. c. 18.

A Salaries, s. 1

Parishes		Clerks of Peace.		Clerks of Magistrates
Kingston, now	......	£600		
Port Royal, now	......	120		
St. Andrew,	......	160		
St. David,	......	120		
St. Thomas ye East	......	200		
Portland	......	120	......	80
St. George,	......	120		
Metcalfe,	......	160		
St. Catherine	......		......	120
St. John,	......	400	......	80
St. Dorothy,	......			
St. Thomas ye Vale,	......	160	......	96
St. Mary, ..	......	200	......	120
St. Ann ..	......	200	......	120
Clarendon	......	200	......	120
Vere	......	120	......	80
Manchester	......	200	......	120
St. Elizabeth	......	200	......	120
Westmorland,	......	200	......	120
Hanover, ..	......	200	......	
St. James, ..	......	200	......	120
Trelawny, ..	......	200	......	120

B Clerks of the Peace fees, s. 2

	£	s.	d.
Drawing indictment and attending trial, recording proceedings and all other business connected therewith.	3	0	0
In case of private prosecutions when not required by the parties prosecuting to act	2	0	0
Taking depositions or examinations, in all other proceedings, per sheet of 160 words, not connected with the above	0	1	6
Entering records, making copies and extracts, per legal sheet of 160 Words......	0	1	0
Each Certificate to be annexed to proceedings	0	2	6
Taking recognizance each person	0	1	0
Venire facias for each Court..	0	2	6
For each Calendar not exceeding 3 for each Court ..	0	4	0
Entering every order of Court	0	1	0
Each copy	0	0	6
Making out and signing each Subpœna or Summons to witness....	0	0	9
Each copy	0	0	3
All proceedings to be returned on Writ of Certiorari or Mandamus per sheet of 160 words..	0	1	0
Servants' Wages, Information and Summons	0	4	6
Attending at trial, and all other work connected therewith	0	3	0
Warrant of Distress	0	3	0
Fees under Petty Debt Act, according to the provisions of that Act			

C Clerks of the Magistrates fees, s. 3

	£	s.	d.
For every deposition on information	0	2	0
Summons or Warrant when required	0	2	0
Each Copy	0	1	0

	£	s.	d.
Attendance at the trial of each case, including the examination of witnesses, and entering record, and all matters connected therewith	0	3	0
Affidavit to ground Search Warrant and Warrant	0	4	0
Affidavit and Warrant for articles of the peace and good behaviour	0	4	0
Each Notice	0	0	9
Each copy	0	0	3
Each Summons or Subpœna for witness	0	0	9
Each copy	0	0	3
Taking recognizance each person	0	1	0

Clerk of the Supreme Court and Crown.

The offices consolidated and the holder to be called clerk of the Supreme Court and Crown, 20 V., c. 22, s. 1. *Offices consolidated*

No person eligible except a Barrister of three years, or a Solicitor of six years standing in the Courts of the island, 20 V., c. 22, s. 2. *Qualification*

He shall before acting, under penalty of £600 for omission, enter into recognizance, in £1000 and two sureties in £500 each, before the Chief Justice, for the faithful and due discharge of the duties of his office, to be approved of by the Attorney-General, and signed before the Chief Justice at the time of entering into security, and on being attested by him to be recorded immediately in the Secretary's Office. The production of the record shall be evidence in all cases, 20 V., c. 22, s. 3. *Security*

He shall within one month after the death or insufficiency of any surety, enter into fresh security, first giving to the Attorney-General four days' notice, in writing, of his intention, with the names and additions of his intended sureties, to be taken and recorded, and be evidence as before directed— 20 V., c. 22, s. 4. *Fresh Security*

No member of the Legislative Council or Assembly, or officer accountable to the public shall be accepted as surety, 20 V., c. 22, s. 5. *Persons ineligible as sureties*

All process of the Supreme Court shall be signed by the Clerk of the Supreme Court and Crown as heretofore, and shall not require the signature of the Chief Justice or other Judge, 20 V., c. 22, s. 6. *signature of process*

Not to be permitted to practise in any Court of this island, 20 V., c. 22, s. 7 *Not to practice*

He shall keep his office in St, Jago de la Vega, and keep it open for the use of the public, from 7, a. m. to 3, p. m., every day, Sundays and Holidays excepted, and shall attend for the discharge of his duties on all such days unless prevented by sickness or other reasonable causes, Penalty. £30— 20 V., c. 22, s. 8. *Office and office hours*

During the continuance of the Act, all fees heretofore payable to the Clerk of the Court or Crown shall be abolished, and all Acts, so far as they relate to s fees, repealed, 20 V., c. 22, s. 9. *Fees abolished*

Penalty for asking, demanding, taking, or receiving by himself or any person for him, any fee or gratuity, £50, and he may, in the discretion of the Supreme Court be declared incapacitated to act, 20 V., c· 22. s. 10. *Penalty for taking fees*

Instead of fees, there shall be set upon all papers, writings, process and proceedings, out of the Supreme or Circuit Courts, or office of the Clerk of the Supreme Court and Crown, the Stamps in Schedule, in addition to other Stamps, 20 V. c. 22, s. 12. *Stamps in lieu of fees*

He shall be allowed in lieu of fees, the annual sum of £800 (to be reduced to £600 after death, removal or resignation of the present holder, 27 V S. 1, c. 4, s. 3.) to be paid by the Receiver General, quarterly, 20 V c. 22, s. 14. *Salary*

And be paid £40 per annum, for contingent expenses of office, not otherwise provided, payable quarterly, 20 V. c. 22, s. 15. *Contingencies*

He shall employ an efficient Clerk to assist him in the ordinary duties of his office, and in receiving, filing and preserving the records, and whose duty it shall also be to enter up and record all orders of the Supreme and Insolvent Debtors' Courts, when required, and of Judges in Chambers, and make and enter the necessary and accustomed indices and alphabets of records, and also to record all documents and proceedings not otherwise provided for. Salary to be paid by Receiver-General, on certificate of the Clerk of the Supreme Court and Crown, £200 payable quarterly, 20 V. c. 22, s. 16. *Clerk, his duties and salary*

Recording Judgments &c. Office copies, remuneration for

Also persons to enter up and record all the Judgments, inquisitions, writs, indictments and other proceedings required by law, or the practice of the Supreme Court, to be entered up and recorded, and the making of office copies when required, and allow for the same at the rate of 4½d for every 160 words. or figures, to be paid from time to time, by the Receiver General, on certificate of the Clerk of the Supreme Court and Crown, endorsed on an account verified on oath by the person entitled to be paid, 20 V. c. 22, s. 17.

Books for records

The Receiver General on requisition of the Clerk of the Supreme Court and Crown, shall procure and supply all such books as are from time to time required for recording or entering documents, 20 V. c. 22, s. 19.

Back alphabets

The Clerk of the Court shall keep regular and just Rack Alphabets of Judgments obtained in the Supreme or Circuit Courts, penalty £300; 20 V. c. 22, s. 20.

Public records, access thereto

All proceedings, civil and criminal, declared to be public records, and the Clerk of the Court shall keep all records in his office, and all books and documents open for inspection by the public, during office hours, and any person shall be entitled to make and take copies of proceedings and documents free of charge, except the fee for searching, where demandable, 20 V. c. 22, s. 21.

Records of writs and returns

He shall keep in his office, books, in which to enter and set down on the return of writs from the Provost Marshal's Office into his the names of plaintiffs or defendants, with their addition, the amount of debt or damages, the costs of suit and of delay, and the levy endorsed on the back of each writ, with the names of the persons who subscribe each direction to levy. Each entry shall specify the Court at which the writ is returnable, with the return thereto.

Evidence

Such books to be received as books of record, and the same or a transcript therefrom of any of the writs therein entered, duly authenticated by the Clerk of the Supreme Court and Crown, shall be received as evidence, as also of the original Judgment when lost or mislaid, 20 V. c. 22, s. 22.

Assignments of Judgments

He shall keep a separate book for recording assignments of Judgments, 20 V. c. 22, s. 23.

And on any assignment being recorded, shall make or cause &c., a note in the margin of the record of the Judgment assigned, the name of the assignee, and date of assignment, and shall not knowingly suffer to issue out of his office, any writ on any such Judgment except by the party entitled to such assignment or his attorney-at-law, 20 V. c. 22, s. 24.

Provost Marshal's Schedule under 43 G. 3, c. 20, s. 18

Each Schedule delivered by the Provost Marshal to him, under 43 G. 3, c. 20, s. 18, shall be recorded in a book, for the purpose, and each original carefully kept, with the date of filing endorsed thereon, penalty £50, 20 V. c. 22, s. 25.

Fees to public officers to be allowed in taxation of costs

He shall tax and allow to each party in his bill of costs, all fees paid to the Provost Marshal and Clerks of Circuit Courts, authorized to be received by them, 20 V. c. 22, s. 26.

He shall cause all proceedings recorded in his office, to be carefully examined, penalty £30, 20 V. c. 22, s. 27.

Satisfactions

He shall enter every satisfaction of Judgment delivered to him at his office on the margin of the record of the Judgment, and keep a book called " a satisfaction book" wherein to be entered alphabetically, dockets of such satisfactions, 20 V. c. 22, s. 28.

Posteas

The Attorney of the party entitled to Judgment, shall at the time of taxing his bill of costs, file a postea of such Judgment, bearing the Stamp required by Schedule, 20 V. c. 22, s. 29.

Returns of satisfactions to the Provost Marshal

He shall, within 20 days after each Supreme Court, return under his hand to the Provost Marshal's Office, a certificate of every satisfaction of Judgment, entered in his office, 20 V. c. 22, s. 31.

Further duties

He shall attend the sittings of the Supreme Court and Judges in Chambers, tax bills of costs on proceedings between party and party, and between

Office copies &c to be delivered within 5 days

Solicitor and client, and file all papers, proceedings or documents to be filed in his office, and cause to be prepared, office copies and exemplifications required, and deliver them within 5 days from the day of which they are ordered, 20 V. c. 22, s. 32.

Leave of absence Deputy

The Governor may grant him leave of absence, not exceeding 12 months at any one time, provided that on each occasion, a person qualified as by this act is required, be appointed by the Governor, to discharge the duties, during his absence, 20 V. c. 22, s. 33.

Stamp Duty on his Commission, shall be £30 only, 20 V. c. 22, s. 34.   *Stamp on Commission*

Any person taking down any book of record, in the office, from the shelf or place in which it is kept, and not returning it to its own proper place, shall forfeit 40s., recoverable before a Justice of St. Catherine 20 V. c. 22, s. 36.   *Taking down and not returning books to place*

Persons not admitted Attorneys, nor the authorized Clerk or agent of an admitted Attorney, who make searches in the Office, or take any extract or docket from the records or documents, shall pay a fee of 1s. for every 3 hours, or less time they are occupied, for which the Clerk of the Court and crown shall give a receipt upon a stamp of equal value, 20 V. c. 22, s. 37.   *Fees for searches.*

A fair written table of stamps imposed by this act shall be prepared, and placed in a conspicuous part of the office, and so kept for public inspection. Penalty £20, 20 V. c. 22, s 38.   *Table of stamps.*

The penalties imposed on the Clerk of the Court and crown for neglect of duty, shall be recovered by attachment, to be issued by the Supreme Court on application of the Attorney General, or by any party aggrieved, and the proceeds applied to the use of the public, 20 V. c. 22, s. 39.   *Recovery &c. of penalties.*

In force for 7 years, 20 V. c. 22, s. 42.

Continued to 19th March, 1871, 27 V. S. 1, c. 4, s. 1.

SCHEDULE TO 20 V. c. 22.

On each declaration of the 1st class	......	......	0	4	0	*Table of stamps, s. 38.*
" " 2nd class	......	......	0	2	0	
" Postea of Judgment of 1st class	......	......	0	6	0	
" " 2nd class	......	......	0	3	0	
" Writ to be returned, with Inquisition in extent	......		0	5	0	
" Inquisition for each writ included therein.	......		0	3	0	
" Other Writ......	......	......	0	3	0	
(Writs of summons, arrests, replevin, subpœna in criminal						
cases, and habeas corpus excepted)						
" Writ of subpœna in civil cases, when the names of three						
witnesses only may be inserted	......		0	1	0	
" Special Writ of Venire Facias	......		0	7	6	
" Certificate under Seal	......		0	7	6	
" " not under Seal	......		0	1	6	
" Attested Order	......		0	1	6	
" Manucaption	......		0	3	0	
" On each information filed in the Crown Office, at the						
instance of a private prosecutor	......		3	0	0	
" Commission for taking Affidavits			3	0	0	
" Other Commission	......		0	3	0	
" Bill of Costs	......	......	0	3	0	
" Memorandum or minute of a judgment to be registered						
under 8 V. c. 48.	......		0	1	0	
" Office Copies on each sheet of folio post containining 24						
lines	......	......	0	1	6	

Clerk of the Warrants.

His fees for drawing a Warrant for the Seal, 4s. 4½d. currency. 10 Ann c. 4, s. 32.

Coin.

No payment shall be deemed good but in current coin of gold or silver, unless where both parties agree for payment in sugar, or other produce, 24 G. 2. c. 19, s. 9.   *Payments to be in gold and silver.*

The Doubloon shall be a legal tender at £3 4s., the silver dollar at 4s. 2d. [but not its subdivisions, 5 V. c. 28.] and the gold coins of Great Britain and Ireland to any amount at the rates they pass current at in Great Britain and Ireland, 3 V. c. 39, s. 10.   *Legal tenders,.*

The British silver crown, half crown, shilling and six p , legal tenders to any amount. All coins under six pence, viz : 4d., 3d., 2d., 1½d, only to the extent of 40s., in any one payment. 7 V. c. 51.

Payment of several notes at once.

When payment is demanded of several bank notes, or other engage-ments, at the same time, reference shall be had to the sum of the whole amount demanded, and a tender of silver separately on each note shall not be legal, 1 V. c. 21, s. 3.

Copper.

Copper coin of the United Kingdom shall be current, and a legal tender for one payment at one time not exceeding 12d. or other amount to be declared by royal proclamation, 6 V. c. 40.

Counterfeiting current foreign coin.

Coining, falsifying, falsely forging or counterfeiting, impairing, dimin-ishing, scaling, washing, clipping, filing or lightening any money, or coins of foreign realms, made current by any Act of this Island, or law, or sta-tute of England or Great Britain, or at any time after to be current or gene-rally, by consent, taken and received as such, felony, 14 G. 3, c. 18, s. 1.

Punishable with penal servitude for 4 years, 19 V. c. 29, s. 1, 21 V, c. 14, s. 3.

Buying or selling or having clippings.

Any person buying or selling or knowingly having in his possession any clippings or filings of the current coin or money shall forfeit the same, and £500 (£300 sterling) one moiety to the informer, to be recovered by ac-tion of debt, &c., with costs, and be branded on the right cheek, R., and be imprisoned until the fine is paid, 14 G. 3 c. 18, s. 2.

Any Justice may enter any house, room, workshop, or other place of any suspected person, and search for all tools and utensils used in coun-terfeiting such coins and all counterfeit coin, clippings, and filings of current coin or money, and, on refusal to permit a search, may with the as-sistance of constables, break open any door, box, trunk, chest, cupboard, or cabinet to search for such tools, &c., and if any are found, seize, as well the tools, &c., as the persons in whose possession they are found, and commit them, to be dealt with according to law, 14 G. 3, c. 18, s. 3.

Importing coun-terfeit coin.

Any master, supercargo, or other person importing, or causing to be imported, any false, base, forged, or counterfeit gold money, or coin, resembling any of the coins of foreign realms now, or to be current, or received by general consent, knowing the same to be false &c., guilty of Felony, 14 G. 3, c. 18, s. 4.

Punishment as above, 19 V. c. 29, s. 1. 21 V. c. 14, s. 3.

Suspected coin,

When any piece of gold or silver coin is offered in payment, and seems base or counterfeit to the person to whom it is offered, he may carry it to any Magistrate, who, on its appearing in his judgment to be base or counterfeit, may cause it to be cut into two equal parts as nearly as may be, and delivered back to the person offering it in payment, 14 G. 3 c. 18, s. 9.

Uttering counter-feit coin.

Any person convicted of any offence below felony of uttering any coun-terfeit money, knowing it to be counterfeit, either of the Queen's coins, or of the coins of foreign realms, which are, or may be current by law or com-mon consent, may be sentenced to imprisonment, with or without hard la-bour and solitary confinement, 1 V. c. 28, s. 4.

Collectors of Dues.

Short Title.

Tax Collection Act, 1864, 27 V. S. 1, c. 31, s. 1.

Appointment.

All duties imposed by any Act, now or to be in force, the collection of which is not provided for (arrears of taxes outstanding on the rolls of Collec-tors of Taxes, or of arrears, excepted) shall be collected by the Clerk of the Vestry, or other person appointed by the Governor, to be called "Collector of Dues," and whom he may dismiss for misconduct, or if Clerk of the Ves-try also, divest him of the office of Collector of Dues, 27 V. S. 1, c. 31, s. 2.

Holders to con-tinue.

Present holders of office shall continue unless removed for misconduct, 27 V. S. 1, c. 31, s. 3.

Neglect of duty.

For every neglect of duties not otherwise provided for, he shall forfeit not exceeding £10, nor less than £5, 27 V. S. 1, c. 31, s. 4.

Collectors who on removal from office do not forthwith deliver accounts on oath, sworn before a Justice, of the monies collected by him since the last account, and of those remaining uncollected, mentioning the names of the persons by whom owing, the amount and description of property in respect of which they are due, or who do not pay over all monies, from time to time received, to the Receiver General, shall be proceeded against by the Clerk of the Peace, who, on receipt of a certificate from the Receiver General that the removed Collector of Dues has failed to comply with the requirements of this Act, shall procure a Justice's warrant to apprehend and bring the defaulter before two Justices, who, upon production and inspection of such certificate, and in the absence of proof to their satisfaction that the requirements of the law have been complied with, shall commit the offender to the common gaol, until he has given in his accounts and made payment, 27 V. S. 1, c. 31, s. 5. *Enforcement of accounts and payment on removal.*

He may, with consent of his sureties, appoint a deputy, to perform the duties and exercise the functions of his office, and revoke any appointment, whose name shall be publicly exhibited in his office, and for whom he and his sureties shall be responsible, 27 V. S. 1. c. 31, s. 6. *Deputy.*

Upon the death or removal of any collector, his and sureties' liabilities shall cease, except in respect of previous defaults. He shall be deemed in default in any case in which within his knowledge, any tax or instalment had fallen due and might have been previously enforced upon proof thereof, 27 V. S. 1, c. 31, s. 7. *Liability.*

He shall give public notice of the rates of taxes, and times of payment as the Executive Committee shall direct, 27 V. S. 1, c. 31, s. 8. *Notice of rates.*

He shall give such information and assistance, with reference to this act, and the license and regulation duties, and other acts under which he receives taxes, as may be required from him, by any taxpayer, 27 V. S. 1, c. 31. s. 9. *Information to taxpayers*

And shall notify to the Receiver General, the names of persons in arrear for taxes, who are recipients of public or parochial salary, or entitled to money from the Treasury, and the Receiver General shall retain the amount of such taxes, 27 V. S. 1, c. 31, s. 10. *To notify taxes in arrear, to Receiver General, by recipients of public monies*

Before acting and within the time appointed by the Governor and Executive Committee, he shall enter into bond, with two sureties, who may limit their respective liabilities, in the sum to be approved of by the Governor &c. Form Schedule A, except Kingston, when the part of the condition applicable to Stamps need not be inserted, and the Governor &c., may require new or further security, 27 V. S. 1, c. 31, s. 11. *Security*

The present collector shall enter into fresh bonds, or on failure by any person, now or to be appointed, the Governor may make a fresh appointment 27 V. S. 1, c. 31, s. 12.

Each surety shall subscribe a declaration before a Justice, that he is worth the sum for which he has consented to be surety, over and above his debts and liabilities, to be endorsed on the bond, 27 V. G. 1, c. 31, s. 13. *Justification*

Every bond shall. within the time for giving security, be delivered to the Receiver General, to be recorded at the public expense, and shall be subjected to Stamp Duty. The production of the bond, probate and declaration or the record or an attested copy, shall be prima facie evidence of execution, 27 V, S. 1, c. 31, s. 14. *Bonds to be recorded Evidence*

The Island Secretary shall keep a separate book, for recording bonds of the Crown, also an index, 27 V. S. 1, c. 31, s. 15.

In any action upon any security bond, it shall suffice for assignment or suggestion of breaches, to deliver particulars of breaches, Form B, or to that effect, with alterations or additions, as the case requires. And the Jury shall assess the damages, and interest shall be recovered thereon, from the first day of the Court, at £10 per cent, per annum. Upon any further breach, the same shall be assigned, and further damages assessed, and interest at that rate recovered, 27 V. S. 1, c. 31, s. 16. *Suggestions of breaches* *£10 per cent interest*

Upon the filing of any declaration. and entry in a book by the Clerk of the Court, the lands, of which the Collector and his sureties are or may afterwards be seized or entitled to, for any interest, or may have any disposing power, shall be charged with and bound by the bond, and all damages thereafter to be assessed, as if a Judgment had been entered up and registered 27 V. S. 1. c. 31, s. 17. *Lands bound from filing declaration*

On affidavit that a Collector has neglected to pay, or account for, any money received by him, a Judge may issue an attachment to the Provost Marshal, or his Deputy, to arrest the person, and seize and secure the goods, chattels, and personal property of the Collector, wherever discovered and to be found. In case his accounts are not duly delivered, or the monies detained by him *Attachments against Collectors* are not paid to the Receiver General, within 14 days after seizure, or if the sale be not stayed, by order of a Judge, to sell and dispose of the same, or sufficient to pay the sum due and unaccounted for, and costs, and restore the overplus if any, to the Collector or person entitled, 27 V. S. 1, c. 31, s. 18.

Stay of execution bail

The Collector may apply to a Judge, upon affidavit, to be admitted to bail, or to stay the execution or sale, to enable him to make application to the Supreme Court, to discharge the same, who may make order accordingly 27 V. S. 1, c. 31, s. 19.

Delivery up of bond

Upon full performance of the conditions of the bond of any collector, and upon his discharge, in writing, by the Executive Committee, the bond shall be delivered up, and satisfaction entered, at the public expense, on the record of the Bond, and of any Judgment thereon, 27 V. S. 1, c. 31, s. 20.

Damages for injuries &c.

No action shall be brought, nor shall any Collector be accountable for any loss, deterioration or injury to goods or property levied or distrained on, except for wilful negligence, ill usage, or injury, 27 V. S. 1, c. 31, s. 32.

Persons making distress not trespassers, for irregularity
Receivers

Nor shall the person making the distress by reason of any irregularity, be deemed a trespasser ab initio, 27 V. S. 1, c. 31, s. 33.

The Collector may proceed for the recovery of taxes, or arrears 2d moiety, penalty or costs, notwithstanding the property is in receivership or the party an officer of the Court, without application to the Court of Chancery, 27 V. S. 1, c. 31, s. 34.

Indigent persons

Where any person in possession of a house, whether as owner or otherwise, is poor and indigent, and unable to pay the tax, or more than a portion, the Collector may refrain from enforcing payment until he has transmitted to the Executive Committee, a statement of the case, name of the party, amount due, description of the house, and any evidence he has of the poverty of the person, or his inability to pay the whole tax, 27 V. S. 1, c. 31, s. 35.

Examinations

And may examine on oath the person liable, and any other person willing to give information respecting his circumstances, and take down the statements to be forwarded, with his recommendation, for the decision of the Executive Committee, 27 V. S. 1, c. 31, s. 36.

Relief

The Executive Committee may institute further enquiries, and when satisfied that the person is poor and unable to pay the taxes or the whole, may direct the Collector not to levy for the taxes or the whole, and the tax shall not be a charge on the house, nor shall any subsequent occupier be liable for the unpaid taxes, 27 V., S. 1, c. 31, s. 37.

Replevin Security, &c

Before a writ of replevin issues for goods distrained on for taxes, the claimant shall file an affidavit, shewing how they are not liable, and the grounds on which the adverse claim is grounded, and procure a Judge's Order for its issue, an attested copy whereof shall be served with the copy declaration, and the Provost Marshal, or his Deputy, before execution, shall require the joint and several bond of the plaintiff, and two sureties to be approved of by the Provost Marshal or his deputy, and the Collector, in a penalty to the Collector sufficient to cover the value of the goods, and £50 for probable costs conditioned for payment of the sum distrained for, and of the costs of distress and defence, or for a return of the goods and payment of the defendants' costs in case of judgment against plaintiff, or of non-suit or discontinuance, and unless the attested copy order is sent with the copy declaration, or bond be delivered, the Provost Marshal or his deputy shall abstain from executing the writ, 27 V., S. 1, c. 31, s. 38.

Not to abate by defendant's death
Limit for trial

An action of replevin shall not abate by death of defendant, but shall be continued by suggestion and substitution of the person on whom his rights devolve. It shall be tried at latest within two court's after issue joined, unless the Supreme Court or Judge of the District Circuit retain the same for sufficient cause on oath, or it is continued at the defendants instance, and unless so tried it shall be peremptorily discontinued without order, and if the amount distrained for, and cost of suits be not paid, or the goods returned and costs paid, upon demand, the Collector may enforce the penalty of the bond against the party and his sureties without prejudice to his other remedies for costs, 27 V. S. 1, c. 31, s. 39.

Pleadings to actions for distresses, &c.

To actions against Collectors or others for any distresses, or other acts in the execution of his duty, the defendant may, with the plea of not guilty, make avowry of, or justify the taking or other act charged and allege generally that it was made or done by virtue of this or any other act in that behalf, without setting forth any other matter or circumstance constituting such justification, and the plaintiff may reply "de injuria", and on the trial the whole matter relied upon by both parties may be given in evidence—27 V. S. 1, c. 31, s. 40.

In any action to recover the value of a distress sold, no more damages than the net proceeds of sale after payment of all expenses shall be recoverable, unless the plaintiff prove that by fraud or want of care the distress has been sold at an under value, or that before the sale he had given written notice to the Collector, or person distraining, of his intention to replevy within a time to be mentioned, not exceeding 14 days from the taking, and had required the sale to be delayed to enable him to replevy, and tendered a reasonable sum to cover the additional expenses occasioned thereby, and the sale was, notwithstanding, proceeded with before the expiration of the time— 27 V., S. 1, c. 31. s. 41. *Damages*

Actions shall be brought within six calendar months after the accruing of the cause of action, and shall be defended at the expense of the public, unless the Judge or Court certify the costs of defence ought to be borne by the defendant personally, 27 V., S. 1, c. 31, s. 42. *Actions*

Persons neglecting or refusing to perform duties, or guilty of any offence not provided against, shall be liable to a penalty not exceeding £5— 27 V., S. 1, c. 31, s. 43. *Penalties*

Penalties shall be summarily recoverable before two Justices, and in default of payment the offenders may be committed until paid, and when paid shall be transmitted to the Receiver-General, to the credit of the revenue, 27 V. S. 1, c. 31, s. 44. *Recovery*

The Justices may award the informer not more than a moiety of the penalty, 27 V., S. 1, c. 31, s. 45. *Informer*

The provisions of this Act shall apply to the collection and enforcement of all taxes, duties and penalties raised or imposed by any other Act not specifically providing for their collection, 27 V., S. 1, c. 31, s. 46. *Extension*

In force until 31st July, 1870, 27 V., S. 1, c. 31, s. 47. *Duration*

Collectors shall be allowed to retain £6 per cent commissions from all duties and moneys received by them, 28 V., c. 28, s. 30. *Remuneration*

And £40 per annum salary on the Governor's Warrant in addition, 28 V., c. 28, s. 34. *Salary*

They shall not interfere in the election of any member of Assembly, or procure any vote to be recorded for any person at any such election, or influence any person to register as a voter in any parish. Penalty £50 for the first offence, and £200 for any future offence, to be recovered in a summary manner, under any Act of this island, 23 V., c. 28, s. 50. *Elections*

Nor be eligible to be nominated for, or elected to a seat in the Assembly, 25 V. c. 28. *Not to be of Assembly.*

SCHEDULE.—27 V. S. 1, c. 31.

A.
Security bonds, s 11.

JAMAICA, SS.

Know all men by these presents, that we
of the parish of   in the county of
and island aforesaid   and
are jointly and severally held, and firmly bound unto our sovereign lady the Queen, her heirs and successors, in the sum of
lawful money of Jamaica, to be paid to our said sovereign lady the Queen, her heirs and successors, for the use of the government of this island, for which payment, to be well and truly paid [made], we bind ourselves, and each of us, and any four, three, or two of us, and the heirs, executors, and administrators of us, and of each of us, and of any four, three, or two of us jointly, severally, and respectively, firmly by these presents. Sealed with our seals.

Dated this   day of   one thousand eight hundred and sixty-
Whereas the above named   · having been appointed the collector of dues and stamp duties for the parish of
has been required to enter into the security prescribed by law for the faithful discharge of such duties.
Now the condition of the above bond is such, that if the above named while and so long as he shall continue and be the collector of dues and stamp duties for the said parish of

M

and at such respective times, and in such manner as are respectively prescribed by any act or acts, now or hereafter to be in force, shall collect, and duly account for, and pay over to the receiver-general all and every the taxes, duties, charges, impositions, and monies which shall be payable to, or receivable by him as such collector of dues and stamp duties as aforesaid, from any person or persons whomsoever; and, in case of neglect or omission of any person or persons to give in a true and correct account of all real and personal property possessed by him or them, liable to any such tax, duty, charge, or imposition, or in case of non-payment by any person or persons of any such tax, duty, charge, or imposition to which he or they may be liable, shall duly enforce the powers of such act or acts against those who shall make default; and if the said   do and shall duly account for all stamps, and stamped paper, and printed forms, which shall from time to time be delivered to him by the receiver-general, in pursuance of the "Stamp Duty Act, 1862," and shall from time to time be sold, or remain on hand respectively, and also account for, and pay over all monies received by him for, or on account of the sale of such stamps, and of such paper, and printed forms respectively, as fixed by the "Stamp Duty Act, 1862," or the schedule thereto, and if he shall render such account to the receiver general, as that officer shall direct, and shall pay over the monies so received by him at the periods fixed for the payment of other monies received by him as collector of dues, then this obligation shall be void, otherwise the same shall remain in full force and virtue : Provided, That the liability of the said   as one of the sureties of the said   shall not exceed pounds, nor shall the liability of the said   as another of such sureties, exceed the sum of   pounds, nor that of the said   the other of such sureties, exceed the sum of   pounds, exclusive of interest, costs, and charges respectively attaching to each.

—————————————(seal.)
—————————————(seal.)
—————————————(seal.)
—————————————(seal.)

Sealed and delivered in the presence of

Memorandum this   day of   annoque domini one thousand eight hundred and sixty-   personally appeared before me, the subscribing witness to the execution of the foregoing bond who being duly sworn, made oath that he was present, and did see the therein named   severally and respectively duly sign, seal, and deliver the same bond, for the purposes therein mentioned.

—————————

Justice of the Peace for the parish of

—————— . ——

11.
Particulars of
branches. s, 16.

In the Supreme Court—To wit.

Regina vs. A. B.

The following are the breaches of the condition of the bond or writing, obligatory in the declaration in this cause mentioned, on account of which the several sums understated are sought to be recovered in this action ; that is to say :

For not duly accounting to the receiver-general for the following sums collected and received by the said   as collector of dues, (and of stamps) of the parish of   viz :

(Insert particulars.)

For not duly paying over to the receiver-general the following sums collected and received by the said   as collector of dues (and of stamps) of the parish of   viz :

(Insert particulars.)

For not collecting and getting in the following sums payable to or receivable by him, as collector of dues (and of stamps), from divers persons within the parish of   viz :

(Insert particulars.

For not enforcing the powers of the acts of the legislature against divers persons who made default in the returns of property possessed by them, liable to taxes under the provisions of the acts in that behalf, amounting, in the whole, to the sum of '   on the   day of last past, viz :

(Insert particulars.)

For not enforcing the powers of the acts aforesaid against divers persons who made default by non-payment of divers taxes and monies which they were liable to pay, amounting, in the whole, to the sum of on the   day of   last past, viz :

(Insert particulars.)

For not accounting for divers sums of other monies come to the hands of the said   as collector of dues of the said parish of and amounting, in the whole, to the sum of on the   day of   last past, viz :

• (Insert particulars.)

For not paying over to the receiver-general divers sums of other monies come, &c., (in the last item.)

For not (here state any other breach, and add as many other breaches as may have been committed.)

Dated this   day of

———

Combinations.

If any person, by violence to the person or property, or by threats or intimidation, or by molesting, or in any way obstructing another, force or endeavor to force, any other person, hired or employed in the agriculture or in any manufacture trade or business, or in domestic service, or as a boatman, or porter, or in any other occupation in which they have been usually employed, to depart from his hiring, employment or work, or to return his work before it is finished, or prevent, or endeavor to prevent, any such person, not being hired or employed, from hiring himself to, or accepting work from any person, or use or employ violence to the person or property of another, or threats or intimidation, or molest, or in any way obstruct another, to force or induce such person to belong to any club or association, or contribute to any common fund, or to pay any fine or penalty on account of his not having complied, or of his refusing to comply with any rules, orders, resolutions or regulations made to obtain an advance, or to reduce the rate of wages, or alter or lessen the hours of working, or decrease or alter the quantity of work, or to regulate the mode of carrying on any manufacture, trade, or business, plantation or property, or its management. or if any person by violence, to the person or property, or by threats or intimidation, or by molesting, or in any way obstructing another, force or endeavor &c. any such person to make any alteration in his mode of regulating, managing, conducting or carrying on such manufacture, trade or business, plantation or property, or to limit the number or description of his workmen, journeymen or servants, or the number of apprentices of any manufacturer or tradesman, every person so offending or aiding, abetting or assisting therein, shall, on conviction before two Justices, be imprisoned only, or to kept to hard labor and solitary confinement for not exceeding three months; but no offence shall be tried, or punishable unless complained of within three calendar months, 3 V. c. 30, s. 1. *(marginal note: Illegal combinations)* *(marginal note: Complaints with in 3 months)*

This act shall not subject to any punishment, persons who meet together to consult upon and determine the rate of wages they will demand for their work, or the hours or time they will work, or who enter into any agreement, verbal or written, among themselves, to fix the rates or prices they shall demand, or the hours or times they will work. Persons so meeting or entering into any such agreement, shall not be liable to any prosecution or penalty, 3 V. c. 30, s. 2. *(marginal note: Legal meetings and agreements, workmen &c.)*

Nor any persons who meet to consult upon and determine the rates of wages or prices they will pay to their journeymen, workmen or servants, for their work, or the hours or times of working, or who enter into any agreement, verbal or written, among themselves, for fixing the rates of wages or prices they shall pay to their journeymen &c., and who are also exempted from prosecution or penalty, 3 V. c. 30, s. 3. *(marginal note: Employers)*

Evidence of offenders   Offenders may equally with others be compelled to give evidence for the prosecution against any other persons, and having given their testimony, shall be indemnified from any prosecution for having offended in the manner wherein or relative to which they give testimony, 3 V. c. 30, s. 4.

Witnesses   Justices may summon and enforce attendance of witnesses, 3 V. c. 30, s. 5.

Conviction . Appeal,   Convictions shall be transmitted to the next (Circuit Court) Appeal, 3 V. c, 30, s. 6,

---

Commissions of Attornies, &c.

Of Attornies, Trustees &c.]   Of Attornies or Agents of Absentees, Trustees, Guardians, Executors and Administrators, arising from their receipts, payments, transactions, management and disposals of the rents, profits, produce, and increase of the Estates and interests for which they are concerned, £6, per cent, including factorage commission for supplies made in the island for real estate, 24 G. 2, c. 19, s. 8.

On receiving and remitting monies   Commission on receiving and remitting monies lent, or remaining at interest in the island, and the interest, £5 per cent, viz. £2 10s for receiving, and £2 10s for remitting, 24 G. 2, c. 19, s. 8.

Penalty for demanding or receiving more, £100 (£60 sterling) recoverable by action of debt, half to the informer, 24 G. 2, c. 19, s. 8.

Factors   Not to extend to commissions for the sale of commodities sent to this Island from Great Britain or elsewhere, 24 G. 2, c. 19, s. 8.

Commissions de bene esse.

How obtainable, and when available on the trial   In any action on its being shewn to a Judge upon oath or affirmation that a material witness is sick, or about to depart from this island, or, from any other circumstance, a party is in danger of losing his testimony, the Judge shall issue a commission to take the examination de bene esse, under his hand and seal, without other signature, to be tested the day it issues, directed to such person or persons as he deems proper, and if more than one commissioner, the power shall be joint, and several; and if upon the trial it is shewn in evidence, or on affidavit, or affirmation by a Quaker, that a witness so examined is dead, off the island, or otherwise unable to attend to testify in court the examination under the commission shall be read in evidence, provided reasonable notice has been given of the taking of such examination— 38 G. 3, c. 23, s. 4,

Costs   The costs of the application for a commission de bene esse, and of the proceedings thereon, shall be costs in the cause, unless otherwise directed, 8 V., c. 28, s. 23.

Commissions Foreign.

Costs of   The costs of applications for, and of the proceedings thereupon shall be costs in the cause, unless otherwise directed, 8 V., c. 28, s, 23.

Commissioners to take Affidavits.

Appointments   The Chief and other Justices of the Supreme Court, or any two of them, the Chief Justice being one, may by commission, under the seal of the court, empower persons in the several parishes and districts to take affidavits in, or concerning any cause, matter, or thing depending, or any wise concerning any of the proceedings of the court, as the Judges used to do, which affidavits shall be filed in the office of the court, and then read and made use of in the court as affidavits taken in court, and shall be of the same force. **Affidavits**

False testimony   Persons forswearing themselves in such affidavits shall be liable to the same penalties as if made and taken in open court. Fee for taking affidavit, 1s. 3d. (9d. sterling), 14 G., 3. c. 3, **Fee**

Not affected by a new appointment of Chief   Such affidavits shall be taken, received, and read, notwithstanding any new appointment of a Chief Justice after the date of the commission— 42 G. 3, c. 26, s. 1.

Registration.   Commissions shall be registered by the Clerk of the Crown, viz.:—the name and addition of the Commissioner, and the date of the commission shall be inserted in a list to be by him kept for the purpose, which he is to have always ready in court, to produce when required, 42 G. 3, c. 26, s. 2.

No affidavit shall be received or read unless the commission has been registered, and the Clerk of the Crown, once in every year, at least, shall cause the list of Commissioners to be published [in "The Jamaica Gazette, by Authority," 8 V., c. 46] for one month, 42 G. 3, c. 26, s. 3.

No affidavit to be read unless appointment registered

Lists to be published annually

Commissioners during their appointment shall be amenable to the Supreme Court for their conduct, 42 G. 3, c. 26, s. 4.

Persons forswearing themselves in any affidavit before a Commissioner shall be guilty of perjury, 42 G. 3, c 26, s, 5,

Perjury

Affidavits before them may be used in Circuit Courts, 19 V., c, 10, s. 45.

Affidavits may be used in Circuit Courts

Commissions Special for Trial of Offences.

For trial of treasons, conspiracies, or administering unlawful oaths, may be issued by the Governor to the Chief Justice, Judge of the Court of Vice-Admiralty, if a barrister of 5 years standing at the bar of this island, and the Judges of the Supreme Court, authorising any three or more of them, of whom the Chief Justice or Judge of the Vice Admiralty Court shall be one, to try such offences by a Jury to be returned before them by the Provost Marshal, in whatever county committed, and the Provost Marshal, having notice of such commission, shall forthwith warn and return the like number of Jurors as he is by law required to return for the Grand or Assize Courts, 4 G. 4 c. 13, s. 6.

For trials of treasons, conspiracies, unlawful oaths

The Governor may issue under the broad seal, Special Commissions of Oyer and terminer, as often as he deems expedient, to the Chief Justice, or, in his absence, the Senior Assistant Judge of the Supreme Court, and such other persons as he may appoint, three to form a quorum, of whom the Chief Justice, or Senior Assistant Judge, shall be one, 5 W. 4 c. 18, s. 1.

For trials of offences generally.

When and to whom to be issued.

The Justices and Commissioners shall enquire by the oaths of good and lawful men of the county into which the Commission issues, of all crimes and offences mentioned in such commissions committed in such county, and shall hear and determine the same, and cause to be done therein what to Justice appertains, according to the laws and customs of this island, 5 W, 4 c. 18, s. 2.

Their powers

The Provost Marshal, on notice from the Chief Justice or Senior Assistant Judge that a Special Commission has been issued, shall cause a panel of 60 Jurors to be struck from the last Jury list returned of persons qualified to serve in the county, and summon or cause, &c., the Jurors so struck to attend on the day and at the place where the Special Commission is to be opened and held. Penalty for each neglect £500 (£300 sterling) to be enforced by attachment out of the Supreme Court on application of the Attorney General, 5 W. 4 c. 18, s. 3.

Provost Marshal to strike and summon Jury.

Each Juror shall be summoned 10 clear days, at least before opening the Commission—Penalty for neglecting to attend, £20, (£12 sterling) to be recovered by attachment from the Supreme Court, on application of the Attorney General, 5 W. 4 c. 18, s. 4.

Jurors attendance.

The Provost Marshal and Clerk of the Crown by themselves or deputies shall attend from day to day during the sitting of the Court. Penalty, £500, (£300 sterling) recoverable as above, 5. W. 4 c. 18, s. 5.

Provost Marshal and clerk Court

The Supreme Court may withhold the issuing of an attachment for any penalty, 5 W. 4 c. 18, s. 6.

Withholding attachment.

The Commission shall not expire by reason of the death or removal of the Governor by whom it is issued, but shall continue in force for 6 months after, unless revoked by his successor, 5 W. 4 c. 18, s. 7.

Continuance of commission.

No stamps necessary to any commission or other proceedings under this Act, 5 W. 4 c. 18, s. 8.

No stamps.

Whenever any popular tumults, riots, or breaches of the peace arise, rendering it advisable for the ends of Justice to have such offences adjudicated on by a Jury constituted otherwise than provided in ordinary cases, and the Governor, with the advice of his Privy Council, deems it expedient, he may issue a special commission of oyer and terminer, and gaol delivery, to be held at such place, and for theatrial of such offences as in such commission shall be expressly directed, 23, V., c. 15, s. 1.

In cases of popular tumults, riots, or breaches of the peace.

Such commission shall be directed to the Judges of the Supreme Court, and held before one of them. In case of the inability of any Judge by whom the commission is opened, to discharge the duties, any other Judge named therein shall proceed to the final execution, 23 V. c,. 15, s. 2.

Direction

Jurisdiction

The jurisdiction of the Special Commission shall extend over the whole island, and not be limited to the locality in which its sessions may be held, 23 V., c. 15, s. 3.

Jurors

The Governor, with the advice of the Privy Council shall determine from what parishes the jurors shall be drawn, and thereupon, under the fiat of the Attorney-General, a writ of venire facias shall issue from the Supreme Court to the Provost Marshal, commanding him to summon from the special and common jury panels, in equal proportions of each list, such number of jurors from each of the parishes to be named in the writ, as may be directed, so that the aggregate number shall not exceed 60 in the whole, and the Provost Marshal shall ballot for, and draw the number of names from the list directed. and the aggregate of the names thus struck shall form the jurors, to be returned on the panel, 23 V., c. 15, s. 4.

Authority

The Court thus formed shall have, and exercise all the powers and authorities of the ordinary Court of Assize, Oyer and Terminer and Gaol Delivery, and the jurors to be warned shall be liable to fine and imprisonment, in the discretion of the court, for absence without cause, or for any other contempt or impropriety of conduct during the sitting of the Court— 23 V., c. 15, s. 5.

Companies Incorporated.

Incoporation how effected

Any seven or more persons, associated for any lawful purpose, may, by subscribing their names to a memorandum of association, and otherwise complying with the requisitions of this Act in respect of registration, form an Incorporated Company, with or without limited liability, 27 V., S. 2. c. 4, s. I.

Limited liability

The liability of members may, according to the memorandum of association, be limited either to the amount, if any, unpaid upon the shares respecively held by them, or to such amount as the members may respectively undertake by the memorandum to contribute to the assets in the event of its being wound up, 27 V., S. 2, c. 4, s. 2.

Limitation by shares. Requisites of memorandum.

Where a Company is formed on the principle of having the liability of its members limited to the amount unpaid on their shares (a company limited by shares) the memorandum shall contain :

1 The name of the Company, with the addition of the word "limited", as the last word in the name.

2 The part of the island in which the office is to be situate.

3. The objects for which it is to be established.

4. A declaration that the liability of the members is limited.

5. The amount of capital with which the Company proposes to be registered divided into shares of a certain fixed amount,

Subject to the following regulations :—

1. That no subscriber take less than one share.

2. That each subscriber write opposite to his name the number of shares he takes, 27 V., S. 2, c. 4, s. 3.

Limitation by guarantee. Requisites of memorandum

When a Company is formed on the principle of having the liability of its members limited to the amount they undertake respectively to contribute to the assets, in the event of its being wound up, (a Company limited by guarantee) the memorandum shall contain :

1. The name of the proposed Company, with the word "limited" as the last

2. The part of the island in which the office is to be situate.

3. The objects for which it is to be established.

4. A declaration that each member undertakes to contribute to the assets of the Company, in the event of its being wound up while he is a member, or within one year afterwards, for payment of the debts and liabilities contracted before the time at which he ceases to be a member, and of the costs. charges, and expenses of winding up the Company, and for the adjustment of the rights of the contributories amongst themselves, such amount as may be required, not exceeding a specified amount, 27 V., S. 2, c. 4, s. 4.

Unlimited companies memorandum

When formed on the principle of having no limit placed on the liability of its members (an unlimited Company) the memorandum shall contain :—

1. The name of the proposed Company.

2. The part of the island in which the office is to be situate.

3. The objects for which it is to be established, 27 V., S. 2, c. 4, s. 5,

The memorandum shall be signed by each subscriber, in the presence of, and be attested by one witness at least. It shall bind the Company and members to the same extent as if each had subscribed his name, and affixed his seal, and there were in the memorandum contained on the part of himself, his heirs, executors, and administrators, a covenant to observe all the conditions subject to the provisions of this Act, 27 V., S. 2, c. 4, s. 6. *Signature and effect of memorandum*

Any Company limited by shares may, so far, modify the conditions in its memorandum, if authorized to do so by its regulations as originally framed, or as altered by special resolution, as after mentioned, as to increase its capital by the issue of new shares of such amount as it thinks expedient, or to consolidate and divide its capital into shares of larger amount than its existing shares; but save as aforesaid, no alteration shall be made by any Company in the conditions contained in its memorandum of Association, 27 V., S. 2, c. 4, s. 7. *Modifications of memorandum of Companies limited by shares*

The memorandum may in the case of a company limited by shares, and shall in the case of a company limited by Guarantee, or unlimited, be accompanied, when registered, by articles of association, signed by the subscribers to the memorandum, and prescribing such regulations for the company as they deem expedient, 27 V. S. 2, c. 4, s. 8. *Articles of association of companies limited by shares, or unlimited companies*

The articles of association shall be signed by each subscriber in the presence of and attested by one witness at least, and shall bind the company and members to the same extent as if each had subscribed his name and affixed his seal thereto, and there were contained a covenant on the part of himself his heirs, executors and administrators to conform to all the regulations therein, subject to this act. All monies payable by any member to the company, in pursuance of the conditions and regulations of the company, or any of them, shall be deemed a debt due from the member to the company, 27 V. S. 2, c. 4, s. 9. *Execution and obligation of articles of association*

The memorandum and articles if any, shall be recorded in the Island Secretary's Office, 27 V. S. 2, c. 4, s. 10. *Memorandum and articles to be recorded*

Upon recording the memorandum and articles when required, the subscribers of the memorandum, together with such other persons as may from time to time become members of the company, shall thereupon be the body corporate, by the name contained in the memorandum, and having perpetual succession and a common seal, with power to hold lands. A certificate given by the Island Secretary, that all the requisitions of this act, in respect to registration, have been complied with, shall be conclusive evidence thereof, 27 V. S. 2, c. 4, s. 11. *On recording memorandum and articles when required, company incorporated. Secretary's certificate of registration conclusive evidence*

No company shall be recorded under a name identical with that by which a subsisting company is already registered, or so nearly resembling the same as to be calculated to deceive, 27 V S. 2, c, 4, s. 12. *No two companies to be recorded under the same or resembling names*

The shares or other interest of any member in a company, shall be personal estate, capable of being transferred in manner provided by the regulations of the Company, and shall not be of the nature of real estate. Each share in the case of a company having a capital divided into shares, shall be distinguished by its appropriate number, 27 V. S. 2, c. 4, s. 13. *Shares &c. personal and transferable estate. Shares to be numbered*

The Subscribers of the memorandum shall be deemed to have agreed to become members of the company whose memorandum they have subscribed, and upon registration of the company, shall be entered on the register of members after mentioned, and every other person who has agreed to become a member and whose name is entered on the register, shall be deemed a member 27 V. S. 2, c. 4, s. 14. *Registered subscribers to be deemed members of company*

Any transfer of the share or other interest of a deceased member, made by his personal representative, shall, notwithstanding, he is not himself a member, be of the same validity as if he had been a member at the time of the execution of the instrument of transfer, 27 V. S. 2, c. 4, s. 15. *Transfers of shares &c. of deceased, by personal representative*

Every company shall cause to be kept in one or more books, a register of its members, and there shall be entered therein, the following particulars :— *Particulars of company's register book.*

1. The names and addresses and occupations, if any, of the members, with the addition, in the case of a company having a capital divided into shares, of a statement of the shares held by each member, distinguishing each share by its number, and of the amount paid or agreed to be considered as paid on the shares of each member.

2. The date at which the name of any person was entered in the register as a member.

The date at which any person ceased to be a member.

Penalties

Any company acting in contravention of this section, shall incur a penalty not exceeding £5, for every day during which its default in complying continues. Every director or manager, who knowingly and wilfully authorizes or permits, such contravention shall incur the like penalty, 27 V. S. 2, c. 4, s. 16.

Annual lists of members of companies by shares Particulars to be recorded.

Every company having a capital, divided into shares, shall make once at least in every year, a list of all persons who on the 14th day succeeding that on which the ordinary general meeting, or, if there is more than one ordinary meeting in each year, the first, is held, are members, and such lists shall state the names, addresses and occupations of all the members therein mentioned, and the number of shares held by each, and shall contain a summary specifying:

1. The amount of capital of the company, and number of shares into which it is divided.
2. The number of shares taken from the commencement of the company to the date of the summary.
3. The amount of calls made on each share.
4. The total amount of calls received.
5. The total amount of calls unpaid.
7. The names, addresses and occupations of the persons who have ceased to be members, since the last list was made, and the number of shares held by each of them.

The above list and summary shall be contained in a separate part of the register and completed within 7 days after such 14th day, and a copy shall be forthwith recorded in the Island Secretary's Office, 27 V. S. 2, c. 4, s. 17.

Penalties for default

If any company having a capital divided into shares, make default in complying with this act, with respect to recording such list of members, or summary, within one month, it shall incur a penalty not exceeding £5, for every day during which default continues. Every director and manager knowingly and wilfully authorizing or permitting such default, shall incur the like penalty, 27 V. S. 2, c. 4, s. 18.

Certificates under common seal evidence of title to shares

A certificate under the common seal, specifying any share or shares of stock, held by any member, shall be prima facie evidence of his title thereto, 27 V. S. 2, c. 4, s. 19.

Registers of members to be kept at office when and to whom accessible

The register of members, commencing from the date of registration of the company, shall be kept at the office, except when closed as after mentioned. It shall during business hours, but subject to such reasonable restrictions as the company, in general meeting, may impose, so that not less than two hours in each day, of one day in every week, be appointed for inspection, to be open to the inspection of any member, gratis, and to the inspection of any other person on payment of 1s. or such less sum as the company may prescribe for each inspection. If such inspection is refused, the company shall incur for each refusal, a penalty not exceeding £2, and a further penalty not exceeding £2, for every day during which the refusal continues. Every director and manager, knowingly authorizing or permiting such refusal, shall incur the like penalty, 27 V. S. 2, c. 4, s. 20.

Closing registers temporarily after advertisement

Any company may, upon giving notice by advertisement in some newspaper published within the island, close the register for any time or times, not exceeding in the whole 30 days, in each year, 27 V. S. 2, c. 4, s. 21.

Increase of capital or members to be recorded. Penalty

Where a company has a capital divided into shares, any increase beyond the registered capital, and where a company has not a capital divided into shares, any increase in the number of members beyond the registered number, shall be recorded in the Island Secretary's Office in the case of an increase of capital, within 30 days from the passing of the resolutions authorizing it, in the case of an increase of members, within 30 days from the time the increase was resolved on or took place. In default the company shall incur a penalty, not exceeding £5, for each day during which the neglect continues, and every director and manager, who knowingly and wilfully authorizes or permits such default, shall incur the like penalty, 27 V. S. 2, c. 4, s. 22.

Enforcing rectification of register.

If the name of any person is, without sufficient cause, entered in or omitted from the register of members, or if default is made or unnecessary delay takes place in entering on the register the fact of any person having ceased to be a member, the person or member aggrieved or any member of the company, or the company itself, may by motion in the Supreme Court, apply for an order of Court, that the register may be rectified, and the Court may either refuse such application, with or without costs, or, if satisfied of the Justice of the case, make an order for the rectification of the register, and direct the company to pay all costs of such motion, application or petition, and any damages the party aggrieved may sustain. The Court may in any proceeding under this section, decide on any question relating to the title of any person, party to such proceeding, to have his name entered in or omitted from the register, whether the question arises between two or more members or alleged members, or between any members or alleged members, and the company, and generally the Court may in any such proceeding, decide any question necessary or expedient to decide for the rectification of the register, 27 V. S. 2, c. 4, s. 23.

When any order is made rectifying the register, the Court may, by its order direct the rectification to be recorded in the Island Secretary's Office, 27 V. S. 2, c. 4, s. 24. *Order of rectification to be recorded.*

The register of members shall be prima facie evidence of any matters directed or authorized to be inserted therein, 27 V. S. 2, c. 4, s. 25. *Register prima facie evidence.*

If a company is wound up and dissolved, every present and past member shall be liable to contribute to the assets, to an amount sufficient for payment of the debts and liabilities and costs, charges and expences, of the winding up, and of the sums required for the adjustment of the rights of the contributories amongst themselves with the qualifications following : *Liability to contribution in case of dissolution.*

1. No past member shall be liable to contribute to the assets, if he has ceased to be a member for one year, or upwards, prior to the commencement of the winding up.

2. Nor in respect of any debt or liability contracted after he ceased to be a member.

3. Nor unless it appears to the Court, that the existing members are unable to satisfy the contributions required to be made by them.

4. In the case of a company limited by shares, no contribution shall be required from any member, exceeding the amount, if any unpaid, on the shares in respect of which he is liable as a present or past member.

5. In the case of a company limited by guarantee, no contribution shall be required from any member exceeding the amount of the undertaking entered into on his behalf by the memorandum of association.

6. Act not to invalidate any provision in any policy of insurance or other contract whereby the liability of individual members, upon any such policy or contract is restricted, or whereby the funds of the company are alone made liable in respect of such policy or contract.

7. No fund due to any member in his character of a member by way of dividends, profits or otherwise, shall be deemed to be a debt of the company, payable to such member, in a case of competition between himself and any other creditor, not a member; but any such sum may be taken into account for the purposes of the final adjustment of the rights of the contributories amongst themselves, 27 V. S. 2, c 4, s. 26.

Every Company shall have an office to which all communications and notices may be addressed. Any company carrying on business without such an office shall incur a penalty not exceeding £5 for every day business is so carried on, 27 V. S. 2, c. 4, s 27. *Office.*

Notice of the situation of the office, and of any change therein, shall be given in some newspaper published in this island. Until it is given the company shall not be deemed to have complied with the provisions with respect to having an office, 27 V. S. 2, c. 4. s. 28. *Notice of situation and change.*

Every limited company whether by shares or guarantee shall paint or affix, and keep, &c., its name on the outside of every office or place in which its business is carried on, in a conspicuous position, in letters easily legible, have its name engraven in legible characters on its seal, and name mentioned in legible characters in all notices, advertisements, and other official publications of such company, and in all bills of exchange, promissory notes, endorsements, cheques, and orders for money or goods, purporting to be signed by or on behalf of such company, and in all bills of parcels, invoices, receipts, and letters of credit of the company, 27 V. S. 2, c. 4. s. 29. *Publication of name of limited company on office notices, bills, invoices, &c.*

Under penalties. Any limited company not painting and affixing, and keeping &c., its name in manner directed, shall be liable to a penalty not exceeding £1., for not so painting or affixing its name, and for every day during which the name is not so kept, painted, or affixed, and every director or manager, knowingly, and wilfully authorizing or permitting such default shall be liable to the like penalty. If any director, manager, or officer, or other person on its behalf uses or authorizes the use of any seal, purporting to be a seal of the company, whereon its name is not so engraven, or issues, or authorizes the issue of any notice, advertisement or other official publication of such company, or signs, or authorises to be signed on its behalf, any bill of exchange, promissory note, endorsement, cheque, order for money or goods, or issues or authorizes to be issued, any bill of parcels, invoice, receipt, or letter of credit of the company wherein its name is not mentioned in manner aforesaid, he shall be liable to a penalty of £50, and be further personally liable to the holder of any such bill of exchange, promissory note, cheque, or order for money or goods, for the amount thereof,, unless duly paid by the company, 27 V. S. 2, c. 4, s. 30.

To keep registers of mortgages, and charges affecting their property open to creditors and members—Penalty. Every limited company shall keep a register of all mortgages, and charges, specifically affecting property of the company, and enter therein in respect of each a short description of the property, the amount of charge created, and the name of the mortgagees or persons entitled ; if any property is mortgaged or charged without such entry being made, every director, manager, or other officer, who knowingly, and wilfully authorizes or permits the omission, shall incur a penalty not exceeding £50. The Register shall be open to any creditor or member, at all reasonable times, and if inspection is refused, any officer refusing, and every director and manager, authorizing, or knowingly and wilfully permitting such refusal, shall incur a penalty not exceeding £5., and a further penalty not exceeding £2 for every day during which the refusal continues, 27 V. S. 2, c. 4, s. 31.

Limited banking and Insurance companies, &c. to exhibit half yearly statements of capital liabilities and assetts—Penalty. Every limited banking company, and every insurance company, and deposit, provident or benefit society, under this Act, shall before it commences business, and also on the first Monday in February and August in every year, during which it carries on business make a statement (Schedule Form A.,) or as near as circumstances admit, and a copy shall be put up in a conspicuous place in the office, and in every branch office or place where their business is carried on, under penalty not exceeding £5 for every day during which default continues, and every director and manager, knowingly and wilfully authorizing, or permitting such default, shall incur the like penalty, 27 V. S. 2, c. 4. s. 32.

Companies not by shares to keep registers of names addresses and occupation of directors and managers. Every company not having a capital divided into shares, shall keep at its office a register containing the names and addresses, and the occupations, of its directors or managers, 27 V. S. 2. c. 4. s. 33.

Penalties. Any such company making default, shall incur a penalty not exceeding £1. for every day during which the default continues, and every director and manager, knowingly, and wilfully authorizing or permitting such default, shall incur the like penalty, 27 S. 2 c. 4, s. 34.

Notes and bills of exchange. A promissory note or bill of exchange, shall be deemed to be made, accepted or endorsed on behalf of a company, if made, &c., in its name, by any person acting under its authority, or if made, &c, by or on behalf, or on its account, by any person acting under its authority, 27 V. S. 2 c. 4, s. 35

Persons knowingly carrying on business when company is less than 7 liable for whole debts. If any company carries on business when the number of its members is less than 7, for six months after the number has been so reduced, every person who is a member during the time it so carries on business, after such period of 6 months, and is cognizant of the fact that it is doing so with fewer than 7, shall be severally liable for the payment of the whole debts contracted during such time, and may be sued for the same, without the joinder of any other member, 27 V. S. 2. c. 4, s. 36.

General meetings. A general meeting of every company shall be held once at least in every year, 27 V. S. 2. c. 4, s. 37.

Power to alter regulations by special resolution. Subject to this Act, and the conditions in the memorandum, any company may, in general meeting from time to time, by passing a special resolution as after mentioned, alter all or any of the regulations in the articles of association, or make new regulations to the exclusion of or in addition to all or any of its regulations, and any such made by special resolution, shall be of the same validity as if originally contained in the articles, and subject in like manner to be altered or modified by any subsequent special resolution, 27 V. S. 2. c. 4, s. 38.

A resolution shall be deemed special whenever a resolution has been passed by a majority of not less than three fourths of the members for the time being entitled according to the regulations to vote, present in person, or by proxy (where proxies are allowed by the regulations) at any general meeting of which notice, specifying the intention to   such resolution has been duly given, and such resolution has been confirmed by a majority of such members for the time being entitled to vote, present in person or by proxy, at a subsequent general meeting of which notice has been duly given, and hold at an interval of not less than 14 days nor more than one month from the date of the meeting at which such resolution was first passed ; And at any meeting in this section mentioned, unless a poll is demanded by at least 5 members, a declaration of the chairman, that the resolution has been carried, shall be conclusive evidence of the fact without proof of the number or proportion of the votes ; recorded in favor or against the same. Notice of any meeting shall be deemed duly given and the meeting duly held, when done in manner prescribed by the regulations. In computing the majority when a poll is demanded, reference shall be had to the number of votes each member is entitled to by the regulations, 27 V. S. 2, c. 4, s. 39.

Special resolution what confirmation thereof. Notices of General meetings.

How majority of votes to be computed.

In default of any regulations as to voting, every member shall have one vote ; in default of any regulations as to summoning general meetings, a meeting shall be held to be duly summoned, of which 7 days notice in writing has been served on every member ; in default of any regulations as to the p   to summon meetings, 5 members shall be competent, and in default of any regulations as to who is to be chairman of such meeting, any person elected by the members present shall preside, 27 V. S. 2. c. 4, s. 40.

In default of regulations.
Summoning general meetings. &c.
In default of regulations.

A copy of any special resolution that is passed shall be recorded in the Island Secretary's Office. If not so recorded within 30 days from confirmation, the company to incur a penalty not exceeding £2 for every day after the expiration of the 30 days, during which it is omitted to be recorded. Every director and manager knowingly and wilfully authorizing, or permitting such default shall incur the like penalty, 27 V. S. 2, c. 4, s. 41.

Copies of special resolutions to be recorded.—Penalty

Where articles of association have been recorded, a copy of every special resolution for the time being in force shall be annexed to, or embodied in every copy of the articles to be issued after the passing of the resolution. Any company making default shall incur a penalty not exceeding £1 for each copy, in respect of which default is made, and every director and manager knowingly and wilfully authorizing, or permitting such default shall incur the like penalty, 27 V. S. 2, c. 4, s. 42.

And annexed to copies of articles subsequently issued—Penalty.

Any company may by instrument in writing, under its common seal, empower any person, either generally or in respect of any specified matter, as its attorney, to execute deeds on its behalf, in any place out of this island, and any deed signed by such attorney on behalf of the company, and under his seal, shall bind the said company and have the same effect as if it were under their common seal, 27 V. S. 2 c. 4, s. 43.

Attorneys to execute deeds.

Any summons, notice, order, or document, required to be served upon the company, may be served by leaving it or sending it through the post in a prepaid letter addressed to the company at their office, 27 V. S. 2 c. 4, s. 44.

Service of summons, &c. on company by post.

The document shall be posted in time, to admit of its being delivered in due course of delivery within the period if any prescribed for the service, and in proving service, it shall be sufficient to prove that it was properly directed and put as a prepaid letter into the Post Office, 27 V. S. 2 c. 4, s, 45.

Proof of service.

Any summons, notice, order, or proceedings, requiring authentication by the company, may be signed by any director, secretary, or other authorized officer, and need not be under the common seal, and may be in writing or print, or partly in writing, and partly in print—27, V. S. 2, c 4, s. 46.

Authentication of the company's summons, &c.

Penalties shall be recovered before two Justices, under 13 V. c. 35, or any other Act in force in respect to summary proceedings,— 27 V. S. 2, c. 4, s. 47.

Recovery of penalties

Who may direct the whole or any part to be applied in payment of the costs, or in rewarding the person upon whose information, or at whose suit the penalty has been recovered, and subject to such direction, it shall be paid to the Receiver-General, to the credit of the island, 27 V. S. 2, c. 4, s. 48.

Minutes of proceedings, evidence thereof as also of appointment of directors, &c.

Every Company shall cause minutes of all resolutions and proceedings of general meetings, and of the Directors or Managers, where there are such, to be entered in books, from time to time provided, for the purpose. Any such minute if purporting to be signed by the Chairman of that, or the next succeeding meeting shall be received as evidence in all legal proceedings, and until the contrary is proved, every general meeting or meeting of directors or managers, in respect of the proceedings of which minutes are so made, shall be deemed to have been duly held and convened, and all resolutions or proceedings duly passed, and all appointments of directors, managers, or liquidators shall be deemed valid, and all acts done by them valid, notwithstanding any defect afterwards discovered in their appointments or qualifications, 27 V. S. 2, c. 4, s. 49.

Security for costs by limited Companies

Where a limited company is plaintiff, or pursuer in any action, suit, or other proceeding, any Judge having jurisdiction may, if it appears by credible testimony, there is reason to believe if the defendant succeeds the assets will be insufficient to pay his costs, require security for costs, and stay proceedings until it is given, 27 V. S. 2, c. 4, s. 50.

Actions for calls

In any action or suit by the company against any member to recover any call, or other moneys due in his character of member, it shall not be necessary to set forth the special matter, but sufficient to allege that the defendant is a member, and is indebted to the company in respect of a call made, or other monies due, whereby an action or suit hath accrued to the company, 27 V. S. 2, c. 4, s. 51.

SCHEDULE.

Half yearly statements of limited Banking and Insurance Companies, s. 32

The capital of the company is divided into   shares of each

The number of shares issued is   Calls to the amount of pounds per share have been made under which the sum of pounds has been received.

The liabilities of the company on the first day of January (or July) were

    Debts owing to sundry persons by the company.
    On judgment £
    On specialty £
    On notes or bills £
    On simple contracts £
    On estimated liabilities £

The assets of the company on that day were
    Government or Island Securities (stating them) £
    Bills of Exchange and Promisory Notes £
    Cash £
    Other securities £

If the company has no capital divided into shares, the portion of the statement relating to capital and shares must be omitted.

Companies Winding Up.

"Contributory" defined

"Contributory" shall mean every person liable to contribute to the assets of a company, in the event of its being wound up, and in proceedings to determine who are to be deemed contributory prior to the final determination shall include "any person alleged to be contributory", 28 V. c. 42, s. 1.

His liability

The liability of a contributory, in the event of a company being wound up, shall be deemed to create a debt in the nature of a specialty accruing due from such person at the times when his liability commenced, but payable at the times when calls shall have been, or shall be made for enforcing such liability, but shall not increase his original liability, 28 V. c. 41, s. 2.

Insolvent contributories, Proof of debts. Assignee to admit proof or pay the sum due.

In case of the insolvency or bankruptcy of a contributory, it shall be lawful to prove the estimated value of his liability to future calls, as well as calls already made, and the official or other assignees of the contributory shall be deemed to represent him, and may be called upon to admit the proof against his estate, or otherwise to allow to be paid out of the assets in due course of law such sum as shall be due from the insolvent, &c. in respect of his liability to contribute to the assets of the company being wound up, 28 V., c. 42, s. 3.

In case of the death of a contributory his perso   s,   Liability of per.
sonal representa
tives and husband
heirs, and devisees, in a due course of administration, a   the
marriage of a female contributory, her husband, during the continuance of
the marriage, in the same sum as she would have been liable if not married,
shall be liable to contribute to the assets of the company, and be deemed
contributories accordingly, 28 V. c. 42, s, 4.

It is immaterial whether the insolvency of the contributory happen be-   *Period of insol-vency immaterial*
fore he is placed on the list of contributories, 28 V., c. 42, s. 5.

A company may be wound up as after defined under the following cir-   *Circumstances under which Company may be wound up*
cumstances :—

1. When it has passed a special resolution requiring it to be wound up.

2. When it does not commence business within a year from its incorpo-
   ·ration, or registration, or suspends business for the space of one
   year.

3. When the members are reduced in number to less than 7.

4. When the company is unable to pay its debts.

5. When the court is of opinion it is just and equitable, that the company should be wound up, 28 V. c- 42, s. 6.

A Company shall be deemed unable to pay its debts.   *When unable to pay its debts.*

1. Whenever a creditor, by assignment or otherwise, to whom the company is indebted, at law or in equity, in a sum exceeding £50, then
   due, has served on the company, by leaving the same at the registered or head office, a demand under his hand, requiring it to pay
   the sum due, and it has for 3 weeks succeeding the service, neglected
   to pay or to secure or compound for the same to the reasonable
   satisfaction of the creditors.

2. Whenever execution or other process, issued on a judgment, decree or
   order obtained in any court in favor of any creditor in any court of
   law or in equity, in any proceedings instituted, by such creditor
   against the company, is returned unsatisfied in whole or in part

3. Whenever it is proved to the satisfaction of the court that the company is unable to pay its debts, 28, V. c. 42, s. 7.

The Judges of the Supreme Court with the powers of a court of equity   *Supreme Court to administer the act with the powers of a court of equity.*
shall be the Judges to administer this act, and the term " Court" through-
out shall mean Supreme Court; and any Judge may do in Chambers any   *Judge in Chambers.*
Act the Court is authorized to do, 28 V. c. 42, s. 8,

Any application to wind up a company shall be by petition. It may be   *Application to be by petition.*
presented by the company, or by any one or more creditors or contributories
or by all or any of the above parties together or separately. Every order   *By whom presented.*
on a petition shall operate in favor of all the creditors, and contributories, as
if made upon the joint petition of a creditor and a contributory. 28 V. c.   *Operation of order.*
42, s. 9.

A winding up shall be deemed to commence at the presentation of the   *Commencement of winding up.*
petition, 28 V. c. 42, s. 10.

The Court at any time after the presentation, and before making an   *Stay of proceedings against company.*
order for winding up the Company, upon application of the company or of
any creditor or contributory may restrain further proceedings in any action, suit, or proceeding, against the company, upon such terms as the
Court thinks fit, 28 V. c. 42, s. 11.

Upon hearing the petition, the Court may dismiss it with or without   *Order on petition.*
costs, and adjourn the hearing conditionally or unconditionally, and may
make any interim order, or any other order it deems just, 28 V. c. 42, s. 12

When an order has been made for winding up a company, no suit, ac-   *After order no proceeding to be taken without leave of Court.*
tion, or other proceeding shall be proceeded with or commenced against
them except with leave of the Court, and subject to such terms as it may
impose, 28 V. c. 42, s. 13.

The Court may, at any time after an order for winding up upon applica-   *Court may stay proceedings after winding up order.*
tion, by motion of any creditor or contributory, and on proof, to its satisfac-
tion, that all proceedings in relation to such winding up, ought to be stayed,
make an order staying the same, either altogether, or for a limited time, on
such terms and subject to such conditions as it deems fit, 28 V. c. 42, s. 14.

When a winding up order has been made of a company limited by   *Unpaid capital of share companies limited by guarantee to be assets—Liabilities of members.*
guarantee, and having a capital divided into shares, any share capital not
called up shall be assets, and a debt of the nature of a specialty due to the
company from each member to the extent of any sums unpaid on any shares
held by him, and payable at such time as may be appointed by the court, 28
V. c. 42, s. 15.

Court to regard wishes of creditors and contributories.

The Court may, as to all matters relating to the winding up, have regard to the wishes of the creditors or contributories, as proved to it by any sufficient evidence, and may, if it thinks it expedient, direct meetings of the creditors or contributories, to be summoned held, and conducted as the Court directs, for the purpose of ascertaining their wishes, and may appoint a person to act as chairman, and report the result of the meeting ; in the case of creditors, regard is to be had to the value of the debts due to each ; of contributories, to the number of votes conferred on each by the company's regulation, 28 V. c. 42 s. 16.

Meetings to ascertain their wishes

Liquidators

For conducting the proceedings in winding up and assisting the Court, upon or after a petition has been filed, it may appoint a liquidator or liquidators, either provisionally or otherwise. When more than one are appointed, the Court shall declare whether any act is to be done by all, or any one or more, also whether any, and what security is to be given by any ; if no liquidator is appointed, or during any vacancy all the property shall be deemed to be in the custody of the Court, 28 V. c. 42, s. 17.

Appointment and directions respecting.

When none, property to be in the custody of the Court.

They may resign or be removed—remuneration.

Any liquidator may resign, or be removed by the Court on due cause shown, and any vacancy filled by the Court. There shall be paid to the liquidator, such salary or remuneration by way of per centage or otherwise, as the Court directs, and if more than one are appointed to be distributed among them, in such proportions as the Court directs, 28 V. c. 42, s. 18.

Description.

Duties.

They shall be described by name, and the style of the liquidator or liquidators of the particular company, and not by their individual names alone, and shall take into their custody, or under their control, all the property, effects, and things in action to which the company is, or appears entitled, and perform such duties in reference to winding up, as the Court imposes, 28 V. c. 42, s. 19.

Powers-

Bring actions, &c

The liquidator, with the sanction of the Court, may

Bring or defend any action, suit, or prosecution, or other legal proceeding civil or criminal, on behalf of the company, in his name and style of office ;

Carry on business

Carry on the business as far as necessary, for the beneficial winding up ;

Sell estate

Sell the real and personal, and moveable property, effects, and things in action by auction or private contract, with power to transfer the whole, or sell in parcels;

Execute deeds &c

Do all acts and execute in his name and style of office, on behalf of and for the company, all deeds, receipts, and other documents, and when necessary use the company's seal ;

Prove, &c. on Insolvent estate of contributories.

Prove rank claim, and draw a dividend in the matter of the insolvency, or bankruptcy of any contributory, against his estate ;

Administer to deceased contributories

Take out if necessary, in his name, and style of office, letters of administration to any deceased contributory, and do any other act necessary for obtaining payment of any monies due from such contributory or his estate ;

Other necessary acts

Do all other things necessary for winding up the affairs of the company, and distributing its assets, 28 V. c. 42, s. 20.

The court may authorize him to exercise any power without its sanction.

The Court may provide by any order, that the liquidator may exercise any of the above powers without its sanction or intervention, 28 V. c. 42, s. 21.

Solicitor

He may, with the sanction of the Court appoint a solicitor to assist him in the performance of his duties, 28 V. c. 42, s. 22.

List of contributories, collection and application of assets

As soon as may be, after making any order for winding up, the Courts shall settle a list of contributories with power to rectify the register of members when required, and to cause the assets of the company to be collected and applied in discharge of its liabilities, 28 V. c. 42, s. 23.

Classification of contributories

In settling the list, the Court shall distinguish between contributories in their own rights, and contributories as representatives of or liable to the debts of others. Not necessary when the personal representative is on the list, to add the heirs or devisees of the contributory, but they may be added if the Court thinks necessary, 28 V. c. 42, s. 24.

Notice to be given to parties to shew cause against being settled

No person shall be made a contributory unless notice in writing be given or sent to him, or in case of his absence to his attorney or agent in this island, to show cause against his being settled as a contributory on the list, at least 14 days before it is settled, 28 V. c, 42, s. 25.

Service on absentee, &c

The Court may direct how service of notices and other proceedings shall be effected, in cases where parties are absentees and unrepresented, or cannot be found after reasonable enquiry, 28 V. c. 42, s. 26.

The court may after order for winding up require any contributory set-tled on the list, trustee, receiver, banker, or agent, or officer of the Company to pay, deliver, convey, surrender, or transfer forthwith, or within such time as the court directs, to, or into the hands of the liquidator any sum or balance, books, papers, estate, or assets which happen to be in his hands for the time being, and to which the Company is prima facie entitled, 28 V., c. 42, s. 27. *Order for transfer, &c: to liquidator of property to which company is prima facie entitled*

And may after order for winding up make an order on any contributory settled on the list, directing payments to be made, in manner in the order mentioned, of any monies due from him, or from the estate of the person he represents, to the company, exclusive of any money he, or the estate may be liable to contribute by virtue of any call made, or to be made by the court in pursuance of this Act, and it may, in making the order when the company is not limited, allow the contributory, by way of set off, any monies due to him, or the estate he represents, from the company on any independent dealing, or contract with the company, but not any monies due to him, or a member of the company in respect of any dividend or profit. When all the creditors of any company whether limited or unlimited are paid in full, any monies due on any account to any contributory from the company, may be allowed to him by way of set off against subsequent calls,— 28 V., c. 42, s. 28, *Contributories must pay up calls, or debts* *Set off*

Also after the order for winding up, and before or after it has ascertained the sufficiency of the assets, make calls, and make order for payment by contributories, settled on the list, to the extent of the liability for payment of all, or any sums it deems necessary to satisfy the debts and liabilities, and the costs, charges, and expenses of winding it up, and for the adjustment of the rights of the contributories amongst themselves, and may in making a call take into consideration the probability that some may partly or wholly fail to pay their portions, 28 V., c. 42, s. 29. *Orders for calls*

May also order any contributory, purchaser or other person from whom money is due to the company, to pay the same into the Receiver-General's Office to the account of the liquidator, and the order may be enforced as if it had directed payment to the liquidator, 28 V., c. 42, s. 30. *For payment into the Receiver General's Office*

If any person, made a contributory either in his own right or as personal representative of a deceased contributory, makes default in paying the sum ordered, execution may issue upon the order as upon an order in pursuance of 8 V., c. 48 (See judgments, &c.) against the contributory or the assets of the deceased, and if the execution in the case of a deceased contributory is not effectual, proceedings may, with the sanction of the court, be taken in Chancery for administering his personal and real estate, and of compelling payment thereout of the money due, 28 V.. c. 42, s. 31. *Enforcement by execution* *Proceedings in Chancery against estate of deceased contributories*

Any order upon a contributory shall, subject to the provisions for appealing, be conclusive evidence that the monies, if any thereby appearing to be due or ordered to be paid, are due, and all other pertinent matters stated in the order, are to be taken to be truly stated as against all persons and in all proceedings, with the exception of proceedings against the real estate of any deceased contributory, in which case it shall only be prima facie evidence for charging his real estate, unless his heirs or divisees were on the list of contributories when it was made, 28 V., c. 42, s. 32. *Order evidence of contents*

The court may fix a certain day or days on, or within which creditors are to prove their debts or claims, or to be excluded from the benefit of any distribution made before such debts are proved, 28 V., c. 42, s. 33. *Fixing times for proof of debts*

It shall adjust the rights of the contributories amongst themselves, and distribute any surplus amongst the parties entitled, 28 V., c. 42, s. 34. *Adjustment of contributories inter se*

It may in the event of the assets being insufficient to satisfy the liabilities, make an order as to payment thereout of the costs and expenses of winding up in such order of priority as it thinks just, 28 V., c. 42, s. 35. *costs*

When the affairs have been completely wound up, the court shall make an order that the company be dissolved from the date of such order, and it shall be dissolved accordingly, 28 V., c, 42, s. 36. *Order for dissolution*

The court may, after an order for winding up, summon before it any officer of the company or person known or suspected to have in his possession any of the estate or effects of, or supposed to be indebted to the company, or any person whom the court deems capable of giving information concerning the trade-dealings, estate, or effects of the company, and may require him to produce any books, papers, deeds, writings, or other documents in his custody or power relating to the company, and if any person so summoned, after being tendered a reasonable sum for his expenses, refuses to come before the court at the time appointed, having no lawful impedi- *Power over Officers, persons in possession of property documents, &c., or indebted to the company, to compel examination*

ment (made known to the court at the time of its sitting, and allowed by it)

Liens

the court may cause him to be apprehended and brought before it for exami-. nation; nevertheless, where any person claims any lien on papers, deeds, or writings, or documents produced by him, such production shall be, without prejudice to such lien, and the court shall have jurisdiction in the winding

None on books or accounts

up, to determine all questions relating to lien. No person shall have or claim any lien on the books or accounts, 28 V., c. 42, s. 37.

Examinations

The Court may examine upon oath, either by word of mouth, or upon written interrogatories, any person appearing or brought before it, concerning the affairs, dealings, estates, or effects of the company, and may reduce into writing his answers, and require him to subscribe them, 28 V. c. 42, s. 38.

Arrest of contributories and seizure of property

May, before or after an order for winding up, on proof that there is probable cause for believing any contributory is about to quit the island, or otherwise abscond, or to remove or conceal any of his goods, for the purpose of evading payment of calls, or for avoiding examination in respect of the affairs of the company, cause him to be arrested, and his books, papers, monies, securities, for money, goods, and chattels, to be seized and him and them to be safely kept, until such time as the Court orders, 28 V. c. 42, s. 39.

Powers additional to those subsisting at law or in equity

Any powers conferred upon the Court, shall be in addition to and not restrictive of any other powers subsisting at law or in equity of instituting proceedings against any contributory or the estate of a contributory or against any debtor of the company, for the recovery of any call or other sums du , and such proceedings may be instituted accordingly, 28 V. c. 42, s. 40.e

Enforcement of orders

All orders may be enforced in the same manner as those in the Supreme Court or Court of Chancery in any proceeding or suit before them, and for the purposes of this act, the Court shall, in addition to the ordinary powers of the Supreme Court, have the same powers for enforcing any orders made by it as the Court of Chancery in relation to matters within its jurisdiction, 28 V., c. 42, s. 41.

Appeals from orders of a single Judge

Appeals from any order or decision made before a single Judge may be made to the Supreme Court sitting in banco in the same manner and subject to the same rules and conditions as are required in cases of new trials in matters within the ordinary jurisdiction of the Supreme Court, 28 V. c. 42, s. 42.

Rules for proceedings

The Supreme Court may, as often as circumstances require, make such rules concerning the mode of proceeding to be had for winding up a company as may seem necessary, but until made, the Court or Judge may, by the order on the petition or upon summary application afterwards, give such directions, not inconsistent with this act, for carrying out the provisions thereof, in respect of the particular company, being or being sought to be wound up, 28 V. c. 42, s. 43.

Transactions between the commencement of and order for winding up, void unless otherwise ordered

Whenever a company is being wound up, all dispositions of the property effects and things in action of the company, and every transfer of shares or alteration of the status of the members, made between the commencement of the winding up, and the order for winding up, shall, unless otherwise ordered, be void, 28 V. c. 42, s. 44.

Books &c. prima facie evidence as between contributories

When being wound up, all the books, accounts and documents of the company, and of the liquidator, shall, as between the contributories, be prima facie evidence, of the truth of all matters purporting to be therein recorded, 28 V. c. 42, s. 45.

Inspection by creditors and contributories

After order for winding up, the Court may make such order for the inspection by the creditors and contributories of the books and papers, as it thinks just, and any books and papers in possession of the company, may be inspected by creditors or contributories in conformity with the order, but not further or otherwise, 28 V. c. 42, s. 46.

Assignees may sue or defend in their own names

Any person to whom any thing in action of the company is assigned in pursuance of this act, may bring or defend any action or suit, relating thereto, in his own name, 28 V. c. 42, s. 47.

Contingent debts and claims sounding in damages proof of

In the event of any company, being wound up, all debts payable on a contingency, and all claims against it, present or future, certain or contingent, ascertained or sounding only in damages, shall be admissible in proof, a just estimate being made so far as is possible of the value of such as are subject to any contingency or sound only in damages, or for some other reason do not bear a certain value, 28 V. c. 42, s. 48.

The liquidator may, with the sanction of the Court, pay any classes of creditors in full, or make such compromise or other arrangement, as he deems expedient with creditors or persons claiming to be so, or having or alleging themselves to have any claims, present or future, certain or contingent, ascertained or sounding only in damages against the company, or whereby it may be rendered liable. 28 V. c. 42, s. 49.

Payments in full —Compromises to or with creditors

Or with such sanction may compromise all calls and liabilities to call, debts, and liabilities capable of resulting in debts, and all claims, whether present or future, certain or contingent, ascertained or sounding only in damages, subsisting or supposed to subsist between the company and any contributory or alleged contributory, or other debtor or person apprehending liability to the company, and all questions in any way relating to or affecting the assets, or the winding up upon the receipt of such sums, payable at such times and generally upon such terms as may be agreed upon, with power for the liquidator to take any security for their discharge, and to give complete discharges in respect of all or any such calls, debts or liabilities, 28 V. c. 42, s. 50.

Compromises with contributories & others

When being wound up, any attachment, sequestration, distress, or execution put in force against the estate or effects of the company, after the commencement of the winding up. shall be void, 28 V. c. 42, s. 51.

After commencement of winding up attachment, &c void

Any such conveyance, mortgage, delivery of goods, payment, execution or other act relating to property as would, if made or done by or against an individual, be deemed in the event of his insolvency to have been made or done by way of undue or fraudulent preference of his creditors, shall if made, or done by, or against any company, be deemed, in the event of its being wound up, to have been made or done by way of undue or fraudulent preference of its creditors, and invalid.—For the purposes of this Act the presentation of a petition for winding up shall be deemed to correspond with the act of insolvency in the case of an individual 28 V., c. 42, s. 52.

Undue preferences

Presentation of petition equivalent to act of insolvency

When in the course of winding up, it appears that any past or present director, manager, or officer, or liquidator has misapplied, or retained in his own hands, or become liable or accountable for any monies of the company, or been guilty of any misfeasance or breach of trust in relation to the company, the court may on application of any liquidator, creditor, or contributory, notwithstanding the offence is one for which the offender is criminally responsible, examine into his conduct and compel him to re-pay any such monies with interest after such rate as the court thinks just, or to contribute such sum to the assets by way of compensation in respect of such misapplication, retainer, misfeasance, or breach of trust, as it thinks just— 28 V., c. 42, s. 53.

Power of court to order re-payment of monies misapplied, &c.

If any director, officer, or contributory of any company wound up, destroys, mutilates, alters, or falsifies any books, papers, writing, or securities, or makes, or is privy to the making of any false or fraudulent entry in any register book of account, or other document belonging to the company, with intent to defraud or deceive any person, the offender shall be guilty of a misdemeanor, and on conviction be liable to imprisonment not exceeding two years, with or without hard labour, 28 V., c. 42, s. 54.

Fraudulent destruction of books, &c. or documents, false entries

Misdemeanor

When any order is made for winding up, if it appear in the course of such winding up that any past or present, director, manager, officer, or member has been guilty of any offence in relation to the company, for which he is criminally responsible, the court may, on application of any person interested in such winding up, or of its own motion direct the liquidator to institute and conduct prosecutions, and order the costs and expences to be paid out of the assets, 28 V., c. 42, s. 55.

Prosecutions at the expence of the assets

Wilfully and corruptly giving false evidence upon any examination upon oath, or in any affidavit, deposition, or solemn affirmation in, or about the winding up of any company or otherwise in any matter arising under this Act, punishable as perjury, 28 V., c. 42, s. 56.

Perjury

The Act shall apply to all companies incorporated under any Act of this island, all partnerships as bankers under Act authorized to sue by their public officer or otherwise, all mining and cost book companies established under any Act, and all other companies limited or otherwise which derive their powers under any Act, whether such corporations, partnerships, or companies have been or shall be appointed, formed, or established under any present or future Act, save where they previously derived their powers under any Statute of the United Kingdom, 28 V., c. 42, s. 57.

Application of Act

Complexional Distinctions.

Abolished   All the free brown and black population of this island shall be entitled to all the rights, privileges, immunities, and advantages to which they would have been entitled if born of, and descended from white ancestors— 1 W. 4, c. 17, s. 2.

Constables.

Justices' Warrants against any person on board ship, may be directed to and executed by them, fee, 3s. currency, 35 C. 2. c. 4, s. 7

Fees for serving warrants, 1s. 3d. currency, 10 Ann, c. 4, s. 17.

Constabulary Force.

Short title   Short title, "The Constabulary and Reward Fund Act," 1864— 27 V., S. 1, c. 30, s. 1.

Appointment at Special Sessions   The Justices of each parish, including Kingston, shall at a Special Session convened for the purpose, from time to time, appoint fit persons, male inhabitants, willing to serve as constables under this Act within the parish, and as constables generally, if need be. No person convicted of any felony or fraudulent offence, shall be appointed a special constable— 27 V., S. 1, c. 30, s. 2.

Session to be advertised   The Clerk of the Peace shall notify every special session convened for such purpose by advertisement in the "Gazette", 27 V., S. 1, c. 30, s. 3.

Number of constables   For every 100 persons resident in each parish, not more than one constable shall be appointed, 27 V., S. 1, c. 30, s. 4.

Head constables   The Justices may appoint out of every 10 such constables, one head constable, to be designated accordingly, 27 V., S. 1, c. 30, s. 5.

Chief constable to be appointed by Governor   The Governor may, from time to time, appoint out of the constabulary force, or the rest of the population in each parish, and in addition to the others, one chief constable for every parish, and for the City and Parish of Kingston, as a distinction for highly meritorious conduct, and the Governor's Secretary shall notify every appointment of chief constable to the Custos, 27 V., S. 1, c. 30, s. 6.

Dismissal or suspension   Any constable, other than a chief constable, may be dismissed or suspended, on satisfactory cause, by order of a majority of justices at a special sessions; any chief constable, by order of the Governor, notified to the Custos, 27 V., S. 1, c. 30, s. 7.

Exemption   After 12 months' service, any constable shall be entitled to be exempted, on notifying his claim to the Custos, 27 V., S. 1, c. 30, s. 8.

Notice of death, &c.   In case of the death, resignation, or quitting the parish, of any constable other than a chief constable, the Inspector of Police shall give notice thereof to the Custos and Justices, through the Clerk of the Peace, who shall immediately notify the same to the Custos, 27 V., S. 1, c. 30, s. 9.

Elections on suspension, &c.   In case the justices suspend or dismiss any constable, they shall proceed with as little delay as possible, to appoint a successor. On suspension or dismissal of a chief constable, the Governor may appoint a successor— 27 V., S. 1, c. 30, s. 10.

Oath of office   Each constable shall, before acting under his appointment, take the following oath, to be administered by a justice:

I, A. B. do swear that I will well and truly serve the Queen, as a constable, under the Constabulary Act, one thousand eight hundred and sixty-four, 27 V., c. 30, for the parish of   , and as a constable generally,—So help me God, 27 V., S. 1, c. 30, s. 11.

Rolls and correction   The Clerk of the Peace shall keep a roll of the names, at full length, and the calling, or occupation, and residence of each constable, from time to time appointed, and keep exposed in his office a copy of such roll, and furnish the Inspector of Police with a copy for each police station in the parish, and on any person ceasing to be a constable, shall erase his name, calling, or occupation, and residence, and insert in the roll, and copy in his office the names at full length, calling, or occupation, and place of residence of any person appointed in his room, notifying the same to the Inspector, from time to time, who shall thereupon correct the copies at the several police stations accordingly, 27 V., S. 1, c. 30, s. 12

The Inspector shall, with the approval of the Custos, determine and define convenient districts in which constables may be warned to serve, and such warning may be given by any constable or policeman by order of the Inspector, 27 V., S, 1, s. 13. *Districts*

The Clerk of the Peace shall report to the Governor all appointments, suspensions, dismissals, resignations, and deaths, and publish the same, from to time, in the " Gazette", 27 V., S. 1, c. 30, s. 14. *Clerk of the Peace to report appointments, &c. to the Governor and Gazette them*

His fee, 1s. for each person appointed for one year, to be paid by the Receiver-General on the Governor's Warrant, 27 V., S. 1, c. 30, s. 15. *Clerk of Peace's fee*

The duties of his office shall be explained to each constable on his being appointed or sworn into office by the justices present, 27 V., S. 1, c. 30, s. 16. *Explanation of his duties*

The Governor in Executive Committee shall, from time to time, frame, amend, or rescind rules for the government of the constabulary, and fix the establishment of grades or ranks in the force, a printed copy, of which rules with a statement or explanation of their duties shall be provided by the Executive Committee, at the expense of the fund established under this Act, and be given to every constable, 27 V., S. 1, c. 30, s. 17. *Rules and explanation of duties to be provided for them*

Each constable shall be furnished with a constable's warrant according to form to be printed and furnished at the expense of the fund, and filled up and completed in writing, agreeably to the instructions, 27 V. S. 1, c. 30, s. 18. *Warrant.*

And shall also be provided at the public expense, with a baton and such distinguishing badge as the Governor shall direct, and head constables and chief constables, may be supplied with such distinctive marks on their batons and badges, as the Governor may direct, 27 V. S. 1, c. 30, s. 19. *Baton and badge*

Every chief constable shall receive his warrant, baton and badge from and be sworn into office before a bench of Justices in Petty Sessions, assembled by direction of the Custos, in the district where he resides, and in the presence of such head constables, as shall attend, and who shall be entitled, on certificate of the Justices present, and Governor's warrant, to one full day's pay each, for such attendance, 27 V. S. 1, c. 30, s. 20. *To be sworn.*

Such constables warrant, batons and badges, shall be delivered to the Inspector or Sergeant in charge of the nearest police station, by any constable who ceases to hold office or quits the parish, or by the representatives, widow or next of kin, of any deceased constable, or by any person in possession thereof. Any person knowingly or wilfully detaining any such warrant &c. shall be liable to a penalty, not exceeding 40s 27 V. S. 1, c. 30, s. 21 *Warrants, batons and badges, to be delivered upon death, &c,*

Each constable shall when acting, unless required to act by any sudden emergency, wear his badge, and carry his warrant, and baton, and exhibit them if required, 27 V. S. 1, c. 30, s. 22. *Badge, baton and warrant, to be worn and exhibited when on duty.*

And shall be under the orders of the Custos and Justices, and for disobedience of any lawful order of a Justice, or other wilful omission or refusal of duty, shall be subject to a penalty, not exceeding 40s. Any constable proved, directly or indirectly, to have frustrated or impeded the ends of Justice, shall be dismissed, and not again-eligible to the Office, 27 V. S. 1, c. 30, s. 23. *Disobedience of orders.*

They shall muster once in every year at the Court House, on a day to be fixed by the Custos, to be inspected by the Custos and Magistrates. Each constable so mustering, shall receive 1s. 6d., the head constable 2s. 6d. and the chief constable 3s. for such day's muster 27 V. S. 1, c. 30, s. 24. *Annual musters. Pay to constables present.*

14 Days notice of the day for muster, shall be given in each parish, by posting bills or otherwise, as the Custos may consider desirable, 27 V. S. 1, c. 30, s. 25. *Notice*

Every constable while holding office, shall be invested with all the powers and authorities incident to the office of constable, at common law, and policeman under any act now or to be in force, and if need be, in the execution of his duty, may act in all respects in any other parish, as fully as in that for which he is appointed, 27 V. S. 1, c. 30, s. 26. *Their powers.*

The Governor in case of any riot or disturbance, actual or apprehended, or other occasion, may cause the constables or so many as he thinks necessary, to be called out and to continue on duty, in their or any other parishes, until the cause for which their services were required has ceased to exist, 27 V. S. 1, c. 30, s. 27. *How to be called out of parish.*

In case of any riot or disturbance or other emergency, actual or apprehended, any Justice in other parishes, and in Kingston the Custos, may order on duty for such period or extended period as may be necessary, either within the parish or in any adjoining parish, such number of constables, and if need be, the Chief Constable also, as in his judgment may be requisite for the service to be performed, 27 V. S. 1, c. 30, s. 28. *In case of emergency.*

To act under Inspector or other officer of police.

Where Constables or any Chief Constable, are ordered or called out on duty, they or he shall be under the command of the Inspector or other officer in command of the Police Force, if any on the spot, and be subject to the orders of the Custos, or other Justices in like manner as the Police, 27 V. S. 1, c. 30, s. 29.

Service of process not civil.

Presence at whippings.

Each Constable (except a Chief Constable) may by order of a Justice, or in Kingston of the Custos, be employed to serve or execute, or to assist in the service or execution of any warrant, summons or other process, except in civil matters. Any Chief or Head or other Constable (not exceeding two altogether, residing in any district, wherein has been committed any offence for which whipping may by law, now or hereafter, be inflicted, when summoned or ordered by any visiting Justice of the Prison, wherein the punishment is to be inflicted, shall attend thereat, and be paid for such attendance as for any other service, 27 V. S. 1, c. 30, s. 30.

See s. 33.

Protection in cases of legal proceedings.

Every Constable shall have the like protection, rights and privileges, in case of and before the commencement of any action or other proceeding at law, as a Constable at common law, or a Policeman under any act, now or to be inforce, may be entitled to claim, 27 V. S. 1, c. 30, s. 31.

Obstructions.

Wounding, assaulting, resisting or obstructing any Constable in the execution of his duty, punishable as for wounding &c., a Constable at common law, or a policeman under any act, now or to be in force in the execution of his duty, 27 V. S. 1, c. 30, s. 32.

Pay.

Every Constable shall be entitled for each day, or part of a day, for which his services are required, (except in the yearly muster) to be paid on the Governor's warrant, out of the treasury, not exceeding 4s to a Chief or Head Contable, and 2s Cd to any other, 27 V. S. 1, c. 30, s. 33.

On justices' certificate.

On certificate of the Justice by whom ordered or called out on duty, which shall shew the service, period and rate of daily pay, the form of certificate to be provided out of the fund, and furnished by the Executive Committee, through the Inspector of Police, 27 V. S. 1, c. 30, s. 34.

Through Inspector of Police.

Every such certificate shall be delivered by the constable in whose favor it is given to the Inspector or nearest Sergeant of Police of the parish. The Inspector shall collect and transmit the certificates to the commissioner for examining the public accounts at the period when he forwards the bills for the police pay of his division, and shall together with such pay draw from the Receiver-General the amount certified by the commissioner to be payable, and for payment of which the Governor's warrant shall be issued, and shall, at each monthly district Court, or in Kingston at the first Court of Petty Sessions, after drawing the same, pay, or cause to be paid to the several constables, the sums to which they are entitled, 27 V. S. 1 c. 30, s. 35.

Additional pay for extraordinary conduct.

The Governor in his discretion may direct, and the Receiver-General on his warrant shall pay any additional sum to any chief or head or other constable who distinguishes himself by extraordinarily active and meritorious conduct, 27 V. S. 1 c. 30, s. 36.

When disabled on service.

As also any further sum to any chief or head, or other constable who has been injured or disabled in the execution of his duty, as also for medicines, or medical or surgical attendance on them, 27 V. S. 1 c. 30, s. 37.

Meritorious services.

And any sum directed by any such warrant to be paid to any policeman, constable, or other person for meritorious service rendered for the public benefit, 27 V. S. 1 c. 30, s. 38.

Limit of expenditure.

The expenditure shall not to exceed £1200 in any year, and an account thereof shall be laid before the Assembly, within 28 days after opening each Session, 27 V. S. 1 c, 30, s. 39.

Extortion.

Any constable who extorts money by directly or indirectly threatening to execute, or use his office against any person, or directly or indirectly threatens to execute or use his office against any person with intent to extort money from him, shall forfeit not exceeding 40s., and be imprisoned with or without hard labour in the discretion of the convicting Justice for not more than 30 days, and be further imprisoned until payment of the penalty, 27 V. S. 1, c. 30, s. 40.

Recovery, &c. of penalties.

Penalties shall be recovered under 13 V. c. 35, or any other act, now or to be in force relating to summary convictions, and carried to the credit of the general revenue, 27 V. S. 1 c. 30, s. 41.

Interpretation.

Unless there is something repugnant or inconsistent " Constable," shall mean any chief, head, or other constable, 27 V. S. 1 c. 30, s. 42.

Constables warrant. s. 18.

JAMAICA, ss. parish of

To   residing at   in the said parish of appointed and sworn a constable, under the " Constabulary and reward fund Act, 1864."

These are to authorize and require you the said   in her Majesty's name in all things, and at all times for such period as you shall continue to be a constable under the said Act, to act in such office and capacity of constable thereunder, and as a conservator of the peace and constable generally, and with all the powers and authorities' incident to the office of constable at common law and policeman, under any Act which may now or hereafter be in force in this island, agreeably to the provisions of the said constabulary and reward fund act, 1864.

Given under our hands this   day of   one thousand eight hundred and

       A. B., Custos or senior magistrate, for the parish of

By Order • E. F., Clerk of Peace for parish of

Constables, Special.

Appointment by Custos or Mayor of Kingston.

The Custos, or next senior magistrate, residing or being at the time in any parish, in his absence, and the Mayor of Kingston, or in his absence the senior Alderman, may, from time to time appoint by precept under their hands, any householders, or others residing within the parish, to be special constables within the respective parishes or the immediate neighbourhood for such time and as to them seems necessary for the preservation of the public peace, and the prevention or suppression of all tumults, riots or felonies, and administer to them not only the usual oaths, administered by law to all special constables, but also the following oath :—

Oaths.

I, A. B., do swear that I will well and truly serve our Sovereign Lord, the King, in the office of Special Constable for the parish of without favor or affection, malice, or ill will, and that I will to the best of my power, cause the peace to be kept and preserved, and prevent all offences against the persons and properties of his Majesty's subjects, and that while I continue to hold the said office, I will to the best of my skill and knowledge, discharge all the duties thereof faithfully, according to law.—So help me God.

Not to affect powers of justices in case of actual tumults, &c.

But nothing herein shall alter, affect, or abridge any power of any Justices to appoint special constables in cases of actual tumults, riot, or felony. No such appointment shall operate as an exemption from doing duty in the militia, except while any special constable is in the actual performance of any duty as such, 4 W. 4 c. 29, s. 1.

Qualification, enrolment, and subscription of oaths.

Every special constable so to be appointed, shall qualify and enrol himself, and take the oaths within such time as shall be fixed by the person appointing him, and his name or mark shall be signed or made by himself to such oaths in the presence of the person appointing him, or of the Clerk of the Peace, on a roll to be kept for the purpose, whereon shall be designated his calling or occupation and place of residence, and a correct list shall from time to time be registered and exposed in the office of the Clerk of the Peace, as part of his duty. For any default in not qualifying and enrolling himself as provided, he shall forfeit £20, (£12 sterling) to be levied on his goods, by warrant under the hand and seal of the person appointing him, and so on toties quoties, or as often as he receives a fresh appointment, and makes default, and which new appointment may immediately follow the penalty of the preceding appointment, 4 W. 4, c. 29, s. 2.

Penalties

To be provided with staff and weapons
Return thereof

Such Special Constable shall at the expense of the parish, be provided with a staff of office, and such necessary weapons as the Justices and Vestry and Common Council of Kingston deem fit, and upon his appointment ceasing, or removal from the parish, such staff and weapons, in good order, shall be by him delivered up to the Clerk of the Peace, under a penalty of £5 (£3 sterling) to be recovered and applied as after provided, and upon his death, shall be delivered to the Clerk of the Peace, and recoverable from any person, in a summary manner, by warrant under the hand of any Justice of the parish, 4 W. 4, c. 29, s. 3.

When to be called out

All Custodes or Senior Magistrates, Mayor or Senior Alderman, respectively, shall have power, on reasonable apprehension of any intended tumult, riot or felony (of the reasonableness of which apprehension they are to be sole Judges, on whatever evidence or information they may receive) or upon any actual tumult, riot or felony, to call upon the immediate active aid and assistance of all or any such Special Constables, for its prevention or suppression. And every such Special Constable, so called upon, and not promptly obeying the call, or not promptly acting under the lawful orders of the party calling upon him, without sufficient excuse, shall incur the penalty of £20 (£12) to be recovered and applied as after provided, and shall also be liable to be indicted for a misdemeanor, 4 W. 4, c. 29, s. 4.

Penalty on not obeying call

When in the absence of Custos Mayor &c

In the absence of the Custos or Mayor, or Senior Magistrate or Alderman, where it is made to appear to two Justices or Aldermen and Common Councilmen, by the information on oath, of one or more respectable inhabitants, or is within their own knowledge, that any tumult, riot or felony, has taken place, or is likely to take place, and may reasonably be apprehended, such Justices may call upon, by warrant or precept in writing under their hands, or by a verbal summons or personal citation conveyed by a Constable, or any respectable person, all such Special Constables residing within the neighbourhood of such actual or apprehended tumult, riot or felony, to act as Special Constables, for such time, and as to the Justices, shall seem necessary for the preservation of the public peace, and prevention or suppression of any tumult, riot or felony, 4 W. 4, c. 29, s. 5.

Recovery &c. of penalties

All penalties shall be recoverable by attachment in the Supreme or [Circuit] Courts, grounded on affidavit, after the Court has considered any affidavits on the part of the party complained of, justifying or explaining his conduct, and the Judges may award costs on either side. Offences shall be complained of within 6 months. Any person appointed a Special Constable, may appeal to the Governor, so as the appeal be made and notice given to the Custos, Mayor, Magistrate or Alderman, who made such appointment, within 14 days after, and he shall not in the meantime be exempted from duty, 4 W. 4, c. 29, s. 6.

Appeal against appointment

Voluntary acceptance

No person by law exempted, shall be prevented from voluntarily accepting the appointment and being sworn and enrolled, and thereupon he shall be subject to all the duties and penalties other Special Constables are liable to, 4 W. 4, c. 29, s. 7.

Powers

Special Constables shall have all the powers and authorities, incident to the office of Constable, for the preservation of the public peace, the apprehending offenders, and the suppression or prevention of all tumults, riots and felonies, and if need be in the performance and prosecution of their duty may act in all respects in any adjoining parish, but in the neighbourhood only of that in which they reside, and only so far as may be necessary, as effectually as in the parish in which they are enrolled, 4 W. 4, c. 29, s. 8.

Contingent and Executory Interests, Rights of entry, Future Interests.

Disposition by will

Devisable; See Wills, 3 V. c. 51, s. 3.

By deed, &c

Any person may convey, assign or charge by any deed, any contingent or executory interest, right of entry for condition broken, or other future estate or interest he is entitled to or peremptorily entitled to in any freehold or leasehold land or personal property, or any part of such interest, right or estate, and every person to whom any such interest &c., shall be conveyed or assigned, his heirs &c., shall be entitled to stand in the place of the person by whom conveyed &c., and have the same interest &c., or such part as is conveyed &c., and the same actions and remedies as the person originally entitled, his heirs &c. would have been entitled to, if no conveyance, assignment or other disposition had been made. But no person is empowered to dispose of any expectancy as heir, or heir of the body inheritable, or as next of kin, under the statutes for the distribution of the estates of intestates of a living person, nor any estate &c., to which he may become entitled under any deed, or under the will of any living person, and no deed shall by force of this act, bar or enlarge any estate tail, further than it would have done, if it had not been passed. No chose in action shall by this act be made assignable at law, 8 V. c. 19, s. 4.

Expectancies estates' tail choses in action

After 30th June, 1845, no estate in land, shall be created by way of contingent remainder, but every estate which would before that time have taken effect, as a contingent remainder, shall take effect, if in a will or codicil as an executory devise, and if in a deed as an executory estate, of the same nature and having the same properties as an executory devise, and contingent remainders existing under previous deeds, wills or instruments, shall not fail or be destroyed or barred, merely by reason of the destruction or merger of any preceding estate or its determination by any other means than the natural effluxion of the time of the preceding estate, or some event on which it was in its creation limited to determine, 8 V. c. 19, s. 6. *Contingent remainders, executory estates*

Copyright.

All books lawfully imported, shall be duty free, 22 V. c. 21, s. 2. *Books duty free*

Subject to this act, reprints of any printed books, first composed or written or printed, or published in the United Kingdom, may be lawfully imported for sale or hire, 22 V. c. 21, s. 3. *Reprints may be imported*

On the importation of any reprint of such book, at the time, protected by the law of copyright, there shall be paid an ad valorem duty, on the bona fide price of such reprint of 20 per centum, 22 V. c. 21, s. 4. *On an ad valorem duty of 20 per cent*

Such duty shall not be paid on newspapers or other regular periodicals, containing extracts only, from such books, 22 V. c. 21, s. 5. *Exemptions*

After collection by the proper officers, the duty shall be paid into the Treasury Chest of the Commissariat Department, with a detailed account thereof quarterly, in order to be duly paid over to the registered proprietor of the copyright, 22 V. c. 21, s. 6. *Appropriation of duty*

Before the reprint of any book is made liable to ad valorem duty, the book shall have been duly registered, or other the requisitions in respect thereto complied with, as the nature of the case may require according to the provisions of any act of the Imperial Parliament relating to copyright, 22 V. c. 21, s. 7. *Registration*

Every reprint imported or brought, sold, hired, published or exposed to sale, or let to hire, contrary to this act, shall be forfeited and sold, one half of the proceeds to be applied to the use of the officers of Customs, or other appointed officers seizing the same, and the other half to the registered proprietor of the copyright of the book from which the reprint is made, and every offender duly convicted before two Justices of the parish, where the seizure is made (who are empowered to try the same, according to the then or any act providing for the recovery of petty debts) shall forfeit £5, and double the value of every copy of such reprint, which he imports or causes to be imported, or knowingly sells, publishes or exposes for sale or lets, or hires or has in his possession for sale or hire, contrary to this act, 22 V. c. 21, s. 8. *Forfeitures and penalties*

Such penalty may be enforced by distress warrant of any Justice, and in case of a return that no sufficient goods of the defendant can be found, any Justice may commit the defendant to any Jail, for not exceeding 3 calendar months, unless the penalty and all costs and charges of the distress and of the commitment (the amount being stated in such commitment) are sooner paid, and of every such penalty, the sum of £2 shall be to the use of the officers of Customs, or other appointed officers, and the remainder paid into the Treasury Chest, of the Commissariat Department, and remitted to the use of the proprietor of the copyright, as provided for payment of the duty, 22 V. c. 21, s. 9. *Enforcement and application*

At the time of the entry of any reprint, the officers passing shall stamp it, and the Collector of Customs at Kingston shall furnish the form of stamp necessary, 22 V. c. 21, s. 10. *Stamp on reprints*

Short Title, the copyright protection act, 1858, 22 V. c. 21, s. 12. *Short title*

" Book" shall include volume, pamphlet, sheet of letter press, sheet of music, map, chart, plan, and periodically published review, 22 V. c. 21, s. 13. *Interpretation*

Coroners.

Inquest

Upon any body being found dead in any parish, the Coroner shall upon the first notice or information to him given, cause the body to be viewed and au inquisition taken thereon, agreeably to the laws of England, and act in every thing relative thereto agreeable to such laws, 11 G. 3, c. 15.

Coroners for St. Thomas in the Vale St. John, St Dorothy and St David

For remedying the inconveniences of several parishes being included in one precinct, the Governor shall cause writs to be issued in the usual manner for the election of a coroner for each of the parishes of St Thomas in the Vale, St. John, St. Dorothy and St. David, who shall possess the same powers, and be obliged to discharge all the duties of the office of coroner agreeably to the laws of England, and of this island, and under the same penalties as any coroner heretofore elected for any precinct, 41 G. 3 c. 13, s. 2.

Whenever any vacancy of the office of coroner of either of these parishes happens, the Governor shall cause a writ to be issued for the election of another coroner as usually practised upon the vacancy of the office heretofore in any precinct, 41 G. 3 c. 13, s. 3

Two Coroners for Port Royal

The Governor shall cause a writ to be issued for the election by the freeholders of Port Royal of another coroner, whose residence shall be in the interior of the parish, and when any vacancy happens by the death or departure from this island of either of the coroners, a new writ shall issue for the election of another in his room, so that there be always a coroner resident in the town, and another in the interior of the parish, 41 G. 3 c. 13, s. 4.

Omission to give notice of sudden death &c on any property, misdemeanor

The owner, manager, or overseer, of any property who shall omit to inform the coroner or in his absence from home or sickness, a Justice, of the death of any person who dies suddenly, or is slain, drowned, wounded, or poisoned, or dies by any cause or in any manner otherwise than according to the common course of nature, on such property, shall be indicted for misdemeanor, and subject to such punishment by fine or imprisonment, or both, as the Court may award, such fine not to exceed £500 (£300 sterling) nor imprisonment 6 months, 58 G. 3, c. 23, s. 1.

Gaolers to give notice of all deaths

See 17 V. c, 23

The keeper of every gaol who omits to inform the coroner, or in his absence, &c, a Justice, of the death of any person who dies in such gaol, by any cause or in any manner, shall be subject to such prosecution and punishment as before mentioned, 58 G. 3, s. 2.

Bodies of persons dying suddenly &c not to be buried or removed in less than 24 hours

Persons dying in confinement elsewhere than in Gaol

No body of any person who may die suddenly or be slain, &c., shall be buried or removed in less than 24 hours after it has been found dead, unless ordered by the coroner or justice acting in his absence, and any person burying or removing any such body without its being so ordered shall be subject to prosecution and punishment as before mentioned. No body of any person who dies by any sort of death in any place of confinement, other than a gaol shall be buried or removed, until an inquest is held thereon, and any person burying or removing such body shall be subject to prosecution and punishment as before mentioned, 58 G. 3 c. 23, s. 3.

Affidavit to be annexed to proceedings before less than 12 Jurors

When a coroner cannot collect a full jury of 12 to form inquests, he shall annex to the proceedings an affidavit of his having used his best endeavours to obtain a full jury, but could procure the number only named in the inquisition, 58 G. 3 c. 23, s. 8.

Act not further to alter the law relating to Coroners

Nothing herein shall alter, vary, or annul any acts of this island or the laws of England respecting coroners and their duties, or any proceedings against, them or touching their office except as hereby altered, 58 V. c. 23, s. 9.

On inquests for manslaughter &c to take and return evidence recognisances & inquisition and sign and certify and return them to the Crown

Every coroner upon any inquisition before him taken whereby any person shall be indicted for manslaughter, or murder, or as an accessory to murder before the fact, shall put in writing the evidence given to the Jury before him, or so much as is material, and shall have authority to bind by recognizance all such persons as know or declare anything material touching the manslaughter, or murder, or the offence of being accessory to murder, to appear at the next [Circuit Court], at which the trial is intended to be, to prosecute or give evidence against the party accused, and shall certify and subscribe the evidence, and all such recognizances and inquisitions before him taken, and deliver them to the Clerk of the Crown, 8 G. 4 c. 22, s. 4.

Penalty

If any coroner offend contrary hereto, the Court, to whose officer any such evidence, recognizance, or inquisition ought to have been delivered, shall upon examination and proof of the offence, in a summary manner set such fine upon him as it thinks meet, 8 G. 4 c. 22, s. 5.

No person being coroner of any city or parish shall sit or vote at any meeting of, or be a member, either as a magistrate or otherwise, of the corporate body of Kingston or of any Vestry, and every election of any coroner, as a member of the Corporation of Kingston, or as a Vestryman or Churchwarden of any parish shall be ipso facto void, 10 V. c. 12, s. 2.

Not to be elected a member of Corporation of Kingston or Vestryman or Churchwarden, nor vote as a Magistrate

The Governor may at any time during the prevalence of any endemic or epidemic disease, with the advice of the Privy Council, issue a Royal proclamation prohibiting the holding of any coroner's inquest upon the body of any person dying within any prison, hospital, or public institution, whose death is certified, by an entry in one of the books of the institution, under the hand of the medical attendant, to have been occasioned by any such prevailing disease, 17 V. c. 23.

Dispensation with inquest in Prisons, Hospitals, &c during epidemic diseases

The Governor may, whenever he thinks fit, give leave to any person filling the office of coroner to be absent from this island, for any period not exceeding 12 calendar months at any one time, 17 V. c. 38, s. 1.

Leave of absence

And may appoint a deputy coroner to act in the place, and discharge the duties of any coroner, to whom leave of absence is given, and such appointment shall be made upon such terms and conditions as to the Governor seems fit, 17 V. c. 38, s. 2.

Deputy

Whenever a vacancy happens in the office of coroner, no person shall be eligible to the office, unless he is a legally qualified practitioner, in physic, or and surgery, and such medical practitioner shall, after having been elected to permanently reside and practice in the parish in which he is elected coroner, 19 V. c. 17, s. 1.

Medical Practitioners to be elected when they offer themselves

If any p s other than a duly qualified medical practitioner is elected and returned coroner, (except under the circumstances after mentioned) such election shall be ipso facto void, and a new writ shall thereupon issue, 19 V. c. 17, s. 2.

And any other election to be void

In case no duly qualified practitioner offers himself as a candidate or desires to be elected a coroner, within 6 days before or after the issuing of the writ of election any other person may be elected coroner, 19 V. c. 17, s. 3.

If no practitioner offer any other person may be appointed

Where any coroner, from ill health, absence from the parish or otherwise, is unable to perform his duty, any Justice of the parish on receiving information of the death of any person from any cause otherwise than by the common course of nature, or of any body being found dead within his jurisdiction shall issue his warrant for warning a Jury, and proceed to hold an inquisition on the body as if he were coroner, and shall exercise the like duties, liabilities, powers and authorities as the coroner, but no Justice shall be entitled to any fee or mile money for issuing such warrant or holding any such inquest, 20 V. c. 9.

Justices to hold Inquests when Coroners are unable to do so

The several coroners shall be paid monthly or quarterly, the salaries set opposite to their respective parishes, 23 V. c. 19, s. 1,

Salaries See Schedule, title, Vestries

Such salaries to be instead and in full of all fees to which they may be entitled, under any act in force, and of commutation for mile money, and printed forms, and it shall not be lawful for the Vestry of any parish to pay any coroner mile money or allowance for forms, 23 V. c. 19, s. 2.

In full of fees &c

Whenever a coroner is required to perform the duties of a sheriff in the execution of any writ, he shall be entitled to be paid a fee of £3 3s, and mile money at the rate of 2s 6d., for every mile he has to travel from his place of residence to the place he is required to go to execute such writ, which the plaintiff shall be bound to pay the coroner before he proceeds to the execution of such writ, and the defendant shall be required to pay such fee and mile money as parcel of the damages and costs of the writ executed upon him, 23 V. c. 19, s. 3.

Fees as sheriff

Act in force until 31st March, 1867, 23 V. c. 19, s. 5.

Duration

Costs.

In suits at law and equity for the recovery of monies lent upon mortgage, or specialty, where the defendant opposes, or sets up a defence, and the plaintiff obtains a judgment or decree for such money, or for the lands and premises upon which the monies were lent, the defendant shall not only pay to the plaintiff the usual taxed costs of suit, but be further liable to such fees as the plaintiff has paid to counsel in the prosecution of the same, and for the

At law or in equity in suits on mortgage or specialty

P

travelling charges and expenses of witnesses subpœnaed by the plaintiff to give evidence in the cause, and all such further charges as the plaintiff, or his attorney, or agent in this island, shall, by affidavit, make appear to have been by him laid out and expended in the cause, to be taxed as costs of increase. Upon application of the defendant in case the costs so taxed appear unreasonable the court may moderate the same, 24 G. 2, c. 19, s. 1.

Counsel's fees
Costs of remittance on advances payable in Great Britain

The counsel for the plaintiffs shall, if demanded, give a certificate under their hands of the fees by them received in any such cause, to be produced upon taxation. And for monies lent or advanced by merchants, factors, or others residing in Great Britain, or by persons residing in this island, and the moneys lent or advanced, agreed to be paid in Great Britain, whether by parol or in writing, the defendant against whom judgment or decree is obtained shall not only pay the costs as above mentioned, but also be liable to such further costs and charges as the plaintiff, his attorney, or agent, executor, or administrator shall make appear by affidavit to the taxing officer, he has sustained or may sustain by remitting the monies so lent or advanced to Great Britain, to be taxed as costs of increase, but the court may, on application of the defendant, moderate the same, 24 G. 2, c. 19, s. 2.

Cost on frivolous writs of Error

If after judgment for the plaintiff in any action the defendant sues any writ of error to annul the judgment and it is afterwards affirmed, or the writ of error discontinued or the plaintiff in error is nonsuit therein, the defendant in error upon certificate of any three of the Judges constituting such court that there was not a reasonable cause for suing such writ of error, and that the same was frivolous and brought merely for delay and vexation, the party bringing the writ of error shall pay to the defendant in error double the costs he has laid out to be taxed on affidavit of himself, his agent, or attorney as costs of increase by the Clerk of the Court of Errors, to be added to the costs of the court below, but the court of errors may moderate the same, 24 G. 2, c. 19, s. 3.

Where damages do not amount to 24s see 5 V. c 50, s. 2, 22 V. c. 28

If upon any action, personal, not being for any title or interest of lands nor concerning the freehold or inheritance of any lands, it appears to the Judges that the debt or damages to be recovered shall not amount to 40s. (24s. sterling) or above, the Judge before whom the action is pursued shall not award, nor the Clerk of the Court tax for costs to the plaintiff any more costs than the debt or damages amount to, but less at their discretions—1 G 3, c. 21

Costs of increase See 24 G 2, c 19, s 2

Where the defendant against whom judgment is obtained (upon open or settled account of any person resident in Great Britain or Ireland against an inhabitant of this island) sets up any defence, he shall be chargeable with costs of increase as heretofore, unless the Judges before whom the action is tried see cause for disallowing the same, and make order accordingly—29 G, 3, c. 13, s. 2.

On actions generally

The plaintiff in every action in the Supreme Court (except as after excepted) in which he recovers damages, shall be entitled to costs out of purse expended in prosecuting his suit, as costs of increase, to be taxed as between party and party, and shall have such process and execution for recovery of the same as plaintiffs have for the recovery of costs of suit, 5 V., c. 50, s. 1.

Damages under 40s. see 13 G. c 20, 22 v c 28

Where the debt or damages, recovered in any personal action, does not amount to 40s. the Clerk of the Court, shall not tax any more costs than the sum recovered unless the Judge, before whom the cause is tried within 10 days after the termination of the Court at which the action is tried, certify on the record, that in his opinion, costs to be taxed as aforesaid, or some specified sum ought to be allowed to the plaintiff, 5 V. c. 50, s. 2.

Defendants costs

If the plaintiff, after appearance by the defendant, is non suited, or a verdict after trial pass against him, the defendant shall have Judgment to recover his costs incurred in defending the action, when taxed as between party and party, and shall have such process and execution for recovering the same against the plaintiff as plaintiffs have on Judgments against defendants, 5. V. c. 50, s. 3.

Actions for penalties

The act shall not extend to actions for the recovery of any penalty or debt, under any act of this island, or statute of the Imperial Parliament in force, unless costs are expressly given by the act or statute under which the action is brought, 5 V. c. 50, s. 4.

In any action against two or more defendants, and any one or more has a nolle prosequi, entered, or on the trial have a verdict, every such defendant shall have Judgment for and recover his reasonable costs, unless in case of a trial, the Judge within 10 days after the trial, in open Court, certify upon the record under his hand, that there was reasonable cause for making him a defendant in such action, 5 V. c. 50. s. 5. Nolle prosequi or verdict, for some defendants

The plaintiff or defendant, in whose favor, upon any demurrer, Judgment is given, shall be entitled to his reasonable costs, and have execution thereof accordingly, 5 V. c. 50, s. 6. Demurrer

The Judges shall make rules for the payment of costs by a plaintiff discontinuing his action, after appearance by the defendant, as shall seem proper, 5 V. c. 50, s. 7. Discontinuance

The Judges on all applications to the Court sitting in Banc, shall in their discretion make such order, as to payment of costs, as shall seem reasonable, 5 V. c. 50, s. 8. Applications in banc

No costs shall be recoverable until first taxed by the Clerk of the Court or his Deputy, 5 V. c. 50, s. 9. To be taxed

The Clerk of the Court or his Deputy, in the taxation of final costs, either for plaintiff or defendant, shall, if required by the opposite party, deduct from the gross amount of the debt or damages, costs of suit or costs of increase, any interlocutory costs obtained by him in the progress of the cause; and Judgment shall be entered up for the balance in favor of the party on whose side the balance appears, and he shall have execution thereof accordingly, 5 V. c. 50, s. 10. Set off of interlocutory costs on final taxation and Judgment to be entered for the balance

So much of any clause, enactment or provision, in any acts of a local or personal nature, whether the same are public or private aets, whereby double or treble, or any other than the usual costs between party and party may be recovered, is repealed, and in lieu thereof the usual costs between party and party, and no more, shall be recovered, 8 V. c. 28, s. 21. Double and treble costs in local &c acts

As also in any public acts not local or personal, and instead of such costs, the parties heretofore entitled under such last mentioned acts to such double, treble or other costs, shall receive such full and reasonable indemnity as to all costs, charges and expences incurred in or about any action, suit or other proceeding, as shall be taxed by the proper officer in that behalf, subject to be reviewed in like manner and by the same authority as any other taxation of costs, 8 V. c. 28, s. 22. In general public acts

In actions wherein the plaintiff recovers a sum exceeding £30, he shall be entitled to recover costs, according to the scale by which the Clerk of the Court is now guided in taxing bills of costs in actions within the jurisdiction of the Supreme Court. In all actions on contracts wherein the plaintiff shall not recover more than £30, and in all actions of trespass not being in ejectment [as to which see that title, 25 V. c. 46, s. 13] of trover or case not being for malicious prosecution, libel, slander, seduction or criminal conversation, wherein he shall recover no more than £10, he shall only be entitled to costs at the rate of one moiety of the said charges. Where the plaintiff establishes a claim beyond £30, but the verdict is reduced by set off below the limit of £30, there shall be marked on the record in Court, the amount found for the plaintiff, and the sum proved by the defendant, under his set off, and the balance struck and stated on the record shall be the verdict of the Jury, and the Clerk of the Court shall thereupon tax and award to the plaintiff costs according to the scale of the Supreme Court. In actions of detinue and replevin, if the value of the property involved in issue exceed £30, the plaintiff shall be entitled, irrespective of the amount of the verdict, to the costs of the Supreme Court, 19 V. c. 10, s. 36. Scale of costs Damages exceeding or not above £30

Trespass &c. £10

Sett off

Detinue Replevin

In all personal actions, wherein the plaintiff seeks by his declaration to recover a greater sum than £30, and Judgment is given for the defendant, or the plaintiff discontinues his action, the defendant shall be entitled to full costs according to the higher scale above indicated, but in all personal actions, in which the plaintiff restricts his demand to £30, or under, the defendant shall, if he succeed, be entitled only to costs on the lower scale, and upon every action so restricted, the plaintiff shall at the head of his declaration and on the endorsement signify such restriction by the words. "Action in the second class for thirty pounds or under" or in words of the like effect, 19 V. c. 10, s. 37. Scale of defendant's costs

Costs where cause of action determinable in an inferior court, see 28 V. c. 35, s. 5.

No person prosecuting any cause of action in the Supreme Court, which might have been determined in an inferior Court, shall recover any greater costs that he would have been entitled to in case he had sued in such inferior Court; act not to apply to causes of action, on which the inferior Court has refused to adjudicate. Nor shall any plaintiff be entitled to costs, by reason of any privilege as attorney or officer of the Supreme Court, 22 V. c. 28.

In ejectment

No more costs shall be taxed to the plaintiff in ejectment than would have been recoverable under 25 V. c. 46, unless a special verdict is found and endorsed on the record, that the land is of greater annual value than £12, and is produced to the officer at the time of taxation, 25 V. c. 46, s. 13.

Crown entitled to, see Customs, 17 V. c. 2, s. 28

In all informations, actions, suits or other proceedings, before any court or tribunal, by or on behalf of the Crown against any Corporation or person in respect of any lands or hereditaments, or of any goods or chattels belonging or accruing to the Crown, or in respect of any money due to Her Majesty by virtue of any act of the Imperial Parliament or of this island, for any public or parochial service, the Attorney General shall be entitled to recover costs, where Judgment is given for the Crown, in the same manner and under the same rules, regulations and provisions as may be in force touching the payment or receipt of costs in proceedings between subject and subject, such costs to be paid to the Receiver General, to the credit of the public, 26 V. S. 2, c. 15, s. 1.

Costs against the crown

If in any such information &c., Judgment is given against the Crown, the defendant shall be entitled to recover costs in like manner, and subject to the same rules and provisions as though such proceeding had been between subject and subject, provided the presiding Judge certify on the record that in his opinion the case is one in which the defendant is entitled to his costs and the Executive Committee shall direct the Receiver General to pay them out of any money voted by the Legislature for that purpose, 26 V. S., 2 c. 15, s. 2.

The proceedings in all such suits shall, as far as applicable, be regulated by the rules of pleading and practice in suits between subject and subject, and the Judges of the Supreme Court may, from time to time, frame further rules for the practice in such cases, 26 V. S. 2, c. 15, s. 3.

Litigation of suit when plaintiff or defendant is unable to answer for costs

If it be established to the satisfaction of a Judge, that any plaintiff or defendant is unable to answer for the costs of a suit instituted or defended by him, the Judge shall order that unless security for costs be given, the suit shall be litigated by affidavits on both sides, before any Judge or before the Court, and shall be thus determined, unless the Judge or Court, upon the materials thus disclosed, see fit to refer the question to the ordinary mode of trials, 28 V. c. 35, s. 1.

Award of non suit &c or damages

And the Judge or Court, in any action so litigated on affidavits, may award a nonsuit or verdict for the plaintiff or defendant, and for such damages as the justice of the case requires, 28 V., c. 35, s. 2.

Relief from costs of vexatious action

If an action be instituted vexatiously without previous demand of payment or satisfaction, the defendant may, on payment into court of the sum admitted to be due, move the court, or a Judge, on affidavit, to be relieved of the costs, and if the Judge or court deem it to have been vexatiously instituted without an opportunity having been afforded of settling the same, the defendant shall be relieved of the costs, 28 V., c. 35, s. 3.

Actions on Judgment

In an action on a judgment no costs shall be taxed to the plaintiff unless the Judge before whom it is tried, or the court above, certify that a case of necessity for such further action has been established, 28 V., c. 35, s. 4.

Where more than one remedy was open

In the taxation of costs, if more than one remedy be open to a suitor, and he pursue the more costly course, only such costs shall be taxed as the less costly course would have entailed, 28 V., s. 35 s. 5.

Unnecessary statement in Supreme court pleadings

No costs shall be allowed for any statements in pleadings in the Supreme Court rendered unnecessary by this Act, 28 V., c. 37, s. 1.

Counties.

Division of Island

Division of the island into the Counties of Middlesex, Surry, and Cornwall, 31 G. 2, c. 4, s. 1.

Boundaries see parishes

Their boundaries shall be as laid down in Robertson's Maps, published in 1804, 50 G. 3, c. 15.

But somewhat altered by the establishment of Manchester by 55 G. 3, c. 23—Metcalfe, 5 V. c. 44.

Court of Chancery.

All Chancery process except attachments may be served by any person as heretofore, 10 Ann, c, 4, s. 24.

Service of process

The Provost Marshal's fees for every commitment and releasement out of Chancery shall be each 2s, 6d. (1s. 6d. sterling), for serving all writs issuing out of the Court of Chancery, to him directed, 2s. 6d. (1s. 6d. sterling) each, besides mile money, 10 Ann, c, 4. s. 8.

Provost Marshal's fees
See 8 G. 2, c. 5, s. 2

For a bail bond on any writ of attachment or other process out of the Court of Chancery, 5s (3s. sterling) for executing a writ of ne exeatinsula, 10s. (6s. sterling) and mile money, and for a bond taken thereon, 5s. (3s sterling), 8 G 2, c. 5, s. 3.

See 8 G. 2, c. 5, s. 2

The Registrar in Chancery, and Clerk of the Patents shall continue to collect all fees heretofore accustomed to be payable to the Chancellor in respect of any proceedings, matter, or things had, made or done in, or issuing out of the said offices, and render an account of, and pay over to the Receiver-General all sums so received by him, 3 V., c, 65, s. 6.

Chancellor's fees

The Chief Justice shall by virtue of his appointment be an Assistant Judge to the Governor in his office of Chancellor, in the discharge of the judicial functions of the office, and be called the Vice Chancellor of Jamaica, 19 V., c. 10, s. 2.

Chief Justice Vice Chancellor

The Chief Justice and Vice Chancellor, shall, as Vice Chancellor, have full power and authority to hear and determine all causes, matters, and things depending in the Court of Chancery, either as a Court of Law, or as a Court of Equity, and exercise all the powers, authority, and jurisdiction in all matters and things which the present Vice Chancellor under any law at present in force has, or of right ought to have, 19 V., c. 10, s. 9.

His powers as Vice Chancellor

In case of the illness or absence of the Chief Justice, the Governor may appoint any one of the Assistant Judges to discharge his duties as Vice Chancellor, 19 V., c. 10, s. 14.

When an Assistant Judge may act

The Court of Chancery may, if they think fit, upon special motion of the complainant in open court in any suit concerning lands in this island, and any charge lien judgment or incumbrance thereon, or any money vested in any Island Security, Public Shares in Public Companies or concerns in this island, or the dividends on produce thereof, founded upon affidavit and such other documents as may be necessary to ascertain the residence of the party, and the particulars mentioned to identify such party and his residence, and specifying the means by which service may be authenticated, and especially where the defendant is resident out of the United Kingdom, whether there are any British Officers, civil or military, appointed by, or serving under Her Majesty, residing at, or near the place, order that service of subpoena, or letter missive to appear and answer upon the party in the manner thereby directed, or in case the court deems fit upon the receiver, steward, agent, or other person receiving or remitting the rents of the lands, if any, in the suit mentioned returnable at such time as the court directs. shall be good service on the party, and afterwards, upon an affidavit of such service had, may order an appearance to be entered for him, at such time and manner, as the court directs, and thereupon proceed upon such service as fully and effectually, as if it had been duly made within the jurisdiction, 6 V., c. 56, s. 1.

Subpoena on persons beyond the jurisdiction

With the subpoena or letter missive served under any such order a copy of the prayer of the bill shall be served on the defendant. No process of contempt shall be entered upon any such proceedings, nor any decree made absolute without special order on special motion. It shall not be compulsory on complainant to serve with process or bring before the court any parties further or otherwise than he is now by law or the practice of the court required to do, 6 V. c. 56, s. 2.

Copy prayer of bill. Contempt process, &c.

Where it appears upon affidavit to the satisfaction of the court that a defendant wherever resident cannot, by reasonable diligence be personally served with the subpoena or letter missive to appear and answer, or that upon enquiry at his usual place of abode he could not be found to be served, and there is just ground for believing he secretes or withdraws himself, or abstains from being duly represented by power of attorney, so as to avoid the service of the process of the court, the court may order that the service of the subpoena and a copy of the prayer of the bill shall be substituted in such manner as the court thinks reasonable and directs by such order, 6. V. c. 56, s. 3.

Substituted service.

Recitals in 'decrees or orders. Office copies of portions of proceedings.

Any person may take an office copy of so much only of any decree, order, report, or exceptions as he requires, and unless the court otherwise specially direct no recitals shall be introduced in any decree or order but the pleadings, petitions, notice, report, evidence, affidavits, exhibits, or other matters or documents on which they are founded shall merely be referred to. The Vice Chancellor, with the consent of the Chancellor, may make rules and regulations as to the form of such decrees and orders as he deems advisable for their proper drawing up and carrying this act into effect in regard thereto, 6 V. c. 56, s. 4.

Alterations in writs, proceedings &c.

The Vice Chancellor with consent of the Chancellor, may by rules or orders to be made within 2 years [from 31st December, 1842,] make such alterations as seem expedient in the forms of writs and commissions, and the mode of sealing, issuing, executing and returning them, also in the forms of and mode of filing bills, answers, depositions, affidavits, and other proceedings, and in the form and mode of taking discovery by answer in writing, or otherwise, in the form and mode of pleading, and in the form and mode of taking evidence, and generally in the form and mode of proceeding to obtain relief, in the general practice of the court, with relation thereto, and in the form and mode of proceeding before the masters, and in the form and mode of drawing up, entering, and enrolling orders and decrees, and in making and delivering copies of pleadings and other proceedings, and may make such regulation as to the taxation, allowance, and payment of costs, and for altering, superintending, controlling, simplifying, and regulating the business and practise of the court, and its several officers, and otherwise for carrying into effect such alterations as to them may seem proper, 6 V. c. 56, s. 5.

Rules to be laid before legislature.

Which rules and regulations were to be laid before the Council and Assembly, and have the force and effect of enactments unless either the Council or Assembly should resolve that the whole, or any part ought not to continue in force, in which case the whole or the part included in the resolutions should cease to be obligatory, 6 V. c. 56, s. 6.

Notice on judgment, &c., creditors, before making them defendants.

Whenever in any suit to obtain a decree or order for the sale of any lands, or any interest therein, or for the sale or distribution of any other property, it appears there is any judgment, recognizance, decree or order of any court of equity, rule of a court of common law, or order of an insolvent's debtors court, which would or ought to be a charge on or in any manner affect such land or other property (see judgments, &c., 8 V, c. 48, s. 10, 14—16,) the plaintiff may, before the persons entitled to receive the sum appearing to be secured thereby are made defendants, cause notice in writing to be served upon them, or in case of absence from the island upon their lawful attornies (the service whereof in the same manner as a writ of subpœna to answer is by the practice of the court required to be served shall be sufficient) apprizing them of the institution and object of the suit and stating shortly the lands and property sought to be sold or distributed, and requiring the persons to whom notice is addressed, or who may be entitled to receive, or be interested in the sum secured by such judgment, &c., within 15 days after service, to cause a notice in writing to be served on the solicitor of the plaintiff (whose name and place of business shall be stated at the end of the notice the plaintiff is allowed to serve) informing him whether they require to be made defendants in respect of their demand, and stating that if they do not reply to such notice within the time they will be made defendants. and in case no notice is served by the person or persons

In case notice is not replied to or they require to be made defendants.

claiming to be entitled, or interested in reply to the plaintiff's notice or they require to be made defendants, the plaintiff shall be at liberty to amend his bill by making them defendants, which amendments may be made with-

Amendment of bill and consequences.

out prejudice to the proceedings theretofore had in such suit, against other parties, and shall not be considered an amendment within the meaning of any rule, or order of the court, and the persons so added as parties, by reason of the service of any such notice by them, or in consequence of not having replied to the plaintiff's notice, shall not be entitled to be paid any costs in the

costs.

suit, unless the court by special order, or by a decree, direct costs to be paid to them, 11 V. c. 34, s. 1.

Judgment, &c, creditors may file claims in master's office.

Judgment, &c., creditors may go before the master in the cause after decree to account, or any order made directing an account to be taken of the debts, charges, or incumbrances affecting such land or property, whether such judgment, &c., is claimed to be a charge on such land or property, prior or subsequent to that of the plaintiff, and file a charge in his office in such suit, claiming the sum alleged to be due thereon; and every person after filing such charge shall be considered a party in the suit so as to be entitled to object or except to the master's report in the same manner as if he had been made a party by the service of process, 11 V. c. 34, s. 2.

In every decree by which an account of debts or incumbrances is directed, the Registrar shall insert a direction to the master to report the relative priorities of the demands which may be proved under it, or by virtue of this act, before him, and the master shall report such priority accordingly, (although such direction is omitted) ; and when any surplus of the produce of any sale, after paying the plaintiff's demand and costs, and any costs that may be awarded to defendants or creditors, and the demands prior to, or contemporaneous with that of the plaintiff, remain in court, the same shall be distributed among the creditors who may have proved their demands in the cause on any judgment. &c. subsequent to that of the plaintiff, according to the respective priorities, if the court so order ; and any creditor, so proving a demand subsequent to that of the plaintiff, may, in case any part of the lands or property, the subject of the suit, remains unsold after discharging the plaintiff's demand and all demands prior thereto, and any costs decreed or ordered to be paid, apply to the court for an order directing a sale of such unsold lands, or of a competent part for payment of the demands subsequent to that of the plaintiff, which have been proved, and the court may accordingly direct such sale if of opinion that such creditors or any of them would be entitled to have their demands raised by a sale of such lands or property, or may direct a receiver to be appointed or continued over such unsold lands or property for the benefit of such subsequent creditors, and distribute the funds to be received by such receiver accordingly, 11 V. c. 34, s. 3.

Masters to report the relative priority of claims proved before him, whether so directed or not by the decree

Sales and distribution for the benefit of creditors subsequent to plaintiff.

Receivers of unsold lands, &c.

If the plaintiff does not cause notice to be served, and without serving the same, makes any person interested in or entitled to such judgment, &c., a party, he shall not be allowed, without a special order or decree, any portion of the costs occasioned by making him a defendant, and shall be liable if the court so direct to pay the costs of such party; and any other costs occasioned by making him a defendant. The plaintiff shall whenever any notice is served by him, cause an affidavit of service to be made and filed within two months after service, 11 V. c. 34, s. 4.

Costs of or occasioned by making judgment, &c. Creditors defendants without notice Service of notice to be filed.

In any suit already instituted, creditors as aforesaid may without answering or appearing at the hearing, go into the master's office in manner and for the purposes aforesaid, and this act shall extend, as far as circumstances will permit, to any such creditor, and any costs unnecessarily occasioned by either the plaintiff requiring an answer, or the creditor putting in an answer or appearing at the hearing, or otherwise, shall be in the discretion of the court, in order to be thrown upon the party by whose act it is occasioned, 11 V. c. 34, s. 5.

Judgment. &c. creditors in existing suits.

To diminish expense in the inrolment of decrees and orders, no part of the statements or allegations in any bill, answer, petition, affidavit or report shall be recited or stated in any inrolment, but it shall be sufficient to state therein the filing of the bill or petition, or service of the notice of motion, the names of the parties, the prayer of the bill or petition, or notice of motion, the filing of the several answers and other pleadings or proceedings and reports, whether confirmed or not, and the short purport or effect of any decree or order made, had, put in, or taken before the date of the decree or order inrolled and leading thereto, 14 V. c. 52.

Inrolments.

In any case where a suit is now pending, or may be instituted in the Court of Chancery, by way of bill or information, any person who would have been entitled to file the same may apply to the court, by petition, for the relief which might have been prayed for by such bill or information, and service of notice of such petition shall be made, as after provided, upon such persons as the petitioner thinks fit, but with power to the court, from time to time, to direct any further service of the same, and service of such notice being made, the person served shall from the time of service become a party to the proceeding, and be bound in all respects thereby in the same manner as if a bill or information had been filed and the person had appeared to a subpœna to appear and answer, 15 V. c. 16, s. 1.

Petitions may be substituted for bills

Service of notice.

Jurisdiction on petion so extensive with that on bill

The court shall have in any matter brought before it, upon petition, the same jurisdiction, powers, and discretion as it could have exercised in a suit by way of bill, or information, and the same powers for enforcing the production of documents required for the purposes of the suit, as if a bill or a cross-bill had been filed, and all orders in any such matter may be made in the same manner, whether on motion or otherwise, and have the same authority and effect, and may be enrolled in the same manner, and be binding upon the same persons, under whatsoever disability they may be, and may be enforced by the same or any such process, and be subject to re-hearing and appeal in the same manner as if made in a suit so instituted, and every order in the nature of a decree shall have the same effect as a decree; and every petition presented under this Act shall have the same effect in making any infant a ward of court, as a bill filed in the matter; and every such petition shall have the same effect as a bill in equity, as well with respect to general proceedings as with respect to proceedings for redemption under Acts relating to ejectment for non-payment of rent, and in suits to foreclose mortgages, and to perpetuate the testimony of witnesses according to the rules and regulations now in force or in use, in respect to depositions taken in such suits, 15 V., c. 16, s. 2.

Applications to stay proceedings on petition, and for the institution of a suit in the ordinary way—costs security

If any person interested, or claiming to be interested, in the matter of any such petition, or whose rights may be injuriously affected by the order to be made on such petition, desire the relief sought in a suit to be prosecuted in the ordinary way, he may, at any time, apply to the court, upon motion in a summary way, for an order directing that the matter of such petition or any part thereof be not further proceeded with under this Act, or that a suit with respect thereto may be instituted or proceeded with in the ordinary way; and thereupon the court shall make such order as is just; but the costs of all parties to be occasioned by any such application, shall (except so far as the court otherwise specially directs) be paid and borne by the person applying, and the court may, by any such order, require such security as it thinks fit to be given by the applicant for answering the additional costs, if any, to be occasioned by reason of such suit or other proceeding being instituted— 15 V,, c. 16, s. 3.

Verification by affidavit

Every petition shall be verified by affidavit annexed thereto or subscribed at the foot thereof in the form, or to the effect in Schedule— 15 V., c. 16, s. 4.

Interrogatories to be answered

Upon presenting such petition, the petitioner may annex to his petition interogatories to be answered by the respondents, or such of them as be requires to answer the same, or he may, with leave of the court after mentioned, file such interrogatories at any later stage of the proceedings —15 V., c. 16, s. 5.

Respondents enterrogatories to petitioners

The respondents may annex to their affidavits in answer, or may otherwise file interrogatories to be answered by the petitioners or any of them, touching the matters alleged in such affidavit or petition, and that whether they file a cross-petition or not, or they may file interrogatories at a later stage, 15 V., c. 16, s. 6.

When leave of the court required to file interrogatories

Except as may be otherwise provided by general orders, no such interogatories shall in either of the cases last mentioned be filed without leave of the court first obtained upon motion or petition, supported by affidavit, and which may be made exparte or otherwise as the court may direct— 15 V., c. 16, s. 7.

Answers to enterrogatories, in forcing same objections to answering.

Until, and except so far as shall be otherwise provided by any rule or order the practice as to answering and enforcing an answer to such interrogatories, shall be the same as upon a bill or cross-bill filed, except that the answer shall be taken in the same way as an affidavit. The person required to answer any interrogaties shall, on being served with a copy, be subject to the same obligation as to answering, and the court may exercise the same powers for enforcing such answer, and the production of documents therein referred to, as if a bill or cross-bill had been filed against such person, and he had been served with subpœna to answer the same, and had appeared thereto, or an appearance had been entered for him under 6 V., c.56, s. 1, (sup). Every such person shall be entitled to the benefit of the same, or the like objection to answering any such interrogatories as he might have insisted on, by way of plea or demurrer, in a suit instituted in the ordinary way— 15 V. c. 16, s. 8.

Every petition shall be entitled "Cause petition under the Court of Chancery Regulation Act, 1851," and shall be heard as causes are now heard, and every such petition, and all affidavits and interrogatories and answers to interrogatories in the matter of any such petition shall be filed in the office of the Registrar, as bills and answers are now filed, and such petitions, affidavits, and answers shall be bound up in books, as bills and pleadings are now entered, subject to such regulations and orders as the court shall make 15 V., c. 16, s. 9.

Title of petition &c., filing proceedings

Any person (the direction of the Master in the case of persons under disability, as after directed, being first obtained) may present a petition to the court, stating any documents, facts, or circumstances relating to any matter falling within the jurisdiction of the court by way of special case, and praying for the opinion of the court thereon, and the court shall give judgment on such petition, which shall bind all such persons as the court shall direct, and, in default of direction, all the persons who presented it, and have the same effect as a declaration made by decree in a suit to which they were parties, and shall be subject to rehearing and appeal as other petitions under this act, and where the opinion of the Court is desired in any matter in which any infant, idiot, lunatic or married woman is interested, the master in rotation shall direct the presenting of the petition by way of special case on behalf of such infant &c., which direction shall be conclusive 15 Vic. c. 16 s. 10.

Petitions by way of special case

Every such special case shall concisely state such facts and documents, as may be necessary to enable the Court to decide the question raised, and at the hearing, the Court and parties may refer to the whole contents of such documents, and the Court shall be at liberty to draw from the facts and documents stated, any inference the Court might have drawn therefrom if proved in a cause, 15 Vic. c. 16, s. 11.

The Court may, in any suit or in any matter pending or being heard before it, or in any examination or investigation before a master in ordinary, direct the whole or any part of the evidence, whether given by the parties or any other person, to be taken either viva voce on oath before the Court or master, or upon affidavit, instead of upon interrogatories or in addition to interrogatories, or may direct further express and specific interrogatories, to be answered by any petitioner, respondent, or witness, or in addition to an examination upon interrogatories, and the Court shall exercise all the powers for enforcing the attendance of any witness in whatever part of the island he may reside, to be examined before the Court or masters in any such matters, as it might exercise for enforcing attendance to be examined upon interrogatories according to the ordinary practice 15 Vic. c. 16 s. 12.

Evidence how to be taken

In taking accounts for the administration of the estate of any deceased person, debts may be proved before the Master by the executor or administrator. If any creditor, after notice of such proof having been made, attempt to establish any larger amount, the same shall be at the peril of any costs which may be awarded against him by the master, 15 V., c. 16, s. 13.

Executors may prove debts, costs of attempts to establish a larger amount

Service of notice of any petition, shall, until and except as may be otherwise provided by general order, be subject to the same regulations as apply to the service of a subpœna or letter missive in any suit, and the court shall have all the same powers with respect to ordering the service of notice of any such petition out of the jurisdiction of the court, or otherwise, as under any Act, or by the constitution of the court, it has, or may exercise with respect to the service of a subpœna or letter missive in a suit instituted by way of bill or information, but after such service all other services with respect to any matter pending under such petition or consequent thereon shall be made upon such persons and in such manner as the court shall direct, and with respect to   s who have absconded or cannot be found, shall be sufficiently made by such advertisement or publications as the court may direct; and every such service, advertisement, or publications, so directed by the master shall be valid and conclusive, to the same extent, and in the same manner, and upon, and against the same parties or persons as the service according to the practice of the court of any subpœna letter missive, or petition in equity would have been, 15 V., c. 16, s. 14.

Service of notice of proceedings

See 6 V. c. 56

By advertisement

The Court may direct the consolidation, or make other order for c on together of any two or more proceedings relating to, or connecti the same trust or estate, whenever such order appears expedient c. 16, s. 15.

Q

Proceedings on transmission of interest

If any transmission take place by death, marriage, or otherwise, of the interest of any party to any proceeding, whether by bill or information in the ordinary course, or under this Act, any party interested may bring before the court the person to whom the interest has been transmitted either by a petition or suggestion at the foot of the original bill, information, or petition, and notice to such person, and service of such notice being made, he shall, from the time of service, become a party to such proceeding, and be bound, in all respects, in the same manner as if an order for revivor or a supplemental decree had been made, without the necessity for any order of revivor or supplemental decree. If the   served be under disability,

Persons under disability

the matter shall be specially brought before the court by affidavit, and the court shall thereupon make such order as is just, 15 V., c. 16, s. 16.

General orders

Receivers

The Vice Chancellor, with the consent of the Chancellor may, from time to time, make and alter, and annul general orders for carrying the purposes of this Act into effect, and regulating the practice thereunder, and the duties and powers of receivers, and the allowance to be made to them for ensuring the better and more efficient management of estates under the control of the court, 15 V., c. 16, s. 17.

To be laid before the Council and Assembly

Which shall be laid before the Council and Assembly immediately after the making and issuing thereof, if then sitting, if not within five days after the next meeting, 15 V., c. 16, s. 18.

Pending suits

In any suit or information now pending, on the application of parties, or either of them, plaintiffs or defendants in the cause, upon motion or petition with due service, the Vice Chancellor may extend the provisions of this Act, so far as may be applicable to proceedings in such manner as may be provided by general orders, 15 V., c. 16, s. 19.

SHORT TITLE.—The Court of Chancery Regulation Act, 1851—15 V., c. 16, s. 20.

Interpretation

"Person" shall include Corporation, and the Attorney-General, in the case of Charities, or of information at the suit of the Crown, 15 V., c. 16, s. 21

SCHEDULE.

In the matter of the petition of—

Affidavit in verification of cause petition, s. 4

I, A. B., the petitioner in the above written (or annexed as the case may be) petition, make oath, and say that so much of the above written (or annexed as the case may be) petition, as relates to my own acts and deeds, is true, and so much thereof as relates to the acts and deeds of any other person, I believe to be true.

Sworn, &c.

Conveyances on mortgages by infants of lands charged with debts or legacies by order of court
See with reference to the necessity of conveyances 28, V., c. 36, s. 14

In suits for the payment of any debts of any person deceased, to which their heirs or devisees may be subject or liable, or of any legacies bequeathed in any will, and thereby charged upon, or made payable out of any real estate, where the court decrees the estates liable to such debts or legacies, or any of them to be sold, or any of such charges to be raised by mortgage of any such estates, and by reason of the infancy of any such heir or devisee, an immediate conveyance thereof, or charge thereon, cannot, as the law at present stands, be compelled, the court may direct, and if necessary compel such infants to convey or charge the estates so to be sold or mortgaged by proper assurances to the purchasers or mortgagees as the court shall direct, and every such infant shall make such conveyance or mortgage accordingly and the assurance shall be as valid and effectual as if the person were at the time of executing, 21, 18 V., c. 58, s. 2.

Conveyances, &c of devised lands in settlement, charged with debts or legacies under decree

Where lands are devised in settlement by persons whose estates are liable to the payment of their debts or legacies, whereby such devise is vested in any person for life or other limited interest with any remainder, limitation, or gift, over which may not be vested, or may be vested in some person from whom a conveyance or other assurance cannot be obtained, or by way of executory devise, and a decree is made for the sale thereof, or for raising a sum of money by mortgage thereon, for the payment of such debts or legacies, or any of them the court may direct any such tenant for life, or other person having a limited interest, or the first executory devisee thereof, to convey, release, mortgage, charge, assign, surrender, or otherwise assure the fee simple, or other the whole interests so to be sold, or charged to the purchasers or mortgagees as the court thinks proper, and every such conveyance, &c., shall be as effectual as if the person who made the same were seized of the fee simple or other whole estate, 18 V. c. 58, s. 3.

When any sale or mortgage is made in pursuance of this act the surplus if any of the monies raised after answering the purposes for which they were raised. and after defraying all reasonable costs and expenses, shall be considered in all respects of the same nature, and descend or devolve in the same manner as the estate or the lands so sold or mortgaged, shall belong to the same persons, be subject to the same limitations and provisions, and be applicable to the same purposes as such estate or such lands would have belonged, and been subject and applicable to, in case no sale, &c., had been made, 18 V. c, 58, s. 4. *Surplus monies & lands, devolution of*

Where any infant directed to execute any conveyance, &c., is of tender years, and unable to execute the same, the court, on due evidence of such fact may direct the Registrar, or in his absence any other person the court thinks proper to appoint in the place of the infant, to execute the same, and the assurance shall be as effectual as if the infant had executed it, 18 V c. 58, s. 5. *Infants of tender years.*

All monies part of the funds of any suit or proceeding in or appropriable by the court shall be paid by the party liable into the Public Treasury, to the "Chancery Fund Account," to the credit of the particular suit or proceeding, subject to the orders of the court, 27 V. S. 2, c. 3, s. 1. *Chancery fund account*

No person shall pay or advance to any master or officer, nor they receive from any person on account of fees or costs, any money, part of the funds, except under an order from the court for the purpose, but the same shall be paid directly into the Treasury by the person to pay, 27 V. S. 2, c. 3, s. 2. *No payment to master or officer.*

The court may, in such way as they think fit, obtain the assistance of accountants, engineers, surveyors, actuaries, and other scientific persons, the better to enable it to determine any matter at issue, in any cause or proceeding, and act upon their evidence or certificate, 27 V. S. 2, c. 3, s. 3. *Accountants, engineers, &c.*

Their allowances in lieu of fees shall be regulated by the taxing master, subject to an appeal to the court, whose decision shall be final, and shall be taxed as costs in the cause, 27 V. S. 2, c 3, s. 4.

Where the matter in dispute or corpus of the estate does not exceed in value £200, the court may order costs to be taxed at the rate of one moiety of those allowed to masters and solicitors, 27 V. S. 2, c. 3. s. 5 *Costs, property not exceeding £200, See 28 V. c. 36, sec. 3.*

For simplifying and cheapening the procedure in Chancery, petitions of course and orders thereon are abolished, and the practice assimilated to that at common law, by filing in all such cases, side bar rules, with the Registrar, embodying the terms of such orders, as on petitions of course would have been entered up, 28 V. c. 36, s. 1. *Side bar rules, substituted for petitions of course.*

Which shall be engrossed on the size of paper prescribed by the rules of the court for interlocutory proceedings, and the Registrar, if the rule be in form, shall subscribe his name thereto in affirmance, and it shall be filed and operate as an order in terms of the rule, 28 V. c. 36, s. 2. *To be engrossed on interlocutory proceedings paper. Signed by the Registrar and filed, & operate as an order.*

Where the value of the subject matter of a suit is below the amounts under stated there shall be charged by Attorneys, Counsel, masters, and others deriving fees therefrom, the proportion of costs specified in the undermentioned scale, viz. :— *Scales of fees in respect of the value of the subject matter of suit.*

Where of or below the limit of—

£50—one fourth of the fees now payable, and causes in this class shall be styled as of the fourth class.

£100—one third of the fees now payable, and causes in this class shall be styled as of the third class.

£150—one half the fees now payable, and causes to be styled as of the second class.

Causes above that value shall rank as of the first class, and entitled to the full scale of charges, 28 V. c. 36, s. 3.

The stamps on process within the scale shall also be abated proportionably in the above ratio with regard to fees, 28 V. c. 36 s. 4. *Abatement on stamps.*

If a suit instituted in any particular class is found at any stage to appertain to a higher class, the same shall not be affected, but the parties (unless the court order the same to be borne exclusively, or in certain proportions by parties in default) shall, on demand of the Registrar, make up the difference of stamps in respect of all papers and proceedings filed or taken by them in the cause as after mentioned, 28 V. c. 36, s. 5. *Provision in respect of additional stamps on transfer of a suit to a higher class.*

To be impressed on a satisfaction piece to be entered up.
The additional stamps to be exacted shall be impressed on a satisfaction piece to be signed and entered up by the Registrar in the cause, stating the transfer of the suit from one class to a higher one, and the sum payable in respect thereof, and the amount of stamps impressed on the satisfaction piece, 28 V. c. 36, s. 6.

The additional stamps shall be allowed to the parties on taxation, 28 V. c. 36, s. 7.

Surplusage. enforcement of brevity. Costs.
Either party to a suit may, by motion, compel the opposite party to expunge all unnecessary surplusage or impertinencies, and if the charge be established, the court shall refer it to the Registrar to strike out unnecessary allegations, and in order to enforce brevity in the proceedings, the Registrar, on the taxation of costs, shall have due regard to the rules against prolixity, and disallow all charges incurred by their violation, 28 V. c. 36, s. 13.

Authenticated copy of order of confirmation of sale to divest the estates of parti e s bound, and vest them in the purchaser.
On a decree for sale of lands, an authenticated copy of the order of confirmation of the sale, under the seal of the court, and stamped with the adva- lerem duty, as on a conveyance, shall be sufficient to divest the estate of all parties to the suit within the jurisdiction, and bound by the decree, and to vest the same in the purchaser, according to the terms and limitations to be embodied in the order of confirmation of sale, 28 V. c. 36, s 14.

When a Justice may discharge the ministerial functions of a master.
In parishes where there is not to be found any master to discharge the ministerial functions of such office, the same may be discharged by any Jus- tice of the Peace, 28 V. c. 36, s. 12.

Courts of Common Pleas and Quarter Sessions.

Abolition of Courts and their jurisdiction transferred to Supreme and Circuit Courts.
The offices of Chairman of Quarter Sessions, and Chief Judge, and the judicial functions of the Assistant Judges of the Courts of Common Pleas abolished, and the judicial powers, duties, and authorities of the Chairmen and Judges of such Courts determined, and their jurisdictions, powers, and rights, transferred to the Supreme and Circuit Courts, 19 V. c. 10, s. 17.

Court of Ordinary.

Chief Justice surrogate.
The Chief Justice as Vice Chancellor shall sit with the Ordinary of this island as surrogate thereof whenever required, 19 V. c. 10, s. 10.

Assistant Judge when to act.
In case of his illness or absence, the Governor may appoint any Assistant Judge to discharge the duties of surrogate, 19 V. c. 10, s. 14.

Rules and orders.
The Ordinary may make and enforce rules and orders in the court for regulating the mode of proceeding, and the practice to be observed in all business to be done in the court, 6 V, c. 55, s. 1.

Attachment.
And may enforce by attachment, under his hand and seal, to be directed to the Provost Marshal. all orders and decrees he shall establish or declare in all causes or proceedings in the Court of Ordinary, 6 V. c. 55, s. 2.

Costs.
And may decree and direct the payment of costs by the party who, in his opinion, ought to bear the same, and the order for payment of such costs (which are to be taxed by the Clerk of the Court of Ordinary) shall be enforced by attachment under the hand and seal of the Ordinary as before directed, 6 V. c. 55, s. 3.

Commissions to examine witnesses abroad.
The court may order commissions to issue for the examination of wit- nesses on oath, at places out of this island, by interrogatories or otherwise, and, by the same or subsequent orders, give such directions, touching the time, place and manner of such examination, and all other matters and cir- cumstances connected therewith as may appear reasonable, 6. V. c. 55, s. 5.

Proceedings to impeach the validity of wills.
In case of any will or testamentary paper, propounded for probate in solemn form, or of any will or testamentary paper admitted to probate in common form, any person, having an interest in the estate forming the sub- ject of such will, or asserting the right of the Crown by escheat, by sanction of the Attorney General, may, by petition on oath, supported by such affida- vits as he may be liable to obtain, impeach the will or testamentary paper so propounded for probate either in solemn or in common form, or so proved in common form; and if in the opinion of the court, and upon the petition and the affidavits in support, and in answer to the application there does not ap- pear sufficient and satisfactory evidence to substantiate and uphold the exe- cution and publication of the testamentary paper. and the court deem fit, they may proceed in either of the modes after prescribed, 18 V. c. 34, s. 1.

The court may, in the case of any contested will or administration, proceed to determine the questions in dispute or in issue upon affidavits, or under a commission or commissions upon interrogatories and depositions, and examinations in writing, and upon oath before a commissioner or commissioners appointed by the court and named in the commission, according to the rules of the court, or the court may examine viva voce and on oath before the court, the parties, and all witnesses or such of them as it deems necessary or directs, and shall have power, from time to time, to issue summonses for, and to enforce the attendance of all parties or witnesses before the court, and any commissioner shall have the like powers of issuing summonses for enforcing the attendance of the parties and witnesses, and a disobedience to any summons shall involve the penalties of a contempt of court; but every witness before he is liable to be proceeded against for a contempt shall have had his necessary expences paid or tendered, 18 V., c. 34, s. 2.

Proceedings by affidavits. Examinations under commission, or by viva voce. Examination of parties and witnesses. Enforcing attendance.

Instead of disposing of the questions before it, the court may, in its discretion, direct an issue to a court of common law to try and determine the fact of the due execution or otherwise of any testamentary paper in question, and, together with an attested copy of the order directing such issue, the clerk of the court shall annex and transmit the testamentary paper in issue to the clerk of the court of common law to which the issue is directed, to be kept among the records of his office for inspection and reference by the parties and their witnesses, and for exhibition and production to and before such court at the trial of the issue, 18 V., c. 34, s. 3.

Direction of an issue to a court of common law, and transmission of order and testamentary paper in dispute

The issue so directed shall be the only record necessary before the court of law, and if directed to the Supreme Court, the issue shall indicate the County (Circuit Court, 19 V. c. 10) in which the same shall be tried, and whether by a special or a common jury, and the filing thereof with the Clerk of the Court in vacation shall be sufficient to entitle the parties to proceed to trial thereon, as if it had been filed in the preceding term of the court, 18 V. c. 34, s. 4

Such issue to be the only record & indicate the county for trial, and whether by special or common jury

Together with the verdict of the jury and the record of the issue directed, there shall be returned to the Court of Ordinary the notes of the evidence taken by the judge presiding at the trial, with his opinion as to the propriety or otherwise of the verdict, and unless any points are reserved for argument in the court of common law before the judges of that court, such return shall be made forthwith after trial, 18 V., c. 34, s. 5.

Return to the Court of Ordinary if no points reserved on trial

The court of common law, where any point has been reserved, may award a new trial of the issue as in other cases within the jurisdiction of courts of common law, and upon the final determination of the issue, the evidence and proceedings at all the trials which have been had shall be certified and returned into the Court of Ordinary, 18 V., c. 34, s. 6.

Award of new trial by common law court proceedings at all trials to be returned to the Court of Ordinary

All the powers and authorities exercisable by the courts of common law in cases within their ordinary jurisdiction may be exercised in the matters so referred to them, 18 V., c. 34, s. 7.

Notice of trial may be served by either of the parties to the issue upon the other, within the time and according to the rules of the court of law in which the issue is depending, 18 V., c. 34, s. 8.

Notice of trial

Upon the return being made to the Court of Ordinary, final judgment may be awarded by such court, and the costs of all proceedings in the suit, and of the issues shall be in its discretion, 18 V., c. 34, s. 9.

Final judgment

The frame of the issue and of the return may be in the form or to the effect following :—

Forms

In the Court of Ordinary of Jamaica,
}
A. vs. B.

In a cause Testamentary

Between I A, of , claiming as ("relator on behalf of the Crown, and with the sanction of Her Majesty's Attorney-General" "as one of the next of kin of, &c." "as the heir-at-law of &c." or as the case may be) the promovent

and

C. B. of , the Executor named in the paper writing hereunto annexed, purporting to be the last will of L. M., late of &c., deceased (as the case may be) the respondents

On motion and prayer of Mr. of Counsel with the (respondent.)

It is ordered that an issue be directed (to the Supreme Court of Judicature,) and it is hereby accordingly directed to the said court to try and determine by a (common or special jury, as the case may be, of the County of
Precinct or pa
rish, 19 V. c. 10
[whether the paper writing hereunto annexed, marked A,] or if more than one describing and distinguishing them) was in due form of law, executed and published by the said deceased L M as, and for his last will and testament, and the question (or "questions") for the opinion of the court and jury is (or "are")

First whether &c.
Second whether &c.

True copy,

W. G. S.
Clerk of the Court of Ordinary, L. S.

FORM OF THE RETURN THERETO.

In the Supreme Court   A. vs. B. in a cause testamentary between &c. (as in the issue directed.)

Pursuant to the issue directed from the Court of Ordinary of this island, to this Court, the same was on the   day of   18
tried before a common (or special) Jury of the   and upon such trial the following evidence was given and received:

Here set forth the notes in extenso of the Judge, trying the cause with all documentary evidence, other than the testamentary paper or papers in issue.

And upon that evidence, the Jury were thus charged by the presiding Judge   set forth the charge.

And upon that evidence, and upon that charge (if any, the following exceptions were tendered by the Counsel of the respondent or promovent, and upon the exceptions to his charge, the presiding Judge, directed the Jury that &c or refused to charge the Jury, as required in the exceptions) whereupon the Jury by their verdict found unanimously (or by a majority of nine to three, as the case may be,)

See new Title,
Jury

First—That &c.
Second—That &c.

And afterwards to wit; at a Supreme Court, held on the first Monday of   upon the points, so, as aforesaid reserved at the trial, (as the case may be) a motion for a new trial was made, and (after argument granted, refused or discharged as the case may be.)

(If a new trial was granted, proceed, as before, to set forth the proceedings thereon.)

And the said presiding Judge, doth report the verdict of the Jury to be a correct and proper verdict (or otherwise as the case may be.)

The foregoing is a true and correct return to the issue directed to the Supreme Court of Judicature of this island, by the Court of Ordinary of this island.

Given under my hand and seal of the said Supreme Court, this day of   Annoque Domini, 18

A.B. Clerk of the Supreme Court, 18 V. c. 34, s. 10.

As the 19. V. c. 10, has abolished the Courts of Common pleas, issues can now only be transmitted to the Supreme Court for trial at the Circuit Courts established by that act.

Court, Supreme.

The Judges of the Supreme Court shall have cognizance of all pleas, civil, criminal and mixed, as fully to all intents as the Courts of King's Bench, Common pleas and Exchequer in England have or ought to have, 33 C. 2, c. 23, s. 1. Jurisdiction

And shall have authority and Jurisdiction, as fully as the Court of Exchequer in England, to hold pleas on the Equity side thereof, in all matters touching Her Majesty's Revenue, imposed or to be imposed by any law of this island, 17 G. 3, c. 27.

The Judges shall be empowered to make, order and establish, all such rules and orders for the more orderly practicing and proceeding in the Court, as fully to all intents and purposes, as all or any of the Judges of the Courts of King's Bench, Common pleas, and Exchequer in England legally do, 33 C. 2, c. 23, s. 4. Rules and orders

And that no person shall be damnified by mistake of his lawyer, for matter of form only, the Judges shall, at all times on motion made in Court, order amendments, and shall not upon arrest of Judgment or writ of error, for matter of form only, reverse any Judgment whatsoever, 33 C. 2, c. 23, s. 5. Amendments, see 27 V. S. I, c. 14, s 11, 28 V c. 37, s. 2

All summonses shall be delivered to the party, or left at their dwelling, 14 days before the Court, by a sworn marshal, otherwise it shall be deemed no service and the defendant by it not bound to appear. and all replevins, Foreign Attachments at the Supreme Courts and arrests be served at any time as heretofore, 33 C. 2, c. 23, s. 10. Service of process

For the future all summonses, issuing out of the Supreme Court, against any persons in Port Royal, shall be delivered 14 days before each Court, as in other parishes, otherwise the same shall not be allowed sufficient service, 8 G. 2, c. 5, s. 16. Port Royal

Upon summons duly served, and defendant not appearing, Judgment shall go by default, provided the Provost Marshal, or his lawful deputy, shall appear in open Court, and there depose upon oath that the party against whom Judgment shall go by default, has been legally summoned, fourteen days before the court, 33 C. 2, c. 23, s. 7. Of summons to be sworn to. Default For service in vacation. See 8 V. c. 28, s. 20

Any Judge may hold a court to call over the list and establish the service of actions, and to transact that particular business and. no other, 19 V. c. 31, s. 1. Establishing service.

All actions that may by law be brought in the Supreme Court shall be brought and filed there, and the declaration shall have the name of the county in which the cause of action arises endorsed on the back of the declaration, and wrote also in the margin, and such process service and proceedings be had and held upon such actions as now are, until judgment obtained by demurrer, default, nil dicit non sum informatus, or otherwise, or until issue is joined on the same, 31 G. 2, c. 4, s. 5. Venue & change of venue.

The Judges may, upon proper cause shewn either by the plaintiff or defendant, direct the trial of the cause in which the application is made to be had in any other county than that in which the venue is laid, 34 V. c. 65, s. 25. Change of.

In all actions, for the recovery of money secured by any bond, bill, note, or other negotiable security, the plaintiff may lay the venue in any county, although the cause of action arose in another, 8 V. c. 28, s. 8. Negotiable securities.

The venue in all actions shall be transitory, and shall be laid in the margin of each declaration, and of each copy thereof, and be endorsed thereon respectively, and the 31st G. 2, c. 4, and all other acts, or parts of acts inconsistent herewith, as to the places of trial of all causes of action, whether local or transitory are repealed, provided that before trial the Supreme Court shall on sufficient cause shewn by a defendant, and after trial on sufficient cause shewn by either plaintiff or defendant, bring back or change the venue in any action, 22 V. c. 39, s. 4. Transitory in all actions.

Bringing back or change of venue.

In all cases of criminal prosecutions, the Judges may, on application either on behalf of the crown or of the accused, and on good cause shewn, change the venue and remove trial from any one [Circuit] Court to another, 22 V, c. 39, s. 3. In criminal prosecutions.

All informations on actions, for the breach or violation of any act of Parliament or of this island relating to trade and navigation, or for laying any duties and customs on the importation of any goods, wares, and merchandize, Informations liable in the Supreme Court only.

and all informations for land under the "Quit Rent Act," and all escheats shall be tried in the Supreme Court only, 31 G. 2, c. 4, s. 13. *

Customs, duties, &c.

All suits or proceedings at the suit of the crown for the recovery of any duty or penalty, or the enforcement of any forfeiture under any act relating to the customs, may be sued for in any court of law, or equity, or in the Court of Vice Admiralty, in the name of the Attorney General or of some officer of Customs, (see Customs) 17 V. c. 2, s. 28.

Frauds, &c., i n Assizes.

In cases of Judgment, in civil suits, in the Assizes, the Supreme Court shall have cognizance of all complaints of fraud, surprise, or irregularity, or for any other matter for which complaint may be made in the Supreme Court, in cases of judgment given in the Supreme Court itself, in like manner as in cases of judgment given in the Supreme Court, such complaints not having come under previous discussion or decision in the Assize Courts of Surry or Cornwall, 44 G. 3, c. 22, s. 1.

Judge in Chambers

One of the Judges during the sitting of the court shall attend in the office of the Clerk of the Court, or at some other convenient place in the town of St Jago de la Vega, daily, or as there shall be occasion, to dispose of all motions of course, and such other matters as are disposed of by the Judges of the Queen's Bench in England in Chambers, 3 V. c. 65, s. 12.

Motions for new trials, or to set aside nonsuit.

All motions for new trials, or for liberty to enter or set aside a nonsuit, shall be made before the Judges of the Supreme Court and not elsewhere, 3 V. c. 65, s. 21.

3 days notice in causes t r i e d i n Kingston Courts in January, 28 V. c. 33 s 5. See C i r cuit Courts.

Such motions shall be made within the first 4 days of the sitting of the Supreme Court next after the trial of the cause in which the motion is made, and not afterwards, and no notice of such motion shall be necessary in the Assizes, provided 14 days notice of such application is given to the opposite party, previous to the Supreme Court, next after the trial, 3 V. c. 65, s. 22.

Certiorari

Writs of Certiorari shall be moved for before and made returnable into the Supreme Court, and not elsewhere, 3 V. c. 65, s. 23.

Issue in vacation Rules to be made for enforcing.

The Judges may make and establish, and alter, amend and rescind rules for the return forthwith, after service, by the Provost Marshal and his deputies, of the service of actions, and for establishing such services before a Judge in vacation, and requiring the entering of appearances, and the pleading thereto by the defendants, and for enforcing the making up of the issue, and authorizing amendments, from time to time, in the proceedings, at periods when the Court is not sitting. Before such rules become effectual they shall be solemnly promulgated in open Court, in the Supreme Court in Banco, and the period at which they are to come into operation shall be stated, and the Clerk of the Supreme Court shall cause all rules from time to time made, to be fairly entered at length in the order book of the Court, as of the day on which they were pronounced, and to be published in the several newspapers in which the official and public advertisements are required to be inserted once at least in each week, for 4 consecutive weeks thereafter, 8 V. c. 28, s. 20.

And laid before Legislature See now, 19 V. c. 10, s. 20.

All rules made under this act shall be laid before the Council and Assembly immediately after the making and issuing if then sitting, if not, 5 days after their next meeting, and be as binding as if enacted, unless either body resolve they ought not to continue in force, in which case the part included in the resolution shall cease to be binding. If not laid before the Council and Assembly within the time limited they shall, after its expiration, be void, 8. V. c. 28, s. 24.

How constituted

The Supreme Court shall be constituted of the Chief Justice and any one or more of the [3] Assistant Judges to be appointed as after mentioned (s. 13) but no Judge shall sit in review of any decision of his own, and if the Chief Justice shall, owing to ill-health or any other unavoidable cause, be absent, the business of the Court shall be carried on by any two or more remaining Judges, 19 V. c. 10, s. 6.

---

* As there is now no Jury process returnable in the Supreme Court, this clause as relates to trials of any issue of fact must be necessarily modified.

The Sessions shall be holden in the Court House, at St. Jago de la Vega, 3 times a year, on the 1st Monday in February, June and October, with all the powers, authority and jurisdiction provided by this act, together with all such other powers, authority and jurisdiction as are now vested in the Court. Except so far as its constitution power and jurisdiction are altered by this act, the Supreme Court shall continue to exercise all powers &c., now vested in or exercised by the Court, 19 V. c. 10, s. 7.

Sessions.—Commencement-powers

Each Session shall be continued from day to day until and during the 2d Saturday after the commencement. No Sessions shall be deemed null, or be determined by reason of the attendance of only one Judge either on the first day or any other day of the period appointed for the sitting, but the Court shall thereupon be lawfully and effectually constituted for the purpose of establishing the service of actions and process, and disposing of motions of course, and moving for orders nisi, and for the argument and disposal of other matters which by consent may be taken before a single Judge, and the Court shall be adjourned from one day to any other day, during such period, by proclamation in open Court, 19 V. c. 10, s. 8.

Duration

The Judges or any three of them may, within 3 months after their appointment, make and frame general rules and regulations for facilitating the proceedings and business of the Supreme and [Circuit] Courts respectively, which shall be of force in the Courts unless altered and amended by the Legislature at its next Session, and shall at such next Session be laid before the Legislature by the Executive Committee, 19 V. c. 10, s. 20.

General rules

The Judges shall from time to time, during the sitting of the Court, rescind, alter, vary or amend the rules and regulations framed under 19 V. c. 10, and laid before the Legislature, or make other rules for facilitating the proceedings of the Supreme and other Courts established by that act, 20 V. c. 12.

Power to vary rules

The entire original jurisdiction in or over, and for entertaining civil actions, heretofore inherent in and exercised by the Supreme Court and the several Courts of common pleas, whether concurrently or exclusively, shall be vested in the Supreme Court alone. In the commencement of an action, it shall not be necessary for the Clerk of the Court to certify any copy declaration to be served on the defendant, it shall be certified by the Attorney or plaintiff who issues the same, and left with the Deputy Marshal of the parish in which it is to be served, 19 V. c. 10, s. 24.

Jurisdiction over actions

Copies, declarations for service

The powers and authorities, heretofore vested in the Courts of Quarter Sessions, by any law either of this island or of England, over the Clerks of the Peace, shall vest in and be exercised by the Judges in the Supreme Court, in respect of their suspension or discharge from office, 19 V. c. 10, s. 32.

Powers over Clerks of the Peace

In actions by default, the damages of which are susceptible of computation, and do not result from injuries to the person or reputation of the plaintiff, it shall not be necessary for him to assess his damages before a Jury, but if he has endorsed on his action, and on the copy for service on the defendant a specification and the particulars of his debt or demand, or of the damages or compensation claimed by him, and therein notify his intention to assess, the damages before the Clerk of the Supreme Court, he shall be at liberty to produce the affidavit of himself, or of his witnesses, or of both, in proof of his debt or claim to damages, and the Clerk of the Court, or in case of disagreement or doubt, any Judge in Chambers, on reference by the plaintiff, may adjudge and award such damages within the limits of the claim endorsed on the action as to the Clerk or Judge seems meet, but in case of doubt as to the amount to be awarded on such affidavit, the Judge shall refer the assessment to a Jury of the venue, 19 V. c. 10, s. 35.

Assessments of damages in certain actions by default

By Clerk of Supreme Court

Judge in chambers

Reference to a Jury

Court, Supreme, Pleadings.

All statements in pleading shall be made briefly and concisely, and statements which need not be proved, such as time, quantity, quality and value, where immaterial, the statement of losing and finding, and bailment in actions for goods or their value, the statement of acts of trespass having been committed with force and arms, and against the Peace of Our Lady the Queen, of promises which need not be proved, as in indebitatus counts, and mutual promises to perform agreements, and all statements of a like kind shall be omitted, and no costs whatsoever shall be allowed for any statement by this act rendered unnecessary, 28 V. c. 37, s. 1,

Statements in pleadings which need not be proved, to be omitted

And no costs allowed therefore

R

Objection by way of demurrer Judgment to be given according to the very right

Either party may object by demurrer to the pleading of the opposite party, on the ground that it does not set forth sufficient ground of action, defence or reply, as the case may be, and where issue is joined on the demurrer, the Court shall proceed and give Judgment according as the very right of the cause and matter in law appears to them without regarding any imperfection, omission, defection or lack of form, and no Judgment shall be arrested, stayed or reversed for any such imperfection &c., 28 V. c. 37, s. 2.

And not arrested for lack of form

Objections by special demurrer no longer available

No pleading shall be deemed insufficient for any defect which could heretofore only be objected to by special demurrer, 28 V. c. 37, s. 3.

Pleadings framed to embarrass, may be struck out or amended Costs

If any pleading be so framed as to prejudice, embarrass or delay the fair trial of the action, the opposite party may apply to the Court or a Judge, to strike out or amend it, and the Court or a Judge, shall make such order respecting the same and the costs of the application, as they see fit, 28 V c. 37, s. 4.

Profert oyer

It shall not be necessary to make profert of any deed or other document mentioned or relied on in any pleading, and if made, it shall not entitle the opposite party to crave oyer, or set it out upon oyer, 28 V. c. 37, s. 5.

Setting out documents in pleadings.

A party pleading in answer to any pleading in which any document is mentioned or referred to, may set out the whole or such part as is material, and the matter so set out shall be deemed part of the pleading in which it is set out, 28 V, c. 37, s 6.

Performance of conditions precedent

The plaintiff or defendant may aver performance of conditions precedent generally, and the opposite party shall not deny the averment generally but shall specify in his pleading, the condition or conditions precedent, the performance of which he intends to contest, 28 V. c. 37, s. 7.

Commencement and conclusion of declarations not in ejectment

Every declaration other than in ejectment, shall commence as follows, or to the like effect :

In the Supreme Court　　　　　　Term 18　　　, Venue A.B.
　　by E.F. his attorney, (or in person as the case may be) sues C.D. for
　　(here state cause of action)
and shall conclude as follows, or to the like effect :

And the plaintiff claims　　　　　　pounds (or if the action is brought to
　　recover specific goods, the plaintiff claims a return of the said
　　goods, or their value and　　　　　　pounds for their detention) 28 V.
　　c. 37, s. 8.

Commencement of declaration after plea of nonjoinder

Where after a plea in abatement of the nonjoinder of another person, as defendant, the plaintiff, without having proceeded to trial on an issue thereon commences another action against the defendants, in the action in which the plea in abatement was pleaded and the persons named in such plea as joint contractois, or amends by adding the omitted defendants, the commencement of the declaration, after stating the Court and term, shall be in the following form, or to the like effect :

Venue A.B. by E.F. his attorney (or in his own proper person &c.)
　　sues C.D. and G.H. which said C.D. has heretofore pleaded in abatement, the nonjoinder of the said G.H. for &c. 28 V. c. 37, s. 9.

Libel or slander

In actions for libel and slander, the plaintiff shall be at liberty to aver the words or matter complained of were used in a defamatory sense, without any prefatory averment to shew how they were in such sense, and the averment shall be put in issue by the denial of the alleged libel or slander, and where the words or matter set forth, with or without the alleged meaning, shew a cause of action, the declaration shall be sufficient 28 V. c. 37, s. 10.

Title and date of pleadings after declaration

Every pleading subsequent to the declaration, shall be entitled in the Court, and of the day of the month, and year when pleaded, and shall bear no other time or date, 28 V. c. 37, s. 11.

Express color abolished

Express color shall no longer be necessary in any pleading, 28 V. c. 37, s. 12.

Also special traverses

Nor special traverses, 28 V. c. 37, s. 13.

Allegation of actionem non, precludi non &c., or prayer of judgment, unnecessary

In a plea or subsequent pleading, it shall not be necessary to use any allegation of actionem non or actionem ulterius non, or to the like effect, or any prayer of Judgment, nor in any replication or subsequent pleading, any allegation of precludi non, or to the like effect, or any prayer of Judgment, 28 V. c. 37, s. 14.

commencement of plea, avowry &c.

No formal defence shall be required in a plea or avowry, or cognizance, and it shall commence as follows, or to the like effect :

The defendant by   his Attorney (or in person, or as the case may be) says that (here state first defence.)

It shall not be necessary to state in a second or other plea or avowry or cognizance, that it is pleaded by leave of the Court or a Judge, or according to the form of the statute, or to that effect, but each shall be written in a separate paragraph, and numbered and commence as follows, or to the like effect : *2nd or other pleas &c*

And for a second (&c.) plea, the defendant says that (here state 2nd. &c.) defence,

or if pleaded to part only, then as follows, or to the like effect :

And for a second (&c.) plea to (stating to what it is pleaded) the defendant, says that &c. *Where pleaded in part*

And no formal conclusion shall be necessary to any plea, avowry, cognizance or subsequent pleading, 28 V. c. 37, s. 15. *Formal conclusions unnecessary*

Any defence arising after the commencement of any action, shall be pleaded according to the fact, without formal commencement or conclusion, and any plea which does not state whether the defence set up arose before or after action, shall be deemed to be a plea of matter arising before action, 28 V. c. 37, s. 16. *Plea of matter subsequent to action*

In cases where a plea puis darrein continuance has heretofore been pleadable in Banco, or at Circuit, the same defence may be pleaded with an allegation that the matter arose after the last pleading, and may, when necessary, be pleaded at the Circuit or Assize Court, but no such plea shall be allowed unless accompanied by an affidavit that the matter thereof, arose within 8 days next before the pleading of such plea, or unless the Court or a Judge otherwise order, 28 V. c. 37, s. 17. *Plea puis darrein continuance* *Affidavit to accompany plea*

When money is paid into Court, such payment shall be pleaded in all cases as near as may be in the following form, mutatis mutandis. *Payment into court* *See payment of money into court, 8 V. c. 28, s. 10. Justices, 13 V. c. 15, s. 10.*

The defendant by   his Attorney (or in person &c.) (if pleaded in part, say as to £   parcel of the money c'a med) brings into Court the sum of £   and says that the said sum is enough to satisfy the claim of the plaintiff in respect to the matter herein pleaded to, 28 V. c. 37, s. 18.

No rule or Judges order to pay money into Court shall be necessary except in the case of one or more of several defendants, but the money shall be paid to the proper officer, who shall give a receipt in the margin of the plea, and the sum shall be paid out to the plaintiff or to his Attorney, upon a written authority from the plaintiff on demand, 28 V. c. 37, s. 19. *No order to pay necessary except in the case of one or more of several defendants*

The plaintiff after delivery of the plea may reply, by accepting the sum so paid into court, in full satisfaction, and discharge of the cause of action in respect of which it has been paid in, and in that case may tax his costs, and in case of non payment, within 48 hours, may sign judgment for his costs so taxed, or he may reply that the sum paid into court, is not enough to satisfy his claim in respect of the matter to which the plea is pleaded, and if an issue thereon is found for the defendant he shall be entitled to judgment and his costs of suit, 28 V. c. 37, s. 20. *Proceedings by plaintiff after payment.*

Where the causes of action may be considered to partake of the character both of breaches of contract, and of wrongs, any plea which is good in substance shall not be objectionable on the ground of its treating the declaration either as framed for a breach of contract or for a wrong, 28 V. c. 37, s. 21. *Pleas to actions partaking of the character of breaches of contract and wrongs.*

All pleadings capable of being construed distributively shall be taken distributively, and if issue is taken thereon, and so much as is sufficient answer to part of the causes of action proved is found true by the jury, a verdict shall pass for the defendant in respect of so much of the causes as is answered, and for the plaintiff in respect of so much as is not so answered, 28 V. c. 37, s. 22. *Pleadings capable of being construed distributively.* *Verdict thereon*

A defendant may either traverse generally such of the facts in the declaration as might have been denied by one plea, or may select or traverse separately any material allegation in the declaration, although it might have been included in a general traverse, 28 V. c. 37, s. 23. *General or separate traverses, of facts in declaration.*

A plaintiff may traverse the whole of any plea or subsequent pleadings of the defendant, by a general denial or, admitting some part, deny all the rest, or deny any one or more allegations, 28 V. c. 37, s. 24. *In pleadings of defendant.*

A defendant may, in like manner, deny the whole or any part of a replication or subsequent pleading of the plaintiff, 28 V. c. 37, s. 25. *In subsequent pleadings of plaintiff.*

Joinder of is-
sue.

Either party may plead in answer to the plea or subsequent pleading of his adversary that he joins issue thereon, which joinder may be as follows, or to the like effect :—

> The plaintiff joins issue upon the defendant's first (&c. specifying what or what part) plea.
> The defendant joins issue upon the plaintiff's replication to the first (&c., specifying what) plea.

When plaintiff
may add a join-
der for defendant

Which form of joinder shall be deemed a denial of the substance of the plea, or other subsequent pleading, and an issue thereon, and where the plaintiff's pleading is in denial of the pleading of the defendant, or some part of it, he may add a joinder of issue for the defendant, 28 V. c. 37, s. 26.

Pleading and
demurring to-
gether by leave
affidavit.

Either party may by leave of the court or a Judge, plead and demur to the same pleading at the same time, upon an affidavit by the party, or his attorney, if required by the court or a Judge, to the effect that he is advised and believes he has just grounds to traverse the several matters proposed to be traversed by him, and that the several matters sought to be pleaded by way of confession and avoidance are respectively true in substance and in fact, and that he is further advised and believes that the objections raised by such demurrer are good and valid objections in law. The Court or Judge in their discretion shall direct which issue shall be first disposed of, 28 V. c. 37, s. 27.

Court &c. to or-
der, which issue
shall be first dis-
posed of.

Several pleas by
plaintiff or de-
fendant by leave
of court.

The plaintiff in any action may, by leave of the Court or a Judge, plead in answer to the plea or the subsequent pleading of the defendant, as many several matters as he thinks necessary to sustain his action, and the defendant may, by leave of the Court or Judge, plead in answer to the declaration or other subsequent pleading of the plaintiff, as many several matters as he thinks necessary for his defence, upon an affidavit of the party making the application, or his attorney, if required by the Court or Judge, to the effect that he is advised, and believes he has just ground to traverse the several matters proposed to be traversed by him, and that the several matters sought to be pleaded as aforesaid, by way of confession and avoidance are respectively true in substance and in fact. The costs of any issue either of fact or law shall follow the finding or judgment upon such issue, and be adjudged to the successful party, whatever may be the result of the other issues, 28 V. c. 37, s. 28.

Affidavit.

Costs of each
issue of fact or
law.

No rule neces-
sary to plead seve-
ral matters after
Judge's order.

No rule of court for leave to plead several matters shall be necessary where a Judge's order has been made for the same purpose, 28 V. c. 37, s. 29.

Objections to
pleading several
matters to be
heard before a
Judge.

Objections to the pleading of several pleas, replications, or subsequent pleadings, or several avowries or cognizances, on the ground that they are founded on the same ground of answer or defence, shall be heard upon summons before a Judge, 28 V. c. 37, s. 30.

New as sign-
ment.
Effect of

One new assignment only shall be pleaded to any number of pleas, to the same cause of action, and shall be consistent with, and confined by the particulars delivered in the action, if any, and shall state that the plaintiff proceeds for causes of action, different from all those which the pleas profess to justify, or for an excess over and above what all the defences set up in such pleas justify, or both, 28 V. c. 37, s. 31.

Pleas to new as-
signments.

No plea already pleaded to the declaration shall be pleaded to such new assignment, except a plea in denial, unless by leave of the Court, or a Judge, which shall only be granted upon satisfactory proof that the repetition of such plea is essential to a trial on the merits, 28 V. c. 37, s. 32.

Demurrer and
joinder

The form of a demurrer except in cases herein specifically provided for, shall be as follows or to the like effect :—

Statement of
ground in margin.
Setting aside.

The defendant by his attorney (or in person, &c.,) or plaintiff, says that the declaration (or plea, &c.,) is bad in substance ; and in the margin some substantial matter of law intended to be argued, shall be stated, and if delivered without such statement, or with a frivolous statement, it may be set aside by the Court or a Judge, and leave be given to sign judgment for want of a plea. The form of a joinder shall be as follows, or to the like effect :—

> The plaintiff (or defendant) says, that the declaration (or plea, &c.,) is good in substance, 28 V. c. 37, s. 33.

Where an amendment of any pleading is allowed, no rule or notice to plead shall be necessary, but the opposite party shall be bound to plead to the amended pleading, within the time specified in the original rule, or within 4 days after amendment, whichever last expires, unless otherwise ordered by the Court or Judge. In case the amended pleading has been pleaded to before amendment, and is not pleaded to de novo, within 2 days after amendment, or such other time as the Court or Judge allows, the pleadings originally pleaded shall stand, and be considered as pleaded in answer to the amended pleading, 28 V. c. 37, s. 34. *Time for pleading after amendment.*

Where already pleaded to, and not pleaded to de novo within two days or other time allowed, original pleadings to stand.

The forms in schedule shall be sufficient, and those and the like forms may be used with such modifications as may be necessary to meet the facts of the case, but it shall not be erroneous or irregular to depart from the letter of such forms so long as the substance is expressed without prolixity 28 V. c. 37, s. 35. *Forms or modifications.*

The signature of counsel shall not be necessary to any pleading, 28 V. c. 37, s. 36. *Counsels signature unnecessary*

This Act shall not affect the statute 8 and 9, Wm. 3 c. 11., for the better preventing frivolous and vexatious suits as to the assignment or suggestion of breaches, or as to judgment for a penalty as a security for damages in respect of further breaches, 28 V. c. 37, s. 37. *Not to affect suggestions of breaches or further breaches.*

No entry or continuance by way of imparlance, curia advisari vult vice-comes non misit breve, or otherwise, shall be made upon any record, postea, or entry of judgment, nor shall it be necessary to allege that the original record is transmitted to the court, and the assessment of costs by the Jury, and of nominal damages on actions of the nature of actions of debt shall not be necessary, but it shall be sufficient to enter the pleadings on the record, in their order according to date, and when necessary the award of a Jury in the terms following : Therefore, let a Jury come, &c., and concluding with the postea and judgment, 28 V. c. 37, s. 38. *Entries of judgment & Omissions*

What sufficient

Actions and proceedings pending at the commencement of the Act, may be carried on to judgment, and execution enforced according to the law and practise under which they were authorized and undertaken, and would continue to be regulated if this Act had not been passed, 28 V. c. 37, s. 39. *Pending actions unaffected.*

The provisions of all Acts not inconsistent with this, and applicable to the altered mode of proceeding shall remain in force, and be applied thereto, 28 V. c. 37, s. 40. *Acts not inconsistent to remain in force and be applied hereto.*

Nothing in this Act shall tend to prevent the same evidence being hereafter given under the general issue as might previously be given, 28 V. c. 37, s. 41. *Evidence may be given under the general issue as heretofore*

To come into operation 1st May, 1865, and to be cited as "The Common Law Pleading Act, 1865," 28 V. c. 37, s. 42. *Commencement and short title*

SCHEDULE.

Forms of Pleadings.—Statements of Causes of Action.

ON CONTRACTS.

1. Money payable by the defendant to the plaintiff, for (these words, "money payable, &c.," should precede money counts like 1 to 13, but need only be inserted in the first) goods bargained and sold by the plaintiff to the defendant. *Goods bargained and sold*

2. Work done, and materials provided by the plaintiff for the defendant at his request. *Work and materials*

3. Money lent by the plaintiff to the defendant. *Money lent*
4. Money paid by the plaintiff for the defendant, at his request. *Money paid*
5. Money received by the defendant for the use of the plaintiff. *Money received*
6. Money found to be due from the defendant to the plaintiff on account stated between them. *Account stated*

7. A messuage and lands sold and conveyed by the plaintiff to the defendant. *Land sold and conveyed*
8. The good-will of a business of the plaintiff, sold and given up by the plaintiff to the defendant. *Good-will of business*
9. The defendant's use by the plaintiff's permission of messuages and lands of the plaintiff. *Use of land*

Fishery.   10. The defendant's use by the plaintiff's permission of a fishery of the
                plaintiffs.

Hire.   11. The hire of (as the case may be), by the plaintiff let to hire to the de-
                fendant.

Freight.   12. Freight for the conveyance by the plaintiff, for the defendant, at his re-
                quest, of goods in ships.

Demurrage   13. The demurrage of a ship of the plaintiff kept on demurrage by the de-
                fendant.

Payee against   14. That the defendant on the   day of   A.D.   by his
payer.   promissory note, now overdue, promised to pay to the plaintiff
                £   (two) months after date, but did not pay the same.

Indorsee against 15. That one A. W. &c., (date) by his promissory note now over due, pro-
indorser.   mised to pay to the defendant or order £   (two) months after
Promissory note.   date, and the defendant endorsed the same to the plaintiff and the said
                    note was duly presented for payment, and was dishonored, whereof
                    the defendant had due notice but did not pay the same.

Drawer against 16. That the plaintiff, on, &c., (date) by his bill of exchange, now overdue,
acceptor. Bill of   directed to the defendant, required the defendant to pay to the plain-
Exchange.   tiff, £   (two) months after date, and the defendant accepted
                    the said bill but did not pay the same.

payee against   17. That the defendant on, &c., (date) by his bill of exchange directed to A.
drawer, after dis- required A. to pay to the plaintiff £   (two) months after date,
honor by drawee   and the said bill was duly presented for acceptance, and was dis-
                    honored, of which the defendant had due notice but did not pay the
                    same.

Promise to mar- 18. That the plaintiff and defendant agreed to marry one another, and a
ry generally   reasonable time for such marriage has elapsed, and the plaintiff has
                    always been ready and willing to marry the defendant, yet the de-
                    fendant has neglected and refused to marry plaintiff.

On a day elapsed 19. That the plaintiff and defendant agreed to marry one another, on a day
                    now elapsed, and the plaintiff was ready and willing to marry the
                    defendant on that day, yet the defendant neglected, and refused to
                    marry the plaintiff.

Sale of horse on 20. That the defendant, by warranting a horse to be then sound and quiet
warranty   to ride, sold the said horse to the plaintiff, yet the said horse was not
                    then sound and quiet to ride.

On charter to   21. That the plaintiff and the defendant agreed, by charter party, that the
load   plaintiff's ship, called "The Ariel" should, with all convenient speed,
                    sail to R, or so near thereto as she could safely get, and that the de-
                    fendant should there load her with a full cargo of tallow or other
                    lawful merchandize, which she should carry to H, and there deliver,
                    on payment of freight £   per ton, and that the defendant should
                    be allowed ten days for loading, and ten for discharge, and ten for de-
                    murrage, if required, at £   per day, and that the plaintiff
                    did all things necessary on his part to entitle him to have the agreed
                    cargo loaded on board the said ship at R, and that the time for so do-
                    ing has elapsed, yet the defendant made default in loading the agreed
                    cargo.

Letting house   22. That the plaintiff let to the defendant a house, No.   street,
                    Kingston, for seven years, to hold, from the   day of   A D
                    18   at £   a-year, payable quarterly, of which rent
                    quarters are due and unpaid.

Letting by deed— 23. That the plaintiff, by deed, let to the defendant a house, No.
breach of covenant street, Kingston, to hold for seven years, from the   day of
to repair   A D, 18   , and the defendant, by the said deed, covenanted
                    with the plaintiff well, and substantially to repair the said house,
                    during the said term (according to the covenant), yet the said house
                    was during the said term out of good and substantial repairs.

For wrongs Independent of Contract.

Trespass by cat- 24. That the defendant broke and entered certain land of the plaintiff,
tle   called "The Big Field", and depastured the same with cattle.

Assault and im- 25. That the defendant assaulted and beat the plaintiff, gave him into cus-
prisonment   tody to a policeman, and caused him to be imprisoned in a police
                    office.

26. That the defendant debauched and carnally knew the plaintiff's wife. Criminal conversation

27. That the defendant converted to his own use, or wrongfully deprived the plaintiff of the use and possession of the plaintiff's goods, that is to say, iron, bricks, household furniture, (or as the case may be.) Conversion

28. That the defendant detained from the plaintiff his title deeds of land called Belmont, in the parish of , in the County of that is to say (describe the deeds.) Detinue

29. That the plaintiff was possessed of a mill, and by reason thereof was entitled to the flow of a stream for working the same, and the defendant, by cutting the bank of the said stream, diverted the water thereof away from the said mill. Diversion of a stream of water

30. That the plaintiff was the first and true inventor of a certain new manufacture, that is to say of "certain improvements in the manufacture of Sulphuric Acid," and thereupon Her Majesty Queen Victoria (or his Excellency , Captain-General and Governor-in-Chief of Her Majesty's said island of Jamaica, in the name, and on behalf of Her Majesty Queen Victoria) by letters patent, under the broad seal of this island, granted the plaintiff the sole privilege to make, use, exercise, and vend the said invention within the said island, for the term of 14 years, from the day of A D, 18 , subject to (here state any condition which the said letters patent were granted subject unto), and the plaintiff did within the time prescribed fulfil the said condition, and the defendant during the said term did infringe the said patent rights. Infringment of patent rights

31. That the defendant falsely and maliciously spoke and published of the plaintiff, the words following, that is to say " he is a thief", (if there be any special damage, here state it with such reasonable particularity as to give notice to the defendant of the peculiar injury complained of for instance), whereby the plaintiff lost his situation as a penkeeper (or as the case may be) in the employ of A Slander

32. That the defendant falsely, and maliciously printed, and published of the plaintiff, in a newspaper, called, the words following, that is to say, " he is a regular prover under insolvencies". the defendant meaning thereby that the plaintiff had proved, and was in the habit of proving fictitious debts against the estates of insolvents, with the knowledge that such debts were fictitious. Libel

COMMENCEMENT OF PLEA.

33. The defendant by his attorney (or in person) says (here state the substance of the plea.)

34. And for a second plea the defendant says (here state the second plea.)

PLEAS IN ACTIONS ON CONTRACTS.

35. That he never was indebted as alleged (this plea is applicable to declarations like those numbered 1 to 13. Never indebted

36. That he did not promise as alleged (this plea is applicable to other declarations on simple contracts, such as those numbered 18 to 21, it would be unobjectionable to use " did not warrant", " did not agree" or any other appropriate denial.) Did not promise

37. That the alleged deed is not his deed. Not his deed

38. That the alleged cause of action did not accrue within six years (state the period of limitation applicable to the case) before this suit. Action did not accrue within six years

39. That the plaintiff, at the commencement of this suit was, and still is indebted to the defendant in an amount equal to the plaintiff's claim for (here state the cause of set off, as in a declaration) (see terms ante) which amount the defendant is willing to set off against the plaintiff's claim. Set off

PLEAS IN ACTION FOR WRONGS INDEPENDENT OF CONTRACT,

40. That he is not guilty. Not guilty

41. That he did what is complained of by the plaintiff's leave. Leave

42. That the plaintiff first assaulted the defendant, who thereupon necessarily committed the alleged assault in his own defence. Self-defence

Right of way   43. That the defendant, at the time of the alleged trespass was possessed of land, the occupiers whereof for twenty years before this suit enjoyed as of right and without interruption, a way on foot and with cattle from a public highway over the said land of the plaintiff to the said land of the defendant, and from the said land of the defendant over the said land of the plaintiff, to the said public highway, at all times of the year, for the more convenient occupation of the said land of the defendant, and that the said alleged trespass was a use by the defendant of the said way.

REPLICATIONS.

Joinder of issue   44. The plaintiff takes issue upon the defendant's first, second, &c. pleas.

45. The plaintiff as to the second plea, says (here state the answer to the plea as in the following forms :—

Set off did not accrue within six years   46. That the alleged set off did not accrue within six years before this suit.

Removal of defendant while trespassing, after refusal to leave plaintiff's land   47. That the plaintiff was possessed of land whereon the defendant was trespassing, and doing damage, whereupon the plaintiff requested the defendant to leave the said land, which the defendant refused to do and thereupon the plaintiff gently laid his hands on the defendant in order to remove him, doing no more than was necessary for that purpose, which is the alleged first assault by the plaintiff.

Traverse of right of way   48. That the occupiers of the said land did not for twenty years before this suit enjoy, as of right, and without interruption the alleged way.

NEW ASSIGNMENT.

Where plaintiff does not proceed for the trespasses admitted   49. The plaintiff, as to the   , and   pleas says, that he sues not for the trespasses therein admitted, but for trespasses committed by the defendant, in excess of the alleged rights, and also in other parts of the said land, and on other occasions, and for other purposes than those referred to in the said pleas.

Where plaintiff replies, and new assigns   If the plaintiff replies, and new assigns, it may be as follows :—

50. And the plaintiff, as to the   , and   pleas, further says, that he sues not only for the trespasses in those pleas admitted, but also for, &c.

If the plaintiff replies, and new assigns to some of the pleas, and new assigns only to the other, the form may be as follows :—

51. And the plaintiff, as to the   , and   pleas, further says, that he sues not only for the trespasses in the   pleas (the pleas not replied to) admitted, but also for the trespasses in the plea (pleas replied to) admitted, and also for, &c.

Criminal Punishment.

Felonies not specially punishable   Persons convicted of felony not punishable with death, shall be punished as prescribed by the acts specially relating thereto. Where no punishment is specially provided, they shall be punishable under this act, and liable to imprisonment not exceeding one year, 9 G. 4, c. 19, s. 5,

Sentence of imprisonment on persons undergoing sentence   Where sentence is passed for felony on a person already imprisoned under sentence for another crime, the Court may award imprisonment for the subsequent offence, to commence at the expiration of the imprisonment to which he was previously sentenced, 9 G. 4, c. 19, s. 6.

Punishment after previous conviction Felonies   Persons convicted of any felony, not punishable with death, committed after a previous conviction for felony, shall be liable to imprisonment, not exceeding two years, 9 G. 4, c. 19, s. 7.

Offences punishable with hard labour and solitary confinement   When any person is charged with an offence a degree below felony, and is convicted in any Court of record of uttering any counterfeit money, knowing it to be so, either of the Queen's coins, or of the coins of foreign realms, current in this island by law or common consent, or any aggravated assault, or any riot, or aggravated breach of the Peace, by unlawfully entering the premises of any person, or keeping a common gaming house, or common bawdy house, or a common ill-governed and disorderly house, or assisting at any seditious meeting, or maiming or injuring any person by furious driving, riding, galloping or racing, or inciting to mutiny by endevouring to seduce a soldier or a seaman, from his allegiance, or embezzling the Queen's Stores, or slanderous words to a Magistrate in the due discharge of the duties of his office, or disturbing public worship, or rioting or striking in or within the precincts of an open Court, or beating, or ill-treating apprentices, or selling cloth falsely marked or put up, he may be sentenced to imprisonment, with or without hard labor and solitary confinement, for such term as the Justices deem meet, 1 V. c. 28, s. 4.

No Court shall direct any offender to be kept in solitary confinement for longer than one month at a time, or three months in one year, nor shall it be in darkness, unless specially ordered, and not beyond 6 days, 1 V. c. 28, s. 5. *Duration of solitary confinement*

When any person is convicted of any of the offences following, as an indictable misdemeanor viz., any cheat or fraud, punishable at common law, any conspiracy to cheat or defraud, or to extort money, or goods, or falsely to accuse of any crime, or to obstruct, prevent, pervert or defeat the course of public Justice, any escape or rescue from lawful custody, on a criminal charge, any public and indecent exposure of the person, any indecent assault, or any assault occasioning actual bodily harm, any attempt to have carnal knowledge of a girl under 12 years of age, any public selling or exposing for public sale, or to public view, of any obscene book, print, picture or other indecent exhibition, the Court may sentence the offender to imprisonment for any term, now warranted by law, and if the Court deem fit, to be kept to hard labor during the whole or any part of the term of imprisonment, 16 V. c. 15, s. 29. *Offences punishable with hard labor*

Persons convicted of any offence for which the punishment of death may be awarded by any law of this island, but for which offence they would not be liable to such punishment by the laws of Great Britain, shall be adjudged to be felons, and punished as persons convicted of the same offence would by law, be punishable in England, and all acts and parts of acts whereby the punishment of death is imposed for the commission of any offence not now punishable with death by any law of Great Britain, is absolutely repealed, 19 V. c. 29, s. 2. *Punishment of death repealed. Offences to be punished according to the law of Great Britain.*

Cruelty to Animals.

Any person wantonly and cruelly beating, illtreating, abusing or torturing any horse, mare, filly, gelding, bull, ox, cow, heifer, steer, calf, mule, ass, sheep, lamb, dog, or other cattle or domestic animal, whether the owner or not, convicted before a Justice, shall forfeit not exceeding 60 shillings, nor less than 5 shillings with costs, or the Justice may commit him not exceeding 60 days, with or without hard labour, without prejudice to any other remedy any party aggreived may have, 25 V. c. 10, s. 1. *To horses, cattle, domestic animals*

Any constable or the owner, or his agent, upon view of such cruelty, or upon the information of any other person who declares his name and place of abode to the constable, may secure, and forthwith, without other authority, convey any offender before a Justice, who shall forthwith examine upon oath any witnesses who appear to give information, 25 V. c. 10, s. 2. *Apprehension of offenders*

Keeping or using any house, room, pit, ground or other place for Cock-fighting, or preparing cocks or other animals for fighting, penalty not exceeding £5 nor less than 10s, with cost, for every day &c., to be recovered before any justice. The person who acts as manager, &c., or receives money for admission, or assists in any such fighting or preparation for fighting, shall be deemed the keeper, and liable to the penalties imposed on him, 25 V. c. 10 s. 3. *Cockfighting*

Any person, by himself or agent, catching, taking, or driving any horse or other animal from any property or place, without the consent or permission of the owner or party in possession, shall, on conviction before two Justices, forfeit not exceeding £10, and, in default of immediate payment, be committed to the nearest prison to hard labor, not exceeding 90 days, besides being liable to an action at the suit of the party aggreived—The person acting as agent shall be competent to give evidence if the Justice consider, from the information that he acted under the delusion of the employers authority to take and use the animal, 25 V. c. 10, s. 4. *Catching &c. animals on properties*

One moiety of the penalty shall be paid to the informer, who shall be a competent witness, 25 V. c. 10, s. 5. *Penalty*

Cryers of Courts.

Fees, Supreme Courts

Fees of the cryer of the Supreme Court, for every witness sworn 7½d (4½d stg.), and for calling out the defendant when the action goes by default 1s 3d (9d stg.), 10 Anne c. 4, s. 4.

Circuit Courts

The judges shall appoint the cryer of each Circuit Court. Each Judge on Circuit may remove him and fill up vacancies. Such cryers shall attend at the courts to which they are appointed as often as they are held. Their salaries in each of the courts of the Home Circuit shall be £20 per annum, in other courts £10 per annum, to be paid by the Receiver-General on certificate of a judge, 19 V. c. 10, s. 33. To same effect, 23 V c. 19, s. 1.

Currency Assimilation.

Currency of the United Kingdom to be that of this island.

The currency of the united Kingdom shall be that of this island, and all receipts, payments, contracts, securities, dealings, and matters relating to money, made or done in this island, shall be according to such currency, 3 V. c. 39, s. 1.

Rate of conversion in respect of previous transactions, &c.

All gifts, &c., and all debts, under any specialty or simple contract, &c., relating to money, before the commencement of this act with reference to the currency of this island, shall be paid and accounted for at the rate of £100 of the currency of the United Kingdom, for every £166 13s. 4d. of the present currency, in the coins and at the rates they are declared legal tenders, 3 V. c. 39, s. 2.

All duties, taxes, rents, and revenues to the Crown, and all penalties and values, where expressed in money by any laws in force, antecedently to this Act, shall be deemed of the previous currency, and be converted into the currency of the United Kingdom at the rate beforementioned, 3 V. c. 39, s. 3.

Transactions in foreign currency.

Not to prevent any gift, &c., or any matter or thing relating to money, from being made or had according to the currency of foreign countries, 3 V. c 39, s. 8.

Franchises, &c., under previous acts,

Nor to affect any franchise, right, benefit, privilege, or advantage resulting from the possession of lands, rents, or property of the value mentioned in any previous act in force, 3 V. c. 39, s. 11.

Commencement.

Act to take effect after 31st December, 1840, 3 V. c. 39, s. 12.

Customs.

Foreign vessels driven in by stress of weather. Supply of necessaries. As to drawback, 28 V. c. 10, s. 11.

The master of every French, Dutch, and other foreign ship coming into port, on pretence of being drove in by stress of weather, want of provisions, or other disabilities, shall, within 24 hours after coming, wait upon the Governor, and discover upon oath the occasion of his coming in, and his necessary wants, and the quantities of money, bullion and goods he has on board, under penalty of the forfeiture of the ship (which oath the Governor may administer) and direct the naval officer, (office abolished 10 G. 4, c. 13.,) immediately to supply him with necessaries, at the cheapest rates they are to be sold for, which the master shall pay for out of the money he has on board, and if he has none, then out of such part of his cargo as shall be sufficient to answer his necessary occasions, 12 G. 1 c. 11, s. 1.

Sale of cargo for necessaries.

But no more goods than to supply what necessaries he wants, over and above his money, and that by leave of the Governor, and by public outcry, first fixing up 3 days notice in the 3 towns of St. Jago de la Vega, Port Royal, and Kingston, under penalty of the forfeiture of the ship and cargo, 12 G. 1 c. 11, s. 2.

Liabilities in port

Every French, Dutch, or Spanish ship shall be subject to such port charges, visitations, rules, and orders as ships of Her Majesty's subjects, 12 G. 1 c. 11, s. 3.

Ports of entry and clearance.

Kingston, Savanna-la-Mar. Montego Bay, and Port Antonio, made ports of entry and clearance, 31 G. 2, c. 19.

Prize ships and goods.

All ships and goods taken and brought into this island, and condemned as prize, during hostilities with any foreign state, shall be liable to the payment of such imposts and duties, and subject to the rules, regulations, penalties, and forfeitures to which the same sorts of ships and goods may be liable, 44 G. 3 c. 10, s. 1.

But not to permit any sugars, rum, taffia, or coffee, condemned as prize, to be sold for consumption in this island, but the same shall be actually and bona fide exported within six months from the time of sale, under the penalty of £1000 (£600 sterling) on the purchaser, and forfeiture of the goods, 44 G. 3 c. 10, s. 2.

Sugars, rum, taffia, coffee.

On the arrival of any prize, the agents for the captors shall, under penalty of £1000 (£600 sterling), within ten days after it is libelled in the Court of Vice Admiralty, report or enter the same in the Receiver-General's Office, and at the same time, under the like penalty, enter into a bond to the Receiver-General (for which report, entry or bond, no fees shall be demanded) for the amount of all imposts, and duties payable on prize goods, within 6 days after the account sales have been recorded, in the office of the Registrar of the Court, or the actual and bona fide sale and delivery of such dutiable prize goods, provided the period does not exceed 6 months, 44 G. 3 c. 10, s. 3.

Prize agents to give bond to the Receiver General for duties.

The Registrar, or acting deputy, shall, within 6 days after the account sales are recorded in his office, deliver to the Receiver-General a copy, under penalty of £500 (£300 sterling) for which he shall receive from him £1 10s. (18s. sterling) for each account delivered, to be charged to the account of the duties, 44 G. 3 c. 10, s. 4.

Registrar of Vice Admiralty Court to deliver to the Receiver General copy of account sales.
His fee.

If the agent of the prize goods, within six days after the account sales have been recorded, or the actual and bona fide sale and delivery of such dutiable prize goods, provided the period does not exceed 6 months, make oath, or prove on the oath of the exporter before the Receiver-General (which he may administer) that the goods or any part have been actually and bona fide exported, the Receiver-General shall repay such imposts and duties, received by him, 44 G. 3 c. 10, s. 5.

Return of duties on goods exported.

On any sale of prize goods, the agent shall, under penalty of £500, (£300 sterling) within 6 days after such sales, or within 6 weeks after the actual and bona fide sale and delivery of such dutiable prize goods, provided the period does not exceed six months, deliver in a specific account to the Receiver General, 44 G. 3 c. 10, s. 6.

Accounts to be delivered to the Receiver General by agent after sales.

Penalties recoverable in the Supreme Court by action of debt, &c., one moiety, to the informer, 44 G. 3 c. 10, s. 7.

Recovery, &c., of penalties,

Sugars, introduced into this island, which have undergone any process of refining, whether from molasses or otherwise, shall be deemed to be refined sugar, 4 V. c. 43.

Refined sugar.

On the arrival of any steam vessel, the commander, or next chief officer shall deliver to the Collector and Controller at the port, a manifest of all goods on board, specifying the marks and numbers, the nature and contents of the packages so far as he is able to ascertain, the names of the shippers and consignees, and no goods shall be landed but by their order, and under the regulations established by the Collector and Controller of Kingston, subject to the approval of the Governor, 14 V. c. 56, s. 4.

Steam vessels.

The Ports of Kingston, Montego Bay and Falmouth, shall continue warehousing ports. The Collector and Controller at Kingston, and the Sub-Collectors at Montego Bay and Falmouth, shall, by notice in writing, appoint warehouses at such ports, for the free warehousing and securing of goods, and declare what sorts of goods may be warehoused, and by like notice, may revoke or alter any such appointment or declaration. Every such notice shall be transmitted to the Governor, and published as he shall direct, 17 V. c. 2, s. 1.

Warehousing ports, Kingston, Montego Bay, Falmouth.

The ports of Savanna-la Mar, and Port Maria, shall also be warehousing ports, and their Sub-Collectors shall appoint warehouses as directed by and subject to the conditions in 17 V. c. 2. 20 V. c. 5, s. 7.

Sav la-Mar, Port Maria.

Black River and Annotto Bay shall be warehousing ports, subject to the provisions of 17 V. c. 2. 27 V. S. 1, c. 11, s. 1.

Black River and Annotto Bay.

And that act is extended to the warehouses at those ports, 27 V. S. 1, c. 11, s. 2.

17 V. c. 2 extended to

The present holder shall continue warehouse keeper at Black River, at a salary not exceeding £35 per annum in addition to his salary as Locker and Gauger under the Rum Warehousing Act, and, on any vacancy of the Locker and Gauger, shall discharge the duties at a like salary, 27 V. S. 1, c. 11, s. 3.

Warehouse keepers Black River.

Annotto Bay.

The Locker and Gauger at Annotto Bay, under any act for warehousing rum, shall discharge the duties of warehouse keeper at a salary not exceeding £10 per annum in addition to his salary as Locker and Gauger, 27 V. S. 1, c. 11, s. 4.

Subject to Customs' regulations.

Such warehouse keepers shall be subject to the several provisions, rules, and regulations of the service, 27 V. S. 1, c. 11, s. 5.

Importers may warehouse goods.

Importers may warehouse goods without payment of duty on the first entry, subject to the rules, regulations, restrictions and conditions after contained, 17 V. c. 2, s. 2.

Conditions on which to be warehoused.

Goods so warehoused shall be stowed in such parts or divisions of the warehouse, and as the Collector and Controller shall direct, and the warehouse locked and secured, and opened and visited only at such times and in the presence of such officers, and under such regulations as the Collector and Controller shall direct ; and the goods after being landed shall be carried to the warehouse, or after being taken out of the warehouse for exportation, or for stores, carried to be shipped under such regulations as they shall direct, 17 V. c. 2, s. 3.

General bond by proprietor &c.

Before any g   are entered in any warehouse, in respect of which security by bond or required, the proprietor or occupier, if willing, shall give general security by bond, with two sureties for the payment of the full duties of importation of all such goods as shall, at any time, be warehoused therein, or for the exportation, or shipment thereof as stores, according to the first account taken on landing, and with further condition that no part shall be taken out until cleared upon due entry and payment of duty, or upon due entry for exportation or for shipment as stores, and with further **Particular bonds by importers** condition that the whole of such goods shall be cleared within two years from the first entry. If he is not willing to give such general security, the different importers shall, upon each importation, before the goods are entered to be warehoused, give security by bond with one surety, in respect of the particular goods imported, in double the amount of duty— 17 V., c. 2, s. 4.

Causes of forfeiture of goods warehoused

If goods entered are not duly deposited in the warehouse, or are afterwards taken out without due entry and clearance, or having been entered and cleared for exportation, or for shipment as stores are not duly carried and shipped, or are afterwards re-landed, except with the permission of the proper officer, they shall be forfeited, 17 V., c. 2, s. 5.

Particulars of goods warehoused

Upon entry and landing of goods to be warehoused, the proper officer shall take a particular account of the same, and mark the contents on each package, and enter them in a book to be kept for the purpose, and no goods shall be taken or delivered from the warehouse except upon due entry, and under the care of the proper officers, for exportation or for stores, or on due entry and payment of duty for home use, 17 V., c. 2, s. 6.

Samples

The Collector and Controller may, under such regulations as they see fit, permit moderate samples to be taken of goods warehoused without entry and without payment of duty, except as shall eventually become payable as on a deficiency of the original quantity, 17 V., c. 2, s. 7.

Sorting and re-packing

And permit the proprietor or person having control over the goods, to sort, separate, and pack, and re-pack them, and make lawful alterations or arrangements for their preservation, or for sale, shipment, or legal disposal, as also any parts of the goods separated to be destroyed, but without prejudice to the claim for duty upon the whole original quantity. Any person may abandon whole packages for the duties, 17 V., c. 2, s. 8.

Abandonment for duty

Transfers to other warehouses

Goods warehoused, being first duly entered, may be delivered, under the authority of the proper officer, without payment of duty, for removal to another warehousing port, under bond for their due arrival and warehousing, 17 V., c. 2, s. 9.

Clearance within two years

All goods so warehoused or re-warehoused shall be duly cleared either for exportation or for home consumption, within two years from the first entry for warehousing, and if not so cleared the Collector and Controller shall cause them to be sold, and the produce applied first to the payment of the duties, next of warehouse rent and charges, and the overplus to the proprietor. But they may grant further time for any goods to remain warehoused, 17 V., c. 2, s. 10.

Unless further time granted

' Upon entry outwards of goods to be exported from warehouse, the person entering shall give security by bond in treble the duties of importation on the quantity, or if the goods are prohibited to be imported for home use in double their value, with two sureties, that they shall be landed at the place for which they are entered outwards, or otherwise accounted for, to their satisfaction, 17 V., c. 2, s, 11.

Bond for exportation

The Imperial Act 16 and 17 V., c. 107, so far as relates to the regulation of British possessions abroad shall be in force, 17 V., c. 2, s. 12.

Stat. 16, & 17 V. c. 107 relating to possessions abroad in force

Goods deposited in warehouse, or on board ship shall, on being entered for home consumption, be subject to the duties payable at the time of the passing of such entry on the like sort of goods, except where special provisions are made to the contrary, 17 V., c. 2, s. 13.

Duties payable to be those in force at the time of entry for home consumption

Upon entry of goods to be cleared from warehouse for home use, the duties shall be payable on the quantity taken on the first entry and landing, except as to tobacco, wines, and spirits, the duties whereon shall be charged upon the quantity ascertained by weight or measure at the time of actual delivery, unless there is reasonable ground to suppose any portion of the deficiency or difference has been caused by illegal or improper means, in which case the proper officer shall make such allowance only for loss as he considers fairly to have arisen from natural evaporation or other legitimate cause. 17 V., c. 2, s. 14.

Quantity on which duties to be paid

If the importer make and subscribe a declaration before the Collector and Controller, or proper officer, that he cannot, for want of full information, make perfect entry, they may receive an entry by bill of sight for the packages or parcels, by the best description which can be given, and grant a warrant that they may be landed and secured to the satisfaction of the officer, at the expense of the importer, and may be examined by him in their presence, and within three days after landing, the importer shall make a perfect entry and pay down all duties, and in default the goods shall be taken to warehouse, and if he do not, within one month after landing, make perfect entry, and pay the duties and charges of removal and warehouse rent, the goods shall be sold for payment thereof, and any overplus paid to the proprietor, 17 V., c. 2, s. 15.

Entry by bill of sight

And afterwards perfect entry, or in default goods to be warehoused and sold

If the importer refuses to pay duties, the Collector or Chief Officer of the port shall secure the goods with the casks or other packages, and cause them to be publicly sold, within 20 days at the most after refusal, or at such time and place as the officer shall, by four or more days' public notice, appoint, to the best bidder, and the money applied in payment of the duties, and charges, and any overplus to the importer, or proprietor, or person authorized to receive same, 17 V., c. 2, s. 16.

Sale on refusal to pay duties

Every importer shall, within 14 days after the arrival of the ship, make due entry inwards, and land the goods, and in default the officers may convey them to the warehouse, and if the duties are not paid within three months after the 14 days expired, with all charges of removal and warehouse rent, they shall be sold to pay first, freight and charges, next, duties, and the overplus to the proprietor or person authorized to receive it— 17 V., c. 2, s. 17.

Goods to be entered and landed within 14 days

Sale for duties

Should the importer or consignee neglect or refuse to pass warrants for 5, or, if he does not reside near the port, 12 days after the vessel has entered at the Customs, it being necessary to unload with as little delay as possible, and notwithstanding 17 V., c. 2, s. 17, the consignee or master may pass the necessary warrants for the goods, and thereupon land and place them in a warehouse of his selection, approved of by the officer of Customs, to be kept, until the duties and charges paid by him have been re-paid by the importer or consignee, and such duties and charges with 3s. for each warrant passed, shall be a lien upon all such goods, and shall be paid previous to their delivery by the wharfinger or person in charge of the warehouse, 23 V., c. 10, s. 2.

When consignee or master of the vessel may pass warrants to warehouse goods

All acts to be done by, to, or with the Collector and Controller may be done at any port where there is no Controller with the Collector or principal officer, and be valid, 17, V., c. 2, s. 18.

Principal officer may act where there is no Controller

Forfeitures and penalties on unlawful removal of goods, &c

All vessels, boats, carriages and cattle, made use of in the removal of any goods, liable to forfeiture under any act relating to the Customs or trade and navigation, shall be forfeited, and every person who assists or is otherwise concerned in the unshipping, landing or removal, or in the harbouring of such goods, or into whose hands or possession, they knowingly come, shall forfeit the treble value, or £100, at the election of the officers of the Customs, and the averment in any information, or libel for the penalty, that the officer has elected to sue for the sum mentioned in the information shall be sufficient proof of such election, without further evidence, 17 V. c. 2, s. 19.

Who may make seizures. Penalty for obstructing them

All goods and all ships, vessels &c., liable to forfeiture, may be seized and secured by any officer of Customs, or Navy, or person employed for the purpose, by or with the concurrence of the officers of the Customs, and any person in any way hindering, opposing, molesting or obstructing any officer &c., in the exercise of his office, or any person acting in his aid or assistance, shall forfeit £200, 17 V. c. 2, s. 20.

Collusive seizures, bribes &c

If any officer of Customs, or person duly employed for the prevention of smuggling, makes any collusive seizure, or delivers up, or makes any agreement to deliver up or not to seize any vessel, boat, or goods liable to forfeiture, under this or any act relating to the Customs, or takes any bribe-gratuity, recompense or reward for the neglect or non-performance of his duty, he shall forfeit £300, and be rendered incapable of serving Her Majesty in any office whatever, and every person giving or offering, or promising to give or procure to be given any bribe &c., or make any collusive agreement, with any such officer or person to induce him in any way to neglect his duty, or to do, conceal or connive at any thing whereby the provisions of any such act may be evaded, shall forfeit £200, 17 V. c. 2, s. 21.

Writ of assistance

Under the authority of a writ of assistance, granted by the Supreme Court or Court of Vice Admiralty, having jurisdiction (who are to grant such writ upon application by the principal officers) any officer, taking with him a Peace officer, may enter any building or other place in the day time, and search for, seize and secure any goods liable to forfeiture, and, in case of necessity, break open any doors, chests or other packages. Such writ of assistance when issued, shall be in force during the whole reign in which it is granted, and for 12 months from its conclusion, 17 V. c. 2, s. 22.

Continuance in force

Violent assault on officer &c, employed thereunder see criminal punishment, 9 G. 4, c 19, s 5, 7

By force or violence, assaulting, resisting, opposing, molesting, hindering or obstructing any officer of the Customs or navy, or other person employed as aforesaid, in the exercise of his office, or any person acting in his aid or assistance, felony, punishable at the discretion of the Court, 17 V. c. 2, s. 23.

Custody and disposal of seizures

All things seized as liable to forfeiture, shall be taken forthwith and delivered into the custody of the Collector and Controller, at the Custom House next to the place where seized, who shall secure them, by the means and in the manner provided and directed by the principal officers at Kingston, and, after condemnation, shall cause them to be sold by public auction to the best bidder. The principal officers at Kingston may direct in what manner the p   of the sale shall be applied, or, in lieu of such sale, may direct any of the emolutoebe destroyed or reserved for the public service, 17 V. c. 2, s. 24.

Proof of payment of duties, &c. to lie on claimer

If any goods are seized for non-payment of duties, or other cause of forfeiture, and any dispute arises whether the duties have been paid, or they have been lawfully imported, or lawfully laden or exported, the proof shall be in the owner or claimer, and not on the officer, 17 V. c. 2, s. 25.

Claim how to be entered, to be on oath to the property

False oath, misdemeanor

No claim to any thing seized and returned into any Court, for adjudication, shall be admitted, unless entered in the name of the owner with his residence and occupation, nor unless oath to the property be made by the owner or by his Attorney or Agent by whom the claim is entered, to the best of his knowledge and belief. Making a false oath, a misdemeanor, and punishable as such, 17 V. c. 2, s. 26.

Security for costs

No person shall be permitted to enter a claim, until security has been given in the Court, in a penalty not exceeding £60, to answer and pay the costs occasioned by such claim, and in default, the things shall be adjudged to be forfeited and condemned, 17 V. c. 2, s. 27.

In proceedings at the suit of the Crown, for the recovery of any duty or penalty, or the enforcement of any forfeiture, the parties shall be entitled to recover costs against each other, as if conducted between subject and subject, and the like amendments may be made in such proceedings, by the Judge or Court, as in civil actions, and all duties, penalties and forfeitures, incurred under or imposed by any act relating to the Customs, and the liability to forfeiture of any goods seized, shall, where not otherwise provided, and except as after provided, be sued for, prosecuted, determined and recovered by action of debt, information, or other appropriate proceeding in any Court of law or equity, or in the Court of Vice Admiralty, in the name of the Attorney-General, or of some officer of Customs, 17 V. c. 2, s. 28.

Costs, amendment of proceedings, courts where to be prosecuted. See costs, 26 V., s. 2, c. 15

No writ shall be sued out against, nor a copy of any process served upon any officer of the Customs or Navy, or other person as aforesaid for any thing done in the exercise of his office, until one calendar month after notice in writing, by the Attorney or Agent of the party, containing the cause of action, name and place of abode of the person who is to bring it, and of the Attorney or Agent, and no evidence of cause of action shall be produced except of such as is contained in such notice, and no verdict be given for the plaintiff, unless he prove on the trial that such notice was given, and in default, the defendant shall receive a verdict and costs, 17 V. c. 2, s. 29.

Notice of action

Every such action shall be brought within three calendar months, and be laid and tried in the place or district where the facts were committed, and the defendant may plead the general issue, and give the special matter in evidence, and if the plaintiff become non-suited, discontinue, or if upon verdict or demurrer Judgment is given against him, the defendant shall receive his costs, and have such remedy as defendants in other cases, 17 V. c. 2, s. 30.

Actions within 3 calendar months— General issue, costs of defence

In case any information or suit is tried, for any cause of forfeiture, on account of the seizure, and a verdict is found for the claimant, and it appears to the Judge that there was probable cause of seizure, he shall certify on the record such probable cause, and the certificate shall be a bar, and may be pleaded as such, to any action, indictment or other proceeding against the party making the seizure; and in case any action &c., shall be brought to trial against any person, on account of any seizure (whether any information have been or shall be brought to trial for the condemnation of the same or not) and a verdict given for the plaintiff, if the Court or Judge certify on the record or other written proceedings, that there was probable cause for seizure the plaintiff shall be entitled to no more than 2d damages, nor to any costs, nor shall the defendant in any such prosecution be fined more than 1s.; and the production of such certificate, or a copy verified by the signature of the officer of the Court having charge thereof, shall be sufficient evidence, 17 V. c. 2, s. 31.

Certificate of probable clause pleadable in bar

Available in reduction of damages &c

Evidence

The officer may, within one calendar month after notice, tender amends to the party complaining, or his agent, and plead such tender in bar, with other pleas, and if the Jury find the amends sufficient, they shall give a verdict for the defendant, in which case, or if the plaintiff become nonsuit or discontinue, or Judgment is given for the defendant, he shall be entitled to the like costs as if he had pleaded the general issue only; but if upon issue joined the Jury find that no amends were tendered, or that they were insufficient, or find against the defendant, on such plea or pleas, they shall give a verdict for the plaintiff, and such damages as they think proper, together with costs. The defendant by leave of the Court, at any time before issue joined, may pay money into Court, as in other actions, 17 V. c. 2, s. 32.

Tender of amends

Payment of money into court See Court Supreme pleadings, 28 V. c, 37, s 19.

Penalties and forfeitures recovered under any act relating to the Customs, where not otherwise provided for, shall be paid to the principal officers at Kingston, and divided and paid, after deducting the charges of prosecution two-thirds into the Island Treasury, and the remaining one-third to the person who seizes, informs and sues, 17 V. c. 2, s. 33.

Appropriation of penalties.

Previously or subsequently to the commencement of any prosecution, under any act relating to the Customs, the Governor, if satisfied that the fine, penalty or forfeiture was incurred without any intention of fraud, or that it is inexpedient to proceed, may mitigate or forego altogether, the same, and if commenced, may stop proceedings by directing the Attorney General to enter a nolle prosequi, or otherwise as well with respect to the share of the officer, as to the proportion payable into the Treasury, 17 V. c. 2, s. 34.

Power to mitigate or forego penalties, and stay proceedings, See 17 V. c. 33, s. 4-6

Actions or Suits for recovery of penalties under this or any act relating to the customs, or to trade or navigation, may be commenced within three years after the offence committed, 17 V. c. 2, s. 35.

Limitation of actions &c

False declarations, certificates &c &c see 17, V c 33, s 7

Any person making and subscribing any false declaration, or making or signing any declaration, certificate or other instrument required to be verified by signature only, the same being false in any particular, or making or signing any declaration for the consideration of the commissioners or officers of the customs on any application presented to them, the same being untrue in any particular, or any person being required to answer questions put by the officers, not truly answering such questions, or any person counterfeiting, falsifying, or wilfully using when counterfeited or falsified, any document required by any act (or by or under the direction of the commissioners or officers) or any instrument used in the transaction of any business or matter relating to the customs, or fraudulently altering or counterfeiting any document or instrument, or the seal, signature, initials, or other mark of, or used by the officers of the customs for the verification of any such document or instrument, or for the security of goods, or any other purpose in the conduct of business relating to the customs or order (sic) the control or management of the commissioners or their officers, shall forfeit, £100. 17 V. c. 2, s. 36.

Forfeiture of goods illegally landed, removed from warehouse, concealed &c

If any goods liable to duties are unshipped from any ship or boat, customs or other duties not being first paid or secured, or if any prohibited goods are importrd or brought into this island, or if any goods which have been warehoused or otherwise secured either for home consumption or exportation, are clandestinely or illegally removed from any warehouse or place of security, or if any goods subject to any duty or restriction in respect of importation, or prohibited are found or discovered to have been concealed on board any ship or boat, within the limits of any port, or are found either before or after landing to have been concealed on board any such ship or boat, they shall be forfeited together with any goods found packed with or used in concealing them, 17 V. c. c, s. 37.

Penalties on illegal importation or concealment of goods removal from warehouse, evasion of duties, &c

Every person concerned in importing any prohibited goods, or any goods the importation of which is restricted, contrary to such prohibition or restriction, and whether unshipped or not, or who shall unship or assist, or be otherwise concerned in the unshipping of any goods restricted, and imported contrary to such restriction, or of any goods liable to duties which have not been paid or secured, or who knowingly harbours, keeps or conceals, or knowingly permits, or suffers, or causes, or procures to be harboured, &c. any such goods or any goods illegally removed without payment of duty from any warehouse or place of security, or to whose hands and possession any such goods knowingly come, or who are in any way knowingly concerned in conveying, removing, depositing, concealing, or in any manner dealing with any goods liable to duties, with intent to defraud the revenue of such duties or any part thereof, or who are in any way knowingly concerned in any fraudulent evasion or attempt at evasion of such duties shall forfeit either treble the value of the goods, according to the then market value, or £100, at the election of the officers of customs, and may be detained by

Detention of offenders

any officer of customs or of the army, navy, or marines on full pay, or by any other person acting in their aid or assistance, or duly employed for the prevention of smuggling, and taken before a Justice to be dealt with as after directed. Persons so detained may give security in treble the amount of the

Who may be held to bail or committed

goods, by recognizance or otherwise, to appear at the time and place to be appointed by the Justice, or in default the Justice may order him to be detained in custody in any goal, and to be taken before two Justices at the time and place so appointed, 17 V. c. 2, s. 38.

Or they may be subsequently detained and dealt with

Or if not detained at the time, or if after detention they escape, they may at any time afterwards be detained, and taken before any Justice, and dealt with as if detained at the time of committing the offence, 17 V. c. 2, s. 39.

Jurisdiction of 2 Justices where treble value does not exceed £100

If treble the value of the goods do not exceed £100, two Justices may sentence the offending party to pay treble the value, or £100, or in default of payment may commit the party to any gaol until paid, 17 V. c. 2. s 40.

If above £100 the party to be bailed or committed to answer in the Vice Admiralty Court

When it appears to 2 Justices, before whom any such person is taken, that treble the value of the goods exceeds £100, they may require him to give security in treble the value, by recognizance, or otherwise, to appear before the Vice Admiralty Court and abide by the judgment, sentence, order or decree of that court, and on failure to give such security, shall commit him to any gaol in this island, to abide by the judgment, &c., of that court. Such proceedings to be filed within one calendar month after committal. 17 V. c. 2, s. 41.

Upon the exhibiting any information before a Justice, of any offence for which the party is not liable in the first instance to be detained, the Justice shall issue a summons for his appearance before two Justices, and such summons directed to such party being left at his last known place of residence, or on board any ship to which he belongs, or has lately belonged, shall be sufficiently served, 17 V. c, 2, s. 42.

Summons and service for appearance before two Justices for trial, see s. 38, 39.

Upon his appearance, or, in case of default, upon proof of service 2 Justices may proceed to the examination of the matter in the information, and upon proof thereof, either upon the confession of the party, or upon the oath of one or more witnesses, may convict the party, and in case of non-payment any Justice may commit him to any gaol in the island until the penalty is paid, 17 V. c. 2, s. 43.

Proceedings thereon

When committed for non pa m t of any penalty, or for not giving security, the Gaoler or keeper of the prison shall receive and take charge of and keep in safe custody such committed person, according to the warrant of committal, until discharged in due course of law, 17 V. c. 2, s. 44.

Duty of Gaoler

The Governor may appoint proper officers to execute the duties of the several offices necessary for the due management and collection of import and export duties, and require security for their good conduct therein, who shall hold office during his pleasure, and fill up vacancies, vary their duties, and remove them from one port to another, but not increase the salaries assigned to them, 17 V. c. 33, s. 1.

Appointment &c. of Customs Officers

The Executive Committee shall be commissioners for the management of the Customs throughout the island, subject to the authority, directions and control of the Governor, and shall obey his orders and instructions, issued to them under his hand, 17 V. c. 33, s. 2.

Commissioners of Customs

And shall, as such commissioners, prepare rules and regulations, and make alterations and amendments therein, subject to the Governor's approval, for the general government and direction of the establishment or department, and for the guidance and conduct of all the officers, which shall be in force as soon as sanctioned by the Governor, and copies shall be laid before each branch of the Legislature within 14 days after the meeting of the following session, and until rules are made and sanctioned the establishment and officers shall be directed and governed by the rules hitherto in practice in the department, under the management and control of the commissioners of Customs of Great Britain, 20 V. c. 5, s. 3.

Rules and Regulations

If any dispute arise between any masters or owners of ships, merchants, importers, consignees, shippers, or exporters of goods, or their agents, and any officer of Customs, with reference to the seizure or detention of any ship or goods, or to any apparently accidental omission, inadvertence, or non-compliance with the laws or regulations relating to the Customs, or to the amount of any duties demanded, the commissioners may determine the dispute, subject to the Governor's approval, 17 V., c. 33, s. 4.

Power to determine disputes

If upon consideration of the facts and circumstances the commissioners are of opinion any penalty or forfeiture has been incurred by any master, &c., they may, with the sanction of the Governor, (if of opinion that it should be so) remit and forego or mitigate any such penalty— 17 V., c. 33, s. 5.

Remit or mitigate penalties

A clause precisely the same as 17 V., c. 2, n. 34, 17 V., c. 35, s. 6.

Governor's power to mitigate penalties

Upon examinations and enquiries made by any Commissioners of the Customs for ascertaining the truth of facts relative to the Customs, or to the conduct of officers or persons employed therein, and upon the like examinations and enquiries made by the Collector and Controller of Kingston, or the Sub-Collector of any outport, any person examined before them as a witness shall deliver his testimony on oath, to be administered by such commissioner, collector, &c., and persons convicted of making a false oath, or of giving false evidence on examination shall be guilty of perjury, and liable to the penalties, 17 V. c. 33, s. 7.

Oaths, powers to administer

False evidence

In all cases wherein proof on oath is required in any matter relating to any business under the management of the commissioners, such oath may be administered by either of the commissioners, or by the collector or controller of Kingston, or by the collector at any outport, or by the persons acting for them respectively, 17 V. c. 33, s. 8.

Persons to administer oath; see also 20 V. c. 5, s. 3, 18, 21

Any order, document, instrument, or writing (not being for the payment of money) required to be under the hands, or the hands and seals of the commissioners, being duly attested by any two of them, shall be deemed an order, &c. of the commissioners. Orders for payment of money shall have also the attestation of the Governor, 17 V. c. 33, s. 9.

Attestation of orders, &c.

For payment of money

Orders for payment of debentures or return duties

The Receiver-General shall not pay any monies on debentures on goods exported, or return duties on goods damaged, or any other return duties, until payment has been authorised by the commissioners, 17 V., c. 33, s. 10.

Present appointment and securities to continue in force

All commissions, deputations, and appointments to officers, in force, continued as if granted under this act, and the bonds of themselves and their sureties, for good conduct or otherwise, shall remain in force, 17 V., c. 33, s. 11.

Oath of office

Oath to be taken by persons appointed to any office or employment in the service of the customs under the control and direction of the Governor on admission:—

I A. B. do declare that I will be true and faithful in the execution, to the best of my knowledge and power, of the trust committed to my charge and inspection in the service of the customs of this island, and that I will not require, take or receive any perquisite, gratuity, or reward, whether pecuniary, or of any sort or description whatever, either directly or indirectly, for any service, act, duty, matter or thing done or performed, or to be done or performed in the execution or discharge of any of the duties of my office or employment, on any account whatever, other than my salary and what is or shall be allowed me by law, or by any special order of the Governor for the time being, 17 V. c. 33, s. 12.

Fees perquisites &c see 23 V., c. 12, s. 5

If any officer, clerk, or other person acting in any office or employment in or belonging to the Customs, under the control or direction of the Governor, &c., take or receive any fee, perquisite, gratuity, or reward, whether pecuniary or of any other description, directly or indirectly from any person (not being a person duly appointed to some office in the Customs) on account of any thing done or to be done by him, in any way relating to his office or employment, except such as he shall receive under any order or permission of the Governor, the offender shall, on proof to the Governor, be dismissed ; and if any person not being duly appointed to some office in the Customs, give, offer, or promise to give any such fee, &c., he shall forfeit £100, 17 V., c. 33, s. 13.

Hours of business

The Governor may, by warrant, appoint the hours of general attendance of the commissioners, officers, and other persons in the service at their proper office and places of employment, and may appoint the time during such hours at which any particular parts of their duties shall be performed by them, 17 V., c. 33, s. 14.

Exemptions from civil duties—not to be engaged in trade

No officer, &c., while employed or acting shall be compelled to serve in any corporate, or parochial, or other public office or employment, or to serve on any jury or inquest, or in the militia; nor shall he be engaged in any trade or business, 17 V., c. 33, s. 15,

Holidays

The following and no other days shall be kept as holidays : New Years' Day, Ash Wednesday, Good Friday, Easter Monday, the Queen's Birthday, 7th June, 28th August, Christmas Day and the Day after— 17 V., c. 33, s. 16.

Bills of entries

The person entering any goods, either upon the first importation, or upon clearing from warehouse, or upon exportation, shall deliver to the Collector or Controller, or proper officer, a bill of entry, fairly written in words at length, containing the name of the importer or exporter, and of the ship and master, the place from which arrived, or to which bound, and place within the port where the goods are to be laden or unladen, and the particulars of the quality and quantity of the goods and packages, their marks and numbers, and such other particulars as may be required by the Collector

Copies

Form

or other proper officer, and at the same time, one or more copies of such bill of entry in which all sums and numbers may be expressed in figures, and the particulars shall be written and arranged in such form and manner, and the number of copies such as the Collector or other proper officer shall require, and no other form shall be a valid entry, and such person shall, at the same time, pay down all duties on the goods (except in case of warehousing) and thereupon the Collector and Controller, &c. shall grant the necessary warrant for lading or unlading, 17 V., c, 33, s. 17.

Agents may be required to produce written authority

When any person applies to any Collector or Sub-Collector to transact business on account of any other, of whom he is not the known or recognized agent, the Collector, &c., or person acting in his behalf, may require him to produce a written authority, and in default may refuse to transact such business, 17 V., c. 33, s. 18.

Where the duties on goods imported are charged not according to the weight, rate, gauge or measure, but according to the value, such value shall be taken to be the first cost at the place of shipment, without shipping or other charges, and shall be ascertained by the oath of the importer or of his known agent, as follows :— Advalorem duties ; see also s. 18-20 ; see also Imports 28 V., c. 10, s. 5, 6.
Value 1st cost without charges
Oath

I, A B of, &c., merchant (or agent of C D of, &c., merchant, carrying on business in   , in this island, but at present an absentee therefrom) do hereby make oath that the invoice now produced, and marked with the letter   , and amounting to the sum of   , is the original invoice received in this island, and which was forwarded by Messrs. C F, of. &c., the shippers of the goods contained in   packages, marked and numbered respectively, and imported by me (or the said C D) in the   , master, from   , and set forth in the said invoice, and that I verily believe the price set down in the said invoice opposite to such goods respectively is the current value of the goods at the place at which the said goods were shipped, or from whence the same were imported, and that there has not been to my knowledge or belief any erasure or alteration made in the said invoice, and I further make oath that I am not (or that the said C D is not to my knowledge or belief) in possession of, nor is there to my knowledge or belief now in the island or intended to be sent or agreed to be admitted in account for the said goods any invoice other than the invoice above mentioned and now produced, or any bill of parcels, letters, document, or communication, or charge whatsoever fixing or charging any other price than the price set opposite to the goods respectively in such invoice set forth, and I further make oath that there are not, and is not to my knowledge or belief any goods or article whatsoever contained in the above mentioned packages, or either of them, other than those specified in the above mentioned invoice, and that there are no other goods on board the said vessel imported by, or belonging to me (or the said C D) for which invoices or an invoice have or has not been produced, or warrants or warrant duly passed. So help me God.
  A B.
Sworn before me this   day of   18   G. H., J. P.

Such oath to be in every case taken by the importer, except only when he may be absent from this island, and then by his agent, and shall be administered by the Collector or Sub-Collector at the port of importation, or, in case of the absence of the importer or agent from the port, by a Justice, and shall be attached to the invoice, and produced to the Collector, &c., at the time of paying the duty, and the Collector, &c., shall demand such invoice, with the oath attached, previous to the entry of any goods on which an advalorem duty is due or may attach. Any person convicted of making a false oath, touching any of the facts relating to any such invoice, shall be guilty of perjury, and punished accordingly. The invoice shall distinctly and clearly set forth and describe the mark and number, and contents and value of every package. By whom to be taken
Before whom, see 28 V. c. 10, s. 7.
To be attached to the invoice
Before entry
False Oath

On the oath or declaration of the importer, or his agent, in case of his absence from this island, that no invoice of the articles about to be entered has been received, they shall be examined by two competent persons to be appointed, one by the Collector, &c., the other by the importer, who shall declare on oath, before a justice, their true and real value at the time of importation, and the value so declared shall be that upon which duties shall be charged and paid, 20 V., c. 3, s. 3.

Such oath may be administered as well by the Controller or Inspector of Invoices as by the Collector at Kingston, 28 V., c. 10, s. 7.

Falsifying, erasing, changing, altering or varying any invoice for the purpose of evading the payment of duties, or any portion, a misdemeanor, and liable to punishment by fine or imprisonment as the court shall adjudge, 17 V., c. 33, s. 20.

When it appears by the certificate of the Collector and Controller that the importer or consignee has, in consequence of the non-receipt of any invoice, paid duty to a larger amount than should have been paid, or, upon the landing of any goods upon which duty has been paid according to invoice or estimation, it is discovered there is a deficiency in the weight, measure or gauge of such goods, the Receiver-General shall return the difference of duty (as computed by the Customs) to which he is entitled, 20 V., c. 5, s. 4.

Detention for the use of Government of goods under valued, see s. 19

If upon the examination of any goods entered to pay duty according to value, it appears to the Collector and Controller of Kingston, or Sub-Collector at any other port, that they are not truly valued, they may detain and secure such goods, and within 7 days after final examination by the officer appointed by the Governor to examine goods entered to pay duty according to value at any port, by virtue of a duty-paid-entry, take such goods for the use of the Government, in which case they shall forthwith give notice in writing to the person entering the goods, of their detention, personally, or by leaving it at his place of abode or business, and thereupon draw an order upon the Receiver-General for the value as appears by the invoice, with an addition of £10 per cent, and the duties upon the entry, where any have been paid, and the charges attendant upon their importation, and the amount shall be paid by the Receiver-General to the importer or consignee in full satisfaction of the same ; and the Collector, &c., shall dispose of the goods for the benefit of the Government, and if the produce of the sale exceeds the sum paid and all charges incurred by the Customs, one moiety of the overplus shall be given to the officer who detained the goods, and the other moiety paid to the Receiver General, and carried to account as import duties, 20 V., c. 5, s. 5.

Refund of excess of duties on lumber staves and shingles

Upon certificate from the Customs, shewing an actual delivery of a less quantity of lumber, staves or shingles than stated in the entry, and duty paid thereon, the Receiver-General shall return such difference, if the amount upon the whole cargo is not under £2, 17 V., c. 33, s. 23.

Refund on goods damaged on Voyage

If any goods, the import duty on which was paid at the time of entry, or which were entered to be warehoused, be found at the time of landing to be damaged, the importer or consignee may, within 15 days after landing, report to the Collector, &c., the name of the vessel in which they were imported, and that he intends to claim an allowance for such damage ; and the Collector, &c., on proof that the goods were damaged on board during the voyage, shall grant a certificate setting forth the amount of damage, and the Receiver-General shall return the amount mentioned in the certificate, 20 V., c. 5, s. 6.

Refund on goods abandoned for duties

Pickled fish

When it appears by the certificate of the officers that goods, so deteriorated in quality by damage or otherwise as not to be of the value of the duties paid thereon, have been abandoned and destroyed, the Receiver-General, shall refund the amount of duties paid. In applications for remission of duties for damage under this clause in respect to pickled fish, it shall be sufficient that the certificate of survey states the fish is unmerchantable and unfit for human food, and has been disposed of for agricultural purposes, and has not realized the amount of the duty, which shall be as valid for the remission of duties as if the fish had been actually destroyed ; and such fish shall be destroyed by order of the officers, when it is not satisfactorily proved to them that it is not (sic) to be used for agricultural purposes, 17 V., c. 33, s. 25.

Stores

The master, on arrival, shall include in his manifest a true account of all the provisions, liquors and other articles of store received on board as such and intended for provision or liquor for the crew or passengers, under penalty of £100 ; and no vessel shall be cleared until all the articles so received on board as stores have been satisfactorily accounted for, on oath, and the duties paid on such articles or portions as are not shewn to have been used for stores. Any stores or liquors shewn to any Custom House Officer to be on board at the time of sailing, shall be relieved from duty, 17 V., c. 33, s. 26.

Goods imported for the army and navy free

The Collector, &c., shall permit all articles imported for the army and navy, and consigned by bill of lading to the officer at the head of the Commissariat or Ordnance department, or the naval commanding officer on the station, to be landed and received free from duty, on the production of the bill of lading and certificate of such officer that the articles have been solely imported for the use of the army or navy, 17 V., c. 35, s. 27.

Refund of duties paid by contractor for supplying the army and navy ; see 20 V., c. 5, s. 23-26

The Receiver-General shall refund to the officer at the head of the Commissariat department, the duties paid by contractors supplying articles for the use of the army and navy on importation, on production of a certificate from the officer in command of the army or navy, that they were supplied for such public purpose, 17 V., c. 33, s. 28.

Any officer of the army or in the Ordnance or Commissariat depart. ment on actual duty, and any commissioned officer of H. M's. fleet serving on this station, who imports any wines, brandy or other spirits, or pur- chases from any resident importer or trader, any quantity (not less at one time than 50 gallons) expressly for his private consumption, or for that of any military or naval mess, shall be entitled to a remission of the duties, and the Receiver-General shall remit them, on a certificate from the Collec- tor and Controller of payment on importation, with a certificate from the respective officers claiming the drawback, testifying the quantity of each article, and that it was imported or purchased from an importer, to be named at length, expressly for their private consumption, or of any mili- tary or naval mess, and are in the actual possession of such officer or mess. Such certificate to be countersigned by the officer commanding the forces or fleet, as signifying their approval, 17 V., c. 33, s. 29.

Remission o n wines and spirits for consumption of officers of the army and navy, or ord- nance and Commis- sariat

On application by the consignee or captain of any vessel, bound for any port not a dependency of this island, the Collector, &c., may permit such stores or provisions as appear to him necessary to be cleared from any bonding warehouse, upon the consignee or agent entering into bond, in three times the amount of the duties, that no portion shall be re-landed in this island without notice to the proper officer, and permission first obtained, and upon any portion being landed except as aforesaid, such consignee or agent shall forfeit the penalty, to be recovered in any court of law, 17 V., c. 33, s. 30.

Ships stores clear- ed from warehouse on bond not to re- land them

Upon entry inwards, the officers may permit any goods to be entered as in transitu for any foreign port or port of this island by the same vessel, or may permit their transhipment to other vessels to be conveyed to their destination without payment of duties at the port of transhipment, upon the importer or his known agent entering into bond for payment of duties, if landed, or for their being bonded at the port of destination in this island, under the like conditions and regulations as in the case of goods removed coastwise from one bonding warehouse to another, 23 V., c. 10, s. 1.

Entry in transitu or tranship m e n t without payment of duties

All returns of imports and exports made to the Receiver-General by Sub-Collectors, shall be in the form in the schedule to 9 V., c. 14 (expired) or in any other form in conformity with the rules issued under this act. The master of every vessel entering, shall, in his manifest, together with the marks and number of packages, state their contents to the best of his knowledge, agreeably to the form, 17 V., c. 33, s. 32.

Forms of returns of imports and ex ports to Receiver- General
Manifest

No drawback shall be allowed on any goods which by reason of dam- age or decay become of less value for home use than the amount of such drawback ; and goods so damaged, cleared for drawback, shall be forfeited, and the person who caused them to be cleared shall forfeit £200, 17 V., c. 33, s. 33.

Clearance of goods of less value than the drawback

If any goods cleared to be exported for drawback are not duly ex- ported, or are re-landed (not having been re-landed or discharged, as short shipped, under the care of the proper officers,) they shall be forfeited, together with any ship, vessel, boat, or craft, used in re-landing or carrying them ; and any person by whom, or by whose means or orders such goods were re-landed or carried, shall forfeit equal to treble the value, such and all other forfeitures and penalties under this act to be recovered under 17 V., c. 2. 17 V., c. 33, s. 34.

Not exporting or re-landing good s cleared for draw- back

Such and all other penalties un- der this act recover- able under 17 V. c. 2

If on the exportation of British or other goods for drawback, estimated according to value, the value then affixed is found to be greater than the amount at which they were valued, at the time of importation, and on which import duty was paid, the party claiming the drawback shall forfeit £100, 17 V. c. 33, s. 35.

Valuing f o r drawback beyond the amount on which duty w a s paid

Import goods upon which advalorem duties shall be paid, shall be en- titled, on the exportation, to any port or place abroad, within 2 years of the date of their first importation to a drawback, equal in amount to the ad valo- rem duty paid on importation, upon the production of a like affidavit to that required by the following section, and such viva voce evidence, on oath, as the officers may require to be administered by the Collector in Kingston or Sub-Collector in any other port, to any person brought before him for exa- mination touching the importation and exportation, 20 V., c. 5, s. 9.

Drawback on ex- portation within 2 years, same as duty paid on importa- tion

To whom draw back allowed

No drawback allowed on exportation, unless the goods were entered in the name of the real owner at the time of entry and shipping, or of the actual purchaser and shipper, and who shall make and sign an affidavit (Form Schedule) that they were duly imported by him on the   day of   18   (mentioning the period) or that he purchased the same from the original importer on the   day of   18   and that the ad valorem duty has been paid, and they are intended for shipment on board the   master for   20 V., c. 5, s. 10.

Affidavit

Proceedings to obtain debenture and payment

For the purpose of computing and paying drawback, a debenture (Form Schedule) shall, within 10 days after the sailing of the exporting vessel, be prepared by the party claiming the drawback, accompanied by the affidavits before mentioned, and laid before the Collector, &c., who shall certify to the due entry outwards; and from the value stated in the affidavit, and upon such evidence as may be taken (s. 9,) the amount of duty to be returned shall be computed, and the debenture when signed delivered to the party claiming the drawback, who, upon presenting same, shall receive the amount from the Receiver-General, and the receipt of the owner, merchant or exporter, or his known agent thereon, shall be the Receiver-General's discharge, 20 V., c. 5, s. 11.

Quantities upon which drawback allowed

Upon the exportation of any of the following goods, upon which duties of importation have been paid, without having been bonded, the Receiver-General shall return to the exporter the whole of the duty paid under the above regulations. Not less than 10 barrels of flour, bread or meal, 10 firkins of lard or butter, 10 boxes of candles, 20 boxes of soap, 5 hhds of ale beer or porter, in bulk, or 15 barrels of bottled ale, beer, or porter, 10 barrels of beef, pork or pickled fish, 5 tierces or 25 bags of rice, 5000 lbs. weight of dried fish, 10 barrels of tongues, 5000 feet of lumber, or 5000 shingles shall be exported at one time, 20 V., c. 5, s. 12.

Drawback on bread or biscuits made here

Upon the exportation of any bread or biscuits made in this island from flour imported, the Receiver-General shall return to the exporter the duty paid upon the flour consumed in making such bread or biscuits, upon the production to him of a statement on oath of the quantity of flour used; the duties to be returned not to exceed the duties upon bread or biscuit imported under acts in force at the time of exportation, 20 V., c. 5, s. 13.

Drawback on exports to Grand Caymanas

The drawback or return of duties shall be allowed on the exportation or carriage of goods to the Grand Caymanas, whereon duties are paid as herein provided, and under the like regulations as are herein directed in respect to drawback. In addition to other regulations, before any debenture is signed, a certificate, under the hand and seal of the custos or some known authority at the place, setting forth the marks and numbers of the packages containing the goods whereon drawback is claimed, and stating that such goods have been landed at the Grand Caymanas, shall be produced to the collector, &c., and be presented with the debenture to the Receiver-General, who shall not pay any drawback or return any duties unless such certificate is presented, 20 V. c. 5, s. 14.

Materials for repair of vessels in distress

The provisions of 17 V., c. 33, and 20 V., c. 5, relating to drawback, extended to, and allowed to operate in respect to all materials necessary to be used in the repairs of vessels putting into any harbour in distress for repairs, not exceeding in the aggregate £100, 28 V., c. 10, s. 11.

Altering marks false invoices &c.

Any person altering, with intent to defraud the revenue, any mark of any package, or the weight of any parcel of goods which has been bonded, or who wilfully uses any counterfeited or falsified invoice or document or instrument used in the transaction of any business or matter relating to the customs, shall forfeit £300, 20 V., c. 5, s. 15.

Computation of duties on liquors in bottles

For the better computation of the duties on ale, beer, porter, cider, perry, wines, or spirits in bottles, six reputed quart, or 12 reputed pint bottles, shall be taken to be one gallon, 20 V., c. 5, s. 16.

Remission of duties on oil for lighthouses
Gunpowder for mining
Iron for railways or tramways

The commissioners on proof that any quantity of oil has been imported or purchased for the use of any light-house, gunpowder exclusively for mining purposes, iron exclusively as rails, chairs, and points for a railway or tramway, may direct the Receiver General to re-pay to the commissioners of the light-house, or the importers or purchasers of gunpowder for mining purposes or iron as aforesaid, the duty paid upon the quantity so imported or purchased, 20 V., c. 5, s. 17.

See Traction Engines, 26 V., S. 2, c. 19, s. 3.

On Traction Engines

The Inspector of Invoices at Kingston (when there shall be one), or the officer who, in his absence, or when there shall be none; is appointed by the Governor to examine goods entered to pay duty according to the value, at Kingston, or at any port (and the Governor is authorised to appoint such officers), shall examine every invoice previous to warrants being passed and the duty paid, and ascertain and certify the correctness ; and no invoice shall be received, nor warrant passed for any goods mentioned in any invoice not so certified ; and if any such inspector or officer see reason to doubt the accuracy or correctness of the value placed upon any goods mentioned in any invoice, he shall require the importer or consignee to attend at the custom house, and examine him on oath (which the Collector or Sub-Collector shall administer), touching such goods and invoice, and the value thereof, and on all points relating thereto, 20 V., c. 5, s. 18.

Powers and duties of inspector of invoices, or officer to examine goods liable to ad-valorem duties ; see also s. 3 Inspector of invoices and assistant, see Imports 28 V., c. 10, s. 5, 6.

The Inspector, or other officer, shall, out of every shipment, or importation of goods to or by any person, subject to ad valorem duty, open one package at least, and, if he think it necessary, all or any number of the packages, and examine and count, or cause, &c., the contents of every package so opened, giving 48 hours' notice to the importer or consignee who may attend at the opening and examination, and should such goods or any portion be found upon examination to be under value, or under price in the invoice or entry, the Collector and Controller at Kingston, upon the report of the inspector or other officer to that effect being made to them, or the Sub-Collector at any other port upon his own view, may, instead of detaining such goods, and, by virtue of a duty-paid entry, taking the same for the use of the Government (s. 5, sup.), cause the same, as stated by the invoice, or on the entry, to be increased to such amount as may seem necessary, and the importer or consignee shall, within 5 days after the increase of value has been intimated to him, pay the duties at such increased value, and in default of such payment, the goods shall be sold at such time and place as the Collector, &c., shall direct, and the proceeds, after deducting the duty, and all charges incurred by the officers, applied (as directed in the concluding portion of 17 V., c. 23, s. 22, repealed by 20 V., c. 5, s. 1. See s, 5, sup. directing the distribution.) Notwithstanding the payment by any importer or consignee of duty upon any goods at the increased value, or the sale of the goods by the officers, the importer or consignee shall, if the commissioners are of opinion his intention was to defraud the revenue, be liable to a penalty of £500, to be recovered under 17 V., c. 2. 20 V., c. 5, s. 19.

Increase value, and in default of payment of duties, on increased value, sell the goods

Penalty in addition

If any inspector (sic) or consignee, upon any examination, wilfully and corruptly give false evidence, or answer, he shall be guilty of perjury, and punishable accordingly, and if he refuses or neglects to attend, or refuses to give evidence or answer in obedience to any requisition by the Inspector of Invoices or Sub-Collector, he shall be subject to the like penalties, and to be enforced as in cases of summary trials before Justices against persons refusing or neglecting to attend or give evidence, 20 V., c. 5, s. 20.

False evidence —refusal to attend or give evidence

In the absence of a Justice, the chief acting officer, at any port other than Kingston, may administer oaths, or accept of declarations required by any act to be in force relating to the Customs, or to their entry or clearance of goods, or the warehousing or exportation of the same, 20 V., c. 5, s. 21.

Administration of oaths, see 17 V., c. 33, s. 7. 8 ; 20 V., c. 5, s. 3

In all disputes between any importer or consignee and officer respecting the value of any goods, the commissioners may determine the same, 20 V., c. 5, s. 22.

Commissioners to determine disputes

Whenever horned cattle are imported for the use of the naval or military service, the duties which may be enforced at the period of importation shall be paid by the contractor importing, 20 V. c. 5, s. 23.

Duties on cattle for the army and navy contracts

Any contractor for the supply of fresh beef for the use of the army or navy, shall be entitled to a refund of the duties paid on importation of the stock, if at the time of application for refund he delivers to, and leaves with the Receiver-General an affidavit, sworn to before a Justice, with a certificate of the officer at the head of the Commissariat Department, or in charge of the victualling depot, in respect of the quantity of meat supplied by the contractor for the consumption of the forces, 20 V., c. 5, s. 24.

Refund of duties

Affidavit to ob tain

Form of affidavit :—

I, A. B., contractor for the supply of fresh beef to Her Majesty's army (or navy) do solemnly swear that　　　　　head of horred cattle, imported by me on the　　　　day of　　　　in the　　　　(name of vessel) from　　　　　　　(name the place whence imported) and on which a duty of 30s. per head has been paid by me, have been slaughtered for the use of Her Majesty's service, according to the terms of my contract, and not otherwise ; and I do further swear that no portion of the flesh or carcase, with the exception of the head, heart, pluck, feet, tallow, and hides of such cattle or any of them, as to the best of my knowledge and belief, have been sold, or been delivered for consumption to any person or persons not being entitled to receive and consume the same under the terms of my contract.—So help me God.

Note.—Should any portion of the meat be sold to prevent its spoiling, let the same be stated, and a proportionate reduction must be made by the contractor from the duty claimed to be refunded

And I hereby claim a refund of the undermentioned amount of duty, viz : On　　　　　　head of imported stock, slaughtered as above stated, at　　　　per head　　....　　....　　£

Less one fifth of the above, being the average value of the head, heart, pluck, feet, tallow, and hides, sold by me as above stated　....　....　....　£

Amount of refund duty claimed　....　　....　£

Sworn to before me at　　　Jamaica this　　　day of　　　18

Signature of Magistrate.

Certified that　　　pounds weight of fresh beef have been supplied by Mr.　　　the contractor for her Majesty's　　at　　　between the 1st and　　　of　　　18

Commissariat, Jamaica, Kingston,　　　18

Signature of Officer—20 V. c., 5, s. 25.

Selling flesh not accounted for

If any contractor, by himself, his servant or agent, sell or permit to be sold, any portion of the flesh not being accounted for in the preceding certificate or affidavit, he shall, on conviction before 2 Justices, forfeit treble the amount of duty on the cattle in respect of which he claimed such refund ; and if he falsely depose to the affidavit, he shall, on conviction, suffer the penalties of wilful perjury, 20 V., c. 5, s. 26.

False deposition.

Salaries of officers

There shall be pai to the several officers during the continuance of this Act, the salaries in the schedule annexed, in lieu of all fees for any services or duties, 23 V., c. 12, s. 1.

The Clerk in Kingston receiving a salary of £275 per annum, being £25 in addition to the £250 in schedule, shall continue to receive, in addition to the salary of £250, a further sum of £25 per annum, so long as he continues to hold his present appointment, 23 V., c. 12, s. 2.

Such salaries, and the sums for the remuneration of additional Tide-Waiters, shall be paid monthly to the Collector and Controller at Kingston, and Sub-Collector at each port by the Receiver-General, upon the Governor's warrant, 23 V., c. 12, s. 3.

Additional Tide-Waiters

Besides the four Tide-Waiters at Kingston mentioned in the Schedule, the Collector and Controller at Kingston may employ and sanction the employment when necessary of any number of persons to act as Tide-Waiters in Kingston and any other principal　　　, and each person so employed shall be paid at the rate of 8s. per day, for every day or part of a day he shall serve ; but no person shall serve as such, until he has taken an oath, which the Collector at Kingston, or Sub-Collector at any other port, may administer :

Oath

I., A. B., do swear that I will faithfully and zealously perform the duties of a Tide-Waiter, and without fear, favor or affection, fee or reward, and uninfluenced and unrestrained by any expectation or consideration whatsoever, inform against every person whom I shall know to be evading or attempting to evade any of the revenue laws of this island, and that I will use all diligence to discover and make known any attempt to evade such laws, or any of them. So help me God, 23 V., c. 12, s. 4.

If any officer demand or receive any fee for any service performed by Penalties on demanding &c. fees
him as such, he shall forfeit £400, to be recovered by action of debt or information, one moiety to the person suing, upon recovery of which penalty, the party suing or prosecuting shall be entitled to his whole costs, out of purse, as between attorney and client to be taxed, 23 V., c. 12, s. 5.

In case of refusal, wilful omission, or neglect on the part of any officer to Neglect of duty &c.
perform any duty of his office on entering or clearing any vessel, or in delivering any necessary document or paper, he shall forfeit not exceeding £60 nor less than £20, to be recovered before two Justices, and, in default of payment, the Justices shall commit the offender to gaol, not exceeding three months, nor less than six weeks, unless he sooner pay the penalty, 23 V., c. 12, s. 6.

The Collector and Controller of Kingston shall take security from the Security
officers in such sums and such number of sureties as may be deemed sufficient by the Executive Committee to her Majesty, for the due accounting for such monies and the faithful discharge of their duties. The present officers who have already given security need not enter into fresh security, but the existing security shall continue in force, 23 V., c. 12, s. 7.

A sum not exceeding £1500 shall be paid on the warrant of the Governor by the Receiver-General, in quarterly porcions to the Collector and £1500 per annum for incidental expenses
Controller at Kingston, for incidental expenses of the establishment of the island, who shall make a return every quarter of the expenditure for incidental expenses to the Executive Committee, 23 V., c. 12, s. 8.

The Health Officers' fees, under 4 V., c. 32, s. 29, shall be recovered and Health officers' fees
received by the Collector and Controller at Kingston and Sub-Collectors at other ports, and paid over to the Receiver-General, in the same manner as the import duties, 23 V. c. 12, s. 9.

Nothing herein shall prevent the abolition of any office, or reduction of Abolition of offices &c.
any salary during the continuance of this Act,—the salaries saved, to lapse into the general fund of the island, 23 V., c. 12, s. 18.

The Governor need not issue a new commission to any person holding Existing commissions to remain in full force
any office, but the existing commissions shall remain of force and effect, 23 V., c. 12, s. 19.

Act to continue until 31st March, 1867, and notwithstanding its expiry, Duration of act
any offences may be punished and penalties enforced, 23 V. c. 12, s. 22.

The powers possessed by the harbour masters, of going on board any Export of articles of war
vessel about to depart from the island, and examining it for the purpose of preventing the export of articles of war, prohibited by proclamation, are also conferred upon the officers of Customs, 25 V. c. 23, s. 3.

SCHEDULE A.—20 V., c. 5.

No.

JAMAICA.

Custom-House, Form of debentures 9.

These are to certify that   has made oath according to law, and otherwise proved to our satisfaction that the several goods specified on the back of this debenture, and set forth in the affidavit (or affidavits) hereunto annexed, have been sold for the purpose of exportation, and it having been made to appear to us from the certificate of the shipping officer that the said goods have been duly exported, we further certify that the amount of drawback on this debenture is   pounds   shillings and   pence.

Collector.

Controller.

To   the Receiver General.

U

Affidavit where exporter was also the importer s. 10

I,   do hereby make oath, that the several packages of British or other goods specified on the back hereof, and entered to be exported on the   for   were duly imported by me in the   and the import duty of   per cent. duly paid on the   day of   18

I do further make oath, that the value now affixed to the said goods is the real and true value upon which the duty was paid at the time of importing the said goods into this island. So help me God.

Sworn before me this   day of   18

No. 1.

Of exporter not claiming drawback, s. 10

I,   do hereby make oath, that the several packages of British goods specified on the back hereof, were purchased by me from the parties whose names are set opposite thereto, and that the said goods are intended for exportation in the   master for   —So help me God.

Sworn before me this   day of   18

No. 2.

Of claimant of drawback, s. 10

I,   do hereby make oath, that the several packages of British or other goods set forth in the affidavit of   were sold by   to the said   and that the said goods were duly imported by   on the   and the import duty duly paid thereon: I do further make oath, that the value now affixed to the said goods is the real and true value upon which the duty was paid at the time of importing the said goods into this island.—So help me God.

Sworn before me this   day of   18

No.

Certificate of custos of Grand Caymanas. s. 14

Grand Caymanas.   }
Place where Certificate Given. }

These are to certify that it hath been proved to my satisfaction that the several goods contained in   packages, marked and numbered respectively   and brought from the port of   in the island of Jamaica, in the   whereof   is master, have been landed at   Grand Caymanas.

Given under my hand and seal at   Grand Caymanas, the
     of   18

           Signature   Seal

Custos (or other known authority.)

SCHEDULE to 23 V, c. 12.

INCLUDING REMUNERATION FOR THE COLLECTION OF THE SEVERAL TONNAGE DUTIES AND HEALTH OFFICERS' FEES.

KINGSTON —Collector	......	......	£800
Comptroller	......		400
One Clerk, at	......		275
Two Clerks, at each	......		250
One Clerk, at	......		225
One Clerk, at	......		210
One Clerk, at	......		200
One Clerk, at	......		175
One Clerk, at	......		130
Landing Surveyor	......		300
First Waiter and Searcher		......	250
Second ditto ditto	......	......	200
Third ditto ditto	......	......	175
Fourth ditto ditto	......	......	175

KINGSTON—Fifth Waiter and Searcher	......	£175
Sixth ditto ditto	......	175
Warehouse Keeper	......	250
Assistant ditto	......	175
First Locker	......	130
Second Locker	......	125
Third Locker	......	125
Inspector of Invoices		300
Sub-Collector at Old Harbour	......	250
Tide Surveyor at Port Royal	......	100
Four Tide-Waiters, at each		·120
PORT MORANT—Sub-Collector, Waiter and Searcher		250
Clerk	......	130
MORANT BAY—Sub-Collector, Waiter and Searcher		225
PORT ANTONIO—Sub-Collector, Waiter and Searcher		150
PORT MARIA—Sub-Collector	......	250
Clerk and Landing Waiter	......	130
ANNOTTO BAY—Sub-Collector	......	225
FALMOUTH—Sub-Collector	......	400
Landing Surveyor	......	250
First Waiter and Searcher		200
Second ditto ditto	......	175
Clerk and Warehouse Keeper	......	120
RIO BUENO—Sub-Collector	......	150
SAINT ANN'S BAY—Sub-Collector	......	250
MONTEGO BAY—Sub-Collector and Warehouse Keeper		400
Waiter and Searcher, and Landing Tide Surveyor		225
Clerk and Warehouse Keeper	......	175
LUCEA—Sub-Collector	......	250
SAVANNA-LA-MAR—Sub-Collector	......	250
Clerk and Landing Waiter	......	150
BLACK RIVER—Sub-Collector	......	250

Deaths by Neglect, &c., Compensation.

When death is caused by wrongful act, neglect or default, which would have entitled the party injured to damages if death had not ensued, the person who would have been liable shall be liable to an action for damages, although the death was caused under circumstances amounting in law to felony, 10 V., c. 6, s. 1. *Actions when maintainable*

For the benefit of the wife, husband, parent and child of the deceased and to be brought by his executor or administrator, the Jury may give damage proportioned to the injury resulting to the parties for whose benefit the action is brought, which amount, after deducting the costs not recovered from the defendant, shall be divided amongst those parties in such shares as the Jury find, 10 V., c. 6, s. 2. *By whom and for whose benefit and in what proportions divisible*

No more than one action shall lie, and it shall be commenced within 12 calendar months after the death, 10 V., c. 6, s. 3. *But one action to lie, and within 12 months after death*

In such action, the plaintiff shall, with the declaration, deliver to the defendant or his attorney, a full particular of the persons on whose behalf the action is brought, and the nature of the claim in respect of which damages are sought to be recovered, 10 V., c. 6, s. 4. *Particulars of persons interested and claim to be delivered with declaration*

"Persons" shall apply to bodies politic and corporate; "Parent" shall include father and mother, grand-father and grand mother, and step-father and step-mother; and "Child," son and daughter, grand-son and grand-daughter, and step-son and step-daughter, 10 V., c. 6, s. 5. *Interpretation*

Deeds.

To be acknowledged or proved and recorded to pass a freehold or grant a lease for above 3 years
· A deed in due form of law, made, and within three months after date, acknowledged by the parties, or proved by the oath of a witness, and recorded at length in the office of enrolments within 3 months shall be valid, without livery, seisin, attornment, or any other act or ceremony in the law; and no deed made without such acknowledgment, or proof and enrolment, shall pass any freehold or inheritance, or grant any lease for above 3 years, 33 C. 2, c. 12, s. 1.

Sales under power to persons here proved and recorded before conveyance from the proprietor recorded to be good
If any person here lawfully empowered make sale of any lands or freehold to any person in this island, and the deeds are duly proved and recorded, before any conveyance from the proprietor is here recorded the deed made and passed here shall be effectual, 33 C. 2, c. 12, s. 3.

Lands conveyed by deed as effectually as by fine and recovery if made for valuable consideration 33 c. 2 c. 22 s. 3, repealed
Bills of sale, deeds and conveyances heretofore made and duly executed, acknowledged, proved and recorded, pursuant to 33 C. 2., c. 22, although no valuable consideration be therein inserted, and all deeds and conveyances to be made for valuable considerations of lands in this island (excepting by infants and persons of nonsane memory), shall pass and convey the lands as fully as any real estate in Great Britain can pass by fine and recovery, 10 Ann, c. 12, s. 3.

Secretary to give receipts for deeds &c. and endorse the date
The Secretary, his Deputies or Clerks, shall immediately upon bringing any deed or writings into the office, sign and give a receipt to the persons demanding the same, and paying for recording, and underwrite, or indorse the day of their being entered, and they shall be deemed to be enrolled from the time of the entry, 10 Ann, c. 4, s. 2.

And record same within 90 days
And record them within 90 days, 56 G. 3, c. 19, s. 3; 60 G. 3, c. 28, s. 1.

Deeds executed in the island not recorded within 90 days after date postponed to bona fide deeds for valuable consideration duly recorded
Deeds executed in this island for lands shall be duly proved or acknowledged and recorded within 90 days after date, or stand void against other purchasers or mortgagees bona fide for valuable consideration, who prove and record their deeds within the time prescribed, 4 G. 2, c. 5, s. 5.

But available against the first vendor &c.
If any vendee, or mortgagee omit to prove and record his deed within the time, and pursuant to the form prescribed, but afterwards does so, no second sale, or mortgage being made, it shall be good, 4 G. 2, c. 5, s. 6.

Time within which deeds executed out of the island must be recorded
Deeds and conveyances executed out of this island shall be proved or acknowledged and recorded within (6, extended by 16 G. 2, c. 5 to 12) calendar months after their date, and within 90 days after the arrival of the ship which brought the same, otherwise to stand void with respect to other purchasers or mortgagees bona fide, for valuable consideration, but still to preserve and maintain a right and title against the vendor or mortgagor and their heirs, in case the first vendee or mortgagee shall, at any time, duly prove and record their deeds and conveyances, no second or other deed or conveyance being in the meantime proved or acknowledged and recorded in favor of any other person, 4 G. 2., c. 5, s. 7; 16 G. 2, c. 5.

Penalties on vendors or mortgagers executing deeds without noticing previous mortgages
If any vendor or mortgager of lands, &c., in this island execute a second or other deed, or conveyance or sale of the same lands, &c. other than to the first vendee, or a second or other deed of mortgage, without having taken notice of the first or prior mortgages with which the lands stand charged at the time of executing the deed, he shall be tried and punished, and subject to the forfeitures and penalties by the laws of England, provided against persons who execute mortgages without taking notice of prior mortgages, 4 G. 2, c. 5, s. 8.

Deed &c. in Secretary's Office 20 years, to be destroyed
All deeds and other papers (except last wills and testaments) that have been recorded and have remained in the Secretary's Office for 20 years, shall be destroyed by the Secretary, 21 G. 3, c. 23, s. 5.

Partitions, Exchanges, Assignments See partition, 8 G. 1, c. 5
No pa or exchange or assignment of any freehold or leasehold land should be valid at law, unless made by deed, except in cases where partition is authorized to be made under the act in force, 8 V., c. 19, s. 2.

Effect of the words " Grant and Exchange"
Neither the word "grant" nor the word "exchange" in any deed shall have the effect of creating any warranty or right of re-entry, or covenant by implication, except where by any act of this island it is or shall be declared the word "grant" shall have that effect, 8 V., c. 19, s. 5.

Need not be indented. Persons not parties may take benefit under
It shall not be necessary in any case to have a deed indented; and any person, not a party to any deed, may take an immediate benefit under it, in the same manner as he might under a deed poll, 8 V., c. 19, s, 9.

Deeds, Probate.

Deeds executed in Great Britain or Ireland, shall be proved on the oath or affirmation of the subscribing witness or witnesses, or acknowledged by the parties before the Mayor or Chief Magistrate of any city, borough, or town corporate in Great Britain or Ireland, and certified under the Common Seal, 27 V., S. 1, c. 17, s. 1.

Deeds executed in any of the dominions, territories, colonies, dependencies or possessions of the Crown, shall be proved on the oath or affirmation of the subscribing witness, or acknowledged by the party before the Governor, or the Commander-in-Chief, or a Judge, or the Mayor or Chief Magistrate of any city or town, or a Notary Public, or any officer, civil or military, holding a commission under the Crown, either under the Imperial or Colonial Government, and certified under his hand and official seal, and where a seal is not appropriated to his office, under the private seal of such functionary, the certificate stating that no official seal exists, 27 V., S. 1, c. 17, s. 2.

Deeds executed in any foreign state whatever, shall be proved or acknowledged before her Majesty's Ambassador, Envoy, Minister, Charge d'Affaires, or Secretary of Embassy or Legation, exercising his functions in such state, or before H. M's. Consul-General or Consul, or any Vice-Consul, or Acting Consul, or Consular agent exercising his functions in such foreign state, and certified under his hand and seal, used in his public capacity, or under the hand and private seal of such functionary if there be no public seal, the absence of which is to be certified, 27 V., S. 1, c. 17, s. 3.

When by statute or ordinance having the force of law in any part of the United Kingdom, a declaration is substituted for an oath or affirmation, the subscribing witness may prove the execution by such declaration, in lieu of oath, 27 V., S. 1, c. 17, s. 4.

Deeds executed in the island shall be proved on the oath or affirmation of the subscribing witness, or acknowledged by the party, before the Governor, a Judge of the Supreme Court, or a Justice of the Peace, and bear the true temporal and local date, 26 V. S. 1, c. 17, s. 5.

Where the right or property of any woman under coverture is intended to be conveyed, released, or extinguished, she shall be examined separately and apart from her husband by the person who takes and attests the probate or acknowledgment, and the examination certified as in England or this island, 27 V. S. 1, c. 17, s. 6.

A deed may be executed in any place, whether subject to the Crown or not, and proved and acknowledged, and the separate examination of any married woman may be taken in this island, or any other place where the witness or party may be, according to the provisions of this act having reference to the place where taken, and be as effectual as if proved or acknowledged at the place of execution, 27 V., S. 1, c. 17, s. 7.

Where more than one witness attests the execution by one party or more, it shall be sufficient to prove the execution by one of such subscribing witnesses, 27 V. S., 1, c. 17, s. 8.

Any Deed proved or acknowledged previously to this act as hereby required, shall be valid, 27 V., S. 1, c. 17, s. 9.

Not to render it imperative or necessary to prove or acknowledge any deed not previously required to be proved, &c., nor to alter the existing rules of law or equity, as to the effect and operation of any deed which, although required, may not be so proved or recorded, 27 V., S. 1, c. 17, s. 10.

Defamation.

In any action for defamation, the defendant (after notice in writing of his intention to the plaintiff at the time of filing or delivering the plea), may give in evidence, in mitigation of damages, that he made or offered an apology to the plaintiff before the action, or as soon afterwards as he had an opportunity of doing so in case it was commenced before there was an opportunity of making or offering such apology, 14 V., c. 34, s. 1.

[marginal notes:] Probate of deeds executed in Great Britain or Ireland — In the dependencies of the crown — In foreign states — Declaration in lieu of oaths — In this island — Women under coverture — Probate by one attesting witness sufficient — Deeds already proved — Deeds not previously requiring probate — Offer of apology in mitigation

Plea that libel was inserted without malice or gross negligence and an apology or offer of an apology with payment of money into court, Replication

In an action for a libel in any public newspaper or other periodical publication, the defendant may plead that it was inserted without actual malice and without gross negligence, and that before the action, or at the earliest opportunity afterwards, he inserted in such newspaper or periodical a full apology for the libel, or if the newspaper, &c., should be ordinarily published at intervals exceeding one week, had offered to publish the apology in any newspaper, &c., to be selected by the plaintiff, and upon filing such plea may pay into Court, money, by way of amends, which shall be of the same effect, and available in the same manner and to the same extent, and subject to the same rules and regulations as to payment of costs as in personal actions, and the plaintiff may reply generally, denying the whole of such plea ; but any such plea, without at the same time making a payment of money into Court by way of amends, shall be deemed a nullity, 14 V., c. 34, s. 2.

Publishing or threatening, &c., a libel, or proposing to abstain, &c. to extort money

Publishing or threatening to publish any libel, or directly or indirectly threatening to print or publish, or proposing to abstain from, or offering to prevent the printing or publishing of any thing touching any other person with intent to extort any money, or security, or valuable thing from such or any other person, or with intent to induce any person to confer or procure for any person any appointment, or office of profit or trust: penalty, imprisonment, with or without hard labor, for not exceeding three years. Not to affect any law respecting the sending or delivery of threatening letters or writings, 14 V., c. 34, s. 3.

Publishing libel knowing it to be false

Maliciously publishing any defamatory libel, knowing it to be false: penalty, imprisonment in the common gaol for not exceeding two years, and fine, 14 V. c. 34, s. 4.

Publishing libel

Maliciously publishing any defamatory libel : penalty, fine or imprisonment, or both, such imprisonment not to exceed one year, 14 V., c. 34, s. 5.

Plea of Justification to indictment and replication—and enquiry thereunder—may be in addition to not guilty

On the trial of any indictment or information for a defamatory libel, the defendant having pleaded as after mentioned, the .truth of the matters charged may be enquired into, but shall not amount to a defence, unless it was for the public benefit they should be published, and to entitle the defendant to give evidence of their truth he shall allege their truth as required in pleading a justification to an action for defamation, that it was for the public benefit they should be published, and the particular facts by reason whereof it was so, to which plea the prosecutor may reply generally, denying the whole. If after such plea the defendant is convicted, the court in pronouncing sentence may consider whether his guilt is aggravated or mitigated by the plea, and by the evidence given to prove or disprove the same. The truth of the matters charged in the libel shall in no case be enquired into without such plea of justification. In addition to such plea, the defendant may plead " not guilty:"

Not to prejudice any defence under plea of not guilty

The act shall not take away or prejudice any defence under the plea of not guilty, which it is now competent to the defendant to make to any action or indictment, &c., for defamatory words or libel, 14 V., c. 34, s. 6.

When the defendant may prove the publication was without his authority, and did not arise from want of care on his part

When upon the trial of any indictment, &c. for libel, under the plea of not guilty, evidence is given, which establishes a presumptive case of publication against the defendant by the act of any other person by his authority, he may prove that the p l a was made without his authority, consent or knowledge, and did obtcation from want of due care or caution on his part, 14 V., c. 34, s. 7.

Costs on indictment &c.

In case of any indictment, &c., by a private prosecutor for any defamatory libel, if judgment is given for the defendant, he shall be entitled to recover his costs from the prosecutor ; and upon a special plea of justification, if the issue be found for the prosecutor, he shall be entitled to recover from the defendant the costs sustained by him by reason of such plea ; such costs of the defendant or prosecutor to be taxed by the officer of the court, 14 V., c. 34. s. 8,

Enforcement and registration

Where a general verdict of guilty or not guilty is returned on the trial of any indictment, &c., to which a plea of justification is filed under 14 V., c. 34, the costs when taxed shall be paid by the private prosecutor or defendant to the other, and may be enforced, by attachment, under the seal of the Supreme Court, or by writ of venditioni, in the form now used for the enforcement of judgments, and may be registered under 8 V., c. 48, and be a lien upon the lands of the parties liable, 18 V., c. 44.

Deodands.

There shall be no forfeiture of any chattel for having moved to or caused the death of man. No coroner's jury shall find any forfeiture of any chattel, which moved or caused the death of the deceased, or any deodand whatever ; nor shall it be necessary, in any indictment or inquisition for homicide, to allege the value of the instrument which caused the death of the deceased, or that it was of no value, 10 V., c. 7.

Abolished

No allegation of value in indictments or inquisitions, see 16 V. c. 15, s. 25.

Dissenters' Marriages.

Marriages solemnized by Dissenting Ministers under the regulations after mentioned shall be valid, 4 V., c. 44, s. 2.

When valid

Banns of marriage may be published in any place of religious worship, or before any public congregation, in an audible manner, sometime during public divine service, on a Sunday, in the face of the congregation, to which both or one of the parties is considered to be attached, and shall contain the Christian or other name and surname, and place of abode of each of the parties, and be so published for three Sundays preceding the solemnization of the marriage, during the morning service if there be service in the morning, and if not, then during the evening service, and if the parties are of different congregations, the banns shall be published before each of the congregations to which they belong, whether in the same parish or not, and where the banns have been published in different places, the officiating minister, under a penalty of £30 sterling at either of the places, shall, at the request of both, or either of the parties, give a certificate of the banns having been published in the place of which he is an officiating minister, and on its production to the minister of the other place, or of such certificates to any other such minister, he may solemnize matrimony between the parties, according to the form and ceremony in use by the persuasion to which he belongs. When the form is other than than that of the United Church, each of the parties shall, in some part of the ceremony, make the declaration according to Schedule A., 4 V., c. 44, s. 3.

Publication of banns in the face of the congregations to which both belong, certificates

Solemnization upon receipt of certificates
Declaration where form is not that of the Church of England

No minister shall be obliged to publish banns between any persons, unless they, two days at least before the first publication, deliver, or cause, &c., to be delivered to him, a notice of their true Christian and other names and surnames, and a description of their place or respective places of abode ; and no minister shall solemnize any marriage after 6 calendar months from the last publication of banns, but the publication shall be void, and the banns must be re-published, 4 V., c. 44, s. 4.

Notice before publication to minister, of names and abode of parties

Marriage to be within 6 months from last publication of banns

No minister who solemnizes any marriage after publication of banns between persons, both, or one of whom (not being a widower or widow) at the time of marriage is under legal age, shall be responsible or liable for having solemnized such marriage without the consent of the parents or guardians, or other persons whose consent is required by law, unless such parent, &c., or one of them, forbid the marriage, and give notice to the minister before he has solemnized the same; and in case the marriage is forbidden, and notice given, the publication of the banns shall be absolutely void, 4 V., c. 44, s. 5.

Liability of minister who solemnises marriage after banns, between persons under age

If marriage forbidden, banns void

The Governor may issue licenses to marry to any Dissenting Minister which shall authorize the solemnization of the marriage by any minister by whom it could have been solemnized, if banns had been published— 4 V., c. 44, s. 6.

Licenses to marry

Wantonly, maliciously, or frivolously forbidding the publication of banns or the solemnization of marriage, without lawful and sufficient cause and authority : penalty, a fine not exceeding £10 sterling, or imprisonment in gaol, not exceeding two months, at the discretion of two Justices, 4 V., c. 44, s. 7.

Wantonly forbidding banns

Marriages shall be solemnized in the presence of two witnesses besides the minister, and immediately after an entry shall be made in a marriage register book, to be kept for the purpose, in which it shall be expressed that the marriage was had by banns or license, and if both or either of the parties married by banns were under age, and not a widower or widow, that it was had with the consent of the parents or guardians, or person having lawful authority to withhold consent, and be signed by the minister with his proper addition, and by the parties married, and attested by the

Requisites to marriage registration in duplicate and recording, see 26 V. s. 2, c. 10.

two witnesses, [form Schedule B] and at the same time before the parties, depart, a duplicate original register shall be made, signed, and attested, [form Schedule C] and left in the hands of the minister, and within six calendar months transmitted to the Island Secretary, to be filed and recorded **Copies evidence** and safely preserved in his office. Such original register, and every copy certified under the hand of the Island Secretary, shall be evidence of the facts therein recorded, when necessary, to give evidence of the marriage, 4 V., c. 44, s. 9.

Neglect in registration, copying or transmission Any minister who solemnizes any marriage under this Act, and is guilty of negligence or wilful default in the registration or copying of the entries, and transmitting them, shall be guilty of a misdemeanor, and punished by imprisonment, not exceeding 12 months, 4 V., c. 44, s. 10.

Searches and certified copies All persons may search the original register book and file of duplicate registers in the presence of the person having the care of them, or his deputy, and have a true copy of any entry, certified, under the hand of the minister or officer having the custody of the original or duplicate, to be a true copy in the form of the duplicate original register, except that it shall be headed certified copy (or copies) of original (or duplicate original) marriage register (as the case may be), and shall be dated on the day, month and year when delivered, 4 V., c. 44, s. 11.

Fees The fees in Schedule D shall be demandable and paid by the parties, applying, before the performance of the duty to which they relate, 4 V., c. 44, s. 12.

Erasing &c. entries. Forging &c. registers or certified copies Unlawfully, wilfully and maliciously erasing, obliterating or destroying or causing or procuring, &c., any original or duplicate original register : felony,—imprisonment in the common gaol or house of correction, for not exceeding two years. Unlawfully or wilfully forging, or altering or falsely making, or causing, or procuring or permitting, &c., any such original or duplicate original register or certified copy, or knowingly or wilfully delivering, offering, uttering, or putting off any false, forged or altered copy : imprisonment in such gaol, or house of correction, for not exceeding 3 years, and not less than 6 months, 4. V., c. 44, s. 13.

Registers of marriages by ministers not of the Church of England previous to this act Within 6 months after the act came into operation, all ministers not of the Church of England, who had been accustomed to marry in their chapels and elsewhere, and to keep a register of the names of the parties, their residence, and the date when the ceremony was performed, together with the names of witnesses in some cases, were required to send a copy of such registries, certified, by the oath of the parties having charge of the original registers, as true and faithful copies of the registers in their possession, to the office of the Island Secretary, there to be kept and recorded, and an examined copy of the registry or record was declared evidence, in all courts, of such marriage, 4 V., c. 44, s. 14.

Copies under 3 V. c. 67 All copies of registers already returned into the Secretary's Office, under th [repealed] Act, 3 V., c. 67, shall be valid from the date thereof, 4 V., c. 44, s. 15.

Confirmation of previous marriages All marriages solemnized at any time by Dissenting Ministers, before this Act, and so registered and returned into the Secretary's Office, declared to be as good and valid as if they had been performed according to the rites of the Church of England, 4 V., c. 44, s. 16.

Exemption from stamps All returns and documents, recorded in the Secretary's Office exempted from stamps, 4 V., c. 44, s. 17.

Verified and corrected copies of existing registers to be recorded and kept. Certified copies The better to preserve evidence of marriages so registered, and to facilitate the proof thereof, every person in whose custody any register lawfully was or should be, was required within 6 months after the passing of the Act to make, or cause to be made, a fair and correct copy of every such register, and of entry therein, and examine, verify and correct (if and where found incorrect,) by the original, any such copy of a register kept by the persuasion to which he belongs, and make a declaration, as follows :

Declaration to be annexed I, A. B., (describe the persuasion to which he belongs) do hereby solemnly, sincerely and truly declare, that I have carefully examined this copy, beginning the day of (month and year), and ending on the day of (month and year) and containing pages and entries of marriages, with the original register, and I believe the same to be throughout a true and faithful copy of the original register, of which it purports to be a copy. "A. B."

Which declaration was required to be entered and signed at the end of the copy to which it related, and the copy securely sealed up, and sent to the Island Secretary to be recorded and kept with the registers of marriages in his office, where they may be searched ; and every copy of entry therein, certified under his hand to be a true copy, shall be of the same force and effect as any certified copy made by him, and which he is required to make, and may receive payment for as in other cases, 4 V., c. 44, s. 18.

Any Minister wilfully making and signing any such declaration, know-ing it to be false, shall, on conviction, suffer the penalties of perjury, 4 V., c. 44, s. 19.

False Declaration

Any person who wilfully detains from the possession of the officiating and acknowledged minister of any congregation of Christians within this island, the register of marriages of persons attached to, or performed by the minister attached to that congregation, shall be guilty of a misdemeanor and shall be imprisoned not exceeding 12 calendar months, 4 V., c. 44, s. 23.

Detaining register from minister

SCHEDULE to 4 V., c. 44.

"I do solemnly declare that I know not of any lawful impediment why I, A. B., may not be joined in matrimony to C. D., here present," (and each of the parties shall say to each other) " I call upon these persons here present to witness that I, A. B. do take thee, C. D. to be my lawful wedded wife (or husband)"

A
Declaration by parties, s. 3

Original Register of Marriages solemnized by Ministers of the Denomination in the Parish (Circuit or Station) of

B
Original Register s. 9

No.	When Married.	Names and Surnames.	Ages.	Condition.	Rank or Profession.	Residence at the time of Marriage.	After Banns or Licence.	Consent. By whom given.
1	1st December, 1838.	Jno. Jones Ly. Gyles	Full Age. Minor	Bachelor. Spinster	Carpenter.		After Banns.	 Henry Gyles, the Father.

Married at   by me, A. B., Minister.

This marriage was solemnized between us. { John Jones. } In pre-
{ Lucy Gyles. } sence of us. { C. D.
{ E. F.

Duplicate Original Register of Marriages Solemnized by Ministers of the Denomination, in the Parish (Circuit or Station) of
Precisely similar to Schedule B, with the addition at foot
" Examined with the original register by, and found to be correct."
A. B.

C
Duplicate, s. 9

For registering a marriage, and transmitting the duplicate original to the Island Secretary 0 2 0
For every certified copy of entry of marriage as aforesaid   0 1 0

D
Fees demandable, s. 12

Ministers of religion transmitting duplicate original registers of marriages required by 4 V , c. 44, s. 9 to be transmitted to the Secretary's Office to be filed and recorded, need not count the words, or do more than certify that they are the duplicate original registers left with them—26 V., s. 0, c. 10, s. 1.

Duplicate registers transmitted to the Secretary's Office need not be counted

The filing and recording of which shall be paid by the public—26 V., S 2, c. 10, s. 2.

To be recorded at the public expense

Distresses for Rent and Taxes.

Costs of distresses for rent under £20 currency

No person making any distress for rent, where the sum demanded and due does not exceed £20 (£12 sterling), nor any person employed in making or doing any act in the course of such distress, or for carrying the same into effect, shall take or receive out of the produce of the goods distrained upon and sold, or from the tenant or landlord, or any other person, any other costs and charges than set forth in the Schedule and appropriated to each act done, nor for any thing mentioned in the Schedule unless really done, 1 V., c. 25, s. 1.

Penalty for taking more. Summary recovery

If any person levy, take, or receive, or retain, or take from the produce of any goods sold, any other or greater costs and charges than are mentioned in such Schedule, or make any charge for any thing mentioned therein, and not really done, the parties aggrieved may apply to a justice of the parish where the distress was made, or in any manner proceeded in, for redress of the grievance, who shall summon the persons complained of, examine into the complaint, and hear the defence, and may adjudge treble the amount of the monies unlawfully taken to be paid by the person so having acted to the complainant, with full costs, and in case of non-payment shall forthwith issue his warrant to levy the same, by distress and sale, and in case no sufficient distress can be had, shall, by warrant under his hand, commit the party until the order or judgment is satisfied, 1 V., c. 25, s. 2

Evidence

Power to summon witnesses, and compel them to give evidence— Penalty not exceeding 40s. (24s. sterling) 1 V., c. 25, s. 3,

Costs of dismissal

The Justice, if he finds the complaint not well-founded, may order costs not exceeding 20s. (12s. sterling) to be paid to the party complained against, which order shall be carried into effect, and levied and paid in the manner, and with the like power of commitment as before directed.

Landlord

No Justice shall make any order or judgment against the landlord for whose benefit any distress is made, unless he has personally levied such distress. No person aggrieved by any distress for rent, or by any proceedings had in the course thereof, or by any costs and charges levied upon him in respect of the same, shall be barred from any legal or other suit or remedy, except so far as any complaint preferred under this Act shall be determined by the order of the Justice, and which order and judgment may be given in evidence under the plea of the general issue, 1 V., c. 25, s. 4.

Forms and proof of orders of Justices

Forms of orders and judgments which may be proved before any court by proof of the signature of the Justice, 1 V., c. 25, s. 5.

Notices of distress and charges, whatever the amount of rent

Every person who levies any distress whatsoever, immediately after shall give to the person upon whose goods the distress is made a list, in writing, of all the goods then distrained upon, with the names of the persons in whose behalf the distress is made, in which shall be stated the day of the month and year in which it was made, with the day on which the distress, if not otherwise satisfied, is to be sold ; (and in case any person cannot conveni-

Service

ently be served with such list at or immediately after the time of distress, it shall be posted the same day on the principal door of the premises on which the distress is made) and shall give a copy of his charges, and of all the costs and charges of any distress whatsoever, signed by him, to the persons on whose goods any distress shall be levied, although the amount of the rent demanded exceed £20 (£12 sterling), 1 V., c. 25. s. 6.

Act extended to distresses for rates and taxes

All the rules and regulations, clauses, provisions, penalties and matters, shall extend, and be put in execution so far as applicable, with respect to any church rates, distresses or levy made for land tax, assessed taxes, poor rates, highway rates, taxes, impositions or assessments whatever, in all cases where the sum demanded and due shall not exceed £20 (£12 sterling), and in all cases where the whole of the several sums, sought to be levied by distresses for any such taxes, &c., at the same time, shall not exceed £20 (£12 sterling), 1 V., c. 25, s. 7.

SCHEDULE.

Form of order and judgment for complainant s. 2, 5

In a matter of the complaint of A. B., against C. D., for a breach of the provisions of an Act of the first year of the reign of Her Majesty Queen Victoria, entitled " An Act to regulate the costs of distresses, levied for payment of small rents, rates and taxes.

I, E. F., a Justice of the Peace for the parish of   do order and adjudge that the said C. D. shall pay to the said A. B,, the sum of as a compensation and satisfaction for unlawful charges and costs, levied and taken from the said A. B., under a distress for (rent or taxes as the case may be,) and the further sum of for costs on this complaint.

(Signed.)   E. F.

In a matter (as above).

Where the complaint is dismissed as unfounded, with or without costs

. I, E. F., a Justice of the Peace for the parish of do order and adjudge that the complaint of the said A. B., is unfounded (if costs are given,) and I do further order and adjudge that the said A. B., shall pay unto the said C. D., the sum of for costs.

(Signed.)   E. F.

	Cncy.	equal to Sterling.	
Levying distresses	5s.	3s.	Costs and charges on distresses, s 1
Man in possession, per day	4s. 2d.	2s. 6d.	
Appraisement, whether by one valuer or more, 6d in the £ on the value of goods.			
Stamp (the lawful amount)			
All expenses of advertisement, if any such	15s.	9s.	
Catalogues, sale and commission, and delivery of goods 1s in the £. on the nett produce of the sale.			

The executors or administrators of any lessor or landlord, may distrain upon the lands demised for any term, or at will, for the arrearages of rent due to such lessor or landlord in his life time, in like manner as he might have done in his lifetime, 8 V., c. 28, s. 15.

Distress by executors for rent in landlord's lifetime

Such arrearages may be distrained for after the end or determination of the term or lease at will, in the same manner as if it had not been ended or determined; but the distress must be made within 6 calendar months after the determination and during the continuance of the possession of the tenant from whom the arrears became due; and all the powers and provisions in the statutes, relating to distresses for rent, shall be applicable to distresses so made, 8 V., c. 28, s. 16.

To be made within 6 months of the determination of tenancy and during tenants' possession

---

Dividing Fences.

Any person possessed of any lands, settlement, buildings or premises, having no dividing fences, or insufficient ones, may require, by a notice in writing in the form annexed, the owner or occupant of the adjoining lands or premises where such fences are wanted, or the guardian, atttorney or agent of the owner, to assist in making, or repairing any, or all of the dividing fences between them, 15 V., c. 22, s. 1.

Notice to assist in making or repairing

In case any such owner, guardian, attorney, or agent or occupier, refuse or fail to comply with such notice within 14 days after service, or in case the parties cannot agree upon their respective proportions, the person making the requisition may apply to a Justice to summon, by his warrant, three neighbouring freeholders as a Jury, who shall be sworn by the Justice to ascertain the propriety of the requisition, and what sort of fence will be most proper for the situation, or if the existing fence be an old one what repairs are necessary, or whether it would be necessary to substitute a new fence, and the jury being so sworn, and having viewed the premises, shall make return in writing of the particulars to the Justice, and thereupon the person making such requisition, under order of the Justice, may proceed in laying out, making or repairing, or removing and reinstating the fence agreeably to the return of the jury. When the work is completed, a jury of 3 freeholders, shall in like manner be summoned by the same or some other Justice, and being duly sworn to fix the price, and to consider the particular convenience such fence may be to either party, shall proceed to consider and determine the same accordingly, and if they find the fence and repairs to be more beneficial to one party than to the other, they shall regu-

Application on refusal

To a Justice to summon a jury to ascertain the propriety of the requisition

Proceedings and return

Jury to be summoned to apportion the expenses

Proceedings to enforce payment

late and apportion the expense accordingly. In case of refusal or of failure, by either party, to pay his proportion of the expense within ten days after the same is ascertained, the same or any other Justice (such refusal or

By distress

failure having been declared on oath to be administered by such last mentioned Justice,) shall issue his distress warrant to any constable, to compel payment, by sale of the goods of the person refusing or failing, which sale shall take place 10 days after the distress, unless otherwise agreed to by the parties, or

Or action

the party refusing or failing to pay his proportion may be proceeded against by action of debt, for the recovery of the amount for which he shall so have been declared liable, 15 V., c. 22, s. 2.

NOTICE OF REQUISITION.

Notice of requisition, s, 1

Under and by virtue of the provisions of an Act, 15 Victoria, chapter 22.

I hereby require you to assist in making or repairing the dividing fence between   settlement, plantation, buildings or land (as the case may be) and   settlement, plantation, buildings or land (as the case may be) in such equitable proportion as may be agreed on.

After requisition the party debarred from claiming damage for distress, or impounding stock

If any person who has been duly called upon according to law to make, renew or repair a line fence, refuse or neglect to do so, he shall be debarred from claiming damage for trespass, and from impounding the stock of the person who had made the requisition, under a penalty of 20s., to be recovered

Penalty

in a summary manner before two magistrates, 15 V., c. 11, s. 24.

How enforceable

To be levied upon the goods of the offender, and in default of goods the Justices shall sentence the party to be imprisoned, not exceeding 60 days 15 V., c. 11, s. 25.

Dormant Securities.

After 20 years void

All bills, bonds and mortgages, judgments and other writings obligatory, whereon no payment is made, or which are not legally demanded within 20 years from the time they became due, or from the last payment,

Persons under disability

thereon, shall be null and void, but the limitation shall not extend to persons under 21, women under coverture, or persons of unsound memory, provided they bring their actions within three years after their disability is removed, 29 G. 3, c. 13, s. 4.

Droghers.

Lien for freight

Owners or masters may detain, out of any parcel of goods brought from any outport to Kingston, as much as the freight amounts to, on refusal of the consignee to pay, and have them valued by a Justice of Kingston, and may detain so much of the value as will pay the freight, returning any overplus to the consignee, 31 G. 3, c. 3, s. 2.

Liability of shipper in Kingston

For goods carried from Kingston to an outport, the owner or master may demand from the shipper after delivery, according to the tenor of the

Summary recovery

receipts or bills of lading, the amount of freight, and on his refusal, may complain to two Justices of Kingston, who, under the penalty of £20 (£12 sterling) shall hear the complaint, and, on proof, issue their warrant to a constable, of distress and sale, after five days' notice. Fees of distress 1s. in the pound on the monies arising from the sale, 31 G. 3. c. 3, s. 3.

Shipper from out ports

Owners or masters may agree with the shipper for freight from one outport to another, and on landing them, or afterwards on refusal to pay, may complain to a Magistrate of the parish where the shipper resides, who, under penalty of £20 (£12 sterling) shall hear the complaint, and on proof, proceed as the Magistrates of Kingston are directed, and the constables shall proceed and be entitled to the same perquisites as those of Kingston, 31 G. 3, c. 3, s. 4.

Receipts or bills of lading to be given

Merchants, factors, wharfingers, or others shipping goods from Kingston to an outport, or from an outport to Kingston, or from one port to another, shall deliver the g   by weight, gauge, measure, quantity or condition to the master, and make two or more receipts or bills of lading, one of which with the invoice shall be transmitted to the consignee or his agent, on pain of forfeiting the value of the goods lost through their neglect; and the master shall sign such receipts or bills of lading, under penalty of £50 (£30 sterling); but no merchant, &c., shall unnecessarily delay him to sign them, 31 G. 3, c. 3, s 5.

Wharfingers at Kingston or outports shall weigh, gauge, measure, count and examine, according to their quality, all goods shipped and landed at their wharves immediately on landing, and enter the same with their weight, gauge, measure, quantity and condition in their wharf books, which they are required to keep, charging according to the established rates, under penalty of £50 (£30 sterling.) Wharfingers and others employed in shipping goods to Europe, shall weigh, gauge, &c., the goods at the shipping or elivery, and make regular entries in their books, 31 G., 3 c. 3, s. 6. Duties and liabilities of wharfingers
On shipments to Europe

Masters shall sign two or more receipts or bills of lading, for goods received on freight at any outport, to be carried to Kingston, 31 G., 3, c. 3, s. 7. Receipts or bills of lading in duplicate

· Every master shall clear out at the proper offices every time he sails from Kingston, in which clearance shall be set forth, on oath, the port to which he has engaged to carry goods on freight, to be administered by the proper officer, and shall not, under penalty of £50, (£30 sterling) stop at any other port, &c., without having been first at the ports cleared out for, and shall stop at the several ports in regular succession, stress of weather or other unavoidable accident excepted ; in which case he shall, within 48 hours after arrival at any port for which he had not cleared out, make a regular protest upon oath before a magistrate, setting forth the cause or necessity of putting in, 31 G. 3 c. 3, s. 8. Clearance. Ports to be visited in order

Any Master selling or disposing of (or not delivering at the port where they were deliverable) any goods taken on board on freight, shall forfeit treble the value to the owner, recoverable by action of debt, 31 G. 3, c. 3, s. 9. Sale of goods taken on freight

Every master, under penalty of £50 (£30 sterling) shall land and deliver goods carried on freight at the port specified in the receipts or bills of lading, and on failure to deliver every parcel taken on board on freight, according to the weight, gauge, measure, quantity and condition by which he received them, shall forfeit treble the value of the goods he fails to deliver at the port of delivery to the owner, recoverable by action of debt, 31 G. 3, c. 3, s. 10. Penalties for non-delivery at ports of landing

Every master signing receipts or bills of lading for proof rum, and not delivering it of sufficient proof to sink oil of olives, shall forfeit £10, (£6 sterling) for every puncheon or cask so delivered, to be recovered in a summary manner before 2 Magistrates of the parish where landed, on complaint on oath of the proprietor or consignee, his agent or factor, who are to hear and proceed on the complaint in the manner the Justices of Kingston are before directed, under penalty of £20 (£12 sterling), and the constable shall proceed and be entitled to the same perquisites as in Kingston, 31 G. 3, c. 3, s. 11. Adulterating rum

Every master spoiling or adulterating Madeira or other wines, taken on board on freight, by mixing any other liquid therewith, or in any other manner, shall forfeit double the value of the pipe or cask of wine, recoverable as above, on complaint of the proprietor, his factor or agent. Similar provisions as to Justices and Constables, 31 G. 3, c. 3, s. 12. Wines

No part of the Act shall extend to boats employed by the inhabitants of Kingston or Port Royal, to fetch plantains and other provisions for the use of the towns, but they may transport goods from port to port in their usual manner, 31 G., 3, c. 3, s. 13. Extent of act

Merchants, factors, wharfingers or others receiving and delivering goods at Passage Fort or Port Henderson to be sent to Kingston, and goods delivered at Kingston to be sent to Passage Fort and Port Henderson, shall have the weight, gauge, &c., ascertained, as well on the receipt as at the delivery, on pain of forfeiting the value of the goods lost or deficient through their neglect, and each boatman or master of a vessel, carrying goods between Kingston, Passage Fort and Port Henderson, shall under Penalty, of £50 (£30 sterling, give a receipt or bill of lading for the goods received on board, or forfeit treble the value of the goods he fails to deliver, to be recovered as in cases between Kingston and outports. Boatmen &c. signing receipts or bills of lading for proof rum, to be carried from Passage Fort or Port Henderson to Kingston, and not delivering it in like good order, or spoiling or adulterating Madeira or other wines, to be carried from Kingston to Passage Fort or Port Henderson, shall be liable to the same penalties, to be recovered in the same manner as directed in cases between Kingston and the outports, 31 G. 3, c. 3, s. 14. Passage Fort ; Port Henderson

War

In time of war, £50 per cent may be demanded for freight of goods on the sum allowed in table of rates, 31 G. 3, c. 3, s. 15.

Recovery &c. penalties

Penalties not otherwise declared shall be recoverable in the Supreme Court, one moiety to the informer, 31 G. 3, c. 3, s. 16.

Fort pass unnecessary

Droghers and ships' boats clearing coastwise shall have free egress from one port to another, without any fort pass being required, 3 V., c. 41.

Education, Competitive Examinations.

Commissioners

The Governor, the Lord Bishop of Jamaica (or in his absence the Bishop of Kingston, or other Coadjutor or Suffragan Bishop, 22 V., c. 23, s. 3) the President of the Council, the Speaker of the Assembly, and five other persons to be nominated by the Governor, shall be Commissioners for enquiring and examining into, and ascertaining the state and progress of education and industrial instruction among the industrial classes of inhabitants, and of distributing, in aid of schools already or to be established for the benefit of such classes, in such proportions as to them may seem expedient, such sums as may by this or any subsequent Act of the Legislature be placed at their disposal for such purpose, upon the conditions after imposed, 8 V., c. 40, s. 1.

Board of education

The Commissioners (three a quorum) of whom the Governor to be one, shall be named "The Board of Education", 8 V. c. 40, s. 2.

Conditions on which aid may be afforded to schools

£1000 was placed at their disposal, 8 V., c. 40, s. 3.

The Board shall not apply any p   of the sum p   at their disposal (except as after excepted) to the purchase or lease of land, lor the erection, repair lease or purchase of buildings, or to the use of any school, industrial or otherwise, not originally established and in operation by means of funds other than those provided by this Act, or to any school, unless the master first signifies to the board, in writing, his consent that a committee may visit the school and examine into its state and system, and into the acquirements, industrial, and otherwise, and the progress and knowledge of the scholars, and also consent to afford all information respecting the school, desired by the board, or to any school in which it is not proved that the Holy Scriptures are habitually read and explained to the scholars, or to any school where the number of scholars who attend on the average of days do not amount to at least 20, 8 V., c. 40, s. 4.

No more than £50 to be applied to any school in the same year

Nor shall they apply for any school, except as after excepted, exceeding £50 in one year, 8 V., c. 40, s. 5.

Normal school of industry

The Board were authorized to apply £300 to be expended in whatever manner they might deem most conducive to the effective establishment of a Normal School of Industry, 8. V., c. 40, s. 6.

Competitive examination
Board of public examiners

The Governor may appoint five persons to be a board of Public Examiners, fill up vacancies, and revoke appointments, 25 V., c. 6, s. 1.

Quorum, Chairman

Three to be a quorum. Any member may be elected chairman, and in his absence any member present may be selected to preside as chairman, 25 V., c. 6, s. 2.

The Board may call in the aid of qualified persons to assist them in conducting examinations and otherwise, 25 V., c. 6, s. 3.

Duties of board

Duties of the Board:—

1. To frame and publish regulations to be observed by candidates for examination, which must be approved by the Governor and Executive Committee.

2. To examine in each year, in Kingston, or cause to be examined at other convenient towns by assistant examiners, at times and places to be fixed by six months' previous notice, candidates in reading and writing, including writing from dictation, arithmetic, English language and grammar, Biblical knowledge, Geography, History, including local history, popular science, school management, ancient and modern languages, and other subjects as may be decided upon.

3. To keep a record of the candidates, shewing the name, age, place of birth and residence of each, and the result of his examination, mentioning the particular avocation or employment, if any, for which he has shewn special aptitude.

4. To grant certificates of qualification to candidates whose examination as to fitness, and whose testimonials as to moral character have been found satisfactory, who shall be classed in three classes, and receive certificates of the first, second or third class, according to their merits, 25 V., c. 6, s. 4

Every person who obtains any such certificate, and is employed as a teacher in any school, supported or assisted by grant for educational purposes, shall receive payment, on the warrant of the Governor, out of such fund. *Additional grants to teachers of schools who have obtained certificates*

A teacher who has obtained a certificate of the 1st class, per annum, £10

Second class, ... £7 10s.
Third class, ... £5

In addition to any benefit from any other grant out of such fund in aid of the school in which he is emplyed, 25 V., c. 6, s. 5.

After the third annual examination, no grant shall be made out of such fund in aid of any school which has not been placed under the charge of a teacher who has obtained a certificate, 25 V., c. 6, s. 6. *After 3rd annual examination no grant to be made to a school not under a certificated teacher*

The Governor may appoint any assistant examiner or other competent person in each County to inspect and report annually upon the state of any schools receiving aid from the public funds, and the 'progress they have made since the last report, distinguishing whether they are under the charge of masters holding certificates or not, with such other remarks as may seem necessary; a copy to be laid before each branch of the Legislature and the Board of Examiners, 25 V., c. 6, s. 7. *Assistant examiner to report on schools*

In case the proficiency of any person who obtains a certificate of the first class is considered by the examiners to merit special recommendation, he shall, on application for, and producing the certificate and special recommendation be deemed a meritorious candidate for employment in the public service, 25 V., c. 6, s. 8. *Special recommendation for proficiency*

The Governor and Executive Committee may appropriate out of any fund voted for educational purposes not exceeding £250 annum for expenses or charges for procuring the services of qualified persons to assist the board, and otherwise about the examinations, and inspecting and reporting upon the schools, 25 V., c. 6, s 9. *Funds to meet expenditure*

Ejectments, Lands of Small Value.

Any person lawfully entitled to any lands, the annual value whereof does not exceed £12, upon which any other has entered, or is in adverse possession, may proceed for its recovery before 2 Justices, 25 V., c. 46, s. 1. *Summary proceedings. Annual value not exceding £12*

The summons (Schedule A) shall be the process for initiating proceedings, and upon proof of service of a copy, at least 12 days before that fixed for the hearing, on the person sought to be ejected, the Justices may hear the complaint, 25 V., c. 46, s. 2. *Summons*

The warrant (Schedule B) shall be the process for giving possession to the party who has proved his case, and shall be issued forthwith after judgment, and continue effective until fully executed, 25 V., c. 46, s. 3. *Warrant*

The stamps shall be 2s. on the summons, 2s. on the warrant, and 6d. on each original subpœna, and no other, 25 V., c. 46, s. 4. *Stamps*

The fees shall be 10s. 6d. to the Clerk of the magistrates for filling up and issuing the summons, attending the trial, and taking down notes of evidence; 3s. for filling up and issuing the warrant; and 1s. for each original subpœna; and 3d. for each copy, allowing for the purposes of this clause and of the stamp duty three copies to each original; and 1s 6d for recording the judgment, 25 V. c. 46, s. 5. *Fees*

All process shall be served by the police, except the warrant to levy costs, which shall be executed by the Collector of Petty Debts, and his surety bond shall include the duties hereby required of him, and his securities shall be liable for their performance, 25 V., c. 46, s. 6. *Service and execution of process*

The Justices may award costs, to the extent of the fees and stamps, and £1 1s. for an Attorney-at-Law, if one attends; and the expenses of such witnesses as have attended, and were material, according to a scale to be fixed by a Special Session of Justices, to be convened for the purpose as occasion requires, to the party succeeding, which shall be recoverable by distress warrant, (Schedule D) 25 V., c. 46, s. 7. *Costs*

Subpœnas shall be in the form Schedule C, and witnesses refusing or omitting to attend without reasonable cause, or to give evidence, may be proceeded against and punished under 13 V., c. 35, 25 V., c. 46, s. 8. *Subpœna witness*

Evidence, deeds, copies of recorded documents

An original deed, shewing on its face that it was proved and recorded, may be received in evidence, without calling the attesting or any other witness, and plain copies of documents of record in any public office, accompanied by an affidavit, sworn before a Justice of any parish by two persons stating that they carefully examined such copies with the original records, and that such copies are true and correct, 25 V., c. 46, s. 9.

Power to adjudicate upon questions of title &c.

The justices may adjudicate upon any question of title, possessory or otherwise, and also as to the continuance or termination of a tenancy, and in all respects exercise as ample jurisdiction as the superior courts, in respect of lands of greater annual value, 25 V., c. 46, s. 10.

Disputed value

The value, if disputed, shall, in the first instance, be established, and determined by the justices upon evidence, and the portion of land claimed shall alone be valued, 25 V., c. 46, s. 11.

Equitable title

Any person equitably entitled may proceed and recover against a wrong-doer, and the legal title shall only be allowed to intervene or prevail as between the legal and equitable owners, 25 V., c. 46, s. 12.

Costs on ejectments in Supreme Court where land is not found to be of greater annual value than £12

In no case shall more costs be allowed or taxed to a plaintiff or lessor of the plaintiff recovering in ejectment in the Supreme Court, than would be recoverable and taxable under this act, unless a special verdict is found, and endorsed on the record that the land recovered is of greater annual value than £12, and to be produced to the taxing officer, 25 V., c. 46, s. 13.

Endorsement of finding of Justices on summons Record

The Justices shall endorse their finding on the back or folding of the original summons, and sign the same, which shall be preserved in the office of the Clerk of the Magistrates; and for a further record, each Clerk of the Magistrates shall keep a bound book of printed forms, (Schedule A) and immediately after every adjudication, one of such forms shall be carefully filled up in exact accordance with the original summons as disposed of, and in the margin shall be copied, opposite the form so filled up, the endorsements and remarks of the Justices, and the day of the issuing of the warrant, if judgment is found for the claimant, and a correct back and fore-alphabet shall be kept and brought up at all times, within one week, 25 V., c. 46, s. 14.

Fore and back alphabets

Appeal

The right of appeal shall prevail in proceedings under this Act, 25 V., c. 46, s. 15.

Forms

The forms in schedule, or to the like effect, shall be sufficient, and no proceedings shall be quashed for defect of form, 25 V., c. 46, s. 16.

Interpretation

"Land" shall mean and include houses, buildings and other corporeal hereditaments, 25 V., c. 46, s. 17.

SCHEDULE TO 25 V., c. 46.

JAMAICA, ss.

Name of Parish or Precinct..

Summons, s. y

Take notice, that it is the intention of   of the parish of   (labourer or merchant as the case may be), to apply under the provisions of the act of the legislature of this island, entitled "An Act to repeal the third Victoria, chapter thirty-three, and the twenty-first Victoria, chapter ten, relating to summary recovery of lands of small value, and to make other enactments in lieu thereof," to two of Her Majesty's Justices of the Peace, on   the   day of   one thousand eight hundred and   at the Court House, at   at the hour of eleven of the clock in the forenoon, or at any time between that hour, and the hour of three of the clock in the afternoon of the same day at which the Justices may attend, to enquire into and adjudicate on the claim of the said   to have possession delivered to him of the piece or parcel of land, with the buildings thereon, situate in the said parish of   and containing by estimation   acres   roods and perches, 'or   feet, and butting and bounding, (state the boundaries as correctly as can be), which said land and premises, are claimed by the said   as (state the estate claimed) ; and take further notice that in the event of your not appearing, the case will be heard and determined in your absence.

Given under my hand this   day of   186
(as the case may be)

(To be signed by any Magistrate of the parish
in which the case is to be heard).

To   of the parish of
(labourer or merchant, as the case may be),
the person now in possession of the land
and premises above-mentioned and described.

JAMAICA, SS.

B
Warrant to de-
liver possession,
s. 3

Name of Parish or Precinct.

Whereas, upon the complaint of (name of claimant), heard and adjudicated before us, the undersigned Justices of the Peace of the parish
of   on the   day of
186   it was adjudged and determined that the said
     is legally entitled to the possession of
the piece or parcel of land with the buildings thereon, situate in the
said parish of   and containing by estimation,
     acres,   roods, and
     perches, or   feet, and butting and
bounding (state the boundaries as correctly as can be) which said
lands and premises are claimed by the said   as
(state the estate claimed) : These are therefore, in her Majesty's
name, to authorize and require you forthwith to proceed to the lands
and premises in question, and with such force as may be necessary
to take and deliver posession of the said lands and premises to the
said   or to such agent as may attend on his behalf to receive such possession.

A. B.   }   Justices adjudi-
C. D.   }   cating.

To the Police of the parish of

JAMAICA, SS.

C
Notice to give
evidence, s. 8

Parish or Precinct.
To   (Witnesses name and description.)
These are to require you to appear and give evidence at the Court
House, at   in the parish of   at
o'clock on   the   day of   186   in a matter in which   of the parish of   seeks to recover
possession of certain lands and premises situate in the said parish of
     from   the person now in possession
thereof, on the part and behalf of the said claimant (or defendant) :
therefore fail not at your peril.

Given under my hand this   day of   in the year of our
Lord, 186

(To be signed by any Magistrate of the parish
in which the case is to be heard.)

Name of Parish or Precinct.

D
Distress for costs
s. 7

To   Collector of Petty Debts for the parish of
You are hereby required, on sight hereof, forthwith to levy the sum of
     pounds, being the amount of costs adjudged against
     in favor of   on the disposal of a certain applica-
tion of the said   against the said   under the
provisions of the act of the legislature of this island, twenty-fifth
Victoria, chapter forty-six. entitled an Act to repeal the third Victoria, chapter thirty three, and the twenty-first Victoria, chapter ten,
relating to summary recovery of lands of small value, and to make
other enactments in lieu thereof, together with the further sum of
two shillings for executing this distress, and poundage at the rate
of one shilling in the pound on the amount of costs hereby directed
to be levied upon the goods, except the necessary wearing apparel and
tools of trade of the said   , and you are also required to sell the

X

goods so distrained within the space of one week from and after such levy ; and out of the proceeds thereof to satisfy the said of the amount of the said costs, and to retain to yourself the sum of two shillings, and the poundage, and to return any overplus to the said and you are hereby further required, in default of finding sufficient goods whereon to levy the whole of the said costs, and the said sum of two shillings, and the poundage, to arrest the said by the body, and imprison him for the space of ten days in the nearest gaol, unless the amount directed to be levied respectively, or so much thereof as thou canst not levy, be sooner paid ; and, for so doing, this shall be your sufficient warrant.

Given under our hands this day of in the year of our Lord, 186

A. B. } Adjudicating
C. D. } Justices.

Emblements.

When writ to issue In cases of emblements the Judges may, upon cause shewn in open court, upon affidavit containing the names of the parties liable, issue, or cause, &c. out of and returnable into the Supreme Court, a writ of enquiry to the Provost-Marshal, to warn 24 good and lawful men of the neighbourhood (each of whom to have a freehold of the value of £10 (£6 sterling) per annum, at the least, to meet on the premises at a day by him to be appointed, then and there by the oaths of 12 of such freeholders, to be chosen by ballot from such as attend, being sworn in presence of a Justice (to be warned and attending for the purpose) to view, examine and enquire, and, on full consideration, determine the quantity, share and proportion for emblements of the crop on the ground at the death of the person under whom they are claimed, and the names of the parties liable thereto, and appraise and value the same in the following form :—

Form of writ George the Third, &c., to the Provost-Marshal General of our said island, greeting :

Whereas it hath been represented to the Judges of our Supreme Court of Judicature, that A. B, of, &c. departed this life possessed of all that, &c. (setting forth the premises), and whereas C. D., of, &c., the Executor of the said A B (or Administrator as the case may be) hath made it appear to the satisfaction of the Judges of our Supreme Court of Judicature that he is well entitled to emblements of the crop on the ground at the time of the death of the said A B ; and we being willing that what is just and right should be done, do command you, that you warn, or cause to be warned, twenty-four good and lawful men of the neighbourhood of the said premises, each of whom to have a freehold of the value of £10 (£6 sterling) per annum, at the least, to meet on the said premises on some certain day by you to be appointed, and then and there by the oaths of twelve of the said freeholders by you to be chosen by ballot from amongst so many of the said twenty-four freeholders to be warned as shall attend, being first sworn in the presence of one or more of His Majesty's Justices of the Peace by you to be warned, and attending for that purpose, well and truly to view, examine, enquire, and, on full consideration of all circumstances, justly determine the quantity, share and proportion of the crop on the ground at the time of the death of the said A. B., and the name or names of the party or parties liable to such emblements, and truly to appraise and value the same according to the best of their judgments and consciences ; and having so done, you are to make due return thereof, openly and distinctly, under your hand and seal, and the hands and seals of such twelve freeholders as aforesaid into our Supreme Court of Judicature on the, &c., witness, &c., 25 G. 3, c. 1, s. 1.

14 days' notice of execution The Provost-Marshal shall not execute the writ until after 14 days notice, at least, of the execution, in writing, signed by him ; and before he enters upon the execution he shall cause the service to be proved by affidavit, sworn before the Justice, which affidavit and original notice he shall annex to his return, 25 G. 3, c. 1, s. 2.

Upon the return filed, the court may adjudge the party suing out the writ the amount of the valuation and appraisement, to be paid within such time as the court directs, and may enforce judgment by writs of execution (abolished, 19 V., c. 10, s. 39,) and venditioni according to the usual course, from which no writ of error, appeal, &c., shall be allowed. The parties against whom the writ issues, or their attornies, upon the return, and during the same Court, may appear and enter into security to deliver to the parties entitled to emblements within such time as the Court directs, at the usual barquadier or shipping place of the estate, produce in kind to the amount of the appraisement, in sufficient casks or usual packages, free from all deductions, to be valued by 3 persons, one to be named by the Court, and the other two by the parties or their attornies. Where the lands lie in several parishes, distinct writs shall issue for each parish, and be separately executed and returned. The Provost-Marshal may appoint a deputy, by warrant under his hand and seal, to execute the same, to be annexed to the return. His fees shall be the same as for the return of other inquests, 25 G. 3, c. 1, s. 3.

Award of payment and execution

Security for delivery of produce

Distinct writ for each parish

Provost Marshal may act by deputy
Fees

No person shall enter on the lands of another for emblements, or have any ingress, egress or regress for the same, 25 G. 3, c. 1, s. 4.

No entry for emblements.

Emblements shall be confined to the crop next succeeding the death of the person under whom they are claimed, if he die before the beginning of the crop, but if during the crop, then only to the crop taking off at the time of his death. When the tenant for life dies during the time of taking off the crop, the Jury shall take into their consideration the expense of putting in the plant canes to be cut the next year, and make a reasonable allowance to the person entitled to emblements, 25 G. 3, c. 1. s. 5.

to Crop applicable emblements. Allowance for plant cane

If the tenant for life is off the island at his death, or the person entitled to emblements is absent from this island, so that no writ is issued while the crop is on the ground, or during the time it is taking off, the person absent may issue such writ after the crop is taken off, and have the full benefit thereby, upon giving evidence to the Jury under the writ of the value of the crop taken off, 25 G. 3, c. 1, s. 6.

When writ may issue after crop taken off

The monies or goods returned upon writs on account of emblements, shall not be affected by or made applicable to prior writs against the persons in remainder or reversion, 25 G. 3, c. 1, s 7.

Levies not applicable to priority

If any person summoned either as Magistrate or Juror, at least 14 days before that on which the writ is to be executed, neglects or refuses to attend, the Provost-Marshal or his Deputy shall, under the penalty of £20 (£12 sterling), to be recovered as other penalties against the Provost-Marshal or his Deputy, return into Court the names and places of abode of such defaulters, with an affidavit of the service, and the Court shall fine each defaulter, and compel payment as is usually done respecting Jurors to attend the Supreme Court. [See Juries warned on writs, 43. G. 3, c. 28.] And the Jurors shall be protected in their persons from all mesne and judicial process during their attendance, and in going to and returning from the place of execution, 25 G. 3, c. 1, s. 8.

Penalties on Magistrate or Jurors neglecting to attend &c.

The Act 25 G., 3 c. 1, was not intended to confine the right to emblements to an executor or an administrator of a tenant for life, or to abridge or defeat the rights of any persons entitled to emblements in respect of any other estate according to the laws of England, but only to direct the manner in which emblements should be ascertained and set out to the parties entitled thereto, 53 G. 3, c. 26, s. 1.

To what cases 25 G. 3. c. 1 applicable

The Regulations in 25 G., 3, c. 1, s. 5–6., shall extend to the case of any persons entitled to emblements according to the laws of England, 53 G. 3, c. 26, s. 2.

25 G. 3, c. 1, s 5, 6 extended to all cases of emblements

Error, Writs of.

No execution shall be stayed upon writ of error or supersedeas for reversing any judgment in any action, or bill of debt upon single bond, or upon any obligation for payment of money only, or upon any action for rent, or any contract or bond to the King, or in any action upon the case or promises for payment of money, actions of trover, covenant, detinue and trespass, or in any action personal, sued in the Supreme or any Court of Assize, unless the person in whose name the writ of error is brought, or some person representing him in this island, other than the attorney-at-law, with

Security before stay of execution in personal actions

two sureties over and above the security given in the office of the Register in Chancery, shall be bound to the party for whom judgment is given by
recognizance, to be acknowledged in the same court or before the Chief Justice, or, in his absence, an Assistant Judge of the Supreme Court, in double
the sum adjudged to be recovered in the judgment, to prosecute the writ of
error with effect, and also to satisfy and pay, if the judgment be affirmed,
the debts, damages and costs upon the former judgment, and all costs and
damages to be awarded for the delaying of execution, or upon any discontinuance in default of the plaintiff, or non-pros or non-suit therein. 17 G.
3, c. 16, s. 1.

In dower, parti-
tion or ejectment Nor in writs of error upon any final judgment after verdict, or by default in any writ of dower or partition, or in any action of ejectione firmæ,
without similar additional security, conditioned that if the judgment is affirmed in the writ of error, or the writ be discontinued in default of the plaintiff,
or he be non-suit or non-pros, the plaintiff shall pay such costs, damages
and sums of money as shall be awarded, upon or after such judgment affirmed, discontinuance, non-suit or non-pros, 17 G. 3, c. 16, s. 2.

Writs of cuqui-
ry as to mesne,
profits and waste The Court, wherein execution ought to be granted, shall issue a writ to
enquire, as well of the mesne profits as of the damages by any waste
committed after judgment in dower, partition, or in ejectione firmæ, and
upon the return, judgment shall be given, and execution awarded for such
Cases not within
act. mesne profits and damages, and also for costs of suit. This act shall not extend to any writ of error to be brought by an executor or administrator,
nor to any action popular, or any other action upon any penal law or statute,
nor to any indictment, presentment, inquisition, information or appeal, 17
G. 3, c. 16, s. 3.

See Privy Council Note.

––––––

Escheats.

The value of the
real estate to be
enquired of In writs of Escheat. the Provost-Marshal shall be commanded to enquire
by a jury of 12 free and lawful men, upon their oaths (they then being on the
premises), the true value of all the real estate which any person dying
without heirs was, at the time of his death, seized of; and after office found
Conditions up-
on which land to
be granted and returned into the Supreme Court and judgment recorded, the Governor
may pass a grant of the escheated estate under the broad seal, provided a
clause be inserted that the grant shall be void in case any right heir appears and claims the same, and legally approves himself to be heir, within
3 years after the date of the patent, and that the value of the escheated
estate, as it was appraised at, shall be secured to be paid into the Treasury
after the expiration of 3 years from the date of the patent; if no heir in the
meantime obtain the same, by the person to whom the Governor grants it,
Valuation to be
paid out of trea-
sury to the heir at
any time and the treasurer or receiver shall pay the sum the escheated estate was
valued at, out of the Treasury, unto or for the use of such heir who claims
and approves himself to be heir, before any other payment, (which
proof of the heir's title shall be made by any public attestation or otherwise, as shall be believed to be evidence by the Judges and Jury) to be recovered at any time without limitation, 33 C. 2, c. 22, s. 2.

Patentee to be
paid for improve-
ments within 3
years before the
heir enters Where any true and valuable improvements are made on escheated lands
by the patentee during the 3 years, the heir, before entering, shall satisfy
to him all such charges as the Chancellor adjudges to be reasonably expended, with interest, 33 C. 2, c. 22 s. 4.

Lands to be
proclaimed for 3
courts before of-
fice found Every parcel of land to be escheated after office found, shall be cried
out in the last proprietor's name 3 times every second Tuesday of the Grand
Court during its sitting, for 3 Courts successively, before judgment pass for
the King, and no patent shall be granted otherwise, or, if so, it shall be
void, 6 G. 2, c. 7, s. 5.

Qualification of
Jurors

Valuations

One-third allow-
ed patentee Upon Escheats for land, the jury shall consist of freeholders to the
value of £10, (£6 sterling) per annum, at least, in the parish where the
land to be escheated is, who shall value on oath, according to the real value
at the time of valuation, one-third of which value shall be allowed the
grantee or patentee towards defraying the charges he shall be at in obtaining the land, 6 G. 2, c. 7, s. 6.

To be tried in
the supreme court Escheats shall be tried in the Supreme Court only, 31 G. 2, c. 4, s. 13.

Persons who obtain Escheats shall, before they obtain a Patent, repair to the Receiver-General's office, and enter into bond with 2 securities, payable in 3 years to the Crown, for the sums due to H. M. for the lands escheated, for which bond the Receiver-General is to receive 10s. (6s. sterling,) and shall charge the persons entering into such bonds, with the amount, in the public books of the revenue, 31 G. 2, c. 18, s. 1.

Escheat bonds to be entered into

And grant to the person a certificate to the Clerk of the Patents that he has entered into bond with security, upon producing of which the Clerk of the Patents shall issue out the Patent, and no Patent shall be granted otherwise, or, if so, it shall be illegal and void, 31 G. 2, c. 18, s. 2.

On Receiver-General's certificate Patent to issue.

Persons who obtain Letters of Preference shall, within 3 months after, proceed to perform the conditions, under penalty of £1000 (£600 sterling,) which the Solicitor of the Crown is directed to recover in an information or action for debt for the use of the Government of this island, 56 G. 3, c. 24, s. 1.

Penalty for omission to perform conditions of letters of preference

Escheat Bonds shall be recorded in the Secretary's Office, and the record, or an attested copy, is declared evidence, 56 G. 3, c. 24, s. 2.

Bonds to be recorded

No Letters of Preference shall issue from the office of the Governor's Secretary, until the application has been filed 14 days, under penalty of £50 (£30 sterling), 3 G. 4, c. 13, s. 9.

Letters of preference

All revenue from Escheats shall be paid to the Receiver-General, and form part of the fund appropriated by 17 V., c. 29, s. 36.

Revenue from part of the permanent Revenue Fund.

All Escheat monies heretofore collected and paid to the Governor, shall be collected by the Registrar in Chancery, and paid to the Receiver-General for the use of the public, 15 V., c. 17, s. 2.

European Assurance Society.

Their guarantee may be taken from persons now holding or to be appointed to public offices or employments, instead of the security already taken or required by the acts now or to be in force, 27 V., S. 1, c. 35.

Their guarantee may be taken as security for public officers

Evidence.

The records of Letters Patent, enrolled in the Secretary's Office, of deeds duly executed and proved, or acknowledged, and enrolled in the said or any other office of record, and the records or enrolment of any wills, duly executed and proved before the Governor by one or more of the subscribing witnesses, shall be evidence of the persons titles to any lands or estates, real or personal claimed thereunder, and allowed in all courts of law or or equity, as if the originals were produced, proved and read in Court, 4 G. 2, c. 5, s. 2.

Record of patents, deeds and wills and copies

The exemplifications of wills made in Great Britain or Ireland, or any other of H. M's. colonies or dominions, and sent over to this island (after probate, according to law in the several Dominions and Colonies) under the seal of the prerogative Court of Canterbury, or under the seal of the Archbishop or Lord Mayor of Dublin, or any Archbishops in their respective dioceses in England or Ireland, or the Mayor, Provosts or Bailiffs, of any other Corporation or body politic, or under the seal of any of the said Dominions or Colonies, and afterwards recorded in this island, shall be sufficient evidence, and read and allowed as such, of the title of the parties claiming any lands or estates under such wills so exemplified in all courts of law or equity, 4 G. 2, c. 5, s. 3.

Exemplifications of wills

The probate of any will taken before any officer authorized to take probate of wills in any of the United States, and exemplified under the seal of the State where probate has been taken, shall be as effectual as if probate had been taken before the Ordinary of this island, 34 G. 3, c. 11, s. 2.

In the United States

The Record or office copy, authenticated by the Secretary or his deputy, of powers of attorney duly executed and recorded, shall be allowed and read in evidence in all courts, as if the originals themselves were actually proved, produced and read. Not to exclude the actual proof, production, and reading in evidence of original powers, 8 V., c. 42, s. 1.

Records &c. of powers of attorney

Certificate of previous conviction for felony, see 20 V. c. 19, s. 8

On an indictment for any felony, not punishable with death, committed after a previous conviction for felony, it shall be sufficient to state that the offender was at a certain time and place convicted of felony, without otherwise describing the previous felony, and a certificate containing the substance and effect only, omitting the formal part of the indictment and conviction for the previous felony, purporting to be signed by the Clerk of the Crown or his deputy, shall, upon proof of the identity of the offender, be sufficient evidence of the first conviction, without proof of the signature or official character of the person appearing to have signed the same, 9 G. 4, c. 19, s. 7.

Of sentences or orders of transportation or banishment, see 20 v. c. 19, s. 2, 8

In case of any prosecution for any escape, attempt to escape, breach of prison, or rescue, either against the convict or against any other person concerned therein, or aiding, abetting or assisting the same, a copy, properly attested, of the commitment, shall after proof that the person is the same that was committed, be sufficient evidence that he was so committed, 1 V., c. 28, s. 14.

For escape, prison breach &c, See 20 v. c 19, s, 8

On any indictment for being found at large, or for rescuing, attempting or assisting in rescuing any offender from custody, or conveying, or causing to be conveyed any disguised instrument for effecting escape, or arms to any such offender, the Clerk of the Court or other officer having the custody of the records, where sentence or order of transportation or banishment has been passed, or the Governor's Secretary shall, at the request of any person on Her Majesty's behalf, give a certificate, signed by him, containing the effect and substance, only omitting the formal part of every indictment and conviction of the offender, and of the sentence or order for his transportation or banishment, which certificate shall be sufficient evidence of the conviction and sentence or order, and be received in evidence, 1 V., c. 28, s. 17.

Certificates of indictments on trials for perjury or subornation, see 20 V. c.19, s. 8

A certificate containing the substance and effect only (omitting the formal part) of the indictment and trial for any felony or misdemeanor, purporting to be signed by the Clerk of the Court, or other officer having the custody of the records of the Court where the indictment was tried, or by the deputy (for which certificate a fee of 6s 8d, and no more, shall be demanded) shall, upon the trial of any indictment for perjury or subornation of perjury, be sufficient evidence of the trial of such indictment for felony or misdemeanor, without proof of the signature or official character of the person appearing to have signed the same, 16 V., c. 15, s. 23.

Endurance of punishment to have the effect of a pardon, except &c.

Where any person has been convicted of felony, not punishable with death, and has endured the punishment to which he was adjudged, the punishment shall have the effects and consequences of a pardon as to the felony, but not so as to prevent or mitigate any punishment to which the offender might otherwise be lawfully sentenced on any subsequent conviction for any other felony, 7 V., c. 5, s. 1.

Endurance of punishment, restoration of competency in cases of misdemeanor, except perjury or subornation

When any offender, convicted of any misdemeanor (except perjury or subornation of perjury) has endured the punishment to which he was adjudged, he shall not be deemed by reason of such misdemeanor an incompetent witness in any Court or proceeding, civil or criminal, 7 V., c. 5, s. 2.

Witnesses not incapacitated from crime or interest, except in case of perjury or subornation

No person offered as a witness shall be excluded by reason of incapacity from crime or interest from giving evidence, either in person or by deposition, according to the practice of the Court, on the trial of any issue joined, or of any matter or question, or on any enquiry in any suit, action or proceeding, civil or criminal in any Court, or before any Judge, Jury, Coroner, Magistrate, Officer or person having by law or consent of parties authority to hear, receive and examine evidence, but every person so offered shall be admitted to give evidence, on oath, or solemn affirmation where receivable, notwithstanding he may have an interest in the matter in question, and notwithstanding he may have been previously convicted of any crime or offence (perjury and subornation of perjury excepted); but not to render competent the husband or wife of any party, nor to repeal any provisions in 3 V., c. 51 (Wills).

Husband and wife, see 22 V., c. 16, s. 3, 4 Wills Defendants in equity

In Courts of equity, any defendant may be examined as a witness, on behalf of the plaintiff or of any co-defendant, saving just exceptions, and any interest he may have in the matters in question in the cause shall not be deemed a just exception to his testimony, but only as affecting or tending to affect his credit as a witness, 7 V., c. 31, s. 1.

Pending suits

Act not to affect any suit, action or proceeding, already brought or commenced, 7 V., c. 31, s. 2.

On the trial of any issue joined, or of any matter or question, or on any enquiry arising in any suit, action or other proceeding in any Court of Justice, or before any person having by law or by consent of parties authority to hear, receive, and examine evidence, the parties and the persons in whose behalf any such suit, &c., may be brought or defended, shall (except as after) be competent and compellable to give evidence, either viva voce, or by deposition, according to the practice of the Court, on behalf of any party to the suit, &c., 22 V., c. 16, s. 2. *Parties to the record &c.*

Not to render any person who in any criminal proceeding is charged with the commission of any indictable offence, or any offence punishable on summary conviction, competent or compellable to give evidence for or against himself, or to render any person compellable to answer any question tending to criminate himself, or in any criminal proceeding to render any husband competent or compellable to give evidence for or against his wife, or any wife for or against her husband, 22 V., c. 16, s. 3. *Persons charged with criminal offences, criminating question — Husband and wife*

Nor shall apply to any action, suit or proceeding, in any Court of common law for criminal conversation, or any action for breach of promise of marriage. 22 V., c. 16, s. 4.

Nor shall repeal any provision in 3 V., c. 51, (Wills). 22 V., c. 16, s. 5. *Wills*

The Judges may, within 3 years, make regulations, by general rules in term, or in vacation, touching the voluntary admission, upon application at a reasonable time before the trial, of one party to the other, of all written or printed documents or copies intended to be offered in evidence on the trial by the party requiring such admission, and touching the inspection before admission is made, and the costs to be incurred by the proof of such documents or copies on the trial, in case of the omitting to apply for such admission, or the not producing of such documents or copies for the purpose of obtaining admission, or of the refusal to make such admission, which rules shall be binding in all courts of common law, and of the like force as if enacted by the legislature, 8 V., c. 28, s. 9. *Admission of documents in evidence*

Rules to be laid before the Legislature, 8 V., c. 28, s. 24. (See Court, Supreme). *To be laid before the legislature*

When any action or other legal proceeding is pending, the Supreme Court, and each of the Judges, on application by any litigant, may compel the opposite party to allow him to inspect all documents in his custody, or under his control, relating to such actions, &c., and, if necessary, to take examined copies, or to procure the same to be stamped, in all cases in which previous to this act a discovery might have been obtained by a bill or other proceeding in a court of equity, at the instance of the party applying, 20 V., c. 19, s. 1. *Compulsory production of documents for inspection, or to take copies or stamp same*

When any certificate, official or public document, or document or proceeding of any corporation or joint stock, or other company, or any certified copy of any document, bye-law, entry in any register or other book, or of any other proceeding, is receivable in evidence of any particular in any Court of Justice, or before any legal tribunal, or the Legislative Council or House of Assembly, or any committee of either, or in any judicial proceeding, the same shall be admitted in evidence, provided they purport to be sealed or impressed with a stamp, or sealed and signed alone as required, or impressed with a stamp, and signed as directed by the respective acts, without any proof of the seal or stamp, where a seal or stamp is necessary, or of the signature, or of the official character of the person appearing to have signed the same, and without any further proof thereof in every case in which the original record could have been received in evidence, 20 V., c. 19, s. 2. *Documents admissable without proof of seal, signature or official character*

All Courts, Judges, Justices, Masters in Chancery, Taxing and Computing Officers of Courts, Commissioners judicially acting, and other Judicial officers, shall take judicial notice of the signature of any of the equity or common law Judges of the superior Courts at Westminster, and of the Judges of the Supreme Court of Chancery and Court of Ordinary, attached or appended to any decree, order, certificate or other judicial official document, 20 V., c. 19, s. 3. *Judicial notice of signatures of Judges of supreme courts of Westminster or this island*

Copies of private acts of Parliament, if purporting to be printed by the Queen's printer, and of private acts of the Legislature, if purporting to be printed by the printer to the Legislature, and of the journals of either house of the Legislature, and of royal proclamations, purporting to be printed by the printers to the Crown or to the Legislature, shall be admitted as evidence, without any proof that they were so printed, 20 V., c. 19, s. 4. *Printed copies of private acts, Journals of either House, and Royal proclamations*

Proclamations, treaties, acts of state and judicial proceedings of foreign states or British colonies

Proclamations, treaties and other acts of State of any foreign State, or of any British colony, judgments, decrees, orders, and other judicial proceeding, of any Court of Justice in any foreign State or British Colony, and affidavits, pleadings, and other legal documents filed or deposited in any such Court, may be proved in any Court of Justice, or before any person having, by law or by consent of parties, authority to hear, receive, and examine evidence, either by examined copies or by copies authenticated as after mentioned, viz.: If the document be a proclamation, treaty, or other act of State, the authenticated copy must purport to be sealed with the seal of the foreign State or British Colony to which the original document belongs. If it be a judgment, &c , of any foreign or Colonial Court, or an affidavit, &c., filed or deposited in any such Court, the authenticated copy must purport to be sealed with the seal of the foreign or Colonial Court to which the original document belongs, or in the event of the Court having no seal, to be signed by the Judge or one of the Judges of the Court, who shall attach to his signature a statement in writing on the copy, that the Court whereof he is a Judge has no seal; but if any authenticated copies purport to be sealed or signed as before directed, they shall be admitted in evidence in every case in which the original could have been, without any proof of the seal or of the signature, or of the truth of the statement, attached thereto, or of the judicial character of the person appearing to have made such signature and statement, 20 V., c. 19, s. 5.

Forgery &c. of documents &c.

Forging any document, or the seal, stamp or signature of any such document, or tendering in evidence any such document, with a false or counterfeit seal, stamp or signature thereto, knowing the same to be false or counterfeit: felony, liable to imprisonment not exceeding 3 years, nor less than 1 year, with hard labour; and whenever any such document has been admitted in evidence, the Court or person who admitted

Documents may be impounded

it may, at the request of any party against whom it is admitted, direct it to be impounded and kept in the custody of an officer or other person for such period, and subject to such conditions as to the Court or person shall seem meet. Persons charged with committing any felony may be dealt with, indicted, tried, and, if convicted, sentenced, and his offence may be laid and charged to have been committed in the county, district or place in which he was apprehended or in custody, and every accessory before or after the fact may be dealt with, &c., in any county, &c., in which the principal offender may be tried, 20 V., c. 19, s. 6.

British Register

Every register of a vessel, kept under any act relating to the Registry of British vessels may be proved, either by production of the original, or by an examined copy, or by a copy purporting to be certified under the hand of the person having the charge of the original, and who is required to furnish such certified copy to any person applying at a reasonable time for the same, upon payment of 1s.; and every such register or copy, and certificate of registry, purporting to be signed as required by law, shall be received in evidence as prima facie proof of all the matters contained or recited in such register, when the register or such copy is produced, and of all the matters contained or recited in, or endorsed on such certificate of registry when the certificate is produced, 20 V., c. 19, s. 7,

Certificates of conviction or acquittal

When in any proceeding whatever, it may be necessary to prove the trial and conviction or acquittal of any person charged with any indictable offence, it shall not be necessary to produce the record of the conviction or acquittal of such person, or a copy, but it shall be sufficient that it be certified or purport to be certified under the hand of the Clerk of the Court or other officer having the custody of the records of the Court, where such conviction or acquittal took place, or by his deputy, that the paper produced is a copy of the record of the indictment, trial, conviction and judgment or acquittal, as the case may be, omitting the formal parts, 20 V., c. 19, s. 8.

Copies or extract of books or documents of a public nature

Whenever any book or other document is of such a public nature as to be admissible in evidence on its mere production from the proper custody, and no statute exists which renders its contents provable by means of a copy, any copy or extract shall be admissible in evidence, if it be proved to be an examined copy or extract, or it purport to be signed and certified as a true copy or extract by the officer to whose custody the original is entrusted, and who is required to furnish such copy or extract to any person applying at a reasonable time for the same, upon payment of a reasonable sum, not exceeding 6d for every folio of 90 words, 20 V., c. 19, s. 9.

If any officer authorized or required to furnish any certified copies or extracts, wilfully certify any document as being a true copy or extract, knowing it is not so, he shall be guilty of a misdemeanor, and be liable, on conviction, to imprisonment not exceeding 18 months, 20 V., c. 19, s. 10. *False Certificate*

Every Court, Judge, Justice, Officer, Commissioner, Arbitrator or other person now or hereafter having, by law or by consent of parties, authority to hear, receive and examine evidence, may administer an oath to all such witnesses as are legally called before them, 20 V., c. 19, s. 11. *Courts and persons having authority by law &c., to hear evidence, may administer oath to witnesses*

"British Colony" shall apply to all possessions of the British Crown, wheresoever and whatsoever, other than Great Britain and Ireland, 20 V., c. 19, s. 12. *Interpretation*

Act not to affect any pending suit, 20 V., c. 19, s. 13. *Pending suits*

Executive Committee.

The Governor may, under his sign manual, appoint, not exceeding 3 members of the House of Assembly and one member of the Legislative Council, to be an Executive Committee, for his assistance in the general administration of the finances, and execution of the duties hereby directed, and may revoke any such appointment, and, subject to the restrictions in this act, make other appointment. If any member forfeits, resigns or loses his seat in the Legislative Council or Assembly, except as after provided. or accepts any other office of emolument, his appointment shall ipso facto cease. During a dissolution of the House of Assembly, no member shall be disqualified by reason of his not being a member of Assembly, 17 V., c. 29, s. 15. *Appointment on members*

When any member of Assembly is appointed a member of the Executive Committee, his seat in the House shall not thereby become vacant, 17, V., c. 29, s. 16. *Not to vacate seat in assembly*

No person shall be appointed a member of the Executive Committee who is the holder of any office of emolument, nor shall any member of the Executive Committee be qualified to hold any other office of emolument while so, 17 V., c. 29, s. 17. *Not to hold any other office of emolument*

The Executive Committee shall assist the Governor in preparing the annual estimates, in levying and disbursing the public monies, and in the general administration of the finances. and, when required, collectively and individually, shall advise and assist the Governor in the general administration of the affairs of this island, and, when required, by a minute under the hand of the Governor, shall give their opinions and views in writing, and at large, on all matters submitted to them, and shall also, when required in writing, advise on, prepare and perfect all estimates, ways and means, papers, messages, answers, bills and other proceedings which the Governor deems advisable to be submitted or communicated to either branch of the Legislature or to any person. And the Governor may, by minute, to be published in the Gazette by Authority, and transcribed in the books of the Executive Committee, direct that the service of any particular parts of the general administration be performed by any particular member, and vary the service, and each member to whom such particular service is appointed shall execute and perform it accordingly; but the Executive Government shall continue to be discharged by the Governor, and on his responsibility as heretofore, either when he has acted alone, or with the advice of his Privy Council. And nothing herein shall vest in the Executive Committee any power of appointing to any office, but the whole patronage and the right of making appointments shall continue as heretofore, 17 V., c. 29, s. 18. *Their duties in reference to Annual Estimates, finances and general administration. Estimates, bills, communications, &c. to the legislature, Particular branches of administration &c.* *Governor's responsibility and patronage*

The members of the Executive Committee, shall, in the Legislative Council and Assembly, be the official organs of intercommunication between the Governor and such Houses, and for the authoritative disclosure of the policy of the Government on all questions political, financial and administrative which become the subject of consideration and discussion, 17 V., c. 29, s. 19. *Official organs of communication with the legislature*

Each member while he holds office shall receive from the Treasury a salary in Schedule A (£800), and the Executive Committee shall be paid £200 per annum in full discharge of all contingencies of office, 17 V., c. 29, s. 20. *Salaries and contingencies*

Y

The Executive Committee Board of Audit

The Governor and members shall constitute a body, to be called "The Executive Committee," and the Executive Committee shall constitute a Board of Audit, or a portion of a Board of Audit, appointed under any act, 17 V., c. 29, s. 21.

Commissioners of Accounts

The Governor may, by minute, name any two members to perform the duties, and be clothed with the powers of the late Commissioners of Accounts, under 15 G. 3, c. 4, * or any other acts imposing duties on, or giving powers to the Commissioners of Public Accounts, and shall perform all other duties of the Commissioners of Public Accounts, 25 V., c. 37, s. 1.

Board of Works

The Governor and any two members of the Executive Committee, shall perform all the duties, and be permanently clothed with the powers vested in the Commissioners under 15 V., c. 18; but not authorizing them to expend any other sums than shall be granted by the Legislature for the purposes in that act mentioned, 17 V. c. 29, s. 22. †

Governor may originate votes of money through the Executive Committee

The Governor may exercise his power of proposing or originating any vote of money in the House of Assembly, by message, or through the Executive Committee as organs of Government, or one of them, under the direction and upon the sole responsibility of the Government, 17 V., c. 29, s. 23.

They may exercise their powers as commissioners of accounts during session

The duties and powers transferred from the Commissioners of Public Accounts to the Executive Committee shall exist, and be exercised as well during the Session as during any adjournment or prorogation, 17 V., c. 29, s 24.

And notwithstanding a dissolution

And notwithstanding the Assembly is dissolved, 17 V., c. 29, s. 25.

Powers of present Boards of Accounts and Works to cease

The powers of the Commissioners appointed under the Acts 15 G. 3, c. 4, and 15 V., c. 18, shall cease, 17 V., c. 29, s. 27.

Commissioners of Customs

The Executive Committee shall be Commissioners of Customs. (See Customs, 17 V., c. 33, s. 2, 4, 5), 20 V., c. 5, s. 2.

Leave of absence

The Governor may give leave of absence, for the benefit of his health, to any member, not exceeding 6 months at one time, but not so as to prevent him from being present during the sitting of the Legislature : and no more than one member shall be absent at the same time. The leave of absence to be free of Stamp Duty, 25 V., c. 37, s. 2.

Secretary

The Governor may appoint a Secretary to the Executive Committee (and fill up vacancies), whose duties, in addition to the custody of all books, papers and documents appertaining to the Executive Committee, shall be defined by a minute of the Governor, with the advice of the Executive Committee, which duties the Secretary is required to perform, 17 V., c. 29, s. 28.

The Governor may remove the Secretary, and appoint another in his place. Every removed Secretary shall deliver to such person, and within such time as the Governor shall appoint, all books, papers and documents in his custody, and upon neglect or refusal, shall incur a penalty of £300, recoverable summarily before 2 Justices, 17 V., c. 29, s. 29.

To be Clerk of Privy Council

He shall be Clerk of the Privy Council. (See Privy Council, 17 V., c. 29, s. 14.)

His salary

The Secretary shall, while he holds office, be entitled to a salary of £400 per annum, in Schedule A, by quarterly payments, 17 V., c. 29, s. 30.

Also an additional salary of £200, 20 V., c. 16.

Their duties under 15 G. 3, c. 4

* The Members of Assembly shall be Commissioners, during the intervals of the sittings, to settle and adjust the public accounts with the Receiver-General, as also the several accounts of all funds and taxes, and to look into and count over the cash in his office belonging to the public, 15 G. 3, c. 4.

Powers permanently conferred upon the Executive Committee as a Board of Works
To expend monies granted for public buildings
Make Contracts
Examine persons
Send for books, &c.
Order the digging stones
Making satisfaction

† The powers thus permanently conferred were given under the temporary Act, 15 V., c. 18, limited to endure until 31st December, 1854, and appear to be (in the absence of temporary enactments) as follow :—

To expend the monies granted for erecting, repairing and altering the buildings belonging to the public; to make contracts with workmen and others for materials, workmanship and labor, and hire laborers; to send for and examine persons upon oath, and also all books, papers, vouchers and writings they require, 15 V., c. 18, s. 1.

To order the digging out and carrying away earth or stones, for the use of the buildings, out of lands not in cultivation, and not enclosed as a garden or a yard, on making satisfaction therefor : the amount, in case of disagree

And a further additional salary of £150, 25 V., c. 38.

The Governor, with the advice of the Executive Committee, shall appropriate one or more rooms in one of the buildings belonging to the Public in St. Jago de la Vega, to be used exclusively as an office by the Executive Committee and their Secretary, and to be a place of deposit for all books, papers and documents belonging to such Committee, 17 V., c. 29, s. 31.

Executive Committee Office

The Executive Committee incorporated for the purposes only herein specified, by the name of the "Executive Committee of Jamaica," and shall have a Common Seal, and have, purchase, receive and hold lands, rents, &c. of what nature or quality soever, and sell, demise or dispose of the same, sue and be sued, &c., 22 V., c. 33. s. 1.

Their incorporation for certain purposes

The purposes of incorporation shall be only such as are or shall be authorized by any act, and for holding any lands to be hereafter conveyed to the body corporate by any officers of state having authority as such, to transfer the same, or which may hereafter be given, conveyed or devised for the use and benefit of the public, 22 V., c. 33, s. 2.

Purposes of incorporation

The possession and right of p   e   n of all lands, &c., now held in trust for or to the use of the crown for the benefit of the people of this island, or charged to such absolute use or benefit, may be recovered, maintained, asserted and vindicated, with the sanction, and in the name of the Executive Committee of Jamaica, for all intents and purposes as if the fee simple were vested in them, 22 V., c. 33, s. 3.

They shall exercise their powers only upon the trusts, and for the purposes hereafter to be or now authorized or directed by some act of the Legislature, or in accordance with the terms of the will, deed or instrument charging them with such public trust, 22 V., c. 33, s. 4.

Trusts

Executors and Administrators.

Executors, when the will of any testator is exhibited to be proved, shall answer, on oath, to the value and circumstances of the testator's testamentary estate to the best of their knowledge, and, at the discretion of the Ordinary, not only take the oath of an executor, but give security to return an inventory of the estate, with an appraisement, on oath, within the time limited by the Ordinary. The examination and oath shall be taken before persons authorized by dedimus, where the party is indisposed, or incapable to attend through age or other infirmity, and where the Ordinary thinks fit to grant the dedimus, 10 Ann, c. 18, s. 1.

Executor's value of estate, security to return an inventory and appraisement

Dedimus

When the value of personal property, of which administration is sought to be obtained from the Ordinary, is sworn to as not exceeding £100, the papers to be obtained from the Court for perfecting administration shall be exempted from all Stamp Duties and fees called the Ordinary's fees, 27 V., s. 1, c. 16, s. 8.

Value under £100

---

ment, to be settled by 3 Justices, not being commissioners nor interested, 15 V., c. 18, s. 6.

To be settled by justices

Except as after, when work is to be done, publicly to advertise for proposals and estimates, and accept the most reasonable and advantageous, 15 V., c. 18, s. 8.

Contracts to be advertised for

No contract to be made unless security is given for its due performance, 15 V., c. 18, s. 9.

And security given for performance

All bonds to be proved as deeds are, and delivered to the Clerk of the Board, and to be good evidence, without producing the attesting witness, 15 V., c. 18 s. 10.

Probate &c. of Bonds

Not to order any work to be done or payment made, except it has been contracted for, and performed agreeably to contract previously advertised, unless the work does not exceed £10, and is required so immediately as to render it impracticable to delay the performance until contracts can be advertised for, 15 V., c. 18, s. 11.

No work to be done without contract, unless under £10 and urgent

When the Commissioners have reason to believe that any person has been guilty of any fraud or misconduct in obtaining any contract, or improper or negligent performance of any work they may order that such person shall be prevented from accepting or being interested in or proceeding any public contract or work for such time as they think fit, 15 V., c. 18, s. 26.

Fraudulent contractors

When the value sworn to by the executor or executrix of any deceased person shall not exceed £100, the documents to prove the will, granting letters testamentary and dedimus to return inventory, shall be exempted from all stamp duties and Ordinary's fees, 27 V., S. 1, c. 16, s. 9.

Pleas—not admissions of assets
To actions by creditors of the deceased, executors or administrators may plead such bars as their testators or intestates might, if living, have pleaded. No such pleas shall be received as conclusive evidence of the admission of assets in defendant's hands, notwithstanding their notice or knowledge of other demands against the estate at the time of pleading, 16 G. 3, c. 15, s. 2.

Footing of Judgments in point of priority. Rule of Executors
Executions duly lodged for any judgments whatever against executors or administrators, within the 2 next Courts after pleading the rule of executors allowed to them by the Supreme Court, (and which shall be pleaded generally against every creditor) shall be exactly on the same footing of priority as if taken together the first Court, 29 G. 3, c. 13, s. 3.

Taking possession of deceased's property without qualifying
Any person taking possession of, and in any manner administering any part of the personal estate and effects of any person deceased, without obtaining probate of the will or letters of administration within 6 calendar months after his decease, or 2 calendar months after the termination of any suit, respecting the will or the right to letters of administration, if any, not ended within 4 calendar months after the death:

Penalty
penalty £100, 6 V., c. 55, s. 4.

Recovery &c.
To be recovered in the Supreme Court by action of debt, &c., with full costs, one moiety to the informer, 13 V., c. 38.

Actions by and against for torts in testator's lifetime
An action of trespass or trespass on the case (as the case may be), may be maintained by executors or administrators for injury to the real estate of the deceased, committed in his lifetime, for which an action might have been maintained by him if committed within 6 calendar months before, and the action is brought within one year after his death, as also against executors or administrators for any wrong committed by the deceased in his lifetime to another, in respect of his property, real or personal, so as the injury was within 6 months before the death, and the action brought within 6 calendar months after the executors

Damages payable on footing of simple contract debts
or administrators have taken upon themselves the administration of the estate, and the damages to be recovered shall be payable in like order of administration as simple contract debts, 8 V., c. 28, s. 1.

Debt on simple contract
Actions of debt on simple contract shall be maintainable against them, 8 V., c. 8, s. 7.

Liability for costs
In actions brought by them in right of the testator or intestate, unless the Court or a Judge otherwise order, they shall be liable to pay costs to the defendant, in case of being non-suited, or a verdict passing against the plaintiff, and in all other cases in which they would be liable, if suing in their own right upon a cause of action accruing to themselves; and the defendant shall have judgment for such costs, to be recovered in like manner, 8 V., c. 28, s. 14.

Renouncing executors discharged of trust and not to be joined in actions &c. after disclaimer recorded
Any person named an executor, who has not in any way acted or interfered with the testator's estate, and executes and records in the Secretary's Office a deed of renunciation and disclaimer of the office and appointment, shall immediately, on the record thereof, be absolutely relieved and discharged of the trust, and shall not be joined as a plaintiff or a defendant in any action, suit or proceeding, 24 V., c. 24, s. 1.

Not to be afterwards entitled to probate
The execution and recording of such deed shall be an abandonment and surrender of all right, title, interest and claim to the office and appointment of executor under the will, and the party shall not afterwards be entitled to claim, or have probate granted to him, 24 V., c. 24, s. 2.

Extent, Writ of

When to issue)
In actions against any person, his Executors or Administrators, and judgment obtained in the Supreme Court, in case nulla bona is returned, the plaintiff may issue a writ for sale of the defendant's lands in the following form:—

Form of writ. Which the supreme court is empowered to alter by 8 V., c. 48, s. 17, and has done so, adapting the form to the extended powers of execution under s. 5
The King to the Provost-Marshal, greeting:

Whereas we have lately commanded thee by our writ, that of the goods and chattels, real and personal, of A. B., thou shouldst levy or cause to be levied, the sum of   , of good and lawful money of this island, as also   for costs of suit, which

C. D. in our Court recovered against the said   , by virtue of which writ thou didst return unto us that the said A, B. had no goods and chattels, real and personal, in this island, whereon thou couldst levy the said   and costs, and the said C D. having prayed of us a fit remedy against the messuages, plantations, lands and tenements of the said A. B., for satisfaction of the said   and costs, we therefore command thee, that of the messuages, plantations, lands and tenements of the said A. B. within this island, thou take to the value of the said   and costs, by the appraisement of 12 good and lawful (men) being freeholders and planters of the neighbourhood of such messuages plantations, lands and tenements, by thee to be summoned to meet upon the said premises for that purpose, and that possession and seisin thereof to the said C. D., thou cause to be delivered on such appraisement for satisfaction of the said   and costs, or so much as the value and appraisement thereof shall extend, to hold to him the said C. D, his heirs and assigns, in fee simple, or for such estate as the said A. B. had in the same; but if the said C. D. shall refuse to accept such possession and seisin of the said messuages, plantations, lands and tenements according to the said appraisement, that thou deliver possession and seisin of the said messuages, plantations, lands and tenements according to the said appraisement to any other person or persons whatsoever that shall pay down the amount of such appraisement, to be held by such other person or persons, his or their heirs and assigns, in fee simple, or for such estate as the said A. B. had in the same, and that thou make return of the particular premises so appraised and delivered to the said C. D., or such other person or persons, and of the appraisement thereof, under the hands and seals of the said 12 good and lawful men into our Supreme Court of this said island, together with this writ; but if no other person or persons whatsoever shall, upon the refusal of the said C. D., pay down the amount of such appraisement, or if thou canst not find any messuages, plantations, lands and tenements of the said A. B. in this island wherewith to satisfy, in part or in all, the said and costs, that then thou make a return thereof into our said Supreme Court of Judicature the   in   next, together with this writ   Witness,   24 G. 2, c. 19, s. 4.

The Provost-Marshal before he execute such writ shall receive directions in writing from the plaintiff upon which of the messuages, plantations, lands and tenements he shall execute it; but the plaintiff shall not direct any set of works or any part, or any capital, messuage or appurtenances to be valued, except the whole cultivated and improved lands usually occupied therewith are directed to be valued, 24 G. 2, c. 19, s. 5.

Instructions for execution

Upon receipt of the writ, the Provost-Marshal shall give 14 days' notice to the defendant, and summon a Jury of 24 planters or freeholders residing near the lands to be extended, out of which 12 shall be sworn by the Provost-Marshal, to value the same. In case the defendant, within 6 calendar months after the appraisement, pay or cause, &c., to the plaintiff or other person the full sum at which the same was valued, with interest, he shall be obliged to accept payment, and re-justate the defendant in possession, and do such further acts as shall be required by the defendant, at the defendant's costs. The act shall not impeach the right of any person, other than the defendant, or of any prior incumbrancer in law or equity by virtue of any lien, but all persons having such right or lien antecedent to the judgment, shall have the full benefit thereof; and in case there are two or more writs of execution against the same person of a concurrent right, the messuages, &c., shall be to the use and benefit of all the plaintiffs, nor shall the act debar any plaintiff from the benefit of any other writs he is by law entitled to for the recovery of any monies due him either before or after issuing the writ, but he shall be entitled to all remedies for recovery of such monies as if this act had never been made, 24 G. 2, c. 19, s. 6.

Notice of execution. Jurors

Right of redemption

Rights of prior incumbrancers

Plaintiffs' other remedies

The 24 G. 2, c. 19, s. 6, shall mean, that upon receipt of such writs, the Provost Marshal shall give 14 days notice to defendant, his executors or administrators, 7 V., c. 42.

Notice of execution to be given to the defendant, his executors or administrators

Extension of remedy under writ of extent

The Provost-Marshal or other officer to whom any writ of extent or any precept is directed, shall make and deliver possession unto the party suing, of all lands, tenements, rents and hereditaments the person against whom the writ is sued, or any person in trust for him was seized or possessed of at the time of [s. 16, registering] the judgment, or at any time afterwards, or over which such person at the time of registering, or at any time afterwards, has any disposing power which he might, without the assent of any other person exercise for his own benefit, which lands, &c., by force of such extent, shall accordingly be held and enjoyed by the party to whom the extent is made and delivered, 8 V., c. 4, s. 8.

Falmouth Water Company.

Incorporation

Incorporation of " The Falmouth Water Company" for supplying the town and shipping of Falmouth with water from the Martha Brae River, Capital £20,000 (12,000 sterling), divided into 400 shares of £50 (£30 sterling) each, 40 G. 3, c. 29, 26 V. S. 2, c. 17.

Rates payable by householders a n d ships

Every person in the possession or occupation of a House or tenement in the town of Falmouth, shall yearly pay to the use of the Corporation, or the person appointed by them, 2s. in the pound upon the rent or annual value of the House or tenements as fixed and rated by the Justices and Vestry of Trelawny, payable half-yearly. The Justices and Vestry shall annually make a fair estimate and rate of all Houses in the town, to be entered in the Vestry book, that the sum payable to the Corporation may be known and the Corporation duly paid. And for every vessel (King's ships, and those employed in H. Majestys' Service excepted) coming into the Harbour, at the rate of 6d (currency) for every ton, such imposition not to affect any drogher or turtler, or any vessel forced into the harbour by an enemy, or by receiving damage at sea, or otherwise by wind and weather or other accident, unless such vessel make use of the water; but no vessel of above 25 tons burthen, shall be admitted as a drogher or turtler within the proviso, 40 G. 3. c. 29, s. 14.

Destroying Aqueducts &c., felony

Wilfully and maliciously demolishing, breaking down, destroying, setting on fire, or filling up any aqueduct, trench, canal, wall, mound, dam, gutter or pipe, by means of or through which the stream of water runs or is conveyed, or any reservoir constructed for confining or preserving the water, or any erection, building, work, engine, instrument or means for the conserving and applying of such water to and for the purposes of this act, or any part of any such aqueduct, &c., felony, without benefit of clergy, 40 G. 3, c. 29, s. 17.

Punishment

The punishment of death is taken away, and the party shall be punished in the same manner as a person convicted of the same offence would by law be punishable in England, 19 V., c. 29, s. 2.

Using water without paying the duties, diverting the water

No person, other than such as are chargable with, and pay the duties, shall use any part of the stream of water in such aqueducts, canals, trenches, gutters, pipes and reservoirs, nor shall any person, without license from the Corporation, divert the water or any part from its place or course: penalty, £50 (£30 sterling), to be recovered by action of debt in the Supreme Court by the Corporation to its own use, with full costs, to be taxed, besides being liable in damages to the Corporation, 40 G. 3, c. 29, s. 18.

Polluting, or obstructing the course of the water, injury to aqueducts &c.

Putting, placing, throwing or casting, or causing, &c., into any of such aqueducts, canals, trenches, gutters, pipes or reservoirs, or other means of containing and conveying such water, any earth, stones, ashes, dirt, dust, rubbish, filth or other matter, whereby the Water may be polluted, injured or affected as to its uses or quality, or doing any other act by means of which the free passage or course of the stream of water through such aqueducts, &c. may be obstructed or hindered, or whereby any other nuisance or annoyance may be occasioned or happen to the water, or doing any other mischief, injury or damage to any of the aqueducts, canals, trenches, walls, mound, dams, gutters, pipes, reservoirs, erections, buildings, works, engines, instruments, or means for taking up, containing and conserving the water: penalty, £100 (£60 sterling), to be recovered as above, besides being liable in damages, 40 G. 3, c. 29, s. 19.

All penalties concerning the recovery of which no particular direction   Penalties
is given, shall, if not paid on demand, be recovered and levied by distress and
sale, by warrant of a Justice, not a member of the Corporation, to be granted
upon information upon oath, and the penalties when recovered, paid to such
persons as the Corporation appoint, for its use, and the warrant shall contain
a clause that in case a sufficient distress cannot be found, the offender be
taken by the body, and committed to the common Gaol, not exceeding 28
days, without bail or mainprize, unless the penalty and charges be sooner
paid and satisfied, 40 G. 3. c. 29, s. 20.

All penalties to be fixed by the Corporation for the non-observance,   Under bye-laws
non-performance or breach of the bye-laws, ordinances and regulations
thereof, shall be recovered, and levied, and applied as under the preceding section, 40 G. 3, c. 29, s. 21.

In cases of damage to the aqueducts, canals, trenches, pipes or gutters,   Damages not ex-
or other matter where the Corporation do not seek for damages exceeding   ceeding £12 stg.
£20 (£12 sterling), the same may be recoverable before any justice, not a
member, who, upon complaint on oath, is required to issue a warrant to all
or any of the constables to empannel and return, at a time and place to be inserted (the time to be within 10 days after the application), 12 good and lawful men, of whom any three upon their oaths (which the Justice is empowered to administer) shall try the complaint, and enquire of and assess damages, and give their verdict under their hands to such Justice, who, upon
such application, is also required to issue another warrant, directed in like manner, requiring the person complained of to be taken and brought before him,
at the time and place inserted in the warrant for empannelling and returning
the inquest, and shall, upon receiving such verdict, commit the party convicted, until he has paid to the Corporation the damages so assessed, with
such costs as the Justice thinks proper to award 40 G. 3, c. 29, s. 22.

No proceeding before a Justice shall be vacated or quashed for want   Want of form
of form, 40 G. 3, c. 29, s. 23.

No action shall be commenced for any thing done in pursuance of this   Actions
Act, until 30 days' notice has been given, or after satisfaction or tender has
been made to the party aggrieved; or, after 9 months, the defendant may
plead the general issue and give the special matter in evidence; and if it
appear to be so done, or that the action has been commenced after the time
limited, or in any other manner than directed, the Jury shall find for the
defendant, and upon a verdict for the defendant, or if the plaintiff is nonsuit
or discontinue, after appearance, or if upon demurrer judgment is given
against the plaintiff, the defendant shall recover his full costs, to be taxed,
and have the like remedy as defendants have in other cases, 40 G. 3,
c. 29, s. 24.

In cases of recovery of any penalty or damages under this Act, the plain-   Costs
tiff shall have judgment for his full costs, to be taxed, 40 G. 3, c. 29, s. 25.

In case of any action of replevin for any distress, the defendant may   Replevin for dis-
plead the general issue, and give the special matter in evidence, and that   tresses
the distress was taken in pursuance and by the authority of this Act. Similar provision for costs, in case the Jury find for the defendant, &c., as in
preceding clause, 40 G. 3, c. 29, s. 26.

If any Provost-Marshal or Deputy, Justice or Vestryman, make default   Penalties for neg-
in any matter required to be done, he shall forfeit £50 (£30 sterling), to be   lect of duty
recovered by action of debt by the Corporation to its own use, with full
costs, to be taxed. If any constable make default, or neglect his duty, he
shall forfeit £20 (£12 sterling), to be recovered, levied and applied as mentioned in sec. 20, and if any person returned upon any inquest neglect his
duty (without a reasonable cause to be shewn in writing, upon oath, to and
allowed by some Justice in writing under his hand), he shall forfeit £10
(£6 sterling,) to be recovered, &c., as last mentioned, 40 G. 3,
c. 29, s. 27.

The Directors of the Company may, under the seal of the Corporation,   Appointment of
at any meeting of the Board, appoint a bailiff or bailiffs for the collection of   water bailiffs
the water dues, and, at discretion, dismiss them and appoint others, 26 V.
S. 2, c. 17, s. 1.

Water rates shall be collected and received by the bailiffs so appointed,   To collect rates
26 V. S. 2, c. 17, s. 2.

Proceedings for rates

On the refusal of any person to pay water-rates, the Directors may sue for and recover the amount due, either in the Petty Debt Court, or by action in the Supreme Court, according to the amount of the rates, 26 V. S. 2, c. 17, s. 3.

Defence that supply of water was not duly made

On the hearing of any Summons or at the trial of any action, the defendant may set up a defence, that the supply of water had not been duly made, and unless it be shewn to the satisfaction of the Justices or of the Jury, that such non-supply or insufficient supply occurred from causes over which the Corporation had no control, they may reduce or negative the claim, 26 V., S. 2, c. 17, s. 4.

Justices members of the corporation not to sit

No Justice, being a shareholder, shall sit and adjudicate in any case brought by the Corporation for rates, 26 V., S. 2, c. 17, s. 5.

Fasts.

7th June, earthquake

Every 7th June (the Anniversary of the Great Earthquake, 1692), unless it falls on the Lord's day, and then the day following shall be set apart and observed as an anniversary day of fasting and humiliation, and the inhabitants shall upon that day annually resort to some usual place where prayers and preaching are used to be ministered, and there orderly and devoutly abide during the celebration of Divine Service, by prayers, preaching, singing of Psalms, &c., 5 W. and M., c. 1, s. 1.

Ministers to give notice the preceding Sunday, and provide a suitable sermon

Every Minister shall give notice to his parishioners in the Church, or other place of Divine Worship, at morning prayer, the Sunday next before the 7th June, for the observation of that day, and provide a Sermon suitable to every occasion, 5 W. and M. c. 1, s. 2.

Exercising trade &c. on that day

No person by themselves or servants, shall do, or cause, &c., any manner of work in their trade, calling or plantation, and no shop, tavern, coffee or punch-house, shall be kept open on that day, on penalty of 40s (24s sterling) for every person by himself or servant so offending, to be recovered before a Justice, one half to the Churchwardens for the use of the parish, and the other half to the informer, 5 W. and M., c. 1, s. 3.

28 August, 2 storms

Precisely similar enactments for the observance of an Anniversary Fast on 28th August, in commemoration of two most dreadful and amazing storms, 1712 and 1722, 9 G. 1, c. 1.

Fines, Forfeitures, Recognizances, Debts to the Crown.

Estreats in the Supreme Court

All fines, amerciaments, sums of money paid on account or in satisfaction of the same, wherein H. M. or the Royal Revenue is interested, imposed or forfeited in the Supreme Court and not taken off or remitted during the sitting, and not before estreated, shall be estreated and certified by the Clerk of the Crown to the Attorney-General, that process may issue for levying the same, and to the Receiver-General within twenty days after every Supreme Court, by delivering to them respectively schedules or estreats, upon

Upon Oath

oath as after directed, of all such fines, &c., with the names and additions of all persons charged with and liable to the same: penalty £100 (£60 stg.), 1 G. 3, c. 13, s. 1.

Form

And before delivery the Clerk of the Crown shall take the following oath :—

> You shall swear that these estreats now by you produced, are truly and carefully made up and examined, and that all fines, amerciaments, recognizances and forfeitures, and all sum and sums of money paid on account or in lieu and satisfaction thereof, which were set, imposed or forfeited, and in right and due course of law ought to be escheated, are to the best of your knowledge, understanding and belief therein contained, and that in the same estreats are expressed and set forth all such fines, amerciaments and forfeitures as have been paid into Court, and the name and names of such person or persons to whom the same were paid, without any wilful or fraudulent discharge, omission, misnomer or other defect whatever.—So help you God.

Which oath the Judges, or one of them, shall administer, and certify on every estreat that it was duly administered according to the form—1 G. 3, c. 13, s. 3.

In case no fine, &c., be set, &c., or they are all remitted and taken off, during the sitting, the Clerk of the Crown shall certify the same upon oath to the Attorney-General and Receiver-General within the time before limited, under like penalty of £50 (£30 stg.), 1 G. 3, c. 13, s. 4. *Where no fine &c. set or all remitted*

No Clerk of the Crown shall spare, take off, discharge, respite, or wittingly or willingly conceal any indictment, fine, issue, amerciament, forfeited recognizance, or other forfeiture, or any sum paid on account thereof, unless by order of the Court, under penalty of £50 (£30 stg.), and loss of office, and to be for ever incapable of exercising the same, 1 G. 3, c. 13, s. 5. *Concealing &c. fines &c.*

The Clerk of the Supreme Court and Crown shall, within twenty days before every Supreme Court, certify and deliver to the Attorney-General and Receiver-General a schedule, containing true dockets of all judgments obtained as of the preceding Court on informations or actions, wherein the whole or any part of the moneys belongs to H. M., or is applicable to the revenue, distinguishing what part belongs to H. M.: penalty £60, 20 V. c. 22, s. 30. *Dockets of judgments in which the crown is interested*

Recoverable by attachment, on application of the Attorney-General, for the use of the public, 20 V. c. 22, s. 39.

The Provost-Marshal shall, on or before the first Monday in every Supreme Court, deliver to the Attorney-General and Receiver-General a list of all actions, writs and processes, mesne or judicial, lodged in his office, wherein H. M. or the revenue are in any way interested, with a true copy of the returns thereto, and of all moneys and effects thereupon levied by him, or levied on other writs, and applicable to the discharge of the debts due to H. M., or otherwise received by him on account of any fines, forfeitures, debts or dues to H. M., and within three days after the delivery of such lists, pay, or cause, &c., to the Receiver-General, all sums so levied and received, under penalty of £200 (£120 stg.), 1 G. 3, c.13, s. 7. *Provost Marshal to deliver lists of process wherein the Revenue is interested, and pay over monies*

He shall deliver to the Attorney-General and Receiver-General, on the first Thursday of every Supreme Court, a true list of all fines and monies received by him in which H. M. and the revenue are in anywise, interested, 19 V., c. 31, s. 14.

In case any fine, &c., or any sum on account, or in lieu of the same, is levied or received by the Provost-Marshal or any Deputy, or Clerk of the Crown, or by any person by their appointment, or consent, and certified and estreated as paid, or returned "levied," and not paid by the Provost-Marshal or Clerk of the Crown to the Receiver-General, according to the directions before given, the Provost-Marshal or Clerk of the Crown neglecting or delaying to pay shall be liable to all writs or processes for the immediate levying and recovering the same, as any other debtors to H. M., which the Attorney-General shall cause to be issued, on a certificate to him by the Receiver-General of every default, 1 G. 3, c. 13, s. 8. *Liabilities of Provost Marshal and clerk of the crown*

The Receiver-General shall keep distinct books wherein to enter, or cause &c., on the debtor side, true copies of all estreats and dockets of judgment to be delivered to him by the Clerk of the Crown, Clerk of the Supreme Court and Clerks of the Peace, and on the opposite or creditor side, from time to time, all sums received on account, and all other discharges, whether by virtue of the Royal Prerogative, or otherwise: penalty £100 (£60 stg.), and which shall be deemed public books belonging to the Office, 1 G. 3, c. 13, s. 9. *Receiver-General to keep accounts of estreats and dockets of judgement, see 21 V., c. 23*

Penalty upon the Attorney-General refusing or neglecting to do his duty, £100 (£60 stg.), 1 G. 3, c. 13, s. 10. *Attorney General's neglect of duty*

All penalties shall be recovered by action of debt, &c., one moiety to him who shall sue, 1 G. 3, c. 13, s. 11. *Recovery &c. of penalties*

All recognizances, or sums to be paid in lieu or satisfaction of them, taken or imposed by any Justice, shall be certified by such or any other Justice, in writing, to the Clerk of the Peace, who shall prepare a list containing the names, residences, trades, professions or callings of the parties, and the sum forfeited by each, which he shall present to the Judge on the first day of each ensuing Circuit Court, and the Judge shall enquire into such recognizances, and direct the Clerk of the Peace to prepare a roll of such (or of the sums payable in satisfaction of each) as have been forfeited, shewing the cause of forfeiture; and the Clerk of the Peace shall also insert all fines and recognizances, set and imposed, and taken by the Judge at such Court, which have been forfeited or not remitted, and all other fines and recognizances forfeited, or imposed by or for the non-appearance at, or absence or departure from such Court without leave by any person bound to attend as juror, pro. *Recognizances &c. certified by justices, list laid before Circuit Judge / Rolls to be prepared by the Clerk of the Peace*

Z

And copy for warded with writs of discharge to the Provost Marshal
secutor, defendant or witness, and within twenty-one days after adjournment, forward to the Provost-Marshal a copy of such roll, with writs of distingas and capias, form Schedule A (varying the writ according to the circumstances of each case), signed by the Judge, which writs shall be his authority, or that of his Deputy, for distraining without delay on the goods of the persons mentioned therein, for the sums set forth as payable by them, and for taking into custody their bodies in case they are not paid, or sufficient goods cannot be found to satisfy them. Every person so taken into custody shall be lodged in the Gaol or nearest prison until the next Circuit Court, to abide the judgment of the Court, unless he sooner pay. Every writ shall run, and may be executed in any part of this island in which the party may be found; but if he has removed or fled into any other parish, the writ shall be endorsed by a Justice of the parish in which the party is found, on the application of the Provost-Marshal or his Deputy, prior to execution— 21 V., c. 23, s. 1.

Execution see s. 6

Duplicates to be forwarded to the Receiver-General
Every Clerk of the Peace shall, within 30 days after each Circuit Court, forward to the Receiver-General a duplicate copy of every roll delivered to the Provost-Marshal, and of every return made by him or his Deputy on the first day of such Court, setting forth therein the cause of discharge in every case in which any person has been discharged by the Court from payment of any recognizance, &c., and the answer of every Deputy-Marshal why any recognizance, &c. had not been paid or recovered, 21 V., c. 23, s. 2.

On oath
The Clerks of the Peace shall, previous to the delivery of any roll to the Provost-Marshal or Receiver-General, make oath before a Justice, to be endorsed on the back of the roll, as follows :—

I, A. B., do swear that this roll has been carefully made up and examined, and that all recognizances taken and recognized at the parish (or precinct) of   which have become forfeited and ought to be paid, and all fines and recognizances imposed and taken by the Judge in the Circuit Court, held in the parish (or precinct) of   on the   day of   , have been inserted in the same, and that it also contains all such sums of money as have been received by me, either in Court or otherwise, on such fines and on forfeited recognizances, without any fraudulent discharge or omission whatsoever.   A. B.

Sworn before me at   the   day of   18

C. D., Justice of the Peace, 21 V., c. 23, s. 3.

Clerk of the Peace to pay receipts to the Receiver-General
Every Clerk of the Peace shall, within 20 days after each Circuit Court, pay over to the Receiver-General all sums received by him on account of the aforesaid fines and recognizances, 21 V., c. 23, s. 4.

Notices of recognizance to be given to persons & sureties
Every Justice, before whom any recognizance is entered into, shall give, or cause, &c., to each of the persons or sureties entering into recognizance at the time of doing so, a written or printed paper of notice, in the form or to the effect mentioned in Schedule B, adapting the same to the particular circumstances of each case, mentioning the names in full, the profession, trade or occupation of every person entering into recognizance, and the parish or place of his residence, 21 V., c. 23, s. 5.

Discharge from custody of persons giving security to appear next Circuit Court
If any person on whose goods the Provost-Marshal or his Deputy is authorized to levy any forfeited recognizance, &c., tender security to him for his appearance at the next Circuit Court to abide its decision, and to pay the same, with such expenses as the Court shall order, the Provost-Marshal or his Deputy may discharge from his custody the person giving such security, 21 V., c. 23, s. 6.

Non appearance

Forfeited
In case any such person shall not appear, the Judge may forthwith issue a bench warrant to bring the person before him, and deal with the recognizance of the sureties as in cases of other forfeited recognizances; and the person making default shall, when taken under the bench warrant, be dealt with as if he had been brought up under a writ of distringas and capias, 21 V., c. 23, s. 7.

New rolls &c. from court to court
The Judge shall, at the opening of each Court, cause to be inserted in a new roll, all forfeited recognizances, &c., included in any previous roll, and not levied or accounted for by the Provost-Marshal or his Deputy, or from the payment of which the parties have not been discharged by the Court or otherwise according to law, and cause a copy of such new roll to be

issued to the Provost-Marshal, with writs for execution, and a duplicate to be forwarded to the Receiver-General, made up, signed and sworn to, in all respects in like manner and within the like time, and with the like liability on the Clerk of the Peace to pay over all sums received by him on account of any forfeitures in any such roll, as is directed in respect to any other roll of forfeited fines and recognizances, and the Judge shall continue so to act from Court to Court, until it is ascertained to the satisfaction of the Court, that every person in default has not any goods whereon to levy, or cannot be found, 21 V., c. 23, s. 8.

The Provost-Marshal shall return every writ of distringas and capias directed to him, and the roll attached thereto, to the Circuit Court on the first day of its sitting, and shew which of the writs have been executed, and the manner, and within 10 days after the rising of such Court, pay over to the Receiver-General every sum of money received by him on account of such writs, under penalty of £100, to be recovered in a summary manner by application to the Supreme Court; and the Provost-Marshal, or his Deputy, shall be examined on oath by the Judge, on the first day of the sitting, or any subsequent day, touching the execution of all such writs forwarded to him previous to its meeting, 21 V., c. 23, s. 9.

Returns and payments to the Receiver General

Examination of Provost Marshal or Deputy

The Judge of the Circuit Court, before whom any person so committed to prison or bound to appear is brought, shall enquire into the circumstances of the case, and, at his discretion, order the discharge of the whole or any part of the forfeited recognizance, &c., such order to be in form (Schedule C.,)and signed by the Clerk of the Peace, and be a discharge of such person from such recognizance, &c.; and where the party has been imprisoned, the Judge may remand him to the same custody, for such period as he shall direct, or order him to be discharged from custody, and may award costs to be paid by the party discharged as to him seems just. Whenever any recognizance has been entered into before a Justice to keep the Peace, or for good behaviour, or to appear, or as bail for the appearance of any person before a Justice, or for the performance of other act before or within the cognizance or jurisdiction of any justice, and is broken by non-appearance or non-performance, or not doing of any act, or it is made to appear from a conviction, on the information of any credible person, that any recognizance for good behaviour, or to keep the peace, has been broken, any Justice may sign and issue a writ of distringas and capias (Form A)., varying the writ according to the circumstances of each case, and which writ shall be executed by the Provost-Marshal or his Deputy as any other writ may be, and the Clerk of the Magistrates shall send to the Receiver-General a docket of every such writ within 5 days after the issuing, and shall be entitled to the like fees thereon as are reserved to the Clerk of the Peace on any other writ under this Act, and the Provost-Marshal shall make return to the next Circuit Court of every writ so issued, and the manner of its execution, at the like time, and shall pay over to the Receiver-General every sum of money received by him or his Deputy on any such writ, within the like period, and under the like penalty and be subject to the like examination as provided in respect to other writs; and any writ not executed shall be included in any new roll to be issued by the Judge of the Circuit Court, and the duplicate, in all respects, in like manner, within the like time, and with the like liability to pay over all money received on account of such writs, as provided in respect to other non-executed writs; and every writ issued by any Justice shall be in all respects subject to the provisions of this Act so far as applicable, 21 V., c. 23, s. 10.

Discharge from fines &c.

Remand or discharge from custody
Costs

Distringas &c. by justices

Docket thereof to the Receiver-General

Provost Marshal's returns to Circuit Court

The Clerk of the Peace shall be entitled to a fee of 2s. 6d. for each writ so issued, and 2s. 6d. for each legal sheet of 160 words which such rolls shall contain, including the returns thereto, and 2s. 6d. for every discharge of any forfeited recognizance or fine, which he shall retain out of any monies received by him; and the Provost-Marshal or his Deputy shall be entitled to the usual fees and commissions on all writs issued under this act. If the Provost-Marshal or his Deputy, or the Clerk of the Peace refuses or neglects to perform any duty, act or thing imposed on or required from them by this Act, they shall forfeit £60, to be recovered in a summary manner, by application to the Supreme Court, with the costs of the application 21 V., c. 23, s. 11.

Fees, Penalties— Clerk of the Peace, Provost Marshal

Every penalty shall, when recovered, be paid over to the Receiver General to the use of the public, 21 V., c. 23, s. 12.

Application of penalties

The Fines and Recognizances Recovery Act, 1857, 21 V., c. 23, s. 14.

Short Title

Stamp duties &c. As to the duties of the officers of Circuit Courts and Magistrates with reference to the duties and penalties in respect of unstamped or insufficiently stamped instruments, and their returns along with those of fines, see Stamps, 28 V., c. 9, s. 45-48.

SCHEDULE TO 21 V., c. 23.

Distringas and Capias, A., s. 1, 10

Victoria, by the grace of God, of the United Kingdom of Great Britain and Ireland, Queen, and of Jamaica, lady defender of the faith, &c.

To the Provost-Marshal-General, greeting :

You are hereby required and commanded to levy the sum of pounds, upon the goods and chattels of , of the parish of , &c., and have the money ready for payment at the next Circuit Court, to be paid over in the manner directed by an Act, made and passed in the 21st year of our reign, entitled "An Act to facilitate the recovery of forfeited recognizances and pecuniary fines;" and if you cannot levy the said sum of pounds, by reason of there being no goods or chattels to be found belonging to the said , then that you take the body of the said , and lodge him in the gaol or prison of the said parish of , or the gaol and prison nearest thereto, there to await the decision of the Judge, at the Circuit Court for the parish, (or precinct) of , unless the said shall give sufficient security for his appearance at such Court, and have you then and there this writ.

Witness , Esquire, Judge of the Circuit Court for the parish (precinct) of at the day of in the year of our reign.

[Seal.]

WHERE THE WRIT IS ISSUED BY ANY JUSTICE OF THE PEACE.

Witness , Esquire, Justice of the Peace in and for the parish (or precinct) of , at in the said parish (or precinct) this day of , in the year of our Lord, 185

[Seal.]

Notice of recognizance, B, s. 5

Parish to wit.

Take notice that you of are bound in the sum of pounds, and your sureties of, &c., in the sum of pounds each, to appear at the Circuit Court for the parish (or precinct) of to be holden at on the day of next, (or as the case may be in matters of summary jurisdiction) and unless you personally make your appearance accordingly, the recognizance entered into by yourself and sureties will be forthwith evied on you and them.

Dated the day of 18

Signed by the Justice of the Peace.

Mitigation or discharge from fine, C. s 10

To the Provost-Marshal General, and all whom it may concern :—

Whereas hath appeared before the Judge of the Circuit Court for the parish (or precinct) of (as the case may be) held at on the day of , and hath made it appear to the satisfaction of the said Judge that he should be relieved from the payment of the sum of pounds (or if the penalty is mitigated, state from what part thereof) : (here state the nature of the fine or forfeiture). Be it therefore remembered that the said is by the said Court discharged from the said fine (or recognizance as the case may be ; or if mitigated, state from what part), and from the writ issued thereon against him.

Dated the day of

By order of the Court,

Signed by the Clerk of the Peace.

Fire.

When a fire breaks out at Port Royal or any other town, two or three of the chief military or civil officers of the town or parish may give directions for the pulling down or blowing up any houses by them adjudged meet to be pulled down, &c., for preventing the further spreading of the same, and if the pulling down, &c., any such house by any such direction shall be the occasion of stopping the fire, or it stops before it comes to the same, the owners shall receive satisfaction, and be paid by the rest of the inhabitants whose houses are not burnt, who are empowered to make rates for the raising and levying such sums as shall be thought convenient by the Justices and Vestrymen. If the house where the fire first begins and breaks out is adjudged fit to be pulled down, the owner shall receive no satisfaction, 33 C. 2, c. 17, s. 2. *Pulling down &c., houses, to stop fire, compensation*

See 21 V., c. 44, s. 15, Title Parishes

Where parishes are provided with proper fire engines and the necessary implements, hose and sockets, the Justices in session shall meet yearly to elect 7 inhabitants of the principal town as Firewardens, two at least to be Justices residing in the town, or within half a mile, and the other 5 to be householders residing in the town, who shall be denominated "The Firewardens for the current year," and shall take and subscribe the following oath, to be administered by a Justice. Where two Justices do not reside in or within half a mile of the town, the Justices may elect one Justice so situated, and in failure of one, then 7 householders, resident within the town. *Annual appointment of firewardens in parishes provided with engines &c*

I, A, B., do swear that I will well, faithfully and impartially, and to the best and utmost of my power and ability, execute and discharge the office of Firewarden for the town of   , in the parish of   for the current year, as directed by an act of the Governor, Council and Assembly of Jamaica, entitled "An act for the better protection of public property and of the property of the inhabitants of the towns in the several parishes of this island from accidents and dangers by fire."—So help me God., 24 V., c. 2, s. 1. *Their oath*

In case any person refuses to take upon him the office, and shall not, within ten days after notice in writing of his election given by the Clerk of the Magistrates take and subscribe the oath, he shall forfeit not exceeding £5, nor less than £1, for the use of the poor, to be recovered before 2 Justices, and in default of payment such fine shall be enforced by levy on his goods. Any reasonable excuse, on oath, shall be taken and accepted by the Justice issuing the warrant, 24 V., c. 2, s. 2. *Penalty for refusing to take oath* / *Without excuse*

The Justices in Special Session shall immediately after the election of Firewardens, proceed to the election of officers from such elected Firewardens, and prepare rules and regulations for the guidance of the Fire Company, 24 V., c. 2,, s. 3. *Election of officers, rules*

And in case of the death or removal of any Firewardens, shall elect others in their place, 24 V., c. 2, s. 4. *Vacancies*

Parishes for which there are special enactments relating to the protection of property against fire; and the establishment of Firewardens, shall be exempt from the provisions of this act, 24 V., c. 2, s. 5. *Parishes having special enactments*

Principal town shall mean towns and villages in which there shall be the Court-House or other building, the property of the public, 24 V., c. 2, s. 6. *Principal town*

Any person who, by the negligent use or management of fire in any place, endangers any buildings, lands, cultivated plants, fences or other property, or who uses or carries any lighted pipe, segar, firestick, torch or flambeau, whereby injury may of shall result to any buildings, &c., shall, on conviction before 2 Justices, forfeit and pay a fine not exceeding £10 and costs, or be committed to be imprisoned only, or imprisoned and kept to hard labor for not exceeding 90 days, 25 V., c. 30. *Negligent use or management of fire*

Fishing and Fowling.

Any inhabitant of the City and Parish of Kingston or its vicinity, may make use of nets or seines for catching fish in the harbour and its vicinity, and the coasts adjacent, or in any of the rivers or streams of running water emptying themselves into the harbour of Kingston, or in any lagoons, or still waters that have communication therewith, having or containing meshes in the bunt or centre of the dimentions of 3 quarters of an inch from knot *Fishing in Kingston Harbour—Nets* to knot, provided the bunt or centre does not exceed the length of 16 fathoms, 44 G. 3, c. 19, s. 1.

No person shall make use of any false bottom cod or pouch, or put any seine or net (though of legal size), or mesh upon or behind the others, in order to catch the small fry or breed of fish, which would have passed through any single net of the meshes before described, or use any other illegal or unwarrantable practice to injure or destroy the small fry or breed of fish, 44 G. 3, c. 19, s. 2.

Penalties

Penalty, (besides forfeiting the net or seine, and which shall be destroyed by order of any convicting Magistrate.) not less than £5 (£3 sterling), and not exceeding £20 (£12 sterling), to be recovered before three Magistrates, and enforced by warrant, to the use of the informer, 44 G. 3, c. 19, s. 3.

Destruction by poison or intoxication
Nets
To same effect, 23 V., c. 5, s. 8
Harbours

No person shall, by himself or servant, destroy any fish in any harbour, bay, creek or river, by any method of poisoning or intoxication, or make use of any seine, net or engine for catching fish in any harbour, bay, river, creek or pond, with less meshes than one and a quarter inches between knot and knot* except cast-nets and shrimp-nets, which shrimp-nets shall not be above two and a half fathoms long, and no person shall join 2 or more shrimp-nets together for the purpose of fishing, or for catching fish or otherwise, 8 G. 4, c. 14, s. 1.

Nor Turtle Eggs

No person, by himself or servant, shall destroy any turtle eggs in any part of this island, or any island or key belonging to the same, 8 G. 4, c. 14, s. 2.

Quails, Ringtails or Baldpates

Or kill any quails, ringtails or baldpate pigeons in the months of March, April, May, June, July or August, 8 G. 4, c. 14, s. 3.

Offenders shall, on conviction before any Magistrate, forfeit not exceeding £20 (£12 sterling), to be recovered by warrant, one half to the poor of the parish, and the other half to the informer, and in default of payment, the offender shall be imprisoned for not exceeding 20 days, by warrant, 1 G. 4, c. 15, s. 4.

Wears or stops

No person, by himself or agent, shall make any wears or stops over any river or pond, unless the land on both sides belong to him, or if he is owner of one side only, with the consent or agreement of the owner of the land on the other side. No person shall make any wear or stop within 100 yards on

Near fordings
any public fording, 6 V.. c. 39, s. 1.

Penalties

Any person making stops and wears in rivers wherein they have no right of property, shall, on summary conviction, upon the complaint of the owner, or his agent or attorney, before 2 Justices be liable to costs, and a penalty not exceeding £1, under pain of imprisonment with or without hard labour for not exceeding 10 days, unless sooner paid, 6 V., c. 39, s. 2.

Using seines &c. upon the ground or sea beach of persons having a right of property ; see Patents, 35 C. 2, c. 12, s. 1

If any person unlawfully and wilfully use any dredge, seine, net or other engine, or drag the same on the ground or sea-beach of any person having a right of property therein, without the consent of the owner, the offender, being convicted before 2 Justices, shall be deemed an offender against the provisions of this act, and subject to a fine, not exceeding £1, 6 V., c, 39, s. 4.

Penalties

All penalties shall be recovered before 2 Justices and enforced in default of payment, by imprisonment, with or without hard labor, for not exceeding 10 days, unless the penalties be sooner paid; and shall be awarded one half to the informer, and one half to the Churchwardens for the use of the poor, 6 V., c. 39, s. 5.

---

* This clause does not appear to affect 34 G. 3, c. 19.

The 8 G. 4, c. 14 repeals 10 Ann, c. 16, and re-enacts (as does also 25 V., c. 5, s. 8) its provisions respecting the size of the meshes, but the 44 G. 3, c. 19 recites that it had been found from experience that nets for the taking of fish, wholly made with meshes of the dimensions directed by 10 Ann 16, are inadequate to the taking of divers kind of small but full grown fish, with which the harbour of Kingston and its vicinity, and the coasts adjacent abound, and whereby the poorer classes of the inhabitants of Kingston and its vicinity are deprived of a cheap and wholesome article of sustenance, and then proceeds to enact ut supra.

Parties feeling aggrieved by any conviction may appeal, 6 V., c. 39, s. 6. *Appeal*

Any inhabitant of the parish may be a witness under 6 V., c. 39, 7 V., c. 23, s. 1. *Inhabitants may be witnesses*

As also any informer ; but if be give testimony, he shall not be entitled to any portion of the penalty, but the whole shall go to the treasurer for the use of the poor, 7 V., c. 23, s. 2. *Also [i]nformers, but not entitled to any part of the penalty if examined*

No proceeding under 6 V., c. 39, shall be quashed for want of form, 7 V., c. 23, s. 3. *Want of form*

Forcible Entry and Detainer.

If a writ of certiorari is granted (except during the sitting of the Supreme Court, and returnable forthwith), before the Justice has completed all proceedings before him upon any complaint of forcible entry and detainer, or forcible detainer, he shall complete all the proceedings, and restore the party ousted to his possession, where entitled, and then return all proceedings, 14 G. 3, c. 17, s. 1. *Justices to complete proceedings before making return to certiorari*

No proceedings shall be set aside for want of form, if the facts are proved to the satisfaction of the Court, 14 G. 3, c. 17, s. 2. *Want of form*

In case the person aggrieved, after restitution, bring any action for damages, as well in respect to his lands as to the produce, stock, household, goods, furniture and plantation utensils, upon or belonging to the premises, and recover damages, the Court shall give judgment for double the damages, besides costs, 14 G. 3, c. 17, s. 3. *Double damages, costs*

Foreign Attachment.

Upon any declaration disclosing the special matter to the Chief Judge of the Supreme Court (or an Assistant Judge, 9 G, 4. c. 24, s. 4.) that the debtor is either gone off this island, or that upon process already taken out against him a non est inventus has been returned, an attachment shall issue, commanding the Provost-Marshal or his Deputy to attach such moneys, goods, chattels or debts in the hands of the possessors of the same, be they attorney, wife, servant or any other person, and also to require them to appear at the next Court to shew cause why the money, &c., or so much as will satisfy the debts demanded should not be delivered to the plaintiff, at which day, if the possessor or debtor, be they attorney, &c., be convicted by confession, verdict or otherwise, that the monies, &c., do properly belong to the person gone off the island or otherwise absent, and if the plaintiff, before or after proof made, swear in open Court that his debt is true, and that directly or indirectly no part of what he demanded is satisfied, and give security in double the sum to restore the same with treble damages, or so much as shall at any time afterwards be disproved, the plaintiff shall have judgment to recover the debt out of the money, &c., attached ; but if any appear as attorney to the debtor, and put in bail to answer the action, and pay the condemnation, the attachment, &c. shall be dissolved, and proceedings had according to the common law ; but, if the possessor or owner, be they attorney, &c., after attachment laid on them in the respective hands, dispose thereof towards payment of any other debts, before that for which such attachment was laid is satisfied, or the attachment dissolved, he shall make satisfaction to the plaintiff out of his own estate, 33 C. 2, c. 23, s. 8. *In what cases they may issue* *Proceedings thereon* *Dissolving the attachment* *Paying away monies &c. after attachment*

In debts not exceeding 40s. (24s. stg.), upon complaint to any Justice that the debtor is gone off this island, or otherwise absent, he may issue a warrant of attachment, to be levied by the Constable in the manner before prescribed, and to be immediately determined by the Justice, 33 C. 2, c. 23, s. 9. *Debts not exceeding 24s*

Foreign attachments may be served at any time before the Court, 33 C. 2, c. 23, s. 10. *Time of service*

Any Assistant Judge may grant fiats for issuing writs of attachment, and in all things act as the Chief-Justice, 9 G. 4, c. 24, s. 4. *Assistant Judges may grant fiats, &c.*

Forgery.

Falsely making, forging or counterfeiting, or causing or procuring, &c., or willingly acting or assisting in the false making, forging or counterfeiting any deed, will, testament, codicil or testamentary writing, bond writing obligatory, bill of exchange, island certificate, receiver-general's check, promissory note for the payment of money, endorsement, assignment or acceptance of any bill of exchange or promissory note for the payment of *Deed, wills, bonds, bills, notes, &c., undertakings, warrants or orders, acquittances, receipts, accountable receipts, &c.*

money, or any undertaking, warrant or order for the payment of money, or any acquittance or receipt either for money or goods, or any accountable receipt either for money or goods, or for any note, bill or other security for the payment of money, or any warrant, order or request for the delivery or transfer of goods, or for the delivery of any note, bill or other security for the payment of money, with intention to defraud any person whatever, or uttering or publishing as true any false, forged or counterfeited deed, will, &c., knowing the same to be false, forged or counterfeited, felony; imprisonment not exceeding 3 years, 4 V., c. 46, s. 2, with or without hard laber, or with or without solitary confinement, s. 12, or penal servitude not less than 4 and not exceeding 8 years, 21 V., c. 14, s. 3.

Transfers of shares, powers of attorney, personating owners, dividends

Forging or altering, or uttering, knowing the same to be forged or altered, any transfer of any share or interest, of or in any stock or annuity or other public fund now or hereafter transferable at the Bank of England, or at either of the Banks of Jamaica, or of or in the capital stock of any body Corporate, Company or Society, whether established by prescription, charter or legislative enactment, or any private company or society whatever, or forging, altering or uttering, knowing the same to be forged or altered, any power of attorney or other authority to transfer any share or interest of or in any such stock, annuity, public fund or capital stock, or to receive any dividend payable in respect of any such share or interest, or demanding, or endeavouring to have any such share or interest transferred, or to receive any dividend payable in respect thereof by virtue of any such forged or altered power of attorney or other authority, knowing the same to be forged or altered with intent in any of such cases to defraud any person whatever, or falsely and deceitfully personating any owner of any such share, interest or dividend, and thereby transfering any share or interest belonging to such owner, or thereby receiving any money due to such owner as if such person were the true and lawful owner, felony: imprisonment not exceeding 2 years, 4 V., c. 46, s. 3, with or without hard labour or solitary confinement, s. 12, or penal servitude from 4 to 6 years, 21 V. c. 14, s. 3.

Name of attesting witness

Forging the name or handwriting of any person as or purporting to be a witness attesting the execution of any power of attorney or other authority to transfer any share or interest of or in any such stock, annuity, public fund or capital stock, or receive any dividend payable in respect of any such share or interest, or uttering or using any such power of attorney or other authority with the name or handwriting of any person forged thereon as an attesting witness, knowing the same to be forged, felony: imprisonment not exceeding 2 years, 4 V., c. 42, s. 4, with or without hard labour and solitary confinement, s. 12, or penal servitude 4 years, 21 V., c. 14, s. 3.

False dividend warrants

If any clerk, officer or servant of, or other person employed or entrusted by any body corporate, company or society, whether established by prescription, charter or legislative enactment, or any private company or society whatever, knowingly makes out or delivers any dividend warrant for a greater or less amount than the person on whose behalf it is made out is entitled to, with intent to defraud any person whatever: felony. Punishment as last above, 4 V., c. 46, s. 5, 12; 21 V., c. 14, s. 3.

Personating bail

Acknowledging before any Court, Judge or other person lawfully authorized, any recognizance or bail in the name of any other person not privy or consenting to the same, whether such recognizance or bail in either case be or be not filed: felony, imprisonment not exceeding 2 years, 4 V., c. 46, s. 6, with or without hard labor and solitary confinement, s. 12, or penal servitude, 4 to 6 years, 21 V., c. 14, s. 3.

Having forged bank notes, bills, or bank post bills &c. in possession

Without lawful excuse, the proof whereof shall lie upon the party accused, purchasing or receiving from any other person, or having in one's custody or possession any forged bank note, bank bill of exchange, or bank post bill, or blank bank note, blank bank bill of exchange, or blank bank post bill, knowing the same to be forged: felony. Punishment as last above, 4 V., c. 46, s. 7, 12; 21 V., c. 14, s. 3.

Registers of baptisms, marriages or burials, &c.

Knowingly and wilfully inserting, or causing or permitting to be inserted in any register of baptisms, marriages or burials, made or kept by the rector, curate, or officiating minister of any parish or district, or by the registrar, any false entry of any matter relating to any baptism, marrage or burial, or forging or altering in any such register any entry of any matter relating to any baptism, marriage or burial, or uttering any writing as and for a copy of an entry in any such register of any matter relating to any baptism, marriage or burial, knowing such writing to be false, forged or altered, or uttering any entry in any such register of any matter relating to any baptism, marriage or burial, knowing such entry to be false, forged or altered, or uttering any copy of such entry knowing such entry to be false, forged or altered, or wilfully destroying, defacing, or injuring, or causing or permitting, &c., any such register, or any part thereof, or forging or altering, or uttering, knowing the same to be forged or altered, any license of marriage: felony. Punishment as last above, 4 V., c. 46, s. 8-12; 21 V., c. 14, s. 3.

No Rector, Curate, Officiating Minister of any parish or district, or the Registrar who discovers any error in the form or substance of the entry in the register of any baptism, marriage, or burial respectively by him solemnized, shall be liable to any penalty, if within one calendar month after the discovery, in the presence of the parent or parents of the child baptised, or of the parties married, or in the presence of two persons who attended at any burial, or in the case of the death or absence of such respective parties, then in the presence of the Churchwardens, he correct the entry according to the truth, by an entry in the margin of the Register, without any alteration or obliteration of the original entry, and sign the entry in the margin, with the day of the month and year when the correction is made ; such correction and signature to be attested by the parties in whose presence they are made. In the copy of the Register to be transmitted to the Registrar of the Diocese, the Rector, Curate or Officiating Minister shall certify the corrections so made by him, 4 V., c. 46, s. 9. *Correction of Register*

Knowingly and wilfully inserting, or causing or permitting to be inserted in any copy of any Register directed or hereafter to be directed to be transmitted to the Registrar of the Diocese, any false entry of any matter relating to any baptism, marriage or burial, or forging or altering, or uttering, knowing the same to be forged or altered, any copy of any Register to be transmitted, or knowingly and wilfully signing or verifying any copy of any such Register, which is false in any part, knowing it to be false : felony. Imprisonment as above, 4 V., c. 46, s, 10-12, or 4 years' penal servitude, 21 V., c. 14, s. 3. *False entries in copies of register to be transmitted to the registrar*

Every principal in the second degree, and every accessory before the fact to any felony, shall be punishable as the principal in the first degree. Every accessory after the fact, with imprisonment, not exceeding 2 years, 4 V., c. 46, s. 11, with or without imprisonment and solitary confinement, s. 12. *Accessories*

After conviction for any offence for which imprisonment may be awarded, the offender may be sentenced to be imprisoned with or without hard labour, and also directed to be kept in solitary confinement, not exceeding one month at any one time, nor 3 months in any one year, 4 V., c. 46, s. 12. *Hard labor, solitary confinement*

In indictments for forging or uttering any instrument, it shall be sufficient to describe it by any name or designation by which it is usually known, or by the purport, without setting out any copy or fac simile, or otherwise describing it, or the value, 16 V., c. 15, s. 5. *Description of instrument in indictment Superseding, 4 V., c 46, s. 13*

It shall be sufficient in any indictment for forging, uttering, offering, disposing of, or putting off any instrument whatsoever, to allege that the defendant did the act with intent to defraud, without alleging his intent to be to defraud any particular person, and on the trial it shall not be necessary to prove an intent to defraud any particular person, but shall be sufficient to prove that the defendant did the act charged with an intent to defraud, 16 V., c. 15, s. 8. *Intent to defraud*

In any prosecution by indictment or information. either at common law, or under any Act against any person for forging any deed, writing, instrument or other matter, knowing it to be forged, or of uttering or disposing of any deed, &c., knowing it to be forged, or of being accessory before or after the fact to any such offence, if a felony, or for aiding, abetting or counselling the commission of any such offence, if a misdemeanor, no person shall be deemed an incompetent witness in support of the prosecution, by reason of any interest he has, or is supposed to have in respect thereof, 4 V., c. 46, s. 14. *Interested witness*

A A

Custody, po
session, person

Where the having any matter in the custody or possession of any person is expressed to be an offence, if he have any such matter in his personal custody or possession, or knowingly and wilfully have any such matter in any dwelling house or other building, lodging, apartment, field or other place open or enclosed, whether belonging to or occupied by himself or not, and whether it be had for his own use, or for the use or benefit of another, such person shall be deemed to have such matter in his custody or possession ; and where the committing any offence with intent to defraud any person is made punishable by this Act, "person" shall include Her Majesty or any foreign Prince or State, or any body corporate, or any company or society of persons not incorporated, or any person or number of persons who may be intended to be defrauded, whether residing or carrying on business in this island or elsewhere, in any place or country, whether under the dominion of Her Majesty or not, 4 V., c. 46, s. 15.

The rest of the
section supersed-
ed by 16 v., c, 15,
s. 8, sup.

Admiralty ju-
risdiction

Any offence punishable under this Act, committed within the jurisdiction of the Admiralty, may be dealt with, enquired of, tried and determined in the same manner as any offence committed without their jurisdiction, 4 V., c. 46, s. 16.

Forts and Barracks transferred to Executive Committee.

The Secretary-at-War was authorized to transfer, by way of gift to the Executive Committee for the use of the public of the island, the Forts, Barracks, Messuages, Lands and Hereditaments mentioned in the Schedule, and the Ordnance Guns, Gun-carriages, and materials for military defence belonging thereto, 25 V., c. 4.

SCHEDULE.

NAME.	POST OR WORK.	ACRES.	ROODS.	PERCHES.
Port Antonio	Barracks and Fort George	6	1	14
Port-Maria	Fort Haldane			
Rio Bueno	Fort Dundas			
Falmouth	Barracks and Fort Balcarres	2	1	30
Maroon Town	Barracks	400	0	0
Montego-Bay	Barracks and Fort Montego	4	2	34
Lucea	Barracks and Fort Charlotte	9	1	26

Free Schools.

JAMAICA FREE SCHOOL.

Drax's free
school

The sum of £11,200 currency, with some arrears of interest, accepted in full discharge of the donation and bequest under the will of Charles Drax, for a Free School or Hospital for the support, maintenance and education of 8 poor boys and 4 poor girls, was vested in certain persons, incorporated as the Trustees of Drax's Free School, to be invested in the purchase of land and securities for the establishment and support of a Free School for 8 poor boys and 4 poor girls, belonging to the inhabitants of St Ann's, and if the funds would admit, a larger number in proportion to the revenue, 43 G. 3, c. 32.

Surrendered
and transferred
to

The Trustees of Drax's Free School having purchased Walton Pen in St. Ann's, with a mansion house and buildings, capable, with a small additional expense, of receiving 50 Scholars, and having £6,500 in ready money belonging to the School, and being desirous to surrender the pen and monies to be invested for the use of a general institution as a seminary for the liberal education of youth, the pen and all the real and personal estates, monies and securities in their possession were transferred for the establishment at Walton Pen of a free Grammar School, 48 G. 3, c. 25, s. 1.

The Jamaica
Free School
Trustees

For the maintenance and education of poor Scholars, to be called "The Jamaica Free School," and for the ordering, directing and conducting all matters relating thereto, the Governor, the President and Members of the

Council, the Speaker and Members of the Assembly, the Chief-Justice and Attorney-General, together with 12 persons named [Parochial Trustees, 7 W. 4, c. 30, s. 6.] were appointed Trustees and Governors for the direction and management, and incorporated as "The Trustees and Governors of the Jamaica Free School," 48 G. 3, c. 25, s. 2. *Incorporated*

In case of the death of the [Parochial] Trustees, or their successors, or their absence from the island for 2 years or upwards, or resignation, or in case of the neglect or omission of any Governor and Trustee, not a member of the Council or Assembly, to attend any 4 consecutive quarterly meetings at the School House in the course of the year, unless prevented by sickness or other unavoidable cause, the Governor, President of the Council, Speaker, Chief-Justice, [Bishop, 7 W, 4, c. 30, s. 6-7. or in his absence, Suffragan, 22 V., c. 23, s. 3, and Attorney-General, 7 W. 4, c. 30, s. 6-7,] or any 3 of them, upon notice, in writing, under the hand of 2 Trustees, may appoint persons to fill up vacancies, 48 G. 3, c. 25, s. 3. *Vacancies, how to be filled up*

The Trustees incorporated by the name of "The Trustees and Governors of the Jamaica Free School," are empowered to receive donations, devises and bequests, and to sell and demise lands, sue and be sued, and to have a Common Seal for conveying or demising hereditaments, and doing other matters relating to the Corporation. Any 7 Trustees may change same, 48 G. 3, c. 25, s. 4. *Incorporation Powers of trustees to take, sell and demise lands*

The Trustees, or any 3 of them, may treat with the Trustees of, or other persons having charge over charitable donations for the foundation of Free Schools, for a transfer of unapplied property, which such Trustees or persons, or a quorum, are authorized to make, after 3 years have elapsed from the time limited by the donor for carrying into effect the charitable uses for which such property was devised, given or bequeathed, and after the agreement for transfer has been laid before the Chief-Justice, Attorney-General and Speaker, and a certificate has been signed by them, or two of them, and recorded in the Secretary's Office, that the views and intention of the original donor and founder have been defeated or become ineffectual, and it is fit to transfer the property in question to the Trustees of the Jamaica Free School, which certificate shall also state in whom the patronage or right to appoint Scholars in respect of the transfer ought to vest, in conformity with the will or intention of the original founder, or agreeable to the laws of this island, where such views have become ineffectual, 48 G. 3, c. 25, s. 5. *To treat for transfer of other donations for schools*

If the intentions are not carried out within 3 years after the time limited by the donors or devisors, and no treaty can be made und rendered effectual for the transfer, upon notice, signed by the Speaker, Chief-Justice, and Attorney-General, or any two of them declaring their opinion that the assignment and transfer ought to be made, after 6 months. the donations and property shall be vested in the Trustees for the purposes of this Act, and they may enforce an account, and payment of the balance appearing due from the heirs, executors, &c., of the donors or devisors, or the persons who have intermeddled with, or received any monies on account of any such charities, 48 G. 3, c. 25, s. 6. *When transfer to be compulsory*

All trust-funds of the School shall be invested in the Receiver General's Office, and bear £8 per cent per annum interest, (48 G. 3, c. 5, s. 7,) and be carried to a separate account with the Trustees, 48 G. 3, c. 25, s. 8. *Investment of property in the Receiver-General's office at 8 per cent*

In consideration of the surrender from the Trustees of Drax's Free School, the Justices and Vestry were empowered to nominate 10 Scholars, to be maintained and educated at the School. Donors of real or personal property of the value of £3000 (£1800 sterling), or £300 (£180 sterling) per annum, shall become life Trustees, with the right of nominating three Scholars, and assigning the trust and right by deed or will for ever, and in that proportion, upwards or downwards, for every £1000 (£600 sterling), or £100 (£60 sterling) per annum, and in respect of every sum of £1000 (£600) transferred by any Trustee or Trustees under this Act, a right of nominating one Scholar, to be exercised by the persons certified to be entitled to the enjoyment of the right by the Chief-Justice, Attorney-General, and Speaker, or any two of them, 48 G. 3, c. 25, s. 9. *Donations and consequent rights of nomination of scholars, and to be trustees*

The powers of the Governor of recommending, nominating, and appointing Scholars extended to any class of free persons, 7 W. 4, c. 30, s. 8. *Scholars*

The Trustees and Governors, or any 7, shall, once a year, during the annual session of the Legislature, meet in St. Jago de la Vega, to examine *Annual meetings in Spanish Town* the state of the Free School, and for giving orders and directions, and making laws respecting its government, as to them or the major part seems meet, 48 G. 3, c. 25, s 11.

Annual Accounts Before whom the accounts of the receipts and expenditure of the institution shall be laid by the Head Master, 7 W. 4, c. 30, s. 5.

Quarterly meetings at School-house Three or more Trustees and Governors shall form a Board of Visitors, to meet at the School-House on 25th March, 24th June, 25th September, and 20th December in each year, or if either of those days fall on a Sunday or on Good Friday, or holiday, on the day following, and at every quarterly meeting, examine and enquire into any neglects, miscarriages, irregularities or misconduct, or mismanagement of the Head or Under-Masters or scholars,

Enquirers and powers with power to suspend them until the opinion of a general meeting can be taken thereon, and thereupon the Trustees shall immediately summon by public advertisement in the "Jamaica Gazette," a general meeting in Spanish-Town within 14 days, to take into consideration the circumstances, and report fully thereon, and the decision of the general meeting shall be final; the meeting to consist of, at least, 13, and to be advertized for toties quoties, until a meeting takes place, 7 W. 4, c. 30, s. 1.

Report to general meetings

Extraordinary meeting Besides annual meetings, any three Governors and Trustees may call extraordinary meetings, by 14 days' advertisement, and three or more shall form a Board of Visitors, with the powers given above to investigate the matter for which the meeting was convened, and, if occasion require, to proceed as before, 7 W. 4, c. 30, s. 2.

Quarterly accounts The Chairman of the quarterly meetings shall draw on the Receiver-General for the amount of the accounts passed thereat, 7 W. 4, c. 30 s. 5.

Bye-laws by annual meeting The Governors and Trustees may, at their annual meeting, make bye-laws and ordinances for the better management of the School, and government of the Head-Master, Under-Master and Scholars, 7 W. 4, c. 30, s. 4.

by meeting at school-house Any 3 or more assembled at the School-House, may make additional bye-laws, to be submitted to a general meeting in Spanish-Town, convened as directed by 7 W. 4, c. 30, and when approved of by them shall be binding, and may also amend, vary and alter bye-laws, to be submitted to and approved of by a general meeting before being acted upon, 5 V. c. 25, s. 5.

Appointment &c. of head and other masters, removal of scholars The appointment and dismissal of Head-Master and Under-Masters and removal of Scholars shall be in the hands of the Trustees, or the majority, at their annual meeting in Spanish-Town, or general meetings to be summoned, 7 W. 4, c. 30, s. 3.

Head-master's qualifications The Head-Master shall be a Clergyman, in Priest's orders, of the Church of England, and a Bachelor of Arts of 3 years standing, of such degree in one of the Universities of Great Britain, 5 V., c. 25, s. 1.

Private pupils And may take private pupils, not exceeding 30, into the School, upon terms to be made by him with their parents or guardians, but no private pupil shall be received, unless the expenses are paid half-yearly, in advance, 5 V., c. 25, s. 4.

Appointment of masters in case trustees neglect If the Trustees or the major part refuse or omit to elect a Head or other Master within 21 days after a vacancy, the Governor, President of the Council, Speaker, Chief-Justice and Attorney-General, or any 3 of them may elect, 48 G. 3, c. 25, s. 15.

All persons employed in the School as assistants or servants shall be exempt from Militia duties, and all service on juries, not exceeding 5 in number 48 G., 3, c. 25, s. 14.

Perpetual annuity of £996 A perpetual annuity of £996 secured to the Charity, in lieu of investments of £12,451; 28 V. c. 23.

MANCHESTER DISTRICT SCHOOL.

Trustees The Custos (or in his absence from the parish, the senior resident Magistrate, s. 28) of Manchester, the Members, Rector and Churchwardens, together with two Tax-payers, qualified as mentioned in s. 6, and to be elected annually, or as vacancies occur, for and from each of the (3) districts created under 1 V, c. 34, and 9 V, c. 44, constituted Trustees and Governors for the establishing, maintaining, management and superintendence of the District Schools, 19 V., c. 39, s. 1.

Annual election and qualification of district trustees The election of Tax-payers as Trustees shall be made by the electors duly registered and qualified to vote for Members of Assembly, and the annual election take place at the time, and under the regulations for annual elec.

tions of Churchwardens and Vestrymen, and no person shall be eligible as such Trustee, unless he be assessed for, and has actually paid direct taxes in his own right not less than £3, be resident in the district for which he is nominated, and is not in arrears for any taxes at the time of election, 19 V. c. 39, s. 6.

If any elected Trustee dies, leaves the island, or ceases to be domiciled in the District, or becomes insolvent, his office shall thereupon become vacant, 19 V., c. 39, s. 7.

And the Custos shall summon the voters of the parish to meet on a fixed day, within ten days after the summons. at an hour and place within the district for which the vacancy exists, to supply it, 19 V., c. 39, s. 8.

But no proceedings of the Trustees shall be vitiated or affected by the existence of any vacancy, 19 V., c. 39, s. 9.

The Trustees and Governors incorporated as "The Trustees of the District Schools of Manchester," with power to take lands on lease or purchase, and to sell or exchange same, to have a Common Seal, to be kept by the Custos or senior resident Magistrate, and to make and alter bye-laws and ordinances for the regulation of the Corporation and persons in its employ, and of the administration of the trusts, 19 V., c. 39, s. 2.

The principal sum of £2744, with interest from 30th March, 1855, at £8 per cent. per annum (being 25-82d part of £9000), then standing at the credit of the Trustees of the Vere Free Schools in the Receiver-General's office, the proportion allowed to Manchester subject to a reduction, to be ascertained as directed by s. 5, but not exceeding £80, was directed to be credited to an account to be opened with the Trustees under this Act, who should stand possessed of such principal sum and interest for carrying out the Trusts, which sum of £2743 should continue to carry interest at £8 per cent., (£219 10s 4d) per annum, but not to authorize the Trustees to draw on the Receiver-General to pay any sums beyond the annual interest, and all monies already or to be paid to the Receiver-General under 18 V., c. 54 (Vere District School) shall be placed to the credit of the same account. and follow and be subject to the Trusts of the £2744, 19 V. c. 39, s. 3.

The Trustees of the Vere District School were further directed, within 14 days after the receipt of any monies on account of rents, rent-charges, or arrears issuing out of or chargeable on any real estate which belonged to the Trustees of the late Vere Free School, under penalty of £10 each for each default, to be recovered as after provided, (see s. 26) to pay to the Receiver-General 25-82d part of every such sum, to be held to the credit of the account with the Trustees of this Act, 19 V., c. 39, s. 5.

And the Receiver-General is directed to pay to the order of the Trustees all such monies, not being monies received on the arbitration or compromise of claims under 18 V., c. 54, to be by them applied in the same way, and subject to the directions in 19 V., c. 39, concerning the interest of £2744 and other annual funds, 24 V., c. 9.

Immediately after the annual election of the Trustees, the Custos shall call a meeting, giving notice in two consecutive numbers of the Gazette, or, if none, in any newspaper, and repeat his calls by other notices until a meeting is held, 19 V., c. 39, s. 10.

All meetings shall take place at the Court-House at Mandeville, 19 V., c. 39, s. 11.

At the first annual meeting, the Trustees shall elect a Chairman, then resident in the parish, 19 V., c. 39, s. 12.

In case of his absence, the Board may elect a Chairman pro tempore, and proceed with business. No less than 5, inclusive of the Chairman, shall constitute a Board, 19 V., c. 39, s. 13.

The Trustees shall meet once a quarter, on 28th March, June, September and December, or within 28 days, and may have special meetings, notice in writing of each special meeting being given by the Clerk of the Boards, affixing same to the outside of the door of the Parish Church 8 days before that appointed, and the Chairman shall direct the Clerk to summon such special meeting on the requirement of 3 Trustees, or without a requisition, if he deems proper. The Board may adjourn, 19 V., c. 39, s. 14.

The Trustees shall keep a Book containing a statement of all the real and personal property of the Trust, and separate books of accounts, and of their proceedings, 19 V., c. 39, s. 15.

Marginal notes:

Vacancies

How to be filled up

Not to vitiate proceedings

Incorporation Powers to purchase and sell lands
Have a common seal
Make bye-laws

Funds of schools £2744 in Receiver General's office

Carrying interest at £8 per cent to which interest and further payments under 18 V., c. 54, the trustees' drafts are limited

Application of further payments

Monies received on arbitration or compromise of claims

Annual meeting Notice

Meetings at Court House

Chairman

Chairman, pro tem
5 a quorum

Quarterly and special meetings Notice

Adjournment

Books of property, accounts and proceedings

Drafts on Receiver-General	The Receiver-General shall keep a separate account of the monies belonging to them, and pay the interest and dividends to their orders, drawn and signed at the meetings, in the presence of the Board, by the Chairman, and countersigned by the Clerk, 19 V., c. 39, s. 16.
Annual account To be examined Signed And forwarded to the Governor to be audited.	An annual account shall be stated to 28th September by the Clerk, and laid before the next meeting, of the receipts and disbursements for the preceding year, at full length, which, after being examined by that or any subsequent meeting, shall, when found correct, be signed by the Chairman, and countersigned by the Clerk, and forthwith forwarded to the Governor to be audited by a Public Board of Audit, or Auditor of Public Accounts, 19 V,. c. 39, s. 17.
Enforcing payment of rents, rent charges, and arrears, upon refusal of Vere trustees Appropriation Indemnity	If on application of the Trustees, in pursuance of a resolution of a Special Meeting, the Trustees of the Vere District Schools decline to exercise the powers vested in them (by 18 V., c. 54), they may, with the consent of the Governor, institute proceedings at law or in equity, in the name of the Vere Trustees, for the recovery of any rents, rent-charges or arrears, formerly payable to the Trustees of the Free Schools of Vere, or to the Justices and Vestry or Churchwardens of that Parish for the use of the poor, to which the Trustees of the Manchester District Schools are equitably entitled, which, when recovered, shall be appropriated in like manner as if proceedings had been taken by the Vere Trustees, first tendering to the latter an indemnity against costs, to be approved of by the Governor, 19 V., c. 39, s. 18.
School houses For persons resident in the parish Course of instruction Children not of the Established Church	The Trustees may purchase, or take on lease such sites, and build, keep in repair and furnish School-Houses thereon in the parish as they think necessary, and the funds will admit, to be free to all persons residing in the parish, over 5 and under 15, whom the Trustees select to be instructed in the lower branches of education, such as reading English, and so much of writing and arithmetic as to enable them to perform accurately and with despatch the duties of an ordinary business life, and to receive religious instruction, according to the principles of the United Church ; and they may cause to be imparted to the Children practical instruction in agricultural, mechanical and other industrial occupations. Children of parents of other denominations than the United Church may be admitted, and shall not be obliged to conform to, or be taught the tenets of the Established Church, 19 V., c. 39, s. 19.
Teachers Removal	The Trustees shall appoint Teachers, and fix their salaries, who shall be members of the Established Church, and shall not receive any other fee or reward without the leave of the Trustees according to their regulations, and may remove them at pleasure, but upon manifest neglect of duty, or for grossly immoral conduct, they are required forthwith to dismiss any Teacher, 19 V., c. 39, s. 20.
School books and other articles	The Trustees shall select, and introduce, and supply the Scholars with uniform class-books, and also furnish the Schools with other proper articles and apparatus, 19 V., c. 39, s. 21.
Bye-laws Alterations and amendments	And make rules and by-laws for their conduct and proceedings, also for the prosperity, order and discipline of the Schools and Teachers, and the security and preservation of the School-Houses and other trust property, which may be revised, altered or amended at a special meeting, due notice of the intended alteration, and of the substance thereof, being given in the summons, 19 V., c. 39, s. 22.
What teachers qualified	Every Teacher shall be deemed qualified who holds a certificate under the hands of the Bishop, or of two beneficed Clergymen, or of any Normal School to be established, stating their belief that the person is well qualified in respect to moral character, learning and ability, to teach in any District School in the parish of Manchester, 19 V., c. 39, s. 23.
Trustees' custody, &c. of school houses, accounts and documents	The Trustees shall be charged with the custody and safe keeping of the district School-Houses, as also of all account books, papers, vouchers and documents, and may each, at all reasonable times, visit and examine the School-Houses, and inspect and take copies or extracts of accounts, &c., at the place where they direct them to be kept, 19 V., c. 30, s. 24.
Annual report to the Governor	They shall make a report up to 28th September in each year, and transmit same to the Governor within 20 days after, signed and certified by the majority of the Trustees making it, specifying the number of Schools established, the daily average of Children taught in each during the preceding year, the names and salaries of the Teachers, the conditions of the School-

Houses, the state of the funds, and any other necessary information, 19 V., c. 30, s. 25.

The Governor may authorize any public Inspector of Schools, or in his absence, any other person, to visit the Schools and report thereon, who shall have free access and egress, and may at all reasonable times inspect and take copies or extracts from all accounts, &c., at the place where they are kept. Penalty for wilfully preventing or obstructing such inspection, or making of extracts, or wilfully neglecting the duty of giving the Inspector access to any documents, not more than £5, to be recovered before two Justices of Manchester, and the whole to be paid to the Trustees in furtherance of their Trust, 19 V., c. 39, s. 26. Inspection

No Teacher shall be eligible to sit in Vestry, or act as a Trustee, and his election as Vestryman, Churchwarden or Trustee shall be void, 19 V., c. 39, s. 27. No teacher to be a trustee, vestryman or churchwarden

A perpetual annuity of £219 10s. 5d. secured to the Schools in discharge of the investment of £2744, 28 V., c. 23. Perpetual annuity of £219 10s 5d

MANCHESTER FREE SCHOOL.

The inhabitants of Manchester were empowered to establish a Public Free School or Schools in Manchester for the education of free children of either or both sexes, inhabitants of Manchester, to be called "The Manchester Free School," and the Justices and Vestry were required to set apart a portion of the parish lands, a diagram whereof to be recorded in the Secretary's Office, and thereupon the land shall be vested in the Trustees, 5 G. 4, c. 20, s. 1. Establishment Parish land allotted therefor And vested in trustees

For ordering and conducting matters relating to the School, the Custos, the resident Members of the parish, the Rector and Churchwardens, the 4 senior Magistrates actually residing, certain persons by name [all dead], and 6 other Freeholders and inhabitants of the parish to be annually elected by the Freeholders on the same day and time, and in manner, and subject to the like qualifications as Vestrymen, were appointed Trustees and Governors for erecting the School and for its direction and management, also of the funds subscriptions and bequests already and to be given, and incorporated as the Trustees and Governors of the Manchester Free School, with powers to hold, sell, demise and lease land, and have a Common Seal, 5 G., 4, c. 20, s. 2. Trustees Incorporation

The Governor, President of the Council, Speaker, Chief-Justice, Attorney-General and Bishop of Jamaica [in whose absence, the Suffragan, 22 V., c. 23, s. 3 Clergy] are appointed Visitors, to enquire and examine into the management and conduct of the Schools, and the funds and their application, and to do all acts appertaining to the office of Visitors, 5 G., 4, c. 20, s. 3-4. Visitors

Five or more Trustees shall form a General Court, the major part of whom are invested with the full power of the corporation, provided the Custos or a member for the parish, or one of the 4 senior Magistrates, or one of the Churchwardens be one of the number forming the General Court, 5 G., 4, c. 20, s. 5. Quorum of trustees

The Trustees may purchase or acquire lands in Manchester, and build thereon houses and other buildings for the School, and for the dwelling, use and reception of the Masters Mistresses, Ushers, Assistants, servants, and children of the School, and endow the same in proportion to their revenues, and may appoint Masters, Mistresses or Ushers of the tenets of the Church of England, and other assistants, servants and persons, and appoint their salaries, stipends, perquisites, or other remunerations, 5 G. 4, c. 20, s. 6. Trustees may purchase or acquire land Appoint masters, &c. Salaries, &c.

They shall elect and receive into the School as many poor Children (inhabitants, or whose parents or reputed parents were inhabitants of Manchester) as may be thought proper in proportion to the revenue, under the regulations of the General Court, and upon any misdemeanor, inability or other sufficient cause, or on their attaining 14, may remove them and elect others; repair uphold and enlarge the buildings in proportion to the revenue; and they, or a Committee appointed at a General Court, may visit the Free School, and reform and redress disorders and abuses, 5 G. 4, c. 20, s. 7. Scholars Removal, 14 Uphold buildings Reform abuses

They may also make, revoke and amend bye-laws and ordinances for the government of the Corporation, Masters, &c. servants and children, for Bye-laws

To be approved of by the Visitors auditing the accounts, settling and arranging the stipend, salaries, remunerations, allowances and maintenance, but which shall not be in force until approved of by the Visitors. or any three of them, of whom the Governor shall be one, and ther approval notified to the Custos by the Governor's Secretary, 5 G. 4, c. 20, s. 8.

Censure removal &c. of masters &c. The Trustees may, upon complaint of misbehaviour and neglect, or other reasonable and sufficient cause, censure, suspend, deprive or remove the Masters, Mistresses, Ushers, servants or others at a General Court, by writing, under their seal, and may also by writing, under their seal, elect persons properly qualified to fill vacant places, 5 G. 4, c. 20, s. 9.

Treasurer, his duties and power They may also, if deemed necessary, appoint a respectable inhabitant to be Treasurer, at a salary, to keep the books of account, and produce them at every meeting, if demanded by any member present, receive and collect the income and funds, as also all sums due or left or given, and to grant releases and discharges in the name of the Corporation, and to have the custody **To have custody of the seal Removal** of the seal, and deliver same to the succeeding Treasurer, to be accountable to the Corporation for his receipts, payments and disbursements, and to be removeable at any time, by order made at any meeting or General Court, and the General Court may afterwards choose another, 5 G. 4, c. 20, s. 10.

Accounts to be annually balanced Annual and other meetings Purposes thereof The accounts of debiture and expenditure shall be made up and balanced every year to the end of the preceeding year, and the Trustees shall call and hold, once at least a-year in the early part, and otherwise as occasion requires, a General Court, to audit and settle all accounts, and examine into any neglects or irregularities, and perform any duties or business. The Court shall be holden at the School-House, between sunrise and sunset, and the Trustees present shall audit the accounts, make all proper examinations and enquiries, and perform all duties and business, and may adjourn. Public **Notice of meetings** notice of the time and place, signed by 3 Trustees, to be affixed on the door of the Court-House for 7 days immediately previous to that of meeting 5 G. 4, c. 20, s. 11..

Investment of funds The Trustees shall invest all monies to come to their hands by public or private donations, grants, bequests, devises, benefactions and subscription, and all monies and rent for which they may not have any immediate use, for the purposes of the School, in the island funds, at £6 per cent. per annum, the interest (and also the principal when wanted for the School) to be paid by the Receiver-General to the order of the Trustees, or any 5 of them, out of any unappropriated monies, 5 G., 4, c. 20, s. 12.

Not to keep in their hands, &c., any property of the corporation They shall not keep in their hands above 30 days, nor use or borrow any of the monies, or buy, sell, rent or lease to one another any of the lands settled, purchased or given to the use of the Corporation, 5 G. 4, c. 20, s. 13.

Penalties Persons offending, or acting contrary to the Act, shall forfeit £50 (£30 sterling), one-third to the Crown, one-third to the Free School, and one-third to the informer, to be recovered by action of debt, &c., 5 G. 4, c. 20, s. 14.

Filling up vacant offices on neglect In case of a vacancy in the office of Master, Mistress, Usher or servant, and the Trustees for six weeks omit or neglect, or refuse to elect, the Visitors, or any 3 (of whom the Governor shall be one), may elect proper and qualified persons, 5 G. 4, c. 20, s. 15.

Election of trustees on neglect If any Trustees die, or resign or depart from the island, and the Freeholders of Manchester for 12 calendar months omit or, neglect or refuse, the Governor may, under his hand and seal, appoint Trustees in the place of those so deceased, resigned or departed this island, 5 G., 4, c. 20, s. 16.

Justices and Vestry may contribute annually out of taxes The Justices and Vestry may apply not exceeding £500 (£300 sterling) per annum out of the Parish Tax, in aid of the funds, to be paid to the Trustees or their Treasurer, or person appointed by them to receive the same, 5 G. 4, c. 20, s. 17.

Annual meeting of visitors and trustees in St. Jago de la Vega The Visitors and Trustees, or any 7, may once a-year during the Session of the Legislature, meet in St. Jago de la Vega, to examine into the state of the School, and for giving orders and directions, and making laws respecting its government, 5 G. 4, c. 20, s. 18.

Incidental expenses The Trustees may, on of the funds, pay all incidental charges and expences, 5 G. 4, c. 20, s. 19t

MANNING'S FREE SCHOOL.

The Custos of Westmoreland, the members of Assembly for the Parish, **Trustees** three of the Senior Magistrates present at any Meeting, the Rector and any 5 Freeholders, elected on the 1st Monday in August in each year, appointed Trustees for the direction and management of the Free School, and of the devise and bequest made by Thomas Manning, and of all subscriptions, devises and bequests to be given for the use of the Free School (5 a quorum); the **5 a quorum** Custos, or one of the Members, or one of the 3 Senior Magistrates actually residing therein being of the number, 9 G. 3, c. 4, s. 2.

At any future election of any Freeholder, the Trustees shall be elected by **Electors** such persons as appear by the Electoral List of the Parish for the current year, qualified to vote for Members of Assembly, 28 V., c. 6, s. 1.

Any Freeholder whose title has been recorded prior to this Act, shall be **Freeholders whose** competent to vote at any such election, upon the production to the Return- **deeds are already** ing Officer of such recorded deed, or a copy certified by the Island Secretary, **recorded** 28 V., c. 6, s. 2.

The Trustees shall be Trustees of the Free School, and of all messuages **Incorporation** and hereditaments which are or shall be given by any person, or purchased by the Trustees for the use of the Free School, and be incorporated as " The Trustees of Manning's Free School," 11 G. 2, c 9, s. 2.

With power for them, or the major part of them, to place out at interest **Powers** donations, to lease, purchase, sue and be sued, and have a Common Seal, en- **Seal** graven " Charity," with a sucking child at her breast, and another in her **To be kept by the** arms, which shall be kept by the Custos, 11 G. 2, c. 9, s. 3. **custos**

Also to build a proper house and out-offices, and endow the same in pro- **School house** portion to their revenues, and in the meantime hire one for the dwelling **Masters** use of one or more Masters and Ushers for instructing youth without charge, in reading, writing, arithmetic, Latin, Greek, mathematics, and any other parts of learning the Trustees think proper, and for the abiding, dwelling and **Scholars** use of poor children of Westmoreland, and maintaining and providing them with necessaries. The Masters and Ushers shall be appointed by them, pro- **Appointment and** vided they are of the religion of the Church of England, and removable **removal of master,** upon misbehaviour or disability. And, within 30 days after any vacancy, **&c.** they shall appoint by writing, under their Common Seal, 11 G. 2, c. 9, s. 5.

Also to receive into the Free School as many children of the parish as **Of scholars** they think proper, in proportion to the revenues, and upon misbehaviour or inability, or upon attaining 14, to remove them and receive others, and ex- pend such sums in proportion to the revenues, in repairing, upholding or en- **Repair &c., of** larging the School and buildings as they think necessary, 11 G. 2, c. 9, s. 6. **buildings**

Also, under their Common Seal, to make ordinances for the government **Ordinances** of the Shoolmasters, Ushers and Scholars, and for settling their stipends and allowances, not repugnant to the prerogative or laws; also to visit the **Reformation of** School, and reform disorders and abuses, 11 G. 2, c. 9, s. 7. **abuses**

Not to keep in their hands, above 30 days, or apply to their own benefit, **Not to derive any** or borrow, on interest, any monies of the Free School, nor to buy, sell or **benefit from the** lease to one another any of the lands, 11 G. 2. c. 9, s. 8. **trust**

Offenders in anything shall forfeit £50 (£30 sterling), one-third to the **Penalties and** Crown, for the support of the Government of the island, one-third for the **recovery** use of the Free School, and the other third to the informer, to be recovered by action of debt, &c., 11 G. 2, c. 9, s. 9.

A perpetual annuity of £471 3s. 3d. secured to the School in lieu of an **Perpetual annu-** investment of £7852 14s. 8d., 28 V., c. 23. **ty of £471 3s 3d**

MUNRO AND DICKENSON'S FREE SCHOOL AND CHARITY.

The Custodes and Rectors of St. Elizabeth and Manchester, the **Trustees** Members of Assembly for St. Elizabeth, the Honorable John Joseph Arthur Shakspeare, Raines Waite Smith, Peter McLaren, Thomas Haffenden, and Isaac Isaacs, were appointed " The Governors and Trustees of Munro and Dickenson's Free School and Charity," and in- **Incorporation** corporated by that name, (three to be a quorum for the transac- **Quorum** tion of business) and to exercise the powers and authorities, so far **Powers** as not repealed by this Act, given under [the private and unprinted Act, 6 G. 4] for the sale of the real estate and slaves of Robert Hugh Munro and Caleb Dickenson, respectively, and investing the same in the funds and

B B

applying the same to the charitable purposes of their wills, and for other purposes, 18 V. c. 53, s. 1-2.

Governor to fill up vacancies of non-official trustees

In case of the death, resignation, refusal to act, absence from the island, removal out of the limits of St. Elizabeth, at the date of the will of Robert Hugh Munro [i. e., before the establishment of the parish of Manchester, 55 G. 3, c. 23] or other vacancy in the office of the non-official Trustees, or in case any such Trustee becomes an official Trustee, the Governor, by any writing under his hand, to be entered on the minutes, may appoint any person resident within the limits, to succeed to and supply the vacancy, and who shall thereupon be a Trustee, 18 V., c. 53, s. 25.

To be reported to him by the chairman

The Chairman shall report to the Governor every such vacancy within 30 days after, 18 V., c. 53, s. 26.

Neglect to attend meetings of trustees

If any non-official Trustee for the space of one year refuses or neglects to attend the legal meeting of the Trustees, such non-attendance shall be a resignation, 18 V., c. 53, s. 27.

Funds transferred to trustees

The principal sum of £23,337 4s. 3d., the sum of £2804 15s., balance of interest to the credit of the Trustees of the Charity in the books of the Receiver-General, as of 10th October, 1854, and all further interest were transferred to and vested in the Trustees of this Act; and the Trustees for sale under the recited Act (6 G. 4,) were required from time to time to account for and pay over to them for the purposes of this Act, all monies to arise from the sale, or rents and profits of the real estate of the testators, 18 V., c. 53, s. 3.

Previous trusts at variance with this act

All previous trusts, and the recited Act, or so much as relates to the monies to be derived from the sale and rents and profits of the real estate, and to the above principal sum and interest, as well accrued as accruing, in so far as such trusts or Act interfere with the object and purposes of this Act, shall cease, 18 V., c. 53, s. 4.

Trustees not to withdraw the principal of £23,337 4s. 3d. Interest only to be drawn

The Trustees shall not withdraw from the Public Treasury, or use or apply any portion of the principal sum of £23,337 4s. 3d., and the interest of the monies only may be drawn by them, and used for the purposes of this Act, 18 V., c. 53, s. 5.

To invest proceeds of sale and rents of unsold lands and donations

Vary securities

Interest only to be dealt with

They shall invest, at interest, in the public funds of this Island, or of the United Kingdom, as to them appears expedient, all monies coming to, or to be received by or paid to them from the sale or the rents and profits of the remaining real estate of the Testators, or from public or private donations, grants or subscriptions, with power to vary the securities, and the interest only of the investments shall be drawn or dealt with by them for the purposes of this Act, 18 V., c. 53, s. 6.

Sites for schools and alms houses

The Trustees were required to determine upon and select a convenient and healthy site or sites within the former limits of St. Elizabeth, for the erection of a School or several Schools for poor boys, and a School or several Schools for poor girls [and for an Alms-House, or Alms-Houses ; see 25 V., c. 22], and, for that purpose, to select any parts of the unsold lands of the testators, and to erect and build thereon, or to repair, enlarge and improve buildings already thereon, or to contract for the purchase, exchange, lease or rent of lands required, and for erecting, repairing, enlarging and improving buildings thereon, and to keep in repair and furnish such buildings for the Schools and Alms-Houses, 18 V., c. 53, s. 7. To enable them to do so, the balance of interest on 10th March, 1855, subject to the drafts of previous Trustees, was placed at their disposal, 18 V., c. 53, s. 8.

Balance of £280,415

Instead of alms-houses, money may be otherwise appropriated for the poor

The Trustees were empowered to appropriate the funds made applicable for the establishment and maintenance of Alms' Houses towards the support otherwise of poor persons, who would be qualified for admission into an Alms-House. (i. e., the poor and necessitous, resident within the ancient limits of St. Elizabeth,) 25 V., c. 22, s. 1.

Investment for building fund account

Application of interest to repair of buildings

Also to invest, at interest, in Island or British Public Securities £646 17s. 5d., or other balance in the Receiver-General's books to the credit of the Building Fund Account, and employ the interest to accrue towards the repairs of the School-Houses and buildings, or re-invest and accumulate same, but not to use for repairs any part of the capital, 25 V., c. 22, s. 2.

Such monies to be applied, as well for relief of poor persons as for repairs of School-buildings, subject to the bye-laws already or to be made in or about the affairs of the Schools, and for appointing the poor and necessitous persons to be admitted for relief, and for ordering the means and system of administering such relief, and otherwise for the management of the Charity; accounts of which monies, and their appropriation, shall be kept, stated and audited, and reports made of the poor, and of their relief, and of the School-Houses, as prescribed by 18 V., c. 53, so far as applicable, which Act, except as altered or amended, is to be followed, as governing the proceedings of the Trustees, 25 V., c. 22, s. 3.

And relief of the poor
Subject to bye-laws

Accounts and reports

This Act shall be read as incorporated with 18 V., c. 53, as hereby amended, 25 V., c. 22, s. 4.

Act incorporated into 18 V. c. 53.

The Trustees shall perpetually maintain within the ancient limits of St. Elizabeth, one or more Schools for poor boys, and one or more Schools for poor girls, for the separate reception, maintenance and education of poor boys and girls resident within such limits (and Alms-Houses, the proportion for which is now applicable to the maintenance otherwise of the poor, resident within the ancient limits), 18 V., c. 53, s. 9.

Schools for boys and girls within the ancient limits of the parish

And shall elect, for admission into the Schools, to be separately maintained and educated, such poor boys and girls as to them shall seem most eligible, and to such number in the aggregate as each School is capable of maintaining, &c., and as having regard to (the maintenance of the poor) the funds at their disposal shall permit, 18 V., c. 53, s. 10.

Election of boys and girls

Also to receive into the Schools such number of Day Scholars, boys and girls, resident within the ancient limits as can conveniently be educated, with those to be maintained and supported, and, if practicable, to establish District Schools for the reception of Day Scholars within the limits, and appoint thereto Masters and Mistresses, and pay them salaries or remuneration, 18 V., c. 53, s. 11.

Day scholars

They may also admit into the Schools the children of persons residing within the limits, willing to pay for their education, either as Day Scholars or otherwise, to such number as they may by any bye-law determine, and fix the amount to be paid for each child, and appropriate to the Master or Mistress a portion of the money received for each as they think fit, for maintenance and education, or education alone, and apply the residue to the general purposes of the Act appropriable as the annual interest, 18 V., c. 53, s. 12.

Children of parents willing to pay for their education
Appropriation of the monies to be paid

For carrying on, conducting and maintaining the Schools and (poor), and keeping up the buildings and furniture, the Trustees may appropriate the interest of the investments, or so much as may be necessary, 18 V., c. 53, s. 13.

Repairs and furniture of schools

The annual accruing interest now producing £1400 and upwards, shall be distributed in the proportions, not exceeding £200, for maintenance of (the poor), not exceeding £800, for keeping up and maintaining the Schools for the reception, education and maintenance of poor boys and girls, and the surplus for repairs and furniture, and towards keeping up and supporting Schools for Day Scholars, 18 V., c. 53, s. 14.

Proportional distribution of interest

The Masters and Mistresses, Officers and servants, shall be appointed by the Trustees, who may at pleasure remove or suspend them, and whose qualification shall be in the discretion of the Trustees, 18 V., c. 53, s. 15.

Appointment and removal of masters &c.

Reporting vacancies of Masters, Mistresses or Matrons to the Governor within 30 days after, and appointments or new appointments within 14 days after, (18 V., c. 53, s. 26). In case of failure, to appoint within 2 months after vacancy, the right shall lapse to the Governor 18 V., c. 53, s. 39.

Reports to the Governor of removal

The Trustees may make, revoke and amend bye-laws and rules for better governing, ordering, and establishing the Corporation and Free Schools, Masters, &c., and persons employed in and about the Schools, and the poor children and others to be educated in the same, and the (poor) as seems most proper for the objects of the charity, and for auditing the accounts, and otherwise for its general management and direction, but which shall have no force until 2 months after a copy, certified as the Governor shall direct, has been laid before him, unless he in the meantime signify his approbation thereof, 18 V., c. 53, s. 16.

Bye-laws

Governor's approval

Governor's disallowance

The Governor may at any time before or after any bye-law has come into operation, certify to the Trustees his disallowance, and, if it be in force, the time at which it shall cease, and none disallowed without having been in operation shall have any force, or, if in force at the time of disallowance, it shall cease at the time limited in the notice, save so far as any penalty has been already incurred, 18 V., c. 53, s. 17.

Clerk

The Trustees may appoint, and, at pleasure, remove a Clerk, and from time to time define his duties, and out of the annual income pay him a salary, allowance or recompense yearly or otherwise for his time and trouble, and on his removal, or in case of his death, resignation, incapacity, departure from the island, or ceasing to reside within the ancient limits, appoint another, toties quoties, 18 V., c. 53, s. 18.

Annual accounts to be kept

The Trustees shall keep a book in which to enter the accounts of all monies received and paid in furtherance or in the general management of the Charity, and which shall distinctly and separately shew what monies have been received or paid in the purchase, if made, of sites, and in the erection, repairs, enlargement or improvement, or furnishing of buildings, under the head of "The Building Account;" and also the receipts and payments for salaries, and the support and maintenance of the poor boys and **And balanced** girls, and poor and necessitous persons, and otherwise in the general management, under the separate head of "The General Management Account," to be made up and balanced to 28th September, in each year, 18 V., c. 53, s. 19.

And audited annually

They shall also cause an account to be made up to 28th September, shewing the transactions at length, keeping separate in the account the Building Account and General Management Account, audited at a Meeting, adjourned **And copies sent to the Governor. Inspectors of accounts and books Their powers** if necessary for the purpose, and signed by the Chairman, and countersigned by the Clerk, and send a copy, within 60 days after the 28th September, to the Governor, who may appoint persons to inspect their accounts and books, and any person, so authorized at all reasonable times, on producing his authority, may examine the books, accounts, vouchers and documents of the Charity, at the place they are directed to be kept, and take copies or extracts, 18 V., c. 53, s. 20.

Annual report to the Governor of charity

And on 28th September, or within 60 days, shall render to the Governor, a report, in writing, signed by the Chairman, stating the number of Schools established and in operation, and their localities; the number of boys and girls, and their age, admitted for education and maintenance, into the respective Schools; the number and ages of the day-scholars, boys and girls, specifying to what Schools respectively admitted; and the number and age of those for whose education, or education and maintenance payment is made; the amount for each child, and how appropriated; the names and salaries, or other remuneration allowed to the Masters and Mistresses to each School; the numbers, sex and age of the poor persons, [maintained]; the names of the matrons, nurses and other officers, and servants employed in the Charity, their salaries or remuneration; also the situation, state, and condition of the buildings; the branches of education and industry taught in each School; the time at which they commenced operation, if established within the preceding 12 months, and, if for any time, when suspended or not in operation, and the reasons or occasion; with such other particulars as they think proper, or the Governor may in writing require, 18 V., c. 23, s. 21.

Further reports

They shall also, when required by direction in writing of the Governor, render a report in writing, on any matter relating to the state and condition and general management of the Schools, and [poor] in the form and manner he directs, 18 V., c. 53, s. 22.

Inspector to visit and examine schools, &c.

The Governor may, when he thinks necessary, authorize any public Inspector of Schools, or other person, to visit the Schools, and enquire and examine into the state and condition, conduct, management and discipline, and into any neglects, miscarriages, or irregularities of **Also to enquire into the state &c. of the poor** any Masters, Mistresses or Scholars, and may also appoint persons to enquire into the state, condition and management of the [poor], and into any neglects or irregularities of the Matrons, Nurses, or **Their powers** servants; and any person so authorized, on producing his authority at reasonable times, shall have access to the Schools, and examine Masters, Mistresses, Scholars, Matrons, Nurses and servants, and have access to the books, &c., and may take copies of extracts, 18 V., c. 53, s. 23.

Persons wilfully obstructing any such Inspector, or other person in the execution of his duty, shall, on conviction before a Justice, forfeit £5, and in default of payment immediately, or within such time as he appoints, the same or any other Justice having jurisdiction in the place where the offender is or resides, may commit him for 30 days, to be determined on payment of the penalty, which shall be returned to the ensuing [Circuit Court] in the usual manner, 18 V., c. 53, s. 24. *Obstructing them*

The Trustees shall meet for the ordinary discharge of business quarterly, on 28th March, June, September and December, or within 20 days thereafter, on the day for which they are summoned by the Chairman, or on a vacancy, 3 Trustees, 18 V., c. 53, s. 28. *Quarterly meetings*

And Extraordinary or Special Meetings may be ordered by the Chairman when he sees occasion, or on requisition of 3 Trustees, specifying the purpose, and the Chairman shall, within 7 days after, sign and issue a notice for such meeting, 18 V., c. 53, s. 29. *Special meetings*

Any business may be transacted at Ordinary Meetings, but no order for money shall be drawn for, other than the ordinary expenses of management, unless at a previous meeting, or unless a full and clear particular of the items and amounts for which drafts are to be made, be stated in the notice for the meeting, and no business shall be transacted at any Special Meeting unless specified in the notice, and no orders for money shall be drawn at any special meeting, except on some special emergency, to be stated in the notice, 18 V., c. 53, s. 30. *Business at ordinary and special meetings, orders for money*

Any Ordinary or Special Meeting may be adjourned if the business then ready, or for which it has been convened, is not completed, 18 V., c. 53, s. 31 *Adjournment*

Every meeting shall be convened by notice in writing, signed by the Chairman, or, on a vacancy, by 3 Trustees, or by the Clerk, under authority of the Chairman or 3 Trustees, specifying the place, day and hour; and in case of an Extraordinary Meeting the purpose. A copy, attested by the Clerk, shall be given to each Trustee, or left at his place of residence, addressed to him, at his usual or last known place of abode 14 days at least before, 18 V., c. 53, s. 32. *Notices of meetings*

Meetings shall be held at the Court-House, Black-River, or at one of the School-Houses, specified in the notice, 18 V., c. 53, s, 33. *Places*

The Custos of St. Elizabeth shall be ex-officio Chairman, and preside at all meetings where present, and do all other acts a Chairman is directed to do, 18 V., c. 53, s. 34. *Chairman*

In case of a vacancy, or of his absence from the island, or ceasing to reside within the ancient limits, the Trustees, at a meeting to be specially called, may elect a Chairman during such vacancy, &c., 18 V., c. 53, s. 35. *On vacancy, &c., trustees to elect one*

In the absence of the Chairman, the Trustees present may elect a Chairman pro tem, 18 V., c. 5 3s. 36. *Chairman, pro tem*

All orders for money drawn shall be fully entered on the minutes, and signed at such meetings by the Chairman, and counter-signed by the Clerk, who shall immediately after transmit to the Receiver-General or Officer a copy of the minute, 18 V., c. 53, s. 37. *Order for money to be entered, &c. on minutes Signature Copy minute to be sent to officer to pay*

The Trustees shall cause a book to be kept, in which the minutes of their proceedings shall be written, and the minutes or draft shall be signed by the Chairman before the Board adjourns, 18 V., c. 53, s. 38. *Minutes*

The School premises and Alms-Houses exempted from all public and parochial taxation, 18 V., c. 53, s. 40. *Exemption from taxes*

A perpetual annuity of £1400 4s. 7d. secured to the Charity in lieu of the investment of £23,337 4s. 3d., 28 V., c. 23. *Perpetual annuity of £1400 4s 7d*

RUSEA'S FREE SCHOOL, HANOVER.

The Custos of Hanover, the Members for the parish, three Senior Magistrates present at any meeting, and actually resident in the parish, the Rector, Churchwardens, any person who should in his life time by deed or otherwise give £600 (£360 sterling), or to that amount in lands, or an annual sum of £30 (£18 sterling), for the use of the Free School, with any 6 Freeholders qualified to vote for Members in Assembly, to be chosen by a majority of the Freeholders present, who are so qualified, between 8 and 12 A. M. on the third Tuesday in February in each year, (the poll to be taken by any Freeholder present) appointed Trustees for the direction and man- *Trustees* agement of the Free School, and the devise and bequest of Martin Rusea and of all subscriptions, donations, devises and bequests, given or to be given for the use of the Free School ; 7 shall be a quorum, of whom the Custos, one of the members, one of the resident Magistrates, the Rector, or one of the Churchwardens to be of the number present. If the Freeholders neglect to chose 6 Trustees, a quorum of 7 or more of the other Trustees are empowered to act as fully as if they had been chosen, 18 G. 3, c. 18, s. 2.

Quorum

Omission to elect 6 trustees

Incorporation Powers

The Trustees incorporated as " The Trustees of Rusea's Free School," with power to purchase, sell and demise lands, 18 G. 3; c. 18, s. 3.

And to place out at interest, on good security, any donations and subscriptions in money. The Common Seal to be kept in the hands of the Custos, or in case of his death or absence from the island, of the Senior Resident Magistrate, 18 G. 3, c. 18, s. 4.

Course of instruction

Also to erect or hire, and enlarge and repair, a house for the use of Masters and Ushers, for instructing poor children in reading, writing, arithmetic, Latin, Greek, mathematics, or any other part of learning the Trustees or the major part of a quorum think proper, with power to appoint, and at pleasure to remove Masters, Ushers, servants and others, and appoint their salaries, perquisites and other rewards, and do all other things necessary or convenient for effecting the purposes intended, 18 G. 3, c. 18, s. 6.

Masters, &c.

Scholars

The Trustees are also empowered to receive into the Free School as many poor children (those of Hanover to be always preferred) as they think proper in proportion to the revenue, and on misbehaviour, inability or other cause, or on their attaining 16, to remove them and receive others, 18 G. 3, c. 18, s. 7.

Bye laws

Also to make bye-laws, and to revoke and amend them for the government of the Corporation and Schoolmasters, officers, servants, and children, and for auditing the accounts, 18 G. 3. c. 18, s. 8.

Contribution out of parish taxes

The Justices and Vestry were also empowered to apply not exceeding £500 (£300 sterling) per annum, out of the Parish Tax towards the Free School, to be paid to the Trustees, or any person appointed by them, 18 G. 3, c. 18, s. 9.

Incidental expenses

The Trustees were further empowered to discharge all incidental expenses, 18 G. 3, c. 18, s. 10.

Perpetual annuity of £270

A perpetual annuity of £270 secured to the School in lieu of an investment of £2700, 28 V., c. 23.

St. Andrew's Free School.

Establishment

Power given to establish on 2¼ acres of land near Half-Way Tree, given by Nicholas Lawes, with a messuage and buildings thereon, convenient for the purpose, a Free School, for the abiding, dwelling and use of one or more Schoolmasters and Ushers of the Church of England, for instructing, without charge, in reading, writing, Latin, Greek, Hebrew, arithmetic, merchants' accounts and mathematics, children of the parishes of St. Andrew and Kingston, and the children of all who settle to the value of £5 (£3 stg.) or pay £50 (£30 stg.) for the improvement and advancement of the School, to be called " St. Andrews Free School ;" and 7 persons named, of the parishes of St. Andrew and Kingston, were appointed Governors, upon the death, resignation, or departure from the island of any of whom, others of the same parishes, within three months after, shall be chosen by the rest of the Governors or the major part of them, and incorporated as " The Governors of the Free School of St. Andrew," to hold the Free School and all lands and gifts to be given or purchased for the use of the School, and to have a Common Seal for making leases and doing other things, with power to them, or the major part, to appoint Schoolmasters and Ushers, and receive into the School as many poor children as they think fit, to be maintained in proportion to the revenues ; to repair, uphold, and enlarge the buildings, make rules and ordinances under the Common Seal for the government of the School, and of the Masters, Ushers and children, their stipends, and all monies for maintenance not repugnant to any ecclesiastical canons or constitutions of the Church of England ; also to visit the School, reform and redress disorders and abuses, and censure, suspend and deprive Schoolmasters, Ushers and children ; but not to buy, sell, rent or lease for their own benefit any of the lands. In case of the refusal or neglect of the surviving or remaining Governors within 3 months, the Governor of the island may, by letters patent under the broad seal, appoint such persons as he thinks fit to be Governors in the place of those deceased, resigned, or departed from this island, 7 W. 3, c. 1.

Course of education

Trustees

Incorporation

Powers

Governor may supply vacancies if the remaining Governors neglect

ST. JAGO DE LA VEGA FREE SCHOOL.

The President of the Legislative Council, the Speaker of the Assembly, the Members, Custos, Rector and Churchwardens of St. Catherine, the Attorney General, and 3 persons qualified to be returned and sit as Members of Assembly residing in St Catherine, to be elected by the ex officio Governors, were incorporated as the Governors of the Free Grammar School of St. Jago de la Vega, and the sum of £1000 (£600 sterling), devised by Peter Beckford, and all real and personal property, the property of the Free School and Governors, as appointed under the repealed Act, 17 G. 2, c. 10, vested in them, with powers to sue and be sued, have and alter a Common Seal, hold real and personal estate not exceeding £1000, appoint Masters, Mistresses, Teachers, Tutors and Subordinates, allowing them a suitable compensation, and to make bye-laws for the management of its property, and the regulation of its affairs, pecuniary, scholastic or otherwise, 27 V., S. 1, c. 19, s. 2-3. *Trustees* *Incorporation Property* *Powers*

Any 5 may form a Court, the major part of whom are invested with full powers, 27 V., S. 1, c. 19, s. 4. *Quorum*

The site of the present building, and all other real estate may be exchanged or sold, and the proceeds invested in the purchase of other premises in a more favourable situation in the town of St. Jago de la Vega, or to erect a building, suitable for a School, and the accommodation of the Masters, 27 V., S. 1, c. 19, s. 5. *New site for school*

Two annuities, and all arrears of £40 (£24 sterling), and £50 (£30 sterling,) charged by the will of Thomas Barrett, on a Pen in St. Catherine, and by Mary Baldwin, on Tamarind Grove Pen, with all powers for recovery of same, vested in the Corporation, 27 V., S. 1, c. 19, s. 6. *2 annuities and arrears vested in them*

The sum of £600 in the Receiver-General's office, at £10 per cent, interest vested in them, with authority to receive the annual interest of £60 in half-yearly payments, 27 V., S. 1, c. 19, s. 7. *Also £600 in the Receiver-General's Office at £10 per cent*

The Receiver-General shall receive from them such sums as they shall desire to invest, at 6 per cent per annum, in half-yearly payments, 27 V., S. 1, c. 19, s. 8. *Receiver General to receive further Investment at £6 per cent.*

Poor children, those of St. Catherine always to have the preference, have a right to be educated in the Free School, in the Latin and Greek tongues, writing, arithmetic, geography, mathematics, and general mechanical and practical knowledge, and such other branches of education in addition as the Governors shall direct to be taught, without charge ; such children to be admitted in conformity to such conditions as the Governors in their general Court shall impose, 27 V., S. 1, c. 19, s. 9. *Admission of children (those of St. Catherine to be preferred). Course of education. Free of charge*

The Master of the Free School shall act as Secretary, and keep the minute and other books, without further remuneration than is fixed for the Master, 27 V., S. 1, c. 19, s. 10. *Secretary*

The Secretary was directed to summon a general meeting by notice to the ex officio Governors, to be served personally, or left at their residence, one week before the day fixed for the meeting, by the police, for the election of the three elective Governors, and in case no meeting then took place, forthwith to summon another for the purpose; and so for three months, every notice to state the hour of meeting, and all meetings, until the Schoolhouses should be repaired, or a new one purchased or erected, to be held in the Vestry-room of St. Catherine, afterwards in the School-House, and once in every year afterwards the Secretary shall cause an election to take place of 3 Governors according to the above provisions. The meeting to be first called during the first week in March. No out-going elective Governor shall be disqualified for re-election, and any vacancy occurring during the year, shall be filled up according to the above provisions, as soon as practicable. Any elected Governor shall become disqualified to continue in office for any of the causes by law declared disqualifications for any Members of Assembly, Churchwarden or Vestryman continuing to be such, 27 V., S. 1, c. 19, s. 11. *Meetings and choice of elective Governors* *Place of meeting.* *Time* *Vacancies Disqualifications*

If the Governors refuse or neglect to have any election, or to fill up a vacancy in the number of the Governors within 3 months, the Governor of the island may nominate persons qualified, and the Corporation shall not be dissolved by reason of the vacancy, 27 V., S. 1, c. 19, s. 12. *In case of 3 months' neglect, the Governor may fill up vacancies*

All deeds and proceedings shall be exempt from Stamp Duty, 27 V., S. 1, c. 19, s. 13. *Exemption from stamps*

A perpetual annuity of £60 settled upon the School in lieu of the in-vestment of £600, 28 V., c. 23.

ST. JAMES' FREE SCHOOL.

Parochial taxes
for free schools . The Justices and Vestry of St. James were empowered, at the time of laying the Parish Tax, to raise, in the same manner and under the same authority, not exceeding £1400 (£840 sterling,) per annum, to be appropriated for the sole purpose of establishing and maintaining a School or Schools in the parish for the education of youth of either or both sexes, to be called the St. James' Free Schools, 46 G. 3, c. 27, s. 1.

Justices and ves-try prohibited from raising taxes   It shall not be lawful for the Justices and Vestry of any parish to levy or impose any tax under any Act heretofore giving authority, 21 V., c. 44, s. 15.

But may include item in estimates of expenditure, see title "Vestries"   They may, however, include in their estimate of expenditure, items for parochial Schoolmasters, and rent of School-Houses, and any other expenditure sanctioned by any Act of the Legislature, 27 V., S. 1; c. 7, s. 32. Schedule A.

Trustees   For ordering and conducting all matters relating to the Schools, the President of the Council, the Speaker of the Assembly, the Custos, representatives in Assembly, the Rector and Churchwardens, the three Senior Magistrates next to the Custos, and actually residing in the parish, for the time being, together with 3 Freeholders of the parish, to be annually elected at the time of electing Churchwardens and Vestrymen, and in the same manner, and if the Custos is one of the representatives, then 4 Freeholders are to be elected instead of 3, shall be Trustees for the direction and management of the Free Schools, and of the fund to be so raised, and of all the subscriptions, donations, devises and bequests to be given for the Free Schools; 5 of the Trustees to be a quorum to do business, the major part of whom at any meeting, shall be invested with full power, provided a notice of their intended meeting be advertised [in the newspaper printed in the parish, or if none, in that printed nearest to the parish] 2 weekly insertions at the least, 46 G. 3, c. 27, s. 1.

As to filling up vacancies, see s. 9

Now Jamaica Ga-zette, see title

Also the Bishop of Jamaica, in his absence, the Suffra-gan Bishop, see "Clergy," 22 V., c. 23, s. 3   To whom the Bishop of Jamaica was added, with all powers vested in the others, 11 G. 4, c. 4, s. 2.

Incorporation and powers   The Trustees, incorporated as "The Trustees of the St. James' Free Schools," for laying out the fund, and any donations, bequests, devises, benefactions and subscriptions, and other monies, and for governing the Free Schools, and carrying the Act into execution, and may hold lands, sell, demise, lease or assign their funds, securities, possessions or hereditaments, and purchase other estate, real or personal, provided, that on every alienation or transfer of the trust-property, the equivalent or consideration-money be invested to the same uses as the property conveyed or assigned; and have a Common Seal, 46. G. 3, c. 27, s. 2.

Donors when to be also trustees   Any person who, in his lifetime, by deed or otherwise, gives £1000 (£600 stg.) or to that amount in lands, or gives and secures to the Corporation during the existence or continuation of the Schools, an annual sum of £100 (£60 stg.) in aid of the fund, shall become a Trustee with all the powers hereby granted, 46 G. 3, c. 27, s. 3.

To purchase or lease houses for schools for—1st, children of St. James; 2nd, those of other parishes   The Trustees or any 5, convened as before enacted, may lease or purchase land, or build a proper house or houses, with out-houses, or hire one to be appropriated and used as Free Schools, to be devoted in the first place for the reception and education of as many poor white [and other, 11 G. 4, c. 4, s. 1-3] children of the parish, as the Trustees or any 5 think fit, and in the next place as many others as they see proper, 46 G. 3, c. 27, s. 4.

Appoint masters, &c. Treasurer, officers and servants Salaries, &c. Power of removal Generally   And may also appoint one or more Masters, Mistresses or Ushers of the principles of the Church of England, for teaching the children, also a Treasurer, officers, servants and others, and appoint salaries, perquisites, and other rewards for their labour and service, with power to remove and displace them if they improperly conduct themselves, and generally to manage, transact and determine all such other matters, as to them or a quorum shall appear necessary or convenient for carrying on the purposes intended:

Purchase cloth-ing for children   they may import from the United Kingdom, or purchase in the island, decent and good clothing for the poor children, also desks, benches, tables, and

Furniture, school-books, stationery   other furniture, school-books, and other stationery, and upon the children

Remove children   attaining a sufficient age, or having received a sufficient education to be determined by the Trustees, may 'remove or discharge them and receive others, and may expend such sums as in proportion to the revenue and expenses may be convenient, in apprenticing the children, or such of them, and to such professions, occupations or manual trades as they see fit, and in repairing, maintaining, upholding or enlarging the Schools and buildings, and they, or a quorum or a Committee to be appointed at a meeting, may visit the Schools, and order, reform, and redress all disorders and abuses, 46 G. 3, c. 27, s. 5. *[margin: Apprentice them | Uphold buildings | Visit schools and reform abuses]*

And may make bye-laws for the better governing, ordering and establishing the Corporation and Free Schools, Masters, &c., Treasurer, officers, &c., and poor children, disposing of the funds, auditing accounts and directing payment thereof, and revoke, amend and alter same, not contrary to the prerogative or laws. The children to be brought up in the Protestant religion, and the principles and tenets of the Church of England, and none other, 46 G. 3, c. 27, s. 6. *[margin: Make bye-laws | Children to be educated in the tenets of the Church of England]*

They shall not for their private benefit, in their own names, or of others in trust for them, buy, sell, rent or lease any of the lands, or keep in their hands above 30 days, or apply to their own use, or take or borrow upon interest, any money of the Free Schools, but shall place all moneys out at interest upon good security, 46 G. 3, c. 27, s. 7. *[margin: Not to derive any benefit from the trust property | Monies to be invested at interest]*

Offenders against this Act shall forfeit £200 (£120 sterling,) one-third to the Crown for the Island Government, one-third for the Free Schools, and the other third to the informer, to be recovered by bill, &c., with full costs, to be taxed, 46 G. 3, c. 27, s. 8. *[margin: Penalties]*

If any Trustee annually elected, die or depart this Island, the surviving Trustees shall give public notice thereof, and appoint a day within 30 days after his death or departure for the election of another, 46 G. 3, c. 27, s. 9. *[margin: Vacancies in case of elective trustees]*

The accounts shall be made up every year to 28th December, and at the next meeting of the Vestry, under penalty of £5 (£30 sterling) on the Treasurer, laid before them for their inspection, and with a view to their raising a less sum than £1400 (£840 sterling) for the Institution for the ensuing year, if they see fit, 46 G. 3, c. 27, s. 10. *[margin: Accounts to be made up yearly to 28th December, and submitted to the vestry]*

TITCHFIELD FREE SCHOOL.

350 Acres of land previously granted for the purpose of a common for the benefit of the inhabitants of the Town of Titchfield, Portland, vested in "The President of the Legislative Council, the Members of the Executive Committee, the Speaker of the Assembly, the Custos and Members of Assembly, the Rector, and the 4 resident senior Magistrates, and the 2 Churchwardens of Portland, as Trustees of the Free School, of whom the Custos shall be the Chairman, 19 V., c. 40, s. 1. *[margin: Land appropriated for | Trustees]*

And who shall continue a Corporation by the same corporate name of "The Trustees of the Titchfield Free School," and use the same Common Seal, and have the like powers, so far as not altered or affected by this Act, as were given to the Trustees in 26 G. 3, c. 7, s. 1, 19 V., c. 40, s. 2. *[margin: Incorporation Powers]*

The Trustees were incorporated as "The Trustees of the Titchfield Free School; and the 350 acres of land vested in them for erecting a Free School, and as a fund for its endowment and support, 26 G. 3, c. 7, s. 2, with power to demise or lease the lands, and to have a Common Seal for making demises or leases, and doing all other things appertaining to the Corporation, in which Seal shall be engraven Apollo directing Youth to the Temple of Fame, erected on a steep hill, Fame sounding a Trumpet on the top of the Dome, with the motto "Virtute et eruditione", and to be deposited with the Custos, 26 G. 3, c 7, s. 3. *[margin: Powers of previous trustees | Common seal | To be deposited with the custos]*

Also to build a Free School-House, with proper out-houses, and endow the same in proportion to their revenues, and in the meantime, hire one for the dwelling and use of one or more Masters or Ushers for instructing youth, without charge to their parents, in reading, writing, arithmetic, Latin, Greek, mathematics and any other branches of learning the Trustees think proper, with power to them, or the major part of them, to appoint properly qualified persons of the Christian religion and Church of England; upon misbehaviour or disability, to remove them, and fill up vacancies within 3 months, by writing, under their Common Seal, 26 G. 3, c 7, s 4. *[margin: Power to build free schools | Masters and ushers | Removal filling up vacancies]*

C C

To receive children Removal Repair of buildings	To receive into the Free School as many children as they think proper in proportion to the revenues, the children of inhabitants of the town to be preferred, and on misbehaviour or inability, or on attaining 18, to remove them and receive others; and to expend such sums in proportion to the revenues, in repairing, maintaining or enlarging the School and buildings as they think requisite, 26 G. 3, c. 7, s. 5.
Ordinances, see 19 V., c. 40, s. 3	Also under their Common Seal to make rules and ordinances for the government of the School, and the Masters, Ushers and Children, and settling their stipends and allowances, not repugnant to the prerogative or the laws; also to visit the School, and reform and redress disorders and abuses, 26 G. 3, c. 7, s. 6.
Not to benefit from the trust property	Not to keep in their hands for above 30 days, or apply to their own use, or borrow at interest, any moneys of the Free School, nor buy, sell, rent or lease to either of themselves, or to any other for their private use, any of the lands aforesaid, or any other lands given, settled or purchased for the uses aforesaid, 26 G. 3, c. 7, s. 7.
Penalties and recovery	Offenders shall forfeit £500 (£300 sterling), one-third to the Crown for the Island government, one-third for the use of the Free School, one-third to the informer, to be recovered by bill, &c., 26 G. 3, c. 7, s. 8.
Rules and ordinances Suspension Power to annul	No rule or ordinance hereafter made by the Trustees, for the ordering and governing of the School, or the Masters, Ushers and children, or the servants or persons employed by the Trustees about the affairs of the School or of the Trust, and for settling their stipends and allowances, shall have any effect, until 2 calendar months after a true copy thereof, certified as the Governor shall direct, has been laid before him, unless he in the meantime signifies his approbation; and he may at any time, before or after it has come into operation, certify to the Trustees his disallowance, and if then in force, fix the time at which it shall cease to be in force, and it shall cease to be in force from the time limited in the notice of disallowance, 19 V., c. 40, s. 3.
Trustees' accounts	The Trustees shall keep a book in which the accounts of all moneys received and paid in furtherance or in the general management of the trust, shall be fairly and clearly entered, shewing the date when the purpose or occasion for which, and the name of the person from or to whom it has been received or paid; and which shall also distinctly and separately shew what moneys have been received, or paid in the purchase (if made) of sites for the Sobocls, and in the erection, repairs, enlargement or improvement and furnishing of the buildings required by this Act and 26 G. 3, c. 7, and the accounts shall be made up and balanced the 30th September in each year, 19 V., c. 40, s. 4.
To be audited And signed Copy to be sent to the Governor. Persons to examine books, &c.	They shall cause an account of the receipts, payments and disbursements of the Trust to be made up, and stated each year to 30th September, showing the transactions at length, distinguishing and keeping entirely separate what is received and paid in respect of the building account, from those in respect of the general management account, and have the same duly audited by a meeting, adjourned if necessary for the purpose, and signed by the Chairman, and send a copy within 60 days after 30th September to the Governor, who, if he thinks fit, may appoint persons to inspect the accounts and books, and any person so authorized may at all reasonable times, upon producing his authority, examine the books, accounts, vouchers and documents of the Charity at the place where they are directed to be kept by the Trustees, and take copies or extracts, 19 V., c. 40, s. 5.
Trustees' reports to the Governor	The Trustees shall, when required by any requisition or direction of the Governor, render a report in writing, on any matter relating to the state and condition and general management of the Trust, in such form as he directs, 19 V., c. 40, s. 6.
Inspector of schools' report	The Governor may, when he thinks necessary, authorize any Public Inspector of Schools, or any other person he thinks proper, to visit the School, and enquire and examine into its state, condition, conduct, management and discipline, and into any neglects, miscarriages or irregularities of the Masters, Mistresses or Scholars; any person so authorized, upon producing his authority, may at all reasonable times have access to the School, examine the Masters, &c., and have access to the books, papers, &c., at the place where they are directed to be kept, and take extracts and copies, 19 V., c. 40, s. 7.

Wilfully obstructing any Inspector or other authorized person; penalty £5, on conviction before a Justice, or in default of payment immediately or within such time as the Justice appoints, the same or any other Justice, where the offender is or resides, may commit him to prison for 30 days, determinable on payment. The penalty to be returned to the ensuing [Circuit Court] in the usual manner, 19 V., c. 40, s. 8.

Wilful obstruction

The Trustees shall meet for the ordinary discharge of business every quarter, on 31st March, 30th June, 30th September and 31st December, or within 20 days after, on the day for which they are summoned by the Chairman, or in the vacancy of the office by 3 Trustees, but no such meeting shall be held, or any proceedings thereat be valid, unless composed of 3 Trustees, 19 V., c. 40, s. 9

Quarterly meetings

Quorum

In case of the Chairman's absence, the Trustees shall appoint a Chairman pro tempore, by whom the minutes and acts done at the meeting shall be signed, 19 V., c. 40, s. 10.

Chairman pro tem

The Trustees shall cause a book to be kept, in which the minutes or entries of the proceedings shall be written, and the minute or drafts signed by the Chairman, or Chairman pro tem, before the Board adjourns, 19 V., c. 40, s. 11.

Minute book

The Titchfield Free School Amendment Act, 1856, 19 V., c. 40, s. 13.

Short title

VERE DISTRICT SCHOOLS.

The Custos (or in case of his absence from the parish, the senior Magistrate resident therein, s. 31), the Members of Assembly for the parish, the Rector, (Island Curates, 19 V., c. 38, s. 1, also all Clergymen of the Established Church, appointed or to be appointed to officiate in any Church or Chapel of the Established Church in Vere while they hold such appointments, 28 V., c. 29, s. 1.) and Churchwardens, with 2 Tax-payers, qualified as after mentioned, and to be elected annually, or as vacancies occur, for and from each of the (2) Districts, created under 1 V., c. 34, and 9 V., c 44. shall be Trustees and Governors for the establishing, maintaining, management and superintendence of the District Schools contemplated by this Act, 18 V., c. 54, s. 1.

Trustees

S. 5

The election of Tax-payers as Trustees shall be made by the electors, duly registered and qualified to vote for Members of Assembly, and the annual election take place at the time and under the regulations for annual elections of Churchwardens and Vestrymen; and no person shall be eligible as such Trustee unless he be assessed for, and have actually paid direct taxes in his own right to an amount not less than £3, be resident in the District for which he is nominated, and not in arrears for any taxes at the time of election, 18 V., c. 54, s. 5.

Annual election and qualification of district trustees

If any elected Trustee dies, leaves the Island, or ceases to be domiciled in the District for which he was elected, or becomes insolvent, his office shall become vacant, 18 V., c. 54, s. 6.

Vacancies

And the Custos shall summon the voters to meet on a fixed day, within 10 days after such summons, at an hour and place specified within the vacant District, to supply it, 18 V., c. 54, s. 7.

How to be filled up

No proceedings of the Trustees shall be vitiated or affected by any such vacancy, 18 V., c. 54, s. 8.

Not to vitiate proceedings

The Trustees and Governors incorporated as "The Trustees of the District Schools of Vere," with power to take lands on lease, or purchase, sell or exchange same, to have a Common Seal, to be deposited with the Custos or senior-resident Magistrate, and make, and alter, and abolish bye-laws and ordinances for the regulation of the Corporation and persons in its employ, and the administration of the Trusts, 18 V., c. 54, s. 2.

Incorporation

The principal sum of £6256 (being 57-82d parts of £9000 standing at the credit of the Trustees of the Vere Free School in the Receiver-General's books), the proportion allotted to Vere was directed to be transferred to the credit of an account to be opened with the Trustees, who should stand possessed thereof, to carry out the Trusts hereby imposed; such sum to continue to carry interest at £8 per cent. per annum, but not to authorize the Trustees to draw, or the Receiver-General to pay any sums, beyond the annual interest, 18 V., c. 54, s. 3.

Transfer by Receiver-General of £6256

To the order of the trustees

At £8 per cent. interest, interest only to be drawn

Legal estate in real property previously in the trustees of the Vere Free School vested in them

The Trustees were also endowed with all the legal estate in real property previously vested in the Trustees of the Free School of the parish of Vere, and with all the rights and powers they might have lawfully exorcised, with all the benefit of, and to be bound by the covenants made with and by those Trustees, but within 14 days after the receipt of any moneys on account of rents, rent-charges or arrears, must pay to the Receiver-General 25-82d parts, upon Trusts to be declared, 18 V., c. 54, s. 4.

Application of 25-82d parts

Now vested in the trustees of the Manchester District schools, see title

Annual meeting after election of trustees

Immediately after each annual election of Trustees, the Custos shall call a meeting of the Trustees, g i g notice in two consecutive numbers of the Gazette by Authority, or, if none, then in any newspaper, and in default of such meeting being held, shall repeat his calls by other notices, until a meeting is held, 18 V., c. 54, s. 9.

Chairman

At every such meeting, the Trustees shall elect from among themselves a Chairman, then resident in the parish, 18 V., c. 54, s. 10.

Place of meeting

For the transaction of business, the Trustees shall meet at the present School-House near the Alley, or at one of the other School-Houses to be established, as the Trustees may direct, and in case of the Chairman's absence, the board shall elect a Chairman pro tem, and proceed with the business to be brought before it, 18 V., c. 54, s. 11.

Chairman pro tem

3 trustees a quorum

For the transaction of the business of the Trust, any 3 Trustees, including a Chairman, shall constitute a Board, 19 V., c. 38, s. 2.

Quarterly meetings

special meetings, notice of

On requirement of 3 trustees, or by chairman

The Board shall meet once a quarter, on 28th March, June, September and December, or within 20 days after, and may have special meetings as often as necessary, due notice in writing of each special meeting being given by the Clerk affixing the same to the outside of the door of the Parish Church for the space of 8 days immediately before that appointed, and the Chairman shall direct the Clerk to summon special meetings on the requirement of any 3 Trustees, or he may call one without such requisition if he deems it proper. The Board may also adjourn as often as necessary, 18 V., c. 54, s. 12.

Adjournment

Meetings to be convened by notice if not held on quarter days

18 V., c. 54, s. 12

Any Chairman, on failure of a quarterly meeting on any of the days specifically appointed for the meeting, may fix any day after the lapse of 8 days, and within 20 from the day so specifically mentioned, notice to be given as in case of special meetings, 19 V., c. 38, s. 3.

Books to be kept, of property, accounts and proceedings

The Trustees shall cause a book to be kept, containing a statement of all the real and personal property belonging to them, or to be vested in them for the Schools, and shall also cause to be kept separate books of the accounts of the institution, and of their proceedings, 18 V., c. 54, s. 13.

Accounts to be kept by Receiver-General, payment o trustees' orders

Accounts to be annually examined by a board

Signed and countersigned, and transmitted to the Governor to be audited

Inquiries and proceedings to recover outstanding property

The Receiver-General shall keep a separate account of the moneys in his hands belonging to the Trustees, and pay the interest and dividends to their orders, to be drawn and signed at the meetings, and in presence of the Board by the Chairman, countersigned by the Clerk, 18 V., c. 54, s. 14.

An annual account shall be stated up to 28th September by the Clerk, and laid before the next meeting, shewing the receipts and disbursements for the previous year at full length, which, after being examined by that or a subsequent meeting, shall, when found correct, be signed by the Chairman and countersigned by the Clerk, and forthwith forwarded to the Governor, to be audited by a Board of Audit, or Auditor of Public Accounts, 18 V., c. 54, s. 15.

As to interposition of the trustees of Manchester district schools &c., 24 V. c. 9

With Governor's consent

Exemption from stamp

The Trustees shall cause enquiry to be made into all sums of money, donations or other property, real, personal. or mixed, due or to become due to the Trust, whether given to the Churchwardens or to the Justices and Vestry, or otherwise, so as they be available for the purposes of the Trustees, and shall be entitled to proceed at law or in equity to recover the same in their corporate name ; and all reasonable costs incurred shall be allowed in their accounts, but to be instituted and continued with consent of the Governor, and not liable to Stamp Duty, 18 V., c. 54, s. 16.

Reference to arbitration and compromise of claims

Apportionment, &c., of receipts

i. e. 57-82d parts for vere schools, 25-82d for Manchester district school, see that title

The Trustees may refer to arbitration, or compromise any claims to any arrears of rent-charge or annuity, or any sums now or to be due, and accept in lieu and satisfaction such principal sums as they think proper, with the consent of the Governor, or as may be awarded by arbitration, or any Court having jurisdiction, and on payment of such principal sums, to release as well the parties as the lands liable, the principal sums received to be paid into the Receiver-General's office rateably, to be apportioned according to the conditions and trusts declared of the £9000, the interest and dividends of the portion alloted to Vere to be paid to the Trustees, and form part of the annual funds of their Trust, 18 V., c. 54, s. 17.

The Trustees may, as they require, draw, and the Receiver-General pay to them all such sums as have already been or may hereafter be paid by them to the credit of their account, for rents, rent-charges or arrears or otherwise, to be applied for the purpose of carrying out the Trusts of 18 V., c. 54, and may invest any surplus moneys at any time in their hands, or at their credit, for which they have no immediate use, in the Island Treasury, at the rate of £6 per cent. per annum, and apply the interest, as well as the principal of such surplus money, or any part, from time to time, for carrying out the Trusts, 28 V., c. 29, s. 2. *(margin: Trustees' drafts; Investment of surplus moneys)*

Not to affect the rights of the Trustees of the District Schools of Manchester, 28 V., c. 29, s. 3. *(margin: Not to affect the rights of Manchester schools)*

The Trustees may purchase or take on lease as many sites for District School-Houses, in addition to that near the Alley, and build, hire or purchase, keep in repair and furnish School-Houses thereon, in the parish, as they think necessary, and as the funds at their disposal admit, and which shall be free to all persons residing in the parish over 5 and under 15, whom the Trustees select to be instructed in the lower branches of education, such as reading the English language, and so much of writing and arithmetic as to enable them when they come into active life to perform accurately and with despatch the duties of an ordinary business life, and also of receiving religious instruction according to the principles of the United Church of England and Ireland; and may also cause to be imparted to the children practical instruction in agricultural, mechanical and other industrial occupations. Children of parents of other denominations may be admitted, and shall not be obliged to conform to, or be taught the tenets of the Established Church, 18 V., c. 54, s. 18. *(margin: Sites of Schools; Free Scholars; Education; Religious instruction; Agricultural, &c., instruction; Children not of the Established Church)*

The Trustees may also appoint Teachers and fix their salaries, who shall be members of the Established Church, and shall not receive any other fee or reward for teaching in the Schools without the leave of the Trustees according to their rules and regulations. They may remove any Teacher at their pleasure, and upon his manifest neglect of duty or grossly immoral conduct, are required to dismiss him, 18 V., c. 54, s. 19. *(margin: Teachers of Established Church. Salaries, see s. 22; Removal)*

The Trustees shall select and introduce uniform Class-books, and supply the Scholars therewith, and furnish to the Schools other necessary articles and apparatus, 18 V., c. 54, s. 20. *(margin: Books and other articles)*

And may make regulations and bye-laws for the conduct of the Board, the prosperity, order and discipline of the Schools and the Teachers, and the security and preservation of the School-Houses and other property, which may be revised, altered or amended at any special meeting, due notice of any intended alteration, and the substance being given in the summons calling the meeting, 18 V., c. 54, s. 21. *(margin: Bye-laws; Amendments, &c.)*

Every Teacher shall be deemed qualified who holds a certificate from the Bishop or 2 beneficed Clergymen, or any Normal School, under the hands of the persons granting the same, and shall state their belief that the person is well qualified in respect to moral character, learning and ability to teach any District School in the parish of Vere, 18 V., c. 54, s. 22. *(margin: Qualified teachers, see s. 19)*

The Trustees shall be charged with the custody and safe keeping of the School-Houses, as well as of the account books, papers, vouchers and documents belonging to the Trust, and each of them may, at reasonable times, visit and examine the School-Houses, and inspect and take copies and extracts of accounts, &c., at the place they are directed by the Trustees to be kept, 18 V., c. 54, s. 23. *(margin: Trustees to have custody of school-houses, accounts books, &c.)*

They shall make a report up to 28th September in each year, and transmit same to the Governor within 20 days after, signed and certified by a majority of the Trustees making it, and shall specify the number of Schools established, the daily average number of Children taught in each School during the preceding year, the names and salaries of the Teachers, the condition of the School-Houses, the state of the funds, and any other information they deem necessary, 18 V., c. 54, s. 24. *(margin: Annual report to the Governor)*

The Governor may authorize any Public Inspector of Schools, or, in his absence, any other person, to visit the Schools as often as he thinks necessary, and to report thereon, and who shall have free access to, and egress from such Schools, and may at all reasonable times inspect, take copies or *(margin: Inspectors of schools, or others to inspect and report upon the schools. Their powers)*

Penalty for obstructing

extracts of accounts, &c., at the place where they are directed to be kept; penalty on persons wilfully preventing, obstructing such inspection or making extracts, or wilfully neglecting the duty of access to documents, not more than £5, to be recovered before 2 Justices, and paid to the Trustees for the furtherance of the Trusts, 18 V., c. 54, s. 25.

No teacher to be a Vestryman, Churchwarden or Trustee

No Teacher shall be eligible to sit in Vestry, or to act as a Trustee, and his election as Vestryman, Churchwarden or Trustee shall be void, 18 V., c. 54, s. 26.

Perpetual Annuity of £500 9s 7d

A perpetual annuity of £500 9s. 7d. secured to the School in lieu of the investment of £6256, 28 V., c. 23.

WOOLMER'S FREE SCHOOL.

Trustees appointed by 9 G. 2, c. 6

The President or Commander-in-Chief [i. e., the Governor], the 4 senior Counsellors, the Speaker of Assembly, the Chief-Justice, the Custos, 4 senior Magistrates, and Rector of Kingston, and 6 of the inhabitants of the parish, such as the Freeholders should annually elect, with Michael Atkins, the surviving executor of John Woolmer, were appointed Trustees for the direction and management of the donation [under the will of John Woolmer], and of all subscriptions, donatives, devises and bequests, to be afterwards given to or for the use of the Free School, 9 G. 2, c. 6, s. 1.

Additional trustees under 15 G. 3, c. 14

The Representatives in Assembly for Kingston, and the Churchwardens and Vestrymen for the parish were appointed Trustees, to be incorporated into, and taken as part of the Corporation instituted by 9 G. 2, c. 6, and added to the Trustees in that Act, appointed with the like powers, and subject to the like duties and penalties; the 6 annual Trustees, inhabitants of the parish, to be elected by the Freeholders annually on the second Thursday in January, when they are by law summoned and met to choose Vestrymen and other Parochial Officers for the current year, 15 G. 3, c. 14, s. 2.

Superintendence under 18 V., c. 61, s. 19 Repealed acts, 41 G. 3, c. 29, s. 10, 8 V. c. 39, s. 13, in all respects the same

The Common Council of [Kingston] shall have the superintendence, regulation, direction, administration and management of "Woolmer's Free School," and of all the business, concerns and affairs of that institution, and the nomination and appointment of all Officers, Teachers and servants whatsoever necessary to be employed, anything in any former Act of this island to the contrary hereof in anywise notwithstanding, 18 V., c. 61, s. 19.

Incorporation

The Trustees shall be Trustees of the Free School, and of all lands and hereditaments to be given by any person, or purchased by the Trustees for the School, and shall be incorporated as "The Trustees of Woolmer's Free School," and hold lands, gifts and devises for the benefit thereof, 9 G. 2, c. 6, s. 2.

Powers over property Seal

And shall place out at interest, on security, any donations or subscriptions, demise and lease hereditaments, and have a Common Seal for making demises, and doing all other things concerning the Corporation, in which

Custody, 15 G. 3, c. 14, s. 3

shall be engraven the Sun breaking through a cloud, 9 G. 2, c. 6, s. 3.

To build and endow school-house, Course of instruction Appointment and removal of master and ushers Ushers to be of the Church of England

They may erect a proper house with out-offices, and endow the same in proportion to their revenues, for the dwelling and use of one or more Masters, and Ushers for instructing youth without charge, in- reading, writing, arithmetic, Latin, Greek, the mathematics and any other parts of learning the Trustees think proper, and may appoint Masters and Ushers, provided they be of the Church of England, and upon misbehaviour or disability, remove them, and within 3 months after any voidance, by writing, under their Common Seal, appoint others qualified as above, 9 G. 2, c. 6, s. 5.

Scholars

And receive into the Free School as many children as they think proper in proportion to the revenues; and upon misbehaviour or inability, or on attaining 18, remove them, and receive others; and in proportion to the revenues, may repair, maintain, uphold or enlarge the School and buildings, 9 G. 2, c. 6, s. 6.

Rules and ordinances Visiting schools Reform abuses

May, under the Common Seal, make rules and ordinances for the government of the School, the Masters, Ushers and children, and for settling their stipends and allowances, not repugnant to the prerogative or law, and may visit the School, and reform disorders and abuses in the government and management, 9 G. 2, c. 6, s. 7.

Trustees not to benefit by the trust

They shall not keep in their hands above 30 days, or apply to their use, or borrow on interest any sums of money given to or for the use of the Free School, or to become due for interest or rent, nor shall they buy, sell or lease any of the lands or hereditaments, 9 G. 2, c. 6, s. 8.

Offenders against the Act shall forfeit £500 (£300 sterling), one-third to the Crown for the government of the Island, one-third to the Free School, and one-third for the informer, to be recovered by bill, &c., 9 G. 2. c. 6, s. 9. *Penalties*

The Trustees at their first meeting after the second Thursday in January in each year, which shall be on the third Thursday, shall elect and choose some reputable housekeeper inhabiting the parish to be the Treasurer for the current year, whose duty it shall be to attend all meetings, keep a set of books containing the accounts, produce them at every meeting if demanded by a member present, and receive and collect the income and funds, and all sums due or left, or given to the Corporation, and give releases and discharges for them, lease or rent lands, place out at interest monies received by him, and advance same to such persons for the purposes, and upon such securities as directed by order of a meeting of Trustees, confirmed by the succeeding meeting, all bonds, securities and leases to be made and taken in the name of "The Trustees of Woolmer's Free School" only, and the monies to be made payable and reserved to them only. He shall have the custody of the Seal, and deliver it to his successor, and be accountable to the Corporation for his receipts, payments and disbursements, and removable by order of any meeting confirmed by the next, 15 G. 3, c. 14, s. 3. *Treasurer His duties and power* *Custody of seal Accountability and removal*

In case of his death, departure from this Island, or removal from office, the Corporation may, at their next meeting, appoint another reputable house-keeper in the parish, who shall continue Treasurer till the succeeding annual election, and be subject to the like duties, liable in all respects, and have the same powers as the Treasurer annually to be elected, 15 G. 3, c. 14, s. 4. *Vacancies*

The Treasurer shall be entitled to a salary, to be fixed by an order of the first meeting of the Corporation after his election, 15 G. 3, c. 14, s. 5. *Salary*

All meetings, except that on the 3rd Thursday in January, shall be convened by public advertisement, signed by the Treasurer or 3 Trustees, which notice shall be at least 5 days before, 15 G. 3, c. 14, s. 6. *Meetings Notice of*

And shall be held at the Free School house, or at Kingston Church, according to the notice given, between 8 and 12, a. m., 15 G. 3, c. 14, s. 7. *Place of holding*

Any 9 Trustees convened and met, shall be a quorum to make and confirm orders, and transact all business, 15 G. 3, c. 14, s. 8. *9 Trustees, a quorum*

A Perpetual Annuity of £1500 (£900 sterling) settled upon the Trustees, in consideration of their delivering up to be cancelled Island Certificates to the amount of £16000 (£9600 sterling), payable half-yearly by the Receiver-General out of any unappropriated public monies, (40 G. 3, c. 33), which has been increased to the sum of £1044, 28 V., c. 23. * *Perpetual annuity of £900 sterling* *Increased to £1044*

Friendly Societies.

Any number of persons in one or more counties or parishes, may form themselves into a Society to raise, by subscription of members, or by voluntary contributions or donations, a fund for the mutual relief and maintenance of the Members, their Wives, or Children or other relations in sickness, infancy, advanced age, widowhood or other natural state or contingency, whereof the ocurrence is susceptible of calculation by way of average, and to make rules for the government not repugnant to the laws of the United Kingdom, or of this Island, or of this Act, and to impose reasonable fines on Members, and amend or annul rules, 6 V., c. 27, s. 1. *Objects of societies*

The Society, before confirmation of their rules, shall, by rules, declare the purposes for which they are established, and to which their moneys, and the proportions and purposes in or for which they shall be applied, and under what circumstances any Member or other person may become entitled, and the rules shall be enforced, and the moneys not diverted or misapplied by any Treasurer, Trustee, Officer or Member, under such penalty as the Society shall by rule impose, 6 V., c. 27, s. 2. *Purposes of establishment, &c., to be declared by rules*

---

* In extinguishment of the annuity under 40 G. 3, c. 33, and of a subsequent investment of £2400 sterling, at £6 per cent. interest.

Rules to be certified by Savings' Bank Barrister

Two transcripts of all rules, signed by three Members and countersigned by the Clerk or Secretary, shall be submitted to the Barrister appointed to certify the rules of Savings' Banks, who shall advise with the Clerk or Secretary, if required, and give a certificate on each, that they are in conformity to law and this Act, or point out in what points repugnant: His fee, £1 12s ; one of which, when certified, shall be returned to the Society, and the other transmitted to the Clerk of the Crown or his Deputy, if the Society embrace a County, but if a Parish, to the Clerk of the Peace, to be laid before the next (Circuit Court, 19 V., c. 10), to be without motion allowed and filed without fee, and, when certified, shall be binding, 6 V., c. 27, s. 3.

Barristers' fees

The Barrister shall be entitled to no further fee for any alteration, or amendment of any rules upon which one fee has been already paid him within three years. If any rules, alterations or amendments are sent, accompanied with an affidavit of being a copy of any enrolled rules, &c., of any other Society, the Barrister shall certify and transmit them without fee, C V., c. 27, s. 4.

Power to confirm rules on Barristers, refusal to certify

If the Barrister refuses to certify all or any rules, the Society may submit them to the (Circuit Court), with the reasons assigned for rejection, and the (Circuit Court) may confirm and allow them notwithstanding, 6 V., c. 27, s. 5.

Settlement of disputes by arbitration Justices See s. 29, 31.

When the rules provide for a reference to arbitrators, and it appears to a Justice, upon complaint of a Member, or of any person on account of such member, that application has been made to the Society, or the Steward, or other Officer, to have any dispute so settled by arbitration, and has not within 40 days been complied with, or that the arbitrators have refused or neglected to make any award, the Justice may summon the Trustee, Treasurer, Steward or other officer against whom the complaint is made, and 2 Justices may determine the matter in dispute, as if the rules had directed any matter in dispute should be decided by Justices, 6 V., c. 27, s. 6.

Expelled members

If any Member is expelled, and the arbitrators or Justices award or order he shall be re-instated, they may award or order in default of such re-instatement to the Member expelled a reasonable sum, which, if not paid, shall be recoverable from the Society or the Treasurer, &c., in the same way as monies awarded by arbitrators, 6 V., c. 27, s. 7.

Rules to be entered in book for inspection

No Society shall have the benefit of this Act, unless all the rules are entered in a book, to be kept by an Officer open for the inspection of Members, and fairly transcribed, and the transcript deposited with the Clerk of the Crown or his Deputy, or Clerk of the Peace, but not to prevent any alterations or repeal, or making new rules as shall be provided, which shall not be in force until entered and certified, and a transcript deposited with the Clerk of the Crown, &c., nor until confirmed, 6 V., c. 27. s. 8.

Rules to be binding Evidence of

All rules in force entered and confirmed shall be binding on the Members, officers, and contributors and their representatives, who shall have notice thereof by such entry and contribution [confirmation], and the entry or transcript, or an examined copy, shall be evidence. No certiorari or other process shall be allowed to remove any rules ; and true copies of transcripts shall be made without fee, except at the rate of 1s. 6d. for every 160 words, 6 V., c. 27, s. 9.

Alteration of rules

No confirmed rules shall be altered, rescinded or repealed, unless at a general meeting, convened by public notice, written or printed, signed by the Secretary, President or other principal officer or Clerk, in pursuance of a requisition by 7 Members (which requisition and notice shall be publicly read at the two usual meetings of the Society to be held next before such General Meeting for the purpose of alteration or repeal, unless a Committee has been nominated for the purpose at a general meeting convened in manner aforesaid, in which case the Committee shall have the like power to make such alterations or repeal), and unless made with the consent of three-fourths of the Members present, or of such Committee, 6 V., c. 27, s. 10.

Rules to specify places of meeting and powers of members, officers &c Alteration of places of meeting

The rules shall specify the places to hold meetings, and provisions with respect to the powers and duties of the Members at large, and of the Committees or Officers. Any Society may alter their places of meeting, upon notice to the Clerk of the Peace 7 days before or after removal, signed by the Secretary or principal officer and 3 Members, such place to be within the County or parish in which the rules are enrolled, 6 V., c. 27, s. 11.

The Society may, at any usual meeting, or by their Committee, elect a Steward, President, Warden, Treasurer or Trustee, and Clerks and other Officers for such time and purposes as shall be fixed by the rules, and fill up vacancies. The Treasurer, &c., appointed to any office, touching the receipt, management or expenditure of money (if required by the rules) shall become bound in a bond (Form Schedule), with two sureties, for the faithful execution of his office, and rendering an account according to the rules, and in all matters lawful, to pay obedience to the same, in such penalty as the major part of the Society at any such meeting deem expedient to be given to the Clerk of the Crown or Peace, without fee, and in case of forfeiture, may be sued for in his name for the use of the Society, they indemnifying him from costs. Bonds not chargeable with Stamp Duties, 6 V., c. 27, s 12. *Election of officers* *Security* *No stamp*

The Society may appoint any Committee, the number to be declared in the rules, and delegate to them all or any of the powers given by this Act, their powers being declared in the rules confirmed and filed. Where a Committee is appointed for any particular purpose, their powers shall be reduced to writing, and entered in a book by the Secretary or Clerk, and a majority shall be necessary to concur in any act of such Committee, who shall act in the name of the Society, and their acts and orders under the powers delegated to them shall have the same force as those of the Society at a general meeting. Their transactions shall be entered in a book belonging to the Society, and liable to the review. allowance or disallowance and control of the Society, as by their general rules confirmed and filed directed, 6 V., c. 27, s. 13. *Committees*

The Treasurer and Trustee shall, with the consent of the Society, to be testified as directed by general rules, lay out such of the moneys of the Society as its exigencies shall not immediately call for, on real securities, or in the purchase of real estate, to be approved of and taken in the name of the Treasurer or Trustee for the time, or invest them in the Public Treasury, or any Savings'-Bank or Chartered Bank of this island, but not otherwise, in the name of the Treasurer or Trustee, and with such consent, may alter, tranfer or sell the same, the dividends, interest and proceeds to be brought to account and applied according to the rules, 6 V., c. 27, s. 14. *Treasurer Investment of funds*

Any person who receives any moneys, effects or funds, or is entrusted with the disposal, management or custody thereof, or of any securities, books, papers or property relating to the same, shall, upon demand, or notice in writing, in pursuance of any order of the Society or Committee, give in his accounts at the usual meeting of the Society, or to such Committee, to be examined and allowed or disallowed, and, on the like demand or notice, pay over all the moneys in hand, and assign and deliver the securities, &c., to the Treasurer or Trustee, or as the Society or Committee shall appoint; and in case of neglect, the Society may, in the name of the Treasurer or Trustee, or other principal officer, petition the Chancellor, who may proceed in a summary way, and make such order, upon hearing all parties concerned, as seems just, which shall be final : and all assignments, sales and transfers in pursuance thereof good, 6 V., c. 27, s. 15. *Accountability* *Chancery Jurisdiction*

When any Trustee is out of the jurisdiction, idiot, lunatic or of unsound mind, or it is unknown or uncertain whether living or dead, or refuses to convey or assure to the person nominated in his stead, either alone or with any continuing Trustee, the Chancellor may appoint a person in his name to convey, &c., which shall be valid, 6 V., c. 27, s. 16. *In cases of transfers of land*

When any Trustee of transferable stock, &c., is absent, &c., bankrupt, insolvent or lunatic, &c., the Chancellor may direct the Receiver-General, Secretary, Deputy, Manager or other officer of the Treasury, Savings' Bank or Chartered Bank to transfer such stock, &c., into the name of such person as the Society shall appoint, and pay over to him the dividends, &c.; and when one or more only, and not all the Trustees are absent, &c., the Chancellor may direct the others who shall be forthcoming, ready and qualified to act, to transfer the stock, &c., and receive and pay over the dividends as the Society shall direct, which transfers and payments shall be valid, 6 V., c. 27, s. 17. *Stock*

No fee or gratuity shall be demanded or taken by any officer of such Court ; and, on petition, the Judge may appoint Counsel and a Practitioner to carry on the petition on behalf of the Society, without fee or reward, 6 V. c. 27, s. 18. *No fees to officers of court, counsel or solicitor*

Orders for transfers of securities

Where orders are made for transfer of securities, &c., transferable at the Treasury or Savings' Bank, or Chartered Bank, the persons to be named shall be the Receiver-General, Secretary, Deputy Secretary or Manager, except where one or more Trustees are ordered to transfer without the concurrence of the others, 6 V. c. 27, s. 19.

Discharges for acts done thereunder

This Act shall be a full discharge to the Receiver-General, &c., for acts done pursuant thereto, and their acts shall not be impeached in any Court to their detriment, 6 V. c. 27, s. 20.

Preference of demands of Society over other debts

If any person entrusted with keeping the accounts, or having any moneys, deeds or effects of the Society, die, become insolvent, or have any extent, execution, attachment, &c., against his lands, goods, &c., or make any assignment, disposition or conveyance, for the benefit of his creditors, heirs, assignees or other persons having legal right, the Sheriff or other officer shall, within 40 days after, demand, in writing, by order of any Society or Committee assembled at any meeting, deliver and pay over all moneys and things belonging to the Society to such person as the Society or Committee appoint, and pay out of the estate, assets or effects, real or personal of such person, all moneys remaining due, which he received by virtue of his office or employment before any other debts, or the money directed to be levied is paid over to the party issuing the process, and such assets, lands, &c., shall be bound to the payment accordingly, 6 V., c. 27, s. 21.

Property vested in Treasury for the time

Powers in civil and criminal proceedings relating to society

All real and personal estate, securities, rights and claims of the Society shall be vested in the Treasurer or Trustee for the time, for the benefit of the Society, and Members according to their interests, and after the death or removal of any Treasurer or Trustee, shall vest in his successor without any assignment or conveyance, except the transfer of stock or securities in the Treasury, Savings' Bank or Chartered Banks, and for all purposes of action or suit, criminal or civil, shall be deemed and stated to be the property of the Treasurer or Trustee, in his proper name, without further description; and he may bring or defend actions or suits, civil or criminal, touching the rights of the Society, if duly authorized, with the consent of a Meeting of the Society or Committee, in his proper name, without other description; and no proceeding shall abate by his death or removal, but may be proceeded with in the name of the successor, who shall pay or receive costs as if the suit had been commenced in his name, for the benefit of, or to be reimbursed from the funds of the Society, 6 V. c. 27, s. 22.

Members competent witnesses

Members shall be competent witnesses in actions, indictments, &c., and proceedings before Justices, notwithstanding any interest they may have, 6 V., c. 27, s. 23.

Responsibility of treasurer for losses

No Treasurer, Trustee or other officer shall be liable to make good any deficiency in the funds, unless he declares, by writing, to be deposited and registered with the rules of the Society, that he is willing to be so answerable, and each of them, or they, may collectively limit their responsibility to a sum specified in such writing; but they shall be personally responsible for all moneys actually received by them on account of the Society, 6 V., c. 27, s. 24.

Payments after decease of members

Payment after the decease of a member to any person who at the time appears to the Trustees entitled to the effects of a deceased intestate Member, shall be valid with respect to any demand of any next of kin, or representatives of such Member against the funds of the Society or the Trustees; but they shall have remedy against the person who received the same, 6 V., c. 27, s. 25.

If not exceeding £30 without letters testamentary or administration

If any Member die entitled to not exceeding £30, the Trustees or Treasurer, if satisfied there is no Will left, and no Letters of Administration will be taken out, may pay the same according to the rules, and if there are none, may divide the same among the persons entitled to the effects of the deceased, without Letters Testamentary or of Administration, 6 V., c. 27, s. 26.

Powers of justices in case of fraudulent imposition on funds

For more effectually preventing fraud and imposition on the funds by any officer, Member or person, being or representing himself to be a Member, or the Nominee, Executor, Administrator or Assignee of a Member, or any other person who, by any false representation or imposition, fraudulently obtains possession of any moneys of the Society, or having in his possession any sum belonging to the Society, fraudulently withholds the same, and for which offence no especial provision is made in the rules, any Justice of the parish within which the Society is held, upon complaint of an Officer of the Society, may summon the party before 2 Justices, who, upon proof of the fraud, shall convict him, and award double the amount of the money fraudulently obtained or withheld, to be paid to the Treasurer for the purposes of the Society, with costs, not exceeding 10s. If the money is not paid within the time specified in the order, the Justices may issue a warrant of distress, and in default of distress, shall commit the offender to hard labor not exceeding 3 calendar months. Not to prevent the Society from proceeding by indictment or complaint, but no party shall be so proceeded against if a previous conviction has been obtained, 6 V., c. 27, s. 27.

Not to prevent proceedings by indictment

No Society shall, by any rule at a general meeting or otherwise, dissolve, so long as the intents and purposes remain to be carried out, without the votes of consent of 5-6ths in value of the existing Members, to be ascertained as after mentioned, and that of all persons then receiving or entitled to receive relief from the Society, either on account of sickness, age or infirmity, to be testified under their hands individually or respectively. For the p   of ascertaining the votes of 5-6ths in value, every Member shall be entitled to one vote, and an additional vote for every five years he has been a Member, but none shall have more than 5 votes in the whole. In all cases of dissolution, the intended appropriation or division of the funds or property shall be stated in the proposed plan of dissolution prior to the consent. No Society shall, by any rule, direct the division of the stock, or any part, other than for carrying into effect the general intents and purposes of the Society, declared and confirmed as aforesaid, but all rules for dissolution and distribution contrary to the rules confirmed and filed, shall be void ; and in the event of division or misappropriation of the funds without the consent declared to be requisite, the Trustee or other Officer, or person aiding or abetting therein, shall be liable to the like penalties as provided for in cases of fraud, 6 V., c. 27, s. 28.

Dissolution

Ascertaining votes

Provision shall be made by the rules, whether a reference of every matter in dispute between any Society or person acting under them, and any individual Member, or person claiming on account of any Member, shall be made to Justices of the parish, or to arbitrators to be appointed as after-directed, and if to be referred to arbitration, certain arbitrators shall be named and elected at the first meeting of the Society or general Committee, to be held after the enrolment of its rules, none of the arbitrators being beneficially interested directly or indirectly in the funds of the Society, of whom a certain number, not less than 3, shall be chosen by ballot in each case of dispute, the number and mode of ballot being determined by the rules, and the names of the arbitrators entered in the book of rules ; and in case of the death, refusal or neglect of any or all the arbitrators to act, the Society or General Committee may, at their next meeting, appoint one or more to act in the place of those dying, &c., and the award made by the arbitrators, or the major part of them, shall be in the form annexed, and conclusive without appeal, or being subject to the control of any Justice, nor removeable into any court of law, nor restrainable by injunction ; and in case of refusal to comply with the decision, any Justice, upon proof of the award, and the refusal to comply therewith, on complaint by or on behalf of the party aggrieved, may summon the party, and any two Justices may proceed to make order therein, and if the money awarded and costs, not exceeding 10s., be not immediately paid, may, by warrant, cause the sum and costs to be levied by distress, or by distress and sale of the moneys, goods, chattels, securities and effects belonging to the party, or to the Society, with all further costs and charges attending the distress and sale or other legal proceeding, returning the surplus, if any, to the party, or to the Society, or one of the Treasurers or Trustees, and in default of such distress being found, or such legal proceeding being ineffectual, then to be levied by distress and sale of the proper goods of the party or officer of the Society so neglecting or refusing, by other legal proceedings, together with such further costs and charges as aforesaid, returning the surplus, if any, to the owner. Whatever sum shall be paid by any officer so levied on his property or goods, in pursuance of the award of the arbitrators or order of the Justices, shall be re-paid, with all damages to him, out of the mo-

Rules to provide for references to arbitrators or justices

Awards conclusive and enforceable by justices

Order
Warrant of distress

neys belonging to the Society, or the first moneys to be thereafter received, 6 V., c. 27, s. 29.

Powers of justices where disputes are to be decided by them

If it is directed by the rules, that any matter in dispute shall be decided by Justices, any Justice, on complaint of any refusal or neglect to comply with the rules by any Member or officer, may summon the party complained of, and 2 Justices may determine the complaint according to the rules ; and if they adjudge any sum to be paid by the party complained of, and he does not pay the money to the person, and at the time specified, shall enforce their award in the manner directed, in case of neglect to comply with the decision of arbitrators, 6 V., c. 27, s. 30.

Their sentences final

The sentences, orders, and adjudications of Justices shall be final, and not subject to appeal, nor removable into a court of law, or restrainable by injunction, 6 V., c. 27, s. 31.

Society may recieve donations

Any Society may receive donations, which shall be applicable to the general purposes, in like manner as contributions of Members, and not otherwise, 6 V., c. 27, s. 32.

Minors members

Minors may become Members, execute instruments, give acquittances, and enjoy the privileges, and be liable to the responsibilities of Members of matured age, if admitted with the consent of their Parents, Masters or guardians, 6 V., c. 27, s. 33.

Annual statements, Copies

The rule shall provide that the Treasurers, Trustees, Stewards or other principal officer shall, once a-year at least, prepare or cause, &c., a general statement of the funds and effects of the Society, specifying in whose custody or possession they are then remaining, with an account of the moneys received and expended by or on account of the Society since the publication of the preceding periodical statement, attested by two Members appointed Auditors, and countersigned by the Clerk or Secretary ; and every member shall be entitled to receive from the Society a copy of such statement, on payment of such sum as the rules require, not exceeding 6d., 6 V., c. 27, s. 34.

5 yearly returns of sickness and mortality

Every Society established or to be established, shall, within 3 months after the expiration of the month of June, and so again within 3 months after the expiration of every further period of 5 years, transmit to the Clerk of the Peace a return of the rate of sickness and mortality experienced by the Society, within the period of 5 years, according to form in Schedule, a copy of which shall be annexed to the rules, 6 V., c. 27, s. 35.

To be transmitted to the Governor and Assembly

Which returns shall be transmitted at the periods mentioned to the Barrister by whom the rules were certified, and be by him transmitted to the Governor and House of Assembly when sitting, 6 V., c. 27, s. 36.

Further returns

The Barrister, within one month after the expiration of September, and so again within 3 months after the expiration of every further period of 5 years, shall transmit to the Governor a list of the Societies enrolled during such period, specifying their names, the places where established, date of enrolment and time of ceasing to exist (if such case should arise), and a copy of the returns of sickness and mortality, a copy of which, with the Schedule attached, shall be laid before the Assembly within 1 month, if the House is sitting, or within one month after they next sit, 6 V., c. 27, s. 37.

No fees on oaths

No fee shall be charged to any Member for any oath he may be legally required to make before a Magistrate to obtain payment of his sick-pay or allowance 6. V., c. 27. s. 39.

SCHEDULE.

Security bonds A

Know all men by these Presents, that we, A. B., of   (Treasurer or Trustee, &c.) of the   Society, established at   in the parish of   , in the county of   , and C. D. of   and G. H. of   , as sureties on behalf of the said A. B.) are jointly and severally held and firmly bound to E. F., the present

Clerk of the Peace for the parish or city (as the case may be) of   in the sum of   , to be paid to the said E. F. as such Clerk of the Peace or his successor, or Clerk of the Peace of the said (city or parish) for the time being, or his certain Attorney, for which payment, well and truly to be made, we jointly and severally bind ourselves, and each of us, by himself, our, and each of our heirs, executors and administrators firmly by these presents. Sealed with our Seals.

Dated the   day of   , in the year of our Lord, 18

Whereas the above bounden A. B. hath been duly appointed (Treasurer or Trustee, &c.) of the   .   Society, established as aforesaid, and he, together with the above bounden C. D. and G. H. as his sureties, have entered into the above-written bond, subject to the condition hereinafter contained. Now therefore the condition of the above-written bond is such, that if the said A. B. shall and do, justly and faithfully, execute his office of Treasurer (or Trustee) of the said Society, established as aforesaid, and shall and do render a just and true account of all moneys received and paid by him, and shall and do pay over all the moneys remaining in his hands, and assign and transfer, or deliver all securities and effects, books, papers and property of, or belonging to the said Society in his hands or custody to such person or persons as the said Society shall appoint according to the rules of the said Society, together with the proper or legal receipts, or vouchers for such payments, and likewise shall and do in all respects, well and truly and faithfully perform, and fulfil his office of Treasurer (or Trustee, &c.,) to the said Society according to the rules thereof, then the above-written bond shall be void, and of none effect, otherwise shall be and remain in full force and virtue.

We, the major a of the arbitrators, duly appointed by the   Society, established at   in the parish of   , in the county of   , do hereby award and order that A. B., (specifying by name the party or the officer of the Society), do, on the   day of   pay to C. D. the sum of   (or we do hereby re-instate in or expel A. B. from the said Society, as the case may be) | Awards B

Dated this   day of   18

E. F.
G. H.

SCHEDULE C.

Returns of sickness and mortality, C

List of Members of the   Society, held at   , established on the

with a Return of the Sickness and Mortality experienced therein for the period of five years, commencing

and ending

Names.	Trade or Profession.	Date of Birth.	Date of Admission into the Society.	Date of becoming a full Member.	For what time entitled to Relief on account of Sickness.								For what time entitled to Relief on account of Superannuation.								Date of Death.	Place of Residence at time of Death.	Remarks.
					In 18		In 18		In 18		In 18		In 18		In 18		In 18		In 18			
					Weeks.	Days.	Weeks.	Days.	Weeks.	Days.	Weeks.	Days.	Weeks.	Days.	Weeks.	Days.	Weeks.	Days.	Weeks.	Days.		

Gaming, Lotteries, Raffles, Loose and Disorderly Persons.

If any person having received a License to retail Liquors, keep or suffer any common gaming in their houses, they shall forfeit £10 (£6 sterling) and whosoever shall, by false dice, or other fraud or deceit, win any money or other things, shall forfeit treble the value, on conviction. No sum exceeding 40s. (24s. sterling) won at any game, or betting on the side of any, shall be recoverable; and all bonds, contracts and securities for above the sum won as aforesaid shall be void, 33 C. 2, c. 5, s. 3.

Retailers not to suffer common gaming in their houses. Winning money by false dice, &c. No more than 24s stg. recoverable for moneys won at any game or betting

Penalties shall be one-half to the informer who sues in any Court of Record, 33 C. 2, c. 5, s. 5.

Recovery and application of penalties

Any person erecting, setting up, continuing or keeping any office or place under the denomination of a sale of houses, lands, plate jewels, goods or other things, by way of lottery, or by lots, tickets, numbers or figures, cards, raffle or dice, or making, printing, advertising or publishing, or causing to be made, &c., proposals or schemes for advancing small sums of money, by several persons, amounting in the whole to large sums to be divided among them by chances of the prizes in such lottery, or delivering out, or causing or procuring, &c., tickets to the persons advancing such sums, to entitle them to a share of the money so advanced according to such proposals or schemes; or exposing to sale any houses, &c., by any game, method or device, depending upon, or to be determined by any lot or drawing, whether out of a box or wheel, or by cards, raffle or dice, or by any machine, engine or device of chance of any kind, shall, upon conviction before 2 Justices, upon oath of a witness, or upon view of such Justice or Justices, or confession, forfeit £200 (£120 sterling) to be levied by distress and sale, and suffer imprisonment not exceeding 3 months; and until the fine is paid, to be applied when recovered after deducting the reasonable charges of prosecution, one moiety to the informer, or, if convicted on the view of 2 Justices, the moiety shall not go to the Justices, but to the poor of the parish, 13 G. 3, c. 19, s. 7.

Making or publishing proposals for lottery

Penalty

All persons who purchase any ticket or share, or be adventurers in any lottery or sale as aforesaid, shall, on conviction as above, forfeit £20 (£12 sterling), to be recovered and applied as before, 13 G. 3, c. 19, s. 2.

Adventures

All sales of houses, &c., by any game at dice or raffle, lottery, machine, engine or other device, depending upon, or to be determined by chance or lot, shall be void, and the houses, &c., set up to sale shall be forfeited to such person, who shall sue for the same in the Supreme Court, 13 G. 3, c. 19, s. 3.

Sales by lottery void. And the property forfeited to him who will sue

Power of appeal, 13 G. 3, c. 19, s. 4.

If any person is convicted of erecting, setting up, maintaining or keeping any lottery, or exposing to sale any houses, &c., by any lottery or other device, or in either of them shall adventure, and has not sufficient goods whereon to levy the penalties, and does not immediately pay the penalty, or give sufficient security for the same, the Justices may commit him to the County Goal for not exceeding 3 months, 13 G. 3, c. 19, s. 5.

Imprisonment in default of goods

If any Justice neglect or refuse to do what is required of him, he shall forfeit £10 (£6 sterling) to be recovered before any one Justice, one moiety to the person who shall sue, the other to the poor; the prosecution to be commenced within 6 months after refusal, 13 G. 3, c. 19, s. 6.

Justice refusing to act

Any action against any person for anything done under this Act shall be commenced within 3 calendar months after, and be laid in the county where the cause of action arises. The defendant may plead the general issue, and give the special matter in evidence, If the Plaintiff become non-suited or discontinue, or if upon verdict or demurrer judgment is given against him, the Defendant (instead of treble costs, shall receive such full and reasonable indemnity as to all costs, charges and expenses incurred in and about the action as shall be taxed, subject to be reviewed as any other taxation of costs, 8 V. c. 28, s. 22,) and shall have remedy as in other cases therefore, 13 G. 3, c. 19, s. 7.

Protection from actions

No person shall, by himself, deputy, servant or other person, for his gain or lucre, erect, set up, continue or keep, hold, occupy, exercise or maintain

Penalty on keepers of gaming houses

any common gaming-house or other place for playing at the games of shovel-board, pharoh, ace of hearts, passage and hazard, or for playing at any games with cards, or with any machine or device of chance of any kind (billiards, backgammon, skittles, nine-pins and bowls only excepted) under penalty, recoverable before a Justice, not exceeding £200 (£120 sterling) nor less than £10 (£6 sterling), or imprisonment in the County Goal (or nearest prison, see Prisons, 20 V.. c. 11, s. 42), not exceeding 6 months, nor less than 3 months, or both fine and imprisonment, such sums to be levied by distress and sale, and after deducting the reasonable charges of prosecution, to be applied, one moiety to the informer, and imprisonment enforced by warrant of one Justice, 39 G. 3, c. 7, s. 2.

On persons using and haunting such houses and playing or betting

Every person using and haunting any of the said houses and places, and being there adventurers in any of the games of shovel-board, &c., cards, or at any game played with any machine, &c., or therein playing, setting at, staking, or pointing at or betting on the side of or against such as play at any such game, (billiards, backgammon, and the other games now played with the backgammon tables, skittles, nine-pins and bowls only excepted) shall, on conviction before a Justice, forfeit not less than £10 (£6 sterling), and not exceeding £100 (£60 sterling), or suffer imprisonment in the County Gaol, [see sup. s. 2.] for not less than 5 days and not exceeding 30 days, such sums to be sued for, recovered and disposed of as aforesaid, 39 G. 3, c. 7, s. 3.

Certiorari, want of form

No complaint shall be removed by certiorari or other process into the Supreme Court, until judgment has been given, nor shall any conviction or judgment be set aside for want of form, in case the fact alleged in the conviction is proved to the satisfaction of the Court, 39 G. 3, c. 7, s. 4.

What private houses to be deemed common gaming houses for lucre

All private houses and other places where loose and dissolute persons meet, and where the games before-mentioned, some or one of them are played at or carried on, and riots or disorders are committed, shall be deemed common gaming-houses for lucre, and all persons haunting and playing at any of the games there shall be liable to the penalties, 39 G. 3, c. 7, s. 10.

Justices may enter houses and arrest the keepers and frequenters, see 7 V., c. 14, s. 12; 18 V., c. 46, s. 2

Every Justice, on information upon oath, may enter into houses and places where such games are holden, exercised, used, occupied or played at, and as well the keepers as also the persons there haunting and resorting and playing, arrest and imprison, 39 G. 3, c. 7, s. 11.

Penalties on justices and goalers neglecting their duty

If any Justice neglect or refuse to do what is required of him by this Act, he shall forfeit £20 (£12 sterling), and if any Deputy-Marshal, or keeper of any County Gaol neglect or refuse to receive any prisoner sent to him by warrant of a Justice to be imprisoned, or shall not keep him within the walls during the whole of the time prescribed by such warrant, he shall forfeit £100 (£60 sterling), one moiety of which penalties shall go to the informer, to be recovered by action of debt, &c., 39 G. 3, c. 7, s. 12.

Prosecutions

All prosecutions shall be commenced within 6 months, 39 G. 3, c. 7, s. 13.

Raffles and lotteries public nuisances

All games and lotteries to be determined by the chance of cards and dice, and proposals or schemes for the sale of plate, jewels, goods and other things, to be determined by raffles, by mathematical engines or machines and by other indirect ways, are common and public nuisances, and all grants, patents and licenses for such lotteries void, 39 G. 3, c. 7, s. 14.

And patents, &c. void
Penalties on makers of lotteries

No person shall publicly or privately exercise, keep open, show or expose to be played at, drawn at or thrown at, or shall draw, play or throw at any such lottery, either by dice, lots, cards, balls or any other numbers or figures, or any other way, or shall expose to sale any house, land, plate, jewels or other goods by any lottery, game, method or device, depending on or to be determined by any lot or drawing, whether out of a box or wheel, or by cards or dice, or by any machine, engine or device of chance of any kind, and every person that shall exercise, expose, offer or shew to be played, thrown or drawn at, any such lottery, play or device, upon conviction before one Justice shall forfeit £100 (£60 sterling), to be levied by distress and sale, by warrant of 2 Justices, which forfeitures, after deducting the charges of the prosecution, shall be applied, one moiety to the informer, 39 G. 3, c 7, s. 15.

All adventurers in any lottery or sale, shall forfeit £10 (£6 sterling), to be recovered, applied and disposed of as the forfeiture last-mentioned, 39 G. 3, c. 7, s. 16.

On adventurers

If any suit be brought for anything done under this Act, the Defendant may plead the general issue, "not guilty," and give the special matter in evidence, that it was done under this Act, and if it appear to be so done, or if the action is brought after the time limited, the Jury shall find a verdict for the Defendant, or if the Plaintiff become non-suited, or suffer a discontinuance, or a verdict pass against the Plaintiff, the Defendant shall have [treble costs ; see however Costs, 8 V., c. 28, s. 21], and the like remedy as Defendants in other cases, 39 G. 3, c. 7, s. 17.

Protection against actions

If two or more persons make oath, in writing before a Magistrate, that any house, or room or place is kept and used as a common gaming-house, or that any parties have assembled, or are to assemble in any house, premises or other place, for the purpose of gambling, such and any other Magistrate to be associated with him may, by order in writing, authorize any Constables to enter into any such house, &c., whether by day or night, with all necessary assistants, (and if required, to use force for the purpose of effecting such entry, whether by breaking open the door or otherwise,) and to take into custody all persons found therein, and to seize all tables and instruments of gaming, and all moneys and securities for money found in such house, &c. and take the persons, instruments of gambling and moneys so found before such or any two Magistrates, 7 V., c. 14, s. 12.

Power of magistrates to order constables to enter houses, &c., and apprehend persons, &c.

Every person so found being the owner or occupier of any such house, &c., shall, on conviction, be liable to a penalty of not less than £20 nor more than £40, to be recovered before 2 Magistrates, or may, in the discretion of 3 Magistrates, be committed with or without hard labour, for not less than 6 weeks nor more than 3 months, and, upon conviction, all the moneys and securities for money, and the monies which the tables and instruments of gaming shall be sold for, (which sale the convicting Magistrates are authorized to order) after deducting all charges on condemnation and sale, shall be paid to the Treasurer for the use of the parish, and every other person found in such premises without excuse shall be liable to a penalty not more than £5, 7 V., c. 14, s. 13.

Penalties on keepers and others
For the enforcement, &c. of penalties, see Towns and Communities, 7 V., c. 14, s. 26

It shall not be necessary, in support of any information for gaming, or suffering any games or gaming in, or for keeping or using or being concerned in the management or conduct of a common gaming-house, to prove that any person found playing at any game therein was playing for any money, wager or stake, 7 V., c. 14, s. 14.

Proof that party was playing for money, &c., unnecessary under act

For the more effectual suppression of gaming, and for restraining the idle assembling of persons in disorderly houses, and in lone and unfrequented places and elsewhere, any Justice, on complaint [on oath ; see Justices, 13 V., c. 35, s. 2-10,] of any Policeman or other person, that any house, room, shop or place is a place of common resort for idle and disorderly persons, may order it to be entered by any Policeman or Constable, who may take into custody any persons gambling in such house, &c., and carry them before any Justice, to be holden to bail to appear and answer any charge against them, and in default of security, committed to gaol until they can be brought for trial, 18 V., c. 46, s. 2.

Power of Justice to order police to enter houses, &c. and take into custody persons gambling

Any Policeman or Constable may take into custody any idle and disorderly persons found assembled in any thoroughfare, street, lane or public place in the neighbourhood of any house, wharf, tavern or other premises, or in any street, or other public place in any city or town, who, upon being desired by him to retire, or disperse and leave the place, refuse or neglect immediately to do so, and carry them before any Justice to be holden to bail, or committed as above, 18 V., c. 46, s. 3.

Police may take into custody disorderly persons refusing to disperse

Any 2 Justices may hear and determine complaints against parties who have been held to bail or committed, and upon proof that the parties apprehended are known to be loose and idle, or disorderly persons, and without any visible means of subsistence, may either call upon them to find sureties for good behaviour for 3 calendar months, or commit them to the nearest district or other prison or penitentiary, to be kept to hard labour not exceeding 30 days, 18 V., c. 46, s. 4.

Who may be required to find sureties or be committed

Powers of police to enter gaming houses, &c.

Any Policeman or Constable, on view of, or who has good reason to believe that any loose, idle or disorderly persons assembled in any house, room, shop, yard or other premises, known, kept or used as a gaming or gambling house, have assembled for the purpose of gambling, may take into custody the persons so found assembled, and carry them before any Justice, to be holden to bail, or committed as before, 18 V., c. 46, s. 5.

And who may, upon proof that they were engaged in, or assembled for the purpose of gambling, be committed

Proof that parties were playing for money, &c. unnecessary

Two Justices may hear and determine complaints against such offenders, and upon proof that they were engaged in gambling, or were assembled for the purpose of gambling, may commit and sentence them to imprisonment, with hard labour in the nearest district or other prison, or in the general penitentiary for not exceeding 60 days. It shall not be necessary to prove that they were playing for any money, wager or stake, 18 V., c. 46, s. 6.

Conviction not to be quashed for want of form, or removed into the Supreme Court

No conviction or appeal shall be quashed for want of form, or be removed by certiorari or otherwise into the Supreme Court, 18 V., c. 46, s. 8.

Appeal

Parties aggrieved may appeal, 18 V., c. 46, s. 9.

Governor.

Fees

His fees on letters of naturalization, 35 C. 2., c. 3, s. 2   £5   (£3 Stg.)
His Clerk, for writing it   ....   10s   (6s ")
For confirmation of patent on re-survey, 2 Ann., c. 7, s. 3   ....   10s   (6s. ")
For every oath taken before him as Governor or Ordinary, 10 Ann, c. 4, s. 22   ....   1s 3d (9d ")

Fees of the Great Seal, 10 Ann, c. 4, s. 20 :—

For the Seal for every 100 acres of land patented   10s.   (6s ")
(and so in proportion for a greater or lesser quantity)
Foot-land not exceeding 50 feet square, adding two sides of the square together ....   5s   (3 ")
Every 100 feet or other number above 50   10s   (6s ")
Every order granted for taking up land per 100   2s 6d (1s 6d")
(and so in proportion for a greater or lesser number of acres.)
Sealing a writing of execution of a decree, subpœna or other process   ....   7½d (4½d ")

Salary

His permanent salary £1500, 17 V. c. 29, Sch. A.

Also a further permanent salary of £2000 (£1200 sterling,) 37 G. 3, c. 9., but the latter Act (as also 36 G. 3, c. 32, and 2. G.4, c. 17, both already repealed by 6 V., c. 35) were repealed by 18 V., c. 17, s. 1.

Fees transferred to the public

All fees of the Courts of Chancery and Ordinary, and Escheat and other moneys heretofore collected and paid to the Governor, shall be collected by the Registrar of the Court of Chancery and Island Secretary, and paid to the Receiver-General for the use of the public, 18 V., c. 17, s. 2.

Duration

Until 10th October, 1856, or for such longer period as payment of £3500, on account of the salary to be provided for the Governor is made by the British government, 18 V., c. 17, s. 3.

Perpetual annuity, £6400

Since which Act a perpetual annuity of £6400 has been granted to the Crown, in commutation for the debt due to the Government on the £200,000 loan, under statute, 2 and 3 W. 4., c. 125, and Act, 4 W. 4, c. 2, to be applied in payment of such expenses of the government, and of objects connected therewith, and local improvements here as the Governor may direct, in pursuance of instructions from one of her Majesty's Principal Secretaries of State, 26 V., s. 2, c. 1.

His powers as Ordinary, or with respect to presentations to Churches or Chapels, not controlled, abridged or altered by the Clergy Act, 22 V. c. 23, s. 1. (See title, Clergy).

The commissions or appointments of the First and Second Aid-de-Camp to the Captain-General or Commander-in-Chief, shall not be liable to or chargeable with the additional stamp of £140 (£84 sterling), under 3 G. 4., c. 13, 7 W. 4., c. 35.

Governor's Aide-de-Camp and Private Secretary.

The Governor may apppint any person who has been or is an Officer in the Army, to be Aide-de-Camp and Secretary, and remove him and make a new appointment; salary £300 per annum, payable on the warrants of the Governor, with the advice of the Executive Committee, 27 V., S. 1, c. 20, s. 1.

In force until 31st March, 1869, 27 V. s. 1, c. 20, s. 2.

Governor's Secretary.

Provision made for his salary to the extent of £1200 per annum, 17 V., c. 29, Schedule A. *Salary*

So much of 3 G. 4, c. 13, as relates to the amount of his salary repealed, and he shall be paid under 17 V., c. 29, £1200 per annum, and no more, in satisfaction of all fees under any other Act, and shall continue in respect to such salary, liable to the penalties by 3 G. 4, c. 13, imposed for taking or demanding any fee, sum of money or reward, other than such salary, 18 V., c. 30.

Penalty £500 (£300 sterling), to be recovered by action of debt, one moiety to the informer, and be further incapacitated to bear his office of Secretary, 3 G. 4, c. 13, s. 1. *Penalty for taking fees, &c.*

Besides the duties under any Stamp Act to be in force, there shall b paid for the following Commissions, Appointments, matters and things, the rates mentioned by means of Stamps to be affixed, 3 G. 4, c. 13, s. 2. *Additional stamps*

	CURRENCY.	STERLING.
For every Commission as General in the Militia	£50 0	£30 0
Colonel	25 0	15 0
Major	15 0	9 0
Captain	10 0	6 0
Lieutenant	5 10	3 6
Ensign or Cornet	3 5	1 19
Adjutant	3 5	1 19
Quarter-Master	3 5	1 19
Surgeon	10 0	6 0
Privateers' Commission	30 0	18 0
Presentation to a Benefice	25 0	15 0
Surveyors' Commission, (22 V., c. 40, s. 6)		
Order for Surplusage Land	10 0	6 0
Fiat for Lands on the Quit-Rent Act	5 0	3 0
Special order for Land	5 0	3 0
Common order for "	5 0	3 0
Order for Foot Land in Titchfield	5 0	3 0
Fiat for Land	20 0	12 0
Letters of Preference for an Escheat	1 0	0 12
Fiat on ditto "	1 0	0 12
Fiat for Writ to elect a Coroner	15 0	9 0
Appointment of a Curate	5 0	3 0
Island Barrack-Master	20 0	12 0
Health Officer	10 0	6 0
Physician to a County Gaol	20 0	12 0
Leave of absence to Members of Council or Custos	20 0	12 0
Pilots' Warrant	10 0	6 0
Commission of Custos Rotulorum	50 0	30 0
Of Magistrate or Justice, when by Writ of Association	5 0	3 0
Chief-Justice	100 0	60 0
Leave of absence to	50 0	30 0
Assistant Judge, when by Writ of Association	10 0	6 0
Attorney General	50 0	30 0
Judge of the Court of Vice-Admiralty	30 0	18 0
Receiver-General	50 0	30 0
Provost-Marshal	50 0	30 0
Clerk of the Supreme Court	50 0	30 0
Registrar in Chancery	50 0	30 0
Secretary of the Island	50 0	30 0

	CURRENCY.		STERLING.	
For Agent-General......	£ 50	0....	£ 30	0
Commissary-General of Regulars	50	0....	30	0
Clerk of the Crown	15	0....	9	0
Public Messenger	20	0....	12	0
Crown Surveyor	20	0....	12	0
Assistant Commissary-General, Regulars	20	0....	12	0
Commissioner of Stamps	20	0....	12	0
Master in Ordinary in Chancery	50	0....	30	0
Master Extraordinary	15	0....	9	0
Flags of Truce	20	0....	12	0
Harbour-Master	15	0....	9	0
Interpreter of Foreign Languages	5	0....	3	0
Armourer	5	0....	3	0
Adjutant-General (exempted, 9 V., c. 35, s. 61.)				
Quarter-Master-General	100	0....	60	0
Deputy Adjutant-General	150	0....	90	0
Deputy Quarter-Master-General	150	0....	90	0
Barrack-Master-General	150	0....	90	0
Deputy	150	0....	90	0
Muster-Master-General	150	0....	90	0
Deputy	150	0....	90	0
Judge Advocate-General	50	0....	30	0
Deputy	150	0....	90	0
Deputy Judge-Advocate	10	0....	6	0
Aide-de-Camp to the Commander-in-Chief (except 1st and 2nd, 7 W. 4, c. 35	140	0....	84	0
Island Engineer	20	0....	12	0
Physician-General	100	0....	60	0
Surgeon-General	100	0....	60	0
Apothecary-General	100	0....	60	0
Every Deputy of the 3, above	100	0....	60	0
Surveyor of Public Works	50	0....	30	0
Order to a Minster to publish in Church an intention to apply for a Private Bill	10	0....	6	0
Marshal and Sergeant of Mace to the Court of Vice-Admiralty	20	0....	12	0
Collector of the Customs	20	0....	12	0
Controller of the Customs	10	0....	6	0
Land and Tide Surveyor	10	0....	6	0
Surveyor and Admeasurer of Shipping	10	0....	6	0
Waiter and Searcher	5	0....	3	0
Water-Bailiff	5	0....	3	0
Order to Land and sell Cargo of any Foreign Vessel	6	0....	3	12
Letters of Preference to Escheat Property of a felon convict	20	0....	12	0
Island Storekeeper	30	0....	18	0
Commissary of Militia	100	0....	60	0
Superintendent of Ordnance Stores	100	0....	60	0
Superintendent of Pioneers and working parties, or of Signals and Beacons, Miner-General or Deputy, or Assistant to any of the 3 last, each	200	0....	120	0
Leave of absence to Attorney General	20	0....	12	0
" " Advocate-General	20	0....	12	0
" " Judge of the Court of Vice-Admiralty	20	0....	12	0
" " Acting Receiver-General	20	0....	12	0
" " Registrar in Chancery	20	0....	12	0
" " Island-Secretary	20	0....	12	0
" " Agent-General	10	0....	6	0
" " Quarter-Master General	25	0....	15	0
" " Deputy Adjutant-General	15	0....	9	0
" " Deputy Quarter-Master-General	15	0....	9	0
" " Barrack-Master-General	15	0....	9	0
" " Deputy	15	0....	9	0

			CURRENCY.		STERLING.	
Leave of absence to	Muster-Master-General		£ 15	0....£	9	0
"	"	Judge Advocate-General	15	0....	9	0
"	"	Deputy Judge Advocate-General	15	0....	9	0
"	"	Physician-General	15	0....	9	0
"	"	Surgeon-General	15	0....	9	0
"	"	Apothecary-General	15	0....	9	0
"	"	Deputy Physician-General	15	0....	9	0
"	"	Deputy Surgeon-General	15	0....	9	0
"	"	Deputyl Apothecary-General	15	0....	9	0
		Collector of Customs	10	6....	6	0
		Controller of Customs	5	0....	3	0
		Each Public Officer not before specified	10	0....	6	0

3 G. 4, c. 13, s. 2.

The Stamps imposed on Commissions in the Militia shall be impressed on Commissions of the same rank and description of persons arriving in this island claiming to have rank in the Militia, 3 G. 4, c. 13, s. 3. **Militia Commissions brought to this island**

In addition to the Stamp on Certificates by the Governor of persons having duly qualified under appointments by Her Majesty or the Commissioners of Her Majesty's Customs, there shall be imposed an additional Stamp equal in amount to the fees that would be paid on such appointments if granted by the Governor. No Officer of the Militia shall be compelled to pay twice for the same rank, on any change of Governor or otherwise, 3 G. 4, c. 13, s. 4. **Appointments to the Customs** **Militia Commissions**

All powers, provisions, rules, methods, articles, clauses, penalties and forfeitures, distribution of penalties and other matters prescribed by any Act imposing Stamp Duties, to be passed, and their application by the Receiver-General, shall (as far as applicable) be of force with relation to the duties hereby imposed, and be put in execution for raising and applying such duties, 3 G. 4, c. 13, s. 5. **Powers of future Stamp Acts extended to enforce the duties hereby imposed**

All Commissions, Appointments, matters and things on which a Stamp is hereby imposed, not stamped as directed, shall be void, and any Secretary who issues any such Commission or Appointment, or does any matter or thing not stamped as aforesaid, shall forfeit £500 (£300 sterling), to be sued for, recovered and appropriated as before directed, 3 G. 4, c. 13, s. 6. **Commissions, &c. not stamped as directed, void**

If any person counterfeit, or forge any stamp or mark, provided or made in pursuance of this Act, or counterfeit or resemble the impression upon any paper, parchment or vellum with such counterfeit mark or impression, knowing it to be counterfeited, or shall utter or sell any paper, &c., with a counterfeit mark or stamp thereon, knowing it to be counterfeit the offender shall be adjuged a felon, and shall suffer death, 3 G. 4, c. 13, s. 7. **Forgery of Stamps &c** **Felony**

The punishment of death repealed, and the party shall be pu   d in the same manner as a person convicted of the same offence would by law be punishable in England, 19 V., c. 29, s. 2. **Punishment**

The Secretary shall, under penalty of £50 (£30 sterling), deliver to the parties entitled thereto all commissions and appointments, in case they are applied for within 24 hours after they have been signed by the Governor, and after the amount imposed by this Act and the Stamp Act now (sic) in force thereon have been tendered to him, and shall, under a like penalty, deliver all other papers required from his office, but to which the Governor's signature is not necessary, within 7 days after they have been approved of by the Governor, 3 G. 4, c. 13, s. 8. **Penalty for delaying the delivery of papers**

No letters of preference shall issue from the office until the application has been filed 14 days; penalty on Secretary £50 (£30 sterling), 3 G. 4, c. 13, s. 9. **For delivering out letters of preference until 14 days after application filed**

Gregory's Charity, St. Catherine.

A messuage and land in St. Jago-de-la-Vega vested in the Chief-Justice, and the Custos, and Rector of St. Catherine, to be sold, and the proceeds invested in their names, the interest and profits to be applied towards the maintenance and support of poor persons from any part of the island, and putting poor boys and girls apprentices, and giving portions in marriage with poor girls from any part of the island in their discretion, 33 G. 3, c. 14

£144 Perpetual annuity   A Perpetual Annuity of £144 secured to the Charity in lieu of a deposit of £2400, 28 V., c. 23.

Gunpowder and Fire-Arms.

No more than 4lbs. of Gunpowder to be kept on any estate, &c., without a li cense
Penalties
   No person shall keep more than 4lbs. of gunpowder at one time on any estate or plantation, penn, settlement, or dwelling house, or other place, except he receive a License from the Common Council or Justices and Vestry for special purposes: penalty not exceeding £5 (£3 sterling), 3 V., c. 43, s. 10.

One-half to the informer, and the other half for the benefit of the poor, or other parochial purposes, 3 V., c. 43, s. 11.

Recoverable before 2 Justices, by distress and sale. In default of goods, they may commit the offender, with or without hard labour, not exceeding 10 days, 3 V., c. 43, s. 12.

Bonds of master of vessels and drog- gers
(As to payment of duties and Ware housing in the magazine, Port Royal, see Imports, 28 V., c. 10, s. 12, 13)
Place of deposit
   The Master of every Vessel arriving in any port having Gunpowder or Fire-Arms on board, and the Master of every drogher having, &c., shall at the time of entry become bound to the Queen in a bond, with two sureties, in the Secretary's Office, in £200, that he will not land or permit, or suffer to be landed any such Gunpowder or Fire-Arms, without a License, under the hand of the Custos, Mayor or a Justice of the parish or precinct in which such port of entry is: penalty, forfeiture of his Vessel, her guns, tackle, ammunition and apparel, and the Custos, or Mayor or Justice is required to direct the Gunpowder or Fire-Arms when landed, to be lodged in the Fort or Magazine nearest to the port, or some place of security approved of by him, 19 V., c. 14, s. 1.

No Gunpowder &c., to be sold, &c., without license
   No person shall deal in, sell or barter by himself, or any servant or agent, under a penalty not exceeding £100 nor less than £20, any Gunpowder or Fire-Arms before he has obtained a License. Form A., 19 V., c, 14, s. 2.

Justices in Special Session to grant li- censes
   The Justices in Special Sessions shall grant such Licences at the times and in manner as Licenses to retail Spirits; and the Special Sessions for granting Licenses shall be summoned and held in the like manner, with the like notice, and the like number of Justices, and under the like penalties on the Custos and Clerk of the Peace as Special Sessions for granting Licenses to retail Spirits, 19 V., c. 14, s. 3.

Applications for licenses
   All applications for Licenses shall be made in writing, and lodged with the Clerk of the Peace 5 days previous to the Special Sessions, 19 V., c. 14, s. 4.

Delivery of license
   The Clerk of the Peace shall not, under penalty of £30, deliver any License to any   until the application has been granted, nor until he has given Bond parish £100, with one Surety. Form, 19 V., c. 14, s. 5.

Receipt for license and Stamp duty to be kept with Clerk of the Peace
   For every License there shall be paid £1, and the person licensed shall leave with the Clerk of the Peace at the time of executing the Bond the receipt of the Receiver-General or Collector of Taxes, or District Collector, for the amount, (Form B) and £1 10s. for commutation of Stamp Duty paid to the Receiver-General, &c., or the Clerk of the Peace shall not deliver the License, 19 V., c. 14, s. 6.

Moneys to be paid to the Receiver General
   The moneys received by Collectors or District Collectors for Licenses and Stamp Duties, shall (the commission having been first deducted) be paid over to the Receiver-General within 14 days after receipt, under penalty of £20, 19 V., c. 14, s. 7.

The Receiver-General shall carry all moneys paid to him, the Stamp Duties to the credit of the public, the Licenses to the credit of the parishes, 19 V., c. 14, s. 8.

The Clerk of the Peace shall transmit to the Receiver-General and Collector or District Collector, within 10 days after each Special Session, a return of the number of Licenses granted, with the names of the persons: penalty £20; and under a like penalty shall transmit a copy for publication in the Gazette within 10 days, 19 V., c. 14. s. 9.

Clerk of the Peace to make and publish returns of licenses

And shall, under a penalty not exceeding £30 nor less than £10, keep a separate book for entering and recording all Receipts, Bonds and Licenses, and under the like penalty cause a list of the names of all persons who have obtained Licenses to be fairly transcribed and set up in the most public part of his office. When the price of any License and Stamp Duties have been paid to any Collector or District Collector, the Clerk of the Peace shall, within 10 days after the receipt has been left with him, transcribe and transmit the original receipt to the Receiver-General, 19 V., c. 14, s. 10.

Record receipts bonds and licenses and exhibit lists of persons licensed

The person receiving the License shall pay 10s. to the Clerk of the Peace for his trouble in performing all the duties required of him. Penalty on making any additional charge, £20, 19 V., c. 14, s. 11.

His Fee

Every License must be taken out within 14 days from the day it was granted; failing which, such person's right to take out the same, or any other Liecuse during the current year, shall be forfeited, 19 V., c. 14, s. 12.

Licenses to be taken out within 14 days

Every License shall continue in force for one year, or from the granting thereof until the 5th April of the next succeeding year, 19 V., c. 14, s. 13.

And continue until 5 April succeeding

Every person licensed to sell Gunpowder or Fire-Arms shall, in order to prevent danger, keep all his Gunpowder, except one barrel at a time, in the Fort or Magazine, or a place of security approved of by the Custos or Mayor, or Justice nearest to his place of residence, and the Captain of the Fort and others having the custody of the Magazines, or the persons having charge of such Gunpowder, shall keep the Powder, and deliver it out only under an order of the Custos or Mayor, or the resident senior Magistrate, in the absence of the Custos, as occasion requires under the penalty of £30, for which he shall receive from the owner at the rate of 2s. per barrel capable of (28 V., c. 10, s. 14) containing not more than 100 pounds weight of Gunpowder, 1s. for every half barrel, (capable of) containing not more than 50 pounds weight, and 6d. for every quarter barrel, (capable of) containing not more than 25 p n weight, whether such Gunpowder is loose or in tin cannisters, 19 V. ça. 14; 28 V., c. 10, s. 14.

Gunpowder except one barrel to be kept at the fort

Duties and fees of Captains of forts &c

Upon information, on oath, that Gunpowder or Fire-Arms are deposited or suspected, &c., in any Vessel, house, store or any improper place, and in any quantity contrary to this Act, any Justice shall issue his warrant to cause search to be made in the suspected Vessel, &c., and any Gunpowder or fire-arms there found contrary to this Act, shall be forfeited for the use of the parish, and the master of the Vessel, or occupier of the house or premises, shall, in a summary manner before 2 Justices, forfeit not exceeding £30, to be applied to the use of the parish, or the offender shall be imprisoned for not exceeding 3 months, as to the Justices shall seem fit, 19 V., c. 14, s. 15.

Search warrant for Gunpowder or Fire Arms. Penalties

Fee Harbours, 23 Vic., c. 5, s. 7.

Every person who shall have any Gunpowder or Fire-Arms in his possession for sale or otherwise, shall, on or before the 28th March in each year, give in, upon oath, to the Clerk of the Peace an account of all which may be then in his custody, power or possession, and an account of what may have been expended, sold or otherwise disposed of by him, from the time of the passing of this Act until the 28th March in every year, and the purposes for which they have been expended or sold, or disposed of, under a penalty not exceeding £10, 19 V., c. 14, s. 17.

Annual returns

Penalties may be recovered before 2 Justices, one half to the informer, (who shall be competent to give evidence), and the other half to the poor of the parish, and upon non-payment, may be enforced under 13 V., c. 35, or any other Act in force at the time the penalty is inflicted, 19 V., c. 14, s. 18.

Penalties

Act in force until 31st March, 1870, 19 V., c. 14, s. 19.

Duration

Act not to alter or abridge the power of the Governor to entrust any person with Gunpowder and Fire-Arms for public purposes, 19 V., c. 14, s. 20.

Not to affect, Governor's power to entrust persons with Gunpowder, &c.

The Gunpowder and Fire-Arms Act, 1856, 19 V., c. 14, s. 21.

Short title

SCHEDULE.

License, A., s. 2

JAMAICA, ss.

At a Special Sessions of the Peace held in and for the Parish of
on the   day of   in the year of our
Lord one thousand eight hundred and   for that purpose, A.
B. of the said parish having been approved of as a Dealer in Gunpowder and Fire-Arms in such parish, and having duly entered into bond
and paid the tax required by law, These are to License the said
to deal in and dispose of Gunpowder and Fre-Arms according to the provisions of the Gunpowder and Fire-Arms Act, 1856, from the
day of   one thousand eight hundred and   to the
day of   in the year of our Lord one thousand eight hundred and
        Dated this   day of   18

Receipt B., s. 6

JAMAICA, ss.

I certify that   has duly paid into my hands the sum of
                        for a License under the Gunpowder and Fire-Arms
Act, 1856, and Stamp Duty thereon.
        Dated this   day of   18
                        A. B., Receiver-General or Collector (or
                        District Collector) of Taxes for the Parish of

Bond, C., s. 6

JAMAICA, ss.

Know all men by these Presents, That we   of the parish
of   dealer in Gunpowder and Fire-Arms, and   of
the parish of   are held and firmly bound unto our Sovereign
Lady the Queen, her heirs and successors, to which payment well and
truly to be made and done, we bind ourselves, and each of us, and the
heirs, executors and administrators of us, and of each of us jointly and
severally, firmly by these presents. Sealed with our seals, and dated
the   day of   one thousand eight hundred and
        Whereas at a Special Session of the Peace holden in and for the parish
of   aforesaid, on the   day of   last, the
above-bounden   was approved of as a dealer in Gunpowder and
Fire-Arms from the   day of   until the   day of
        next ensuing, and the above-bounden   was also ap-
proved of as the surety of the said
        Now the condition of the above-bond is such, that if the above-
named   his executors or administrators do not, and shall not
with an evil intent, sell, or barter, give or otherwise dispose of, under any
pretext or means whatsoever, any Gunpowder or Fre-Arms, or suffer any
person or persons in his service or employ, or under his direction or authority, to sell or barter, or give or otherwise dispose of, under any pretext or
means whatsoever, any Gunpowder or Fire-Arms, and do and shall once in
each and every year, on or before the 28th day of March, return to the
Clerk of the Peace of the said parish of   a general account on oath of all such Gunpowder or Fire-Arms as shall have been
in his possession, and shall have been sold or bartered, or otherwise disposed of by him during the said year, and do, and shall in all things conform himself to all and every the provisions, clauses, articles, matters and
things mentioned and contained in the Act of the 19th Victoria, chapter
14, being the "Gunpowder and Fire-Arms Act, 1856," then the above obligation to be void and of none effect.
        Sealed and delivered in the presence of   Seal.
                                                                Seal.

Hackney Carriages.

What are

Carriages with two or more wheels, used for standing or plying for hire
in any street or road, in any city or town, or the neighbourhood, whatever
the form or construction, or the number of persons it is calculated to convey,
or number of horses by which they are drawn, shall be deemed Hackney
Carriages, and may be so described, 10 V. c. 29, s. 1.

Proprietor's name
and abode to be
left with Clerk of
the Peace

The proprietor shall, before he commences to ply for hire, leave at the
office of the Clerk of the Peace, an account, in writing, of his Christian and
surname, and place of abode, in words, at length, and as often as, and within
7 days after his place of abode is changed ; penalty, 40s, 10 V., c. 29, s. 2.

Before any Hackney Carriage is used and employed or let to hire, the proprietor shall paint, or cause, &c., in straight lines, in a conspicuous place on the right or off side, the Christian or initials and Surname at full length and place of abode of the Proprietor or Principal Proprietor, and the number of persons to be carried, in words at length, " to carry Persons", 16 inches to be allowed to each person. Where more than one Carriage is held by the same Proprietor, each shall be numbered with a distinguishing number, and the letters and numbers painted in legible characters of black or white (whichever most differs from the color of the ground whereon painted), the letters at least one inch in height and of proportionate breadth, and shall be re-painted as often as any part becomes obliterated or defaced : Penalty, 40s, 10 V., c. 29, s. 3.

And painted on carriage, with the number of persons it is licensed to carry

When complaint is made against the Driver, any Justice may summon the Proprietor personally to appear and produce the Driver to answer, and if he neglect or refuse, without a reasonable excuse, he shall forfeit 40s as often as summoned until the Driver is produced. On the second or subsequent summons, the Justices may hear the complaint in the absence of the Proprietor and Driver, or either, and on proof of the offence, may give judgment against the Proprietor for the penalty, 10 V. c. 29, s. 4.

Proprietor may be summoned to appear and produce driver

The pecuniary penalties and costs, unless the Driver pays them, may be levied by distress and sale of the goods of the Proprietor, and for want of sufficient distress, the Proprietor may be committed not exceeding 2 calendar months, unless sooner paid, 10 V., c. 29, s. 5.

Liability for driver

Every Proprietor who pays any penalty or costs by reason of any offence of the Driver, may recover the same from the Driver in a summary manner, and on complaint before a Justice, he shall enquire into the same, and cause the sum which appears to have been paid, to be levied by distress and sale of the goods of the Driver, and for want of sufficient distress, may commit him for not exceeding 2 calendar months unless sooner paid, with or without hard labor. If the Driver has been previously convicted of the offence for which the penalty and costs have been paid by the Proprietor, such proceedings shall be taken against the Driver upon the conviction, as if they had not been paid by the Proprietor, and upon recovery shall be re-paid to him, 10 V., c. 29, s. 6.

Liability over of driver

In case of dispute between Proprietor and Driver, upon complaint of either, any Justice shall determine the same, and order compensation to either party, and in case of non-payment, cause the same to be levied by distress and sale, and for want of sufficient distress, may commit the party for not exceeding 2 calendar months, unless sooner paid, 10 V., c. 29, s. 7.

Dispute between proprietor and driver

The Driver of every such carriage shall, if required by any person hiring (unless he have a reasonable excuse, to be allowed by the Justice), drive it to any place he is required within the limits of the city or town : Penalty, 40s, 10 V., c. 29, s. 8.

Driver bound to take up passengers

Every Hackney Carriage found standing in any street or place, unless actually hired, shall be deemed to be plying for hire, although not on any standing or place appropriated for carriages for hire, and the Driver shall go with any person desirous of hiring it, to any place within the limits or bounds, and on the hearing of any complaint against the Driver for refusal, shall adduce evidence of being actually hired at the time, and on failure shall forfeit 40s, 10 V., c. 29, s. 9.

Unless actually hired, which he must prove

If the Driver in civil and explicit terms declare that the Carriage is actually hired, and is afterwards summoned, and on the hearing produces evidence that it was actually and bona fide hired, and it shall not appear that he used uncivil language, or improperly conducted himself to the party by whom he is summoned, the Justice may order such party to make him compensation for his loss of time in attending to make his defence, and in default of payment, may commit the party for not exceeding one calendar month unless sooner paid, 10 V. c. 29, s. 10.

Compensation if summoned, although hired, for refusal

The Proprietor or Driver may stand and ply for hire, and drive on the Lord's Day, and if he do so, shall be compellable to do the like work as on any other day of the week, 10 V., c. 29, s. 11.

Lord's day

The Proprietor or Driver may demand and take for hire the rates and fares in either of the Schedules A and B, calculated for time or distance, at his option, if the hirer require him to wait with the Carriage, either before he drives off or while using it, 10 V., c. 29, s. 12.

Fare, rate of

F F

Refusal to pay fare—Injuring carriage

If any person refuse or omit to pay the Driver for the hire, or defaces or injures any Carriage, any Justice may grant a summons, or if necessary, [in which case the complaint must be on oath, 13 V., c. 35, s. 2], a warrant for bringing before him, or any other Justice, the defaulter or offender, and, on proof on oath, may award reasonable satisfaction to the party complaining for his fare or damages and costs, and also compensation for loss of time, and, on refusal, may commit the offender for not exceeding one calendar month, unless the amount is sooner paid, with hard labour, if he think fit, 10 V., c. 29, s. 13.

Refusal to drive for legal fare with expedition

If the Driver refuse to go with any person desirous of having his carriage for the legal fare, or refuse to drive with reasonable expedition, or if the Proprietor or Driver exact or demand for the hire more than the proper sum, such Proprietor or Driver shall forfeit 40s., 10 V., c. 29, s. 14.

No agreement for more than proper fare valid

No agreement with any driver for payment of more than his proper fare, where not required to go beyond the limits, shall be binding on the person making the same, but he may, notwithstanding, refuse on discharging the Carriage the payment of any sum beyond the proper fare, or if he actually pays more, whether in pursuance of any agreement or not, he may, on complaint against the Driver before a Justice, recover back the sum paid beyond the fare, and the driver shall forfeit, as a penalty for exaction, 40s., and in default of re-payment of the excess, or payment of the penalty, the Justice may forthwith commit the Driver to prison for not exceeding one calendar month, unless sooner paid, 10 V., c. 29, s. 15.

Agreement for less than proper fare

If the Proprietor or Driver, or other person on his behalf, and with his consent, agree before-hand with any person hiring to take for any job less than the rate of fare, the Proprietor or Driver shall not exact or demand more than the sum agreed for: Penalty, 40s., 10 V., c. 29, s. 16.

Compellable to carry the full number painted on carriage or less

The Driver shall, if required by the hirer, carry the number of persons painted on the Carriage, or any less number at the hirer's option, and, on refusal. shall forfeit 40s, 10 V., c. 29., s. 17

Waiting for hirer deposit

Where the Driver is required to wait, he may demand and receive a reasonable sum as a deposit over and above his fare, to be accounted for when the Carriage is finally discharged, and if any Driver who has received a deposit refuses to wait, or goes away, or permits the Carriage to be driven, or taken away without the consent of the person making deposit, before the expiration of the time for which the sum deposited is a sufficient compensation, according to the rates and fares in Schedule B,, or on the final discharge of the Carriage refuses to account for the deposit, he shall forfeit 40s., 10 V., c. 29, s. 18.

Property left in carriage

The Driver of any Carriage, wherein any property is left by any person hiring. shall within 4 days after, carry it in the state he finds it, and leave it with the Clerk of the Peace: Penalty, £20. The Clerk of the Peace shall forthwith enter in a book to be kept at the office, the description of the property, name and address of the Driver, and the day on which it is brought (fee for entry, 2s. 6d.), and the property shall be returned to the person proving to the satisfaction of a Justice that it belonged to him, previously paying such fee and other expenses, with a reasonable sum to the Driver. If not claimed by, and proved to belong to some person within one year after deposit (having been advertised in some public newspaper circulating in the city or town by the Clerk of the Peace), the property shall be delivered up to the Driver, if he apply within one calendar month after the year; or in default of application, any Justice may cause it to be sold, and the proceeds, after deducting the fee and expenses, shall be paid to the Receiver-General to the public account, 10 V., c. 29, s. 19.

[Carrying others when whole carriage hired

If the Proprietor or Driver of any Carriage, the whole of which is hired, permit or suffer any person to ride or be carried in, upon, or about such carriage without the express consent of the person hiring, he shall forfeit 20s., 10 V., c. 29, s. 20.

Standing across the street or alongside other carriage—refusing to give way—taking away fare

If any Proprietor or Driver stand or ply for hire with any Hackney Carriage, or suffer it to stand across any street, or common passage or alley, or alongside of any other hackney Carriage, or two in a breadth, or feed the horses in any road, street or common passage, save only with corn out of a bag, or if the Driver refuses to give way if he conveniently can to any private Coach or Carriage, or obstructs or hinders the Driver of any other Hackney Carriage, in taking up or setting down any person, or wrongfully in a forcible or clandestine way, takes away the fare from any other who, in the judgment of any Justice before whom complaint is heard, shall appear to be fairly entitled to such fare, the offender shall forfeit 20s. 10 V., c. 29, s. 21.

The Common Council of Kingston and Justices and Vestry shall define the limits of the city or town in which Carriages shall ply, and appoint proper places where they may stand and ply for hire, and make order for regulating the number of Carriages to stand in such places, the distances from each other, the times at and during which they may stand and ply for hire, and orders and regulations for the better ordering and regulating such carriages and the Drivers and others having the management, and may alter, amend or repeal the same, and cause them to be advertised in a newspaper circulating in the city or town, and a copy hung up for public inspection in the office of the Clerk of the Peace, before they or any of them shall be carried into effect or be considered as repealed. In case the Driver or person having the management of any Hackney Carriage p m it to stand for hire in any place not appointed, or at or for any other or any longer time than appointed, or in any other manner offends against the rules, &c., to be made, the person who so places it, or if not known, the owner shall forfeit not exceeding £5, to be paid, after deducting such part as shall be adjudged to the informer, to the Receiver-General. No such rules, &c., shall be in any respect repugnant to, or inconsistent with the laws, or any of the provisions of this act Act, 10 V., c. 29, s. 22. *(margin: Ordnances, &c. respecting limits, stands, &c.; Advertisement, &c.)*

If the Driver leave any Carriage unattended in any street, road, or at any place of public resort or entertainment, whether hired or not, any officer of Police, Constable or other Peace Officer may drive away and deposit the same with the horses at some place of safe custody, and the Driver shall forfeit 20s for such offence, and in default of payment upon conviction, and of the expenses of taking and keeping the Carriage and Horses, the same with the harness or any of them shall be sold by order of the convicting Justice, and after deducting the penalty and costs and expenses, as well of the proceedings as of the taking, keeping and sale, the surplus shall be paid to the Proprietor, 10 V., c. 29, s. 23. *(margin: Leaving carriage unattended)*

If the Proprietor, Driver, or person having charge, by intoxication, or by wanton and furious driving, or other wilful misconduct, injures or endangers any person in his life, limbs or property, or makes use of abusive or insulting language; or is guilty of other rude behaviour to any person, or assault or obstructs any officer of Police, Constable or Peace Officer in the execution of his duty, the offender shall forfeit £6, and in default of payment, be committed not exceeding 2 calendar months, 10 V., c. 29, s. 24. *(margin: Intoxication, furious driving, misconduct, abusive language, rude behavior, obstructing police, &c)*

If any Driver or assistant is summoned or brought before a Justice to answer any complaint, which is afterwards withdrawn or quashed or dismissed, or the Defendant acquitted, the Justice may order the complainant to pay him compensation for his loss of time, and in default of payment may commit him for not exceeding one calendar month unless sooner paid, 10 V., c. 29, s. 25. *(margin: Compensation for loss of, time in case complaint dismissed)*

Pecuniary penalties shall be distributed, one moiety or less, with costs, to the informer, 10 V. c, 29, s. 26. *(margin: Distribution of penalties)*

SCHEDULE A.

RATES AND FARES FOR DISTANCE.

For every person conveyed for any distance within the limits or bounds of any city or town 0 0 6

Where the whole Carriage is taken by the hirer, he shall pay a sum equal to 6d. for each person the same is capable or represented to be capable of carrying with convenience.

For every person conveyed beyond the limits or bounds (except where a special agreement is entered into an additional sum beyond 6d., of 0 0 3

Where the whole is taken, and no special agreement entered into, the hirer shall pay an additional 3d. for each person it is capable and represented to be capable of carrying with convenience.

But not compulsory to ply beyond the limits or bounds.

SCHEDULE B.

RATES AND FARES FOR TIME.

For any time within and not exceeding 30 minutes	......	......	0 2 0
Above 30 minutes, and not exceeding 45	......	......	0 3 0
Above 45 minutes, and not exceeding one hour		......	0 4 0

For any further time exceeding one hour, at the rate of 1s. for every 15 minutes completed, and 1s. for any fractional part of 15 minutes.

Such fares being in full for the hire of the whole Carriage, and the Driver compellable to carry the full number of persons it is represented to be capable of carrying, or any lesser number, at the option of the hirer.

If the Driver is required to go beyond the limits, and no special agreement, and the hirer does not require to take back himself or any passengers, the Driver shall be entitled to 1s. additional to return.

But not compulsory on any Driver to go beyond the limits.

Harbours.

Taking ballast from reefs off Port Royal, see 23 V , c. 5, s. 11
No person shall fetch, or cause to be fetched in any boat vessel or canoe, from the reefs or shoals, or dig up any stones below high water-mark from the eastermost and southernmost part of any of the keys lying off Port-Royal, and no stones, small or great, be fetched or taken up for ballast, or any other use from the eastermost side of the Point of Port-Royal, so far as Plumb-Point, on penalty of £10 (£6 sterling], 33 C. 2, c. 17, s. 4.

One-third to the Crown, one-third to the Churchwardens for the use of the parish, and one-third to the informer, recoverable by action of debt, &c., 33 C. 2, c. 17, s. 6.

Sinking wrecks or throwing ballast in Road of Kingston See 23 V,. c. 5, s. 8. 10
No wreck shall be sunk, or ballast thrown into the road of Kingston to the eastward of the westend of the town, nor to the westward of the east part of Kingston, 8 Ann, c. 8, s. 4.

Bouying channel from Port Royal to Kingston
The parish of Kingston may, as often as there is occasion, buoy or stake out the Channel between Port-Royal and Kingston, at the costs of Kingston, 8 Ann, c. 8, s. 6.

Damaging buoys
Whosoever, by himself or his servant, willingly or maliciously cuts away, or pulls up any such buoy or stake, shall forfeit £50 (£30 sterling), one-half to him who shall sue in the Supreme Court, 8 Ann, c. 8, s. 7-8.

Foreign Vessels
Every French, Dutch or Spanish Ship, or other vessel arriving in any harbour, &c., shall be subject to such Port-charges, visitations, rules and orders as the vessels of Her Majesty's subjects trading hither are, 12 G. 1, c. 11, s. 3.

Injuring buoys, &c., in Port Royal Harbour or Channels Obstructing vessels sailing in or out
If any person makes fast, or hangs on, or secures any fishing or other boat to any bouy, stake or mark, on any of the shoals or quays in or about the Harbour of Port-Royal, or the Channels leading into the Harbour, or causes any obstruction to any vessel sailing into or out of the Harbour, by surrounding with boats any of such buoys, stakes or marks, or breaks down, removes, pulls up, cuts away, injures, destroys any of them or any stave or vane attached or affixed thereto, he shall, on conviction before 2 Justices of Port-Royal, forfeit, not exceeding £5 (£3 sterling) and costs, or be committed not exceeding 30 days, and, at the discretion of the Justices, over and above such fine, or notwithstanding such imprisonment, all costs and expenses for repairing or re-erecting such buoy, &c., the amount to be fixed by the Justices, who may take evidence thereof on oath, and enforce payment with costs by distress and sale, and, in default of goods, may commit the offender not exceeding 30 days, 3 V., c. 36.

Harbour masters fees collection
The Receiver-General shall be relieved from the collection of Harbour-Masters' fees, which are to be collected by themselves, 18 V., c. 24, s. 1.

No vessel shall be cleared out of the Customs until a certificate of payment, signed by the Harbour-Master or his Deputy, is produced by the Master to the principal Officer, in form annexed : penalty £50, recoverable in the Supreme Court. In case of the absence of the Harbour-Master or his Deputy, the Master, prior to clearance, may pay the fees to the principal Officer, who shall receive and account for them to such Harbour-Master.— Where the Harbour-Master is in receipt of a salary from the Vestry, no fees shall be demanded or taken by him so long as he continues to receive such salary, 18 V., c. 24, s. 2.

Harbour-Master's Office, port of   , one   Certificate
thousand eight hundred and

These are to certify that   the Master or Commander of
the   named the   has paid the Harbour-
Masters' fees at this port of clearance.

To   , Harbour-Master.

The Common Council of Kingston may make ordinances relative to
the Harbour, and the duties of the Harbour-Master, Water-Bailiff, and all offences, evils and inconveniences touching the Harbour, without prejudice
to the right of the Governor to appoint the Harbour-Master, 18 V.,
c. 61, s. 15.   Kingston Harbour Regulations

The Harbour of Kingston shall include all the body of water between   Extent of
the shores in the parishes of Kingston and Port-Royal, to the eastward of
Kingston, and the shores in the parishes of Kingston, St. Andrew and St.
Catherine to the westward of Kingston, and the Palisadoes or shores in
the parish of Port-Royal, and extending from the head of the harbour to
Passage Fort in St. Catherine and to Gallows' Point in Port-Royal, and
from this latter to the southernmost point of The Twelve Apostles' Battery,
18 V., c. 61, s. 16.

The Governor may, by writing, under his hand and seal, appoint a   Harbour master appointment
Master-Mariner or other efficient person as Harbour-Master. Upon a vacancy
in any of the ports mentioned in Schedule A., remove them, and fill up vacancies, 23 V., c. 5, s. 1.

Every Harbour-Master shall perform the undermentioned duties in the   Duties [In harbors generally
port or parish for which he is Harbour-Master :   Oath of office

1. Take and subscribe an oath of office before a Justice, to be lodged with
the Clerk of the Vestry.

> I do swear, that I will faithfully and impartially, and to the best of my
> ability and judgment, perform as Harbour-Master for the port (or
> parish of)   the duties imposed upon me by " Harbours' Re-
> gulation Act, 1859," and which shall be imposed by any regula-
> tions to be issued by the Governor in Executive Committee,
> under the authority of the same.

2. Any Harbour-Master hereafter appointed, shall, in person, except pre-   Acting in person or by deputy, residence See s. 16
vented by illness, and if already appointed, by himself or deputy, per-
form the duties, and reside at the port, or within 5 miles ; if for more
than one Port in some part of the parish convenient for visiting the
several Ports, and particularly the principal one.

3. Appoint, in writing, when necessary, the place in the Harbour where   Deposits for ballast, &c
ballast, rubbish, earth, stone, and gravel, or any other useless and unserviceable thing shall be thrown and left from any Vessel.

4. Direct and regulate the position, moving, unmoving and removal of every   Position of Vessels
Vessel.

5. Take charge of every Vessel on fire, and give direction for preventing   Vessels on fire
the spread of, and for extinguishing such fire.

6. Furnish the Captain of every Vessel trading beyond the Tropics within   Harbour regulations
24 hours after anchoring, and the Captain of every Vessel trading
within the Tropics, twice every year, in January and July, or as soon
after as practicable, with a printed copy of the Harbour Regulations,
or such parts of this Act as the Commissioners for each Port consider
necessary and provide for the guidance of each Captain, 23 V., c. 5, s. 2.

The Harbour-Master for Kingston shall perform the undermentioned   In Kingston
duties, acts and things in addition to all others :

1. He shall demand from the Captain of every Vessel entering with Gun-   Gunpowder
powder, within 24 hours after delivery of the Harbour Regulations, the
receipt of the officer in charge of the Magazine at Fort-Charles for
such Gunpowder.

2. He shall see that every Vessel in Harbour is at all times moored not less   Moorings
than 50 fathoms from the nearest wharf, (except between 1st August and
30th November, inclusive, during which time not less than 150 fathoms)
and is unloaded and loaded by boats, except whilst discharging or taking in cargo alongside a Wharf as after provided.

Unloading &c

3. That no Vessel approaches or remains within a less distance for the purpose, or on pretence of loading or unloading goods on or from any wharf until it is ready for her reception alongside.

4. Nor remains alongside longer than :—a Vessel under 150 tons burthen, for 4 working days; above 150, and under 200 tons, for 6 working days; from 200 to 250 tons, 8 working days; above 250, for 12 working days; but if any Vessel, within the period allowed, complete her loading or unloading, she shall be immediately removed. If any Vessel has not completed her unloading or loading, and there is no other ready to unload or load at the same wharf, such Vessel may continue until she has completed, or there is another Vessel ready to come alongside to unload or load.

5. That when the business of any wharf is incommoded or obstructed by more than one Vessel being moored at a neighbouring wharf, the Vessel first moored at the neighbouring wharf is removed, if the time allowed has expired, if not, that the Vessel which arrived last is removed until the time allowed the first Vessel expires.

Anchoring, making fast, &c

6. That every Vessel while lying alongside any wharf has at all times a fit and proper anchor out in a south-easterly direction from her bow at a distance of not less than 30 fathoms.

7. That no Vessel has a bow-fast or stern-fast attached or fixed to any wharf when not unloading or loading thereat.

8. That no Vessel is allowed to swing within 200 fathoms of any wharf, and every Vessel anchored or lying within that distance has out at all times a sufficient anchor a-head in the direction east-south-east from the Vessel with a sufficient cable, and a proper kedge-anchor a-stern, in a direction west-north-west from the Vessel, with a sufficient hawser attached with buoys, fastened to such anchor and kedge-anchor, by buoy ropes, not exceeding in length the depth of the water, where they lie by more than one fathom.

9. That no Vessel has at any time, her anchor acockbill, or hanging over the bows, but properly fished to the bow, so as not to injure any boat or craft passing the Vessel, or taken on deck if necessary, or required by the person in charge of any wharf, while the Vessel is lying alongside. 23 V., c. 5, s. 3.

Liabilities of Harbour Master

Every Harbour-Master who from ignorance or neglect moors or places any Vessel in a position to occasion damage to it, or any other Vessel or wharf, shall be liable to make good the damage and may be proceeded against by action of debt in the Supreme Court, 23 V., c. 5, s. 4.

Every Harbour-Master who omits, neglects or refuses to do and perform the several duties, matters and things required by this Act, or any regulation issued by the Governor in Executive Committee to be done by him, shall forfeit not exceeding £50, and may be removed from his appointment, 23 V., c. 5, s. 5.

Fees See 18 V., c. 24.

The Harbour-Masters of the several ports or parishes in Schedule A, shall be entitled to the fees and salaries set opposite the port or parish in Schedule B, to be payable, collected and received as now, 23 V., c. 5, s. 6.

Offences in Kingston Harbour

Every Captain or other person committing any of the following offences in the harbour of Kingston, shall forfeit not exceeding £60, or suffer imprisonment, with hard labor, not exceeding 3 months :

Ballast

1. Who shall take up or carry away, without the permission of the Harbour-Master, any earth, sand, stones or ballast from the Palisadoes.

Gunpowder

2. Who shall not within 24 hours after he has anchored his Vessel, deposit all the Gunpowder therein at Fort-Charles, or within 24 hours after he has received the Harbour Regulations, and on demand of the Harbour-Master, produce to him a receipt from the officer in charge of the Magazine therefor.

3. Who shall receive any Gunpowder, or knowingly permit the same to be received on board in the Harbour.

Flying jibboom &c., to be close rigged, &c

4. Who shall not, within 48 hours after dropping anchor, have the flying jib-boom and main-boom of his Vessel close rigged in, and her sprit sail yard on deck, or fore-and-aft under the bow-sprit, and shall not so continue whilst the Vessel is within 200 fathoms from the nearest wharf, 23 V., c. 5, s. 7.

Every Captain or other person who commits any of the following offences in any Harbour, shall forfeit not exceeding £60, or suffer imprisonment, with or without hard labour, not exceeding 3 months : In any harbour

1. Refusing or neglecting to moor, unmoor, remove or place any Vessel at the time and in the manner directed by the Harbour-Master. Not mooring, &c. as directed

2. Obstructing or hindering the mooring, unmooring, removal or placing of any Vessel in any Harbour ordered by the Harbour-Master. Obstructing the mooring, &c.

3. Obstructing any Harbour-Master in the discharge of any duty imposed by this Act, or any regulation issued by the Governor in Executive Committee. Obstructing Harbour Master

4. Throwing or casting into, or depositing in, or causing, &c., in any Harbour or part thereof, other than the places appointed by the Harbour-Master for the reception, any ballast, rubbish, earth, stones and gravel, or other useless or unserviceable article. Throwing ballast, &c.

5. Throwing, casting or letting go, or causing, &c., in any Harbour, or leaving, or causing to be left on the shore, without permission of the Harbour-Master, the carcass of any animal, either from on board of any Vessel in, or from any part of the shore of such Harbour Throwing carcasses, &c.

6. Suffering the dead body of any human being, or the carcass of any animal to remain on board of any Vessel more than 12 hours. Dead bodies, carcasses on board

7. Dropping anchor at any time between 1st December and 31st July inclusive, less than 50 fathoms ; or between 1st August and 30th November inclusive, at a distance less than 100 fathoms from the nearest Wharf. Dropping anchor within distances

8. Allowing pitch, tar, turpentine or other combustible matter, to be boiled or heated on board of any Vessel, or in any Boat, unless the Boat is moored at least 30 fathoms distant from the nearest Vessel and Wharf. Combustibles

9. Burning, scorching, or paying, or allowing the side or bottom of any Vessel to be burned, &c., at any place in any Harbour, other than a careening place, or place appointed by the Harbour-Master for the purpose. Paying sides, &c.

10. Kindling, or permitting a fire to be kindled on board of any Vessel in any other than a proper iron fire-place or caboose, or kindling or permitting any fire to be kindled or kept burning after 8 at night. Fires

11. Beating, blowing or using, or permitting, &c., on board of any Vessel, any drum, trumpet, horn or other noisy instrument, to the disturbance or annoyance of any of the inhabitants of any city or town binding on or adjacent to the Harbour. Drums, &c

12. Employing or causing, &c., or permitting to remain on board of any Vessel, any indentured Apprentice, or immigrant laborer under contract, without the permission of his master or employer. Apprentices Immigrants, &c.

13. Removing any Vessel from one wharf to another, or from any other place to a wharf without having previously informed the Harbour-Master, and received his direction in respect to such removal. Removing Vessels

14. Discharging, or causing, or permitting, &c., any Fire-Arms on board any Vessel (a Steam Vessel whose anchor is about to be weighed preparatory to her departure excepted). Firearms

15. Refusing or neglecting whenever a Boat is passing to or from any wharf to which a Vessel is attached by a bow or stern-fast to slacken the same, so as to permit its passage, or whenever a Boat is vered a-stern of any Vessel, to haul such Boat up close a-stern whenever any other Vessel happens to be passing. Slackening bow or sternfast, &c.

16. Using any net or seine for catching fish, (shrimp nets excepted) having meshes in any part of less dimensions than 1¼ inch between knot and knot. Nets or seines

17. Using any net or seine for catching shrimps of a greater length than 2½ fathoms, or joining 2 or more of such nets or seines. Shrimp nets

18. Cutting, breaking, or untying the rope or chain by which any buoy is held to or connected with any anchor, place or thing, or setting loose any buoy from any anchor, &c., to which it has been attached. Loosing buoys

19. Using an unlicensed or unregistered Boat which shall not belong to any Vessel in the Harbour, nor be carrying freight from or to the Harbour for the Vessel to which such Boat belongs, 23 V. c. 5, s. 8. Unregistered boats

Wilfully sinking vessels

Every person who wilfully sinks any Vessel, or causes, &c., in any Harbour without having first obtained the permission of the Commissioners for the Harbour, in writing, under their hands, or that of their Clerk, shall forfeit £500, and be liable besides to answer in damages to the Commissioners for all expenses incurred by them in removing such Vessels, and all damages occasioned by sinking the same, 23 V., c. 5, s. 9.

Accidental sinking

If any Vessel is accidentally sunk, and the owner or consignee fail to remove it out of the limits of the Harbour, or to such part as the Harbour-Master appoints, within 3 months after he is required, in writing, by the Harbour Master to do so, the Vessel shall become forfeited to the Commissioners, who shall remove it at the expense of the Parish, and dispose of the Vessel or materials saved by public outcry, and the moneys, when received, shall be paid to the Receiver-General for the use of the parish, 23 V., c. 5, s. 10.

Ballast, &c. from reefs

If any person dig up or carry away any stones, sand or ballast from any reef or breakwater by which any Harbour is protected, he shall forfeit not exceeding £20, or suffer imprisonment, with or without hard labor, not exceeding 30 days, 23 V., c. 5, s. 11.

Commissioners

The Common Council of Kingston and the Vestries of the parishes in Schedule A shall be Commissioners for carrying this Act into effect in such parishes, 23 V., c. 5, s. 12.

Persons incapable of holding office

If any person who is a Member of the Committee for any parish, or interested in any wharf in any port, as Owner, Lessee, Tenant or Wharfinger, is appointed Harbour-Master for such Port, Parish or Harbour, his appointment shall be void. If a Harbour-Master become a Commissioner, or interested in any Wharf, he shall be taken to have resigned his appointment, and the Governor shall in either case appoint some other person to fill the vacancy, 23 V., c. 5, s. 13.

Committees of Commissioners

Differences between the Harbour-Master and any person respecting the mooring, unmooring or removal of any Vessel from one part of any Harbour to another, or from or to any wharf, shall be adjusted by three Members of the Committee for the Harbour, which Committee the Common Council and Vestry shall appoint at the commencement of every year, or at each quarterly Vestry, and shall consist of persons residing at or near the Port for which they are a Committee; but no Member of any Committee shall act in any case where he is in any way concerned or interested, 23 V., c. 5, s. 14.

Deputy Harbour Masters

If any Harbour-Master hereafter to be appointed is unable to attend to his duties from illness or otherwise, he may appoint a Deputy, 23 V., c. 5, s. 15.

To be appointed by the Governor Remuneration

Subject to the previous approval of the Governor. The Governor in Executive Committee shall fix any portion of the emoluments of the Office, not exceeding one-half for his Deputy's services, 23 V., c. 5, s. 16.

Fees on coasting vessels Kingston and St. Thos. East

After the death, resignation or removal of the Harbour-Master of Kingston or St. Thomas in the East, the fees of their successors on coasting Vessels shall not exceed 1s 6d per quarter, 23 V., c. 5, s. 17.

Penalties, recovery

Penalties not exceeding £60, shall be proceeded for and recovered before the Justices in Petty Sessions, and payment enforced under the provisions of any Act now or to be in force for the recovery of small debts. Penalties, exceeding £60, by action of debt. When recovered such penalties shall be pa a e, one moiety to the informer, who shall be a competent witness, 23 V.ycb5, s. 18.

App n men under repealed Acts declared valid and confirmed, 23 V., c. 5, s. 19i t ts

Interpretation

Harbour-Master substituted for, and to be understood in the same sense as Water-Bailiff in repealed Acts; Captain, the Master or person at the time in charge of the Vessel; Boat, shall include Canoe and other Crafts without a deck; Vessel, Ship, Barque, Brig, Schooner, Sloop, or other Craft with a deck, whether propelled by steam or otherwise; Harbour, Roadstead or Harbour, 23 V., c. 5, s. 20.

Short title

Harbours Regulation Act, 1859, 23 V., c. 5, s. 21.

SCHEDULE.

Parishes and Ports for which Harbour-Masters may be appointed, s. 1.

PARISHES.	PORTS.	PRINCIPAL PORTS.
Kingston..........	Kingston............................	
St. Thos. in the East	Morant Bay, Port Morant and Man-chioneal......................	Morant Bay.
Metcalfe..........	Annotto Bay........................	
St. Mary..........	Port Maria, Oracabessa & Rio Nuevo	Port-Maria.
Trelawny	Falmouth and Martha Bræ	Falmouth.
Hanover..........	Lucea and Green Island............	Lucea.
St. James.........	Montego Bay........................	
St. Elizabeth......	Gravesend..........................	
St. Dorothy	Old Harbour, Salt River and Cla-rendon Bay......................	Old Harbour.
Westmoreland.....	Savanna-la-Mar.....................	
St. Ann..........	St.Ann's Bay, Ocho Rios & Rio Bueno	St. Ann's Bay.
Portland..........	Port Antonio.......................	
Manchester........	Alligator Pond.....................	

Fees and salaries B., s. 6

PARISHES.	DESCRIPTION OF VESSEL.	Vessels trading North of the Tropic of Cancer, each Voyage.	Vessels trading between the Tropics, each Voyage.	Coasting Vessels, payable quarterly	Annual Salary.
		£ s. d.	s. d.	s. d.	
Kingston	Ship or 3 masted Vessel................	1 12 0	16 0		
	Brig or Brigautine...	1 4 0	12 0		
	Schooner or Sloop.....	0 16 0	8 0		
	Coasting Vessel......			8 0	
St. Thomas in the East	Ship. &c..............	1 16 0	18 0		
	Brig, &c..............	1 4 0	12 0		
	Schooner, &c........	0 18 0	9 0		
	Coasting Vessel......			6 0	
Metcalfe.............	Ship, &c..............	0 9 0	4 6		£30
	Brig, &c..............	0 6 0	3 0		
	Schooner, &c.	0 4 6	2 3		
	Coasting Vessel......			1 6	
St. Mary.............	Same Fees............				£60
Trelawny............	Same Fees...........				£84
Hanover.............	Ship, &c..............	0 9 0	4 6		£36
	Brig, &c..............	0 6 0	3 0		
	Schooner, &c........	0 4 6	2 3		
St. James.............					£36
St. Elizabeth.........	Same Fees as Hanover				
St. Dorothy..........	Ship, &c.............	0 18 0	9 0		
	Brig, &c.............	0 9 0	4 6		
	Schooner, &c........	0 6 0	3 0		
Westmoreland .... ⎫ St. Ann............ ⎪ Portland............ ⎬ Manchester........ ⎭	Same Fees as Metcalfe.				

Hawkers and Pedlars.

To be licensed

No Hawker, Pedlar or other person shall go from place to place, or from house to house, to sell any goods or article of traffic (except as after) without a License from the Common Council of Kingston and the Justices and Vestries of other parishes, 4 V., c. 11, s. 2.

Annually—fee

Before any Hawker, &c., shall carry about or expose for sale any goods, &c., (except as herein) he shall take out and pay for a License to the Clerk of the Common Council or Vestry, not exceeding £4 sterling, for the use of the parish, and 3s. sterling as a fee to the Clerk for the License, which shall only continue in force for one year from date. No License shall be granted to any person unless he produce to the Common Council or Justices and Vestry, at the time of application, a certificate of good character, signed by two Justices, and which License shall extend only over the parish for which it is granted, 4 V., c. 11, s. 3.

Registers

Receiver-General

The Common Council and Justices and Vestry shall direct their Clerks to keep a register, in which all Licenses, and the names of the persons obtaining them shall be inserted, and the Clerks shall receive the sum fixed for every License, and keep an account thereof, and pay the same over once in every quarter to the Treasurer for the use of the parish, and in default of payment shall forfeit £30 sterling, to be recovered by warrant of distress of 2 Justices, and shall be forthwith dismissed from his office, 4 V., c. 11, s. 4.

Copies to be furnished to police

The Clerks of the Common Council and Vestries shall, once in every quarter, forward a copy of the Register, signed and certified as correct, to the Chief Police Officer, to be kept in a conspicuous part of the Police Station-House for the use and guidance of the policemen of the parish, 4 V., c. 11, s. 5.

Penalty for selling out of parish for which licensed

If any Hawker, &c., not having a License, goes from place to place, or from house to house, for the purpose of selling any goods, &c., (except as excepted) or opens an occasional room or shop, and exposes for sale, by retail or otherwise, any goods or other articles of traffic, except &c., in any town, parish, or place, other than that in which he usually resides, and so evades the payment of any public or parochial taxes, he shall, on conviction before 2 Justices, forfeit not exceeding £6. sterling and costs, and in default of immediate payment, his goods shall be forfeited and sold at public outcry to defray the penalties and costs, 4 V., c. 11, s. 6.

Exceptions

Act not to prohibit any person from selling any bread, fresh-fish, milk, fruit, vegetables or provisions, or to limit the real workers or makers of any goods, or their children, apprentices or known agents, or servants usually residing with them, only, from carrying about or exposing to sale, and selling by retail or otherwise, any goods, &c., of their own making, 4 V., c. 11, s. 7.

Interpretation of

Provisions shall be taken to signify ground provision or vegetable roots, or other vegetables, commonly known by the term "Bread-kind," and not pickled, salted or preserved victuals, or any other articles of food imported; but pickled, salted and preserved, or smoked victual, actually and bona fide manufactured in this island, may be sold, 6 V., c. 30.

Selling, &c. without license

Any person not having a License, travelling from place to place, or from house to house, for the purposes aforesaid, shall forfeit not exceeding £4 sterling, to be recovered before 2 Justices, and in default of immediate payment, the goods, &c., found in his possession, shall be levied upon, and sold at public outcry to pay the fine, 4 V., c. 11, s. 8.

Seizure of goods and detention of pedlar

Any Constable or Peace Officer may seize and detain any Hawker, Pedlar or other person found travelling from place to place or house to house, and trading without a License, or who, being so found, refuses or neglects, on demand, to produce his License, and carry him before a Justice, who shall examine into the facts, and upon proof that the person had so traded, and upon demand had produced no License, may convict and sentence him to pay not exceeding £2 sterling, with costs, and in default of immediate payment, enforce the same, by warrant of distress of the goods, &c., and sell a sufficient part to satisfy the penalty and costs at public outcry for the use of the parish, 4 V., c. 11, s. 9.

If any person produce or shew any forged or counterfeit License, he shall, on conviction before 2 Justices, forfeit not exceeding £6 sterling, for the use of the parish, or in default of immediate payment of the fine and costs, be committed with or without hard labour, not exceeding 30 days, 4 V., c. 11, s. 10. **Forged licenses**

In case any person lend or hire any License, or trade with, or under color of any License granted to any other person, or in which his real name has not been inserted as the person to whom it was granted, the offender shall forfeit not exceeding £6 sterling, to be recovered in a summary manner, with costs, as before directed, 4 V., c. 11, s. 11. **Lending, &c. license**

If any Constable or Peace Officer refuse or neglect to aid and assist in the execution of this Act, he shall, on conviction, forfeit not exceeding £6 sterling, to be recovered and applied as before mentioned, 4 V., c. 11, s. 12. **Penalty on constable, &c. not enforcing act**

In cases where the penalty is recoverable before 2 Justices, one moiety shall be applied for the benefit of the parish, and the other to the informer, who shall be a competent witness. The penalty in case of non payment to be recovered as before provided, 4 V., c. 11, s. 13. **Application of penalties**

Appeal, 4 V., c. 11, s. 14. **Appeal**

All suits and prosecutions shall be commenced within 3 months, 4 V., c. 11, s. 15. **Commencement of proceedings**

No proceedings shall be quashed or appealed against for want of form. Licenses, Warrants, Warrants of Distress and Sale, and Convictions shall be in the forms annexed, or words to the like effect, 4 V., c. 11, s. 16. **Want of form**

FORM OF LICENSE.

Venue.—This is to certify that A B, of the parish of   hath been this day duly licensed, as a fit and proper person to hawk and peddle in the parish of   any goods, wares, merchandize or other articles of traffic for the space of one year from the date hereof or this License, being transferable to any other person. **Form of License,**

Given under our hands (sic) this   day of
To be signed by the Clerk of the Common Council or Vestry.

Highways not Main Roads.

A Board of " Commissioners of Highways and Bridges for the parish of   " shall be established in each parish, with p we by such name to sue and be sued, enter into deeds, contracts and o agreements, which, when entered into by them and signed, or in the case of Deeds, signed and sealed by 3 Commissioners on behalf of any Board, shall be valid, 25 V., c. 18, s. 2. **Commissioners**

Such Board shall consist of the Custos or senior acting resident Magistrate, the resident Members of the Legislative Council, the Members of Assembly for the parish, 2 resident Justices for each of the Districts named in Schedule A, or if there be none, such 2 Justices residing in an adjoining District, or if in any precinct there be no such resident Justices in the particular parish, the Justice or Justices may be taken from any other parish of the precinct, and one resident Tax-Payer or a Householder, paying taxes annually, not less than [20 s., 27 V., S. 1, c. 26, s. 1] for each District, not a Justice, if none resident, then from any other District nearest the one to be represented at the Board, to be annually elected by the Justices in Special Sessions, except in Kingston, where the Board shall consist of the Custos or senior acting resident Magistrate, the Mayor and 2 Justices for and resident in each District, and one Alderman and one Householder or Tax-Payer in each District, paying taxes as aforesaid, to be annually elected by the Justices in Special Sessions, 25 V., c. 18, s. 3. **How composed**   **In Kingston**

The Custos shall be the Chairman, and, in his absence, the senior Magistrate present shall act as such, 25 V., c. 18, s. 4. **Chairman**

Each Board shall have the exclusive care, management, control and superintendence of all Highways, Roads, Thoroughfares, Streets, Lanes, Aqueducts and Bridges in the parish, except the roads transferred to the Main Road Commissioners, 25 V., c. 18, s. 5. **Powers**

A Special Session shall be called by the Custos, or, in his absence, senior resident Magistrate, by notice in the "Jamaica Gazette," at least 5 **Elective commissioners** days before that of meeting, within 14 days after 1st February, and the Justices so assembled shall elect Commissioners, whose names shall be entered in the Minute-Book kept by the Clerk of the Peace, and published in the "Jamaica Gazette," 25 V., c. 18, s. 6.

Quorum—meetings at Court House

No less than 5 Members shall constitute a Board for the transaction of business, except where the Commissioners exceed 18, and then not less than 7, and where they do not exceed 9, 3 shall suffice. The Commissioners shall hold their meetings at the Court-House, 25 V., c. 18, s. 7.

Quarterly and special meetings

The Commissioners shall meet once in each quarter on the third Wednesday in January, April, July and October, or other convenient day in the same week; but every Quarterly Meeting on any other day shall be convened as a Special Meeting, so that if no Quarterly Meeting is convened for any other day, it shall take place on the third Wednesday, without special notice. Special Meetings shall be convened by the Chairman, or, in his absence or refusal, by any 3 Commissioners, whereof 5 days' notice in writing shall be given to each Commissioner by their Clerk, specifying the day and hour, 25 V., c. 18, s. 8.

Clerk salary

The Commissioners at a Special Meeting shall appoint the Clerk to their Board, with power to remove him. Salary not exceeding £30 per annum, by quarterly or monthly payments, on warrant of the Governor, 25 V., c. 18, s. 9.

Orders for payment of accounts

All orders for payment of accounts for expenditure shall be signed by the Chairman and 4 Commissioners, where the Board is constituted by 7 or 5, and by 2, in addition to the Chairman, where constituted by 3, and countersigned by the Clerk, 25 V., c. 18, s. 10.

Vacancies

In case of death, absence from the island exceeding 3 calendar months, or removal from the parish, or resignation of any Commissioner, the vacancy shall be filled up with all convenient speed, but no election shall be made by the Justices in Special Session unless notice is published in the "Gazette by Authority," at least 7 days before the meeting. If any vacancy is occasioned by the appointment of a Commissioner to be Custos, or any Commissioner becoming Senior resident Magistrate, a new election shall be made in his room, 25 V., c. 18, s. 11.

Duty of the Commissioners :

Duties of commissioners
Record in Clerk of the Peace's office of highways

1. To cause Roads intended to be used as Highways, which have been laid out, but not completed or described, or have been generally used for 20 years but not recorded, to be fully ascertained, described, and entered of record in the office of the Clerk of the Peace in so far as not already done.

Road districts

2. To divide their parish into Road Districts, corresponding in extent with the Districts Schedule A.

Annual returns of roads to be submitted to the legislature

3. To prepare and submit annually to the Executive Committee, to be laid before the Legislative Council and Assembly, returns of Roads, classifying them into Carriage Roads of the first class; ditto of the second class; Bridle Roads of the first class; ditto of the second class; the number of miles of which each Road consists, and its termini; the total expenditure laid out on each during the year, their state and condition at the date of return; whether repairable under contract or not, if so, the particulars and duration of the contract, and probable amount of expenditure for the ensuing year; also statements of alterations, new Roads and Bridges constructed during the year and the expenditure incurred in consequence; also of further alterations recommended of existing Roads and Bridges, and new Roads and Bridges required, and probable expenses beyond the probable expenditure, to keep the present Roads and Bridges in repair : such Returns to be made up to the 30th September preceding; and such further returns as the Executive Committe may require.

Apportionment of funds to roads, &c.

4. To allot, at the time and in proportions to be ascertained as directed (s. 13), and where required, after taking evidence as provided (s. 14), the sums appropriated to be expended in repairs and alterations of existing Roads, and in the formation of new Roads, and in the construction and repair of Bridges and Water-courses, after reserving not less than £20 per cent. per quarter on the amount allotted, to meet Clerk's salary, unforseen expenses, and for repairs of unforseen injuries by extraordinary floods and accidents.

5. To cause and authorize the survey of new Roads, and give directions for repairing Roads, Streets, Bridges, Highways and Water-courses, and for the immediate removal of nuisances, and the prosecution of offences, and to direct that all metalled portions of the Road shall not exceed 16 feet in width in great thoroughfares, nor be less than 10 feet in any case.

Surveys, repairs, nuisances, prosecutions, metalling

6. To inspect and audit all accounts for expenditure, and pass the necessary orders, to be signed and countersigned as directed (s. 10), for payment by the Receiver-General, and at least once in each quarter to inspect and audit the accounts of the Waywardens, 25 V., c. 18, s. 12.

Audit and pass accounts   Also way warden's accounts

The residue of the moneys to be paid to the Receiver-General for Licenses [on Drays, Carts, Water-Carts, Wains, Wagons, Spring-Carts, and Hackney or other Carriages, and in respect of Carriages, Horses and Asses, after deducting £20 per cent. for Main Roads, s. 32] raised in each parish, shall be applied and appropriated to the repair and improvement of the roads, under the management and superintendence of the Commissioners of each parish, and be carried to the credit of a separate account by the Receiver-General with them, 25 V., c. 12, s. 33.

Read funds

The Main Road Revenue arising from Road, Stock, Carts and Wheels in any parish possessing no Main Road, shall be expended on the improvement of the chief Carriage Roads and Bridges of such parish as its Commissioners of Highways, &c. shall determine, 25 V., c. 12, s. 10.

In parishes possessing no main road

The Commissioners at their first Quarterly Meeting in January, shall fix a per centage for each District, by which the appropriation within the year shall be made for the repairs, maintenance or formation, or construction of Roads and Bridges, such per centage to be fixed with reference to the mileages, traffic, existing state of repair, and other circumstances or requirements, exigencies or claims of the localities where new Roads or Bridges are required, upon evidence to be taken where required as after provided (s. 14), or otherwise upon the best information the Commissioners can obtain, 25 V., c. 18, s. 13.

At meeting in January to fix per centage of appropriation for each district

If two or more Householders or Tax-Payers to the annual value of £2 each, require, by written notice to the Clerk, at or before the January Quarterly Meeting, of which requisition, and the names of the persons making it, a minute shall be made by the Clerk, the Commissioners shall, before fixing the per centage, take evidence of any persons who appear before them, on oath or otherwise, which oath the Chairman may administer, touching the state of any of the Roads, such evidence to be taken down in writing by the Clerk, and upon such evidence, where it has been required, or otherwise upon the best information they can obtain, the Commissioners shall fix the per centage, 25 V., c. 18, s. 14.

Evidence to be taken before fixing per centage on requisition

The Collector of Dues, within 5 days after each quarter, shall make return to the Commissioners of the sums, under the respective heads of Taxes and Duties, collected and transmitted to the Receiver-General during the quarter expired, applicable to Road purposes, which the Clerk shall lay before them at their first Quarterly Meeting after receipt, 25 V., c. 18, s. 15.

Quarterly returns from Collector of Dues of remittances to the Receiver-General for road purposes

The Receiver-General, at the commencement of each quarter, shall communicate to the Clerk the sum the Commissioners will be entitled to expend and draw for the preceding quarter for Road purposes, not being more than ¼ of the annual revenue of the parish for Parochial Roads (see s. 12) 25 V., c. 18, s. 16.

Receiver-General's quarterly communication of items at credit for parochial roads

Also accounts, either by statement or pass-book, shewing payments and receipts during each quarter, stating the names of parties in whose favour orders are drawn, and the amounts, 21 V., c. 4, s. 23.

Also of receipts and payments

The Governor, with the advice of the Executive Committee, may sanction the Commissioners to draw to the extent, if necessary, of the whole sum at their credit, (see s. 12) payable on the Governor's warrant to their order, for repairing extraordinary damage, 25 V., c. 18, s. 17.

Drafts for extraordinary damage

The Receiver-General shall annually make up and furnish to the Executive Committee, for the Legislative Council and Assembly, a statement, to 10th October, of the amounts allotted, and of the orders of the Commissioners paid by him for Road purposes in each parish, and the balances applicable to their orders, 25 V. c. 18, s. 18.

Receiver General's annual account for legislature

The Commissioners may enter into contracts for repairing and keeping in repair for one or more years, any Roads or Bridges, or portions thereof;

Contracts for repairs of roads, &c. limits of outlay

the moneys payable in any one year under contracts not to exceed the sum alloted to the Roads, &c. The subject of contract and the repairs shall be subject to the inspection and approval of the Way-Wardens and Commissioners. The Commissioners shall not lay out nor direct the expenditure of a larger m, in the whole, in any one year, than has been appropriated, 25 V., su 18, s. 19.

Mile Marks Guide Posts
The Commissioners shall cause mile-marks of stone, wood or iron to be erected on such roads as they think proper, at a distance of one mile from each other, with legible inscriptions; and also guide-posts at the intersections of such Roads as they think proper, and guide-posts in water-courses to shew the height of water therein; and keep in repair all such as have been erected, 25 V., c 18, s. 20.

Way-Wardens
And shall also appoint as many Way-Wardens as they deem necessary in each District, who shall perform the duties hereby imposed. Every Way-Warden shall be resident near, and interested in the condition of the Road for w   he is appointed, and removable for neglect of duty, 25 V., c. 18, s. 21. hich

Duties
Duty of Way-Wardens:—

Superintendance, disbursements and removal of nuisances
1. To superintend the repairing of the Highways, Streets and Bridges within the district, and the performance of all works ordered by the Commissioners; to disburse moneys furnished by the Commissioners, and cause the removal of nuisances.

Plans and estimates
2. To prepare, or cause to be prepared, plans of Roads and estimates required by the Commissioners.

Mile Marks Guide Posts
3. To see that the Mile-marks and Guide-posts are kept up in good order, and the Guide-posts in the Water-courses properly marked.

Attend meetings
4. To attend all Quarterly Meetings and other meetings when required, and take instructions relating to Roads.

Notice of encroachments, &c.
5. To give immediate notice to the Clerk, of all encroachments, nuisances and infringments of this Act.

Accounts and Vouchers
6. To prepare and submit his accounts and vouchers once at least in each quarter, and whenever required, 25 V., c. 18, s. 22.

Altering or discontinuing roads, laying out new roads
Any 6 Freeholders may apply to the Commissioners to alter or discontinue, or to lay out a new Road, in writing, signed by the applicants, accompanied by a plan, 25 V., c. 18, s. 23.

Notices to owners &c. of lands
Before the Commissioners come to any determination on any application, they shall cause 7 days' notice, in writing, to be given to the occupants and owners of the land through which the proposed alterations or new Road are to pass, as also to those through whose lands any Road then runs, of the time and place of meeting to decide thereon, at the expense of the applicants, 25 V. c., 18, s. 24.

Meeting Certificate and plan to be exhibited
They shall meet at the time specified, and at such meeting, or an adjournment, hear reasons for or against the application, and, if they determine to entertain it, either wholly or in part, make out and subscribe a certificate of their determination, to be deposited with the Clerk of the Peace, containing or accompanied by a plan of the Road and intended alterations, or of the Road to be discontinued, or the new Road, furnished by the applicants, copies of which the Clerk of the Peace shall exhibit on the Court-House door, for at least 21 days before that appointed for the meeting of the Jury, 25 V., c. 18, s. 25.

Jury to be summoned
Any Justice who, as a Commissioner, signs the certificate, may issue his warrant to a Policeman or Constable to summon 13 Freeholders or Householders of the neighbourhood paying taxes to the extent of 20s. annually, whether of the same or of any adjoining parish, able to read and write, not being interested in the lands through which the Road proposed then runs, or through which it is proposed the alterations shall be made, or any proposed new Road would run, to attend at a place and time to be mentioned, at least 21 days after that on which a copy of the certificate has been exhibited, 25 V., c. 18, s. 26.

Jury of 7 to be sworn
If 7 appear, they shall be sworn, by any Justice then present, to examine the proposed alterations or new Road, or Road to be discontinued, and ascertain whether such alterations or new Road are necessary or expedient and useful as a Road of public, or as a Road of private communication, or whether it will be expedient and useful to discontinue such Road, and in the

case of a new Road, or of alteration, if it appears to them to be so, after they have gone over and inspected the same, that they will, according to the best of their skill and judgment, assess the damages to be sustained by the making or alterations of such Road, and determine the several matters according to equity and good conscience, without undue bias, partiality or favor. The decision of the Jury or a majority shall be received and certified by the Justice to the Commissioners, (see s. 29.) If 7 do not appear, the Justice shall fine each absent Juror, not less than 20s., nor more than 40s, unless satisfactory reasons are given for such absence to be recovered as after mentioned, (s. 90) 25 V., c. 18, s. 27. Fine on absent jurors

In case any such Jury cannot be formed, from non attendance or other cause, another warrant may be issued, and another day fixed, and so on until a Jury is formed. The Clerk of the Peace shall put up and exhibit on the Court-House door, at least 7 days' notice of the day appointed for such further meeting, 25 V., c. 18, s. 28. Further juries

The 7 who appear and are sworn shall examine the route of such Highway, and, if satisfied, find by their verdict that the alteration of any existing Road is necessary and proper, or the new Road is necessary and proper, or that such Road ought to be discontinued, and assess the damages to be sustained by the making or altering of any Road, and make and subscribe a certificate to such effect, to be also subscribed by the Justice, and delivered to the Commissioners, 25 V., c. 18, s. 29. Duty of jurors on findings

The Commissioners and owners and occupiers of the land through which any new Road or alteration passes, may agree upon the amount of damages, and for a release of all claim to damage, and the Jury shall not be sworn to assess, nor shall assess any damages, the subject of agreement. No new Road or alteration shall be opened, or worked, or used until the damages have been paid or tendered, except with the sanction of the owner of the soil. The agreement and release shall be filed and recorded in the office of the Clerk of the Peace, and the same, or assessment of damages shall preclude owners or occupiers from further claim to damages. In case of the absence of the owner or his representative, or where the owner is not known, the damages shall be paid to the Receiver-General, and kept by him without interest until claimed by the party entitled, 25 V., c. 18, s. 30. Agreements respecting damages Agreement on assessments. Absence, &c. of owner

When any person is the owner of any land over which a new Road or alteration is made, and also of the soil of any portions of the Road proposed to be altered or discontinued, in whole or in part, the Jury who assess the damages shall take into consideration the value of the Road, or part to be abandoned, to the owner, and the benefit to result to him therefrom, and deduct the same from the damages which otherwise would have been assessed; and the owner of the land so abandoned may enclose it, 25 V., c. 18, s. 31. Matters to be considered on assessment of damages

All damages fixed by agreement, or awarded, shall be paid out of the funds to be allotted and appropriated for the Highways. Nothing herein shall authorize the commencement of the alteration of any Road, or the laying out of any new Road, or the expenditure of any money therefor, or for payment of any damages, until funds have been appropriated for the purpose by the Legislature, 25 V. c. 18, s. 32. Funds out of which damages payable. No expenditure until funds are appropriated by the legislature, see s. 40, par. 9

If the Commissioners of any adjoining parish, before a Jury is impanelled, give notice, in writing, to the Commissioners of the parish in which proceedings are pending for alteration, laying out of a new Road, or discontinuance, that the same will prejudicially affect the Roads of such adjoining parish, they shall not be further proceeded with until the Commissioners of the adjoining parish consent to the continuance of the pending proceedings; and in the event of their not doing so, the Executive Committee, on reference to them, shall decide whether the proposed alteration or new Road, or discontinuance, shall take place, 25 V. c. 18, s. 33. Objections of commissioners of adjoining parish

When application is made to the Commissioners for any Private Road and they are of opinion it is reasonable, the same mode of proceeding shall be adopted as in the case of a public Highway, but the damages awarded, and the expenses of the Road and its maintenance shall be paid by the applicant, 25 V., c. 18, s. 34. Applications for private roads

Every Private Road when laid out, shall be for the use of the applicant, heirs and assigns, but not converted to any other use; and the applicant shall be compelled to keep up proper fences on each side, 25 V., c. 18 s. 35. Private roads

Persons conceiving themselves aggrieved by any refusal or determination to entertain any application, or the finding of the Jury, may, within 60 days after the refusal or finding, appeal to the Circuit Court; but an appeal by one person, and a decision thereon shall not conclude any other person who appeals within the limited time, and has not been heard, 25 V., c. 18, s. 36.

No appeal shall be heard until after the time limited, nor shall the Judge of the Circuit Court pronounce any Judgment until he has heard all pending appeals; and after hearing all such appeals, the Judge shall pronounce one Judgment embracing the whole subject, 25 V., c. 18, s. 37.

Such appeal shall be in the form of a petition to the Appellate Judge, signed by the Appellant, or his agent, and briefly state the grounds on which made, and whether brought to reverse the determination entirely, or only a part, and what part. Notice of appeal, and of the time when it would be heard, shall be given to the Commissioners, and at least one of the persons who opposed the same before them, when the determination appealed from was against an application sanctioned by the Commissioners, or if an appeal from their determination, and a finding of the Jury thereon, then notice shall be also given to one or more of the applicants. Notice shall be served, at least 30 days before the day appointed for the hearing, on one of the Commissioners, either personally, or by leaving the same at his dwelling-house; and the service on any applicant shall be in like manner, 25 V., c. 18, s. 38.

The Appellate Judge shall have power to compel the attendance of witnesses, and examine them upon oath or affirmation, and to adjourn the hearing. His decision shall be reduced to writing, and signed, and conclusive, and be recorded in the Clerk of the Peace's office, 25 V., c. 18, s. 39.

When the determination of the Commissioners to alter an existing Road or lay out a new Road, and the finding of the Jury is confirmed on appeal, or the time for appealing is expired without an appeal, and it has received the sanction of the Legislature, by the grant of moneys to carry out and complete same, they may give to the owner or occupant of any enclosed, cultivated or improved lands through which the intended alterations or new Road will pass, 90 days notice, in writing, of their intention to open and work the Road, to enable him to remove his fences and erect such new fences as he thinks necessary; but shall not commence to open or work such alterations or new Road, until the expiration of the notice, without their consent, nor until the damages awarded by the Jury have been paid or tendered, and have received the sanction of the Legislature. Penalty £50, upon each Commissioner who assents to the opening or working of any such alteration or renewed Road, to be recovered in an action of debt by each person aggrieved. Not to subject any Commissioner to any penalty for any temporary alteration or deviations rendered necessary in consequence of any temporary injury or accident to any Highway, 25 V., c. 18, s. 40.

The Clerk of the Peace shall be paid by the applicant for laying out, altering, or discontinuing any Road:

To drawing out the necessary proceedings, and attending the Jury	£1 1 0
Each mile he is required to travel, to be reckoned from Court House, ...	0 1 0
Recording all proceedings, for every 160 words	0 1 0
Attested copy of the proceedings to be recorded in any other parish, or for any other purpose, for every 160 words	0 1 0

No other fees shall be demanded or received by him, except in cases of appeal, when he shall be entitled to the like fees as are payable in cases of appeal from summary adjudications of Justices, 25 V., c. 18, s. 41.

Every public Highway already or to be laid out, but not opened and worked, at the public or parochial expense, within 10 years from the time of being laid out, and not opened and worked by means of funds authorized by the Legislature within the like period, shall cease to be a Road for any purpose, unless worked and kept in repair by any private person using such Road, in which case such person, his heirs and assigns, continuing to repair the same, shall be entitled to continue the use of the same, by himself, his servants, carriages, and horses, and stock, 25 V., c. 18, s. 42.

All public Highways now in use, of which a record has been made in the office of the Clerk of the Peace, shall be deemed public Highways, and only to be altered or discontinued by proceedings under this Act, unless not-worked for the period before mentioned, 25 V., c. 18, s. 43.

On application of 6 Freeholders, in writing, to any Justice, stating they intend to lay the plan of a new Road, or alterations and improvements of any Road, before the Commissioners, he shall granta warrant to authorize the person employed by them to enter upon all lands and properties, to take the levels, and make the necessary traverses and surveys, to enable him to make the plans and sections of the new Road or alterations. Any person obstructing such survey, shall be liable to fine not exceeding £5, on conviction before 2 Justices, 25 V., c. 18, s. 44. *Authority to enter lands so as to make plans*

The Commissioners, when about to alter or repair any Road or Bridge may apply to the Governor and Executive Committee for authority to require the services of the Civil Engineer of the County, who, on the authority being obtained, shall prepare and finish such plans, specifications and estimates, and give such supervision and examination, and in all respects perform such duties, in respect of such Roads and Bridges, as are required in respect of Main Roads, 25 V., c. 18, s. 46. *Services of County Engineer*

The width of all public Carriage Roads made or to be laid out by the Commissioners, shall be, if practicable, 24 feet, when made through open ground, 60 feet through standing wood, 40 feet when the wood is only on one side; and no private Road shall be more than 40 feet wide, 25 V., c. 18, s. 49. *Width of carriage roads*

All Streets to be laid out in any Town shall be not less than 40 feet wide and Lanes not less than 20 feet wide, 25 V., c. 18, s. 50. *Of streets, lanes*

The Commissioners may order the Way-wardens to open all Carriage Roads to the width before mentioned, which shall have been used as public Highways for 20 years, 25 V., c. 18, s. 51. *Enlargement of highways to such widths*

When a Highway has been encroached upon by fences, the Commissioners may order such to be removed, so that the highway may be of the breadth before enacted, at the cost of the party who made the encroachment, or of any person claiming under him, giving notice, in writing, to the party. &c., to remove such fences forthwith, such notice to specify the legal breadth of the Road, the extent of the encroachment, and the places where it exists, 25 V., c. 18, s. 52. *Encroachments, see s. 63*

If the party, &c., do not remove it within 14 days after service of notice, he shall forfeit 5s. for every day after the expiration of the notice during which the fences continue unremoved, or until removed by the Commissioners, besides the expense of removal, to be recovered, as penalties imposed by this Act, 25 V., c. 18, s. 53. *Penalty for non-removal*

Any tree falling into any Highway, so as to cause obstruction thereon, shall be removed by the owner or occupier of the land from which it fell within 24 hours after notice to remove; if he neglect, any Way-warden or Commissioner may cause it to be removed at his expense, and he shall be liable to a penalty of 5s. for every day after the expiration of the notice, during which it remains unremoved; such p a and expenses to be recovered as other penalties. Any person wilfully placing any tree or other obstruction on any Highway, shall be liable to a penalty not exceeding £5, 25 V., c. 18, s. 54. *Removal of fallen trees, placing obstructions on highway*

Cutting down any tree on land not occupied by the person, so as to fall into any Highway, river or stream, unless by order or consent of the owner or occupier: Penalty, not exceeding £5 nor less than £1, 25 V., c. 18, s. 55. *Falling trees into highways, &c. by persons not occupants*

Cutting, or causing to be cut down any tree so as to fall into any river, stream or water course, or obstruct any Road or fording, or divert the river course, so as to encroach upon or injure or tend to injure any public Highway or Bridge, and not removing the same within 24 hours after notice: Penalty not exceeding £5, 25 V., c. 18, s. 56. *Falling trees into river, &c.*

The owner or occupier, or his agent, attorney or overseer, of the land next adjoining to any Road or Bridge, shall cut, prune or lop the fences, and also the branches of trees, bushes or shrubs, growing in or near such fences, (the same not being in any garden or orchard, walk or avenue, to any house, nor an ornament or shelter to a house, unless it hang over the Road or Bridge, so as to impede or annoy any carriage or person travelling thereon) in such manner that it be not prejudiced by the shade, nor the sun and wind excluded to its damage, or if he neglect to do so within 14 days after notice, in writing, by any Commissioner, Way-warden or other person, authorized for the time, the Way-warden or other person shall cause the same to be cut, pruned or lopped, and the owner or occupier, *Lopping fences, &c. adjoining*

H H

agent, &c., shall pay the expenses, and in default, they may be recovered, with costs, if any, as any p a ty; not to apply to roads passing through unfenced rune of woodland, ез61V., c. 18, s. 57.

Swinging gates

No swinging or other gates shall be allowed on any public Highway laid out since 28 February, 1851, or to be laid out, unless a written permission to erect them has been previously obtained from the Commissioners. Not to give or recognize any right to erect any such gates, or to interfere with any rights now enjoyed or possessed by any parties who have erected or have the right to erect gates on roads running through their lands. The Commissioners are not authorized to grant permission to erect any gate across any Post-road, 25 V., c. 18, s. 58.

Wanton injuries to bridges

Wantonly injuring any Bridge being an Highway: Penalty, not exceeding £60 nor less than £20, or imprisonment with or without hard labour, not exceeding 90 days, nor less than 30, 25 V., c. 18, s. 59.

Drains, materials for repairs from waste lands or from enclosed &c., lands

The Way-wardens or persons employed in conducting, and superintending the repairs of any Road, Street or Bridge or private Road, annually repaired at private expense, and kept open for the use of the public, may cut drains on lands adjoining, to carry off the water collected, and dig and carry away any gravel-stone, sand or other materials, out of any savannah, unenclosed or open land, river or gully, being waste land in or near thereto, proper for draining, repairing or amending the same, without paying anything therefor; they levelling, or causing to be levelled all holes and pits where materials are dug and carried away, and, where sufficient materials cannot be conveniently obtained from any savannah, waste and unenclosed or open land, rivers or gullies in the neighbourhood, may, by order of the Commissioners, cut drains, and dig and carry away any materials out of the grounds or enclosures of any person, (not being the ground whereon any house stands, garden or yard, planted walk or avenue to any house, or any parcel of provision ground) wherein such drain is necessary for keeping the Road in good order, or wherein such materials are to be found, and carry away so much as the Way-wardens, or persons so employed, judge requisite, paying such rates for materials and damage as the Commissioners judge reasonable. Persons molesting, hindering or obstructing the Way-wardens, or any person so employed, or the persons under their command, in cutting any drains, or in digging or carrying away materials, shall forfeit not exceeding £10, 25 V., c. 18, s. 60.

Taking away materials for repairs, &c.

Any person, without the consent of the Way-wardens or Commissioners, taking away any materials purchased or gathered for the repair or use of any Road, &c., or any materials out of any q a or pit, without their permission, shall forfeit not exceeding £10. Not to prevent any person in possession of the land on which the quarry or pit is, from digging and removing materials for his own use, 25 V., c. 18, s. 61.

Damages by Water Companies

If any corporation, Society, or Company for supplying any City, Town, or other place with water, dig, or cause to be dug in any Road, &c., any trenches or holes for laying down or repairing any water-pipe or plug, or thing connected therewith, and keep, or cause, or permit to be kept open longer than reasonably requisite, or cover over or fill up, or cause or permit it to be covered over or filled up in an imperfect manner, or occasion and suffer, or permit any damage thereto by reason of the imperfect state or want of repairs of any such pipe, &c., such Corporation, &c., shall forfeit not more than £20 nor less than £5, over and above the expenses in their repair, 25 V., c. 18, s. 62.

Penalty not exceeding £10 for any of the following offences :—

Mile marks

1. Removing, destroying, injuring or defacing any Mile-mark.

Guide Posts

2. Injuring or defacing any description affixed to any Guide-post, or destroying or injuring such Guide-post, or any Guide-post in any water course.

Obstructing water courses, dragging logs, &c.

3. Injuring any Highway, by obstructing or diverting any Creek, Water-course or sluice, or by drawing logs stones, or things of weight, on the surface of any Road or Bridge, otherwise than upon wheel carriages.

Obstructing highway or drains

4. Obstructing any Highway, or filling up or placing any obstruction in any Water-course or ditch constructed for passing water across or under, or for draining the water from any Highway.

Riding, &c. on foot paths

5. Riding, driving, leading, or drawing any animal or vehicle upon any footpath or causeway, for the use or accommodation of foot passengers, or wilfully doing or causing any injury to be done to the same.

6. Using any drag, joggle, or other instrument, for retarding the descent of any wheel carriage down any hill, in such manner as unnecessarily and wilfully to destroy or injure the surface of any Highway. *Drags and joggles*

7. Upon any Highway or side, killing, slaughtering, burning, dressing or cutting up any beast, swine, calf, lamb or other cattle, except horned stock injured in the carriage of produce, or otherwise, which in such case may be slaughtered and removed. *Killing, &c. cattle on*

8. Depositing any dead carcase or any rubbish, on any Road or place adjacent thereto, to the annoyance of persons using such road; or in towns, depositing the same in any other place than appointed by the Commissioners or other competent authority, 25 V., c. 18, s. 63. *Carcasses, rubbish*

Any person depositing any dead carcase, offal or night soil, in any place appointed by the Commissioners or other competent authority, for the deposit of dirt and rubbish, shall effectually bury or burn the same under a like penalty, 27 V. S. 1, c. 26, s. 2. *Carcasses, offal, &c, buried or burnt*

9. Leaving any wagon or other wheel carriage upon any Street or Highway, or on the side thereof, without a person in the custody or care thereof, longer than necessary to load or unload, except in cases of accident, or in cases of accident longer than necessary to remove same, or not placing same, with or without beasts of draught harnessed or yoked thereto, during the time of loading or unloading, as near to one side of the street or Highway as possible. *Leaving carriages in streets, &c.*

10. Making any hedge or other fence at the side of any Street or Highway so as to reduce the breadth below the prescribed limit. *Fences encroaching on, see s. 49 51*

11. Depositing any loose earthsand, brick or rubbish against any wall or excavation for a foundation-wall, or fence, piazza, or bridge, in any Street, Highway or Road, or creating or causing any nuisance on any Road, Street or Thoroughfare, and refusing or neglecting to remove the same after having been required to do so by the Commissioners, or a Way-warden. *Deposits of earth, &c., nuisances*

12. Using or carrying any lighted firestick or torch on or about any Road, Street, Lane, Path or Thoroughfare, whether public or private. *Fire sticks, torches*

13. Driving any horse, gelding, mare, filly, mule or donkey, loaded or unloaded, along any mountain bridle Road, and neglecting to lead the same on passing any traveller riding. *Not leading horses, &c. on mountain bridle road*

14. Allowing any swine to be at large on any Highway, 25 V., c. 18, s. 63. *Swine*

Any Commissioner or Way-warden may destroy, or cause to be destroyed, any swine found at large on any Highway, 25 V., c. 18, s. 64. *Destruction of swine*

Making or erecting any wall, or building upon or near to any Street or Highway, so as to reduce or limit the breadth : Penalty, not exceeding £60 nor less than £20. The Commissioners may remove the wall or building forthwith, 25 V., c. 18, s. 65. *Encroachments by walls or buildings*

The Commissioners for St Elizabeth, out of the Parochial Highways Funds, shall provide for the cleaning, clearing and keeping navigable the Black River; and all the powers and rules vested and charged upon the Commissioners, Way-wardens or other officers or persons, employed or authorized by them, and all penalties, liabilities and other obligations imposed by this Act in respect to any Roads or Bridges, may be exercised, imposed or charged and enforced, so far as applicable in respect to the Black River, for the purpose of cleaning, clearing and keeping it navigable 25 V., c. 18, s. 66. *Black River ; St. Elizabeth*

Wilfully felling any trees, or casting or causing the same to be cast, or any cane-trash or earth, or other thing, into the Black River, whereby the navigation may be stopped or impeded : Penalty, £60, one half to be paid to the Receiver-General to the credit of the Commissioners, to be expended in cleaning, clearing and keeping the River navigable, the other moiety to the informer, 25 V., c. 18, s. 67. *Impeding the navigation*

No deed, contract or agreement, or proceeding by or with the Commissioners, shall be subject to Stamp Duty, 25 V., c. 18, s. 88, *Exemption from stamp duties*

No Commissioner or Way-warden shall be entitled to any remuneration or fee for his services, 25 V., c. 18, s. 89. *No remuneration to commissioners or way wardens*

All penalties shall be recovered before 2 Justices, not Commissioners. In default of payment, offenders may be imprisoned, with or without hard labour, not exceeding 6 calendar months, unless sooner paid, and penalties *Recovery &c. of penalties*

Apprehension of
offenders

Commencement
of prosecutions

Forms

25 V., c. 12, partly
incorporated here-
with.   See s. 13-23,
36 28, 30, 40, 41, 47
Duration

shall be paid to the Receiver-General, in aid of the funds for the general
Road expenditure of the parish. The Justices may adjudge not exceeding
one moiety to any persons who have contributed to the conviction of any
offender in such proportions as they think fit, 25 V., c. 18, s. 90.

Any Commissioner, Way-warden, Constable, Policeman or Peace Officer, or person called to his assistance, may take into custody without
warrant, any person who, within view of any such Commissioner, Way-
warden, Constable, Policeman or Peace Officer, commits any offence in this
Act, to be dealt with according to 24 V., c. 11, s. 36-39, or either of those
sections (Police Act) as the circumstances require, 25 V., c. 18, s. 91.

Prosecutions shall be commenced within 3 calendar months, and not
later. 25 V., c. 18, s. 92.

The Forms in Schedule may be used so far as applicable, and may be
modified or altered as circumstances require, 25 V., c. 18, s. 93.

The provisions of the Main Road Act, 25 V., c. 12, so far as applicable,
shall be incorporated with, and read as part of this Act, 25 V., c. 18, s. 94.

Act in force until 31st March, 1869, 25 V., c. 18, s. 95.

SCHEDULE, 25 V., c. 18.
COUNTY OF MIDDLESEX.

Parishes and
dicts, A. s. 3, 19

PARISHES.	DISTRICTS.	PARISHES.	DISTRICTS.
St. Catherine,	Trinity.	St. Ann,	Dry Harbour.
	Ramsay.		Alexandria.
	Caymanas.		Seville.
St. John,	Luidas.		Pedro.
	Guanaboa.		Ocho Rios.
St. Dorothy,	Marlie.		Moneague.
	Esquiral.	Vere,	Yarmouth.
St. Thos. ye Vale,	Trinity.		Moreland.
	St. Thomas.	Clarendon,	Ludlow.
	Harewood.		Mocho.
	St. Faith		Chapelton.
St. Mary,	Retreat.		Lime Savanna.
	Bagnolds.	Manchester,	Mile Gully.
	Port Maria.		Mandeville.
			Snowden.

COUNTY OF SURRY.

Kingston,	No. 1 West Division	St. Thos. ye East,	Morant.
	No. 2 East Division		Blue Mountain.
	No. 3 Parish.		Bath.
St. Andrew,	St. Christopher.		Plan-Garden-River
			Manchioneal.
	St. James.	Portland,	St. Margaret.
	St. Joseph.		Titchfield.
	Liguanea.		St. Mark.
Port Royal,	Dallas.		Aberdeen.
	Metcalfe.	St. George,	Buff Bay.
			Belcarras.
	The Town.		Hope Bay.
St. David,	Wellington.	Metcalfe,	Maxwell.
	Easington.		Scot's Hall.
			Annotto Bay.

COUNTY OF CORNWALL.

St. James,	Rose Hall.	Hanover,	Green Island.
	St. James.		Lucea.
	Montpelier.		Interior.
	Marley.	Westmoreland,	St. Paul's.
	Springfield.		Trinity.
	Belfont.		Savanna-la-Mar.
Trelawny,	Falmouth,		St. Peter's.
	Good Hope.		St. John.
	Rio Bueno.		St. Thomas.
	Swanswick.	St. Elizabeth,	Black River.
	Ulster Spring.		Lacovia.
	Stewart Town.		Goshen.
			Santa Cruz.

At a meeting of the Commissioners of Highways for the parish of , held at the Court-House in the said parish, the day of A. B. was nominated, elected and appointed Clerk of such Board of Commissioners during the pleasure of the said Commissioners, and the salary to be allowed to the said Clerk was fixed at the sum of pounds per annum, payable by quarterly payments on the
(To be signed by the Chairman and two Commissioners).

Appointment of clerk, s. 9

At a meeting of the Commissioners of Highways for the parish of , held at the Court-House in the said parish, on the day of A. B., of &c., was nominated, elected and appointed a Way-warden for the district of the said parish, for the purpose of carrying into execution in such district the provisions of the Act or Acts now or hereafter to be in force respecting Highways, and the said A. B. is hereby required and enjoined faithfully and truly to execute his said office.
(To be signed by the Chairman and two Commissioners.)

Appointment of way-wardens, s. 21

Take notice, That you were at a meeting of the Commissioners of Highways for the parish of , held at the Court-House of the said parish on the day of elected and chosen one of the Way-wardens for the district of that parish, and you are faithfully and truly to execute the office of Way-warden, according to the directions of the Act or Acts now, or hereafter to be in force.
Dated the day of
To A. B., of

Notice of appointment, s. 21

> C. D., Chairman.
> E. F., Commissioner.
> G. H., Commissioner.

At a meeting of &c.
Whereas it hath been made to appear to the said Commissioners that the common Highway, in a certain place called in the district of the said parish, hath been encroached upon by fences erected thereon by one A. O., which it is necessary should be removed ; we do hereby give you notice to remove such fences forthwith, which said fences extend feet, or thereabouts, upon and along such Highway, the legal breadth of which Highway is feet, and which encroachment extends for the whole length of the said fence, and can only be removed by erecting the said fence feet to the of the place where the same now stands, and such encroachment exists at , otherwise proceedings will be taken against you according to law.
To A. O., of &c. or
To A. P., of &c. claiming under the said A. O.
(To be signed by the Chairman and two Commissioners.)

Notice to remove encroachment by fences, s. 54

In pursuance of the directions given by an Act, passed in the twenty-fifth year of the reign of Queen Victoria, chapter 18, I, A. B., of &c., one of the Way-wardens of the district of the parish of do hereby give you notice forthwith to (stating the nuisance complained of, and requiring its removal), on a certain part of the Queen's Highway, lying between and , in the said district and parish, to the obstruction and annoyance of the said Highway.
Dated this day of
To C. D., of

Waywardens notice to remove nuisances, s. 54, &c.

> A. B., Way-warden.

At a meeting, &c.
Whereas it has been represented to us, that there are not sufficient gravel, stone, sand or other materials to be conveniently obtained from any savannah, waste, or unenclosed or open land, rivers, or

Summons to show cause why way-wardens should not enter to dig for materials upon enclosed lands, s. 60

gullies, in the neighbourhood of (the Road, Street, or Bridge, as the case may be, describing same,) in the district of the said parish, but that such materials may be conveniently obtained from grounds and enclosures in your occupation, (called and known by the name of and , or otherwise, describing the same, not being the ground whereon any house stands or any garden, yard, planted walk or avenue to any house, or any parcel of provision ground) : We do hereby give you notice to appear before the said Commissioners at the Court-House in the said parish, between the hours of , and of the noon of the day of , to shew cause why we should not make our order, authorizing and empowering the Way-wardens of the said district, or other persons employed in conducting and superintending the repairs of such Road, Street or Bridge, as the case may be, any or either of them, to dig and to carry away any gravel, stone, sand, or other materials out of the said grounds or enclosures in your occupation, (not being the ground whereon any house stands, garden or yard, planted walk or avenue to any house, or any parcel of provision ground), whereon any such materials shall be found, and, from time to time, to carry so much thereof as they, any or either of them shall judge requisite for keeping in repair, and amending such (Road, Street or Bridge), paying such rates for such materials, and the damage done to the owners and occupiers respectively of the grounds where and whence the same shall be dug and carried away, as the Commissioners for the time being shall judge reasonable.

Given under our hands on behalf of the said Commissioners, the day and year first above written.

　　　　　　　　　　　　· (Three Commissioners.)

To A. B., of 　　　　&c.

　　　　　　　　　——

At a meeting, &c.

Order authoriz-
ing their taking
materials, s. 60 Whereas A. B., of &c. having been duly summoned to appear before us to shew cause why we should not make the order herein contained, and having appeared before us accordingly, (" or having sent his steward or agent,' " or " C. D. on his behalf, to attend us on that occasion," or " but not having appeared," or " E. F., the owner of the lands hereinafter mentioned having appeared," or " having sent his steward or agent," or " G. H., on his behalf to attend us on that occasion") we have heard what has been alleged, and taken the matter into consideration, and are of opinion, and therefore hereby order, authorize and empower the Way-wardens of the , district of the said parish for the time being, and other the persons employed or to be employed in conducting and superintending the repairs of (' ' Road, Street or Bridge, as the case may be, describing the same) any or either of them, to dig and to carry away any gravel, stone, sand or other materials out of the grounds or enclosures in the occupation of the said A. B., called and or otherwise describing the same), (not being the ground whereon any house stands, garden or yard, planted walk or avenue to any house, or any parcel of provision ground, whereon any such materials shall be found, and from time to time to carry so much thereof, as they, any or either of them shall judge requisite for keeping in repair and amending such Road, Street or Bridge) paying such rates for such materials, and for the damage done to the owners and occupiers respectively of the grounds where and whence the same shall be dug and carried away, as the Commissioners for the time being shall judge reasonable.

Given under our hands on behalf of the said Commissioners, the day and year first above written.

　　　　　　　　　　　　(Three Commissioners.)

Abolition of Tolls Tolls abolished on and after 1st October, 1863, and the Commissioners of the respective Boards directed to sell the toll-houses and lands attached thereto; and apply the proceeds to the credit of the Board to which they belonged, the signature and seal to any title deed and acknowledgement of the receipt of the purchase money, by the Secretary of any Board, sufficient to vest in the purchaser a valid title, 26 V., S. 2, c. 8.

The Governor and Executive Committee were authorized to appropriate out of the loan of £27,000 to be raised under this Act, to the account of the " Parochial Roads Loan," not exceeding in the whole £5000, in such sums as the Executive Committee might direct, of which not exceeding £2000 should be appropriated for repairs of Parochial Roads, not being Main Roads, damaged by the floods in November 1863, and not exceeding £3000 for the formation of new, and re-construction of other Parochial Roads, not Main Roads as next mentioned, 27 V., S. 1, c. 24 s. 5. Appropriation of £6000.

And not in any other manner or for any other purpose, 27 V., S. 1, c. 24, s 6s

The Executive Committee shall fix and determine the allotments of the £5000 on account of Parochial Roads, in such amounts or appropriations as may seem advisable, upon consideration of the representations already or to be made by the Local Boards of Highways and Bridges, as to the damages occasioned by recent floods and as to the necessity of assistance being given in forming new, or reconstructing existing Roads extensively used for purposes of traffic, 27 V. S. 1, c. 24, s. 7. Roads to which to be allotted

Detailed accounts of the expenditure of the loan monies to be laid before the Assembly. 27 V., S. 1, c. 24, s. 8. Accounts to be laid before the Assembly.

The Governor and Executive Committee were authorized to use out of the Treasury not exceeding £3000, for damages occasioned by the May floods, 1864, to Parochial Roads and Bridges, 27 V. S. 2, c. 6, s. 1. Further allotment of £3000.

Accounts of which to be laid before the Assembly, distinguishing the amounts expended for temporary repairs, from those for permanent repairs, made up to the latest period, 27 V., S. 2, c. 6, s. 2.

Hogs and Goats.

When any Hog or Goat is found in any cane-piece, mill-yard, coffee-piece, corn-piece, provision-ground, grass-piece, pasture or other land, without the consent of the owner or person in possession, the owner or his attorney, overseer or penkeeper, or the person in possession or charge, or any person employed thereon, may kill or cause, &c. every such hog or goat, and deliver the carcase to the owner, upon application, if made within 4 hours after, but if not, the person who killed, or caused it to be killed, may dispose of the carcase as he thinks proper, without being liable to any penalty or damage, 22 V., c. 17, s. 2. Found in Cane Pieces, &c. may be destroyed.

Any two Justices at the first Petty Session Court in January, April, July and October, and at a Petty Session to be held at such other times as they think proper, may direct the sergeant or some policeman in any city, town or village, to give notice, by printed or written bills posted on the entrance doors of the Court-House, police stations and market house, and in or near the market-places where there is no market-house, and in such other manner as they think best, that all Hogs and Goats found at large in the streets or lanes, or in any burial-ground or church-yard, will, after the expiration of 7 days from the date of the first notice so posted or given, be taken up and destroyed, 22 V., s. 17, s. 3. Destruction of Hogs and Goats found in the Streets

Every Hog or Goat found at large or tethered in any street, lane or public place, shall be forfeited by the owner, and may be killed or seized and appropriated to his own use, by any person employed as after stated to destroy or seize the animal before it can regain the premises of its owner and be claimed to be protected by him, 22 V., c. 17, s. 4. Destruction of

The owner of any Hog or Goat found in any street, lane or public place, or the person who claims to protect any hog or goat found at large. and pursued into his premises, shall be liable on summary conviction before any Petty Session to a penalty of not exceeding 40s. or imprisonment not exceeding one calendar month, 22 V., c. 17, s. 5. Penalty for protecting them.

If the Inspector of Police, whenever necessary, shall employ any requisite number of persons to destroy or remove or to seize all Hogs and Goats found at large, or tethered in any street, &c., and their remuneration shall be fixed and regulated by the Justices in Petty Sessions, and on due proof of the Employment of Persons to destroy and seize,

performance of the duty, the Justices shall direct their Clerk to pay out of the fines collected, the remuneration fixed to the persons entitled, 22 V. c. 17, s. 6.

Owner may reclaim on payment of 10s.

The owner of any Hog or Goat seized or killed by the means aforesaid, may immediately on its capture, and before its disposal by the person seizing reclaim the animal, or its carcase, on payment of 10s, 22 V., c. 17, s. 7.

Obstruction.

Any person offering, or causing obstruction to any other while engaged in the pursuit, capture or destruction of any such animal, shall be liable, on conviction before 2 Justices, to a penalty not exceeding £5, or imprisonment, with or without hard labor, not exceeding 60 days 22, V., c. 17, s. 8.

Interpretation.

The expressions " Hogs and Goats" shall mean and include all animals of their respective kinds, 22 V., c. 17, s. 9.

Police to protect persons employed.

The Inspector shall direct the police to protect persons employed to seize and destroy Hogs and Goats whilst so employed, and also in carrying away for their own use all Hogs and Goats so seized or destroyed, 22 V., c. 17, s. 10.

Holidays in Public Offices.

None shall be observed or kept except the days mentioned in Schedule A. and B., the days to be set apart for the observance of the Birthday of Her Majesty, her heirs and successors, and such days as shall by Proclamation of the Governor be specially appointed to be observed as Holidays or Fast Days, 8 V., c. 30.

SCHEDULE A.

Island Secretary's Office.	New Year's Day and the day following.
Registrar in Chancery.	Ash-Wednesday, Good-Friday, Easter Monday and Tuesday, Christmas Day, and two days after, 7th June and 28th August.
Provost-Marshal-General.	
Clerk of the Supreme Court.	

SCHEDULE B.

Receiver-General and Stamp Office, and all other Public Offices in Kingston.	New Year's Day, Ash-Wednesday, Good-Friday, Easter Monday, Christmas Day, and the day following, 7th June, 28th August.
Customs.	
Holidays to be kept by the Customs,	Queen's Birthday and same as in Schedule B., 17 V., c. 33, s. 16.

Horses and Cattle.

Stoned Horses.

No person shall put to pasture, or suffer to run at large at any common savannah or waste ground, any stoned-horse not of the height of 14½ hands, and 3 years old and upwards, to be measured from the lowest part of the hoof of either of the forefeet, to the highest part of the withers, and every hand to contain 4 inches of the standard, on pain of forfeiting the horse, 26 V. S. 1, c. 3, s. 1.

Any person who finds any such stoned-horse at pasture, or running at large, may seize and take it before a Justice to have it measured in view of such Justice, and if found not to be of the height, the horse shall be forfeited to and the property immediately vested in the person taking up the same (on his making oath as to the time and place where the horse was taken up,) unless the owner or some person on his behalf, tender to him £1 for each horse, in which case it shall (being first castrated, and the owner paying the expense) be restored, 26 V. S. 1. c. 3, s 2.

Glandered, &c., Horses, &c.

No person shall put to pasture or suffer to run at large any horse, mare or gelding, or any mule or ass infected with scab, mange, farcy or glanders, upon any common, pasture, savannah or waste ground or highway, street or lane. Penalty not exceeding £6 to be recovered before 2 Justices, 26 V. S. 1, c. 3, s. 3.

Any person who knowingly put in or turns upon any pasture, common savannah or waste ground, highway, street or lane, any horse, &c. having the farcy, glanders, or other infectious disease shall forfeit not exceeding £6, recoverable as aforesaid; but not to prevent any pe n injured from bringing his action for the damage sustained, 26 V. S. ₹sec. 3, s. 4.

₹On due proof by competent witnesses, that any horse, &c., is infected as aforesaid, being made before a Magistrate, he shall order the beast to be destroyed, 26 V. S. 1, c. 3, s. 5.

The Executive Committee shall provide Queen's Purses of £105 each, to be run for on 2nd Tuesday in March, 1866, over Black River Course ; in 1867, over Savanna-la-Mar Course ; in 1868, over Falmouth Course, the best of three mile heats under the usual regulations at Races for H. M's Plates in Great Britain, at the following weights, viz: 3 years old, 7 stone ; 4 years old, 8 stone ; 5 years old, 8 stone, 7 lbs. ; 6 years old, 8 stone, 12 lbs ; aged, 9 stone, with the usual allowance of 3lbs to Mares and Geldings. As also purses of £105 each to be run for in like manner, on the 3rd Tuesday in April, 1866, over the Manchester Course ; 1st Tuesday of August, 1867, over the St. Ann's Course, 3rd Tuesday of December, 1868, over Spanish Town Race Course, or such other Course in St. Catherine as the Stewards of the Races may agree on, under the rules, regulations and weights before directed, as also a purse of £105, in 1865, 1866, 1867 and 1868, on the 2nd Tuesday of December, over the Kingston Course, under the above rules, &c., or if there is no Course, in either of the above places, at the time, the Judge of the Race may appoint it to be run over the Course nearest and most convenient. No horse shall be allowed to win more than 2 Queen's Purses under this or any former Act. The Custos shall appoint the Judge, or if not he shall be chosen by a majority of the persons (or by some person for each on their behalf,) in whose names the horses are entered, and the Judge shall give the owner of the winning horse, a certificate that he is entitled to the Queen's Purse, to be paid by the Receiver-General on being endorsed by 2 Members of the Executive Committee. No Queen's Purse shall be allowed unless it is shewn to the Executive Committee, that at the meeting there were at least 4 other bona fide Purses or Cups raised, run for, and paid, worth at least £20, exclusive of Stakes paid by the owners of running horses ; in the event of any parish failing to comply with which terms the Executive Committee may transfer the Purse to some other parish in the same County the following year, 26 V. S. 1, c. 3, s. 6. 26 V, S. 2. c. 11.

Queen's Purses

The Receiver-General shall pay 20 Guineas on 20th January in each year, during the continuance of this Act, and the year after its expiry, to the breeder of the heaviest Ox, Heifer or Cow slaughtered previously to 31st December, which, when slaughtered, exclusive of the suet, heart, liver, lights, head, tongue, tail, feet, entrails, hide and all offals, exceed 1450 pounds weight, first producing a certificate sworn to, and specifying separately the weights, as well of the several quarters, as of each part above excluded, to be ascertained by actual weighing in the presence of the Clerk of the Market, or of a Justice, where there is none, 26 V. S. 1, c. 3, s. 7.

Prize Oxen

The Receiver-General shall pay on 31st of December in each year, £30 to the importer or importers of each of the first 4 entire horses, of either of the Cleveland Bay, Clydesdale, Suffolk, Punch breed or American breed, not less than 3 nor above 6 years, nor under 15 hands height, imported in each year; £20 for each of the first 4 mares, not less than 3 nor above 5 years, nor under 15 hands, of either of the above breeds ; £20 for each of the 4 first bulls, of either the Shorthorn, Devon, Sussex or Hereford breeds, of not less than 18 months nor over 3 years old, and after having been at least 3 months in the island ; and £10 for each of the first 3 rams, of the Southdown or Leicester breed, that has been in the island for 3 months ; the breed of the horses, mares, bulls and rams to be certified by competent persons in Great Britain or America, the certificates to accompany them on importation, and the importers to produce them to the Custos, Members, and 2 other Magistrates of the parish in which they are imported, any 3 of whom on being satisfied that they are such as are contemplated, shall so certify to the Receiver-General, and he shall, on the warrant of the Governor, pay the premium to the importers, their agents or representatives, 26 V. S. 1, c. 3, s. 8.

Prize Horses, Mares, Bulls, and Rams

£100 shall be paid annually to the Agricultural Society in any parish which first proves to the Executive Committee that they have raised by individual contributions an equal sum for the importation of cattle for the improvement of the breed in this island, 26 V. S. 1, c. 3, s. 9.

£100 to Agricultural Society

I I

Penalties Penalties shall be enforced by distress warrant of a Justice ; or upon a return that sufficient goods cannot be found, the Defendant may be committed for 20 days, unless sooner paid, one moiety to the informer, 26 V., S. 1, c. 3, s. 10.

Duration In force until 31st December, 1866, 26 V., S. 1, c. 3, s. 11.

Husband and Wife, Conveyances by.

Validity of All Bills of Sale and Conveyances made by Husband and Wife, and acknowledged and recorded, shall be valid against all persons as if they had passed by fine and recovery in any of the Courts of Westminster, 33 C. 2, c. 22, s. 3.

Immigrants.

Interpretation " Immigration Agent" shall include any person appointed by the Governor to act as Agent-General or Sub-Agent; "Immigrant," all persons introduced under this Act; "Indian Immigrant," any Immigrant introduced from the British possessions in the East Indies ; "Asiatic Immigrant," any Immigrant introduced from any other part of the Continent or Islands of Asia, (including China, 23 V., c. 29, s. 1) except the British possessions in the East Indies ; "African Immigrant," any Immigrant from the African Continent or Madagascar, or any other Island adjacent to the Coast of the African Continent inhabited by the negro race ; "Indenture," all contracts of service, whether by indenture, or otherwise declared valid; "Indentured Immigrant," any Immigrant under indenture, who has not completed his industrial residence ; "Employer," the proprietor, including any Body Corporate, Company or Association interested in the cultivation of Estates, or the manufacture of agricultural produce, or Manager, Attorney, Overseer, or other person having the direction of or chief authority upon any Sugar, Coffee, or other plantation, breeding penn, or pimento walk upon which any Immigrant may be employed. The Lessee or Tenant of any Estate shall, during the continuance of his lease or agreement, be deemed a proprietor, 22 V., c. 1, s. 1.

Agent-General and Sub-agent The Governor may appoint and remove an Agent-General and Sub-Agents of Immigration to act within the limits or districts specified in their appointments. Each Sub-Agent shall be also an Inspector of Immigrants, 22 V., c. 1, s. 2.

Agent-General's salary The Governor and Executive Committee may direct payment to the Agent-General of £500 per annum, out of the funds chargeable with his **Treasury, 22 V., c. 1, s. 2** salary, 27 V., S. 2, c. 8.

Sub agent's remuneration And to each Sub-Agent not less than 2s. and not exceeding 6s. for each Immigrant, per annum, placed under his care, to be calculated with regard to their number and location, 24 V., c. 16, s. 3.

Security Sub-Agents shall give security to account, and be allowed commissions on their collections, to pay the premium to the Guarantee Society, 27 V., S. 2, c. 5, s. 20.

Agents abroad The Governor, with the sanction of H. M. Government, may appoint Agents at ports of emigration from which Immigrants may be embarked under regulations, and fix their remuneration not exceeding in any year £3000, 22 V., c. 1, s. 3.

Ports of Emigration And by proclamation or notice in the Gazette, and, if he thinks fit, London Gazette, and any newspaper out of the Island, name the ports or places from which Immigration is permitted, and the conditions under which it may be carried on, 22 V., c. 1, s. 4.

Proportion of sexes He shall make provision for the introduction of such a proportionate number of Immigrants of both sexes as may be fixed by H. M's. Government, 22 V., c. 1, s. 5.

Contracts before arrival If any Immigrant from Madeira, the Azores, the Canaries or the Cape de Verde Islands, or Europe, the West Indies, the United States or British Provinces of North America, or from any port or place from which Immigration is permitted, before arrival, contracts with any person to perform service in this island, the contract, when approved of and countersigned by the Immigration Agent, and subject to such alterations as he may make, with the consent of parties, shall be valid for not exceeding 3 years. Except as after mentioned, no contract shall be approved and countersigned unless it is signed with the names or marks of the contracting parties, and purports to be attested by a Justice, whose signature shall be attested by a notary public, or by a notary public in the first instance, or British Consul or some other person approved by, or acting under H. Majesty's Government, one of whom shall certify that the parties entered into it voluntarily and with a full understanding of its meaning, nor unless the Immigration Agent is satisfied the Immigration has been carried on in accordance with all existing regulations of the Imperial Government and of the Legislature, 22 V., c. 1, s. 6

To be approved by the Immigration Agent

If the Immigration Agent is not so satisfied, or finds the contract not to be so signed and attested, he shall report to the Governor, who may, notwithstanding, direct him to approve and countersign it, 22 V., c. 1, s. 7.

Governor may direct the Agent to approve

In case any Immigrant other than an Asiatic or Indian, before embarkation, has consented to enter, upon arrival, into a contract with any employer the Immigration Agent may select, for not exceeding 3 years, such consent being shewn by certificate of the Government Immigration Agent, or by an agreement signed by the Immigrant, and witnessed by a notary consul or other officer, the Immigration Agent may indenture him to any employer the Governor thinks fit. No assignment shall take effect until the employer and Immigrant or Immigration Agent on his behalf, have executed an Indenture m (No. 4), or as may be approved of by the Governor, 22 V., c. 1, s. 8 For

Contracts of service to employers to be selected by the Immigration Agent
Chinese 5 years, 25 V., c. 35, s. 8, also Indians and liberated Africans, 27 V., 8. 2, c. 5, s. 1, 7 Indenture

No contract for service unless otherwise provided for by any Act relating to Immigration shall be binding for any period exceeding 3 years, 23 V., c. 31, s. 2.

Duration of contracts

The Agent-General shall, when directed by the Governor, cause a notice to be published in the Gazette by authority (Forms No. 1, 2), requiring proprietors and managers to make application to him for such Immigrants as they desire to indenture upon their arrival, and to notify the names and residences of each proprietor, the estate, the number wanted, the description of the buildings in which they are to be located, and the country or place from which he is desirous they should be introduced, and to express the willingness of the proprietor to accept the services of so many as shall be allotted to him, not exceeding the number applied for immediately after their arrival, which application the Agent-General shall submit to the Governor and Executive Committee with a view to arrangements being made for the introduction of the required number, or as many as practicable, 22 V., c. 1, s. 9.

Notices for application for Immigrants

Every applicant refusing to accept the services of the Immigrants allotted to him under 22 V., c. 1, s. 9, shall forfeit, in lieu of other moneys under that Act, a sum equivalent to £1 for each year every such Immigrant would otherwise be indentured for him, with the cost of food and lodging incurred by the Island between the arrival of the Immigrant and the transfer of his services, to be ascertained and fixed by the Agent-General, and the whole or such amount as the Governor sees fit to direct shall be immediately enforceable, 24 V., c. 16, s. 2.

Liabilities of applicants

The Agent at any port of emigration shall transmit to the Agent-General by the vessel in which the Immigrants are shipped, and other ordinary means of communication, a return of the age, as near as can be ascertained, of every Immigrant shipped, and such other particulars as the Governor directs, 22 V., c. 1, s. 10.

Reports of age, &c. from agents abroad

Passage money shall be paid only for such as are landed alive, 24 V., c. 16, s. 1.

Passage money

If any Immigrant is not immediately provided with employment, the Immigration Agent shall provide him with food and lodgings at the expense of the Island until indentured, to be re-paid by the person to whom he is indentured, 22 V., c. 1, s. 13.

Food and lodging before indentured

The Governor may make regulations, to be binding upon employers, respecting the food and clothing to be provided for Immigrants during their first 3 months of service, and respecting their lodging, medicine, and medical care, also during the continuance of their indentures, and respecting other matters necessary for carrying this Act into effect, to be published in the Jamaica Gazette, 22 V., c. 1, s. 14.

Food, clothing, medical attendance, &c. after indenture

Every Immigrant, in the absence of express agreement, shall, during

Allowances during illness

illness, receive, instead of wages, such allowances as the state of his health requires, or as may be directed by any regulation to be issued and published by the Governor, 22 V., c. 1, s. 15.

Medical officer, sick to be brought before him

The person in charge of every estate on which Immigrants are employed shall cause, to be brought before the medical officer, at each periodical visit, every indentured Immigrant upon such property, whom he believes, or who reports himself to be labouring under any disease or malady, or suffering from any bodily injury or hurt, or in any respect to require medical or surgical treatment, 27 V., S. 2, c. 5, s. 10.

Register book to be kept by him in Hospital

Every medical practitioner charged with the care of attendance on Immigrants, shall keep in each hospital or room set apart for the sick, a book in which to record his visits, and a Register Book (Form) and a Case Book (Form,) and enter in the Register Book the name, age, sex, and race of each Immigrant under his care in such hospital, and further state in the Case Book the nature of the disease or injury from which the patient is believed or alleged to be suffering, the remedies and diet prescribed by him in each case, and the result; and the Immigration Agent of the district shall have access to such Register and Case Books at any time between 7 a.m. and 6 p.m., 22 V., S. 2, c. 5, s. 11.

Reports.

The medical man attending, when required by the Governor, shall make general or special reports or returns in reference to the Immigrants under his care, and to all matters respecting their sanitary state, and enter or allow to be entered, a copy of any such report or return on the Estates' Hospital Book, 27 V., S. 2, c. 5, s. 12.

Public Hospital Dues,

No employer shall be subject to any charge for hospital dues, on account of any Immigrant under indenture to him, unless sent or taken to the hospital by his direction or consent; and the charge per diem, in such case, shall not exceed 1s., 27 V., S. 2, c. 5, s. 13.

Register

The Agent-General shall keep a register (Form No. 3) for separate classes of Immigrants arriving, distinguishing each class by a particular alphabetical letter, and insert therein the names of all Immigrants of each class arriving, and number each by a particular number, commencing with No. 1 and proceeding by regular numerical progression, and distinguish under different heads the letter, number, name, age, sex and country of every Immigrant, the time when, place whence, and vessel in which he arrived, the cost of passage, whether introduced by means of the unappropriated residue of the £100,000 loan raised under 15 V., c. 20 and 16 V., c. 25, or of loans under other Acts, (specifying them) or by the private means of the employer or other person (naming him), and the average cost of importation, (stating such average cost in the column, 24 V., c. 16, s. 10) and whether entitled or not to a return passage; also the name of the employer to whom indentured on arrival, and the moneys, if any, advanced to him previously to his arrival and to be re-paid out of his wages, and such further particulars as the Governor directs; and shall furnish to each Sub-Agent full particulars in respect of every Immigrant located in or transferred to his district, 22 V., c. 1, s. 16.

Annual returns of employers

The employer shall, on or before 13th October in each year, make a Return, (Form No. 5) to the 30th September preceding, of the names and numbers of all such Immigrants as have been in his employment at any time during the past year, with the date and cause (as far as may be known) of all deaths, and the number of births, and the names of all who have left the estate during such preceding year, to the Agent-General, who shall insert the particulars in the Register to be kept by him; and the Agent-General shall,

And Agent General

at the end of every year terminating on 30th September, furnish the Governor with an abstract return, in triplicate, of the number, sex, increase and decrease of all Immigrants in the Island who have not completed their industrial residence; also of each sex arrived within the previous 12 months, the ships and date, to be furnished on or before the 10th November, and laid before the Legislative Council and Assembly, 22 V., c. 1, s. 17.

Indenturing Indian Immigrants, see 27 V., S. 2, c. 5, s. 7

Every Indian Immigrant, arriving before 12th October, 1864, was required to be assigned by indenture, (Form No. 4), for a period of 2 years, and might, within one month after the expiration of that period, be re-indentured to any other employer whom he might select, for a further period of one year, and within one month after the expiration of the third year, and on payment of £5 might demand a certificate of industrial residence, or within such period as might be prescribed by the Governor, before the expiration of such third year, signify to the Immigration Agent his desire to be re-indentured to any other employer whom he might select, for one year from the termination of his existing indenture, and the Agent should re-indenture him accordingly; and if he should fail to make such payment or require such re-indenture, his original indenture or re-indenture should be deemed to be extended for one year, 22 V., c. 1. s. 18.

And might, within one month after the expiration of his 4th years' service, on payment of £2 10s., demand a certificate of industrial residence, or might require, and be re-indentured for a 5th year; and if he fails to do so, his last indenture should be deemed to be extended for such 5th year, 22 V., c. 1, s. 19. *Asiatic Immigrants. As to Chinese, see 23 V., c 29, s. 4; 25 V. c. 36, s. 8*

The Immigration Agent may assign any Asiatic Immigrant, on his arrival, for not exceeding 5 years, according to the terms of any contract into which he enters before arrival. At the expiration of the 2nd and every other year, the Immigrant may require the Agent to transfer him to some other employer, whom he may select, for the remainder of the period, or on payment of all advances before arrival, and of £3 per ann. for every year wanting to complete 5 years' residence, to release him from his indenture, and give him a certificate of industrial residence, such assignment and transfer to be made by indenture, as nearly as may be, in (Form 4), or such other as may be approved of by the Governor, and determinable, at the request of the Immigrant, in like manner as the original assignment, 22 V., c. 1, s. 20.

In making any assignment, the Agent shall not separate husbands from wives, nor children under 15 from their parents or natural protectors, 22 V., c. 1, s. 21. *Husbands and wives and children*

Husbands and wives, and children, shall be included in one indenture, and one contract entered into, as to all so included, for payment of the sums chargeable, 24 V., c. 16, s. 8.

So much of 22 V., c. 1, s. 8, and s. 11, 12, 59, 60, 61, 62, 63, and other sections of the same or any other Act relating to the payment by employers of the cost of importation, and incidental expenses, repealed, except where otherwise provided, 24 V., c. 16, s. 28. *Contracts for payment of sums chargeable against employers*

Form No 9 of the Schedule referred to in the repealed sections 59, 60, and Forms Nos. 10 and 11, referred to in s. 68, of 22 V., c. 1, cancelled, and in lieu, Forms Nos. 1, 2. and 3 substituted, subject to alterations or modifications in the case of Chinese Immigrants, as circumstances require, 24 V., c. 16, s. 7.

For providing funds for importation, and the re-payment of moneys borrowed under the "Immigration Loan Act, 1858," (22 V., c. 3.) there shall be levied and paid the moneys after mentioned, in lieu of those provided by any Act, except the Export Duties under 15 V., c. 39, 24 V., c. 16, s. 5. *Immigration Funds*

The employer shall, at the time of entering into indenture, pay to the Immigration Agent all moneys incurred for food and lodging of every Immigrant indentured after 3 days from the time notice is given of the allotment to him (such time in case of personal service to run from the day after notice is given, or, in case of notice through the Post Office of the district, from the day after that on which such notice is deliverable at such Post Office,) 24 V., c. 16, s. 6. *Payment by employers annually and otherwise*

Instead of the annual payments by 24 V., c. 16 directed, the employer of every Immigrant already or to be allotted, except in the case of liberated Africans free of cost, shall pay in advance for every year's service of every Immigrant of or above 12 years, £1 10s., and for every year's service of every child under 12, 15s., and shall enter into a like contract, (except as to the amounts of annual payments) as directed by 24 V., c. 16. (Form No. 1) to secure in advance the respective annual payments for each year subsequent to the first; but employers of Immigrants already indentured might subscribe a memorandum of agreement in the form annexed, to be annexed to or endorsed on the contracts entered into under 24 V., c. 16, which should be valid to secure the annual payments in advance therein mentioned or indicated, 25 V., c. 35, s. 1. *Increased annual payments See as to liberated Africans, 28 V., c. 3* *Memorandum on contracts already entered into*

In case of refusal or neglect, then the Immigrants were to be allotted to some other employer, 25 V., c. 35, s. 3. *On neglect to make payments, &c' indenture may be determined*

Indentures to lessees

All existing provisions shall remain in operation for payment of moneys incurred or to be incurred for food and lodging, 25 V., c. 35, s. 4.

Indentures to lessees

No Immigrant introduced by the Government shall be indentured to a lessee or tenant, unless the owner is a party to the indenture or contract for payment of the expenses of introduction, and [or] the lease or agreement has a longer period to run than the indenture, or the lessee enters into separate security to provide for payment of such expense, and for the location and maintenance of such Immigrants, to be approved of by the Governor and Executive Committee, 22 V., c. 1, s. 22.

Death of employer, &c., right to services of Immigrant, transfer

If the employer die, or the Estate mentioned in the contract is determined, forfeited, alienated or devised, the person who becomes entitled to such Estate shall be entitled to the services of the Immigrant during the residue of his indenture. For the purpose of deciding any dispute as to the title to the Estate and the services of the Immigrants, the person actually in possession shall be deemed entitled, but the services of an indentured Immigrant may be transferred, with his consent, to any other Estate belonging to the same employer; a memorandum of the transfer to be endorsed on the contract and signed by the Immigration Agent, 22 V., c. 1, s. 23.

Cancelling indentures and re indenturing

The Immigration Agent may, with the sanction of the Governor, cancel the indenture of every Immigrant, in respect of whom any money remains unpaid for 3 months, or for 1 month after a distress warrant has issued for want of goods whereon to levy; or the indenture of any Immigrant who being paid according to the quantity of his work, has not received work sufficient, in the opinion of the agent, to enable him to earn a reasonable amount of wages; or in case any immigrant has been ill-used by his employer, or of neglect of duty or breach of contract on the part of any employer, in addition to any other penalty or forfeiture, 22 V., c. 1, s. 24.

Insufficient accommodation, proved misconduct, or Governor's directions

If the Agent-General reports that the accommodation provided for any Immigrant is bad or insufficient, or any proved misconduct of the employer towards any Immigrant, or if, on any other ground, the Governor considers it requisite, he may direct the Agent-General to cancel the indenture, and also those of every other Immigrant indentured to such employer, and indenture them to others, and from the date of such indenture, the preceding employer shall be released from any future pecuniary or other liability. The

Period of re indenture

term of service under any new indenture, shall not, with the time of past service, exceed the period for which he was previously bound, 23 V., c. 31, s. 1.

At employer's request

The Immigration Agent may, with the sanction of the Governor, at the request of any employer and Immigrant, cancel any indenture for the purpose of re-indenture, 22 V., c. 1, s. 25.

Re-indenture without Immigrant's consent

Any Immigrant whose indenture has been cancelled, may (without his consent) be re-indentured, not exceeding the unexpired period, 22 V., c. 1, s. 26.

Absence from service, compensation, see 27 V., S. 2, c. 5, s. 14, 15

No Indian or Asiatic Immigrant, who deserts or absents himself from service, otherwise than from illness, while under indenture, for periods amounting together to more than one month in each year, shall be entitled to a certificate of industrial residence, until he has further served under indenture for the period of absence or desertion, unless he give a money commutation, 22 V., c. 1, s. 27.

Whenever an Immigrant is required to make good time lost from absence or desertion, he may, with the sanction of the Immigration Agent, commute by a money payment to the employer, to be fixed by the Agent, subject to the decision of the Governor, in case either party is dissatisfied with

During imprisonment

his award. Absence while undergoing imprisonment to be made good by service or compensation, 22 V., c. 1, s. 28.

Industrial residence. Since 19th Oct. 1684, see 27 V., S. 2, c. 5, s. 1.

In the case of Immigrants under 12, residence in the island shall, for completing industrial residence, be equivalent to residence under indenture; immediately after that age, they shall be liable to be indentured by the Agent-General for the then residue of their term, and to the privileges and obligations of an indentured Immigrant. The Agent-General shall determine the period at which the Immigrant attains 12, according to the best evidence or information he can obtain, 22 V., c. 1, s. 29.

Immigrant's title to certificate of

All Immigrants, other than Indian or Asiatic, shall be entitled, after 3 years' residence, to demand from the Agent a certificate of industrial residence, unless it is recorded in his office, or otherwise appears that such Immigrant has deserted or absented himself from service, otherwise than from illness, while under indenture, for periods amounting together, during the 3 years, to more than 3 months, in which case he shall not be entitled to such certificate until he has further served for the period of absence or desertion, or given a money compensation, 22 V., c. 1, s. 30.

Any Asiatic or Indian Immigrant who has served 5 years under indenture, or made money payments in lieu of service, may demand a certificate of industrial residence, (Form No. 6), 22 V., c. 1, s. 31. Asiatic and Indian

Immigrants born out of the British Dominions, who obtain or become entitled to a certificate of industrial residence shall be immediately entitled to all the privileges of a natural born British subject, 22 V., c. 1, s. 32. Naturalization

Every Immigrant who has received, or become entitled to such certificate, may abandon service, and demand from the Immigration Agent a passport, (Form No. 7, altered by 27 V. S. 2, c. 5, s. 4) which, as well as the certificate, shall be signed and given gratis, but no Immigrant shall depart the island without such passport, 22 V. c. 1, s. 33. Passports

Every Indian Immigrant on production of his passport, may depart at his own expense, or, after 10 years' residence, be entitled to a back-passage at the expense of the island to the port in India from which he emigrated, provided he claim such back-passage, within 18 months after it becomes due, unless he has, with the sanction of the Governor, foregone such right in consideration of a grant of land, or money payment, or partly of a grant of land, and partly of a payment in money. The Governor shall give each applicant at least 3 months' notice, as precise as circumstances render possible, of the period at which the passage will be offered him, 22 V., c. 1, s. 34. Return passages

The Governor may authorize the Immigration Agent to grant a certificate of exemption from industrial service (Form No. 8) to any Immigrant who, from sickness, accident or other cause, appears incapable of labour, and may send any Indian Immigrant back, at the expense of the fund provided, to the port whence he emigrated, at any time afterwards, 22 V., c. 1, s. 35. Certificate of exemption

Every Indian who becomes entitled to a back-passage, shall receive, out of the fund provided, 25s. for every 6 months he is detained, 22 V., c. 1, s. 36. Demurrage back-passage

In respect of ships leaving with return Immigrants, the Agent shall perform all the duties imposed on Immigration Agents in England by the Passengers' Act, 1855, of the Imperial Parliament, or any other Passengers' Act in force, 22 V., c. I, s. 37. Passengers' Acts

The Immigration Agent shall collect and take po s i of the property of any Immigrant dying, and, with the sanction of the Governor, deliver it to any person who establishes a right thereto, or, in the absence of any such person, turn the property into money, and pay the proceeds into the Island Treasury, to be remitted to the persons in India, or elsewhere, entitled, 22 V., c. 1, s. 38. Property of deceased Immigrants

The Governor may make all regulations for giving effect to the last section. Any person contravening such regulations, liable, on conviction, to a penalty not exceeding £5, 22 V., c. 1, s. 39. Regulations relating thereto

Every indentured Immigrant, in the absence of express agreement, and except in case of illness, shall be bound to work upon, or in the service of the estate mentioned in his indenture for 9 hours of each day, except Sundays, Good Friday, New-Year's Day and Christmas Day, and such other days to be observed as festivals, according to the national customs of the class to which he is registered as belonging, as the Governor shall appoint, 22 V., c. 1, s. 40. Hours of labour, holidays
Chinese, see 25 V., c. 35, s. 8

The Immigration Agent may enter upon any estate where Immigrants are employed, and inspect their condition, and require a muster of those on the estate, and shall, at such periods as the Governor directs, visit and inspect every estate whereon they are employed, 22 V., c. 1, s. 41. Inspection by agent

Every employer shall, within 24 hours after it comes to his knowledge that any Immigrant has deserted, report such desertion at the nearest Police Station, stating the distinguishing letter, and number, and names, with the date of indenture, and every other information likely to facilitate his apprehension; and the Police shall circulate such report among the several stations throughout the island. Employers failing to comply, shall forfeit not exceeding £5, 22 V., c. 1, s. 42. Reports of desertion

Absence from estate, apprehension

The employer or any servant of his, the Immigration Agent, or any Police Constable, or Rural Constable, may stop, without a warrant, any African, Indian, or Asiatic Immigrant at any time (except Sundays, or holidays, or festivals) found during the hours of work more than 2 miles from the estate, and if he fail to produce, upon being required, a certificate of exemption or of industrial residence, or a written ticket of leave, signed by his employer, may take him back to the estate, or if he refuses to disclose the name of the estate, then shall take him forthwith to some neighbouring Justice, who shall forthwith enquire into the case, and unless satisfied that the Immigrant has completed such residence, or obtained such exemption, or is absent with leave, shall make order for his immediate committal to the nearest prison, (not a County gaol) with or without hard labour not exceeding 30 (27 V., S. 2, c. 5, s. 15) days, 22 V., c. 1, s. 43.

Desertion to be recorded in plantation book, and accessible to Immigration Agent

The manager of every estate, within 24 hours of his having knowledge of the desertion of any Immigrant, shall make entry and record thereof, and of the particulars, (Form) ; such record to be kept on the estate, and accessible to the Immigration Agent at any time between 7 a. m. and 6 p. m., 27 V., S. 2, c. 5, s. 14.

Desertion After 3 months, employer not chargeable, or in case of return entitled to abatement, nor while undergoing of imprisonment

In case of desertion or absence from service for 3 months, the employer shall not be chargeable for such Immigrant after such 3 months, or in case of his return to service, only in proportion to the period of service after such return, nor shall he be chargeable for any period during which the Immigrant may be undergoing imprisonment, 27 V.; S. 2, c. 5, s. 16.

Penalties on employers, &c.

Every employer who omits to make the annual return, (s. 17), every person who, by act or omission, obstructs the Immigration Agent in entering upon any plantation where any Immigrant is employed, or in enquiring into the condition of any Immigrant, (s. 41) shall, on conviction, forfeit not exceeding £20, 22 V., c. 1, s. 44.

On Immigrants

Every Immigrant who, during his indenture, without lawful excuse, absents himself from his work, (s. 40, 43) shall forfeit his claim to wages and allowances for the time he absents himself, and, on conviction, shall be imprisoned in the nearest prison, (not a County gaol) and kept to hard labor for not exceeding 14 days, 22 V., c. 1, s. 45.

Loss or damage of employers' property

If any Immigrant, by negligence or improper conduct, lose, throw away, endanger or damage the property of his employer, or endanger such property by a careless or improper use of fire, or cruelly illuse any cattle, or live stock belonging to his employer, or entrusted to his care, or by negligence occasion them to be cruelly illused, he shall, on conviction, be punished by imprisonment, with or without hard labor, not exceeding 30 days, 22 V., c. 1, s. 46.

Improper use of certificates or passports

Any Immigrant who falsely or fraudulently pretends that he has completed his industrial residence, or uses, gives or lends any certificate or passport for any fraudulent purpose, or wilfully counterfeits or alters any certificate or passport, shall, on conviction, be imprisoned with hard labor for not exceeding 3 months, 22 V., c. 1, s. 47.

Harbouring, penalty

Every person harbouring or employing any Immigrant under indenture, or inveigling or enticing him to quit or desert from his legal service, shall be deemed guilty of an offence, and on conviction before 2 Justices shall pay a fine not exceeding £5, or be imprisoned with or without hard labour not exceeding 3 months, as the Committing Justices shall adjudge ; the fine when pa   to be appropriated to the credit of the Further Immigration Fund, 1868, 27 V. S. 2, c. 5, s. 17.

Damages to employer

Every person who harbours or employs any Immigrant under indenture, shall, in addition to such fine, pay to the employer by way of damages at the rate of 4s. for every day the Immigrant has been employed by him. In case of any such Immigrant being employed on an estate, it shall be sufficient to support a conviction, to prove that the Immigrant has been employed thereon while under the personal charge and superintendence of the person charged ; such damages to be recovered as any money ordered to be paid under any Act, for the time in force, respecting summary convictions and orders by Justices, 27 V., S. 2, c. 5, s. 18.

22 V., c. 1, s. 48, repealed except proviso

Except the proviso 22 V., c. 1, s. 48, repealed, but the proviso kept in force, 27. V., S. 2, c. 5, s. 19.

If any employer states upon oath before a Justice that he has reasonable cause to suspect any Immigrant is harboured, concealed or employed on the premises of any person, such Justice may grant a warrant to search for, and bring him and the person by whom he is harboured, &c., before him, to be dealt with as provided, 22 V., c. 1, s. 48.

Search Warrant

Every Master or person in charge of any vessel, who knowingly receives or harbours on board any Immigrant who has not duly obtained his passport, with the intention of carrying him out of this island, or any person who aids and abets the departure of any such Immigrant, shall, on conviction, forfeit not exceeding £20 for each, 22 V., c. 1, s. 49.

Carrying away Immigrants without passports

All offences and breaches of any stipulation or engagement in any indenture, on the part of either employer or Immigrant, for which no punishment is otherwise provided, may be heard and determined by the Immigration Agent, and, on conviction, be punishable, in case of any employer, by fine, not exceeding £5, and in default of payment, imprisonment not exceeding one month, and in case of any Immigrant, imprisonment, with or without hard labour, not exceeding one month, 22 V., c. 1, s. 50.

Jurisdiction of Immigration Agent

Every Indenture, Contract, Document or other proceeding, or any copy thereof, or any extract from the Register to be kept by the Agent-General, certified by or purporting to bear the signature of any Immigration Agent, shall be received as prima facie evidence of the original, and of the truth of the contents, 22 V., c. 1, s. 51.

Evidence

All Appointments, Documents and legal Instruments required or made evidence by this Act shall be exempted from Stamp Duty, 22 V., c. 1, s. 52.

Exemption from Stamp duty

As also under this or any other Acts, then or thereafter to be passed respecting Immigrants, 24 V., c. 16, s. 27.

All penalties and forfeitures shall be sued for and recovered by the Agent-General in the name of the Queen, in a summary manner, before the Immigration Agent of the parish in which they are incurred, and the aggregate amount of penalties in respect of any number of Immigrants under indenture to the same employer under one information. The penalties and forfeitures to be pa   by an employer shall be recovered by distress and sale of the goods and chattels to be found on the estate, on which a landlord might distrain for rent in arrear, and shall not be repleviable except under an order of a Judge, to be made upon affidavit before a Justice or Commissioner of the Supreme Court, disclosing such special circumstances as would, if proved on the trial of the replevin, warrant a verdict in the plaintiff's favour. Every Immigration Agent who enforces any provisions of this Act shall be deemed to have been acting as, and entitled to the protection afforded by Law to a Justice acting in the execution of his office. All pecuniary penalties when recovered, shall be paid over to the Receiver-General to the credit of the New Immigration Fund. No goods distrained on shall be sold before the lapse of 14 days after distress. If any person, otherwise than by the authority of the person making such distress, removes, during any part of the 14 days, any of the goods distrained on, from the premises whereon made, he shall be liable to a further penalty of equal amount to that for which the distress was made, 22 V., c. 1, s. 53.

Recovery of penalties before Immigration Agent

Replevin

In cases of conviction for absence or desertion, the Immigration Agent may award to any Policeman, Constable, or other person who has been active in the apprehension of any Immigrant, not exceeding 6d. for each mile he had to travel, from the place where the Immigrant was apprehended to the residence of the nearest Justice, nor 5s. in the whole for each Immigrant, and grant him a certificate of the sum awarded, signed by the Agent, and countersigned by the Clerk of the Peace or Magistrates' Clerk, which shall be payable on the Governor's warrant, at the Treasury, out of the Constabulary Reward Fund, 22 V., c. 1, s. 54.

Reward for apprehending deserters

On complaint by employer or Immigrant, the Agent may, in addition to any other order, award to the Immigrant the whole or such proportion of wages as he thinks reasonable, or authorize the employer to retain the whole or any specified portion, 22 V., c. 1, s. 55.

Wages, payment and abatement, &c.

On complaint of any Immigrant for non-payment of wages, or damages for breach of contract, or misconduct, the Agent may make a proportionate abatement out of any sum to be awarded to such Immigrant, for such days or times as he shall be proved to have been, without the consent of his employer, absent from, or neglecting his service or work, and also for the value of any

K K

damage done to his property through the misconduct, negligence or carelessness of such Immigrant; but no Immigrant whose wages have been abated for absence, shall be required to give any further service for the period of absence, 22 V., c. 1, s. 56.

Time for complaint, &c.

Except where otherwise directed, no complaint, by employer or Immigrant, against the other, shall be entertained, unless preferred within 30 days; and on the hearing, no abatement or deduction shall be made from the amount determined to be due to either party, by reason of any misconduct of which he was guilty at any time exceeding 30 days before the institution of the complaint, 22 V., c. 1, s. 57.

Sentences of imprisonment to be returned to Agent General

Whenever any indentured Immigrant is sentenced, by any Court or Justices, to imprisonment for any offence against the criminal law, the proper officer shall, within one calendar month from the date of sentence, forward to the Agent-General a return, setting forth as accurately as may be the distinguishing letter and number, and name of the Immigrant, the name of the Estate on which he is indentured, the offence and term of imprisonment, 22 V., c. 1, s. 58.

Immigrants at private expense, contracts to be dispensed with

The Immigration Agent shall dispense with the execution of any contract for payment of expenses, with respect to Immigrants introduced otherwise than by the Island Government, and shall endorse upon the contract of service that the cost of introduction has been fully paid and discharged by the employer, and upon the transfer at any time of such services, with the assent of the parties, shall make a similar endorsement. Such employers and Immigrants shall be amenable to this Act, in all other respects applicable to industrial Immigrants and their employers, 22 V., c. 1, s. 64.

Re-payment of advances

The employer of any Indentured Immigrant shall pay to the Agent the amount mentioned in the Indenture as advanced to such Immigrant, previous to his embarkation, either by an immediate payment, or by half-yearly instalments, at the rate of 1s. per week, at his option ; and shall be entitled to deduct the same by weekly instalments from his wages, to be paid by the Immigration Agent into the Treasury, to the credit of the Further Immigration Fund, 1861, 22 V., c. 1, s. 65 ; 24 V., c. 16, s. 19 ; 25 V., c. 35, s. 5.

Refusal to fulfil contracts for Immigrants

Every Proprietor or Manager, who has made application for, and afterwards refuses or neglects to enter into indenture and contract, shall forfeit and pay to the Immigration Agent for every Immigrant allotted to him whom he refuses or neglects to indenture, equal to £1 for each year the Immigrant would otherwise have been indentured to him, and cost of food and lodging, as ascertained and fixed by the Agent-General, 24 V., c. 16, s. 2.

The Governor may remit or mitigate any such forfeiture, 22 V., c. 1, s. 66.

Agency

Every person deputed to manage any Estate under Power of Attorney, recorded in the Secretary's Office, shall be deemed the authorized agent of his principal for the purposes of this Act, in the absence of express provision to the contrary in such power, but without prejudice to any right of action of the principal against any Agent who has contravened or acted without or against his instructions, 22 V., c. 1, s. 67.

Lien and recovery of moneys payable for immigrants

All moneys payable to the Immigration Agent in respect to any Indentured Immigrant, or for refusal or neglect to execute an indenture, shall be a first charge on the Estate in respect of which the Immigrant is, or, but for such refusal or neglect, would be under indenture, and may be enforced by warrant of distress and sale (Forms Nos. 2 and 3, 24 V., c. 16) to be directed by the Agent-General or Sub-Agent of the district, or to any Policeman of the parish where the same is required to be executed, without any previous information or summons, and the aggregate amount of penalties in respect of any number of Immigrants, recoverable by distress warrant, to be executed upon the same Estate, may be included in one warrant. As against mortgagees or other incumbrancers, or purchasers of property sold for payment of any mortgage or other incumbrance, after they have entered into possession, no greater amount of arrears shall be enforceable, and raiseable as a **See 25 V., c. 35, s. 1** first charge on any Estate than the two last half-yearly instalments actually due next before such entry, 22 V., c. 1, s. 68.

£100,000, Immigration Loan appropriations

All moneys received from the employers of Immigrants, introduced by means of moneys raised under 15 V., c. 39, and 16 V., c 25., shall be paid by the Agent-General, within one week after receipt, to the Receiver-General, and carried to the credit of the "£100,000 Immigration Loan, New Sinking Fund," and remitted under warrant of the Governor, with the advice of the Executive Committee, to be invested under those Acts as part of the Sinking Fund established under them, 22 V., c. 1, s. 69.

All moneys received from employers of Immigrants, introduced by means of moneys raised under any Act to be passed, shall be paid, one week after receipt by the Agent-General, to the Receiver-General, 22 V., c. 1, s. 70.

Other appropria-tions to further Im-migration Fund Account 1861

To the credit of "The Further Immigration Fund Account, 1861," 24 V., c. 16, s. 22; 25 V., c. 35, s. 5.

The Receiver-General shall close "The New Immigration Fund Account," under 22 V., c. 1, s. 70, and open a new account in his books, "The Further Immigration Fund Account, 1861," to which to transfer the balance of that account, 24 V., c. 16, s. 22.

For raising a fund to meet the expense of a return passage for Indian Immigrants, who entitle themselves to claim a return passage to the ports from which they embarked, or for the permanent colonization of such and any other Immigrants, the Agent-General shall, on or before 10th November in each year, furnish to the Receiver-General and the Governor a return, shewing, as far as practicable, the total number of Immigrants, of all classes, introduced by means of moneys raised under Acts for raising funds within the previous 10 years, alive in the Island on the preceding 30th September, and thereupon the Governor, with the advice of the Executive Committee, shall, by warrant, direct the Receiver-General to set apart and carry a sum, equal to 20s. for every Immigrant appearing to be alive in this Island on that day in each year, out of any unappropriated public moneys, to the credit of an account in his books, "The Immigrants' Colonization and Return Passage Fund," 22 V., c. 1, s. 71.

Return passage, &c.; colonization fund
Chinese, 23 V., c. 29, s 10
Liberated Afri-cans, 25. V., c. 19, s. 7

Investment

To be invested at interest in securities in this Island, or the public funds of Great Britain, and the interest accumulated until money is wanting for the purchase of lands, or for return passages, 22 V., c. 1, s. 72.

The Receiver-General shall pay thereout, warrants of the Governor, with the advice of the Executive Committee, on account of the purchase of land for the colonization of Immigrants, or as a money-commutation in lieu of back-passages of Indian Immigrants, and the further sums required for payment of back-passages. And for providing back-passages, the Governor may direct the Receiver-General to advance moneys from the general revenue, to be re-paid out of the fund when there is sufficient money at its credit, 22 V., c. 1, s. 73.

The Receiver-General shall carry to the credit of the same account, £5000 out of the surplus moneys arising from the Export Duties, under 15 V., c. 39, after providing for Interest and Sinking Fund on so much of the loan as has been raised, 22 V., c. 1, s. 74.

Whenever a sufficient number of Immigrants require to have lands granted to them, the Governor and Executive Committee may contract for the purchase, in fee simple, of lands in the proximity of estates, whereon Immigrants are located, or other lands suitable; the title to be taken in the name of H. M.; and the Governor may, with the like advice, grant any lands, or the right and title of H. M. to any lands which have become forfeited for non-payment of land tax, or quit rents, or otherwise, for the purposes of this Act, 22 V., c. 1, s. 75.

Purchases of land

Every Indian Immigrant who has completed an industrial residence of 5 years, at the least, desirous to commute his right to a back-passage for a grant of land or money, shall be entitled to claim, through the Agent-General, a grant of 10 acres of land, purchased as aforesaid, and a grant or patent for 10 acres shall be made out and given to him, and he be put into possession by the Agent of the District; and the Governor may, at the request of the Immigrant, direct payment of a money equivalent in lieu of the whole or a portion of the land, in which case a lesser quantity only of land, as may be agreed upon, shall be granted; but no Indian Immigrant shall be entitled to such grant or money-payment, until he has completed an industrial residence at least of 5 years. The provisions of this section shall have no effect until her Majesty's Government sanction the principle of commutation, 22 V., c. 1, s. 76.

Commutations for back-passage

The Governor, with advice of the Executive Committee, may give or grant to any Immigrant whatsoever, by way of reward for meritorious conduct, not exceeding one acre of land, for each year of industrial residence

Grants as rewards

under indenture, in consideration of faithful performance of duties thereunder, 22 V., c. 1, s. 77.

Diagrams to grants

Grants and Patents shall have annexed a plat or diagram, laid out after actual survey by the Crown Surveyor of the County, 22 V., c. 1, s. 78.

Cost of title

The cost of surveying shall not exceed 30s. for every 10 acres, 22 V., c. 1, s. 79.

To be delivered free of arrears of land tax and expense of title

Such lands shall be discharged of all arrear of land tax and quit rents, and the grant and survey made, and all the expenses paid at the charge of the "Immigrants' Colonization and Return Passage Fund," and recorded and delivered to the Immigrant free of expense, which expenses to be paid under the Governor's warrant by the Receiver-General, 22 V., c. 1, s. 80.

Exemption from taxes

Persons receiving a grant or patent of land shall be exempted from all direct taxes, charges and assessments, public and parochial (taxes by way of License or on wheel carriages, horsekind or horned stock excepted) for 3 years after, 22 V., c. 1, s. 81.

Permissive occupation of lands

The Immigration Agent, with the sanction of the Governor, may permit any Immigrant, during industrial residence, to occupy, any lands purchased or acquired, for such time and on such conditions as the Governor shall determine, so as not to interfere with the discharge of his services, and no such Immigrant shall be liable to any direct public or parochial tax or charge in respect of such permissive occupation, 22 V., c. 1, s. 82.

Recovery of possession

At any time after the expiration of 30 days after notice in writing, signed by an Immigration Agent, requiring the delivery up of possession of any land he may have been permitted to occupy has been served upon any Immigrant, or upon his wife, widow, child, or other member of his family, of the age of 16 years or upwards, or in case no person be found in the occupation, then after the expiration of 30 days after notice affixed to and left upon some conspicuous part of the premises, if possession has not been delivered up agreeably to the requirement of such notice, the Immigration Agent having first summoned the defendant to appear before him, may, by warrant under his hand (form No 12), order any Policeman, Constable or Peace Officer to enter upon any such lands, and any dwelling-house and buildings thereon, and remove every person found thereon or therein, together with his goods, and put any person, appointed by the Immigration Agent, in possession ; and any Immigrant or other person who, after possession has been so obtained, either by voluntary delivery or compulsory process, knowingly takes or holds possession of any such lands, shall, on conviction, be liable to be imprisoned, with or without hard labour, not exceeding 3 months, 22 V., c. 1, s. 83.

Forms

The Forms in Schedule or Forms to the like effect shall be valid, 22 V., c. 1, s. 84.

Short title

Short Title, "The Immigration Act, 1858," 22 V., c. 1, s. 86.

CHINESE IMMIGRANTS INTRODUCED AT PRIVATE EXPENSE.

Inspection on board ship

Upon the arrival of any ship having Chinese laborers on board, the Immigration Agent-General and Health Officer shall forthwith proceed on board, and, with the assistance of such officer, ascertain, by personal inspection of the vessel and passengers, and papers furnished the Master under the "Chinese Passengers' Act, 1855" of the Imperial Parliament, whether its provisions have been complied with or not, and report to the Governor on the state of the vessel and treatment of the passengers, and whether there appear to be grounds for proceeding against the Vessel or Master, and upon all other such matters as the Governor may direct, 22 V., c. 2, s. 1.

Contracts

The provisions respecting contracts are superseded by 25 V., c. 35, s. 8, which see infra. "Chinese introduced by the Island Government," except as herein set out.

The contract, on arrival, shall be submitted to the Agent-General, who may make alterations for the benefit of the laborer, to make them conformable to the conditions, and record and countersign them ; and no contract or altered contract shall be binding on any laborer until so countersigned. Every contract shall be deemed an indenture, and, during its currency, every Chinese laborer an Immigrant within 12 V., c. 1, 22 V., c. 2, s. 3.

If it is established before any Sub-Agent or Inspector of Immigrants, on complaint by any Chinese laborer, that he is not provided by his employer with sufficient work to enable him to earn a just amount of wages according to the current rate under his contract, he shall report the same to the Governor, who shall declare the contract to be cancelled, and thereupon the Immigration Agent, with the sanction of the Governor, shall cause the laborer to be indentured to some other employer on the terms, as near as may be, of the contract, for not exceeding the unexpired period of his term of service, 22 V., c. 2, s. 4. *Cancelling and re-indenturing, see 23 V., c. 31, s. 1*

All sums received by the Agent-General from any Chinese laborer under s. 3, shall be paid by him to the person who defrayed the expense of introduction, subject to a rateable deduction, in case the Government paid any part of the expense, 22 V., c. 2, s. 5.

"Governor," "Immigration Agent-General," "Written Contract," "Plantation" and "Employer," shall bear the meaning assigned in 22 V., c. 1, 22 V., c. 2, s. 6. *Interpretation*

CHINESE INTRODUCED BY THE ISLAND GOVERNMENT.

The provisions of "The Immigration Act, 1858," (22 V., c. 1), "The Immigration Loan Act, 1858," (22 V., c. 3), and "The Immigrants' Industrial School Act, 1858," (22 V., c. 8), applicable to Asiatic Immigrants, extended to Immigrants introduced by the Government of this Island, and to Immigrants and other children introduced under this Act, except as altered hereby, 23 V., c. 29, s. 1. *Acts extended to*

Chinese Immigrants shall be distinguished as a separate class by the letter G, and numbered, commencing No. 1, in regular numerical progression, 23 V., c. 29, s. 2. *Distinguishing letter*

Their indentures shall be made in conformity with their contracts previously to embarkation; and the Form of the indenture, 22 V., c. 1, Sched. No. 4, altered accordingly, 23 V., c. 29, s. 3. *Indentures*

Notwithstanding anything to the contrary in any Act relating to Chinese Immigrants, all written contracts for the performance of labor or service of agriculture in this Colony, made by or with the authority of the Emigration Agent, in China, with any Chinese Immigrant, shall be binding on the parties for the period named, not exceeeding 5 years from the day of landing, and shall be signed with the name or marks of the contracting parties, or of persons lawfully acting on their behalf, and attested by the Emigration officer at the port of embarkation, who shall declare that the Immigrant parties signed the same voluntarily, and with a due understanding of their effect; and every signature purporting to be that of an Emigration Officer, shall be held to be genuine without proof, but persons disputing it may prove the signature is not genuine. Every contract shall conform to the following conditions: *Conntract 5 years*

1 The Contract shall secure the Immigrant the same rate of wages, for the same proportionate quantity of work, as may be paid to unindentured laborers working on the estate or otherwise, and secure to the Immigrant wages at the rate of 4 dollars per calendar month with sufficient food, on condition that he works 7½ hours each day except Sundays, with a reservation of 5 holidays in each year to be fixed by the Governor. *Conditions*

2. It shall bind the employer to furnish to the Immigrant, free of charge, suitable lodging, and, when sick, suitable and sufficient medicines and nourishment, medical attendance and hospital accommodation.

3. Authorize the employer to deduct 1 dollar per mensem from the wages of any such Immigrant, in re-payment of any advance certified to have been made to him in China by the Agent, and also to deduct from the wages of any Immigrant who may assign a portion to any party in China, a sum equal to such portion in each month.

4. The contract may be terminated by the Immigrant at the end of each year from the commencement, on payment, for each unexpired year of the term, of a sum equal to one-fifth of the amount paid for his passage; and the Immigrant may change his employer at the end of the third and fourth years.

And all provisions in any other Act to the like effect as any foregoing condition shall be read as herewith consolidated, 23 V., c. 35, s. 5.

Certificate of industrial residence

Any Chinese Immigrant desirous of determining his Indenture, on payment to the Agent-General (of the necessary sum under 25 V., c. 35, s. 8, part 4), shall be released absolutely from indenture, and be immediately entitled to a certificate of industrial residence, 23 V., c. 29, s. 4.

Payments in China

If any indenture contain a stipulation for payment of any portion of wages for the benefit of the Immigrant's parents or family in China, the same shall be retained by the employer, and pai by monthly instalments through the Immigration Agent, into the public dreasury, to be transmitted to an Agent in China, for payment to the proper persons; and the Governor may make the necessary regulations for giving effect to this provision, 23 V., c. 29, s. 5.

How enforced

Payment of such moneys may be enforced in the summary manner, provided by 22 V., c. 1, s. 68, and the warrant of distress and sale may be signed by the Agent-General, or Sub-Agent. Form :—

Whereas default has been made in payment of the portion of wages of Chinese Immigrants located on   estate in the parish of   reserved to be paid to me for transmission to China for the benefit of their parents, or families, that is say monthly instalments to the   day of   instant of each equal to   under indenture dated the   day of   One thousand eight hundred and   with an Immigrant named
(G. 15) as also   monthly instalments to the day of   each equal to   under indenture dated the   day of   One thousand eight hundred and   with an Immigrant named
(G. 18) which several instalments amount in the aggregate to the sum of   These are therefore to command you to levy the said sum of   by distress of any goods and chattels to be found upon the said estate in the said parish upon which a landlord might distrain for rent in arrear, and if within fourteen days next after such distress by you taken, with or without previous appraisement, the said sum, and the charges of distraining and keeping the same shall not be paid, then that you do sell the said goods and chattels, so by you distrained, and out of the money arising from such sale, that you do retain the charges of distraining, keeping and selling the same goods and chattels, and pay the said sum to me, to be accounted for under the provisions of the "Chinese Immigration Act, One Thousand Eight Hundred and Fifty Nine," or any other Act in force relating to Chinese Immigrants, returning the surplus, on demand, to the proprietor, overseer, or manager of the said Estate.

Given under my hand, this

To any Policeman of the parish of   day of   23 V., c. 29, s. 6.

Females and children under 12 free settlers

Every Chinese female and child under 12, introduced, who shall not be bound to serve under indenture, shall be deemed a free settler, and the expense of introduction paid in the first instance, out of the moneys raised under 22 V., c. 3; 23 V., c. 29, s. 7.

Age how determined

The Agent-General shall determine the age of every child, supposed to be under 12, according to the report or return of the Agent in China, or otherwise, according to the best evidence on information he can obtain, 23 V., c. 29, s. 8.

Proportion of women and children

The proportion of Chinese women and children under 12, to be introduced, with reference to the number of male Immigrants, shall be such as may be fixed by H. M'F. Government, 24 V., c. 16, s. 4.

Agent General's return to include Chinese

The returns of Immigrants to be furnished by the Agent-General, on or before 10th November in each year to the Governor and Receiver-General, [22 V., c. 1, s. 7], shall contain Chinese Immigrants, at the time of their introduction, bound, or liable to serve under indenture, and also Chinese women and children introduced under this Act, within the previous 15 years, alive in this Island, on the preceding 30th September; and the returns as to such women and children shall be made in such form as the Governor directs, and a like sum as is required to be carried to the credit of

Fund to meet expenses of introducing women and children

"The Immigrants' Colonization and Return Passage Fund," for every Immigrant within the 22 V., c. 1, shall be carried to the credit of the same fund, for every Chinese Immigrant, woman and child, appearing by the return to have been so introduced (and alive,) out of any unappropriated public moneys, and the amount appropriated and invested, and the interest accumulated as directed by 22 V., c. 1, s. 72, to form a fund for paym·nt of the principal and interest of the moneys to be raised for introducing such Chinese women and children, 23 V., c. 29, s. 10.

Interpretation

"Immigration Agent," " Immigrant," " Asiatic Immigrant," " Indenture" and " Employer,' shall have the same meaning as is assigned by 22 V., c. 1 ; 23 V., c. 29, s. 11.

Short title

" The Chinese Immigration Act, 1859," 23 V., c. 29, s. 12.

Appropriation of moneys rece i v e d for Chinese

. All moneys received and paid over by the Agent-General to the Receiver-General, under 23 V., c. 29, shall be carried to the credit of " The Further Immigration Fund Account, 1861," 24 V., c. 16, s. 21.

LIBERATED AFRICANS.

Indenture.

In the absence of orders in Council, and until some other Officer, civil or military, is appointed by H. M., the Agent-General of Immigration shall, under the Governor's orders, previous to condemnation, receive, protect and provide for, and, after condemnation, indenture persons condemned under the Statutes for the abolition of the Slave Trade, not enlisted as soldiers, sailors or marines, whatever their age, to any employer, within 22 V., c. 1, upon the terms therein authorized ; and any indenture by the Agent-General shall be of the same force as if the party had himself, when of full age executed it under that Act ; and such persons may be re-indentured, and their services pass and be transferred in like manner as the services of indentured Immigrants, provided the person to whom the Estate is aliened, demised or devised, signify, by endorsement upon the indenture, his willingness to become the employer, or, in case. of refusal, they may be re-indentured, 22 V., c. 4, s. 1.

Duration

None shall be indentured or re-indentured longer than 3 years, or until he reaches 18, 22 V., c. 4, s. 2.

When supposed to be under 18, the Agent-General, shall fix the age at the date of the indenture, and endorse the same thereon, and, in default, the indenture shall determine at the expiration of 3 years, 22 V., c..4, s. 3.

Parties subject to 22 V., c. 1

Subject to the jurisdiction under the Statutes of the Court of Vice-Admiralty, every such person when indentured, and his employer, shall be amenable to 22 V., c. 1 ; 22 V., c. 4, s. 4.

Advances for maintenance

The Governor, with the advice of the Executive Committee, may, by warrant, direct the Receiver-General to advance from the Treasury any money, required for the maintenance and support of such persons previously to condemnation and indenture, 22 V., c. 4, s. 5.

Naturalization

All such persons heretofore or to be brought into this Island after condemnation and indenture, shall be deemed natural born subjects, and capable of holding and transmitting real and personal estate, 22 V., c. 4, s. 7.

Expenses of removal to this island of liberated Africans

The Governor may direct payment out of the funds available for the introduction of Immigrants, of all expenses to be incurred from 1st April, 1862, in the removal to this Colony of liberated Africans from the places where originally landed, including expenses reasonably incidental to their protection and care after arrival, and before assignment to employers, 25 V., c. 19, s. 1.

Indenture duration since 12 Octr ., 1864, see 27 V., S. 2, c. 5, s. 6-9

Every liberated African so introduced, may be indentured by the Immigration Agent to any employer the Governor thinks fit, for not exceeding 3 years, or such time as may elapse until 18, but not to take effect until the Employer and Immigrant, or the Immigration Agent on his behalf, has executed an Indenture, 22 V., c. 1, Form No. 4, or in such other form as may be approved by the Governor, 25 V., c. 19, s. 2.

Age

When supposed to be under 18, the Immigration Agent shall, according to the best evidence or information he can obtain, fix his age at the date of the indenture, and endorse the same thereon, or, in default, the indenture shall determine 3 years from the date, 25 V., c. 19, s. 3.

Annual and other payment

Every Employer shall pay to the Immigration Agent all expenses for food and lodging as provided by 24 V., c. 16, (s. 6) in respect to other Immigrants, and £1 10s. in advance for the 1st year's service, of every liberated African of the age or supposed age of 18 or upwards, and 15s

In advance for the 1st year's service of every African under that age, included in such indenture, and shall also enter into contract in form similar to Form 24 V., c. 16, mutatis mutandis, for payment of £1 10s. in advance for each subsequent year of service for each African of 18, and 15s. in advance for each subsequent year for each under that age, until he attain such age, to be paid on the day next after that of the expiration of the previous year of service, as provided in respect of the annual payments for other Immigrants, 25 V., c. 19, s. 4.

Africans introduced before 1 April, 1862

Such annual payments shall not be payable in respect to any liberated Africans introduced free of cost prior to 1st April, 1862. All such Africans may be indentured according to the other provisions of this Act, but the Employer shall not be required to enter into contract, nor be liable for payment of any moneys further than the cost of their maintenance and support, and incidental to their protection and care, between the period of arrival and being indentured, the amount to be fixed by the Governor, and collected by the Immigration Agent, from the Employer at the time of entering into indenture, 25 V., c. 19, s. 5.

Payments to be made to the credit of the further immigration fund account, 1861

All moneys to be paid by Employers shall be paid over by the Immigration-Agent to the Receiver-General, to the credit of "The Further Immigration Fund Account, 1861," by 24 V., c. 16, established, 25 V., c. 19, s. 6.

To be included in annual return under 22 V., c. 1, s. 71

The Immigration Agent shall include in the return under 22 V., c. 1, s. 71, all Liberated Africans introduced within 10 years preceding the date; and the like sum of 20s. and from the like moneys, shall be appropriated, annually, on account of every such African alive in this island at that date, as is required on account of any other Immigrant, to the credit of "The Immigrants' Colonization and Return Passage Fund," and invested and accumulated, 25 V., c. 19, s. 7.

Parties subject to Immigration Acts

Every Employer and Indentured African, shall be entitled and subject to the rights, privileges, duties, obligations and penalties in any Act now, or to be in force, relating to Immigrants, and their provisions observed and enforced as to the recovery of annual and other payments, and in every other respect, except any right to a return passage, and as otherwise provided, 25 V., c. 19, s. 8.

Certificate of industrial residence

Every Liberated African, after residence of 3 years, or such other time as shall elapse until he reach 18, shall be entitled to demand from the Imgration Agent, a certificate of industrial residence, unless it be recorded in his office, or otherwise appear that he has deserted or absented himself from service, otherwise than from illness, while under indenture, for periods amounting together, during the term, to more than 3 months, in which case he shall not be entitled to such certificate until he has further served under indenture for the period of absence or desertion, or given a money compensation in lieu, 25 V., c. 19, s. 9.

Reduced rates 20s and 10s Half-yearly

Employers of Liberated Africans, already or to be indentured, shall pay for their services at the respective annual rate of 20s. and 10s, in lieu of 30s. and 15s, to be made in half-yearly instalments, 28 V., c. 3, s. 1.

Times of payment

The first payment in the case of those already indentured shall be made six months after the termination of the current year of service, and in the case of those hereafter indentured, six months after the date, 28 V., c. 3, s. 2.

Enforcement

Every instalment, in case of default, shall be recovered with the like power, and by the like proceeding as the charge or rate reduced, except that it shall not be payable or recoverable in advance, 28 V., c. 3, s. 3.

Refund of any excess of payments

The Receiver-General shall, on the warrant of the Governor, refund any excess of payments beyond the reduced rates, which may be made after the passing, but before the coming into operation of this Act, 28 V., c. 3, s. 4.

Incorporated with other acts

Act to be read as incorporated with a part of any other act in force relating to Liberated Africans, 28 V., c. 3, s. 5.

Royal assent

Not to come into operation until the Royal assent has been signified and proclaimed, 28 V., c. 3, s. 6.

Immigration after 12th October, 1864.

After the coming into operation of this Act, (12th October, 1864) the Immigration Agent may assign, under the provisions of 22 V., c. 1, as hereby modified and extended, for not exceeding 5 years, the services of any Indian Immigrant Laborer, aged 12 years or upwards, to be introduced by the Government; and the period of service shall be computed from the date of arrival, or, having been under 12 when he arrived, from the period of his attaining that age, as nearly as can be ascertained, 27 V., S. 2, c. 5, s. 1. *Indians to be assigned for 5 year's* *Children under 12*

On compliance with the terms of his indenture of service for 5 years, by any Indian Immigrant subject to indenture under this Act, he shall be entitled to a passport, having the effect of that provided for under 22 Vic., c. 1 ; 27 V., S. 2, c. 5, s. 2. *Passport*

Deserters or absentees for any other cause than illness, for periods, or a period of more than one month for each year of indenture, shall not be entitled to a return passage, as provided by 22 V., c. 1, until they have further served, under indenture, for the period of absence or desertion, unless they give a money commutation in lieu, as thereby prescribed regarding industrial residence, 27 V., S. 2, c. 5, s. 3. *Deserters—return passage*

The form of passport may be varied from that of 22 V., c. 1, by substituting the words " having completed a service of 5 years under indenture according to " The Immigration Amendment Act, 1864," for "having obtained his certificate of industrial residence," 27 V., S. 2, c. 5, s. 4. *Form of passport*

The Governor may grant a free return passage to any such Indian Immigrant under this Act, who, from sickness, accident, or other cause, appears to him incapable of labor, 27 V., S. 2, c. 5, s. 5. *Free return passages*

All Liberated Africans to be hereafter introduced (12 October, 1864) shall be divided into two classes, the first to include those who, upon inspection of the Immigration Agent and Health Officer of the Port, are considered of or above 15 years of age, the second, those under 15, 27 V., S. 2, c. 5, s. 6. *Liberated Africans classification*

Those of the 1st class shall be indentured to the employer to whom they may be allotted, for 5 years. The Governor and Executive Committee may discharge any indentured Liberated Africans at the expiration of 3 years from the date of indenture, and upon doing so, shall release their employers from the proportionate part of the annual charges payable by them, 27 V., S. 2, c. 5, s. 7. *1st class indenture*

Those of the 2nd class shall be indentured until 20, according to Form D, or such other as the Governor and Executive Committee may direct. Those of the 2nd class shall be allowed one afternoon besides Sunday, in each week, to be appointed by the Governor, for receiving education and religious instruction. Any Manager or person in charge of an estate, preventing the attendance of any such African, at any school, on any such afternoon, or obstructing the minister of the parish, or any minister of religion, or licensed schoolmaster, authorized by the Governor in visiting and instructing any such African, or neglecting or refusing to provide a fit place, if required by the Inspector of schools, for the communication of such instruction, shall forfeit 20s, to be recovered on complaint of the Inspector of schools, or any one authorized by him, in writing, 27 V., S. 2, c. 5, s. 8. *2nd class indenture. Time for education and religious instruction*

Every enactment except s. 2 and 3 of 25 V. c. 19, providing for the introduction of Liberated Africans, shall apply to both classes, the age of 15 being substituted for 18, and the indenture, by this Act directed, being followed for Liberated Africans of the 2nd class, and in respect to their right to certificates of industrial residence; the term of 5 years substituted for 3 years, 27 V., S. 2, c. 5, s. 9. *Extension of 25 V., c 19 to*

The Governor in Executive Committee, may appoint Interpreters for carrying out the Immigration Acts, not exceeding one in each district, and fix a scale of pay and allowance to be defrayed out of the Immigration Fund. Any Immigrant liable to indenture, or indentured Immigrant, with the consent of his employer, shall be eligible, and, if appointed, his services, pro tempore, shall be taken in lieu of industrial indentured service, 27 V., S 2, c. 5, s. 21. *Interpreters*

L L

Not to affect pre-
vious contracts,
&c., &c.

Not to affect any contract or requirement in relation to industrial service, and its incidents, as to any Immigrant introduced previously to the passing of this Act, 27 V., S. 2, c. 5, s. 22.

Short title

The Immigration Amendment Act, 1864, 27 V., S. 2, c. 5, s. 23.

Except as modi-
fied, &c., previous
Acts incorporated

Except as by this Act modified, extended or altered, the Acts relating
to Immigration shall be read as part of, or incorporated with this Act, and
shall continue, or be applicable to Employers and Immigrants, 27 V., S.
2, c. 5, s. 24.

FORMS

18

Notice to persons
requiring immi-
grants, 22 V., c. 1,
s. 9

Proprietors, or Managers of Estates, desirous of indenturing Immigrants on their arrival in this Island, are requested to notify to me
the name and residence of the Proprietor, the Estate on which it is
proposed to indenture Immigrants, the number of Immigrants wanted
for such Estate, the particular description of the building or buildings,
in which such Immigrants are to be located, and the country or
place from which the Proprietor is desirous such Immigrants shall be
introduced; such notification to be in the form annexed to " The Immigration Act, 1858," or as nearly thereto as circumstances will permit, otherwise no attention will be paid to the application.

A. B., Agent-General of Immigration.

18.

Sir,

Application for
immigrants, 22 V.,
c. 1, s. 9; 24 V.
c. 16, s. 9

Pursuant to the notice in the Gazette by Authority, dated
18   , I beg to intimate to you, on behalf of my constituents, A. B., of   C. D., of &c,, (describing each
Proprietor) the Proprietors of   Sugar Estate, or
otherwise, (according to the nature of the property, naming it) in the
Parish of   , that they are desirous to
indenture on that Estate   Immigrants to
be introduced from (here specify the class of Immigrants, and
country, or if desirous of the services of any description of Immigrants
" any country or place the Governor may think proper") and on behalf of my constituents, I hereby express their willingness to accept
the services of so many of such Immigrants as shall be allotted to
them, not exceeding the number above applied for, upon the terms
and conditions of " The Immigration Act, 1858," immediately after
the arrival of such Immigrants, or that they will forfeit and pay to
the Agent-General of Immigration for the time being, a sum equal
to one pound for each year every Immigrant allotted to them would
otherwise be indentured to them, together with the cost of food and
lodging incurred by the Island between the time of the arrival of
every such Immigrant and the transfer of his services to some other
person, to be ascertained and fixed by the Agent-General of Immigration, and the description of the building in which the Immigrants are
to be located is as stated hereunder. My power of attorney bears
date (specify date) and is recorded in the Secretary's Office, libro
folio

I am, &c.,

E. F., Attorney to the above named.

To G. H., Esquire, Agent-General of
Immigration.

Register of Immigrants introduced into the Island of Jamaica, under the Immigration Act, 1858.

Distinguishing Letter.	Ditto Number.	Name of Immigrant.	Age.	Sex.	Country.	Time of Arrival.	Place whence Shipped.	Vessel.	Cost of Passage.	Average cost of Importation.	Whether entitled to a Return Passage or not.	At whose expense introduced.	To whom indentured.	Estate on which located.	Advances to be repaid out of Wages.	Date of Death.	Date of Certificate of Industrial Residence.	Date of Passport.	Port from which Passport returned to be cancelled.	REMARKS.

DISTINGUISHING LETTER.—1. Of Immigrants from Great Britain, the British West Indies and possessions in North America - - - - A
2. Of Immigrants from the United States of America - - - - - B
3. Of Immigrants from Madeira, the Azores, the Canaries, and the Cape de Verde Islands - - - C
4. Of Indian Immigrants - - - - - D
5. Of Asiatic Immigrants - - - - - E
6. Of African Immigrants - - - - - F

Other Classes, with distinguishing letters, may be added, if requisite.

7. Chinese (23 V., c. 29, s. 2) - - - - - G

JAMAICA, ss.

This indenture made the   day of   , 185   , between A. B., Immigrant laborer, (A. No.   ) or C. D., Immigration Agent of this colony, on behalf of A. B. &c., of the one part, and E. F. of   in the said Island   of the other part, witnesseth, That in virtue of " The Immigration Act, 1858," and in consideration of the covenants on the part of the said E. F., hereinafter contained, he the said A. B. doth hereby bind himself to the said E. F. for the term of   years, to be computed from the date hereof; and doth hereby covenant with the said E. F., his heirs and assigns, that he the said A. B. will, during the said term, or the continuance of these presents, truly and faithfully serve the said E. F., his heirs and assigns, as laborer on   estate, in the parish of   , according to the laws and regulations made, or hereafter to be made, concerning Immigrant laborers in this Island; and the said E . F . doth hereby covenant with the said A. B. that the said E. F., will, during the said term, or the continuance of these presents, provide the said A. B with suitable and sufficient lodging, medicine, and medical atten- dance, (a) and during three months from the date of this indenture' with food and clothing, according to the annexed scale; and such medicine, medical attendance, food and lodging, shall be in conformity with the laws or regulations made, or hereafter to be made, concern- ing Immigrant laborers in this Island; and also will pay wages to the said A. B. (b) during the next three months, at the rate of   per diem, and after the expiration of three months at the same rate which may be at the time paid to the laborers not under written agreement, working on said estate, according to the quantity of work performed, being at the rate of not less than   per subject nevertheless to deductions, at the following rate, per (" week" or " month," as the case may be,) viz:—

	£	s.	d.
Medical Attendance			
Lodgings			
Re-payment of Advances, amounting in all to			
Total deductions per (week)			

In witness whereof, we have hereunto set our hands.

A. B., or C. D.
E. F.

N. B.—The passages between brackets, lettered (a) and (b) may be omit- ted, if the Immigration Agent shall see fit. If they are inserted, the Immi- gration Agent must add a scale of food.

Return for the year commencing 1st October, 185 , ending 30th September, 185- Returns, 99 V., s
    of the entire number of Immigrants located on Estate, 1, s, 17
    in the parish of , the property of

DISTINGUISHING LETTERS OF CLASS.

	A		B		C		D		E		F	
	Males.	Females.	Males.	Females.	Males.	Females.	Males.	Females.	Males.	Females.	Males.	Females.
Number at last Return												
Increase by Birth												
" by Transfer from other Estates												
" by Return of Deserters absent at date of last Return												
Decrease by Death												
" by Transfer to other Estates												
" by Desertion												

SPECIFICATION OF BIRTHS.

Name of Infant.	Date of Birth.	Sex.	Name of Father.	His Distinguishing Letter and Number.	Name of Mother.	Her Distinguishing Letter and Number.

Specification of Deserters Returned, who were Absent at Date of last Return.

Names of Deserters.	Sex.	Distinguishing Letter and Number.	Date of Desertions during Year.	Date of Returns during Year.

IMMIGRATION,

SPECIFICATION OF DEATHS.

Names of De- ceased.	Sex.	Distinguishing Letter and Number.	Date of Death.	Cause of Death.

SPECIFICATION OF DESERTERS DURING THE YEAR.

Names.	Sex.	Distinguishing Letter and Number.	Dates of Deser- tion.	Dates of Re- turn during year.

I, A. B., owner of Estate, the property of do hereby declare that the above five returns contain, to the best of my knowledge and belief, returns of the number of Immigrants on the said Estate, on the 1st day of October, 185 , the date of the last return, and on the 1st day of October, 185 , as also of the increase and decrease since the last return, arising from births or deaths, transfers from, or to other Estates; the return of deserters absent therefrom on the preceding 1st October, but who afterwards returned to the Estate; as also of cases of desertion from the Estate during the year ending 30th September, 185

A. B.

Declared by the above-named A. B., before me,
this day of 185

J. P.

Certificate of industrial residence, 22 V., c. 1, s. 31 These are to certify, that (A 21), an Immigrant introduced into this Island from , on the day of 18 , having served under indenture for the full period of years of industrial residence, is now at liberty to abandon service, and is freed and discharged from all obligations of industrial residence or of service, except the obligation to obtain a passport, previous to his leaving the Island, under " The Immigration Act, 1858," or any other Act relating to Immigration.

(Signed) A. B., Agent-General of Immigrants. (or as the case may be.)

Passport, 22 V., c 1, s. 33 ; 27 V., B, 2, c. 5, s. 4 These are to certify that (A 21), an Immigrant introduced into this Island from , on the day of , having obtained his certificate of industrial residence, and having applied to me for a passport, is entitled to depart from this Island ; and the master or other person in charge of any vessel, is hereby authorized and empowered to receive such Immigrant on board his vessel, for the purpose of carrying him off this Island, taking from the said Immigrant this passport, and depositing the same with the officer of Her Majesty's Customs of the port from which the vessel may clear, in order that the same may by such officer be returned to the Agent-General of Immigration to be cancelled.

(Signed).

[Or having completed a service of 5 years under indenture, according to "The Immigration Amendment Act, 1864,"] 27 V., S. 2, c. 5, s 4.

I do hereby certify, that   (A. 22) an Immigrant introduced into this Island from   , hath been by direction of the Governor, exempted from further industrial residence, in consequence of (state the cause).

22 V., c. 1, s. 35

We A. B., and C. D., of, &c., by G .H., of   our true and lawful attorney, duly authorized in this behalf, do hereby contract and engage with the Agent-General of Immigration, or the Sub-Agent of the district wherein the parish of   shall be situate, for the time being, in respect of   (A. 21) an Immigrant from   indentured to the said   for   years, by indenture of equal date herewith, and located on   estate, in the said parish of   to pay to such Agent-General, or Sub-agent for the time being, at the rate of* one pound ten shillings in advance for each year of service, subsequent to the first year during which such indenture shall continue in force, the first of such annual sums to be paid on the   day of   . 18 · and the moneys hereby intended to be secured shall be deemed a prior charge upon the said   estate, and shall be recovered and enforced under the provisions of "The Immigration Act, 1858," or any other Act in force relating to Immigrants.

Contract for payment of expenses, 24 V., c 16, s. 6; 25 V., c. 35, s. 1

As witness our hands, this   day of

A B.
C. D. } By G H., their attorney.

Whereas default hath been made in payment of the several instalments due, under contracts entered into by A. B. of   C, D. of &c., in respect of Immigrants located on   Estate, in the parish of   that is to say, an instalment of one pound,† ten shillings, payable in advance for the year to end on the · day of under contract, dated - day of in respect of, an Immigrant named   (A. 21) an instalment of one pound ten shillings each, payable in advance for the year to end on the   day of under contract dated the   day of   in respect of three Immigrants named   (B. 21)   (B. 22)   (B. 23) and which several instalments amount in the aggregate to the sum of'   pounds : These are therefore to command you to levy the said sum of   pounds, by distress of any goods or chattels to be found upon the said   Estate, in the said parish, upon which a landlord might distrain for rent in arrear; and if, within 14 days next after such distress by you taken, with or without previous appraisement, the said sum, and the charges of distraining and keeping the same shall not be paid, then that you do sell the said goods and chattels so by you distrained, and out of the money arising by such sale, that you do pay the said sum of   pounds to me, to be accounted for under the provisions of "The Immigration Act, 1858," or any other Act or Acts in force relating to Immigration; returning the overplus, if any,

Authority to [distrain for instalments due, 24 V.- c. 16, s. 7.

---

* In case of children under twelve years of age, the rate should be stated at fifteen shillings per annum for each child.

N. B. If the Immigrant has been re-indentured, insert " originally indentured to   by indenture dated the   day of   and then located on   Estate, but now re-indentured to the said   for   years, to be located on   Estate, in the said parish, by indenture of equal date herewith," and proceed as above.

N. B. If the re-indenture is only for one year, no contract for payment of expenses will be necessary, as the year's instalments will be paid in advance on execution of the re-indenture.

† Or "fifteen shillings," in case of a child under twelve years of age.

on demand, to the Proprietor, Overseer or Manager of the said Estate, after retaining the charges of distraining and keeping such distress.
Given under my hand, this   day of   18
To any Policeman of the parish of

Authority to distrain after neglect to enter into indenture, 24 V., c 16, s 7

Whereas   Immigrants from   having been allotted to
A. B.   C. D. of, &c., for the purpose of being indentured on
          Estate, in the parish of   pursuant to their application of
date   day of   (through E. F., their attorney), to G.
H., Esquire, the (then) Agent-General of Immigration, the said
have neglected and refused to enter into indenture, and contract in respect of such Immigrants, and have forfeited and become liable immediately to pay the sum of   pounds, being the amount which they would have been required to pay, and enter into contract to pay, if they had entered into indenture and contract in respect of each of such Immigrants, in accordance with such application, and have also forfeited and become liable to pay the further sum of   pounds, which I have ascertained and fixed as the cost of food and lodging of such Immigrants, incurred by the Island between the time of their arrival and the transfer of their services, and which several sums amount in the aggregate to the sum of   , which forfeiture and sum of
£   His Excellency the Governor has been pleased to mitigate and reduce to the sum of   (if such be the case). These are therefore, &c., as in the preceding form, filling up the amount to be distrained for, with the full amount of forfeiture, or the mitigated sum, if the same shall be reduced.

Contract with Chinese laborer introduced at private expense, 22 V., c. 2

It is agreed between A. B., Chinese labourer, and C. D., acting on behalf of E. F., Proprietor of the plantation (s) (X and Z) in the Island of Jamaica, that A. B. shall serve the said E. F. on (one of) the said plantation (s) in the growing or manufacturing of articles. the produce of such plantation (s) for the term of 5 years, from the day on which A. B. shall land in Jamaica : Provided always, that it shall be lawful for A. B. to terminate the said agreement at the expiration of 3 years, on payment of the sum of £10, or at the end of 4 years, on the payment of the sum of £5 : And it is further agreed, that E. F. shall pay to A. B. the same rate of wages as is paid to the labourers not under contract or indenture, working on the same plantation, not being less than at the rate of   a day (which wages shall be paid on the last day of every week), and that E. F. shall supply A. B., free of cost, with suitable lodgings, and with such medicines and medical attendance and hospital accommodation as A. B. may need when sick : And it is further agreed, that if the said plantation shall come into the possession of any other person than the said E. F., A. B. shall be bound to serve such other person, if required to do so on the same plantation, and on the above terms : And it is further agreed that E. F. may deduct from the wages of A. B., at the rate of 4s. a month, the total sum of (not more than £2 8s.) which A. B. acknowledges himself to have received in advance before leaving China.

Sec 25 V., c. 35, s, 8

To be filled up by the agent of the party introducing the laborer

Hospital Register, 27 V., S, 2, c. 5, s. 11

| Date. | Name. | SEX. | | Age. | Race. | Disease. | Result. | Date. | Remarks. |
		M.	F.						

Date.	Name.	Sex.		Age.	Race.	Disease.	Diet.	Remedies, Directions, Medical Comforts.
		M.	F.					

No.	Description of Immigrant.	Name.	Sex.	Age.	Date of Indenture.	Plantation from which deserted.	Date of Desertion.	Date of return to Service.	Remarks.

No.   Ship   day of

Indenture of minor
Liberated Africans
27 V., S. 2, c. 5, s. 8

This indenture, made on the   day of
in the year one thousand eight hundred and sixty
between   Immigration Agent in the Colony of
Jamaica, for and on behalf of   alias   a
Liberated minor African, of the age of   years, and recently
sent to this Colony under the authority of Her Majesty's Government,
for the purpose of being located and settled in the said Colony, of the
one part, and   as Proprietor (or otherwise, as the
case may be), of   Estate, in the Parish of   in
the County of   in the said Colony, as employer, of the
other part, Witnesseth, that by virtue of the Statute in such case
made and provided, and in consideration of the covenants, promises
and agreements, on the part and behalf of the said employer of the
said Liberated African hereinafter contained, he, the said Immigration
Agent, by these presents doth indenture, place and bind the said Liberated African to and with the said   , employer, to serve
him for the term of   years, to be computed from the day
of the date of these presents; and doth hereby, for and on behalf of
the said Liberated African, to and with the said employer, covenant,
promise and agree that the said Liberated African, shall and will
during all and every part of the said term, truly and faithfully serve
the said employer as a laborer on the said Estate, and the said
employer doth hereby covenant, promise, and agree to and with
the said Immigration Agent for and on behalf of the said liberated
African, that he, the said employer, shall and will, until the
said Liberated African shall have attained the age of fifteen
years, find and provide the said Liberated African with suitable and
sufficient diet, clothing, tools, or implements of work, lodging, and,
when sick, medicine, nourishment, hospital accommodation and medical attendance, in a like and equal manner with the rest of the
Africans under the age of fifteen years indentured in this Colony,
and according to the laws in such case made and provided, and according to all other laws which may hereafter be made, touching or

M M

concerning Africans under the age of fifteen years, indentured in the said Colony ; and shall allow to the said Liberated African, during the continuance of these presents, for education and religious instruction, such one afternoon, in every week, as shall be appointed or assigned by the Governor of the said Colony, for the time being, for such purpose.

In witness whereof the said Immigration Agent for and on behalf of the said Liberated African, and the said employer, have hereunto set their hands, on the day and year first above written.

Signature of Employer.
Signature of Immigration Agent.

EDUCATION.

Short title

"The Immigrants' Industrial Schools' Act, 1858, 22 V., c. 8, s. 1.

Children may be sent to industrial schools

Any Immigration Agent may order the child of any Immigrant under indenture, with the consent of such Immigrant, or any Immigrant's child, being an orphan, or abandoned by his parents, to be sent to any Certified Industrial School, where conveniently situated, to be fed, taught, employed, maintained and taken care of, as native children, 22 V., c. 8, s. 2.

Returns of children sent

When any Agent orders a child to be sent to a Certified Industrial School, he shall, within 14 days after giving the order, make a return, in duplicate, to the Agent-General, of the sex, name and age, and of the date of the order, countersigned by the Manager of the School, one copy to be transmitted by the Agent-General to the Secretary of the Executive Committee within 7 days after receipt, 22 V., c. 8, s. 3.

Teachers of Immigrants

The Governor may sanction the employment of any competent native Christian Immigrant as a Teacher or Instructor of Immigrants, in the proportion of not exceeding one in 500 Immigrants, and make remuneration for such services out of the funds applicable for Immigration purposes, at such rate as, with the advice of the Executive Committee, he deem reasonable, 24 V., c. 16, s. 30.

FURTHER IMMIGRATION FUND ACCOUNT, 1861.

Moneys to be carried to credit

All moneys received and paid by the Agent-General to the Receiver-General, shall be carried by him to the credit of "The Further Immigration Fund Account, 1861," 24 V., c. 16, s. 21 ; 25 V., c. 19, s. 6 ; 25 V., c. 35, s. 5.

As also the surplus moneys under 15 V., c. 39, 24 V., c. 16, s. 25.

And surplus moneys on account of duties under this Act, 24 V., c. 16, s. 16-18.

Account to be opened

The Receiver-General shall close the new Immigration Fund Account under "The Immigration Loan Act, 1858," (22 V., c. 3) and open and keep an account, "The further Immigration Fund Account," and carry to the debit and credit all the balances at the debit and credit of the account to be closed, and all other moneys to be received or paid under this Act, and any Acts recited or referred to (22 V., c. 1, c. 3, 23 V., c. 29), to be payable out of the account to be closed, shall be payable out of any moneys from time to time at the credit thereof, 21 V., c. 16, s. 22.

Limit of moneys to be due for immigration purposes

The utmost of moneys to be borrowed under 22 V., c. 3, and 24 V., c. 16, on the loan or succession of loans authorized by those Acts, or either of them, is limited to the total sum of £150,000, over and above the moneys at the credit of "The Further Immigration Fund Account, 1861," 25 V., c. 35, s. 6

Surplus

If in any year there is a surplus of the moneys to the credit of the above fund, and those to be invested, after meeting the payments of interest and sinking fund and all other charges, the Governor, with the advice of the Executive Committee, may apply such surplus for Immigration purposes, 24 V., c. 16, s. 24.

Short title

The Further Immigration Act, 1861, 24 V., c. 16, s. 31.

Immigrant Settlements.

Power to form companies for promoting

Provisions enabling any number of persons, not less than 20, in any Parish, to form Incorporated Joint Stock Companies, to be called "The   Company," for promoting Agricultural settlements of lands by Immigrants, upon subscribing a sufficient quantity of stock, divided into 1000 shares, of not more than £10, nor less than £1 each, after payment of 1-5th of each share to the Treasurer, and registration for the purchase of lands to be sold to Immigrant settlers, and for making loans not exceeding £25 each, at £10 per cent. per annum, to settlers, 25 V., c. 20.

Import Duties.

From the passing of this Act, (22 December, 1864,) the duties in Schedules shall be raised, levied and paid to Her Majesty for the Government of the Island, upon the articles imported and enumerated. The articles with the word "Free" set opposite, shall be admitted free of duty, with the exception of Schedule B, the duties on which shall be deemed to be levied from 9 December, 1864, 28 V., c. 10 s. 1. *Duties payable.*

Each hogshead, puncheon or tierce, imported and containing coals manure, or other article not liable to duty, shall be charged with the duty on shooks. All packages containing goods subject to ad valorem duty, shall be free of such or any other duty, 28 V., c. 10, s. 2. *Hogsheads, &c. containing goods*

The duties shall be levied, recovered and received by the Officers of the Customs, under the regulation and powers of the Imperial Act, 16 and 17 V., c. 107, or any subsequent Imperial Act as relates to the British possessions, 28 V., c. 10, s. 3. *Enforcement of duties*

The moneys, the produce of duties received, shall be paid by the Customs' Officers every week to the Receiver-General, or into any Bank as provided by law, and applied as after directed, 28 V., c. 10, s. 4. *To be paid over weekly to the Receiver-General or a Bank*

The Governor may appoint to the Customs' establishment, at the port of Kingston, an Inspector of Invoices, and also an Assistant, and remove any already or to be appointed. *Inspector of Invoices and Assistant* It shall be their duty, or of one of them, to examine every invoice of goods imported into such port previous to warrants being passed and duty paid, and ascertain and certify their correctness; and no invoice shall be received, or warrant passed, not so certified. If he see reason to doubt the correctness of the value placed upon any goods in any invoice, he may examine such merchandize, and require the importer or consignee to attend at the Custom-House, and, in the presence of the Collector or Controller, examine him on oath (which they are respectively authorized to administer), touching the goods, and invoice, and value, and on all other points relating thereto. The existing appointments shall continue, but subject to this Act. The Sub-Collectors at the several ports shall exercise, and be charged and vested with the like duties and powers, and may administer, where necessary, the like oath, 28 V., c. 10, s. 5. *Their duties* / *No invoice to be received, or warrant passed unless certified* / *May examine the importer or consignee* / *On oath* / *Existing appointments; Sub-Collectors to exercise the like duties*

Assistant Inspector's salary, £200, to be paid on the Governor's warrant, 28 V., c. 10, s. 6. *Assistant Inspector's salary*

The Receiver-General shall annually reserve, out of the duties to be collected and paid to him, £30,000, to be appropriated to the liquidation of the public debt, and £25,000 towards defraying certain expenses of the Government, as appropriated by 17 V., c. 29, s. 38-42; 28 V., c. 10, s. 8. *Appropriation of £30,000 and £25,000 of duties towards 17 V., c. 29*

The residue of duties in Schedules A. & B., shall be applied to the use of the public, 28 V., c. 10, s. 9. *Residue of duties in Sch. A. B. (as to C. see s. 17)*

The Executive Committee may, if they think proper, upon proof that any materials or articles imported and subject to duty are intended to be exclusively used in the erection, or for the repairs, or in the service of any place for religious worship, direct the Officers of Customs at the port of entry, to admit same to entry without payment of duty, or for the Receiver-General, on the Governors's warrant, to re-pay to the importer the amount of duty paid, 28 V., c. 10. s. 10. *Exemption from duties, articles for places of religious worship*

On proof to the satisfaction of the Executive Committee that any quantity of gunpowder has been imported or purchased solely and exclusively for mining, blasting, or road purposes in the Island, the Receiver-General, on the Governor's warrant, shall re-pay to the person or company who imported or purchased gunpowder for the purpose, the amount of duty paid, 28 V., c. 10, s. 12. *Remit of duties on gunpowder*

The importer of gunpowder may warehouse same in the Magazine of Port Royal, without payment of duty on the first entry, subject to the regulations in 17 V., c. 2 or any other warehouseing Act, but not to be delivered, except upon a delivery order, signed by the Collector and Con- *Warehousing Gunpowder, Port Royal Magazine* troller, and specifying the name of the person to or for whom any such powder is to be delivered, the quantity deliverable, and such other particulars as the Collector and Controller deem necessary. Nothing herein shall in any way interfere with or counteract any law, or regulation in force or practice for the Government, or regulation of the Magazine at Port Royal, or the Officers in charge of Fort Charles, 28 V., c. 10, s. 13.

Remit of duties on coals (nugatory coals being free, see schedule) The Governor, by his warrant, may direct the Receiver-General to refund all sums satisfactorily shewn to have been paid by or on account of the Royal Mail Steam Packet Company, or any other Company or individual, for duties on coals brought for the use of Steam Vessels carrying mails, and on coals not imported for nor used in internal consumption ; and no duty shall in future be chargeable on coals brought for the purpose aforesaid, or not intended to be used for internal consumption, 28 V., c. 10, s. 15.

Notwithstanding the expiration or repeal of 25 V., c. 8, or any subsequent Act (26 V., c. 4, s. 2, and 27 V., c. 6, s. 1, the 3 Acts repealed by 28 V., c. 11), raising or continuing a supply by a duty on articles imported, and for their appropriation, or the expiration or repeal of this Act, any offence against either, or penalty incurred, may be proceeded for, recovered and enforced, 28 V., c. 10, s. 16.

Application of duties In addition to the duties in Schedule A, there shall be raised, levied and paid the duties in Schedule B. to be applied to the general revenue, and, in addition, to be applied to Main Road purposes, the duties in Schedule C., 28 V., c. 10, s. 17.

Short title The Import Duties Act, 1864, 28 V., c. 10, s. 18.

Duration In force until 31st March, 1867, as regards Schedule A., until 31st March 1866, as regards Schedules B. and C., 28 V., c. 10, s. 19.

Schedule A.
Appropriation, s. 17

SCHEDULE A.

	£	s.	D.
Ale, per tun	5	7	0
Asses, per head	0	5	0
Bacon, per cwt.	0	10	0
Barley (not being Pearl Barley) per bushel	0	0	3
Beef, dried, per cwt.	0	10	0
Ditto, salted or cured, per barrel of 200 lbs.	0	10	0
Beans, per bushel	0	0	3
Beer, per tun	5	7	0
Birds		Free.	
Books, printed, and printed Papers, including Maps		Free.	
Bread or Biscuit, per cwt.	0	6	0
Bricks, per 1000	0	4	0
Bullion		Free.	
Butter, per cwt.	0	9	0
Calavances, per bushel	0	0	3
Candles, Composition, per box of 56 lbs.	0	7	0
———— Tallow, per box of 56 lbs.	0	2	6
———— Wax or Spermacetti, per box of 56 lbs.	0	10	0
Cattle, neat, per head	0	10	0
Carriages, Carts, & Waggons, used for Agricultural purposes		Free.	
Cheese, per cwt.	0	10	0
Cider, per tun	4	7	0
Clothing, Army and Navy, and undress		Free.	
Coals		Free.	
Cocoa, per cwt.	0	10	0
Coffee, per cwt.	1	0	0
Coin		Free.	
Coke		Free.	
Corn, Indian, per bushel	0	0	3
Cotton Wool		Free.	
Diamonds		Free.	
Dogs		Free.	
Dyewoods		Free.	
Drawings		Free.	
Engravings, and Lithographs, and Photographs		Free.	
Fish, dried or salted, per cwt.	0	2	6
———— fresh		Free.	
———— smoked, not otherwise enumerated or described, per cwt	0	4	0

	£	s.	D.
Fish, alewives, pickled, per barrel	0	2	0
—— Herrings, pickled, per barrel	0	2	0
—————— smoked, per box of 25 lbs.	0	0	6
—— Mackerel, pickled, per barrel	0	4	0
—— pickled, not otherwise enumerated or described, p. barl.	0	4	0
—— Salmon, smoked, per cwt.	0	10	0
———————— wet or salted, per barrel	0	10	0
Flax	Free.		
Flour, rye, per barrel	0	8	0
Flour, wheat, ——	0	8	0
Fruits, fresh	Free.		
Goats, per head	Free.		
Guano, and any other Manure	Free.		
Gums	Free.		
Gunpowder, per lb.	0	0	6
Hams, per cwt.	0	10	0
Hand Machines for preparing Fibre, spinning Cotton, or Wool	Free.		
Hay and Straw	Free.		
Hemp	Free.		
Hides, raw	Free.		
Horses, Mares and Geldings, per head......	0	8	0
Hogshead's Shooks, each	0	0	6
Hydraulic Presses, and Printing Presses	2	0	0
Ice	Free.		
Iron, Galvanized, per £100 value	4	0	0
——, ditto for Roofing, and every kind of Iron Roofing, Doors, and Shutters	Free.		
Indigo, per pound	0	0	3
Lard, per cwt.	0	5	0
Leeches	Free		
Matches, Lucifers, and others, per gross of twelve dozen boxes, each box to contain one hundred sticks, and boxes containing any greater or lesser quantity, to be charged in proportion..	0	5	0
Malt Dust	Free.		
Marble, in slabs or blocks, per £100 value...	4	0	0
Machines, (horse-power), per £100 value......	4	0	0
Meat, fresh	Free.		
——, salted, or cured, per barrel of 200lbs.	0	10	0
Meal, not Wheat, per barrel	0	1	0
Mills, whether for grinding Canes, Paint, Coffee, Corn, or grain of any kind, or for sawing Boards, raising Water, or are set in motion by steam, horse, wind, or water-power, per £100 value	4	0	0
Molasses	Free.		
Mules, per head	0	8	0
Necessaries, (Army and Navy) including Mess Plate and Furniture, Band Instruments. to be certified by the Military and Naval Commanding Officers, as requisite or necessary	Free.		
Oats, per bushel	0	0	3
Oil Cakes, whole, or in powder, and other prepared food for Animals	Free.		
Oil, per gallon	0	0	4
Patent Fuel	Free.		
Pans for boiling Sugar, whether of Copper or Iron, per £100 value	4	0	0
Pease, (not being Split Pease) per bushel	0	0	3
Perry, per ton	4	7	0
Pipes for conveying fluids, per £100 value	4	0	0
Plants, growing	Free.		
Ploughs, Plough-harrows, and Harrows, Cultivators, Clod-crushers, Horse Hoes, Dibbles, Sewing Machines, and parts thereof, four per cent			
Pork, salted or cured, per barrel of 200lbs.	0	10	0
Porter, per tun	5	7	0
Poultry	Free.		

		£	s.	D.
Puncheon Shooks, each..		0	0	6
Pumps for raising water, per £100 value		4	0	0
Railway Truck Wheels, per £100 value		4	0	0
Resins and Rosin			Free.	
Rice, per cwt.		0	2	0
——, undressed, per bushel		0	1	0
Salt, per cwt.		0	0	1
——, Rock			Free.	
Sarsaparilla •.....			Free.	
Sausages, dry or pickled, per cwt.		0	10	0
Sheep...			Free.	
Slates			Free.	
Soap, per box of 56lbs		0	3	0
Soda, Ash, or Sub-soda			Free.	
Specimens, illustrative of Natural History, Mineralogy, and geology			Free.	
Spirits, Brandy, per gallon		0	7	0
—— Gin, per gallon....		0	6	0
—— Rum, produce of, & imported from British possessions per gallon		0	6	0
—— Whiskey, per gallon		0	5	0
—— of Wine, Alcohol, and all other Spirits, Cordials, or compounds, per gallon		0	8	0
Stills, or any part of a Still, per £100 value		4	0	0
Steam engines, or part thereof, per £100 value		4	0	0
Sugar, refined, per lb		0	0	2
—— unrefined, per cwt		0	10	0
Swine			Free.	
Tallow, Grease, Tallow Grease, or Grease and Slush			Free.	
Tea, per lb		0	1	6
Tierce Shooks		0	0	6
Tiles, Marble, per £100 value •......		4	0	0
——, eartben			Free.	
Tobacco, manufactured, including Cavendish, for every pound weight		0	0	6
—— on every 100lbs. weight of unmanufactured		1	1	0
—— Cigars, for every pound weight...		0	2	6
Tongues, dried per cwt..		0	10	0
——, salted or cured, per barrel of 200lbs		0	10	0
Tortoiseshell			Free.	
Tow....			Free,	
Turtle			Free.	
Uniforms, prescribed by her Majesty's regulations, or any Law of this Colony..			Free.	
Vegetables, fresh			Free.	
Wax, Bees			Free.	
Wheat, per bushel		0	0	4
Wines, whether in bulk or bottled, per tun		15	0	0
Wood, for one thousand feet of Pitch Pine Lumber, by superficial measurement of one inch thick		0	12	0
——, for every one thousand feet of White Pine Lumber, or other Lumber, by superficial measurement of one inch thick		0	8	0
——, Shingles, Cypress, more than 12 inches in length, per 1000		0	4	0
——, Wallaba Shingles		0	4	0
——, Boston Chips, and all Shingles, not otherwise enumerated, or described, per 1000		0	2	0
——, Woodhoops, per 1000		0	2	0
——, a e and Heading, red or white Oak, or Ash, per 1000St v s		0	4	0
Wire, Iron, for fences ; and Wire Fencing ; and Iron Standards and Hurdles, and Tomb Railings, per £100 value		4	0	0
And after these rates for any greater or less quantity of such Goods respectively.				

				£	s.	D.	
On all other Goods, Wares, Merchandize, Plantation supplies and effects of every description, not previously enumerated, for every £100 value	......			12	10	0	

SCHEDULE B.

				£	s.	D.	
Rice, per 112 lbs.	......	......		0	0	6	Appropriation, s. 1
Tobacco, manufactured, per lb.	......	......		0	0	2	
Ditto, unmanufactured, per lb.	......	......		0	0	1½	
Cigars, per lb.	......	......		0	0	6	
Snuff, per lb.	......	......		0	0	6	
Shingles, per 1000	......	......		0	1	0	
Meal, per barrel	......	....		0	1	0	

SCHEDULE C.

			£	s.	D.	
On each cwt. of Codfish	......	......	0	1	0	Appropriation, s 1
Ditto gallon of Brandy	......	......	0	1	0	
On each gallon of Wine (in bottle)	......	......	0	0	9¾	
Ditto ditto ditto (in bulk)	.	......	0	0	3¾	
Ditto ditto Gin	......	......	0	2	0	
Ditto ditto British Spirits	.....	......	0	3	0	
Ditto barrel Beef	......	.....	0	4	0	
Ditto ditto Pork	......	.....	0	4	0	
Ditto ditto Tongues		......	0	4	0	
Ditto cwt. Rice	......	......	0	1	0	
Ditto bushel of Wheat	......	......	0	0	4	
Ditto pound of manufactured Tobacco		......	0	0	2	
Ditto ditto Leaf or unmanufactured Tobacco		......	0	0	1½	

Indictments.

In any Indictment or information wherein it is requisite to state the ownership of property, real or personal, belonging to or in the possession of more than one person, whether partners in trade, joint-tenants, parceners or tenants in common, it is sufficient to name one and to state the property to belong to him and another or others, as the case may be, and whenever it is necessary to mention for any purpose, any partners, joint-tenants, parceners or tenants in common, so to describe them. This provision extended to all Companies and Trustees, 8 G. 4, c. 22, s. 6. *[Allegation of ownership of partners, &c.]*

No indictment or information shall be abated by reason of any dilatory plea of misnomer, or of want of addition, or of wrong addition of the party, if the Court is satisfied by affidavit or otherwise, of the truth of the plea, but in such case, they shall forthwith cause it to be amended according to the truth, and call upon the pa   to plead, and proceed as if no such dilatory plea has been pleaded, 8 G. 4, c. 22, s. 7. *[Dilatory Pleas]*

No judgment shall be stayed or reversed for want of a similiter, nor by reason that the Jury process has been awarded to a wrong officer upon an insufficient suggestion, nor for any misnomer or misdescription of the officer returning such process, or of any of the Jurors, nor because any person has served upon the Jury who has not been returned as a Juror by the Provost-Marshal or other officer ; and where the offence charged has been created or subjected to a greater degree of punishment by any Act, the indictment, &c., after verdict, shall be sufficient to warrant the punishment, if it describe the offence in the words of the Act, 8 G. 4, c. 22, s. 9. *[Defects cured after Verdict. Description of offence in words of the Act]*

If any person arraigned for treason, felony or piracy, plead not guilty, he, by that plea, without any other form, puts himself upon the country for trial, and the Court shall, in the usual manner, order a Jury for his trial, 9 G. 4, c. 19, s. 1. *[Not Guilty]*

If he stand mute of malice, or will not answer directly, the Court may order the proper officer to enter a plea of "not guilty" on his behalf, which shall have the same effect as if he had actually pleaded it, 9 G. 4, c. 19, s. 2. *[To be entered for person a standing mute of malice, &c.]*

Whenever any Act of this island relating to any offence, punishable upon Indictment or summary conviction, in describing or referring to the offence *[Singular number, masculine gender]* or subject matter, on or with respect to which it is committed, or the offender or party affected or intended to be affected by the offence, uses words importing the singular number, or masculine gender only, it shall be understood to include several matters and persons, and females as well as males, unless otherwise specially provided, or there be something in the subject or context repugnant to such construction, 9 G. 4, c. 19, s. 8.

Offences on boundaries of parishes, &c., or begun in one and completed in another

Where any felony or misdemeanor is committed on the boundaries of 2 or more parishes or counties, within 500 yards thereof, or is begun in one parish or county and completed in another, it may be dealt with, enquired of, tried, determined and punished in any of such parishes or counties, in the same manner as if actually and wholly committed therein, 5 V., c. 29, s. 1.

During journeys

When committed on any person, or on or in respect of any property, on or upon any coach, wagon, cart or other carriage, employed in any journey, or on any person, or on or in respect of any property on board any vessel whatever, employed on any voyage or journey upon any navigable river, canal, or inland navigation, it may be dealt with in any parish or county through any part whereof such coach, &c., passed in the course of the journey or voyage. Where the side, centre or other part of any highway, or the side-bank, centre or other part of any river, canal or navigation constitutes the boundary of any two parishes or counties, the felony or misdemeanor may be dealt with, enquired of, &c., in either of the parishes or counties, through or adjoining to, or by the boundary of any part whereof such coach, &c., passed in the course of the journey or voyage, 5 V., c. 29, s. 2.

Amendment of variances on trial

Whenever on the trial of any Indictment for felony or misdemeanor, there appears to be any variance between the statement in the Indictment and the evidence offered in proof thereof in the name of any country, city, parish, township, or place mentioned or described in the Indictment, or in the name or description of any person, body politic or corporate, alleged to be owner of any property, real or personal, the subject of any offence charged therein, or in the name or description of any person, body politic or corporate, therein alleged to be injured or damaged, or intended to be injured or damaged by the commission of such offence, or in the Christian or surname, or both or other description of any person, or of any matter or thing therein named or described, or the ownership of any property, the Court, if it consider the variance not material to the merits, and that the defendant cannot be prejudiced in his defence on such merits, may order the Indictment to be amended according to the proof by an officer of the Court, both in that part where the variance occurs, and in every other part which it becomes necessary to amend, on such terms, as to postponing the trial before the same or another Jury as the Court thinks reasonable, and after any such amendment, the trial shall proceed, whenever to be proceeded with, in the same manner in all respects, and with the same consequences, both with respect to the liability of witnesses to be Indicted for perjury or otherwise, as if no variance had occurred. In case the trial is had at nisi prius, the order for the amendment shall be endorsed on and returned with the record, and thereupon such papers, rolls or other records of the Court from which it issued, as it may be necessary to amend, shall be amended accordingly by the proper officer. In all other cases, the order for the amendment shall either be endorsed on the indictment, or engrossed and filed together with it among the records of the Court. Where the trial is postponed, the Court may respite the recognizances of the prosecutor and witnesses, and of the defendant and his sureties accordingly, on which the prosecutor and witnesses shall be bound to prosecute and give evidence, and the defendant to attend, to be tried without fresh recognizances, as if originally bound to appear and prosecute, or give evidence at the time and place to which the trial is postponed. Where the trial is to be had before another Jury, the Crown and the defendant shall be entitled to the same challenges as before the first Jury was sworn, 16 V., c. 15, s. 1.

Verdict, &c.

Every verdict and judgment given after the making of any amendment, shall be of the same force as if the Indictment were originally in the form in which it was after amendment, 16 V., c. 15, s. 2.

Drawing up record

If it become necessary for any purpose to draw up a formal record, in any case where an amendment has been made, the record shall be drawn up in the form in which it was after amendment, without taking notice of the fact of such amendment having been made, 16 V., c. 15, s. 3.

In any Indictment for engraving, or making the whole or any part of any instrument, matter or thing, or for using, or having the unlawful possession of any plate or other material, upon which the whole or any part of any instrument, matter or thing has been engraven or made, or for having the unlawful possession of any paper upon which the whole or any part of any instrument, matter or thing has been made or printed, it shall be sufficient to describe the same by any name or designation it is usually known by, without setting out any copy or fac simile of the whole or any part, 16 V., c. 15, s. 6.

Indictment for engraving, &c., or unlawful possession of plate or paper. General description sufficient

In all other cases wherever necessary to make any averment in any Indictment as to any instrument, whether it consists wholly or in part of writing, print or figures, it shall be sufficient to describe it by any name or designation it is usually known by, or by the purport, without setting out any copy or fac simile of the whole or any part, 16 V., c. 15, s. 7.

As also in other cases of instruments, &c.

If, on the trial of any person charged with any felony or misdemeanor, it appear to the Jury upon the evidence, that the defendant did not complete the offence charged, but is guilty only of an attempt to commit same, he shall not be entitled to be acquitted, but the Jury may return a verdict that the defendant is not guilty of the felony or misdemeanor charged, but is guilty of an attempt to commit the same, and thereupon he shall be liable to be punished, as if he had been convicted upon an indictment for attempting to commit the particular felony or misdemeanor charged; and no person so tried shall be liable to be afterwards prosecuted for an attempt to commit the felony or misdemeanor for which he was tried, 16 V., c. 15, s. 9.

On indictments for felony or misdemeanor, defendant may be found guilty of an attempt to commit the offence

If, on the trial of any person for any misdemeanor, it appears the facts amount in law to a felony, he shall not be acquitted of the misdemeanor; and no person tried for such misdemeanor shall be liable to be afterwards prosecuted for felony on the same facts, unless the Court think fit to discharge the Jury from giving any verdict upon such trial, and to direct him to be indicted for felony, in which case he may be dealt with in all respects as if he had not been put upon his trial for such misdemeanor, 16 V., c. 15, s. 12.

Indictments for misdemeanor where the facts amount to felony

In every Indictment in which it is necessary to make any averment, as to any money or note of the Treasury, or of any Bank of this Island, it shall be sufficient to describe such money, or Treasury or Bank Note, simply as money, without specifying any particular coin, or Treasury or Bank Note; and such allegation, as far as regards the description of the property, shall be sustained by proof of any amount of coin, or of any Treasury or Bank Note, although the particular species of coin of which the amount was composed, or the particular nature of the Treasury or Bank Note is not proved, 28 V.. c. 15, s. 1.*

Money, to include Bank or Treasury Notes

It shall not be necessary to state any venue in the body of any Indictment, but the County, Parish, or other jurisdiction named in the margin, shall be taken to be the venue for all the facts stated in the body. Where local description is, or shall be required, it shall be given in the body of the Indictment, 16 V., c. 15, s. 24.

Venue

No Indictment for any offence shall be held insufficient for want of the averment of any matter unnecessary to be proved, nor for the omission of the words " as appears by the Record" or, " with force and arms," or, " against the peace," nor for the insertion of the words " against the form of the statute," instead of " against the form of the statutes," or vice versa, nor for that any person mentioned therein is designated by a name of office or other descriptive appellation, instead of his proper name, nor for omitting to state the year at which the offence was committed, where time is not of the essence of the offence, or for stating the time imperfectly, nor for stating the offence to have been committed on a day subsequent to the finding of the Indictment, or on an impossible day, or a day that never happened, nor for the want of a proper or perfect venue, or proper or formal conclusion, nor for want of or imperfection in the addition of any defendant, nor for want of the statement of the value or price of any matter or thing, or the amount of damage, injury or spoil, in any case where the value or price, or the amount of damage, injury or spoil is not of the essence of the offence, 16 V., c. 15, s. 25.

Technical nicities supersedes 8 G. 4, c. 22, s. 9

---

* This enactment was originally part of 16 V., c. 15, s. 18., the whole of which section was inadvertently repealed by 27 V, s 1, o. 32. The mistake does not appear to have been completely rectified.

Objections to be by demurrer or motion to quash before the Jury is sworn; amendment

Every objection to any Indictment for any formal defect apparent on it sface, shall be taken by demurrer, or motion to quash the Indictment, before the Jury is sworn, and not afterwards; and the Court before which the objection is taken, may, if thought necessary, cause the Indictment to be forthwith amended in such particular by some officer of the Court or other person, and thereupon the trial shall proceed as if no such defect had appeared, 16 V., c. 15, s. 26.

Traverse Adjournment.

No person prosecuted shall be entitled to traverse, or postpone the trial of any Indictment found against him. If the Court, on application of the person so indicted, or otherwise, is of opinion he ought to be allowed a further time to prepare for his defence, or otherwise, the Court may adjourn the trial to the next subsequent Session, upon such terms as to bail, or otherwise, as to it seems meet, and respite the recognizances of the prosecutor and witnesses accordingly, in which case they shall be bound to attend to prosecute and give evidence at such subsequent Session, without entering into fresh recognizance, 16 V., c. 15, s. 27.

Certiorari

Unless a writ of Certiorari for removing the Indictment into the Supreme Court is delivered at such Session, before the Jury is sworn for the trial, 5 V., c. 48, s. 1.

Before bill found

Such writs of Certiorari may be applied for and issued before Indictment found in the like cases, and in the same manner, and upon the same terms and conditions as if the writ were applied for after Indictment found, 5 V., c. 48, s. 2.

Highways

Act not to extend to any prosecution by Indictment for the non-repair of any Bridge or Highway, 5 V., c. 48, s. 5.

Interpretation

In this Act, Indictment shall include information, inquisition and presentment, as well as Indictment, and also any plea, replication or other pleading; and any nisi prius record. "Finding of the Indictment," shall include "the taking of an inquisition," "the exhibiting of an information," and "the making a presentment." Any word importing the singular number, or masculine gender, several persons and parties, as well as one, females as well as males, bodies corporate, as well as individuals, and several matters and things, as well as one. "Property," shall include goods, chattels, money, valuable securities, and every other matter or thing, whether real or personal, upon or with respect to which any offence may be committed, 16 V., c. 15, s. 30.

Appeal from conviction at Circuit Court, security, postponement of sentence, &c.

If any person, convicted upon an Indictment for a felony or misdemeanor, before any Circuit Judge, conceive himself damnified by the misdirection of the Judge, or by the improper reception or rejection of evidence and has objected at the trial to the ruling of the Court, in either of these respects, the record shall be returned by the proper officer into the Supreme Court, and the person making the objection may move there for a new trial, or if he deem the Indictment or information contains no sufficient charge of an offence punishable, or that there has been a mis-trial, he may move in the Supreme Court, after requiring the proper officer to return the record into the Supreme Court, for a reversal of the judgment of the Court by which he was sentenced, if any has been given, or if it has been delayed, he may move for a writ of prohibition against proceeding to judgment on such Indictment and conviction. Not to deprive any party to any suit or proceeding of his right to tender a bill of exceptions to the ruling or charge of any Judge. The person so intending to appeal, either in arrest of judgment or for a new trial, shall, before the final adjournment of the Court before which the trial was had, enter into security (to be fixed by the Judge, according to a scale to be fixed by the rules of the Court, or until rules are framed at the discretion of the Judge) to enter his appeal for the then next Supreme Court within the time allowed by its rules. Where the trial is had within 14 days before the then next sitting, the party shall have until the session of the Supreme Court next succeeding to enter his appeal. The Judge, if he see fit, may postpone the passing of sentence, or respite the judgment, consequent on the conviction, until the decision of the Supreme Court can be obtained, 19 V., c. 10, s. 43.

Industrial Schools.

Industrial Schools Act, 1857, 21 V., c. 41, s. 1. Short title

" Police," shall include or mean Parish Constables or other Peace Interpretation Officers; " Justices," any two or more Justices acting together; " Child," any boy or girl, in the opinion of the Justices under 16; " Certified School," any School or Institution certified under this Act; " Managers," the Directors, Managers, or other persons who have the management or control of any Certified Industrial School; " Parent," any person legally liable to maintain a child, and also any person upon whom an order of affiliation has been made and not quashed; " Parish," any city or town, 21 V., c. 41, s.2.

The Governor, with the advice of the Executive Committee, may enter Certified Industrial Schools into arrangements with the Managers of any School in which Industrial training is provided, and in which children are fed as well as taught, for the reception, maintenance, instruction, care and employment of any poor and vagrant children, and the Governor may grant a certificate under hand accordingly, and thenceforth the School shall be a " Certified Industrial School," 21 V., c. 41, s. 3.

The Governor shall direct a report of the condition and regulations of Annual Reports Withdrawal of certificate every Certified Industrial School, to be made to him at least once a year by such person as he appoints; and if upon such report. the Governor in Executive Committee is dissatisfied with the condition or regulations of the School, he may withdraw his certificate, and upon notice of withdrawal to the Managers, the School shall cease to be a Certified Industrial School from the time specified in the notice, 21 V., c. 41, s. 4.

When any child is found in want and distress, or soliciting alms, or Destitute children may be sent to a Certified School for a week, notice to parents, &c. wandering in the streets or highways, or sleeping therein, or in any unenclosed piazza or unoccupied house or outbuildings, or not having any home or settled place of abode, or lawful and visible means of subsistence, whether such child have parents or any guardian, or adult relative living or not, any person may bring, or cause, &c., any such child before the Justices, who, on receiving satisfactory proof of such condition or vagrancy, may order him, provided there be any certified Industrial School, to be sent there for not exceeding one week, and direct enquiries to be made, and notice (Form A.) given to the parent or guardian, or nearest adult relative, if any can be found, or to the person with whom the child is, or was last known to have been residing, of the circumstance, and that the matter will be enquired into at the time and place mentioned in the notice, 21 V., c. 41, s. 5.

At which time and place any Justices may make full enquiry into the Discharge of child, delivery to his parents, &c., sending him to a school matter, and may order the child to be discharged altogether, or if the parent (or where the child is an orphan, the guardian or nearest adult relative) be found, may, on proof of the child having been found in any such circumstances as aforesaid, deliver him up to the parent, or, if an orphan, guardian, &c., on his giving an assurance in writing (Form B.), that he will be responsible for the good behaviour of the child for not exceeding 12 months, and, in default of such assurance, may, by writing, under their hands and seals, (Form C.) order the child to be sent for education and training to any Cer- Of the parents religious persuasion, if any, in that or an adjoining parish tified Industrial School. If within the parish where the child was taken into custody, or any adjoining pa   , there is any Certified Industrial School, conducted on the principles of the religious persuasion, to which the parent, in the opinion of the Justices, belongs, and the Managers are willing to receive him, the child shall be sent to such School, and no other, 21 V., c. 41 s 6.

If the child, after such assurance is given, be brought up again as having Penalty on parents, &c. if child be found under similar circumstances been found under such circumstances as aforesaid, within the period for which the parent, &c , has become responsible for his good behaviour, the Justices may inflict a fine upon him, not exceeding 40s., should it be proved to their satisfaction that the last mentioned act has taken place through the neglect of the parent, &c., 21 V., c. 41, s. 7.

If the parent, &c., objects to the School to which the child has been Removal to another school on request of parent, &c. sent or ordered, and proposes some other Certified Industrial School, and proves that the Managers of it are willing to receive the child, and if on any other than religious ground, pays or finds security to pay any expenses incurred in consequence of his objection, any Justice of the parish where the child was taken into custody, shall order (Form D.) the child to be sent to the School proposed by the parent, &c., 21 V., c. 41, s. 8.

Discharge of child on suitable employment or other sufficient cause

On the application of the parent, &c., or of the Managers, any Justices of the parish in which the School is situate, or where such parent resides, if satisfied that a suitable employment in life has been provided for the child, or that there is otherwise sufficient cause, may discharge (Form E.) the child from the Certified Industrial School before the expiration of the period for which he had been sent there, or may order his removal from one Certified Industrial School to another (Form F.), or may order him to be discharged altogether, 21 V., c. 41, s. 9.

Or on good security

On good security being given at any time by the parent, or by any other person, any two Justices of the County in which the School is situate, or of the Parish where such parent resides, shall order (Form G.) the child to be discharged. The security shall be in such amount as the Justices determine, or may be rejected, on proof that the security has been previously rejected or forfeited, 21 V., c. 41, s. 10.

Governor may order discharge on security

On application of the parent, or guardian, or nearest adult relative, or of any other person, on security being found for the future good behaviour of any child, the Governor may order the child to be discharged, and the sufficiency of such security shall be in his judgment, and his order may be mutatis mutandis in the form or to the effect of the (Form G., 21 V., c. 41), 22 V., c. 32, s. 1.

No child to be detained beyond 16

No person shall be detained in any such School beyond 16, against his consent, 21 V., c. 41, s. 11.

Absconding

If any child, whether lodging in the School or elsewhere, before attaining 16, or being discharged, wilfully absconds or neglects his attendance, any Justice of the Parish in which the School is, or in which the child is re-taken, may, by writing under his hand and seal, order him to be sent back to the School, and to be detained until he attains 16, or for such shorter period as the Justices (sic) think fit, 21 V., c. 41, s. 12.

Repeated desertion

In case of any child absconding, or repeatedly deserting from any such School, the Managers may cause to be inflicted on him moderate whipping, or confine him in solitary confinement, and place him on bread and water for such period as they think advisable, 22 V., c. 32, s. 2.

Enticing away or harbouring children

Any person who directly or indirectly withdraws a child from the School, or induces him to abscond previous to his attaining 16, or being duly discharged, or who knowingly conceals or harbours him, or prevents his return, shall be liable to a penalty not exceeding £2, to be recovered before 2 Justices in or near the place where the offence was committed, or where the offender may at the time happen to be, under 13 V., c. 35, or other Act relating to summary proceedings, 21 V., c. 41, s. 13.

Service at place of abode

The leaving of any notice, or summons, or order at the usual or last known place of abode of the party to whom it is directed, shall be sufficient service, 21 V., c. 41, s. 14.

Children left destitute on the parish, or whose parents cannot maintain them, may be sent to a School

Whenever application is made to any Churchwarden, or the Justices and Vestry of any parish, for the maintenance for, or assistance in maintaining any child, on the ground of its having no parent in the Island, or alive, or the parent being unable to maintain, or having deserted or abandoned such child, the Justices may direct it to be taken from the applicant, or person in whose custody it is, and placed in the Certified Industrial School of the parish, or nearest parish, 21 V., c. 41, s. 15.

Judges and Justices in petty sessions may send children under 16 to a Certified School after conviction

The Judge of any Court and the Justices in Petty Sessions, when any child under 16 is charged with any offence, may refrain, upon conviction, from passing sentence, and direct, by an order, in writing, that he be taken to the Certified Industrial School nearest the place where he was convicted, the Managers of which shall be willing to receive him, to be kept for such period as may be directed in such order, 21 V., c. 41, s. 16.

To be kept apart as far as practicable from other children, and employed as the Governor, &c. may direct

The Governor and Executive Committee may direct that every child sent to any such School by the order of any Judge or Justices, after conviction for any offence other than vagrancy, shall be kept separate and apart, so far as practicable, from any other children, and employed in such manner as shall appear best to the Governor, with such advice, 21 V., c. 41, s. 17.

Regulations respecting religious teaching

In every Industrial School, a book shall be kept by the Managers, to which access shall be had at all reasonable hours, in which the religious denomination of the child, when admitted, shall be entered; and upon the representation of the parent, or, in case of an orphan, of the guardian or nearest adult relative of any inmate, a Minister of the religious persuasion of the in mate, at certain hours to be fixed by the Managers, may visit such schools, to afford religious assistance to such inmate, and instruct him in the principles of his religion, 21 V., c. 41, s. 18.

A duplicate of the order under which any child is ordered to be sent to a Certified Industrial School shall be sent to the Managers, and be a sufficient warrant for the detention, 21 V., c. 41, s. 19.

Duplicate order to be sent with child to the School

In every case in which a child is sent by a Judge or Justices to a Certified School, they shall state in the order for admittance, the amount to be paid to the person taking the child, as compensation for his trouble, not exceeding 5s., which the Managers are authorized to pay, and take credit for in their account with the Public, 21 V., c, 41, s. 20.

Fee to the person taking the child to the school to be stated in order and charged to the public

Where the child is sent to a Certified School by the order of a Judge or Justices, the Governor and Executive Committee may direct payment to the Managers, out of the annual fund voted for the Penitentiaries and Prisons' Department, of such or any part of such sum as would be payable for the maintenance in any Penitentiary or Prison of such child, if he had been sentenced to imprisonment therein, instead of being sent to such School, 22 V., c. 32, s. 3.

The Governor, &c. may order payment to the school out of prisons' fund, the maintenance of children sent by the Judges or Justices to the Certified School

The Governor and Executive Committee may direct payment by the Receiver-General to the Managers of any Certified Industrial School to which any child shall be sent under 21 V., c. 41, of not exceeding 5d. per day for each child, to be made monthly or quarterly as the Governor directs, 23 V., c. 24, s. 1.

Also of other children sent

Whenever it is necessary to prove that any Industrial School is duly certified or sanctioned, the production of an attested copy of the Certificate shall be sufficient evidence. The production of the original, or a duplicate of the order under which any child has been sent, or is detained, or a copy of such order, with a memorandum, signed by the Manager or Superintendent, or Master or Matron of any such School, that the young person named in such order was duly received into, and is at the signing thereof detained in such School, or has been otherwise disposed of according to law; and the production of the original or duplicate of any order made upon the parent, or a copy certified by the Clerk to the Justices making the same, shall in all proceedings be sufficient evidence, without proof of the signatures or official characters of the Justices or other persons, 21 V., c. 41, s. 22.

Certain certificates duplicates, &c. evidence.

Whenever the Governor and Executive Committee grants a Certificate to any Industrial School, they shall, within one calendar month, cause a notice to be published in the "Jamaica Gazette," which shall be sufficient evidence of the fact; and whenever the Governor, with the notice (sic) aforesaid, withdraws the Certificate, they shall, within one calendar month, give notice of withdrawal in the "Gazette," 21 V., c. 41, s. 23.

Publication of certificates to schools and withdrawal

The several forms in the Schedule, or any forms to the like effect, shall, in all cases, be sufficient. No summons, notice or order shall be invalidated for want of form only, 21 V., c. 41, s. 24.

Forms
Want of form

SCHEDULES.—21 V., c. 41.

To C. B., of the parish of

I hereby give you notice, pursuant to section five of the "Industrial School Act, 1857," that a child, named A. B., apparently about years of age, the son of (or who has been residing with) you the said C. B., has been taken into custody, for having been on the day of , in the parish of , found (in the words of this Act), and that the matter will be inquired into on the day of , at o'clock in the forenoon, at , before such Justices of the Peace for the said parish as may then be there, who may make such order on you the said C. B., to be dealt with according to the said Act as they may think fit; the said A. B. is in the meantime detained in the , at by order of a Justice of the Peace.

Notice to parent, &c. that child is in custody, A. s. 5

Dated this   day of   185

M. N., Constable or Inspector of Police.

Assurance for child's good behavior. B. s. 6

Whereas a child, named A. B., the son of C. D., has been proved a vagrant: I, C. D., hereby undertake to be responsible for the good behaviour of the said child, for the period of   months from the day of the date thereof.

Order sending child to an Industrial School, C. s. 6

To wit.   }   To the Constable of   , and to the Managers
          }   of the Certified Industrial School at

Whereas a certain child, named A. B,, about   years of age, was this day brought before us, two of Her Majesty's Justices of the Peace for the parish of   , for that he, on the day of   , at   , was found in the act of vagrancy, (or as the case may be in section five): And whereas we have made full enquiry into the matter, pursuant to the "Industrial Schools' Act, 1857," and no satisfactory assurance has been given for the future proper care and good behaviour of the said child: Now therefore we, the said Justices do, pursuant to section six of the said Act, order you the said Constable to take the said child, and him safely convey to the   Certified Industrial School, at   ; and there to deliver him, together with this order ; and we do hereby command you, the said Managers, (it appearing to us that you are willing to receive him therein), to receive the said child into your charge in the said School, and there to detain, educate and train him for the period of   from the date hereof.

Given under our hands and seals, this   day of   at   , in the pa   aforesaid.
(Signatures and seals of Justices.)

Order changing school, D. s. 8

To the Managers of the   Certified Industrial School at
            , and to the Managers of the   Certified Industrial School at

Whereas a certain child, named A. B., about   years of age, was on the   day of   , by order of two of Her Majesty's Justices of the Peace for the parish of   , pursuant to the "Industrial School Act, 1857," taken to the   Certified Industrial School at   , there to be detained for the period of   from the said day of   and he is now detained therein (if so): And whereas, C. B., according to the provisions of the said Act, entitled to chject, has objected to the said School, and has proposed the   Certified Industrial School at   , and proved to me, the undersigned, one of Her Majesty's Justices of the Peace for the parish of   where the child was taken into custody, that the Managers of the   Certified Industrial School at   are willing to receive the said child, and the said C. D. has also complied with the other conditions of section eight of the said Act; These are therefore, pursuant to section eight of the said Act, to order you, the said Managers of the   Certified Industrial School at   to deliver up the said child forthwith to the Certified Industrial School at   ; and you the said Managers of the said last mentioned School, are hereby required to receive the said child into your charge in the said School, and there to detain, educate and train him for the period of   from the   day of

Given under my hand and seal, this   day of   at   , in the parish aforesaid.

J. S., (L.S.)

Order for discharge on employment being found, E. s. 9

To the Managers of the   Certified Industrial School at

Whereas a certain child, named A, B., about   years of age, was on the   day of   , by the order of two of Her Majesty's Justices of the Peace for the parish of   , made pursuant to the "Industrial School Act, 1857,

taken to the   Certified Industrial School at   ,
there to be detained for the period of   ,from the day of
    ., and he is now detained therein* . And whereas it appears
to us, two of Her Majesty's Justices of the Peace for the parish of
    in which the School is situate, (or in which the parent, or
guardian or nearest adult relative of the said child resides) that
suitable employment in life has been provided for the said child (or
there appears to us, &c., sufficient cause for the discharge of the
said child): These are therefore, pursuant to section twelve of the
said Act, to command you, the said Managers, forthwith to discharge the said child, and to deliver him into the charge of
who brings this order.

Given under our hands and seals, this   day of
   at   in the parish aforesaid.

            (Signatures and seals of Justices.)

———

To the Managers of the   Certified Industrial School at   *Order changing*
     , and to the Managers of the   Certified Industrial   *school on assurance*
School at   *of future good be-*
                                               havior, F. s. 9

(Proceed to the asterisk* in the Form E, and then say): And whereas
it appears to us desirable that the said child should be removed
from the said   Certified Industrial School to the said
    Certified Industrial School, (the Managers of which said last
mentioned School being willing to receive the said child therein):
These are therefore, pursuant to section nine of the said Act, to
order you, the said Managers of the   Certified Industrial School at   , to deliver up the said child forthwith
to the   Certified Industrial School, or to any person authorized by them to receive the child at   ; and you, the
said Managers of the said last mentioned School, are hereby required to receive the said child into your charge in the said School,
and there to detain, educate and train him for the period of
from the   day of

Given under our hands and seals, this   day of
   at   in the parish aforesaid.

           (Justices signatures and seals.)

———

(Proceed to the asterisk* in the Form E, and then say): And whereas   *Order for dis-*
good security has been found before us, two of Her Majesty's Jus-   *charge on security*
tices of the Peace for the parish of   , in which the   *for good behavior,*
School is situate (or in which the parent, or guardian, or nearest   *G. s. 10*
adult relative of the said child resides), for the future good behaviour of the said child: These are therefore, pursuant to section
ten of the said Act, to command you, the said Managers, forth-
wth to discharge the said child, and to deliver him into the charge
of   who brings this order.

Given under our hands and seals, this   day of
   at   in the parish aforesaid.

         (Signatures and seals of Justices.)

The Managers, or a majority, of any Certified Industrial School, with the   *Power of mana-*
consent of the Governor, may bind apprentice to any householder any child   *gers to apprentice*
at the expiration of the period for which he has been placed in the School   *children*
(or before, if the child has attained 13 years) who is an orphan, or whose parents, guardian or nearest adult relative are unable or unwilling to make provision for his future care and support, 25 V., c. 2, s. 1.

Such binding shall be for not more than 5 nor less than 3 years, by in-   *· For not more than*
denture, or other contract, in writing, in or to the effect of the Form annexed,   *5 nor less than 3*
to be executed in triplicate by the Managers, or a majority, on behalf of the   *years: indenture,*
apprentice, and by the Master, one of which shall be kept by the Managers,   *&c. to be in tripli-*
one by the Master, and one by the apprentice, either of which shall be ad-   *cate*
missible as evidence in any suit or proceeding, and shall contain covenants

on the part of the Master for the maintenance and support of the apprentice, and for the payment of the wages or allowance agreed on, and for his training and education in the handicraft, trade, business, or mystery, or other industrial employment, agricultural or domestic, to which he is bound, 25 V., c. 2, s. 2.

Complaints against apprentices

Any two Justices of the parish in which the apprentice is employed, shall hear and determine any complaint brought by any Master against his apprentice; for misdemeanor, misconduct, negligence or absence from service; and, on due proof, shall punish the offender, by abating all or any part of his wages or allowance, or by imprisonment, not exceeding three months and the infliction of any punishment shall not cancel the binding, 25 V., c. 2, s. 3.

Against Masters !

Any two Justices shall also hear and determine any complaint brought by any apprentice against his Master for non-payment of his wages, or allowance, or for ill-usage, and shall order payment of the wages or allowance due such apprentice, and in case of proved ill-usage, shall impose on the Master a fine not exceeding £10, and costs, and in default of immediate payment, adjudge him to be imprisoned for not exceeding 3 months unless sooner paid, and may, in addition, order the apprentice to be discharged, and the indenture or contract to be cancelled, or assign the apprentice for the unexpired term of his apprenticeship to some other Master, to be approved proved of by the Managers, 25 V., c. 2, s. 4.

Masters and apprentices may be examined on oath

The Justices may examine, on oath, any Master, or apprentice, or other person coming before them as complainant or defendant, 25 V., c. 2, s. 5.

Apprentices not to be discharged or assigned by masters without consent of managers

No Master shall, without the consent of the Managers, or a majority, put away, or discharge or transfer his apprentice, whether the apprentice consent or not, 25 V., c. 2, s. 6.

Powers of managers to assign apprentice in case of death or absence of master

If any Master, before the expiration of the term of service, die or leave the Island, and remain absent 6 months without having made provision to the satisfaction of the Managers for carrying out the terms of the indenture, they, or a majority, may assign such apprentice for the unexpired term, to any other householder, and such assignment shall be subject to all the provisions of this Act, 25 V., c. 2, s. 7.

Proceedings to be under 13 V., c. 35, &c.

All remedies and proceedings for enforcing any order, adjudication or conviction, shall be under 13 V., c. 35, and the Acts in aid thereof, (see Justices), 25 V., c. 2, s. 8.

Proceedings exempt from Stamp Duty

All matters and proceedings under this Act shall be exempt from Stamp Duty, 25 V., c. 2, s. 9.

———

Indenture of apprenticeship s. 2

JAMAICA, SS.

Know all men by these presents, That A. B., C. D., &c., the Managers (or as the case may be, the majority of the Managers of the Industrial School for boys or girls) situate in the Parish of   duly certified according to the provisions of the "Industrial Schools' Act, 1857," by and with the consent of the Governor of this Island, do put and place E. F., aged   years, an inmate of the said School, duly placed in the said School under the provisions of the said Act, for whose future care and support no provision has been made by his parents, guardians or relatives, apprentice to G. H. of the Parish of   with him to dwell and serve from the day of the date of these presents for the term of   years thence ensuing, during all which term the said apprentice his said Master shall faithfully serve in all lawful business according to his power and ability, and honestly, orderly and obediently in all things, demean and behave himself towards his said Master during the said term ; and the said (Master) [for himself, his executors and administrators, doth covenant and agree to and with the said Managers and every of them, their, and every of their successors for the time being by these presents, that he the said (Master) the said apprentice in the art, trade or mystery of   (or as the case may be, in the business or occupation or calling of   ) or other industrial employment, agricultural or domestic, shall and will teach and instruct, or cause to be taught or instructed in the best way and manner that he can, and shall and will during all the term aforesaid find, provide, and allow unto the said apprentice sufficient meat, drink, apparel, lodging, medical attendance, and all other things necessary and fit for an apprentice. (Here insert any other special or additional covenant.)

In witness whereof the said parties hereto have hereunto set their hands and seals this day of , in the year of our Lord One Thousand Eight Hundred and

Sealed and delivered in the presence of

Infants.

The Chancellor or Vice-Chancellor, upon hearing the petition of the mother of any Infant, in the sole custody or control of the father, or of any person by his authority, or of any guardian after his death, and affidavits filed in support of or in answer to such petition, may make order for the access of the petitioner to such Infant at such times, and subject to such regulations as he deems convenient and just; and if the Infant be within the age of 7 years, may make order that it be delivered to and remain in the custody of the petitioner until that age, subject to such regulations as he deems convenient and just, 17 V., c. 39, s. 1. *Order for mother, access to her infant or custody*

Affidavits in support of, or in answer to such petition shall be filed in the office of the Registrar of the Court of Chancery, within such time and under such regulations as are directed by the rules of the Court, 17 V., c. 39, s. 2. *Filing affidavits*

In applications, the Chancellor, &c., may receive any petition or affidavit, sworn before any Master in Ordinary or Master Extraordinary; and any person who deposes falsely and corruptly shall be guilty of perjury, 17 V., c. 39, s. 3. *How to be sworn. Perjury*

All orders shall be enforced by process of contempt of the Court, 17 V., c. 39, s. 4. *Orders to be enforced by contempt process*

Where any action, suit or other proceeding for the payment of debts, or for any other purpose, is commenced or prosecuted by or against an Infant under 21, either alone or together with any other person, the parol shall not demur, but the action, &c., shall be prosecuted and carried on in the same manner, and as effectually as actions or suits heretofore by or against Infants, where, according to law, the parol did not demur, 18 V., c. 58, s. 1. *Parol demurrer taken away*

Inheritance.

"Land" shall extend to Messuages and all other Hereditaments, whether corporeal or incorporeal, and whether Freehold or of any other tenure, and whether descendible according to the common law (sic), and to money to be laid out in the purchase of Land, and to Chattels, and to other property transmissible to heirs, and also to any share of the same Hereditaments and Properties, and to any estate of Inheritance, or for life or lives, or other estate transmissible to heirs, and to any possibility, right or title of entry or action, and any other interest capable of being inherited, and whether in possession, reversion, remainder, or contingency; "the Purchaser," the person who last acquired the land otherwise than by descent, or by escheat or partition, by the effect of which the land becomes part of, or descendible as other land acquired by descent; "Descent," the title to inherit land by reason of consanguinity, as well where the heir is an ancestor or collateral relation, as where he is a child or other issue; "Descendants" of any ancestor, shall extend to all persons who must trace their descent through such ancestor; "the person last entitled to Land" shall extend to the last person who had a right thereto, whether he did or did not obtain the possession or the receipt of the rents and profits; "Assurance," any deed or instrument (other than a will) by which any Land is conveyed or transferred at Law or in Equity, 3 V., c. 34, s. 1. *Interpretation— land* *Purchaser* *Descent* *Descendants* *Person last entitled* *Assurance*

In every case descent shall be traced from the purchaser; and that pedigree may never be carried further back than the circumstances of the case and nature of the title require, the person last entitled to the Land shall be considered the purchaser, unless it be proved that he inherited, in which case the person from whom he inherited shall be considered the purchaser, unless it be proved that he inherited; and in like manner the last purchaser from whom the Land is proved to have been inherited, shall be considered the purchaser, unless it is proved that he inherited, 3 V., c. 34, s. 2. *Descent to be traced from the last purchaser. Who to be deemed such*

O O

To take as devisee
under will; and as
purchasers under
assurances

When any Land has been devised, by any testator who dies after 31 July, 1840, to the heir, or to the person who shall be the heir of such testator, such heir shall be considered to have acquired the Land as a devisee and not by descent; and when limited by any assurance, executed after 31 July, 1840, to the person or to the heirs of the person who shall thereby have conveyed the same Land, such person shall be considered to have acquired the same as a purchaser; and shall not be considered entitled as of his former estate, or part thereof, 34 V., c. 4, s. 3.

Similar provisions
under cases of limitations to the heir
or heirs of the body
of an ancestor

When any person has acquired any Land by purchase, under a limitation to the heirs, or heirs of the body of any of his ancestors, in an assurance executed after 31 July, 1840, or under a limitation to the heirs, or to the heirs of the body of any of his ancestors, or under any limitation having the same effect in the will of any testator who departs this life after 31 July, 1840, such Land shall descend, and the descent be traced as if the ancestor named in the limitation had been the purchaser, 3 V., c. 34, s. 4.

Descent from a
brother or sister to
be traced through
the parent

No brother or sister shall be considered to inherit immediately from his or her brother or sister, but every descent from a brother or sister shall be traced from the parent, 3 V., c. 34, s. 5.

Lineal ancestor
may be heir, and
where there is no
issue, of the purchaser, in preference to others

Every lineal ancestor shall be capable of being heir to any of his issue ; and where there is no issue of the purchaser, his nearest lineal ancestor shall be his heir in preference to any person who would have been entitled to inherit, either by tracing his descent through such lineal ancestor, or in consequence of there being no descendants of such lineal ancestor, so that the father shall be preferred to a brother or sister, and a more remote lineal ancestor to any of his issue other than a nearer lineal ancestor or his issue, 3 V., c. 34, s. 6.

Paternal ancestors and their descendants to be preferred to the maternal ancestors, and
among them males
to females—No
female maternal ancestor to inherit until males have failed

None of the maternal ancestors of the person from whom the descent is to be traced, nor any of their descendants shall be capable of inheriting, until all his paternal ancestors and their descendants have failed ; and no female paternal ancestor of such person, nor any of her descendants shall be capable of inheriting until all his male paternal ancestors and their descendants have failed ; and no female maternal ancestor of such person, nor any of her descendants shall be capable of inheriting until all his male maternal ancestors and their descendants have failed, 3 V., c. 34, s. 7.

On failure of male
paternal ancestors,
the descent to be
traced through the
mother of the more
remote paternal ancestor and her
descendants

Where there is a failure of male paternal ancestors of the person from whom the descent is to be traced and their descendants, the mother of his more remote male paternal ancestor, or her descendants shall be the heir or heirs of such person, in preference to the mother of a less remote male paternal ancestor or her descendants, and where there is a failure of male maternal ancestors of such persons and their descendants, the mother of his more remote male maternal ancestor and her descendants, shall be heir or heirs of such person, in preference to the mother of a less remote male maternal ancestor and her descendants, 3 V., c. 34, s. 8.

Any person related to the person from whom the descent is to be traced, by the half blood, shall be capable of being his heir, and the place in which any such relation by the half blood shall stand in the order of inheritance, so as to be entitled to inherit, shall be next after any relation in the same degree of the whole blood and his issue where the common ancestor shall be a male, and next after the common ancestor where such common ancestor is a female ; so that the brother of the half blood on the part of the father shall inherit next after the sisters of the whole blood, on the part of the father and their issue ; and the brother of the half blood, on the part of the mother, shall inherit next after the mother 3 V., c. 34, s. 9.

When the person from whom descent is to be traced has had any relation who, having been attainted, died before the descent took place, such attainder shall not prevent any person from inheriting land, who would have been capable of inheriting the same by tracing his descent through such relation if he had not been attainted, unless the land has escheated in consequence of such attainder before 1 August, 1840, 3 V., c. 34, s. 10.

This Act shall not extend to any descent which took place on the death of any person who died before 1 August, 1840, 3 V., c. 34, s. 11.

Where any assurance executed before the 1 August, 1840, or the will of any person who died before 1 August, 1840, contains any limitation or gift to the heir or heirs of any person, under which the person answering the description of heir is entitled to an estate by purchase, the person who would have answered the description if this Act had not been made, is declared entitled by virtue of such limitation or gift, whether the person named as ancestor were living on or after 1 August, 1840, 3 V., c. 34, s. 12.

Initials and Contractions.

In actions upon Bills of Exchange or Promisory Notes, or other written instruments, any of the parties to which are designated by the initial letter or letters, or some contraction of the Christian or first name, or names, it shall be sufficient in every affidavit to hold to bail, and in the process of declaration to designate such persons by the same initial letter or letters, or contraction of the Christian or first name or names, instead of stating them in full, 8 V., c. 28, s. 6.

Description by in affidavits to hold to bail and process of declaration

---

Insane Prisoners

Where it is given in evidence, upon the trial of any person charged with treason, murder or felony, that he was insane at the commission of the offence, and is acquitted, the Jury shall find specially whether he was insane at the time, and declare whether he was acquitted on account of insanity ; and if they find he was insane at the time, the Court shall order him to be kept in strict custody, in such place and manner as to the Court shall seem fit, until the Governor's pleasure is known, and thereupon the Governor may give order for his safe custody, as he sees fit, 1 V., c. 28, s. 2.

Powers of the Governor to dispose of persons, acquitted of felony on account of insanity
See 25 V., c. 9, s. 13

If any person indicted for any offence is insane, and upon arraignment found so to be by a Jury impannelled for that purpose, so that he cannot be tried, or if upon the trial he appears to the Jury to be insane, the Court may direct such finding to be recorded, and order him to be kept in strict custody until the Governor's pleasure be known ; and if any person charged with any offence is brought before any Court, to be discharged for want of prosecution, and appears to be insane, the Court may order a Jury to be impannelled to try his sanity, and if they find him insane, may order him to be kept in strict custody in such place and in manner as the Court deems fit, until the Governor's pleasure is known ; and in all cases of insanity so found, the Governor may give such order for the safe custody of such person during his pleasure, in such place and in such manner as he deems fit, 1 V., c. 28, s. 3.

Persons found to be insane upon arraignment or on trial, or when brought up to be discharged for want of prosecution
See 25 V., c. 9, s. 13

All persons of unsound mind charged with felony, and acquitted on account of insanity, or found to be insane at the time of arraignment, shall be confined in the New Lunatic Asylum, 25 V., c. 9, s. 13.

All such persons to be confined in the new Lunatic Asylum

When any person under sentence in the General Penitentiary or other prison, becomes insane or of unsound mind, and the Surgeon or Medical Officer of the prison deems it proper he should be removed to the Lunatic Asylum for safe keeping and for treatment, it shall be his duty forthwith to certify the same to the Governor, 24 V., c. 22, s. 1.

Prisoner under sentence becoming insane

Who, on receipt of the Certificate, shall sign and transmit his Warrant to the Superintendent, to deliver up the prisoner to the proper authorities at the Lunatic Asylum, 24 V., c. 22, s. 2.

Removal to the Lunatic Asylum

As soon as any transferred lunatic prisoner becomes sane, or of sound mind, the Medical Officer of the Lunatic Asylum shall certify the same to the Governor, 24 V., c. 22, s. 3.

His recovery to be certified to the Governor

And the Governor shall forthwith sign and transmit his Warrant to the Inspector and Director of the Asylum, either to discharge the person, if his period of sentence has expired, or, if not, to transfer him back to the Penitentiary or prison from whence he came, there to remain for the unexpired period of his sentence, 24 V., c. 22, s. 4.

Who shall direct his discharge, if sentence has expired, or return to prison

---

Interest, Usury.

Merchants, factors and others residing in Great Britain, who lend or advance moneys in Great Britain to persons in this Island, at the time, are entitled to an Interest of £5 per cent. per annum, 24 G. 2, c. 19, s. 12.

£5 per cent. interest on British loans

Notes and Orders carrying Interest shall carry interest after judgment upon the principal sum, at the same rate they bore before judgment, until the whole principal is satisfied, 14 G. 3, c. 28, s. 13.

Interest on Judgments upon notes and orders

On judgments of British creditors

When Judgment is obtained upon an open or settled account of any person resident in Great Britain or Ireland, against any inhabitant of this Island, Interest, at £5 for every £100 by the year, shall be allowed from the first day of the Court in which judgment is obtained on the principal sum, until satisfied, and the plaintiff, his Attorney, Executors, Administrators or Assigns, may mark and sign, or cause, &c. a levy upon all process to be thereon issued accordingly, 29 G. 3, c. 13, s. 1.

On judgments on simple contract debts generally

When Judgment is obtained on open or settled account, or other simple contract debt, Interest at £6 per cent. by the year shall be allowed from the first day of the Court in which judgment is obtained, on the damages assessed until satisfied, and the plaintiff, his Attorney, Executors, &c., may mark and sign, or cause, &c., a levy for such damages with Interest upon all process to be thereon issued accordingly, 51 G. 3, c. 5.

Repeal of Usury Laws

24 G. 2, c. 19, s. 10, and 25 G. 2, c. 14. s. 1, and all existing Laws against Usury, repealed, 18 V., c. 48, s. 1.

Without prejudice to existing rights or liabilities

Not to prejudice or affect the rights, or remedies, or diminish or alter the liabilities of any person in respect of any act done previously, 18 V., c. 48, s. 2.

Where current rate recoverable

Where interest is now payable upon any contract, express or implied for payment of the legal or current rate of Interest, or where upon any debt or sum of money, Interest is now payable by any rule of Law, the same rate of Interest shall be recoverable as if this Act had not been passed, 18 V., c. 48, s. 3.

Interpleader.

Defendant having no interest may obtain an order upon a third party claiming an interest to appear and maintain or relinquish his claim, and for a stay of proceedings against him; costs, &c.

Upon application by or on behalf of any defendant sued in the Supreme Court in any action of assumpsit, debt, detinue or trover, before plea by affidavit or otherwise, showing that he does not claim any interest in the subject matter of the suit, but that the right is claimed, or supposed to belong to some third party who has sued or is expected to sue for the same, and that the defendant does not in any manner collude with such third party, but is ready to bring into Court, or to pay or dispose of the subject matter of the action as the Court or a Judge may order, the Court or a Judge may make rules and orders, calling upon such third party to appear and state the nature and particulars of, and maintain or relinquish his claim, and upon such rule or order to hear the allegations as well as of such third party as of the plaintiff, and in the meantime to stay the proceedings, or the action, and finally to order such third party to make himself defendant in the same or some other action, or to proceed to trial in one or more feigned issue or issues, and also to direct which of the parties shall be plaintiff or defendant on the trial, or with the consent of the plaintiff and such third party their Counsel or Attornies, to dispose of the merits of their claims, and determine the same in a summary manner, and to make orders as to costs and all other matters, 7 V., c. 32, s. 1.

The decision of the court final

The judgment in any such action or issue, as may be directed by the Court, or Judge, and the decisions of the Court and the Judges in a summary manner shall be conclusive against the parties, and all persons claiming under them, 7 V., c. 32, s. 2.

Third party barred of his rights as against defendant; costs as between him and plaintiff

If the third party does not appear, upon such rule or order, to maintain or relinquish his claim, being duly served, or neglects or refuses to comply with any rule or order to be made after appearance, the Court, or a Judge, may declare him, and all claiming under him, to be barred from prosecuting his claim against the original defendant, his executors or administrators, saving the right or claim of such third party against the plaintiff, and thereupon make such order between such defendant and the plaintiff as to costs and other matters as may appear just, 7 V., c. 32, s. 3.

Orders to be made in open court; rescinding Judge's orders

No order shall be made except in open Court, and during the regular sittings of the Court. All orders made by any single Judge may be rescinded or altered by the Court in Banc, within a reasonable time from the making as other orders by a single Judge, 7 V., c. 32, s. 4.

Judge may himself refer application to the court

If, upon application to a Judge, or in any later stage of the proceedings, he thinks the matter more fit for the decision of the Court in Banc, he may refer it to them, and thereupon the Supreme Court shall dispose of the same, as if the proceeding had originally commenced by rule of the Supreme Court, 7 V., c. 32, s. 5.

When any claim is made by Assignees of Insolvent Debtors, or other persons, not being the parties against whom process is issued, to any goods or property taken or intended to be taken in execution under process, or the proceeds or value, the Court (upon application of the Provost Marshal, his Deputies or other Officer, made before or after the return of such process, and as well before as after action brought against such Provost-Marshal &c.,) may call before them, by rule of Court, as well the party issuing such process as the party making such claim, and thereupon exercise for the adjustment of such claims, and the relief and protection of the Provost Marshal, &c., the powers before contained, and make such rules and decisions as appear just according to the circumstances. The costs to be in the discretion of the Court, 7 V., c. 32, s. 6.

Proceedings on claims against Provost Marshal, &c. arising out of the execution of process; costs

All rules, orders, matters and decisions, except affidavits, may, together with the declaration, be entered of record in a separate book, to be kept exclusively for the purpose, and regularly indexed by the Clerk of the Court with a note in the margin, expressing the true date of entry, that the same may be evidence in future times, if required. To secure and enforce the payment of costs, every rule or order shall have the effect of a judgment, except only as to becoming a charge on lands; and if any costs are not paid within 15 days after notice of the taxation and amount to the party ordered to pay the same, his Agent or Attorney, a writ or writs of execution (in the form or nature of the writs of Venditioni Exponas, now in use, adapted and changed according to the case) may issue for the same, together with the costs of such entry, and of the execution, and shall be returnable in the Court, to be held next after the day on which they are sued out, and bear test, on the day of issuing, and not as of any term or sittings; and the Provost Marshal or his Deputies, or other Officer executing any such writ, shall be entitled to the same fees, and no more, as upon any similar writ grounded upon a judgment, 7 V., c. 32, s. 7.

Proceedings to be recorded in a separate book and indexed, with date of entry in margin

Enforcement of costs by venditioni

[Provost Marshal's fees

Island Curates' Fund.

The Receiver-General shall deduct and retain, out of each quarterly sum he is called upon to pay to the order or demand of any Curate, or the Chaplain of the General Penitentiary, £6 6s., 8 V., c. 38, s. 1.

Quarterly deductions of £6 6s from stipends]

No lapse of stipend by the default of any Island Curate or Chaplain, or otherwise, shall affect the Fund, but the Receiver-General shall, quarterly, apply to the Fund the deduction authorized, whether there be any lapse or not, 8 V., c. 38, s. 4.

Whether there be a lapse of stipends or not

Every person to be appointed an Island Curate, not having resided in the Island, and officiated as a Clergyman of the Church of England for 5 years next preceding his appointment, shall appear in Kingston before he enters on his duties, and be examined by the Medical Officer of the Institution; and if it appear from a report, under the hand of such Medical Officer that the life is bona fide, and apart from all technical objections, uninsurable, and would be rejected by any Assurance Office, according to the rules that govern Life Assurance, the Trustees may limit the claim of the family of such Curate on the Fund, by directing that all payments, with their accumulated interest, be returned at his death to his family, provided he leaves any within the degrees of relationship, and within the ages to which the benefits of the Fund extend. If the party whose life is declared to be uninsurable, in the event, survive five years from his admission, his family shall be entitled to the benefits of the Fund to all intents, 15 V., c. 20, s. 5.

Limitation of the claims of the family of Island Curates whose lives are uninsurable

The Trustees were permitted to admit, as members, Stipendiary Curates, desirous of participating in the benefits of the Fund after a residence of 2 years immediately preceding admission in Jamaica, or elsewhere within the Tropics, to a certain extent, and upon certain conditions, 8 V., c. 38, s. 12, 13, 14, ptly.

Stipendiary Curates

But these provisions are repealed, but not so as to defeat or limit any right or interest any Stipendiary Curate might have acquired, who should still remain a Member; and his widow and children are entitled to every advantage to which they would otherwise have been entitled, 15 V., c. 20, s. 5.

Curates, members of the fund, becoming Stipendiary Curates may retire and receive an equitable sum from the fund, or may continue a contributing member on the same terms as if he had continued an Island Curate

If any Island Curate, a Member of the Fund, become a Stipendiary Cu. rate, he shall be at liberty either to continue a Member or to retire. If here. tires, on giving notice as required (by 8 V., c. 38) to be given by an Island Cu. rate on becoming a Rector, he shall receive from the Fund such sum as may be considered equitable, to be ascertained as in the case of a Member becoming a Rector. If such Stipendiary Curate shall not pay to the Receiver-Ge. neral on account of such Trust Funds, a like amount as would have been de. ducted from his salary if he had remained an Island Curate, and at the times the Receiver-General was authorized to deduct the same, or within 20 days after, he shall be considered to have retired from the Fund. Such Stipen. diary Curate shall make the like returns, and in all respects be liable to the provisions of this Act, and of 8 V., c. 38, and 14 V., c. 35, as if he still continned an Island Curate, 15 V., c. 20, s. 1.

The provisions of 8 V., c. 38, and 14 V., c. 35, shall extend and be applicable to every person who, having been an Island Curate, becomes a Stipendiary Curate, and remains a Contributing Member of the Fund, 15 V., c. 20, s. 2.

Similar provision in the case of any member of the fund becoming a Rector

If any Member become a Rector, he may either continue or retire, and if he retires and gives notice in writing to the Secretary of the Trustees of his intention so to do, he shall receive such a sum from the Fund as the Trustees, under the advice of the Actuary, consider equitable. If he receive any payment of his stipend from the Receiver-General without the deduction, he shall be considered to have retired. If he elect to continue a Member, he shall give notice to the Secretary, and also to the Receiver-General, who shall in such case continue to deduct from the stipend of the Rector the quarterly sums authorized to be deducted out of the stipend of the Curates and Chaplain, and, the Rector shall, so far as regards his interest, make the Returns, and be, in all respects, subject to the provisions herein, as if he had continued a Curate, 8 V., c. 38, s. 15.

Members resigning their appointments to receive an equitable sum from the fund

If any Member, at any time resign his appointment in this Island, and give notice of resignation to the Secretary, and if any Stipendiary Curate, being a Member of the Fund, become an Island Curate, such Member so resigning, and such Stipendiary Curate, shall receive such a sum from the Fund for his interest, as the Trustees, under the advice of their Actuary, consider equitable, 8 V., c. 38, s. 16.

Or may continue contributing members

Or though he resign, or cease to hold his appointment, he may continue a Contributing Member, provided he pay to the Receiver-General, on account of such Trust Fund, a like amount as would have been deducted if he. had retained his appointment, and at such times as the Receiver-General is authorized to deduct the same from the stipends of Members, or within 20 days after. In the event of failure to pay such amounts, or any of them within the time limited, the interest or claim on the Fund to which his widow and children would be entitled, if the payments had been continued until his death, shall be forfeited, 19 V., c. 16, s. 1.

Deprived Curates

As to the continuance of the claims of the widow and children of deprived Curates, see Clergy, 22 V., c. 9, s. 33-34.

The unappropriated fund to remain in the Receiver-General's hands to accumulate at interest

So much of the Fund as shall be unappropriated, shall remain in the hands of the Receiver-General as a Loan to the Public, to be applied to the uses of the Government, for which Loan the Receiver-General was di. rected to pay, and allow to the Trustees interest, quarterly, at the rate of £1 10s. per quarter, and, at the end of every quarter, to add unappropriated interest to principal, 8 V., c. 38, s. 5.

The above clause was repealed and re-enacted, allowing interest annually at the rate of £6 per cent. per annum on the sum then invested, and also at the end of each year the addition of the unappropriated part of such interest to the principal of the Fund; but in respect of all further capital to be invested, allowed only £4 per cent. per annum for interest, 18 V., c. 20.

Present rate of interest

The Receiver-General shall pay and allow to the Trustees interest at the rate of £6 per cent. per annum from 1st January, 1862, on the principal sum at their credit on that day, and the like rate of interest on all further capital and Reserved Appropriable Fund or Unappropriated Fund invested subsequently. 25 V., c. 34, s. 1.

Such part of the interest as is unappropriated during any year, shall, at the end of the year, be added to the capital, and bear interest at the rate allowed by this Act, 25 V., c. 34, s. 2.

No interest shall be allowed after 1st January, 1862, under 8 V., c. 38, or 18 V., c. 20, 25 V., c. 34, s. 3.

The Sums directed to be retained by or paid to the Receiver-General and the accruing interest, with the moneys in the Receiver-General's hands, under the repealed Acts, 6 V., c. 50, and 7 V., c. 65, were directed to be vested under the name of " The Island Curates' Fund" in the Lord Bishop of Jamaica (in whose absence the Coadjutor Bishop, 22 V., c. 23, s 3, Clergy), the President of the Council, the Chief-Justice, the Vice-Chancellor, the Speaker of the House of Assembly, the Attorney-General, the Members of Assembly for St. Catherine, Kingston, Port-Royal and St Andrew for the time, and all the Island Curates and Chaplain of the Penitentiary (and all other Contributing Members, 15 V., c. 20, s. 4) for the time being, and they, or any 3 of them (although there be no Lay Trustee present 14 V., c. 35, s. 4) were appointed Trustees to retain and hold the Fund, and, to receive from, and the Receiver-General shall pay to their order, (Form) the sums from time to time required, and the Trustees, with the assistance of an Actuary, shall direct, manage and appropriate the Fund to the best advantage for the benefit of the widows and children of the Island Curates and other Members of the Fund, 8 V., c. 38, s. 3 ; 14 V., c. 35, s. 4 ; 15 V., c. 20, s. 4 ; 22 V., c. 23, s. 3.

Trustees of fund

The Trustees shall hold, at least, 4 meetings a year in Kingston, on the first Thursday in January, April, July and October, for the purpose of transacting business ; and all orders on the Receiver-General for payments out of 'the Fund shall be in the Form aforesaid, and drawn and signed at such Quarterly Meetings by at least 3 Trustees (no Layman required, 14 V., c. 35, s. 4), and also by the Secretary, 8 V., c. 38, s. 11.

Quarterly Meetings

The Trustees were directed at their first Quarterly Meeting to appoint one of their own body to be their Secretary, at such a salary, to be paid out of the Fund as they should think proper, 8 V., c. 38, s. 6.

Secretary

They were also directed to convene a General Meeting of Trustees, by public advertisement (see now Jamaica Gazette, 8 V., c. 46, 14 V., S. 1, c. 4), for the purpose of electing an Actuary of the Fund, provided the day appointed for the General Meeting should be at least one month after the first publication of such advertisement, and the Actuary should be an Actuary of one of the Life Assurance Societies in London, and be paid for his services out of the Fund, 8 V., c. 38, s. 7.

Actuary

The Secretary shall be selected from among the Contributing Members and not otherwise, 14 V., c. 35 s. 6.

The Actuary or Secretary shall only be removable at a General Meeting convened for the purpose, in pursuance of a resolution of a Quarterly Meeting, and in the manner pointed out for the election of the first Actuary, and upon the removal of any Actuary or Secretary, the Trustees shall at such General Meeting, and upon their death or resignation at the first Quarterly Meeting after, appoint another, 8 V., c. 38, s. 8.

Removal

The Trustees were directed to appoint some Resident Medical Practitioner (in Kingston, 15 V., c. 20, s. 5), to be the Medical Adviser of the Institution, and to be paid out of the Funds for every report the usual fee paid by an Insurance Office for a similar report. On his death, removal or resignation the Trustees shall fill up the vacancy at their next meeting, 15 V., c. 20, s. 6.

Medical Officer

Contributing Members were required to make out and transmit to the Secretary Annual Returns as to the state of their families, and in case any member whose stipend was paid by or through the Receiver-General, omitted to make such return after 3 several applications, in writing, by the Secretary, in the 3 several months after 31 March, it was provided he should pay a fine of £10 to the Fund, which the Receiver-General was directed to deduct from the next quarterly payment, after notice from the Trustees to make the deduction, 8 V., c 38, s. 14.

Return of families of members to be made to Secretary

On or before 31 March in every alternate year, a return shall be made by every Member of the Fund to the Secretary, stating such information as to the ages or marriages of their children, according to Form in Schedule A., and a copy of the Form shall be sent from the Secretary by the Post to each Member, on or before 31 January, 1859, and in each alternate year afterwards, 14 V., c. 35, s. 3.

From which he shall prepare and transmit to the Actuary returns at intervals not exceeding 7 years

The Secretary from time to time, but at intervals not exceeding in the furthest 7 years, shall prepare and transmit to the Actuary for his guidance and information, the several forms in Schedule B. C. D. and E. accurately from the returns transmitted to him, 14 V., c. 35, s. 5.

A scheme of distribution of the annual allowances to the widows and children of deceased Island Curates and Chaplain for a period of 7 years was fixed by 8 V., c. 38, s. 9.

And the Actuary prepare septennial schemes of distribution to be presented to and confirmed by the trustees

The scheme of distribution shall be submitted by the Trustees to the Actuary for readjustment at the expiration of every 7 years, and if it require any variation, it shall be made by a certificate, in writing, of the Actuary, to be presented and confirmed at the next Quarterly Meeting of the Trustees after receipt. Such variation shall be framed upon the most correct calculations which the circumstances admit, and so that the interest of all claimants upon the Fund, whether in possession or expectancy, may be secured, 8 V. c. 38, s. 10.

Claimants on the funds and their interests therein

To entitle the widow and orphan children of any deceased Member of the Fund to a share of the benefit, they, or their guardians, if infants, shall produce to the Trustees a certificate from the Justices and Vestry in Vestry assembled, of the Parish in which the Member held his appointment, certifying the number, ages and other circumstances affecting the claims of such widows and orphans applying. No widow or daughter of any Member shall receive any share or benefit after her marriage, nor any son after he has attained 21, 8 V., c. 38, s. 17.

Children of deceased Members, whose mothers shall be dead, shall be considered as first class orphans, and those whose mothers shall be alive, as 2nd class orphans. Daughters after attaining 25, shall be entitled to allowances as 2nd class orphans only, whether their mothers are living or not, 8 V., c. 38, s. 18.

Widows and children of Curates deceased since 31 December, 1842

If any Island Curate has died since 31 December, 1842, his widow and children shall be entitled to the same benefits as if he had died after this Act, 8 V., c. 38, s. 19.

Children born before their father became a licensed clergyman of the diocese

No child of any person hereafter to be appointed an Island Curate, born brfore the father became a licensed Clergyman in this Diocese, shall be entitled to claim or receive any share, or to participate in any of the advantages of the Fund, 14 V., c. 35, s. 1.

Those born before he became a member of the fund —

The children of any person becoming a Member, born after their father entered into Holy Orders, and whilst he was a Clergyman licensed in this Diocese, but before he became a Member of the Fund, shall be entitled to one-half the share and benefit according to the class to which they belong, which would have been heretofore allowed to them, unless the father, at the time of his decease, has been a Member and Subscriber for 10 years, in which case they shall be entitled as fully as if this Act had not passed, 14 V., c. 35, s. 2.

Annual returns to Assembly

The Trustees shall, at the Quarterly Meeting in October, prepare and sign a report, to be laid forthwith before the House of Assembly, if in Session, or, if not, within a fortnight after the commencement of its then next Session, which report shall set out and explain the state of the Fund for the preceeding 12 months, and the names and ages of the parties, having allowances therefrom, the amounts and also the particulars connected with the same who have ceased to have allowances since the last report, and shall also state the purport and effect of the opinion and advice given by the Actuary on the several points submitted to him, 8 V., c. 38, s. 20.

SCHEDULE TO 8 V., c. 38.

FORM OF ORDER TO THE RECEIVER-GENERAL.

Order to Receiver-General

Pay to the order of   the sum of   being for (here state the purpose of the order)

Dated this   day of   18

A. B. ⎫
C. D. ⎬ Trustees of the Island Curates' Fund.
E. F. ⎭

G. H., Secretary.

SCHEDULE TO 14 V., c. 35.

Form A, to be furnished every Two Years by every Member to the Secretary.

Name.	Date of Birth.	Place of Birth.	Date of becoming a Subscriber to the Fund.	Date of Marriage.	Date of Decease	Place of Decease.	Disease which caused Death.
Rev. A. B.	9th Mar., 1806	Germany	March, 1843	11th Jan., 1838			
C. D. his Wife,	20th Dec., 1820	Jamaica		11th Jan., 1838			
Issue							
E. F.	29th April, 1839	Jamaica.			2nd Aug., 1846	Jamaica	Fever.
G. H.	25th Dec., 1840	"			17th May, 1840	Jamaica	Congestion of Brain
K. L.	27th June, 1842	"					
M. N.	16th Jany., 1846	"			17th Sept., 1846	Jamaica	{ Convulsions from Teething.
R. S, 2nd Wife.	10th Sept., 1828	"		2nd Feb., 1848			
Issue, &c.							

N. B.—This information is to cover the whole period of Life, and not to extend simply to the period in which the Fund has been instituted.

Additional Form B. to be periodically furnished by Secretary to Actuary.
A list of those Members who have died since the institution of the Fund.

Particulars to be ranged under the same heads as before.

Additional Form C. to be furnished periodically by Secretary to Actuary.

A list of those Members who have ceased to belong to the Trust since its institution, from other causes, except death.

Particulars under same heading as before, with the additions, "Date from which the Member ceased to belong to the Fund," and "amount of money restored out of the Fund."

Additional Form D. to be furnished periodically by the Secretary to the Actuary.

A list of all Annuitants deceased since the institution of the Fund.

Particulars under same heading as before.

Additional Form E. to be furnished periodically by the Secretary to the Actuary.

A list of all existing Annuitants upon the Fund.

Particulars under 3 first headings as before, and also under the following headings, " Date of becoming an Annuitant," " Place of Residence."

Advances for purchase of lands and houses for Island Curacies

Subject to the proviso after contained, the Trustees may appropriate so much of the capital as is requisite in the purchase of houses and lands attached, or of houses alone, for the accommodation and use of the Island Curates requiring them, and to be attached to their Curacies, subject to the regulations and restrictions after contained. The Trustees shall reserve and retain in their hands, not less than £1500 of the capital of the Fund, after payment of the several annuities and claims charged thereon, 11 V., c. 16, s. 1.

Particulars to be submitted to the Vestry

Whenever any Island Curate is desirous of purchasing a house with lands, or a house alone, to be attached to his Curacy, he shall, at his own expense, procure and lay before the Justices and Vestry of the parish, or in Kingston before the Court of Common Council, at any meeting, a full and just specification of the property proposed to be purchased and attached, and of its particular locality, and setting forth the exact or estimated distance from the Chapel at which he is officiating, accompanied by a note or memorandum, in writing, under the hand of the proprietor, detailing the terms and conditions on which, and the consideration for which the property is to be sold, and the nature of the title as far as ascertainable, 11 V., c. 16, s. 2.

And forwarded to the Governor and Bishop

If the Justices and Vestry, or Common Council approve of the proposed purchase, and by a resolution in due form, attested under the hand of their Clerk, certify that the site and locality are eligible for the performance of the Spiritual duties of such Island Curate, and that the premises are in their estimation worth the sum demanded, regard being had to their state of repair at the time, such Island Curate shall forward the resolution, with the specification, and all other the information directed to be laid before the Justices and Vestry, to the Governor, and also to the Bishop, for their sanction and approval, 11 V., c. 16, s. 3.

Loan for purchase and title

If the Governor and Bishop approve of the purchase, and testify their approval, in writing, by countersigning the resolution, and the Island Curate forward the same, so signed and countersigned, and all the papers required to be laid before the Justices and Vestry, &c., to the Trustees, they may, if to them it seem advisable, but not otherwise, at any Quarterly Meeting, lend out of the capital of the Fund, not exceeding for any one Island Curacy £600, for the purchase and immediate repair (if repair be necessary), or for the purchase alone of the property. Before the Loan is made, the Trustees shall be satisfied of the validity of the title, in all respects, at the expense of the Island Curate, who shall also bear all expenses attendant upon the preparation and recording of the title and otherwise, so as no expenses whatever in reference to any proposed or complete purchase be thrown upon the Trustees. And the title shall be taken in the name of the Bishop and his Successors, as Trustees, upon Trust, for the sole use, benefit and accommodation of the Incumbent of the Island Curacy for the time, and to be attached to such Island Curacy accordingly for ever, 11 V., c. 16, s. 4.

Receiver-General to deduct £7 8s per annum from stipend for 20 years

Whenever the Trustees have made such loan, and signify the same, in writing, under the hand of their Secretary, to the Receiver-General, he shall retain, out of the next and every succeeding quarter's stipend of the Island Curate, in respect of whose Curacy the advance has been made, at the rate of £8 16s., (afterwards reduced to £7 8s., 19 V., c. 16, s. 2,) per annum for every £100 so advanced, and shall continue to make such deduction for 20 years, computed from the day on which such advances were actually made, 11 V., c. 16, s. 5.

The moneys so retained the Receiver-General shall restore and carry to the credit of the Fund, and allow interest quarterly, at the rate of £6 per cent per annum, towards re-payment of the loan, and of the accrued and accruing interest 11 V., c. 16, s. 6. *Interest to be allowed on money retained under 11 V., c. 16*

Afterwards the Receiver-General was directed to allow interest on £7 8s., at the rate of £4 per cent per annum, towards re-payment, 19 V., c. 16, s. 2. *Afterwards reduced; see 8 V., c. 38, s 5. 18 V., c 20 25 V., c. 34*

When it appears to the satisfaction of a Board of Trustees, on the representation of any Island Curate or otherwise, that the property requires repairs, they may advance a loan, not exceeding £200, subject to the provisions, restrictions and regulations before contained, and to be re-paid by the same means and in the same manner as before provided, in payment of such necessary repairs, on proof, to their satisfaction, that the repairs have been fairly and bona fide done, and the amount required expended on the premises; and the Receiver-General shall pay the amount accordingly to the Island Curate, upon presentation of an order of the Trustees, certified by their Secretray. In case of any one Curacy, the amount of any outstanding loan for the purchase, and of any additional loan for the repair of the same house, shall never exceed £600, 11 V., c. 16, s. 7. *Loans for repair / Limit of Loan*

When it appears to the satisfaction of the Trustees on the representation of the Incumbent Island Curate or otherwise, that the premises, in cases where houses and lands are already attached to Island Curacies, require repair, they may, in their discretion, appropriate out of the Fund by way of loan, not exceeding in the case of any one Curacy, £200, for such necessary repairs. Proof shall be previously given to their satisfaction of the necessity of such repairs in the first instance, and that the required sum has been fairly and bona fide expended on the premises, and the Receiver-General shall pay the moneys appropriated by the Trustees to the Island Curate upon their order, certified by the Secretary, 11 V., c. 16, s. 8. *Loans for repairs of premises already attached to Island Curacies—limit*

Such loans shall be subject to the restrictions and regulations before contained, and re-paid by the same means, and in the same manner as provided in reference to the moneys advanced in the purchase of lands and houses for Island Curacies, 11 V., c. 16, s. 9.

No Island Curacy which contracts a debt to the Fund, shall be converted into any other than the station of an Island Curate, until the debt has been fully discharged, 11 V., c. 16, s. 10. *Premises to continue Island Curates' Station until debt is discharged*

No Deed or Instrument to be made and executed in pursuance of, or for the purposes of this Act, shall be liable to any Stamp or other Duty, 11 V., c. 16, s. 11. *Exemption from Stamp Duties*

Jamaica Gazette by Authority.

The Commissioners of Public Accounts shall contract for printing and publishing, in Kingston or St. Jago de la Vega, and circulating a separate Newspaper, 8 V., c. 46, s. 1. *Contract for publication*

Distinct from all other papers, and called "The Jamaica Gazette by Authority," and entirely to consist of, without other matter, all Government, Militia, Public and Parochial Orders, Notices, Returns and Advertisements of every description, published under the authority of the Governor, the Council or Assembly, or by order of the Court of Chancery, the Supreme Court, Insolvent Courts, or by the direction of any Board of Commissioners or Trustees under any Act for any public service, or by the authority and direction of the Justices and Vestry of any Parish, or the Corporation of Kingston, or any Officer of Militia in command; all Notices; Returns and Advertisements required to be published by any Public or Parochial Officer by any Act; all Insolvent Debtors' Notices; all Notices and Advertisements under the Insolvent Debtors' Act, and any Act connected therewith, and all other Advertisements of a Public or Parochial nature, directed to be published by any Act, 0 V., c. 40, s. 2. *To be a distinct paper Contents*

Days of publica- tion — distribution limited	And which shall be published and issued on Thursday, or such other day in each week as the Commissioners of Public Accounts direct, and circulated by the Contractor immediately upon the publication, postage being paid by him, to and among the Governor, his Secretary, all Members and Officers of the Council and Assembly, Magistrates, Inspectors and Sub-Inspectors of Police, the Churchwardens and Vestrymen, and the Clerks of the Vestry and of the Peace, the Members of the Corporation of Kingston and the Clerk of the Common Council, the Collectors and Sub-Collectors of the Customs, the Receiver-General and his Deputies, the Heads of Departments in the Naval, Military and Civil Service, and such other Public and Parochial Officers and persons as the Commissioners of Public Accounts direct. The total number of copies not to exceed 1500, and the Contractor shall not be required to furnish to any of the persons more than one copy, 8 V., c. 46, s. 3.
Charges of publi- cation Circulation and Postage	All copies shall be circulated, and all Advertisements inserted and published at the cost of the Contractor, and without any further claim against the Public or the Council, any Public or Parochial Authority or individual, or for the expense of transmission by the post, or for the postage of letters containing or relating to such Advertisements, or any charge or expense, other than and except the remuneration under his contract, 8 V., c. 46, s. 4.
Tenders — Con- tracts for 5 years	When necessary, the Commissioners shall, by Advertisement, call for Sealed Tenders for Printing and Publishing such Newspaper, and its distribution and circulation, and accept any Tender, and conclude any agreement they think most eligible. They shall not contract for a less term than 5 years, beyond which any Contract shall not be valid. No parties offering to contract, or proposing to be security for any Contractor, or who are concerned directly or indirectly in any Contract, shall sit or vote when it, or any matter connected therewith, is before the Commissioners 8 V., c. 46, s. 5.
Notice of Meet- ings	Notice of every Meeting at which Tenders are to be received, shall be given by Public Advertisement, at least 30 days before the day appointed, 8 V., c. 46, s. 6.
Security	To secure the due performance of any agreement, the Contractor shall enter into bond to the Crown, with one or more Sureties, to be approved of by the Commissioners, in £2000, 8 V., c. 46, s. 7.
Contract — Bond Stamps	Every Contract shall be by Deed, which, and the bond for performance, shall be exempt from Stamp Duty, and recorded in the Secretary's Office, 8 V., c. 46, s. 8.
Payment	The Receiver-General shall pay to the order of the Commissioners, out of any moneys unappropriated, the amount of the remuneration agreed upon and fixed on any such Contract, in the proportions, and at the times the Commissioners appoint for payment, 8 V., c. 46, s. 9.
Annulment of con- tract	In case of failure, non-performance or non-observance by any person, of the terms of his Contract, the Commissioners may immediately break off and annul any Contract, and may again, either before or after rescinding any Contract, advertize for new Tenders, and Contract anew for the publication, distribution and circulation of such Newspaper, taking security for the performance of the Contract. But not to affect the right of the Commissioners of proceeding against any Contractor and his Sureties for any breach of Contract, 8 V., c. 46, s. 10.
Advertisements directed by previous acts to be made in the Gazette	All Public and Parochial Anthorites, Officers, Commissioners and Trustees, shall publish in such newspaper, in lieu and instead of any other, all Advertisements necessary in the course of their business or duty, directed by previous Acts, and for such number of times, and as required to be published, and publication in such Newspaper shall be a compliance with such Acts, 8 V., c. 46, s. 11.
Otherwise not valid	No Advertisement, Notice or Communication of a public nature from any Public or Parochial Authority, or Officer, or Board, whose Advertisements are required to be inserted in the Newspaper, shall be valid, unless published as directed, 8 V., c. 46, s. 12.
Prerogative not affected	Not to interfere with the Royal Prerogative, 8 V., c. 46, s. 13.
Publication of advertisements, &c. during non exis- tence of Gazette	The Commissioners of Public Accounts may, when there is no existing contract under the 8 V., c. 46, or if the publication of the " Jamaica Gazette by Authority," from any cause, ceases or determines, appoint any one or more Newspapers published in Kingston, in which Advertisements of a public

nature shall be published, which shall, during the non-existence of any Contract, or the non-publication of such Newspaper be sufficient; and it shall not be necessary to publish the Advertisements upon any other day in such week than Thursday, or such other day as they direct, 14 V., S. 1, c. 4, s. 1.

Jamaica Mutual Life Assurance Society.

Certain powers of suing and being sued, and other privileges conferred upon them, but without incorporating them, 8 V., c. 13.

8 V., c. 13, s 18, which enabled them to invest their Funds in the Receiver-General's Office, at £6 per cent. per annum interest, repealed, 18 V., c. 47.

Limited powers conferred upon them
Powers to make investments in Receiver-Gen eral's Office repealed

Jamaica Railway Company.

Incorporation, powers and privileges of the Company, for establishing and maintaining a Railway from Kingston to Spanish-Town, thence to the Angel's Pen, 7 V., c. 25.

Incorporated

Powers of the Legislature to purchase the Line after the expiration of 20 years, from 1st January, 1845, or to reduce the Fares or Tolls, guaranteeing £15 per cent. per annum profit to the Proprietors, 8 V., c. 12.

Clauses more especially affecting the Public:—

The Master or Owner of every Barge, Float, Boat or Vessel, passing under any Bridge built by the Company, shall make satisfaction to them for any damage or injury, 7 V., c. 25, s. 9.

Damages by barges, &c. to the company's bridges

No Shareholder shall be liable for any debt of the Company beyond his share of unpaid capital, 7 V., c. 25, s. 27.

Extent of Shareholders' liabilities

The Company may demand and recover for Carriages not belonging to them, moved, or propelled upon the Railway, for conveyance of Passengers or Cattle, Animals or other live or dead Stock, and otherwise, or of Produce, and any Articles, Matters or things at a rate or Toll not exceeding:

Tolls demandable for use of road

For all Dung, Compost, and all Soils of Manure, Lime and Limestone, and for all Undressed Materials for the repair of Public Roads or Highways, per ton, per mile £0 0 6

Coals, Coke, Culm, Charcoal, Cinders, Hay, Grass, Firewood, Building, Pitching and Paving Stones, Dressed Bricks, Tiles, Slates, Clay, Sand, Iron; Stone, Pig, Bar, Rod, Hoop, Sheet and all other descriptions of Wrought Iron and Castings, not manufactured into Utensils, or other Articles of merchandize, per ton, per mile 0 0 9

Sugar, Coffee, Rum, Pimento, Grown Corn, Salt, Saltfish, Salted Provisions, Flour, Cheese, Candles, Soap, Dyewoods, Earthenware, Lumber, Staves, Shingles, Deals, Metals, except Iron Nails, Anvils, Vices and Chains, per ton, per mile 0 0 10½

Cotton and other Wool, Hides, Drugs, Manufactured Goods and other Wares, Merchandize or Things, per ton, per mile 0 1 0

Every person conveyed in or upon any Carriage per mile...... 0 0 4

Every Parcel, not exceeding 28 pounds for any distance 0 0 6
" " Not exceeding 100 pounds 0 1 0

Every Horse, Mule, Ass or other Beast of draft or burden, and and for every Ox, Cow, Bull, or Neat Cattle, conveyed in or upon any Carriage per mile.. .... 0 0 3

Every Calf, Sheep, Lamb, Goat or Pig so conveyed, per mile.. 0 0 1

Every Carriage of whatever description so conveyed, not adapted and used for travelling on a Railway, and not weighing more than one ton, carried on a Truck or Platform, per mile 0 0 6

Every such Carriage weighing more than one ton, per ton, per mile, and so in proportion for every fraction of a ton...... 0 0 9

Every Carriage not belonging to the Company, but properly adapted for use on the Railway, to be approved of by their Engineer, not weighing more than one ton, moved or propelled by the motive power used on the Railway, per mile .. £0 0 6

Every Carriage of like description above one ton weight, per ton, per mile, according to weight, charging for all fractional parts below 112lbs. as 112lbs. 0 0 6

7 V., c. 25, s. 73.

Company's rates for carriage. General Lien. Justices to determine disputes : See s. 84, 85—8 V., c. 12, s. 5.
The Company may carry passengers, produce, goods, cattle and other animals, and demand and recover for such carriage and conveyance, in addition to the rates and tolls before authorized, such sum as the Company or Directors may fix and require, and shall have a general lien in respect of the conveyance of all produce, cattle, &c., carried by them, and may seize and detain any produce, cattle, &c., carried by them, not only for the carriage of the particular produce, &c., but also of any other produce, &c., therefore carried, then due from the persons by or to whom they are addressed, until payment is made, as well for any general balance, as of the sum due for the carriage of the articles seized, with reasonable charges for seizure and detention ; and if not redeemed within 10 days, they may be appraised and sold as in case of distresses for rent. In case of dispute concerning the amount due, or the charges, it shall be ascertained and determined as in cases of disputes respecting rates and tolls due to the Company, and the Justice determining the dispute, shall have the like power to award and enforce payment of the costs as in such cases, 7 V., c, 25, s. 74.

No greater tolls to be charged by company or any other person than the company are authorized to demand
Neither the Company, nor any person using the Railway as a carrier, shall demand or take a greater amount of toll, or make any greater charge for the carriage of passengers or g , than they are authorized to demand ; and, upon payment of the tolls demandable, all persons shall be entitled to use the Railway, with carriages properly constructed, subject to the regulations of t he Company, by virtue of the powers conferred upon them, 7 V., c. 25, s. 75e

Power to reduce and raise tolls
The Company may reduce the rates, and afterwards raise them, so that they shall not, at any time, exceed the amount authorized, 7 V., c. 25, s. 76.

Tolls to be charged equally to all persons
All tolls for the use of the Railway, and all tolls for carriages and the use of locomotive power, shall be charged equally to all persons, whether per mile, or per ton per mile, or otherwise, in respect of all passengers, and of all goods, &c., of alike description, conveyed or propelled by a like carriage or engine passing in the same portion of the line of Railway, under the like circumstances ; and no reduction or advance in any tolls shall be made directly or indirectly, in favor, or against any particular Company or person travelling upon, or using the same portion of the Railway, 8 V., c. 12, s. 5.

Lists of tolls, &c. to be exhibited
The Company shall cause to be painted on boards, and affixed, and continued and renewed as often as obliterated or defaced, in some conspicuous place at the commencement and termination of the Railway, in large and legible characters, an account or list of the several rates or tolls the Company direct to be taken, and of the prices to be taken for the carriage of passengers, articles, matters or things upon the Railway ; and in case any owner or master of, or person having or assisting in the charge of any Carriage, or any Collector of rates, tolls, or sums, demands or takes more than the amount therein specified, he shall forfeit not exceeding £20, 7 V., c. 25, s. 80.

Tolls to be taken only while exhibited
The Company shall not demand or take any rates, tolls or sums, except during such time as the board on which they are painted remains affixed, 7 V., c. 25, s. 81.

Defacing, &c. boards on which bye-laws, tolls, &c. are painted
If any person wilfully pulls down, defaces or destroys any board whereon any bye-laws, orders, or rules, rates, tolls or sums are painted, or concurs or aids therein, he shall, on conviction, forfeit to the Company not exceeding £50, 7 V., c. 25, s. 82.

Duties of Collectors
Every Collector shall place his Christian and surname painted on a board in legible characters in the front or other conspicuous part of the place at which any rates, tolls or sums are collected or received, wherein he shall be on duty, immediately on his coming on duty, each of the letters of such names to be at least 2 inches in length, and of a breadth in proportion, and painted either in white letters on a black ground, or in black let-

ters'on a white ground, and continue the same so placed during the whole time he is'on duty, If any Collector omit so to do, .or demand or take a greater or less rate than he is authorized by this Act, or the orders and resolutions of the Company in pursuance thereof, or demand or take a rate, &c., from any person who is exempt from payment, and claims such exemption, or refuses to permit, or will not permit any person to read, or hinders any person from reading the inscription on the board, or refuses to tell his Christian or surname to any person who demands the same, or having paid the legal rates, &c., or in answer to such demand gives a false name, or upon the legal rate, &c., being paid or tendered, unnecessarily detains, or wilfully obstructs or prevents any passenger from passing on the Railway, or makes use of any scurrilous or abusive language to any passenger, or to any Treasurer, Clerk, Engineer or other Officer of the Company, such Toll-Collector shall forfeit not exceeding £10, 7 V., c. 25, s. 83.

The rates, &c., authorized to be taken, shall be paid to such persons at such places, upon or near the Railway, and in such manner and under such regulations as the Directors, by notice to be annexed to the account or list of rates, &c., direct ; and in case of a refusal or neglect, on demand, to pay such as have acrued due to the person appointed to receive them, the Directors may, in case such rates, &c., amount to £50 or upwards, sue for and recover the same, by action of debt, or upon the case in any Court of Record, or the person to whom they ought to have been paid, may, whether they amount to £50 or not, seize the articles, matters or other things, in respect whereof any such rates, &c., ought to be paid, or any part thereof, and the carriages laden therewith, and detain them until payment is made, with reasonable charges for such seizure and detention ; and if they are not redeemed within 10 days, they shall be appraised and sold, as in cases of distress for rent. In case such rates, &c., do not amount to £50, the Company shall not sue by action of debt, or on the case, but they shall be recovered by distress and sale only, 7 V., c. 25, s. 84. *Regulations respecting the payment and enforcement of tolls, &c.*

If any dispute arise concerning the amount of the rates, &c., due to the Company, or the charges of distress, the Collector, or person distraining, may detain such distress, or, as the case may require, the proceeds of sale, until the amount of the rates, &c., due, or the charges are ascertained by a Justice acting within his jurisdiction, who, upon application, shall examine the matter, upon oath of the parties or other witness, and determine the amount, and may assess and award such costs to be paid by either of the parties to the other as he thinks reasonable, and, in case of non-payment, on demand, such costs shall be levied by distress and sale, by warrant of such Justice, 7 V., c. 25, s. 85. *Disputes respecting rates, &c. to be determined by a Justice, costs*

If any person wilfully throw, place, scatter, or drop any gravel, stone rubbish, or other matter or thing upon any part of the Railway, unless by authority of the Company, or wilfully obstruct or prevent any person in the execution of this Act, or do any act to obstruct the free passage of the Railway, he shall forfeit not exceeding £100, nor less than 40s., 7 V., c. 25, s. 89. *Obstructions to railway*

If any person wilfully, and to the injury of the undertaking, or of the Company, injure, break, throw down, destroy, steal, or take away any part of the Railway, or other works or materials, he shall be liable to the like penalties as in cases of felony, and the Court was empowered to cause him to be transported for 7 years, or, in mitigation, award such sentence as the Law directs in cases of simple Larceny, 7 V., c. 25, s. 90. *Injuring or stealing any part of the railway or works*

Transportation has been abolished, and 4 years' penal servitude substituted for 7 years transportation, 21 V., c. 14, s. 3.

All persons may pass along the Railway with carriages properly constructed as directed, upon payment only of such rates, &c., as shall be demanded by the Company, not exceeding those before mentioned or referred to, provided the motive power is of the same description as that used by the Company ; and such persons shall be subject to the rules and regulations, as to speed or otherwise, which are made by the Directors, by virtue of the powers herein granted, 7 V., c. 25, s 97. *Passage with carriages properly constructed on payment of tolls,*

If any person (except the Company, their agents and servants, and by them only, for the purposes of the Railway), ride, lead or drive, or cause, &c., or aid or assist, &c., upon such Railway, without the license and consent of the Company, any Horse, Mule or Ass, or lead or drive, or *Riding or driving beasts upon railway* cause, &c., or aid or assist, &c., any cow or other neat cattle, sheep, swine or any other beast or animal (except only in directly crossing the same, at places to be appointed for the purpose, and except only in passing across the same, for the necessary occupation of the lands through which the Railway is laid), he shall forfeit not exceeding £15, 7 V., c. 25, s. 98.

Passing on foot upon railway

If any person pass, or travel on foot upon the Railway (except for the purpose of attending any carriage under his care, and except any Officer or other person in the employ of the Company, and also except the owners or occupiers of lands and premises adjoining the Railway, their servants and workmen, in passing across or along the same, as before authorized to and from their lands), he shall forfeit not exceeding £10, 7 V., c. 25, s. 99.

The Company to fence off railway from adjoining lands

The Company shall, at their own charges, after any land is taken for the use of the Railway or other works, divide, and separate and keep the same constantly divided and separated from the lands adjoining, with good and sufficient posts, rails, hedges, ditches, mounds or other fences, in case the owners at any time desire the same to be fenced off, or the Company think proper to fence them off, instead of erecting gates across, and shall make and maintain all necessary gates and stiles in such fences, the gates being made to open towards such lands; and in every such case the powers and regulations before contained, with respect to the gates and other works, shall extend and apply to the making and maintaining of such fences, and the gates and stiles therein, 7 V., c. 25, s. 102.

Service of notice to the Company

In cases where it is necessary to serve any summons, demand, notice, writ or other proceeding at Law or in Equity upon the Company, service upon any Director, or the Manager or Treasurer, or left at the office of the Manager, or Treasurer, or Company, shall be sufficient, 7 V., c. 25, s. 104.

Notices by Company

Where it is necessary for the Company to give notice to any body corporate or person, it may be in writing, in print, or partly in writing and partly in print, and be signed by a Director, or by the Clerk of the Company or Treasurer, without being required to be under the Common Seal, and be delivered to such person, or left at his last or usual place of abode, or be delivered to some member of the Corporation, or left at his last or usual place of abode, or to some Clerk or other Officer of the Corpation, or left at his office, or last or usual place of abode, except where any other mode is directed, 7 V., c. 25, s. 105.

Recovery of compensation, &c. from Company

When any money is by any Justice ordered to be paid as compensation or satisfaction for any materials or costs, or for any damage, or injury done, or committed by the Company, or any person acting under their authority, and the money is not paid by the Company to the party entitled, within 30 days after demand, in writing, has been made from the Company, in pursuance of the direction or order of such Justice, and in which demand the order of the Justice shall be stated, the amount shall be levied and recovered by distress and sale of the goods vested in the Company, or of their Treasurer, for the time, under a warrant, under the hand and seal of such Justice, on application for the purpose by the party entitled to receive the money. The Treasurer may retain out of any money he receives, all damages, costs and expenses he is put unto, 7 V., c. 25, s. 111.

Recovery and application of penalties

All penalties and forfeitures imposed by this Act, or by any bye-law, rule or order made in pursuance thereof, (the manner of levying and recovery whereof is not otherwise directed), may, in case of non-payment, be recovered in a summary way, by the order and adjudication of two Justices, and afterwards be levied, as well as the costs, if any, on non-payment, by distress and sale, and where not directed to be otherwise applied, shall be paid, one moiety to the informer, and the remainder to the Treasurer of the Company, unless incurred by the Company, when they shall be paid one moiety to the informer, and the remainder to the Churchwardens for the benefit of the poor, and if not forthwith paid, the Justices shall order the offender to be detained in safe custody, until return can be conveniently made to such warrant of distress, unless he gives security by way of recognizance for his appearance before them, or some other Justices on the the day appointed for the return of such warrant (not more than 8 days from the taking security); but if upon the return it appear that no sufficient distress can be had whereon to levy the penalties and costs, and they are not forthwith paid, or if it appear that the offender has not sufficient goods whereupon the penalties, &c., could be levied, if a warrant of distress issued, they need not issue the same, but may, by warrant, commit him for not exceeding 3 calendar months, or until the penalty is sooner paid, with costs, or until he be otherwise discharged by due course of law, 7 V., c. 25, s. 112.

In cases where damages or charges are authorized to be paid, and the manner of ascertaining the amount is not specified or provided for the amount, in case of non-payment or dispute, shall be ascertained and determined by two Justices, who are authorized to investigate the same, on oath or otherwise; and where any damages or charges are directed to be paid in addition to any penalties for any offence, the amount, in case of non.payment or dispute, shall be settled and determined by the Justices, who, on non-payment of the damages, shall levy the same by distress and sale in manner directed for levying penalties, 7 V., c. 25, s. 113. 2 Justices to as-certain damages and charges

The Justices may summon the parties complained of, and hear and determine the matter, although no information, in writing, has been exhibited, and such proceedings shall be as valid, as if an information in writing had been exhibited, 7 V., c. 25, s. 114. Justices may pro ceed on summons without informa-tion in writing

The Custos or senior Magistrate of Kingston, St. Catherine or St. Andrew, and a Justice of either parish acting within his jurisdiction, may appoint fit persons, nominated by the Manager and Treasurer, or 3 Directors, to be Special Constables within the Railway and other works, and every person so appointed shall make a declaration before a Justice, duly to execute the office of Constable for the premises; and every person, so appointed and sworn, shall have power to act as a Constable for the preservation of the peace, and the security of persons and property against felonies and unlawful acts within the limits of the premises, and shall have all powers authorities, protections and privileges for apprehending offenders, as well by night as by day, and for doing all acts for the prevention, discovery and prosecution of felonies and other offences for the preservation of the peace, as Constables; and the Justices, on proper representation of the Company or Manager, or the Manager and Treasurer, or 3 Directors, may dismiss or remove any such Constable, and thereupon all powers, &c., vested in him shall cease, 7 V., c. 25, s. 115. Special Constables

Any Collector, Surveyor, or other officer of the Company, or any Police officer or Constable, and such persons as he calls to his assistance, may seize and detain any person unknown to such Collector or Surveyor, or other officer who commits any offence against this Act, and convey him before a Justice for the parish, without any warrant or other authority than this Act, and such Justice shall proceed immediately to the hearing and determining of the complaint, 7 V., c. 25, s. 116. Securing tran sient offenders

The Justices may cause the information (where one is taken in writing or in print), and the conviction to be drawn up according to the following Forms, or to the same effect :— Information and conviction

FORM OF INFORMATION.

Be it rememembered, that on the   day of
A. B. of   informeth me (or us)   of Her
Majesty's Justices of the Peace for the Parish of
that   of (here describe the offence, with the time and place) contrary to an Act, passed in the seventh year of the reign of Her Majesty Queen Victoria, entitled "An Act for making and maintaining a Railway from Kingston to Spanish Town, with liberty to continue the same to the Angel's Pen or Plantation, situate in the Parish of Saint Catherine, and for other purposes, which hath imposed a forfeiture of   for the said offence.
        Taken the   day of   before me (or us).

The Forms are very defective, and it would be advisa-ble to adopt those given by 13 V., c. 35

FORM OF CONVICTION.

Be it remembered, that on the   day of   A. B. is convicted before me (or us)   of Her Majesty's Justices of the Peace for the Parish of   (specifying the offence, and the time and place when and where the same was committed as the case may be), contrary to an Act, passed in the seventh year of the reign of Her Majesty Queen Victoria, entitled (here insert the title of the Act, see sup.)
        Given under my hand and seal (or our hands and seals), the day and year first above written   7 V., c. 25, s. 117.

Q Q

Distresses, &c. not unlawful for want of form, nor parties trespassers ab initio, &c.

No distress shall be deemed unlawful, nor any party making the same a trespasser, on account of any defect, or want of form in the summons, conviction, warrant of distress or other proceeding, nor shall such party be deemed a trespasser ab initio on account of any irregularity afterwards committed by him, but all persons aggrieved by such defect or irregularity, may recover satisfaction for the special damage in an action upon the case, 7 V., c. 25, s. 118.

Appeal

Parties may appeal from summary convictions, 7 V., c. 25, s. 119.

Evidence of Bye laws

In cases of prosecution for offences against the rules, bye-laws, orders and regulations of the Company, the production of a written or printed paper purporting to be rules, &c., and authenticated by having the Common Seal of the Company affixed thereto, shall be evidence of the existence of such rules, &c.; and it shall be sufficient to prove they have been made public, by exhibiting in a conspicuous place at the termini of the Railway, and upon any toll-house of the Company, a written or printed copy, 7 V., c. 25, s. 120.

" at of Form

No proceedings shall be quashed or vacated for want of form, or be removed certiorari or other proceeding into any Court of Record, 7 V., c 25, s. 12ly

Protection from actions

No action or other proceeding shall be brought against any person for any thing done in pursuance of this Act, or in the execution of the powers or authorities, or any of the orders made, given or directed, in, by or under this Act, unless 28 days previous, notice in writing is given by the party intending to commence and prosecute such action, &c., to the intended defendant, nor unless it be brought or commenced within 6 calendar months, or in case there shall be a continuation of damage within 3 calendar months after the doing or committing such damage has ceased, nor unless laid and brought in the County or place where the matter in dispute or cause of action arose; and the defendant may plead the general issue, and give this Act, or the Deed of Settlement, or the special matter in evidence at the trial, and that the same was done by the authority of this Act, and if it appear to have been so done, or that such action, &c., has been brought otherwise than as directed, the Jury shall find for the defendant, upon which verdict, or if the plaintiff become non-suited, or suffer a discontinuance of his action, &c., after the defendant has appeared, or a verdict pass against the defendant, or if upon demurrer or otherwise, judgment be given against the plaintiff, the defendant shall have costs, and the same remedy for recovering them as in other cases, 7 V., c. 25, s. 122.

Tender of amends

No plaintiff shall recover in any action for any irregularity, trespass or other wrongful proceeding, made or committed in the execution of this Act, if tender of sufficient amends has been made before action brought; and in case none have been made, the defendant may, by leave of the Court, at any time before issue joined, pay into Court such sum as he thinks fit, whereupon such proceedings, order and adjudication, shall be had and made by the Court, as in other actions where defendants are allowed to pay money into Court, 7 V., c. 25, s. 123.

Statements of Traffic

The Company shall publish, or cause once at least in each of the Kingston daily papers, quarterly (see Jamaica Gazette, 8 V., c. 46, s. 11), a true and correct statement and account of the number of passengers, carriages, horses, mules, asses, neat cattle, sheep, goats and pigs, and the number of tons weight of goods, wares and merchandize, carried and conveyed by them during each quarter, under a penalty of £20, to be recovered in a summary manner before two Justices of Kingston, by distress and sale of the Company's goods, 7 V., c. 25, s. 125.

Jamaica Spa.

Directors

The Governor, Council and Assembly for the time being were incorporated by the name of the Directors of the Jamaica Spa, and 250 acres of land in St. Andrew, with a Chalybeate Spring thereon, vested in them upon trust, to sell same, except 20 acres adjoining to the Spring, which should remain inalienable for the use of the Public, and with power to appoint officers, and make rules and ordinances for their government and that of the Spa, 16 G., 3, c. 20.

Exchange of lands with Silver Hill

The Directors were empowered to exchange the 20 acres reserved by 16 G., 3, c. 20, for land of Silver Hill Plantation, in the neighbourhood of, and commodious to the Spring, 54 G. 3, c. 18.

Jews.

Persons professing the Jewish Religion are entitled to exercise and enjoy the same rights, privileges, immunities and advantages to which other natural born subjects are entitled, 11 G. 4, c. 16, s. 2.

Entitled to the same rights as natural born subjects

Also 9 G. 4, c. 28, s. 1

Not to affect any title to real estate, or other right or title of any person of the Jewish Religion, or of persons claiming under persons of the Jewish Religion, 11 G. 4, c. 16, s. 3.

Whenever any person professing the Jewish Religion presents himself to take the oath of abjuration, the words " Upon the true faith of a Christian" shall be omitted in administering it, and the taking and subscribing the oath without those words shall be sufficient, 2 W. 4, c. 2.

May omit " Upon the true faith of a christian," from the oath of abjuration

Judges.

No person appointed a Judge shall execute, or officiate his place or office until he take the oaths of allegiance and supremacy in open Court, nor directly or indirectly ask, demand or receive any other profit, benefit or advantage from any Clerk of the Court, or other person whatsoever, under color or pretence of his place, office or authority, but what is allowed them by the Acts of this Island, under a penalty of £500 (£300 stg.) 33 C. 2, c. 23, s. 3.

Judges to be sworn ; see 42 G. c. 19 ; 19 V., c. 12, s. 3

Not to receive any profit but what is allowed by Acts

One moiety to the Crown, and the other to the informer, 33 C. 2, c. 23, s. 20.

The Judges shall not be removed from executing their offices but by H. M's. pleasure, signified under the Seal (sign) Manual, and until H. M's. pleasure for removal is signified, their Commissions shall remain in full force, 21 G. 3, c. 25. s. 1.

Removal of Judges

The Governor may, with the advice and consent of (a majority of a Board of 57 G. 3, c. 17) Council, upon good and sufficient cause, suspend any Judge from executing his office until H. M's. pleasure is known, the Governor sending to H. M. a full and true state of the cause of suspension in order for the Royal determination, and delivering to the Judge, at the time of suspension, a true copy, signed by the Governor, in order that he may be able, by himself or his agents, to make his defence before H. M. against his being displaced, if he think proper, 21 G. 3, c. 25, s. 2.

Suspension

The offices of Chief Justice and Assistant Judges of the Supreme Court were vacated, and the Governor was empowered to appoint, under the Broad Seal a Barrister who had practised 5 years at least at the Bar of this Island, or at the Common Law Bar of Great Britain or Ireland, at any time previous to his appointment, to be the Chief Justice of this Island, and who shall preside in the Supreme Court, and exercise all such powers, and discharge all such duties as appertain to his office, 19 V., c. 10, s. 1.

Appointment, &c. of Chief Justice

The Chief Justice shall also be Vice-Chancellor. Upon a vacancy occurring in such offices by death, resignation, or in any other manner, the Governor may appoint some other person qualified as aforesaid in his place, and the Stamp on every Commission shall be £100, 19 V., c. 10, s. 2.

Who is to be Vice Chancellor
Stamp on Commission ; see 28 V., c. 9

The Chief Justice and Vice-Chancellor, previous to his commencing to execute any of the duties of either of his offices, shall take the following oath, in addition to the oath of allegiance and other oaths or declaration required by law to be taken by persons entering on office, which the Governor shall administer :—

Oaths of Office

I, A. B. do solemnly and sincerely promise and swear that I will duly and faithfully, to the best of my skill and power, execute the offices of Chief Justice and Vice-Chancellor of this Island. So help me God, 19 V., c. 10, s. 3.

The salary of the Chief Justice and Vice-Chancellor shall be £1800 a year, payable quarterly, out of the sum appropriated by 17 V., c. 29, Schedule A: towards payment of Judical Salaries, by warrant of the Governor, as directed by that Act. No person shall be entitled to receive such salary, unless qualified as before mentioned, 19 V., c. 10, s 4.

Salary

Removal of chief Justice and Assistant Judges

The Chief Justice and Vice-Chancellor, and Assistant Judges, shall not be removable or removed from their offices, or either of them, otherwise than according to the provisions of 21 G. 3, c. 25, and 57 G. 3, c. 17, nor shall they be suspended from the exercise of their offices by the Governor, except with the advice and consent of a majority of a Board of Privy Council, 19 V., c. 10, s. 5.

Appointment, &c. of Assistant Judges

The Governor shall appoint, by Commission under the Broad Seal, 3 Barristers who have been in actual practice, and have actively practised 3 years at the least at the Bar of this Island, or at the Common Law Bar of Great Britain or Ireland at any time previous to their appointment, to be Assistant Judges of the Supreme Court, and they shall exercise all such powers, and discharge such duties as appertain to their office, 19 V., c. 10, s. 13.

Chief Justice to preside in Home Circuit, an Assistant Judge over one of each of the others
Stamp on Commission of Assistant Judge ; see now 28 V., c. 29, superseding 2 W. 4, c. 1)

The Chief Justice shall, by virtue of his office, be the Judge who presides in the Courts to be held in the Home Circuit, and the 3 Assistant Judges shall each preside in the Courts to be held in some one of the other Circuits. The Governor shall fill up vacancies. Stamp upon Commissions, £70. In case of the illness or absence of the Chief Justice, the Governor may appoint any Assistant Judge to discharge his duties, whether as Chief Justice, Vice-Chancellor, Surrogate or Judge of the Courts of the Home Circuit, 19 V., c. 10, s. 14.

Oaths of Assistant Judges

Every Assistant Judge shall, before entering upon the duties of his office, take and subscribe the oath of allegiance, and also take and subscribe the oaths and declarations at present taken by persons entering into office as Assistant Judges and Justices of Assize, 19 V., c. 10, s. 15.

Salaries

The salary of each Assistant Judge shall be £1200 a year, payable out of the sum appropriated by 17 V., c. 29, Schedule A., towards the payment of Judicial salaries, and by warrant of the Governor as directed by that Act. No person shall be entitled to receive such salary, unless qualified as before mentioned, 19 V., c 10, s. 16.

Exception

Provision was made for one appointment of a person who had practiced for 3 years at the Equity Bar of England, 24 V., c. 5.

Leave of absence Substitutes

The Governor may grant leave of absence for not exceeding one year to any Judge, provided some properly qualified person, according to this Act, can be found to fill the office, and discharge the duties of such absentee, and who shall be thereupon appointed by the Governor in his stead. Such Judge shall, during his absence, be entitled to the moiety only of his salary, and the other moiety shall, by warrant of the Governor, be paid to the person acting. The Stamp on the Commission to the Substitute of the Chief-Justice shall be £20 ; to the Substitute of an Assistant Judge, £15 ; and there shall be no Stamp on the Commission of a Substituted Vice-Chancellor, 19 V., c. 10, s. 49.

Absence 3 months beyond leave

If any Chief-Justice or Assistant Judge, shall, at any time, be absent from this Island for exceeding 3 months after the expiration of his leave of absence, or depart without leave, his salary shall cease, and he shall be considered to have vacated or resigned his office, and the Governor may appoint another in his stead, 19 V., c. 10, s. 50.

Disqualifications; see also 47 G. 3, c. 13, s. 4

No Chief-Justice or Assistant Judges shall be capable of being elected, or of sitting as a Member of the Assembly, or of any Parochial Board, or hold or act under any Power of Attorney for the management of any Estate, or Plantation, or practice at the Bar in any Court, or otherwise, professionally, 19 V., c. 10, s. 51.

Powers of the Judges

Where any act or matter is required to be done or performed, or power exercised by a Judge of the Supreme Court, or by a Chairman of Quarter Sessions, in any Statute not expressly repealed by this Act, and not repugnant to its provisions, such Act shall, notwithstanding the abolition of the office of Chief and Assistant Judge of the Supreme Court, and of the office of Chairman of Quarter Sessions, be done and performed by the Judge of the District Court, or by the Judge of the Supreme Court as the case may be, within whose jurisdiction such matter would come, in accordance with the provisions of this Act, 19 V., c. 10, s. 54.

Short Title

Judicial Amendment Act, 1855, 19 V., c. 10, s. 58.

Judgments of Courts.

When Judges give the reasons for their judgment they shall be copied into a book

When the Judges of the Supreme Court, the Vice-Chancellor, the Judges of the West India Incumbered Estates' Court, or the Court of Appeal from the summary Jurisdiction of Magistrates, shall deliver to the Clerk or Registrar of the Court, their reasons, in writing, for any judgment, the Clerk or Registrar shall copy the same into a substantially bound book in his office, to be kept for reference by all Members of the Legal Profession, without payment of any fee, and by any other person, on payment of any fee payable for consulting the Records, 28 V., c. 14, s. 1. For reference

In any case wherein it is signified to the Court that the judgment is intended to be appealed against, a written copy of such reasons shall be delivered in reasonable time to the Clerk of the Court, or the Registrar, as the case may be, 28 V., c. 14, s. 2. Written reasons shall be delivered, when it is signified to the Court that the decision will be appealed from

Upon payment of the fee, for copying work in the office of the particular Court, any party may obtain an office copy of any such written Judgment or decree, certified by the Officer, 28 V., c. 14, s. 3 Charge for certified copies

Judgments, Decrees, Orders.

All Judgments obtained on Bond, Promissory Note, Bill of Exchange, or on any account or cause of action whatever, and passed or paid away, may be assigned in manner following :— Assignments of judgments

    Be it remembered, that I, A. B., have this   day of   in the year of our Lord   assigned unto C. D., his Heirs, Executors and Administrators, a Judgment obtained in   Grand Court for the sum of   by   against   on his (Bond, Note, Bill of Exchange, or as the same may be), and that there is now due thereon the sum of   principal money. the sum of   for interest and   costs of suit, and I have received the sum of   in full consideration thereof. Form

Such assignment shall be recorded in the Office of the Clerk of the Supreme Court, 14 G. 3, c. 28, s. 6.

The Clerk of the Supreme Court and Crown shall keep a separate book for recording Assignments of Judgments, 20 V., c. 22, s. 23. Record

And on any Assignment being recorded, shall make, or cause to be made, a note in the margin of the record of the Judgment, of the name of the Assignee and date of Assignment, and shall not knowingly suffer to issue out of his office any writ on any such Judgment, except by the party entitled to the Assignment, or his Attorney-at-Law, 20 V., c, 22, s. 24. To be noted on margin of record of judgment, & writs to be issued by Assignee

The Clerk of the Supreme Court and Crown shall keep back alphabets of Judgments obtained in the Supreme or Circuit Courts. Penalty, £300, 20 V., c. 22, s. 20, to be recovered on application of the Attorney General or party aggrieved, and the proceeds applied to the use of the Public, 20 V., c. 22, s. 39. Back Alphabets

All Judgments obtained and verdicts entered up in the Middlesex, Cornwall and Surry Assize Courts, shall be deemed and entered up in the Office of the Clerk of the Supreme Court as Judgments of the Supreme Court, immediately preceding the Assize Court in which the verdict was obtained, 3 V., c. 65, s. 18. Judgments of Assizes to be entered as of preceding Supreme Court

Immediately upon Judgment being entered up in the Supreme Court, the party in whose favor it passed may issue his writ to the Provost-Marshal, who shall immediately proceed to execute the same, according to its exigency, and upon the sale of any levy made thereunder, pay over the proceeds, deducting his legal commission, to the party issuing it, 19 V., c. 10, s. 39. Immediate execution

All Judgments against any person shall, from (the Registry, s. 15) in the Office of the Clerk of the Supreme Court, operate as a charge upon all lands, &c., of or to which he was at the time of (registration), or at any time afterwards shall be seized, possessed or entitled, for any estate or interest at Law or in Equity, whether in possession, reversion, remainder or expectancy, or over which, he at the time or afterwards, shall have any disposing power, which he might, without the assent of any other person, exercise for his own benefit, and be binding against him, and all persons claiming under him, and be also binding as against the issue of his body and all other persons whom he might, without the assent of any other person, cut off and debar from any remainder, reversion and other interest in or out of any such lands. No Judgment shall have preference or priority over any unrecorded Deed, appearing by the probate to be prior in point of date, such Deed not being a voluntary settlement where the possession has gone consistent therewith, nor Liens of judgments on lands prevent a valid title from being acquired against Judgment Creditors by the effect and operation of the possessory laws of this Island, 8 V., c. 48, s. 10.

Stock or Shares

If any person against whom Judgment is entered up has or is entitled to any Government, Island or other stock funds or annuities, or any stock or shares of or in any public Company in this Island (whether incorporated or not), standing in his name, in his own right, or in the name of any person in trust for him, any Judge, on application of any Judgment Creditor, may order that such stock funds, annuities or shares, or such of them, or such part as he thinks fit, shall stand charged with the payment of the amount for which Judgment has been entered up, and all interest due thereon, which order shall entitle the Judgment Creditor to all such remedies as he would have been entitled to, if the charge had been made in his favor by the Judgment Debtor. No proceedings shall be taken to have the benefit of such charge, until after the expiration of 3 calender months from the date of the order, 8 V., c. 48, s. 11.

Order exparte only in the first instance to be made absolute

Every such order shall be made in the first instance ex parte, and without notice to the Judgment Debtor, and be an order to show cause only, and shall restrain the Directors of such Bank or Company, or the Receiver-General, from permitting a transfer, or making payment of any dividends or interest thereon in the meantime, and until the order is made absolute or discharged, and if after notice to the person to be restrained, or in the case of Corporations, to any authorized Agent, and before the order is discharged or made absolute, such Corporation or person permit any transfer to be made by the Judgment Debtor, the Corporation or person shall be liable to the Judgment Creditor for the value or amount of the property charged and transferred, or such part as is sufficient to satisfy the Judgment; and no disposition of the Judgment Debtor, in the meantime, shall be valid or effectual against the Judgment Creditor. Unless the Judgment Debtor, within a time to be mentioned in such order, shew to a Judge sufficient cause to the contrary, the order after proof of notice thereof to the Judgment Debtor, his procuration Attorney or Agent, shall be made absolute. Any Judge, upon the application of the Judgment Debtor or any person interested, shall have power to discharge or vary such order, and in all cases to award such costs as he thinks fit, 8 V., c. 48, s. 12.

Benefit of charge forfeited, if debtor taken in execution before it is realized

If any Judgment Creditor who has obtained any charge, or is entitled to the benefit of any security afterwards, and before the property charged or secured has been converted into money or realized, and the produce applied towards payment of the Judgment Debt, cause the person of the Judgment Debtor to be taken or charged in execution upon such Judgment, he shall be deemed to have relinquished all right to the benefit of the charge or security, and shall forfeit the same, 8 V., c. 48, s. 13.

Decrees, Orders, Rules, to have effect of judgments, and the powers of the Judges extended to Courts of Equity and Insolvency See Title Interpleader, 7 V., c. 32, s. 7

All decrees and orders of Courts of Equity, and all rules of Courts of Common Law, and all orders of the Court of Insolvency, whereby any sum of money, or any costs, charges or expenses are payable to any person shall have the effect of Judgments in the Supreme Court, and the persons to whom they are payable shall be deemed Judgment Creditors within the Act, and all powers given to the Judges of the Supreme Court, with respect to matters depending in the same Court, may be exercised by Courts of Equity, with respect to matters therein depending, and by the Court of Insolvency, and all remedies given to Judgment Creditors are in like manner given to persons to whom any money or costs, charges or expenses, are by such orders or rules directed to be paid, 8 V., c. 48, s. 14.

Registers of judgments, decrees, wills and orders

No Judgment of the Supreme Court, nor any Decree or order of any Court of Equity, nor any rule of a Court of Common Law, nor order in the Court of Insolvency, shall, by virtue of this Act, affect any lands, &c., as to purchasers, mortgagees or creditors, unless and until a memorandum or minute containing the name and the usual or last known place or abode, and the title, trade or profession of the person whose estate is intended to be affected, and the Court, and the title of the cause or matter in which such Judgment, Decree, or order or rule was obtained or made, and the date thereof, and the amount of the debt, damages, costs, or moneys thereby recovered or ordered to be paid, is left with the the Clerk of the Supreme Court, who shall forthwith enter the same particulars in a book, in alphabetical order, by the name of the person whose estate is intended to be affected, 8 V., c. 48, s. 16.

altered the se-

Such new or altered Writs may be sued out of the Courts of Law, Equity and Insolvency, as may by such Courts be deemed necessary or expedient for giving effect to the provisions of the Act, and in such forms a, the Judges think fit to order. Their execution shall be enforced as the execution of similar Writs is now enforced, or as near thereto as the circumstances admit. And any existing Writ, the form of which is in any manner altered in persuance of this Act, shall nevertheless be of the same force as if no alteration had been made therein, except so far as the effect is varied by this Act, 8 V., c. 48, s. 17.

Act extended to Aliens, Denizens and Women, 8 V., c. 48, s. 19. Aliens, &c.

The Plaintiff in any Judgment, or his Executor Administrator, Assignee, or Attorney, on receiving full satisfaction and payment of all sums due to the Plaintiff, within three months after receiving satisfaction on any Judgment, to be recovered after the passing of this Act, and after request, in writing, by the defendant, or his Attorney or Agent, shall give, in writing, under his hand, sufficient authority to the Clerk of the Supreme Court to enter satisfaction on the margin of the record of such Judgment, under penalty of £60 to the party injured, to be recovered by action of debt in the Supreme Court, 27 V, S. 1, c. 27, s. 2. Satisfactions
Penalty

Taxed Costs shall be recoverable between plaintiff and defendant, as in other cases between party and party, 27 V., S. 1, c. 27, s. 3. Costs

Where Plaintiffs have been fully paid the sums due on Judgments recovered by them, and have died without entering satisfaction, the Judges at any sitting of the Supreme Court, may order the Clerk of the Court to enter satisfaction on such Judgments, the defendant, his Heirs, Executors or Administrators, proving to the Court that the Judgments have been fully paid; and where it appears that only part of a Judgment has been paid to the plaintiff in his lifetime, the Judges may, on proof thereof, and the balance being paid to the Executor, Administrator or Assignee of the Plaintiff, order satisfaction to be entered, 11 G. 3, c. 20, s. 2. When Court may order satisfaction to be entered by the Clerk after Plaintiff's death

The Clerk of the Supreme Court and Crown shall enter every satisfaction of Judgment delivered to him at his office on the margin of the Record of the Judgment to which the satisfaction refers, and keep a book, called "A Satisfaction Book," wherein shall be entered, alphabetically, dockets of such satisfactions, 20 V., c. 22, s. 28. Entry of satisfaction margin of judgment and in Satisfaction Book

And within 20 days after each Supreme Court, under penalty of £30, (recoverable by attachment on application of the Attorney-General or party aggrived, for the use of the Public, s. 39), for each offence, return, under his hand into the Provost-Marshal's Office, a certificate of every satisfaction of Judgment entered in his Office, 20 V., c. 22, s. 31. Returns of satisfactions to Provost Marshal

The Provost-Marshal, within 10 days after every Grand Court, under penalty of £500 (£300 sterling) for every neglect, shall return into the office of the Clerk of the Court, lists properly attested, under his hand, of all such writs as are from Court to Court returned satisfied into his office ; and the Clerk of the Court shall record the same in a book to be kept for that purpose, and by virtue thereof, enter satisfaction on the margin of the records of the Judgments on which such writs were issued, 14 G. 3, c. 28, s. 15. Provost Marshal's returns of satisfactions to the Clerk of the Court to be recorded and entered on margin of judgment

The Provost-Marshal, under penalty of £100 (£60 sterling) [recoverable in the Supreme Court, one moiety to the informer, s. 19], for every neglect or refusal, shall make entry in his books, of the writs returned to him by the Clerk of the Supreme Court, being satisfied, on being paid by the defendant in the writ, his Attorney, Executors or Administrators, 2s. 6d. (1s. 6d. sterling) for each satisfaction, 14 G. 3, c. 28, s. 16. Provost Marshal to enter in his book satisfactions on judgments returned to him by Clerk of the Court—fee

Judgment as in case of Non-Suit.

Where Issue is joined in any Action in the Supreme Court, and the plaintiff neglects to bring it on to be tried for two Courts after issue joined, the Judges may, at any sitting of the Court after such neglect, upon motion in open Court (due notice thereof having been given), give the like Judgment for the defendant as in cases of non-suit, unless upon just cause and reasonable terms they allow any further time or times for the trial of such issue, and if the plaintiff neglect to try it within the time or times so allowed, such Judgment shall immediately thereupon pass for the defendant, the costs to be taxed, and otherwise awarded, as in cases of Judgment upon non-suit. Such Judgment shall be of the like force as Judgment upon non-suit, and no other, 6 V., c. 31. May be moved for if action not tried within 2 Courts after issue, further time, effect of judgment

Juries.

No Judgment after verdict, upon any indictment or information for any felony or misdemeanor, shall be stayed or reversed by reason that the Jury process has been awarded to a wrong officer upon an insufficient suggestion, nor for any misnomer or misdescription of the officer returning such process, or of any of the Jurors, nor because any person has served upon the Jury, who has not been returned as a Juror by the Provost-Marshal or other Officer, 8 G. 4, c. 22, s. 9.

When and how trial by Jury may be dispensed with

In any civil action where the Crown is not a party, if all the parties signify to the Court their consent to dispense with trial by Jury of any issue, and to substitute the Judge, he shall hear and decide upon the evidence, subject to all such proceedings for reversal or alteration which verdicts are subject to, 15 V., c. 9, s. 3.

Qualification of Jurors

Exemptions

Every male (except as after excepted) between 21 and 60, who is able to read and write, shall be qualified and liable to serve on Juries in the several Courts. Members of the Council and Legislative Council, Custodes, Pilots actuallly serving, Wharfingers when actually employed, persons who from poverty are unable to attend, and persons following such professions and callings as by the laws of Great Britain would exempt them, shall be exempted, and shall not be inscribed in the after mentioned list, 19 V., c. 23, s. 2.

Disqualifications

No man not a natural born subject shall be qualified to serve, except as after provided for; and no man attainted of treason, or convicted of any felony or infamous crime, shall, unless pardoned, be qualified to serve on any Jury or Inquest in any Court, or upon any occasion whatever, 19 V., c. 23, s. 3.

Lists of persons qualified to serve to be prepared by Clerk Vestry

The Justices and Vestry, on or before 10th February in each year, shall cause their Clerk to prepare and make out in alphabetical order, a list of every man residing within their parishes, qualified and liable to serve on Juries, with the Christian or first name, or names and surname written at full length, and his title, quality, calling or business, distinguishing such as are Justices and such as are qualified to serve as Members of Assembly, by writing the words, "Justice of the Peace," or "qualified to serve as a Member of Assembly" opposite the name of each person intended to be distinguished; and the Clerk of the Vestry shall prepare and make out such lists according to the best information he is able to procure, under penalty of £5 for the omission of every name, which, but for his wilful default or negligence, he might have inserted therein, 19 V., c. 23, s. 4.

And transmitted to the Provost Marshal, Common Jury Lists

The Clerk of the Vestry shall, under a penalty of £50, transmit the list to the Provost-Marshal on or before 20th February. Immediately upon receipt of each list, the Provost-Marshal shall, under a penalty of £100, make up and enter in a book a separate list, to be called "The Common Jury List," for each parish or precinct, of the names in alphabetical order of every person mentioned therein who is not a Justice of the Peace, nor qualified to sit as a Member of Assembly, who shall form the panels of Common Jurors to serve in each of the Courts under the Judicial Amendment Act, 1855 (19 V., c. 10) for the ensuing year, commencing on the 20th May, 19 V., c. 23, s. 5.

Clerks of the Peace to furnish Provost Marshal with lists of resident Justices, special Jury lists

The Clerk of the Peace shall, under a penalty of £50, on or before 20th February, make a Return to the Provost-Marshal of all persons then in the Island holding Commissions of the Peace for and resident in such parish, under a penalty of £5 for every omission; and the Provost-Marshal shall, under a penalty of £100, immediately upon the receipt of the Return, make up therefrom, and from the list made by each Clerk of the Vestry, and enter into a book a separate list to be called "The Special Jury List" for each parish or precinct, of the names in alphabetical order of all such Justices and other persons, who, not being Justices, are qualified to sit in the Assembly, 19 V., c. 23, s. 6.

Copies of lists to be returned to Clerks of Circuit Courts

The Provost-Marshal shall, on or before 20th May, under penalty of £100, return true copies of the lists of Common Jurors and Special Jurors into the office of the Clerk of each Circuit Court; and no alteration, addition or omission shall be made by the Provost-Marshal, or any other persons in such lists, under a penalty of £100 for every addition, &c., 19 V., c. 23, s. 7.

The Clerk of the Supreme Court shall, at least 21 days before each Supreme Court, seal and issue to the Provost-Marshal a Writ of Venire Facias for each Circuit Court then immediately following, in the Form annexed A., 19 V., c. 23, s. 8. *Writs of Venire for Circuit Courts*

The Provost-Marshal shall, under penalty of £100, on or before the 1st day of each Supreme Court, strike and make up a panel of Jurors for each of the Courts to be holden immediately after each Supreme Court, and return a true copy of the panel into the office of the Clerk of each Court, and also warn the Jurors in such panels to attend such Courts, and each Venire Facias, with the panel annexed, shall, immediately after the termination of each Court, be returned with all other Records by the Clerk into the Supreme Court, 19 V., c. 23, s. 9. *Panels of Jurors, warning them* *Venire and Panel to be returned after Court to the Supreme Court*

Every panel of Jurors to be returned by the Provost-Marshal (except that for the precinct of Kingston) shall contain the names of 40 persons resident in the parish or precinct, taken from the Special and Common Jury Lists, in the proportions, viz.: 15 from the Special Jury List; and where there shall not be 15 names on that List, then whatever number there is upon it, and 25, or the number required to make up 40, from the Common Jury List. The Grand Jury, when sworn, shall consist of not less than 9 of the persons named in such panel, who shall first appear, upon being called, (21, V., c. 25, s. 6,) and the remainder of the 40 shall serve as Common Jurors, 21 V., c, 25, s. 2. *Panels* *Grand Jury; see s. 6; 19 V., c. 23, s 19*

Each Writ of Venire Facias, to be issued after 1st April, 1865, for the precinct of Kingston, shall require the Provost-Marshal to summon 90 Jurors at each Court, and each panel shall contain the names of 90 persons, 30 from the Special Jury List, and 60 from the Common Jury list of the precinct, taken indifferently and in due proportion from the several parishes constituting or to constitute that precinct, 28 V., c. 33, s. 2. *Venire and Panel for Kingston*

The Grand Jury in the Home Circuit shall, in all cases, except capital cases, consist of not less than 7, and not more than 9; and 7 shall, in all such cases, except as aforesad, find a True Bill, 28 V., c. 33, s. 8. *Grand Jury— Home Circuit*

A Jury, whether Special or Common, qualified as required, consisting of 7 persons only, may be impanelled for the trial of any issue in any civil suit, or upon an information for the recovery of money at the instance of the Crown, or of any person on its behalf, and the Courts shall receive a verdict of 5 only, of whom the foreman, should he agree to that verdict, may be one, if such 5 persons, by their foreman, whose duty it shall be to deliver such verdict, declare they are agreed, and such verdict, when so delivered, shall have the same ferce as if the whole Jury had concurred. In delivering the verdict the foreman shall declare in the presence of the Jury that 5 of their number have agreed. But nothing in this section shall extend to informations at the suit of the Crown, or by any one in its behalf, for the recovery of any penalty, 19 V., c. 23, s. 11. *In civil proceedings Jury to consist of 7, 5 of whom may return verdict*

A Jury of 7 may be empanelled for the trial of any felony or misdemeanor, but a verdict shall not be received unless unanimous. Not to alter or affect the course of trial heretofore in use, in cases of treason, murder, or other capital felony, 19 V., c. 23, s. 16. *Jury of 7 whose verdict must be unanimous in all criminal cases except treason and capital felonies*

The proviso to 19 V., c. 23, s. 16, is only intended to require, that on any indictment for treason, murder, or other capital felony, 12 Jurors, at least, shall form the Grand Jury, by whom the indictment is found, and on the trial 12 Jurors shall be empanelled. In all other respects capital felonies shall be tried as other criminal cases, and be subject to the provisions relating to the trial of criminal offences, 21 V., c. 25, s. 6.

On the trial of any criminal or civil case, the Court, on the request of the prosecutor or the defendant in any indictment, or of any party to a suit, shall require the Jury to be balloted for by the Clerk or other Officer, and thereupon such Jury shall be chosen by ballot, subject to all rights of challenge, 21 V., c. 25, s. 7. *Juries may be ballotted for*

No person arraigned for any felony, except for murder, or other capital felony, or for treason, shall be admitted to any peremptory challenge, beyond 7, and in capital cases, no peremptory challenge shall be allowed beyond 12, 19 V., c. 23, s. 17. *Peremptory challenges*

In any Inquest wherein the Queen is a party, if they that sue for the Queen will challenge any Jurors, they shall assign of their challenge a cause certain, and the truth of such challenge shall be enquired of according to the custom heretofore observed, 19 V., c. 23, s. 18 *The Crown must assign a cause of challenges*

Fine on absent Jurors

If any man having been summoned does not attend, or being thrice called, does not answer to his name, or if any such, or any talesman, after having been called, is present, but does not appear, or, after appearance, wilfully withdraws, the Court shall set a fine upon every such man or talesman making default (unless some reasonable excuse is proved by oath or affidavit) to the amount of £1 at least, and not exceeding £10, 19 V, c. 23, s. 19.

Talesmen

When a full Jury shall not appear, or when after appearance of a full Jury, by challenge on behalf of the Queen, or of any party, the Jury is likely to remain untaken, for default of Jurors, the Court, upon request made for the Queen by any one authorized or assigned by the Court, or on request made by the parties, plaintiff or defendant, or their Attornies, in any action or suit, shall command the Provost-Marshal or proper officer for him, to name and appoint, as need requires, so many of such able men of the parish or precinct then present, as shall make up a full Jury, and the Provost-Marshal, or other person for him, shall, at such command of the Court, return such men duly qualified as are present, or can be found to serve, and annex their names to the former panel. When a Special Jury has been struck, the persons to serve as talesmen and to complete the Jury, shall be such as have been empanelled upon the Common Jury panel, if a sufficient number can be found, and the Queen, by any one so authorized or assigned, and every the parties aforesaid, shall have their respective challenges to the Jurors so added, and the Court proceed to the trial with the Jurors before empanelled, and the talesmen added, as if they had been returned upon the panel, 19 V., c. 23, s. 20.

Jury de medietate

Not to deprive any Alien, indicted of any felony or misdemeanor, of the right of being tried by a Jury composed in part of Aliens; but on the prayer of every Alien so indicted, the Court shall direct the Provost-Marshal or proper officer for him, to return such a number of Aliens, if they can be found in the parish or precinct where the trial is to be had, as that the Jury may consist of 4 Aliens, and 3 other Jurors qualified as required; and no Alien shall be liable to be challenged for want of qualification, but may be challenged for cause, 19 V., c. 23, s. 21.

Penalties

All penalties shall be recovered before 2 Justices, and paid to the Receiver-General, 19 V., c. 23, s. 23.

SCHEDULE.

Venire Facias, 19 V., c. 23, s. 6   JAMAICA SS.

Victoria, by the Grace of God of the United Kingdom of Great Britain and Ireland, Queen, and of Jamaica, Lady Defender of the Faith, &c.

To the Provost-Marshal-General of the said Island, greeting :—

We command you that you cause to come before us at our to be holden at the   of   in the (Parish or Precinct)   aforesaid for the (Parish or Precinct) on the   day of ·   next, between the hours of 9 and 10 in the forenoon of the same day   good and lawful men of the said (Parish or Precinct) of   who, as Jurors, shall do and execute all such things as shall be then and there given them in charge, and enjoined them on our behalf, and then and there to try for us all such issues, and do and execute all such matters and things as shall be given them in our behalf, and also then and there to try all such issues as shall be given them in charge between party and party, and to assess all such damages as shall be brought before them, and also to enquire for us of and concerning all such matters and things as shall be then and there given in charge and enjoined on our behalf, and also to enquire of and concerning the several matters contained in our Writs of enquiry concerning lands related against for the non-payment of (Land Tax and 21 V., c. 34 s. 31,) Quit Rents, and that you and your sufficient Deputies be then and there present to do and execute all such things as shall be thought necessary for our service, and have thou then and there this Writ, with the return thereof, and the names of the Jurors, and fail not at your peril   Witness   Chief Justice of the said Island, and Chief Judge of the said Supreme Court of Judicature, at Saint Jago de la Vega, the   Monday in in the   year of our reign.

Juries, Special.

The Supreme Court may, in any action or suit wherein issue in fact has been joined, on the application of any plaintiff or defendant, or at the instance of the Attorney-General, or the prosecutor or defendant in any prosecution for a misdemeanor in such Court, order a Special Jury to be struck, 20 V., c. 14, s. 2.

To be taken from the Special Jury List of the parish and or suit, made up under 19 V., c. 23, s. 7. 20V., c. 14, s. 3.

The party obtaining the order shall serve on the Attorney of the opposite party, if he has appeared by Attorney, otherwise on such party, and leave with the Provost-Marshal and Clerk of the Supreme Court respectively a copy, with a notice of his intention to proceed and strike a Special Jury at the office of the Clerk of the Court, on a day to be named in such notice, which shall be, for the Home Circuit Courts of Kingston and St. Catherine, at least 5 days, and for the several other Courts, at least 14 days before the day for holding the Court at which the suit, or information or indictment is to be tried, and every such notice in the Home Circuit shall be served at least 24 hours, and in other cases 4 days before the time appointed, 20 V., c. 14, s. 4.

Each Special Jury shall consist of 21 persons, and shall (in the presence of the parties or of their Attornies, if they attend, or if not in their absence) be ballotted for by the Clerk of the Court at the time and place appointed, and for that purpose the Provost-Marshal shall, on the day before the time appointed for striking such Jury, furnish to the Clerk of the Court a copy of the Special Jury List of the precinct or parish. If there be an insufficient number of Jurors qualified to serve returned on the Special Jury List, the number to make up 21 shall be ballotted for from the Jurors, not being Special Jurors, returned in the panel warned to attend the Circuit Court, 20 V., c. 14, s. 5.

From the 21 names so ballotted for, each party, or his Attorney, in any civil suit, and the defendant and Clerk of the Crown, in any information or indictment, shall strike out 5 names by one at a time, the party obtaining the order, or the Clerk of the Crown beginning first, and the remaining 11 shall be the panel of Special Jurors struck and returned for the trial, 20 V.; c. 14, s. 6.

Within 2 days after the panel is so struck, the party obtaining the order shall deliver to the Provost-Marshal, or his Deputy, a copy, with the panel containing the names of the 11 Jurors struck, certified by the Clerk of the Court, and thereupon the Provost-Marshal or his Deputy shall warn the persons set down to attend at the Court at which the suit, &c., is to be tried; and the first 7 Jurors who appear shall be the Jury empanelled to try the suit, &c.. For the performance of his duty, the Provost-Marshal shall be paid by the party obtaining the Special Jury, £2 2s., 20 V., c. 14, s. 7.

In case the opposite party, or his Attorney, refuse, neglect, or fail to attend, the party at whose instance the order was obtained, may proceed to strike the same, the Clerk of the Court acting on behalf of the absent party, until the number of Jurors be reduced from 21 to 11, 20 V., c. 14, s. 8.

In case the suit, &c., is not tried at the Court for which the Special Jury was struck and warned, the parties may apply for and obtain a new order for striking another Special Jury, which shall be struck in like manner, and so on, from Court to Court, until the suit, &c., is tried or disposed of, 20 V., c. 14, s. 9.

Every person who serves upon any Special Jury, shall be allowed 10s. 6d., to be paid by the party applying for it, 20 V., c. 14, s. 10.

The party who applies shall pay the fees for striking, and all expenses of trial by such Special Jury, and shall not have any further allowance for the same, upon taxation of costs, than he would be entitled to if the cause had been tried by a Common Jury, unless the Judge, immediately after the trial, certify in open Court upon the back of the record, that the cause was a proper one to be tried by a Special Jury, 20 V., c. 14, s. 11.

All proceedings and matters in 19 V., c. 23, relating to Special Juries, and for obtaining and enforcing their attendance, and for making up a full Jury at the trial, shall continue in force, except where expressly altered by this Act. (See Juries,) 20 V., c. 14, s. 12.

Marginal notes:
When a Special Jury may be ordered

To be taken from Special Jury List

Notice of striking Jury

How composed

How struck

How warned

1st 7 who appear to be the Jury to try

Provost Marshal's Fee

Proceeding to strike Jury in the absence of the opposite party

Fresh orders for Special Juries to be obtained from Court to Court till trial

Fees of Jurors

Costs of Special Jury

19 V., c. 23 extended to

Juries Warned on Writs, &c.

Penalties for non-attendance

If any person summoned or warned, refuse or neglect to attend at any proceeding under the Statutes of forcible entry and detainer, or at the execution of any Writ of extent emblements, partition or escheat, he shall forfeit to the party aggrieved, not exceeding £50 (£30 stg.) nor less than £10 (£6 stg.) to be enforced in the Supreme Court, by order and attachment, with full costs, to be taxed. If any person warned, and not attending as a Juror, shall, without being called upon so to do, by the first day of the Supreme Court next after, show sufficient excuse for such non-attendance, to the Court, by affidavit filed in the Office of the Clerk of the Crown, he shall not incur the penalty. And it shall be a sufficient excuse that he is 60, 43 G. 3, c. 28.

Justices of the Peace.

Enforcement of Fines

Where Justices in Petty Sessions are invested with power to inflict a pecuniary fine, and whether or not a particular mode of enforcement in default of payment be prescribed by distress on the goods, or by imprisonment, the Justices may direct the penalty and costs to be enforced, in default of payment, either directly by imprisonment, as may be directed by the Act under which the conviction takes place, with or without hard labor, or indirectly by the like imprisonment with or without hard labor, in default of goods whereout to satisfy the penalty and costs, 21 V., c. 9. s. 1.

Award and enforcement of compensation for non-performance of orders

Where they are invested with power to make an order otherwise than for the payment of money, they may, in their discretion, award that in default of the performance of the matter they are empowered to enjoin to be done, the defendant shall pay to the complainant such sum as they award as compensation for default of performance, and to direct, as before provided, the enforcement of such order, and of the costs, if adjudged, either directly by imprisonment for not exceeding one calendar month, or indirectly by the like imprisonment for the like term, in default of goods whereout to satisfy the sums adjudged to be paid as compensation and costs, 21 V., c. 9, s. 2.

Proceedings to ascertain amount of costs ; enforcement of order

Whenever any such order shall have been heretofore made, the person claiming the benefit thereof may issue a summons to the person charged in such cause before 2 Justices of the parish in which the original adjudication was made, why, in default of performance of the original order, the Justices should award to the complainant such sums as they think a fair compensation in default of the performance of the matter or thing directed to be done by the original order ; and the Justices may adjudicate on such complaint, and award such compensation, and enforce the same with costs (if adjudged) by imprisonment directly or indirectly as before provided, 21 V., c. 9, s. 3.

Imprisonment to run from capture

Where imprisonment is directed, it shall begin to run only from the date of the capture of the offender or defendant, and the officer directing (effecting) the capture, shall endorse on the warrant the date of caption, 21 V., c. 9, s. 4.

Stamp on private summons ; those at instance of the Police not chargable with stamp

The Stamp on each private summons may be impressed substitutionally on the information. No information or summons sued out by a Policeman, complaining of the infraction of any Public Act, shall be charged with a stamp, 21 V., c. 9, s. 5.

Adjudication by one Justice with consent

With the consent of the informer, complainant or plaintiff, and of the defendant, in any case of summary jurisdiction, a single Justice may adjudicate, 21 V., c. 9, s. 6.

One Justice may establish service and assess damages by default

In default of 2 Justices to form a Court of Petty Sessions, any single Justice may establish service of all civil cases ; and where service is established and no appearance entered, one Justice may assess the damages by default, 21 V., c. 9. s. 7.

Or adjourn

In all cases, civil or criminal, one Justice may adjourn the hearing, 21 V., c. 9, s. 8.

Extent of Act

Act extended to all Acts passed or to be enacted, conferring summary jurisdiction on Justices, 21 V., c. 9, s. 9.

Subpœnas to parishes beyond jurisdiction

Any Justice may issue subpœnas to witnesses, into a different Parish from that in which the proceedings are pending, and any such subpœna, when endorsed by a Justice of the Parish in which it is sought to be put into operation, may be served therein (upon tender of reasonable expenses, and disobedience shall entail the same consequences as in cases of subpœnas served within the jurisdiction of the Justice issuing it, 21 V., c. 9, s. 10.

No Justice shall demand or receive any fee for the performance of any act or duty required of him in that capacity ; and 10 Ann c. 4, s. 16, and all other Acts g vi g fees to Justices, so far as relates to such fees, are repealed, 21 V., c. 31.i n

Fees abolished

Justices of the Peace, Indictable Offences.

Where a charge or complaint (A) is made before a Justice, that any person has committed, or is suspected to have committed any treason, felony, or indictable misdemeanor, or other indictable offence, within the limits of his jurisdiction, or that any person guilty or suspected to be guilty of having committed any such crime or offence elsewhere is residing or being, or is suspected to reside or be within the limits of his jurisdiction, such Justice shall issue his warrant (B) to apprehend him, and to cause him to be brought before such or any other Justice or Justices for the same parish, to answer to such charge or complaint, and to be further dealt with according to law.— The Justice to whom the complaint is preferred, instead of a warrant in the first instance, may issue his summons (C) to such person, requiring him to appear before him or such other Justice or Justices as may be present at a time and place to be mentioned, and if after service he fail to appear, such or any other Justice may issue a warrant (D) to apprehend and cause such person to be brought before such or some other Justice or Justices for the Parish to answer to the charge, and be further dealt with according to Law. But not to prevent any Justice from issuing the warrant first mentioned at any time before or after the time mentioned in the summons for the appearance of the accused, 13 V., c. 24, s. 1.

Complaints of an indictable offence; warrant for the party's apprehension

Or a summons in the first instance

And if not obeyed a warrant may be issued

Summons not to prevent the issue of a warrant in the meantime

Where any indictment is found by the Grand Jury in any (Circuit Court, 19 V., c. 10) against any person then at large, and whether he has been bound by recognizance to appear to answer to the same or not, (the Clerk of the Circuit Court, 19 V., c. 10) at which the indictment is found shall, after the Sessions, upon application of the prosecutor, or of any person on his behalf, and on payment of a fee of 1s. 6d. if such person has not already appeared and pleaded to the indictment, grant to such prosecutor or person a certificate (E.) of such indictment having been found, upon production whereof to any Justice for any parish in which the offence is alleged to have been committed, or in which the person indicted resides, or is, or is supposed or suspected to be or reside, he shall issue his warrant (F) to apprehend the person indicted, and to cause him to be brought before him or any other Justice or Justices for the same parish, to be dealt with according to law ; and afterwards, if such person be apprehended and brought before any Justice, he shall, upon its being proved upon oath or affirmation, that the person apprehended is the same person who is charged in such indictment, without further inquiry or examination, commit (G.) him for trial, or admit him to bail as after mentioned ; or if such person so indicted is confined in any Gaol for any other offence, the Justice shall, upon its being proved upon oath or affirmation, that the person so indicted, and the person so confined in prison, are the same, issue his warrant (H.) directed to the Gaoler or Keeper of the prison, commanding him to detain such person in his custody until by H. M's. writ of Habeas Corpus he shall be removed for the purpose of being tried upon the indictment, or otherwise be removed or discharged out of his custody by due course of law, 13 V., c. 24, s. 2.

Warrant to apprehend a party against whom an indictment is found

Proceedings upon apprehension

Any Justice may issue any warrant as aforesaid, or any such warrant on a Sunday as well as on any other day, 13 V., c. 24, s. 3.

Warrants may issue on Sunday

Where a Justice for any parish is also a Justice for any other parish, he may act as such for the one parish, while he is residing, or happens to be in the other, on all matters before or after mentioned, and all his acts and the acts of any Constable or Officer in obedience thereto, shall be as valid as if such Justice were at the time in the parish for which he acts, and all Constables and other officers for the parish for which the Justice so acts, are required to obey his warrants, orders, directions, or acts, and to perform their several offices and duties in respect thereof, under the penalties to which any Constable or other officer may be liable for a neglect of duty ; and any such Constable or peace officer, or other person apprehending or taking into custody any person offending against law, and whom he

A Justice for two parishes may act for one while in the other

And apprehended offenders in the one parish taken before him in the other

ought to apprehend in any such parish, may take and convey him before any such Justice for such parish, while in such other parish, and the Constables, &c., and other persons shall act in all things as if the Justice were within the parish for which he acts, 13 V., c. 24, s. 4.

No warrant to issue in the first instance without information in writing on oath Summons upon parol information

Where a complaint is made before a Justice, if it be intended to issue a warrant in the first instance, an information and complaint (A) in writing, on the oath or affirmation of the informant or of some witness in that behalf, shall be laid before him. Where it is intended to issue a summons instead of a warrant, it shall not be necessary that the information be in writing, or be sworn to, or affirmed, but it may be by parol merely, and without oath or affirmation. No objection shall be allowed to any information for any alleged defect in substance, or in form, or for any variance between it and the evidence on the part of the prosecution, 13 V., c. 24, s. 5.

No objection for alleged defects, &c. in information

Upon information Justice to issue summons or warrant

Upon such information, the Justice receiving it may issue his summons or warrant, to cause the person charged to be and appear before him, or any other Justice or Justices for the parish, to be dealt with according to law ; such summons (C) shall be directed to the party charged, and state shortly the matter of the information, and require the party to appear at a certain time and place before the Justice who issues it, or such other Justice or Justices as may then be there, to answer to the charge, and to be further dealt with according to law, and shall be served by a Constable or Peace Officer, by delivering it to the party personally, or if he cannot conveniently be met with, then by leaving it with some person for him at his last or most usual place of abode, and the Constable, &c. who served it shall attend at the time and place, and before the Justices, to depose, if necessary, to the service. If the person does not appear, he may issue his warrant (D) for apprehending the party, and bringing him before such or some other Justice or Justices to answer the charge, and to be further dealt with according to law. No objection shall be allowed to any summons or warrant for any alleged defect, in substance or in form, or for any variance between it and the evidence on the part of the prosecution; but if any such variance appear to the Justice to be such, that the party has been deceived or misled, he may, at the request of such party, adjourn the hearing to some future day, and, in the meantime, remand or admit him to bail, 13 V., c. 24, s. 6.

Summons

Service and proof

In default of appearance a warrant shall issue

No objection for defects, &c. in summons or warrant, but Justices may adjourn the hearing

Signature direction and execution of warrant

Every warrant (D) to apprehend any person charged with any indictable offence, shall be under the hand of the Justice, and may be directed either to any Constable, or other person, or generally to the Constable of the parish within which it is to be executed, without naming him, or to such Constable, and all other Constables or Peace Officers in the parish, or generally to all the Constables or Peace Officers within such parish, and shall state shortly the offence on which it is founded, and name, or otherwise describe the offender, and order the persons to whom it is directed to apprehend the offender and bring him before such or some other Justice or Justices for the parish, to answer to the charge, and be further dealt with according to law ; and it shall not be necessary to make the warrant returnable at any particular time, but it may remain in force until executed, and may be executed by apprehending the offender at any place within the parish, or in case of fresh pursuit, at any place in the next adjoining parish, and within 7 miles of the border of such first mentioned parish, without having such warrant backed (see 23 V., c. 16, s. 1) ; and where the warrant is directed to all Constables or other Peace Officers within the parish within which the Justice issuing the same has jurisdiction, any Constable, &c. for such parish may execute the warrant in any parish within the jurisdiction for which such Justice acted when he granted it, as if it were directed specially to such Constable by name, and notwithstanding the place in which the warrant is executed is not within the parish for which he is Constable or Peace Officer. No objection shall be allowed to any such warrant for any defect in substance or in form, or for any variance between it and the evidence adduced on the part of the prosecution before the Justices ; but if any such variance appear to such Justice to be such, that the party charged has been deceived or misled, he may, at the request of such party, adjourn the hearing to some future day, and, in the meantime, remand or admit him to bail, 13 V., c. 24, s. 7.

No objection for alleged defects, &c.

If the person is not found within the jurisdiction of the Justice, or if he escape, go into, reside, or be, or be supposed or suspected to be in any other parish out of the jurisdiction of·the Justice issuing the warrant, any Justice of the parish into which he escapes or goes, or in which he resides, or is, or is supposed or suspected to be, upon proof alone being made, on oath, of the handwriting of the Justice issuing such warrant, may make an indorsement (I) on such warrant, signed with his name, authorizing its execution within his jurisdiction, and which indorsment shall be sufficient authorit to the person. bringing it, and to all other persons to whom it was originally directed, and.also to all Constables, &c., of the parish where it is indorsed, to execute the same in such other parish, and to carry the person against whom the warrant was issued, when apprehended, before the Justice who first issued it, or before some other Justice in and for.the same parish, or some Justice of the parish where the offence, in the warrant mentioned, appears therein to have been committed. If the prosecutor, or any of the witnesses upon the part of the prosecution, are then in the parish where the person is apprehended, the Constable or person who apprehends him may, if so directed by the Justice backing such warrant, take and convey him before such or some other Justice of the same parish, who may take the examinations of such prosecutor or witnesses, and proceed as after directed, (s. 15) with respect to persons charged before a Justice with an offence alleged to have been committed in another parish than that in which such persons are apprehended, 13 V., c. 24, s. 8.

Backing warrants and authority conferred thereby for execution ; see 23 V., c. 16, s. 1, 3.

Examination of prosecutor and witnesses if in the parish where the person is apprehended

Every summons or warrant, issued by any Justice, may be served or executed out of the parish, by the policeman or constable to wl. m it is directed, or any other policeman or constable, and shall have the same force as if originally issued or subsequently indorsed by a Justice having jurisdiction in the parish where it is served or executed, 23 V., c. 16, s. 1.

Summons or warrants may be executed out of the parish as if backed

Any Justice before whom any person is brought under a warrant, who is apprehended in another parish than that in which the offence was committed, may take bail, by recognizance, for his appearance before the Justices of the parish in which the offence was committed, in such amount as the Justice thinks fit, 23 V., c. 16, s. 3.

Persons may be bailed in the parish where apprehended

All warrants given by Justices against any person on board any ship or vessel, shall be directed to the Provost-Marshal or his Deputy, or any Constable of the place, according to the tenor of the warrant, who are required to execute the same, and shall receive 3s. (1s. 9½d stg.) 35 C. 2, c. 4, s. 7.

Warrants on board ship

If it is made to appear to any Justice, by the oath or affirmation of any credible person, that any person within his jurisdiction, is likely to give material evidence for the prosecution, and will not voluntarily appear as a witness against the accused, such Justice shall issue his summons (K.) to such person, under his hand, requiring him to appear at a time and place mentioned, before him or such other Justice or Justices as shall then be there, to testify what he knows concerning the charge against the accused ; and if he neglect or refuse to appear, and no just excuse is offered for his neglect or refusal, then (after proof upon oath or affirmation of service upon him, either personally, or by leaving the same with some person at his last or most usual place of abode) the Justice or Justices before whom he should have appeared, may issue a warrant, (L. 1) under his or their hands, to bring him at a time and place to be mentioned, before him or them, or such other Justice or Justices as shall then be there, to testify as aforesaid, and which warrant may, if necessary, be backed, in order to its being executed out of the jurisdiction of the Justice, or if such Justice is satisfied by evidence upon oath or affirmation, that it is probable such person will not attend to give evidence without being compelled, instead of issuing such summons, he may issue his warrant (L. 2) in the first instance, and which. if necessary, may be backed ; and if on the appearance of the person summoned, either in obedience to the summons, or upon being brought by virtue of the warrant, he refuse to be examined upon oath or affirmation concerning the premises, or refuse to take such oath or affirmation or, having taken it, refuse to answer questions put to him, without any just excuse, any Justice present, and having jurisdiction, may by warrant (L. 3) under his hand, commit the person so refusing to Gaol for not exceeding 7 days,

Summons to witnesses for prosecution

Warrant in case of default

Warrant in the first instance

Commitment of witnesses, &c. refusing to be examined

unless he, in the meantime, consent to be examined and answer, 13 V., c. 24, s. 9.

Examination of witnesses upon oath in the presence of accused, who may ask questions to be put into writing, &c.

Where any person appear, or is brought before any Justice, charged with any indictable offence committed within this Island, or whether he appear voluntarily upon summons, or has been apprehended with or without warrant, or is in custody for the same, or any other offence, he shall, before he commits the accused, or admits him to bail, in the presence of the accused, who shall be at liberty to put questions to any witness produced against him, take the statement (M) on oath or affirmation of those who know the facts and circumstances of the case, and put the same into writing ; and such depositions shall be read over to, and signed by the witnesses who have been examined, and by the Justice or Justices taking the same : and the Justices before whom the witness appears, shall, before he is examined, administer to him the usual oath or affirmation ;

When depositions receivable in evidence on trial

and if upon the trial of the accused, it be proved, upon the oath or affirmation of any credible witness, that any person whose deposition has been taken as aforesaid, is dead, or so ill as not to be able to travel, and if also it be proved that it was taken in the presence of the accused, and that he, or his Counsel or Attorney, had a full opportunity of cross-examining the witness, then if the deposition purport to be signed by the Justice, by or before whom it purports to have been taken, the deposition may be read as evidence in such prosecution, without further proof, unless it be proved such deposition was not, in fact, signed by the Justice. 13 V., c. 24, s. 10.

After examinations the accused to be cautioned, and statement taken down

After the examination of all the witnesses on the part of the prosecution is completed, the Justice, or one of the Justices shall, without requiring the attendance of the witnesses, read or cause to be read to the accused, the depositions taken against him ; and shall say to him these words, or words to the like effect : " Having heard the evidence, do you wish to say anything in answer to the charge ? You are not obliged to say anything, unless you desire to do so ; but whatever you say, will be taken down in writing, and may be given in evidence against you upon your trial." And whatever the prisoner then says in answer, shall be taken down in writing, (N) and read over to him, and shall be signed by the Justice or Justices, and kept with the depositions, and transmitted with them as after mentioned ; and afterwards, upon the trial of the accused, may, if necessary, be given in evidence against him, without further proof, unless it be proved that the Justices purporting to sign, did not in fact sign the same. The Justice, before the accused makes any statement, shall state to him, and give him clearly to understand that he has

Warning to accused

nothing to hope from any promise of favor, and nothing to fear from any threat which may have been holden out to him, to induce him to make any admission or confession of his guilt ; but that whatever he then says, may be given in evidence against him upon his trial, notwithstanding such

Other evidence of admissions or statements admissible

promise or threat. Not to prevent the prosecutor in any case from giving in evidence any admission or confession, or other statement of the accused made at any time, which by law would be admissible, 13 V., c. 24, s. 11.

Place of examination not an open Court

The room or building in which the Justice takes such examinations and statement, shall not be deemed an open Court for that purpose ; and such Justice, in his discretion, may order that no person have access, or be or remain therein without his permission, if it appear to him that the ends of Justice will be best answered by so doing, 13 V., c. 24, s. 12.

Recognizances of prosecutor and witnesses

The Justice before whom any witness is examined, may bind, by recognizance (O 1) the prosecutor and every such witness, to appear at the next [Circuit] Court at which the accused is to be tried, then and there to prosecute, or to prosecute and give evidence, or to give evidence, as the case may be, against the accused ; which recognizance shall particularly specify the profession, art, mystery, or trade of every person entering into or acknowledging it, together with his Christian and surname, and the parish in which he resides ; and being duly acknowledged by the person, shall be subscribed by the Justice and a

Notice thereof Transmission of papers to officer of Court where trial is to be

notice (O 2) thereof, signed by him, shall, at the same time, be given to the person bound thereby. And the several recognizances, with the written information (if any), the depositions, the statement of the accused, and the recognizance of bail, if any, shall be delivered by the Justice, or he shall cause them to be delivered to the proper officer of the

Court, in which the trial is to be had, before or at the opening of the Court, on the first day of its sitting, or at such other time as the Judge who is to preside at the trial orders. If any witness refuse to enter into, or acknowledge such recognizance, the Justice may, by his warrant (P 1), commit him to the prison for the parish in which the accused is to be tried, to be safely kept, until after the trial, unless, in the meantime, he enter into recognizance before a Justice for the parish in which the prison is situate. If afterwards, from want of sufficient evidence or other cause, the Justice before whom the accused is brought, does not commit him, or hold him to bail, he or any other Justice of the parish may, by order, (P 2) direct the keeper of the prison where the witness is in custody, to discharge him; and such keeper shall thereupon forthwith discharge him 13 V., c. 24, s. 13.

Commitment of witnesses refusing to enter into recognizance

To be discharged if the accused is not committed or bailed

If from the absence of witnesses or other reasonable cause, it become necessary or advisable to defer the examination, or further examination of the witnesses, for any time, the Justice before whom the accused appears, or is brought, may, by his warrant (Q. 1) from time to time, remand him for such time as he deems reasonable, not exceeding 8 clear days, to the prison in the parish, or if the remand be for not exceeding 3 clear days, may verbally order the Constable, or person in whose custody the accused is, or any other Constable or person to be named by the Justice, to continue or keep him in his custody, and to bring him before the same or some other Justice as shall be there acting, at the time appointed for continuing such examination. Any Justice may order the accused to be brought before him, or any other Justice, at any time before the expiration of the time for which he is remanded, and the Gaoler or officer in whose custody he is, shall obey such order, or instead of detaining the accused in custody during the remand, any Justice before whom he appears or is brought, may discharge him, upon his entering into a recognizance, (Q. 2. 3.) with or without a surety, conditioned for his appearance at the time and place appointed for the continuance of such examination, and if he do not afterwards appear at the time and place, he, or any other Justice present, upon certifying (Q. 4) on the back of the recognizance the non-appearance of the accused, may transmit it to the Clerk of the Peace, to be proceeded upon as other recognizances; and such certificate shall be sufficient prima facie evidence of such non-appearance of the accused, 13 V., c. 24, s. 14.

Prisoner's remand not exceeding 8 days by warrant

Or verbally in custody of constable, &c. for not exceeding 3 days

Remand under recognizance

If party does not appear recognizance to be to be transmitted to Clerk of the peace

When a person appears, or is brought before a Justice, in the parish wherein he has jurisdiction, charged with an offence alleged to have been committed in any parish wherein the Justice has not jurisdiction, he shall examine such witnesses, and receive such evidence in proof of the charge, as shall be produced before him within his jurisdiction, and if in his opinion such testimony and evidence is sufficient proof of the charge, shall commit him to the prison for the parish where the offence is alleged to have been committed, or admit him to bail, and bind over the prosecutor, if he has appeared, and the witnesses, by recognizance accordingly, but if the testimony and evidence is not sufficient to put the accused upon his trial, he shall bind over such witnesses as he has examined, by recognizance, to give evidence, and shall by warrant, (R) under his hand, order the accused to be taken before some Justice or Justices in and for the parish where the offence is alleged to have been committed, and at the same time deliver the information and complaint, and the depositions and recognizances taken by him, to the Constable or Officer who has the execution of the last mentioned warrant, to be delivered to the Justice before whom he takes the accused, and which depositions and recognizances shall be deemed to be taken in the case, and treated as if taken before such last mentioned Justice, and shall, together with such depositions and recognizances as he shall take, be transmitted to the Clerk of the Court where the accused is to be tried before mentioned, if the accused is committed or admitted to bail. If such last mentioned Justice shall not think the evidence sufficient to put him upon his trial, and discharges him without holding him to bail, every recognizance taken by the first Justice shall be void, 13 V., c. 24, s. 15.

Duty of Justice before whom a person is charged with an offence committed out of his jurisdiction as to examinations and commitment, &c., and bind over witnesses

Or transfer of accused and documents to the parish where offence committed

To be returned as part of the proceedings if the accused is committed or bailed for trial

If accused is afterwards discharged the recognizances by first Justice shall be void

Where any person appears, or is brought before a Justice, charged with any felony, or with any assault, with intent to commit any felony, or with any attempt to commit any felony, or with obtaining, or attempting to obtain property by false pretences, or with

Discretionary power to admit to bail in felonies or certain misdemeanors

a misdemeanor, in receiving property stolen, or obtained by false pretences, or with perjury, or subornation of perjury, or with concealing the birth of a child, by secret burying or otherwise, or with wilful or indecent exposure of the person, or with riot, or with assault, in pursuance of a conspiracy to raise wages, or assault upon a Peace Officer in the execution of his duty, or upon any person acting in his aid, or with neglect or breach of duty as a Peace Officer. or with any misdemeanor, for the prosecution of which the costs may be allowed out of the Public Funds, such Justice may, in his discretion admit such person to bail, upon his procuring and producing sufficient surety or sureties to ensure the appearance of the accused to be tried; and thereupon he shall take the recognizance (S. 1-2) of the accused and his surety or sureties, conditioned for his appearance, at the time and place of trial, and that he will then surrender and take his trial and not depart the Court without leave. Where a person charged with any indictable offence is committed to prison to take his trial at any time afterwards, and before the first day of the Court, or before the day to which it may be adjourned, the Justice or Justices who signed the warrant for his commitment may admit the accused to bail, or if of opinion that for any of the offences before-mentioned the accused ought to be admitted to bail, shall, in such cases, and, in all other cases of misdemeanor, certify (S. 3) on the back of the warrant of commitment his or their consent to such accused being bailed, stating also the amount of bail to be required; any Justice attending, or being at the prison where the accused is in custody, on production of such certificate may admit him to bail, or if it is inconvenient for the sureties to attend at the prison, to join with the accused in the recognizance of bail, the committing Justice may make a duplicate of such certificate (S. 4), and upon the same being produced to any Justice of the same parish, he may take the recognizance of the sureties, in conformity with the certificate, and upon the recognizance being transmitted to the Keeper of the Prison, and produced with the certificate on the warrant of commitment to any Justice at such prison, he may take the recognizance of the accused, and order him to be discharged out of custody as to that commitment. And where any person is charged before any Justice with any other indictable misdemeanor, such Justice, after taking the examinations in writing, instead of committing him to prison, shall admit him to bail, or if he has been committed to prison and applies to any Visiting Justice of such prison, or any other Justice for the parish, before the first day of the Court at which he is to be tried, or before the day to which it may be adjourned to be admitted to bail, such Justice shall accordingly admit him to bail; and where he is admitted to bail by a Justice other than the Committing Justice, the Justice admitting him to bail shall forthwith transmit the recognizance or recognizances to the Committing Justices, or one of them, to be transmitted with the examinations to the proper officer. No Justice shall admit any person to bail for treason, nor shall he be admitted to bail, except by order of the Supreme Court, or a Judge in vacation, 13 V., c. 24, s. 16.

Where a Justice admits to bail any person in any prison, he shall send to, or cause to be lodged with the Keeper, a warrant of deliverance (S. 5) under his hand, requiring the Keeper to discharge him, if he be detained for no other offence, and upon such warrant of deliverance being delivered to or lodged with such Keeper, he shall forthwith obey it, 13 V., c. 24, s. 17.

When all the evidence offered on the part of the prosecution against the accused has been heard, if the Justice is of opinion that it is not sufficient to put him upon his trial, he shall forthwith order him, if in custody, to be discharged as to the information then under enquiry; but, if in his opinion, the evidence is sufficient to put the accused upon his trial for an indictable offence, or if the evidence raises a strong or probable presumption of the guilt of the accused, he shall, by his warrant (T. 1) commit him to the prison to which by Law he may be committed, within which the Justice has jurisdiction, to be there safely kept, until thence delivered by due course of Law, or admit him to bail, 13 V., c. 24, s. 18.

The Constable or other person to whom the warrant of commitment is directed, shall convey the accused to the prison mentioned in the warrant, and there deliver him with the warrant to the Keeper, who shall thereupon give such Constable, &c., a receipt (T. 2) for such prisoner, setting forth the state and condition in which he was when delivered into his custody, 13 V., c. 24, s. 19.

Marginal notes:

Bail after commitment

Persons charged with other misdemeanors to be bailed

The Justice admitting to bail shall transmit the recognizance to a committing Justice to be sent to the proper officer

No bail for treason

Warrant of deliverance

Discharge, commitment or admission of defendant to bail after evidence heard

Prisoner to be delivered to the keeper with the warrant—his receipt

After all the examinations have been completed, and before the first day of the Court, at which any person committed or admitted to bail is to be tried, such person may require and be entitled to have from the Officer or person, having the custody of the same, copies of the depositions on which he has been committed or bailed, on payment of a reasonable sum, not exceeding at the rate of 1s. 6d. for each folio of 160 words, 13 V., c. 24, s. 20. *Defendant's right to copy of depositions*

The Forms in Schedule, or to such effect, shall be valid, 13 V., c. 24, s. 21. *Forms*

All Acts or parts of Acts, inconsistent with this Act, repealed, 13 V., c. 24, s. 23. *Repeal of Acts*

In all cases, civil and criminal, one Justice may adjourn the hearing, 21 V., c. 9, s. 8. *One Justice may adjourn*

SCHEDULE.—13 V., c. 24.

To WIT:

The information and complaint of C. D., of   (laborer, &c.) taken this   day of   in the year of our Lord, 18   : before the undersigned, (one) of Her Majesty's Justices of the Peace, in and for the said (Parish) of   who saith that (&c., stating the offence.) *Information, A, s. 1-5*

Sworn before (me), the day and year first above mentioned at

                      J. S.

To the Constable of   and to all other Peace Officers in   the said (Parish) of *Warrant to apprehend, B, s. 1*

Whereas A. B. of   (laborer, &c.) hath this day been charged, upon oath, before the undersigned (one) of Her Majesty's Justices of the Peace in and for the said parish of, for that he, on   at.   did (&c., stating shortly the offence) : These are therefore to command you, in Her Majesty's name, forthwith to apprehend the said A. B., and to bring him before (me) or some other of Her Majesty's Justices of the Peace in and for the said (parish), to answer unto the said charge, and to be further dealt with according to Law.

Given under my hand, this   day of in the year of our Lord   at   in the parish aforesaid,

                      J. S.

To A. B. of   (laborer.) *Summons, C, s. 1, 6*

Whereas you have this day been charged before the undersigned, (one) of Her Majesty's Justices of the Peace in and for the said (parish) of   for that you, on   at (&c., stating shortly the offence) : These are therefore to command you, in Her Majesty's name, to be and appear before me on at   o'clock in the forenoon, at or before such other Justice or Justices of the Peace for the same (Parish) as may then be there, to answer to the said charge, and to be further dealt with according to Law : Herein fail not.

Given under my hand, this   day of in the year of our Lord   at   in the parish aforesaid.

                      J. S.

To the Constable of   and to all other Peace Officers of the said parish of *Warrant where summons disobeyed, D, s. 1-7*

Whereas on the   last past, A. B., of (laborer) was charged before the undersigned (one) of Her Majesty'

Justices of the Peace in and for the said (parish) of
for that (&c., as in summons) : And whereas (I) then issued (my)
summons to the said A. B., commanding him, in Her Majesty's name)
to be and appear before (me) on   at
o'clock in the forenoon, at   or before
such other Justice or Justices of the Peace for the same (parish) as
might then be there to answer to the said charge, and to be further
dealt with according to law : And whereas the said A. B. bath neglected to be or appear at the time and place appointed in and by
the said summons, although it hath now been proved to me, upon
oath, that the said summons was duly served upon the said A. B. :
These are therefore to command you, in Her Majesty's name, forthwith
to apprehend the said A. B., and to bring him before me, or some
other of Her Majesty's Justices of the Peace in and for the said (parish)
to answer to the said charge, and to be further dealt with according
to law.

Given under my hand, this   day of
          in the year of our Lord   at   in the
          parish aforesaid.

                                                            J. S.

Certificate of indictment being found, E, s. 2

I hereby certify that at (a Court of Oyer and Terminer, and General
Gaol Delivery, holden in and for the (county or parish, as the
case may be), of   at
              , in the said (county or parish) as the case may
be), on   a bill of indictment was
found by the Grand Jury against A. B. therein described, as A. B.
late of   (laborer, &c.) for that he (&c., stating
shortly the offence), and that the said A. B. hath not appeared or
pleaded to the said indictment.

          Dated this   day of   18

                                        J. D.
                              Clerk of the Crown, or
                    Clerk of the Peace of and for the said parish.

Warrant to apprehend person indicted, F, s. 2

To the Constable of   and to all other Peace Officers
in the said parish of

Whereas it hath been duly certified by J. D., Clerk of the Crown (or
Clerk of the Peace, of and for the parish of
that (&c., stating the certificate): These are therefore to command you,
in Her Majesty's name, forthwith to apprehend the said A. B., and to
bring him before (me) or some other Justice or Justices of the Peace in
and for the said (parish) to be dealt with according to law.

Given under my hand, this   day of
          in the year of our Lord   at
          in the parish aforesaid.

                                                            J. S.

Warrant of commitment of person indicted, G, s. 2

To the Constable of   and to the keeper of the (Common
Gaol or other Prison) at   in the said parish of

Whereas by (my) warrant under my hand, dated the
day of   after reciting that it had been certified by
J. D. (&c. as in the certificate) (I) commanded the Constable of
                    and all other Peace Officers of the said parish, in Her
Majesty's name, forthwith, to apprehend the said A. B., and to bring
him before (me) the undersigned, (one) of Her Majesty's Justices of
the Peace in and for the said (parish), or before some other Justice or
Justices of the Peace in and for the said (parish), to be dealt with according to law : And whereas the said A. B. hath been apprehended
under and by virtue of the said warrant, and being now brought before (me), it is hereupon duly proved to me, upon oath, that the said
A. B. is the same person who is named and charged in and by the

said indictment : These are therefore to command you, the said Constable, in Her Majesty's name, forthwith to take, and safely convey the said A. B. to the said (Common Gaol, or other Prison) at
           in the said (parish), and there to deliver him to the keeper thereof, together with this precept: And I do hereby command you, the said keeper, to receive the said A. B. into your custody in the said (Common Gaol, or other Prison); and him there safely to keep, until he shall be thence delivered by due course of law.

Given under my hand, this   day of
   in the year of our Lord   at
   in the parish aforesaid.

                                                      J. S.

To the Keeper of the (Common Gaol, or other Prison), at
           in the said parish of

Warrant to detain person indicted already in custody, H. s. 2

Whereas it hath been duly certified by J. D. Clerk of the Crown, (or Clerk of the Peace, of and for the Parish of
   ), that, (&c., stating the certificate) : And whereas (I am) informed that the said A. B. is in your custody in the said (Common Gaol, or other Prison), at   aforesaid, charged with some offence or other matter, and it being now duly proved upon oath before (me) that the said A. B. so indicted as aforesaid, and the said A. B. in your custody as aforesaid, are one and the same person : These are therefore to command you, in Her Majesty's name, to detain the said A. B. in your custody, in the (Common Gaol, or other Prison) aforesaid, until, by Her Majesty's writ of habeas corpus, he shall be removed therefrom, for the purpose of being tried upon the said indictment, or until he shall otherwise be removed or discharged out of your custody by due course of law.

Given under my hand, this   day of
   in the year of our Lord   at
   in the Parish aforesaid.

                                                      J. S.

To WIT :

Indorsement in backing a warrant, I. s. 8

Whereas proof upon oath hath this day been made before me, one of Her Majesty's Justices of the Peace for the said (parish) of
   that the name of J. S. to the within warrant subscribed, is of the handwriting of the Justice of the Peace within mentioned : I do therefore hereby authorize W. T. who bringeth to me this warrant, and all other persons to whom this warrant was originally directed, or by whom it may lawfully be executed, and also all Constables and other Peace Officers, of the (parish) of
   to execute the same within the said last mentioned (parish) and to bring the said A. B., if apprehended, within the same (parish) before me, or before some other Justice or Justices of the Peace of the same parish, to be dealt with according to law.

Given under my hand, this   day of
           18

                                                      J. L.

To E. F. of   (laborer.)

Summons of witness. K. s. 9

Whereas information hath been laid before the undersigned (one) of Her Majesty's Justices of the Peace in and for the said (parish) of
   that A. B. (&c. as in the summons or warrant against the accused), and it hath been made to appear to me upon (oath) that you are likely to give material evidence for the prosecution) : These are therefore to require you to be and to appear before me on   next, at   o'clock in the forenoon, at   or before such other Justice or Justices of the Peace for the same parish as may then be there,

.to testify what you shall know concerning the said charge so made against the said A. B. as aforesaid. Herein fail not.

> Given under my hand, this
> in the year of our Lord
> . in the parish aforesaid.

day of
-at

J. S.

Warrant where witness has not obeyed summons, L. 1, s. 9

To the Constable of   and to all other Peace Officers in the said (parish) of

Whereas information having been laid before the undersigned, (one) of Her Majesty's Justices of the Peace in and for the said (parish) of that A. B. (&c. as in the summons), and it having been made to appear to (me) upon oath that E. F. of laborer) was likely to give material evidence for the prosecution, I did duly issue my summons to the said E. F., requiring him to be and appear before me on   at or before such other Justice or Justices of the Peace for the same parish as might then be there, to testify what he should know respecting the said charge so made against the said A. B. as aforesaid. And whereas proof hath this day been made before me, upon oath, of such summons having been duly served upon the said E. F. : And whereas the said E. F. hath neglected to appear at the time and place appointed by the said summons, and no just excuse has been offered for such neglect: These are therefore to command you to bring and have the said E. F. before me, on   at o'clock in the forenoon, at   or before such other Justice or Justices of the Peace for the same (parish) as may then be there, to testify what he shall know concerning the said charge so made against the said A. B. as aforesaid.

> Given under my hand, this
> in the year of our Lord
> the parish aforesaid.

day of
at

in

J. S.

Warrant for a witness in the first instance, L. 2, s. 9

To the Constable of   and to all other Peace Officers in the said (parish) of

Whereas information hath been laid before the undersigned, (one) of Her Majesty's Justices of the Peace in and for the said (parish) of that, (&c., as in summons), and it having been made to appear to (me), upon oath, that E. F. of (laborer) is likely to give material evidence for the prosecution, and that it is probable that the said E. F. will not attend to give evidence without being compelled so to do : These are therefore to command you to bring, and have the said E. F. before me, on   at o'clock in the forenoon, at   or before such other Justice or Justices of the Peace for the same (parish), as may then be there, to testify what he shall know concerning the said charge so made against the said A. B. as aforesaid.

> Given under my hand, this
> in the year of our Lord
> in the parish aforesaid.

day of
at

J. S.

Warrant for commitment of witness refusing to be sworn or to give evidence, L. 3, s. 9

To the Constable of   and to the Keeper of the Common Goal or other Prison at   in the said Parish of

Whereas A. B. was lately charged before the undersigned, (one) of her Majesty's Justices of the Peace in and for the said parish of for that, (&c., as in summons), and it having been made to appear to (me) upon oath, that E. F. of was likely to give material evidence for the prosecution, I duly issued my summons to the said E. F., requiring him to be and appear before me, on   at or before such other Justice or Justices of the Peace as should then he there, to testify what he should know concerning the said charge so made against the said A. B. as aforesaid, and the said E. F. now appearing before me (or being brought before me by virtue of a warrant in that behalf, to testify as aforesaid), and being required to make oath or affirmation as a witness in that behalf, hath now refused so to do (or being duly sworn as a witness, doth now refuse to answer certain questions concerning the premises which are here put to him), without offering any just excuse for such his refusal: These are therefore to command you, the said Constable, to take the said E. F., and him safely to convey to the (Common Goal, or other Prison) at in the parish aforesaid, and there deliver him to the said Keeper thereof, together with this precept ; and I do hereby command you, the said Keeper of the said (Common Gaol or other Prison) to receive the said E. F. into your custody in the said (Common Gaol or other Prison), and him there safely keep for the space of days for his said contempt, unless he shall, in the meantime, consent to be examined, and to answer concerning the premises ; and for your so doing this shall be your sufficient warrant.

Given under my hand, this   day of
in the year of our Lord   at
in the parish aforesaid.

                     J. S.

———

To WIT :

The examination of C. D. of   (Planter), and E. F.   Depositions, M of   (laborer), taken on (oath) this   s. 10
day of   in the year of our Lord
at   in the parish aforesaid, before the undersigned (one) of Her Majesty's Justices of the Peace for the said (parish), in the presence and hearing of A. B., who is charged this day before (me), for that he the said A. B., on
at   (&c., describing the offence as on a warrant of commitment.)

This deponent C. D. on his (oath) saith as follows, (&c., stating the deposition of the witness as nearly as possible in the words he uses. When his deposition is complete let him sign it.)   And this deponent E. F. upon his oath saith as follows : (&c.)
The above depositions of C. D. and E. F. were taken and sworn before me, at   on the day and year above mentioned.

                     J. S.

———

A. B. stands charged before the undersigned, (one) of Her Majesty's   Statement of accused, N, s. 11
Justices of the Peace in for the (parish) aforesaid, this
day of   in the year of our Lord   for that
he the said A. B. on   at   (&c., as in the caption of the depositions), and the said charge being read to the said A. B., and the witnesses for the prosecution C. D. and E. F. being severally examined in his presence, the said A. B. is now addressed by me, as follows :—" Having heard the evidence, do you wish to say anything in answer to the charge ? You are not obliged to say any thing unless you desire to do so, but whatever you say will be taken down in writing, and may be given in evidence against you upon your trial." Whereupon the said A. B. saith as follows :

(Here state whatever the prisoner may say, and in his very words, as nearly as possible. Get him to sign it if he will.)

                     A. B.

Taken before me, at   the day and year first
above mentioned

                     J. S.

Recognizance to prosecute or give evidence, O 1, s. 13

Be it remembered, that on the   day of,
in the year of our Lord   C. D.
of   in the parish of
personally came before me, one of Her Majesty's Justices of the
Peace for the said parish, and acknowledged himself to owe to our
Sovereign Lady the Queen the sum of   of good
and lawful money of this Island, to be made and levied of his goods
and chattels, lands and tenements, to the use of our said Lady the
Queen, her heirs and successors, if he the said C. D. shall fail in the
condition indorsed.
Taken and acknowledged the day and year first above mentioned
at   before me.
                                                        J. S.

───────

Condition to prosecute

(circuit court for 19 V., c. 10)

The condition of the within written recognizance is such, That whereas
one A. B. was this day charged before me, J. S., Justice of the
Peace within mentioned, for that (&c., as in the caption of the depositions) : If therefore he the said C. D. shall appear at the next
[Court of Oyer and Terminer, or General Gaol Delivery for
the County of   (or at the next Court
of general Quarter Sessions of the Peace], to be holden in and for (the
parish) of   * and there prefer, or cause to be
preferred, a bill of Indictment for the offence aforesaid against the
said A. B., and there also duly prosecute such Indictment then the
said recognizance to be void, or else to stand in full force and virtue.

Condition to prosecute and give evidence

Same as the last Form to the asterisk, * and then thus :—And there
prefer, or cause to be preferred, a bill of Indictment against the said
A. B. for the offence aforesaid, duly prosecute such Indictment, and
give evidence thereon, as well to the Jurors who shall then inquire
of the said offence, as also to them who shall pass upon the trial of the
said A. B., then the said recognizance to be void, or else to stand in
full force and virtue.

Condition to give evidence

Same as the last form but one to the asterisk,* and then thus :—
" And there give such evidence as he knoweth, upon a bill of Indictment to be then and there preferred against the said A. B. for
the offence aforesaid, as well to the Jurors, who shall there enquire of the said offence, as also to the Jurors who shall pass upon
the trial of the said A. B., if the said bill shall be found a true
bill, then the said recognizance to be void, or else to stand in full
force and virtue."

TO WIT :

Notice of recognizance to be given to the prosecutor and his witnesses, O 2, s. 13

(Circuit Court for 19 V., c. 10)

Take notice, that you, C. D. of   are bound in the sum
of   to appear at the next [Court of
Oyer and Terminer, or General Gaol Delivery for the county of
                    (or at the next Court of general Quarter
Sessions of the Peace] to be holden at
and then and there (prosecute and) give evidence against A. B.
and unless you then appear there, and (prosecute and) give evidence accordingly, the recognizance entered into by you will be
forthwith levied on you.
            Dated this .   day of   18
                                            J. S.

───────

Commitment of witnesses for refusing to enter into recognizance P 1, s. 13

To the Constable of   and to the Keeper of the
(Common Gaol or other Prison) at   in the
said parish of
Whereas A. B. was lately charged before the undersigned, (one) of
Her Majesty's Justices of the Peace in and for the said parish of
                    for that (&c., as in the summons
to the witness), and it having been made to appear to (me) upon
oath that E. F. of   was likely to give
material evidence for the prosecution (I) duly issued (my) summons
to the (said E. F., requiring him to be and appear before (me) on
            at   or before

such other Justice or Justices of the Peace as should then be there, to testify what he should know concerning the said charge so made against the said A. B. as aforesaid ; and the said E. F. now appearing before (me), or being brought before (me) by virtue (of a warrant in that behalf, to testify as aforesaid), hath been now examined by (me) touching the premises, but being by (me) required to enter into a recognizance, conditioned to give evidence against the said A. B., hath now refused so to do: These are therefore to command you, the said Constable, to take the said E. F., and him safely to carry to the (Common Gaol, or other Prison) at in the parish aforesaid, and there deliver him to the said Keeper thereof, together with this precept ; and I do hereby command you the said Keeper of the said (Common Gaol or other Prison), to receive the said E. F. into your custody in the said Common Gaol or other Prison, there to imprison and safely keep him until after the trial of the said A. B. for the offence aforesaid, unless, in the meantime, such E. F. shall duly enter into such recognizance as aforesaid, in the sum of pounds, before some one Justice of the Peace for the said parish, conditioned in the usual form, to appear at the next [Court of Oyer and Terminer, or General Gaol Delivery (or General Quarter Sessions of the Peace), to be holden in and for the [county or parish] of and there to give evidence before the Grand Jury upon any Bill of Indictment which may then and there be preferred against the said A. B. for the offence aforesaid, and also to give evidence upon the trial of the said A. B. for the said offence, if a true Bill should be found against him for the same.

(Circuit Court to be holden in and for the said parish)

Given under my hand, this   day of
in the year of our Lord   at
in the parish aforesaid.

J. S.

————

To the Keeper of the (Common Gaol or other Prison) at
in the parish of

ubsequent order to8 discharge witness, P. 2, s. 13

Whereas by (my) order, dated the   day of
(instant), reciting that A. B. was lately before then charged before (me) for a certain offence therein mentioned, and that E. F. having appeared before me, and being examined as a witness for the prosecution in that behalf, refused to enter into a recognizance to give evidence against the said A. B., and I therefore thereby committed the said E. F. to your custody, and required you safely to keep him until after the trial of the said A. B. for the offence aforesaid, unless in the meantime he should enter into such recognizance as aforesaid: And whereas for want of sufficient evidence against the said A. B., the said A. B. has not been committed or holden to bail for the said offence, but on the contrary thereof has been since discharged, and it is therefore not necessary that the said E. F. should be detained longer in your custody: These are therefore to order and direct you, the said Keeper, to discharge the said E. F. out of your custody, as to the said commitment, and suffer him to go at large.

Given under (my) hand, this   day of   in the year
of our Lord   at   in the parish aforesaid.

J. S.

————

To the Constable of   and to the (Keeper of the Common
Gaol or other Prison) at   in the said parish
of

Warrant remanding a prisoner, Q 1, s. 14

Whereas A. B. was this day charged before the undersigned, (one of Her Majesty's Justices of the Peace in and for the said (parish) of for that, (&c., as in the warrant to apprehend), and it appears to me to be necessary to remand the said A. B.: These are

T T

therefore to command you, the said Constable, in Her Majesty's name, forthwith to convey the said A. B. to the (Common Gaol or other Prison) at   in the said (parish), and there to deliver him to the Keeper thereof, together with this precept ; and I hereby command you, the said Keeper, to receive the said A. B. in your custody in the said (Common Gaol or other Prison), and there safely keep him until the   day of   instant, when I hereby command you to have him at   at o'clock in the forenoon of the same day, before me, or before such other Justice or Justices of the Peace for the said (parish) as may then be there, to answer further to the said charge, and to be further dealt with according to law, unless you shall be otherwise ordered in the meantime.

Given under my hand, this   day of   in the year of our Lord   at   in the parish aforesaid.

J. S.

Recognizance of bail, instead of remand on adjournment of examination, Q. 2, s. 14

Be it remembered, That on the   day of in the year of our Lord   A. B. of   labourer, L. M. of   gentleman, and N. O. of planter, personally came before me, one of Her Majesty's Justices of the Peace for the said (parish), and severally acknowledged themselves to owe to our Lady the Queen the several sums following : that is to say, the said A. B. the sum of   and the said L. M. and N. O. the sum of   each, of good and lawful money of this Island, to be made and levied of their several goods and chattels, lands and tenements, respectively, to the use of our said Lady the Queen, her heirs and successors, if he the said A. B. fail in the condition endorsed.

Taken and acknowledged the day and year first above mentioned, at before me.

J. S.

Condition

The condition of the within written recognizance is such, that whereas the within bounden A. B. was this day (or on   last past), charged before me, for that, (&c., as in the warrant:) And whereas the examination of the witnesses for the prosecution in this behalf is adjourned until the   day of   instant. If therefore the said A. B. shall appear before me on the said day of   instant at   o'clock in the forenoon, or before such other Justice or Justices of the Peace for the said (parish) as may then be there to answer (further) to the said charge, and to be further dealt with according to law, then the said recognizance to be void, or else to stand in full force and virtue.

Notice of recognizance to be given to the accused and his sureties. Q. 3, s. 14

Take notice that you, A. B., of   are bound in the sum of   and your sureties, L. M. and N. O., in the sum of each, that you, A. B., appear before me, J. S., one of her Majesty's Justices of the Peace for the (parish) of   in the   day of instant, at   o'clock in the forenoon at   or before such other Justice or Justices of the Peace for the same (parish) as may then be there, to answer further to the charge made against you by C. D., and to be further dealt with according to law ; and unless you, A. B., personally appear accordingly, the recognizance entered into by yourself and sureties will be forthwith levied on you and them.

Dated this   day of   18
J. S.

Certificate of non appearance to be indorsed on recognizance, Q. 4, s. 14

I hereby certify that the said A. B. hath not appeared at the time and place in the above condition mentioned, but therein hath made default, by reason whereof the within written recognizance is forfeited.

J. S.

To W. T., Constable of and to all other Peace
Officers in the said parish of

Whereas A. B. of (laborer), hath this day
been charged before the undersigned (one) of Her Majesty's Justices of
the Peace in and for the said parish of for that
(&c., as in the warrant to apprehend) : And whereas (I) have taken
the deposition of C. D., a witness examined by (me) in this behalf,
but inasmuch as (I) am informed that the principal witnesses to prove
the said offence against the said A. B. reside in the (parish) of C. where
the said offence is alleged to have been committed : These are therefore
to command you, the said Constable, in Her Majesty's name, forthwith
to take and convoy the said A. B. to the said (parish) of C., and there
carry him before some Justice or Justices of the Peace in and for that
(parish), and near unto the (parish of)
where the offence is alleged to have been committed, to answer further to the said charge before him or them, and to be further dealt
with according to law : And (I) hereby further command you, the
said Constable, to deliver to the said Justice or Justices the information in this behalf, and also the said deposition of C. D., now given
in your possession for that purpose, together with this precept.

Given under my hand, this day of
in the year of our Lord at in
the parish aforesaid.

J. S.

Be it remembered, That on the day of
in the year of our Lord
A. B. of laborer, L. M. of gentleman, and N. O. of planter, personally came
before (us), the undersigned two of her Majesty's Justices of the Peace
for the said (parish), and severally acknowledged themselves to owe
to our Lady the Queen the several sums following : (that is to say) the
said A. B. the sum of and the said L. M. and N. O.
the sum of each, of good and lawful money
of this Island, to be made and levied of their several goods and chattels, lands and tenements respectively, to the use of our said Lady
the Queen, her heirs and successors, if he the said A. B. fail in the condition indorsed.

Taken and acknowledged the day and year first above-mentioned, at
before us.

J. S.
J. N.

The condition of the within written recognizance is such, That
whereas the said A. B. was this day charged before (us), the Justices within mentioned, for that (&c., as in the warrant) : If there
fore the said A. B. will appear at the next [Court of Oyer and Terminer and General Gaol Delivery (or Court of General Quarter Sessions of the Peace], to be holden in and for the (county of or parish of) and there surrender himself-
into the custody of the Keeper of the (Common Gaol or other Prison)
there, and plead to such indictment as may be found against
him by the Grand Jury, for or in respect of the charge aforesaid,
and take his trial upon the same, and not depart the said court
without license, then the said recognizance to be void, or else to
stand in full force and virtue.

Take notice, that you, A. B. of are bound
in the sum of and your (sure-
ties L. M. and N. O.) in the sum of each,
that you, A. B. appear, &c., (as in the condition of the recognizance)
and not depart the said court without leave, and unless you, the
said A. B., personally appear and plead, and take your trial ac-

cordingly, the recognizance entered into by you and your sureties shall be forthwith levied on you and them.

Dated this   day of   18

                                J. S.

Certificate o con sent to bail by committing Jus- tices, indorsed on commitment, S. 3, s. 16

I hereby certify, that I consent to the within named A. B. being bailed by recognizance, himself in   and (two) sureties in   each.

                                J. S

The like on a se parate paper, S. 4, s 16

Whereas A. B. was, on the   committed by me to the (Common Gaol or other Prison) at   charged with (&c., naming the offence shortly): I hereby certify that I consent to the said A. B. being bailed by recognizance, him- self in   and (two) sureties in   each.

Dated the   day of   18

                                J. S.

To the Keeper of the (Common Gaol or other Prison) at in the said parish of

Warrant of deli verance on bail bee ing given for a prisoner already committed, S. 5, s. 17

Whereas A. B. late of   laborer, hath, before (us two) of Her Majesty's Justices of the Peace in and for the said parish, entered into his own recognizance, and found suf- ficient sureties for his appearance at the next [Court of Oyer and Terminer and General Gaol Delivery (or Court of General Quarter Sessions of the Peace), to be holden in and for the county of, or]

(Circuit Court to be holden in and for)

parish of   to answer our Sovereign Lady the Queen, for that, (&c., as in the commitment), for which he was taken and committed to your said Common Gaol or other Prison): These are therefore to command you, in Her said Majesty's name, that if the said A. B. do remain in your custody in the said (Common Gaol or other Prison) for the said cause, and for no other, you shall forthwith suffer him to go at large.

Given under our hands, this   day of   in the year of our Lord   at in the parish aforesaid.

                                J. N.
                                J. S.

Warrant of com mitment, T. 1, s. 18

To the Constable of   and to the Keeper of the (Common Gaol or other Prison) at in the said parish of

Whereas A. B. was this day charged before me, J. S., one of Her- Majesty's Justices of the Peace in and for the said (parish) of   on the oath of C. D., of   planter, and others, for that (&c. stating shortly the offence): These are there- fore to command you, the said Constable of   to take the said A. B., and him safely to convey to the (Common Gaol or other Prison) at   aforesaid, and there to de- liver him to the Keeper thereof, together with this precept; and I do hereby command you, the said Keeper of the said (Common Gaol or other Prison) to receive the said A. B. into your custody in the said (Common Gaol or other Prison), and there safely keep him until he shall be thence delivered by due course of law.

Given under my hand, this   day of   in the year of our Lord   at in the parish aforesaid.

                                J. S.

I hereby certify, that I have received from W. T., Constable of the body of A. B., together with a warrant, under the hand of J. S., Esquire, one of Her Majesty's Justices of the Peace for the parish of   and that the said A. B. was (sober, or a the case may be), at the time he was so delivered into my custody.

P. B.,

Keeper of the Common Gaol or other Prison.

Justices of the Peace, Summary Convictions or Orders.

Where an information is laid before one or more Justices, that any person has committed, or is suspected to have committed any offence or act within their Jurisdiction for which he is (or hereafter may be, 18 V., c. 57, s. 1.) liable by law upon summary conviction before a Justice or Justices to be imprisoned, or fined or otherwise punished, and also where a complaint is made to any such Justice or Justices, upon which he or they have (or shall have, 18 V., c. 57, s. 1.) authority by law to make any order for the payment of money or otherwise, such Justice or Justices shall issue his or their summons (A) directed to such person, stating shortly the matter of information or complaint, and requiring him to appear at a time and place before the same or some other Justice or Justices of the parish to answer to the information, &c., and to be further dealt with according to law, and such summons shall be served by a Constable, or Peace Officer or other person to whom it is delivered, upon the person to whom it is directed, by delivering the same to the party personally, or leaving it with some person for him at his last or most usual place of abode ; and the Constable, &c. who serves it, shall attend at the time and place, and before the Justices, to depose if necessary, to the service. Not to oblige any Justice to issue any summons, where the application for any order of Justices is by law to be made ex parte. No objection shall be allowed to any information, complaint or summons, for any alleged defect therein in substance or in form, or for any variance between the information, &c., and evidence on the part of the informant or complainant at the hearing, but if the variance appear to be such that the party has been received or misled, the Justices may, upon such terms as they think fit, adjourn the hearing to some future day, 13 V. c. 35, s. 1.

If the person does not appear before the Justices at the time and place mentioned, and it appears to him, by oath or affirmation, that it was served a reasonable time before that appointed for appearing, such Justice or Justices, upon oath or affirmation, substantiating the matter of such information, &c., may issue a warrant (B) to apprehend the party summoned, and bring him before the same or some other Justice or Justices, to answer to the information, &c., and to be further dealt with according to law, or may, upon oath or affirmation substantiating the information, instead of a summons, issue, in the first instance, a warrant (C.) for apprehending the person, and bringing him before the same or some other Justice or Justices to answer to the information, and to be further dealt with according to law, or if where a summons is issued, and on the day and at the time and place appointed, the party fails to appear, then if it be proved, on oath or affirmation to the Justice or Justices then present, that such summons was duly served a reasonable time before that appointed for his appearance, they may proceed ex parte to the hearing, and to adjudicate thereon, as fully as if the party had personally appeared, 13 V., c. 35, s. 2.

Every warrant to apprehend a defendant to answer, &c., shall be under the hand of the Justice issuing it, and may be directed either to any Constable, or other person by name, or generally to the Constable of the parish with in which it is to be executed, without naming him, or to such Constable, and all other the Constables of the parish within which the Justice has jurisdiction, or generally to all the Constables within such last mentioned parish, stating shortly the matter of the information, &c., and name, or otherwise describe the person against whom it is issued, and shall order the Constable or person to whom it is directed, to apprehend the defendant, and bring him before one or more Justices as the case requires of the same parish to answer, and to be further dealt with according to law. It shall not be necessary to make such warrant returnable at any particular time, but it may remain in force until executed, and may be executed by apprehending the defendant at any place within the parish within which the Justices issuing it have jurisdiction, or in case of fresh pursuit, at any place in the next adjoining parish or place, within 7 miles of the border of such first mentioned parish, without having such warrant backed as after mentioned; and in all cases where the warrant is directed to all Constables or Peace Officers in the parish within which the Justice has jurisdiction, any Constable, &c. ; for any parish within the jurisdiction for which such Justices acted when granting the warrant, may execute it, as if it were directed specially to such Constable by name, and notwithstanding the place in which it is executed is not within the parish for which he is Constable, &c., and such of the provisions and enactments in 13 V., c. 24, (s 8-9) as to the backing of any warrant, and the indorsement thereon by a Justice or other officer, authorizing the person bringing such warrant, and all other persons to whom it was originally directed, to execute the same within the jurisdiction of the Justice or officer making such indorsement as are applicable to this Act, shall extend to all such warrants, and to all war-

Defects in warrant, variances between it and evidence
rants of commitment issued under this Act, as fully as if repeated and made parts of it. No objection shall be allowed to any such warrant for any alleged defect in substance or in form, or for any variance between it and the evidence on the part of the informant or complainant, but if any such variance appear to be such that the party apprehended has been thereby deceived or misled, the Justices, upon such terms as they think fit, may ad-

Adjournment and committal or discharge on bail
journ the hearing to some future day, and in the meantime may commit (D) the defendant to the house of correction, or other prison, lock-up-house or place of security, or to such other custody as they think fit, or discharge him upon his recognizance (E.), with or without surety at their discretion, conditioned for his appearance at the time and place at which the hearing is ad-

Forfeited recognizance
journed. Where a defendant is discharged upon recognizance, and does not afterwards appear at the time and place mentioned, the Justice who has taken the recognizance, or any other then there present, upon certifying (F.) on the back of the recognizance his non-appearance, may transmit the recognizance to the Clerk of the Peace of the parish within which it was taken, to be proceeded upon as other recognizances; and such certificate shall be sufficient prima facie evidence of his non-appearance, 13 V., c. 35, s.3.

Execution of summons out of parish without endorsement
Every summons or warrant for the apprehension of any person charged with any offence issued by any Justice in any parish, may be served or executed out of the parish by the Policeman or Constable to whom it is directed, or any other, and shall have the same force as if it had been originally issued, or subsequently endorsed by a Justice having jurisdiction in the parish where it is served or executed, 23 V., c. 16, s. 1.

Taking bail out of parish for appearance
Any Justice before whom any person is brought under a warrant, who is apprehended in another parish, may take bail by recognizance, for his appearance before the Justices of the parish in which the offence was committed, in such an amount as he thinks fit, 20 V., c. 16, s 3.

Warrants against persons on board ship
Warrants given by Justices against any person on board any ship or vessel, may be directed to the Provost-Marshal or his Deputy, or any of the Constables of the place, according to the tenor of the warrant. Fee for executing, 3s. (1s 9d stg.), 35 C. 2, c. 4, s. 7.

Description of property of partners &c.
In any information, &c., or the proceedings therein, in which it is necessary to state the ownership of any property belonging to or in the possession of partners, joint-tenants, parceners, or tenants in common, it shall be sufficient to name one of, and to state the property to belong to the person so named, and another or others, as the case may be, and whenever necessary to mention for any purpose any partners, &c., it shall be sufficient so to describe them ; and whenever in any information, &c., or the proceedings thereon, it is necessary to describe the ownership of any work or building, made, maintained or repaired at the expense of any parish, or of any materials for the making, altering or repairing of the same, or of any goods provided at the expense of any parish, they may be described as the property or goods of the Churchwardens, other than Kingston, when they shall be described as the property or goods of the Mayor, Aldermen and

See now Highways, 25 V., c. 18, s. 9. Main Roads, 21 V., c 32, s. 5-7
Commonalty of the city and parish of Kingston, and all materials and tools provided for the repairs of Highways at the expense of any parish may be described in like manner, 13 V., c. 35, s. 4.

Every person who aids, abets, counsels or procures the commission of any offence now or hereafter punishable on summary conviction, shall be proceeded against and convicted, either together with the principal offender, or before or after his conviction, and shall be liable, on conviction, to the same forfeiture and punishment as such principal, and may be proceeded against and convicted, either in the parish where such principal offender may be convicted. or in that in which such offence of aiding, abetting, counselling or procuring has been committed, 13 V., c. 35, s. 5. *Aiders and abettors*

Such provisions and enactments in 13 V., c. 24, (s. 4), whereby a Justice for one parish may act for the same while residing, or being in any other parish of which he is also a Justice as are applicable to this Act, shall be incorporated into and extend to all Acts required of, or to be performed by Justices under this Act, 13 V., c. 35, s. 6. *Powers of Justice to act for one parish in another of which he is also a Justice*

If it is made to appear to any Justice, by the oath or affirmation of any credible person, that any person within his jurisdiction is likely to give material evidence in behalf of the prosecutor, or complainant or defendant, and will not voluntarily appear to be examined as a witness, he shall issue, his summons (G. 1) to such person, under his hand, requiring him to be and appear at a time and place therein mentioned, before him or some other Justice or Justices for the same parish as shall then be there, to testify what he knows concerning the matter of the information, &c.; and if any person so summoned, neglect or refuse to appear, and no just excuse be offered, then (after proof, upon oath or affirmation of service, either personally or by, leaving it for him with some person at his last or most usual place of abode, and that a reasonable sum was paid or tendered to him for his costs and expenses) the Justice before whom he should have appeared may issue a warrant (G. 2) under his hand, to bring him at a time and place to be therein mentioned before him, or before such other Justice as shall then be there, to testify as aforesaid, and which warrant may, if necessary, be backed as before mentioned, in order to its being executed out of the jurisdiction of the Justice, or if satisfied by evidence, upon oath or affirmation, that it is probable such person will not attend to give evidence without being compelled to do so, then, instead of a summons, he may issue his warrant (G. 3) in the first instance, and which, if necessary, may be backed. If, on his appearance, either in obedience to the summons, or upon being brought up by virtue of the warrant, such person refuse to be examined upon oath or affirmation concerning the premises, or refuse to take such oath or affirmation, or having taken it, refuse to answer such questions concerning the premises as shall then be put to him without any just excuse for refusal, any Justice present may, by warrant (G. 4) under his hand, commit the person so refusing. to the Common Goal or other Prison for the parish, not exceeding 7 days, unless he, in the meantime, consent to be examined and answer, 13 V., c. 35, s 7. *Summons to witness* *If not obeyed, warrant* *Backing warrant 13 V., c. 24, s. 8 9* *Warrant in first instance*

In cases of complaint upon which a Justice may make an order for the payment of money or otherwise, the complaint need not be in writing, unless required by some particular Act upon which it is framed, 13 V., c. 35, s. 8 *When complaints must be in writing*

Any variance between the information and the evidence in support thereof, as to the time at which the offence or act is alleged to have been committed, shall not be material, if it be proved the information was in fact laid within the time limited for laying it, nor as to the parish within which it is alleged to have been committed, if it is proved to have been committed within the jurisdiction of the Justice by whom the information is heard and determined. If any such variance, or any variance in any other respect between the information and evidence appear to the Justice to be such that the party charged has been deceived or misled, he may, upon such terms as he thinks fit, adjourn the hearing to some future day, and, in the meantime, commit (D.) the defendant to the Gaol, or other Prison or place of security, or to such other custody as he thinks fit, or discharge him, upon entering into recognizance (E) with or without surety, for his appearance at the time and place to which the hearing is adjourned. Where a defendant is discharged upon recognizance, and does not afterwards appear, the Justice who took it, or any Justice then there present, upon certifying (F) upon the back of the recognizance his non-appearance, may transmit the recognizance to the Clerk of the Peace of the parish within which it was taken, to be proceeded upon as other recognizances. The certificate shall be sufficient prima facie evidence of such non-appearance, 13 V., c. 35, s. 9. *Variances, adjourning, hearing, &c*

Complaints and Informations need not be on oath unless warrant issue in first instance

Every complaint upon which a Justice is authorized by law to make an order, and every information for any offence or act punishable upon summary conviction, unless some particular Act otherwise require, may be made or laid without oath or affirmation, except where the Justice issues his warrant in the first instance to apprehend the defendant; and in every case where a warrant issues in the first instance, the matter of such information shall be substantiated by the oath or affirmation of the informant, or by a witness on his behalf, before any warrant is issued. Every such complaint shall be for one matter of complaint only, and not more, and every information for one offence only, and no more, and may be made or laid by the complainant or informant in person, or by his Counsel or Attorney, or other person authorized on that behalf, 13 V., c. 35, s. 10.

Counsel or Attorney

Within what time to be laid

Where no time is limited for making any complaint, or laying any information in the Act relating to each particular case, it shall be made or laid within 6 calendar months from the time the matter arose, 13 V., c. 35, s. 11.

Hearing

Every such complaint and information shall be heard, determined and adjudged by one, two or more Justices as directed by the Act upon which it is framed, or other Act in that behalf, and if there be no such direction, by one Justice; and the room or place in which the Justice sits, shall be deemed an open and public Court, to which the public generally may have access, so far as it can conveniently contain them, and the party against whom the complaint is made, or information laid, admitted to make his full answer and defence, and to have the witnesses examined and cross-examined by Counsel or Attorney on his behalf; and every complainant or informant may conduct his complaint or information, and have the witnesses examined and cross-examined by Counsel or Attorney on his behalf, 13 V., c. 35, s. 12.

Proceedings in default of defendant's appearance

If at the day and place appointed in the summons the defendant does not appear when called, the Constable or person who served him shall declare, upon oath, in what manner he served it, and if it appear that he duly served it, the Justice may proceed to hear and determine the case in defendant's absence, or upon his non-appearance, may issue his warrant as before directed (S. 2), and adjourn the hearing until he is apprehended, when he shall be brought before the same or some other Justice, who shall either by his warrant (H) commit the defendant to the Common Gaol, or other Prison or place of security, or if he think fit, verbally, to the custody of the Constable or person who apprehended him, or to such other safe custody as he deems fit. and order him to be brought at a certain time and place before such Justice as shall then be there, of which order the complainant or informant shall have due notice. If at the day and place appointed, the defendant appear voluntarily, or is brought by virtue of any warrant, then if the complainant or informant having had notice, do not appear by himself, his Counsel or Attorney, the Justice shall dismiss the complaint or information, unless for some reason he think proper to adjourn the hearing upon such terms as he thinks fit, in which case he may commit (D.) the defendant in the meantime to the Common Gaol, or other Prison or place of security, or to such other custody as the Justice thinks fit, or may discharge him, upon his entering into a recognizance (E) with or without surety, conditioned for his appearance at the time and place to which the hearing is adjourned; and if he do not afterwards appear at the time and place mentioned, such any other Justice then there present, upon certifying (F.) on the back of the recognizance the non-appearance of the defendant, may transmit such recognizance to the Clerk of the Peace of the parish within which the offence is laid to have been committed, to be proceeded upon as other recognizances, and the certificate to be prima facie evidence of such non-appearance; but if both parties appear, either personally or by their respective Counsel or Attorneys, before the Justice who is to hear and determine the complaint or information, he shall proceed to do so, 13 V., c 35, s. 13.

Course of proceeding on hearing

Where the defendant is present, the substance of the information or complaint shall be stated to him, and he shall be asked if he have any cause to shew why he should not be convicted, or why an order should not be made, against him as the case may be; and if he thereupon admit its truth, or shew no cause, or no sufficient cause why he should not be convicted, or why an order should not be made against him, the Justice present shall convict him, or make an order against him accordingly; but if he do not admit its truth, shall proceed to hear the prosecutor or complainant, and such witnesses as he may examine, and such other evidence as he may adduce in support of his information or complaint, and also to hear the defendant, and such witnesses as he may examine, and such other evidence as he may adduce in his defence, and also to hear such witnesses as the prosecutor or complainant may examine in reply, if the defendant has examined any witness, or given any evidence other than as to his defendant's general character, but the prosecutor or complainant shall not be entitled to make any observations in reply upon the evidence given by the defendant, nor the defendant to make any observations upon the evidence given by the prosecutor or complainant in reply ; and the Justice having heard what each party has to say, and the witnesses and evidence adduced, shall consider the whole matter, and determine the same, and convict or make an order upon the defendant, or dismiss the information or complaint as the case may be ; and if he convict or make an order against the defendant, a minute or memorandum shall then be made, for which no fee shall be paid, and the conviction (I. 1-3) or order (K. 1-3) shall afterward be drawn up by the Justice in proper form, under his hand, and he shall cause it to be lodged with the Clerk of the Peace, to be filed among the Records of (the Circuit Court, 19 V., c. 10.,) or if he dismiss it, he may, if he thinks fit, being required, make an order of dismissal of the same (L), and give the defendant a certificate (M), which afterwards, upon being produced without further proof, shall be a bar to any subsequent information or complaint for the same matters against the same party. If the information or complaint negative any exemption, exception, proviso or condition in the act on which it is framed, the prosecutor or complainant need not prove such negative, but the defendant may prove the affirmative in his defence if he would have advantage of the same, 13 V., c. 35, s. 14.

Exemptions, &c. negatived in information, &c, to be proved by defendant in his defence

Every prosecutor (notwithstanding any pecuniary interest in the result, 22 V., c. 16), and complainant, whatever his interest may be in the result, shall be a competent witness to support such information or complaint. Every witness shall be examined upon oath or affirmation, which the Justice is authorized to administer, 13 V., c. 35, s. 15.

Competency of witness, testimony on oath, &c

Before or during the hearing, any one Justice, or the Justices present, may adjourn the hearing to a time and place to be then appointed, and stated in the presence and hearing of the party or parties, or their Attorneys or Agents present, and in the meantime may suffer the defendant to go at large, or may commit (D.) him to the Common Gaol or other Prison, or place of security in the parish, or to such other safe custody, as he thinks fit, or may discharge the defendant, upon his entering into a recognizance (E.) with or without surety, at his discretion, conditioned for defendant's appearance at the time and place to which such hearing or further hearing is adjourned ; and if either or both of the parties do not appear personally or by Counsel or Attorney, the Justice present may proceed to such hearing or further hearing, as if they were present, or if the prosecutor or complainant does not appear, may dismiss such information or complaint with or without costs. Where a defendant is discharged on recognizance, and does not afterwards appear, the Justice who took the recognizance, or any other then there present, upon certifying (F.) on the back of the recognizance the non-appearance of the accused, may transmit it to the Clerk of the Peace, to be proceeded upon as other recognizances. The certificate shall be sufficient prima facie evidence of such non-appearance, 13 V, c. 35, s. 16.

Adjournments

In all cases of conviction where no particular form is given by the Act creating the offence or regulating the prosecution, and in all cases of conviction upon Acts hitherto passed, whether any particular Form is given or not, the Justice who convicts may draw up his conviction on paper, in such one of the Forms of conviction (I. 1-3) in Schedule as is applicable, or to the like effect , and where an order is made, and no particular Form is given by the Act, and in all cases of orders under any Act hitherto passed, whether any particular Form is given or not, the Justice may draw it up in such one of the Forms of Orders (K. 1-3) in Schedule as is applicable, or to the like effect. Where by any Act authority is given to commit a person to prison, or to levy any sum upon his goods by distress for not obeying any order, the defendant shall be served with a copy of the minute of such order before any warrant of commitment or distress issues ; but such order or minute shall not form any part of the warrant of commitment or distress, 13 V., c. 35, s. 17.

Form of convictions and orders

Copy minute of order to be served

Costs

In all cases of summary conviction, or of orders, the Justice may award and order therein that the defendant pay to the prosecutor or complainant such costs as to him seems just; and where instead of convicting or making an order he dismisses the information or complaint, he may, by his order of dismissal, order the prosecutor or complainant to pay to the defendant such costs as to him seems just, and the sums allowed for costs shall be specified in such conviction or order, or order of dismissal, and recoverable in the same manner and under the same warrants as any penalty or sum of money therein adjudged to be paid is to be recoverable ; and where there is no penalty or sum to be recovered, such costs shall be recoverable by distress and sale of the goods of the party, and in default of distress, by imprisonment, with or without hard labour, for not exceeding 10 days, unless sooner paid, 13 V., c. 35, s. 18.

As to Justices' powers to award and enforce pa m of compensation in default of performance in cases of orders other than for payment of money, see 21 V., c. 9, s. 2.

Distress Warrant

Where a conviction adjudges a pecuniary penalty or compensation to be paid, or an order requires the payment of a sum of money, and by the Act it is to be levied upon the goods of the defendant, by distress and sale, and also in cases where by the Act no mode of raising or levying such penalty, compensation or sum of money, or of enforcing payment is stated or provided, the Justice making such conviction or order, or any other for the same parish, may issue his warrant of distress (N. 1 2) for levying same, in writing, under his hand; and if after delivery of such warrant of distress to the Constable to whom directed, sufficient distress is not found

Backing

within the jurisdiction of the Justice granting it, then on proof alone being made, on oath, of the handwriting of such Justice before any Justice of any other parish, such Justice of such other parish shall thereupon make an indorsement (N. 3) on such warrant, signed with his hand, authorizing its execution within the limits of his jurisdiction, by virtue of which warrant and indorsement the penalty, or sum and costs, or so much as may not have been before levied or paid may be levied by the person bringing it, or by the persons to whom it was originally directed, or by any Constable or Peace Officer of the last mentioned parish, by distress and sale of the

Where warrant would be ruinous to defendant or his family, or he has no goods

goods of the defendant in such other parish. Whenever it appears to any Justice to whom application is made for any such warrant of distress, that its issue would be ruinous to the defendant or his family, or wherever it appears to him by defendant's confession or otherwise, that he has no goods whereon to levy such distress. he may, instead of issuing such warrant of distress, commit the defendant to the Common Gaol, or other Prison within his jurisdiction, to be imprisoned, with or without hard labor, for such time and in such manner as by law the defendant might be so committed in case such warrant of distress had issued, and no goods could be found, to levy such penalty, or sum and costs, 13 V., c., 35, s. 19.

In case of distress Justice may suffer defendant to be at large, or detain him in custody until return of warrant, or take security for his appearance at time of return

Where a Justice issues any such warrant of distress, he may suffer the defendant to go at large, or verbally, or by a written warrant in that behalf, order the defendant to be detained in safe custody until return is made to such warrant of distress, unless he give security, by recognizance or otherwise, for his appearance before him at the time and place appointed for the return of such warrant of distress, or such other Justice as may then be there. Where a defendant gives security by recognizance, and does not afterwards appear at the time and place mentioned, the said, or any Justice then there present, upon certifying (F.) on the back of the recognizance the non-appearance of the defendant, may transmit such recognizance to the Clerk of the Peace, to be proceeded upon as other recognizances. Such certificate shall be sufficient prima facie evidence of non-appearance, 13 V., c. 35, s. 20.

Commitment in case of insufficient distress

If at the time and place appointed for the return of any such warrant, the Constable return (N. 4) that he could find no goods or chattels, or no sufficient goods or chattels whereon he could levy the sum or sums therein mentioned, together with the costs of levying, the Justice before whom it is returned shall issue his warrant of commitment (N. 5) under his hand, directed to the same or any other Constable, reciting the conviction or order shortly, the issuing of the warrant of distress and return, and requiring such Constable to convey the defendant to the Common Gaol or other Prison or place of security of the parish, and there to deliver him to the keeper, and requiring the keeper to receive the defendant, and there imprison him, or to imprison him and keep him to hard labor in the manner and time di. rected by the Act on which the conviction or order was founded, unless the sum or sums adjudged to be paid, and all costs and charges of the distress, and also of the commitment (the amount being ascertained and stated in such commitment) be sooner paid, 13 V., c. 35, s. 21.

In all cases of convictions or orders, where the Act on which they are founded provides no remedy, in case it be returned to a warrant of dis. tress, that no sufficient goods of the party can be found, the Justice to whom it is made, or any other, may, by his warrant, commit the defendant to the Common Gaol, or other Prison or place of security, for not exceeding one calendar month, unless the sums adjudged to be paid, and all costs and charges of the distress and of the commitment (the amount being ascer. tained and stated in such commitment) be sooner paid, 13 V., c. 35, s. 22.

Commitment where remedy given by the Act

In all cases where the Act by virtue of which a conviction for a penalty, or compensation, or an order for payment of money is made, makes no provision for its being levied by distress, but directs that if it is not paid forthwith, or within a certain time therein mentioned, or to be mentioned in such conviction or order, the defendant shall be imprisoned, or imprisoned and kept to hard labor for a certain time, unless sooner paid, it shall not be levied by distress, but if the defendant do not pay the same with costs, if awarded, forthwith, or at the time specified in such conviction or order, the Justice making it, or any other, may issue his warrant of commitment (O. 1-2) under his hand, requiring the Constables to whom it is directed to take the defendant to the Common Gaol or other Prison, or place of security for the parish, as the case may be, and there to deliver him to the keeper, and requiring the keeper to receive and there to imprison him, or to imprison and keep him to hard labor as the case may be, for such time as the Act directs, unless the sums adjudged to be paid, and also all costs and charges are sooner paid, 13 V., c. 35, s. 23.

Commitment in the 1st instance

Where a conviction does not order the payment of any penalty, but that the defendant be imprisoned, or imprisoned and kept to hard labor for his of. fence, or where an order is not for the payment of money, but for the doing of some other act, and directs that in case of the defendant's neglect or refusal to do such act, he be imprisoned or imprisoned and kept to hard labor, and the defendant neglects or refuses to do such act, the Justice making it, or some other, may issue his warrant of commitment (P. 1-2) under his hand, and requiring the Constables to whom it is directed to take and convey the defendant to the Common Gaol or other prison or place of security for the parish as the case may be, and there to deliver him to the keeper, and re. quiring the keeper to receive the defendant, and imprison him, or imprison him and keep him to hard labor, as the case may be, for such time as the Act directs. In all such cases where, by the conviction or order, any sum for costs is adjudged to be paid by the defendant to the prosecutor or com. plainant, the sum may, if the Justice think fit, be levied by warrant of distress, (P. 3-4) and, in default of distress, the defendant may be commit. ted (P. 5.) to the same Common Gaol or other Prison or place of security, to be imprisoned not exceeding one calendar month, to commence at the termina. tion of the imprisonment he shall then be undergoing, unless such sum for costs, and all costs and charges of the distress and commitment be sooner paid, 13 V., c. 35, s. 24.

Commitment where conviction or order is not for pen. alty or payment of money — enforce. ment of costs; see 21 V., c. 9, c. 2 3

Where a Justice, upon any information or complaint, adjudges the de. fendant to be imprisoned, and he is then in prison undergoing imprison. ment upon a conviction for any other offence, the warrant of commitment for such subsequent offence shall be forthwith delivered to the Gaoler to whom directed ; and the Justice issuing it may award therein that the im. prisonment for such subsequent offence commence at the expiration of the imprisonment to which the defendant had been previously adjudged or sen. tenced, 13 V., c. 35, s. 25.

Commencement of sentence of im. prisonment for sub. sequent offence

Where any information or complaint is dismissed with costs, the sum awarded for costs in the order of dismissal may be levied by distress (Q. 1) on the goods of the prosecutor or complainant ; and in default of distress, or of payment, such prosecutor or complainant may be committed (Q. 2) to the Common Gaol, or other Prison or place of security, for not exceeding 10 days, unless such sum, and all costs and charges of the distress, and of the commitment, (the amount being ascertained and stated therein,) be sooner paid, 13 V., c. 35, s. 26.

Costs of dismissal enforcement

Payment to constable having distress warrant, or to keeper of prison of penalty, &c. ; a discharge

In all cases where any person pays or tenders to the Constable having the execution of the warrant of distress, the sums mentioned, with expenses to the time of payment or tender, he shall cease to execute the same ; and where any person is imprisoned for non-payment of any penalty or other sum, he may pay or cause to be paid to the Keeper of the Prison, the sum in the warrant of commitment mentioned, together with the costs, charges and expenses, if any, therein also mentioned ; and the Keeper shall receive the same, and discharge him, if he be in his custody for no other matter, 13 V., c. 35, s. 28.

Any one Justice may act in all matters preliminary to or after hearing

In all cases of summary proceedings before Justices upon any information or complaint, one Justice may receive the information or complaint, and grant a summons or warrant thereon, issue his summons or warrant to compel the attendance of any witnesses, and do all other acts and matters preliminary to the hearing, even where by the act the information or complaint must be heard and determined by two or more Justices, and after the case has been heard and determined one Justice may issue all warrants of distress or commitment thereon. Not necessary that the Justice who so acts before or after the hearing shall be the Justice or one of the Justices by

Where 2 or more Justices are required they must be present and acting together during the whole of the hearing

whom the case is heard or determined. Where by Act it is or shall be required that any information or complaint be heard and determined by two or more Justices, or that a conviction or order shall be made by two or more Justices, such Justices must be present, and acting together during the whole of the hearing and determination of the case, 13 V., c. 35, s. 29.

Forms

The Forms in Schedule, or Forms to the like effect, shall be valid, and it shall not be necessary that they be, or purport to be made under seal, 13 V., c. 35, s. 31.

Extension of 13 V., c. 35 to subsequent Acts giving summary jurisdiction

All the provisions, remedies and Forms prescribed and given by 13 V., c. 35, extended. wherever applicable, to all Statutes and Acts of the Legislature since enacted and hereafter to be passed, and under which a summary jurisdiction has been or shall be given to Justices, 18 V., c. 57, s. 1.

The Forms to that Act may be adapted to meet the varying circumstances of each case in their application, and may be simplified in their frame and language, provided the substance and effect be preserved, 18 V., c. 57, s. 2.

Constables or Gaolers to pay moneys to Magistrates' Clerks, who are to pay the proportions applicable to parties and account to Collector of Dues weekly for residue, Magistrate's Clerk and Gaolers to render Monthly Accounts to Clerk of Vestry

Wherever upon any summary conviction or order of adjudication by Justices, any Constable or other person receives any penalty or sum of money, he shall pay the same to the Clerk of the Magistrates ; and if any person committed to prison upon any conviction or order for non-payment of any penalty or sum thereby ordered to be paid, desires to pay the same and costs before the expiration of the time for which he is so ordered to be imprisoned by the warrant of commitment, he shall pay the same to the Gaoler or Keeper of the Prison, who shall forthwith pay the same to the said Clerk ; and all sums received by such Clerk, which shall be payable under the judgment or conviction, or under the provisions of the Act in that behalf to the parties, complainant or informant, or otherwise, shall forthwith be paid in the proportions, and according to the directions of the judgment, or conviction or Act, and all other sums so received applicable to any Parochial use or purpose, shall, by such Clerk, in his next weekly or other settlement as after provided, be paid to the (Collector of Dues, 27 V., S. 1, c. 31) of the parish. Every such Clerk and every Gaoler or Keeper of a Prison, shall keep a true and exact account of all such moneys received by him, of whom, and when received, and to whom, and when paid, in the Form, Schedule T. to 13 V., c. 35, annexed, or to the like effect ; and once in every month render a fair copy of every such account to the Clerk of the Vestry, to be laid before the Justices and Vestry, or in Kingston to the Clerk of the Common Council, to be laid before them on or before the 10th of the ensuing month : penalty, £5, to be recovered under 13 V., c. 35, 18 V., c. 57, s. 4.

As to the Stamps and penalties received in the Magistrates' Courts, see Stamps, 28 V., s. 9, s. 45-48.

Clerk Magistrates to make payments to the Collector of Dues weekly, and exhibit his receipt to the Justices at Weekly Sessions. Exhibit accounts monthly

The Clerk of the Magistrates shall weekly pay over to the (Collector of Dues) the fines and penalties paid to and received by him during the preceding week, and exhibit to the Justices at each weekly or other Session in the Parochial Town, the receipt therefor, and every month submit to the Justices at the first Petty Sessions, the original account (to be entered and contained in a Record Book to be kept for the purpose), verified on oath, of all such moneys received by him, and therewith produce the Record Book of all summary adjudications made by the several Courts of Petty Sessions held in the parish during the preceding month, 18 V., c, 57, s. 5.

The Police Officer of each parish shall also, on the 1st day of each month, make a return, on oath, of all distress warrants issued by the Justices in Petty Sessions in the course of each preceding month, shewing the execution of each warrant, or the reason or causes for the non-execution; and the monies to be levied by them shall be forthwith paid over to the Clerk of the Magistrates, to be by him accounted for and paid over to (t) Collector of Dues) and other parties entitled thereto, in the proportions directed by such process, 18 V., c. 57, s. 6.

Police Officer's Monthly Accounts, Receipts to be paid to Magistrates' Clerk

The respective Gaolers and Keepers of Prisons to whom commitments of prisoners for default of payment of fines have been directed, on the 1st day of each month, shall make out a list, verified on oath, of all prisoners committed in the course of the preceding month, to their custody, for non-payment of fines inflicted by the Justices in Petty Sessions; such returns shall state the amounts, if any, paid to procure the release of every prisoner released before the expiry of the term, and disclose in what cases imprisonment, in default of payment, has been fully undergone, and during the currency of the imprisonment, and until its final completion or full payment of the fine, the commitments in course of operation shall be continued in each succeeding monthly return. The monies paid to procure the release of prisoners, shall be received and paid by the Gaoler to the Clerk of the Magistrates, to be by him accounted for, and paid over to the [Collector of Dues]. Such returns shall be laid before the Justices in Petty Sessions, at their first Sessions in each Parochial Town in each month, and by them at such first Sessions duly investigated and compared, and when audited and found to be correct, shall be signed by the Justices, and deposited with the Clerk of the Magistrates, to be preserved among the records of his office, 18 V., c. 57, s. 7.

Gaolers' Monthly Returns — Receipts to be paid to Magistrates' Clerk

Returns to be investigated by the Justice, and signed if correct

It shall be the duty of (the Collector of Dues) once in each week before the Petty Sessions, to demand (if the Clerk of the Magistrates has made default in) payment of the fines of the preceding week, and on non-payment, to make complaint to the Justices, 18 V., c. 57, s. 8.

Collector of Dues to make complaints to Justices of non-payments in any week

The Returns, Lists and Receipts, shall not be subjected to Stamps, 18 V., c. 57, s. 9.

Returns, &c. exempt from stamps

Each Justice, Clerk of the Magistrates, Gaoler, Police Officer or (Collector of Dues) failing or neglecting to do and perform any of the duties or requirements of this Act, shall forfeit not exceeding £5, to be recovered before 2 Justices, 18 V., c. 57, s. 10.

Penalties

Any person interested in the execution of any distress warrant, may assume the defence of any action against any Police Officer or other person, in respect of the execution of any such warrant, 18 V., c., 57, s. 11.

Defence of actions on execution of distress warrants

In civil and criminal cases, one Justice may adjourn, 21 V., c. 9, s. 8.

Adjournments

SCHEDULE—13 V., c. 35.

To A. B. of

Summons to defendant upon an information or complaint, A, s. 1

Whereas information has this day been laid (or complaint hath this day been made) before the undersiged (one) of Her Majesty's Justices of the Peace in and for the said parish of
for that you (here state shortly the matter of the information or complaint) : These are therefore to command you, in Her Majesty's name, to be and appear on   at   o'clock in the forenoon at   before such Justices of the Peace for the said parish as may then be there to answer to the said information (or complaint) and to be further dealt with according to law.

Given under my hand, this   day of
in the year of our Lord   at   in the
parish aforesaid.

J. S.

Warrant where the summons is disobeyed, B, s. 2

To the Constable of   and to all other Peace Officers in the said parish of

Whereas on   last past, information was laid (or complaint was made) before the undersigned (one) of Her Majesty's Justices of the Peace in and for the said parish of for that A. B. (&c., as in the summons): And whereas I then issued my summons unto the said A. B., commanding him in Her Majesty's name, to be and appear on   at o'clock in the forenoon, at   before such Justices of the Peace for the said parish as might then be there, to answer to the said information (or complaint): and to be further dealt with according to law : And whereas the said A. B. hath neglected to be or appear at the time and place so appointed in and by the said summons, although it hath now been proved to me, upon oath, that the said summons hath been duly served upon the said A. B.: These are therefore to command you, in Her Majesty's name, forthwith to apprehend the said A. B., and to bring him before some one or more of Her Majesty's Justices of the Peace in and for the said parish, to answer to the said information (or complaint), and to be further dealt with according to law.

Given under my hand, this   day of in the   year of our Lord, 18.
at   in the parish aforesaid.

                                    J. S.

Warrant in the first instance, C, s. 2, 13

To the Constable of   and to all other Peace Officers in the said parish of

Whereas information hath this day been laid before the undersigned, (one) of her Majesty's Justices of the Peace in and for the said parish of   for that A. B. (here state shortly the matter of the information), and oath being now made before me, substantiating the matter of such information : These are therefore to command you, in Her Majesty's name, forthwith to apprehend the said A. B., and to bring him before some one or more of Her Majesty's Justices of the Peace in and for the said parish, to answer to the said information, and to be further dealt with according to law.

Given under my hand, this   day of in the year of our Lord   at in the parish aforesaid.

                                    J. S.

Warrant of committal for safe custody during an adjournment of the hearing, D, s. 3, 9, 13, 16

To W. T., Constable of   and to the Keeper of the (Common Gaol or other Prison) at

Whereas on   last past, information was laid (or complaint was made) before the undersigned (one) of Her Majesty's Justices of the Peace in and for the said parish of for that (&c., as in the summons): And whereas the hearing of the same is adjourned to the   day of instant, at   o'clock in the forenoon, at and it is necessary that the said A. B. should, in the meantime, be kept in safe custody : These are therefore to command you, the said Constable, in Her Majesty's name, forthwith to convey the said A. B. to the (Common Gaol or other Prison), at and there deliver him into the custody of the Keeper thereof, together with this precept; and I hereby command you, the said Keeper, to receive the said A. B. into your custody in the said (Common Gaol or other Prison), and there safely keep him until the   day of   instant, when you are hereby required to convey and have him, the said A. B., at the time and place to which the said hearing is so adjourned as aforesaid, before such Justices of the Peace for the said parish as may then be there, to answer further to the said infor mation (or complaint), and to be further dealt with according to law.

    Given under my hand, this   day of
        in the year of our Lord, 18   at
        in the parish aforesaid.

                                     J. S.

Be it remembered, that on   A. B. of   Recognizance for the appearance of the defendant where the case is adjourned or not at once proceeded with E, s. 8, 9, 12, 13.
    laborer, and L. M. of   planter, personally
came before the undersigned (one) of Her Majesty's Justices of the
Peace in and for the said parish of   and
severally acknowledged themselves to owe to our Sovereign Lady
the Queen, the several sums following ; (that is to say), the
said A. B. the sum of   and the said L. M. the sum of
            of good and lawful money of this island, to be
made and levied of their several goods and chattels, lands and tenements respectively, to the use of our said Lady the Queen, her
heirs and successors, if he, the said A. B., shall fail in the condition
endorsed.

   Taken and acknowledged the day and year first above-mentioned, at
                    before me.

                                       J. S.

The condition of the within written recognizance is such, that if the
said A. B. shall personally appear on the   day of
               instant, at   o'clock in the fore-
noon, at   before such Justices of the Peace for
the said parish as may then be there, to answer further to the information (or complaint) of C. D., exhibited against the said A. B., and
to be further dealt with according to law, then the said recognizance to be void, or else to stand in full force and virtue.

Take notice, that you A. B., are bound in the sum of   Notice of such re-cognizance to be given to the defen-dant and his surety
           and you L. M. in the sum of
            that you, A. B. appear personally on
           at   o'clock in the forenoon, at
           before such Justice of the Peace for the said parish as
shall then be there, to answer further to a certain information (or
complaint) of C. D., the further hearing of which was adjourned to
the said time and place ; and unless you appear accordingly, the recognizance entered into by you, A. B, and L. M., as your surety, will
forthwith be levied on you and him.

Dated this   day of   18
                                     J. S.

I hereby certify that the said A. B. hath not appeared at the time and   Certificate of non-appearance to be endorsed on the re-cognizance, F, s. 8, 9, 12, 13, 16, 20
place in the said condition mentioned, but therein hath made default,
by reason whereof the within written recognizance is forfeited.

                                   J. S.

To E. F., of   in the said parish of   Summons of [a witness, G 1, s. 7
   Whereas information was laid (or complaint was made) before the
undersigned (one) of Her Majesty's Justices of the Peace in and
for the said parish of   for that)&c., as in
the summons), and it hath been made to appear to me, upon (oath),
that you are likely to give material evidence on behalf of the (prosecutor, or complaint, [complainant] or defendant) in this behalf :
These are therefore to require you to be and appear on
           at   o'clock in the forenoon, at
before such Justices of the Peace for the said parish as may then

be there, to testify what you shall know concerning the matter of the said information (or complaint).

Given under my hand, this   day of
       in the year of our Lord, 18   at
       in the parish aforesaid.

                                J. S.

Warrant where witness has not obeyed summons, G 2, s. 7

To the Constable of   and to all other Peace Officers in the said parish of

Whereas information was laid (or complaint was made) before the undersigned (one) of Her Majesty's Justices of the Peace in and for the said parish of   for that (&c., as in the summons), and it having been made to appear to me, upon oath, that E. F. of   in the said parish, laborer, was likely to give material evidence on behalf of the (prosecutor), I did duly issue my summons to the said E. F., requiring him to be and appear on   at   o'clock in the forenoon of the same day, at   before such Justices of the Peace of the said parish as might then be there, to testify what he should know concerning the said A. B., or the matter of the said information (or complaint) : And whereas proof hath this day been made before me, upon oath, of such summons having been duly served upon the said E. F., and of a reasonable sum having been paid (or tendered) to him for his costs and expenses in that behalf : And whereas the said E. F. hath neglected to appear at the time and place appointed by the said summons, and no just excuse hath been offered for such neglect : These are therefore to command you to take the said E. F., and to bring and have him on   at   o'clock in the forenoon, at   before such Justices of the Peace for the said parish as may then be there, to testify what he shall know concerning the matter of the said information (or complaint).

Given under my hand, this   day of
       in the year of our Lord, 18
       at   in the parish aforesaid.

                                J. S.

Warrant for a witness in the first instance, G 3, s. 7

To the Constable of   and to all other Peace Officers in the parish of

Whereas information was laid (or complaint was made) before the undersigned (one) of Her Majesty's Justices of the Peace in and for the said Parish of   for that (&c., as in the summons), and it being made to appear before me, upon oath, that E. F. of   (laborer), is likely to give material evidence on behalf of the (prosecutor) in this matter, and it is probable that the said E. F. will not attend to give evidence without being compelled so to do : These are therefore to command you to bring and have the said E. F. before me, on   at   o'clock in the forenoon, at   or before such other Justices of the Peace for the said parish as may then be there, to testify what he shall know concerning the matter of the said information or (complaint)

Given under my hand, this   day of
       in the year of our Lord, 18   at   in the parish aforesaid.

                                J. S.

Commitment of witness refusing to be sworn or to give evidence, G 4, s. 7

To W. T., Constable of   in the said parish of and to the Keeper of the (Common Gaol or other Prison) at

Whereas information was laid (or complaint was made) before the undersigned (one) of Her Majesty's Justices of the Peace in for the said (Parish) of   for that (&c., as in the summons), and one E. F. now appearing before me, such Justice as aforesaid, on   at

and being required by me to make oath or affirmation as a witness in that behalf, hath now refused so to do- (or being now here duly sworn as a witness in the matter of the said information or complaint, doth refuse to answer certain questions concerning the premises, which are now here put to him), without offering any just excuse for such refusal: These are therefore to command you, the said Constable, to take the said E. F., and him safely convey to the (Common Goal or other Prison), at ,
aforesaid, and there deliver him to the said Keeper thereof, together with this precept; and I do hereby command you, the said Keeper of the said (Common Goal or other Prison), to receive the said E. F. into your custody in the said (Common Gaol or other Prison), and there imprison him for such his contempt, for the space of   days, unless he shall, in the meantime, consent to be examined, and to answer concerning the premises; and for your so doing this shall be your sufficient warrant.

Given under my hand, this   day of
in the year of our Lord, 18   at   in the parish aforesaid.

J. S.

————

To   Constable of   and to the Keeper
of the (Common Goal or other Prison), at

Warrant to remand a defendant when apprehended, II. s. 13

Whereas information was laid (or complaint was made) before the undersigned (one) of Her Majesty's Justices of the Peace in and for the said parish of   for that, (&c., as in the summons or warrant): And whereas the said A. B. hath been apprehended under and by virtue of a warrant upon such information (or complaint), and is now brought before me as such Justice as aforesaid; These are therefore to command you, the said Constable, in Her Majesty's name, forthwith to convey the said A. B. to the (Common Goal or other Prison), at   and there to deliver him to the said Keeper thereof, together with this precept; and I do hereby command you, the said Keeper, to receive the said A. B. into your custody in the said (Common Goal or other Prison), and there safely keep him until   next, the
day of   instant, when you are hereby commanded to convey him at   .
at   o'clock in the forenoon of the same day, before such Justices of the Peace of the said parish as may then be there, to answer to the said information (or complaint), and to be further dealt with acccording to law.

Given under my hand, this   day of
in the year of our Lord, 18   at   in the parish aforesaid.

J. S.

————

To WIT:

Be it remembered, That on the   day of   in the
year of our Lord   at   in the said parish of
A. B. is convicted before the undersigned (one) of her Majesty's Justices of the Peace for the said parish, for that (he, the said A. B., &c., stating the offence, and the time and place when and where committed), and I adjudge the said A. B. for his said offence, to forfeit and pay the sum of   (stating the penalty, and also the compensation, if any), to be paid and applied according to law; and also to pay to the said C. D. the sum of   for his costs in this behalf; and if the said several sums be not paid forthwith, (or on or before   next),* I order that the same be levied, by distress and sale of the goods and chattels of the said A. B.; and in default of sufficient distress,* I adjudge the said A. B. to be imprisoned in the Common Gaol or other Prison, at   in the said parish, (there to be kept to hard labour) for the space of

Commitment for a penalty to be levied by distress, and in default of sufficient distress, imprisonment, II s. 14–17

V V

unless the said several sums, and all costs and charges of the said distress, (and of the commitment) shall be sooner paid.
Given under my hand, the day and year first above-mentioned, at in the parish aforesaid.

J. S.

* Or, where the issuing of a distress warrant would be ruinous to the defendant or his family, or it appears that he has no goods whereon to levy a distress, then, instead of the words between the asterisks,** say, "then inasmuch as it hath now been made to appear to me (that the issuing of a warrant of distress in this behalf would be ruinous to the said A. B. and his family," or " that the said A. B. hath no goods or chattels whereon to levy. the said sums by distress), I adjudge, &c." as above, to the end.

Conviction for a penalty, and in default of payment, imprisonment I 2, s. 14-17

To WIT :

Be it remembered, That on the   day of in the year of our Lord   at   in the said parish, A. B. is convicted before the undersigned (one) of Her Majesty's Justices of the Peace for the said parish, for that he, (the said A. B., &c., stating the offence, and the time and place when and where it was committed), and I adjudge the said A. B. for his said offence, to forfeit and pay the sum of   - (stating the penalty, and the compensation, if any), to be paid and applied according to law ; and also to pay the said C. D. the sum of for his costs in this behalf; and if the said several sums be not paid forthwith (or on or before   next), I adjudge the said A. B. to be imprisoned in the (Common Gaol or other Prison) at. in the said parish, (and there to be kept to hard labour) for the space of   unless the several sums shall be sooner paid.
Given under my hand the day and year first above-mentioned, at in the parish aforesaid,

J. S.

Conviction when the punishment is by imprisonment, &c., I 3, s. 14-17

To WIT :

Be it remembered, That on the   day of   in the year of our Lord   in the said parish, A. B. is convicted before the undersigned (one) of Her Majesty's Justices of the Peace for the said parish, for that (he, the said A. B., &c., stating the offence, and the time and place when and where committed), and I adjudge the said A. B., for his said offence, to be imprisoned in the (Common Gaol or other Prison), at   in the said parish, (and there kept to hard labour) for the space of   , and I also adjudge the said A. B. to pay the said C. D. the sum of for his costs in this behalf; and if the said sum for costs be not paid forthwith (or on or before   next), then* I order that the said sum be levied by distress and sale of the goods and chattels of the said A. B. ; and in default of sufficient distress in that behalf,* I adjudge the said A. B. to be imprisoned in the said (Common Gaol or other prison', and there kept to hard labour for the space of to commence at and from the termination of his imprisonment aforesaid, unless the said sum for costs shall be sooner paid.
Given under my hand the day and year first above-mentioned, at in the parish aforesaid.

J. S.

* Or, where the issuing of a distress warrant would be ruinous to the defendant or his family, or it appears that he has no goods whereon to levy distress, then, instead of the words between the asterisks,** say "inasmuch as it hath now been made to appear to me (that the issuing of a warrant of distress in this behalf would be ruinous to the said A. B. and his family," or "that the said A. B, hath no goods or chattels whereon to levy the said sum for costs by distress), I adjudge, &c.'

To wit :

Be it remembered, That on   complaint was made before the undersigned (one) of Her Majesty's Justices of the Peace in and for the said parish of   for that (stating the facts entitling the complainant to the Order, with the time and place, when and where they occurred), and now at this day, to wit, on
at   the parties aforesaid appear before me, the said Justice, (or the said C. D. appears before me the said Justice, but the said A. B. although duly called, doth not appear by himself, his Counsel or Attorney; and it is now satisfactorily proved to me, on oath, that the said A. B. has been duly served with the summons in this behalf, which required him to be and appear here at this day, before such Justices of the Peace for the said parish as should now be here, to answer the said complaint, and to be further dealt with according to law ;) and now, having heard the matter of the said complaint, I do adjudge the said A. B. (to pay the said C. D. the sum of
forthwith, or on before   next, as the Act may require) ; and also to pay to the said C. D. the sum of   for his costs in this behalf ; and, if the said several sums be not paid forthwith (or before   next,) * I hereby order that the same be levied by distress and sale of the goods and chattels of the said A. B., and in default of sufficient distress in that behalf, * I adjudge the said A. B. to be imprisoned in the (Common Gaol or other Prison), at * in the said parish, (and there kept to hard labour) for the space of   , unless the said several sums, and all costs and charges of the said distress (and of the commitment), shall be sooner paid.

Given under my hand, this   day of   in the year of our Lord   at   in the parish aforesaid.

J. S.

*Or, where the issuing of the distress warrant would be ruinous to the defendant or his family, or it appears that he has no goods whereon to levy a distress, then, instead of the words between the asterisks*** say "then, inasmuch as it hath now been made to appear to me (that the issuing of a warrant of distress in this behalf would be ruinous to the said A. B. and his family," or "that the said A. B. hath no goods or chattels whereon to levy the said sums by distress), I adjudge, &c.

———

To wit :

Be it remembered, That on   complaint was made before the undersigned (one) of Her Majesty's Justices of the Peace in and for the said parish of   for that (stating the facts entitling the complainant to the Order, with the time and place when and where they occurred), and now, at this day, to wit on
at   the parties aforesaid appear before me, the said Justice (or the said C. D. appears before me, the said Justice, but the said A. B. although duly called, doth not appear by himself, his Counsel or Attorney, and it is now satisfactorily proved to me on oath, that the said A. B. has been duly served with the summons in this behalf, which required him to be and appear here on this day before such Justices of the Peace for the said parish as should now be here, to answer the said complaint, and to be further dealt with according to law) ; and now having heard the matter of the said complaint, I do adjudge the said A. B. (to pay to the said C. D. the sum of
forthwith, or on or before   next, or as the Act may require) ; and also to pay to the said C. D. the sum of
for his costs in this behalf ; and if the said several sums be not paid forthwith (or on or before   next), I adjudge the said A. B. to be imprisoned in the (Common Gaol or other Prison), at   in the said parish, (there to be kept to hard labor) for the space of   , unless the said several sums shall be sooner paid.

Given under my hand, this   day of   in the year of our Lord,   at   in the parish aforesaid.   J. S.

Order for any other matter where the disobeying of it is punishable with imprisonment, K 3, s. 14-17

To wit :

Be it remembered, That on   complaint was made before the undersigned, (one) of Her Majesty's Justice of the Peace in and for the said parish of   for that, (stating the facts entitling the complainant to the order, with the time and place when and where they occurred; and now at this day, to wit, on   at   the parties aforesaid appear before me, the said Justice (or the said C. D. appears before me, the said Justice, but the said A. B. although duly called doth not appear by himself, his Counsel or Attorney: and it is now satisfactorily proved to me, upon oath, that the said A. B. has been duly served with the summons in this behalf, which required him to be and appear here at this day, before such Justices of the Peace for the said parish as should now be here to answer to the said complaint, and to be further dealt with according to law) and now, having heard the matter of the said complaint, I do therefore adjudge the said A. B. to (here state the matter required to be done); and. if, upon a copy of a minute of this order being served upon the said A. B. either personally, or by leaving the same for him at his last or most usual place of abode, he shall neglect or refuse to obey the same, in that case, I adjudge the said A. B. for such his disobedience, to be imprisoned in the (Common Gaol or other Prison), at   in the said parish (there to he kept to hard labor) for the space of   , (unless the said order be sooner obeyed, if the act authorize this); and I do also adjudge the said A. B. to pay to the said C. D. the sum of   for his costs in this behalf; and if the said sum for costs be not paid forthwith (or on or before   next). I order the same to be levied by distress and sale of the goods and chattels of the said A. B. (and in default of sufficient distress in that behalf, I adjudge the said A. B to be imprisoned in the said (Common Gaol or other Prison), (and there kept to hard labor) for the space of   to commence at and from the termination of his imprisonment aforesaid, unless the said sum for costs shall be sooner paid.

Given under my hand, this   day of
    in the year of our Lord,   at
    in the parish aforesaid.

                     J. S.

Order of dismissal of an information or complaint, L, s. 14

To wit :

Be it remembered, that on   information was laid (or complaint was made) before the undersigned (one) of her Majesty's Justices of the Peace in and for the said parish of   for that, (&c., as in the summons to the defendant), and now, at this day, to wit, on   at   both the said parties appear before me in order that I should hear and determine the said information (or complaint) (or the said A. B. appeareth before me, but the said C. D., although duly called, doth not appear), whereupon the matter of the said information or (complaint) being by me duly considered, it manifestly appears to me that the said information (or complaint) (is not proved, and*) I do therefore dismiss the same (and do adjudge that the said C. D. do pay to the said A. B. the sum of   for his costs, incurred by him in his defence in this behalf; and if the said sum for costs be not paid forthwith) or on or before   ), I order that the same be levied by distress and sale of the goods and chattels of the said C. D. ; and in default of sufficient distress in that behalf, I adjudge the said C. D. to be imprisoned in the (Common Gaol or other prison), at   in the said parish, (and there kept to hard labor) for the space of   unless the said sum for

---

* If the informant or complainant do not appear, these words may be omitted.

costs, and all costs and charges of the said distress and of the commitment, shall be sooner paid.

Given under my hand, this in the year of our Lord in the parish aforesaid.

day of at

J. S.

I hereby certify, That an information (or complaint) preferred by C. D. against A. B., for that, (&c., as in the summons), was this day considered by me, one of Her Majesty's Justices of the Peace in and for the parish of and was by me dismissed with costs.

Certificate of dismissal, M, s. 14

Dated this day of 18

J. S.

To the Constable of the said parish of and to all other Peace Officers in

Warrant of distress upon an order for the payment of money, N 2, s. 19

Whereas A. B., late of (laborer), was on this day (or on last past), duly convicted before the undersigned (one) of Her Majesty's Justices of the Peace in and for the said parish of for that, (stating the offence as in the conviction), and it was thereby adjudged that the said A. B. should, for such his offence, forfeit and pay, (&c., as in the conviction), and should also pay to the said C. D. the sum of -for his costs in that behalf; and it was hereby ordered, that if the said several sums should not be paid (forthwith), the same should be levied, by distress and sale of the goods and chattels of the said A. B., and it was thereby also adjudged, that in default of sufficient distress, the said A. B. should be imprisoned in the (Common Gaol or other Prison) at in the said parish (and there kept to hard labour) for the space of unless the said several sums, and all costs and charges of the said distress, and of the commitment, should be sooner paid: And whereas the said A. B. being so convicted as aforesaid, and being (now) required to pay the said sums of and hath not paid the same, or any part thereof, but therein hath made default: These are therefore to command you in Her Majesty's name, forthwith to make distress of the goods and chattels of the said A. B.; and if within the space of days next after the making of such distress, the said sums, together with the reasonable charges of taking and keeping the distress shall not be paid, that then you do sell the said goods and chattels so by you distrained, and do pay the money arising by such sale unto the Clerk of the Justices of the Peace of the parish, that he may pay and apply the same as by law is directed, and may render the overplus, if any, on demand, to the said A. B.; and if no such distress can be found, then that you certify the same unto me, to the end that such further proceedings may be had thereon as to the law doth appertain.

Given under my hand, this in the year of our Lord, in the parish aforesaid.

day of at

J. S.

To the Constable of in the said parish of and to all other Peace Officers

Warrant of distress upon a conviction for a penalty, N 1, s 19

Whereas on last past, a complaint was made before the undersigned (one) of Her Majesty's Justices of the Peace in and for the said parish of for that, (&c., as in the order), and afterwards, to wit, on at the said parties appeared before me (or as in the order), and thereupon having considered the matter of the said complaint, I adjudged the said A. B. to pay to the said C. D. the sum of on or before the then next, and also to

pay to the said C. D. the sum of   for his costs
in that behalf; and I thereby ordered that if the said several sums
should not be paid on or before the said   then next, the
same should be levied by distress of the sale of the goods and chattels
of, the said A. B., and it was adjudged, that in default of sufficient
distress in that behalf, the said A. B. should be imprisoned in
the (Common Gaol, or other Prison), at   in the
said parish (and there kept to hard labour) for the space of
unless the said several sums, and all costs and charges of the distress,
(and of the commitment,) should be sooner paid: And whereas the
time in and by the said order appointed for the payment of the said
several sums of   ·   and
hath elapsed, but the said C. D. hath not paid the same, or any part
thereof, but therein hath made default": These are therefore to command you, in Her Majesty's name, forthwith to make distress of the
goods and chattels of the said A. B.; and if within the space of
                    days after the making of such distress, the said
last-mentioned sums, together with the reasonable charges of taking
and keeping the said distress, shall not be paid, that then you do sell
the said goods and chattels so by you distrained, and do pay the
money arising from such sale unto   the
Clerk of the Justices of the Peace for the parish of
that he may pay and apply the same as by law directed, and may
render the overplus, if any, on demand, to the said A. B.; and if no
such distress can be found, then that you certify the same unto me,
to the end that such proceedings may be had therein, as to the law
doth appertain.

Given under my hand, this   day of
      in the year of our Lord,   at
      in the parish aforesaid.

                                        J. S.

Endorsement in
backing a warrant
of distress N 3, s. 19 To WIT:

Whereas proof upon oath hath this day been made before me, one of
Her Majesty's Justices of the Peace in and for the said parish of
                    that the name of J. S. to the within warrant
subscribed, is of the hand-writing of the Justice of the Peace within mentioned; I do therefore authorize W. T., who bringeth to me
this warrant, and all other persons to whom this warrant was originally directed, or by whom the same may be lawfully executed,
and also all Constables and other Peace Officers of the said parish of   to execute the same within the said parish of

Given under my hand, this   day of   18
                                        J. B.

Constables' return
to a warrant of dis-
tress, N 4, s. 21

I, W. T., Constable of   in the parish of
            do hereby certify to J. S., Esquire, one of Her Ma-
jesty's Justices of the Peace for the said parish, that by virtue of
this warrant, I have made diligent search for the goods and chattels
of the within mentioned A. B., and that I can find no sufficient
goods or chattels of the said A. B. whereon to levy the sum within
mentioned.

Witness my hand, this   day of   18
                                        W. T.

Warrant of com-
mitment for want
of distress, N 5, s. 21

To the Constable of   and to the Keeper of the
            (Common Gaol or other Prison), at   in the
said parish of
Whereas, (&c., as in either of the foregoing distress warrants, N., 1—2;
to the asterisk* and then thus:) And whereas afterwards, on the
            day of   in the year
aforesaid, I, the said Justice, issued a warrant to the Constable of
            commanding him to levy the said sums of
            and   by distress and sale of

the goods and chattels of the said A. B. : And whereas it appears to me, as well by the return of the said Constable to the said warrant of distress, as otherwise, that the said Constable hath made diligent search for the goods and chattels of the said A. B., but that no sufficient distress whereon to levy the sums above mentioned could be found : These are therefore to command you, the said Constable of   to take the said A. B., and him safely to convey to the (Common Gaol, or other prison) at aforesaid, and there deliver him to the said Keeper, together with this precept ; and I do hereby command you, the said Keeper of the said (Common Gaol or other Prison) to receive the said A. B. into your custody in the said (Common Gaol or other Prison) there to imprison him (and keep him to hard labour) for the space of   unless the said several sums, and all the costs and charges of the said distress (and of the commitment), amounting to the further sum of   shall be sooner paid unto you the said Keeper, and for your so doing this shall be your sufficient warrant.

Given under my hand, this   day of
      in the year of our Lord,   at
      in the parish aforesaid.

                                                J. S.

To the Constable of   and to the Keeper of the
(Common Goal or other Prison), at   in the said
parish of

Whereas A. B., late of   (laborer), was on this day duly convicted before the undersigned, (one) of Her Majesty's Justices of the Peace in for the said parish, for that (stating the offence as in the conviction), and it was thereby adjudged that the said A. B., for his said offence, should forfeit and pay the sum of
(&c., as in the conviction), and should pay to the said C. D., the sum of   for his costs in that behalf; and it was thereby further adjudged, that if the said several sums should not be paid (forthwith), the said A. B. should be imprisoned in the (Common Goal or other Prison), at   in the said parish (and there kept to hard labour) for the space of unless the said several sums (and the costs and charges of commitment), should be sooner pa   : And whereas the time in and by the said conviction appointed for the payment of the said several sums hath elapsed, but the said A. B. hath not paid the same, or any part thereof, but therein hath made default : These are therefore to command you, the said Constable of   to take the said A B. and him safely to convey to the (Common Gaol or other Prison), at   aforesaid, and there to deliver him to the Keeper thereof together with this p   ; and I do hereby command you, the said Keeper of the said (Common Gaol or other Prison), to receive the said A. B. into your custody, in the said (Common Gaol or other Prison), there to imprison him (and keep him to hard labor) for the space of   unless the said several sums (and the costs and charges of commitment), (amounting to the further sum of   ) shall be sooner paid ; and for your so doing this shall be your sufficient warrant.

Warrant of commitment upon a conviction for a penalty in the first instance, O 1, s. 23

Given under my hand, this   day of
      in the year of our Lord,   at
      in the parish aforesaid.

                                                J. S.

To the Constable of   and to the Keeper of the (Common Gaol or other Prison), at   in the said parish of

Whereas on   last past, complaint was made before the undersigned (one) of her Majesty's Justices of the Peace in and for the said parish of   for that (&c., as in the order), and afterwards, to wit, on   at the parties appeared before (me), the said Justice (or as it may be in

Warrant of commitment on an order in the first instance, O 2, s. 23

the order), and thereupon having considered the matter of the said complaint, I adjudged the said A. B. to pay to the said C. D. the sum of   on or before the   day of   then next, and also to pay to the said C. D. the sum of   for his costs in that behalf, and I also thereby adjudged that if the said several sums should not be paid on or before the   day of   then next, the said A. B. should be imprisoned in the (Common Gaol or other Prison) at   in the said parish, (and there kept to hard labor) for the space of   unless the said several sums should be sooner paid: And whereas the time, in and by the said order appointed for the payment of the said several sums of money hath elapsed, but the said A. B. hath not paid the same or any part thereof, but therein hath made default : These are therefore to command you, the said Constable of   to take the said A. B., and him safely convey to the said (Common Gaol or other Prison) at   aforesaid, and there to deliver him to the Keeper thereof, together with this precept ; and I do hereby command you, the said Keeper of the said Common Gaol or other Prison) to receive the said A. B. into your custody in the said (Common Gaol or other Prison), there to imprison him (and keep him to hard labour) for the space of   unless the said several sums (and the costs, and charges of commitment), amounting to the further sum of   ) shall be sooner paid unto you the said Keeper ; and for your so doing this shall be your sufficient warrant.

Given under my hand, this   day of   in the year of our Lord,   at   in the parish aforesaid.

               J. S.

——

Warrant of commitment on conviction where the punishment is by imprisonment, P 1, s. 24

To the Constable of   and to the Keeper of the (Common Gaol or other Prison), at   in the said parish of

Whereas A. B., late of   (laborer). was this day duly convicted before the undersigned (one) of her Majesty's Justices of the Peace in and for the said parish of   for that, (stating the offence as in the conviction), and it was thereby adjudged that the said A. B. for his said offence should be imprisoned in the (Common Gaol or other Prison), at   in the said parish (and there kept to hard labour) for the space of   These are therefore to command you, the said Constable of   to take the said A. B., and him safely convey to the Common Gaol or other prison, at   aforesaid, and there to deliver him to the Keeper thereof, together with this precept ; and I do hereby command you, the said Keeper of the said (Common Gaol or other Prison), to receive the said A. B. into your custody in the said (Common Gaol or other Prison), there to imprison him (and keep him to hard labour) for the space of   and for your so doing this shall be your sufficient warrant.

Given under my hand, this   day of   in the year of our Lord   at   in the parish aforesaid.

               J. S.

——

Warrant of commitment on an order where the disobeying of it is punishable by imprisonment, P 2, s. 24

To the Constable of   and to the Keeper of the (Common Gaol or other Prison) at   in the said parish of

Whereas on   last past, complaint was made before the undersigned (one) of Her Majesty's Justices of the Peace in and for the said parish of   for that, &c., as in the order), and afterwards, to wit, on   at   the said parties appeared before me (or as it may be in the order), and thereupon having considered the matter of the said complaint, I adjudged the said A. B. to (&c., as in the order), and that if upon a copy of the minute of that order being duly served upon the said A. B., either personally, or by leaving the same for him at his last or most usual place of abode, he should neglect or refuse to obey the same, it was adjudged that in such case the said A. B. for such his disobedience, should be imprisoned in the (Common Gaol or other Prison), at in the said parish, (and there kept to hard labour) for the space of (unless the said order should be sooner obeyed): And whereas it is now proved to me, that after the making of the said order, a copy of the minute thereof was duly served upon the said A. B., but he then refused (or neglected) to obey the same, and hath not as yet obeyed the said order:" These are therefore to command you, the said Constable of to take the said A. B., and him safely to convey to the (Common Gaol or other Prison), at aforesaid, and there to deliver him to the Keeper thereof, together with this precept; and I do hereby command you, the said Keeper of the said (Common Gaol or other Prison), to receive the said A. B. into your custody in the said (Common Gaol or other Prison), there to imprison him (and keep him to hard labour) for the space of , and for so doing this shall be your sufficient warrant.

Given under my hand, this   day of
in the year of our Lord   at
in the parish aforesaid.

J. S.

To the Constable of   and to all other Peace Officers in
the said parish of

Warrant of distress for costs, upon a conviction where the offence is punishable by imprisonment, F 3, s. 24

Whereas A. B. of (labourer), was on last past, duly convicted before the undersigned (one of Her Majesty's Justices of the Peace in and for the said parish, for that (stating the offence as in the conviction), and it was thereby adjudged that the said A. B. for his said offence should be imprisoned in the (Common Gaol or other Prison), at in the said parish, (and there kept to (hard labour) for the space of and it was also thereby adjudged that the said A. B. should pay to the said C. D. the sum of for his costs in that behalf; and it was thereby ordered, that if the said sum of for costs should not be paid (forthwith), the same should be levied by distress and sale of the goods and chattels of the said A. B.; (and it was adjudged that in default of sufficient distress in that behalf, the said A B. should be imprisoned in the (Common Gaol or other Prison), (and there kept to hard labour) for the space of to commence at and from the termination of his imprisonment aforesaid, (unless the said sum for costs, and all costs and charges of the said distress, and of the commitment, should be sooner paid) : And whereas the said A. B. being so convicted as aforesaid, and being required to pay the said sum of for costs, hath not paid the same, or any part thereof, but therein hath made default:" These are therefore to command you, in Her Majesty's name, forthwith to make distress of the goods and chattels of the said A. B.; and if within the space of days next after the making of such distress, the said last-mentioned sum, together with the reasonable charges of taking and keeping the said distress, shall not be paid, that then you do sell the said goods and chattels so by you distrained, and do pay the money arising from such sale to the Clerk of the Justices of the Peace for the parish of that he may pay the same as by law directed, and may render the surplus, (if any), on demand, to the said A. B.; and if no such distress can be found, then that you certify the same unto me, to the end that such proceedings may be had therein as to the law doth appertain.

Given under my hand, this   day of   in the
year of our Lord,   at
the parish aforesaid

J. S.

X X

Warrant of distress for costs upon an order where the disobeying of the order is punishable with imprisonment, P 4, s. 24

To the Constable of   and all other Peace Officers in
the said parish of

Whereas on   last past, complaint was
made before the undersigned or e) of Her Majesty's Justices of the
Peace in and for the said parish of   for that, (&c.,
as in the order) ; and afterwards, to wit, on   at
the said parties appeared before me as such Justice as aforesaid,
(or as it may be in the order), and thereupon, having considered the
matter of the said complaint, I adjudged the said A. B. to (&c., as in
the order), and that if, upon a copy of the minute of that order being
served upon the said A. B., either personally, or by leaving the
same for him at his last or most usual abode, he should neglect or
refuse to obey the same, I adjudged that in such case the said A. B.
for such his disobedience, should be imprisoned in the (Common
Gaol or other Prison), at   in the said parish, (and there
kept to hard labour) for the space of   (unless the
said order should be sooner obeyed), and I thereby also adjudged the
said A. B. to pay to the said C. D. the sum of   for his
costs in that behalf ; and I ordered, that if the said sum for costs
should not be paid (forthwith), the same should be levied of the
goods and chattels of the said A. B, (and in default of sufficient distress in that behalf, I thereby adjudged that the said A. B. should
be imprisoned in the said (Common Gaol or other Prison), (and there
kept to hard labour) for the space of   to commence
at and from the termination of his imprisonment aforesaid, unless the
said sum for costs, and all costs and charges of the said distress, and of
the commitment, should be sooner paid) : And whereas, after the
making of the said order, a copy of the minute thereof was duly
served upon the said A. B., but the said A. B. did not then pay, nor
hath he paid the said sum of   for costs, or any part
thereof, but therein hath made default : These are therefore to command you, in Her Majesty's name, forthwith to make distress of the
goods and chattels of the said A. B. ; and if, within the space of
days next after the making of such distress, the said
last mentioned sum, together with the reasonable charges of taking
and keeping the said distress, shall not be pa , that then you do sell
the said goods and chattels so by you distrained, and do pay the
money arising from such sale to   the Clerk of the
Justices of the Peace for the parish of   that he may pay
the same as by law directed, and may render the overplus, if any,
on demand, to the said A. B. ; and if no such distress can be found,
then that you certify the same unto me, to the end that such proceedings may be had thereon as to the law doth appertain.

Given under my hand, this   day of
in the year of our Lord,   at
in the parish aforesaid.

J. S.

————

Warrant of com-
mitment for want
of distress in either
of the last 2 cases,
P 5, s. 24

To the Constable of   and to the Keeper of
the (Common Gaol or other Prison), at   in the
said parish of

Whereas, (&c., as in the last two forms respectively to the asterisk (*)
and then thus)   And whereas afterwards,
on the   day of   in the year aforesaid,
I, the said J. S., issued a warrant to the Constable of
commanding him to levy the said sum of   for costs, by
distress and sale of the goods and chattels of the said A. B. : And
whereas it appears to me, as well by the return of the said Constable to the said warrant of distress, as otherwise, that the said Constable hath made diligent search for the goods and chattels of the said
A. B., but that no sufficient distress whereon to levy the sum above
mentioned could be found : These are therefore to command you, the
said Constable of   to take the said A. B., and him
safely to convey to the (Common Gaol or other Prison), at
aforesaid, and there deliver him to the Keeper thereof, together with
this precept : And I do hereby command you, the said Keeper of the
said (Common Gaol or other Prison), to receive the said A. B. into

your custody in the said (Common Gaol or other Prison), there to imprison him (and keep him to hard labor) for the space of unless the said sum, and all costs and charges of the said distress (and of the commitment), amounting to the further sum of shall be sooner paid unto you, the said Keeper; and for your so doing this shall be your sufficient warrant.

Given under my hand, this   day of
  in the year of our Lord   at
  in the parish of

             J. S.

To the Constable of   and to all other Peace Officers in
 the said parish of

  Whereas on   last past, information was laid (or complaint was made) before the undersigned (one) of Her Majesty's Justices of the Peace in and for the said parish, for that (&c., as in the order of dismissal); and afterwards, to wit, on at   both parties appearing before me in order that I should hear and determine the same, and the several proofs adduced to me in that behalf being by me duly heard and considered, and it manifestly appearing to me that the said information (or complaint) was not proved, I therefore dismissed the same, and adjudged that the said C. D. should pay to the said A. B. the sum of for his costs incurred by him in his defence in that behalf, and I ordered that if the said sum for costs should not be paid (forthwith), the same should be levied of the goods and chattels of the said C. D. (and I adjudged, that in default of sufficient distress in that behalf, the said C. D. should be imprisoned in the (Common Gaol or other Prison), in the said parish (and there kept to hard labour for the space of   unless the said sum for costs, and all costs and charges of the said distress, and of the commitment, should be sooner paid, (*): And whereas the said C. D. being now required to pay unto the said A. B. the said sum for costs, hath not paid the same, or any part thereof, but therein hath made default: These are therefore to command you, in Her Majesty's name, forthwith to make distress of the goods and chattels of the said C. D.; and if, within the space of   days next after the making of such distress, the said last mentioned sum, together with the reasonable charges of taking and keeping the said distress shall not be paid, that then you do sell the said goods and chattels so by you distrained, and do pay the money arising from such sale to the Clerk of the Justices of the Peace for the said parish of   that he may pay and apply the same as by law directed, and may render the overplus (if any), on demand, to the said C. D.; and if no such distress can be found, then that you certify the same unto me, to the end that such proceedings may be had therein as to the law doth appertain.

Given under my hand, this   day of
  in the year of our Lord,   at
  in the parish aforesaid.

             J. S.

Warrant of distress for costs upon an order for dismissal of an information or complaint, Q 1, s. 26

To the Constable of   and to the Keeper of the
 (Common Gaol or other Prison), at   in the said
 parish of

  Whereas, (&c., as in the last form to the asterisk (*), and then thus):
" And whereas afterwards, on the   day of in the year aforesaid, I, the said Justice, issued a warrant to the Constable of   commanding him to levy the said sum of   for costs, by distress and sale of the goods and chattels of the said C. D.: And whereas it appears to me, as well by the return of the said Constable to the said warrant of distress, or otherwise, that the said Constable hath made diligent search for the goods and chattels of the said C. D., but that no sufficient distress whereon to levy the sum above mentioned could be

Warrant of commitment for want of distress in the last case, Q 2, s. 26

found : These are therefore to command   , the said Constable
of   to take the said C. D., and him safely
convey to the (Common Gaol or other Prison), at   aforesaid,
and there deliver him to the said Keeper thereof, together with this
precept ; and I do hereby command you, the said Keeper of the said
(Common Gaol or other Prison), to receive the said C. D., into your
custody in the said (Common Gaol or other Prison), there to imprison
him (and keep him to hard labor) for the space of
unless the said sum, and all costs and charges of the said distress,
(and of the commitment), amounting to the further sum of
shall be sooner paid unto you, the said Keeper ; and for your so doing
this shall be your sufficient warrant.

Given under my hand, this   day of
        in the year of our Lord,   at
        in the parish aforesaid.

                                        J. S.

Monthly Returns, 18 V., c. 57, s. 4

ACCOUNT OF CLERK OF THE PEACE, AND OF THE KEEPER OF THE (COMMON GAOL, OR OTHER PRISON.)

Monthly Return to the Justices and Vestry of the Parish of (or to the Common Council of the City and Parish of Kingston), of Fines, Penalties, and Sums of Money received by the Clerk of the Peace, (or by the Keeper of the Common Gaol, or other Prison, at) and how applied, from the day of 18 to the 31st day of the same Month.

Name of Party Convicted.	Date.	Offence.	Costs.	Amount thereof paid.	Fine.	Amount thereof paid.	Amount of Fine received for Parish.	Amount of Fine otherwise applied.	Punishment when Fine not paid.	Names of Convicting Magistrates.	Reasons of non-payment, or other observations.

(Signed)

(Clerk of the Peace, or Keeper of the Common Gaol, or other Prison.)

Justices, Actions against.

For acts within his jurisdiction; Case in which malice and want of probable cause to be alleged and proved

Every Action to be brought against any Justice for any act done by him in the execution of his duty as such, with respect to any matter within his jurisdiction, shall be an Action on the case, as for a Tort.; and in the declaration, it shall be expressly alleged that the act was done maliciously, and without reasonable and probable cause : and if at the trial upon the general issue, the plaintiff fail to prove the allegation, he shall be nonsuit, or a verdict be given for the defendant, 13 V., c. 15, s. 1.

For acts without or in excess of jurisdiction

When action not maintainable

For any act done by a Justice in a matter of which by law he has not jurisdiction, or in which he exceeds his jurisdiction, any person injured thereby, or by any act done under any conviction or order made, or warrant issued by such Justice in any such matter, may maintain an Action against him in the same form and in the same case as he might have done before this Act, without making any allegation in his declaration that the act complained of was done maliciously, and without reasonable and probable cause. No such Action shall be brought for any thing done under such conviction or order, until it has been quashed, either upon appeal or upon application to the Supreme Court ; nor shall any Action be brought for any thing done under any such warrant which has been issued by such Justice to procure the appearance of such party, and has been followed by a conviction or order in the same matter, until it has been quashed as aforesaid ; or if such warrant is not followed by any conviction or order, or if it be a warrant upon an information for an alleged indictable offence, nevertheless if a summons were issued previously to, and was served upon the person, either personally or by leaving it for him with some person at his last or most usual place of abode, and he did not appear according to the exigency of such summons, no Action shall be maintained against such Justice for anything done under such warrant, 13 V., c. 15, s. 2.

Where conviction by one and warrant thereon by another Justice

Where a conviction or order is made by one Justice, and a warrant of distress or commitment is granted thereon by another bona fide, and without collusion, no Action shall be brought against the Justice who granted such warrant, by reason of any defect in the conviction or order, or for any want of jurisdiction in the Justice who made it ; but the Action, if any, shall be brought against the Justice who made the conviction or order, 13 V., c. 15, s. 3.

Application to and order of Supreme Court upon Justice to do an act ; no action maintainable

Where a Justice refuses to do any act relating to the duties of his office as such, the party requiring it to be done may apply to the Supreme Court, upon an affidavit of the facts, for a rule, calling upon such Justice, and also upon the party to be affected by such act, to shew cause why it should not be done ; and if after due service of the rule, good cause is not shewn against it, the Court may make it absolute, with or without, or upon payment of costs ; and the Justice on being served with such rule absolute, shall obey the same, and do the act required ; and no Action or proceeding shall be commenced or prosecuted against him for having obeyed such rule and done the act required, 13 V., c. 15, s. 4.

No action for anything done under warrant by reason of defect in conviction confirmed on appeal

Where a warrant of distress or commitment is granted by a Justice upon any conviction or order, either before or afterwards confirmed upon appeal, no Action shall be brought against him for anything done under it by reason of any defect in the conviction or order, 13 V., c. 15, s. 5.

Setting aside proceedings

Where it is enacted that no Action shall be brought under particular circumstances, if any Action is brought, a Judge may, upon application of the defendant, and upon an affidavit of facts, set aside the proceedings, with or without costs, 13 V., c. 15, s. 6.

Commencement of action

No action shall be brought against any Justice for anything done in the execution of his office, unless commenced within 6 calendar months next after the act complained of was committed, 13 V., c. 15, s. 7.

Notice of action

Nor commenced until one calendar month after a notice, in writing, of such intended action has been delivered to him, or left for him at his usual place of abode, by the party intending to commence such action, or by his Attorney or Agent, in which notice the cause of action, and the court in which it is intended to be brought shall be clearly and explicitly stated, and on the back shall be endorsed the name and place of abode of the party intending to sue, and also the name and place of abode or of business of the Attorney or Agent, if served by one, 13 V., c. 15, s. 8.

The venue shall be laid in the (parish or district, 19 V., c. 10) where the act complained of was committed, and the defendant allowed to plead the general issue, and give any special matter of defence, excuse or justification in evidence under such plea at the trial, 13 V., c. 15, s. 9.

Venue—General issue

After notice and before action commenced, the Justice may tender to the party-complaining, or to his Attorney or Agent, such sum as he thinks fit as amends for the injury complained of in the notice, and after action commenced, and at any time before issue joined, may, if he has not made such tender, or in addition to such tender, pay into court such sum as he thinks fit, which tender and payment of money into court, or either, may afterwards be given in evidence by the defendant under the general issue, and if the jury are of opinion the plaintiff is not entitled to damages beyond the sum or sums so tendered and paid into Court, they shall give a verdict for the defendant, and the plaintiff shall not be at liberty to elect to be non-suit, and the sum, if any, paid into Court, or so much as is sufficient to satisfy the defendant's costs shall be paid out of Court to him, and the residue to the plaintiff, or if where money is paid into Court, the plaintiff elect to accept it in satisfaction, he may obtain from any Judge of the Court an order that it be paid out of Court to him, and that the defendant pay him his costs, to be taxed, and thereupon the action shall be determined, and the order be a bar to any other action for the same cause, 13 V., c. 15, s. 10.

Tender and payment of money into Court

If at the trial the p ai t ff do not prove that the action was brought within the time limited, lomt that notice was given one calendar month before action commenced, or if he does not prove the cause of action stated in such notice, or that it arose in the place laid as the venue in the margin of the declaration, he shall be nonsuit, or the Jury shall give a verdict for the defendant, 13 V., c. 15, s. 11.

In what cases non suit or verdict for defendant

Where the plaintiff is entitled to recover, and proves the levying or payment of any penalty or sum under any conviction or order as parcel of the damages he seeks to recover, or if he prove he was imprisoned under such conviction or order, and seeks to recover damages for such imprisonment, he shall not be entitled to recover the amount of such penalty or sum, or any sum beyond, as damages for such imprisonment, or any costs of suit whatsoever, if it be proved that he was actually guilty of the offence, or that he was liable to pay the sum he was ordered to pay, and with respect to such imprisonment that he had undergone no greater punishment than that assigned by law for the offence of which he was convicted, or for non-payment of the sum he was ordered to pay, 13 V., c. 15, s. 12.

Damages

If the plaintiff recover a verdict, or the defendant allow Judgment to pass against him by default, such plaintiff shall be entitled to costs, as if this Act had not been passed, or if in such case it be stated in the declaration that the Act complained of was done maliciously, and without reasonable and probable cause, the plaintiff, if he recover a verdict for any damages, or if the defendant allow Judgment to pass against him by default, shall be entitled to full costs, to be taxed as between Attorney and Client; and in every action against a Justice for anything done by him in the execution of his office, the defendant, if he obtain Judgment upon verdict, or otherwise in all cases, shall be entitled to his full costs, to be taxed as between Attorney and Client, 13 V., c. 15, s. 13.

Costs

Kingston Aqueduct.

The Members of Assembly for St. Andrew and Kingston, and the Justices and Vestry of Kingston were incorporated as " The Trustees of the Kingston Aqueduct," to hold lands, donations, subscriptions, &c., with power to enter into lands in St. Andrew and Kingston, and dig and cut through the same, or any highways, canals, drains, trenches, and gutterings, and build and throw up mounds, dams or walls, to convey the torrents of water occasioned by rains, overflowing of rivers and otherwise, into the sea, and preventing the waters from running into and damaging the streets, lanes, and houses in Kingston, and running into low grounds, or becoming stagnant therein and noisome to the neighbourhood, for which compensation is to be made, 36 G. 3, c. 24.

Commissioners incorporated Their powers (See now Highways and Main Roads)

Kingston Corporation.

Incorporation and powers

The Freeholders and other inhabitants of the City and parish of Kingston, duly qualified according to law to vote in the election of Members of Assembly, incorporated by the name of "The Mayor, Aldermen and Commonalty of the City and Parish of Kingston," with power to sue and be sued, have a Common Seal, and alter the same, and continue to hold any real and personal estate now held and heretofore purchased or acquired by them for the use of the Corporation, and capable of accepting, purchasing and holding any estate, real or personal, and may sell and convey lands of the Corporation for such reasonable sums as may be expedient, or accept other lands in exchange, and apply the moneys arising from such sales for the use and purposes of the Corporation as to them seem expedient, 18 V., c. 61, s. 2.

Race Course

The Mayor, &c., by their corporate name were empowered to purchase and hold land in St. Andrew, called the Race-Course, and any other land and real estate within this Island, for the public use, benefit and purposes of the Corporation ; and the Magistrates, Constables and other Officers of Justice of Kingston, to have full power to execute and exercise their present powers, duties and functions in and upon the Race-Course, as if the lands were within and part of the city and parish of Kingston ; such Race-Course to be at all times open from 5 a. m., until 8 p. m., for the use and recreation of the public, and not to be built upon by any person, 49 G. 3, c. 28, s. 1.

Court House, lands held for use of the poor

A parcel of land in Orange Street, as also a lot of land in Church street, devised for the use of the poor, and also some part of a parcel of land purchased for a Court House for transacting parochial business, binding on Duke-Street, Water-Lane and Harbour-Street, (now part of the present Court Houses) were vested in the Justices and Vestrymen for the time being, with power to rent, lease or demise the same at will, from year to year, or for not exceeding 14 years, for the highest rent that can be obtained, and apply the rents and profits towards supporting the poor of the parish, and any surplusage of the annual rents towards the contingent charges of the parish, 27 G. 3, c. 5.

Mayor, Aldermen and Common Councilmen

One Mayor, 12 Aldermen and 12 Common Councilmen shall be chosen and elected as after directed, 18 V., c. 61, s. 3.

Leases of land to the corporation

The Corporation may demise and lease any of their lands to any person or body corporate, and also lands from any persons or body corporate for the public use, benefit and purposes of the Corporation, for not exceeding 21 years, and apply the moneys to arise therefrom in such manner, for the use and purposes of the Corporation, as to them shall seem expedient, 18 V., c. 61, s. 5.

Triennial election of Mayor

On the 2nd Wednesday in January after the passing of this Act, and on the 2nd Wednesday in January in every third year afterwards, the freeholders and other persons qualified to vote for Members of Assembly for the city and parish shall assemble at such public place within the city, as the Mayor, or in his absence, sickness or default, the first or senior Alderman upon the roll, or in his default, any other Alderman, according to seniority, shall appoint, and then and there, by plurality of votes or voices, elect out of the Mayor and Aldermen for the time being, and such persons as have been Mayor or Aldermen at any time before, one person to be Mayor, who shall thereupon enter upon and continue in his office until the next triennial election of Mayor. In case any Alderman whose term of office may not be ending on that day is elected Mayor, the freeholders and other electors shall assemble and meet at such public place in the city, and such time as the Mayor, &c., shall appoint, and by plurality of votes, elect and choose out of the freeholders an Alderman in his room for so much of his term of office as is unexpired, 18 V., c. 61, s. 6.

Annual election of 4 Aldermen

On the 2nd Wednesday in January in each year, such freeeholders and other electors shall assemble at such public place as the Mayor, &c., shall appoint, and then and there, by plurality of votes, elect out of the freeholders of the parish 4 Aldermen in the room of the 4 Aldermen whose term of office expires at such respective periods, who shall thereupon enter upon and continue in their office for 3 years and no longer, unless re-elected ; and upon such election the Aldermen elected (not being Aldermen who had retired in rotation, and who shall, on re-election, retain the order and seniority they enjoyed before their retirement) shall be put upon the roll next after the Aldermen then already on the roll, the immediate order and seniority of the Aldermen then being elected for the first time, being determined as between themselves by lot, 18 V., c. 61, s. 7.

On the 2nd Wednesday in January in each year such freeholders and other electors shall assemble at such place to be appointed as in the case of the election of Aldermen, and then and there, by plurality of votes, elect, out of the freeholders of the parish, 4 Common Councilmen in the room of the 4 Common Councilmen whose term of office expires, who shall thereupon enter upon and continue in their office for 3 years, and no longer, unless re-elected. In case of an election of Alderman, any Common Councilman for the time being shall be eligible to be an Alderman. In case of an election or appointment to any office by the Common Council, any Alderman or Common Councilman willing to accept the appointment, may be elected. In case any Common Councilman is elected an Alderman, or any Alderman or Common Councilman is elected to any office, the freeholders and electors shall assemble at such time and place as the Mayor &c. shall appoint, and then and there by plurality of votes elect, out of the freeholders, an Alderman or Common Councilman in the room of the Alderman or Common Councilman elected to any office, or of the Common Councilman elected to be an Alderman, for so much of his term of office as may be unexpired, 18 V., c. 61, s. 8. Annual election of 4 Common Councilmen

Common Councilmen eligible to be Aldermen Aldermen or Common Councilmen may be elected to offices Vacancy to be filled up by new election

The qualification to vote at any election of Mayor, Aldermen, or Common Councilmen, or of any officer to be elected by the voice of the electors, shall be similar to, and regulated and governed by the laws, for the time in force for declaring and regulating the qualification of voters for Members of Assembly, 18 V., c. 61, s. 9. Qualification of voters

No person shall be eligible to the office of Mayor, Alderman or Common Councilman, who has not been assessed for direct taxes in Kingston, in his own right, for the year immediately preceding his election, to the amount of £3, and who has not actually paid the taxes, or such portion as at the time of election was due by him, 18 V., c. 61, s. 10. Eligibility as Mayor, &c. £3 taxes

No candidate shall be nominated as Mayor, Alderman, or Common Councilman, who does not possess the qualifications required; and the Recorder, or persons taking the poll, are prohibited from receiving the nomination of any candidate who does not produce at the poll, and previous to his nomination, a certificate from the Clerk of the Common Council that he has been assessed for direct taxes in Kingston, in his own right, for the preceding year, in the amount of £3, and receipts of the [Collector of Dues] shewing he had actually paid such taxes, or the portion due at the time of election, 18 V., c. 61, s. 11. Qualification to be produced before nomination

Nor be capable of sitting or voting, until he has produced to the Recorder, or a Justice, previous to taking the oaths, (s. 22) a certificate and receipts as above, 18 V., c. 61, s. 12. And before taking oaths

If any member of the Common Council becomes bankrupt, or is declared an Insolvent Debtor, or takes the benefit of any law for the discharge of any Insolvent Debtor from his debts, or becomes a public defaulter, or is convicted of felony or infamous crime, he shall be disqualified to sit; and the voters shall meet at such places and time as the Mayor, &c. appoints, by plurality of votes, to elect from the qualified inhabitants a person in his room for the remainder of his term of office, 18 V., c. 61, s. 13. Disqualifications

Every election shall commence between 8 and 9 a. m., and be kept open until 4 p. m., and the poll shall be taken by the Recorder, or other persons appointed by the Mayor, &c., who shall enter the names of the persons elected in a book for the purpose. The Mayor, &c., may appoint any number of polling places, with competent persons to act, as may be necessary for completing the elections within the time. Not to prevent the closing the Poll with the general consent of the candidates, where an election is contested, previous to 4 o'clock, and where not contested, 2 hours after opening it. The Recorder, &c., in case of obstruction or riot may adjourn the poll to a future day, of which he shall then and there give notice, and proceed on the day of adjournment to complete the election within the hours before limited, and again adjourn if further obstruction be offered, until concluded without obstruction. In every case of election, whether by the electors or Common Council, where two or more candidates having each a larger number of votes than the others, Elections opening and closing poll; adjournment in case of riot

quality of Vote

each have the same number of votes for any office, it shall be determined by lot which is to be considered duly elected, 18 V., c. 61, s. 14.

Common Council Ordinances. The Mayor, Aldermen and Common Councilmen, for the time, shall be called "The Common Council of the City and Parish of Kingston," who, or any 7 (of whom the Mayor and one Alderman, or 2 Aldermen, to be part) shall have power to make bye-laws, ordinances and regulations relative to

Fires, Firewardens Preventing and extinguishing Fires, for the appointment of Firewardens, and raising, organizing and directing a sufficient force or complement of men for working Fire Engines, and compelling the service of competent men as officers of Engines, and as firemen, and enforcing their attendance on duty when called upon in the City and Parish.

Wells, Pumps, &c Making better, ordering, preserving, and keeping the public Wells, Fountains, Pumps, and Aqueducts (that at Rock Fort excepted.)

Night Watch Establishing a nightly watch.

Streets (See now Highways, 25 V., c. 18, s. 3, 5 &c. Laying out new Streets, Squares and places, and extending the present Streets, and for amending, repairing, and keeping in good order all Streets, Lanes, Alleys, Squares, Places, and Highways, and relative to encroachments and impediments therein, and other offences, evils and inconveniences.

Dangerous, &c., Trades Dangerous, noisome or offensive trades in particular Streets and places.

Harbour The Harbour, and Duties of the Harbour Master, and offences, evils, and inconveniences touching the Harbour, without prejudice to the Governor's right to appoint the Harbour-Master.

Markets Markets, but not to extend to regulating, or ascertaining the price of any commodity or article brought for sale, nor to affect the right of the office of Clerk of the Market.

Lighting Lighting the City and Parish in the night.

Seamen Soldiers Foreigners Regulating Seamen, Soldiers, and Foreigners in respect to their being in the streets, or elsewhere than in their ships, quarters, residences, or lodgings in the night time and otherwise, as may appear expedient for preserving the peace.

Taverns Retailers Taverns, Grog-Shops, Punch and Tippling Houses, and Retailers.

Play houses, &c Play-Houses and places of public amusement.

Crimp houses Crimp Houses and Crimps.

Hawkers and Pedlars Hawkers, Pedlars, and Higlers.

Forestalling and regrating Forestalling and regrating.

Drays, Carts, &c Drays, Draymen, Water Carts, Wains, Waggons, and other Carriages used in the transport and carriage of goods, grass, wood, or fruit, for sale, or employed for hire, their owners and workers.

Places where to ply Places whereon, whence, and wherein, such owners, workers and carriages shall ply and carry, and be worked, and their licensing.

Wherries Boats Wherries and Boats, Wherrymen and Boatmen, in the Harbour.

Canoes fishing and plying for hire Registering and Licensing of Fishing and other Canoes plying in the Harbour.

Putrid, &c., provisions Putrid and damaged or decayed provisions and commodities. The places where goods shall be exposed for sale.

Sale of Goods Obstructions on piazzas and thoroughfares by goods there improperly exposed.

Obstructions on Piazzas Decayed buildings, huts, vacant lots of land.

Decayed buildings Vacant lands nuisances Nuisances in the City and Parish or Harbour, and their abatement.

Hogs and Goats Hogs and Goats at large.

Fireworks and Firearms Firing of squibs, rockets, fireworks, guns, pistols, or fire-arms,

Furious riding and driving, Breaking horses Riding or driving horses or cattle furiously or negligently, and breaking horses.

Conducting and driving horned and other cattle and stock in, into or through the City and parish. *Driving stock*

Flying Kites. *Kites*

Warning meetings of Common Council, times and places of meeting, absence, leaving without cause, and generally for ordering and regulating the business of the Corporation, and members and officers, and enforcing their attendance. *Warning, &c, Common Council Officers*

Any other matters which may concern the good government and police of the City and Parish. *Good Government*

Such by-laws and ordinances not to be repugnant to the prerogative or the laws in force : and the Common Council or any 7, of whom the Mayor and one Alderman or 2 Aldermen to be part, may appoint in such ordinances reasonable penalties for non-observance, non-performance, or breach, not exceeding, if a fine, £60, or if imprisonment, 3 calendar months with or without hard labor. Not necessary to affix the Corporation Seal to any ordinance. 18 V., c. 61, s. 15. *Not to be reprignant to law, Penalties*

The Harbour of Kingston shall include all the water between the shores in Kingston and Port Royal to the Eastward of Kingston and the shores in Kingston, St. Andrew, and St. Catherine, to the Westward of Kingston, and the Palisades or shores in Port Royal, and extending from the Head of the Harbour to Passage Fort, in St. Catherine, and to Gallows Point in Port Royal, and from the latter to the Southernmost point of the Twelve Apostles Battery, 18 V., c. 61, s. 16. *Harbour of Kingston*

Offenders against the ordinances shall be tried before 2 Justices, and on conviction the adjudication shall be enforced, in case of a fine (unless forthwith paid) to be levied by distress and sale by warrant under the hand and seal of one or more of the convicting Justices, and when levied or paid, paid over to the Treasurer or Bankers of the city and parish to the use of the Corporation, the overplus to the party, the charges being deducted, such charges to be fixed by the Common Council. The warrant shall contain a direction that in case a sufficient distress cannot be found, the offender be taken by the body and stand committed for a time to be mentioned, not exceeding 3 calendar months without bail or mainprize, and with or without hard labour, unless the fine and charges are sooner paid; and in case of adjudication of imprisonment, the offender shall be committed by warrant of one or more convicting Justices for the time to be adjudged to the Common Gaol, House of Correction or Penitentiary, with or without hard labor. Persons convicted may appeal, 18 V., c. 61, s. 17. *Trial of offences Punishments* *Appeal*

The Common Council on the 1st Monday in January, in each year, shall elect by plurality of votes a Recorder to assist in preparing ordinances and advise the Common Council in all matters of law, a Solicitor, 2 Churchwardens, and in case of a vacancy, (see Vestry 16 V., c. 43,) Clerk of the Common Council, (who shall be appointed out of inhabitants householders of the city and parish), so many Constables as the Common Council deem necessary, a Sexton, Beadles, Organists of the several Churches and Chapels and such other Officers as they deem necessary, (all to be appointed out of the inhabitants of the city and parish) and may fill up vacancies as they occur. No officer shall act as a Justice while he holds office, under pain of dismissal. Not to affect the right of the Custos to appoint a Clerk of the Peace, The Common Council may for good cause remove officers and appoint others for the remainder of their term of office, and may give leave of absence for a reasonable time, the party providing to their satisfation a sufficient deputy to perform the duties during his intended absence, 18 V., c. 61, s. 18. *Election of officers. Recorder Solicitor 2 Churchwardens Clerk of Common Council Constables Sexton Beadles Organists And others Officers not to act as Justices Clerk of the Peace Removal of officers Leave of absence*

The Common Council shall have the superintendance, regulation, direction, administration and management of Wolmers Free School, the Poor House and Parochial Hospital, and the business and affairs of those Institutions, and the nomination and appointment of all officers teachers,, and servants, 18 V., c. 61, s. 19. *Woolmer's Free School, Poor House, Parochial Hospital*

The Common Council may establish and put into execution, regulations and provisions concerning security to be entered into by all or any officers for the execution of their offices, and discharge of the trusts reposed in them, and appoint and alter their remuneration, 18 V., c. 61, s. 20. *Officers security Remuneration*

Oaths of Mayor,
&c

Recorder, Church-
warden, Coroner,
Collector of Dues
Roman Catholics,
Jews
See oaths, 26 V.,
s. 2, c. 3
Roman Catholics,
10 G. 4 c, 12
Senior Alderman,
to act in case of
Mayor's death, &c

Every person elected Mayor, Aldermen or Common Councilmen, before sitting or voting in the Common Council, shall take and subscribe the oaths
of allegiance, supremacy and abjuration, to be administered by the Recorder
or in his absence by a Justice. Persons appointed Recorder, Churchwarden or Coroner or Collector of Taxes, shall take and subscribe an oath
for the faithful discharge and execution, of their office before a Justice.—
Roman Catholics or Jews need not take, or subscribe any other oaths, than
the oath of allegiance or such as may be established by law, 18 V., c. 61, s. 22.

In case of absence, sickness, or death of the Mayor, the first or senior
Alderman or any other according to Seniority, may execute the duties and
trusts belonging to the office, 18 V., c. 61, s. 23.

Penalty for not
taking office after
election

If any person elected Mayor Alderman or Common Councilman, and
having notice from the Clerk of the Common Council, for 10 days, refuses,
neglects or delays to take upon himself and execute the office, the Common
Council may assess or levy a fine upon him as to the office of Mayor, not
exceeding £100, Alderman or Common Councilman not exceeding £50,
and another election shall take place without further notice to the person so
refusing or neglecting. Any person so fined, shall not be again nominated or
elected at the election consequent upon his refusal, &c. The fine, if not
paid, shall be levied by distress and sale by warrant under the hand of the
Mayor or any Alderman, and paid to the Treasurer or Bankers for the use
of the Corporation, and any overplus rendered, on demand, to the party, deducting charges, 18 V., c. 61, s. 24.

New election in
case of death, ab-
sence, or change of
residence, beyond
4 miles of Mayor

In case the Mayor, dies, goes off the island, changes or alters his permanent residence beyond 4 miles from the parish Church within the time
for which he has been elected, he shall be ineligible to be nominated and
elected, and the qualified male inhabitants shall assemble at such places
and time as the first or senior Alderman upon the roll, or in his default, any other Alderman according to seniority, shall appoint, and by
plurality of votes, elect out of the Aldermen, or persons who have been
Aldermen duly qualified, another May or for the remainder of the term of
office, 18 V., c. 61, s. 25.

Similar provision in case of the death, &c., of an Alderman or Common
Councilman. The Common Council may grant leave of absence to any
member for not exceeding 3 calendar months, and his seat shall not be vacated,
but not more than 2 members of the Corporation shall be absent on leave
at the same time, 18 V., c. 61, s. 26.

Similar provision for the new election of Recorder, Solicitor, Churchwardens, or Clerk of the Common Council in case of death, going off the
island without leave of the Common Council, or change of permanent residence beyond 4 miles from the Church, from out of the inhabitants, householders, or in case of any other officer from out of the inhabitants of the
city and parish, 18 V., c. 61, s. 27.

The Common Council shall be summoned and held so often and at
such public places within the city as the Mayor appoints, and if, upon the
requisition of 5 members, the Mayor, &c. refuses or neglects to call a meeting,
any two Aldermen may summon a meeting at such place and time as to

them seem expedient. The Common Council or any 7 may fine any officer or member who, after notice, fails to appear or attend without reasonable cause to be allowed by them, or who is guilty of rude and contumacious behaviour, whereby the business of any meeting is obstructed or prevented, or leaves the Court previous to an adjournment without leave of
the Chairman, so as no fine for any one default exceed £5, the fine to be
levied by distress and sale, &c., as directed, s. 24, 18 V., c. 61 s. 28.

Open and unoc-
cupied lands, no-
tice to enclose

When owners or p   in possession and entitled to any open and
unoccupied lots of land are unknown, the Common Council may cause notice
to be served upon them, to enclose, or cause them to be enclosed, and if
they neglect or refuse to enclose them within 60 days after service, and
they remain open, immediately after the expiration of the 60 days, the offender shall, upon conviction, before 2 Justices, forfeit not exceeding £2,
and in case of refusal or non-payment of any such sum, within such period as
the Justices direct, they or any other 2 Justices may issue their warrant to
levy the same and costs and charges by distress and sale, rendering the
overplus to the offender, 18 V., c. 61, s. 29.

The Common Council, if the owner, &c., after the expiration of the notice, has neglected, or refused to enclose, or in the event of his being unknown, may cause all such open und unoccupied lots or spaces of land to be enclosed, as they think fit, and enter into possession, and after notice given as directed, cause them or any of them to be sold at public outcry, or by private contract for the most money that can be had, and invest the money as after provided, and enter into, sign, seal, and deliver all necessary conveyances to purchasers, which shall be conclusive upon all persons. Notice of intention to enclose and sell shall be given to the owner or person in possession or 'entitled, if known, at least 3 calendar months before putting up or offering them for sale; if not known, notice shall be given in any two of the daily newspapers, for at least 3 calendar months previously, and after that period such sales or contracts for sale shall be conclusive against all persons, and the Common Council may receive from purchasers the sums for which they are sold, which after deducting the costs and expenses attending the enclosing and sale, shall be paid to the Receiver General to answer the claims of persons entitled to receive the same 18 V., c. 61. s. 30.

Sale and conveyance Notices. Investment of purchase money

No Action shall be commenced for any thing under this or any other Act concerning the order and Police of the City and Parish, or the Ordinances, after a sufficient satisfaction or tender, or until 30 days notice in writing to the person against whom it is intended to be brought, or after 6 months next after the thing done. The defendant may plead the general issue, and give the special matter in evidence, and that it was done under such Acts or Ordinances; and if so, or if the Action has been commenced after the time, or in any other manner than directed, the Jury shall find for the defendant; and upon a verdict, or if the plaintiff is nonsuited, or discontinues after appearance, or if upon demurrer judgment is given against him, the defendant shall recover full costs, to be taxed, and have the like remedy as defendants in other cases, 18 V., c. 61, s. 31.

Protection in case of actions

In case of an Action of Replevin for any distress taken in pursuance of this or any other Act or Ordinance as above, the defendant may plead the general issue, and give special matter in evidence, and that it was taken under such Acts or Ordinances; and if so, the Jury shall find for the defendant, &c., as in s. 31, 18 V., c. 61, s. 32.

In case of replevin

The Common Council may, from time to time, include in the Ways, and Means of the City and Parish, all expenses incurred in carrying out this Act, 18 V., c. 61, s. 33.

Expenses under this act to be included in ways and means

Kingston Gas Company.

Power given to William George Astwood, Esquire, to form a Company for the purpose of manufacturing and supplying Gas for lighting the Streets and Public and Private Buildings of the City of Kingston, with exclusive privileges for 21 years, (s. 43), the Company to have a Capital of at least, £20,000, of which at least, £10,000, one-half, shall be subscribed for before any of their powers are put in force, (s. 3), the works to be commenced on or before 1st March, 1866, and ready for use in the portion of the City circumscribed by, and including North Street in the North; West Street in the West; Little Port-Royal Street, Port-Royal Street and Harbour Street in the South, and Wildman Street and High Holborn Street in the East, on or before 1st March, 1869, (s. 11.) If from any cause the Company fail to deliver a full and sufficient supply of Gas for the space of 6 months continually, their powers shall cease, (s. 12), the maximum rate for every 1000 cubic feet of Gas supplied, and meter-rent to be fixed and allowed by the Governor or by Arbitration on the completion of the undertaking, (s. 57), and subject to amendment at any time after the first 3 years, (s. 58), and with power to the Legislature after 21 years, from 1st January, 1866, to revise the rates and charges, so as to reduce the net profits to not less than 15 per cent. per annum, (s. 59), 28 V., c. 40.

Power to establish

Capital

Works

Supply

Rates, &c

Kingston and Liguanea Water Works' Company.

Company Incorporated for supplying the City of Kingston and Liguanea with Water from Hope River, as the "Kingston and Liguanea Water Works' Company," 22 V., c. 36.

Incorporation

Exclusive privileges

The Company shall have the exclusive right and privilege of supplying the City of Kingston with Water for 21 years, from 31st December, 1858 and of laying, making, enlarging, altering, completing and maintaining all Water Works aqueducts, Reservoirs, Gutters, Pipes and other necessary Works, 22 V., c. 36, s. 12.

Powers for upholding works, distributing water, &c

For distributing the Water to the different inhabitants, the Company, their Agents, Officers, workmen and servants may maintain their present works, and dig and break up the soil and pavements, brickways of any road, street or lane, highway, foot paths, commons, alleys, passages and public places within and near to the City and Parish of Kingston and St. Andrew, and sink and lay Pipes, Tanks and other conveniences, put stop-cocks or plugs or branches from pipe to pipe in such places through yards, or brick or stone walls, and alter the position of, and repair, relay and maintain such pipes, tanks, stop-cocks and plugs, and do all acts they think necessary and convenient for completing, repairing and using the Works, and may uphold their present, and also make houses and other works, and all such cisterns, ponds, basins, main-pipes, haud-pipes, stand-pipes, service-pipes, branches of lead and other metal pipes, cocks, chambercocks in common valves, fire-plugs, air-plugs, fire-cocks, main feeders, janapers and pumps as the Company think requisite' and divert, alter, repair, widen, enlarge, amend and discontinue the same, doing as little damage as may be in the execution of the powers granted and making full satisfaction for any damages occasioned to the party injured, 22 V., c. 36, s. 38.

Agreement for supply of water, enforcement, stop page

Such of the inhabitants of the City of Kingston and district of Liguanea and others as are desirous of having Water from the Water Works laid into their yards and premises, shall apply to the Company or Directors and agree with them for the quantity of Water to be delivered to the applicant daily and the weekly rate or price to be paid for such water (not exceeding 2s. per week for each 100 gallons, s- 33), and sign or attach his name to a book called the Order Book, and therein agree as to the rate according to the quantity the Company agrees to supply during a prescribed period, at which the Water may he laid on the district in which the house or premises are ; such persons paying quarterly, monthly or weekly as agreed on. If any rate or sum is in arrear, the Company may charge the rate payer or occupier with the original price of the Pipe and Cock, and the expenses of laying down the same ; and the rate in arrear with the original cost of the Pipe and Cock, and the expense of laying the same down, shall be recovered by the Company by distress and sale of the goods of such rate payer, or of any person found on the premises, and in case the goods are fraudulently removed, the Company may, by their bailiff or other officer, follow them as goods fraudulently removed to avoid payment of rent ; and all the powers and remedies are given to the Company to levy for rates on the premises supplied with Water, as landlords possess for recovery of rents by law ; and the Directors may cause the Pipes leading to the defaulter's premises to be separated from the Main Pipe or Aqueduct, and cause the Water to cease from running thereto. If any person lay or cause any leaden or other pipe or gutter to communicate with any such Aqueduct or Main Pipe of the Company without their consent, he shall forfeit and pay to the Company, not exceeding 20s for every day such Pipe so remains or has been used, 22 V., c. 36, s. 39.

Entry to inspect premises supplied Obstruction

The Manager, Engineer or Bailiff, or other person acting under the authority of the Company or Directors, may at all reasonable times in the day, enter into any yard, house, &c. supplied with water or wherein the Company's Pipe is laid, to inspect and examine if there be any waste, undue diversion, or improper appropriation of the Water, or if refused admittance or entrance for such inspection or examination, or on being admitted obstructed in, or prevented from making it, the Company may cut and turn off, and cause the Water from such house, &c., and if it has been already cut off, but the Pipes still remain, any Magistrates may direct in writing a Policeman to accompany such officer, and ensure a peaceable and quiet inspection, 22 V., c. 36, s. 40.

Ground broken to be restored and fenced off by the company

When any ground is broken up or opened in any Street, Lane, or Road, by the Company, or any person employed by them for laying, taking up, or repairing any Aqueduct, Main Pipe or Communicating Pipe, they shall fill in, or cause, such ground, and remove any rubbish occasioned by the opening or breaking up the same, as soon as conveniently may be, and in the meantime cause such ground to be fenced or guarded so as not to be dangerous to passengers and cattle ; and if there be any wilful or negligent delay in the Company or their Agents, the parties offending shall forfeit not exceeding £5, 22 V., c. 36, s, 41

When it is found necessary to lay down pipes in, upon, or under any part of any public or turnpike road, they shall be laid down on the sides of the road only ; and, if laid down otherwise, or in case any pipe happen to burst or break, or cause the water to injure any road, the commissioners or proper officers of the road shall give notice to the company, or their agents, to take up or remove, or repair the same; and, if they neglect or refuse, for the space of 48 hours after notice, to commence to repair or remove the same, the company shall forfeit and pay to the Churchwardens of the parish in which the pipe has burst or broken and caused such injury to the road, £5 ; to be recovered from the manager, clerk or agent to the company as after stated, 22 V., c. 36, s. 42. *Pipes to be laid on sides of roads. Burst pipes to be removed, &c*

See Highways, 25 V., c. 18, s. 62

Bathing in any dam, reservoir, aqueduct, water-way, feeder or pond, the property of the company ; washing any dog or other animal therein; throwing or casting any dog, cat, or other animal, or any filth, dirt or other noisome or offensive thing ; washing or cleansing any clothes, cloths, wool or leather, skins of sheep or lambs, or hogs, or goats, or other animal, or any noisome or offensive thing in any such dam &c. or causing or suffering the water or drainings of any sink, gutter, sewer or drain to run or be conveyed thereinto, or causing any other annoyance to be done to the water therein, whereby the water may be soiled fouled, or corrupted : Penalty, not exceeding £50, 22 V., c. 36, s. 43. *Fouling or corrupting water*

Any person taking or using or causing or permitting, or suffering, &c. any water from any reservoir, aqueduct or pipe, or any water which has flowed or been taken out of same without the previous consent of the company ; any person, supplied by them under any contract or agreement, giving, letting, selling, or in any way disposing of, on any pretext to any other person any such water or any part thereof, or any person wilfully letting off or causing to run to waste any water from any such aqueduct or pipe shall forfeit to the company, not exceeding £10, and the company may take or cut off the water supplied from the house,&c. of the persons offending; but not to subject any person supplied with water to any forfeiture or penalty for suffering [supplying] any person with any quantity of water in case of fire, or during any time the pipe or cocks belonging to any person supplied by the company are out of repair. Such pipe or cocks to be repaired as soon as may be after any damage happens thereto, 22 V., c. 36, s. 44. *Taking or permitting company's water to be used or water*

All fines, penalties and forfeitures, imposed by this act, or by any rule, order or bye law in pursuance thereof, the manner of levying and recovering whereof is not particularly directed, shall, in cases of non-payment, on conviction, be levied by distress and sale of the goods of the offender, by warrant under the hand and seal of any justice of the parish wherein the offence is committed or the offender is or resides, which warrant the Justice shall issue, upon the confession of the party or evidence of any credible witness, on oath. All fines, &c. the application whereof is not particularly directed, shall be paid to the treasurer or directors, and the overplus after deducting the fines, &c., and the expense of distress and sale, shall be rendered to the owner ; and, if not forthwith paid, such Justice may, by warrant under his hand and seal, commit the offender to the Common Gaol, or General Penitentiary, for not exceeding 4 calendar months, unless the fine, &c., and all reasonable charges attending the recovery, be sooner paid, 22 V., c. 36, s. 45. *Recovery, &c. of Penalties*

FORM OF CONVICTION,

FOR ANY OFFENCE AGAINST THIS ACT, OR AGAINST ANY BYE-LAWS, RULES, ORDERS, OR REGULATIONS OF THE COMPANY.

Conviction

Be it remembered, that on this   day of in the year of the reign of   A. B. is convicted before me   one of Her Majesty's Justices of the Peace for the Parish of   having, (as the offence shall be). And I (or we, the said do adjudge him (her or them) to forfeit and pay for the same the sum of •

Given under (our or) my hand and seal the day and year aforesaid, 22 V., c. 36. s. 46.

Irregular distress

Where any distress is made for any sum to be levied by virtue of this Act, it shall not be deemed unlawful, nor the party making it a trespasser, on account of any defect or want of form in the information, summons, conviction, warrant of distress, or other proceedings relating thereto, nor shall the party distraining be deemed a trespasser, ab initio, on account of any irregularity afterwards done by him; but the party aggrieved shall recover full satisfaction for the special damage, in an action on the case, 22 V., c. 36, s. 47.

Protection from actions

No plaintiff shall recover in any action for anything done, or omitted to be done under this Act, unless notice in writing has been given to the defendant, or left at his last or usual place of abode, 21 days before action commenced, of such intended action, signed by the Attorney of the plaintiff, specifying the cause of action, nor shall the plaintiff recover if tender of sufficient amends have been made to him or his Attorney, by or on behalf of the defendant before action brought, and if none has been made, the defendant may, by leave of the Court, before issue is joined, pay into Court, such sum as he thinks fit, whereupon such proceedings, order, and judgment shall be had, made, and given by the Court, as in other actions where the defendant is allowed to pay money into Court, 22 V., c. 36, s. 48.

Limitation of action, General issue, Costs

Every such action shall be brought or commenced within 6 calendar months next, after the fact committed, or in case there be a continuation of damages, then within 6 calendar months next after it has ceased, and not afterwards, and be laid and brought in the parish where the matter in dispute or cause of action arises, and not elsewhere, and the defendant shall plead the general issue, and give this Act, and the special matter in evidence, and if the act appear to have been done or omitted to be done by virtue, or under color of this Act, or the action is brought before the expiration of 21 days next after notice, or after sufficient satisfaction made or tendered, or after the time limited, or is brought in any other parish, the Jury shall find for the defendant; or if the plaintiff becomes non-suit or discontinue after the defendant has appeared, or if a verdict pass against him or upon demurrer, or otherwise Judgment is given against him, the defendant shall have double costs, and the same remedy as for costs in other cases, 22 V., c. 36, s. 49.

Notice to be served on Chairman Actions by one against Chairman

Where the Company or Directors are mentioned, either to sue or be sued, it shall be sufficient to send out any action or institute any proceeding in the name of the Chairman of Directors for the time being, and sufficient to serve such Chairman alone with the necessary notices in all actions sent out or suits instituted against the Company, 22 V., c. 36, s. 50.

Removal of company's property Resistance

Where pipes are laid into any house, &c., and the parties or owners in possession have discontinued taking or paying for the use of the water, or have forfeited their right, the agents of the Company under a written authority from the Chairman, may enter and take up, and remove any pipe, or other property belonging to the Company, and on any resistance being made to such agent, the parties shall forfeit three times the value of the pipes, and the expenses of laying them, to be recovered as before provided, 22 V., c. 36, s. 51.

Evidence of bye-laws

In prosecutions for offences against the Bye-laws of the Company, the production of a written or printed paper, purporting to be such, and authenticated by having the Common Seal of the Company affixed, shall be evidence of their existence, and it shall be sufficient to prove that they have been made public, by the exhibition of a written or printed copy, in a conspicuous place at the office of the Company, 22 V., c. 36, s. 60.

Water rates and debts recoverable under Petty Debt Act if not exceeding £10

Where the amount of rates in arrear, together with the authorized costs charges and expenses do not exceed £10, whether the Company are or are not able to find goods whereon to levy, they may, at the option of the Company, be sued for and recovered, with all costs and charges against the party in arrear, and charged with such charges, costs and expenses, by and in the name of the Chairman, in like manner as proceedings may now be had for the recovery of debts not exceeding £10, and all other sums due and to be due to the Company, on any account, whether on bond, bills, or open account or otherwise, not exceeding £10, and whether an original sum or a balance, shall be recoverable and enforceable as debts, under the Petty Debt Act, but in every such process the plaintiff shall be described as Chairman of the Directors of the Company, 22 V., c. 36, s. 61.

If from any cause the Company fail to deliver to the city of Kingston a full and sufficient supply of water for 6 months continually, all the powers and privileges granted to them shall cease, 22 V., c. 36, s. 62.

Failure to deliver water for 6 months, see s 67

After 21 years next following 1st January, 1859, if the net rate of profits of the Company, beyond the costs and expenses incurred bona fide in carrying on and managing the Company, are then at least equal to 15 per cent per annum on their capital outlay, the Legislature may, at any time thereafter, purchase the right of water and water-works, and their lands, hereditaments and appertenences, at the price or rate of not less than 25 years of such net annual profits, calculated upon the average of the 3 years preceding such purchase, 22 V., c. 36, s. 63.

Legislative right to purchase

The Legislature may, from time to time as expedient, after the expiration of the 21 years, in case the profits for 3 years prior thereto have exceeded 15 per cent on the capital outlay, revise the rules and charges for the supply of such water, in such manner as in their judgment shall be calculated to reduce the net profits to not less than 15 per cent per annum, 22 V., c. 36, s. 65

Revision of rates

Nothing in the Act shall prevent the Legislature from making or authorizing such further arrangements as they may consider expedient for the supply of the city of Kingston, or any part with water, in case the Company fail for a period of 6 months continuously to supply the city with such quantity of good and wholesome water as shall appear to the Legislature to be sufficient, or if the Company shall not at all times furnish its supply at such rate as the Legislature deem reasonable, 22 V., c. 36, s. 67.

Legislative interposition in case of Company's failure

Their accounts, and disbursements and profits shall be kept in regular books, and a summary published once a year in the "Gazette," or such newspapers as the Directors direct. In case of dispute as to the actual amount of profits in any given year, the matter may be referred to the arbitration of two persons to be elected, one by the Governor, and the other by the Company or Directors, with power to the arbitrators, in case they disagree, to appoint any umpire, whose award shall be final, 22 V., c. 36, s. 68.

Accounts To be advertized yearly Ascertainment of profits by arbitration

The reservoirs and other works, and the Company in respect thereof, shall not be rated, charged or assessed for the payment of any public or parochial taxes, 22 V., c. 36, s. 64.

The Company exempted from taxes

The Act shall not confer any exclusive right or privilege in any other place than the city of Kingston and its limits, 22 V., c. 36, s. 66.

Exclusive privileges confined to the city of Kingston

Throwing any ballast, gravel, stone, mud, broken bottles, the dead carcase of an animal, blood, putrid meat, filth, night soil or rubbish into any part of the water-works, reservoirs, aqueducts, trenches, waters, water courses or feeders, or into the Hope River, or into any stream or rivulet feeding the Hope River, or into any dam, gutter or pipe for conveying water from the Hope River, used or to be used by the Company for the purpose of this Act, or knowingly, willingly or maliciously breaking, throwing down or injuring any of the iron pipes, lead pipes, plugs, fire cocks or any other works erected, made or maintained for the purposes of the Company, or by virtue of this Act, or injuring any part thereof, or wasting or letting off any water therefrom : felony ; imprisonment, with hard labor, in the General Penitentiary, for not exceeding 3 years, or, in mitigation, the Court may award such sentence as the law directs in cases of injury to property, 22 V., c. 36, s. 69.

Throwing ballast &c, into the works, Hope River or feeders. Injury to works, &c

Kingston Police Magistrate.

The Governor shall appoint from among the Barristers of not less than 3 years standing, or Attorneys-at-Law of not less than 5 years standing in this Island, a Police Magistrate for the City and Parish of Kingston, who shall, before entering upon his duties, take the oaths prescribed for Justices of the Peace, and shall thereupon have magisterial jurisdiction within the City and Parish, and enjoy all the immunities and protection, and be subject to the penalties of other Justices ; and upon a vacancy occurring by death, resignation, forfeiture of office or suspension, the Governor may appoint another qualified person, 21 V., c. 27, s. 1.

Appointment

Vacancy

He shall not, unless with the sanction of the Governor, reside at a greater distance than 3 miles from Kingston, nor absent himself from his Court longer than 2 days at any one time, except during illness, or on leave of the Governor ; and shall appoint, a Deputy qualified as aforesaid, to be

Residence Absence

approved of by the Governor, to act during his absence on leave, 21 V., c. 27, s. 2.

Daily sitting He shall sit daily at the Court House in the City, or other place assigned by the Custos, or, in his absence, the Senior Magistrate, 21 V., c. 27, s. 3.

Quarterly returns He shall make a Return to the Governor, quarterly, within 21 days after 31st March, 30th June, 30th September and 31st December, of all cases tried before him, and convictions thereunder, and how adjudicated, distinguishing the character of each offence, and the sex and age of each offender, 21 V., c. 27, s. 4.

Salary He shall be paid under the Governor's Warrant a salary of £500, in lieu of all fees, by quarterly payments, 21 V., c. 27, s. 5.

Stamps The proceedings mentioned in the Schedule issued for adjudication in Kingston, shall be impressed with the Stamps therein mentioned, over and above any others which may require to be impressed, 21 V., c. 27, s. 6.

Duration In force until 31 December, 1868, 21 V., c. 27. s. 8.

STAMPS ON PROCESS.

	S.	D.
Under Petty Debt Act On every original Summons	0	6
Each Subpœna or Summons to witness, to contain the names of not more than 3 witnesses	0	6
Every Distress Warrant	1	0
Every Bond for Security of Damages where time is granted	1	0
On other proceedings Every information or complaint, not being an information by a Police Officer, and for a public offence	0	6
Every recognizance to appear and answer, for each party recognized	1	6
Every recognizance to keep the peace, or be of good behaviour, for each party recognized	2	0
Each Subpœna or Summons to a witness, to contain names of not more than 3 witnesses	0	6

Kingston Slip Dock.

Commissioners 3 a quorum The Governor, with the Executive Committee, and 5 Commissioners to be appointed by him, any 3 of whom, exclusive of the Governor, at any meeting summoned by him, may be a quorum, are empowered:

To appropriate lands 1. To appropriate such portion of the lands of the Lunatic Asylum in Kingston as are sufficient for a Slip Dock, Buildings and Workshops, or if deemed advisable, to purchase as much land as may be requisite, and to wall in and enclose the lands.

And erect a Slip Dock, Machinery and buildings 2. To cause to be erected on the lands a Slip Dock and Machinery for hauling up and receiving Steam and other Vessels of at least 3000 tons registered tonnage, in a safe and proper manner, of such plan, construction and materials, and with such buildings and conveniences as shall be fitting for the accommodation of tradesmen and others engaged in the examination and repairs of any vessel placed on the Slip, and for the safe custody of all stores and materials belonging to such vessels, and required for their repair.

Advertise for tenders 3. To invite, by advertisements in two London newspapers, 2 newspapers and the "Gazette" in this Island, and 2 newspapers in New York, tenders for the construction of the Slip Dock and buildings, according to detailed and complete working specifications and plans, to be carefully prepared and submitted for inspection, and subject to the supervision of any Engineer to be employed as after provided, and **Not exceeding £35,000** accept the most eligible tender or tenders, not exceeding £35,000 in the whole, inclusive of the prices of convict labour, and all materials that can be supplied from Rock Fort lands, and by the General Penitentiary, at rates and prices to be fixed by the contractor and Inspector of Prisons, or in case of disagreement by a third person to be appointed by them, or if, after 7 days' notice, either refuse or neglect to join in any such appointment, then to be appointed by the other, and the third person's decision to be final.

4. To contract with, and take security from the persons whose tender is accepted for the whole or any part of the works, by joint and several bond from the contractor, with 2 or more approved sureties, in a sum to be fixed by the Governor, Executive Committee and Commissioners for securing the completion of the works or 'parts contracted for, subject to supervision as provided for, and require new or additional security as they deem proper. *Contract and take security*

5. To procure in duplicate from Bell and Miller, Engineers, Glasgow, carefully prepared, detailed and complete working specifications and plans of the works to be performed, and cause them to be submited to the persons desirous of tendering, and pay therefor not exceeding £1000. *Procure plans, &c. to be submitted to persons desiring to contract Cost*

7. To authorize the employment of any number of convicts in the Penitentiary in the erection of the buildings or works, the quarrying, taking away and using stones from the public lands at Rock Fort, and applying dressed stones, bricks and lime from the Penitentiary for the performance of the works, a correct account of the quantity and value of the labor and materials to be kept by the Inspector of Prisons, and paid by or charged against the respective contractors at the rates and prices to be fixed, 28 V., c. 39, s. 1. *Convict labor and materials from Rock Fort and the Penitentiary Account to be kept*

Upon the completion of the Slip Dock and buildings, the Governor, Executive Committee and Commissioners may advertize the same to be leased for not exceeding 7 years, and accept the most advantageous offer, but with a covenant that the Lessee shall keep the Slip Lock, machinery, and buildings in repair, and security to be approved of by the Governor, with the advice aforesaid, for the rent of the Slip Dock, and keeping and delivering up the same in good order at the end of the term, 28 V., c. 39, s. 3. *Lease of Slip Dock, &c. Security*

If there is no offer to lease, or none it would be advisable to accept, the Governor, &c., or any 5 (the Governor to be one) may make arrangements for working the Slip Dock, and may employ the necessary officers and servants at reasonable salaries and wages, until other provision or direction is made on the meeting of the Legislature next after its completion, 28 V., c. 39, s. 4. *Arrangements for working on public account*

The Receiver General shall— *Receiver General to keep—*

1. Keep two accounts, one, " the Slip Dock Debenture Account," (as to which see Loans Kingston Slip Dock), also, " the Slip Dock Account," in which he shall credit all moneys received for rent, or the use and occupation or working of the Slip and buildings, and debit all moneys paid for their construction and erection, and the purchase of lands, if necessary, and otherwise, 28 V., c. 39, s. 5. *1. The Slip Dock Debenture Account 2 The Slip Dock Account*

The Executive Committee shall lay before the Assembly annually, within 20 days after the assembling of the Legislature, an account in detail, made up to the end of the financial year, shewing all moneys received and paid by the Receiver-General on account of the Slip Dock, and a statement in detail of the progress of the works to the first day of the Session, 28 V., c. 39, s. 8. *Accounts to be annually laid before the legislature*

The Governor may direct, if the Slip Dock is not leased, and shall make it a condition in every lease, that H. M.'s ships of war shall at all times have the preference in the use of the Slip Dock, on H. M.'s government contributing such proportion of the cost of erection, including lands and buildings, as the Governor and Executive Committee shall agree upon, with the Lords Commissioners of the Admiralty, 28 V., c. 39, s. 9. *H. M's Vessels to have preference in use*

The Governor and Executive Committee may enter into engagements with the Lords Commissioners of the Admiralty for entering into, carrying out, and obtaining the satisfactory completion of contracts for the construction of the Slip Dock, works and buildings, and for regulating the use and providing for the proper supervision and maintenance of the Slip Dock works and buildings. The amount for which the Island shall be liable in the whole shall not exceed £40,000, to be raised under this Act. Copies of all engagements with the Lords Commissioners of the Admiralty shall be laid before the Council and Assembly as early as possible, 28 V., c. 39, s. 10. *Contract with the Admiralty Island liability limited to £40,000*

Proceedings to acquire lands, &c. In case of neglect or refusal, or incapacity, or impediment on the part of any person interested in any land necessary to be purchased, to treat or agree for the sale thereof, or of any right of easement, the Governor and Executive Committee may take the like proceedings for acquiring such land, or right, or easement, as under the Prisons' Consolidation Act, 20 V. c. 11, s. 6–9 ; the Governor, with the advice of the Executive Committee being taken as the authorities or functionaries to proceed, instead of the Executive Committee, 28 V., c. 39, s. 11.

If a question of title occur, the money may be placed in the Receiver General's Office If any question arise as to title to any land or easement taken, the Governor and Executive Committee may cause the money payable to be placed in the Receiver-General's office to the credit of the persons interested, describing them as far as can be, subject to the control and disposition of the Supreme Court, 28 V., c. 39, s. 12.

Applications to the Supreme Court Upon the application of any person making claim to the money, or any portion, or any interest in the land, &c., the Supreme Court shall, in a summary way, and after such notice as it deems fit, and to such persons as it may direct, order distribution according to the respective interests of the claimants, and make such other order as seems fit, 28 V., c. 39, s. 13.

Prima Facie title On any question of title, the persons in possession as owners, or in receipt of the rents, or use of any right or easement, as being entitled thereto at the time of the land, &c. being taken, shall be deemed lawfully entitled; until the contrary is shewn, and, unless shewn, the parties in possession, receipt or user, and all parties claiming under them, or consistently with their possession, shall be deemed entitled to, and be paid such money, 28 V., c. 39, s. 14.

Land, &c. vested in Executive Committee All land, &c. taken shall vest in the Executive Committee, for the purposes of this Act: pursuant to 22 V., c. 23 ; 28 V., c. 39, s. 15.

Payments for works Out of any moneys applicable, the Governor, by his Warrant, with advice of the Executive Committee, shall direct payment of any sums required for the works, 28 V., c. 39, s. 16.

Notice of meetings No meeting shall be held, except on 2 days' notice from the Secretary to the Board, to be left with or sent through the Post to the Governor, each Member of the Executive Committee and each Commissioner, 28 V. c. 39, s. 17.

Exemption from Import Duties All materials, implements and things imported, shall be admitted free of duty, on direction of the Governor and Executive Committee, 28 V., c. 39, s. 18.

Tonnage Dues Every Vessel resorting to the Port of Kingston for the sole purpose of repairs, or being hauled up on the Slip Dock, shall be exempt from Tonnage Dues ; and in case they afterwards enter and clear outwards with cargo, or having brought cargo enter inwards, the same or any part shall be charged with Tonnage and other Dues, under 23 V., c. 12, and 46 G. 3, c. 28, on her whole tonnage, or under 24 V., c. 3, on the measurement of the tonnage occupied by the outward cargo, or from which cargo shall be actually landed, subject to those Acts, 28 V., c. 39, s. 20.

Kingston Thoroughfares.

Limits The Works authorized by this Act shall be executed within the limits from East to West, from the line of Hanover Street to Orange Street, both inclusive, and from the line of the parish of St. Andrew to the Sea, on North and South lines, respectively, within the Eastern and Western limits, 28 V., c. 24, s. 1.

Commissioners ; 3 a quorum Any 2 Members of the Executive Committee, the Custos, the Mayor and Members for Kingston, shall be Commissioners, 3 a quorum :

For reconstruction of Streets 1. To cause to be reconstructed the several streets, cross-streets and lanes, within the above limits, by such methods, and with such materials and workmanship as may appear best calculated to obtain and secure the convenient and permanent use of the streets, cross-**To lead off rain waters, and ultimately sewage** streets and lanes, and to provide for leading off the rain-waters which fall in or flow down the same, and eventually to lead off also the refuse and sewage waters issuing or flowing from the houses built, or to be built within the limits.

2. To remove, destroy, alter, divert, stop up or abate any stairs, steps, enclosures, posts, piles or other encroachments, obstructions, materials and things, or such parts as in the judgment of the Board shall be necessary to remove, &c., erecting or providing other suitable steps, or stairs in the stead of any so removed or stopped up, so as to equalize the width and height of the several causeways or piazzas in, and to restore the original width by law prescribed of the streets, &c., and to make the same available for general and convenient use as public thoroughfares. *Remove and reconstruct encroachments*

3. To cause such drains, pipings, sewer-gratings and water-tables to be constructed, and such parts of the streets, cross-Streets and lanes, to be laid out for carriage ways, and such part for foot passengers as shall be requisite or proper. *Construct drains, &c., carriage and foot ways*

4. To enter upon and take any land, or any right of user or enjoyment right of way or other right, or easement of, out of, over upon or in connection with any land belonging to the city or any person, and to make and complete, and keep in repair and good order from time to time on such land, such works as may be requisite for the more complete drainage of the rain and sewage waters of the City, making compensation to any person having interest in any land, or in respect of any right therein taken for the purposes of this Act. *To make works for drainage on lands* *Making compensation*

5. To take (in case of neglect, or refusal or incapacity, or any impediment on the part of any person interested in any land, to treat or agree for the sale thereof, or any right of easement therein or thereout) the like proceedings for acquiring the land, right or easement, as are provided to be taken under the Prisons' Consolidation Act, 20 V., c. 11, s. 6, to 9, inclusive, which so far as applicable are incorporated herein, the Board being taken to be the authorities to proceed instead of the Executive Committee, 28 V., c. 24, s. 2. *To take up lands* *Under powers of 26 V., c. 11, s. 6-9, (Prisons)*

The Governor and Executive Commitee may— *Powers of Governor and Executive Committee to authorize the labor of convicts in penitentiary*

1. Authorize the employment of any number of convicts in the Penitentiary, the quarrying, taking away and using any quantity of stones from the public lands at Rock Fort, and the supplying of such quantities of dressed stones, bricks and lime from the Penitentiary as are necessary ; a correct account of the quantity and value of such labor and materials being kept by the Inspector of Prisons. *The use of materials from Rock Fort Quarry* *Stones broken from penitentiary* *The Inspector of Prisons keeping account*

4. Out of the moneys applicable by warrant, to direct payment to the order of the Commissioners of such sums as may be required for the works, 28 V., c. 24, s. 3.

The Receiver-General shall— *Receiver General's duties*

I. Keep an account, "The Kingston Streets Account," in which to credit all moneys collected under this Act, whether by sale of bonds or debentures, or for taxes or duties, or the annual sum charged on the estimates of expenditure, and debit all moneys paid for the construction and execution of works, or for payment of interest, or principal of any loan moneys, 28 V., c. 24, s. 6.

If any question arise as to the title of any person having interest in any land which, or any right or easement in which shall be taken, the Governor and Executive Committee shall cause to be deposited the money payable, in respect thereof, with the Receiver-General, to be placed to the credit of the persons interested in the land, describing them as far as can be, subject to the control and disposition of the Supreme Court, 28 V., c. 24, s. 8. *Deposit of purchase money where the title is in question, subject to the disposition of the Supreme Court*

Upon application by any person making claim to the money deposited, or any portion, or any interest in the land, or right, or easement therein, in respect whereof it has been deposited, the Supreme Court, shall in a summary way, and after such notice as to them seems fit, and to such persons as they direct, order distribution of the moneys according to the respective interests of the claimants, and make such order as seems fit, 28 V., c. 24, s. 9, *Proceedings on applications therefor*

On any question of title, the persons in possession as owners, or in receipt of the rents, or in the user of any right or easement, as entitled thereto at the time of the land, &c., being taken, shall be deemed lawfully entitled, until the contrary be shown to the satisfaction of the Court, and unless the contrary be shown, the parties in possession, &c., and those claiming under them, or consistently with their possession, shall be deemed *Persons in possession to be deemed entitled until the contrary is shewn* entitled to the money deposited, and it shall be paid and applied accordingly, 28 V., c. 24, s. 10.

Land to vest in the Executive Committee

All land, or any right or easement therein, taken under this Act, shall vest in the Executive Committee, under 22 V., c. 23, enabling them to hold and maintain the title to any property or estate for the benefit of the public, 28 V., c. 24, s. 11.

Commissioners of Highways not to interfere

Notwithstanding any thing to the contrary in any Act, no Commissioners of Highways and Bridges, as a Board, or otherwise, collectively or individually, or any Surveyor, Inspector, Way-warden, or other Officer or Agent, shall in any manner interfere with, obstruct, hinder, or impede the execution of the works, or any part thereof, authorized; and any person offering or making any such interference, &c., shall, on conviction, in a summary way, forfeit not exceeding £10, to be enforced, in case of default in payment, according to any Act relating to summmary proceedings before Justices, 28 V., c. 24, s. 12.

The Board to make rules for the guidance of their proceedings, &c.

The Board (s. 2) shall have power to make rules and regulations for the guidance of their proceedings, and for the control and superintendence of the persons employed by them, and generally for carrying out the provision of the Act, 28 V., c. 24, s. 14.

Land Tax and Quit Rents.

Quit rents Land tax

Holders of land shall continue to pay ½d. of money current previous to the 31st December, 1840, for every acre of land other than foot land, and for foot land at the rate of ½d. of like money per foot, for 2 sides of the square added together, as a certain established Quit Rent and acknowledgment to H. M., and such further sum in addition as will amount to 1d. sterling for each acre on which Quit Rents are payable by the acre : and the like sum of 1d. of like money for each foot of land, to be calculated as aforesaid, for which Quit Rents are payable by the foot, and for a fractional part of an acre or foot, the like sum of 1d., 8 V., c. 16, s. 1.

Annual returns

All persons in possession of land, whether as sole or part owners, or lessees in their own right, or in right of their wives, or as mortgagees in possession, guardians or trustees, shall, by themselves or one of their Attorney or Agent, or Overseer, or principal servant in charge or management, yearly, on 28th March, or within 20 days after, or such other time as shall be appointed by law for making returns of other taxable property, give in, or cause &c., to the Common Council of Kingston, or Justices and Vestry, a return in writing of the quantity in possession, or under the charge of the person making the return, with a declaration subjoined to the effect following, if the return be the only return of lands made by him within the parish for the current year :—

> I, A. B., do solemnly and sincerely declare that the above return is in all respects, to the best of my knowledge and belief, a just and true return of all lands in my possession, or under my charge, within the Parish of

Or if the person making return as owner or otherwise, be required to make more than one return of lands within the same parish, he shall annex to every return a declaration to the effect following :—

> I, A. B., do solemnly and sincerely declare that the above and other returns made, or intended to be made by me, contain to the best of my knowledge and belief, in all respects, just and true returns of all lands in my possession, or under my charge, in the Parish of

To be made before any Justice within the Island, whether appointed for the parish where the lands are situate or not, or before the Clerk of the, Vestry of the Parish where they are situate. Wilfully making a false declaration a misdemeanor, 8 V., c. 16, s. 2.

Returns and payment to be annually made

No person, except as after mentioned, (who redeemed the Land Tax under s. 11-18 while they were in operation) shall be exempted from the liability to pay the Land Tax although not assessed ; but it shall be the duty of every person to make the annual returns required by law of the lands in his possession, or under his charge, to the Clerk of the Vestry, and once in each year, by himself or agent, to pay to the Receiver-General such Land Tax, and obtain an acquittance and discharge therefor, 21 V., c. 34, s. 7.

Land tax no longer redeemable

After 1st January, 1862, no Land Tax due or chargeable on any land shall be redeemable; but all lands whereon land has been up to that day redeemed, shall remain redeemed and exempt from such tax, 24 V., c. 26, s. 5.

To be paid to Collector of Dues

Every person in possession of land as owner, tenant, or in any other character, shall on the 1st August, or within 10 days after, pay to the Collector of Dues of his parish the full amount of the tax, without deduction for discount, and obtain from him an acquittance thereof, 28 V., c. 28, s. 3.

Lists of persons who have redeemed land tax, and of the land redeemed to be exposed on Court House

Every Clerk of the Vestry shall keep in his office, and expose for public inspection in some conspicuous part of the Court House, true and correct alphabetical lists of all persons who have redeemed the Land Tax and the lands in respect whereof the tax has been redeemed in his parish by persons making payments to him, and add to such lists the names of all persons, and the lands in his parish, in respect whereof the tax has been redeemed at the Receiver-General's office, 21 V., c. 34, s. 21.

Certificate of redemption or payment of land tax to be annexed to deeds or patents before recording

The Island Secretary shall not record any Deed relating to land, except leases, the probate whereof bears date subsequently to the passing of 21 V., c. 34, [31st December, 1857] or any Patent which bears date subsequently, unless a certificate to the effect of the form annexed of the Collector of Dues of the parish where the land is situate, which the Collector is required to give, she..ing that the Land Taxes have been paid or redeemed, is annexed thereto, or endorsed thereon, that the island tax has been redeemed, or that all arrears for the then preceding 5 years, payable on the land therein comprised, have been fully paid and discharged; and the Island Secretary shall record such certificates with the Deed or patent to which it refers, and be entitled to a fee at the rate of 1s. 6d. per legal sheet of 160 words, or fractional parts thereof, 26 V., S. 2, c. 21, s. 2.

FORM OF CERTIFICATE.

Certificate

JAMAICA ss.

Parish of   day of   186

I hereby certify that the Land Tax has been redeemed, (or that all Land Tax has been paid for 5 years last past, to the day of   186   ) on   acres of land, situate in the parish of   known as

C. D.

Collector of Dues for parish of

Quarterly returns from Island Secretary to the Receiver General of recorded deeds and patents
To same effect, 8 V., c. 16, s. 8

The Island Secretary shall, immediately after the expiration of each quarter, transmit to the Receiver-General a docket of every Deed relating to land (except Leases) the probate whereof bears date previously to this Act or Patent of Land bearing previous date, brought into his office to be recorded during such quarter, on which the Land Tax is not redeemed, setting forth the names of the purchasers or patentees, and of the grantors, the name of the parish, quantity of land and boundaries, as also any distinguishing name, situation or number, or other description, if any, and shall be entitled to demand from the party bringing the Deed or Patent, 1s. 6d. for his trouble in making out and transmitting the docket, and 3s. to the Receiver-General, 21 V., c. 34, s. 23.

Fees

Receiver General's fees to be carried to the Main Road Fund

The Receiver-General's fees, so long as his services are paid by a salary, and the contingences of his office defrayed at the expense of the Island, shall be carried to the credit of the Main Road Fund account, 21 V., c 34, s. 36.

Certificates, &c. evidence
Exempt from Stamps

Every certificate of redemption, or the record or an office copy, shall be received as evidence in all Courts, and on all Judicial proceedings, and such certificates shall be exempted from Stamp Duty, 21 V., c. 34, s. 25.

Certificates of lands on which 20 years taxes are due to be made to the Governor, &c.

If after the expiration of 5 years, there are any lands on which the Land Tax is not redeemed, the Receiver-General shall from time to time certify to the Governor and Executive Committee all lands on which 20 years Land Tax and Quit Rents have been in arrear and unpaid, in order that they may be proceeded against as forfeited for non-payment, 21 V., c. 34, s. 26.

Proceedings for the forfeiture of lands for the benefit of the public

Upon receipt of Directions from the Governor and Executive Committee, the Receiver-General shall furnish to the Attorney-General a certificate, (Form No. 3) of the non-payment of such Land Tax (including Quit Rents), specifying the quantity and description of the land, and the name of the original or last patentee, and that the Quit Rents and Land Tax in respect of such lands, for the space of 20 years and upwards, have been, and are in arrear and unpaid, and become the relator on behalf of Her Majesty in any proceedings which shall be thereupon commenced and prosecuted for the forfeiture of such lands for the benefit of the public. But not to affect the rights of any person who shall have already obtained a certificate, 21 V., c. 34, s. 27.

Proceedings at the instance of individuals

See s. 36

After 5 years, any person desirous of proceeding to enforce the forfeiture of any lands on which Land Tax and Quit Rents for 20 years are in arrear and unpaid, may pay to the Receiver-General a sum equal to 20 years Land Tax and Quit Rent in respect of such lands, which shall entitle him to a certificate (Form No. 3) from the Receiver-General to the Attorney General, that such person hath paid to him 20 years Land Tax and Quit Rents in respect of the land, specifying the quantity and description, and name of the original or last patentee, for which he shall be entitled to a fee of 1s 6d. No person shall be entitled to any such certificate in respect of lands, the Receiver-General has been directed to proceed against for the benefit of the public, previously to the tender of 20 years' Land Tax and Quit Rent, 21 V., bl 34, s. 28.

Attorney General's further writ of enquiry

The Attorney-General shall, upon production of any such certificate, issue his precept or fiat, for which he shall be entitled to a fee of £1 8s 6d, to the Clerk of the Supreme Court, to prepare and issue one or more writs of enquiry as the case requires, returnable at the Court of the parish or precinct wherein the lands may be situate, to be holden after the then ensuing Supreme Court, which writ the Clerk of the Supreme Court shall, on receipt of such precept, make out and issue to the following effect:

Form of writ

JAMAICA, ss.

County

Parish

Victoria, by the Grace of God of the United Kingdom of Great Britain and Ireland, Queen, and of Jamaica, Lady Defender of the Faith, &c.

To the Provost-Marshal of this our Island of Jamaica, greeting:

Whereas A. B., our trusty and well beloved our Receiver-General of our said Island, (or A. B. of the parish of   as the case may be) hath related to our trusty and well beloved our Attorney-General for our said Island, that his late Majesty   by his letters patent, bearing date the   day of   in the year   did grant unto C. D., his heirs and assigns,   acres of land, situate, lying and being in the parish of   butting and bounding   (and if the case so require, Which said land hath been transferred to, and now forms part of the said parish of   naming the parish in the venue), and that the Quit Rents and Land Tax in respect of the said lands, for the space of 20 years and upwards before the issuing of this our writ, have remained and have been in arrear and unpaid: (If at the instance of a private relator: And whereas the said A. B. hath paid to our trusty and well beloved our Receiver-General in the said Island the sum of   being the amount of 20 years' Land Tax and Quit Rents in respect of such land). And whereas it is our royal will and pleasure to be satisfied of the truth of the said premises: Now we command thee, that by thyself or thy lawful deputies, thou dost warn seven good and lawful men of our parish (or precinct) of   to be and appear before our Judge of our Circuit Court for the parish (or precinct) of   on the   in   next at   then and there to enquire whether or not the said lands were granted to the said C. D., and whether or not the Land Tax and Quit Rents in respect of the said lands have remained, and have been in arrear and unpaid for the space of 20 years next, before the issuing of this our writ; And we also command thee, that thou return this writ in all things duly executed, with the names of the persons by thee warned, to our said Judge of our said Circuit Court for the said parish (or precinct) of   to be holden at   the day of   next

Witness, the Honorable   Chief Judge, &c.

21 V., c. 34, s, 29.

The Provost-Marshal shall return such writ to the Circuit Court, endorsed as follows: Return thereof

The execution of this writ appears by the return of Her Majesty's Writ of Venire Facias to me directed, returnable this present Circuit Court, for the parish (or precinct) of

Given under my hand and seal, this   day of   for which he shall be entitled to a fee of 9d, 21 V., c. 34, s. 30. Fee

In all Writs of Venire Facias to be issued after the 5 years, returnable at the several Circuit Courts, the following words shall be inserted: Venire Facias

"And also to enquire of and concerning the several matters contained in our Writs of Enquiry, concerning lands related against, for the non-payment of Land Tax and Quit Rents," 21 V., c. 34, s. 31.

On the second Tuesday of the Supreme Court, as of which such Writs shall bear teste and be issued, and on the first day of the Circuit Court where such Writs are returnable, they shall be proclaimed, and afterwards, during the sitting of the Circuit Court, a Jury returned as aforesaid shall be empanelled, charged and sworn, to enquire of the truth of the several points in the Writ, and the Judge shall receive all such legal evidence as shall be produced to the Jurors, touching the premises, and the Receiver-General's certificate shall be received as prima facie evidence of the truth of the contents, and the Jurors shall return their verdict concerning the several points to be enquired into, in writing, indorsed on or annexed to the Writ, 21 V., c. 34, s. 32. Proclamations

Jury

Evidence

Receiver General's certificate p r i m a facie evidence
Verdict

The Judge of the Circuit Court shall transmit the Writ and Verdict to the office of the Clerk of the Supreme Court, who shall file the same, and insert an Abstract in a Table, to be kept in some public part of his office, in the following manner:— To be transmitted to the Clerk of the Supreme Court to be filed
Abstract to be exhibited

INFORMATIONS FOR FORFEITED LANDS.

Day Writ Issued.	Relator.	Original or last Patentee.	Place and Quantity.	Final Judgment when to pass.

21 V., c. 34, s. 33.

3 A

Further procla-mations

Upon the filing of the return of each writ and inquisition, and producing the same at the Supreme Court, the Attorney-General shall cause proclamation to be made of such return on the 2nd Tuesday of such Court, and also at the Circuit Court of the parish or precinct where it was made returnable, to be holden next after, 21 V., c. 34, s. 34.

After proclama-tions if the Inquisi-tion is not traversed final judgment

After such Return has been proclaimed in two successive terms of the Supreme Court, and also in two successive sittings of the Circuit Court, if no person traverse the Inquisition, and put in his claim at the same time, or pray time to enter such traverse and claim on the second Tuesday of the Supreme Court next succeeding the last Proclamation, final judgment shall be pronounced for the Queen; and thereupon if the Receiver-General has been the relator, the Governor shall be entitled to grant and dispose of the same as after provided; or if any private person has been the relator, on producing a docket of such judgment (which the Clerk of the Supreme Court shall make out and deliver) a Patent shall issue and pass the Seal of this Island, to vest the lands in the relator, his heirs and assigns, which shall be a perpetual bar to all former grantors or claimants under the person in whom the same shall be found to have been vested, whether by devise or purchase or otherwise, but against no other person claiming under any other title, 21 V., c. 34, s. 35.

Patent
Effect of

R. G's. Clerk

For the performance of the additional duties imposed upon him, the Receiver-General may appoint an additional Clerk in his Office, at a salary not exceeding £250 per annum, with powers to remove him, 21 V., c. 34, s. 37.

Form of Certifi-cate, 21 V., c. 34, s. 37-28

CERTIFICATE

Of Non-payment of Land and Quit-Rent Taxes.

Jamaica, s.s.

Parish.

I, A. B., Receiver-General of the said Island, do hereby certify, that his late Majesty,   by his letters patent, bearing date   did grant unto C. D. (the original or last Patentee), his heirs and assigns, acres of land, situate, lying and being in the parish of   , butting and bounding, &c., ; and that Quit Rents and Land Tax in respect of the said lands for the space of 20 years and upwards, are in arrear and unpaid (a); and I am directed by his Excellency the Governor to become the Relator on behaf of Her Majesty in proceedings for the forfeiture of such lands (u).

Given under my hand, this   day of

To the Honorable Her Majesty's Attorney-General.

Landlord and Tenant.

Tenants, &c. holding over after demand and notice, to pay double the yearly value

Tenants for life, lives or years, or persons coming into possession of lands, under or in collusion with them, wilfully holding over after the determination of the term, and after demand and notice in writing for delivering possession by their Landlords or Lessors, or the persons to whom the remainder or reversion belong, or their Agents, shall pay, during the time they hold over or keep the persons entitled out of possession, to such persons, their executors, &c., double the yearly value of the land for so long as they are detained, to be recovered by action of debt wherein the defendant shall be obliged to give special bail, against the recovery of which penalty there shall be no relief in Equity, 25 G. 3, c. 7, s. 1.

Tenants holding over after notice to quit
Supersedes 25 G. 3, c. 7, s. 2

In case any Tenant (having power to determine his lease by notice to quit) gives notice of his intention to quit at a time mentioned, and does not accordingly deliver up possession at the time, he, his executors or administrators shall from thenceforward pay to the Landlord or Lessor double the

---

(a a) Or as the case may be, and E. F. of, &c., hath paid me the sum of pounds being the amount of 20 years' Land Tax and Quit Rents in respect of such land to entitle him to become the Relator in proceedings for the forfeiture thereof.

Sec. 26-35, supersede 9 G. 3, c. 9, s. 1, 11-13, which regulated proceedings on forfeitures for non-payment of Quit Rent.

rent or sum he should otherwise have paid ; to be levied, sued for and re-covered at the same time and manner as the single rent before giving notice ; and the double rent shall continue to be paid during all the time the Tenant continues in possession, 1 V., c. 26, s. 15.

The Landlord, where the agreement is not by Deed, may recover a rea-sonable satisfaction for the lands, &c., held. or occupied by the defendant, in an action on the case for use and occupation ; and if in evidence on the trial, any parol, demise or any agreement, not by deed whereon a certain rent is reserved, appears, the Plaintiff shall not be non-suited, but may make use thereof as an evidence of the quantum of the damages to be recovered, 1 V., c. 26, s. 12.

Action for use and occupation where no agreement by deed

Where Tenant for life dies before, or on the day on which rent was re-served or made payable upon any demise or lease, which determined on the death of Tenant for life, his executors or administrators may, in an ac-tion on the case, recover from the under-Tenants the whole, or a portion of the rent according to the time the Tenant for life lived of the last year or quarter, or other time in which the rent was growing due, making all just allowances, or a proportionable part respectively, 1 V., c. 26, s. 13.

Executors, &c. of tenant for life, may recover a propor-tionable part of last year's, &c. rent on leases which deter-mine on his death Supersedes 25 G. 3, c.7, s. 3

Where the term or interest of any Tenant under a lease or agreement in writing for any term or number of years certain, or from year to year, has expired, or been determined either by Landlord or Tenant, by regular notice to quit, and the Tenant, or any holding and claiming under him, re-fuses to deliver up possession, after lawful demand in writing, made and signed by the Landlord or his agent, and served personally upon, or left at the dwelling house or place of abode of such Tenant or person, and the Landlord proceeds by ejectment, he may, at the foot of the declaration, ad-dress a notice to the Tenant or person, requiring him to appear in Court on the first day of Term, to be made defendant, and to find such bail if or-dered by the Court, and for the purposes after specified ; and upon his ap-pearance, or in case of non-appearance, on making the usual affidavit of service of the declaration and notice, the Landlord producing the lease or agreement, or a counterpart or duplicate, and proving the execution by affidavit, and upon affidavit that the premises have been actually enjoyed under the lease or agreement, and the interest of the Tenant has expired, or been determined by regular notice to quit, (as the case may be), and possession has been lawfully demanded, may move the Court for a rule for the Tenant or person to shew cause within a time to be fixed by the Court, on a consideration of the situation of the premises, why the Tenant or person upon being admitted defendant, besides entering into the common rule, and giving the common undertaking, should not undertake, in case a verdict pass for the plaintiff, to give him a judgment, to be entered up against the real defendant, of the term next preceding the time of trial, and also why he should not enter into recognizance by himself, and 2 sureties in a reasonable sum, conditioned to pay the costs and damages to be recovered by the plaintiff ; and the Court, upon cause shewn, or upon affidavit of service of the rule, in case no cause is shewn, may make it absolute in whole or in part, and order the Tenant or person, within a time to be fixed upon on consideration of all the circumstances, to give such undertakings, and find such bail, with such conditions, and as shall be specified in the rule, or the part made absolute ; and in case the party neglects and lays no ground to induce the Court to enlarge the time for obeying it, upon affida-vit of service of the order, an absolute rule shall be made for entering up judgment for the plaintiff, 1 V., c. 26, s. 1.

When on eject-ment, the Landlord may require securi-ty for costs and damages from de-fendant

When it appears on the trial of any ejectment by Landlord against Tenant, that the Tenant or his Attorney has been served with notice of trial, the plaintiff shall not be nonsuited for default of defendant's appearance, or of confession of lease, entry and ouster, but the production of the con-sent rule and undertaking of the defendant shall be sufficient evidence thereof, and the Judges at the trial shall, whether he appear or not, permit the plaintiff, after proof of his right to recover possession of the whole or any part of the premises, to go into evidence of the mesne profits from the expiration or determination of the Tenant's interest, to the time of the verdict, or some preceding day, to be specially mentioned therein ; and the Jury finding for the plaintiff shall give their verdict upon the whole matter, both as to the recovery of the whole or part of the premises, and the damages to be paid for mesne profits. But not to bar the Landlord from an action for mesne profits from the verdict, or day specified therein,

Defendant con-cluded by confes-sion of lease ; entry and ouster in con-sent rule damages by way of mesne profits to be asses-sed ; recovery of subsequent mesne profits

down to the day of delivery of possession of the premises recovered, 1 V., c. 26, s. 2.

Costs

Where the Landlord proceeds under this Act, and the Tenant has found bail, and he fails, the Tenant shall (instead of double costs, receive such full and reasonable indemnity as to all costs, charges and expenses, incurred in and about the action as shall be taxed, subject to review as any other taxation, 8 V., c. 28, s. 22.) Act not to prejudice any right of action or remedy Landlords already possess, 1 V., c. 26, s. 3.

Other remedies not prejudiced

No goods taken in execution to be removed until payment of arrears of rent not exceeding 1 year

No goods on Lands leased for life or lives, term of years at will or otherwise, shall be taken in execution, unless the party at whose suit it is sued out before removal, pays the Landlord or his bailiff all sums due for rent at the time of the taking, provided the arrears do not amount to more than one year's rent, or if so, the party paying one year's rent may proceed to execute his judgment, and the Provost-Marshal, or other Officer, may levy and pay to the plaintiff, as well the money paid for rent as the execution money, 1 V., c. 26, s. 4.

Distress on goods fraudulently removed for arrears of rent

In case any Tenant or Lessee fraudulently or clandestinely conveys away, or carries off the premises his goods, to prevent the Landlord or Lessor from distraining for arrears of rent due, he, or any person by him empowered, within 30 days after removal, may take and seize the same wherever found, as a distress for the arrears, and sell or otherwise dispose of them as if they had been distrained upon the premises. But no Lessor, Landlord or other person, entitled to arrears of rent, shall take or seize any goods sold bona fide, and for a valuable consideration, before seizure, to any person not privy to such fraud, 1 V., c. 26, s. 5.

Liability of tenant his aiders and abettors for double the value recoverable by action of debt

Any Tenant or Lessee fraudulently removing and conveying away his goods, and any person wilfully and knowingly aiding, or assisting him in such fraudu'ently conveying away, or carrying any part of his goods, or in concealing them, shall forfeit and pay to the Landlord or Lessor double the value of the goods by them respectively carried off, or concealed, by action of debt, wherein no more than one impartance shall be allowed, 1 V., c. 26, s. 6.

Or if not exceeding £50 before 2 Justices

Where the goods do not exceed the value of £50, the Landlord, his bailiff, servant or agent, may exhibit a complaint, in writing, against the offender before two Justices of the parish residing near the place whence the goods were removed or found, not being interested in the lands whence they were removed, who may summon the parties, examine the fact and witnesses, and in a summary way determine whether such persons be guilty, and enquire of the value of the goods by them respectively Fraudulently carried off or concealed, and upon full proof of the offence, by order, may adjudge the offenders to pay double the value to the Landlord, his bailiff, servant or agent, at such time as they appoint ; and if the offenders, having notice of the order, refuse or neglect to do so, may, by warrant, levy the same by distress and sale, and for want of distress, commit them to the House of Correction to hard labor, without bail or mainprize, for 6 months, unless the money is sooner satisfied. Parties may appeal, 1 V., c. 26. s. 7.

Power to break open houses, &c. to distrain

Where any goods fraudulently or clandestinely conveyed or carried away, are placed or kept in any house, barn, building, stable, out-house, yard-close, or place locked up, fastened or otherwise secured, so as to prevent their being taken and seized as a distress for arrears of rent, the Landlord or Lessor, or his steward, bailiff, receiver or other person empowered to take and seize as a distress for rent such goods (first calling to his assistance the Constable or other Peace Officer of the parish, or place where they are suspected to be concealed, who are required to assist, and in case of a dwelling house, oath being first made before a Justice of a reasonable ground to suspect the goods are therein), in the day time, may break open any such house, &c., and take and seize the goods for the arrears of rent, as they might have done if they had been put in any open place or field, 1 V., c. 26, s. 8.

Distress on stock depasturing upon any common appendant or appurtenant, growing produce, &c.

Every Lessor or Landlord, his steward, bailiff, receiver, or person empowered by him, may take and seize as a distress for arrears of rent, any cattle or stock of their Tenants feeding or depasturing upon any common, appendant or appurtenant, or any ways belonging to all or any part of the premises demised or holden, also all sorts of fruits, produce, manufacture, or other product growing, or making or made, or any part of the estate so demised or holden, as a distress for arrears of rent ; and the same may cut, gather, make, cure, carry and lay up, when ripe, in the barns, buildings or other proper place on the premises, or if there be none, in any other barn building, or proper place, which he shall hire or procure as near as may be, and in convenient time to appraise, sell or dispose of the same, towards satisfaction of the rent and charges of distress, appraisement and sale, in the same manner as other goods ; and the appraisement shall be taken when cut, gathered, cured, and made, and not before. Notice of the place where they are lodged or deposited shall be given, within one week after, to the Lessee or Tenant, or left at his last place of abode, and if after any distress of fruits, &c., and at any time before they are ripe and cut, cured or gathered, the Tenant or Lessee, his Executors, Administrators, or Assigns, pay, or cause to be paid, the whole rent then in arrear, with the full costs and charges of making the distress, and occasioned thereby, then and upon payment or lawful tender whereby the end of the distress will be fully answered, the same and every part shall cease, and the fruits, &c., be delivered up, 1 V., c. 26, s. 9.

Any person lawfully taking any distress for any kind of rent, may impound, or otherwise secure the distress of what nature or kind soever, in such place or part of the premises chargeable with the rent, as is most convenient, and appraise, sell and dispose of them upon the premises, in like manner as may be done off the premises ; and any person may come and go to and from the place where any distress is impounded and secured, to view, appraise and buy, and carry off or remove them on account of the purchaser ; and if any pound breach or rescous is made of any goods or stock distrained for rent, and impounded or otherwise distrained, the person guilty thereof, or aiding or assisting, shall be indicted and punished as of or a misdemeanor, and make restitution in damages in a civil action, 1 V., c. 26, s. 10. *(margin: Impounding distress on premises, right of ingress and egress ; poundbreach rescous)*

The Court may, where ejectment is brought against a Tenant who holds, or has held possession under a sub-letting or under-letting from any other person, suffer the Landlord to make himself defendant, by joining with the Tenant in case he appear, but if not, judgment shall be signed against the casual ejector for want of appearance ; but if the Landlord of any part of the lands desire to appear and enter into the consent rule, the Court shall permit him, and order a stay of execution upon the judgment against the casual ejector, until further order, 1 V., c. 26, s. 11. *(margin: Making Landlord a defendant to ejectment proceedings with or without tenant)*

If any Tenant at a rack rent, or where the rent reserved is fully 3-4ths of the yearly value of the demised premises, who is in arrear for ½ year's rent, deserts them, and leaves them uncultivated or unoccupied, so as no sufficient distress can be had to countervail the arrears, two Justices having no interest in the demised premises, at the request of the Lessor or Landlord, his bailiff or receiver, may go upon, and view the same, and affix, or cause, &c., on the most notorious part of the premises, notice in writing, what day (at the distance of 14 days at least) they will return to take a second view ; and if upon the second view, the tenant or some person on his behalf does not appear and pay the rent in arrear, or there is not sufficient distress upon the premises, the Justices may put the Landlord in possession, and the lease to the Tenant as to any demise only, shall from thenceforth become void. Such proceedings of the Justices shall be examined in a summary way at the next (Circuit Court, 19 V., c. 10,) in which the lands lie, and if in Middlesex, by the Judges at the next Grand Court, who may order restitution to be made to the Tenant, with his expenses and costs, by the Lessor or Landlord, if they see cause ; and in case they affirm the act of the Justices, may award costs not exceeding £5 (£3 stg.) for the frivolous Appeal, 1 V,, c. 26, s. 14. *(margin: When 2 Justices may put Landlord in possession if half year's rent in arrear and the tenant deserts the premises ; review by Circuit Court or Supreme Court in Middlesex)*

Where any distress is made for any kind of rent justly due, and any irregularity or unlawful act is afterwards done by the party distraining, or his agent, the distress shall not be unlawful, or the party making it a trespasser, ab initio ; but the party aggrieved may recover full satisfaction for the special damage, and no more, in an Action of Trespass, or on the case, at his election, with full costs ; but he shall not recover in any such Action, if tender of amends were made by the party distraining, or his agent, before Action brought, 1 V., c. 26. s. 16. *(margin: Remedy of party justly distrained on for subsequent irregularities or unlawful acts)*

In actions against Landlords, &c. they may plead the General Issue; costs

In Actions of Trespass, or upon the case, against any person entitled to rents, his bailiff or receiver, or other person, relating to any entry upon the premises chargeable, or to any distress or seizure, sale or disposal of any goods thereon, the defendant may plead the general issue, and give the special matter in evidence; and if the plaintiff become nonsuit, discontinue, or have judgment against him (in lieu of double costs; costs to be taxed under 8 V., c. 28, s. 22, see s. 3), 1 V., c. 26, s. 17.

Avowries and cognizance; costs

All defendants in replevin may avow or make cognizance generally that the plaintiff in replevin, or other tenant of the lands whereon the distress was made, enjoyed them under a grant or demise at such a certain rent during the time wherein the rent distrained for accrued, which rent was then and still remains due, without further setting forth the grant, tenure, demise, or title of the landlord or lessor, and if the plaintiff become nonsuit, &c., as in s. 17, 1 V., c. 26, s. 18.

Replevin bonds on distresses for rent, Assignments

The Provost-Marshal and officers to execute replevins shall, in very replevin of a distress for rent take, in their own names from the plaintiff, and two responsible persons as sureties, a bond in double the value of the goods distrained (to be ascertained by the oath of a witness not interested in the goods or distress to be administered by him), and conditioned for prosecuting the suit with effect and without delay, and for duly returning the goods and chattels distrained, in case a return shall be awarded, before any deliverance be made of the distress. And the Provost-Marshal or officer taking any such bond at the request and costs of the avowant, or person making cognizance, shall assign such bond to him by endorsing the same, and attesting it under his hand and seal, in the presence of two credible witnesses, which may be done without any stamp, provided the assignment so endorsed be duly stamped before action brought, and, if forfeited, the avowant or person making cognizance, may bring an action, and recover in his own name, and the Court, may, by rule of Court, give such relief to the parties upon the bond as is agreeable to justice and reason, and such rule shall have the effect of a defeazance, 1 V., c. 26, s. 19.

Larceny and Similar Offences.

Interpretation Document of title to goods

In the interpretation of this Act, "Document of Title to Goods" shall include any bill of lading, warehouse-keeper's certificate or order for the delivery or transfer of any goods or valuable thing bought and sold, note, or any other document used in the ordinary course of business, as proof of the possession or control of goods, or authorizing, or purporting to authorize either by endorsement or by delivery, the possession (possessor) of such document to transfer or receive any goods thereby represented or therein mentioned or referred to."

Document of title to lands

"Document of Title to Lands," shall include any deed, map, paper or parchment, written or printed, or partly written and partly printed, being or containing evidence of the title, or any part of the title to any real estate, or to any interest out of any real estate.

Trustee

"Trustee" shall mean a Trustee on some express trust, created by some deed, will or instrument, in writing, and include the heir or personal representative of any such Trustee, and any other person upon or to whom the duty of such trust has devolved or come; and also an Excutor and Administrator, and an official Manager or Assignee, or other like officer, acting under any p e en or future Act relating to Joint Stock Companies or Insolvency, 27 Va S4, 1 c. 33, s. 1.

And shall also include Receiver of the Court of Chancery and other officers of the Courts of Law and Equity of this Island, the Guardians of infants, the Provost-Marshal and his deputies, the Collector of Petty Debts and their deputies, Bailiffs employed to distrain for rent, and the Treasurers or recipients of property for any public, civil, parochial or eleemosynary purpose, or for any other person or persons or association of persons, 28 V., c. 15, s. 2.

Valuable security

"Valuable Security," shall include any order or other security whatever, entitling or evidencing the title of any person or body politic to any share or interest in any public stock or fund of this Island, or of the United Kingdom, or of any foreign state, or in any fund of any Body Corporate, Company or Society within this Island, or the United Kingdom, or in any foreign state or country, or to any deposit in any Bank, as also any debenture, deed, bond, bill, note, warrant, order or other security whatsoever for money, or for payment of money, whether of this Island or of Great Britain or Ireland, or of any foreign state, and any document or title to lands or goods as before defined.

"Property", shall include every description of real and personal property, money, debts and legacies, and all Deeds and Instruments relating to or evidencing the title or right to any property, or giving a right to recover or receive any money or goods, and shall also include, not only such property as was originally in the possession or under the control of any party, but also any property into or for which the same may have been converted or exchanged, and anything acquired by such conversion or exchange, whether immediately or otherwise.

For the purposes of this Act, the "Night" shall be deemed to commence at 7, p. m., and to conclude at 6, a.m. of the next succeeding day; "Month" shall mean calendar month, 27 V. S. 1, c. 33, s. 1.

Every Larceny, whatever the value stolen, shall be deemed of the same nature, and subject to the same incidents as Grand Larceny was before 4th March, 1837, and be dealt with, enquired of, tried, determined and punished as heretofore, in any Court which has now the power to try such offences or Larcenies, and also to try and punish all accessories thereto, 27 V., S. 1, c. 33, s. 2.

Any bailee of any chattel, money or valuable security, fraudulently taking or converting the same to his own use, or the use of any person other than the owner, although he shall not break bulk or otherwise determine the bailment, shall be guilty of Larceny, and may be convicted thereof on any indictment for Larceny: but this section shall not extend to any offence punishable on summary conviction, 27 V., S. 1, c. 33, s. 3.

Persons convicted of Simple Larceny, or any felony made punishable like Simple Larceny (except in cases otherwise provided for), shall be kept in penal servitude for 3 years, or imprisoned not exceeding 2 years, with or without hard labor, and with or without solitary confinement, 27 V., S. 1, c. 33, s. 4.

It shall be lawful to insert several counts in the same indictment against the same person for any number of distinct acts of stealing, not exceeding 3, committed by him against the same person within 6 months, from the first to the last of such acts, and to proceed thereon for all or any of them, 27, V., S. 1, c. 33, s. 5.

If, upon the trial, it appears that the property alleged to have been stolen at one time was taken at different times, the prosecutor shall not by reason thereof be required to elect upon which taking he will proceed, unless it appear there were more than 3 takings, or that more than the space of 6 months elapsed between the first and last of such takings. In either of such last mentioned cases, the prosecutor is required to elect to proceed for such number of takings, not exceeding 3, as appear to have taken place within 6 months from the first to the last, 27 V., S. 1, c. 33, s. 6.

The offence of Simple Larceny, committed after a previous conviction for felony, whether upon an indictment, or under any Act authorizing 2 or more Justices in Petty Sessions to convict for any Simple Larceny, shall be punishable by penal servitude for not exceeding 10 years, nor less than 3, or imprisonment for not exceeding 2 years, with or without hard labor, and with or without solitary confinement, 27 V., S. 1, c. 33, s. 7.

The offence of Simple Larceny, or any offence hereby made punishable like Simple Larceny, after a previous conviction of any indictable misdemeanor under this Act, shall be punishable by penal servitude for not exceeding 7 years, nor less than 3, or imprisonment not exceeding 2 years, with or without hard labor, and with or without solitary confinement, 27 V., S. 1, c. 33, s. 8.

Stealing any horse, mare, gelding, colt or filly, mule or ass, or any bull, cow, ox, heifer or calf, or any ram, ewe, sheep or lamb, pig or goat: felony, Penal servitude not exceeding 14 years, nor less than 3, or imprisonment not exceeding 2 years, with or without hard labor, and with or without solitary confinement, 27 V., S. 1, c, 33, s. 9.

Wilfully killing any animal, with intent to steal the carcase, skin, or any part of the animal so killed: Felony, punishable as upon a conviction of stealing, provided the offence of stealing the animal so killed would have amounted to Felony, 27 V., S. 1, c. 33, s. 10.

Property

Night
Month

Larceny, incidents of

By bailers

Simple Larceny—punishment

3 Acts of stealing in one indictment

Property taken at different times, election

Larceny after previous conviction for felony

For misdemeanor

Stealing horses, cattle, sheep, pigs, goats

Killing animals with intent to steal

Birds, dogs, and mals in confinement

Stealing any bird, or any dog, or any other beast or animal ordinarily kept in a state of confinement, or for any domestic purpose, not being the subject of Larceny at Common Law, or wilfully killing any such bird or beast, or animal, with intent to steal the same, or any part thereof, punishable before 2 Justices, by commitment to the Common Gaol or District Prison, or General Penitentiary, to be imprisoned only, or to be imprisoned and kept to hard labor for not exceeding 6 months, or by forfeiture and payment over and above the value of the bird, beast or other animal, of not exceeding £20, inclusive of costs. If after a previous conviction of any such offence against this or any former Act, the offender shall be committed to the General Penitentiary, or nearest District Prison, to hard labor for not exceeding 12 months, as the convicting Justices think fit, 27 V., S. 1, c. 33, s. 11.

Skin or Plumage

If any such dog or the skin, or bird, or the plumage, or beast, or the skin, or animal, or any part is found in the possession, or on the premises of any person, any Justice may restore it to the owner; and any person in whose possession, or on whose premises such dog, or the skin, or such bird, or the plumage, or beast, or the skin, or animal, or any part thereof is found, (such person knowing the dog, &c., has been stolen, and the plumage is that of a stolen bird, or the skin that of a stolen dog, or a stolen beast, or the part that of a stolen animal) shall, on conviction before a Justice, be liable for a first offence to such forfeiture, and for every subsequent offence, to such punishment as any person convicted of stealing any dog, &c., is made liable by the last preceding section, 27 V., S. 1, c. 33, s. 12.

Fish, Crabs, or Turtle

Unlawfully and wilfully taking or destroying any fish, crabs, cray-fish, oysters or turtle, in any water which runs through, or is in any land adjoining or belonging to any person, the owner of such water : a misdemeanor. Unlawfully and wilfully taking and destroying, or attempting to take or destroy any fish, &c., in any water, not being such as before mentioned, but which is private property : punishable before one Justice, by forfeiture and payment, over and above the value of the fish taken or destroyed (if any), of not exceeding £5, 27 V., S. 1, c 33, s. 13.

Stealing for destroying valuable securities

Stealing, or, for any fraudulent purpose, destroying, cancelling, or obliterating the whole or any part of any valuable security, other than a document of title to lands : Felony of the same nature, and in the same degree, and punishable in the same manner as if the person had stolen any chattel of like value, with the share, interest or deposit to which the security so stolen relates, or with the money due on the security or secured thereby, and remaining unsatisfied, or with the value of the goods or other valuable thing represented, mentioned or referred to in or by the security, 27 V., S. 1, c. 33, s. 14.

Document of title to Lands

Stealing, or, for any fraudulent purpose destroying, cancelling or obliterating, or concealing the whole or any part of any document of title to lands : Felony, penal servitude for 3 years, or imprisonment not exceeding 2 years, with or without hard labor, and with or without solitary confinement. In any indictment for any such offence relating to any document of title to land, it shall be sufficient to allege it to be, or to contain evidence of the title, or of part of the title of the person, or of some one of the persons having an interest, whether vested or contingent, legal or equitable in the real estate to which it relates, and to mention the real estate or some part thereof, 27 V., S. 1, c. 33, s. 15.

Wills

Either during the life of the Testator. or after his death, stealing or, for any fraudulent purpose, destroying, cancelling, obliterating, or concealing, the whole or any part of any Will, Codicil, or other Testamentary instrument, whether relating to real or personal estate, or both : Felony, penal servitude for life, or not less than 3 years, or imprisonment not exceeding 2 years, with or without hard labor, and with or without solitary confinement. In the Indictment for such offence, it shall not be necessary to allege that such Will, &c., is the property of any person. Nothing in this or the last preceding section, nor any preceding conviction or judgment thereupon shall prevent, lessen or impeach any remedy at Law or in Equity, any party aggrieved might have had if this Act had not passed, but no conviction of any offender shall be received in evidence in any action or suit against him. No person shall be liable to be convicted of any such felonies by any evidence whatever, in respect of any act done by him, if he has, any time previously to being charged, first disclosed such act, on oath, in consequence of any compulsory process of any Court of Law or Equity, in any action, suit or proceeding bona fide instituted by any party aggrieved, or has first disclosed the same in any compulsory examination or deposition before any Court, upon the hearing of any matter in any insolvency, 27 V., S. 1, c. 33, s. 16.

Stealing, or for any fraudulent purpose taking from its place of deposit for the time being, or from any person having the lawful custody, or unlawfully and maliciously cancelling, obliterating, injuring, or destroying the whole or any part of any record, writ, return, panel, process, interrogatory, deposition, affidavit, order or warrant of Attorney, or of any original document belonging to any Court of Record, or relating to any matter, civil or criminal, begun, depending or terminated in such Court, or of any bill, petition, answer, interrogatory, deposition or affidavit, order or decree, or of any original document of, or belonging to, any Court of Equity, or relating to any cause or matter, begun, depending or terminated in any such Court, or of any original document in any wise relating to the business of any office or employment under H. M., and being or remaining in any office appertaining to any Court of Justice, or in any Government or Public Office: Felony; penal servitude for 3 years, or imprisonment not exceeding 2 years, with or without hard labor, and with or without solitary confinement. It shall not be necessary in any Indictment to allege that the article is the property of any person, 27 V., S. 1, c. 33. s. 17. Records, &c.

Stealing or ripping, cutting, severing or breaking, with intent to steal, any glass or woodwork belonging to any building, or any lead, iron copper, brass or other metal, or any utensil or fixture, whether made of metal or other material, or of both respectively, fixed in or to any building, or anything made of metal fixed in any land, being private property, or for a fence to any dwelling house, garden, or in any street, or in any place dedicated to public use or ornament, or in any burial ground: Felony, punishable as in the case of Simple Larceny. In case of any such thing fixed in such street or place as aforesaid, it shall not be necessary to allege the same to be the property of any person, 27 V., S. 1, c. 33, s. 18. Fixtures, &c.

Stealing or cutting, breaking, rooting up, or otherwise destroying or damaging with intent to steal, the whole, or any part of any tree, sapling or shrub, or any underwood growing in any pleasure ground, garden, orchard or avenue, or in any ground adjoining or belonging to any dwelling-house (in case the value of the article or articles stolen, or the amount of injury done exceed £1): Felony, punishable as in the case of Simple Larceny. If growing elsewhere than in any of the situations above mentioned (in case the value or amount of injury exceed £3): Felony, punishable as in case of Simple Larceny, 27 V., S. 1, c. 33, s. 19. Trees, shrubs, &c. in gardens, &c.
Value, &c. exceeding £1
Exceeding £3

Stealing or cutting, &c., with intent to steal the whole or any part of any tree, sapling or shrub, or any underwood wheresoever growing, the stealing or injury done being to the amount of 1s. at the least, the offender, on conviction before 2 Justices, shall forfeit and pay, over and above the value or amount of injury, not exceeding £3. For a second offence, after a conviction under this or any former Act, imprisonment in the General Penitentiary, or nearest District Prison, with hard labor, not exceeding 12 months. For a subsequent offence, after having been twice convicted, whether both or either of the convictions were before or after the Act: Felony, punishable as in case of Simple Larceny, 27 V., S. 1, c. 33, s. 20. In other places
Value 1s at least
Not exceeding £3
After previous convictions

Stealing or cutting, breaking or throwing down, with intent to steal any part of any live or dead fence, or any wooden post, pale, wire or rail, set up or used as a fence, or any stile or gate, or any part thereof respectively: the offender, on conviction before a Justice, shall forfeit and pay, over and above the value of the articles stolen, or the amount of injury done, not exceeding £3, or if after a previous conviction, commitment to the General Penitentiary or nearest District Prison, with hard labor, not exceeding 12 months, 27 V., S. 1, c. 33, s. 21. Fences, posts, &c.
After previous conviction

If the whole or any part of any tree, sapling or shrub, or any underwood, or any part of any live or dead fence, or any post, pale, wire, rail, stile or gate, or any part thereof, being of the value of 1s. at the least, is found in the possession of, or on the premises of any person, with his knowledge, and he being summoned before a Justice shall not satisfy the Justice that he came lawfully by the same, he shall forfeit and pay, over Trees, fences, posts, &c. of the value of 1s for which no satisfactory account is given and above the value of the article so found, not exceeding £2, 27 V., S. 1, c. 33, s. 22.

Stealing plants, &c. in a garden orchard, provision ground or cane-piece, &c. value exceeding 10s

Stealing or destroying, or damaging with intent to steal any tree, plant, root, fruit or other vegetable production growing in any garden, orchard, provision ground, or cane or coffee or pimento field, the value whereof exceeds 10s., punishable as Simple Larceny, 28 V., c. 4, s. 2.

Whipping after previous conviction, 28 V., c. 18
Value not exceeding 10s
See s. 5, and 27 V., S. 1, c. 33, s. 103
After previous conviction ; see 28 V., c. 18, whipping

If the value does not exceed 10s., the offender, on conviction, before 2 Justices, shall be committed to the nearest District Prison, or to the General Penitentiary to hard labor, for not exceeding 6 calendar months. If any person so convicted, afterwards commit any such offence, he shall be guilty of Felony; and liable to the same punishment as for Simple Larceny, 28 V., c. 4, s. 3.

Stealing plants, &c. growing elsewhere
After previous conviction ; see 28 V., c. 18, whipping

Stealing or destroying, &c., any tree, plant, root, fruit or other vegetable production, used for the food of any man or beast, or for medicine, or for distilling, or for dying, or for or in the course of any manufacture, growing on any land, open or enclosed, not being a garden, orchard, provision ground, or cane or coffee or pimento field—commitment, on conviction before 2 Justices, to the nearest District Prison or the Penitentiary, to hard labor for not exceeding 2 calendar months. After a previous conviction : Felony, punishable as above, 28 V., c. 4, s. 4.

Commitment to penitentiary by Justices

The power of commitment to the General Penitentiary shall be exercised only by Justices authorized by the proviso to 27 V., c. 33, s. 103 ; 28 V., c. 4, s. 5.

Prosecutions for offences under this Act shall be deemed public prosecutions, 28 V., c. 4, s. 6.

Robery stealing from prison

Robbing any person, or stealing any chattel, money or valuable security from the person of another : felony : penal servitude not exceeding 14 years, nor less than 3 years, or imprisonment not exceeding 2 years, with or without hard labour, and with or without solitary confinement, 27 V., S. 1, c. 33, s. 25.

Prisoner may be convicted of assault with intent to rob

If, upon the trial of any person upon any Indictment for robbery, it appear to the Jury that the defendant did not commit the crime of robbery, but that he did commit an assault with intent to rob, he shall not be entitled to be acquitted, but the Jury may return as their verdict, that the defendant is guilty of an assault with intent to rob, and, thereupon he may be punished as if he had been convicted upon an Indictment for feloniously assaulting with intent to rob. No person so tried shall be liable to be afterwards prosecuted for the robbery, 27 V., S. 1, c. 33, s. 26.

Assault with intent to rob

Assaulting any person with intent to rob : Felony, except in cases where a greater punishment is provided by this Act ; 3 years' penal servitude, or imprisonment not exceeding 2 years, with or without hard labor, and with or without solitary confinement, 27 V., S. 1, c. 33, s. 27.

Robbery or assault with intent to rob, being armed, and using personal violence

Being armed with any offensive weapon or instrument, robbing, or assaulting, with intent to rob any person, or together with one or more others robbing or assaulting with intent to rob any person, and at the time of, or immediately before, or immediately after such robbery, wounding, beating, striking or using any other personal violence to any person : Felony ; penal servitude for life, or not less than 3 years, or imprisonment not exceeding 2 years, with or without hard labor, and with or without solitary confinement, 27 V., S. 1, c. 33, s. 28.

Sending, &c. threatening letters demanding property, &c.

Sending, delivering, or uttering, or directly or indirectly causing to be received, knowing the contents, any letter or writing, demanding of any person with menaces, and without any reasonable or probable cause, any property, chattel, money, valuable security or other valuable thing : Felony ; the like punishment, 27 V., S. 1, c. 33, s. 29.

Demanding property with menaces or force

With menaces, or by force demanding any property, chattel, money, valuable security, or other valuable thing of any person, with intent to steal the same : Felony ; 3 years' penal servitude, with or without hard labor, and with or without solitary confinement, (sic.) 27 V., S. 1, c. 33, s. 30.

Letters threatening to accuse of crime to extort money, &c.

Sending, delivering or uttering, or directly or indirectly causing to be received, knowing the contents, any letter or writing, accusing or threatening to accuse any other person of any crime punishable by law with death or penal servitude for not less than 7 years, or of any assault with intent to commit any rape, or of any attempt or endeavor to commit any rape, or of any infamous crime as after defined, with a view or intent in any of such cases to extort or gain, by means of such letter or writing, any property, chattel, money, valuable security or other valuable thing from any person: Felony; penal servitude for life, or not less than 3 years, or imprisonment not exceeding 2 years, with or without hard labor, and with or without solitary confinement. The abominable crime of Buggery, committed either with mankind or beast, and every assault with intent to commit the said abominable crime, and every attempt or endeavor to commit the said abominable crime, and every solicitation, persuasitn, promise, or threat offered or made to any person whereby to induce such person to commit or permit the said abominable crime, shall be deemed an infamous crime within this Act, 27 V., S. 1, c. 33, s. 31.

Accusing or threatening to accuse either the person to whom such accusation or threat is made, or any other person of any of the infamous or other crimes lastly before mentioned, with a view or intent in any of the cases last aforesaid, to extort or gain from the person so accused, or threatened to be accused, or from any other person, any property, chattel, money, valuable security, or other valuable thing: Felony; penal servitude for life, or for not less than 3 years, or imprisonment not exceeding 2 years, with or without hard labor, 27 V., S. 1, c. 33, s. 32. Accusing or threatening, &c. to extort money. &c.

With intent to defraud or injure any other person by any unlawful violence to, or restraint of, or threat of violence to, or restraint of the person of another, or by accusing or threatening to accuse any person of any treason, felony, or infamous crime as before defined, compelling or inducing any person to execute, make, accept, endorse, alter, or destroy the whole or any part of any valuable security, or to write, impress, or affix his name, or the name of any other person, or of any company, firm or copartnership, or the seal of any body corporate, company or society, upon or to any paper or parchment, in order that the same may be afterwards made or converted into, or used or dealt with as a valuable security: Felony; penal servitude for life, or for not less than 3 years, or imprisonment not exceeding 2 years, with or without hard labor, and with or without solitary confinement, 27 V., S. 1, c. 33, s. 33. Accusing or threatening, &c to compel execution of papers, &c. to be used as valuable securities

It shall be immaterial whether the menaces or threats be of violence, injury or accusation, to be caused or made by the offender, or by any other person, 27 V., S. 1, c. 33, s. 34. Nature of threat immaterial

Breaking and entering any church, chapel, meeting-house, or other place of Divine worship, and committing any felony therein, or being in any church, &c., committing any Felony therein, and breaking out of the same: Felony; penal servitude for life, or not less than 3 years, or imprisonment not exceeding two years, with or without hard labor, and with or without solitary confinement, 27 V., S. 1, c. 33, s. 35. Sacrilege, breaking in or out of church, &c. or place of divine worship

Entering the dwelling-house of another with intent to commit Felony or being in such dwelling-house, committing any Felony therein, and in either case breaking out of the dwelling-house in the night (see s. 1), shall be deemed Burglary, 27 V., S. 1, c. 33, s. 36. Entering dwelling house to commit felony; felony in dwelling house, and breaking out in night, burglary

Persons convicted of Burglary, shall be liable to penal servitude for life, or not less than 3 years, or imprisonment not exceeding 2 years, with or without hard labor, and with or without solitary confinement, 27 V., S. 1, c. 33, s. 37. Punishment of burglary

No building, although within the same curtilage with any dwelling house, and occupied therewith, shall be deemed part thereof for any of the purposes of this Act, unless there be a communication between such building and dwelling-house, either immediate or by means of a covered or enclosed passage leading from the one to the other, 27 V. S. 1, c. 33, s. 38. What buildings parts of dwelling house

Entering any dwelling-house in the night, with intent to commit any Felony therein: Felony; penal servitude not exceeding 7 years, nor less than 3, or imprisonment, not exceeding 2 years, with or without hard labor, or with or without solitary confinement, 27 V., S. 1 c. 33, s. 39. Entering a dwelling house in the night with intent to commit felony

Breaking and entering any building, and committing any Felony therein, such building being within the curtilage, of a dwelling house, and occupied therewith, but not part thereof according to the provision before mentioned, or being in any such building, committing any Felony therein, and breaking out of the same: Felony; penal servitude not exceeding 14 years, nor less Breaking into or out of a building without the curtilage but not part of a dwelling house, and committing felony than 3, or imprisonment not exceeding 2 years, with or without hard labor, and with or without solitary confinement, 27 V., S. 1, c. 33, s. 40.

Breaking into a house, shop, &c., and committing felony, or committing felony and breaking out

Breaking and entering any dwelling-house, school-house, shop, warehouse or counting-house, and committing any Felony therein, or being in any dwelling-house &c., committing any Felony therein, and breaking out of the same : Felony ; penal servitude not exceeding 14 years, nor less than 3 years, or imprisonment not exceeding 2 years, with or without hard labor, and with or without solitary confinement, 27 V., S. 1, c. 33, s. 41.

Breaking and entering a dwelling house, church, chapel, &c., shop, &c. with intent to commit a felony

Breaking and entering any dwelling-house, church, chapel, meeting-house or other place of Divine worship, or any building within the curtilage, school-house, shop, warehouse or counting-house, with intent to commit felony therein : Felony ; penal servitude not exceeding 7 years, nor less than 3, or imprisonment not exceeding 2 years, with or without hard labor, and with or without solitary confinement, 27 V., S. 1, c. 33, s. 42.

Being found by night armed, with intent to break, &c. any buildings, or with implements of house-breaking or disguised, misdemeanor

Being found by night armed with any dangerous or offensive instrument, with intent to break or enter into any dwelling-house or other building whatsoever, and to commit any Felony therein, or being found by night having in one's possession, without lawful excuse (the proof of which shall be upon the person) any pick-lock, key, crow-jack, bit, or other instrument of house-breaking, or being found by night with one's face blacked, or otherwise disguised, with intent to commit any Felony, or being found by night in any dwelling or other building whatsoever with intent to commit any Felony therein : Misdemeanor, penal servitude for 3 years, or imprisonment not exceeding 2 years, with or without hard labor, 27 V., S. 1, c. 33, s. 43.

After previous conviction for felony or misdemeanor, felony

Persons convicted of any Misdemeanor in s. 43. committed after a previous conviction either for Felony or Misdemeanor, shall be liable on such subsequent conviction to penal servitude not exceeding 10 years, nor less than 3 years, or imprisonment not exceeding 2 years, with or without hard labor, 27 V., S. 1 c. 33, s. 44.

Stealing in a dwelling house of the value of £3

Stealing in any dwelling-house any chattel, money or valuable security, to the value in the whole of £3 or more : Felony ; penal servitude not exceeding 14 years, nor less than 3 years, or, imprisonment, not exceeding 2 years, with or without hard labor, and with or without solitary confinement, 27 V., S. 1, c. 33, s. 45.

With menaces and putting in bodily fear

Stealing any chattel, money, or valuable security in any dwelling house, and by any menace or threat putting any one being therein in bodily fear : Felony ; penal servitude not exceeding 14 years, nor less than 3, or imprisonment not exceeding 2 years, with or without hard labor, and with or without solitary confinement, 27 V., S. 1, c. 33, s. 46.

Stealing goods in process of manufacture, value 10s

Stealing to the value of 10s. any goods or articles of manufacture, whilst laid, placed, or exposed during any stage, process, or progress of manufacture in any building, field, or other place : Felony ; penal servitude not exceeding 14 years, nor less than 3, or imprisonment not exceeding 2 years, with or without hard labor, and with or without solitary confinement, 27 V., S. 1, c. 33, s. 47.

Exportable produce to the value of 1s found under search warrant without a satisfactory account

If any Sugar already manufactured, or in the process of manufacture, or any Coffee or Pimento, Ginger or other valuable Produce commonly used for exportation in the Island, being of the value of 1s. at the least, is, by virtue of a Search Warrant, to be granted as after mentioned, (S 87) found in the possession of any person, or on his premises, with his knowledge, and such person, being taken before a Justice, shall not satisfy the Justice that he came lawfully by the same, he shall, on conviction, forfeit and pay, over and above the value of the article so found, not exceeding £6, 27 V., S. 1, c. 33, s. 48.

Stealing in a Vessel or from a wharf

Stealing any goods or merchandize in any vessel, canoe or boat of any description whatsoever, in any haven or port of entry, or discharge, on any navigable river, or in any creek or basin belonging to, or communicating with such haven or port, or river, or stealing any goods or merchandize, from any wharf or quay : Felony ; penal servitude not exceeding 14 years, nor less than 3, or imprisonment not exceeding 2 years, with or without hard labor, and with or without solitary confinement, 27 V., S. 1, c. 33, s. 49.

Plundering or stealing any part of any ship or vessel in distress, or wrecked, stranded, or cast on shore, or any goods, merchandize, or articles of any kind belonging to such ship or vessel: Felony; penal servitude not exceeding 14 years, nor less than 3, or imprisonment not exceeding 2 years, with or without hard labor, and with or without solitary confinement; and the offender may be indicted and tried either in the parish or precinct in which the offence is committed, or any next adjoining, 27 V., S. 1, c. 33, s. 50.

If any goods, merchandize or articles of any kind belonging to any ship or vessel in distress, or wrecked, stranded or cast on shore, are found in the possession of any person with his knowledge, or on the premises of any person with his knowledge, and such person, being taken or summoned before a Justice, shall not satisfy him that he came lawfully by the same, they shall, by order of the Justice, be forthwith delivered over to, or for the use of the rightful owner, and the offender, shall, on conviction by him, be committed to the Common Gaol or District Prison, or General Penitentiary, to be imprisoned only, or to hard labor, not exceeding 6 months, or forfeit and pay, over and above the value, not exceeding £12, 27 V., S. 1, c. 33, s. 51.

If any person offer or expose for sale any goods, merchandize or articles unlawfully taken, or reasonably suspected to have been taken from any ship or vessel in distress, or wrecked, stranded or cast on shore, any person to whom they shall be offered for sale, or Officer of Customs or Peace Officer, may lawfully seize the same, and with all convenient speed, carry the same, or give notice of such seizure to some Justice; and if the person who has offered or exposed the same for sale being summoned, does not appear and satisfy the Justice that he came lawfully by such goods, merchandize or articles, they shall, by his order, be forthwith delivered over to, or for the use of the rightful owner, upon payment of a reasonable reward (to be ascertained by the Justice) to the person who seized; and the offender shall, on conviction by him, either be committed to the Common Gaol, District Prison or General Penitentiary, to be imprisoned or kept to hard labor for not exceeding 6 months, or else shall forfeit and pay over and above the value of the goods, merchandize or articles, not exceeding £12, 27 V., S. 1, c. 33, s. 52.

Whosoever being a Clerk or servant, or being employed for the purpose, or in the capacity of a Clerk or servant, steals any chattel, money or valuable security belonging to, or in the possession or power of his Master or employer, shall be guilty of Felony: penal servitude not exceeding 14 years, nor less than 3 years, or imprisonment not exceeding 2 years, with or without hard labor, and with or without solitary confinement, 27 V., S. 1, c. 33, s. 53.

Whosoever being a Clerk or servant, or being employed for the purpose or in the capacity of a Clerk or servant, fraudulently embezzles any chattel, money or valuable security delivered to, or received or taken into possession by him for, or in the name, or on the account of his Master or employer, or any part thereof, shall be deemed to have feloniously stolen the same from his Master or employer, although not received into the possession of such Master or employer, otherwise than by the actual possession of his Clerk, servant, or other person so employed: penal servitude not exceeding 14 years, nor less than 3 years, or imprisonment not exceeding 2 years (with or without hard labor, and with or without solitary confinement, 27 V., S. 1, c. 33, s. 54.

Whosoever being employed in the Public Service of Her Majesty, or being a Constable or other person employed in the Police of any city, parish, precinct or place, shall steal any chattel, money or valuable security belonging to, or in the possession or power of her Majesty, or intrusted to or received, or taken into possession by him by virtue of his employment, shall be guilty of Felony: penal servitude not exceeding 14 years, nor less than 3, or imprisonment not exceeding 2 years, with or without hard labor, and with or without solitary confinement, 27 V., S. 1, c. 33, s. 55.

Whosoever being employed in the Public Service of Her Majesty, or being a Constable, or employed in the Police of any County, City, District or place whatsoever, and intrusted, by virtue of such employment, with the receipt, custody, management or control of any chattel, money or valuable security, embezzles any chattel, money or valuable security intrusted to, or received or taken into possession by him by virtue of his employment, or any part, or in any mannner, fraudulently applies or disposes of the same, or any part, to his own use or benefit, or for any purpose, except for the Public Service, shall be deemed to have feloniously stolen the same from Her Majesty : penal servitude not exceeding 14 years, nor less than 3, or imprisonment, not exceeding 2 years, with or without hard labour. Offenders against this or s. 55, shall be dealt with, indicted, tried and punished, either in the county or place in which they are apprehended, or are in custody or have committed the offence ; and in every case of Larceny, embezzlement or fraudulent application or disposition of any chattel, money or valuable security in this, or s. 55, in the Warrant of Commitment and Indictment, the property may be laid in H. M., 27 V., S. 1, c. 33, s. 56.

3 Distinct acts of embezzlement may be charged in one indictment; description of money or valuable security; embezzlement

For preventing difficulties in the prosecution of offenders, in any case of embezzlement, fraudulent application or disposition before mentioned, it shall be lawful to charge in the Indictment and proceed for any number, not exceeding 3 distinct acts of embezzlement, or of fraudulent application or disposition committed against Her Majesty, or against the same Master or employer, within 6 months from the first to the last act. In any Indictment where the offence relates to any money or valuable security, it shall be sufficient to allege the embezzlement or fraudulent application or disposition to be of money, without specifying any particular Coin or valuable security; and such allegation, so far as regards the description of the property, shall be sustained if the offender is proved to have embezzled or fraudulently applied or disposed of any amount, although the particular species of Coin or valuable security, of which such amount was composed, is not proved, or if he is proved to have embezzled or fraudulently applied or disposed of any piece of Coin or valuable security, or any portion of the value, although such piece of Coin or valuable security may have been delivered to him, in order that some part of the value should be returned to the party delivering the same, or to some other person, and such part has been returned accordingly, 27 V., S. 1, c. 33, s. 57.

Persons indicted for embezzlement may be found guilty of larceny; or those indicted for larceny of embezzlement

If upon the trial of any person indicted for embezzlement, or fraudulent application or disposition, it is proved that he took the property in any such manner as to amount in law to Larceny, he shall not be entitled to be acquitted, but the Jury may return as their verdict that he is not guilty of embezzlement or fraudulent application or disposition, but is guilty of Simple Larceny, or of Larceny as a clerk, servant, or person employed for the purpose or in the capacity of a clerk or servant, or as a person employed in the public service, or in the Police, as the case may be; and thereupon he shall be liable to be punished as if he had been convicted upon an Indictment upon such Larceny   If upon the trial of any person indicted for Larceny, it is proved that he took the property in any such manner as to amount in law to embezzlement or fraudulent application or disposition, he shall not be entitled to be acquitted, but the Jury may return as their verdict, that he is not guilty of Larceny, but is guilty of embezzlement, or fraudulent application or disposition, as the case may be; and the person may be punished as if convicted, upon an Indictment for such embezzlement, &c.; and no person so tried for embezzlement, &c., or for Larceny, shall be liable to be afterwards prosecuted upon the same facts, 27 V., S. 1, c. 33, s. 58.

Larceny by tenants or lodgers

Whosoever shall steal any chattel or fixture let to be used by him or her in or with any house or lodging, whether the contract be entered into by him or her, or her husband, or by any person on behalf of him or her, or her husband : Felony, imprisonment not exceeding 2 years, with or without hard labor, and with or without solitary confinement; and in case

Where value exceeds £5 Indictment

the value exceed £5, penal servitude not exceeding 7 years nor less than 3, or imprisonment not exceeding two years, with or without hard labor and with or without solitary confinement. In every case of stealing any chattel in this section mentioned, an Indictment may be preferred in the common form as for Larceny, and in every case of stealing any fixture in this section mentioned, the Indictment may be in the same form as if the offender were not a Tenant or Lodger; and in either case the property may be laid in the owner or person letting to hire, 27 V., S. 1, c. 33, s. 59.

Fraudulent conversion by bankers, merchants, brokers, attorneys or agents intrusted with moneys, chattels or securities, under written directions, or without authori-

Whosoever having been intrusted, either solely or jointly with any other person as a Banker, Merchant, Broker, Attorney, or other Agent, with any money, or security for the payment of money, with any direction in writing to apply, pay, or deliver such money or security, or any part thereof, (or) of the proceeds, or any part of the proceeds of such security, for any purpose or to any person specified in such direction, in violation of good faith, and contrary to the terms of such direction, in any wise converts to his own use or benefit, or the use or benefit of any person other than the person by whom he was so entrusted, such money, security, or proceeds, or any part ; and whosoever having been intrusted either solely or jointly with any other person as a banker, merchant, broker, attorney, or other agent, with any chattel or valuable security, or any power of Attorney for the sale or transfer of any share or interest in any public stock or fund, whether of the Island or elsewhere, or in any stock or fund of any Body Corporate, Company, or Society, for safe custody or for any special purpose, without any authority to sell, negotiate, transfer, or pledge, in violation of good faith, and contrary to the object or purpose for which it was intrusted to him, sells, negotiates, transfers, pledges, or in any manner converts to his own use or benefit, or to the use or benefit of any person other than that by whom he was so intrusted, such chattel or security or the proceeds or any part, or the share or interest in the stock or fund, to which such power of Attorney relates, or any part: Misdemeanor; penal servitude not exceeding 7 years, nor less than 3, or imprisonment not exceeding 2 years, with or without hard labor, and with or without solitary confinement. But nothing in this section relating to Agents shall affect any Trustee in or under any instrument whatsoever, or any mortgagee of any property, real or personal, in respect of any act done by him in relation to the property comprised in, or affected by any such trust or mortgage nor restrain any Banker, Merchant, Broker, Attorney or other Agent, from receiving any money which is, or becomes actually due and payable upon or by virtue of any valuable security according to its tenor and effect, as he might have done if this Act had not been passed, nor from selling, transferring, or otherwise disposing of any securities or effects in his possession upon which he has any lien, claim, or demand, enabling him by law so to do, unless such sale, transfer or other disposal extend to a greater number or part of such securities or effects than are requisite for satisfying such lien, claim, or demand, 27 V., S. 1, c. 33, s. 60.

ty to sell or pledge, &c., not to affect trustees or mortgagees, or receipts of moneys actually due, or securities or sales &c. to extent of any lien or claim

Whosoever being a Banker, Merchant, Broker, Attorney, or Agent, and being intrusted either solely or conjointly with any other person with the property of any other person for safe custody, with intent to defraud, sells negotiates, transfers, pledges, or in any manner converts or appropriates the same, or any part, to, or for his own use or benefit, or the use or benefit of any person other than that by whom he was so intrusted: Misdemeanor; liable to any of the punishments the Court may award under s. 60, 27 V., S. 1, c. 33, s. 61.

Fraudulent sales &c of property entrusted for safe custody

Whosoever being intrusted, either solely or jointly with any other person, with any power of attorney for the sale or transfer of any property, fraudulently sells, transfers, or otherwise converts the same or any part to his own use or benefit, or the use or benefit of any person other than that by whom he was so entrusted: Misdemeanor; liable to any of the punishments as above, 27 V., S. 1, c. 33 s. 62.

Fraudulent sales &c, of property by persons entrusted with powers of attorney

Whosoever, being a Factor or Agent, intrusted either solely or jointly with any other person for the purpose of sale, or otherwise, with the possession of any goods, or of any document of title to goods (see s. 1), contrary to or without the authority of his principal, for his own use or benefit, or the use or benefit of any other person than that by whom he was so intrusted, and in violation of good faith, makes any consignment, deposit, transfer or delivery of any goods or document of title so entrusted to him as in this section before mentioned, as and by way of a pledge, lien, or security for any money, or valuable security borrowed or received by such factor or agent, at or before the time of making such consignment, deposit, transfer or delivery, or intended to be thereafter borrowed or received ; or contrary to or without such authority, for his own use or benefit, or the use and benefit, of any other person than that by whom he was so intrusted, and in violation of good faith, accepts any advance of any money or valuable security on the faith of any contract or agreement to consign, deposit, transfer, or deliver any such goods or document of title, shall be guilty of a Misdemeanor, and liable to any of the punishments as above. Every Clerk or other person, knowingly and wilfully acting and assisting in making any such consignment, deposit, transfer or delivery, or in accepting or procuring such advance, shall be guilty of Misdemeanor, and liable to any of the same punishments. No such Factor or Agent shall be liable to any prose-

Factors fraudulently obtaining advance on the property of their principals

Clerks wilfully assisting

Cases excepted where the pledge does not exceed the amount of their lien

cution for consigning, depositing, transferring or delivering any such goods, or documents of title, in case they are not made a security for, or subject to the payment of any greater sum than the amount which at the time of such consignment, deposit, transfer or delivery was justly due and owing to such Agent from his Principal, together with the amount of any Bill of Exchange, drawn by or on account of such Principal, and accepted by such Factor or Agent, 27 V., S. 1, c. 33, s. 63.

Definitions of terms

Any Factor or Agent intrusted as aforesaid, and possessed of any such document of title (see s. 1), whether derived immediately from the owner of such goods or otherwise, by reason of such Factor or Agent having been intrusted with the possession of the goods, or of any other document of title **Entrusted** thereto, shall be deemed to have been " intrusted" with the possession of the goods represented by such document of title ; and every contract **Pledge—Lien** pledging or giving a lien upon such document of title shall be deemed a **Possessed** " pledge" of, or " lien" upon the goods to which it relates ; and such Factor or Agent shall be deemed to be ' possessed' of such goods or document, whether in his actual custody or held by any other person, subject to his **Advance** control, or for him, or on his behalf. Where any loan or " advance" is bona fide made to any Factor or Agent intrusted with and in the possession of any such goods or document of title, on the faith of any contract or agreement in writing, to consign, deposit, transfer or deliver such goods or document of title, and such goods or documents of title are actually received by the person making such loan or advance, without notice that the Factor or Agent was not authorized to make such pledge or security, every such loan or advance shall be deemed to be a loan or advance on the security of such goods or document of title within s. 63, though not actually received by the person making such loan or advance till the period subsequent thereto. **Contract or agreement** Any " contract or agreement," whether made direct by such Factor, or with any clerk or person on his behalf, shall be deemed a contract or agreement with **Payment** such Factor or Agent, and any payment made, whether by money or Bill of Exchange, or other negotiable security an " advance," within s. 63 ; and a **Possession, evidence of entrusting unless the contrary is shewn** Factor or Agent in possession as aforesaid of such goods or document, shall be taken, for the purposes of s. 63, to have been intrusted therewith by the owner, unless the contrary be shewn in evidence, 27 V., S. 1, c. 33, s. 64.

Trustees fraudulently disposing of, or destroying property

Whosoever being a Trustee (see s. 1) of any property for the use or benefit, either wholly or partially, of some other person, or for any public or charitable purpose, with intent to defraud, converts or appropriates the same or any part to or for his own use or benefit, or the use or benefit of any person other than such person as aforesaid, or for any other purpose than such public or charitable purpose, or otherwise disposes of, or destroys such property or any part, shall be guilty of a Misdemeanor, and liable to any **No prosecution to be commenced without the sanction of a Judge or the Attorney General** of the punishments last mentioned (s. 60). No proceeding or prosecution for any offence in this section shall be commenced without the Attorney General's sanction. Where any civil proceeding has been taken against any person to whom this section applies, no person who has taken such civil proceeding shall commence any prosecution under this section without the sanction of the Court or Judge before whom such civil proceeding was had, or is pending, 27 V., S. 1, c. 33, s. 65.

Directors, &c. of corporations or public companies fraudulently appropriating property

Whosoever being a Director, Member, or Public Officer, of any Body Corporate or Public Company, fraudulently takes or applies for his own use or benefit, or for any use or purposes (omitted other than the use or purposes) of such Body Corporate or Public Company, any of the property of such Body Corporate or Public Company, shall be guilty of a Misdemeanor, and liable to any of the punishments before mentioned, (s. 60) 27 V., S. 1, c. 33, s. 66.

Or keeping fraudulent accounts

Whosoever being a Director, Public Officer, or Manager of any Body Corporate or Public Company, as such, receives or possesses himself of any of its property, otherwise than in payment of a just debt or demand, and, with intent to defraud, omits to make, or to cause or direct to be made a full and true entry thereof in its books and accounts, shall be guilty of a Misdemeanor, and liable to any of the punishments before mentioned (s. 60) 27 V., S. 1, c. 33, s. 67.

Or wilfully destroying or falsifying books, &c.

Whosoever being a Director, Manager, Public Officer, or Member of any Body Corporate or Public Company, with intent to defraud, destroys, alters, mutilates, or falsifies any book, paper, writing, or valuable security belonging thereto, or makes or concurs in the making of any false entry, or omits or concurs in omitting any material particular in any book of account or other document, shall be guilty of a Misdemeanor, and liable to any of the punishments before mentioned (s. 60), 27 V., S. 1, c. **33**, s. 68.

Whosoever being a Director, Manager, or Public Officer of any Body Corporate or Public Company, makes, circulates or publishes, or concurs in making, circulating or publishing any written statement or account which he knows to be false in any material particular, with intent to deceive or defraud any Member, Shareholder, or Creditor of such Body Corporate or Public Company, or with intent to induce any person to become a Shareholder or Partner therein, or to entrust or advance any property to such Body Corporate or Public Company, or to enter into any security for the benefit thereof, shall be guilty of a Misdemeanor, and liable to any of the punishments last before mentioned (s. 60); 27 V., S. 1, c. 33, s. 69.

Or publishing fraudulent statements

Nothing in any of the last 8 sections (62–69) shall enable or entitle any person to refuse to make a full and complete discovery by answer, or affidavit in answer to any Bill in Equity, or Cause Petition, or to answer any question or interrogatory in any civil proceeding in any Court, or upon the hearing of any matter in bankruptcy or insolvency. No person shall be liable to be convicted of any of the Misdemeanors in such sections mentioned, by any evidence whatever, in respect of any act done by him, if he, at any time previously to his being charged with such offence, has first disclosed such act, on oath, in consequence of any compulsory process of any Court of Law or Equity, in any action, suit or proceeding, bona fide instituted by any party aggrieved, or has first disclosed the same in any compulsory examination or deposition before any Court, upon the hearing of any matter in bankruptcy or insolvency, 27 V., S. 1, c. 33, s. 70.

No person to be exempt from answering any questions or interrogatories in civil proceedings or insolvency, but persons making compulsory disclosures not liable to prosecution

Nothing in the last 9 sections, nor any proceeding, conviction or judgment had or taken thereon against any person under any of them, shall prevent, lessen or impeach any remedy at Law or in Equity, which any party aggrieved might have had if this Act had not been passed; but no conviction shall be received in evidence in any action or suit against him, nor shall affect or prejudice any agreement entered into or security given by any Trustee, having for its object the restoration or re-payment of any trust property misappropriated, 27 V., S. 1, c. 33, s. 71.

No remedy at law or equity affected; convictions not to be received in evidence in any action or suit; no agreement for restoration, &c. of trust property affected

By any false pretence obtaining from any other person any chattel, money or valuable security, with intent to defraud: Misdemeanor, penal servitude for 3 years, or imprisonment not exceeding 2 years, with or without hard labor, and with or without solitary confinement. If upon the trial of any person indicted for such Misdemeanor, it is proved he obtained the property in question in any such manner as to amount in law to Larceny, he shall not be entitled to be acquitted of such Misdemeanor; and no person tried for such Misdemeanor shall be liable to be afterwards prosecuted for Larceny upon the same facts. It shall be sufficient in any indictment for obtaining or attempting to obtain any such property by false pretences, to allege that the accused did the act with intent to defraud, without alleging an intent to defraud any particular person, and without alleging any ownership of the chattel, money or valuable security; and on the trial it shall not be necessary to prove an intent to defraud any particular person, but sufficient to prove that the party did the act charged with an intent to defraud, 27 V., S. 1, c. 33, s. 72.

Obtaining goods, &c. by false pretences

Not to be acquitted because the offence amounts to larceny

Indictment intent to defraud

Whosoever shall, by any false pretence cause or procure any money to be paid, or any chattel or valuable security to be delivered to any other person for the use or benefit, or on the account of the person making such false pretence, or of any other person, with intent to defraud, shall be deemed to have obtained such money, chattel or valuable security within the meaning of the last preceding section, 27 V., S. 1, c. 33, s. 73.

Where the money, &c. is delivered to a 3d person under the false pretence

With intent to defraud or injure any other person by any false pretence, fraudulently causing or inducing any other person to execute, make, accept, indorse or destroy the whole or any part of any valuable security, or to write, impress, or affix his name or the name of any other person, or of any company, firm or copartnership, or the Seal of any Body Corporate, Company or Society, upon any paper or parchment, in order that the same may be afterwards made or converted into, or used or dealt with as a valuable security: Misdemeanor; penal servitude for 3 years, or imprisonment not exceeding 2 years, with or without hard labor, and with or without solitary confinement, 27 V., S. 1, c. 33, s. 74.

Inducing persons by false pretence to execute deeds or other instruments

Receiving stolen property where the principal is guilty of felony

Whosoever shall receive any chattel, money, valuable security or other property, the stealing, taking, extorting, obtaining, embezzling or otherwise disposing whereof amounts to a Felony, either at Common Law or by this Act, knowing the same to have been feloniously stolen, taken, extorted, obtained, embezzled or disposed of, shall be guilty of Felony, and may be indicted and convicted either as an accessory after the fact or for a substantive Felony; and in the latter case, whether the principal felon has or has not been previously convicted, or is or is not amenable to justice. Every such receiver, howsoever convicted, shall be liable to penal servitude not exceeding 14 years, nor less than 3, or imprisonment not exceeding 2 years, with or without hard labor, and with or without solitary confinement. No person, however, tried for receiving as aforesaid, shall be liable to be prosecuted a second time for the same offence, 27 V., S. 1, c. 33, s. 75.

Indictment for stealing and receiving

In any Indictment containing a charge of feloniously stealing any property, counts may be added for feloniously receiving the same or any part, knowing it to have been stolen, and in any Indictment for feloniously receiving any property knowing it to have been stolen, a count may be added for feloniously stealing the same; and where any such Indictment is preferred and found, the prosecutor shall not be put to his election, but the Jury who try the same may find a verdict of guilty, either of stealing the property, or of receiving the same or part, knowing it to have been stolen; and if preferred and found against two or more persons, may find all or any of them guilty, either of stealing the property or of receiving the same or part, knowing it to have been stolen, or one or more guilty of stealing the property, and the other or others guilty of receiving the same, or part, knowing it to have been stolen, 27 V., S. 1, c. 33, s. 76.

Separate receivers may be indicted in same indictment in the absence of the principal

Whenever any property has been stolen, taken, extorted, obtained, embezzled or otherwise disposed of, in such a manner as to amount to a Felony, either at common law or by this Act, any number of receivers at different times of such property or part thereof, may be charged with substantive Felonies in the same Indictment, and tried together, notwithstanding that the principal felon is not included, or is not in custody, or amenable to justice, 27 V., S. 1, c. 33, s. 77.

On indictment for jointly receiving, one or more persons separately receiving parts of the property may be convicted

If on the trial of two or more indicted for jointly receiving any property, it is proved that one or more separately received any part or parts of such property, the Jury may convict upon such Indictment such of the persons as are proved to have received any part or parts of such property, 27 V., S. 1, c. 33, s. 78.

Receiving where the principal was guilty of a misdemeanor

Receiving any chattel, money, valuable security or other property, the stealing, taking, obtaining, converting, or disposing whereof is made a Misdemeanor by this Act, knowing it to have been unlawfully stolen, &c.: Misdemeanor; and the receiver may be indicted and convicted, whether the person guilty of the principal Misdemeanor has or has not been previously convicted, or is or is not amenable to justice. Every such receiver shall be liable to penal servitude, not exceeding 7 years, nor less than 3, or imprisonment not exceeding 2 years, with or without hard labor, and with or without solitary confinement, 27 V., S. 1, c. 33, s. 79.

Receivers where triable

Whoever receives any chattel, money, valuable security or other property, knowing the same to have been feloniously or unlawfully stolen, taken, obtained, converted or disposed of, may, whether charged as an accessory after the fact to the Felony, or with a substantive Felony, or with a Misdemeanor only, be dealt with, indicted, tried and punished, in any parish or precinct in which he has or had any such property in his possession, or in which the party guilty of the principal Felony or Misdemeanor may by law be tried, in the same manner as such receiver may be dealt with, &c., in the parish or n where he actually received such property, 27 V., S. 1, c. 33, s. 80 preci ct

Receiver where the stealing is punishable on summary conviction

Where the stealing or taking of any property is by this Act punishable on summary conviction, either for every offence or for the first and second offence only, or for the first offence only, any person who receives any such property knowing it to have been unlawfully come by, on conviction before a Justice, shall be liable, for every first, second or subsequent offence of receiving, to the same forfeiture and punishment to which a person guilty of a first, second or subsequent offence of stealing or taking such property is by this Act made liable, 27 V., S. 1, c. 33, s. 81.

In case of every Felony under this Act, every principal in the second degree, and every accessory before the fact, shall be punishable in the same manner as the principal in the first degree is by this Act punishable. Every accessory after the fact to any Felony under this Act (except only a receiver of stolen property), shall be liable, on conviction, to imprisonment not exceeding 2 years, with or without hard labor, and with or without solitary confinement. Persons who aid, abet, counsel or procure the commission of any Misdemeanor under this Act, shall be liable to be indicted, and punished as principal offenders, 27 V., S. 1, c. 33, s. 82.

Principals in the 2d degree, and accessories; abettors in misdemeanor

Whosoever shall aid, abet, counsel or procure the commission of any offence punishable on summary conviction, either for every time of commission or for the first and second time only, or for the first time only, shall, on conviction before a Justice, be liable for every first, second or subsequent offence of aiding, &c., to the same forfeiture and punishment a person guilty of a first, second or subsequent offence as a principal offender is made liable, 27 V., S. 1, c. 33, s. 83.

Aiding and abetting offences punishable on summary conviction

If any person guilty of any Felony or Misdemeanor mentioned in this Act, in stealing, taking, obtaining, extorting, embezzling, converting or disposing of, or in knowingly receiving any chattel, money, valuable security or other property, is indicted for such offence by or on behalf of the owner, or his executor or administrator, and convicted thereof, the property shall be restored to the owner, or his representative, and the Court may award Writs of Restitution for the property, or order restitution in a summary manner. If it appears before any award or order is made, that any valuable security has been bona fide paid or discharged by some person or Body Corporate liable to the payment, or, being a negotiable instrument, has been bona fide taken or received by transfer or delivery by some person or Body Corporate for a just and valuable consideration, without any notice or any reasonable cause to suspect that the same had by any Felony or Misdemeanor been stolen, taken, obtained, extorted, embezzled, converted or disposed of, the Court shall not award or order restitution of such security. Nothing in this section shall apply to the case of any prosecution of any Trustee, Banker, Merchant, Attorney, Factor, Broker, or other Agent, entrusted with the possession of goods or documents of title to goods (see s. 1) for any Misdemeanor against this Act, 27 V., S. 1, c. 33, s. 84.

Restitution of stolen property after conviction not applicable to negotiable securities bona fide paid or transferred for value or prosecutions of trustees, &c. entrusted with goods or documents of title to goods

Corruptly taking any reward, directly or indirectly, under pretence, or upon account of helping any person to any chattel, money valuable security or other property, which by any Felony or Misdemeanor has been stolen, taken, obtained, extorted, embezzled, converted or disposed of, as in this Act before mentioned (unless the a t have used all due diligence to cause the offender to be brought to trial for the same) : Felony ; penal servitude not exceeding 7 years, nor less than 3, or imprisonment, not exceeding 2 years, with or without hard labor, and with or without solitary confinement, 27 V., S. 1, c. 33, s. 85.

Corruptly taking reward for helping to the recovery of stolen property without bringing the offender to trial

Whosoever shall publicly advertize a reward for the return of any property which has been stolen or lost, and in such advertisement use any words purporting that no questions will be asked, or shall make use of any words in any public advertisement, purporting that a reward will be given or paid for any property which has been stolen or lost, without seizing or making any enquiry after the person producing such property, or shall promise or offer in any such public advertisement to return to any pawnbroker, or other person who may have bought or advanced money by way of loan upon any property stolen or lost, the money so paid or advanced, or any other sum of money or reward for the return of such property, or shall print or publish any such advertisement, shall forfeit £50 for every such offence, to any person who will sue for the same by action of debt, to be recovered with full costs of suit, 27 V., S. 1, c. 33, s. 86.

Advertising a reward for the return of stolen property, and that no question will be asked or a reward paid without enquiry or advances on the property returned, printing or publishing any such advertisement

Any person found committing any offence punishable either upon indictment or upon summary conviction by virtue of this Act, may be immediately apprehended, without a warrant, by any person, and forthwith taken with such property, if any, before a neighbouring Justice, to be dealt with according to law. If any credible witness prove, on oath before a Justice, a reasonable cause to suspect that any person has in his possession or on his premises any property on or with respect to which any offence, punishable either upon indictment or upon summary conviction has been committed, the Justice may grant a warrant to search for such property, as in the case of stolen goods. Any person to whom any property is offered to be sold,

Persons found committing offences may be apprehended without warrant

Search warrants

Persons to whom property is offered for sale or in pawn may seize the party

pawned, or delivered, if he has reasonable cause to suspect that any such offence has been committed on or with respect to such property, is authorized, and, if in his power, required to apprehend and forthwith to take before a Justice the party offering the same, together with such property, to be dealt with according to law, 27 V., S. 1, c. 33, s. 87.

Persons loitering at night, and suspected of felony

Any Constable or Peace Officer, may take into custody, without warrant, any person he finds lying or loitering in any highway, yard or other place during the night, and whom he has good cause to suspect of having committed, or being about to commit any Felony against this Act, and take him as soon as reasonably may be before a Justice, to be dealt with according to law, 27 V., S. 1, c. 33, s. 88.

Compelling appearance of persons punishable on summary conviction

Where any person is charged, on the oath of a credible witness before a Justice, with any offence punishable on summary conviction under this Act, the Justice may summon the party charged to appear at a time and place named in the summons. If he does not appear accordingly, then (upon proof of the due service of the summons upon such person, by delivering the same to him personally, or by leaving the same at his usual place of abode), the Justice may either proceed to hear and determine the case ex parte, or issue his Warrant for apprehending such person, and bringing him before himself or some other Justice; or the Justice before whom the charge is made, may, if he thinks fit, without any previous summons (unless where otherwise specially directed) issue such warrant, and the Justice before whom the person charged appears or is brought, shall proceed to hear and determine the case, 27 V., S. 1, c. 33, s. 89.

Application of forfeitures and penalties

Every sum of money forfeited on any summary conviction for the value of any property stolen or taken, or for the amount of any injury done (such value or amount to be assessed in each case by the convicting Justice), shall be paid to the party aggrieved, except where he is unknown, and in that case shall be applied in the same manner as a penalty. Every sum imposed as a penalty, whether in addition to such value or amount, or otherwise, shall be paid and applied in the same manner as other penalties recoverable before Justices, in cases where the statute imposing them contains no direction for payment to any person. Where several persons join in the commission of the same offence, and, on conviction, are each adjudged to forfeit a sum equivalent to the value of the property, or amount of the injury, no further sum shall be paid to the party aggrieved than such value or amount, and the remaining sum or sums forfeited shall be applied as any penalty imposed by a Justice as before directed, 27 V., S. 1, c. 33, s. 90.

Where several persons join in commission of the same offence

Commitment for non-payment; scale of imprisonment

In every case of summary conviction, where the sum forfeited for the value of the property stolen or taken, or for the amount of the injury done, or imposed as a penalty is not paid, either immediately after conviction, or within such period as the Justices at the time of conviction appoint, the convicting Justice (unless where otherwise specially directed,) may commit the offender to the Common Gaol or District Prison, or the General Penitentiary, there to be imprisoned only, or to be imprisoned and kept to hard labor not exceeding 2 months, where the amount of the sum forfeited, or the penalty imposed, or both, as the case may be, together with the costs, do not exceed £3; or not exceeding 4 months where the amount with costs does not exceed £6, or not exceeding 6 months in any other case; the commitment to be determinable in each of the cases, upon payment of the amount and costs, 27 V., S. 1, c. 33, s. 91.

Not exceeding 2 months where property, &c. does not exceed £3; 4 months where not exceeding £6; not exceeding 6 months in any other case, determinable on payment

Discharge on first conviction on making satisfaction

When any person is summarily convicted before a Justice against this Act, and it is a first conviction, the Justice may, if he think fit, discharge the offender from his conviction, upon his making such satisfaction to the party aggrieved for damages and costs, or either, as shall be ascertained by the Justice, 27 V., S. 1, c. 33, s. 92.

Summary conviction a bar to other proceedings

In case any person convicted of any offence punishable upon summary conviction by virtue of this Act, has paid the sum adjudged to be paid, with costs, under such conviction, or has received a remission from the Crown, or suffered the imprisonment awarded for non-payment, or the imprisonment adjudged in the first instance, or has been so discharged from his conviction by any Justice, he shall be released from all further or other proceedings for the same cause, 27 V., S. 1, c. 33, s. 93.

Appeal

Nothing herein shall deprive any person who thinks himself aggrieved by any summary conviction, of his right of appeal, under 21 V., c. 22, or any other Act, 27 V., S. 1, c. 33, s. 94.

No conviction or adjudication on appeal therefrom shall be quashed, for want of Form, or removed by Certiorari into the Supreme Court ; and no Warrant of Commitment shall be held void by reason of any defect, provided it be therein alleged that the party has been convicted, and there be a good and valid conviction to sustain it, 27 V., S. 1, c. 33, s. 95.

Not to be quashed for want of form, &c.

All Actions and prosecutions for anything under this Act, shall be laid and tried in the parish or precinct where the fact was committed, and commenced within 6 months after, and not otherwise : and notice in writing of the Action and cause thereof, given to the defendant one month at least before the commencement of the Action. The defendant may plead the general issue, and give the special matter in evidence. No plaintiff shall recover in any Action, if tender of sufficient amends are made before Action brought, or a sufficient sum paid into Court afterwards, by or on behalf of the defendant. If a verdict pass for the defendant, or the plaintiff become nonsuit, or discontinue after issue joined, or if upon demurrer or otherwise, Judgment is given against the plaintiff, the defendant shall recover full costs as between Attorney and Client, and have the like remedy as any defendant in other cases : and though a verdict is given for the plaintiff, he shall not have costs, unless the Judge certify his approbation of the Action, 27 V., S. 1, c. 33, s. 96.

Protection from action

All indictable offences in this Act, committed within the jurisdiction of the Vice Admiralty of this Island, shall be deemed offences of the same nature, and liable to the same punishments as if committed upon land in this Island, and dealt with, enquired of, tried and determined in any parish or precinct in which the offender is apprehended or in custody. In any Indictment for any such offence, or for being an accessory to any such offence, the venue in the margin shall be the same as if the offence were committed in the parish or precinct, and the offence itself averred to have been committed " on the high seas." If any person is tried and convicted before any Court in this Island for any offence under the authority of this section, he shall be liable to, and shall suffer such punishment, forfeiture or penalty, as he would be subject to in case such offence had been committed, and was enquired of, tried and determined in England, anything in this Act to the contrary notwithstanding. Nothing herein shall alter or affect any of the laws relating to the Government of H. M's. Land or Naval Forces, 27 V., S. 1, c. 33, s. 97.

Offences committed within the jurisdiction of the Vice Admiralty

In any Indictment for any offence punishable under this Act, and committed after a previous conviction or convictions for any Felony, Misdemeanor, offence or offences punishable upon summary conviction, it shall be sufficient after charging the subsequent offence, to state that the offender was at a certain time and place, or at certain times and places, convicted of Felony, or of an indictable Misdemeanor, or of an offence or offences punishable upon summary conviction, (as the case may be) without otherwise describing the previous Felony, Misdemeanor, offence or offences; and a certificate containing the substance and effect only, (omitting the formal part) of the Indictment and conviction for the previous Felony or Misdemeanor, or a copy of any such summary conviction, purporting to be signed by the Clerk of the Circuit Court or other officer, or the Deputy of such other officer, having the custody of the records of the Court where the offender was first convicted, or to which such summary conviction was returned, upon proof of the identity of the person of the offender, shall be sufficient evidence of such conviction, without proof of the signature or official character of the person appearing to have signed it.

Indictment for a subsequent offence. statement and proof of previous offence

The proceedings upon any Indictment for committing any offence after a previous conviction shall be as follows : The offender shall, in the first instance be arraigned upon so much only of the Indictment as charges the subsequent offence, and if he plead " not guilty," or if the Court order a plea of not guilty to be entered on his behalf, the Jury shall be charged in the first instance to enquire concerning such subsequent offence only, and if they find him guilty, or if on arraignment he plead guilty, he shall then and not before be asked whether he had been previously convicted as alleged in the Indictment ; and if he answer he had been, the Court may proceed to sentence him accordingly ; but if he deny or stand mute of malice, or will not answer directly to the question, the Jury shall then be charged to enquire concerning such previous conviction or convictions, and it shall not be necessary to swear them again, but the oath already taken by them shall extend to such last mentioned enquiry. If upon the trial for any such subsequent offence

Proceedings at trial, and enquiry to be confined in the first instance to the subsequent offence

the person give evidence of his good character, the prosecutor in answer may give evidence of his conviction for the previous offence or offences, before such verdict of guilty is returned, and the Jury shall enquire concerning such previous conviction or convictions at the same time they enquire concerning the subsequent offence, 27 V., S. 1, c. 33, s. 98.

Fine and sureties to keep the peace in addition to or in lieu of imprisonment in case of misdemeanor or Sureties to keep the peace, in addition to other punishment in case of felony

When any person is convicted of any indictable Misdemeanor, the Court may, in addition to or in lieu of any of the punishments authorized, fine the offender, and require him to enter into his own recognizance, and to find sureties both, or either, for keeping the peace and being of good behaviour. In case of any Felony, the Court may require the offender to enter into his own recognizances, and to find sureties, both, or either, for keeping the peace in addition to any punishment authorized. No person shall be imprisoned under this clause for not finding sureties, exceeding 1 year, 27 V., S. 1, c. 33, s. 99.

Place of imprisonment

When imprisonment with or without hard labor may be awarded for any indictable offence, the Court may sentence the offender to be imprisoned in the Common Gaol, or to be imprisoned and kept to hard labor in the General Penitentiary, or nearest District Prison, 27 V., S. 1, c. 33, s. 100.

Solitary confinement

When solitary confinement may be awarded, the Court may direct the offender to be kept in solitary confinement not exceeding one month at any one time, and not exceeding 3 months in any one year, 27 V., S. 1, c. 33, s. 101.

Cost of prosecution

The Court before which any indictable Misdemeanor is prosecuted or tried, may allow the costs of the prosecution, as in cases of Felony. Every order for payment shall be made out, and the money paid and repaid upon the same terms and in the same manner as in cases of Felony, 27 V., S. 1, c. 33, s. 102.

Place of imprisonment under summary conviction

When upon any summary conviction, imprisonment without hard labor is awarded, the Justices may commit the offender, if to them it seem fittest, to the County Gaol or nearest District Prison; and when hard labor forms part of any such sentence, the offender shall be committed to the nearest District Prison. The Justices of Kingston, St. Andrew, Port Royal and the Precinct of St. Catherine, may convict and sentence offenders upon summary convictions as by law they may now do, 27 V., S. 1, c. 33, s. 103.

Larceny, &c., Summarily Punishable.

Summary disposal, where the property does not exceed 5s

Where any person is charged before 2 or more Justices in Petty Sessions, with having committed Larceny, and the value of the property does not, in their judgment, exceed 5s., they may hear the charge in a summary manner; and if the person confess it, or the Justices, after hearing the whole case for the prosecution and for the defence, find the charge proved, they may convict and adjudge the party to be committed to the Common Gaol, or Penitentiary, or other Prison, with or without hard labor for not exceeding 90 days. If they find the offence not proved, they shall dismiss the charge, and make out and deliver to the person a certificate, under their hands of dismissal. Forms of Conviction and Certificate, Schedule A. and B., 20 V., c. 3, s. 1.

When above 5s, but not exceeding 10s, with consent

If the property in their judgment is above 5s., but does not exceed 10s., and the person consents, the Justices may determine the charge summarily, and if he confesses, or is convicted, may sentence him to imprisonment as above, not exceeding 6 calendar months, or, if the offence is not proved, may dismiss the charge, and make out and deliver a certificate of dismissal, Forms Schedule C. and D., 20 V., c. 3, s. 2.

Value to be fixed on oath before entering on complaint

The Justices shall, before entering upon any complaint, fix the value, by evidence on oath, 20 V., c. 3, s. 3.

Proceedings where the property exceeds 5s, and party consents

Where the value exceeds 5s. and they propose to proceed summarily, one of them shall state to the person the substance of the charge, and say to him:—Do you consent that the charge against you shall be tried by us, or do you desire that it shall be sent for trial by a jury? And if he consents, they shall reduce the charge into writing, and read it to him, and then ask him whether he is guilty or not. If he say he is guilty, they shall proceed to pass sentence upon him. If he say he is not guilty, they shall take the examinations of all witnesses for the prosecution, and enquire if he has any defence, and if he states he has, hear it, and dispose of the case summarily, 20 V., c. 3, s. 4.

If on the hearing, the Justices are of opinion there are circumstances which render it inexpedient to inflict any punishment, they may dismiss the person without doing so, 20 V., c. 3, s. 5.

If it appear that the offence is one which, owing to a previous conviction or from other circumstances, is fit to be the subject of prosecution by Indictment, or if the value exceed 5s., and the party does not consent to a determination by the Justices, they shall, instead of adjudicating, deal with the case as if the Act were not passed, 20 V., c. 3, s. 6.

Where a person is charged with Simple Larceny, and the property exceeds 10s., but not £10, or stealing from the person, or Larceny as a Clerk or servant, and the evidence, when the case on the part of the prosecution is completed, is, in the opinion of the Justices, sufficient to put the person upon his trial for an Indictable offence, the Justices may, if the case appears to them to be one which may properly be disposed of, and adequately punished under this Act, reduce the charge into writing, read it to the person, and ask him if he is guilty or not of the charge. If he say he is guilty, they shall cause the plea of guilty to be entered upon the proceedings, and sentence him to imprisonment as before (s. 1), for not exceeding 12 calendar months. Form of Conviction, Schedule E. But if he says he is not guilty, or refuses or declines to plead guilty or not guilty, the Justices shall send the case for trial in the usual manner. The Justices, before they ask whether he is guilty or not, shall explain to him, he is not obliged to plead or answer before them at all, and if he do not, he will be committed for trial in the usual course. No sentence shall be for longer than 12 calendar months, 20 V., c. 3, s. 7.

In cases of summary proceeding under s. 1 and 2, the accused may make his full answer and defence, and have all witnesses examined and cross-examined by Counsel or Attorney, and have his case postponed from one Petty Session to another, to enable him to procure the attendance of witnesses or legal adviser, or otherwise upon sufficient cause; but no postponement shall take place after the examination of witnesses for the prosecution has been commenced, 20 V., c. 3, s 8.

The Justices may remand the person for further examination, as under the Acts for the purpose, (See Justices, 13 V., c. 24, s. 14,) 20 V., c. 3, s. 9.

If a person suffered to go at large upon recognizance, do not afterwards appear, the Justices before whom he ought to have appeared, shall certify (under the hands of 2) on the back of the recognizance to the Clerk of the Peace, the fact of non-appearance, and the recognizance shall be proceeded upon as others which become forfeited, and the certificate shall be prima facie evidence of non-appearance, 20 V., c. 3, s. 10.

The adjudicating Justices shall transmit the conviction or a duplicate of the certificate of dismissal with the written charge, the deposition of the witnesses for the prosecution and for the defence, and the statement of the accused to the next Circuit Court for the parish, to be kept by the proper officer among the records. A copy, certified by the officer of the Court, or proved to be a true copy, shall be sufficient evidence to prove a conviction or dismissal in any legal proceeding, 20 V., c. 3, s. 11.

The convicting Justices may order restitution of stolen property in cases where the Court might, 20 V., c, 3, s. 12.

Convictions shall have the same effect as a conviction upon Indictment, save that they shall not be attended with any forfeiture, 20 V., c. 3, s. 13.

Persons who obtain a certificate of dismissal, or are convicted under this Act, shall be released from further criminal proceedings for the same offence, 20 V., c. 3, s. 14.

No conviction, sentence or proceeding, shall be quashed for want of form, nor commitment held void for any defect, if it be alleged that the offender has been convicted, and there is a valid conviction to sustain it, 20 V., c. 3, s. 15.

Not to take away the power of any superior Court, nor defeat the right of appeal, 20 V., c. 3, s. 16.

No proceeding or document shall be liable to Stamp Duty, 20 V., c. 3, s. 17.

" Property," shall include every description of chattels, money, or valuable security, 20 V., c 3. s. 19.

Receivers of sto-len goods—Embezzlement

The Justices shall have the same jurisdiction in respect of offences of receiving goods and chattels knowing them to have been stolen, and of embezzlement of goods and chattels, as in cases of Larceny under 20 V.. c. 3, 27 V., S. 1, c. 13, s. 1.

The provisions of that Act declared applicable to the present, 27 V., S. 1, c. 13, s. 2.

The summary jurisdiction conferred upon two or more Justices under 20 V., c. 3, shall in all cases of a charge after a previous conviction of an offence within such jurisdiction, and specially mentioned in this Act, be annulled ; and the Justices shall take the examination of all witnesses for the prosecution, and if in their opinion a proper case is made out for the consideration of a Grand Jury, they shall transmit them to the Clerk of the Peace of the parish in which they act, for further prosecution at the Circuit Court, 28 V., c. 18, s. 1.

Stealing cultivated growing plants, &c.
Or produce
Horses
Cattle
Sheep Pigs or Goats
Killing with intent to steal the carcase, &c., maiming
Stealing domesticated animals, or those used for food—Feloniously receiving any such property or animals
Act when to come into operation

The cases are, stealing, destroying or damaging, with intent to steal any cultivated plant, root, fruit or other vegetable production used for the food of man or beast, or for medicine or for distillation, dyeing, or for,or in the course of any manufacture growing in any garden, orchard, or provision ground, whether inclosed or not, or in any cane, coffee or pimento field. Stealing any horse, mare, gelding or colt, filly, mule or ass, or any bull, cow, ox, heifer or calf, or any ram, ewe, sheep or lamb, pig or goat, or wilfully killing any of such animals with intent to steal the carcase, skin or any part thereof, or wilfully maiming any of the said animals. Stealing any domesticated animal, or any animal ordinarily used for human food, or feloniously receiving any such property or animals, knowing them to have been stolen, 28 V., c. 18, s. 2.

Act not to come into operation until the Royal assent is advertised in the Jamaica Gazette, 28 V., c. 18, s. 3.

SCHEDULE TO 20 V., c. 3.

Parish or Precinct to wit :—

Conviction, A, s. 1

Be it remembered, that on the   day of   in the year of our Lord   at   in the said parish, A. B. being charged before us, the undersigned   of Her Majesty's Justices of the Peace for the said parish* is convicted before us, for that (he the said A. B., &c., stating shortly the offence, and value, and the time and place when and where committed) ; and we adjudge the said A. B., for his said offence to be imprisoned in the (name place of confinement) in the parish of   , and there kept to hard labor (if hard labor be added) for the space of

Given under our hands the day and year first above mentioned, at   at   , in the parish aforesaid.

                            Signatures of two Justices.

Parish or Precinct to wit :—

Certificate of dismissal, B, s. 1

We   of Her Majesty's Justices of the Peace for the parish of   certify that on the   day of   , in the year of our Lord   at   in the said parish, A. B., being charged before us*, for that (he the said A. B., stating shortly the offence, and value and the time and place when and where alleged to be committed), having summarily adjudicated thereon, we do dismiss the said charge.

Given under our hands this   day of   , in the parish aforesaid.

                            Signatures of two Justices.

Form C, s. 2

Same as Form A., only at the asterisk inserting the following words, viz: " And consenting to our deciding upon the charge summarily."

Form D, s. 2

Same as Form B., only at the asterisk inserting the following words, viz: " And consenting to our deciding upon the charge summarily."

Parish or Precinct.

To wit.

Be it remembered, that on the day of in the year of our Lord at in the said parish, A. B., being charged before us, the undersigned of Her Majesty's Justices of the Peace for the said parish, for that (he the said A. B., &c., stating shortly the offence, and the time and place when and where committed), and pleading guilty to such charge he is thereupon convicted before us of the said offence ; and we adjudge the said A. B., for his said offence to be imprisoned in the ordinary place of confinement at, in the parish of and there kept to hard labor (if hard labor adjudged) for the space of

Given under our hands the day and year first above mentioned at in the parish aforesaid.

Signatures of two Justices.

Laws of England in Force.

Notwithstanding the repeal of 1 G. 2, c. 1, all such Laws and Statutes of England as were at any time before that Act esteemed, introduced, used, accepted, or received as Laws in this Island, shall continue so, except so far as repealed or altered by any Law of this Island, 8 V., c. 16, s. 7.

Laws of the Island.

All original Acts shall be lodged in the Secretary's Office of Enrolments at St. Jago de la Vega ; and the Secretary shall at all office hours be ready to shew them when required, and give copies thereof, or of any clause, 33 C. 2, c. 24, s. 1.

Fees for copies, 2s. 6d. (1s. 6d. stg.), per 160 words, 56 G. 3, c. 19, s. 1 ; 60 G. 3, c. 23, s. 5.

All Acts shall be entered and recorded in a fair book, to be kept for that purpose only. Penalty £100 (£60, stg.) and the entry or a copy, sworn to by the Secretary before a Judge of the Supreme Court, shall be as valid as the original, and pleadable, 10 Ann, c. 4, s. 3.

And shall be recorded within 90 days, 56 G. 3, c. 19, s. 3; 60 G. 3, c. 23, s. 1.

Commissioners to compile, print and publish the Laws: the Chief Justice, President of the Council, Speaker, Attorney General, 5 Senior Assistant Judges of the Grand Court, and Members of the Council and Assembly for the time, 30 G. 3, c. 20, s. 1; 32 G. 3, c. 29, s. 1; 47 G. 3, c. 18, s. 1 ; 59 G. 3, c. 24, s. 1

The Laws, printed and published under the authority of the Commissioners, shall be received as conclusive evidence, 30 G. 3, c. 20, s. 2 ; 32 G. 3, c. 29, s, 2 ; 47 G. 3, c. 18, s. 2.

Copies shall be sent to the Governor, to each Member of the Council and Assembly, the Chief Justice and each Assistant Judge, and to each Clerk of the Peace and Clerk of the Vestry for the use of the parish, 30 G. 3, c. 20, s. 3; 32 G. 3, c. 29, s. 3; 47 G. 3, c. 18, s. 3.

Meetings of the Commissioners shall be held in St. Jago de la Vega during the Session and not otherwise, 59 G. 3, c. 24, s. 2.

The Commissioners so convened may put up to Contract by Advertisement, the collecting, printing and publishing the Laws, accept any Tender and conclude any agreement they think most eligible, in such manner and under such terms as to them seems most advantageous for the public ; but in exercising the power of assigning the copyright, shall not Contract for less than 7 years, nor beyond 14 years, 59 G. 3, c. 24, s. 3.

To secure the performance of any agreement, the Contractor shall enter into bond with one or more securities in £2000 (£1200 sterling.) No person entitled by law to copies shall receive, nor the Contractor charge for more than one copy each, although the person acts in several capacities, 59 G. 3, c. 24, s. 4.

3 D

410

Contracts to be by deed, exempt from stamps & recorded

Execution by Commissioners

Contracts shall be by Deed, exempt from Stamp Duties and recorded in the Secretary's Office; and the execution by 7 Commissioners of any Deed agreed to at a meeting shall be sufficient on the part of the Commissioners, 59 G. 3, c. 24, s. 5.

Assembly may order distribution of copies to others than by law entitled

Besides the persons specifically entitled by law to copies of the Laws, the House of Assembly may by vote or resolution, from time to time, order other persons to be furnished with Laws, which the Contractor shall be bound to do, and be allowed the like rate as other copies are contracted for, 59 G. 3, c. 24, s. 6.

Laws passed after demise of the crown Alteration, &c., during Session

Laws passed after the demise of any former King, before such demise was made known in this Island, shall be in full force, 53 G. 3, c. 9, s. 2.

Acts passed after the commencement of this Act (16th October, 1856), may be altered, amended or repealed in the same Session, 18 V., c. 31, s. 1.

Division into sections — substantive enactments

Acts shall be divided into sections, if there are more enactments than one, which shall be deemed substantive enactments without introductory words, 18 V., c. 31, s. 2.

Citing former Acts

In any Act, when a former Act is referred to, it shall be sufficient to cite the year of the reign; where more Sessions than one in the year, the number of the Session, and the chapter, where more than one, without reciting the title; and the reference, in all cases shall be according to the copies of Acts printed by the Contractor or printer authorized by law to print the same.

Portion of a section

Where it is only intended to amend or repeal a portion only of any section of an Act, it shall be necessary still either to recite such portion, or to set forth the matter intended to be amended or repealed, 18 V., c. 31, s. 3.

Repeal of an Act not to revive Acts thereby repealed unless, &c.

Where any Act repealing in whole or in part any former Act, is itself repealed, the last repeal shall not revive the Act or provisions before repealed, unless words be added reviving them, 18 V., c. 31, s. 4.

Repealed Acts to be in force until the repealing Act comes into operation

When an Act is made repealing in whole or in part any former Act, and substituting other provisions, those repealed shall remain in force until the substituted provisions come into operation, 18 V., c. 31, s. 5.

Definition of words in future Acts Her Majesty

In all Acts, the words "Her Majesty" shall mean Her present Majesty Queen Victoria, her heirs and successors, and the King or Queen regnant of the United Kingdom for the time, his or her heirs and successors.

Governor Legislative Council Assembly Executive Committee

"Governor," the Officer for the time being administering the Government of this Island. "Legislative Council," the Legislative Council of this Island, and the Members of the Legislative Council for the time being. "Assembly," the Assembly of this Island for the time being, and the Members of the Assembly for the time being. "Executive Committee," the Executive Committee appointed, or to be appointed, and the Members of the Executive Committee in this Island for the time being.

Custos

"Custos," where there is no Custos, or where the Custos is absent, shall include the Magistrate next in seniority to the Custos, or the senior Magistrate in the parish, and resident in the parish, and in the habit of acting as a Justice of the Peace therein, and of presiding at the meetings of the Vestry.

Name of office, &c.

The name of office, or the style or title of the officer in respect to every public and parochial office in this Island, shall mean the person holding the office, designated or mentioned for the time being, and the lawful deputy of any officer who may by law act by deputy.

Vestry Justices & Vestry Vestryman

"Vestry" and "Justices and Vestry," shall respectively include and mean the Court of Common Council of the city and parish of Kingston. "Vestryman," shall include and mean Mayor, Alderman and Common Councilman respectively.

Clerk of the Vestry Parish

"Clerk of the Vestry," Clerk of the Common Council. "Parish," the city and parish of Kingston, and any city or precinct.

Supreme Court

"Supreme Court," the Supreme Court of Judicature of this Island.

Justice

"Justice," any Justice of the Peace of the parish or precinct in which any offence is committed, or in which the matter requiring the cognizance of any Justice of the Peace or Magistrate arises.

Apprentice

"Apprentice," shall mean a male or female.

Masculine gender

Words importing the masculine gender, shall include females.

Singular—plural

"The singular," shall include the plural, and the "plural" the singular, and include bodies politic, corporate, and collegiate, aggregate or sole, ecclesiastical and lay, as well as individuals, unless the contrary is expressly provided.

Month

"Month," shall mean calendar month, unless words be added shewing lunar months to be intended.

Computation of time

Where any particular number of days is prescribed by any Act, or mentioned in any rule or order of Court, made in pursuance of any such Act, for the doing of any act or for any other purpose, the same shall be reckoned, in the absence of any expression to the contrary, exclusive of the first, and inclusive of the last day, unless the last day happens to fall on Sunday, Christmas day, Good Friday, Monday or Tuesday in Easter, or a day appointed for a Public Fast or Thanksgiving, in which case the time shall be reckoned exclusive of that day ; also " Land," shall include messuages, tenements and hereditaments, houses and buildings of any tenure, unless where there are words to exclude houses and buildings, or to restrict the meaning of tenements of some particular tenure. " Oath," " swear," and " affidavit," shall include affirmation, declaration, affirming and declaring in the case of persons allowed by law to declare or affirm instead of swearing, 18 V., c. 31, s. 6. *

'Land'

Oath swear Affidavit

All Acts made after the commencement of this Act, shall be deemed public Acts, and judicially taken notice of, unless the contrary is declared, 18 V., c. 31, s. 7.

Public Acts

Act to commence from first day of next Session, (16th October, 1856,) 18 V., c. 31, s. 8.

Commencement— 16th October, 1856

Leases, Agreements, Surrenders.

Guardians may grant Leases by Deed of the real and personal estate of infants, for any term not beyond their minority, at the highest rent and most advantageous conditions they can procure. Not to affect any power given to them by the parents. They shall take security for payment of rent and performance of covenants, 2 W. 4. c. 16 s. 2.

By guardians of infants' Estates

Security

Leases of personal estate shall contain a Schedule of such personalty ; and all leases of infants' properties, and Schedules with the instruments containing the security, shall be recorded in the Secretary's Office, within 3 months after execution, otherwise at the expiration of the 3 months they shall determine, 2 W. 4, c. 16, s. 3.

Schedule

Record

No Lease or surrender in writing of any Freehold or Leasehold land shall be valid as such, unless made by Deed, but any agreement in writing to let or surrender, shall be valid, and take effect as an agreement to execute a lease or surrender, and the person in possession of the land, in pursuance of any agreement to let, may, from payment of rent or other circumstances, be construed to be a tenant from year to year, 8 V., c. 19, s. 3.

To be by deed

Agreement'

Where the reversion of any land expectant on a lease is merged in any remainder or other reversion or estate, the person entitled to the estate into which it has merged, his heirs &c., shall have the like advantage, remedy and benefit against the lessee, his heirs, successors, &c., for non-payment of the rent, or for doing of waste or other forfeiture, or for not performing conditions, covenants or agreements, expressed in his lease, demise or grant, as the person who would for the time being have been entitled to the mesne reversion which has merged would have had if he had not been merged, 8 V., c. 19, s. 10.

Remedies of persons entitled over after a merged reversion expectant on a lease

Whenever any party to any Deed, made according to Form, Schedule 1, or to any other Deed expressed to be made in pursuance of this Act, employs any of the forms of words in column 1 of the 2nd Schedule, and be distinguished by any number therein, the Deed shall have the same effect, and be construed as if the party had inserted the form of words in column 2, and distinguished by the same number ; but it shall not be necessary in the deed to insert any number, 13 V., c. 22, s. 1.

Effect of certain forms of words in deeds expressed to be made in pursuance of this Act

Every such Deed, unless any exception is specially made, shall be held to include all out-houses, buildings, stables, yards, gardens, cellars, edifices and other erections, lights, paths, passages, ways, waters, water-courses, liberties, privileges, easements, profits, commodities, emoluments, hereditaments and appurtenances, whatsoever, to the lands therein comprised, belonging or appertaining, 13 V., c. 22, s. 2.

Words to be held included

Any Deed or part which fails to take effect under this Act, shall be valid, and bind the parties so far as the rules of Law and Equity will permit, 13 V., c. 22, s. 3.

Deed not taking effect under this Act otherwise valid

In taxing any Bill for preparing and executing a Deed under this Act, the Taxing Officer in estimating the charge, shall consider, not the length of the Deed, but only the skill and labor employed, and responsibility incurred in the preparation, 13 V., c. 22, s. 4.

Remuneration for such deeds

' Lands," shall extend to all Tenements and Hereditaments of Freehold tenure, or any undivided part. "Parties," Bodies Politic or Corporate, or Collegiate, 13 V., c. 22, s. 5.

The Schedules, Directions and Forms shall be deemed part of this Act, 13 V., c. 22, s. 6.

FIRST SCHEDULE.

This Indenture made the   day of   one thousand, &c., in pursuance to an Act to facilitate the granting of leases between (here insert parties names) witnesses that the said (Lessor or Lessors) doth (or do) demise unto the said (Lessee,) his (or their) executors, administrators and assigns, all, &c. (parcels) from the   day of   for the term of thence ensuing, yielding therefore during the said term the rent of (here state rent, and mode, and days of payment.) In witness whereof, the said parties hereto have hereunto set t i hands and seals.

SECOND SCHEDULE.

DIRECTIONS AS TO THE FORMS.

1st. Parties who use any of the Forms in the first column, may substitute for "Lessor" or "Lessee" any names; and corresponding substitutions shall be taken to be made in the corresponding Forms in the second column.

2nd. They may substitute the feminine g   for the masculine, or the plural number for the singular in the Terms in the 1st column, and corresponding changes shall be taken to be made in second column.

3rd. They may fill up the blanks in Forms 4 and 5 in the 1st column, with any words or figures, which shall be taken to be inserted in the corresponding blank spaces in the Forms embodied.

4th. They may introduce into or annex to any of the Forms in the 1st column any express exceptions or qualifications, and the like shall be taken to be made in the corresponding Forms in the second.

5th. Where the premises are of freehold tenure, the covenants 1 to 10 shall be taken to be made with, and the proviso 11 to apply to the heirs and assigns of the Lessor. When of Leasehold tenure, to the Lessor, his executors, administrators and assigns.

Column 1.	Column 2.
1. That the said Lessee covenants with the Lessor to pay rent.	1. And the said Lessee doth hereby for himself, his heirs, executors, administrators and assigns, covenant with the said Lessor, that he the said Lessee, his executors, administrators and assigns will, during the said term, pay unto the said Lessor the rent hereby reserved in manner hereinbefore mentioned without any deduction whatsoever.
2. And to pay Taxes.	2. And also will pay all taxes, rates, duties and assessments whatsoever, whether parochial or otherwise, now charged, or hereafter to be charged upon the said demised premises, or upon the said Lessor, on account thereof, excepting all taxes, rates, duties and assessments whatsoever, or any portion thereof. which the Lessee is or may be by law exempted from.

COLUMN 1.

COLUMN 2.

3. And to Repair.

3. And also will, during the said term, well and suf-ficiently repair, maintain, pave, empty, cleanse, amend and keep the said demised premises with the appurtenances in good and sub-stantial repair, together with all houses, out-houses, stills, still-houses, stores, store-houses, edifices, barbicues, tanks, and all other build-ings, fixtures and things which, at any time during the said term, shall be erected and made, when, where and so often as need shall be.

4. And to paint outside every year.

4. And also that the said Lessee, his executors, ad-ministrators and assigns will, in every year in the said term, paint all the outside wood-work and iron-work belonging to the said premises, with 2 coats of proper oil colors, in a workman-like manner.

5. And paint and paper inside every year.

5. And also that the said Lessee, his executors, ad-ministrators and assigns will, in every year, paint the inside wood, iron and other works now or usually painted, with 2 coats of proper oil colors, in a workman-like manner, and also re-paper, with paper of a quality as at present, such parts of the said premises as are now papered, and also wash, stop, whiten, or color such parts of the said premises as are now plastered.

6. And to insure from fire in the joint names of the said Lessor and the said Lessee, to shew Re-ceipts, and to build in case of Fire.

6. And also that the said Lessee, his executors, ad-ministrators and assigns, will forthwith insure the said premises hereby demised to the full value thereof, in some respectable Insurance Office, in the joint names of the said Lessor, his executors, administrators and assigns, and the said Lessee, his executors administrators or assigns, and keep the same so insured dur-ing the said term, and will, upon the request of the said Lessor or his agent, shew the receipt for the last premium paid for such Insurance for every current year, and as often as the said premises hereby demised shall be burnt down, or damaged by fire, all and every the sum or sums of money, which shall be recovered or re-ceived by the said Lessee, his executors, admin-istrators or assigns, for or in respect of such In-surance, shall be laid out and expended by him in building or repairing the said demised premi-ses, or such parts thereof, as shall be burnt down or damaged by fire as aforesaid.

7. And that the said Lessor may enter and view state of repair, and that the said Lessee will repair according to notice.

7. And it is hereby agreed, that it shall be lawful for the said Lessor and his agents, at all season-able times during the said term, to enter the said demised premises, to take a schedule of the Fixtures and things made and erected thereupon, and to examine the condition of the said premises; and further, that all wants of reparation, which upon such views shall be found, and for the amendment of which notice, in writing, shall be left at the premises, the said Lessee, his executors, administrators and assigns, within 3 calendar months next after every such notice, will well and sufficiently repair and make good accordingly.

COLUMN 1.

COLUMN 2.

8. That the said Lessee will not use premises as a shop.

8. And also, that the said Lessee, his executors, administrators and assigns, will not convert, use or occupy the said premises, or any part thereof, into or as a shop, warehouse or other place for carrying on any trade or business whatsoever, or suffer the said premises to be used for any such purpose, or otherwise than as a private dwelling house, without the consent, in writing, of the said Lessor.

9. And will not assign without leave.

9. And also that said Lessee shall not, nor will, during the said term, assign, transfer, set over, or otherwise by any act or deed procure the said premises, or any of them to be assigned, transferred, or set over unto any person or persons whomsoever, without the consent, in writing, of the said Lessor, his executors, administrators or assigns first had and obtained.

10. And that he will leave premises in good repair.

10. And further, that the said Lessee will, at the expiration or other sooner determination of the said term, peaceably surrender and yield up unto the said Lessor, the said premises hereby demised, with the appurtenances, together with all buildings, erections and fixtures, now or hereafter to be built or erected thereon, in good and substantial repair and condition in all respects, reasonable wear and tear and damage by fire only excepted.

11. Proviso for re-entry by the said Lessor, on non-payment of rent or non-performance of covenants.

11. Provided always : and it is expressly agreed that if the rent hereby reserved, or any part thereof shall be unpaid for 15 days after any of the days on which the same ought to have been paid, although no formal demand shall be made thereof, or in case of the breach or non-performance of any of the covenants and agreements herein contained on the part of the said Lessee, his executors, administrators, and assigns, then, and in either of such cases, it shall be lawful for the said Lessor at any time thereafter, into and upon the said demised premises, or any part thereof, in the name of the whole, to re-enter, and the same to have again, re-possess and enjoy as of his former estate, anything hereinafter contained to the contrary notwithstanding.

12. The said Lessor covenants with the said Lessee for quiet enjoyment.

12. And the Lessor doth hereby for himself his heirs, executors, administrators and assigns, covenant with the said Lessee, his executors, administrators and assigns, that he and they paying the rent hereby reserved, and performing the covenants herein before on his and their part contained, shall and may peaceably possess and enjoy the said demised premises for the term hereby granted, without any interruption or disturbance from the said Lessor, his executors, administrators or assigns, or any other person or persons lawfully claiming by, from, or under him, them, or any of them.

Tenants for life or in tail, in possession, and Guardians, Trustees or Committees of Tenants for life or in tail, or in fee simple, who are Infants, Lunatics, Idiots, or otherwise incapable of acting for themselves, may, by Deed to be duly proved and recorded, demise and lease the land, or any part, to any person who will improve the same, by erecting or building thereon any new stores, houses or buildings, or by re-building, repairing, enlarging or improving any stores, houses or buildings on the land, or shall covenant and agree so to do within 4 years next after the date of the demise or lease, for any term not exceeding 21 years, to take effect in possession, so as there be reserved the best yearly rents, to be incident to the immediate reversion that can be reasonably gotten, without taking anything in the nature of a fine, premium or foregift, and there be contained therein a condition of re-entry for non-payment, within a reasonable time to be specified, of the rents reserved, and so as the Lessees covenant for the due payment of the rent. A peppercorn or any smaller rent than that to be ultimately made payable, may be reserved during all or any part of the first 5 years of any such term, 28 V., c. 44.

Building or repairing leases by tenants for life, or in tail in possession, Guardians, Trustees or Committees, upon covenant so to do within 4 years

Not exceeding 21 years in possession Best yearly rent to be reserved Condition for re-entry for non payment of rent Nominal or smaller rent may be reserved for first 5 years

Legislative Council.

There shall be within this Island two Legislative Chambers or Houses, a Legislative Council to be composed as after prescribed, and an elective Legislative Assembly, to be called the Legislative Council and Assembly of Jamaica. The Legislative Council shall exercise and enjoy the same powers, privileges, rights and immunities as the present (Privy) Council, when sitting as a Legislative Council, have heretofore exercised and enjoyed, and which of legal right appertain to them as a Legislative Body, with such others as are by this Act conferred, 17 V., c. 29, s. 1.

The then Members of the Council, of whom the Honorable John Salmon and George Price continue declared Members of the Legislative Council, and H. M., by instrument under the Sign Manual may authorize the Governor, in H.M.'s name by instrument under the Broad Seal, to summon other persons qualified as after mentioned, the number not to exceed or be less altogether than 17, and to fill up vacancies at any time within 6 calendar months from the reduction of the number below 17, by death or disqualification. The continuing Members may exercise all the powers; and every person summoned, shall, by virtue of the summons, become a Member. No person shall be summoned who is not of the full age of 21, a natural born subject, or naturalized by Act of Parliament, or under an Act of this Island. When vacancies occur by death, resignation or removal of Members holding offices of emolument, so that their number falls below 5, further appointments may be made, so that not more than 5 at any one time shall be holders of any office of emolument, including the Member of the Executive Committee. No person but the 5 holders of offices shall be summoned, unless he is possessed in his own right, or in right of his wife, of a freehold estate in this Island, producing a clear annual income to him of £300, or pays taxes, public and parochial, to the extent of £30, on real property in this Island, held by him as of freehold in his own right, or in right of his wife, 17 V., c. 29, s. 2,

They shall exercise and enjoy the like political powers and authorities as the House of Lords, of initiating or originating any legislative measures not involving the imposition of taxes, or the appropriation of the public money, 17 V., c. 29, s. 3.

Every Member shall hold his seat for life, subject to the provisions after contained, 17 V., c. 29, s. 4.

But may resign his seat, and upon resignation and acceptance by the Governor the seat shall be vacant, 17 V., c. 29, s. 5.

If any Legislative Councillor, for 2 successive Sessions, fails to attend in Council, without the permission of H. M. or the Governor, signified by him to the Legislative Council, or ceases to be qualified, or becomes bankrupt, or is declared an insolvent, or takes the benefit of any Law relating to Insolvent Debtors, or becomes a public defaulter, or is convicted of Felony or other infamous crime, his seat shall thereby become vacant; and any question arising in respect of such vacancy shall be referred by the Governor to the Legislative Council to be determined. Either the person or the Attorney General may appeal from their determination, and the judgment

Its Powers

Members how appointed

Number

Qualifications Vacancies Holders of office

Non holders of office

Powers of originating Bills

To hold seats for life

Resignations

Disqualifications

Questions on vacancies to be referred to the Legislative Council, with appeal to the Queen in Council

of H. M., with the advice of her Privy Council, shall be final. If any

Absence for more than 2 consecutive years   Member for more than 2 consecutive years, ceases or omits to give his attendance, his seat shall become vacant, notwithstanding any permission or leave of absence given him, 17 V., c. 29, s. 6.

President vacancy   Her Majesty may, under the Sign Manual, authorize the Governor in her name, by instrument under the Broad Seal, when any vacancy arises, by death or otherwise, to appoint another Member to be President, 17 V., c. 29, s. 7.

Salary   The President shall receive from the Public Treasury a salary of £600, 17 V., c. 29, s. 8.

Oath   No Member shall sit or vote until he has taken and subscribed an oath before the Governor or some person authorized by him. Form :—

> I, A. B., do sincerely promise and swear, that I will be faithful and bear true allegiance to Her Majesty Queen Victoria, as lawful Sovereign of the United Kingdom of Great Britain and Ireland, and of this Island, and that I will defend her to the utmost of my power against all traitorous conspiracies and attempts whatever, which shall be made against her person, crown and dignity, and that I will do my utmost endeavor to disclose and make known to Her Majesty, her heirs and successors, all treasons and traitorous conspiracies and attempts which I shall know to be against her, or any of them, and all this I do swear without any equivocation, mental evasion, or secret reservation. And I do further swear, that I am possessed of one of the property qualifications required of a non-official Member of the Legislative Council, by an Act, entitled : " An Act for the better Government of this Island, and for raising a revenue in support thereof." So help me God.

No Member holding any office of emolument shall be required to take so much of the oath as relates to the property qualification, 17 V., c. 29, s. 9.

Affirmation   Members authorized by law may make an affirmation instead of an oath, 17 V., c. 29, s. 10.

Clerk and Officers   They may, as vacancies occur, appoint a Clerk of the Council, and other Officers mentioned in Schedule A, who shall be entitled to the salaries there mentioned, 17 V., c. 29, s. 11.

One of Executive Committee to be a member   One of the Members of the Executive Committee shall be a Member of the Legislative Council, and on forfeiture or resignation of his seat, his appointment as a Member of the Executive Committee shall cease, 17 V., c. 29, s. 12.

Accounts to be laid before them   Accounts in detail of the expenditure and appropriation of all revenue and other moneys placed under the control or direction of the Governor, or of any Body in conjunction with him, or under his authority, or within his control, shall be laid before the Legislative Council within 14 days after the beginning of the Session, after the expenditure and appropriation have been made, 17 V., c. 29, s. 34.

Office of emolument   " Office of emolument :" Any office held under the Crown, or the Government of this Island, or under any Act of Parliament, or of this Island, or under any parochial or other public Body constituted under any Act, 17 V., c. 29, s. 52.

Stamps exemption   No appointments, commissions or orders for money, shall be liable to Stamp Duty, 17 V., c. 29, s. 53.

Salaries

	£		
Salaries—President	600	0	0
Chaplain	60	0	0
Clerk	414	0	0
Librarian	60	0	0
Usher of the Black Rod	270	0	0

17 V., c. 29, Sch. A.

The salary of the present Chaplain, Revd. G. W. Rowe, continued at £120, 17 V., c. 31.

Salaries in lieu of Fees to the President, £100 : Clerk, £60 ; Usher of the Black Rod, £20, 21 V., c. 17, s. 4, Sch.

Ineligibility   Auditors of Public Accounts ineligible, 21 V., c. 1, s. 17.

Also Receiver-General and Book-keeper, 21 V., c. 4, s. 19.

Legislative and other Printing.

The Executive Committee authorized to enter into one or more contracts, upon the most eligible terms, to print the Journals of the Legislative Council, and Minutes of Assembly, with Indexes to be prepared by the Contractor; Bills, Documents, and Papers ordered by the Legislature; Motion Papers and Notices as per Schedule ; Documents and Papers directed by the Executive Committee; and Forms required for the use of the Receiver-General's Office, Customs and Collecting Constables. Such contracts to be for 7 years, and security taken for their due performance, 19 V., c. 3.

Contracts

For 7 years Security

SCHEDULE.

200 Copies of the Daily Journals or Minutes of the Legislative Council.

200 Copies of the Daily Votes, or Minutes of the Assembly.

100 Copies of such Journals, and 100 Copies of such Votes, to be delivered daily, and the other 100 copies of each, to be bound up in Volumes, with the like number of Copies of the Appendix and Index, at the termination of the Sessions.

Preparing or compiling the Index to the Journals of the Legislative Council, and also to the Votes of the Assembly, and printing 100 Copies respectively, to be bound up with such Journals and Votes.

100 Copies of all Bills, Documents or Papers ordered to be printed for the use of the Legislature, or for distribution separately from the Journals or Votes.

75 Copies of Motion Papers, containing the notices given by Members of the Legislative Council and the House of Assembly respectively daily.

All Documents and Papers directed by the Executive Committee, and Forms required by the Receiver-General and Collector of the Customs, for the use of the Receiver-General's Office, the Collecting Constables and the Customs, as often as required.

Lepers.

The Governor and Executive Committee may lease or purchase sufficient lands in convenient localities in Kingston, St. Catherine, St. Andrew, Port Royal or St. David, for the settlement and establishment of persons afflicted with Leprosy or Yaws, or Diseases akin thereto, and for that purpose erect Cottages, Huts or other buildings for their careful and comfortable reception and keeping, due care being taken in every establishment to provide for the complete separation of the sexes ; the buildings for males being divided, and, as far as can be, removed from those for females, and placed on separate parcels of land, if the Executive Committee so advise, 28 V., c. 13, s. 1.

Settlements to be leased or purchased for Lepers, &c.

Separation of sexes

The Governor, as soon as proper places have been provided, to be called the "Lepers' Home," shall appoint a Medical attendant thereto, at a salary of £120 per annum, a Male Superintendent at a salary not exceeding £80 per annum, and a Matron at not exceeding £60 per annum, payable quarterly or monthly as the Governor directs, by warrant, and may remove them, and fill up vacancies, 28 V., c. 13, s. 2.

Medical attendant £120 Superintendent £80 Matron £60

The Superintendent may employ 2 or more male servants to attend upon the male inmates, and for the Matron to employ 2 or 3 female servants to attend upon the female inmates, at wages to be approved of by the Governor in Executive Committee, and paid by Warrant of the Governor ; and the Superintendent and Matron may remove them, and appoint others, 28 V., c. 13, s. 3.

Servants

The Inspector and Director, in conjunction with the Medical Officers of the Public Hospital, shall, subject to the approval of the Governor in Executive Committee, make rules and regulations for the government of the Medical Attendant, Superintendent, Matron, and other Officers, servants and inmates of the respective divisions of the Institution, and may, subject to such approval, rescind, alter, amend and add to, or make new rules, 28 V., c. 13, s. 4.

Rules and Regulations

Visits and reports of Medical Attendant

The Medical Attendant shall visit once a week, and oftener if necessary, and prescribe Medical treatment where necessary, for the inmates, and make a quarterly report to the Governor in Executive Committee, of the state of the inmates, and of the Institution generally, with any recommendations or remarks he thinks fit to submit, with or as part of any such report, 28 V., c. 13, s. 5.

Hospital Inspector's visits and reports

Entries in Visiting Book

Transcripts to be sent to the Governor

Inspector's Salary £60

The Inspector of the Public Hospital, or such other person as the Governor may appoint, shall visit and inspect the Institution and inmates, and report on their condition at least once a month, and oftener, if the Governor requires, and shall make a note of each visit in the Visiting Book to be kept at the Institution, with such observations upon the state of the Institution and inmates, and the conduct of the officers and servants as he thinks proper ; and the Superintendent and Matron shall transmit monthly to the Governor a transcript of such entries. The Inspector shall be paid at the rate of £60 per annum, on the Governor's Warrant, for his services, 28 V., c. 13, s. 6.

Contracts for Stores, &c.

Medicines

He shall take contracts, subject to the approval of the Governor in Executive Committee, for stores, provisions and necessaries for the Institution. Medicines shall be supplied from the Public Hospital, on the requisition of the Medical Attendant, 28 V., c. 13, s. 7.

Duties of Superintendent and Matron with respect to Stores, &c ; their reports

Inspector, &c. to check Stores on each visit

The Superintendent and Matron shall be responsible for the due care and appropriation of all stores, provisions and necessaries supplied to their respective divisions, and shall make reports monthly to the Inspector or other person, &c., of the quantities received, consumption, quantities on hand, and state and condition of stores, &c., and generally of the state of the several divisions of the Institution ; and the Inspector or person, &c., shall on each visit, check the stores, &c., on hand, with the reports, 28 V., c. 13, s. 8.

Admissions of destitute patients

Upon the establishment of the Lepers' Home, any person afflicted with Leprosy or Yaws, or other disease akin thereto, in indigent circumstances, who presents himself to the Medical Attendant, and claims admission, or with a Certificate from a qualified Medical Practitioner that he is afflicted with Yaws or Leprosy, &c., shall be allowed to remain in, and be treated as an inmate of the Institution, 28 V., c. 13, s. 9.

Of persons not in destitute circumstances

Or if not in destitute circumstances, they may become inmates, upon giving security to the Superintendent for payment, monthly, of the cost of maintenance and medical treatment, not exceeding 2s. per day, 28, V., c. 13, s. 10.

Recovery of moneys due for maintenance, &c.

Which moneys shall be recovered by the Superintendent for the time being, or some other person appointed by him, in the same manner as demands under any Act in force for the recovery of small debts, without limitation of amount, 28 V., c. 13, s. 11.

Lepers, &c. convicted of vagrancy or begging may be committed to the Lepers' Home

Payment of expenses

If any person deemed to be afflicted, is found loitering on any road, street, lane, thoroughfare of, or leading to, or from any city, town or village, or wandering about from place to place, and not having any visible means of living, or is found begging, any Policeman or Constable may apprehend and take him before a qualified Medical Practitioner, who, upon being satisfied that he is a Leper, &c. shall certify the same, and be taken thereupon be taken before a Justice who, upon conviction for such vagrancy or begging, shall direct, in writing, under his hand, that the person be committed to the Lepers' Home for not exceeding 28 days, and thereupon he shall be taken to the Lepers' Home, and there received, and kept for such period, and the reasonable expense in taking him before a Medical Practitioner, and to the Lepers' Home, shall be paid by the Superintendent as a charge against the Institution, 28 V., c. 13, s. 12.

Persons so committed leaving during sentence

If any person so committed to the Institution, leave it before the expiration of the period of committal, and is seen wandering about in any street, thoroughfare or public place or way, he or she shall be taken back by the Superintendent or Matron, or any Policeman or Constable, and the Superintendent or Matron shall take measures, under rules and regulations to be, from time to time, made by the Governor in Executive Committee, for the proper keeping them within the bounds of the Institution, 28 V., c. 13, s. 13.

The Receiver-General shall pay, upon the Governor's Warrant, monthly, or otherwise, the sums necessary to meet the expenses of the Lepers' Home, not exceeding £2000 in any year, 28 V., c. 13, s. 14.

Expenses not to exceed £2000 per annum

The Justices and Vestry of any parish or adjoining parishes, other than before named, may, where it seems necessary, include in the annual estimates of expenditure, a sufficient sum for providing for the proper care and keeping of persons afflicted therein ; and where adjoining parishes join in arrangements, the expenses shall be borne rateably according to the number of diseased persons chargeable to each, 28 V., c. 13, s. 15.

Provision in the annual estimates of other parishes for persons afflicted

License and Registration Duties.

On the 1st August, or within 10 days after, in each year, the occupier or possessor of each item of enumerated, not exempted from payment of the Duties, and every person keeping or using Fire Arms shall set forth a statement of such property according to the forms to be supplied by the Collector of Dues, and declare to the truth of such payment, and pay him in respect thereof :

Returns and payment of duties

	£	s.	D.
For every House of the annual value of £12 or upwards, at the rate of 1s. 6d. in the pound	0	1	6
Each head of Horsekind used for any purpose whatsoever upon a Main or Parochial Road	0	11	0
Each head of Horsekind used solely for hire and livery-stable purposes	0	7	0
Each Ass	0	3	6
Each head of Horsekind, Ass or Horned Stock, except those next mentioned, not used on a Main or Parochial Road	0	1	0
Each head of Working Cattle, Horsekind and Asses, used solely in and about the cultivation of estates, plantations or pens, within the confines thereof	0	0	6
Every other Head of Cattle	0	0	6
Every Wheel of a Carriage	0	15	0
Ditto ditto used solely for hire and livery-stable purposes	0	10	0
Each head of Sheep	0	0	2
Each Boat plying for hire, Droghers and Ships' Boats excepted	1	0	0
Each Canoe or Boat, other than a Boat or Canoe plying for fare, Drogher's and other Ship's Boats excepted lying	0	10	0
Each Wheel of a Cart	0	6	0
Ditto ditto Hackney Carriage	1	0	0
Each Fire Arm Registration of and License to use on the premises of the owner	0	2	0
License to keep and use otherwise	0	8	0

28 V., c. 28, s. 1.

And shall, upon payment of the duty, forthwith take out from the Clerk of the Peace the License required ; penalty 40s., 28 V., c. 28, s. 2.

Licenses to be taken out

Every person in possession of land as owner, tenant, or in any other character, shall, on 1st August, or within 10 days after, pay to the Collector of Dues of his parish the full amount of the tax by law imposed thereon, without any deduction for discount, and obtain from him an acquittance thereof, 28 V., c. 28, s. 3.

Land Tax to be paid without discount

Any Assignee of property, liable to tax or duty, which comes to his possession or occupation after 1st August, the tax or duty on which had been previously paid, and the License or acquittance transferred by the Assignor to him, and any person who acquires property after that period in substitution of property of the like description, upon which the duty had been paid, but which had been destroyed, or had become unserviceable, shall not be liable to any tax or duty upon said property, and the tax previously paid, and License or Acquittance therefor, shall protect and renewal to the property so acquired. In every such case the License shall be produced to the Collector of Dues, who shall make a memorandum thereon of the transfer or acquittance, 28 V., c. 28, s. 4.

Assignees of duty paid property, the License for which is transferred
Property acquired in substitution for duty paid property destroyed, &c.
Collector's Memorandum on License

The Assignor of any property for which a License has been obtained shall, upon the the transfer specify in the bill or receipt whether the License is also transferred, and, if so, give the number, date, letter and parish ; in

Particulars to be expressed in bill or receipt to exempt Assignee from duty

In which case the Assignor not entitled to substitute other property

default of which, or if it does not convey the information, the Assignee shall pay the duty and take out a fresh License. The Assignor of property and of the benefit of the License shall not be entitled to occupy or possess any other property in substitution, without paying the duty and obtaining a fresh License for the same, 28 V., c. 28, s. 5.

On death License to inure to personal representatives or Assignee

Upon the death of any person, his License shall inure to his personal representatives or their Assignees for the residue of the term ; and in all cases of assignment of property on which duty has been paid and the License transferred, it shall inure to the Assignee for the residue of the term, 28 V., c. 28, s. 6.

Head of the family responsible

Whenever any property liable to tax or duty belongs to, or is held in Trust for any inmate or member of a family, the head or principal member shall be responsible for payment, and liable to penalties, 28 V., c. 28, s. 7.

Liabilities of occupiers or possessors for portions of a year

Any person who, after 1st August, enters into the occupation of any land or house chargeable with tax or duty, or becomes possessed of any dutiable property not licensed or registered, or whereon duty has not been paid, shall be liable to pay the whole or a portion, according to the time to elapse between the period when he entered into the occupation, or became possessed, and the next recurring period for the payment of the tax or duty ; such time to be computed from the first day of the quarter during which the occupation or possession commenced, at the rate of one-fourth of the whole annual tax for each quarter or fractional part, 28 V., c. 28, s. 8.

Collector may take declarations

The Collector of Dues may take declarations, 28 V., c. 28, s. 9.

Penalty for omitting to pay duties and take out Licenses

Any person omitting to pay the taxes or duty within the time limited, and in the manner prescribed, or to take out the necessary acquittance or License, shall forfeit not less than the amount of the duties evaded ; and shall also be condemned, on conviction, to pay the amount evaded, the charges of the Licenses, and the costs of proceedings to recover them. Any

Any contravention of the Act

person contravening any of the provisions of this Act, shall be liable to a penalty not exceeding £5, 28 V., c. 28, s. 10.

Forms of 13 V., c. 35, applicable

The Forms of conviction and distress and otherwise, under 13 V., c. 35, may be adapted to meet the exigencies of each case under this Act, 28 V., c. 28, s. 11.

Interpretation House

"House," shall mean every inhabited or occupied dwelling house, shop, store, wharf, warehouse, office or place of business of the annual value of £12 or upwards, and shall, for the purpose of valuation, include the out-offices, yards and curtilages, and lands attached ; and, for the purposes of taxation, the true annual value of every house shall, when tenanted at a rent, be taken to be the rent actually payable by the year, and where otherwise occupied, the full yearly rent at which it is yearly and bona fide worth to be let, 28 V., c. 28, s. 12.

Where let in subdivisions

Where a house is let in different sub-divisions, and is occupied by several persons or families, or by the owner, with one or more other persons, and the aggregate rents and value amount to £12 or upwards, it shall be charged with the duties, as if occupied by one person or one family only ; and the landlord or owner shall be deemed, for the purposes of taxation, the occupier, except where the duty has been paid, and the house registered by some other person, 28 V., c. 28, s. 13.

Houses on estates, &c.

Houses on any estate or pen, shall be exempt from the house tax if occupied by the owner or tenant, or his family, or by the attorney, overseer, or other servants of the estate or pen, free of rent ; but if let or rented to any person, or used for any other than the purposes of such estate or pen, they shall be liable to the house tax, 28 V., c. 28, s. 14.

Carriage

"Carriage," shall mean all spring carriages, whether used for the transport of persons on business or pleasure, or used exclusively in the business of a livery stable.

Cart

"Cart," shall mean every cart, dray, wagon or wain, whether on springs or not, used for burthen.

Hackney Carriage

"Hackney carriage" shall mean every wheeled carriage plying for hire in any town, or from one parish to another, for the carriage of passengers, or kept solely for hire and livery stable purpose.

Fire-arms

"Fire-arms" shall mean every musket, fowling-piece, gun or carbine, rifle, pistol, or revolver.

" Horsekind" shall mean every horse, mare, colt, filly, gelding-or mule. Horsekind

" Working cattle," shall mean all bulls, cows, speyed heifers, steers horses, mares, geldings and mules used or worked on or within the limits of an estate, and all horned stock used on estates, and for carrying produce or other commodities for or on account of any estate or plantation. Working Cattle

" Boat," shall mean any canoe, wherry, lighter, or other boat. Boat

" Estate" shall mean any land from which 5 hogsheads or 40 barrels of Sugar, or 35 hundred weight of Coffee are produced, or Pimento to the extent of 25 bags of 120 pounds weight each, as an annual average, is gathered. Estate

"Pen" shall mean any land upon which 40 head of breeding and other stock are kept and licensed. Pen

" Collector of Dues," shall mean any person appointed to get in or receive the duties hereby imposed, 28 V., c. 28, s. 15. Collector of Dues

On payment of the tax or duties, the Collector of Dues shall forthwith make out and deliver to the party paying, a receipt in acknowledgment of payment, and numbered consecutively, in which he shall specify the several items of property for which they are paid, and the respective sums paid thereon, to be forthwith delivered by the party to the Clerk of the Peace, who shall thereupon make out and deliver to the person entitled thereto a License numbered and otherwise in conformity with the receipt, which receipt and License shall be according to the forms the Executive Committee shall direct and supply, 28 V., c. 28, s. 16. Collector's receipts for Taxes

To be exchanged for Clerk of the Peace's License

Forms

The Registration or Licenses to keep and use Fire-arms, shall be personal, and shall not entitle any person not licensed to keep, carry, or use Fire-arms, unless he be the servant of a Licensee for the purpose, and shall carry or use them in his master's service, and within the limits of his property, 28 V., c. 28, s. 17. Fire-arms License personal

Any Policeman or Constable may require the production of his License by any person carrying or using any Fire-arm, otherwise than on public service ; and if not produced, may seize and convey the Fire-arms to the next Court of Petty Sessions of the Justices, who, in case of non-production of a License and satisfactory evidence that it had been obtained prior to the seizure, shall order them to be detained for 10 days, and then sold, unless earlier redeemed, 28 V., c. 28, s. 18. Seizure by Police on non production of Licenses

Detention a n d sale unless redeemed

Every person in possession of a Still on 1st August, shall, within 10 days after, make a return to the Collector, of every Still in his possession, and pay him 20s for each, and 1s. to the Clerk of the Peace, under penalty not exceeding £10 nor less than 40s for each Still not returned ; and the Collector shall grant a receipt for the sums to the party paying them. No Still which has not been used for 6 months previous to 1st August shall be liable to the tax, 28 V., c. 28, s. 19. Still Licenses License 20s to be returned and paid for to Collector of Dues
Not liable if not used for 6 months before 1st August

On production of the receipt to the Clerk of the Peace, he shall deliver to the party a Certificate of Registration in the form the Executive Committee supply, and make a return to the Receiver-General, of all certificates so delivered by him at the period for making returns of other certificates granted by him, 28 V., c. 28, s. 20. C l e r k of the peace's certificate of Registration
Return to Receiver General

The Collector shall at the usual period for making returns of taxes and duties, make a return of all Stills returned to him, and remit therewith all moneys paid to him for the same, 28 V., c. 28, s. 21. Collector's Return

When the duties imposed by this Act amount to or exceed £4, they may be paid by moieties ; the first on or before 10th August, and the 2d on or bfore 10th February succeeding, and on payment of the 1st moiety, and production of the Collector's receipt to the Clerk of the Peace, he shall grant the License, and in like manner, upon payment of the 2d moiety, and production of the receipt, 28 V., c. 28, s. 22. Taxes £4 or more may be paid in moieties

The duties to be paid by moieties shall be entered and registered by the Collector and Clerk of the Peace separately from those paid in full, and the Receipts and Licenses issued and granted for moieties shall have the word " moiety" written or printed legibly on the top and along the margin, and the Clerk of the Peace shall demand and receive only 6d for a License on each moiety, 28 V., c. 28, s. 23. And the receipts and Licenses kept separate
Clerk of the Peace's fee 6d for each moiety

Cart Licenses Hackney carriages, boats, firearms

The Clerks of the Peace shall deliver to the persons entitled, Licenses for Carts, Hackney Carriages, Boats and Fire-arms ; and each License shall state the distinguishing letter assigned by the Executive Committee to the parish for the year, and be marked and distinguished conformably therewith, and be numbered in each separate class with the number assigned thereto in the Collector's receipt, and a separate number shall be assigned

Separate licenses for each cart, hackney carriage and boat Fire-arms

to, and a separate License issued for each Cart, Hackney, Carriage, Boat and Fire-arms ; but any number of Fire-arms may be included in a License for same, 28 V., c. 28, s. 24.

Letter and number to be painted on each cart, &c

The letter and number mentioned in the License shall be painted on the right side of the Cart, Hackney Carriage and bow of the Boat, in legible letters, and numbers of the size of at least 2 inches, in white, on a dark ground, 28 V., c. 28, s. 25.

Exemptions from taxes, in cases of officers of Army and Navy, or School-houses

Houses occupied, and Carriages, Horses and Carts used by Officers of the Army and Navy on actual service, and Houses in which Schools are kept are exempted from taxation, so long as they shall actually be occupied and used by such Officers, or as School-Houses, but no longer, 28 V., c. 28, s. 26.

Railway, &c., trucks and carriages, estate's carts

Railway and Tramway Trucks and Carriages and Carts, used upon an estate or pen, shall not be liable to seizure or payment of tax, so long as they are used exclusively upon such Railway and Tramway, and within the lines and limits of the estate or pen to which they belong, upon any public road running through any such estate or pen, and within the lines or limits, 28 V., c. 28, s. 27.

Duration of license

Each License shall be in force from 1st August to 31st July next, 28 V., c. 28, s. 28.

Attendance of Collector and Clerk of the Peace to receive duties and issue licenses

The Collector of Dues and Clerk of the Peace shall, at each period fixed for payment of Duties, attend on such days and convenient places throughout the parish as the Custos and Justices, or in default, as the Custos shall determine, to receive payment of Duties, and issue Licenses, 28 V., c. 28, s. 29.

Collector's receipts to be numbered and transcribed in numerical order in a book

His returns to Receiver General in September

And monthly afterwards

The Collector shall number in consecutive order each Receipt granted, and transcribe same in numerical order in a book to be kept in his office, in the form prescribed by the Executive Committee, and to be open to public inspection, and shall transmit to the Receiver-General, on or before 30th September, a statement, declared to before a Justice, of the total number of persons who have paid taxes or duties, with the aggregate of each head or division of items of property, and the total amount of payments to 28th September, and within 5 days after each month, transmit a similar statement for the period elapsed since the date to which the last return was made, in such form as the Executive Committee shall from time to time direct, shewing the number in consecutive order of the receipts issued by him during the then preceding month, with the names of the taxpayers, the items of property, and sums paid by each, and the gross aggregate receipts of the month, including Land Tax, and shall, at the same time,

With the amount of receipts less £6 per cent. for his services

transmit to the Receiver-General the full amount of all duties and moneys received by him, deducting £6 per cent. for his services under this Act, 28 V., c. 28, s. 30.

Clerk of the Peace to mark licenses with corresponding number

Additional particulars for carts, &c

Alphabetical record

Monthly copies to be sent to Receiver General

And record book laid before quarterly vestry St. Catherine precinct

The Clerk of the Peace shall mark on each License the number of the corresponding Receipt of the Collector, and on each License in respect of each Cart, Hackney Carriage and Boat, the distinguishing number of the current licensing year. The number of the General Receipt, and the separate number assigned to each shall also be marked on the License therefor. He shall also keep a separate record in alphabetical order, in form prescribed and supplied by the Executive Committee : and within 10 days after the expiration of each month, transmit to the Receiver-General a copy of his record book, shewing the names of, and items of property, and sums paid by each person, declared to before a Justice, and to be before each Quarterly Vestry his record book of Licenses, except in St. Catherine, where the Clerk of the Peace may make a return of the names of the persons who have taken out Licenses during the quarter in each parish of the precinct, 28 V., c. 28, s. 31.

Clerk of the Peace's Fees

The Clerk of the Peace shall be entitled to a fee of 1s. upon each License granted by him, except in cases of moieties to be paid with the Duties to the Collector, who shall account for, and pay over the same to his credit, and at the foot of each receipt, specify the amount of fees so received, 28 V., c. 28, s. 32.

The Collector and Clerk of the Peace shall, for every neglect or default, forfeit not exceeding £5, over and above the amount of Duties not transmitted ; and where the defaulting officer is the recipient of salary from the Treasury, the Receiver-General shall deduct therefrom the amount of the penalty inflicted, 28 V., c. 28, s. 33.

Each Collector shall be paid a salary of £40 per annum on the Governor's Warrant, in addition to the commission of £6 per cent. authorized to be deducted from all moneys collected by him, 28 V., c. 28, s. 34.

Every item of property liable to, but which has not paid Duty or been Licensed and every Cart, Hackney Carriage or Boat, not lettered or numbered according to the register of the parish as directed, and whether being used or not, shall be seized by any Policeman or Constable, and conveyed to a Justice, who may direct the same, and all goods found in the Cart, Hackney Carriage or Boat, so seized (except the party in charge, think fit to remove the goods), to be kept until the case can be adjudicated by the Justices, who may direct the property to be detained until redeemed or sold, 28 V., c. 28, s. 35.

Out of the proceeds the Collector shall be paid the amount of the Taxes or Duties and License, and the cost of taking, keeping and selling the property seized, not exceeding 1s. in the pound, and 4s. to the seizing officer ; and the surplus, if any, shall be returned to the owner, or person from whom the property was taken, 28 V., c. 28, s. 36.

Who may at any time before the sale, redeem the property, by complying with the Act, and paying 4s. to the seizing officer, and the charges on taking and keeping the property not exceeding 1s. per diem. The Collector shall give a receipt as before directed, for the amount of the License when paid to him, and thereupon the necessary License shall be granted by the Clerk of the Peace, upon production of which the property shall be restored ; but any Justice may direct the seizing officer to sell immediately by public outcry, any goods seized of a perishable nature, and apply the proceeds as directed, and notwithstanding such seizure and sale, the penalties for the breach of this Act may be sued for and enforced against the offender, 28 V., c., 28, s. 37.

Any person allowing his License to be used by any other person in contravention of this Act, shall be liable to a penalty not exceeding £10, nor less than £2, and any person using such License shall be liable to a like penalty, 28 V., c. 28, s. 38.

Counterfeiting or forging, or causing, &c., or aiding in counterfeiting or forging any License, Registration Letter, Number or Mark, painting or impression required by this Act, or knowingly uttering, giving or procuring to be given, or making use, or procuring to be made use of, or accepting or receiving any counterfeited or forged License, &c., in any respect or particular : penalty, £10, and imprisonment with hard labor, for not exceeding 6 calendar months, 28 V., c. 28, s. 39.

All penalties and forfeitures, and all Taxes, Dues and Arrears to be paid the Collector, may, instead of the process of distress prescribed by 27 V., c. 31, (s. 21-31) or any Act to be passed for the Collection of Taxes, be recovered before 2 Justices of the parish where the offence or default was committed, or the offender or defaulter resides ; and in case of nonpayment, may be enforced by distress and sale of the offender's or defaulter's goods, or imprisonment not exceeding 3 months, unless such penalty, Taxes, Duties, Arrears and Costs, are sooner paid, and may be enforced under 13 V., c. 35, or other Act in respect to summary proceedings ; and the forms may be adapted to meet the requirements of this Act ; and notwithstanding anything in 13 V., c. 35, the Taxes, Dues, and Arrears, or any of them, and the penalty for omitting to pay the same may be included in, and recovered on one proceeding, 28 V., c. 28, s. 40.

In all legal proceedings, the production of a certificate, purporting to be signed by the Receiver-General, or any Clerk of the Peace or Collector, stating the number and description or the value of property in respect of which the person named appears to have paid Duties, and any book, record, statement or return made by either of those officers in execution of this Act, shall be received as prima facie evidence of the truth of the statements therein ; and any certificate, purporting to be signed as aforesaid, that the person therein named, does not appear, from any document in his office, authorized to occupy or keep, or use any property within the meaning of

Marginal notes:

Neglect of Collector or Clerk of the Peace

Collector's salary

Seizure of unlicensed property and carts, &c., not lettered by a policeman

After disposal

Out of proceeds the taxes and license to be paid to the Collector the costs, and 4s to the seizing officer

Surplus to owner, &c

Conditions on which property may be redeemed

Sale of parishable property

Penalties enforcable

Lending or using licenses

Counterfeiting, &c., licenses, &c

Recovery of penalties, taxes and arrears

Under 13 V., c. 35

In one proceeding

Certificates of Receiver General, Clerks of the Peace and collectors and books, respecting taxable property, prima facie evidence

this Act, or any greater number of any such items respectively than are expressed in any such certificate, shall be also received as prima facie evidence of the truth of the facts therein stated, 28 V , c. 28, s. 41.

Exemptions from stamps

No Receipt or License Registration, Certificate or Process under this Act, shall be liable to Stamp Duty, 28 V., c. 28, s. 42.

Refund of duties overpaid

The Executive Committee may refund any amount of License Duty, which may appear to them to have been overpaid, 28 V., c. 28, s. 43.

Executive committee to determine distinguishing letter for each parish for the year

They shall, in each year, determine, and, by public advertisement in the Jamaica Gazette, communicate to the Clerk of the Peace the distinguishing letter of his parish to be affixed to Licenses for the ensuing licensing period or year, and which shall be the distinguishing letter for the period, and inserted in each License accordingly for the parish, 28 V., c. 28, s. 44.

Remuneration to persons aiding collectors

They may allow a reasonable sum for remunerating any person appointed by the Collector, with their consent, for aiding him in discovering and proceeding against persons in default or in arrear for Duties, and otherwise in assisting in the collection, 28 V., c. 28, s. 45.

False declarations

Wilfully making a false declaration, or knowingly swearing falsely where an oath is required, shall be punishable as perjury, and the prosecution shall be of a public nature, 28 V., c. 28, s. 46.

Inforcement of act notwithstanding its repeal or expiry.

Notwithstanding the repeal or expiry of this Act, all Taxes and Duties payable thereunder, may be enforced, and offences punished, penalties recovered, bonds, recognizances, &c., enforced, and proceedings continued, 28 V., c. 28, s. 47.

Appropriation of certain duties to the general public service

The Duties on Breeding Stock and Working Cattle, Estates, Plantations and Pens, Horsekind and Mules, Sheep, Canoes, Wherries and other Boats, and Houses, and on Fire-Arms and Stills, shall be appropriated towards the general public service, 28 V., c. 28, s. 48.

Forms and books

The Forms and Books required shall be prescribed and supplied to the respective officers by the Executive Committee, 28 V., c. 28, s. 49.

Short title and duration

The License and Registration Duties Act, 1865—In force from 1st August, 1865, until 31st July, 1867, 28 V., c. 28, s. 51.

Light Houses—Morant Point.

commissioners Tonnage duty

The Naval Commander-in-chief, the Commodore or Senior Officer, the Custos and Members in Assembly for Port-Royal, Kingston and St. Thomas in the East, and the Members in Assembly for St. David, or any 5 of them, were appointed Commissioners to erect and maintain the Light-House, and a duty of 6d. (late currency) per ton imposed on all vessels entering and clearing out each voyage at the time of entry, with power to the Commissioners to reduce and again increase rates not exceeding as above, and to

Loan

draw upon the Receiver-General to the extent of £8000 (£4800 stg.) as a loan, bearing £6 per cent. interest, and with power to appoint a Solicitor,

Officers

Clerks and other officers ; the balance of duties, after discharging the annual costs and expenses of maintenance, to be applied in reduction of the interest and principal monies advanced, 3 V., c. 66.

PLUMB POINT NEAR PORT-ROYAL.

The Admiral or Officer commanding on the Station, the Speaker of the Assembly, the Commodore or Senior Officer, other than the Admiral, the Commanding Officers of the Royal Engineers and Artillery, the Custos of Port-Royal, Custos, Mayor and Harbor-master of Kingston, and 8 other persons named, or such persons as shall be appointed by the remaining Commissioners in the room of any such Commissioners, or of any Commissioners to be appointed in their room, who shall die, leave the Island, or become incapable or unfit, incorporated as " The Commissioners of the Plumb Point Light

commissioners

House in Jamaica," with a Common Seal, and appointed Commissioners for its election and maintenance, with power to borrow not exceeding £5000

Loans

by loans on the credit of the taxes, and duties, at £6 per cent. interest, payable half-yearly, the principal not longer than 10 years after the passing of the Act. Vessels entering Port-Royal or Kingston, subject to the payment on

Tonnage dues

Steam Vessels of 2d per ton per register, not demandable oftener than once in 3 calendar months, on other Vessels, 6d per ton on the whole registered Tonnage : the duty in respect of droghers and other Ships, Sloops and Vessels, (other than Steam Vessels) engaged in the coasting trade, or trading within the Tropic of Cancer, to be demandable not ofener than once in 12 calendar months; in respect of all other Vessels on every entry. And after payment of all principal and interest, the Commissioners were empowered to lower and again increase the rates not exceeding the above rates. Besides the persons to be employed in and about the Light House, the Commissioners are empowered to employ a Solicitor and a Clerk, at a salary of £30, 15 V., c. 17.

Officers, &c.

Power was given to the Commissioners to purchase other land, 26 V., S. 2, c. 9 s. 1.

Additional Land

Vessels arriving at Port-Royal to land passengers, or receive orders, or calling off the Port to take Pilots on board, shall not be liable for Light House Dues, 26 V., S. 2, c. 9, s. 2.

Exemptions from Dues

Loan from the Imperial Government, Perpetual Annuity.

The Loan of £200,000 Sterling contracted under 4 W., 4, c. 2, upon which there was due £249,582 0s. 2d on 5th February, 1862, was commuted for a Perpetual Annuity of £6,400, charged on the Duties and sources of revenue mentioned in Schedule to 17 V., c. 29, next after the two sums of £30,000 and £25,000. Such Annuity to become due on 30th June and 31st December, and to be applied in payment of such expenses of the Government of this Island, and of objects connected therewith, and of local improvements here, as the Governor may direct, persuant to the instructions of one of Her Majesty's Principal Secretaries of State; and an account of the expenditure to be laid before the Assembly within the first 2 weeks of each meeting, 26 V., S. 2, c. 1.

Perpetual Annuity of £6,400 in lieu of debt to Parliament on £200,000 loan

Application

Account to be laid before the Assembly

Loans Guaranteed by Government.

IMMIGRATION—£100,000.

Agents were appointed to raise a Loan in Great Britain on the guarantee of the Government, to be applied in promoting the introduction of free laborers (and to the extent of £20,000, the pa men of the return passage of Coolie Immigrants). Not to exceed £100,000, at £4 per cent. interest, payable half-yearly, in London, and redeemable 30th June, 1872, secured by the Duties imposed, and also as a further charge on the gene a revenue. The monies to meet the half-yearly interest, to be remitted by the Receiver-General, as also £2500 a-year for the establishment of a Sinking Fund.

Agents to raise loans

			£	s	D	
Duties imposed on every hogshead of Sugar exported.			0	2	6	*Export Duties charged therewith*
"	"	" puncheon of Rum...	0	2	0	
"	"	" tierce of Coffee	0	2	0	
"	"	" Pimento, per 120lbs.	0	0	4	

Every 3 tierces of Sugar shall be taken to be equivalent to 2 hogsheads, and every 8 barrels to 1 hogshead, and 2 hogsheads of Rum to 1 puncheon, 15 V., c. 39, s. 1–15.

Every package, not a hogshead, tierce or barrel, shall be charged in the proportion it bears to a hogshead of 17 cwt., 24 V., c. 16, s. 17.

£50,000 having been raised, redeemable on 30th June, 1872, the agents were empowered to raise the remaining £50,000 by Debentures, redeemable at the end of 20 years, from the date of their issue, 16 V., c. 25.

The moneys received from the employers of Immigrants, introduced by means of moneys raised under 15 V., c. 39, and 16 V., c. 25, shall be paid by the Agent-General one week after receipt to the Receiver-General, to the credit of the £100,000 Immigration Loan New Sinking Fund, and the Governor and Executive Committee may direct the whole, or portions of the moneys at any time to the credit of that Fund, to be invested as part of the Sinking Fund 22 V., c. 1, s. 69.

Moneys received from employers of Immigrants charged with redemption

30th September. 1864.

At debit of 1st moiety, £50,000; at credit of Sinking Fund, £19568 1 9

,, ,, ,, 50,000 ,, ,, ,, 6745 0 0

3 F

£500,000 LOAN GUARANTEED.

£30,000 annually appropriated for Interest and Sinking Fund; and Import Duties to raise same

So long as the £30,000 to be annually raised and paid for 30 years, and to be appropriated to the liquidation of the Public Debt, and interest, is payable, there shall be raised and paid upon all live and dead stock and goods imported, the Duties enumerated in Schedule C, those in Schedule D. being to be admitted free, 17 V., c. 29, s. 38-40.

To be levied under 17 V , c. 1, notwithstanding its expiry, if there be no other Act regulating the collection of Import Duties ; but if there be any such Act in accordance with the existing Act, and the produce of the Duties shall be paid by the Officers of the Customs every week to the Receiver-General, to be applied (in payment of the £30,000, and and permanent Civil List of £25,000 per annum), 17 V., c. 29, s. 41.

Other provisions may be substituted

The Legislature may make other full provision for the payment and application of such annual sums ; and while other provision is made, the Duties hereby imposed shall cease to be collected, as also while Duties larger or equal in amount are collected and raised under any Act. In any such case, the sums of £30,000 and £25,000 shall be reserved and paid out of the proceeds of the Duties under any such Act, 17 V., c. 29, s. 42.

Appropriation of £30,000 for 30 years for interest and Sinking Fund on Guaranted Loan unless sooner liquidated

There shall be payable out of the Revenue Fund yearly, for 30 years after the proclamation of this Act, £30,000 for paying the annual interest at £4 per cent., and providing a Sinking Fund for the liquidation of the portion of the Public Debt, to be guaranteed by the British Government, which shall be paid by the Receiver-General in discharge of the Governor's Warrants. So soon as the principal, and all interest on the Guaranteed Debt of £500,000, and all necessary expenses are by such means or otherwise liquidated, the payments shall cease, 17 V., c. 29, s. 46.

Debts to be discharged out of loan

The Debts and liabilities in Schedule F. shall be discharged out of the Loan, 17 V., c. 29, s. 50.

Powers to raise and redeem loan and discharge interest at £4 per cent.

For the raising and redemption of the Loan of £500,000 guaranteed by the Imperial Parliament on the security of the Permanent Revenue under 17 V., c. 29, Her Majesty was empowered to appoint Agents in England, to borrow and raise in Great Britain, by Bond, Debenture or otherwise, that sum as the Commissioners of the Treasury should determine, redeemable on 1st June, 1885, for sums not less than £300, at £4 per cent. interest payable in London half-yearly, as also out of the remittances by the Receiver-General, to pay the interest, and annually invest £10,000, and the accruing dividends in the British Funds as a Sinking Fund ; accounts of which to be transmitted to the Governor, through the Colonial Secretary, to be laid before the Assembly, 17 V., c. 35.

30th September 1864 ; at debit of Loan, £500,000.
At credit of SinkingFund, £90,000.

Loans on Island Security.

IMMIGRATION.

Loans to be contracted

The Governor and Executive Committee are empowered to borrow in this Island or Great Britain, not exceeding £50,000 in any one year, for defraying, in the first instance, the expense of introducing Immigrants, at £6 per cent. interest, payable half-yearly, at the Island Treasury, or if drawn in Great Britain, in London. The moneys so raised, and the interest thereon, to be the only charge upon the moneys directed by 22 V., c. 1, to be carried to the credit of "The New Immigration Fund Account," (superseded by The Further Immigration Fund Account, 1861, 24 V., c. 16, s. 22.), and for repayment of which the credit of the Island is also pledged, in case of any deficiency, to discharge the same by such means, and out of such Funds as the Legislature may provide when the deficiency arises, 22 V., c. 3.

Limit

The utmost amount of moneys to be borrowed on the Loan or succession of Loans, is limited to the total sum of £150,000 over and above the moneys at the credit of The Further Immigration Fund Account, 1861, and the moneys to be invested under this Act, 25 V., c. 35, s. 6.

When redeemable

The Bonds and Debentures shall be made redeemable ; one-third of the amount or estimated amount to be required in each year, at the expiration of not exceeding 5 years ; one-third, not exceeding 10 years, and the residue not exceeding 15 years, after the expiration of the year in which the same shall be contracted ; and such principal moneys and interest shall be secured upon The Further Immigration Fund, 1861, and The interest payable half-yearly out of any moneys then at the credit of that Fund or otherwise, under 22 V., c. 3, 25 V., c. 35, s. 7.

All moneys to be paid by employers shall be paid over by the Immigration Agent to the Receiver-General, to the credit of The Further Immigration Fund Account, 1861, 25 V., c. 35, s. 5.

Funds applicable to redemption Further Immigration Fund

For providing Funds for the importation of Immigrants and re-payment of the moneys to be borrowed under 22 V., c. 3, there shall be levied, raised and paid, the funds and moneys after mentioned, in lieu of those set apart by any existing Acts, except the Export Duties imposed by 15 V., c. 39, 24 V. c. 16, s. 5.

Export Duties

For the redemption of the principal moneys to fall due upon the Bonds and Debentures under 22 V., c. 3, there shall be established a Sinking Fund, to which shall be carried and appropriated in each year a sum sufficient to meet their re-payment as they become due; and the Receiver-General, under the Governor's Warrant, shall annually remit such moneys to the Agents in Great Britain, to be invested in the Public Funds, 24 V., c. 16, s. 14.

Sinking Fund

The Duties in Schedule shall be levied and received by the Officers of Customs in the same manner as other Duties of Customs, 24 V., c. 16, s. 15.

Collection of Duties

Distinct accounts of which shall be kept by the Collector and Controller of Kingston and by the Receiver-General ; and the moneys at the credit of the account to be kept by the Receiver-General shall be from time to time transferred to the credit of "The Further Immigration Fund, 1861," as the Governor may direct, 24 V., c. 16, s. 16.

Distinct Account to be kept

Every 3 tierces of Sugar exported shall be taken to be equivalent to 2 hhds., 8 barrels, to 1 hhd. Every other package shall be charged with Duty in the proportion it bears to the hhd. of 17 cwt. Every 2 hhds. of Rum shall be equivalent to 1 phn. Every quarter-cask or other package shall be charged with Duty in the proportion it bears to a phn. of 90 gallons. All Coffee exported in packages other than tierces, shall be charged with Duty in the proportion of 7 cwt. to one tierce ; and every package of Sugar exported, not being a hhd., tierce or barrel, shall be charged with Export Duty, under 15 V., c. 39, in the proportion it bears to the hhd. of 17 cwt., 24 V., c. 16, s. 17.

Computation of packages for duties

During the Financial Year terminating on the 30th September, 1866, after appropriating £8000 for the purposes of this Act, the Receiver-General shall apply any surplus moneys in aid of the expenditure of the several parishes ; and thereafter the whole amount of the Revenue derivable from such Duties shall be exclusively applicable for the purposes of this Act. 24 V., c. 16, s. 18.

Appropriation of Duties

After making full provision for the remittance from time to time of the amounts required to meet the half-yearly Interest on the Bonds and Debentures, under 15 V., c. 39, and 16 V., c. 20, as well as the annual payments provided for the redemption of the principal, as also of any other Principal or interest moneys already charged upon the produce of the Duties, the Receiver-General shall carry the surplus of any year to the credit of "The Further Immigration Fund Account, 1861," for Immigration purposes, 24 V., c. 16, s. 25.

Surplus Duties under 15 V., c. 39

The Export Duties raisable under 15 V., c. 39, and under this Act, shall continue to be raised only so long as there shall be owing or unpaid any moneys for the introduction of Immigrants, or for Loans contracted for their introduction, for payment whereof full provision shall not have been made, 24 V., c. 16, s. 26.

Cesser of Duties

DUTIES ON EXPORTS UNDER 24 V., c. 16.

	£	s.	D.
Every hogshead Sugar..	0	3	0
" puncheon Rum..	0	2	6
" tierce of Coffee..	0	4	0
Pimento, per bag of 120lbs., or on every 120lbs.	0	0	6
Logwood and other Dyewoods, Lignumvitæ, Ebony, and Cocus Wood, per ton, at the rate of..	0	1	0
Ginger, at the rate per cwt.	0	1	0
Beeswax, at the rate per cwt.	0	2	0
Arrowroot, at the rate per cwt.....	0	1	0
Cocoanuts, at the rate of per 1000..	0	1.	0
Honey, at the rate of per cwt.	0	1	0
Mahogany, at the rate of per M. feet, superficial measure	0	5	0

£4000 for Immigration purposes for 1865 to go to General Revenue
The Receiver-General shall, on Warrant of the Governor in Executive Committee, carry to the credit of the General Revenue in reimbursement of so much of £6039 appropriated to account of the Colonization and Back Passage Fund, the sum of £4000, provided by 24 V., c. 16, s. 18, for Immigration purposes for 1864-5, 28 V., c. 45, s. 8.

Chinese women and children
The Governor and Executive Committee were empowered to borrow in this Island or in Great Britain, sufficient to pay the cost of introducing, not exceeding 1000 in any one year, Chinese women and children under 12 (2 children counting, as one woman) as free settlers, in the manner, and with the powers given by 22 V., c. 3, except that the Bonds or Debentures should be redeemable 15 years at furthest after date, the half-yearly interest on which shall be paid out of the Immigrants' Colonization and Return Passage Fund, (22 V., c. 1, s. 71, and 23 V., c 29, s. 10), and remitted as prescribed by (22 V., c. 3, s. 6) ; and the principal moneys discharged out of the amount to be accumulated on such funds, in addition to which the credit of the Island is pledged for re-payment of principal and interest, 23, V., c. 30.

30th September, 1864, at debit of 22 V. c. 3, £12,138.
At credit of Sinking Fund, £1500.

KINGSTON AND ANNOTTO BAY JUNCTION ROAD.

£15,000
The Trustees were empowered to borrow not exceeding £15,000, at not exceeding £6 per cent. interest, payable half-yearly, and the principal to be re-paid within 20 years from the passing of the Act, for repayment of which and interest, the credit of the Island was pledged. 18 V., c. 66.

The Road is now one of the Main Roads under 21 V., c. 32.
30th Sept., 1864, at the debit of Loan, £9900.

KINGSTON SLIP DOCK.

£40,000
The Governor and Executive Committee were empowered to raise in this Island or Great Britain, not exceeding £40,000, to construct a Slip-Dock in Kingston Harbour, at £6 per cent. interest, payable half-yearly, if in this Island, at the Treasury, or if in Great Britain, in London ; and whenever the amount at the credit of the Slip Dock account, after its completion, is more than required to pay one year's accruing interest, to direct the excess or such portion as is considered proper, to be applied to the purchase of Bonds, &c., to be cancelled. Such Bonds, &c., to be redeemable at such times, and in the proportions the Governor and Executive Committee determine, not longer than 25 years after their issue ; and detailed accounts to the end of the Financial Year, shall be laid before the Assembly, within 20 days, shewing all moneys received and paid on account of the Slip Dock, and a statement in detail of the progress of the works to the first day of the Session. The credit of the Island is pledged for re-payment of the Loan and annual interest, 28 V., c. 39, s. 2-5—8-19.

KINGSTON THOROUGHFARES.

£14,500
The Governor and Executive Committee are empowered to raise, for the re-construction of the most inhabited streets and lanes of Kingston, in this Island or Great Britain, by Bond, Debenture or otherwise, not exceeding £14,500, at £6 per cent. interest, payable half yearly, on Bonds, &c., payable in this Island at the Treasury, on those payable in Great Britain, in London : the Bonds, &c., to be redeemable not longer than 25 years after their issue, and after notice of not less than 12 months of the intention to pay them off ; after expiry of which, interest shall cease on those notified to be payable, 28 V., c. 24, s. 2, 3, 7.

Taxes to meet
To provide for payment of the interest and principal of the moneys to be raised, there shall be paid annually the following taxes :—

For each House of the annual value of £12, in every Street, Cross Street and Lane, from Hanover Street to Orange Street, both inclusive, and from the line of St. Andrew to the sea, within

	s	d
those limits	0	7
Each Head of Horse-kind used in the City	3	6
" For Livery Stable purposes	2	6
" Wheel of a Carriage	5	0
" For Livery Stable purposes solely	3	6
" Cart Wheel "	3	0
" Hackney Carriage Wheel	6	8

And there shall be stated annually on the Estimates for the Public Service, and raised as part of the Public Expenditure, £200, 28 V., c. 24, s. 4.

The Rates and Duties shall commence in the present year, and with the items or objects charged therewith, be g en in for and payable at the same periods, and collected by the same Officers, and with the like powers, and subject to the like penalties and fines, for any default, and the like meaning and interpretation of terms and all other provisions of law, as any like Taxes on Houses, Wheels and Stock, under any Act now or at any time in force, or of the last preceding License and Registration Duties Act, but shall not be payable after pa ment of the principal and interest moneys of the Loan, 28 V., c. 24, s. 5. y   *Collection*

The Receiver-General shall—   *Receiver-General's Accounts*

Keep an account, entitled "The Kingston Steeets Account," in which to credit all moneys received and collected, whether by sale of Bonds, &c., or for Taxes and Duties, or the annual sum (£200) charged on the estimates of expenditure, and debit all moneys paid for the construction and execution of works, or for payment of interest or principal of any Loan moneys, and pay out of any money at the credit, or if none, or it is not sufficient, out of any public moneys unappropriated, the half yearly interest on the Bonds, &c., or remit same for payment in Great Britain, 28 V., c. 24, s. 6.

Accounts to be laid before the Assembly within 28 days after meeting, distinguishing the sums paid for interest, and principal, and other accounts of expenditure, 28 V., c. 24 s. 13.   *Accounts to be laid before the Assembly*

MAIN ROADS, &c.

The Governor and Executive Committee were empowered to borrow, either in this Island or in Great Britain by Bond, Debenture or otherwise, not exceeding £50,000, as required for the purposes of this Act, and to appoint Agents to raise money in Great Britain, at an interest not exceeding £6 per cent., payable half-yearly at the Treasury, if payable in this Island, or in London, if payable in Great Britain, and the principal to be redeemable at the furthest at the end of 50 years from date ; the interest to be payable out of any moneys at the credit of the Main Road Fund Account, or, if the same be at any time deficient, to be made good out of any other unappropriated Public Revenue, but to be re-paid out of the first moneys afterwards to come to hand on account of the Main Road Fund, 21 V., c. 34, s. 3-5.   *£50,000*

Similar provisions in respect of a further Loan, not exceeding £40,000, for Main Roads, 24 V., c. 26 s. 1, 2, 4.   *£40,000*

For making provision for the redemption of the Main Road Loans, under 21 V., c. 34, and 24 V., c. 26, in the Financial Year 1885-86, and each subsequent Financial Year, until redemption of such Loans, there shall be appropriated and charged the Estimates of the Public Expenditure, not exceeding £15,000, to be applied by the Governor and Executive Committee in redemption of the principal moneys, according to the numerical order of the Debentures until fully redeemed, 27 V., S. 1, c. 25, s. 2.   *Redemption*

The Governor and Executive Committee may extend the periods for which Debentures have been issued, so as to bring the time of payment within this Act, but so as not to postpone the period of payment beyond 1890, 27 V., S. 1, c. 25, s. 3.   *Extension of Debentures*

This Act incorporated with 21 V., c. 34, and 24 V., c. 26, 27 V. S. 1, c. 25, s. 4.

Power to the Governor and Executive Committee to borrow in this Island or Great Britain, not exceeding £12,000, by Bond, &c., redeemable at furthest at the end of 25 years from their issue ; the interest to be paid half yearly as they fall due on those payable in the Island, and remitted to Great Britain to meet such as are payable there : and not exceeding £300 a-year, to be invested in the British Funds towards a Sinking Fund. The moneys borrowed and interest to be a charge on the general Revenue, and the moneys required on account of principal and interest shall be annually stated in the Estimates, and raised annually as part of the general Public Expenditure, the moneys borrowed to be entered as "The Main Road Further Loan Fund, 1863," and carried to The Main Road Fund Account, under 21 V., c. 34. £10,000 of the Loan to be disbursed solely for re-construction of Roads and building of Bridges ; and detailed accounts   *£12,000*

of the expenditure, and of the a men   of interest and investments, laid
before the Assembly within 28 days after the Session, 26 V., S. 2, c. 5.

£27,000   Similar provisions in respect of a further Loan, not exceeding £27,000,
to be appropriated, £12,000 to the Main Road Further Loan Fund,
£10,000 to the Dry River Bridge Loan account, and £5000 to the Parochial Roads Loan Sinking Fund not exceeding £810 per annum. Detailed
accounts to be laid before the Assembly, 27 V., S. 1, c. 24.

£9,000   A further Loan not exceeding £9000 for re-payment to the Treasury
of advances for repairs of Roads and Bridges under 27 V., S. 2, c. 6, in
consequence of May, 1864, floods. Sinking Fund, £3 per cent. per annum
on amount actually raised, 28 V., c. 26.

30th Sept., 1864, at debit of 1st Loan £50,100

                2d   38,250

                3d   12,000 at credit of Sinking Fund £300

                4th   13,950

PAROCHIAL DEBTS.

£15,000   The Executive Committee were empowered to borrow in the Island, by
Bond, Debenture or otherwise, not exceeding £15,000, to pay off the liabi-
lities of the Local Boards of Health, and arrears of salaries of Parochial
Officers, at £5 per cent. per annum, payable half yearly at the Receiver-
General's Office, redeemable within 10 years, to be met by the several
parishes to which advances should be made, 18 V., c. 60.

30th Sept,, 1864, at debit of Loan, £1500

PAROCHIAL DEBTS AND COLLECTING CONSTABLES' COMPENSATION.

£40,000   The Executive Committee were empowered to raise by Bond, Debenture or otherwise, not exceeding £40,000 at £5 per cent. interest, payable
half-yearly at the Receiver-General's Office (increased to £6 per cent, by
22 V., c. 24, s. 1) to pay off the debts of the several. parishes, and compen-
sate the Collectors of Taxes, whose offices were abolished, (and any surplus
for the expense of Parochial works and repairs of Churches and other
buildings in the parishes, 22 V., c. 24, s. 2) for the payment of the interest
on which and gradual redemption of the principal, £3000 per annum was
appropriated out of the General Revenue to be applied to the payment of
interest in the first place, and the balance to the purchase of bonds, &c., to
be cancelled, or if impracticable to purchase them at par, the balance to be
invested at interest in this Island or in Great Britain until they can be purchased, 21 V., c. 44, s. 1-14.

30th September, 1864 at debit of Loan, £34,050.

PUBLIC LIABILITIES, 1860.

£20,000   The Governor and Executive Committee were empowered to borrow
in this Island or elsewhere by Bond, Debenture or otherwise, not exceeding
£20,000, if required, at interest not exceeding £6 per cent., payable half-
yearly out of any unappropriated moneys in the Treasury, and the principal to be redeemable within 4 years, but no Bond to be issued until the
amount in the Receiver-General's chest falls below £10,000, 24 V., c. 27.

30th September, 1864. Nothing at debit of Loan.

PUBLIC AND PAROCHIAL BUILDINGS AND KINGSTON STREETS.

£15,000   The Governor and Executive Committee were empowered to raise not
exceeding £15,000, upon Bonds or Debentures bearing interest at not exceeding £6 per cent., payable half-yearly at the Island Treasury, for repairing, enlarging and building Churches, Chapels, Court-Houses and other
buildings in the several parishes. Such Debentures to be redeemable at
furthest at the end of 25 years from date, with directions to invest in securities in this Island or in the Public Funds in Great Britain, or in any
Bank in the Island, not exceeding £375 per annum, to accumulate as a
Sinking Fund to be annually stated on the estimates of expenditure and annual accounts of moneys received and paid, laid before the Assembly,
26 V., S. 2, c. 20, s. 7-13.

£17,500   Similar powers were given to raise in this Island or Great Britain a
further Loan not exceeding £17,500 for repairing Public and Parochial
Buildings, and a portion of the Kingston Streets, except that the period of
commencement of the annual investment for the formation of a Sinking
Fund should be as the Governor and Executive Committee might direct,

and the amount should be calculated at £3 per cent. per annum on the amount of the Loan to be from time to time actually raised, 27 V., S. 1, c. 37, s. 1-2 ; 27 V., S. 2, c. 7.

30th September, 1864.
At debit of first Loan, £15,000 ; at credit of Sinking Fund, £23,75.
    „ „   second   6200

TRAM ROADS.

The Governor may take up, by way of Loan, on Debentures for £50 each, not exceeding £100,000, at 6 per cent. interest from date, charged on the General Revenue, and the interest to be paid half-yearly ; annual accounts of which shall be laid before the Legislative Council and Assembly ; and the distribution of the moneys to be taken up is vested in the Main Road Commissioners, 22 V., c. 10, s. 1-8, 10, 11. *£100 000*

Which Debentures shall be redeemable at furthest 21 years after date, but the Governor and Executive Committee may, at any time, on the expiration of 4 years after issue, call in and pay off any Debenture, to be determined by lot as the Governor may direct ; and notice of the distinguishing numbers of those redeemable, shall be given in the "Gazette," and interest shall cease from the day they are redeemable, 25 V., c. 44, s. 2. *Redemption*

Establishment of a Sinking Fund to pay off the principal in 21 years, and any surplus funds, after providing for interest on Loan and Sinking Fund, and 6 per cent. interest on the shares of any Company (see Tram Roads), the surplus to be applied to the redemption of Debentures, 25 V., c. 44, s. 37-38. *Sinking Fund, &c.*

The unrepealed portions of 22 V., c. 10, incorporated, 25 V., c. 44, s. 56. *22 V., c. 10, incorporated*

FORM OF DEBENTURE—22 V., c. 10.

No.   Government of Jamaica—Tram Road Debenture.

This Debenture issued this   day of   in the year of our Lord, 18   entitles the bearer to be paid at the Office of the Receiver-General, the sum of fifty pounds sterling, under the terms of the Act of the twenty-second Victoria, chapter ten, entitled "An Act for encouraging the formation of Tram Roads," with interest on the same, at the rate of six per cent. per annum, from the date hereof, such interest to be paid half-yearly, on the thirty-first day of March, and on the thirtieth day of September in each year, at the Office of the Receiver-General, for which payment of principal and interest the general revenue of the Island stands charged.
Witness our hands this   day of   18
        Members of Executive Committee.
Secretary to Executive Committee.
30th Sept. 1864.—At debit of Loan, £5050.

Lumber Measurers.

Masters of Vessels, Merchants, Supercargoes and others importing Deal or other boards, planks, scantling, or ranging Timbers, shall, under penalty of £30, apply to a sworn Measurer, to attend at the landing, who, within 12 hours, under penalty of 40s, shall attend and measure the same, and by a scratch mark on each board, &c., express the exact quantity according to the bona fide thickness on the square edge of every board, plank, or piece of sawn scantling, by eighths of an inch and not less, and on every piece of hewn scantling or other Timber, by quarters of an inch, and which boards &c.; whether under or over an inch in thickness, shall be so calculated or reduced that the 1000 feet of measurement shall contain equal to 1000 superficial feet of 1 full inch thickness, 9 V., c. 20 s. 1. *Lumber to be measured and marked by sworn measurers* *How to be ascertained*

No person shall be a duly qualified Measurer without first having been examined and appointed by (the Circuit Court, 19 V., c. 10 s. 17), after full examination in open Court, by a competent Lumber Measurer. His fee 20s, to be paid previous to examination by the person to be examined. Fine for non-attendance, 10s, to be enforced by distress warrant : and if the person is found properly qualified, the (Judge) shall administer an oath to him for the faithful discharge of his office, and grant him a certificate.— Clerk of the Peace's fee, 4s Persons qualified under previous Act shall continue so, 9 V., c. 20, s. 2 *Appointment* *Clerk Peace fee*

Acting without being qualified Fees

Attempting to act without being qualified: penalty, £6, 9 V., c. 20, s. 3.

Fees 4s., for every 1000 feet of Lumber he actually measures and marks, 9 V., c. 20, s. 4.

Penalty for falsely marking

Penalty for marking any board, &c., for more or less than is really contained therein, 10s., recoverable before 2 Justices, half to the person who sues, the other half for the use of the poor of the parish, 9 V., c. 20, s. 5.

Lunatic Asylum, New.

Erection

Erected under powers conferred by 7 V., c. 11.

Site and Grounds

And lands acquired for site and grounds under 11 V., c. 33.

Board of Visitors; 5 a quorum

A Board of Visitors, consisting of the Bishop of the Diocese, or, in his absence, the Bishop of Kingston, the Custos and Mayor of Kingston, Inspector of Prisons, Police Magistrate of Kingston, Principal Medical Officers of the Army and Navy, and 5 persons resident in or near to Kingston, (one of the Medical Profession) shall be appointed and removeable by the Governor, for the supervision of the Asylum, but shall not receive any emolument from the Institution, or have any pecuniary interest, direct or indirect in any contract for supplies. 5 to form a Board, 25 V., c. 9, s. 1.

Meetings and duties

The Board shall meet once a quarter, or oftener, at the Institution and inspect the books and accounts, as also the wards, cells, stores, and every other place, and the liquors, provisions, and medicines in store; receive and investigate complaints by and against officers, servants, patients, or inmates, and, if necessary, report thereon to the Governor, and draw up and transmit to him such other reports or returns as they deem necessary, or the Governor calls for: and any Member may call at and inspect the Asylum, or any portion, at any hour of the day or night, and examine any inmate; and the Board may suggest alterations in the rules and regulations, for submission by the Inspector and Director, for the consideration of the Governor in Executive Committee, 25 V., c. 9, s. 2.

Chairman

The Board shall, at a General Meeting, elect annually a Chairman. In his absence, the Members present may elect one pro tem, 25 V., c. 9, s. 3.

Visitors' Book

A Visitor's book shall be kept, in which Members shall enter the dates of their visits, and remarks on the management or regulation of the Institution. Copies to be forwarded weekly to the Governor by the Clerk, 25 V., c. 9, s. 4.

Inspector and Director Chaplain

Duties of Inspector

The Inspector and Director of the Public Hospital, shall be Inspector and Director: the Chaplain of the Penitentiary, the Chaplain. The Inspector's duties and authorities shall be the same as in the Public Hospital ; also to draw up, alter or amend rules and regulations (subject to the approval of the Governor in Executive Committee) for the government and guidance of the Board of Visitors, and all patients, officers, servants, and inmates, and for enforcing cleanliness, temperance, and decent and orderly behaviour. The rules shall be printed and hung up in the Building, and read publicly by the Clerk to the officers and servants, in his presence once a month; and copies subscribed by the officers, attendants and servants, or such as are required ; and such of the Rules as it is deemed expedient shall be published in the "Jamaica Gazette," or any other newspaper; under direction of the Governor in Executive Committee, 25 V., c. 9, s. 5.

Medical Superintendent or t—Medical Officer

The Governor may appoint and remove a Medical Superintendent, and if he deems it expedient, may engage the services of a qualified Medical Officer, trained and accustomed to the modern treatment of the insane, and as occasion requires, make an acting appointment. Any permanently appointed Medical Superintendent shall reside in and devote his entire attention to the Institution ; but in case of an acting appointment, residence and exclusive attention may be dispensed with. The salary of the holder of an acting appointment shall not exceed £300 ; that of a Medical Superintendent, £600 ; and in case of an appointment from abroad, the Governor may allow £60 for expenses of removal, 25 V., c. 9, s. 6.

Inspector's Annual Report for Legislature

The Inspector and Director shall annually prepare, in triplicate, a report to the Governor, to be laid before the Legislature, of the state and condition of the Institution to 30th September, as also of the expenditure and contract prices of the past and requirements for the coming year, to be previously submitted to the Board of Visitors, with the draft reports of the

Medical Superintendent's (s. 18) and Chaplain's (post), both of which the Inspector, &c., shall have copied in triplicate, to be forwarded to the Governor for presentation to the Legislature. The Chaplain shall perform Divine Service at the Institution every Sunday, and as often on week days as practicable, shall visit the sick, and generally administer religious consolation to such of the inmates as the Medical Superintendent considers in a fit state to receive it. But not to prejudice the rights of Ministers of other Religious Denominations from visiting under the Rules and Regulations of the Board of Visitors, approved of by the Governor ; and the Chaplain shall annually, as soon after 30th September as possible, furnish to the Inspector and Director a draft report, 25 V., c. 9, s. 7.

Chaplain's duties

The Governor may, on application of the Board of Visitors, appoint and remove a Consulting Medical Attendant, whose attendance shall be honorary, and without emolument, and who shall be ex officio a Member of the Board of Visitors, 25 V., c. 9, s. 8.

Consulting Medical Attendant

The Governor may also appoint and remove the following Officers who shall be resident on the premises : A Purveyor or Steward, to act as Dispenser and Clerk to the Board of Visitors, salary £120 ; a Warden, salary £100 ; and Matron, salary £84, exclusive of board, washing and servants. The Warden and Matron to be trained and accustomed to the modern treatment and management of the insane ; and in case of an appointment from abroad, the Governor may allow each £25 for expenses of removal, 25 V., c. 9, s. 9.

Purveyor or Steward ; Clerk
Warden ; Matron

The subordinate officers and servants shall be appointed and removed by the Inspector, with the concurrence of the Governor, except the nurses, who shall be appointed with the concurrence of the Medical Superintendent, subject to the Governor's approval. They shall receive salaries not exceeding the sums to be allowed by the Governor in Executive Committee, and may receive rations, or be otherwise dieted daily from or at the Institution, and other perquisites, in addition to, or in lieu of portion of salary, subject to the regulations of the Board of Visitors, 25 V., c. 9, s. 10.

Subordinates

No stores, provisions, wines or other necessaries (except medical stores and materials for domestic or personal clothing, which may be imported with the sanction of the Governor in Executive Committee, without competition,) shall be contracted for or purchased, until after advertisement in the "Gazette" or other newspaper, by direction of the Governor in Executive Committee, calling for tenders ; the most advantageous to be accepted. Contracts and securities shall be entered into with the Executive Committee, and no contract shall inure beyond one year. In cases of emergency, the Inspector may contract for or order supplies immediately required, not exceeding £20 at one time, 25 V., c. 9, s. 11.

Stores, &c. (except medicines and clothing) to be contracted for by tender for 1 year

Persons of unsound mind charged with Felony, and acquitted on account of insanity, or found to be insane at the time of arraignment, or who may be committed or removed to a Lunatic Asylum, shall be confined in the New Lunatic Asylum, 25 V., c. 9, s. 13.

Lunatics charged with felony

Upon information before a Justice that any destitute person, whose relations or friends are unable or unwilling to take charge of him, is wandering at large, and deemed to be insane, and it is dangerous he should be permitted to go at large, he shall issue his Warrant to apprehend and bring him before 2 Justices for examination, who may summon witnesses, and call to their assistance a legally qualified Medical Practitioner ; and if it appears the person is of unsound mind and dangerous, may, by order, cause him to be conveyed to and detained in the Asylum ; which Warrant and Certificate of a Medical Practitioner the he is a fit subject to be confined, and stating the form of the disease shall be left at the Institution with the person. If more than 4 weeks have elapsed since the Medical certificate was granted, a fresh certificate must be obtained after examination. If any person appears to the Medical Superintendent an unfit subject for admission, he may, with or without further consultation with the Consulting Attendant or other Medical man, refuse to receive him, and may send him, if sick or destitute, to the Public Hospital or Poor House, and enter his reasons in the Books of the Institution, a copy of which shall be forthwith transmitted to the Governor by the Inspector. Any person admitted as an inmate may be delivered up to his friends or relations, or upon recovery discharged, if in the opinion of the Medical Superintendent it is safe and expedient to do so, 25 V., c. 9, s. 14.

Destitute insane persons dangerous to be at large

3 G

Cost of conveyance a charge on the Institution

The cost of conveyance of any Lunatic to the Asylum, where expense is incurred, shall be admitted as a charge against the Institution, when certified by the Inspector as just and necessary, and no expenditure or draft on such account shall be made by any Vestry, or allowed, 25 V., c. 9, s. 15.

Other Lunatics may be received at 1s 6d per diem, besides clothing, &c.

The Medical Superintendent may receive as an inmate any insane person, at the instance of any relative or friend willing to pay, and giving security, to be fixed by the Inspector, for payment of the charges for his maintenance and treatment, at the rate of not less than 1s. 6d per diem, and any additional charges for clothing, extra diet or otherwise, and funeral expenses, upon there being left with the Medical Superintendent a certificate signed by 2 legally qualified Medical Practitioners, to the effect that they had each separately, at least on 2 occasions, examined such person as to his mental condition, and that he is, in their opinion, insane, and a fit subject to be confined in the Asylum, Form Schedule B, 25 V., c. 9, s. 16.

Register of Inmates

The Medical Superintendent immediately upon admission, shall make an entry in the Register of Inmates, in the form agreed upon by the Visitors, and sanctioned by the Governor in Executive Committee. The Register shall be regularly entered up, and open to the Inspector and Visitors, 25 V., c. 9, s. 17.

Books to be regularly written up and open to inspection

Medical annual report

The Medical Superintendent, with the assistance of the Dispenser and Clerk, shall keep regularly written up to date, the Books to be fixed upon and provided by the Board of Visitors, and the Medical Superintendent shall keep a full record of daily occurrences, with a written statement of the past (so far as can be obtained) and present history of every inmate, which books shall be open to the Inspector and Visitors ; and the Medical Superintendent shall annually, as soon after 30th September as practicable, prepare a Medical Report of the state of the Institution and its inmates, to be submitted to the Board of Visitors by the Inspector (s. 7), 25 V., c. 9, s. 18.

Statement of deaths

In case of the death of any patient, a statement (Form, Schedule A.) of the death and cause, and the names of any persons present, shall be drawn up and signed by the Clerk and Medical Officer, and a copy transmitted by the Clerk to the Registrar of Deaths for the district, 25 V., c. 9, s. 19.

Destitute discharged patients to be furnished with means to return home

Property of persons admitted

The Inspector, upon the discharge of any destitute patient may furnish him with means to support himself until he can return to his home or friends, not exceeding 1s. per diem, or 8s. in the whole, 25 V., c. 9, s. 20.

If any insane person at the time of admission is possessed of any property, it shall be taken charge of by the Clerk, and full particulars entered in a book by him, and attested by the Medical Superintendent, and shall be liable for his medical attendance, &c., at the rate of 1s. 6d. per diem, and funeral expenses, in case of death, and may be sold by the Inspector to defray same, the surplus to be delivered up to the patient upon his discharge, or, in case of his death, to the parties legally entitled thereto, upon application, 25 V., c. 9, s. 21.

Recovery of moneys due by patients, &c.

All moneys due by or on account of patients or for funeral expenses, shall be recoverable by the Inspector in the Petty Debt Court at Kingston, or of the parish where the defendant resides, at the option of the Inspector, without limitation as to amount ; and for recovery thereof out of the estate and effects of any person of unsound mind, the summons addressed to him may be served upon the Medical Superintendent, and judgment enforced under any Petty Debt Act, except as respects the imprisonment of such person while of unsound mind, 25 V., c. 9, s. 22.

Orders of Justices on relatives or friends, &c. to r payment of dues, &c.

If it appears to 2 Justices that any Lunatic has any estate applicable to his maintenance, and more than sufficient to maintain his family, if any, they may, on application of the Inspector, make an order in writing, under their hands and seals, to the nearest known relative or friend for payment of the Asylum Dues and funeral expenses, or either ; and if not paid within one month after service, they or any other Justices may, by an order under their hands and seals, direct any Collector of Petty Debts or other person, to seize so much of the money, and seize and sell so much of the goods, and take and receive so much of the rents and profits of the lands and tenements of such Lunatic, and of any other income of such Lunatic as may be necessary to pay the dues and expenses, or either, accounting for the same to the same or any other Justices, such dues and expenses, or either, having been first proved to their satisfaction by the certificate of the Inspector, or otherwise, and the amount set forth in such order., If any Trustee or other person having the possession, custody, or charge of any property of the Lunatic, or if any company, or body or person, having in their hands any stock, interest, dividend or annuity belonging or due to the Lunatic, pay the whole or any part to defray the amount set forth in the order, the receipt of the Collector or person shall be a discharge, 25 V., c. 9, s. 23.

All moneys to be received for the Institution shall be paid to the Receiver-General, and be applicable to the expenses of the Institution, and payable under Warrants from the Governor, 25 V., c. 9, s. 24.

Moneys to be paid to Receiver-General

Any Superintendent, Officer, Nurse, Attendant, servant or person employed, striking, wounding, ill-treating or wilfully neglecting any Lunatic, shall be guilty of a misdemeanor and subject to Indictment, or on a summary conviction before 2 Justices, not exceeding £20, nor less than £2, (sic), 25 V., c. 9, s. 25.

Ill-treatment or neglect by officers &c. of Lunatics

Medical Certificates shall be according to Form Schedule B, 25 V., c. 9, s, 26.

Medical Certificates

The Board of Visitors may administer oaths to officers and inmates on enquiries. Persons wilfully giving or procuring, or instigating false evidence, shall be punishable as for perjury or subornation, 25 V., c. 9, s. 27.

Oaths]

New Lunatic Asylum Act, 1861, 25 V., c. 9, s. 28.

Short Title]

SCHEDULES.

I hereby give you notice, that   private (or pauper) patient admitted into this Asylum on the   day of died therein, in the presence of   on the day

Notice of death &c., s. 19

Signature
Clerk of the Asylum.

Dated the   day of   186

I certify that the apparent cause of death of the said as ascertained by post mortem examination (if so) was

Signature

Medical Superintendent of the Asylum.

I, the undersigned (here state the qualification), and being in actual practice as a Medical Practitioner, hereby certify that I, on the day of   at   in the parish (or town) of (in any case where more than one Medical Certificate is required by this Act, here insert, " separately from any other Medical Practitioner," and, if necessary, " on two separate occasions"), personally examined A. B. of   (insert residence and profession, or occupation, if any), and that the said A. B. is a Lunatic (or an idiot, or a person of unsound mind), and a proper person to be taken charge of and detained under care and treatment, and that I have formed this opinion upon the following grounds:—

Medical Certificate, B. s. 14, 16, 26

1. Facts indicating insanity, observed by myself (here state the facts.)

2. Other facts (if any) indicating insanity communicated to me by others, (here state the information, and from whom).

Signed   place of abode.

Dated this   day of   one thousand eight hundred and

Main Roads and Bridges.

The following lines of Roads were transferred to, and placed under the superintendence of the Main Road Commissioners to be managed under this Act :—

Main Roads, 21 V, c. 32

NORTH WESTERN POSTAL ROUTE.

From Kingston to Green Island, by way of Spanish Town, Linstead,

Moneague (by Bolt's Hill) to St. Ann's Bay, Rio Bueno, Falmouth, Montego Bay, Lucea.

SOUTH WESTERN ROUTE.

From Spanish Town to Green Island, by way of Old Harbour, Four Paths, Porus, Mandeville, over the Bull Head Hill, down Spur Tree Hill to Black River and Savanna-la-Mar. From Old Harbour (through Salt River to the Alley, through Sedge Pond), to Milk River Bath to the foot of Bossus Hill.

From Bread Nut Bottom to Chapelton.

From Porus to the foot of the Bogue Hill.

SOUTH EASTERN ROUTE.

From Kingston to Port Antonio, by way of Yallahs, Morant Bay and Manchioneal.

NORTH EASTERN ROUTE.

From Port Antonio to Ocho Rios, and to the intersection of St. Ann's Bay.

MISCELLANEOUS.

Kingston to Gordon's Town.   Moneague to Ocho Rios.

Montego Bay to Savanna-la-Mar, by Ramble and Montpellier.

Dry Harbour to Stewart Town.

Kingston to Annotto Bay.

From Hoghole (St. Thomas in the Vale), through Rio Magna and Nonsuch, to Port Maria, 21 V., c. 32, s. 1.

25 V , c, 12   Also the portion of Road from Hoghole Estate, St. Thomas in the Vale, to the Main Road near Shenton Estate in the same parish.

The Road from the Baptist Chapel in Spanish Town, to the entrance of the Guanaboa Vale at Aylmers, St. Jobu's, and the Road from Worthy Park Estate to the Junction with the Main Road at Ewarton.

See s. 35   The proposed new Road from North to South between Trelawny and St. Elizabeth, and Manchester.

Such part of the Road from the Bogue in St. Elizabeth as leads through Elim, to the Junction of the Main Road at the Tomb-stones near Lacovia Bridge, 25 V., c. 12, s. 34.

That portion of the Road from the Harbour of Port Morant, through Bowden, across the Iron Bridge, to the Main Road at the foot of Quaa Hill leading to Manchioneal, and the portion of the Main Road through Bath from Port Morant to the foot of Quaa Hill, was transferred to the Parochial Road Board, 25 V., c. 12, s. 34.

27 V., g 1, c. 36   But restored as a Main Road, by 27 V., S. 1, c. 36, s. 6.

28 V. c. 30   The Road No. 36 in Hanover, leading from Lucea Bridge over Riley's River, to the Main Road at Glasgow in Westmoreland, 28 V., c, 30.

All grants for opening and making the proposed new Grand Junction Road between Trelawny and St. Elizabeth, and Manchester, shall be under the control and disposal of the Main Road Commissioners, to be appropriated for such purposes, 25 V., c. 12, s. 35.

The superintendence and powers of the Trustees or Parochial Commissioners over the Roads or portions of Roads transferred, were determined, and existing contracts continued, and moneys due or becoming payable by the Trustees or Commissioners, shall be payable out of any outstanding moneys or funds at the disposal of the Governor and Executive Committee under this Act, 21 V., c. 32, s. 2.

Property vested in them   The right, interest and property in the Roads and Bridges, erections, buildings, mile-stones, posts, rails, fences and things provided for them, with the several conveniences and appurtenances and materials, and all materials, tools and implements provided for repairing the Roads, and the scrapings of the Roads shall be vested in the Commissioners; and in all legal proceedings, civil and criminal, it shall be sufficient to state generally that they are the property of the Secretary for the time, 21 V., c. 32, s. 57.

Commissioners   The Commissioners incorporated under the name of the Main Road Commissioners, to sue and be sued, have a Common Seal, and do all other acts appertaining to their Corporate Body, 21 V., c. 32, s. 58.

The Governor and Members of the Executive Committee, or any two of them, shall have and exercise all the powers of Main Road Commissioners, 21 V., c. 32, s. 4. Commissioners

The Chairman of the several Parochial Boards of Commissioners of Highways and Bridges shall be entitled to attend quarterly and other meetings of the Main Road Commissioners, and any Chairman who attends may take part in, and vote upon any discussions or resolutions at such meeting, in respect of any transferred Roads or Bridges situate in the parish for which he is Chairman, but not in respect of any others situate elsewhere, 21 V., c. 32, s. 5. Chairman of parochial Boards

The Governor need not preside at or attend any meeting, except where its purpose is to discuss or determine what money shall be borrowed for the purposes of the Main Road Act, 25 V., c. 12, s. 44. Governor need not be present, except where money is proposed to be borrowed

At least 14 days' notice of all meetings shall be published in the "Gazette" before they are held, 21 V., c. 32, s. 5. Notice of meetings

The offices of County Commissioners abolished, 25 V., c. 12, s. 1. County Commissioners abolished

The Governor may appoint 3 Civil Engineers, to have the care, management, control and superintendence of the Main Roads, removeable at pleasure : salary, £600, in full of travelling and other expenses incidental to the office ; and a Secretary (salary, £250), 21 V., c. 32, s. 3 ; 27 V., S. 1, c. 36, s. 11. Engineers
Secretary

£50 per annum placed at the disposal of the Governor and Executive Committee for contingencies of office, 25 V., c. 12, s. 42. Contingencies

DUTIES OF MAIN ROAD COMMISSIONERS.

To attend Quarterly Meetings, and such further Special Meetings as the Governor directs to be summoned, and to form a Board, to be called "The Main Road Commissioners," and under that name, to discuss and determine what money shall be borrowed under the powers given to the Governor, with the advice of the Executive Committee ; what Reports, Statements, Surveys and Documents furnished by the Engineers shall be adopted ; to what extent alterations shall be made in any Road or Bridge, and what new Road or Bridge it will be expedient to lay out or build ; and to apportion the amount of expenditure to be laid out on each Road for general repairs, as also for the alterations sanctioned to be made on each Road or Bridge, or the laying out and building of new Roads and Bridges, distinguishing the expenditure to be sanctioned under separate heads. Duties of Main Road Commissioners
Moneys to be borrowed
Engineer's reports, &c
Apportionment of Expenditure

To supervise the annual General Return prepared and submitted by the Engineers, and to determine the probable amount of expenditure under separate heads, required for the ensuing year ; what amount may be expected to be met by unexpended grants or funds of any previous year ; what amount it should be recommended to the Legislature to grant towards the proposed expenditure for the ensuing year ; and what sums should be expended out of moneys in the Receiver-General's hands, borrowed under this Act, 21 V., c. 32, s. 4. Supervision of Engineer's annual return
Probable expenditure for ensuing year, and grants to be recommended

The Commissioners of Highways and Bridges in each parish shall, on or before 10th April in each year, elect not exceeding three of their own Body who consent to be Commissioners for the care and superintendence of the Main Roads, who in conjunction with the Custos or Senior Magistrate representing him, shall be called "Local Main Road Commissioners," 25 V., c. 12, s. 2. Local Commissioners

The Members of the Legislative Council, if resident in the parish, and the Members of the Assembly for each parish, shall be ex-officio Members of the Board of Local Main Road Commissioners, and exercise all the authorities and functions vested in other Members of the Board, 27 V., S. 1, c. 36, s. 1 Members of Council and Assembly
Ex Officio Local Commissioners

In case of the death, absence from the Island for more than 3 calendar months, or removal from the parish, or neglect to attend 3 meetings in succession without sufficient excuse, or otherwise to perform the duties under 25 V., c. 12, or on the resignation of any Commissioner, a vacancy shall be occasioned, and filled up with all convenient speed by the election of a new Commissioner, 27 V., S. 1, c. 36, s. 2. Vacancies

The Local Commissioners shall meet from time to time, by notice in writing, signed by 2 Commissioners, of whom the Custos to be one, and any 2 Commissioners form a quorum for the despatch of business, 25 V., c. 12, s. 3. Meetings

The Custos or Senior Magistrate shall order the meeting, and the Clerk shall sign the notice, which is a sufficient summons, 27 V., S. 1, c. 36, s. 3. .

The Clerk to the Parochial Board of Commissioners of Highways and Bridges shall be the Clerk to the Local Main Road Commissioners, and receive £10 per annum additional salary, 25 V., c. 12, s. 4.

DUTY OF LOCAL COMMISSIONERS.

Duties of Local Commissioners

Examination and approval or disapproval of tenders, a n d applications for advances, audit accounts, and lay statements, &c. before the General Board

To aid and assist, and act under the instructions of the General Board of Main Road Commissioners; examine every Tender for work or repairs, or for the supply of materials on any Main Road or Bridge in the parish, and if they approve, countersign it before its adoption, if not, state in writing thereon, or annexed thereto, their objections; and examine or cause, &c., by some competent person if the County Engineer is away, any works or repairs executed or in progress on any account or application for an advance, before attesting and sanctioning payment or any advance; to audit accounts for payment of extra services of persons employed in the absence of the County Engineer; to lay before the General Board of Main Road Commissioners a statement of all Tenders accepted or declined, and of all accounts attested or advances sanctioned; and also of all accounts or applications rejected or objected to, with their reason in every case for declining any Tender, &c.

Examine and approve or disapprove assessments or agreements f o r damages under 21 V., c. 32, s. 16, and forward them

To examine every assessment of or agreement for damages under 21 V., c. 32, s. 16, and cause them to be transmitted to the Main Road Commissioners with their approval, or in case of disapproval, with the particulars of their objections subscribed and signed.

County Engineer's reports and statements

To receive and enter on their Minutes all Statements and Reports from the County Engineer; and in case of rejection of, or objection to any Tender or Account, or application for an advance, they shall decide the course to be followed in the particular matter, and the County Engineer shall govern himself accordingly, 25 V., c. 12, s. 5.

DUTIES OF CIVIL ENGINEERS.

Civil Engineer's duties
To attend meetings of commissioners

To attend all Quarterly and other Meetings of the Main Road Commissioners when required.

Prepare and transmit reports, &c., to them

To prepare and transmit to the Main Road Commissioners all necessary Reports, Statements, Surveys and Documents relating to the Roads under their supervision.

Inspect and report on Main Roads to Commissioners

To visit and personally inspect and report to the Main Road Commissioners on the state of any Road and the Bridges in his County, and on the expediency of making alterations, or of laying out new Roads or building new Bridges, and the probable expenses, wheoever the Main Road Commissioners direct.

Inspect all Roads and Bridges in the County

To visit and personally inspect as often as necessary or required, all the Roads and Bridges throughout the County.

Annual returns

To prepare and submit annually to the Main Road Commissioners a General Return (Form annexed) of all the Roads in the County included in the Schedule, distinguishing them, the number of miles, and the acclivities and declivities, the total amount of expenditure laid out on each, the state and condition of each at the date of the return, whether repairable under con tract or not, if so, the particulars and duration, and probable amount of ex penditure required for the ensuing year; also statements of the alterations made on the Roads and Bridges, and the new Roads and Bridges constructed during the year, and the expenditure in consequence of such alterations, and of such new Roads and Bridges also of the further alterations recommended of existing Roads and Bridges; and the new Roads and Bridges still required, and the probable expenses over and above the probable expenditure required to keep the present Roads and Bridges in repair during the ensuing year, with such further particulars as the Commissioners direct. Such annual returns to be made up to the 30th September preceding.

Allot apportionments allowed by the Commissioners

To allot or apportion the sums appropriated for the repairs of the several Roads, in such proportions to be worked out upon such Roads as the Commissioners direct to be expended in the repairs and alterations of existing, and formation of new Roads, and in the construction or repair of Bridges and Water-courses.

To make the surveys of new Roads when so directed and give directions for and superintend the repairing of the Roads, Bridges and Water-courses, and the immediate removal of all nuisances therefrom, and for the prosecution of such offences as, in his opinion, ought to be prosecuted. *Surveys of new Roads, superintendence of repairs, removal, &c. of nuisances*

To inspect and audit all accounts for expenditure connected with the Roads and Bridges, and to submit them, with his observations, to the Commissioners, in order that, if approved, they may pass orders for payment 21 V., c. 32, s. 6. *Audit of accounts and submission to Commissioners, with remarks*

Each County Engineer shall be a Member of the Board of Local Commissioners in each parish of the County, but shall exercise his vote only as a casting vote when only 2 Commissioners are present, and they differ in opinion, 25 V., c. 12, s. 6. *To be Members of the Local Boards, but not to vote unless, &c.*

Each Engineer, with the sanction of the Main Road Commissioners, may enter into contracts for repairing and keeping in repair for one or more years, any Roads or Bridges, or portion of Roads and Water-Courses, the moneys to be payable in any year thereunder not to exceed the sum apportioned to the Road, Bridge, or portion of Road, the subject of the contract. No Engineer shall expend, or direct the expenditure of a greater sum in the whole on the Roads and Bridges under his superintendence in one year, than has been appropriated by the Commissioners, 21 V., c. 32, s. 7. *Contracts for repairs* *Limitation of expenditure*

Each County Engineer shall, for 4 consecutive weeks, with the sanction of the Main Road Commissioners, advertize in the "Gazette" for persons willing to keep the Main Roads, not then under contract, in order, for 12 months or more, after 1st March, 25 V., c. 12, s. 11. *Annual advertisements for contracts*

Each County Engineer shall submit to the Local Board every tender he receives for work or repairs, and every account and application for an advance, and every assessment or agreement for damages, under 21 V., c. 32, s. 16, for examination; and no tender shall be adopted, or any account or advance audited, unless approved or countersigned by a quorum of Local Commissioners, and they have directed the adoption or payment, 25 V., c. 12, s. 7. *To submit tenders &c., to local commissioners for examination or adoption by them before being acted on*

At the end of each quarter, he shall make a complete inspection of the Main Roads and Bridges in each parish, and make a report in detail to each Local Board, to be forwarded after their inspection, with such remarks as he deems necessary for the guidance or adoption of the General Board of Main Road Commissioners, 25 V., c. 12, s. 8. *Quarterly inspections of roads and reports in detail to local boards with remarks for guidance of general board*

And make up once in each month an account in detail, of all moneys certified by him as expended, verified by solemn affirmation before a Justice, and lodged with the Secretary of the Main Road Commissioners, 25 V. c. 12, s. 12. *Monthly accounts of expenditure certified by him.*

The Governor and Executive Committee may employ any Engineer in any one or more than one County from time to time, and assign any particular Roads, or lines, or sections, for supervision and care, or to be laid out, or formed, or altered by any such Engineer in any one or more than one County, 27 V., S. 1, c. 36, s. 5. *Employment in other counties or on particular roads, &c.*

No Civil Engineer or Local Commissioner shall engage, either directly or indirectly, or be personally interested in any contract for any work on any Road whatsoever, 25 V., c. 12, s. 38. *No Civil Engineer or Local Commissioner to be engaged in contracts*

The Engineer for Middlesex shall be the Chief Engineer of Roads and Bridges, 25 V., c. 12, s. 36. *Chief Engineer*

And the Governor in Executive Committee shall appoint a place in St Jago de la Vega for the Office of the Chief Engineer and Colonial Engineer and Architect, and order it to be fitted up and prepared for the convenient discharge of the duties, 25 V., c. 12, s. 37. *His Office in St. Jago de la Vega*

In case of the death, removal, or absence of any Civil Engineer, the Governor and Executive Committee may require the remaining Engineers to perform the duties, or any part of the duties of the deceased, removed, or absent Engineer, for not exceeding 6 months, and allow remuneration out of the lapsed salary, 25 V., c. 12, s. 39. *Employment to do duties of others on death, &c. remuneration*

Receiver-General to furnish Commissioners with quarterly statements of ordinary main road funds received by him

The Receiver-General shall by the first post, after 1st April, July, October and January, transmit to the Secretary of the Main Road Commissioners, a quarterly statement in detail (Form Schedule) of all the ordinary Main Road Revenue received by him during the previous quarter, as a guide to the Commissioners, to be published in the "Gazette" by the Secretary within 14 days after receipt, 25 V., c. 12, s. 9.

Allotment of funds by the Commissioners

The Commissioners shall allot the Main Road Revenue towards the annual repairs; and any extraordinary funds provided by the Legislature for the formation or further improvement of the Main Roads and Bridges generally, shall be allotted by them for the formation and further improvement of such as in the judgment of the County Engineer and **Revenue to be allotted to parish where there are no main roads** Local Board ought to be made or further improved. The Main Road Revenue from Road, Stock, Carts and Wheels, in any parish possessing no main Road, shall be expended on the improvement of the chief Carriage-Roads and Bridges of such parish, in such manner as the Commissioners of Highways and Bridges of such parish determine, 25 V., c. 12, s. 10.

Appropriation of moneys under License Duties Act; see now 27 V., c. 28

The Receiver-General shall deduct from the moneys to be payable under the Licenses Duties' Act, 25 V., c. 39, for Licenses on Drays, Carts, Water Carts, Wains, Wagons, Spring Carts and Hackney or other Carriages, Horses and Asses, a sum equal to 20 per cent. upon the moneys paid over to him, and carry the same, and also all moneys received for Land Tax or arrears thereof, to the credit of the Main Road Fund, to be applied and appropriated in aid of 21 V., c. 32, and 21 V., c. 34 (Main Roads and Main Road Funds), or any Act in aid, or amendment thereof (the remainder to the Highways, s. 33), 25 V., c. 12, s. 32.

Import Duties Sch. C, 28 V., c. 10

The Duties on Imports in Schedule C. (in force to 31st March, 1866) shall be applied to Main Road purposes, 28 V.; c. 10, s. 17.

Receiver-General's annual accounts to be submitted to the Assembly

The Receiver-General shall make up distinct statements of all moneys received under any Act for Road purposes to the 30th September, and forward them to the Executive Committee, to be laid before the Assembly on or before 1st November, or at its meeting thereafter, 25 V., c. 12, s. 31.

Mile-Marks Guide-Posts
Ditto in water course

Each Engineer, with the sanction of the Commissioners, may cause mile marks of stone, wood or iron to be erected on such Roads as he thinks proper, 1 mile from each other, with such legible inscriptions as he judges necessary; also guide-posts to be erected and kept up at the intersections of such Roads as he thinks proper, and guide-posts in water-courses to show the height of water therein, and keep in repair those already or to be erected, 21 V., c. 32, s. 8.

Duty of Engineers and Waywardens to place posts to mark the lines of dangerous fordings or mouths of rivers

It shall be the duty of the County Engineers and Waywardens of each Road, or the persons acting under their authority, to place posts to mark the line through deep or dangerous fordings, or mouths of rivers, 25 V., c. 12, s. 18.

Alterations
Discontinuance
New Roads
Commissioners
Directions to Engineers
Notice to owners, &c.

The Commissioners may direct any Engineer to alter or discontinue any Road, or lay out a new Road in lieu of, or to complete any Road in progress in the county, 21 V, c. 32, s. 9.

On receipt of directions and before acting, the Engineer shall cause notice, in writing, to be given to the occupants and owners of lands through which the proposed alterations or new Road would pass, and of the lands through which any Road then runs, of the time and place at which he will meet to receive objections and approvals; the notice to be served personally, or by leaving it at the dwelling house of each owner or occupant, at least 7 days before the day appointed, 21 V. c. 32, s. 10.

Discussion at meeting, report of reasons to the Commissioners
Certificate and plans to be deposited with Clerk of the Peace, and copy exhibited on Court House door 21 days before Jury meet

The Engineer shall meet at the time specified, and at such meeting or an adjournment, hear reasons for and against such direction, and transmit a report to the Commissioners; and if they adhere to their directions, wholly or in part, shall make out and subscribe a certificate, to be deposited with the Clerk of the Peace, containing or accompanied by a plan of the Road to be altered, and of the intended alterations, or of the Road to be discontinued, or of the intended new Road, and the clerk of the Peace shall exhibit a copy of the certificate and plan on the door of the Court-House, and keep it so exhibited for at least 21 days before that appointed for the meeting of the Jury to be summoned, 21 V., c. 32, s. 11.

Plans to be produced at meeting

At the Meeting above directed, the Engineer shall produce, and submit for inspection and examination, a plan or section of the Road to be altered, and the intended alterations, or to be discontinued, or of the new Road, 25 V., c. 12, s. 40.

The Engineer who signed the certificate, shall issue his warrant to the Police or Constables to summon 5 Parochial Commissioners of the neighbourhood, whether of the same or of any adjoining parish, having no interest in the lands through which the Road proposed to be altered or discontinued then runs, or in the land through which it is proposed the alterations shall be made, or through which any proposed new Road would run, to attend at a time and place to be mentioned (at least 21 days after that on which a copy of the certificate was exhibited,) 21 V., c. 32, s. 12. 5 Parochial Commissioners to be summoned of that or a neighbouring parish

If three of such Commissioners appear, they shall be sworn by any Justice present, well and truly to examine the proposed alterations or new Road, or Road to be discontinued (as the case requires) according to the best of their judgment and ascertain whether such alterations or new Road are or is necessary, or will be expedient and useful, or whether it will be expedient and useful to discontinue such Road, as the case requires; and in the case of a new Road or of any proposed alterations, if it shall appear to them to be so after they shall have gone over and inspected the same, that they will, according to the best of their skill and judgment, assess the damages to be sustained by the making or alteration of such Road, and determine the several matters according to equity and good conscience, without undue bias, partiality or favor; and their decision shall be received and certified by the Justice to the Engineer. If 3 Jurors do not appear, the Justice shall fine each absentee not less than 20s, nor more than 40s, unless satisfactory reasons are given for absence, to be recovered as after-mentioned, 21 V., c. 32, s. 13. 3 to be sworn as a jury Penalty for non-attendance

In case a Jury cannot be formed from non-attendance or other cause, another warrant may be issued, and another day fixed, and so on, until a Jury is formed. The Clerk of the Peace shall exhibit on the door of the Court House, at least 7 days' notice of the day appointed for the further meeting, 21 V., c. 32, s. 14. Further warrants to summons juries, 7 days notice

The 3 Parochial Commissioners who appear and are sworn, shall personally examine the route, and if satisfied, shall find that the alterations or new Road is, in their opinion, necessary and proper, or in their opinion the Road ought to be discontinued, and shall assess the damages to be sustained by the making or alteration of any Road, and make and subscribe a certificate to such effect, to be also subscribed by the Justice, and delivered to the Engineer. Fees of each Juror and Presiding Justice, 20s, to be paid by an order of the Engineer on the Receiver-General, out of any moneys applicable, 21 V., c. 32, s. 15. Proceedings of Jurors, their fees and that of Justice

The Engineer, subject to the approval of the Commissioners, and the owners or occupiers, may agree upon the amount of damages, and for a release from such owners or occupiers; and thereupon the Jury shall not be sworn to assess, nor shall they assess any damages. Every agreement and release shall be filed and recorded in the Clerk of the Peace's Office, and shall preclude all further claim for damages, 21 V., c. 32, s. 16. Agreement respecting damages See 25 V., c. 12, s. 5.

When any person is owner of any land over which any new Road or alteration is made, and also of the soil of any portions of the Road to be altered or discontinued, in whole or part, the Jury shall take into consideration the value of the abandoned portion to the owner, and the benefit to result to him therefrom, and deduct same from the damages; and the owner may enclose the land so abandoned, 21 V., c. 32, s. 17. Deductions from damages in respect of value of abandoned road to owner, which he may enclose

When the proprietors of any lands agree among themselves to open a new Road through lands belonging to them and actually in their possession, they may apply to the Main Road Commissioners, who may issue a warrant to any Surveyor to lay out the Road at the expense of the parties applying, and on laying it out a Diagram shall be lodged with the Clerk of the Peace, recorded in his Office, and thereafter the Road shall be a Public Road, and subject to any Laws for the maintenance and regulation of Public Roads, 21 V., c. 32, s. 18. Roads at expense of proprietors of lands

All damages fixed by agreement or awarded, shall be paid by the Receiver-General under the Governor's Warrant, out of any moneys applicable, 21 V., c. 32, s. 19. Damages payable by Receiver General

Every person who appeared before the Jury and opposed the application, may, within 14 days after the finding, appeal to the Circuit Judge; but an appeal by one person, and a decision thereon, shall not affect the rights of any other appellant who has not been heard. Appeals shall be regulated by the Law in force regulating appeals from the summary jurisdiction of Magistrates, 21 V., c. 32, s. 20. Appeals

Clerk of the Peace's fees

Drawing out the necessary proceedings and attending the
Jury 1 1 0

Each mile he is required to travel, to be reckoned from the
Court-House of his parish (in the precinct of St. Catherine, to be reckoned from the Court-House in St. Jago
de la Vega) 0 1 0

Recording proceedings, for every 160 words 0 1 0

Making attested copy of the proceedings, if required, to be
recorded in any other parish, or for any other purpose,
for every 160 words 0 1 0

To be paid by the Receiver-General upon the order of the Engineer;
in the case of copies required by any other person, by the party. No
other fees shall be demanded, except in case of appeal, when he shall be
entitled to the like fees as in case of summary adjudications, to be paid as
before-mentioned, 21 V., c. 32, s. 21.

30 days' notice of Engineer's intention to commence work

Whenever the finding in favor of the alteration of an existing, or the
laying out of a new Road has been confirmed on appeal, or the time of
appealing has expired, the Engineer shall give to the owner or occupant of
any enclosed, cultivated or improved land through which the alterations or
new Road will pass, 30 days' notice, in writing, of his intention to open and
work the Road, so as to enable him to remove and erect new fences:
Penalty, £50, to be recovered by Action of Debt by the person aggrieved;
but not to subject any Engineer to any penalty for any temporary alterations or deviations rendered necessary in consequence of any temporary
injury or accident to any Highway, 21 V., c. 32, s. 22.

Width of roads

The width of all Roads already, or to be laid out, shall if practicable
be 24 feet through open ground, 60 feet through standing wood, and 40
feet when the wood is only on one side; but the metal portion of any
Road shall not be more than 16 feet, nor less than 12 feet in width, 21 V.,
c. 32, s. 23.

Removal of encroachments, notice

When any Road has been encroached upon by fences, the Engineer, if
in his opinion necessary, shall order the fences to be removed at the cost
of the party who made them, or the person claiming under him, so that the
Road may be of the breadth before enacted, provided he give notice in
writing to remove such fences forthwith, specifying the legal breadth of the
Road, the extent of the encroachment, and the places where it exists, 21
V., c. 32, s. 24.

Penalty

If not removed within 14 days after service, the party shall forfeit 5s.
for every day, after the expiration of the notice, the fences continue unremoved, or until removed by order of the Engineer, besides the expenses
of removal, to be recovered as penalties, 21 V., c. 32, s. 25.

Erecting walls, &c., to obstruct highway

No person shall make or erect, or place any wall or building, or
fencing or barrier across, upon, or near to any Road, so as to obstruct,
interfere with, or prevent passage thereon, or to reduce or limit the
breadth, under a penalty of not exceeding £60, nor less than £20; and the
Engineer or Local Main Road Board, may remove or cause, &c., such
wall, &c., forthwith, 21 V., S. 1, c. 36, s. 7.

Removal of fallen trees

If any tree fall upon any Road, so as to cause obstruction thereon, in
consequence of any default of the owner or occupier, or a servant acting
by his direction, it shall be removed by the owner or occupier within 24
hours after notice to remove, from the Engineer or a Justice; and if he
neglect, the Engineer, or in his absence a Justice, shall cause it to be
removed at his expense, and he shall be liable to a penalty of 5s. for
every day after the expiration of the notice during which it remains unre-
Wilfully placing obstructions
moved; such penalty and expenses to be recovered as other penalties.
Wilfully placing any tree or other obstruction on any Highway: penalty
not exceeding £5, 21 V., c. 32, s. 26.

Falling trees without consent of owner, &c

Any person cutting down any tree on land not occupied by him, so
as to fall into any Main Road, river or stream, unless by order or consent
of the owner or occupant, shall be liable to a penalty not exceeding £5,
nor less than £1, 21 V., c. 32, s. 27.

Cutting or causing, &c. any tree, so as to fall into any river, stream or water-course within 100 yards of any fording, and obstruct any Road or fording, or divert the river course, so as to encroach upon or injure any such Road, or endanger any Bridge over the River, &c., and not removing it within 24 hours after notice: penalty not exceeding £5, 21 V., c. 32, s. 28.

Cutting down trees into a river, &c., within 100 yards of a fording &c., and not removing after notice

No swinging or other gates shall be allowed on any (Main) Road, except by permission of the Commissioners, and on condition that a watchman is constantly kept to open them when required, 21 V., c. 32, s. 29.

Swinging Gates

But not to affect any existing rights, except on failure to keep a watchman, 25 V., c. 12, s. 41.

Existing rights

Whoever wantonly injures any Bridge shall forfeit not exceeding £60, nor less than £20, or be subject to imprisonment, not exceeding 90 days nor less than 30 days, 21 V., c. 32, s. 30.

Injuring bridges

The Engineer employed in conducting and superintending the repairs of any Main Road or Bridge, may cut and cover, if necessary, Drains on lands adjoining, to carry off the water collected on the Road, and dig and carry away any gravel, stone, sand, or other materials, out of any savannah, uninclosed or open land, river or gully, being waste land in or near such Road or Bridge, proper for draining, repairing or amending the same, without paying for the same; such Engineer levelling, or causing, &c., all holes and pits. Where there are not sufficient materials to be so conveniently obtained, the Engineer may cut drains, and dig and carry away any gravel, &c., out of the grounds or inclosures of any person, (not being the ground whereon any house stands, garden or yard, p a walk or avenue to any house, or any parcel of provision ground) wherein a Drain may be necessary, or materials are found, and to carry so much as the Engineer judges requisite for draining or keeping in repair, or amending such Road, or Bridge, or Drain, paying such rates for materials, and damage to the grounds where and whence dug, or over which carried, as the Engineer judges reasonable. Persons molesting, hindering or obstructing him, or the persons under his command, in cutting or covering any drains, or in digging and carrying away any gravel, &c., shall forfeit not exceeding £10, 21 V., c. 32, s. 31.

Engineer's powers to cut drains, dig and take materials in waste lands without paying

From other grounds; compensation

Obstructing

Taking away, without the Engineer's consent, any materials purchased or gathered for the repair or use of any Road, Bridge or Drain, or out of any quarry or pit, made, dug or opened to get materials for any Road Bridge or Drain: penalty not exceeding £10. Not to prevent the person in possession of the land from digging and removing materials for his own use, 21 V., c. 32, s. 32.

Taking away materials for repairs

If any Coporation, Society or Company for supplying water, digs, or causes, &c., in any Road, any trenches, or holes for laying down or repairing any water-pipe or plug, or other thing connected therewith, and keeps or causes &c., open for a longer period than is reasonably requisite, or covers over, or fills up or causes, &c., in an imperfect manner, or occasions or suffers, or permits to be occasioned any damage or injury to any Road, by reason of the imperfect state or want of repair of any such pipe, &c., or fails while it is undergoing repairs to keep a light thereat after dark, and take all other reasonable precautions to prevent accidents, they shall forfeit not more than £20, nor less than £5, over and above the expense of repairs incurred, 21 V., c. 32, s. 33.

Water Companies keeping open trenches, &c

Any Engineer when necessary to keep any Road or Bridge in good order, may lop or cut down the branches of any tree overhanging it, 21 V., c. 32, s. 34.

Engineer may lop trees

The Owner or Occupier, or his Agent, Attorney or Overseer of the land adjoining any Road or Bridge, shall cut, prune, or lop the fences and branches of trees, bushes or shrubs growing in or near such fences (not being in any garden, or orchard, walk or avenue to any house, nor an ornament or shelter to a house, unless it hang over the Road or Bridge, so as to impede or annoy any carriage or p travelling), so that the Road or Bridge is not prejudiced by the shade or the sun and wind excluded to their damage. On failure whereof, within 14 days after notice in writing by any Local Commissioner in respect of Main Roads, or by the Commissioners of Highways and Bridges, or the Waywardens or persons appointed for the purpose in respect to Parochial Roads, they may cause to be cut, pruned or lopped, and such owner, &c., shall be charged with and pay the charges and expenses of doing so, or in default, they may be recovered with costs, if any, as a penalty, 25 V., c. 12, s. 23.

Owners, &c., to cut fences, trees, &c., hanging over roads or bridges after notice; penalty

Powers of entry by commissioners

And the respective Commissioners, Waywardens, Engineers, or other persons employed, may, in case of default of the owner, &c., enter on any land for the purpose, 27 V., S. 1, c. 36, s. 8.

Penalties not exceeding, £10 for the following offences :—

Mile-marks

Removing, destroying, injuring or defacing any mile-mark, on any Main Road.

Guide posts

Injuring or defacing any description affixed to any guide-post on any such Road, or destroying or injuring such guide-post, or any guide post on any water-course.

Diverting water courses. drawing logs, &c., on roads

Injuring any such Road, by obstructing, or diverting any creek, water-course or sluice, or by drawing logs, stones, or other things of weight on the surface of any such Road or Bridge, otherwise than upon wheeled carriages, or rollers.

Obstructing road or water courses

Obstructing any such Road, or filling up or placing any obstructions in any water-course or ditch constructed for passing water across or under, or for draining the water from any such Road.

Riding, &c., on foot paths or injuring them

Riding, driving, leading or drawing any animal or vehicle upon any foot path, or cause-way made for the use or accommodation of foot passengers, or wilfully doing, or causing injury to be done to the same.

Improper use of drags, &c

Using any drag, joggle or other instrument, for retarding the descent of any wheel carriage down any hill, so as unnecessarily and wilfully to destroy or injure the surface of any such Road.

Killing, &c., beasts on roads

Killing, slaughtering, burning, dressing or cutting up, upon an such Road or Bridge, or the side, any beast, swine, calf, lamb or other cattle, except horned stock injured in the carriage of produce or otherwise, which in such case may be slaughtered and removed.

Carcases, rubbish ; see 27 V., S. 1, c. 36, s, 9

Depositing any dead carcase, or any rubbish on any such Road, or place adjacent thereto, to the annoyance of persons using such road.

Leaving wagons, &c., unattended longer than necessary, or not on one side of the road

Leaving any wagon, or other wheel carriage upon or on the side of any Road without any proper person in the custody or care longer than necessary to load or unload, except in cases of accident (or in case of accident for a longer time than is necessary to remove it), or not placing such wagon or other wheeled carriage with or without beasts of draught, harnessed or yoked thereto, during the time of loading or unloading the same, as near to one side of the Road as possible.

Owner's name and abode on carriages of burden

Using any carriage of burthen without the owner's name and place of abode painted in one or more straight lines, upon some conspicuous part of the right or off side, in large legible letters, not less than 1 inch in length.

Fences reducing breadth of road

Making any hedge or other fence at the side of any such Road, so as to reduce or limit the breadth below that prescribed.

Depositing loose earth, &c.. nuisances and neglect to remove same after notice

Depositing any loose earth, sand, brick, or rubbish, against any wall, or excavation for a foundation wall, or fence or Bridge in any such Road, or creating or causing any nuisance on any such Road, and refusing or neglecting to remove the same after being required by the Engineer or a Justice of any district.

Firestick torches

Using or carrying any fire-stick or torch on or about any such Road 21 V., c. 32, s. 35.

Further penalties not exceeding £10.

Depositing rubbish, &c., on roads or neighbourhood

Depositing any rubbish, filth, offal or night-soil, on any Road thoroughfare, or place adjacent thereto, to the annoyance of persons using the same, or in the neighbourhood.

Depositing night-soil, &c., without burying or burning

Depositing any night-soil or dead carcase or offal, in any place appointed by the Commissioners, or other competent authority, without having it buried, and effectually covered with earth, or burnt, 27 V., S. 1, c. 36, s. 9.

Leaving things on road likely to frighten horses

Leaving any thing on any Road of a nature likely to frighten animals, and thereby cause injury to passengers or property : fine not exceeding 20s. or imprisonment, in default of payment, for 20 days, 25 V., c. 12, s. 13.

Penalties

Penalties recoverable summarily before 2 Justices, not exceeding 40s., and in default of payment, commitment to the Common Gaol or House of Correction, with or without hard labor, not exceeding 30 days, unless sooner paid.

Any driver of any wagon, cart or other carriage, who rides thereon, or on any horse drawing it, not having some other person on foot or on horseback to guide same (such as are driven with reins, and conducted by a person holding the reins of all the horses drawing the same, excepted.)

Drivers riding on carriages or horses not driven with reins

Any driver of any wagon, wain, cart, dray, or other carriage, who rides on the shafts or any other part without having and holding reins attached to each side of the bridle of each beast drawing it, or who leaves the same standing, or travelling on any Road without some person to hold or guide the beasts drawing the same.

Riding on shaft, &c. without holding reins, leaving carriage without some person

Any driver of any carriage whatsoever on any part of any Road, who by negligence or wilful misbehaviour, causes any hurt or damage to any person, horse, cattle or goods conveyed in any carriage on the Road, or who quits the same and goes on the other side of the hedge or fence enclosing the same, or negligently or wilfully is at such distance from the carriage, or in such a situation, whilst it is passing on the Road, that he cannot have the direction and government of the horses or cattle drawing the same.

Causing damage by negligence or misbehavior

Leaving any cart or carriage on such Road so as to obstruct the passage.

Leaving cart &c. on road

Driving or acting as the driver of any wagon, cart or other such carriage not having the owner's name, as by law required, painted and remaining legible thereon, and refusing to tell or discover the true names of the owners or principal owners.

Driving carriages without owner's name, and refusing to tell same

Any driver of any wagon, cart, or other carriage, or of any horses, mules or other beasts of draught or burthen meeting any other wagon, &c., or horses, &c., who shall not keep his wagon, &c., on the left or near side of the Road.

Not keeping left or near side on passing

Wilfully preventing any other person from passing him, or any wagon, &c., or horses, &c., under his care upon such Road or by negligence or misbehaviour preventing, hindering or interrupting the free passage of any person, wagon &c., or horses, &c., on any Road, or not keeping his wagon, &c., or horses, &c., on the left or near side of the Road to allow such passage.

Preventing free passage

Riding on any horse or beast, or driving any carriage furiously so as to endanger the life or limbs of any passenger.

Furious riding or driving to danger of passengers

Every driver offending as aforesaid may, with or without warrant, be apprehended by any person who sees the offence committed, and conveyed before a Justice to be dealt with, and if he refuse to discover his name, the Justice before whom he is taken or complaint is made may commit him to hard labor not exceeding 30 days, or proceed against him for the penalty, by a description of his person and the offence only, without adding any name or designation, but expressing in the proceedings that he refused to discover his name, 25 V., c. 12, s. 14.

Apprehension without warrant refusal to discover name

Any driver of any wagon, wain, cart, dray, or other carriage, who wilfully or wantonly, or through culpable negligence, suffers it to strike against any retaining wall, parapet wall or Bridge, or to pass over or against the banks appertaining to any Road or Bridge, or by negligence or wilful misbehaviour causes any hurt or damage to any such Road or Bridge shall forfeit not exceeding 40s., with costs, to any person who complains; and in default of payment, shall be committed to the nearest Prison, not exceeding 30 days, with or without hard labor, 26 V., c. 12, s. 15.

Injuries to walls, bridges, banks, &c.

Riding, or leading or driving any horse, ass, mule, cattle, swine or carriage, or any single wheel of any wagon, wain, cart, dray or carrriage along any ditch, drain, or water-table, except in case of necessity, alongside of any Road, or wilfully obstructing or doing, or causing any injury or damage thereto, or to any Bridges, posts, rails or fences thereof, or in ploughing, or in the cultivation of any uninclosed lands adjacent to any Road, turning any horse, cattle or other animal upon the same, or by the side, or suffering any water, filth, dirt or other offensive matter to run or flow into or upon such Road from any house, building, erection, lands or premises adjacent, or after having blocked or stopped, any cart, wagon or other carriage in going up a hill or rising ground, causing or suffering it to be or remain on the Road the stone or other thing with which it was blocked or stopped: Penalty not exceeding 50s., over and above the damages occasioned, or in default of payment, imprisonment for 30 days, 25 V., c. 12, s. 16.

Riding or driving along ditch, &c. damaging roads, bridges, posts, rails or fences; running horses, &c. on road in ploughing

Suffering filth, &c. to run from adjacent houses, &c.

Not removing blocks or stops of carts, &c

Seizure and forfeiture of timber, stones, &c. left on any road or bridge unless redeemed

Any County Engineer, Local Main Road or other Commissioner, or Waywarden of any Highway, or any person authorized by either of them, may seize and carry off any timber, stone, dung. rubbish or other matter, or thing laid or left upon any Road or Bridge, or side drain, or ditch thereof, so as to be a nuisance, and sell or dispose thereof as a forfeiture, as the County Engineer, Local Main Road or other Commissioner or Waywarden shall direct, unless the owners redeem same, by payment to the County Engineer, in respect of any Main Road, or to the Clerk of the Commissioners of Highways &c., in respect of other Roads, of not exceeding £5 by way of penalty, such payment to be made to the Receiver-General, or otherwise applied with the sanction of the Main Road Commissioners, or Commissioners of Highways, &c., as the case requires, to the account of the Road.

Applicable

Materials for repairs, &c. of houses or walls

The proprietor or occupier of any land or house may lay down any materials for repairing or re-building any house.or wall immediately adjoining any Road or Bridge, the materials occupying one fourth of the breadth of the Road only, and the proprietor or occupier giving 3 days previous notice, in writing, to the County Engineer, or Local Commissioner or Waywarden, or erecting such fence round them, and fixing and lighting lamps thereon, as the County Engineer, &c., requires.—

Soil, &c. insufficient to defray expenses of removal

If any soil, ashes or rubbish, laid on any Road is insufficient to defray the expense of removal, the person who laid or deposited the same, shall repay to the County Engineer, &c., the money necessarily expended for the removal, to be levied, if not forthwith re-paid, as penalties, 25 V., c. 12, s. 17.

Contractors for repairs to fence and light dangerous places

Every Contractor for the repairs of any Bridge or section of any Road, while the same are dangerous to travellers by night, shall fence them, and cause a light during each night to be conspicuously placed at or near such Bridge or section of Road, to warn them of such danger: Penalty, £5, 25 V., c. 12, s. 19.

Wagons, &c. to be lighted at night

No person in charge of any wagon, cart or dray, shall travel in the dark, unless he have a light placed in some conspicuous part, under penalty not exceeding 20s, and in default of payment, imprisonment with or without hard labor not exceeding 15 days, 25 V , c. 12, s. 20.

Pits, &c. adjoining roads to be fenced in

If any proprietor or occupier, or engineer, or contractor, dig any pit, or make any cut at the side of any Road dangerous to travellers and their animals, and shall not fence them when required by any local or other Commissioner or Waywarden, or other person acting under their, or either of their authority, he shall forfeit not exceeding 20s, for every day it continues unfenced beyond 3 days after he has been required, and after such requisition, the Waywarden or Commissioner may cause it to be fenced at his expense, which, if not paid on demand, shall be recovered as a penalty, 25 V., c. 12, s. 21.

Road through adjoining land during repairs

Compensation

Any County Engineer or Waywarden may make a Road through the grounds (not being the site of a House, nor a Garden, Yard, Court, Plantation, Provision Ground or avenue, to any House or Ground set apart for Building Ground) adjoining to any ruinous or narrow part of any Road to be made use of as a public Road, whilst the old Road is repairing or widening, making recompense to the proprietor or occupier for damages ; and in case the County Engineer or Waywarden and proprietor or occupier differ, the Commissioners of Main Roads, in board assembled, shall hear and determine all questions as to the amount of damages and expense, 25 V., c. 12, s. 22.

Contractors, &c., neglecting to pay laborers on Main Roads

If any Contractor or person intrusted with the superintedence of any repairs or alterations to, or the construction of any Main Road, who is charged with or undertakes the payment of money to any work-people or other persons, for work performed on the Main Roads, fails or neglects to make such payment without a sufficient reason, to the person entitled, he shall, on conviction before 2 Justices, be adjudged to pay to the party complaining, such sums as appear to be due, and shall also forfeit not exceeding £10 ; and if the sum and penalty, with costs, if ordered, are not paid immediately or within such period as the Justices appoint, they may commit him to be imprisoned, with or without hard labor for not exceeding 3 calendar months, unless sooner paid, 27 V., S. 1, c. 36, s. 10.

Tramways on Main Roads

On the advice of the Chief Engineer, that the laying down and maintenance of a Tramway in any locality where the making and repairing of the ordinary Main Road is unusually difficult would be advantageous, the Main Road Commissioners may cause any such Tramway to be laid down accordingly, the expense per mile not to exceed £1000, 25 V.. c. 12, s. 30.

The Main Road Commissioners, on such conditions and security as to *Private Tram-*
them shall seem reasonable, may permit the p   m   of any private Tram- *ways*
way to lay down the same along the side of, in across under or across any
Main Road ; but not so as to interfere with the general traffic or couve-
nience of passengers, 25 V., c. 12, s. 43.

No deed, contract or agreement, or proceeding under this Act, shall be *Exemption from*
subject to any Stamp Duty, 21 V., c. 32, s. 59. *Stamps*

All penalties shall be recovered before 2 Justices, and paid to the Re- *Recovery and ap-*
ceiver-General in aid of the Main Road Fund. The Justices may mitigate *plication of penal-*
penalties, and adjudge not exceeding one moiety to any persons who have *ties*
contributed to the conviction of any offender, in such proportions as they *Mitigation*
think fit, 21 V., c. 32, s. 60.

Any Commissioner, Engineer, Constable, Policeman or Peace Officer, *Apprehension*
and all persons they call to their assistance, may take into custody without *without warrant*
warrant, any person who, within view of any such Commissioner, &c.,
commits any offence in this Act, 21 V., c. 32, s. 61.

The prosecution of offences punishable summarily shall be commenced *Commencement*
within 3 calendar months, 21 V., c, 32, s. 62. *of prosecutions*

The Ma   Road Act, 1857 ; in force until 31st December, 1872, 21 V , *Short Title—Du-*
c. 32, s. 63. in *ration, 21 V., c. 32*

The Main Road Commissioners or Commissioners of any Road, at a *Indictments, pro-*
public meeting, may direct prosecutions by indictment or otherwise, for any *secution by*
nuisance done or continued on any Road under their care, or to recover any
penalty or forfeiture under any Act to be in force, at the expense of the
Road Revenues, to be allowed at a subsequent meeting, 25 V., c. 12,
s. 26.

In case any person resist, or make forcible opposition against any per- *Forcible resist-*
son employed in the execution of this or any future Act for making, amend- *ance, assaults, res-*
ing or repairing any road, or assaults any County Engineer, Local or *cue of distress*
other Commissioner, Waywarden, or Surveyor, in the execution of his
office, or hinders, or makes any rescue of cattle or goods distrained, the offender shall forfeit not exceeding £10, 25 V., c. 12, s. 27.

Any Local or other Commissioner, Secretary, Clerk, Collectors, Sur- *Apprehension of*
veyors or other Officers, and such persons as they call to their assistance, *unknown persons*
may, without warrant, seize and detain any unknown person who commits *without warrant*
any offence, and take him before any Justice for the parish near where the
offence is committed, or the offender is apprehended; and the Justice shall
act with respect to him according to this or any other Act for making or
repairing Roads, 25 V., c. 12, s. 28.

Every penalty imposed by this Act shall be recovered as under 21 V., *Penalties*
c. 32, s. 60, 25 V., c. 12, s. 46.

Unless there is something in the subject or context, repugnant thereto, *Interpretation—*
" Horse" shall mean, Horse, Mare, Golding, Mule or Ass ; " Beast," *Horse, Beast, Cat-*
" Cuttle," any Horned Stock, Sheep Goat or Swine ; " Carriage." any *tle, Carriage, Road,*
Wagon, Wain, Cart, Dray or other Carriage, or Vehicle whatsoever of any *Main Road Act,*
description, and whether with or without springs ; " Road" or " Roads," *Act*
any Main Road, or any Highway or Road whatever ; " Main Road Act,"
as well " the Main Road Act, 1857," as any other Act now or to be in force,
relating to Main Roads ; " Act," any Act now or to be in force, relating to Main Roads or any other Highway or Road whatsoever, 25 V., c. 12,
s. 47.

The Main Road Act Amendment, and General Road Act, 1861, 21 V., *Short Title, 21 V.,*
c. 12, s. 49. *c. 12*

In all actions against any person employed on Main Roads for acts *Protection from*
done in relation to Main Roads, they may plead the general issue, and give *actions*
the special matter in evidence, 25 V., c. 12, s. 50.

This Act may be read as incorporated with, and part of 21 V., c. 32, and *Incorporation of*
25 V., c. 12, 27 V., S. 1, c. 36, s. 13. *27 V., S. 1, c. 36*

Tolls abolished, and the Toll Houses and Land to be sold, 26 V., S. 2, *Tolls abolition*
c. 8.

FORM—21 V., c. 32.

Of General Return of Roads to be annually submitted by the Civil Engineers.

COLUMN.	1.	2.	3.	4.	5.	6.	7.	8.
	Distinguishing No. of Road.	Name, or short description.	No of miles same consists of, and the rate of acclivities and declivities.	Tolls and rent received last year.	State and condition of road.	If repairable under contract or not.	Particulars and duration of contract.	Ordinary expenditure last year.

COLUMN.	9.	10.	11.	12.	13.	14.	15.
	Alterations during year.	Expenditure in consequence.	New roads and bridges constructed.	Expenditure in consequence.	Total expenditure last year.	Expenditure in excess of estimates.	Savings on estimates.

16.	17.	18.	19.	24.
Amount of Toll collections expended on road.	Amount expended from legislative grants.	Amount expended from "Land Tax Loan," &c. under act.	Probable ordinary expenses for ensuing year.	Total probable expenses for ensuing year.
20.	21.	22.	23.	
Further alterations recomended.	Probable expense thereof.	New roads and bridges recommended to be made.	Probable expense thereof.	

3 I

SCHEDULE.—25 V., c. 12.

Quarterly Main Road Fund Account from the _____ day of
18__ to the _____ day of _____ '18__

	Arrears of Land Tax.	Land Tax.	License Duties.
St. Catherine			
St. John................			
St. Dorothy			
St. Thomas in the Vale..			
St. Mary			
Clarendon			
Vere			
St. Ann			
Kingston			
St. Andrew			
Port Royal..........			
St. David			
St. Thomas in the East ..			
Portland............			
St. George..........			
Metcalfe			
St. Elizabeth			
Westmoreland			
Hanover			
St. James			
Trelawney			

RECAPITULATION.

Received for arrears of Land Tax ....
  "   Land Tax ....
Deductions under License Duties Act ....
For Import Duties, 28 V., c. 10. Sch. C.
Expenditure, Cornwall ....
  "   Middlesex................
  "   Surry.................
  "   Salaries................

Re_____ General.

Main Road Fund.

Revenue to be carried to fund and charges thereon
All revenue to arise by virtue of 8 V., c. 16, from the Land, Tax or its redemption under this Act (see Land Tax, &c.,) to be transferred to the superintendance of the Main Road Commissioners, and all annual and other money grants to be made for the maintenance and improvement of the Main Roads and Bridges, shall be _____ the maintenance and improvement thereof, and as a Fund _____ nt of any moneys to be borrowed for that purpose, and the int_____ " reon, 21 V., c. 34, s. 1.

All moneys to be received under _____ id to the Receiver-General, and carried to a general sepa_____ e called the Main Road Fund ; and all moneys to be raise_____ nder this or any other Act relating to Main Roads, to be tran_____ e management of Main Road Commissioners ; and the interest on all moneys so raised, shall be a charge upon the moneys carried to the credit of such Fund, and if it prove insufficient, the credit of the Island shall stand pledged for any deficiency, 21 V., c. 34, s. 2.

All fees received by the Receiver-General under this Act, so long as his services are paid by a salary, and the contingencies of his office defrayed at the Island expense, shall be carried to the credit of the Main Road Fund Account, 21 V., c. 34, s. 36.

Short Title
"The Main Road Fund Act, 1857," 21 V., c. 34, s 40.

Malicious Injuries to Property,

Setting fire to places of Divine worship
Unlawfully and maliciously setting fire to any church, chapel, meeting house or other place of Divine Worship : Felony, penal servitude for life, or not less than 3 years, or imprisonment not exceeding 2 years, with or without hard labor, and with or without solitary confinement, 27 V., S. 1, c. 34, s. 1.

. Unlawfully and maliciously setting fire to any Dwelling-house, any person being therein : Felony, punishment as above, 27 V., S. 1, c. 34, s. 2.

Unlawfully and maliciously setting fire to any house, stable, coach-house, out-house, warehouse, office, shop, mill, store-house, granary, hovel, shed or fold, or to any plantation, pen or settlement, or to any sugar works, or works on any coffee plantation, or to any building, or to any trash-house on any sugar estate, or to any erection used for the purpose of manufacturing or preparing, or for preserving when manufactured and prepared, any of the products of such plantation, pen, settlement or sugar estate, or in carrying on any trade or manufacture, or any branch thereof, whether in the possession of the offender or of any other person, with intent to injure or defraud any person : Felony, punishment as above, 27 V., S. 1, c. 34, s. 3.

Unlawfully and maliciously setting fire to any station, engine-house, warehouse, or other building, or to any bridge belonging or appertaining to any Railway, Tramway, port or harbour : Felony, penal servitude for life, or not less than 3 years, or imprisonment with or without hard labor, 27 V., S. 1, c. 34, s. 4.

Unlawfully and maliciously setting fire to any building other than before mentioned, belonging to the Queen, or to any County, City, Parish or place, or devoted or dedicated to public use or ornament, or erected or maintained by public subscription or contribution : Felony, punishment as last above, 27 V., S. 1, c. 34, s. 5.

Unlawfully and maliciously setting fire to any matter or thing being in, against or under any building, under such circumstances that if the building were thereby set fire to, the offence would amount to Felony : Felony, penal servitude not exceeding 14 years, nor less than 3, or imprisonment not exceeding 2 years, with or without hard labor, 27 V., S. 1, c. 34, s. 6.

Unlawfully and maliciously setting fire to any building other than in this Act mentioned : Felony, punishment as last above, 27 V., S. 1, c. 34. s. 7.

Unlawfully and maliciously, by any overt act, attempting to set fire to any building, or any matter or thing in the last preceding section mentioned, under such circumstances that if the same were set fire to, the offender would be guilty of Felony, (omitted Felony) and being convicted thereof, punishment as last above, 27 V., c. 34, s. 8.

Unlawfully and maliciously, by the explosion of gunpowder or other explosive substance, destroying, throwing down or damaging the whole or any part of any dwelling-house, any person being therein, or of any building whereby the life of any person is endangered : Felony, penal servitude for life, or not less than 3 years, or imprisonment not exceeding 2 years, with or without hard labor, and with or without solitary confinement, 27 V., S. 1, c. 34, s. 9.

Unlawfully and maliciously placing or throwing in, into, upon, under, against or near any building, any Gunpowder or other explosive substance, with intent to destroy or damage any building, or any engine, machinery, working tools, fixtures, goods or chattels, whether or not any explosion take place, or any damage be caused : Felony, penal servitude not exceeding 14 years, nor less than 3, or imprisonment not exceeding 2 years, with or without hard labor, and with or without solitary confinement, 27 V., S. 1, c. 34, s. 10.

If any persons riotously and tumultuously assembled together to the disturbance of the public peace, unlawfully and with force demolish or pull down or destroy, or begin to demolish, pull down or destroy any church, chapel, meeting-house, or other place of Divine Worship, or any house, stable, coach-house, out-house, warehouse, office, shop, mill, barn, granary, shed, hovel or fold, or any building or erection used in farming land, or in carrying on any trade or manufacture, or any branch thereof, or any building other than in this section before mentioned, belonging to the Queen, or to any county, city, parish or place, or devoted or dedicated to any public use or ornament, or erected or maintained by public subscription or contribution, or any machinery whether fixed or moveable, prepared for or employed in any manufacture, or in any branch thereof, or any steam engine or cattle mill, water mill or other engine, or mill for the purpose of manufacture, or for making sugar, or for preparing coffee or other produce, building or erection used in conducting the business of such manufacture, or preparing such produce, or any bridge, wagon, wain, truck for conveying any manufacture whatever from the place where it was prepared : Felony, penal servitude for life, or not less than 3 years, or imprisonment not exceeding 2 years, with or without hard labour, and with or without solitary confinement, 27 V., S. 1, c. 34, s. 11.

Injuries to buildings by rioters

If any persons riotously and tumultuously assembled together to the disturbance of the public peace, unlawfully and with force, injure or damage any such church or chapel, meeting-house, place of Divine Worship, house, stable, coach-house, out-house, warehouse, office, shop, mill, building, erection, machinery, engine, bridge, wagon, wain or truck as in s. 11 mentioned : Misdemeanor, penal servitude not exceeding 7 years, nor less than 3, or imprisonment not exceeding 2 years, with or without hard labor. It upon the trial of any person for any Felony in the last preceding section mentioned, the Jury are not satisfied that the person is guilty thereof, but are satisfied that he is guilty of any offence in this section, they may find him guilty thereof, and he may be punished accordingly, 27 V., S. 1, c. 34, s. 12.

Persons indicted under previous section may be found guilty under this

Injuries by tenants to buildings or fixtures

Whosoever being possessed of any dwelling-house, or other building or part of any dwelling-house or other building held for any term of years, or other less term, or at will, or held over or after the termination of any tenantry, unlawfully and maliciously pulls down or demolishes, or begins to pull down or demolish the same or any pa t, or unlawfully and maliciously pulls down or severs from the freehold, any fixture being fixed in or to such dwelling-house or part thereof : Misdemeanor ; for punishment (see s. 42,) 27 V., S. 1, c. 34, s. 13.

Injuries to manufactures

Unlawfully and maliciously cutting, breaking or destroying, or damaging with intent to destroy, or to render useless any goods or articles of manufacture whilst in any stage, process or progress of manufacture, or by force entering into any house, shop, store, building or place, with intent to commit any of the offences in this section : Felony, penal servitude for life, or not less than 3 years, or imprisonment not exceeding 2 years with or without hard labor, and with or without solitary confinement, 27 V., S. 1, c. 34, s. 14.

Injuries to machinery, &c

Unlawfully and maliciously cutting, breaking or destroying, or damaging with intent to destroy or to render useless, any machine or engine whether fixed or moveable, used or intended to be used for mowing, ploughing or draining, or for performing any other agricultural operation, or any machine or engine, or any tool or implement, whether fixed or moveable, prepared for, or employed in any manufacture whatsoever : Felony, penal servitude, not exceeding 7 years. nor less than 3, or imprisonment not exceeding 2 years, with or without hard labor, and with or without solitary confinement, 27 V., S. 1. c. 34, s. 15.

Setting fire to vegetable productions

Unlawfully and maliciously setting fire to any corn-piece, grass-piece pimento walk, coffee-piece or pasture, or plantation, or of any cultivated vegetable produce whether standing or cut down, or to any part of any wood, coffee or plantation of trees, wheresoever growing : Felony, penal servitude not exceeding 14 years. nor less than 3 years, or imprisonment, not exceeding 2 years with or without hard labor, and with or without solitary confinement, 27 V., S. 1, c. 34, s. 16.

Setting fire to stacks of grain, straw, vegetable produce, coals, charcoal, wood, or bark

Unlawfully and maliciously setting fire to any stack of grain, straw, or of any cultivated vegetable produce, or of coals, charcoal, wood, or bark : Felony, penal servitude for life, or not less than three years, or imprisonment not exceeding 2 years, with or without hard labor, and with or without solitary confinement, 27 V., S. 1, c. 34, s. 17.

Attempts to set fire

Unlawfully and maliciously, by any overt act, attempting to set fire to any such matter or thing as in s. 16 & 17, mentioned, under such circumstances that if the same were thereby set fire to the offender would be guilty of Felony : Felony ; penal servitude, not exceeding 7 years nor less than 3, or imprisonment, not exceeding 2 years, with or without hard labor, and with or without solitary confinement, 27 V., S. 1, c. 34, s. 18.

Damaging trees, &c., in gardens, &c, injury exceeding £1

Unlawfully and maliciously cutting, breaking, barking, rooting up or otherwise destroying or damaging the whole or any part of any tree, sapling or shrub, or any underwood, growing in any pleasure-ground, garden or orchard, or avenue, or in any ground adjoining or belonging to any dwelling house (in case the amount of injury done exceeds £1): Felony, penal servitude for 3 years, or imprisonment not exceeding 2 years, with or without hard labor, and with or without solitary confinement, 27 V., S. 1 c. 34, s. 19.

When growing elsewhere than in any pleasure-ground, &c., (in case the amount of injury done exceed £5): Felony, penal servitude for 3 years, or imprisonment not exceeding 2 years, with or without hard labor and with or without solitary confinement, 27 V., S. 1, c. 34, s. 20. *Growing elsewhere; injury exceeding £5*

Wheresoever growing (the injury done being to the amount of 1s at least) on conviction before a Justice, the offender shall be committed to the Common Gaol or District Prison, to be imprisoned only, or to be kept to hard labor not exceeding one month, or else forfeit and pay over and above the amount of the injury done, not exceeding £3. If after conviction of any such offence against this or any former act, for the second offence, he shall be committed to the Common Gaol or District Prison to be kept to hard labor not exceeding 12 months. After having been twice convicted (whether both or either of such convictions took place before or after this Act); any subsequent offence shall be a Misdemeanor: Imprisonment not exceeding 2 years, with or without hard labor, and with or without solitary confinement, 27 V., S. 1, c. 34, s. 21. *Wheresoever growing; injury 1s, see s. 43-44* *2d Offence* *After 2 convictions*

Unlawfully and maliciously destroying or damaging, with intent to destroy any plant, root, fruit or vegetable production growing in any garden, orchard or nursery ground, on conviction before a Justice, the offender shall be committed to the Common Gaol or District Prison, or General Penitentiary, to be imprisoned only, or kept to hard labor not exceeding one month, or forfeit and pay over and above the amount of the injury done, not exceeding £6. If after conviction of any such offence under this or any former Act: Felony, penal servitude for 3 years, or imprisonment not exceeding 2 years, with or without hard labor, and with or without solitary confinement, 27 V., S. 1, c. 34, s 22. *Plants, roots, fruit or other vegetable produce in garden, &c.; see s. 43-44* *After previous conviction*

Unlawfully and maliciously destroying or damaging, with intent to destroy any cultivated root or plant, used for the food of man or beast, or for medicine, or for distilling, or for dyeing, or for or in the course of any manufacture, and growing in any land, open or enclosed, not being a garden or orchard, or nursery ground, on conviction before a Justice the offender shall be committed to the Common Gaol or District Prison, to be imprisoned only, or kept to hard labor not exceeding one month, or forfeit and pay over and above the amount of the injury done, not exceeding 20s., and in default of payment, with costs, if ordered, shall be committed as aforesaid not exceeding one month, unless payment is sooner made. After conviction of any such offence against this or any former Act, on any subsequent conviction, he shall be committed to the Common Gaol or District Prison, to hard labor not exceeding 6 months, 27 V., S. 1, c. 34, s. 23. *Cultivated roots, or plants for food of man or beast—medicine, distilling, dyeing, &c. in open or enclosed land; see s. 43-44* *On subsequent conviction*

Unlawfully and maliciously cutting, breaking, throwing down, or in any wise destroying any fence of any description, or any wall, stile or gate, or any part, on conviction before a Justice for the first offence, the offender shall forfeit and pay over and above the amount of the injury done, not exceeding £5. After conviction of any such offence against this or any former Act, on any subsequent conviction, he shall be committed to the Common Gaol or District Prison to hard labor not exceeding 12 months, 27 V., S. 1, c. 34, s. 24. *Injuries to fences, walls, stiles, gates* *On subsequent conviction*

Unlawfully and maliciously cutting through, breaking down, or otherwise destroying the dam, flood-gate or sluice, of any fish-pond or of any water which is private property, with intent to take or destroy any of the fish in such pond or water, so as thereby to cause the loss or destruction of any of the fish, or unlawfully or maliciously putting any lime or other noxious material into any such pond or water, with intent thereby to destroy any of the fish therein, or unlawfully and maliciously breaking down or otherwise destroying the dam or flood gate of any well or pond, or any gutter or pipe for the conveyance of water: Misdemeanor, penal servitude not exceeding 7 years, nor less than 3, or imprisonment not exceeding 2 years, with or without hard labor, and with or without solitary confinement, 27 V., S. 1, c. 34, s. 25. *Dams, floodgates* *Gutters, pipes*

Unlawfully and maliciously pulling or throwing down, or in any wise destroying any Bridge (whether over any stream of water or not), or any viaduct or aqueduct, over or under which Bridge, viaduct *Bridges, viaducts aqueducts* or aqueduct, any Highway, Railway, Tramway or Canal passes, or doing any injury with intent, and so as to thereby render such Bridge, viaduct or aqueduct, or the Highway, Railway, Tramway or Canal passing over or under the same, or any part thereof dangerous or impassable : Felony, penal servitude for life or not less than 3 years, or imprisonment not exceeding 2 years, with or without hard labor, and with or without solitary confinement, 27 V. S. 1, c. 34, s. 26.

Toll Bars—Weighing Machines; see s. 42

Unlawfully and maliciously throwing down, levelling or otherwise destroying in whole or in part any turnpipe gate, or toll-bar, or any wall chain, rail, post, bar or other fence belonging to any turnpike gate or toll bar, or set up or erected to prevent passengers passing by without paying any toll directed to be paid by any Act relating thereto, or any house, building or weighing engine erected for the better collection, ascertainment or security of any such toll : Misdemeanor, 27 V., S. 1, c. 34, s. 27.

Railways—Tramways. Putting wood upon, removing rails, &c., diverting points or machinery, shewing or removing signals, other obstructions, &c

Unlawfully and maliciously putting, placing, casting or throwing upon or across any Railway or Tramway, any wood, stone or other matter or thing, or unlawfully and maliciously taking up, removing or displacing any rail, sleeper or other matter or thing belonging to any Railway or Tramway, or unlawfully and maliciously turning, moving or diverting any points or other machinery belonging to any Railway or Tramway, or unlawfully and maliciously making or showing, hiding or removing any signal or light, upon or near to any Railway or Tramway, or unlawfully and maliciously doing, or causing to be done, any other matter or thing with intent in any of the cases aforesaid, to obstruct, upset, overthrow, injure or destroy any engine, tender, carriage or truck using such Railway or Tramway : Felony, penal servitude for life, or not less than 3 years, or imprisonment not exceeding 2 years, with or without hard labour, 27 V., S. 1, c. 34, s. 28.

Engines or carriages on railroads or Tramways, Traction Engines or carriages

By any unlawful act, or by any wilful omission or neglect, obstructing, or causing to be obstructed, any engine or carriage using any Railway or Tramway, or any Traction engine or wagon using any ordinary public Road or aiding or assisting therein : Misdemeanor, imprisonment not exceeding 2 years, with or without hard labor, 27 V., S. 1, c. 34, s. 29.

Electric Telegraph

Unlawfully and maliciously cutting, breaking, throwing down, destroying, injuring or removing any battery, machinery, wire, cable, post or other matter or thing, being part of or being used or employed in or about any Electric or Magnetic Telegraph, or in the working thereof, or unlawfully and maliciously preventing or obstructing in any manner whatsoever the sending, conveyance or delivery of any communication by any such Telegraph : Misdemeanor, imprisonment not exceeding 2 years, with or without hard labor. If it appear to any Justice, on the examination of any person charged with any offence against this section, that it is not expedient to the ends of Justice that it should be prosecuted by indictment, he may proceed summarily, and the offender shall, on conviction, either be committed to the Common Goal, or District Prison or General Penitentiary, to be imprisoned only, or kept to hard labor, not exceeding 3 months, or else shall forfeit and pay not exceeding £10, 27 V., S. 1, c. 34, s. 30.

Cattle, Killing, maiming or wounding

Unlawfully and maliciously killing, maiming or wounding any cattle: Felony, penal servitude not exceeding 14 years, nor less than 3 years, or imprisonment not exceeding 2 years, with or without hard labor, and with or without solitary confinement, 27 V., S. 1, c. 34 s. 31.

Killing, &c. dogs, birds, domesticated animals

Unlawfully and maliciously killing maiming or wounding any dog, bird, beast or other animal, not being cattle, but being either the subject of Larceny at common law, or being ordinarily kept in a state of confinement, or for any domestic purpose, on conviction before a Justice, the offender shall be committed to the Common Gaol or District Prison, or General Penitentiary, to be imprisoned only, or kept to hard labor, not exceeding 6 months, or forfeit and pay over and above the amount of the injury done, not exceeding £12.

After previous conviction

If committed after a previous conviction of any of such offences, commitment to the Common Gaol or District Prison to hard labor for not exceeding 12 months, 27 V., S. 1, c. 34, s. 32.

Setting fire to or destroying ships whether complete or unfinished

Unlawfully and maliciously setting fire to, casting away, or in any wise destroying any ship or vessel, whether complete or in an unfinished state : Felony, penal servitude for life, or not less than 3 years, or imprisonment not exceeding 2 years, with or without hard labor, and with or without solitary confinement, 27 V., S. 1, c. 34, s. 33.

Unlawfully and maliciously setting fire to, or casting away, or in anywise destroying any ship or vessel with intent thereby to prejudice any owner or part owner of such ship or vessel, or of any goods on board, or, any person who has, or shall underwrite any Policy of Insurance upon such ship or vessel, or the freight, or upon any goods on board: Felony, punishment as above, 27 V., S. 1, c. 34, s. 34.

Unlawfully and maliciously, by any overt act, attempting to set fire to, cast away or destroy any ship or vessel under such circumstances that if the ship or vessel were thereby set fire to, cast away or destroyed the offender would be guilty of Felony: Felony, penal servitude not exceeding 14 years, nor less than 3, or imprisonment not exceeding 2 years, with or without hard labor, and with or without solitary confinement, 27 V., S. 1, c. 34, s. 35.

Unlawfully and maliciously placing or throwing in, into, upon, against or near any ship or vessel, any gunpowder or other explosive substance, with intent to destroy or damage any ship or vessel, or any machinery, working tools, goods or chattels, whether or not any explosion take place, and whether or not any injury be effected: Felony, same punishment as above, 27 V., S. 1, c. 34, s. 36.

Unlawfully and maliciously damaging, otherwise than by fire, gunpowder or other explosive substance, any ship or vessel, whether complete or in an unfinished state, with intent to destroy the same, or render it useless: Felony, penal servitude not exceeding 7 years, nor less than 3, or imprisonment not exceeding 2 years, with or without hard labor, and with or without solitary confinement, 27 V., S. 1, c. 34, s. 37.

Unlawfully masking, altering or removing any Light or Signal, or unlawfully exhibiting any false light or signal with intent to bring any ship, vessel or boat into danger, or unlawfully and maliciously doing anything tending to the immediate loss or destruction of any ship, vessel or boat, and for which no punishment is before provided: Felony, penal servitude for life, or for any term not exceeding 2 years (sic), with or without hard labor, and with or without solitary confinement, 27 V., S. 1, c. 34, s. 38.

Unlawfully and maliciously cutting away, casting adrift, removing, altering, defacing, sinking and destroying, or unlawfully and maliciously doing any act with intent to cut away, cast adrift, remove, alter, deface, sink or destroy, or in any other manner unlawfully and maliciously injure or conceal any boat, buoy rope, perch, pile or mark used or intended for the guidance of seamen, or the purpose of navigation: Felony, penal servitude not exceeding 7 years, nor less than 3 years, or imprisonment not exceeding 2 years, with or without hard labor, and with or without solitary confinement, 27 V., S. 1, c. 34, s. 39.

Unlawfully and maliciously destroying any part of any ship or vessel in distress, or wrecked, stranded or cast on shore, or any goods merchandize or articles of any kind, belonging to such ship or vessel: Felony, penal servitude not exceeding 14 years, nor less than 3, or imprisonment not exceeding 2 years, with or without hard labor, and with or without solitary confinement, 27 V., S. 1, c. 34, s. 40.

Sending, delivering or uttering, or directly or indirectly causing to be received, knowing the contents thereof, any letter or writing threatening to burn or destroy any house, barn or other building, or any rick or stack of grain, hay or straw, or other agricultural produce, or any grain; hay, or straw or agricultural produce in or under any building, or any ship or vessel, or to kill, maim or wound any cattle: Felony, penal servitude not exceeding 10 years, nor less than 3, or imprisonment not exceeding 2 years, with or without hard labor, and with or without solitary confinement, 27 V., S. 1, c, 34, s. 41.

Unlawfully and maliciously committing any damage, injury or spoil to or upon any real or personal property, either of a public or private nature, for which no punishment is before provided, the damage, injury or spoil being to an amount exceeding £5: Misdemeanor, imprisonment not exceeding 2 years, with or without hard labor. In case any such offence is committed between 9, p.m. and 6, a.m., penal servitude, not exceeding 5 years, nor less than 3 years, or imprisonment not exceeding 2 years, with or without hard labor, 27 V., S. 1, c. 34, s. 42.

(marginal notes:) Setting fire to or destroying ships or goods on board — Attempting to do so — Placing or throwing explosive substances with intent to destroy or damage any ship machinery or goods — Damaging otherwise than by fire gunpowder or other explosive substance any ship whether complete or unfinished — Making altering, &c. lights or signals, exhibiting false lights, &c. — Cutting away, &c. boats, buoys, &c., piles or marks for guidance of seamen or for purposes of navigation — Destroying, &c. vessels in distress or wrecked, &c. or goods belonging thereto — Threatening letters to destroy property — Injuries to property, real or personal, not specified, not exceeding £5 — If committed between 9 p.m. and 6 a.m.

To any property for which no punishment is provided, punishable before a Justice

Wilfully or maliciously committing any damage, injury or spoil to or upon any real or personal property, either of a public or private nature, for which no punishment is before provided, the offender shall, on conviction before a Justice, be committed to the Common Gaol or District Prison, or General Penitentiary, to be imprisoned only, or with hard labor not exceeding 2 months, or to forfeit and pay not exceeding £5, and also such further sum as shall appear to the Justice to be a reasonable compensation for the damage, injury or spoil so committed, not exceeding £5, which last sum in the case of private property shall be paid to the party aggrieved, and in the case of property of a public nature, or wherein any public right is concerned, the money shall be applied in the same manner as every penalty imposed by a Justice under this Act; and if such sums, with the costs if ordered, are not paid, either immediately after the conviction, or within such time as the Justice at the time of the conviction appoints,

Exceptions Acts under reasonable supposition of right; trespasses in fishing or pursuit of game

he may commit the offender to the Common Gaol or District Prison, to be imprisoned only, or with hard labor not exceeding 2 months, unless such sum and costs are sooner paid. Not to extend to any case where the party acted under a fair and reasonable supposition that he had a right to do the act complained of; nor to any trespass, not being wilful and malicious, committed in fishing, or in the pursuit of game, but every such trespass shall be punishable in the same manner as if this Act had not passed, 27 V., S. 1, c. 34, s. 43.

Extended to injuries to trees saplings, shrubs, and underwood for which no punishment is provided

The provisions in the last section shall extend to any person wilfully or maliciously committing any injury to any tree sapling, shrub or underwood, for which no punishment is before provided, 27 V., S. 1, c. 34, s. 44.

Principal in 2d degree and accessories

In the case of every felony punishable under this Act, every principal in the second degree, and every accessory before the fact, shall be punishable in the same manner as the principal in the first degree. Every accessory after the fact shall be imprisoned for not exceeding 2 years, with or without hard labor, and with or without solitary confinement. Every person aiding, abetting, counselling or procuring the commission of any Misdemeanor punishable under this Act, shall be liable to be proceeded against, indicted and punished as a principal offender, 27 V., S. 1, c 34, s. 45.

Persons loitering during the night may be taken in custody by constable without warrant on suspicion of felony

Any Constable or Peace Officer may take into custody without warrant, any person he finds lying or loitering in any Highway, yard or other place during the night, and whom he has good cause to suspect of having committed, or being about to commit any Felony against this Act, and take him as soon as reasonably may be before a Justice, to be dealt with according to law, 27 V., S. 1, c. 34, s. 46.

Immaterial whether the malice is against the owner or otherwise

Every punishment and forfeiture by this Act imposed on any person maliciously committing any offence, whether punishable upon Indictment or Summary Conviction, shall equally apply and been forced, whether it be from malice conceived against the owner of the property or otherwise, 27 V., S. 1, c. 34, s. 47.

Or that the offender were in possession of the property

Every provision of this Act not before so applied, shall apply to every person who, with intent to injure or defraud any other, does any of the Acts before made penal, although the offender be in the possession of the property against or in respect of which such act is done, 27 V., S. 1, c. 34, s. 48.

Allegation sufficient that the act was done with intent to injure or defraud, and not necessary to prove an intent to injure, &c.; any particular person

It shall be sufficient in any Indictment for any offence against this Act, where it is necessary to allege an intent to injure or defraud, to allege that the party accused did the act with intent to injure or defraud (as the case may be), without alleging an intent to injure or defraud any particular person; and on the trial, it shall not be necessary to prove an intent to injure or defraud any particular person, but it shall be sufficient to prove that the accused did the act charged, with an intent to injure or defraud (as the case may be), 27 V., S. 1, c. 34, s. 49.

Persons found committing any offence may be apprehended without warrant by any peace officer or the owner or his servant

Any person found committing any offence against this Act, whether punishable upon indictment or summary conviction, may be immediately apprehended without a warrant by any Peace Officer, or the owner of the property injured, or his servant, or any person authorized by him, and forthwith taken before some neighbouring Justice to be dealt with according to law, 27 V., S. 1, c, 34, s. 50.

Where any person is charged on the oath of a credible witness before a Justice, with any offence punishable on summary conviction under this Act, the Justice may summon him to appear at a time and place to be named, and if he does not appear, upon proof of service, by delivering the summons to him personally, or by leaving it at his usual place of abode, the Justice may either proceed to hear and determine the case ex parte, or issue his warrant for apprehending such person, and bringing him before himself or some other Justice, or the Justice before whom the charge is made, (may, without any previous summons) unless where otherwise specially directed) issue such warrant, and the Justice before whom the person charged appears or is brought, shall proceed to hear and determine the case, 27 V., S. 1, c. 34, s. 51.

Proceedings on summary convictions

Persons aiding, abetting, counselling or procuring the commision of any offence by this Act, punishable on summary conviction, either for every time of its commission, or for the first and second time only, or for the first time only, shall, on conviction before a Justice, be liable for every first, second or subsequent offence of aiding, &c., to the same forfeiture and punishment to which a person guilty of a first, second or subsequent offence as a principal offender is made liable, 27 V., S. 1, c. 34, s. 52.

Aiders and abettors of offences summarily punishable 1st, 2nd and subsequent offences of aiding

Every sum forfeited for the amount of any injury done shall be assessed in each case by the convicting Justice, and paid to the party aggrieved, except where he is unknown, in which case the sum shall be applied in the same manner as a penalty. Every sum imposed as a penalty by any Justice, whether in addition to such amount or otherwise, shall be paid and applied as other penalties recoverable before Justices where the statute imposing them contains no directions for payment to any person. Where several persons join in the commission of the same offence, and are upon conviction each adjudged to forfeit a sum equivalent to the amount of the injury done, no further sum shall be paid to the party aggrieved than such value or amount ; and the remaining sums forfeited, shall be applied in the same manner as any penalty imposed by a Justice is before directed to be applied, 21 V., S. 1, c. 34, s. 53.

Forfeitures for injuries ; assessment and application

Where several are adjudged to pay for forfeitures for injuries the party aggrieved to receive only one, the rest to be applied as penalty

In every case of a summary conviction under this Act, where the sum forfeited for the amount of the injury done or imposed as a penalty is not paid either immediately after the conviction or other such period as the Justice at the time of the conviction appoints, the convicting Justice (unless when otherwise specially directed), may commit the offender to the Common Goal or House of Correction, to be imprisoned only or kept to hard labor for not exceeding 2 months, where the amount of the sum forfeited, or of the penalty imposed, or of both (as the case may be), together with the costs, do not exceed £5 ; for not exceeding 4 months where the amount with costs do not exceed £10 ; and not exceeding 6 months in any other case. The commitment to be determinable in each case, upon payment of the amount and costs, 27 V. S. 1, c. 34, s. 54.

Enforcement of payment of forfeitures and penalties by commitment

Where not exceeding £5

Where not exceeding £10

Above £10

Where any person is summarily convicted before a Justice of any offence against this Act, and it is a first conviction, the Justice may discharge the offender from his conviction upon his making such satisfaction to the party aggrieved for damages and costs, or either, as shall be ascertained by the Justice, 27 V. S. 1, c. 34 s. 55.

Justice may discharge offender on payment of damages and costs upon 1st conviction

When any person convicted of any offence punishable by summary conviction under this Act, has paid the sum adjudged to be paid with costs under such conviction, or has received a remission thereof from the Crown, or has suffered the imprisonment awarded for non-payment, or the imprisonment in the first instance, or has been discharged from his conviction by any Justice he shall be released from all further or other proceedings for the same cause, 27 V. S. 1, c. 34 s. 56.

Persons summarily convicted when released from further proceedings

In all cases upon any summary conviction under this Act, any person thinking himself aggrieved, may appeal, 27 V., S. 1, c. 34, s. 57.

Appeal from summary conviction,

No such conviction or adjudication on appeal shall be quashed for want of form, or removed by Certiorari ; and no warrant of commitment shall be held void by reason of any defect, if it be therein alleged that the party has been convicted, and there is a valid conviction to sustain it, 27 V., S. 1, c. 34, s. 58.

Which are not to be quashed for want of form, nor any commitment avoided where there is a valid conviction

3 K

Protection from actions

All actions and prosecutions for anything done in pursuance of this Act, shall be laid and tried in the pari or precinct where the fact was committed, and commenced within 6 months after, and not otherwise. Notice in writing of such action, and of the cause, shall be given to the defendant one month at least before the commencement of the action. The defendant may plead the general issue, and give the special matter in evidence; and no plaintiff shall recover, if tender of sufficient amends is made before action is brought, or a sufficient sum paid into court after action by or on behalf of the defendant. If a verdict pass for the defendant or the plaintiff be nonsuit, or discontinue after issue joined, or if upon demurrer or otherwise, judgment is given against the plaintiff, the defendant shall recover full costs as between attorney and client, and have the like remedy for the same as any defendant in other cases, and though a verdict be given for the plaintiff, he shall not have costs against the defendant, unless the Judge before whom the trial is, certify his approbation of the action, 27 V., S. 1, c. 34, s. 59.

Offences committed within the jurisdiction of the Court of Vice Admiralty, how triable and punishable

All indictable offences in this Act committed within the jurisdiction of the Court of Vice Admiralty of this Island, shall be deemed offences of the same nature, and liable to the same punishment as if committed upon land in Jamaica, and may be dealt with, enquired of, tried, and determined in any parish or precinct in which the offender is apprehended or in custody, in the same manner as if the offence had been committed in that parish or precinct. In any indictment for any such offence, or being accessory to such an offence, the venue in the margin shall be the same as if the offence had been committed there, and the offence shall be averred to have been committed on the high seas; and any offender shall be liable and shall suffer such punishment or forfeiture, or penalty, as he would be subject to in case such offence had been committed, and was enquired of, and tried, and determined in England. Not to alter or affect any of the laws relating to the government of H. M.'s land and naval forces, 27 V., S. 1, c. 34, s. 60.

Not to affect the laws relating to land and naval forces

Fines and sureties to keep the peace in what cases

On conviction of any indictable Misdemeanor under this Act, the court may, in addition to, or in lieu of any of the punishments authorized, fine the offender, and require him to enter into his own recognizances, and to find sureties, both or either for keeping the peace, and being of good behaviour. In case of any Felony, the court may require the offender to enter into his own recognizances, and to find sureties, both or either, for keeping the peace, in addition to any punishment by this Act authorized. No person shall be imprisoned under this clause for not finding sureties exceeding one year, 27 V., S. 1, c. 34, s. 61.

Imprisonment on summary conviction without hard labor

With hard labor In Kingston, St. Andrew, and Port Royal and precinct of St. Catherine

When upon any summary conviction, imprisonment without hard labor is awarded, the imprisonment, may be either in the County Gaol or nearest District prison. Whenever hard labor is awarded, it shall be in the nearest District Prison. The Justices for Kingston, St. Andrew and Port-Royal and precinct of St. Catherine, may commit and sentence male offenders to the General Penitentiary, and females to the Female Penitentiary, as they are now authorized by law, 27 V., S. 1, c. 34, s. 62.

Solitary confinement

Whenever solitary confinement is awarded under this Act, the court may direct the offender to be kept in solitary confinement for any portions of his imprisonment, or imprisonment with hard labor not exceeding 1 month at any one time, nor 3 months in any 1 year, 27 V., S 1, c. 34, s. 63.

Costs of prosecution in misdemeanors

The court before which any indictable Misdemeanor against this Act is prosecuted or tried, may allow the costs of the prosecution as in cases of Felony; and the order for payment shall be made out, and the money paid and re-paid upon the same terms and in the same manner as in cases of Felony 27 V., S. 1, c. 34, s. 64.

Pardons to persons imprisoned may issue, although money be payable otherwise than to the crown

The Queen's representative may extend the Royal mercy to any person imprisoned, by virtue of this Act, although for non-payment of money to some person other than the Crown, 27 V., S. 1, c, 34, s. 65.

Mandamus, Prohibition, &c.

Persons claiming right may be called upon to show cause

Powers of Court over

See Interpleader

In any application for a Writ of Mandamus, Prohibition or otherwise, the Supreme Court may make rules and orders, calling not only the person to whom the Writ is required to issue, but all other persons having or claiming any right or interest in or to the matter of the Writ, to shew cause against the issuing and payment of the costs of application; and upon the appearance of such other person, or in default of appearance after service, may exercise all such powers, and make all such rules and orders applicable to the case as are given or mentioned in this Act, 7 V., c. 32, s. 8.

Markets.

44. Lands in Kingston heretofore purchased and used, and appointed for the sale of Fresh Meat, Fish, Vegetables, Provisions and Fruit, and the buildings thereon, shall be vested in the Mayor, Aldermen and Commonalty of the City and Parish of Kingston, and their successors. Lands and Buildings in other parishes where held absolutely in trust for any such parish, shall vest absolutely in the Churchwardens, and where held under lease, shall vest in the Churchwardens for the residue of the term of any existing lease as the assignees of the parties named as lessees, and all further purchases and leases shall be taken in the name of the Churchwardens of the parish of   (naming it), and actions and suits for breach of covenant or contract respecting, or for damage or injury to the market places or buildings or appurtenances, shall be brought by or against the Churchwardens, by such name, and the contracts alleged in such actions laid to have been made by or with them, and be supported by evidence of any valid contract entered into by or with the Justices and Vestry, or other person heretofore lawfully authorized to enter into the same on behalf of any parish. In all criminal or other proceedings, where it is required to allege property in such market-places, buildings or appurtenances, other than in Kingston, where they shall be alleged to be in the Mayor, Aldermen and Commonalty of the City and Parish of Kingston, they shall be stated to be in the Churchwardens of the parish of   The Churchwardens to whose hands any money shall come by virtue of this Act, shall be responsible to the Justices and Vestry; but no Churchwarden shall be personally liable to make good out of his own funds, any moneys recovered in any action or suit against the Churchwardens, 9 V., c. 38, s. 1.

Markets, Lands and Buildings in Kingston vested in the Corporation
In other parishes in the Churchwardens
Actions and suits
Allegation of property
Churchwardens not personally liable for moneys recovered against them

The Common Council of Kingston, and the Justices and Vestrymen of other parishes may purchase or lease land [with the sanction of the Executive Committee, see Vestry, 27 V., S. 1, c. 7,   ] for the erection or extension of markets, and uphold, repair, or improve the same, and make rules for their government, and for the maintenance of good order and cleanliness therein; and all existing rules shall continue in force until altered or varied, 9, V., c. 31, s. 2.

Extension and repair—Good order and cleanliness ; see 11 V., c. 30, s. 2

Subject to the right of appointing Clerks of the Markets in such parishes as H. M. is entitled to make, and its exercise, the Common Council and Justices and Vestry may appoint and remove Clerks of the Markets, and remunerate them by salary, 9 V., c, 38, s. 3.

Appointment and removal of Clerks

And may enter into arrangements with the Governor for the non-exercise of the power of appointment or with the patentee, subject to the Governor's approval, for the non-exercise of his office, except through their nominee, and subject to this Act, 9 V., c. 38, s. 4.

Patentees

And may fix and establish a reasonable Scale of Fees, to be payable at the Markets, by persons resorting thereto, and alter same; and until established those heretofore usually received shall be collected, 9 V., c. 38, s. 5.

Fees ; see 21 V., c. 12

The rents and fees shall be part of the general parochial funds, and the expenses, part of the parochial expenditure, 9 V.. c. 38, s 6.

Rents and fees and expenses part of parochial funds and expenditure

No fresh Meat, Fish. Vegetables, Provisions or Fruit, shall be sold in any City or Town, elsewhere than in the Market place during the hours it is kept open.   Selling, or exposing for sale any fresh Meat, &c., during such hours elsewhere than in the Market : Penalty not exceeding 40s. Not to prevent any person from going from house to house offering for sale or selling Fruit, Provisions or Vegetables during such hours, 9 V., c. 38, s. 7

Sales to be in market place while open
Fruit, Provisions, Vegetables
See as to Kingston, 27 V., S. 1, c. 10

Disobeying or infringing any rule, ordinance or regulation, now or to be made ; Penalty not exceeding £5, 9 V., c. 38, s. 8.

Disobeying Rules

Slaughtering or causing, &c., any Bull, Steer, Cow or other description of neat Cattle for beef or veal, or any Sheep. Lamb, Goat or Kid, or drying or exposing to be dried the skin of any neat Cattle, Sheep, &c., within any Town, other than in such places as the Common Council or Justices and Vestry appoint, or as have been heretofore usually allowed : Penalty not exceeding £5, 9 V., c. 38, s. 9.

Slaughtering cattle, &c. or drying skins in towns

Unwholesome meat, fish and provisions

The Clerks of the Markets shall seize, or cause, &c., any bad or unwholesome Meat, Fish or Provisions, brought into the Market or elsewhere for sale, and cause them and the parties in whose possession they are, and their employers to be brought before 2 Justices, who may direct the Meat, &c., to be destroyed and fine the offenders not exceeding 40s. each, 9 V., c, 38, s. 10.

Prosecutions Appropriation of penalties

Prosecutions shall be commenced within 3 calendar months before 2 Justices, and penalties enforced by distress and sale, or in default of goods, commitment not exceeding 1 calendar month; and all penalties paid in aid of the funds of the parish except such portion as the Justices award to persons informing, and upon whose evidence the conviction is made, 9 V., c. 38, s. 11.

Building, &c. markets other than as established by the Justices and Vestry, or selling therein

Fruit, Provisions or Vegetables from house to house

Building or establishing, or causing, &c., to be established, any Market for the sale of fresh Meat, Fish, Vegetables, Provisions or Fruit, or selling or disposing or permitting or causing to be sold or disposed of, or offering and exhibiting for sale in any such place in any City, Town or Parish, other than the regular Markets established by the Corporation of Kingston, or Justices and Vestry, and subject to the regulation and payment of the fees ordained by them: Penalty £5 for every day or portion of a day, during which the articles are sold or exposed, or offered for sale. Not to prevent any person from going from house to house offering for sale, or selling Fruit, Provisions or Vegetables, 10 V., c. 30, s. 1.

Imperative to Justices and Vestry to provide markets in parishes where there are none

It shall be imperative on the Justices and Vestries in parishes where no Markets are provided, to provide such Markets, establish regulations and ordain scales of fees: Penalty £5 on every Justice and Vestryman neglecting such duty, 10 V., c. 30, s. 2.

Sales, &c. on Piazza

Any person exposing or exhibiting for sale, or selling or permitting to be exposed for sale in or upon any piazza, verandah, wharf or entrance to a wharf, portico or other erection in front of the house or premises occupied by him or in his possession, or in any street in any City or Town, any fresh Meat, Fish, Vegetables, Provisions or Fruit, shall forfeit 10s., 10 V., c. 30, s. 3.

Penalties

Penalties shall be recovered and enforced as under 9 V., c. 38, s 11, 10 V., c. 30, s. 4.

Leases not exceeding 3 years

The Justices and Vestry and Common Council may rent or lease for not exceeding 3 years, as shall appear most advantageous, and for the most money that can be had, the Markets in their parishes, with the rights and appurtenances, and execute and deliver all necessary agreements, demises or leases, 21 V., c. 12, s. 1.

Justices and Vestry may lease suitable market premises

The Justices and Vestry of any parish where there is not any Market building or Premises, may lease suitable premises, 21 V., c. 12, s. 2.

Execution

The signatures of the Custos or presiding Justice, or the affixing, by order of the Mayor or a presiding Alderman at a meeting, the Seal of the Common Council to any agreement, demise or lease for renting or leasing to any person the Market and appurtenances, shall suffice to make it valid; but every agreement, &c., shall be signed or sealed, or directed to be sealed at a meeting of the Justices and Vestry or Common Council, summoned in the usual manner either for the special purpose or for transacting business generally, 21 V., c. 12, s. 3.

Form of lease

Such agreement, demise or lease, shall contain all necessary powers for the recovery of rent in arrear and re-entry, and all usual covenants on the part of a tenant or lessee, and as nearly as circumstances will permit in the form of words in the Schedules to 13 V., c. 22 (Leases) 21 V., c. 12, s. 4.

Description of Lessors

It shall be sufficient to describe the Justices and Vestry, or Common Council as the Justices and Vestry of the parish of (naming it), acting in pursuance of the Market Lease Act, 1857, or the Common Council of the City and Parish of Kingston, acting in pursuance of the Market Lease Act, 1857, 21 V., c. 12, s. 5.

Rent to be paid to the Receiver-General

The moneys to be reserved as rent shall when received be paid over to the Receiver-General for the use of the Government of this Island, 21 V., c. 12, s. 6.

Security

The Justices and Vestry or Common Council may require and take security by bond or otherwise, in such amount, and with such sureties as they think fit, and may from time to time require additional or new security from any person leasing or renting any Market, 21 V., c. 12, s. 7.

The Market Lease Act. 1857, 21 V., c. 12, s. 8. Short Title

As regards Kingston, so much of 9 V., c 38, s. 7 as relates to the sale of fresh Meat, Fish, Vegetables, Provisions or Fruit, elsewhere than the Market place during the hours it is kept open, is repealed, 27 V., S. 1, c. 10 s. 1. As regards Kingston, the prohibiting to sell elsewhere than in the market repealed

Any person desiring to establish a shop for sale of fresh Meat, Poultr, Game, fresh Fish, Vegetables, Provisions or Fruit in Kingston, shall notify his intention to the Clerk of the Common Council at least one month previous to a Quarterly Meeting of the Common Council, and state in writing the situation and intended purpose of such shop. No such shop shall contain more than fresh Meat or Poultry, and Game, or fresh Fish or Turtle and Shellfish or Vegetables, Provisions and Fruit, 27 V., S. 1, c. 10 s. 2. Notice by persons desiring to establish shop for sale of meat, &c.
Shop to contain nothing more

After such publication, the application shall be submitted at their next Quarterly Meeting, where they may direct the City Inspector to visit the premises, and examine and report to the Common Council, whether they are suitable for their intended purpose, and whether supplied with all the necessary requirements and appliances, so as to prevent the same becoming a nuisance to the neighourhood, 27 V., S. 1, c. 10 s. 3. Premises to be examined and reported upon by City Inspector

On the favorable report of the City Inspector, the Common Council shall grant permission to establish the shop; but the person shall be subject to the laws and ordinances regulating the Markets and to the inspection of the City Inspector and Clerk of the Markets, 27 V., S. 1, c. 10, s. 4. Common Council may give permission; conditions

In case of such shop becoming a nuisance to the neighbourhood, or of repeated infraction of the law or ordinance regulating Markets, or resistance to the constituted authorities, the Common Council may revoke such License, 27 V., S. 1, c. 10 s. 5. Revoke permission

Not to authorise any person to exhibit, &c., for sale any such articles in any Piazza, Verandah or Wharf, or other public place, so as to create obstruction or annoyance to inhabitants or passengers, 27 V., c. 10 s. 6. Not to authorise sales, &c. on piazzas

Before any person is entitled to open any shop for the purposes aforesaid, he shall take out a License from the Common Council, and pay such sum as they may determine according to a scale of fees to be fixed by them; the amount to be paid by the Collector of Dues and accounted for by him to the Receiver-General, as part of the parochial revenue, 27 V., S. 1, c. 10 s. 7. License to be taken from Common Council to open there fore

No Lessee shall be eligible to hold the other office of Clerk of the Markets at one and the same time for Kingston, 27 V., S. 1, c. 10 s. 8. No lessee to be also Clerk of the Markets for Kingston

Maroons.

Sale of the forfeited Trelawny town lands directed, with the exception of about 300 acres reserved for the use of the Troops, 36 G. 3, c. 33. 400 Acres Trelawney Town Land

These lands (400 acres) the Secretary at War was authorized to transfer to the Executive Committee for the benefit of the Island, 25 V., c. 4.

The Executive Committee, or any 2 of them, were authorized to make conveyances of the allotments of lands to Maroons, under the repealed Acts, 5 V., c. 49, 7 V., c, 34, 9. V, c. 27, and 13 V., c. 32, for which conveyances had not been made, 19 V., c. 25, s, 1. Conveyances by Executive Committee of lands allotted to Maroons

Form of conveyance, which is not to be valid without a diagram, annexed. Conveyance and diagram exempted from Stamps, 19 V., c. 25, s. 2. Form diagram stamps

In case of disputes between parties, the Executive Committee, or any 2 of them, were empowered to determine same, and convey the land to such one as they should think fit, 19 V., c. 25, s. 3. Executive Committee to determine disputes

The rights and privileges granted to the Maroons by repealed Acts, not affected in any way, 19 V., c. 25. s. 5. Privileges

Maroon Townships Land Allotment Act, 1856, 19 V., c. 25, s. 6. Short Title

---

FORM OF CONVEYANCE.

We, the undersigned being   of the Executive Committee, appointed to grant and convey lands to Maroons for the parish of   do hereby grant and convey unto   his heirs and assigns, all and every the lands consisting of   acres, mentioned, comprised and delineated in the plat or diagram thereof, hereunto annexed, to hold such lands, with their and every of their rights, members and appurtenances, unto and to the use of the said his heirs and assigns for ever. In witness whereof, we have hereunto set and affixed our hands and seals, this   day of one thousand eight hundred and

Marriage.

Revocation of will

The revocation of a previous Will, 3 V., c. 51, s. 13, (see Wills).

No suit to compel marriage

No suit or proceeding shall be had to compel the celebration of any Marriage, by reason of any promise or marriage contract entered into, or of seduction or any other cause ; but not to prevent the recovery of damages for breach of promise of marriage, or seduction, or other cause, 4 V., c. 44, s. 8.

Marriages de Facto.

Provisions for legitimising issue by subsequent marriage of their parents, and declarations between 11 April, 1840, and 22 December 1841

Many Marriages de facto having taken place, but which have never been sanctioned by any public ceremony, or formally registered ; and in many cases the parties having had offspring of such Marriages ; and it being expedient that provision should be made for enabling such persons to confer upon their children the benefit of children born in lawful wedlock, persons having so contracted Marriage, were empowered at any time within 12 months after the passing of this Act (22nd December, 1840) duly to solemnize the marriage ceremony before any Clergyman of the established Church, or in any other manner authorized (see Dissenters' Marriages), and make the declaration attested by the witnesses present, and signed by the Minister, in the form prescribed ; which ceremony should have relation back to the time of the Marriage de facto ; and all their children shall be

Certificates and declarations in duplicate

deemed to have been born in holy wedlock, and enjoy all the rights, privileges and advantages of persons born in lawful wedlock ; to p   e evidence whereof, duplicate original declarations were required, before the parties departed, to be made, signed and attested, to be appended to and kept with the original and duplicate original registers, and for all purposes of evidence deemed part thereof ; and such ceremony was allowed to be performed without Banns or License. Not to defeat any grant previously made by the Crown, 4 V., c. 44, s. 20.

Duplicates to be recorded in Secretary's Office

The Duplicate certificates of de facto Marriages and declaration were authorized to be registered, by parties interested in legitimising their issue, in the Secretary's Office, 4 V., c. 44, s. 21.

As also under previous Act, 3 V., c. 67, s. 17

Provision is also made for recording Duplicate certificates and registration under a similar provision in the the repealed Act, 3 V., c. 67, s. 17 passed 11th April, 1840,* 4 V., c. 44, s. 22.

Martial Law.

Arrests ne exeat insula may be executed

Notwithstanding Martial Law any action or writ of arrest at law, or writ of exeat insula or like process in equity may be sued forth and executed for enforcing payment or securing the debtor, as if Martial Law were not in force : provided it is shown on oath in writing, in addition to the usual affidavit for grounding the action, writ or process, that the defendant is about to depart the Island upon the knowledge, credible information or belief of the deponent ; or in case the debtor actually departs this Island, or is ab

Also Foreign Attachments

sent during Martial Law, writs of foreign attachments may issue against his moneys, goods and chattels in whosoever hands they be or are supposed to be, 11 V., c. 7, s. 1.

Judges, Justices in criminal cases

Coroners

The Chief Justice and Judges of the Supreme Court and Justices of the Peace shall act in all criminal matters, by committing or bailing offenders or binding over parties or witnesses to prosecute ; and Coroners shall execute their office notwithstanding Martial Law, 11 V., c. 7, s. 2.

---

* Provision was thus made for legitimising issue by subsequent Marriages between 11th April, 1840, and 22nd December 1841.

The Judges, Justices, Provost Marshal and Deputies, and Constables may act in cases of forcible entry, and detainer, in signing writs of restitution and possession and in the execution of writs, warrants and other process, 11 V., c. 7 s. 3. **Forcible entry and detainer.**

Landlords may distrain for rent upon giving security. to the amount o the goods distrained on, before a Justice, to make restitution upon a re plevin, thereafter to be brought for the goods, in case judgment is given against them, 11 V., c. 7, s. 4. **Distress for rent Landlord to give security**

Justices and Vestry, Churchwardens, Surveyors of Highways, or Waywardens, shall proceed to the discharge of their duties and the several Constables may collect, levy and distrain for taxes, and shall incur penalties for neglect of duty, 11 V., c. 7, s. 5. **Justices and Vestry, Churchwardens, Waywardens, Collectors of Taxes**

Constables distraining shall give security to the amount of the goods distrained on, before a Justice, to make restitution upon any replevin to be brought in case judgment is given against them, 11 V., c. 7 s. 6. **Security from Collectors**

In force until 31st December, 1857, 11 V., c. 7, s. 7.

Continued until 31st December, 1867, 21 V., c. 20, s. 1.

The Judges may act within their circuits, as the Justices of Assize were, by 11 V., c. 7, empowered to act, 21 V., c. 20, s. 2. **Circuit Court Judges**

Masters in Chancery.

The Vice-Chancellor may, from time to time, make or alter such rules or regulations as he may see fit, for the due, efficient, economical and speedy discharge of the business in the office of the Master. Copies to be laid before the Legislature within 21 days after the opening of the Session after which they are made, 27 V., S. 2, c. 3, s. 6. **Vice Chancellor to make rules for discharge of business.**

In making up their report they shall not embody nor repeat the claims and vouchers lodged with them in their reports, but shall make a schedule of claims propounded before them, distinguishing such sums as are admitted to proof and established, from those which have been disallowed, numbering them consecutively, and referring by a distinguishing number to the proofs and vouchers in their office in support of their report, 28 V., c. 36 s. 8. **Claims and vouchers not to be embodied in reports** **Reference to vouchers**

The practice of issuing several consecutive notices for one and the same act is abolished; and but one peremptory notice for each act shall be allowed in taxation, 28 V., c. 36, s. 9. **One peremptory notice**

As soon as a Master leaves the Island, either party may, by a side bar rule, transfer the cause to the Master next in rotation; and before quitting the Island, each Master shall deposit with the Registrar the papers and documents in all suits referred to and pending before him, 28 V., c. 36; s. 10. **Transfer of causes** **Papers and documents to be deposited with Registrar**

As vacancies occur they shall not be filled up, nor new appointments made, but the duties shall be confined to existing Masters and the survivor; and on their total extinction, the duties theretofore discharged by the Masters shall be performed by the Registrar, who shall be entitled to be remunerated for such extra duties according to the allowance to be from time to time ordered by the court, according to the nature and quality of the services rendered; and the court may direct the employment of accountants, engineers, actuaries or other scientific persons to facilitate the enquiries and references, and act upon their certificates, and make and order such allowance and remuneration as seems just, 28 V., c. 36, s. 11. **Vacancies** **Duties ultimately to be transferred to Registrar** **Scientific persons**

The fee of the Master and Masters extraordinary for taking an affidavit shall be in all cases 1s, irrespective of the classification of the suit; and in parishes where there is not to be found a Master to discharge the ministerial functions of such office, they may be discharged by any Justice of the Peace, 28 V., c. 36, s. 12. **Fee for taking affidavits** **Justice of the Peace may discharge ministerial functions**

Medical Practitioners.

Whenever any legally qualified Medical Practitioner in that capacity attends any Court, or before a bench of Magistrates, to give evidence on behalf of the Crown in any public prosecution or investigation, in obedience to a subpœna or summons issued by the Clerk of the Crown or Peace, the Court may order him, for his attendance, to be paid the fee provided in Schedule A., 13 V., c. 21, s. 1. **Fees for attendance in courts or before Justices as witnesses**

The orders of the Court shall be forthwith made out and drawn upon the Receiver-General, and delivered by the Clerk of the Court to the Medical Practitioner ; those of a Court of Petty Sessions or bench of Magistrates shall be drawn by the Clerk of the Peace or Clerk of the Magistrates, and countersigned by the Clerk of the Vestry or Common Council on the Treasurers of the Parishes. Such orders shall be paid on presentation forthwith to the Medical witness or person authorized to receive the same on his behalf, 13 V., c. 21, s. 2.

Before Coroners

Those attending Coroner's Inquests to give evidence as witnesses or to give evidence and perform a post-mortem examination in obedience to an order or summons from a Coroner, shall be entitled to receive the remuneration or fee in Schedule B, under the Coroner's order on the Receiver. General, to be forthwith paid on presentation, but not for any post-mortem examination, without the previous directions of the Jury, 13 V.c., 21, s. 3.

A., s. 1

SCHEDULES.

	£	s.	d.
Attending to give Professional evidence at Assizes...	2	2	0
For every Mile from his place of Residence to the Court House....	0	1	6
Every day he is in attendance to give evidence	1	1	0
Attending to give Professional evidence before the Magistrates	1	1	0

B., s. 3

	£	s.	d.
Attending to give Professional evidence at any Coroner's Inquest, whereat no post-mortem examination is made by such Practitioner..	1	1	0
For every Mile he is obliged to travel from the place where he is summoned, to that where the Inquest is held	0	1	6
Making post-mortem examination of the body of the Deceased, with or without an analysis of the contents of the stomach or intestines, and for attending to give evidence, the additional fee of	2	2	0

To be elected Coroners ; see Coroner

They are entitled to be elected Coroners if they offer themselves as candidates. 19 V., c. 17.

Registry Office

The Island Secretary shall be the Registrar, and the office of enrolments the Registry Office of duly qualified Medical men, 23 V., S. 1. c. 17, s. 1.

Form of Register

Form of Register, Schedule A, to be kept by him, 23 V., S. 1, c 17, s. 2.

Persons entitled to be registered

Any person who, prior to this Act, was actually practising Medicine and Surgery, or Medicine or Surgery, and was hitherto registered as a duly qualified Medical Practitioner, Licentiate, or extra-Licentiate under any Act, or being a Licentiate or extra-Licentiate of any College under any Act of this Island, or being a Fellow, Licentiate, or extra-Licentiate of any College or Faculty of Physicians or Surgeons, or Society of Apothecaries of the United Kingdom, of any College, Faculty or Society elsewhere, being recognized as such by the General Council of Medical Education and Registration of the United Kingdom, under the Imperial Act, 21 and 22 Vict., (c. 90) cited as the Medical Act, who was actually practising Medicine and Surgery, or Medicine or Surgery prior to this Act, whether hitherto registered or not, shall on production to the Registrar, of a declaration made before a Justice (Form B if hitherto registered, Form C if not) declared to and signed by him, and impressed with a 10s. stamp if already registered, or 20s. if not, be entitled to be registered under this Act as a duly qualified Medical Practitioner, 23 V., S. 1, c. 17, s. 3.

Where not already practising

Any Fellow, Licentiate, or extra-Licentiate, &c., as in the preceding clause described, who shall not have been actually practising, but shall desire to do so, shall on production to the Registrar, of a declaration before a Justice (Form C) declared to, and signed by him, and impressed with a 20s. stamp, be entitled to be registered under this Act, 23 V., S. 1, c. 17, s. 4.

Any person not a Fellow, Licentiate, or extra Licentiate recognized as aforesaid, who has practised prior to this Act, desiring to practice shall, on production by him to the Registrar of a certificate of examination (Form D,) signed by the Members of the Board of examination, and countersigned by the Secretary and impressed with a stamp of £11 11s. be entitled to be registered, 23 V., S. 1, c. 17, s. 5. After examination

Any person wilfully making a false declaration shall be deemed to have committed perjury and be punishable accordingly, 23 V., S. 1, c. 17, s. 6. False declaration

Whenever any Fellow, Member, Licentiate or extra Licentiate of any College, or Faculty of Physicians and Surgeons, or Society of Apothecaries of any College, Faculty or Society, elsewhere than in the United Kingdom, who shall not have been actually practising in this Island prior to 23 V., c. 17, desires to p a ti e Medicine and Surgery, or Medicine or Surgery, and possesses and produces such Diplomas, Certificates and Testimonials as the Board of Examiners consider a sufficient guuarantee for, and passes an examination before, and obtains a certificate from them that he has produced satisfactory Diplomas, &c., and is qualified to practise Medicine and Surgery, or Medicine or Surgery in this Island, such person upon producing to the Registrar a declaration to be made before a Justice, according to Form C, 23 V., c. 17, declared to and signed by him, and impressed with 11 Guineas Stamps, shall be entitled to be registered, and practise as a duly qualified Medical Practitioner, 26 V., S. 2, c. 23, s. 1. Admission after examination of Members of Colleges, &c. not of the United Kingdom Stamped declaration

Before the meeting of the Board, the person about to present himself for examination, shall pay to the Secretary all charges incidental to the meeting, 26 V., S. 2, c. 23, s. 2. Expenses of Board

The certificate shall be the following effect :— Certificate
This is to certify, that   of the parish of
                      on application made by him to us, was on
the   day of   last, examined by us touching his
qualification to practice as a Medical Practitioner; and that at such
examination, he produced before us satisfactory and sufficient Diploma, Certificate or Testimonials, and that having been first duly examined by us, he satisfied us that he is a fit and proper person, and qualified to practice Medicine and Surgery, (or Medicine or Surgery) and that he may be registered under the authority of the " Medical Act, 1859."

To be signed by the Members of the Board, or any 2 of them, and countersigned by the Secretary, 26 V., S. 2, c. 23, s. 4.

To the Registrar under the Medical Act, 1859.

The Registrar, on 1st July and 1st January in every year, or as soon after as practicable, shall cause to be published in "The Jamaica Gazette" an Alphabetical List signed by him, of the several Medical men on the Register, with their places of abode, and Medical title. Fee, 40s., to be paid by Governor's Warrant, 23 V., S. 1, c. 17, s. 7. Lists to be published in the Gazette

A copy of the Gazette shall be evidence of the registration of the persons named therein, 23 V., S. 1, c. 17, s. 8. Gazette evidence

If the name has not been published in the ' Gazette,' a certified copy, under the hand of the Registrar, of the entry of the name of the person in the Register, shall be evidence thereof, 23 V., S. 1, c. 17, s. 9. If name not published, Registrar's Certificate sufficient

Upon the death of any Practitioner upon the Register becoming known to the Registrar, he shall draw a line through, and write " dead" opposite the name, 23 V., S. 1, c. 17, s. 10. To be struck out on death

Any person after registration obtaining a higher degree, or other qualification, shall be entitled to have the same inserted in the Register, in substitution for, or in addition to that previously registered. Fee 10s. to the Registrar, 23 V., S. 1, c. 17, s. 11. Higher degrees to be inserted in register

Every person registered under 23 V., c. 17, or the Imperial Act, 21 & 22 V., c. 90 (the Medical Act), shall be entitled to practice in any part of the Island, and to demand and recover with full costs, reasonable charges for professional advice and visits, and the costs of any Medicine, or Medical or Surgical operations or appliances performed, given, paid or supplied by him to his patients, 23 V., S. 2, c. 1, s. 2. Persons registered entitled to practise and maintain actions

No person shall be entitled to recover any charge, unless he proves at the trial of any issue, or on the assessment of damages in any action by default, or after judgment by demurrer, that he is registered under the Island or Imperial Act, 23 V., S. 2, c. 1, s. 3. But not otherwise to recover any charge

Medical Officers of the army and navy on full pay Medical Officers of the Army and Navy serving in the Colony on full pay, shall be deemed registered under 23 V., S. 1, c. 17 ; 23 V., S. 2, c. 1, s. 4.

"Qualified Medical Practitioner" in previous Acts The words "legally qualified Medical Practitioner," or "duly qualified Medical Practitioner," or any words importing a person recognized by law as a Medical Practitioner or Member of the Medical Profession, when used in any Act now or to be in force, shall be construed to mean a person registered under this Act, 23 V., S. 1, c. 17, s. 14.

Registered Practitioners exempt from serving on juries or parochial offices Every person registered shall be exempt, if he so desires, from serving in the Militia, except in a medical capacity, and on Juries and Inquests, or Corporate and Parochial offices, 23 V., S. 1, c. 17, s. 15.

Alone qualified to hold medical appointments No person shall be elected or appointed to any situation or office, public or parochial, of Coroner, Physician, Surgeon, Medical Officer or Attendant, or as Physician, &c., to any Friendly or other Society for affording relief in sickness, infirmity or old age, or any Life Insurance Company, unless registered ; and the appointment of any person not so registered shall be void, 23 V., S. 1, c. 17, s. 16.

Or give certificates Nor shall any Medical Certificate be valid, unless the person signing is registered, 23 V., S. 1, c. 17, s. 17.

False entries in register If the Registrar wilfully makes, or causes or permits to be made, any false or incorrect entry in any Register, or any alteration in any entry in any Register whereby it shall be falsified : Misdemeanor, imprisonment in any Prison not a County Gaol, not exceeding 12 months, 23 V., S. 1, c. 17, s. 18.

Attempting to procure registration fraudulently, &c. Any person wilfully procuring or attempting to procure himself to be registered under this Act, by making or producing, or causing or procuring to be made or produced any false or fraudulent representation or declaration, either orally or in writing, or by any false or fraudulent Diploma, License, Certificate or other Document, or wilfully and falsely personating any other person, and persons aiding and assisting in so doing : Misdemeanor, imprisonment in any Prison not a County Gaol, not exceeding 12 months, 23 V., S. 1, c. 17, s. 19.

Every person guilty of the following offences, on conviction before 2 Justices, shall forfeit not exceeding £20, or be committed not exceeding 6 calendar months :—

Assuming the name or title of a Medical Practitioner 1. Wilfully and falsely pretending to be, or taking or using the name or title of Physician, Doctor of Medicine, Surgeon, Licentiate, or any other name, title, addition or description, implying that he is registered under either of the recited Acts, or that he is recognized as in the 3rd section of 23 V., S. 1, c. 17, as a Physician, &c., or in any other name, title or designation required by that Act.

Taking any fee, &c. not being registered 2. Not being registered under either of the recited Acts, demanding, taking or receiving any fee or reward from any other person for the performance of any service in any of the said characters or capacities, 23 V., S. 2, c. 1, s. 5.

Appropriation of penalty One moiety of the penalty to be paid to the informer or prosecutor, who shall be a competent witness in support of the prosecution, 23 V., S. 2, c. 1, s. 6.

Board of Examiners The Governor may appoint 5 Medical practitioners (willing to undertake the duty) to form a Board of Medical Examiners (3 a quorum,) for the examination of any person who makes application with a view of being registered, who shall continue in office for 3 years, and no longer, unless reappointed ; and the Governor may fill up vacancies, 23 V., S. 1, c. 1, s. 21.

They may make rules The Board shall elect a Chairman and Secretary, and make regulations as to the place and time of meetings, and for their guidance generally, and for the direction of persons desiring to come before them for examination previous to registration, and may rescind or alter, and make new rules. All such rules to be transmitted to the Governor and Privy Council, and when approved of by them, they shall be binding upon the Board and all other persons, 23 V., S. 1, c. 17 s. 22.

Books—Fees for recording at public expense The Executive Committee shall procure at the public expense when necessary, such books as they consider proper for registering the names and other particulars of Medical Practitioners, and pay the Registrar for recording any Diploma, License or Certificate, or other document required to be recorded in the Registry Office, at 1s. 6d. per 160 words, 23 V., S. 1, c. 17, s. 23.

Each Member of the Board who attends at any meeting for any examination, shall be entitled to be paid under the Governor's warrant 2 guineas on each attendance : and the Secretary shall be paid in addition to the said sum of 2 guineas, 1 guinea for each meeting, to cover the cost of transcribing the Minutes of the Meeting into a proper book, to be furnished by the Executive Committee at the public expense, and of stationery and postages, 23 V., S. 1, c. 17, s. 24.

No appointment to be a Member of the Board shall be construed as an appointment to, or acceptance of an office of emolument within 4 V., c. 19, or 17 V., c. 29, or any other Act, or otherwise, 23 V., S. 2, c. 1, s. 8.

All penalties under this Act shall be recovered before 2 Justices at the instance of any person, 23 V., S. 1, c. 17, s. 25.

The Medical Act, 1859, 23 V., S. 1, c. 17, s. 26.

Except so far as repealed or altered, 23 V., S. 1, c. 17 shall be incorporated with, and read as part of this Act, 23 V., S. 2, c. 1, s. 7.

Margin notes:
- Discovery of penalties.
- Fees, Examiners, &c.
- Appointment of Examiner not to be deemed one of emolument
- Penalties, 23 V. S. 1, c. 17
- Short Title

SCHEDULE TO 23 V., S. 1, c. 17.

Register of Medical Men, A, s. 2

Date of Record.	Name.	Residence.	Diploma, License, Certificate, or other Qualification.	Date of such Diploma, License, other Qualification.	Remarks.

I, A. B., residing in the parish of   in the county of   do hereby declare that I was duly registered according to law on the   day of   and that I am the person whose name appears on the register under the Act, hitherto passed for the registration of duly qualified Medical Practitioners in this Island, and that I was practising Medicine and Surgery (or Medicine or Surgery) in this Island previous to the passing of the Medical Act, 1859.

Margin note: Declaration of person already registered, B, s. 3

(Signed)   A. B.

Declared to before me, this   day of   in the year

C. D., j. p.

I, A. B., residing in the parish of   in the county of   do hereby declare that I am a member of   (here state the College, Faculty, or Society, and was authorized by such College, Faculty or Society) on the   day of   in the year 18   as appears by my Diploma (or License or other document) to practice Medicine and Surgery (or Medicine or Surgery), and that I was practising Medicine and Surgery (or Medicine or Surgery) in the

Margin note: Declaration of person claiming to be registered, C, s. 4 ; see 26 V., S. 2, c. 23, s. 1

Medical Of
of the
navy

parish of   in this Island previous to the passing of the Medical Act, 1859.

Declared before me, this   day of   in the year
    (Signed)   A. B.
    C. D., j. p.

Note—In the case of those who did not practice in this Island previous to the passing of the Act, the words " and that I was not practising Medicine and Surgery, or Medicine or Surgery in the parish of   in this Island previous to the passing of the Medical Act, 1859.

Certificate of
Board of Medical
Examiners, D, .s. 5

This is to certify that   of the parish of   on application made by him to us, was on the   day of   last (or instant) examined by us touching his qualification to practise as a Medical Practitioner, and that at such examination, he satisfied us that he was a fit and proper person, and qualified to practise Medicine and Surgery (or Medicine or Surgery); and that he may be registered under the authority of the Medical Act, 1859.

To be signed by the Members of the Board, or any 2 of them, and countersigned by Secretary.

To the Registrar under the Medical Act, 1859.

Merchant Shipping.

Courts of Enquiry

Purpose

When complaint is made by any owner or other person interested in a British ship or her cargo, or by the consignee in this Island of such ship or cargo, or by the master, mate, or one-third of the crew to the Governor that such ship is lost, abandoned or materially damaged on or near the coast of this Island, or such ship has caused loss or material damage to, or suffered such loss or damage from any other such ship on or near such coast, or by reason of any casualty happening to or on board of any such ship, on or near such coast, loss of life has ensued, or any such loss, damage, abandonment or casualty happened elsewhere, and the captain or mate of

Constitution

the ship alleged to be in fault is in this Island, the Governor may appoint a Court of Enquiry, to consist of not less than 3 persons, nor more than 5, one to be a Naval Officer not under the rank of Lieutenant, and to be nominated by the Commodore or Naval Officer of highest rank then in the Island and on active service ; and such officer so nominated, if he be appointed, shall be President of the Court. The Court shall also comprise one master of a British merchant ship, and one merchant. No consignee or owner shall sit on any enquiry respecting the ship of which he is such consignee or owner, in whole or in part, 27 V., S. 1, c. 18, s. 1.

Notice of complaint

Inquiry

The Court or President shall give reasonable notice to the persons complained against, of the time and place of holding such Court, and at such time and place, proceed to enquire into the allegations of such complaint, and if necessary, may from time to time adjourn such enquiry as to the Court may seem fit ; and after full enquiry, shall make a report to the Governor, for his confirmation or disapproval, 27 V., S. 1, c. 18, s. 2.

Witnesses

The Court may, by summons under the hand of the President, require the attendance of all persons it thinks fit to examine for the purpose of such enquiry and report, and administer oaths to witnesses; and instead of administering an oath, require any witness to make and subscribe a declaration of the truth of the statements made in his examination, 27 V., S. 1, c. 18, s. 3.

Production of books, &c,

The Court may also require and enforce the production of all books, papers or documents it may consider important for its purposes, 27 V., S. 1, c. 18, s. 4.

Expenses

The expenses of witnesses summoned for and attending at any such Court of Enquiry, and also £2 per diem during the sitting of the Court to each member, shall be paid by the Receiver-General, under an order from the President, on the warrant of the Governor, out of the funds raised by Tonnage Duties upon shipping. Witnesses' expenses shall be calculated according to the scale authorized by the Supreme Court, 27 V., S. 1, c. 18, s. 5.

Disobedience of orders

Wilful disobedience or neglect of any lawful order of the Court of Enquiry, or its President, shall subject the offender to a penalty of not more than £5, nor less than £1, 27 V., S. 1, c. 18, s. 6.

. All penalties shall be recoverable before 2 Justices of the Parish in which the contumacy occurred, or the penalties accrued, and shall be paid over to the Receiver-General to the credit of the Tonnage Dues Account, 27 V., S. 1, c. 18, s. 7. Discovery of penalties

Any wilfully false and material oath or declaration shall subject the witness to the penalties of perjury, 27 V., S. 1, c. 18, s. 8. False swearing

Metals, Old.

No person, under a penalty not exceeding £30, shall deal in the purchase and sale, or barter and exchange of any manufactured Iron, Copper, Lead, Brass or other Metallic substance, which may have been already in use, without having been first licensed by the Justices of the parish, 19 V., c. 32, s. 1. Dealers to be licensed

Such License shall be granted, upon the application, in writing, of the person requiring it by the Justices in Special Session, upon their approval of the person, who shall pay therefor to the Collector or District Collector, to be remitted to the Receiver General within 14 days after receipt, £12, and which, unless forfeited, shall continue in force for 1 year, or until 5th April of the next year, 19 V., c. 32, s. 2. Annual license
Tax

At the Special Sessions for granting Spirit Licenses, the applications for Licenses to deal in such Metals or other Metallic substances shall be also disposed of, and from time to time as may be required, the Custos or Senior Magistrate shall convene a Special Sessions to dispose of applications, 19 V., c. 32, s. 3. Special Sessions

Within 10 days after approval of the applicant, the License shall be taken out of the Clerk of the Peace's Office, or in default, the applicant's right to take out the same, or any other License during the current year, shall be forfeited. Clerk of the Peace's fee for same, and all Duties connected therewith, 5s. A list of Licenses shall be publicly exhibited in a conspicuous place in his office by each Clerk of the Peace at the time each License is granted, and a list of every person licensed, within 10 days after its issue, forwarded to the Receiver-General, 19 V., c. 32, s. 4. When to be taken out

Clerk of the Peace's fee

The Collector's receipt for the License Tax of £12, shall be lodged with the Clerk of the Peace before the issue of a License, 19 V., c. 32, s. 5. Lists of licenses

No person shall in any way deal in or trade or traffic, with reference to any Metal, &c., except between 7, a. m. and 6, p. m. of every day of the week other than Sunday, nor otherwise than in his usual place of business, 19 V., c. 32, s. 6. Receipt for license tax to be lodged

Every person selling, bartering or exchanging, or in any way disposing of any Metal or Metallic substance, shall give therewith a bill of parcels, describing his name, residence, description and title to, and the weight and description, price or consideration, use to which it had been heretofore applied, and the place or person from which or whom it had been obtained or severed. No dealer shall take or receive any Metal, &c., without such bill of parcels, which he must keep and produce, on the order of a Justice, or when otherwise called upon in due course of law, 19 V., c. 32, s. 7. Bills of parcels

Every Dealer shall keep a book wherein to enter daily at the time, in separate columns, the particulars as above of each purchase, which facts shall be vouched for by the declaration (Form Schedule) of the person claiming title to dispose of the same before a Justice, and shall be numbered and filed for reference by the dealer receiving same, and referred to by its number in the book opposite to its entry. A false declaration shall involve the persons making or procuring same to the penalties of perjury or subornation; and notwithstanding the form prescribed by 6 V., c. 24 (see oaths), may not be followed, the declaration professed to be taken hereunder shall be held to be taken by virtue of that Act, 19 V., c. 32, s. 8. Books

Notwithstanding the production of the declaration, it shall be the duty of any Dealer to detain articles offered for sale or otherwise, under circumstances raising or warranting a suspicion that they have been improperly obtained, and to deliver them to a Justice or policeman, in order that the party may establish his claim, or be proceeded against for his wrongful possession, 19 V., c. 32, s. 9. Detention of articles offered for sale

Opposite to each entry in the book, there shall be left a blank column or space, in which shall be entered immediately as it takes place, the disposal of each particular article, 19 V., c. 32, s. 10. Entry of disposal

Books and metals to be open to inspection

Such book shall be kept in the dealer's shop, open to the inspection of any Justice or policeman, under the order of a Justice ; and the dealer shall, whenever required, exhibit his book, and the Metals in his possession, to the inspection of the Justice or policeman producing such order, and they may be accompanied by any person required to identify any articles supposed to be in the dealer's possession, 19 V., c. 32, s. 11.

Sign Board

Every dealer shall, within one week after being licensed, put up exposed to public view, a board in the front of his house or shop, over the door towards the public street, lane or road, with his name in full, and the words " Licensed to deal in Metals," in white letters, of not less than 2 inches in size, on a black ground, 19, V., c. 32, s. 12.

Penalties on dealers, &c.

Every person purchasing or selling, or bartering or exchanging, or otherwise dealing in any Metallic substance, convicted of any default in, or neglect, violation or breach of any of the provisions of this Act, shall be liable to a penalty not exceeding £30, to be levied on his goods, and in default of payment to be imprisoned with or without hard labor, not exceeding 3 calendar months, which imprisonment may be awarded in the warrant of distress or by a separate commitment, and put in force in default of full satisfaction by means of a levy, or until the fine or balance is paid ; and the dealer's License shall be forfeited, and the party convicted, whether licensed or not, incapable of being after licensed

On Clerks of the peace and Collector

Clerks of the Peace liable to penalties for default, &c., not exceeding £5 ; Collectors of Taxes not exceeding £20, to be levied, in default of payment, by warrant of distress, Such penalties shall inure, one moiety to the use of the parish, and the other to the informer, who shall be competent to give evidence, 19 V., c. 32, s. 13.

Declarations, &c on shipments

Prior to the shipment of any Metals, &c., from one port to another, or from the Island, the shipper, if a dealer in Metals, shall produce at the Custom House at or nearest the place of shipment, his License, and the bill of parcels, book of entry and declaration, and lodge at the Custom House copies thereof. If the shipper be in possession of an Estate or Plantation, or other place wherefrom the Metal, &c., was severed or taken, he shall lodge a declaration, taken before a Justice, that he is in possession or charge of the Estate, &c., (Form Schedule C.) If the shipper purchased from the person in possession of the Estate, he shall obtain from him the declaration required, with the following words added thereto : " And that the said articles of Metal were by me sold to C. D. of the parish of   on the   day of   18 ." And the shipper shall declare on the back thereof, that the articles of Metal therein mentioned are the same which have been entered for shipment by him, which declaration so endorsed he shall lodge at the Custom House previous to clearance. Making or procuring a false declaration to such effect shall be punishable as perjury or subornation, notwithstanding the form of declaration may not be the form prescribed by 6 V., c. 24 (see oaths), 19 V., c. 32, s. 14.

Forgery false entries, &c

Forgery of, or causing to be forged or counterfeited, any bill of parcels, book, declaration or certificate, or wilfully giving or causing, &c., any false bill of parcels, or keeping or causing, &c., any false book, or making, &c., any false statement or entry in, or copy or extract of or from any bill of parcels or book, or withholding, &c., any entries from, or wilfully altering or falsifying, &c., any bill of parcels, book, copy or extract from, or entry in any particular or respect, the person, his aiders and abettors, may be indicted for a Misdemeanor, and imprisoned in the General Penitentiary with hard labor, not exceeding one year, or in the discretion of two Justices before whom he is brought, he may be proceeded against as for a violation of the provisions of this Act, and be punishable as herein provided, 19 V., c. 32, s. 15.

To what Act is inapplicable

This Act shall not apply to the purchase or barter of Quicksilver, or to Metals in ore or unsmelted, nor to sales or purchases at public Auction, nor sales or purchases effected of estate's Machinery, nor old or other Metals by or from the Proprietors thereof, or their Agents lawfully empowered, except in respect to any shipment of any Metal or Metallic substances as herein provided, 19 V., c. 32, s. 16.

Short Title

Sale and Barter of Metals' Act, 1856, 19 V., c. 32, s. 17.

SCHEDULE.

JAMAICA, ss.

License

At a Special Sessions of the Peace in and for the Parish or Precinct of on the day of A. B., of having been approved of as a fit and proper person to be licensed to deal in old Metals and Metallic substances, the said A. B., is hereby licensed to deal in the purchase and sale, barter and exchange of old Metal and Metallic substances, under the 19 Victoria, chapter 32, in the (Shop) situate at No. in the said Parish from the date hereof, up to and until the 5th day of April in the year 18

Dated ·

C. P., Clerk of the Peace.

———

JAMAICA, ss.

Parish

Declaration, s. 8

I A. B., of do declare that an (old brass cock) measuring in length (describing the article specifically and fully), and weighing · ounces avordupois, is my property, and was by me purchased or imported when new (or otherwise according to the fact) from of, &c., on or about the 18 and has been by me ever since used as (state use to which applied, and place where used, or how and where kept since the purchase, &c.

A. B.

Taken and declared under the Act of the 19th Victoria, chapter 32, being The Sale and Barter of Metals' Act, 1856, at, &c.

C. D., J. p.

———

JAMAICA, ss.

Parish

Declaration on shipment, s. 14

I A. B., &c., of &c., do declare that I am in possession of, or in charge of (state estate, &c., from which Metal taken), and that the articles of Metal (describing them specifically) measuring and weighing (giving measurement and weight fully and particularly) were taken from the said (Estate, &c.,) and were by me (or state any other person according to the fact) imported or purchased in this Island from &c., at, &c., (state place whence, and person from whom imported, or purchased), and has been by me ever since used as (state use to which applied, and place where used, or how and where kept since the purchase, &c.) ·

A. B.

Taken and declared under the Act, 19th Victoria, chapter 32, being The Sale and Barter of Metals Act, 1856, at

C. D., j. p.

———

Military Defences.

No foreigner or other person than natural born subjects shall, without special leave of the Governor, under his hand and seal, enter any of H. M's. fortifications, 12 G. 1, c. 11, s. 3.

Visiting fortifications

Lands set apart from the Crown Reserves and Estates, and placed under the charge of the Officers of the Ordnance or the Governor, for Military Defence, or purchased by or in trust for H. M., or Her Royal Predecessors, or used or occupied for the use of the Ordnance, or for Military Defence, or to be hereafter purchased for those services, vested in the Principal Officers of H. M's. Ordnance, 6 V., c. 34.

Vesting of military defences

Transferred from the Ordnance Officers to the Secretary for War, with authority to empower any Officer of the Ordnance, or any other Civil Department of the Army in this Island, to act for him, 19 V., c. 44, c. 45,

In Secretary for War

Forts at Port Royal, &c.

The Forts and Fortifications of Port Royal, Apostles Battery, Fort Augusta, Fort Clarence, Rock Fort, and Fort Nugent, vested in the Secretary for War, and £600 per annum to be paid to the Principal Commissariat Officer, out of the £750 per annum appropriated by 17 V., c. 29, to the pay of the Officers of Fort Charles, and towards the repairs of that Fort, 26 V., S. 2., c. 2.

Barracks.

6 G. 2, c. 10, s. 5, 6, 9. 10 G. 2, c. 6.	Directed the Building of Barracks in Westmoreland, St. Elizabeth, and on the borders of Clarendon and St. Ann; also at Rio Bueno, between St. James and St. Ann.
22 G. 2, c. 19.	Authorized the erection of a Guard-House and Barrack in Kingston.
12 G. 3, c. 12.	Authorized the sale of land purchased for a Barrack, and the purchase of other land for erecting Barracks in St. Dorothy
23 G. 3, c. 9.	Authorized the sale of Barracks in St. Mary, and the purchase of land in St. Thomas Vale for a Barrack.
32 G. 3, c. 25.	Authorized the enlargement of the Barracks and Barrack Yard St. Jago de la Vega.
31 G. 3, c. 20.	Transferred the repairs of Barracks from the parishes to the public.
42 G. 3, c. 27.	Authorized the purchase of land in the interior and elsewhere for Barracks. Recites the erection of an additional Barrack at Stony Hill, and directs the sale of the old Barrack and 2 acres of land.
47 G. 3, c. 23.	Sewer from the Barrack Yard, Spanish Town, to the Rio Cobre.
36 G. 3, c. 33, s. 3.	300 Acres at the least were directed to be reserved, for the use of H. M's. Troops out of the forfeited Trelawney Town Maroon Lands. 400 acres were transferred to the Executive Committee, under 25 V., c. 4.

Forts

32 G. 3, c. 31.	Montego Bay Fort, St. James, placed on the Island Establishment.
35 G. 3, c. 42.	Forts at Falmouth, Port Morant, Fort Haldane, St. Mary, placed on the Island Establishment.
38 G. 3, c. 20.	Fort at Annotto Bay, St. George, placed on the Island Establishment.
40 G. 3, c. 35.	Fort Clarence (formerly Fort Small), St. Catherine, placed on the Island Establishment.
40 G. 3, c. 36.	Fort Dundas, Rio Bueno, placed on the Island Establishment.
44 G. 3, c. 25.	Exchange of the lands of Fort Balcarres, Falmouth, for lands at Palmeto Point, whereon to erect a new Fort, to be placed on the Island Establishment.
46 G. 3, c. 24.	Purchase of Castile Fort, and 118 acres of land for a Fort on the Island Establishment under the name of ." Fort Nugent."
47 G. 3, c. 17.	Forts on the Island Establishment to be placed in charge of an Officer, Non-Commissioned Officer, or Private of Artillery or White Forces. Officers commanding Forts not to permit vessels to sail until certificates have been lodged with them or the payment of fees and duties. Their fee, 6s. 8d. (4s stg.) on each ship, s. 4; repealed as to droghers, 3 V., c. 41.

| 48 G. 3, c. 22. | Purchase of land at Windsor Point, near the Port of St. Ann, for the erection of Fort Coote, to be placed on the Island Establishment. |
| 57 G. 3, c. 23. | The Forts and Magazines at Lucea, Montego Bay Falmouth, Fort Haldane, Fort Augusta and Port Antonio, placed under the command of Captains—their salaries, fees and perquisites. |

Militia.

The Regiments of Foot Militia shall consist of the following number of Rank and File.— *Foot Militia*

Kingston, 400, and 2 Companies of Artillery of 20 men each.

Port-Royal, 100.

St. Thomas in the East and St. David, 250.

St. Andrew, 150, and 1 Company of Artillery of 16 men.

Portland, 100.

St. George, 100.

Metcalfe, 150.

St. Elizabeth, 250.

Westmoreland, 250, and 1 Company of Artillery of 20 men.

Hanover, 250.

St. James, 300, and 1 Company of Artillery of 30 men.

Trelawny, 300, and 1 Company of Artillery of 30 men.

The Western Interior, 100.

St. Catherine, 200, and 1 Company of Artillery of 20 men.

St. John and St. Dorothy, 150,

St. Thomas in the Vale, 150.

Clarendon, 200.

Vere, 100.

Manchester, 150.

St. Ann's Eastern, 200.

St. Ann's Western, 200, and 1 Company of Artillery of 20 men.

St. Mary, 200. 9 V., c. 35, s. 3.

A Regiment of Cavalry shall be organized in each of the Counties of *Cavalry*
Surry, Middlesex and Cornwall, to be composed as follows :

				Privates.
Surry,	Kingston, 2 Troops of 25 each			
	St. Thomas in the East	Blue Mountain		20
		Port-Morant		20
		Manchioneal		20
	St. David, one Troop	....	..	15
	Portland, one Troop	....		15
	St. George, one Troop	....		15
	Metcalfe, one Troop	....		20
	St. Andrew, one Troop	....		20
Middlesex,	St. Catherine, one Troop	....		30
	St. Thomas in the Vale, one Troop		....	20
	St Mary, one Troop	....		20
	St. Ann's, Eastern	....		20
	Ditto, Western	....		20
	Manchester, one Troop	....		20
	Clarendon, one Troop	....		20
	Vere, one Troop			20
	St. John, one Troop	....		20
	St. Dorothy, one Troop	....		20
Cornwall,	Trelawny, Leeward	....		30
	Ditto, Windward			20
	St. John's, one Troop	....		30
	Hanover, one Troop	....		20
	Westmoreland, one Troop	....		00
	St. Elizabeth, one Troop	....	....	30

3 M

Cavalry Officers

To each Regiment there shall be, 1 Colonel, 2 Lieutenant-Colonels, 2 Majors, 1 Adjutant, 1 Quarter-Master, and 1 Surgeon.

For each Troop, 1 Captain, 2 Lieutenants, 1 Cornet, and 1 Surgeon.

Every Colonel or Commanding Officer recommending to a commision, unless there is a vacancy in the number so limited, shall suffer a fine not exceeding £60. Not to impeach the rank of, or exempt from duty any Officer already appointed, 9 V., c. 35, s. 4.

Infantry Officers

The Officers of each Regiment shall not exceed 1 Colonel, 1 Lieutenant-Colonel, 1 Major, 1 Adjutant, 1 Quartermaster, except the Kingston Regiment, which shall not exceed 1 Colonel, 2 Lieutenant-Colonels, 2 Majors; 1 Adjutant, and 1 Quartermaster. For every 50 men composing any Company of a Regiment, 1 Captain, 2 Lieutenants, 1 Ensign; and for every Company of Artillery, 1 Captain and 2 Lieutenants, for every Regiment, 1 Deputy-Judge Advocate, 1 Chaplain (the Rector or Curate of the parish,), 1 Surgeon and 2 Assistant-Surgeons ; and the Governor may grant commissions, or make promotions under his hand and seal as vacancies occur, and are signified by the General, of the district, or in his absence, by the Senior Officer of the Regiment.

Property qualification for 1st Commission

No first commission shall be granted to any Officer, unless he place in the hands of the Colonel or Commanding Officer, a declaration, on honor, of his being possessed of landed property of the real value of £500, or an annual income of £100, 9 V., c. 35, s. 5.

Existing Commissions

The repeal of previous Acts shall not affect any Commission already granted, 9 V., c. 35, s. 2.

Supernumerary Officers

The senior Officers of each rank in each Regiment shall perform the duties to be performed by Officers of such rank ; and no new Commission shall be granted in any Regiment, until every supernumerary Officer in such Regiment has been placed on active duty, 9 V., c. 35, s. 6.

Persons liable to perform Militia duty; Horse

Every male from 21 to 45, rot exempted by law, shall be liable to perform Militia duty ; and any person possessed of a Horse, of the value of not less than £20, shall be qualified to serve in the Horse Militia, 22 V., c. 43, s. 1. As to retirement of Officers above 55, 9 V., c. 35, s. 56.

Exemptions

EXEMPTIONS.

The Members of the Council, Speaker of the Assembly, Chief Justice, and other Judges of the superior Courts, Receiver General and Clerks in his office, Island Secretary and his Deputy, Registrar in Chancery, Clerk of the Court and Crown, Provost Marshal and his Deputies, Officers of the Customs, of the Prisons, Coroners, Postmaster General and his Deputies, persons in Port Royal permanently employed in the Dock Yard or Victualling Establishment and Naval Hospital, such employment to be proved by Certificate of the senior Naval Officer, the Inspector General, Inspectors and Police Force, Special Constables on Railways, on Certificate on honor of the Director or Manager, Ministers of Religion, and persons duly qualified, actually and habitually employed in piloting and navigaitng Vessels, persons residing in or coming to this Island, who have held commissions under the Sign Manual, or signed by the Lord High Admiral or Commissioners of the Admiralty, or of the Navy Board, or Lord Lieutenant of Counties, or Governors or Lieutenant Governors in the Island and other Dependencies of the Empire as Officers, shall receive rank of junior Officers of their grade, and do duty under their former Regimental rank, on producing, where the Commission has not conferred rank in the regular Military or Naval Service, certificates from the Commanding Officers of having done duty for at least 6 months, and that they have not been degraded by sentence of a Court Martial, or from misconduct been obliged to retire.

Persons holding commissions in the United Kingdom or Dependencies

Medical and Surgical Practitioners Members of Assembly and Justices

Medical and Surgical Practitioners legally qualified (see 23 V., c. 17, s. 15, and all Members of Assembly and Justices) shall be exempt from doing duty in the ranks, 9 V., c. 35, s. 7.

Immigrants

Immigrants exempt for 3 years next after their arrival, except in case of Martial Law, 9 V., c. 35, s. 115.

Annual Returns by persons liable to Militia duty

On 30th April in each year, all persons liable to perform Militia duty, shall give in to the Clerk of the Common Council, or Vestry of the Parish in which they reside, a Return, Forms A and B. Penalty, £2, for each omission, or for making a false return, 22 V., c. 43, s. 2.

The Clerk of the Common Council or Vestry shall keep a book to register the names and qualifications of all persons liable and qualified, keeping distinct registers of the names and qualifications of those qualified to serve in the Horse and Foot, setting forth their nature, and shall attend and produce the register at meetings to ballot for men : Penalty, £10, 22 V., c. 43, s. 3.

Registers to be kept by Clerks of Vestries, &c. and produced at meetings to ballot

Register books shall be provided by the Receiver-General, on the direction of the Governor in Executive Committee, 22 V., c. 43, s. 4.

To be provided by Receiver General

Whenever it appears necessary to the Captain General that a ballot should take place for the embodiment of the Militia, for the service or purposes prescribed by 9 V., c. 35, the Custos shall convene a Special Session of the Peace, to assemble at a convenient time and place, at which 3 Justices shall be a quorum. They shall cause the number of men required to form the quota of the Regiment to be chosen by ballot out of the registers. After the ballot has been taken, such Justices shall make up and sign a list of the names of the persons chosen, (Form C., 9 V., c. 35) to be kept in the office of the Clerk of the Vestry or Common Council ; the persons ballotted for or enrolled shall be deemed Privates of the Foot or Troop and liable to perform Militia duty according as they have been respectively assigned when required by order of the Captain General, until their period of service expires ; and in case of refusal or omission to attend when called upon for Militia duty : penalty, £2, 22 V., c. 43, s. 5.

Ballot by direction of Captain General Special Sessions for
Lists
Penalty

Before proceeding to such ballot, the quorum of Justices shall strike off the names of persons known to them, or satisfactorily shewn at the time to be incapacitated by bodily infirmity, 22 V., c. 43, s. 6.

Incapacitated persons to be struck off before ballot

Any person balloted and enrolled claiming temporary or permanent relief shall produce his claim before a Board of Officers (5 where relief is sought from duty in the Foot, 3 where in the Horse) selected by the Officer Commanding the Regiment or Troop, who may be of the number, and, if so, the President. The presiding officer shall report to the Custos the names of all persons relieved permanently or temporarily, and he shall convene a Special Sessions, to fill up, by the ballot, the vacancies declared by the Board of Officers, and so toties quoties, as the names become reduced by at least 10 in number ; and the Clerk of the Vestry or Common Council shall remove from the Register the names of persons from time to time known to him to have died, 22 V., c. 43, s. 7.

Reliefs by boards of officers Supersedes, 9 V., c. 35, s. 17
To be reported to Custos Further ballots
Names of dead persons to be removed from Register

The Board shall summon, by 2 days previous notice in writing, any competent Physician or Surgeon, being a Military Medical Officer residing at or nearest the place where any Board assemble, to attend the meeting, who, before he begins his examination of the party claiming exemption, shall make the following declaration, to be administered by the President :—

Medical officer to be summoned to attend board to examine applicants for relief Declaration

I   do solemnly declare, that I will, to the best of my ability, faithfully and truly report as to the fitness for service of the man or men about to be submitted to my examination, and that I will not receive from any of them any fee or reward whatsoever for such examination.

The Physician or Surgeon shall be bound to attend, under the like penalties as are inflicted on Officers for non-attendance at Court Martial, to be recovered in a summary manner, 9 V., c. 35, s. 18.

Penalty for non attendance

When the Militia is called out for duty, the Colonel or Commanding Officer of each Regiment or Troop may call upon the Custos to restore by ballot its effective strength, by not less than 10 at one time, if reduced by death or permanent removal from the list or otherwise to such extent from its lawful quota, 22 V., c. 43, s. 8.

When Colonel, &c, may call for ballot

Every person chosen to serve shall, under penalty of £2, for every day's neglect or omission to appear at the time and place appointed for examination, and if on examination, found able and fit for service, shall be enrolled in a roll to be then and there prepared, to serve for 5 years in the Company or Troop he is appointed to, and take the oath following, which any Justice present may administer :—

Persons found fit to serve to be sworn for 5 years ; supersedes 13 V., c. 31, s. 5

I, A. B., do solemnly promise and swear that I will be faithful, and bear true allegiance to Her Majesty Queen Victoria, and that I will faithfully serve in the Militia within this Island for the defence of the same during the time of 5 years for which I am enrolled, unless I shall be sooner discharged, 22 V., c. 43, s. 9.

Substitutes

If any person chosen to serve produces before the Justices at the ballot for his substitute, a man of the same parish or district, able and fit for service, and approved of by them, he shall be enrolled in the Regiment or Troop for which his principal was chosen for 5 years ; and the principal shall be exempt from service for the period, and as if he himself had served. The substitute shall take the following oath, to be administered by any Justice present :—

Oath

I, A. B., do sincerely promise and swear that I will be faithful, and bear true allegiance to Her Majesty Queen Victoria ; and that I will faithfully serve in the Militia within this Island, for the defence of the same during the time of five years, or for such further time as the Militia shall remain embodied, unless I shall be sooner discharged, 22 V., c. 43, s. 10.

Volunteers Supersedes : 3 V, c. 31, s. 5

Where the ballot does not furnish the number of men required, Volunteers may be enlisted by the Colonel or Commanding Officer, on being approved of by a Court of Enquiry appointed by him, as to character and competency, 22 V., c. 43, s. 11.

Arms, Dress and Accoutrements to be as Captain General directs

The arms, dress and accoutrements of the Officers and men of the Foot and Horse, shall be such as the Captain-General directs, subject to H. M's. pleasure, 22 V., c. 43, s. 17.

Issue to Colonels, by order of Commander-in-Chief on representation through General of district

Colonel's liability

No arms or accoutrements shall issue from the public Arsenal to any Colonel for distribution amongst his Regiment, except by a special order of the Commander-in-Chief, on a representation in writing through the General of the district by the Colonel. Every Colonel shall be charged by the Island Storekeeper, in a book to be kept for the purpose, with those issued for the use of his Regiment, until he discharges himself, by rendering a satisfactory account of their distribution or disposal, 9 V., c. 35, s. 23.

Colonel's annual returns of strength of Regiment and Arms and Accoutrements

Also on retiring from command or leaving island

Every Colonel shall once a year, in October or oftener, if required by the Commander-in-Chief, under penalty of £60, to make his return to the General of the district, for transmission to the Adjutant-General, of the actual strength of their Regiments, the number and condition of arms and accoutrements in use of his Regiment, and the number and disposal of all received by him, and the reason of any deficiency for which he is accountable ; and on retiring from the command or leaving the Island, under a like penalty of £60, shall make the like full return of the actual strength of his Regiment, and an account of the arms and accoutrements for which he is accountable as before, within 3 months after retirement, or 21 days previous to going off, 9 V., c. 35, s. 24.

Returns by Captains, &c., of Arms and Accoutrements for which they are accountable

Every Captain or Commanding Officer of every Company of Infantry, or Artillery or Troop of Horse, shall, under penalty of £10, within 10 days after every muster, or 10 days previous to going off the Island, or 10 days after his retiring, promotion or removal from one Company or Troop to another, render to the Colonel, according to the manner and form appointed and prescribed by the Commander-in-Chief, an account of all the arms and accoutrements in use of his Company or Troop, and of all received by him and distributed, and the cause of the deficiency, if any, in the number for which he is accountable, 9 V., c. 35, s. 25.

Purchasers from public Arsenal to make good deficiencies

Any Colonel, with the authority of the Commander in Chief, Captain, &c., or non-Commissioned Officer, or Private, with a certificate from the Colonel, may purchase from the public Arsenal any number of arms and accoutrements to make good what he is accountable for, by paying into the Receiver-General's Office £2 14s. for each set of arms and accoutrements of the Foot, and £4 10s. for the Horse, and upon producing the Receiver-General's receipt, shall receive the same out of the public Arsenal, 9 V, c. 35, s. 26.

Recovery of penalties for deficiencies

Application

The penalties before imposed shall be recovered against Colonels, by warrant, under the hand and seal of the General commanding the District, against Captains, &c., by the Colonel's warrant, against non-commissioned Officers or Privates, by warrant of the Officer commanding the Company, or Troop, or of the Officer accountable for the deficiency for which the fine is incurred, such fines incurred by non-Commissioned Officers and Privates for the deficiencies of arms in the Foot to be received by the Captain, &c., and paid to the Colonel, and by him applied to the purpose of replacing the arms deficient in the different Companies, and the fines on non-Commissioned Officers and Privates of Horse, shall be collected by the Captains, &c., and applied in like manner, 9 V., c. 35, s. 27.

Arms, accoutrements, ball cartridges, paper and flints, nipples and caps, shall be furnished out of the public Stores, upon application in writing by the Colonels to the General of the District, and subject to the approval of the Commander in Chief. In case of the death of any person who has received arms, the property of the public, the person into whose possession they come shall deliver them over forthwith to the Officer commanding the Company of the district in which the deceased resided. Penalty, £10, to be recovered by warrant, under hand and seal of the Colonel, 9 V., c. 35, s. 28. *Arms &c, to be furnished from public stores*

Penalty on persons in possession of Arms of the public, received by deceased persons and not delivered up

Embezzling, selling, losing, by carelessness, or designedly or negligently wasting, spoiling, injuring or using, for any other purposes than those of Military duty, any arms, ammunition, accoutrements, clothing or other articles with which any Regiment or part is furnished: penalty not exceeding £10, or 30 days' imprisonment, by warrant under hand and seal of the Colonel or Commanding Officer, besides being liable in case of embezzlement to be prosecuted at law, 9 V., c. 35, s. 29. *Embezzling, selling losing, &c., Arms, Ammunition, &c*

Prosecution for embezzlement

Knowingly and wilfully buying, taking in exchange, concealing or otherwise receiving any Militia arms or accoutrements, or any public stores or ammunition delivered for the Militia on any pretence: penalty on conviction before a Justice, £3, and if not immediately paid, or there are no sufficient goods whereon to levy, commitment for 15 days, or until the fine is sooner paid, 9 V., c. 35, s. 30. *Buying, concealing, &c. arms or accoutrements, &c.*

All arms, ammunition and accoutrements issued for the Militia, shall be subject to the orders and regulations of the Captain General for their safe-keeping in good order and delivery, to such Officer or other person as he may appoint to receive them, 22 V., c. 43, s. 18. *Arms, &c. subject to Captain General's orders for safe keeping and re delivery*

Any person abusing or embezzling, wasting, spoiling or injuring any arms ammunition, or accoutrements issued for the Militia, and any Officer not making returns of them when required by the Governor, shall be liable to the penalties imposed by 9 V., c. 35, 22 V., c. 43, s. 19. *Abusing, embezzling, wasting, &c. arms, &c., or not making returns, punishable under 9 V., c. 35*

The offences in 9 V., c. 35, s. 29, 30, shall be offences under this Act, and may be proceeded against as Misdemeanors, without prejudice, and in addition to the penalties thereby imposed, 22 V., c. 43, s. 20. *Offences in 9 V., c. 35, s. 29-30 indictable also as misdemeanors*

The Governor, with the advice and consent of the Privy Council, may direct the embodiment of the Militia or any part thereof, and call out the same for drill and exercise, at such times, places and manner as he may appoint, 28 V., c. 38, s. 76. *Embodiment for drill and and exercise by Governor and Privy Council*

Militia Regiments or Companies and Troops, shall be drilled and exercised when embodied at such times and places in their parishes as the Captain General may appoint, not exceeding once in each month, except in cases of great emergency, 22 V., c. 43, s. 12. *Musters for drill*

No Colonel or Captain, &c., of a Troop shall be liable to any suit civil or criminal, for appointing any place of muster, provided it be not in any cultivated ground, common pasture excepted, 9 V., c. 35, s. 35. *Muster Grounds*

The Colonel of the Kingston Regiment may order any musters on the Race Course; and the Colonel of the Port-Royal Regiment may hold its musters for inspection on the Race Course, subject to the power of the Commander-in-Chief for regulating musters, 9 V., c. 35, s. 114. *Muster Ground Kingston and Port Royal Regiments*

Notices of the time and place of exercise shall, by order of the Colonel, be made public by insertion in the 'Gazette,' and by affixing one copy on the door of the Court-House, or such other places as he shall appoint, which shall be sufficient notice to every person belonging to the Regiment, and who shall duly attend accordingly, 9 V. c. 35, s. 36. *Notices of Muster*

The Captain &c., shall select and appoint such men of his Company as are approved of by the Colonel, to serve as Sergeants and Corporals, as to him shall seem most competent, 9 V., c. 35, s. 37. *Appointments of non-commissioned officers*

The Colonel shall form the flank companies, and regulate the Artillery and other companies as to him shall seem best, 9 V., c. 35, s. 38. *Flank Artillery and other companies*

When any Militia-man after enrolment becomes unfit for service, the Colonel may discharge him on the certificate of a Medical Board, 9 V., c. 35, s. 39. *Discharge of Militiamen on certificate of Medical Board*

Upon the death of a private, or his appointment to be a Sergeant, Corporal, or other non-Commissioned Officer, or discharge, the Colonel shall cause the vacancy to be filled up at the first ballot after, 9 V. c. 35, s. 40. *Vacancies to be filled up at next ballot*

Absence from muster by commissioned officers.	Every Colonel absent from muster without a sufficient excuse, to be approved of by the General commanding the District, shall forfeit £10, to be levied by warrant of distress and sale under his hand and seal. Every Officer under the rank of Colonel absent without excuse, approved of by the Colonel or other Commanding Officer of the Regiment, or Captain commanding the Troop, shall forfeit: a Colonel Commandant, £6, a Lieutenant-Colonel, £5, a Major, £4, a Captain, £3, any other Commissioned Officer under the rank of Captain, £2; to be levied by warrant, under the hand and seal of the Colonel or Officer commanding on the occasion. If absent
Subsequent absence	on any subsequent occasion without sufficient excuse, every such Officer shall be liable (in addition to the ordinary penalty, or without such penalty having been enforced) to such punishment, by censure, fine or imprisonment as a general Court Martial shall award, 9 V., c. 35, s. 42.
Returns by Commanding Officers of Companies of foot after each muster, with warrants and excuses to Officer Commanding	Upon every muster or other duty, the Captain, &c., shall, within 5 days and not sooner than 3 days, in respect to the Regiments of St. Catherine and Kingston, and within 10 days, and not sooner than 7 days in respect to other Regiments of Foot, make a return of his Company to the Officer commanding, specifying the number of Officers, non-Commissioned Officers, and Privates present, and the names of absentees and defaulters in arms and accoutrements: penalty, £6, to be levied by warrant under the hand and seal of such Commanding Officer; and every excuse for absence or other default of a non-Commissioned Officer or Private, shall be given into such Captain, &c., within 3 days after the muster or other duty in St. Catherine and Kingston, and within 5 days in respect to other Regiments of Foot, and every such Captain, &c., shall, with his return, deliver to such superior Officer warrants ready for signature against all absentees and others in default, without any excuse given in, and also warrants ready for signature against all absentees and others in default for whom an excuse may be given in, to be accompanied by the excuses; and shall also specifically state all excuses for which warrants are not delivered:
Commanding Officers return to Colonel Field return	penalty, £3, to be levied by warrant under the hand and seal of the Colonel or Officer commanding the Regiment The Officer to whom the return has been made shall, within 5 days thereafter, make a like return to the Colonel or commanding Officer of the Regiment. A return of the number present in each Company under arms at all Regimental Battalion or division musters, shall be made by the Captain, &c., on the field to the senior Officer present, 9 V., c. 35, s. 43.[*]
Returns of Captains &c. of Troop	Captains, &c., of Troop, within 10 days, and not sooner than 7 days after the muster or other duty, shall make a like return under the same penalties, and the Officer to whom the return is made, shall, within 5 days after, make a like return to the Colonel, &c., 9 V., c. 35, s. 44.
Protection from process on day of muster, &c., or within 48 hours before or after	The Provost Marshal or any of his Deputies shall not arrest, detain or molest on any mesne or Judicial process any Commissioned or non Commissioned or Warrant Officer, or Private, Drummer, Fifer, or other musician, or execute any levy or extent on any property, real or personal, of any Officer, &c., engaged in Militia duty, or acting under the orders of the Commander in Chief or other superior Officer, on the day of muster or other duty, nor within 48 hours before or after, provided he has appeared at, or is going to, or returning from muster, under penalty of £60, for every offence knowingly and wilfully committed, to be recovered by action of debt, triable in the county where the cause of action arises by the person aggrieved, to his own use, with full costs, and being further liable to make reparation in damages; and every execution contrary to the spirit of this provision is annulled and declared void, 9 V., c. 35, s. 45.
Disobedience of orders	Every Officer, non-Commissioned Officer or Soldier, of Horse, Foot or Artillery, on any occasion of duty refusing to obey, or not promptly obeying any lawful command of any Officer or non-Commissioned Officer, his superior, shall suffer punishment by fine not exceeding £30, or imprisonment not exceeding 15 days, as either a General or Regimental Court Martial shall award, 9 V., c. 35, s. 46.
Rude, &c., language or behaviour to superior Officer	Every Officer, &c., treating any superior Officer with rude, affronting or contemptuous language, act, gesture or behaviour, when on duty or at any other time in matters arising from or appertaining or referring to Militia duty; fine not exceeding £60, or degradation or imprisonment not

---

[*] The 9 V., c. 35, s. 41, inflicting fines, &c., on non-Commissioned Officers and Privates absent from muster, was repealed by 22 V., c. 43, s. 23, and no other provision has been substituted, thus rendering nugatory the above provisions for punishment of non-attendance.

exceeding 28 days, as a Regimental or General Court Martial may award, 9 V., c. 35, s. 47.

Any Officer or non-Commissioned Officer wilfully or wantonly oppressing, maltreating or ill-using any inferior Officer or Soldier : fine not exceeding £60, or imprisonment not exceeding 28 days as above, 9 V., c. 35, s. 48.

Ill-treatment of inferior officers or men

Any Officer, &c., or Soldier who strikes or draws, or attempts to draw any weapon upon or against, or offers other wrongful violence or force to, or in any wise insults any other Officer, non-Commissioned Officer or Soldier when on duty, or at any other time in matters arising from or appertaining or referring to Militia duty : same punishment. If any complaint under this section or any other herein is made groundlessly, frivolously, vexatiously or wantonly, the complainant shall suffer similar punishment, to be awarded by the Court trying the complaint, 9 V., c. 35, s. 49.

Striking or drawing weapon, or attempting or offering violence or insult
Frivolous complaints generally

Any Officer or Soldier who does not keep silence and conduct himself in an orderly manner when on any duty : fine not exceeding £10, or imprisonment not exceeding 20 days as above, 9 V., c. 35, s. 50.

Not keeping silence, &c. on duty

Whosoever having any person in his employ, or domiciled with him liable to do Militia duty, shall hinder or prevent, or endeavour, &c., by or under threat, persuasion or otherwise, any such person from making any return directed by this Act, or from attending at any meeting or upon occasion of muster or other duty, or upon any sound, beat, alarm, order or notice from repairing to the place of rendezvous with arms in good order : fine not exceeding £60, or imprisonment not exceeding 28 days as above, 9 V., c. 35, s. 51.

Preventing, &c., person in employment or domiciled from making returns, attending meetings, musters, &c

Any Officer drunk, or guilty of riotous or disorderly behaviour on guard, party, muster, or other duty, shall be liable to fines according to their respective grades as before specified, or to degradation or other punishment as a general Court Martial shall award. Any non-Commissioned Officer or Soldier so offending, shall suffer punishment, by fine not exceeding £20, or imprisonment not exceeding 20 days, as a Regimental or General Court Martial shall award, 9 V., c. 35, s. 52.

Drunkenness or riotous behaviour on guard, &c

Any Officer or Soldier giving or sending a challenge to any other when on duty, or arising out of matter appertaining to Militia duty, to fight a duel, or writing or sending, or causing to be sent any letter or other writing, or printed paper in anywise insulting or derogatory to the character and rank of the person addressed, for any offence taken or pretended to be taken on any occasion of duty : fine not exceeding £60, or imprisonment not exceeding 28 days as above, 9 V., c. 35, s. 53.

Sending challenge
Insulting or derogatory letter, &c

Any Commissioned Officer behaving in a scandalous, infamous and improper manner, unbecoming the character of an officer and a gentleman : fine not exceeding £60, or degradation by General Court Martial, 9 V., c. 35, s. 54.

Conduct unbecoming an officer and a gentleman

All disorders and neglects which Officers, non-Commissioned Officers or Privates may be guilty of, to the prejudice of good order and Military discipline not specified : fine not exceeding £60, or imprisonment not exceeding 28 days, by Regimental or General Court Martial, 9 V., c. 35, s. 55.

Disorders and neglects prejudicial to discipline not specified

Any person who holds any Commission, Warrant or Appointment relating to any Military duty or service, shall be subject to all lawful commands of the Commander-in Chief, General or Commanding Officer of a District, and any other superior Officer. Nothing herein shall prevent any Officer above 55 retiring from the Service, or shall prevent his obtaining his discharge from the Captain-General, on sufficient grounds being shewn, 9 V., c. 35, s. 56.

Officers, &c., subject to their superiors
Retirement of Officers over 55. Discharge from Captain General on sufficient grounds

No person shall be appointed Aide-de-Camp to the Commander-in-Chief, unless either a Captain having done duty as such for at least 2 years or a Field Officer ; nor shall any person be appointed to the General Staff, nor to any Brevet rank, unless at the time he be either a Captain having done duty as aforesaid, or a Field Officer. Notwithstanding any such appointment, he shall continue in his Regiment, and no person appointed to any General Staff or Brevet rank shall have any rank annexed for more than one step above his Regimental rank, except only as to the appointment of Aide-de-Camp to the Governor, and Officers in the Adjutant-General's and Quarter-Master General's Departments, 9 V., c. 35, s, 57.

Aide de camp to commander-in-chief
Staff brevet rank ; see s, 104

District Generals

To make annual &c., inspections of regiments

Call for returns under penalties

The Governor may appoint from the Militia, General Officers of Districts, who are authorized to inspect the several Regiments within their Districts, at their usual places of Muster once a-year, and oftener if the Commander-in-Chief direct ; and to call upon the several Colonels or Commanding Officers for all such Returns as seem expedient to be made within 15 days ; Penalty, £30, to be levied by Warrant under the hand and seal of such General Officer, directed to the Provost Marshal, who by himself or Deputy shall execute same, and pay the amount to the Receiver-General, to the credit of the Island.

Not to interfere with internal management, or to change field exercise or movements

Not to confer on such General Officer any right to interfere with the internal management of any Regiment, or to make any change in the Field exercise or movements, so as to vary the same from that practised for the time in the Regular Service, which only is to be used, 9 V., c. 35, s. 58.

When to have a Staff, of whom to consist and how appointed

No General Officer shall have a Staff, unless actually in command of a division of the Militia, or a District, on which appointment he may appoint as his personal Staff, under his hand and seal, and not by Commission, one Brigade Major and one Aide-de-Camp, who shall at the time of appointment be Officers actually doing duty in the Militia, above the rank of Ensign ; and one Secretary, whether he do Military duty or not, who shall continue of the same ranks in their Regiments, and be promoted in their turns, 9 V., c. 35, s. 59.

Staff appointments, what

Every appointment except a General Officer, or to Regimental or to Brevet rank, shall be a Staff appointment, and subject to the provisions concerning Staff appointments, 9 V., c. 35, s. 60.

Adjutant General's commissions free of Stamps

The Commission of Adjutant-General or any other Commission necessary to confer the rank of Colonel upon him, shall be exempted from Stamp Duty, any Act notwithstanding, 9 V., c. 35, s. 61.

Notices of commissions to be published in Gazette

If not taken out within 6 weeks after recommendation notified, Colonel to recommend next senior Officer

Every Commission shall be void, unless the name of the person and rank conferred, and the date, are published by the Governor's Secretary within one month after in the " Gazette," which particulars in an official form, the Secretary must transmit within 7 days after issuing the Commission to the Conductors of the " Gazette" for publication, and they are required to publish on the next publication day after receipt. If any Officer is recommended for promotion, occasioned by a vacancy in the Regiment, and declines to accept of or take his Commission out of office within 6 weeks after it has been notified to him in writing by, or by order of the Colonel, &c., he shall continue to do duty under the Commission he held at the time of such recommendation, and the Colonel shall, under penalty of £30, recommend the next senior Officer, 9 V., c. 35, s. 62.

Death, &c,. of Colonel, &c., to be reported to the district General by Officer next in command

Upon the death of the Colonel or Officer commanding any Regiment, the Officer next in command shall, within 30 days after, report to the General of the District under penalty of £20, to be recovered by Warrant under his hand and seal, 9 V., c. 35, s. 63.

Absence from the island without leave a vacancy

How leave is to be obtained

For what time

The absence of an Officer from the Island on leave, shall not make a vacancy : but if he goes off without leave, if Colonel or Commanding Officer of a Regiment, from the General of the District, or if any other Officer, from the Colonel, &c., it shall make a vacancy, and be filled up : and the Officer on his return shall do duty as junior Officer of the rank he held. Leave may be granted for not exceeding 2 years, but shall be void if the Officer return within the time, 9 V., c. 35, s. 64.

Recommendations to be Officers

The Colonel, &c., may recommend any person to be an Officer in his Regiment qualified as required. (s. 5.) ; and every recommendation shall state specifically the vacancy to be filled up, and how occasioned, and any Colonel, &c. knowingly or without due enquiry into facts, recommending a person contrary to any of the aforesaid provisions, shall forfeit £100, to be levied as after mentioned, 9 V., c. 35, s. 65.

No Officer to resign his Commission without permission of Governor or Court Martial

No Officer shall resign his Commission, unless by permission of the Commander in Chief, or upon cause shewn before a general Court Martial ; but if the cause submitted is adjudged insufficient, he shall be obliged to do duty under his commission, and in case of refusal or wilful neglect, be degraded, and sentenced to serve as a Private; and any Colonel accepting a resignation shall be liable to fine, not exceeding £100, by a general Court Marshal, 9 V., c. 35, s. 66.

When any Officer, either of Brevet rank or otherwise, removes to Notices by Officers of removal into another parish, and Colonels another parish, unless the Militia of both parishes form one Regiment, he shall give notice in writing to his Colonel, and immediately report himself to the Colonel of the Regiment of the parish to which he removes: penalty, £20, to be levied by Warrant under hand and seal of the latter, and in failure of such notification and report for 6 weeks, he shall be further liable to fine, not exceeding £60, or diminution of rank, or degradation to serve in the ranks by a General Court Marshal; and the Colonel of the parish from which the removal is made, shall give notice in writing to the Colonel of the Regiment of the parish to which the removal is made: Penalty, fine not exceeding £30 by General Court Marshal; and Vacancy to be filled up he shall also report such removal to the Governor, and from thenceforth the post shall be vacant, and be filled up by a new Commission. The Colonel of the Regiment of the parish to which the removal is made shall forthwith enroll the Officer, under penalty not exceeding £30, to be recovered by Officer to do duty en seconde in the regiment of the parish, he removes to until a vacancy warrant under the hand and seal of the General of the District, or as a General Court Martial may award, and the Officer shall thenceforth act and do duty en seconde to the Officers of his rank, until a vacancy in his rank happens, to which he shall be appointed without taking out a new Commission, and then he shall come in as the junior of his rank; though in all duties of the line he shall take rank from the date of his Commission, Officers of horse same regiment If any Officer of Horse, other than a Field Officer, remove from one parish to another the Horse of both belonging to the same Regiment, he shall report his removal to the Colonel: penalty, fine, not exceeding £60, as a General Court Martial shall award, and such Colonel shall thereupon make such order concerning such Officer doing duty in the one parish or the other, as the convenience of the individual or the good of the service requires, under penalty of a fine not exceeding £30, as a General Court Martial awards; but if ordered to do duty in the parish to which he removes, the Officer shall do duty according to his rank in the Regiment, and if any Officer thereby becomes supernumerary, he shall continue to do duty in his rank, but under the command of his senior.— Different Regiments When the Horse of the two parishes belong to different Regiments, the case shall be proceeded on as in case of the removal of an Officer of Foot from one parish to another, and under the like penalties. Every Colonel of Foot Residence of Colonels of regiments shall reside in the parish of his Regiment, and every Colonel of Horse in the District of his Regiment, or so near to the Parish or District that he can attend to his duty therein, or shall be liable to have his post vacated by sentence of a General Court Martial. In any case of removal of an Cause may be shewn to the Commander in Chief why an Officer should not come in the new regiment or troop Officer, if cause can be shewn to the satisfaction of the Commander in Chief by the Commanding Officer of the Horse or Foot of the Parish, or District to which the removal is, why any such person ought not to come in as an Officer, he shall not be called upon to do duty in such Parish or District. Port Royal If any Officer, non-Commissioned Officer or Soldier of any Troop remove into Port-Royal, where there is none, he may either join the Troop of an adjoining parish near his residence, or the Regiment of the parish, provided he reports himself to the Captain of the Troop he intends to join, or the Colonel of the Regiment. If the Officer removing is able to Officers removing if able may continue to do duty with their regiments attend to his duty in the parish from which he removes, and actually continues to do duty therein to the satisfaction of the General Commanding the District, he shall not, as long as he continues to do duty be deemed within the forgoing provisions, 9 V., c. 35, s. 67.

The Governor may appoint Courts or Boards of General or Field Officers and Captains, in such number and places as he thinks proper, to en- Boards of Officers to be appointed by the Governor quire into and determine all matters concerning Military duty and regulation required for the good of the Service, who shall have power to summon May summon witnesses and examine, upon oath, all persons required, by notices in form and under the like penalties as are specified for Officers, witnesses and others summoned before Courts Martial. The Deputy Judge Advocate of the Regiment where Deputy Judge Advocate to attend them the Board is ordered to sit, shall attend and record proceedings under the like penalties. Such Court or Board shall be an open Court, and not con- To be an open Court ducted with closed doors, except in the forms customary in Courts Martial, and report proceedings to the Captain General, 9 V., c. 35, s. 71. Report to Captain General

For the trial of all offenders for punishment whereof a General Court Courts Martial. Charges to be submitted, how summoned Martial is required, the Colonel, &c., of a Regiment of Foot or Horse shall submit in writing to the Commander-in-Chief or General of the District, the Charges, who shall direct the time and place of holding, and call upon the Colonels of the several Regiments of the District to name Officers from their Regiments to form the Court, which Courts shall be subject in all respects to the provisions concerning Courts Martial, 9 V., c. 35, s. 72.

Of whom to consist, and rank

Every General Court Martial shall consist of not less than 13, or more than 15 Officers, none under the rank of Captain. When a complaint is by an Officer or person of the Foot, against an Officer or person of the Horse, or vice versa, the Court shall consist of Officers of the Foot and Horse in such numbers as may be most convenient, if it be impossible to have equal numbers of each; and the Officers on all General Courts Martial shall take rank according to the dates of their commission, 9 V., c. 35, s. 73.

Penalties on member or witnesses not attending before General Courts Martial

Power to remit

Every Officer warned as a member of a General Court Martial or witness, not attending, unless prevented by sickness, certified by a Surgeon or Assistant Surgeon, or by any unavoidable accident shewn to the satisfaction of the Court, shall, for every default in respect to a General Court Martial, forfeit not exceeding £30, to be levied by Warrant under the hand and seal of the senior Officer present at the Court, or of the Officer ordering it. The Commander-in-Chief or General of the District may remit any such fine, upon oath, shewing to his satisfaction that the person fined had a good and sufficient excuse for his non-attendance, and could not have made it at the time appointed for the sitting of the Court; and in like manner the Colonel, &c., may remit any such fine inflicted by a Court ordered by him, upon oath shewn as aforesaid, 9 V., c 35, s. 74.

In cases of regimental Courts Martial

Regimental Courts Martial

No Commissioned Officer to be tried by a Regimental Court nor Colonel, &c., deprived of rank unless Court convened by Commander-in-Chief

For the trial of all offences for punishment whereof a Regimental Court Martial is required, the Colonel, &c., may hold, order or summon them as the exigencies of the Regiment require. In no case shall a Commissioned Officer be tried by a Regimental Court Martial, nor a Colonel, &c., be deprived of his rank by sentence of a Court Martial, unless convened by the Commander-in-Chief, 9 V., c. 35, s. 75.

Regimental Courts Martial, how composed and warned

On all Courts proceedings, &c., to be according to the rules of the Army

Regimental Courts Martial shall consist in the Horse of at least 3; in the Foot of at least 5 Commissioned Officers; the members to be warned 5 days inclusive, previous to the time to be holden. On all Courts Martial the proceedings shall be had, and the members shall take rank according to the rules of the Army. No Officer shall be eligible to sit, unless he has taken the usual oaths of allegiance and supremacy, or the oaths required of Roman Catholic (10 G. 4, c. 12) or Jewish (2 W. 4. c. 3) subjects, subsequent to his first Commission before any Judge Advocate or Deputy Judge Advocate, who is authorized to administer the same, 9 V., c. 35, s. 76.

Non attendance of officers on witnesses or regimental Court

Every Officer or witness warned, and not attending any Regimental Court Martial, unless prevented by sickness or inevitable accident, to be certified and shown, as required in the case of a General Court Martial, shall forfeit not exceeding £20, to be levied by warrant under the hand and seal of the President or Senior Officer attending at the Court, or of the Officer ordering it, 9 V., c. 35, s. 77.

Notices of meeting of Court and charge

Consequences of non-appearance without cause

The person to be tried by a General Court Martial shall have 8 days' notice in writing, and by a Regimental Court, 5 days' notice, to be served personally, or left at his residence, of the time and place. and of the charge to be preferred: and if he do not appear or send a satisfactory reason for his absence, or if evidence is given of his keeping out of the way to avoid service, he shall stand convicted, and incur the punishment the Court would have adjudged had his guilt been established upon trial, 9 V., c. 35, s. 78.

Oath of Members

Before any proceedings are had, the Members shall take the following oath before the Judge Advocate-General or his Deputy, or in their absence, by any person appointed by the Colonel or President of the Court to act upon the occasion:—

You shall well and truly try and determine, without partiality, favor or affection, according to evidence in the matter now before you, between our Sovereign Lady the Queen and the offender to be tried; and you shall not upon any account, at any time whatsoever, disclose or discover the vote or opinion of any particular member of this Court Martial, unless required to give evidence thereof as a witness by a Court of Justice in a due course of law.—So help you God.

And the President shall then administer an oath to the Judge-Advocate or Deputy Judge-Advocate or person officiating in the following words:—

Judge Advocate's

You swear that you will not, on any account, at any time whatsoever disclose or discover the vote or opinion of any particular member of this Court Martial, unless required to give evidence thereof as a witness by a Court of Justice in a due course of law.—So help you God, 9 V., c. 35, s. 79.

Every Court Martial may administer an oath to every witness that the evidence he shall give in the matter to be tried shall be the truth, the whole truth, and nothing but the truth. Taking a false oath, or suborning or procuring any other so to do, shall be punishable as perjury or subornation. Any person not in the Militia, who has received written notice to attend as a witness from any Judge Advocate or person acting, or any Officer ordering the Court, and not attending, shall forfeit £100, to be recovered by action of debt triable in the County where the cause of action arises by any person suing, to his own use, with full costs to be taxed, unless he shew upon the trial of the action good cause for non-attendance, and that it was made to the Officer ordering the Court within 14 days from the time appointed for the Court. Any person in the Militia having notice and not attending, shall suffer punishment by fine not exceeding £60, or imprisonment not exceeding 3 months as a Regimental or General Court Martial shall award. Witnesses to have 5 days' notice, served personally, or left at their residence, 9 V., c. 35, s. 80.

Oaths to witnesses
Penalty for non-attendance
When not in the militia
If in the militia
5 Days notice

No sentence shall be given unless concurred in by the majority. The sentence of a Regimental Court Martial prononne by the President shall not be subject to revision or require confirmation, but shall be executed in all things by Warrant under the hand and seal of the President ; but there shall be a right of appeal to a General Court Martial, which, in case of a frivolous, wanton, or groundless appeal may increase the punishment of the Regimental Court, award costs to the party aggrieved by the appeal, and direct compensation by the Appellant to the Judge Advocate, &c., having the trouble occasioned thereby ; the increased punishment, costs and compensation, to be enforced by imprisonment under the Warrant of the President of the General Court Martial. Whoever shall prefer a charge against another, so as to cause him to be prosecuted by a Court Martial, and shall fail to attend and proceed, or to prove his charges, the Court shall, unless sufficient cause is shewn, acquit the person accused, and also proceed as in cases of groundless, &c., complaints (s. 49) and punish the prosecutor accordingly, by fine not exceeding £60, to be levied by warrant under the hand and seal of the President, or by imprisonment, or by both, 9 V., c. 35, s. 81.

Sentences to be of a majority
Of regimental Courts to be executed by warrant of President
Appeal to General Court Martial
Consequences if frivolous
Consequences of frivolous charges

The sentence of a General Court Martial declared by the President, shall not (provided it does not extend to degradation of a Commissioned Officer) be subject to revision or require confirmation, but be in all things executed by Warrant under the hand and seal of the President. All Regimental or General Courts Martial shall be holden in the parish or precinct of their Regiments except in Martial Law, and the minutes shall be regularly kept by the Deputy Judge Advocate officiating : penalty not exceeding £60, or 28 days' imprisonment by General Court Martial; and the minutes shall be open to the inspection of every Officer of the Regiment, 9 V., c. 35, s. 82.

Sentence of General Court Martial not to require confirmation, except in cases of degradation to be executed by President's warrant ; see however 22 V., c. 43, s. 16
Courts Martial to be held in parish, &c., of regiment, except in Martial Law
Minutes

Every Court Martial shall sit not earlier than 8, a. m., nor later than 5 p. m., and shall have power to adjourn according to the necessity of the case, 9 V., c. 35, s. 88.

Time for holding

No Militia Officer or man shall be sentenced to death, except for mutiny, desertion to the enemy, or traitorously delivering up to the enemy any garrison, fortress, post or guard, or for traitorous correspondence with the enemy ; and no sentence of any General Court Martial shall be carried into effect until approved of by the Captain-General or Commander-in-Chief, if there be none, 22 V., c. 43, s. 15.

Sentence of death
To be approved by Captain General, &c. ; see 9 V., c. 35, s. 82

No Officer of the Army shall sit on any Militia Court Martial, 22 V. c. 43, s. 16.

Officers of the Army not to sit

The Colonel, &c., of Foot shall appoint Marshals, who shall act as Marshals to the Troops of the parish or precinct. All Marshals shall be liable to be examined, and answer upon oath to a Court Martial touching the non execution of warrants and non-services of notices and other Militia process sent to them by the Colonel, &c., of Foot, or by the Judge Advocate, or Commanding Officer of Horse ; and if it appear any Marshal has been in any wise negligent in the execution of any warrant or other duty,

Marshal's duties and liabilities

the Court shall impose upon him a fine not exceeding £30, and if not forthwith paid, the President shall issue a warrant under his hand and seal to the Constables of the parish, to take and convey him to the Common Gaol, to be detained for not exceeding 30 days, for default of payment of any one fine, or until it is paid. If any Marshal neglect to attend, or refuse or omit to answer upon oath any question, touching the non-execution of any warrant or other duty, he shall be liable to be fined by the Court not exceeding £60, and in case of non-payment, committed to Gaol not exceeding 2 months under warrant as aforesaid, or the Colonel may dismiss him, and he shall be liable to do duty as a private. No levy shall be made by the Marshal on the day of muster, or for 24 hours before or after. The Colonel, &c., of Foot, or Captain, &c., of Troop, may cause a Regimental Court of Enquiry to be held once in every 3 months, within 10 days after each usual quarter day, if he see occasion, to be composed as in the case of Courts Martial, and persons warned shall be liable to the like penalty as for non-attendance on a Regimental Court Martial, to be levied by Warrant under the hand and seal of the Colonel, &c., of the Regiment, or Captain, &c., of the Troop to which the Officer belongs, directed to the Constables of the parish, at which Court of Inquiry the Colonel, &c., shall produce his account of the receipts and disposal of all fines collected, or monies paid over to him ; and the Members shall be sworn well and truly to enquire touching and concerning the non-execution of all such warrants, of which the Court shall be required to enquire, and well and truly to determine upon any such enquiry, without partiality, favor or affection, by the Judge Advocate or his Deputy, or person appointed to act ; and the Court shall make a report, in duplicate, of the state of the accounts of the Colonel, &c., one copy under the hand of the President within 5 days, to be transmitted by him to the General of the District : penalty, £50, 9 V., c. 35, s, 83.

Not to make levies on day of muster or 24 hours before or after
Quarterly Regimental Courts to examine Accounts
Penalty for non attendance

The Marshal shall only retain to himself as compensation for his trouble in collecting fines one fourth of the amount collected, 15 V., c. 27.

The Marshal, on receipt, shall endorse on each warrant the date at which it came to his hands, and if not able to levy the amount directed within 5 days, may thereupon take the body of the party to the Common Gaol, there to remain for the period specified ; and the Marshal as well as the Keeper of the Gaol, shall notify in writing on the back of the warrants the date at which the party is taken to and received in Gaol, and where issued for imprisonment ; only the Marshal shall proceed forthwith to execute them, and he and the Keeper shall each notify on the back the date at which it was executed, and the prisoner received into custody, where he shall be safely kept for the period specified, 9 V., c. 35, s. 1, 13.

Resisting, or threatening to resist the execution of any warrant, or hindering, obstructing or interrupting a Marshal or person appointed to assist him in the execution of his office, or in anywise impeding or obstructing, or threatening, &c., the execution of a sentence of any Court Martial, or any person in the execution of this Act : fine not exceeding £60, or imprisonment not exceeding 28 days by Regimental or General Court Martial, 9 V., c. 35, s. 85.

To prevent parties against whom warrants are issued from giving up to Marshals some article of property as a levy, not their own goods, and for which actions of replevin are immediately instituted. Where levies are given up upon Militia Warrants, and replevins brought, and on trial a verdict is given for the plaintiff, the Judge before whom it is tried shall grant a certificate of such verdict under his hand, upon production of which to the Colonel or Commanding Officer of the Regiment or Troop, he shall issue a warrant against the party giving up such improper levy for £30, and if not paid within 10 days after demand by the Marshal, he shall take the delinquent to Gaol for 3 calendar months ; and it shall not be set aside for want of form, 9 V., c. 35, s. 86.

Any Deputy Marshal, or person having the care of any Gaol, not receiving or not keeping any person brought to Gaol under sentence of a Court Martial or warrant for the full period specified, shall forfeit not exceeding £60 as a Court Martial may award, to be levied under the hand and seal of the President, 9 V., c. 35, s. 87.

The penalties and fines imposed against Officers, non-Commissioned Officers and Privates where not particularly provided, shall be recovered and levied by distress and sale of the offender's goods, by warrant under the hand and seal of the Colonel, &c., of any Regiment, or of the President of any Court Martial (as the case may be), directed either to the Marshal or any Constable, rendering any overplus on demand, after deducting all necessary charges; and the warrant, in default of goods whereon to levy, shall authorize the Marshal to take the body of the offender, and commit him to the Common Gaol for the space of as many days as are before provided, according to the nature of the offence, 9 V., c. 35, s. 89.

Warrants for fines (except such as are directed to be under the hand of the Governor or Commander in Chief) shall be directed to the Marshal, and paid to the Colonel, &c., and may be applied so far as necessary for procuring drums, fifes, colors, standard and trumpets, for and defraying the clothing of the Band and other incidental expenses of the Regiment, and the overplus to the Receiver-General. The General of the District may cancel any warrant against defaulters in his District upon sufficient cause. Any Marshal making default, in paying over when required by the Colonel, &c., shall be liable to fine or imprisonment as a Court Marshal shall award. Any Colonel or other Officer to whom payments were made, making default in accounting and paying over, after being required by the Receiver-General or General of the District, shall be liable to be tried by a General Court Martial, and be sentenced to pay a fine not exceeding, £100, or to be cashiered, 9 V., c. 35, s. 91.

Warrants for fines, except of Governor, to be directed to Marshals and paid to Colonel
Application of fines

General of district may cancel warrants
Penalties on Marshals not paying over
On Colonels, &c

The Colonel, &c., shall, within 10 days after each usual Quarter-day, send or transmit to the General of the District a copy of the Regimental account, of the receipts and disposal or all money and fines collected or paid over to him, 9 V., c. 35, s. 92.

Colonel, &c., to transmit to General of district quarterly accounts; see s. 85

The Adjutant of each Regiment of Foot, and Junior Commissioned Officer of each Troop shall keep, in a book for the purpose, an exact account of the receipt and application of all fines levied and paid to the Colonel, &c., of Foot, or Captain, &c., of Horse; such book to be open to the inspection of the Officers, and produced to all Courts of Enquiry, under penalty of £20, to be recovered by warrant under the hand and seal of the Colonel, &c., of Foot, or Captain of the Troop, 9 V., c. 35, s. 93.

Adjutant of foot and junior Commissioned Officer of horse to keep books of accounts
To be open to Officers
And produced to Courts of enquiry

Councils of War shall consist of the Governor, Admiral, Captains, and, if none, Senior Officer in port, Members of the Privy Council, Speaker and Members of Assembly, General Officers of Militia and Field Officers of Regiments, not being Officers of the Regular Troops, and no other person shall have a right to sit, debate or vote, thereat; and not less than 21 shall be a quorum of a Council of War, 9 V., c. 35, s. 94.

Councils of war

Quorum

If the Assembly is dissolved, or not in being, and it is necessary before a new Assembly meets to summon a Council of War, the Members of the late Assembly shall have a right to sit, debate, and vote, 9 V., c. 35, s. 95.

If the Assembly is dissolved the late members to sit &c

Martial Law shall not be declared or imposed but by advice of a Council of War, and at the end of 30 days, shall determine ipso facto, unless continued by the advice of a Council of War, 9 V., c. 35, s. 96.

Martial law to be declared by advice of a Council of War, and to cease at end of 30 days, unless continued

The Governor, with the advice of a Council of War may, in the event of disturbance or emergency of any kind, declare any particular parish, district or county under Martial Law, and exempt other parts. Whenever Martial Law is declared or imposed, or the Militia or any part embodied under this clause, they shall be paid :—

Any parish, &c., may be declared under Martial Law
Pay of Militia on duty during

Each Major-General actually doing duty, £4 per day, to cover all expenses of forage, &c.

Colonel of Foot and Horse, £2 10s to cover all expenses.

Field Officer of Foot or Horse, including Major-General's Staff, £1 4s to cover all expenses

Captain, Chaplain, Surgeon, Deputy Judge Advocate and Adjutant, 12s.

Subaltern, including Quarter-Master and Assistant Surgeons, 9s.

Warrant and non-Commissioned Officer of Foot, 4s 6d for pay and rations, Privates including Band, 4s for pay and rations.

Officers and Warrant and non-Commissioned Officers and Privates of the Troop, 3s per day, as rations for one horse, additional.

The bills and amount for rations for non-Commissioned Officers and Privates shall be drawn for by the Colonels, &c., by orders on the Receiver General. The pay of Officers and extra expenses shall be audited and determined by the Commissioners of Accounts, before they become

How to be drawn for and paid

payable. No Officer, Warrant Officer, or Private, not actually and bona fide on duty, shall draw any allowance, 9 V., c. 35, s. 97.

Militia during Martial Law subject to articles of war, relating to H. M. S. Troops, except &c . Every Officer or man shall, during Martial Law, be subject to the Articles of War, and act for punishing mutiny and desertion, and all other laws then applicable to Her Majesty's Troops in this Island, and not inconsistent with this Act, except that no Militia man' shall be subject to any corporal punishment, except death' (see s. 15) or imprisonment for any contravention of such laws, and except that the Captain-General or Commander-in-Chief may direct that any provision shall not apply to the Militia, 22 V., c. 43, s. 13.

Senior Officer present to command
Officers of the Army to take precedence of Militia Officers of equal rank
Colonels under Commission from Commander of the forces Any body of Militia when called out shall be commanded by the Officer highest in rank present, or the senior of Officers of equal rank. Officers of the Army shall always be reckoned senior to all Militia Officers of the same rank, whatever the dates of their Commissions; and Colonels, by Commissions signed by the Commander of the Regular Forces, shall command Colonels of Militia, whatever the date of their Commissions, 22 V., c. 43, s. 14.

Emergencies on which Militia may be embodied In all cases of actual invasion, or upon imminent danger thereof, rebellion, insurrection or other emergency, the Governor (the occasion being first communicated to the Legislature, if sitting, or declared in Council, and notified by proclamation, if no Legislature is sitting or in being), may order the Colonels, &c., with all convenient speed, to draw out and embody all their Regiments and Corps to be raised and trained, or so many and such part as he judges necessary, and in such manner as is best adapted to the circumstances of the danger, and to put them under the command of such general Officers as he is pleased to appoint, and to direct the Forces to be led by their respective Officers into any parts of the Island for repelling and prevention of any invasion, and suppression of any **While embodied subject to articles of war** rebellion or insurrection; and from the time any Regiment, &c., is called out and embodied, until it shall be returned to its parish and disembodied by the Governor's orders, the Officers, &c., and Privates shall be subject to the rules and articles of war in force [under 22 V., c. 43, s. 13], 9 V., c. 35, s. 98.

Colonels, &c., to issue and make public their orders for embodiment The Colonel, &c., to whom any order is directed shall forthwith issue his order for the purpose, and immediately proceed to make same public, in the manner directed for making public notices of the time and place of exercise, (s. 36) 9 V., c. 35, s. 99.

Non-attendance at place of rendezvous desertion
Knowingly concealing persons who ought to attend Any person ordered to be drawn out and embodied (22 V., c. 43, s. 5, &c.), (not labouring under any infirmity or sickness incapacitating him) who shall not appear at the place of rendezvous, and march in pursuance of the order, shall be liable to be apprehended and punished as a deserter; any person harbouring and concealing him, knowing him to be such Militia-man, shall forfeit £60, 3 V., c. 35, s. 100.

Governor may direct regiments, &c., not embodied to be trained and exercised as ordinarily; see 22 V., c. 43, s. 12 If during the time any part of the Militia continues embodied, the Governor deems it expedient that any other part, not actually embodied, should be drawn out to be mustered, trained and exercised for a limited time instead of being embodied for service, he may direct the Colonels, &c., to cause the Militia not actually embodied, or any part, to be drawn out in order to be mustered, &c., in such proportion and for such time, and at such places as to such Colonel, &c., shall seem best, as directed for ordinary training and exercise, and they shall be mustered, &c., accordingly, 9 V., c. 35, s. 101.

When Governor with advice of Council may raise additional forces beyond the number appointed As it may be expedient in cases of actual invasion or imminent danger thereof and of rebellion that the Governor should be empowered to increase without delay the number of the Militia, he may, with the advice of the Council, issue a Royal proclamation, communicating it to the Legislature, if then sitting, or at their first meeting after, and direct thereby that in addition to the number of men required by this Act, there shall be forthwith raised and enrolled in the several Regiments any number of **Duty of Colonels, &c.** men between 21 and 45 as he sees fit. And the Colonel, &c., shall, on the issuing of the proclamation, proceed to raise and enroll such men at the times specified, without regard to regulations relative to the Militia, and the ballotting for and enrolling them, and the men so raised to train and exercise and call out into actual service, and the supplementary Militia hereby directed to be raised as far as can be enforced, as if the number added had been included in the number directed to be raised by this Act, 9 V., c. 35, s. 102.

Neither the whole nor any part of the Militia, shall on any account he carried or ordered out of the Island, but any part of the Militia may be carried or transported by sea from one port or place to another in the Island, 9 V., c. 35, s. 103.

The Governor may bestow and confirm Brevet rank to Officers whose conduct when on actual service he considers deserving of such distinction, 9 V., c. 35, s. 104.

When there is occasion to remove the Militia or any Detachment to Head Quarters, or from one place to another in this Island, the Governor shall give orders for regulating their march as he thinks proper, and the Colonel, &c., may quarter his Officers and men on the nearest plantation, or in such houses or out-houses as may be in his line of march most convenient, without being liable to any action for damages, to procure refreshment for his party, not exceeding 3s. for each man for 24 hours, and impress or cause to be impressed, such a number of wains, carts, horses, mules, cattle shallops, boats, wherries or canoes, as are necessary in such march or removal, giving proper certificates to the persons supplying refreshments, as also to the owners of wains, &c., impressed, to be paid by the Receiver-General after being certified by the Officer commanding, and produced to and approved of by a Board of Commissioners of Public Accounts (Governor in Executive Committee), 9 V., c. 35, s. 105.

No Colonel, &c., who impresses or causes, &c., any carts, &c., shallops, &c., for the purpose aforesaid shall be liable to any suit, civil or criminal, 9 V., c. 35, s. 106.

Upon the conclusion of the particular service for which the impressment is made, the Officer commanding shall return such carts, &c., to the place where they belong, under penalty of double the value, to be determined by 2 Justices in a summary manner, 9 V., c. 35, s. 107.

Any Trooper carrying a despatch, whose horse becomes unserviceable, may impress any horse or mule to enable him to reach his destination, provided he report the impressment to the Commanding Officer of the post whither he is proceeding, whose duty it shall be to return the horse or mule forthwith to the owner under the above penalty, and provided the horse or mule shall not belong to the personal working stock of any Field Officer, actually doing duty in the Militia, 9 V., c 35, s. 108.

It shall be the duty of all Troopers in times of Martial Law, or when the Militia is embodied, or on any sudden emergency or occasion, to carry expresses, except despatches to Port Royal, which are to be left with the main guard at Kingston or Passage Fort, or Port Henderson, who shall forward them to Port Royal, and also in or out of Martial Law to convey and execute within the district of any superior Officer of Cavalry, such orders as he shall issue for assembling Courts Martial, or serving notices for attending any other Military duty, under penalty of a fine not exceeding £60, nor less than £10, by a General Court Martial. It shall not be lawful to send by a Trooper any return muster-roll, or any despatch relative to any Regiment of Foot, unless directed to the Governor or Commander-in-Chief, or to a General Officer of a district. Every person sending a despatch shall write his name on the outside; and no person shall send any despatch by a Trooper of a private nature or otherwise than as before mentioned, under penalty of £60, to be levied by Warrant under the hand and seal of the Commander-in-Chief, nor shall the messenger of public despatches charge any Trooper with any despatch, which by virtue of his office and the salary annexed, he ought to forward: penalty £60, to be recovered by warrant as last aforesaid, 9 V., c. 35, s. 109.

"Commander-in-Chief" shall mean Governor, 9 V., c. 35, s. 110.

Any person sued for anything lawfully commanded or done in execution of this Act, may plead the general issue, and give the special matter in evidence, and if a verdict be found for the defendant, or the plaintiff is nonsuited or discontinue, shall have full costs, to be taxed, 9 V., c. 35, s. 111.

Every Warrant, or non-Commissioned Officer or Private, who in any engagement, with an internal or invading enemy, loses a limb or an eye, or is otherwise wounded so as to be rendered incapable to serve, shall, upon producing a certificate from his Commanding Officer, that he is so rendered incapable to serve, be allowed an annuity of £20 so long as he continues to reside in the Island, and remains unable to do duty, to be paid by the Receiver-General, upon application of the party entitled, and that he is then residing in the parish of and to which application shall be affixed a certificate of the Minister or a Magistrate, or one of the Churchwardens of the parish, that he is then living in the parish ; and if any Warrant, or non-Commissioned Officer or Private, is killed in any such engagement, and leaves a widow, or child, or children lawfully begotten, his widow shall be entitled to receive during her widowhood an annuity of £20, upon the like condition and terms ; and in case of her marriage or death, the annuity shall go to the child or children, in equal shares, until the youngest attains 15, 9 V., c. 35, s. 112.

In case of death to widow or children

All General Officers of Districts, General Staff Officers, Colonels, &c., of Regiments or Detachments, shall be remunerated all sums they pay for postage or otherwise in the discharge of their duties, on being audited by the Commissioners of Accounts (Executive Committee), 9 V., c. 35, s. 116.

Postage and other disbursements

This Act shall continue in force, notwithstanding and during Martial Law, 9 V., c. 35, s. 117.

In force during Martial Law

9 V., c. 35, and 13 V., c. 31, except so far as rerepealed, incorporated, 22 V., c. 43, s. 21.

9 V., c. 35 and 13, V, c. 31

Any penalty by this Act imposed, may be recovered before 2 Justices, and enforced as other summary convictions, or as any penalty for an offence of a like or corresponding nature or class may, by 9 V., c. 35, or 13 V., c. 31, be recovered, and shall be paid to the Receiver General, with power to the convicting Justices to award any part to any informer, who shall be a competent witness, 22 V., c. 43, s. 22.

Recovery, &c., of penalties

In case of invasion or imminent danger thereof, the Governor, with the advice of the Privy Council, and by proclamation in H. M's name, may raise as auxiliary to the Militia, and equip and maintain Volunteer Rifle Corps and Artillery Companies, for the defence of such ports or other places as may be advisable. The Officers and men shall be subject to all regulations, pains and penalties, and have all exemptions and immunities provided in respect to the Militia. The expense not to exceed £2000, and a detailed account of expenditure laid before the Assembly during the first 15 days of the meeting next thereafter, 22 V., c. 43, s. 24.

Volunteer Rifle Corps & Artillery Companies in cases of invasion, &c

All arms, accoutrements, ammunition, uniforms and musical instruments, imported for the use of any Militia or Volunteer Company shall be free of all Import Duties and Town Dues, 28 V., c. 38, s. 27.

Arms, &c. for use of free of duty &c

SCHEDULE.

Registration givings in for horse A., 22 V., c. 43, s. 2

NAME.	Age or probable age.	Occupation.	Place of Abode.	Whether he possesses Horse of not less than twenty pounds value.

For foot B., 22 V., c, 43, s. 2

NAME.	Age or probable age.	Occupation.	Place of Abode.

I,   of   do declare the above Returns under the Act of the twenty-second Victoria, chapter 43, for securing a better registration for the Militia, are true.

Declared before me this
  day of   18
                  J. P.

Name.	Age or probable Age.	Place of Abode.

List of persons ballotted for and enrolled, O. retained from repealed sec 9 V., c. 35, s. 13, by 22 V., c. 43, s. 4

Militia Volunteers.

The Volunteer Militia Act, 1865, 28 V., c, 38, s. 1.   Short Title

The Governor may accept the services of persons desiring to be formed into Volunteer Militia Companies, who offer their services through the Custos of the parish in which they are to be formed, 28 V., c. 38, s. 2.   Tender of service by Volunteers

And may continue the services of those previously accepted, unless and until he thinks fit to disband them. This Act shall apply to every Company as if its services were accepted thereunder, without prejudice to anything already done in relation to or by any such Company, 28 V., c. 38, s. 3.   Existing Companies

A majority of the Commissioned Officers of each Volunteer Company, may receive Volunteers as Non-commissioned Officers and Privates to supply vacancies. No person dismissed from a Company shall be permitted to join another without the Governor's previous sanction, nor shall any person who has left a Volunteer Company be permitted to join any other except on production of a certificate from his former Commanding Officer, to the effect that he knows no reason why the person should not re-enlist, and that he had faithfully discharged his duties when formerly in the service, 28 V., c. 38, s. 4.   Supply of vacancies   Persons who have been dismissed from or have left other companies

Any person holding a Commission in the Militia in any parish, and any other person in any such parish desirous of tendering his services as an Officer of Volunteers of such parish, shall forward to the Custos a notification of his desire to serve, with an affidavit, sworn to before any Justice of the Peace, stating that he is in receipt of an income or salary of not less than   Qualification of Officers

And appointment

£120, per annum, who shall forward the same without delay to the Governor, who is empowered to make all appointments of Commissioned Officers of the Volunteer Force, 28 V., c. 38, s. 5.

Dismissed persons ineligible as officers

No person who has been or may be dismissed from any Militia Regiment or Company, or Corps of Volunteers, shall be eligible to be appointed an Officer, 28 V., c. 38, s. 6.

Officers of Militia may accept lower rank in the Volunteers without prejudice

Any Officer in the Foot or Horse Militia may, if willing, be appointed as an Officer in any Volunteer Company, as of a rank or grade lower than that held by him in the Militia, but shall nevertheless retain his Militia rank so as to entitle him to promotion therein, 28 V., c. 38, s. 7.

First and subsequent appointments

Every person after his first appointment as an Officer may be promoted to a higher rank ; but every first appointment in consequence of any vacancy must be made in the manner prescribed for original appointments from among the persons whose applications are submitted through the Custos, 28 V., c. 38, s. 8.

Commissions to be free of charge notifications in the Gazette

The Commissions shall be free of Stamp duty and every other charge. The issue of all Commissions shall be notified in the " Gazette," and a list of the several Officers of Volunteers, with the dates of their appointments, shall be published once in every 6 months in the " Gazette," 28 V., c. 38, s. 9.

Non Commissioned Officers

The Commanding Officer of every Volunteer Company shall appoint Non-commissioned Officers, and fill up vacancies, and who shall hold their rank during his pleasure, 28 V., c. 38, s. 10.

Qualification for Non-commissioned Officers and privates

In cavalry or mounted rifles

Every person not disabled by bodily infirmity, and possessing an income of £40 per annum, may tender his services as a Non-commissioned Officer or private of any Volunteer Artillery or Rifle Company ; and any person possessed of such qualification, and having a Horse of the value of £15, may tender his services as a Non-commissioned Officer or Private of any Cavalry or mounted Rifle Company, 28 V., c. 38, s. 11.

Honorary members

A majority of the Officers of a Company may admit persons as Honorary Members, but who shall not be included in the muster roll of the Company, nor be subject to Military discipline, nor liable to be assembled with the Volunteers for actual Military duties. They may wear the uniform of the Company, and contribute to its funds. The Officers shall determine on the rank to be held by any Honorary Member, subject to the Governor's approval, 28 V., c. 38, s. 12.

Secretary

The Commanding Officer of any Company may appoint any Officer, Non-commissioned Officer or Honorary Member of his Company, to act as Secretary to the same, 28 V., c. 38, s. 13.

Oath on enlistment

Every Volunteer (except Honorary Members) shall take the following oath :—

> I, A. B., do sincerely promise and swear that I will be faithful, and bear true allegiance to Her Majesty Queen Victoria ; and that I will faithfully serve in the Volunteer Militia of Jamaica, for the defence of the said Island, and the maintenance of order and the public peace therein, during my enrolment in such Volunteer Militia.

Formula signed by party and attested by the Justice conclusive evidence of his being a Volunteer

Which oath may be administered by any Justice of this Island. On the oath being administered to a Volunteer, he shall sign a formula of the oath previously entered in a book to be kept by the Commanding Officer, and the signature shall be attested by the Justice administering the oath, and the entry and signature shall ipso facto be conclusive evidence without further proof of the fact of the party who has taken and signed the oath, being a Volunteer, 28 V., c. 38, s. 14.

Resignation of Officers

No Commissioned Officer shall be allowed to resign without the Governor's sanction upon sufficient reasons, and upon his paying all moneys due or becoming due by him to his Corps or Company, and such further amount as may be laid down in the rules to be promulgated by the Governor, on the recommendation of the Board of Officers, regulating the resignation of Officers.

Retirement of Non-commissioned Officers or privates

Any Non-commissioned Officer or Private may be permitted by a majority of the Officers of his Company to retire when not on actual service, after giving one month's notice to his Commanding Officer of his desire, and delivering up in good order (fair wear and tear only excepted,) all arms, clothing and appointments, being public property, or property of his Company issued to him, and paying all moneys due or becoming due by him under this Act, or any regulations promulgated by the Governor, or any rules of the Company, and thereupon his name shall be struck out of the muster roll by the Commanding Officer, 28 V., c. 38, s. 15

Appeal to 2 Justices whose determination shall be binding

If any Non-commissioned Officer or Private gives notice, and a majority of the Officers refuse to grant him leave to resign, he may appeal to 2 Justices of the parish to which the Company belongs, they not being Volunteers, who shall hear the appeal, and may summon and examine any witness on oath and if it appears to them that the arms, clothing and appointments issued, being public property, or property of his Company or Corps, have been delivered up in good order (fair wear and tear only excepted), or that he has paid sufficient compensation for any damage the articles have sustained, and that all moneys due or becoming due by him under this Act, or the rules and regulations to be issued by the Governor, or the rules of his Company, have been paid, the Justices may order the Commanding Officer forthwith to strike such Non-commissioned Officer or Private out of the muster roll, and their determination shall be binding on all parties, 28 V., c. 38, s. 16.

Disbanding Companies by Governor, formation of others Dismissal of officers, &c To be notified in the Gazette

Any Volunteer Company may be disbanded by the authority of the Governor, who may thereupon authorize the formation of another Company in lieu thereof. The Governor, upon good cause may dispense with the services of any Officer, Non-commissioned Officer or other member of any Company, to be notified in the "Gazette" within 10 days, 28 V., c. 38 s. 17.

Band or Drum Corps

Every Company may form a Band or Drum Corps, either separately or conjointly with another or others, who shall be Members exclusive of the Rank and File, and subject to the same discipline, and shall enjoy the privileges of Volunteers, 28 V., c. 38, s. 18.

Regulations for their Government

And shall be governed as a majority of the Officers of the Company or Companies from time to time determine upon; but such regulations shall not have effect until they have been approved by the Governor and lodged with the Clerk of the Peace, whereupon they shall have the force of law, 28 V., c. 38, s. 19.

Uniform, Arms, &c To be furnished by the Island And to be Island property

The uniform, arms, equipment, accoutrements, ammunition and other stores of the Officers and men shall be such as the Governor directs. The arms, &c., shall be furnished to the Non-commissioned Officers and Privates at the expense of the Island, but shall always remain Island property, 28 V., c. 38, s. 20.

Or if not furnished with uniforms, non-commissioned Officers &c., to be paid an annual commutation Subject to regulations

The Governor shall cause the Non-commissioned Officers and Privates to be furnished with uniforms, at the expense of the public, or pay to each Volunteer an amount annually in commutation of such clothing, subject to any rule or regulation to be promulgated by the Governor, on the recommendation of the Board of Officers, 28 V., c. 38, s. 21.

Officers resigning or dismissed not delivering up Arms, &c.

Every Commanding Officer who on his resignation or dismissal, or within 7 days after, neglects or refuses to hand over to the Officer or Non-commissioned Officer next in command, or person appointed by the Governor, all arms, &c., issued or intrusted to his care, shall be liable to a fine not exceeding £5, nor less than £2, in addition to the value of the articles withheld, 28 V., c. 38, s. 22.

Members of companies not delivering up articles

Every Member who fails to deliver up to the Officer in command, all arms, accoutrements, ammunition, bugles or other articles intrusted to his care, within 7 days after having received intimation of his dismissal, or after his resignation, shall, on conviction, be liable to a penalty not exceeding £5, nor less than 20s. in addition to the value of the articles withheld, 28 V., c. 38, s. 23.

Embezzlement, &c

By Volunteers Other persons

Any Volunteer who embezzles, pawns, sells, loses by carelessness, or designedly or negligently wastes, spoils, injures or uses for any other purposes than those of the Queen, any arms, ammunition, accoutrements or other articles with which any Corps or Company or any part has been or may be furnished at the public expense shall be liable to a fine not exceeding £2, as a Court of Enquiry may direct, in addition to the value. Any Person, other than a Volunteer, guilty of any such acts, shall be liable to a penalty not exceeding £5, in addition to the value, to be recovered as after directed, or to imprisonment in any Gaol, not exceeding 20 days, 28 V., c. 38, s. 24.

Buying from, assisting volunteers to dispose of arms, &c.

Knowingly buying or taking in exchange from any Volunteer, or any person, acting on his behalf, or soliciting or enticing any Volunteer to sell, or knowingly assisting, or acting for any Volunteer, in selling or having in possession or keeping, without satisfactorily accounting for the same, any arms, &c., being public property, or that of any Volunteer Corps or Company, or any public stores or ammunition issued for their use: penalty not exceeding £5, or imprisonment in any Gaol for not exceeding 20 days, 28 V., c, 38, s. 25.

Delivery over of arms, &c after death

In case of the death of any Volunteer or other person who has received any arms, ammunition, accoutrements or other articles belonging to any Company, the person into whose possession they come shall deliver them over forthwith to the Officer commanding the Company to which they belong : penalty, not exceeding £5, in addition to the value, and in default of payment of fine and value, imprisonment in any Gaol for not exceeding 10 days, as the Justices award, 28 V., c. 28, s. 26.

Arms, &c. imported for militia or volunteers free of duty

All arms, accoutrements, ammunition, uniforms and musical instruments, imported for the use of any Militia or Volunteer Company, shall be free of Import Duties and Town Dues, 28 V., c. 38, s. 27.

Drill

Absence

Each Company shall be drilled once at least in every month, on a day and place to be fixed by the Commanding Officer, but the Governor or Commanding Officer may order extraordinary drills or parades when and where he thinks proper. Any member absent without having sent a good excuse in writing, or previously obtained leave of absence from the Commanding Officer, shall be fined in such sums as may be fixed from time to time in the regulations of the Governor issued, on the recommendation of the Board of Officers, 28 V., c. 38, s. 28.

Breach of discipline when on duty

Officers to be placed under arrest non commissioned officers, &c. in custody

If any Volunteer while under arms or on march or other duty, or while engaged in any Military exercise or drill, or while wearing the clothing or accoutrements of his Company, and going to or returning from any place of exercise or assembly of his Company, disobeys any lawful order of any Officer or non-Commissioned Officer, under whose command he then is, or is guilty of misconduct, breach of discipline or insubordination, the Officer in command of the Corps or Company, or any superior Officer in command, may order the offender, if an Officer, under arrest, and if a Non-commissioned Officer or Private, into the custody of any Drill Instructor, or any Volunteer belonging to the same or any other Corps, or Company, but so that the Officer is not kept longer under arrest or custody than during the time the Corps or Company remains under arms or on march, or duty, or assembled or continues engaged in any Military exercise or drill; but such arrest or custody shall not prevent his subsequent trial by a Court of Enquiry, 28 V., c. 38, s. 29.

Court of Enquiry
Administrative junction of Companies
To be otherwise separate
May be mustered together once in 6 months
Inspection by senior officers of the army

Two or more Companies in the same or adjoining parishes may be administratively united on the joint application of the Commanding Officers. Notwithstanding the formation of any administrative Corps, the several Companies shall be deemed separate for all the purposes of this Act. The Governor may direct the muster (not more than once in 6 months) of any Administrative Corps for drill or exercise, 28 V., c. 38, s. 30.

When any Volunteer Company or Corps are on actual service, or are undergoing inspection, or doing other Military duty, the Governor may place them and their Officers under the command of Officers of the Army, senior in rank to every Volunteer Officer present, 28 V., c. 38, s. 31.

Drill Instructors, military

Volunteer

Companies 3 years in existence

The Governor may appoint Drill Instructors from the Army for the Volunteers, to be paid out of the money voted for Militia and Volunteer services at such rates as may be considered reasonable. They shall be subject to the orders of the Commanding Officer of the Company or Corps to which they may from time to time be attached, but amenable only to the Military authorities for any misconduct or breach of Military discipline. But not to prevent the Governor from appointing any efficient Volunteer, on his being declared competent by the Board of Officers, and who shall he paid a like sum as those selected from the Army. No Volunteer Company in existence for 3 years shall be entitled to a Drill Instructor at the public expense, 28 V., c. 38, s. 32.

Annual inspection by an officer of the army
His pay
Cost not to exceed £230

An annual inspection of every Volunteer Corps shall be held by a competent Officer of the Army, to be appointed by the Governor, who shall be paid such sums as the Governor in Executive Committee may award; the whole cost of inspection not to exceed £230, per annum, to be paid out of the money voted for Militia and Volunteer purposes, 28 V., c. 38, s. 33.

The Inspecting Officer shall discharge the duties of Secretary to the Governor in Volunteer and Militia matters, and all orders, directions, and notifications conveyed or signed by the Military Secretary to the Militia or Volunteers, shall be deemed to proceed from the Governor. He shall be assisted in his duties by an Assistant, who shall receive £75 per annum, 28 V., c. 38, s. 34.

Military Secretary
Assistant £75 per annum

The Military Secretary shall hold the Brevet rank of Colonel in the Militia and Volunteers, and be relieved of all Stamp Duties and other charges on his commission as such, 28 V., c. 38, s. 35.

Brevet Rank

The Governor may appoint any Volunteer Officers to act on his Staff for Volunteer purposes, but without remuneration, 28 V., c. 38, s. 36.

Staff appointments

Also annually a Board of Officers to consist of his Military Secretary, and 10 Volunteer Officers, and fill up vacancies. The Assistant to the Military Secretary shall act as their Secretary, and three of the Board shall be a quorum, 28 V., c. 38, s. 37.

Board of Officers
Their Secretary
3 a quorum

The Board of Officers shall make rules and regulations respecting anything directed or authorized, or provided for by regulations, and also such as seem fit (not inconsistent with this act) respecting—

Rules and Regulations

The strength of each Company, as well as the distribution of its Officers, Non-commissioned Officers and Privates.

Strength of the company, &c.

The appointment or promotion of Officers of Administrative Corps or Volunteer Companies.

Appointments &c. of officers

The efficiency of Volunteers, and granting certificates of such efficiency.

Efficiency

The assembling and proceeding of Courts of Enquiry.

Courts of Enquiry

And the full execution of this Act, and the general Government and discipline of the Force.

General Government

All which rules and regulations, when approved of by the Governor in Privy Council, and published in the "Gazette," shall have the force of law, and be quoted as such, in any Court of Enquiry or Court of Law or Equity. The Board may alter or repeal them, subject to such approval and promulgation. All funds voted for Volunteer Militia purposes, shall be distributed by the Governor in Executive Committee, on the recommendation of such Board of Officers, 28 V., c. 38, s. 38.

Their force
May be altered
Distribution of funds

The Governor may order the Volunteers, or any portion to any part of the Island, to aid in its defence, the maintenance of order and the public peace, the protection of property or upholding of the law. The Custos, or, in his absence, the Senior Magistrate of any parish in which any such emergencies arise, may call out the Volunteers of the parish. All requisitions for their services must be made in writing, and signed by the authority, 28 V., c. 38, s. 39.

Ordering Volunteers upon service

When a Corps or Company or any part is called out, every member shall be bound to assemble as directed by his Commanding Officer, and to proceed to the place where his presence is required, and from the time it is called out it shall be deemed on actual service ; and any Officer, non-Commissioned Officer, Private, or other party attached to the same, not incapacitated by infirmity for Military Service (to be established by the certificate of a Medical Practitioner or two Justices), who refuses or neglects to assemble or march, or discharge the duty required of him, shall be deemed a deserter, and tried as soon as convenient thereafter by a Court of Enquiry or Court Martial, 28 V., c. 38, s. 40.

Neglect to assemble and perform duty ; desertion
Triable by Court of Enquiry or Court Martial

Every Commissioned Officer shall, while on actual service, be entitled to the pay and allowances of an Officer of the same rank in the Army, 28 V., c. 38, s. 41.

Pay and allowances of officers

Every Non-commissioned Officer shall, while on actual service, be entitled to 7s 6d. and every private to 5s per day for rations. Members of a Cavalry or Mounted Corps, to 2s in addition for the forage of a horse, to be paid out of the amount voted for Militia and Volunteer purposes, 28 V., c. 38, s. 42.

Non-commissioned officers and privates

When the Militia of any parish are called out in case of war, invasion, insurrection or riot, or imminent danger, the Volunteers of the parish shall be deemed to be included in the order, and be allowed the same amount for

Volunteers to be deemed included in any order, calling out the militia of the parish rations and forage as if specially ordered out by the Governor, Custos or other Magistrate, 28 V., c. 38, s. 43.

Release from active service

After being called out for active service, the Corps shall be deemed released therefrom only by an order, in writing, signed by the Governor, the Custos, or, in his absence, the Senior Magistrate of the parish ; and each Volunteer shall receive the allowance for rations and forage until released from duty, and after the return of his company to its parish, 28 V., c. 38, s. 44.

When subject to the articles of war

See s. 37-38

When on actual Military Service for protection of the Island against invasion, they shall be regulated by, and be subjected to the provisions of the Militia Law, and the Rules and Articles of War then in force ; but on any other emergency, by this Act, and the Regulations promulgated with the sanction of the Governor in Privy Council, 28 V., c. 38, s. 45

Impressment of horses, &c.

Any Volunteer carrying a despatch, or engaged in any other service, may impress any horse or mule, but shall report it to the Commanding Officer of the post, or other authority to whom he is proceeding, who shall return it as soon as convenient to the owner, on the conclusion of the service for which it was impressed, 28 V., c. 38, s. 46.

Courts of enquiry on any matters relative to the companies

The Governor may assemble a Court of Enquiry, composed of Militia and Volunteer Officers, or partly of Officers of the Army and partly Volunteers, to enquire into any matter relative to Companies of any parish, and to record the facts and circumstances ascertained on the enquiry, and report thereon to him, 28 V., c. 38, s. 47.

Complaints against Officers

The Governor, on receipt of a complaint against any Commissioned Officer for misconduct, insubordination or breach of discipline, shall assemble a Court of Enquiry to investigate and report thereon, consisting of 5 Officers of Volunteers selected by him, 28 V., c. 38, s. 48.

Charges against n o n commissioned officers or privates

On a charge of misconduct, &c., against any non-Commissioned Officer or Private, the Commanding Officer of the Company to which the accused belongs, shall summon the Members of the Company to meet and ballot for a Court of Enquiry to investigate the charge, consisting for the trial of a Non-commissioned Officer of 2 Officers and 3 Non-commissioned Officers; of a Private, of 1 Officer, 2 Non-commissioned Officers and 2 Privates, of the same or any other Company or Companies of the parish, 28 V., c. 38, s. 49.

Proceedings of Courts of Enquiry

Witnesses

Non attendance

Absence of accused

The Members convened shall, before proceeding, be sworn faithfully to discharge their duties. The Court shall have power to summon the accused, and any witness whose name has been previously forwarded to the Secretary of the Company, and to examine all witnesses on oath. Any Volunteer who, on being summoned, neglects or refuses to attend and give evidence before any Court of Enquiry, either in his own or any other Company, shall, on proof of the service of such summons, be fined not exceeding £3. Any other person, not exceeding £2, to be imposed on proof of such summons by the President, in his discretion. If the accused absents himself without forwarding to the President an explanation for his absence, satisfactory to a majority of the Members, the complaint shall, on proof of the service of the summons, be investigated in his absence, and the decision acted upon, 28 V., c. 38, s. 50.

Sentence against an officer

Any Court of Enquiry may impose on any Volunteer Officer found guilty on a charge, a fine not exceeding £10, or recommend his dismissal, or both, 28 V., c. 38, s. 51.

A non commissioned officer or private

Or, on finding a Non-commissioned Officer or Private guilty, may impose a fine, not exceeding £5, or dismissal from the Company, or both. In the case of a Non commissioned Officer, the Court may, in lieu of dismissal, recommend his reduction to the ranks, with or without a fine, 28 V., c. 38, s. 52.

For desertion

8. 56 -57

If the charge be for desertion, the Court may sentence, in addition to, imprisonment in Gaol not exceeding 20 days, which sentence the President shall put into execution, by issuing a warrant of commitment, under his hand, directed to the Collector of Petty Debts of the parish, or to any of his lawful deputies, provided the sentence has been confirmed by the Governor or as after directed, 28 V., c. 38, s. 53.

Suspension pending charge

On a charge being preferred against any Officer, Non-commissioned Officer or Private, the Commanding Officer of the Company shall immediately suspend him from his duties, and he shall remain under suspension until his case is adjudicated or otherwise disposed of. In the case of a Com.

manding Officer, the Governor, on receiving a complaint against him, shall immediately suspend him, to remain so until his case is adjudicated, &c., 28 V., c. 38, s. 54.

If any Volunteer make a groundless, frivolous or vexatious complaint against another, so as to cause him to be prosecuted before a Court of Enquiry, the pa y making such complaint shall be liable to a penalty not exceeding £3, which fine the Court before whom the case is heard may impose, but the party so fined shall be entitled to an appeal to the Governor, against such decision; notice thereof to be given to the President within 2 days after the sentence is promulgated, and the grounds of Appeal forwarded to him within 7 days thereafter, for transmittal to the Governor, 28 V., c. 38, s. 55.

Groundless complaints

No sentence made before any Court of Enquiry for dismissal or imprisonment for desertion, shall be carried into execution until confirmed by the Governor, who may annul or commute the same, 28 V., c. 38, s. 56.

Sentence of dismissal or imprisonment must be confirmed by the Governor

Not to prevent any appeal from the decision of a Court of Enquiry to the Governor, notice of which shall be given by the party sentenced, to the President, within 2 days after the decision has been arrived at and promulgated. The Appellant shall, within 7 days, thereafter, forward to the President, for transmission to the Governor, the grounds of his Appeal, 28 V., c. 38, s. 57.

Appeal to the Governor

The Government, or any Parochial Vestry or other Board, Society, Corporation or person, may grant and renew Licenses for the use, during any term of any years, of lands under their control as a target ground for Volunteers; and any Volunteer firing on the same with the sanction of his Commanding Officer shall be held to be in the performance of a lawful duty, 28, V., c. 38, s. 58.

Rifle ranges

Where a foot path crosses or runs inconveniently or dangerously near to any lands purchased or otherwise acquired for a rifle range, it may, with consent of the Board of Highways and Bridges, be stopped up or diverted at the cost of the public, 28 V., c. 38, s. 59.

Pathways across target grounds

No Officer or Member of any Company shall be liable to any suit, civil or criminal, for appointing or using any place for drill or muster, not in any cultivated ground or Guinea Grass-piece, 28 V., c. 38, s. 60.

Muster grounds

Every Volunteer shall be free from arrest on mesne or civil process for 12 hours before and during any parade, muster, drill, ball-practice or other service, by order of the Governor or Officer commanding his Company, and for 12 hours after, 28 V., c. 38, s. 61.

Freedom from arrest

Every Volunteer except Honorary Members, shall be exempt from liability to serve personally or to provide a substitute in the Militia; but a Non-commissioned Officer or Private, not possessed of a certificate of efficiency, shall cease to have the privilege of exemption on his discharge or resignation, unless he quits the Company on account of change of residence, and enrols himself in a Volunteer Company in the parish to which he transfers his residence, within 2 months of ceasing his connexion with the Company to which he was previously attached. No person, who has served 2 years as a Volunteer Officer, or has received a certificate of efficiency, and who has not been dismissed the service, shall be liable to be enrolled as a Non-commissioned Officer or Private in the Militia. The certificate of the Commanding Officer, that the person named is a Volunteer, enrolled in his Company, or the certificate of efficiency, in the case of a party exempt from Militia Duty, except during Martial Law, or other emergency, or the Commission of an ex Officer of Volunteers, shall be conclusive evidence thereof, and secure exemption from Militia Duty for the period specified in this Act, 28 V., c 38, s. 62.

Exemption from Militia duty

Every Volunteer who has obtained a certificate of efficiency, shall, on its production to the Collector of Dues of his parish be relieved of payment of taxes to the extent of 40s. No Registration Tax shall be paid on any horse kept by any Officer or Member of a Cavalry or Mounted Rifle Volunteer Company, on his producing to the Collector of Dues of his parish an affidavit, sworn to before a Justice to that effect, 28 V., c. 38, s. 63.

Relief of Taxes

Two-thirds of the Members of any Company present, at a meeting convened for the purpose by the Commanding Officer, after 10 days' notice, may make regulations for the management of the property, finances,

Financial rules;

To be approved by the Governor and civil affairs of the Company, which, being approved of by the Governor, shall have the force of law, 28 V., c. 38, s. 64.

And lodged with the Clerk of the Peace And which, within 14 days after his approval, shall be lodged with the Clerk of the Peace, and kept among the records of his office, 28 V., c. 38, s. 65.

Alterations, &c. Two-thirds of the Members, after 10 days' notice, may alter or repeal any regulations, subject to the Governor's approval, and after approval, such amendment shall be lodged with the Clerk of the Peace, 28 V., c. 38, s. 66.

Returns of strength, &c. The Governor may require any Inspecting Officer, or Commanding Officer of an Administrative Corps or Company, to make to him returns or reports of their strength and efficiency, or on any other subject connected with the Volunteers he deems requisite, 28 V., c. 38, s. 67.

False Certificate Any Commanding Officer of a Company or Administrative Corps, who knowingly gives a false certificate, shall, besides being dismissed from his appointment, be liable to a penalty not exceeding £20, one moiety to the informer, the other to be appropriated to the use of the Company, or Administrative Corps to which he was attached, 28 V., c. 38, s. 68.

Obstruction &c. on duty Any person who obstructs or assaults any Volunteer whilst in the execution of his duty, shall, on conviction before 2 or more Justices, be fined not exceeding £10, and in default of payment, be imprisoned in any prison, not exceeding 30 days, nor less than 2 days, 28 V., c. 38, s. 69.

Recovery of subscriptions, fines, &c by a Court of Enquiry All subscriptions, fines, penalties, and forfeitures imposed by any Court of Enquiry under this Act, or under any rules, &c., shall be recovered at the instance of the Officer commanding the Company, under any Act relating to the recovery of Petty Debts, but if any Volunteer is imprisoned in consequence of the non-payment of any such subscription, &c., or the absence of goods whereon to levy, he may be released, by order of the Governor or his commanding Officer, before the expiration of the term of imprisonment 28 V., c. 38, s. 70.

Without the intervention of a Court of Enquiry All fines and penalties imposed without the intervention of a Court of Enquiry, shall be recovered before 2 or more Justices, and, if not forthwith paid, levied by warrant of distress, and in default of sufficient distress, the offender shall be imprisoned in any Common Goal (unless where otherwise directed) for not exceeding 30 days, 28 V., c. 38, s. 71.

Appropriation All subscriptions, &c., recovered, shall be the property of the Company to which the person paying the same is or was attached, and be appropriated to its use by a Board of Officers and Non commissioned Officers, annually appointed by the Members of the Company, 28 V., c. 38, s. 72.

Property of company vested in the commanding officer All moneys subscribed by or for the use of any Company, and all effects belonging to any such Company or lawfully used by it, not the property of any individual Officer or Volunteer, and all lands and other property acquired by the Company, shall vest in the Commanding Officer for the time, **Civil and criminal proceedings** and his successors, with power to sue and make contracts and conveyances, and do all other lawful things relating thereto; and any civil or criminal proceedings taken by the Commanding Officer shall not be discontinued or abated by his death, resignation or removal, but may be carried on and completed by his successor. In case of the disbanding of a Company, all **Property of disbanded companies** property previously belonging thereto shall be vested in the Governor for the benefit of the Island, 28 V., c. 38, s. 73.

Exemption from Stamps Want of form All proceedings under this Act, or any rules and regulations shall be exempt from Stamp Duties, and no proceedings shall be quashed for want of Form, 28 V., c. 38, s. 74.

Interpretation "Persons" shall include any set of individuals, or a body corporate or incorporate; "Company," a Volunteer Troop of Cavalry or Mounted Rifles or Artillery, or Company of Rifles; "Corps," Volunteer Companies combined for administrative purposes, or otherwise acting together, or any individual Company, 28 V., c. 38, s. 75.

Officers &c. already appointed or enrolled All Officers appointed under repealed Acts shall continue so, but subject to this Act or Acts to be passed, and all Non-commissioned Officers and Privates and Members of Band or Drum Corps already enrolled, shall continue to serve as Volunteers, subject to the provisions of this Act, 28 V., c. 38, s. 78.

Milk River Bath.

The Members of the Council and Assembly, and the Custos of Vere (as also the Justices, 44 G. 3, c. 29, s. 1), or any three of them, were incorporated as "The Directors of the Milk River Bath," and ½ acre of land, including the Milk River Bath and Buildings vested in them, with power to lease any part for not exceeding 21 years, and apply the proceeds towards increasing the Buildings, and providing necessaries and conveniences for sick and poor people, and with power to appoint and remove for neglect or misdemeanor, officers and servants, and make rules and regulations, not repugnant to the prerogative, or to law, or Ecclesiastical Canons or constitutions of the Church of England. £100 (increased to £300 or £180 stg. 44 G. 3, c. 29. s. 2) granted for sustaining the buildings, and defraying salaries and fees of officers and servants. Any Medical man to be appointed to the Bath, must make oath before he receives his salary, that he has while in health visited the establishment 3 days of the week at least, and report to the House, at their Session, the result of his practice, 33 G. 3, c. 19 ; 44 G. 3, c. 29. *(margin: Incorporation and powers. Grant of £180 stg. Medical Man to visit Bath 3 days in the week. Reports to Assembly)*

The Directors were empowered to purchase additional land contiguous for Buildings, 34 G. 3, c. 25, s. 1 ; 35 G. 3, c. 26. *(margin: Additional Land)*

Mines and Minerals.

No Tax or Impost in respect of Minerals whether of Royal or base Metal, shall be imposed upon the Mines or Ores, or persons working them for 12 years, from 1st January, 1855 ; but not to affect Land and Quit Rent Tax, 18 V., c. 59. *(margin: Exempted from taxes for 12 years)*

Mining Companies.

Provisions for the establishment, registration and management of, with limited liabilities, 17 V., c. 32 ; 18 V., c. 42 ; 22 V., c. 11.

Mining Leases.

Powers given to Corporations, Ecclesiastical or Civil, seized of an Estate of Freehold in possession, Tenants for life with immediate remainder to first and every other son in tail, and for Guardians of Infants, and Committees of Lunatics or Idiots, seized of an Estate of Freehold in possession, with the approbation of the Chancellor of Jamaica, Tenants in dower, or by the curtesy, with the consent of the person seized in reversion or remainder of an Estate of inheritance to grant Leases for 50 years of Mines opened or unopened upon certain conditions (but not mortgagees without the assent of the mortgager). As also persons in possessions under Leases for 99 years, of which not less than 50 years are unexpired, reserving the rights of the Crown, 18 V., c. 32. *(margin: Powers to grant leases for 50 years)*

Mortgages.

Mortgagees having received satisfaction of the monies due, shall enter satisfaction upon the margin of the record of the Mortgage, at the request of the mortgager, which shall release the same, and shall, within 3 months after request, and tender of reasonable charges, repair to the office of enrolment, and make the acknowledgment : Penalty, £50 (£30 stg.) to the party aggrieved, to be recovered in any Court of Record, 33 C. 2, c. 12, s. 4. *(margin: Satisfaction)*

Foreigners or aliens may lend money at lawful interest upon the security of any freehold or leasehold estate, and hold same as an effectual security for the money lent, 13 G. 3, c. 16, s. 1. *(margin: Mortgages to aliens valid)*

On forfeiture of the security and non-payment of the money lent, the legal estate upon which the Mortgage is granted shall vest in the President of the Council, the Speaker of the Assembly, and the Chief Justice for the time, upon the trusts of the original conveyances or securities to the foreigner or alien for the money lent ; and the foreigners, their heirs, &c., may bring and prosecute, by themselves or their attornies, their actions or bills in any court of law or equity, in the names of the trustees beforementioned, for the recovery of the moneys due, by sale or otherwise, as *(margin: On forfeiture legal estate vested in President of the Council, &c., in whose names proceedings may be taken to enforce payment)*

3 P

natural subjects may, and the trustees shall allow their names to be used; but no such foreigner or alien shall be entitled to obtain or enter into the actual possession of any such lands or estates, or to foreclose the equity of redemption, 13 G. 3, c. 16, s. 2.

Foreigner not to enter into possession or foreclose

The Provost Marshal or his Deputy shall not remove any levy on any mules, cattle, stock, carriages, plantation utensils or implements, if the defendant, his overseer, attorney, trustee, executor, &c., or the mortgagee or person claiming title to the levy in virtue of some Mortgage or prior incumbrance, his overseer, &c., within 5 days after the levy, produce to the Provost Marshal or Deputy making the levy, an attested docket, of the Mortgage or other incumbrance, with an affidavit of the defendant, his overseer, &c., or of the mortgagee, &c., his overseer, &c., (sworn before a Judge or any Justice of the Peace) that to the best of his knowledge, information and belief, the mules, &c. whereon the levy is made. are included in the Mortgage or other incumbrance, a docket whereof is produced, or are the increase of the same, and that such Mortgage, &c. is prior to the execution on which the levy is made, in the following Form :—

Levies on mortgaged property not to be removed on production of docket and affidavit

*No. 1.
Form of Affidavit*

I, A. B., of the parish of   in the said Island, owner, (overseer, trustee, &c. as the case may be) do swear that the (here set forth the particulars of the levy, whether mules, cattle, stock, or plantation utensils, as the case may be) levied on by
            Deputy Marshal for the said parish, on the
day of   instant (or last past, as the case may be) on a writ of Venditioni Exponas, at the suit of   against (or by virtue of a writ of replevin, as the case may be) are to the best of this deponent's knowledge, information and belief, either comprised and included, or are the increase of stock comprised and included in a certain Indenture of Mortgage, or other incumbrance, bearing date the   day   from   to an attested docket whereof this deponent produced to the said Deputy-Marshal at the time of his making the aforesaid levy, (or as soon after as this deponent had an opportunity of so doing, as the case may be) ; and this deponent further saith, that to the best of his knowledge and belief, the said Indenture of Mortgage or other incumbrance is prior to the [execution on which the dele and substitute judgment on which the 19 V., c. 10, s. 39] writ of Venditioni Exponas was issued whereon the aforesaid levy was made.

And acknowledgment to deliver unless n replevin is lodged, or 6 days after trial

And do also give to the Provost Marshal or his Deputy an acknowledgment in writing, that the levy has been made, and remains in his hands, and shall be produced or delivered over to the Provost Marshal or his Deputy on the 1st Monday in the succeeding Grand Court, in case no replevin is filed and lodged by the person claiming title under such Mortgage, &c., and in case any replevin is filed, the levy or such part as shall not be recovered by the plaintiff in replevin, shall, within 5 days after trial, he delivered to the Provost Marshal or his Deputy, to be sold if the Court so order ; which acknowledgment shall be in the following Form :—

*No. 2.
Form of Acknowledgment*

I, A. B., of the parish of   in the said Island, owner, (overseer, trustee, &c., as the case may be) do hereby acknowledge that
            Deputy-Marshal for the parish of
aforesaid, did on the   day of   instant, (or last past, as the case may be) levy on (here set forth the particulars of the levy) in my possession on a writ of Venditioni Exponas (if more than one mention them) at the suit of
against   (or by virtue of a replevin at the suit of
against   as the) case may be, and I do also acknowledge that the said levy so made as aforesaid remains in my hands and possession, and that I hold the same ready to be delivered over to the Provost Marshal or his Deputy, agreeable to a law of this Island in such case made and provided. Given under my hand this
day of   one thousand eight hundred and

Replevin to be tried within one Court after brought

The replevin shall be tried within one Court next after that for which it is brought, unless the plaintiff is prevented from trying it by such cause as shall, upon affidavit, appear satisfactory to the Supreme Court, 23 G., 3, c. 14, s. 1.

Consequences of non-delivery

If any person who has given such acknowledgment refuses, declines or omits producing and delivering over such levy at the time and for the purpose declared, and the same is made to appear to the Supreme Court, he shall be liable to be proceeded against by attachment, fine, imprisonment, or otherwise as to the Court shall seem proper, 23 G. 3, c. 14, s. 2.

If in his absence any Overseer or person resident or employed on the property give the acknowledgment, the mortgager, mortgagee or other person in possession shall be bound thereby, as if he had actually signed and given it, an liable to be proceeded against by the Supreme Court, 23 G., 3 c. 14, s. 3.

Mortgager or Mortgagee bound by acknowledgment

Although not to be removed, the levy shall be deemed in the custody of the Provost Marshal or his Deputy; but he shall not be entitled to any consideration by way of Goal fees or other fees or charges, until the levy is delivered over to be sold (if such be the case), and then to Goal fees only from the time of delivery, and to such other fees as the Provost Marshal is legally entitled to upon the sales of levies, 23 G. 3, c. 14, s. 4.

Levy to be considered in custody. Provost Marshal's fees

It shall not be necessary at the trial of such replevin to produce the cattle, &c., but proof at the trial or under any commission or rule of Court that those mentioned in the replevin are also mentioned and comprised in the Indenture of Mortgage or incumbrance produced, shall be sufficient proof of identity, 23 G. 3, c. 14, s. 5.

Need not be produced at trial Evidence of identity

Mortgagees or persons claiming title under the Mortgage, &c., or any claimants under them swearing falsely upon the trial, shall be guilty of and liable to the penalties of perjury, 23 G. 3, c. 14, s. 6.

False swearing

Any Marshal with intent to barrass and distress the debtor or defendant in any writ, or the estate or properly against which any writ is issued, acting contrary to the Act, shall be punishable by line, and imprisonment at the discretion of the Supreme Court, and liable for all such losses, costs, charges, damages and expenses as the defendant or mortgagee, his executors, &c., may sustain by reason thereof, recoverable upon being taxed, and adjudged by the Court in the most summary manner by attachment or otherwise, 23 G. 3, c. 14, s. 7.

Marshal punishable for harassing defendant

Act not to extend to replevins in any other case, 23 G. 3, c. 14, s. 7.

Act not to extend to replevins in other cases

Where action is brought on any bond for payment of money secured, by Mortgage or performance of the covenants therein, or action of ejectment for recovery of possession of any mortgaged lands, there being no suit depending in Chancery for foreclosing or redeeming such mortgaged lands, if the person having right to redeem, and who appears and becomes defendant at any time pending the action, pay to the mortgagee or his attorney, or in case of their refusal, bring into Court all the principal moneys and interest due on such Mortgage, and the costs expended in any suit at law or in equity upon the Mortgage (such principal interest and costs to be ascertained and computed by the Court, or its proper officer, to be appointed for the purpose), the moneys so paid or brought in shall be taken in full discharge, and the Court may discharge the mortgager or defendant from the same, and by rule of Court compel the mortgagee or his attorney, at the cost of the mortgager to assign, surrender or re-convey the mortgaged lands and such estate and interest as the mortgagee has thererein, and deliver up all Deeds, &c., relating to the title to the mortgager, his heirs, &c., or such persons as they may appoint, 25 G. 3, c 10, s. 1.

On actions on Mortgage, Bond, or Covenant or ejectment for Mortgaged lands, the Court on payment may discharge the Mortgage and compel a conveyance, &c

Where any bill or suit is brought in Chancery, to compel the Defendant to redeem any Mortgage, by payment of the money due thereon or the principal and interest due on such Mortgage, with any money due on any incumbrance, or specialty charged or chargeable on the equity of redemption, and in default of payment to foreclose the equity of redemption, the Court of Chancery on application by the defendant having right to redeem, and on his admitting the plaintiff's title, may at any time before the suit is brought to a hearing, make such order or decree as might have been made in a cause regularly brought to hearing, and all parties shall be bound thereby, but the Act shall not extend to any case where the person against whom redemption is prayed by writing under his hand, or that of his Attorney, Agent or Solicitor, to be delivered before the money is brought into the Court of law, to the Attorney or Solicitor, &c. for the other side, insists that the party praying a redemption has not a right to redeem, or that the premises are chargeable with other principal sums than appear on the face of the Mortgage, or are admitted on the other side, nor to any case where the right of redemption in any cause or suit is con-

Where the Court of Chancery may make order in suits to compel a redemption before the suit is brought to a hearing

Act not to extend to cases where the plaintiff insists that the defendant has no right to redeem

troverted or questioned between different defendants in the same cause, nor shall prejudice any subsequent Mortgagee or incumbrances, 25 G. 3, c. 10, s. 2.

Satisfaction, discharge and conveyance of mortgaged land by executor or administrator when valid

When any person entitled to any freehold land by way of Mortgage has departed this life, and his executor or administrator is entitled to the money secured by the Mortgage, and the legal estate is vested in the heir or devisee of the Mortgagee or the heir, devisee, or other assign of such heir or devisee, and possession has not been taken by virtue of the Mortgage, nor any action or suit be depending, such executor or administrator may, upon payment of the principal and interest due to him on the Mortgage, enter satisfaction on the margin of the record in the Secretary's Office, or otherwise may convey by Deed, or surrender as the case may require, the legal estate which became vested in such heirs or devisee, and such entry of satisfaction or conveyance shall be as effectual as if it had been made by any such heir or devisee, his heirs or assigns, 8 V., c. 19, s. 7.

Bonafide receipts of survivors or executors

The bona fide payment to and receipt of the survivor, or survivors of two or more Mortgagees, or the Executors or Administrators of such survivors, shall effectually discharge the person paying from seeing to the application or being answerable for the misapplication of the money, unless the contrary be expressly declared by the instrument creating the security, 8 V., c. 19, s. 8.

Mutual Debts Set Off.

Debts which may be set off

Where there are Mutual Debts between plaintiff and defendant, or if either party sue or be sued as Executor or Administrator, where there are Mutual Debts between the Testator or Intestate and either party, one debt may be Set against the other, and such matter be gi   in evidence upon the general issue, or pleaded in bar as the nature of the case requires, pro-

When not pleaded notice of set off to be given with plea of general issue

vided the manner after prescribed be observed so as at the time of his pleading the general issue where any such Debt of the plaintiff, his Testator or Intestate is intended to be insisted on in evidence, notice be given of the particular sum or Debt intended to be insisted on, and upon what account it became due, or otherwise the matter shall not be allowed in evidence upon such general issue, 10 G. 3, c. 1, s. 1.

Where the action or debt to be set off is on specialty it must be pleaded in bar

In all cases where either the Debt for which the action is brought or the Debt intended to be Set Off accrues by reason of any penalty contained in any bond or specialty, the Debt intended to be Set Off shall be pleaded in bar, in which plea shall be shewn how much is justly due on either side,

Judgment if for plaintiff to be entered only for the sum due on balance

and if the plaintiff recover judgment, shall be entered for no more than appears to be justly due to him after one Debt being Set against the other, 10 G. 3, c. 1, s. 2.

Naval Officer.

Office abolished

His Patent having been revoked, all acts imposing duties or penalties on and establishing fees for the Naval Officer, were repealed, 10 G. 4, c. 13.

Naval Service.

Property vested in the Lords Commissioners of the Admiralty

Property in Lands, purchased at various times, and conveyed in Trust for the Crown, or to be purchased for the use of the Naval Service was vested in the Lords Commissioners of the Admiralty, 26 V., S. 1, c. 2.

The following enactments appear to have been from time to time made, relating to Naval Property.

13 G. 2, c. 11,	Axtell's Pen, St. Andrew, adjoining Port Royal Harbour, for a Hospital.	
29 G. 2, c. 18,	Port Royal Naval Hospital.	
39 G. 3, c. 10,	"	"
59 G. 3, c. 14,	"	"
22 V., c. 7,	"	"
23 V. S. 1, c. 7,	"	"
7 G. 2, c. 4,	Port Royal Dock Yard.	
14 G. 2, c. 2,	"	"
56 G. 3, c. 25	"	"

3⅓ Acres, 2 Roods of Land, were purchased from the Parish of Port Royal, by Alexander Donaldson, contractor for victualling the Navy, for buildings to contain the stores and provisions, and for the accommodation of the agents, clerks, and labourers employed in that service, but no buildings were to be erected within 500 yards of the foot of the Glacis, 41 G. 3, c. 30, s. 7.

A private Act was also passed in 1828, 9 G. 4, to carry into effect an agreement with John Brown, for the purchase of lands and buildings for a Naval Convalescent Hospital.

Naval Stores.

Statute 9 and 10 W. 3, c. 41, for preventing embezzlement of Naval Stores, and Frauds in paying Seamen's Wages declared in force, 32 G. 3, c. 27.

Notaries Public.

The Governor may, by Warrant under his hand and seal, commission and appoint as many persons as he thinks fit to be Notaries Public, to discharge the duties assigned to the Office by the laws of Great Britain, and of this Island, or by the practice of commerce, 28 V., c. 16, s. 1.   *Appointment]*

Before entering upon the duties of his office, each Notary shall, under a dedimus to be issued by the Governor, be sworn well, truthfully and faithfully to discharge such duties, 28 V., c. 16, s. 2.   *To be sworn*

Before noting any protest, where the circumstances appear to the Notary to be suspicious, and not warranting the protest demanded, he shall refuse to act, until, by an order of 2 Justices in Petty Sessions, the person requiring the protest has established a right thereto, and before applying for such order, notice of the application shall be given to the Notary, and such persons, if any in the Island interested in the subject of Protest, 28 V., c. 16, s. 3.   *Protests under suspicious circumstances*

When a protest or other Notarial Act is refused, the Notary shall mark on the Log Book, Bill of Exchange, or other document, his refusal to the effect, "protest refused," with his signature, and date of refusal subscribed, 28 V., c. 16, s. 4.   *Refusal of protest to be marked on document*

It shall be a misdemeanour, punishable by fine or imprisonment with or without hard labour, not exceeding 3 years, or by both fine and imprisonment, for any Notary or other person falsely to certify or propound any statement, document or thing, or fraudulently with intent to deceive, to conceal, withhold or pervert any fact, document or thing, pertinent to the subject of protest or other Notarial Act, 28 V., c. 16, s. 5.   *False certificates or fraudulent concealment, &c, in protests*

Notaries shall be deemed Officers of the Supreme Court, and liable to its summary jurisdiction, and on a certificate from the Court of misconduct, the Governor shall discharge the offender from his Office, 28 V., c. 16, s. 6.   *To be officers of the Supreme Court Discharge from office*

Stamps to be impressed on each Commission, to be counter-signed by the Clerk of the Supreme Court.   *Stamp on Commission*

			£	s.	d.
For the whole Island	....	....	10	0	0
" The City of Kingston	....	....	6	0	0
" Any other Parish	....	....	3	0	0

28 V., c. 16, s. 7.

Instead of the Impressed Stamp of 4s prescribed by the Stamp Act, a 5s Adhesive Stamp may be substituted, if duly cancelled as prescribed, 28 V., c. 16, s. 8.   *Adhesive Stamp 5s Stamps, 28 V., c. 16, s. 34*

Their fees shall be, exclusive of Stamps: *Fees*

For subscribing and sealing a Protest	....	....	0 10	6
Drawing and preparing same if required, per legal sheet of 72 words	....	....	0 5	6
Copies of Documents therein, per legal sheet	....	....	0 2	6

28 V., c. 16, s. 9.

Act not to come into operation until H. M'S. assent has been proclaimed, 28 V., c. 16, s. 10.   *Commencement*

Oaths and Affirmations and Declarations.

Quakers and Moravians

Quakers and Moravians may, in Criminal cases, make solemn affirmation or declaration, instead of taking an oath, in the words : I, A. B., do solemnly, sincerely and truly declare and affirm," which shall be of the same force and effect as if they had taken an oath in the usual form. Making a false affirmation or declaration punishable as perjury, 9 G. 4, c. 19, s. 10.

Declarations substituted

Where by any Act made or to be made relating to the Revenue, the Office of Stamps and the collection of Public and Parochial Taxes, Certificates of the growth and manufacture of produce, or by any official regulation in any department, any Oath or Affidavit might but for this Act be required to be taken or made by any person on the doing of any act, or for the purpose of verifying any book, entry or return, or for any other purpose whatsoever, a declaration may be substituted before a Justice, who is empowered to take and subscribe the same, 6 V., c. 24, s. 1.

The Vestries, Corporation of Kingston, and any other Body Corporate, now authorized to administer or receive any Oath or Affidavit may make bye-laws or orders, directing the substitution of Declarations, unless repugnant to the Laws of the Island, 6 V. c, 24, s. 2.

Oath of allegiance

Act not to apply to the Oath of Allegiance, in any case in which it may be required to be taken by any person appointed to any office, but it shall continue to be required and be administered and taken, 6 V., c. 24, s. 3.

Oaths, &c. in Courts of Justice, and on summary convictions

Nor to any Oath, Affidavit or Affirmation in any Judicial proceeding in any Court of Justice, or in any proceeding for or by way of summary conviction before any Justice, 6 V., c. 24, s. 4.

Fees

Whenever any Declaration is to be made and subscribed, the fees which would have been payable on the taking and making any legal Oath or Affidavit, shall be in like manner payable upon such Declaration, 6 V., c. 24, s. 5.

Form of declaration

When a Declaration has been substituted, or is directed or authorized to be made and subscribed, although not substituted in lieu of an Oath heretofore legally taken, it shall, unless otherwise directed, be in the Form prescribed in Schedule, 6 V., c. 24, s. 6.

False declaration

Wilfully and corruptly making and subscribing any such Declaration, knowing it to be untrue in any material particular, declared a Misdemeanor, 6 V., c. 24, s. 7.

Unauthorized oaths not to be administered

No Justice or other person shall administer, or cause, &c., or allow to be administered, or receive or cause, &c., any Oath, Affidavit or solemn Affirmation, touching any matter whereof he has not jurisdiction or cognizance by some statute in force at the time. Not to extend to any Oath, &c., touching the preservation of the peace, or the prosecution, trial or punishment of offences touching any proceedings before the Council or Assembly, or any Committee thereof, or which may be required by the laws of any foreign country to give validity to instruments to be used there, 6 V., c. 24, s. 8.

Official Oaths

Act not to extend to Oaths, &c., of Governor, Members of Council, or Assembly, Judges, Justices, or Public Officers, upon entering upon or during their continuance in office, 6 V., c. 24, s. 9.

Declarations

A Declaration before a Justice shall be required and taken in lieu of any Oath or Affidavit required under any Act relating to any Highways, &c., or for improving any City, Town or place, or touching any trust relating thereto, 6 V., c. 24, s. 10.

SCHEDULE.

Declaration

I, A. B., do solemnly and sincerely declare that   and I make this solemn declaration, conscientiously believing the same to be true, and by virtue of the provisions of an Act, made and passed in the sixth year of Her Majesty's reign entitled " An Act to abolish Oaths and Affidavits except in certain cases, and to substitute declarations in lieu thereof, and to suppress voluntary and extra-judicial oaths and affidavits.

Taken and acknowledged before me

State Oaths

The Oaths of Allegiance, Supremacy and Abjuration need not be taken by any person upon his election or appointment to any corporate, public or parochial office more than once during the reign of the same Sovereign, nor shall any such person be liable to any penalty, disability or forfeiture for not taking them oftener, 26 V., S. 2, c. 3,

In Acts after the first day of next Sessions (16th October, 1856,) the words "oath," "swear," "affidavit" shall include affirmation and declaration in the case of persons by law allowed to declare or affirm instead of swearing, 18 V. c. 31, s. 6. Interpretation

---

Obeah and Myalism.

When any person is convicted of being a dealer in Obeah or Myalism, or pretending or professing to tell fortunes, or using or pretending to use any subtle, craft or device, by palmistry or any such like superstitious means to deceive or impose on any of Her Majesty's subjects, by means thereof, before 2 Justices, he may be committed to the nearest prison to hard labor not exceeding 3 calendar months; 19 V., c. 30, s. 1. Summary trial and conviction

Or the Justices may send him for trial at the next Circuit Court, where he may be sentenced to imprisonment with hard labor for not exceeding 12 calendar months, and corporal punishment, not exceeding 78 lashes, nor more than 39 lashes, shall be inflicted at one time, and one month shall elapse between each infliction, 19 V., c. 30, s. 2. Punishment on indictment

Any person who for false, crafty, or unlawful purposes shall pretend to the possession of supernatural power, or who by threat, promise, persuasion or action shall induce or attempt to induce any other person to believe he can by the exercise of any such supernatural power, bring about or effect any object or carry out any design of his own, or of any other person, or for the purpose of carrying out any such design or object, shall falsely cunningly or unlawfully make use of omens, spells, charms, incantations or other preternatural devices shall be deemed an Obeah or Myal-man, or a dealer in Obeah, and Myalism, and the words Obeah and Myalism understood to be of one and the same meaning, and the like offence, 21 V., c. 24, s. 1. Meaning of Obeah

Upon information on oath, stating reasons for the belief, that any person is by habit an Obeah or Myal-man, any Justice may issue a Search Warrant, directed to any Constable, to enter the dwelling or other premises of the party by force, if necessary, between sunrise and sunset, and make diligent search for any materials, characters or things, pretended to be possessed of some occult or unintelligible power in assisting dealers in Obeah and Myalism, in their evil practices, and if any be found, to bring them with the party informed against, before the said or some other Justice, who may commit the accused, in default of bail, to the nearest lock-up, or other place of detention, to be brought before the sitting Justices at their next or some other Session ; and any Obeah or Myal-man by habit or repute, convicted before 2 Justices, of having in his possession or on his premises, any charm, character or other thing as aforesaid, shall be sentenced to be imprisoned to hard labor, not exceeding 60 days, 21 V., c. 24, s. 2. Search Warrant, &c. Having in possion charms, &c.

Any person on behalf of himself or on account of any other person, who shall consult any one pretending to be a dealer in Obeah and Myalism, with the intention of doing any person an injury, either in his person, situation or property, or with any criminal intent, not amounting to solicitation to commit felony, or any other crime now punishable by law, shall on conviction before 2 Justices, be sentenced to hard labour, not exceeding 3 calendar months. Any person consulting any person pretending to be a dealer in Obeah and Myalism, to effect by the exercise of his pretended power as an Obeah or Myal-man, any object, or bring about some event, although not injurious to others, nor connected with any criminal intent, but which the consulting party wishes to accomplish by the supposed supernatural agency of Obeah or Myalism, shall forfeit not exceeding 40s exclusive of costs, and in default of payment, at such time as the Justices direct, shall be imprisoned without hard labour not exceeding 30 days, 21 V., c. 24, s. 3. Consulting dealers in Obeah

---

Obligations, 20 Years Dormant.

All bills, bonds, and mortgages, judgments and other writings obliga- Void tory whatsoever, whereon no payment has been or shall be made, or which have not been or shall not be legally demanded within the space of 20 years, from the time they became due, or from the last payment thereon, shall be null and void, to all intents and purposes. But not to extend to any person under 21, women under coverture, or persons of unsound memory, provided they bring their actions to recover any such demand within 3 years after attaining 21, or becoming sole or sane, 29 G. 3, c. 13, s. 4.

Persons under disabilities

Offences against the Person.

Murder

Whosoever is convicted of murder shall suffer death as a felon, 27 V. S. 1, c. 32, s. 1.

Sentence of death Treatment of prisoner after conviction

Upon conviction, the Court shall pronounce sentence of death to be carried into execution as heretofore. The person convicted after sentence shall be confined in some place within the prison apart from all other prisoners, and be fed on bread and water only, and with no other food or liquor, except in case of receiving the Sacrament, or in case of any sickness or wound, when the Medical attendant of the prison may order other necessaries to be administered, and no person but the Goaler and his servants, and the Chaplain and Medical attendant of the prison shall have access to him, without the permission, in writing, of the Court, or of the Provost Marshal or his Deputy. In case the Court think fit to respite the execution of the convict, the Court or a Judge may by a license in writing relax during the period of the respite all or any of the above restraints or regulations, 27 Veriod 1, c. 32, s. 2.

Conspiracy to murder

Conspiring, confederating and agreeing to murder any person, whether a subject of H. M., or not ; soliciting, encouraging, persuading or endeavouring to persuade, or proposing to any person to murder another whether a subject or not, a Misdemeanor : penal servitude for not more than 10 and not less than 3 years, or imprisonment not exceeding 2 years, with or without hard labour, 27 V., S. 1, c. 32, s. 3.

Manslaughter

Whosoever is convicted of Manslaughter, shall be liable to be kept in penal servitude for life, or not less than 3 years, or to imprisonment not exceeding 2 years, with or without hard labor, or pay such fine as the Court awards, in addition to, or without any such other discretionary punishment, 27 V., S. 1, c. 32, s. 4.

Indictment

In any indictment for murder or manslaughter, or for being an accessory, it shall not be necessary to set forth the manner in which, or the means by which death was caused, but it is sufficient in any indictment for Murder, to charge that the defendant did feloniously, wilfully, and of his malice a forethought, kill and murder the deceased, and sufficient in any indictment for manslaughter, to charge the defendant did feloniously kill and slay the deceased, and in any indictment against any accessory to any Murder or Manslaughter, to charge the principal with the Murder or Manslaughter, as the case may be as above, and then to charge the defendant as an accessory, as heretofore, 27 V., S. 1, c. 32, s. 5.

Misfortune Self Defence

No punishment or forfeiture shall be incurred by any person who kills another by misfortune, or in his own defence, or in any other manner without felony, 27 V., S. 1, c. 32, s. 6.

Petit Treason

Every offence which before 7 W. 4 c. 41 would have amounted to petit treason shall be deemed Murder only, and no greater offence ; and persons guilty in respect thereof as principal or accessories, shall be dealt with, indicted, tried and punished as principals or accessories in murder, 27 V., S. 1, c. 32, s. 7.

Offence partially in and partly out of the Island

Where any person being feloniously stricken, poisoned, or otherwise hurt upon the sea, or at any place out of this Island, dies of such stroke, poisoning or hurt in this Island, or being feloniously stricken, &c., at any place in this Island, dies of such stroke, &c., upon the sea or at any place out of this Island, the offence whether Murder or Manslaughter, or being accessory, may be dealt with, enquired of, tried, determined and punished in the parish or precinct in which such death stroke, &c., happens, in the same manner in all respects as if the offence had been wholly committed in that parish or precinct, 27 V., S. 1, c. 32, s. 8.

Administering to or causing to be administered to, or taken by any person any poison or other destructive thing, or by any means whatever; wounding or causing any grievous bodily harm to any person with intent to commit Murder: Felony; penal servitude for life, or not less than 3 years, or imprisonment not exceeding 2 years, with or without hard labour, and with or without solitary confinement, 27 V., S. 1, c. 32, s. 9. Administering poison with intent to murder

By explosion of gunpowder or other explosive substance destroying or damaging any building with intent to commit murder: the like, 27 V., S. 1, c. 32, s. 10. Destroying buildings by explosive substances with intent to murder

Setting fire to any ship, or vessel, or any part thereof, or any part of the tackle, apparel or furniture thereof, or any goods or chattels therein, or casting away, or destroying or attempting to destroy any ship or vessel with intent to commit murder: the like, 27 V., S. 1, c. 32, s. 11. Setting fire to ship or goods or destroying, &c., with intent to murder

Attempting to administer to, or attempting to cause to be administered to or be taken by any person, any poison or other destructive thing, or shooting at any person, or by drawing a trigger, or in any other manner attempting to discharge any kind of loaded arms (see s. 17) at any person, or attempting to drown, suffocate or strangle any p with intent to commit murder, whether any bodily injury be effected or not: the like, 27 V., S. 1, c. 32, s. 12. Attempting to administer, &c., poison or to shoot, drown or to strangle with intent, &c

Attempting to commit murder by any means other than above specified: the like 27 V., S. 1, c. 32, s. 13. Attempting to murder by any other means

Maliciously sending, delivering, or uttering, or directly or indirectly causing to be received, knowing the contents thereof, any letter or writing threatening to kill or murder any person: Felony; penal servitude, not exceeding 10 years, nor less than 3, or imprisonment not exceeding 2 years, with or without hard labor, and with or without solitary confinement, 27 V., S. 1, c. 32, s. 14. Letters threatening to kill or murder

Unlawfully and maliciously preventing or impeding any person being on board of, or having quitted any ship or vessel in distress or wrecked, stranded or cast on shore, in his endeavour to save his life or preventing or impeding any person in his endeavours to save the life of any such persons as in this section first aforesaid: Felony; penal servitude for life, or not less than 3 years, or imprisonment not exceeding 2 years, with or without hard labor, and with or without solitary confinement, 27 V., S. 1, c. 32, s. 15. Preventing from saving life from any ship

Unlawfully and maliciously, by any means wounding, or causing any grievous bodily harm to any person, or shooting at any person, or by drawing a trigger, or in any other manner attempting to discharge any kind of loaded arms at any person with intent to maim, disfigure or disable, or do some other grievous bodily harm to any person, or with intent to resist or prevent the lawful apprehension or detainer of any person: the like, 27 V., S. 1, c. 32, s. 16. Wounding grievous bodily harm, shooting, discharging, &c., fire-arms to maim, disfigure or disable, do bodily harm or prevent apprehension

Any Gun, Pistol or other Arms loaded in the barrel with gunpowder or any other explosive substance and ball, shot, slug or other destructive material, shall be deemed Loaded Arms within this Act, although the attempt to discharge the same may fail from want of proper priming, or from any other cause, 27 V., S. 1, c. 32, s. 17. Loaded arms what

Unlawfully and maliciously wounding, or inflicting any grievous bodily harm upon any other person, either with or without any weapon or instrument: Misdemeanor; Penal servitude for 3 years, or imprisonment not exceeding 2 years, with or without hard labor, 27 V., S. 1, c. 32, s. 18. Wounding, &c., with or without weapon

By any means attempting to choke, suffocate or strangle any other person, or, by any means calculated to choke, &c., attempting to render any other person insensible, unconscious, or incapable of resistance, with intent thereby to enable oneself or any other person to commit, or with intent thereby to assist any other person in committing any indictable offence: Felony; penal servitude for life, or not less than 3 years, or imprisonment not exceeding 2 years, with or without hard labor, 27 V., S. 1, c. 32, s. 19. Attempting to choke, suffocate or strangle

Unlawfully applying or administering to, or causing to be taken by, or attempting to apply or administer to, or attempting to cause to be administered to, or taken by any person any chloroform, laudanum, or other stupefying or overpowering drug, matter or thing, with intent thereby to enable Applying &c, Chloroform, Laudanum or stupefying drugs oneself or any other person to commit, or with intent to assist any other person in committing any indictable offence: the like, 27 V., S. 1, c. 32, s. 20.

Poisoning, &c., so, as to endanger life, &c

Unlawfully and maliciously administering to, or causing to be administered to, or taken by any other person any poison or other destructive or noxious thing so as thereby to endanger the life, or inflict upon such person any grievous bodily harm: Felony; penal servitude not exceeding 10 years, nor less than 3, or imprisonment not exceeding 2 years, with or without hard labor, 27 V., S. 1, c. 32, s. 21.

Or to injure aggrieve or annoy

Unlawfully and maliciously administering to or causing to be administered to, or taken by any other person any poison or other destructive or noxious thing with intent to injure, aggrieve or annoy such person : Misdemeanor ; 3 years penal servitude, or imprisonment not exceeding 2 years, with or without hard labor, 27 V., S. 1, c. 32, s. 22.

Jury may upon trial under s. 21 convict of offence under s. 22

If upon the trial of any person for any Felony under s. 21, the Jury are not satisfied that the accused is guilty thereof, but are satisfied that he is guilty of any Misdemeanor in s. 22, they may acquit him of the Felony, and find him guilty of the Misdemeanor, and thereupon he may be punished as if convicted upon an indictment for such Misdemeanor, 27 V., S. 1, c. 32, s. 23.

Exposing children under 2 years

Unlawfully abandoning or exposing any child under 2 years, whereby its life is endangered, or health is or is likely to be permanently injured : Misdemeanor ; 3 years penal servitude, or imprisonment not exceeding 2 years, with or without hard labor, 27 V., S. 1, c. 32, s. 24.

Burning, maiming, disfiguring, disabling, &c., by explosive substances

Unlawfully and maliciously, by the explosion of gunpowder or other explosive substance, burning, maiming, disfiguring, disabling or doing any grievous bodily harm to any person : Felony ; penal servitude for life, or not less than 3 years, or imprisonment not exceeding 2 years, with or without hard labor, and with or without solitary confinement, 27 V., S. 1, c. 32, s. 25.

Attempting to do so by sending, &c., explosive substance Casting, throwing, &c., corrosive fluids &c Whether bodily injury effected or not

Unlawfully and maliciously causing any gunpowder or other explosive substance to explode, or sending, or delivering to, or causing to be taken or received by any person, any explosive substance, or any other dangerous or noxious thing, or putting or laying at any place, or casting or throwing at or upon, or otherwise applying to any person any corrosive fluid or any destructive or explosive substance, with intent to burn, maim disfigure, or disable any person, or to do some grievous bodily harm to any person, whether any bodily injury be effected or not : Felony ; the like, 27 V., S. 1, c. 32, s. 26.

Throwing wood, &c., on railway or tramway, diverting points, &c., shewing or hiding, &c., signals to endanger safety

Unlawfully and maliciously putting or throwing upon or across any Railway or Tramway, any wood, stone or other matter or thing, or taking up, removing or displacing any rail, sleeper or other matter or thing belonging to any Railway or Tramway, or turning, moving, or diverting any points or other machinery belonging to any Railway or Tramway, or making or shewing, hiding or removing any signal or light upon or near to any Railway or Tramway, or doing or causing to be done any other matter or thing, with intent to endanger the safety of any person travelling, or being upon such Railway or Tramway : Felony ; penal servitude for life, or for any term not exceeding (not less than) 3 years, or imprisonment not exceeding 2 years, with or without hard labor, 27 V., S. 1, c. 32, s 27.

Endangering by unlawful act or neglect, safety on railway or tramway

Endangering or causing to be endangered by any unlawful act, or wilful omission or neglect, the safety of any person conveyed by, or being in or upon a Railway or Tramway, or aiding or assisting therein : Misdemeanor ; imprisonment not exceeding 2 years, with or without hard labor, 27 V., S. 1, c. 32, s. 28.

Assaults Preventing clergy, &c. from performing divine service, &c., arresting them

By threats or force obstructing or preventing or endeavouring to obstruct and prevent any Clergyman or other Minister in or from celebrating Divine Service, or otherwise officiating in any Church, Chapel, Meeting-house, or other place of Divine Worship, or in or from the performance of his duty in the lawful burial of the dead in any Church-yard or other burial place, or striking or offering violence to, or upon any civil process, or, under pretence of executing any civil process, arresting any Clergyman, or other Minister engaged in, or, to the knowledge of the offender, about to be engaged in any of the rites or duties aforesaid, or going to perform the same or returning from the performance thereof : Misdemeanor : imprisonment not exceeding 2 years, with or without hard labor, 27 V., S. 1, c. 32, s. 29.

Assaulting and striking, or wounding any Magistrate, Officer or other person lawfully authorized in or on account of the exercise of his duty, in or concerning the preservation of any vessel in distress, or of any vessel, goods or effects wrecked, stranded or cast on shore, or lying under water : Misdemeanor ; penal servitude for not exceeding 7 years, nor less than 3, or imprisonment not exceeding 2 years, with or without hard labor, 27 V., S. 1, c. 32, s. 30.

Assaulting magistrates, &c., in preservation of vessels in distress or goods

Assaulting any person with intent to commit Felony, or assaulting, resisting or wilfully obstructing any Peace Officer in the due execution of his duty, or any person acting in his aid, or assaulting any person with intent to resist or prevent the lawful apprehension of himself or any other person for any offence : Misdemeanor ; imprisonment, not exceeding 2 years, with or without hard labor, 27 V., S. 1, c. 32, s. 31.

Assaults with intent to commit felony
Peace officers and persons in aid, &c.

Unlawfully and with force hindering or preventing any seaman or person labouring on board any vessel from working at or exercising his lawful trade, busines or occupation, or beating, or using any violence to any such person with intent to hinder or prevent him from working at, or exercising the same, punishable, on conviction before 2 Justices, by imprisonment in the Common Goal, General Penitentiary, or District Prison ; and if in either of the latter, to be liable to be kept, in addition, to hard labor for not exceeding 3 months. No person so punished shall be punished for the same offence under any other law, 27 V., S. 1, c. 32, s. 32.

Assaults, &c., to prevent seamen, &c., from working at trade on board ship

Beating or using any violence or threat of violence to any person, with intent to deter or hinder him from buying, selling or otherwise disposing of, or to compel him to buy, sell, or otherwise dispose of any poultry, hogs, grain, fruit, or fish, or other provisions or food, in any Market or other place, or beating or using any such violence or threats to any person having the care or charge of any poultry, hogs, grain, fruit or fish, or other provisions, whilst in the way to or from any City, Market, Town or other place with intent to stop the conveyance of the same, punishable in like manner as in s. 32, before two Justices ; and persons so punished, not to be punished for the same offence by virtue of any other Law, 27 V., S. 1, c. 32, s. 33.

Assaults to prevent buying or selling in Market or stop the conveyance of goods

Any person unlawfully assaulting or beating any other person, on complaint by or on behalf of any person aggrieved, and on conviction before 2 Justices, may be committed to the Common Gaol or District Prison, or General Penitentiary, with or without hard labor, not exceeding 2 months, or else forfeit and pay a fine, not exceeding, with costs, if ordered, £5 ; and, if not paid immediately after conviction. or within such period as the Justices at the time of conviction appoint, he may be committed as above, unless the fine and costs be sooner paid, 27 V., S. 1, c. 32, s. 34.

Assault or battery

When any person is charged before 2 Justices, with an assault or battery upon any male child whose age does not, in their opinion, exceed 14, or upon any female either on the complaint of the party aggrieved or otherwise, the Justices, if the assault or battery is of such an aggravated nature that it cannot, in their opinion, be sufficiently punished under the above provisions as to common assaults and batteries (s. 34), may proceed to hear the same, in a summary way, and, if proved, commit the offender, who shall be liable to be imprisoned in the General Penitentiary, or in any District Prison, with or without hard labor, or without hard labor in any Gaol, for not exceeding 6 months, or to pay a fine, not exceeding, with costs, £20, and in default of payment, to be imprisoned as aforesaid, not exceeding 6 months, unless sooner paid ; and if the Justices so think fit, in any case, to be bound to keep the peace, and he of good behaviour for not exceeding 6 months from the expiration of such sentence, 27 V., S. 1, c. 32, s. 35.

Assaults on children and females

If the Justices upon hearing any such case of assault and battery under s. 34 or 35, upon the merits, deem the offence not proved, or find the assault or battery to have been justified, or so trifling as not to merit any punishment, and accordingly dismiss the complaint, they shall forthwith make out a certificate under their hand, stating the facts of such dismissal, and deliver it to the party against whom the complaint was preferred, 27 V. S. 1, c. 32, s. 36.

When Justices may dismiss cases under s. 34, 35

Certificate

If any person has obtained such certificate, or having been convicted has paid the whole amount adjudged to be paid, or suffered the imprisonment, or imprisonment with hard labor, awarded, he shall be released from

Release from further proceedings, civil and criminal of persons who have obtained certificates or undergone punishment

Justices to abstain from adjudication, if assault accompanied by attempt to commit felony, or a fit subject for indictment

Or where questions of title arise, &c., or insolvency or execution of process

all further or other proceedings, civil or criminal, for the same cause. In case the Justices find the assault or battery complained of to have been accompanied by any attempt to commit felony, or are of opinion the same is from any other circumstance a fit subject for prosecution by Indictment, they shall abstain from any adjudication, and deal with the case in all respects as if they had no authority finally to hear it. Nothing herein shall authorize any Justices to determine any case of assault or battery, in which any question arises as to the title to any lands, or any interest therein, or accruing therefrom, or as to any insolvency or any execution under the process of any Court of Justice, 27 V., S. 1, c. 32, s. 37.

Punishment on indictment for assaults occasioning bodily harm

For common assaults

Whosoever is convicted upon an Indictment of any assault occasioning actual bodily harm, shall be liable to penal servitude, for 3 years, or imprisonment not exceeding 2 years, with or without hard labor; for a common assault to imprisonment not exceeding 1 year, with or without hard labor, 27 V., S. 1, c. 32, s. 38.

Rape

Rape, Felony : penal servitude for life, or not less than 3 years, or imprisonment not exceeding 2 years, with or without hard labor, 27 V., S. 3, c. 32, s. 39.

Procuring illicit connection with woman or girl under 21

Procuring by false pretences, false representations, or other fraudulent means, any woman or girl under 21 years, to have illicit carnal connection with any man : Misdemeanor ; imprisonment not exceeding 2 years, with or without hard labor, 27 V., S. 1, c. 32, s. 40.

Abusing girl under 9

Unlawfully and carnally knowing (see s. 54,) and abusing any girl under 9 : Felony, penal servitude for life, or not less than 3 years, or imprisonment, not exceeding 2 years with or without hard labor, 27 V., S. 1, c. 32, s. 41.

Under 11

Any girl above 9 and under 11 : Misdemeanor ; penal servitude for 3 years, or imprisonment, not exceeding 2 years, with or without hard labor, 27 V., S. 1, c. 32, s. 42.

Indecent assault Attempt to abuse girl under 11

Whosoever is convicted of any indecent assault upon any female, or of any attempt to have carnal knowledge of any girl under 11, shall be liable to imprisonment, not exceeding 2 years, with or without hard labor, 27 V., S. 1, c. 32, s. 43.

Abduction of heiress or next of kin from motives of lucre

Fraudulent abduction of woman under 21 against with father &c

Offender capable of taking any of her property

Where any woman of any age has any interest, whether legal or equitable, present or future, absolute, conditional, or contingent, or any real or personal estate, or is a presumptive heiress or coheiress, or presumptive next of kin, or one of the presumptive next of kins to any one having such interest, whoever, from motives of lucre, takes away or detains such woman against her will with intent to marry or carnally know her, or to cause her to be married or carnally known by any other person, and whosoever shall fraudulently allure, take away, or detain such woman, being under 21, out of the possession and against the will of her father or mother or of any other person having the lawful care or charge of her, with intent to marry or carnally know her, or to cause her to be married or carnally known by any other person, shall be guilty of Felony : Penal servitude not exceeding 14 years, nor less than 3 years, or imprisonment not exceeding 2 years, with or without hard labour, and incapacity to take any estate or interest, legal or equitable, in any real or personal property of such woman, or in which she has any such interest, or which shall come to her as such heiress, coheiress, or next of kin ; and if any marriage has taken place such property upon conviction shall be settled as the Court of Chancery may, upon any information at the suit of the Attorney-General, appoint, 27 V., S. 1, c. 32, s. 44.

Abduction of any other woman with intent to marry &c

Taking away by force or detaining against her will any woman of any age, with intent to marry or carnally know her, or cause her to be married or carnally known by any other person : Felony ; Penal servitude. not exceeding 14 years nor less than 3, or imprisonment not exceeding 2 years, with or without hard labour. 27 V., S. 1, c. 32, s. 45.

Abduction of unmarried girl under 16

Unlawfully taking or causing to be taken any unmarried girl under 16 out of the possession or against the will of her father or mother, or of any other person having the lawful care or charge of her : Misdemeanour ; imprisonment not exceeding 2 years, with or without hard labour. 27 V., S. 1, c. 32, s. 46,

Leading or taking away unlawfully, either by force or fraud, or decoying or enticing away, or detaining any child under 14, with intent to deprive any parent, guardian, or other person having the lawful care or charge of such child of the possession of such child, or with intent to steal any article upon or about the person of such child, to whomsoever belonging, or with any such intent receiving or harboring any such child, knowing the same to have been by force or fraud led, taken, decoyed, enticed away, or detained as before mentioned ; Felony ; penal servitude not exceeding 7 years nor less than 3 years, or imprisonment not exceeding 2 years, with or without hard labor. No person who has claimed any right to the possession of such child, or is the mother, or has claimed to be the father of any illegitimate child, shall be liable to be prosecuted by virtue hereof on account of the getting possession of such child out of the possession of any person having the lawful charge thereof, 27 V., S. 2, c. 32, s. 47. *Child stealing*

Whoever being married, marries any other person during the life of the former husband or wife, whether the second marriage take place in this Island or elsewhere, shall be guilty of Felony ; penal servitude for not exceeding 4 years, or imprisonment not exceeding 2 years, with or without hard labor. Any such offence may be dealt with, enquired of, and punished in any parish or precinct where the offender is apprehended or in custody, as if it had been there actually committed. Not to extend to any second marriage contracted elsewhere than Jamaica by any other than a subject of H. M., or to any person marrying a second time, whose husband or wife has been continually absent from such person for 7 years then last past. and has not been known by such person to be living within that time, nor to extend to any person who at the time of such second marriage was divorced from the bond of the first marriage, or to any person whose former marriage was declared void by the sentence of any Court of competent Jurisdiction, 27 V., S. 1, c. 32, s. 48. *Bigamy*

May be tried where offender is apprehended Excepted cases

Every woman being with child, who, with intent to procure her own miscarriage, unlawfully administers to herself any poison or other noxious thing, or unlawfully uses any instrument or other means with the like intent, and whoever, with intent to procure the miscarriage of any woman, whether she be or be not with child, unlawfully administers to her, or causes to be taken by her any poison or other noxious thing, or unlawfully uses any instrument or other means with the like intent, shall be guilty of Felony ; penal servitude for life or not less than 3 years, or imprisonment not exceeding 2 years, with or without hard labor, and with or without solitary confinement, 27 V., S. 1, c. 32, s. 49. *Attempts to procure abortion*

Unlawfully supplying or procuring any poison or other noxious thing, or any instrument or thing, knowing it is intended to be unlawfully used or employed, with the intent to procure the miscarriage of any woman, whether with child or not : Misdemeanor ; penal servitude for 3 years, or imprisonment not exceeding 2 years, with or without hard labor, 27 V., S. 1, c. 32, s. 50. *Supplying or procuring poison, or instruments for the purpose*

If any woman is delivered of a child, every person who, by any secret disposition of the dead body, whether the child died before, at, or after the birth, endeavors to conceal the birth thereof, shall be guilty of a Misdemeanor : imprisonment not exceeding 2 years, with or without hard labor. If any person tried for the murder of any child is acquitted thereof, the jury may find, if it so appear in evidence, that the child had recently been born, and that such person did, by some secret disposition of the dead body of such child, endeavor to conceal the birth thereof, and thereupon the Court may pass such sentence as if he had been convicted upon an indictment for the concealment of the birth, 27 V., S. 1, c. 32, s. 51. *Concealing the birth of a child*

Whosoever is convicted of the abominable crime of buggery, committed either with mankind or with any animal, shall be liable to be kept in penal servitude for life or not less than 10 years, 27 V., S. 1, c. 32, s. 52. *Unnatural offences*

Attempting to commit the said abominable crime or being guilty of any assault, with intent to commit the same. or of any indecent assault upon any male person, Misdemeanor : Penal servitude not exceeding 10 years, nor less than 3, or imprisonment not exceeding 2 years, with or without hard labor, 27 V., S. 1, c. 32, s. 53. *Attempt to commit*

When upon the trial of any offence under this Act it is necessary to prove carnal knowledge, it shall not be necessary to prove actual emission *Carnal knowledge defined* of seed, but the carnal knowledge shall be deemed complete upon proof of penetration only, 27 V., S. 1, c. 32, s. 54.

Apprehension by Constable without warrant of suspected persons

Any Constable or Policeman may take into custody, without a warrant, any person he finds lying or loitering in any highway, yard, or other place during the night, and whom he has good cause to suspect of having committed or being about to commit any Felony in this Act mentioned, and take him as soon as reasonable may be before a Justice, to be dealt with according to law, 27 V., S. 1, c. 32, s. 55.

Principals in 2nd degree and accessories

In case of every Felony under this Act, every principal in the second degree, and every accessory before the fact shall be punishable as the principal in the first degree; and every accessory after the fact to any such Felony except Murder, shall be liable to imprisonment not exceeding 2 years, with or without hard labor. Every accessory after the fact to murder shall be liable to penal servitude for life, or not less than 3 years, or to be imprisoned for not exceeding 2 years, with or without hard labor Any person counselling, aiding or abetting the commission of any indictable Misdemeanor under this Act, shall be proceeded against, indicted and punished as a principal offender, 27 V., S. 1, c. 32, s. 56.

Offences within jurisdiction of Vice-Admiralty

Indictable offences in this Act, committed within the jurisdiction of the Vice-Admiralty of this Island, shall be dealt with, enquired of, tried and determined in any parish or precinct in which the offender is apprehended or in custody, as if they had been actually committed there, and in any indictment for any such offence, or for being accessory to such an offence, the venue in the margin shall be the same as if the offence had been committed in such parish or precinct, and the offence shall be averred to have been committed on the high seas. Not to affect any of the laws relating to the government of Her Majesty's Land or Naval Forces, 27 V., S. 1, s. 32, s. 57.

If any person is tried and convicted before any Court in this Island for any indictable offence, under 27 V., S. 1, c. 32, s. 57, he shall be liable to, and suffer such punishment, or forfeiture, or penalty as he would be subject to in case the offence had been committed, and was enquired of, and tried and determined in England, anything in that Act to the contrary notwithstanding, 27 V., S. 1, c. 34, s. 60.

Solitary confinement

When solitary confinement is awarded under this Act, the Court may direct the offender to be kept in solitary confinement for any portions of any imprisonment, or imprisonment with hard labor, not exceeding 1 month at any one time, nor 3 months in one year, 27 V., S. 1, c. 32, s. 58.

Fine and sureties to keep the peace in what cases

On conviction for any indictable misdemeanor under this Act, the Court may, in addition to or in lieu of any punishment authorized, fine the offender, and require him to enter into his own recognizances, and to find sureties both or either, for keeping the peace, and being of good behaviour; and in case of any Felony punishable otherwise than with death, may require the offender to enter in his own recognizances, and find sureties, both or either, for keeping the peace, in addition to any punishment authorized; but no person shall be imprisoned for not finding sureties for more than 1 year, 27 V., S. 1, c. 32, s. 59.

Convictions not to be quashed for want of form

No summary conviction under this Act shall be quashed for want of Form, or removed by Certiorari into the Supreme Court; and no warrant of commitment shall be void by reason of any defect therein, provided it be therein alleged that the party has been convicted, and there is a valid conviction to sustain it, 27 V., S. 1, c. 32, s. 60.

Costs or indictments for assaults

Any person convicted on any Indictment of any assault with or without battery and wounding, or either, may, in addition to any sentence for the offence, be adjudged to pay to the prosecutor his actual and necessary costs and expenses of the prosecution, and such moderate allowance for loss of time as the Court shall, by affidavit or other enquiry and examination, ascertain to be reasonable; and unless the sum awarded be sooner paid, the

Additional imprisonment in case of non payment

offender shall be imprisoned for not exceeding 3 months, in addition to the term of imprisonment, if any, for the offence, 27 V., S. 1, c. 32, s. 61.

Distress and sale for costs

The Court may, by warrant under hand and seal, order such sum to be levied by distress and sale of the goods and chattels of the offender, and paid to the prosecutor, and the surplus, if any, to be paid to the owner; and in case the sum be so levied, the imprisonment awarded until payment shall cease, 27 V., S. 1, c. 32, s. 62.

Parishes.

PARISHES.

Names of the 15 Parishes into which the Island was then divided confirmed, 33 C. 2, c. 18, s. 12.

The boundaries of the several Counties and Parishes shall be as laid down in Robertson's Maps, published 1804, 50 G. 3, c. 15.

Subdivisons of Parishes, 1 V., c. 34 ; 9 V., c. 44.

Names of the several subdivisons, 25 V., c. 18, Schedule A.

Parochial elections for Members of the Common Council of Kingston, Vestrymen and Churchwardens, shall be regulated by this Act, where not inconsistent with the Kingston Corporation Act, 19 V., c. 61, and the Vestry Regulation Act (now 27 V., S. 1, c. 7,) or other Acts regulating such elections, 22 V., c. 5, s. 31.

Not to levy or impose any Tax or Impost, or raise any Loan under any Act now or heretofore giving authority, 21 V., c. 44; s. 15.

The surplus of £40,000 Loan for payment of Parochial Debts, and Collecting Constable's compensation, was directed to be applied for Parochial works and repairs of Churches and Buildings, 22 V., c. 24, s. 2.

The Receiver-General shall apply the surplus proceeds of Export Duties under this Act, in aid of Parochial expenditure, until 30th September, 1866, after deducting for Immigration purposes £4000 for 1865, and £8000 for 1866, 24 V., c. 16, s. 18.

CLARENDON.

Confirmed as a Parish under that name, 33 C. 2, c. 18, s. 12.

Parts of Carpenter's Mountains taken from Clarendon and St. Elizabeth and annexed to Vere, 12 G. 2, c. 6.

Part of Middlesex, 31 G. 2, c. 4, s. 1.

Manchester separated from, 55 G., 3 c. 23.

Lands vested in Trustees for sale, and the proceeds to be invested in other lands, and erecting other Buildings for a School-house, 8 G. 3, c. 12.

The then Workhouse vested in the Magistrates and Vestry for sale, and the Barrack and lands attached vested in them for a Workhouse, 11 G. 4, c. 5.

HANOVER.

Separated from Westmoreland and declared a distinct Parish, 10 G. 1, c. 5, s. 1.

Boundaries, 10 G. 1, c. 5, s. 1 ; 29 G. 3, c. 22 ; 7 V., c. 56.

Part of Cornwall, 31 G. 2, c. 4, s. 1.

Commissioners appointed to sell the lands whereon the then Court-house, Goal and Workhouse were built, and to purchase other lands for a Court-house, Goal, Workhouse, Hospital and Poor-house, 41 G. 3, c. 23, s. 1, 3, 4, 7, 9, 43 G. 3, c. 23.

Commissioners appointed to sell the Goal and Work-house in Lucea, and purchase other lands in the Town for the erection of a new Goal, Work-house and Poor-house, and enlarging the Church yard and Barrack yard, 7 G. 4, c. 15, s. 1-4, 8-10, 12, 14-19.

Lucea.—Appointment of Trustees to improve and enlarge the Town, s. 1-20. Provisions respecting fires and Firewardens, s. 21-33. Discharging fire-arms, in the Town, s. 34. Rubhisb, flying kites s. 35, 48. Open lots, s. 36. Sale of spirits, s. 37. Bell s. 38. Idle and disorderly persons, s. 39. Furious riding and driving, s. 40. Street, pumps, wells, &c., s. 41, 42, 47. Unwholesome provisions, s. 43. Sale of grass, s. 44. Assize of bread, s. 45, 46. Hawkers and Pedlars, s. 53. Hogs and goats, s. 54. Bathing and washing, s. 56. Penalties, protection from actions, &c., s. 57-63, 3 V., c. 50.

KINGSTON.

Separated from St. Andrew, and declared a distinct Parish, 5 W. and M., c. 3, s. 1.

Boundaries from St. Andrew, 5 W. and M., c. 3, s. 1 ; 39 G., 3 c. 34.

Names

Boundaries ; see Title Robertson's maps

Subdivisions

Names of [See Title Highways]

Parochial elections ; see Title Assembly

Power to impose taxes or contract debts taken away

Repairs of buildings, &c

Export duties in aid of expenditure ; see Title Loans on Island Security, Immigration.

Name

Carpenter's mountains

Part of Middlesex

Manchester

School

Workhouse

Established

Boundaries

Part of Cornwall

Court house, &c.

Goal, Churchyard &c

Lucea

Established

Boundaries

3 Members	To send 3 Representatives to the Assembly, 5 W. and M., c. 3, s. 1.
Receiver General's Office	Receiver-General and Island Secretary to keep offices there, 5 W., and M., c. 3, s. 3.
Part of Surry	Part of Surry, of which the Town of Kingston shall be the County-Town, 31 G. 2, c. 4, s. 1.
Gaol	A Goal to be built in Kingston for the County of Surry, 32 G., 2, c. 3, s. 1.
Parish land	Lands in Orange Street and Church Street, and the Court-house, Duke Street and Harbour Street vested in the Justices and Vestry for the use of the poor, 27 G. 3, c. 5.
Town dues	Kingston Town Dues, 11 V., c. 19 ; 18 V., c. 51.
	Such Dues shall not be collected during the continuance of this Act, but the Receiver General shall reserve out of the collections hereunder for the purposes thereof £1,800, 22 V., c. 48.
Sale of lands belonging to Kingston and St. Andrew	Powers of the Common Council and Vestry of St. Andrew to sell lands devised for the use of the poor of both parishes, and invest the proceeds in Island Debentures, 23 V., c. 21.

MANCHESTER.

Established	May-day, Mile-Gully and Carpenter's Mountain Districts separated from Vere, Clarendon and St. Elizabeth, and declared a distinct parish in Middlesex. Boundaries 55 G., 3 c., 23.
Part of Middlesex	
Sale of lands	Power to sell 60 acres of surplus land not needed for Parochial Buildings, 2 W. 4, c. 11.

METCALFE.

Established	Separated from St. Georges and St. Mary, and declared a distinct parish in Middlesex. Boundaries 5 V., c. 44.
Marine Hospital	Annotto Bay Marine Hospital, 1 G. 4 c. 20 ; 5 V., c. 44, s. 16.

PORTLAND.

Titchfield	Allotment of 50 acres of land at Patterson's Point, and 20 acres of Lynch Island for a town, to be granted in lots as foot land, to be built upon, and of 250 acres of land adjoining as a Common thereto, 9 G. 1, c. 8, s. 6-7.
	50 Acres added to the Town of Titchfield, and 100 acres to the Commons, 12 G. 1, c. 10, s. 3.
Free School lands	The Common Lands vested in the Trustees of Titchfield Free School, 26 G. 3, c. 7, s. 1.
Lynch's Island	20 Acres of Land in Lynch's Island vested in the Crown, 3 G. 2, c. 1.
Port Antonio	Port Antonio made a port of entry and clearance, 10 G. 1, c. 8, s. 6
Boundaries	Boundaries of the parish, 8 G. 1, c. 8, s. 1 ; 10 G. 1, c. 8. s. 4; 11 G. 2, c. 5 s. 14.
Part of Surry	Part of Surry, 31 G. 2, c. 4, s. 1.
Patented Land	Lands patented shall be held on the same conditions as in other parishes, 21 G. 3, c. 22,

PORT ROYAL.

Name	Confirmed as a parish under that name, 33 C. 2, c. 18, s. 12.
Patented Lands	Patents for Parade place and 1100 Acres of Land beyond ne Breastwork declared valid, 35 C. 2, c. 12, s. 2.
Wharfing town	Justices and Vestry empowered to wharf and secure the Town towards the sea, and maintain the wharfs, 5 W. & M. c. 4.
Streets	May appoint two scavengers to employ rakers to cleanse the streets, 11 W. 3, c. 4, s. 1.
	Ends of streets not to be wharfed or filled up so as to prevent Canoes, &c., from landing or taking on board water or freight, 11 W. 3, c. 4, s 5.
Fires	For the security of the Town and prevention of Fires the Justices and Vestry may make rules and ordinances to be binding upon the inhabitants under a penalty of 40s. (21s. stg.) recoverable before a Justice, 3 Ann, c. 2, s. 5.

Part of Surry, 31 G. 2, c. 4, s. 1. *Part of Surry*

300 Acres of Land on the Salt River and Rio Cobre, in St. Andrew, *Grass lands* patented in the name of Joseph Hunt for the use of the parish, vested in the Churchwardens for the time being, 3 G. 3, c. 3.

Boundaries from St. Andrew, 14 G. 3, c. 25. *Boundaries* From St. David, 23 G. 3, c. 15.

Appointment of Trustees to sell the 1100 acres of Land patented for *Sale of parish* the parish. Conditions upon which 34 acres, 2 roods, intended to be sold to *land* A. Donaldson for buildings for Naval Stores and provisions are to be enjoyed. Power to build fortifications, &c., thereon, 41 G. 3, c. 30.

Elections of Churchwardens, Vestrymen and Coroner for the Moun- *Elections* tain District, and Parochial Courts and Vestries shall be held at the Court House in the Mountain District. Elections for Members of Assembly and Coroner for the Town, in the Town of Port Royal, 6 W. 4, c. 22.

Town Constables and Night Watch, s. 2; Drunken and Disorderly *Town Police regu-* persons, s. 3; Fires and Firewardens, s. 4-15; Discharging Fire Arms, s. *lations* 16; Filth and Rubbish, s. 71-1; Unwholesome provisions, s. 19-20; Canoes, &c., in streets, s. 21; Scavengers, s. 22; Unenclosed Lands, s. 23-24; Spirits, s. 25; Church Bell, s. 26; Assize of Bread, s. 27-28; Sales of Meat, &c., s, 29; Hogs, Goats, &c., s. 32; Canoes, &c., plying for fare or freight, s. 33-37; Harbour, Concurrent Jurisdiction of Justices of Kingston and Port Royal, s. 39; Apprehension of offenders, Prosecutions within 3 calendar months, Penalties, Costs, Appeals, Convictions, &c., s. 40-53; Protection from Actions, s. 54; Sale and rent of Parish Lands, s. 56-58, 6 V., c. 59.

ST. ANDREW.

Confirmed as a Parish under that name, 33 C. 2, c. 18, s. 12. *Name*

Kingston separated from, 5 W. & M. c. 3, s. 1. *Kingston separated from*

Boundaries from Kingston, 5 W. & M., c. 3, s. 1; 39 G. 3, c. 34. *Boundaries*

Part of Surry, 31 G. 2, c. 4, s. 1. *Part of Surry*

Boundaries from Port Royal, 14, G. 3, c. 25. *Boundaries*

Power of the Vestry and Common Council of Kingston to sell lands *Sale of St. An-* devised for the use of the poor of both parishes, and invest the same in *drew and Kingston* Island Debentures, 23 V., c. 21. *lands*

ST. ANN.

Confirmed as a Parish under that name, 33 C. 2, c. 18, s. 12. *Name*

Part of Middlesex, 31 G. 2, c. 4, s. 1. *Part of Middlesex*

Land purchased by the Parish for a Barrack, under the repealed Act *Sale of land* 1 G. 3, c. 19, vested in the Justices and Vestry for sale or otherwise for the benefit of the parish, 48 G. 3, c. 14.

St. Ann's Bay.—Incorporation of the Justices and Vestry for the purposes *St. Ann's Bay* of the Act, s. 1; Surveyor, Town Clerk and other Officers, s. 2; Penalties on *Police Regulations* Justices, Vestrymen, &c. for non-attendance, s. 3; Fires and Firewardens, s. 4-15; Discharging Fire Arms, s. 16; Filth and Rubbish, s. 17; Unenclosed lots, s, 18; Spirits, s. 19; Draining Swampy Lands, s. 21; Unwholesome Provisions, s. 22; Slaughtering Cattle, s. 26; Purchase and Sale of Lands, Improvement of Town, s. 28-29; Penalties, Recovery, Protection from Actions, &c., s. 31-35, 46 G. 3, c. 26.

Powers of Justices and Vestry to alter the course of Seville River for *Harbour* the amendment of St. Ann's Bay Harbour, 48 G. 3, c. 23.

The Governors and Trustees of the Jamaica Free School empowered *Chapel and Buri-* to convey 2 acres of Walton Pen to the Bishop of Jamaica, and Rector *al ground, Mon eagu* and Churchwardens of St. Ann, for a Chapel and Burial Ground for the use of the inhabitants of the Moneague District, 5 V., c. 25, s. 2.

ST. CATHERINE.

Confirmed as a Parish under that name, 33 C. 2, c. 18, s. 12. *Name*

Part of Middlesex, St. Jago de la Vega, the County Town where the *Part of Middlesex* Supreme Court is to be held, 31 G. 2, c. 4, s. 1.

The Justices and Vestry to cause 500 acres, part of 1235 acres of land, *Common* patented for the use of the inhabitants, nearest the Town, to be laid out for a

Savanna or Common to the Town, and lay taxes for keeping it clean, and to lease or rent out the residue, 20 G. 2, c. 10, s. 1, 2, 4-6.

Leases of parish lands
The Custos and such of the Justices as are Freeholders of the parish, and the Vestrymen and Churchwardens for the time being, incorporated, with power to lease, for not exceeding 99 years, the lands, other than the 500 acres; the lots to be leased as acre-lands not to contain less than 5 acres: the profits to be disposed of by the Vestry in relief of parochial taxes, but not by way of anticipation, 6 G. 3., c. 4.

The lots of foot land leased by the foot to be leased at an annual rent of not less than 2d per foot, calculated upon the measurement of 2 sides to the square, 11 G. 3, c. 14, s. 11.

The lots of acre-land to be leased at such annual rents, and for such term and time as the Justices, Vestrymen, and Churchwardens shall think most beneficial for the parish, 21 G. 3, c. 13.

St. Jago de la Vega
No penguins to be planted in the Town of St. Jago de la Vega, 22 G. 2, c. 6, s. 2.

Justices and Vestry to appoint places of deposit for filth and rubbish, 21 G. 2, c. 8, s. 3.

Night Watch in St. Jago de la Vega, 11 G. 3, c. 14, s. 9, 10.

Poor house
The lands and buildings occupied by the 20th Light Dragoons vested in the Justices and Vestrymen for the erection of a Poor house for the Paupers of the parish, and the transient poor and distressed persons passing through St. Jago de la Vega, 56 G. 3, c. 22.

Court house and Parochial Offices
Rooms to be set apart in the lower part of the building, to be erected on the south side of the square in front of the King's House for the Clerk of the Vestry, Clerk of the Peace and Police Office, to be exclusively disposed of and controlled by the Justices and Vestry, free from all charge for rent or otherwise; and the parish and precinct, when the Assembly is not sitting to have the use of any other apartment suitable for a Court-house for holding parochial courts and meetings, but not to interfere with the Grand Jury, 58 G. 3, c. 17, s. 6.

The Court-house placed under the control and supervision of the Custos of the precinct, 27 V., S. 1, c. 7, s. 29.

Hospital
Powers given to repair the Hospital and Work-House for the use of the precinct, or such of the parishes as should contribute, 6 G. 4, c. 16.

St. Thomas in the Vale
St. Thomas in the Vale separated from the precinct, 5 W. 4, c. 24.

St. Jago de la Vega Police Regulations
St. Jago de la Vega—Fires and Firewardens, s. 2-15; discharging Fire-Arms, s. 16; Filth and Rubbish, s. 17; Unenclosed Lots, s. 18; Spirits and Gunpowder, s. 19-20; Bell to be rung, Idle and Disorderly Persons, s 21 22; furious Riding and Driving, s. 23; Routes of Carriages of Burthen, droves of Cattle, &c., s, 24; Licensed Carriages of burthens, s. 25-28; Unwholesome Provisions, s. 29; Clerk of the Markets, s. 30; Pedlars, s. 34; Hogs and Goats, s. 35; Additional Buildings in Market Places, s. 36; Alterations and Improvements in the Town, s. 38; Surveyors, Town Clerk, and other Officers, s. 39; Justices, Vestrymen, &c., neglecting to attend Meetings, s. 40; Penalties Recovery, &c., s. 41, 42, 50; Protection from Actions, s. 43; costs, s. 44; Washing and Bathing places, s. 48; Seizure of Produce exposed for Sale, and by persons not Householders, s. 49; limits of the Town, s. 50, 5 W. 4, c. 39.

Fletcher's trust
Justices and Vestry to include as an item of parochial expenditure in the Ways and Means, £91 4s. annually, for payment, quarterly, of annuities to 3 poor widows under the will of George Fletcher, and collect the rents of a house. The remaining part of his real estate for the use of the parish, 10 V., c. 45.

ST. DAVID.

Name
Confirmed as a Parish under that name, 33 C. 2, c. 18, s. 12.

Part of Surry
Part of Surry, 31 G. 2, c. 4, s. 1.

Boundaries
Boundaries from Port-Royal, 23 G. 3. c. 15.

Separated from St. Thomas in the East
Separated from the precinct of St. Thomas in the East, and separate Custos and Justices to be appointed, 8 V., c. 8.

ST. DOROTHY.

Name
Confirmed as a Parish under that name, 33 C. 2, c. 18, s. 12.

Part of Middlesex
Part of Middlesex, 31 G. 2, c. 4, s. 1.

St. Elizabeth.

Confirmed as a Parish under that name, 33 C. 2, c. 18, s. 12.   *Name*

Westmoreland separated from, 2 Ann, c. 1, s. 1.   *Westmoreland separated from*

Parts of Carpenter's Mountains taken from St. Elizabeth and Clarendon, and annexed to Vere, 12 G. 2, c. 6.   *Carpenter's mountains*

Part of Cornwall, 31 G. 2, c. 4, s. 1.   *Part of Cornwall*

Powers of the Justices and Vestry to appoint River Wardens, and keep open the navigation of the Black River, 23 G. 3, c. 8, s. 1-16.   *Black River*

Transferred to the Commissioners of Highways and Bridges for the parish, 25 V., c. 18, s. 66.

A piece of land in Black River to be sold, and the proceeds to be applied in the purchase of mountain land in the parish for the Incumbent, for provision grounds, 23 G. 3, c. 8, s. 27-29.   *Glebe land*

(This same piece of land apparently had been previously directed to be sold for a similar purpose, 1 G. 3, c. 5.)

Trustees appointed to complete the building of a Bridge over the Black River, 51 G. 3, c. 18.   *Black River Bridge*

Manchester separated from, 55 G. 3, c 23.   *Manchester*

The Barracks and land belonging thereto vested in the Justices and Vestry for erecting a Court house, and other parochial purposes, 7 W 4, c. 17.   *Court house, &c.*

St. George.

Confirmed as a Parish under that name, 33 C. 2, c. 18, s. 12.   *Name*

Part of Surry, 31 G. 2, c. 4, s. 1.   *Part of Surry*

1 Acre, 3 roods, and 37 perches of land in Douglas Town, near Buff Bay, vested in the Magistrates and Vestry to erect a Church, and lay out a Burial Ground, and 300 acres of land and certain slaves, for the use of the Rector, 41 G. 3, c. 22.   *Church and burial ground*

The 300 acres of land and slaves to be sold, and the proceeds invested in the purchase of suitable lands for a Parsonage, and the interest in the meantime paid to the Rector, 58 G. 3, c. 29.

Metcalfe separated from, 5 V., c. 44.   *Metcalfe separated from*

Compromise with the present Rector, in respect of his claims for Rectory House, Glebe and servants, and fees for burial and otherwise, 25 V., c. 21.   *Rectory*

St. James.

Confirmed as a Parish under that name, 33 C. 2, c. 18, s. 12.   *Name*

Part of Cornwall, 31 G. 2, c. 4, s. 1.   *Part of Cornwall*

Trelawny separated from, 14 G. 3, c. 31, s. 1, 4.   *Trelawny separated from*

Lands purchased for a Church, Church Yard, Burial Grounds, Parsonage, Glebe, Court house, Barracks, Hospitals, or other public or parochial purposes, vested in the Churchwardens of St. James, 33 G. 3, c. 23.   *Church burial ground, &c*

Justices and Vestry empowered to purchase lands and erect a new Court house, as also to purchase one or more parcels of land for Burial Grounds at a reasonable distance from Montego Bay, 36 G. 3, c. 35, s, 19, 22.   *Court house and burial ground, &c., Gaol, &c*

Further powers given for the erection of the Court house, as also a Gaol, Guard House, and Parochial Arsenal, and for the erection of a Bridge over Montego River, 42 G 3, c. 24.

Montego Bay declared the County town, and the Gaol the County Gaol of Cornwall instead of Savanna-la-Mar, 56 G. 3, c. 20, s. 1.   *County Gaol*

The old Barracks and land near Montego Bay vested in the Justices and Vestry for the erection of a Workhouse, (see 60 G, 3, c. 20), 1 G. 4, c. 19, s. 2.   *Work house*

The Justices and Vestry of St. James empowered to convey a sufficient portion of 50 acres of Marley land, purchased by them for a Parochial Chapel, Parsonage House and Burial Ground, for a Parsonage House and Glebe, and dispose of the residue in aid of the parish funds, 6 V., c. 60.   *Marley Chapel, &c*

Montego Bay—Retailers of Spirits, s. 1-7; Fires and Firewardens, s. 8-23; Night Watch, s. 29-37; Repair of Streets, s. 39; Swamps, s. 40-4;   *Montego Bay Police regulations*

Unwholesome Provisions, s. 42-43 ; Churchwardens incorporated, s. 49-50 ; Protection from Actions, Recovery of Penalties, &c.. s. 51-53, 35 G. 3, c. 35·

The Custos, Justices, Vestrymen, Rector and Churchwardens, incorporated and invested with powers for the alteration and improvement ot the Town of Montego Bay, and appointment of officers, s. 1-8, 10-14 ; Firewardens, s. 9 ; Burial of the Dead, s. 23 ; Penalties, Protection from Actions, &c., s. 24-29, 36 G. 3, c. 35.

Marine Hospital	Montego Bay Marine Hospital, 60 G. 3, c. 16.

ST. JOHN.

Name	Confirmed as a Parish under the name, 33 C. 2, c. 18, s. 12.
Part of Middlesex	Part of Middlesex, 31 G. 2, c. 4, s. 1.

ST. MARY.

Name	Confirmed as a Parish under that name, 33 C. 2, c. 18 s. 12.
Part of Middlesex	Part of Middlesex, 31 G. 2, c. 4. s. 1.
Manning's Town	The Justices and Vestry empowered to exchange 90 acres of land devised by Thomas Manning for the use of the poor, with C. N. Baily, for Nibb's Penn, binding on Port Maria, part to be laid out as a Town, to be called Manning's Town, and to erect thereon a Court House and offices for the Clerk of the Vestry, Clerk of the Peace, Collecting Constable, and other public offices, Goal and Workhouse, a Poor-house and Hospital, and Pound. To design and lay out the plan of the Town, and lease the lands so laid out in lots, and also to lease out. but not sell the residue of the land, reserving a sufficient quantity or the right of using the same for the musters and exercise of the Militia, 57 G. 3, c. 20, s. 1, 3, 5, 7, 9-15.
Marine Hospital	Marine Hospital and Aqueduct, 1 G. 4, c. 16.
Metcalfe separated from	Metcalfe.—Separated from, 5 V., c. 44.

ST. THOMAS IN THE EAST.

Name	Confirmed as a Parish under the name of St. Thomas, 33 C. 2, c. 18, s. 12.
Part of Surry	Part of Surry, 31 G. 2, c. 4, s. 1.
Parsonage	The Parsonage and Glebe land vested in the Justices and Vestry for sale. Another more convenient Parsonage House, and sufficient quantity of Glebe land, to be provided for the use and residence of the Rector, 51 G. 3, c, 19.
St. David separated from precinct	St. David.—Separated from the Precinct, 8 V., c. 8

ST. THOMAS IN THE VALE.

Name	Confirmed as a Parish under the name of St. Thomas in the Valley, 33 C. 2, c. 18, s. 12.
Part of Middlesex	Part of Middlesex, 31 G. 2, c. 4, s. 1.
Parochial buildings	Justices and Vestry empowered to purchase lands, and erect a Court House, Goal, Workhouse Poor-house and Hospital, and other Buildings for Parochial purposes, 57 G. 3, c. 26.
Separated from precinct of St. Catherine	Separated from the Precinct of St. Catherine, and separate Custos and Justices to be appointed, 5 W. 4, c. 24.

TRELAWNY.

Separated from St. James	Separated from St. James, and declared a distinct Parish in Cornwall, 14 G. 3, c. 31, s. 1-4.
Part of Cornwall Court house	The Justices and Vestry empowered to sell the Court-house at Martha Brae, and erect a new Court-house in Falmouth, at the place called " The Fort," or to purchase other lands for the purpose, 35 G. 3, c. 28.
Stewart Town	The Justices and Vestry appointed and incorporated as Commissioners, to purchase, not exceeding 50 acres of land appertaining to Foss's Settlement, or to Robert Home Gordon, or in the vicinity, whereon to lay out a Town, in lots, to be called Stewart Town, and establish bye laws and ordinances for the prevention and extinguishment of fire, the laying out streets, &c., repairing the same, removing and preventing nuisances, sup

pressing noxious trades, establishing and regulating a Market, and the trade and traffic in shops, government of Taverns, Grog-shops, Venders and Retailers of Spirits, Hawkers Pedlars and Higlers, and in every other way wherein the Police and well-being of the Town may be concerned : to appoint officers, sell or lease the lots of lands. Proceedings to enforce penalties, &c., 53 G. 3, c. 19, s. 1-3, 5, 10, 12, 14.

Falmouth—Fires and Firewardens, s. 2-17 ; Discharging Fire Arms, s. 18 ; Filth and rubbish, s. 19 ; Unenclosed Lands, s. 20 ; Spirits, s. 21 ; Bell, Drunken and Disorderly Persons, s. 22, 23 ; Furious Riding or Driving, s. 24; Unwholesome Provisions. s. 26 ; Assize of Bread, s. 27-29 ; Of Grass, s. 30 ; Night Watches, s. 31-38 ; Streets, s. 39-40 ; Goats and Hogs, s. 45 ; Hawkers and Pedlars, s. 46 ; Improvements of the Town, s. 49-57 ; Neglecting to attend Meetings of Justices and Vestry, s. 58 ; Recovery, &c., of Penalties s. 59, 73 ; Protection from Actions, s. 70 ; Costs, s. 71 ; Seizure of Produce suspected to be stolen, s. 72, 1 V., c. 27.   *Falmouth*

Justices and Vestry empowered to purchase lands, and build a landing place in Falmouth, solely for the embarkation or disembarkation of persons, 11 V., c. 37.   *Landing place*

Commissioners for erecting 2 Iron Bridges over the Martha Brae River, in lieu of the wooden Bridges on the high Road, from the Rock to Falmouth, 11 V., c. 17 ; 15 V., c. 32.   *Martha Brae bridges*

Falmouth Marine Hospital, 23 V., S. 1, c, 20.   *Marine Hospital*

VERE.

Confirmed as a Parish under that name, 33 C. 2, c. 18, s. 12'   *Name*

Part of Carpenter's Mountains taken from St. Elizabeth and Ciarendon, and added thereto. Boundaries thereof, 12 G. 2, c. 6.   *Carpenter's mountains*

Part of Middlesex, 31 G. 2, c. 4, s. 1.   *Part of Middlesex*

Manchester separated from, 55 G. 3, c. 23.   *Manchester separated from*

The Justices and Vestry to purchase and build a Court-house, and for other Parochial purposes, 51 G. 3, c. 22.   *Court house*

WESTMORELAND.

Separated from St. Elizabeth, 2 Ann, c. 1, s. 1.   *Separated from St. Elizabeth*

Hanover separated from it, 10 G. 1, c. 5, s. 1.   *Hanover separated from*

Boundaries. 2 Ann, c. 1, s. 1 ; 10 G. 1, c. 5, s. 1 ; 29 G. 3, c, 22 ; 7 V., c. 56.   *Boundaries*

Part of Cornwall, Savanna-la-Mar, the County Town, 31 G. 2, c. 4, s. 1   *Part of Cornwall*

County Goal to be built at Savanna-la-Mar, 32 G. 2, c. 3, s. 1.

Montego Bay declared the County Town, and its Goal the County Goal, 56 G. 3, c. 20.

Savanna-la-Mar, casks to be made within squares of brick or stone, s. 5. Buildings not to be covered with thatch, &c., s. 7. Penalties, s. 8, 9, 9 G. 3, c. 4.   *Savanna-la-Mar*

The Goal at Savanna-la-Mar to be sold by the Justices and Vestry, and another built in a more convenient spot in or near the Town, 19 G. 3, c. 19, s. 1.   *Gaol*

Savanna-la-Mar.—Trustees appointed (in consequence of the destruction of the old Town by fire, hurricane and inundation) to lay out the ground called the Savanna, into a new Town whereon to build a Court-house, Market-house, and other Public Buildings. Powers of Trustees to purchase land, s. 1, 2 ; Boundaries, s. 3 ; Powers to lay out streets, &c, build Court-house, control Buildings, &c., buy Fire Engines, &c, Sink Wells, s. 4-7 ; Appoint officers, s. 8 ; Divide the land into lots, of not more than one acre each, and grant leases, not exceeding 99 years, or convey, in fee simple but not more than one acre to any one person, s. 9-12 ; Convey fresh water to the Town, s. 13, 15, 16, 17 ; Cut a canal from the sea to the Town, s. 14; Application of receipts from grants and leases and ground rents, s. 18-19 ; Inoculation for Small-pox, &c., s. 20 ; Penalties Protection from suits, &c., s. 21-26, 21 G. 3, c. 11.   *Savanna-la-Mar*

Marine Hospital, Savanna-la-Mar, 53 G. 3, c. 22.   *Marine Hospital*

Parochial build
ings   Barracks near Savanna-la-Mar vested in the Justices and Vestry-men for a House of Correction, and Poor-house, or other Parochial purposes 7 W. 4, c. 27.

Partition.

Proceedings to ef-
fect   After Summons or other Process in Partition returned, and affidavit of the Provost Marshal, his Deputy or other person, of notice given of the Writ of Partition to the Tenant to the action, or his Attorney or Agent (if to be found in the Island) whose power is recorded one month at least before the issuing of the Writ or Summons, and where the Tenant cannot be found in the Island or any Attorney whose power is recorded to the Tenant in possession, or occupier of the Land whereof Partition is demanded, if any such there be, other than the demandant, and if there be none in possession but the demandant, then a copy of the Summons or other process being left on the premises 14 days at least before the next Court, if the Tenant to the Writ or true Tenant to the Lands do not appear, or cause an appearance to be entered in the Court where the Writ is returnable, then, in default of appearance, the demandant having entered his declaration the Court shall proceed to examine the demandant's title and quantity of his part and purport, and as they find it to be, they shall for so much give judgment by default, and award a Writ to make Partition, whereby such proportion, part and purport may be set out severally, which being executed and returned, and thereon final Judgment entered, the same shall be good, and conclude all persons whatever, their right, title or claim, though not named in the proceedings, nor the title truly set forth. If the Tenant or person concerned, within one year from entering the first judgment, apply to the Court by motion, and shew good matter in bar of the Partition, or that the demandant has not title to so much as he has recovered, the Court may suspend or set aside the Judgment and admit the Tenant to appear and plead; and the cause shall proceed as if no such Judgment had been given; and if the Court upon hearing, adjudge for the first demandant, the first judgment shall stand confirmed, and be good against all persons, 8 G. 1, c. 5.

     And instead of treble costs, shall receive full indemnity, as to costs and expenses, to be taxed, subject to review as any other taxation, 8 V., c. 28, s. 22.

May be made by
precept to Deputy
Marshal   The Provost Marshal may make Partition by precept to a Deputy 19 V., c. 31. s. 15.

Jurors   Attendance of Jurors enforced at the execution of Writ (see Jurors on Writs), 43 G. 3, c. 28.

To be otherwise
by deed   No Partition of Freehold or Leasehold Land shall be valid at Law without Deed, except where authorized by the Law now in force, 8 V., c. 19, s. 2.

Partnerships, Limited.

     Conditions upon which Limited Partnerships may be formed, except for the purpose of Banking or making Insurance, between special Partners, not liable for the debts of the Partnership beyond the sum contributed in cash to the capital of the Copartnership, and 2 or more general Partners liable as now; the general Partners only having power to transact the business of, and sign for, and bind the Partnership, and liable to be sued as if there were no special Partners, 16 V., c. 21.*

Patents.

To be enrolled   All Patents shall be enrolled in the Office of Enrolments within 6 months after sealing, 33 C. 2, c. 12, s. 7.

For fisheries and
Shoal water void   All Patents for Fishery, and shoal water in and about the Harbour of Port Royal and other Harbours, and the water before several persons' land and Royal Mines, the Parade in St. Jago de la Vega, and the

---

     * There seems little probability that this Act will be resorted to, the Incorporated Companies' Act, 27 V., S. 2, c. 4, affording much greater advantages.

Fishery in and between the Rio Cobre and the Salt River in St. Andrew's, declared void, and no such Grant or Patent now or hereafter granted prejudicial to anchorage, navigation or common fishery, shall be good. Owners of land adjoining upon any Harbour, Bay or Creek, may take up the shoal water to make wharfs or bridges, convenient before their own land and none else, and all Patents for shoal water or building of wharfs or bridges before any man's own land shall be deemed good, 35 C. 2, c. 12, s. 1.

A Patent under the Great Seal, and enrolled, shall be evidence of the Patentee's title to the lands or other things granted, and a bar to the rights of the Crown, 2 Ann, c. 7, s. 1. *Evidence*

For all lands within the survey or bounds, any misnomer, misbounding or mistaking of quantity or other error notwithstanding, and such grants shall be taken as strongly against the Crown as the grants of other persons against them, 2 Ann, c. 7, s. 2. *To be liberally construed*

In case either H. M. or the Patentee are aggrieved by a mistake in quantity, a re-survey shall be made by a Surveyor, indifferently sworn between the Crown and the Patentee, or who claimeth in his right before a Justice, and a confirmation of the former grant shall issue under the Broad Seal, reciting the error and reserving for the future the same rent mentioned in the grant, according to the just quantity found by such re-survey; for which, confirmation the Chancellor shall receive 10s. (6s. stg.) and the Clerk of the Patents 8s. currency, and no more, to be paid as all other charges by the party requiring the same ; but no retrospect shall be had to what rent ought to have been paid, be the quantity more or less, 2 Ann, c. 7, s. 3. *Re-surveys*

If any person, by mistake of Surveyors or otherwise, settle upon any land belonging to the Crown, and the same is afterwards found to be so, the person so settled shall be preferred to all other persons, and entitled to a Patent, paying the usual fees only, provided he apply for such Patent, and pay the Quit Rents (and Land Tax, see 8 V., c. 16, s. 1) usually reserved, for such time as he has been possessed thereof as aforesaid, and until the Patent pass the seal, the possessor, his heirs and assigns shall continue in quiet possession, 4 G. 2, c. 4, s. 7. *Persons settling on Crown lands when entitled to Patents*

Patents for Improvements under Acts in Force.

Egan's Sugar, expires July, 1866, 16 V., c. 32, c. 34.
Brandei's   "   "   April, 1867, 16 V., c, 33.

Patents for Inventions.

When any person by himself, or if an Absentee, by his attorney, applies to the Governor by petition, to be lodged at the Executive Committee office, alleging that he has invented or discovered some new and useful act, machine, manufacture, or composition of matter not before known or used in the Island, or some improvement in such invention and discovery, and praying to obtain an exclusive property in such invention or discovery or improvement, and that Letters Patent be granted for the same, the Governor, in the name or on behalf of H. M , with the advice and consent of the Executive Committee, may direct Letters Patent under the Broad Seal to be issued, which shall recite the allegations and suggestions of the petition, and give a short description of the invention, &c., and thereupon grant to the applicant, his executors, &c., for not exceeding 14 years the full and exclusive right and liberty of making, constructing and using, and vending to others to be used, the new invention, &c. ; such Letters Patent shall be signed by the Governor. The Governor in Executive Committee, if they deem it expedient, may insert in the Letters Patent a provision, extending their operation for a further term of 7 years, 21 V., c. 30, s. 1. *Petition for ; Letters Patent] For 14 years 7 years extension*

Before any Letters Patent are signed and issued, the petition, specification and declaration delivered therewith, shall be referred to the Attorney-General, who shall examine same, and may call to his aid such scientific or other person as he thinks fit, and cause to be paid to him by the applicant such remuneration as the Attorney General appoints, not exceeding *Petition, &c , be referred to Attorney General Who may call in aid Remuneration.*

£5, and if satisfied that the application may properly oe granted, and that
the specification describes the nature of the invention, discovery or im-

Certificate

provement, he shall allow the same, and give a certificate of his allowance, and return the petition, specification and declaration, with his certi-

If he does not al low it to certify his reasons

ficate into the Executive Committee office ; and if he does not allow the
application, he shall certify to the Governor his reasons, 21 V., c. 30, s. 2.

Petition to be ac companied with de claration of belief that petitioner is true inventor, &c

Before any person obtains or receives Letters Patent, he or, if an Absentee, his Attorney shall make solemn declaration in writing before a Justice,
that he verily believes he is the true inventor or discoverer of the art, machine, composition of matter or improvement for which he solicites Letters Patent, and that such invention or discovery or improvement has not, to the
best of his knowledge or belief, been known or used in this Island, to be delivered with the Petition, 21 V., c. 30, s. 3

And also with specification

Such Person, or his Attorney, shall also deliver therewith a written description or specification of his invention, and of the manner of using, or process of compounding the same, in such full. clear and exact terms, as to distinguish the same from all other things before known or used in this Island,
and to enable any person skilled in the art or science of which it is a branch,

And model in case of a machine

or with which it is most nearly connected, to make, compound and use the
same ; and in case of any machine, shall deliver a model, and explain the
principle and modes in which he has contemplated the application of that

Drawings, &c

principle, or character by which it may be distinguished from other inventions, and accompany the whole with drawings and written references,

Specimens

where the nature of the case admits of drawings, or with specimens of the
ingredients, and of the composition of matters sufficient in quantity for the

Signature and attestation

purpose of experiment, where the invention is of a composition of matter,
which description or specification shall be signed by such person or his Attor

Dispensation with model

ney, and attested by two witnesses. Where from the complicated nature
of any machinery, the cost of a model may be so grea as to prevent any
ingenious but poor persons from obtaining Patents, the Governor and Executive Committee may dispense with its delivery previous to the granting of any
patent, and the Act; being in other respects complied with, the party shall
be entitled to a Patent in the same manner as if a model had been lodged,
21 V., c. 30, s. 4.

Attorney General's fee

The applicant shall deposit with his petition £5, as fee to the Attorney-
General, on reference of such Petition, 21 V., c. 30, s. 5.

4 weeks advertise ment of application

No Letters Patent shall be granted until notice shall be published in the
"Gazette" and one other newspaper of this Colony, for at least, 4 weeks of the
intention to apply, containing in general terms, the description of the invention or improvement for which they are desired, 21 V., c. 30, s. 6.

To be brought into oper a t i o n in two years

If any Letters Patent are not brought into operation within two years,
they shall be forfeited and thence become void, 21 V., c. 30, s. 7.

Date

Letters Patent may be issued to be sealed and bear date as of the day or
the application, or where the Attorney-General or Governor in Executive
Committee think fit as of the day of the sealing, or any intermediate day, 21
V., c. 30, s. 8.

Of force from date

And shall be of the same force as if actually sealed on the day expressed, 21 V., c. 30, s. 9.

To be applied for within three months

No Letters Patent, save in the case of those discharged or lost, shall issue,
unless applied for within 3 months after the date of filing the Petition, 21
V., c. 30, s. 10.

Grant to executors &c., in case of ap plicant's death

Where the applicant dies during the pendency of his application, Letters
Patent may be granted to his Executors or Administrators at anytime within
3 months after his death, and be of the like force as if they had been granted
to the applicant during his lifetime, 21 V., c. 30, s. 11.

Renewal of lost Patents

In case any Letters Patent are destroyed or lost, others of the like tenor
and effect, and sealed and dated as of the same day, may, subject to the regulations of the Governor in Executive Committee, be issued under the authority of the grant in pursuance of which the original was issued, 21 V., c.
30, s. 12.

Fraudulent pa tents

In case of any Letters Patent obtained in fraud of the true and first Inventor, any Letters Patent granted to the true and first inventor, shall not be
invalidated by such other Letters Patent, or of any use or publication of the

invention subsequent to the granting of such other Letters Patent as last-mentioned, 21 V., c. 30, s. 13.

Where any Letters Patent are obtained for any new and useful invention or discovery, and thereafter another discovers or makes any improvement in the principle or process, and applies for and obtains Letters Patent for the exclusive right of such improvement, the person who obtains a Patent for the improvement, shall not make use or vend the original invention or discovery, nor shall the Patentee of the original invention make use or vend any such improvement. Simply changing the form or proportions of any machine, or composition of matter in any degree shall not be deemed a discovery or improvement within this Act, 21 V., c. 30, s. 14. *Mutual rights in inventions and improvements*

Mere change of form or proportions

No applicant shall be deprived of his right to a Patent in this Colony, upon the like proceedings being had in all respects as in case of an original application for his invention, by reason of his having previously taken out Letters Patent therefor in any other country : provided the invention has not been introduced into public and common use in this Colony prior to his application for a patent therein. The Patent in this Colony shall not continue after the expiration of the Patent granted elsewhere ; and where more than one Patent or like privilege is obtained abroad, immediately upon the expiration or determination of the term which first expires, that in this Colony shall cease. No Letters Patent granted here after the expiration of the term for which such Patent or r g was obtained elsewhere, shall be of any validity, 21 V., c. 30, s. 15p ivile e *Patent here for inventions already Patented elsewhere*

Duration

Any Patentee, his executors, &c., may assign and transfer (the whole) or any part of his right, title or interest, and the assignee having recorded the assignment in the Secretary's Office, shall thereafter stand in the place of the original patentee, as well as to all or the part assigned of the right, privilege and advantage, as also in respect of all or proportionate liability or responsibility as to the Letters Patent, and the invention and discovery thereby secured, and in like manner shall the assignees of any such assignee, stand in the place of the original patentee or inventor, 21 V., c. 30, s. 16. *Assignments*

Letters Patent may, upon the like proceedings in all respects as in case of an original application, be issued by the Governor in Executive Committee to the assignee of any person who has taken out Letters Patent for his invention or discovery in any other country, but not for any invention or discovery made abroad for which no Letters Patent have been there obtained : provided the invention or discovery assigned has not been introduced into public and common use into this Colony prior to the application. The assignee of the Foreign Patent shall file with his application, the assignment duly proved under which he claims a Patent in this Colony, and an affidavit setting forth the date of the Patent abroad, that the article thereby patented has not been in public and common used in this Colony, and that he is the assignee for a good consideration, 21 V., c. 30, s. 17. *Patents to assignees of foreign Patents*

If in any suit or action it is proved or specially found by the verdict that by mistake, accident or inadvertence, and without any wilful default or intent to defraud or mislead the public, a Patentee in his specification has claimed to be the original and first inventor or discoverer of any material or substantial part of the thing patented, but of which he was not the original or just inventor, and has no just or legal title to claim the same, his Patent shall be valid for so much of the invention, discovery or improvement, as is actually his own, provided it be a material and substantial part of the thing patented, and plainly distinguishable from other parts patented without right ; and every such Patentee and his legal representatives and assignees, whether holding the whole or a particular interest in the Patent, may maintain suits at law or in equity for any infringement of such part as is actually the invention or discovery of the Patentee, although his specification may embrace more than he has a legal right to claim ; but if in such case he obtain a verdict or judgment, he shall not be entitled to costs, unless before the commencement of the suit he has filed in the Secretary's office a disclaimer, attested by one witness or more, of the part which was claimed without right. No person bringing a suit shall be entitled to the benefit of this section if, in the opinion of the Court before which the matter is tried, he has unreasonably neglected or delayed to record his disclaimer, 21 V., c. 30, s. 18. *Consequences of including too much in specification without disclaimer without wilful default or fraud*

Effect on costs of suit

3 s

New Patent to be taken out

If any Patent becomes inoperative or invalid by reason of a defective or insufficient description or specification, or by reason of the Patentee claiming in the specification as his own invention more than he had a right to claim, and the error has arisen from mistake, &c., and without any fraudulent or deceptive intention, the Governor in Executive Committee, upon the surrender of such Patent and upon petition therefor, may cause a new Patent to be issued to the Patentee for the residue of the term mentioned in the first Patent, in accordance with the Patentee's amended description and specification. In case of his death or assignment of the original Patent or any fractional interest therein, the right shall vest in his legal representatives to the extent of their respective interests, and the re-issued Patent, with the amended description and specifications, shall have the same operation in law, as though originally filed in the amended form before the issuing of the original Patent, 21 V., c. 30, s. 19.

Disclaimers of part of title to invention, &c., or specification, memorandum of alteration may be recorded with Attorney General's leave

Every Patentee, or his legal representative or assignee, whether holding the whole or any particular interest, may conjointly or separately, as the case may require, enter and record in the Secretary's Office, having first obtained the Attorney-General's leave, certified by his fiat and signature, a disclaimer of any part of either the title of the invention or improvement, or of the specification, stating the reason for such disclaimer; or may, with such leave, enter and record a memorandum of any alteration in the title or specification, not being such disclaimer or alteration as shall extend to the exclusive right granted by the Patent, which disclaimer or memorandum of alteration, being recorded, shall be deemed part of the Patent or specification

Caveat

in all Courts. Any person may enter a Caveat at the Secretary's Office against such disclaimer or alteration, which being entered, and a copy left with the Attorney-General, shall give the party entering the same a right

Disclaimer or alteration not receivable in evidence in pending actions, &c., except scirefacias

to have notice of the application being heard by the Attorney-General. No such disclaimer or alteration shall be receivable in evidence in any action or suit (except in any proceeding by Scire Facias) pending when it was entered, but in every such action or suit, the original title and specification alone shall be given in evidence, and deemed the title and specification of the in-

When to be advertised

vention for which the Patent was granted. The Attorney-General before granting his fiat may require the party applying for the same to advertise his disclaimer or alteration in such manner as to him seems right, and if he so require such advertisement, shall certify in his fiat that it has been duly made, 21 V., c. 30, s. 20.

Costs on alteration or disclaimer

The Attorney-General may, by his certificate, order by, or to whom the costs of any hearing or enquiry for any such alteration, &c., shall be paid, and how and by whom such costs are to be ascertained ; and if not paid within 4 days after the amount is ascertained, the Attorney-General may make an order for payment which may be made a rule of the Supreme Court, 21 V., c. 30, s. 21.

Additions to original description or specification

If an original Patentee desire to add a description or specification of an improvement upon his original invention or discovery, made or discovered by him subsequent to the date of his Patent, he may, upon the like proceedings being had in all respects as in case of an original application, have the same annexed to his original description and specification ; and the Island Secretary shall certify upon the annexed description and specification the time of its being annexed and recorded, and thereafter it shall have the same effect in law as if it had been embraced in and recorded with the original, 21 V., c. 30, s. 22.

Documents to be filed by Secretary of Executive Committee and endorsed and receipts given

Every petition, declaration, and specification, and every certificate or warrant thereon, shall be left at the Office of the Executive Committee, and the day of the delivery and the date of every reference shall be endorsed thereon by the Secretary of the Executive Committee, and an acknowledgment of receipt, either separately or together, as the same may be delivered, shall be given to the petitioner, or person delivering the same, or his

After Letters Patent to be recorded and preserved in Island Secretary's Office
And receipts given
Fees

agent, all which petitions, &c., when Letters Patent are granted, and all Letters Patent, disclaimers and memoranda of alteration and assignments, shall be lodged, filed and preserved in the Secretary's Office, and there recorded in or in continuation of the books of records of Patents hitherto kept; and a receipt shall be given by the Island Secretary, and a registry of such petitions, &c., and of all proceedings thereon, shall be kept at such Office. The Island Secretary's fees for recording every such petition, &c., and for every receipt granted therefor, shall be the like as in cases of Deeds, 21 V., c. 30, s. 23,

.Any person may obtain from the Island Secretary's Office, certified copies of any Letters Patent, petitions, &c., disclaimers, &c., document, &c., connected therewith, or drawing relating thereto, on payment of the like fees as for copies of other documents ; aud such certified copies" shall be evidence, 21 V., c. 30, s. 24.

If reference is made to drawings in any specification, an extra copy shall be left therewith, and bound up in a suitable book, and plain, accurate and sufficient notes of reference to the specification wherewith such drawings have been deposited, shall be made on or annexed to the drawings, aud bound up with them, so that the reference may be easily seen and understood, 21 V., c. 30, s. 25.

The Island Secretary shall cause indexes to all petitions, &c., enrolled or recorded, to be prepared in the Form now used,&c., and such indexes and the books of Record, shall be open to public inspection at the usual times, and on payment of the usual fees in cases of searches, 21 V., c. 30, s. 26.

In any Action for infringment of a Patent, the plaintiff shall deliver with his declaration, concise particulars of the breaches complained of, and the defendant, on pleading thereto, shall deliver with his plea, and the prosecutor in any proceedings, by Scire Facias to repeal Letters Patent, to deliver with his declaration, concise particulars of any objections he means to rely on at the trial in support of his pleas or suggestions of the declaration, in proceedings by Scire Facias, and at the trial no evidence shall be allowed to be given in support of any alleged infringment, or of any objection impeaching the validity of the Letters Patent, which is not contained in the particulars delivered. The places where, and the manner the invention is alleged to have been used or published prior to the date of the Patent, shall be stated in the particulars delivered. A Judge in Chambers may allow the plaintiff, defendant or prosecutor to amend the particulars delivered, upon such terms as he thinks fit. At the trial of any proceedings by Scire Facias to repeal Letters Patent, the defendant shall be entitled to begin and give evidence in support of the Patent, and if evidence is adduced by the prosecutor impeaching its validity, the defendant may reply, 21 V., c. 30, s. 27.

In any action for the infringment of a Patent, the defendant shall not plead any other plea than the general issue, which shall put the plaintiff to such proof in support of his action, and let in such evidence for the defendant as in any action under such plea the defendant may, or the ai iff at present is required to adduce ; nevertheless the defendant may, alongtwith his plea, give notice by endorsement or annexed, of any special defence he might, by the present practice offer under a special plea, and for which he would be required to plead specially. The defendant at the trial shall be bound by such notice, and not be at liberty to go into evidence of any other defence he would by the present rules of pleading be restricted from giving, exept under a plea for the purpose specially pleaded ; and if the plaintiff would, under the present rules of pleading, be entitled to set up one of 2 answers to such special defence, he shall endorse upon his similiter the nature of the answer, and shall at the trial be precluded from entering into evidence in support of any other answer. Not to prevent any party from filing a General or a Special Demurrer, 21 V., c. 30, s. 28.

In any action for the infringment of Letters Patent, the Court, if sitting, or if not, a Judge, on the application of the plaintiff or defendant, may make such order for an injunction, inspection or account, and give such directions respecting the action, injunction &c., and proceedings therein, as to the Court or Judge seems fit, 21 V., c. 30, s. 29.

In taxing the costs in any action, regard shall be had to the particulars delivered, and the plaintiff and defendant shall not be allowed any costs in respect of any particulars, unless certified by the Judge, before whom the trial was had, to have been proved by them, without regard to the general costs of the cause; and such Judge shall certify on the record that the validity of the Patent came in question, and the record with such certificate, being given in evidence in any suit or action, for infringing or proceeding by Scire Facias to repeal the Letters Patent, shall entitle the plaintiff in any suit or action, or the defendant in Scire Facias, on obtaining a decree, decretal order or final judgment to his full costs as between attorney and client, unless the

Judge making the decree or order, or the Judge trying the action or proceeding, shall certify that he ought not to have full costs, 21 V., c.30, s.·30.

3 times the actual damage recoverable

When Letters Patent have been granted, and any person, without the consent of the Patentee, his executors, &c., in writing, makes, devises, uses or sells the thing, invention or discovery, whereof the exclusive right is secured, the offender shall forfeit and pay to the Patentee, &c., a sum equal to 3 times the actual damage sustained, to be recovered with costs, by action on the case founded on this Act in the Supreme Court, 21 V., c. 30, s. 31.

Using the name of a patentee or impressing, &c., the words Patent, &c., without authority

If any person shall write, paint or print, or mould, cast or carve, or engrave or stamp upon anything made, used or sold by him, for the sole making or selling of which he has not obtained a Patent, the name, or any imitation of the name of any other person who has obtained Letters Patent, without leave in writing of such Patentee, or his assigns, or if any person shall, upon such thing not having been purchased from the Pantentee, or some person who purchased it from or under him, or not having had the license or consent in writing of the Patentee or his assigns, write, &c., or otherwise mark the words "Patent," 'Letters patent," "By the Queen's Patent," or any words of the like kind, meaning or import, with a view of imitating or counterfeiting the stamp, mark or other, devise of the Patentee : penalty, £50; recoverable by action of debt, &c. ; one moiety to the person who sues. Not to subject any person to any penalty for stamping, or in any way marking the word "Patent" upon anything upon which a Patent before obtained has expired, 21 V., c. 30, s. 32.

Penalty

Not applicable after expiry of Patent

Forms

The forms in the Schedule may be used and varied as occasion requires, 21 V., c. 30, s. 33.

Stamps

The Stamp duties in Schedule shall be charged, and no others, 21 V., c. 30, s. 34.

Scirefacias

The writ of Scire Facias shall be for the repeal of any Letters Patent under this Act, as the same would be for the repeal of Letters Patent issued under the great Seal in England, 21 V., c. 30, s. 35.

Act to be construed by analogy to the English Patent Laws

If any doubts arise in the construction of this Act, they are to be construed by analogy to the laws now or to be in force in England, relating to Patents, so far as they shall be applicable, 21 V., c. 30, s. 36.

Commissioners

The Governor may, by Warrant under his Sign Manual, free from Stamp duty, appoint Commissioners during his pleasure, and who may be summoned to attend any meeting, and take part in any proceedings of the Governor in Executive Committee in any matter under this Act, 21 V., c. 30, s. 37.

Interpretation

"Invention," "Discovery' and "Improvement" shall mean any manner of new manufacture or new mode of manufacture, the subject of Letter Patent and grant of privilege within the meaning of 21 Jas. 1, c. 3. "Petition," "Declaration," "Reference," "Certificate," "Warrant," "Letters Patent" shall mean instruments in the form and to the effect in the Schedule, subject to such alterations as may from time to time be made under the powers of this Act, 21 V., c. 30, s. 38.

Short title

The Patent Law Amendment Act, 1857, 21 V., c. 30, s. 39.

No British or foreign Patent of effect here without a Patent under this act

No Letters Patent heretofore, or to be obtained in Great Britain or elsewhere, for the exclusive privilege of trade or manufacture, or any invention in connection therewith, shall be of any validity or effect in this Island, unless Letters Patent for the privilege or invention, in respect of which such foreign Letters Patent may have been obtained, are granted and issued under this Act, nor until all its provisions and requirements have been complied with in respect to Letters Patent, 21 V., c. 30, s. 41.

SCHEDULE.

Stamp Duties.

				£	s.	d.
Letters Patent	....	....	....	5	0	0
Petition	....	....	....	0	1	6
Declaration	....	....	....	0	1	6
Specification	....	....	....	0	5	0
Reference	....	....	....	0	0	0
Certificate or Warrant of Attorney-General			....	0	0	0
Disclaimer or Memorandum of Alteration		....	....	0	1	6
Assignment	....	....	....	0	10	0

FORMS.

To His Excellency, &c. &c., (here insert name and title of Governor.)

The humble petition of (here insert name and address of petitioner,) for, &c.

SHEWETH,

That your petitioner is in possession of an invention for

(The title of the Invention.)

which invention he believes will be of great public utility; that he is the true and first inventor thereof, and that the same is not in use by any other person or persons, to the best of his knowledge and belief.

Your petitioner, therefore, humbly prays that your Excellency will be pleased, in the name and on behalf of her Majesty the Queen to grant unto him, his executors, administrators and assigns Her Majesty's Letters Patent for this Island, for the term of fourteen years, pursuant to the statute in that case made and provided.

And your petitioner will ever pray, &c.

I,   of   in the county of   do solemnly and sincerely declare that I am in possession of an invention for, &c., &c.

(The title as in petition.)

which invention I believe will be of great public utility; that I am the true and first inventor thereof, and that the same is not in use by any other person or persons, to the best of my knowledge and belief; and that the instrument in writing, under my hand and seal, hereunto annexed, particularly describes and ascertains the nature of the said invention, and the manner in which the same is to be performed; and I make this declaration, conscientiously believing the same to be true, and by virtue of the provisions of an Act made and passed.

                    A. B.

Declared at   this
day of   A. D.
before me
           , Justice of the Peace.

To all whom these presents shall come:

I,   of   send greeting: Know ye, that I, the said   , do hereby declare the nature of my invention for

(Insert title as in petition.)

and in what manner the same is to be performed to be particularly described and ascertained, in and by the following statement, (that is to say:)

(Here describe the invention.)

In witness whereof, I the said A. B., have heretofore set my hand this day of   A. D.

We attest:
   C. D. of   &c.
   E. F. of   &c.

His Excellency is pleased to refer this petition to Her Majesty's Attorney.
General, to consider what may be properly done therein.

        Secretary to the Executive Committee.

In obedience to his Excellency's command, referring to me the petition
of   , of   , to consider what may be properly done therein, I do hereby certify as follows: that the said petition sets forth that the petitioner

(Allegations of the petition.)

And the petitioner most humbly prays

(Prayer of the petition)

That in support of the allegations contained in the said petition, the declaration of the petitioner has been laid before me, whereby he solemnly declares that

(Allegations of the declaration.)

That there has also been laid before me a specification signed and attested by two witnesses, and also a certificate of the filing thereof.

That it appears that the said application was duly advertised. Upon consideration of all the matters aforesaid, and as it is entirely at the hazard of the said petitioner, whether the said invention is new, or will have the desired success, and as it may be reasonable for his Excellency to encourage all arts and inventions which may be for the public good, I am of opinion that his Excellency may grant Letters Patent unto the petitioner, his executors, administrators, and assigns, for his said invention, within this Island, for the term of fourteen years, according to the statute in that case made and provided, if his Excellency shall be graciously pleased so to do, to the tenor and effect following :

(See forms Letters Patent.)

Given under my hand this   day of   A. D.

Attorney-General, Jamaica.

—

tters patent   Victoria. by the grace of God, of the united kingdom of Great Britain, and Ireland, Queen, and of Jamaica, lady defender of the faith. To all to whom these presents shall come greeting :

Whereas   hath, by his petition, humbly represented unto our Captain-General and Governor-in-Chief of our Island of Jamaica, that he is in possession of an invention for

(Insert title of Invention.)

which the petitioner conceives will be of great public utility ; that he is the true and first inventor thereof, and that the same is not in use by any other person or persons, to the best of his knowledge and belief. The petitioner therefore most humbly prayed that we would be graciously pleased to grant unto him, his executors, administrators, and assigns, our royal Letters Patent, for the sole use, benefit, and advantage of his said invention, within our said Island of Jamaica, for the term of fourteen years, pursuant to the statute in that case made and provided.

And whereas, the said   hath particularly described and ascertained the nature of the said invention, and in what manner the same is to be performed, by an instrument in writing, under his hand, and has caused the same to be duly filed in the office of the Island secretary.

And we, being willing to give encouragement to all arts and inventions, which may be for the public good, are graciously pleased to condescend to the request.

Know ye therefore that we, of our special grace, certain knowledge, and mere motion, have given and granted, and by these presents, for us, our heirs and successors, do give and grant unto the said his executors, administrators. and assigns, our especial license, full power, sole privilege and authority, that he the said his executors, administrators and assigns, and every of them, by himself and themselves, or by his and their deputy or deputies, servants, or agents, or such others as he the said   his executors, administrators and assigns, shall at any time agree with, and no others, from time to time, and at all times hereafter, during the term of years herein expressed, shall and lawfully may make, use, exercise, and vend his said invention, within our said Island of Jamaica, in such manner as to him the said   his executors, administrators, and assigns, or any of them, shall in his or their discretion seem meet ; and that he the said   his executors, administrators and assigns, shall and lawfully may have and enjoy, the whole profit, benefit, commodity, and advantage, and enjoy from

time to time, coming, growing, accruing, and arising by reason of
the said invention, for and during the term of years herein mentioned,
to have, hold, exercise, and enjoy the said licenses, powers, privileges, and advantages hereinbefore granted, or mentioned to be
granted, unto the said   , his executors, administrators, and assigns, for and during, and unto the full end and term
of fourteen years, from the   day of   A. D.
                next and immediately ensuing, and according to the
statute in such case made and provided; And to the end, that he
the said   , his executors, administrators, and assigns,
and every of them, may have and enjoy the full benefit, and the sole
use and exercise of the said invention, according to our gracious intention herein-before declared, we do by these presents, for us, our
heirs and successors, require and strictly command all and every
person and persons, bodies politic and corporate, and all other our
subjects whatsoever, of what estate, quality, degree, name or condition soever, they be, within our said Island of Jamaica, that neither they nor any of them, at any time during the continuance of the said term of fourteen years hereby granted, either directly or indirectly do make, use, or put in practice the said invention or any part of the same, so attained unto by the said
                as aforesaid, nor in anywise counterfeit, imitate, or resemble
the same ; nor shall make or cause to be made, any addition thereto,
or subtraction from the same, whereby to pretend himself, or themselves the inventor or inventors, devisor or devisors thereof, without
the consent, license or agreement of the said   his
executors, administrators or assigns, in writing, under his or their
hands and seals, first had and obtained in that behalf, upon such pains
and penalties as can or may be justly inflicted on such offenders for
their contempt of this our royal command; and further, to be answerable to the said   his executors, administrators,
and assigns, according to law, for his and their damages thereby occasioned ; and moreover, we do by these presents for us, our heirs
and successors, will and command all and singular the Justices of the
Peace, Constables, and all other Officers and Ministers whatsoever,
our heirs and successors for the time being, that they, or any of
them, do not, nor shall at any time during the said term hereby
granted, in anywise molest, trouble, or hinder the said
his executors, administrators, or assigns, or any of them, or his or
their deputies, servants, or agents in or about the due and lawful use
or exercise of the aforesaid invention, or anything relating thereto :
Provided always, and these our Letters Patent are, and shall be upon
this condition, that if, at any time during the said term hereby
granted, it shall be made appear to us, our heirs or successors, or any
six or more of our or their Privy Council of our said Island of Jamaica, that this our grant is contrary to law, or prejudicial, or inconvenient to our subjects in general, or that the said invention is not a
new invention, as to the public use and exercise thereof, or that the
said   is not the true and first inventor thereof within
this Island as aforesaid, these our Letters Patent shall forthwith
cease, determine, and be utterly void to all intents and purposes,
anything hereinbefore contained to the contrary thereof in anywise
notwithstanding : Provided also, that these our Letters Patent or any
thing herein contained, shall not extend or be construed to extend, to
give privilege unto the said   ,   his executors, administrators, and assigns, or any of them, to use or imitate any invention or work whatsoever, which hath heretofore been found out or
invented by any other of our subjects whatsoever, and publicly used
or exercised, unto whom our like Letters Patent or privileges have
been already granted for the sole use, exercise and benefit thereof.
It being our will and pleasure that the said   , his executors, administrators, and assigns, and all and every other person
and persons to whom like Letters Patent or privileges have been
already granted as aforesaid, shall distinctly use and practice their
several inventions, by them invented and found out, according to the
true intent and meaning of the same respective Letters Patent, and
of these presents : Provided likewise nevertheless, and these our
Letters Patent are upon this express condition, that if the said

instrument in writing, filed as aforesaid, does not particularly describe and ascertain the nature of the said invention, and in what manner the same is to be performed ; and also, if the said

his executors, administrators, or assigns, shall not supply or cause to be supplied for our service, all such articles of the said invention as he or they shall be required to supply by the Officers or Commission. ers administering the department of our service, for the use of which the same shall be required, in such manner, at such times, and at and upon such reasonable prices and terms as shall be settled for that purpose by the said Officers or Commissioners requiring the same, that then, and in any of the said cases, these our Letters Patent, and all liberties and advantages hereby granted, shall utterly cease, deter. mine and become void, anything hereinbefore contained to the con. trary thereof in anywise notwithstanding : Provided, that nothing herein contained, shall prevent the granting of Licenses in such manner, and for such consideration as they may by law be granted ; And lastly we do, by these presents for us, our heirs and successors, grant unto the said   his executors, administrators, and assigns, that these our Letters Patent on the filing thereof, shall be, in and by all things, good, firm, valid, sufficient and effectual in the law, according to the true intent and meaning thereof, and shall be taken, construed, and adjudged in the most favorable and benefi. cial sense, for the best advantage of the said   , his executors, administrators, and assigns, as well in all our Courts of Record as elsewhere, and by all and singular the Officers and Ministers whatsoever of us, our heirs and successors, in our said Is. land of Jamaica, and amongst all and every the subjects of us, our heirs and successors within our said Island of Jamaica, notwith. standing the not full and certain describing the nature and quality of the said invention, or of the materials thereunto conducing or be. longing : Provided further, that if the said   '   his heirs, administrators or assigns shall, upon petition, presented to our Captain General and Governor-in-Chief, or Officer administering the Government of our said Island, before the expiration of the term of years hereby granted, show that he or they has or hath been unable to obtain a due remuneration for his or their expense or labor in per fecting the aforesaid invention, and our Captain General and Gov- ernor-in-Chief or Officer administering the Government as aforesaid, in Executive Committee, shall be of opinion, that an extension of the term of years aforesaid, should be granted, it shall be lawful for our Captain-General and Governor-in-Chief, or Officer adminis- tering the Government as aforesaid, to extend the term of years aforesaid, for any further period not exceeding 7 years, and to sign and issue in the name and on behalf of us, our heirs or successors new Letters Patent in the form or of the tenor or effect aforesaid unto the said   his executors, adminis- trators or assigns for the aforesaid invention, for any such further pe- ried not exceeding 7 years as aforesaid accordingly.   And to the end aforesaid, we have caused these, our Letters Patent to be sealed with the Broad Seal of our said Island of Jamaica.

Seal.   Witness his Excellency, &c., &c., &c., Captain General and Governor in Chief, (or administering the Government) of our said Island of Jamaica, and the territories thereon depending,' Chan- cellor and Vice-Admiral of the same at Saint Jago de la Vega, this   day of   Annoque Domini   'and in the   year of our reign.

Paupers.

Purchase of land for
The Corporation of Kingston, and Justices and Vestrymen authorised to contract for and purchase lands in fee simple in their parishes or elsewhere, and to accept gifts or grants of land for the purposes of this act, 7 G. 4, c. 26, s. 1.

Form   of convey- ance
All such Conveyances and Assurances shall be according to the Form following, or as nearly as circumstances will admit :

I (or we)   of .   in consideration of the sum of   to me (or us) paid, do hereby grant and release to the Justices and Ves-

try of   all (describing the premises to be conveyed) and
all my right, title, and interest to, and in the same and every part
thereof, to hold to the said Justices and Vestry of the said parish of
and their successors, to, for and upon the uses, intents and purposes of
a certain Act of the Governor or Council and Assembly of this Island,
made and passed in the 7th year of the reign of his Majesty King
George the Fourth, entitled "An Act to enable the Justices and Vestrymen of the several parishes of this Island, by the acquisition and
settlement of lands, to furnish relief to Paupers, and promote habits of
industry amongst them, to enable the Corporation of the city of Kingston, and the Justices and Vestrymen of the several parishes of this
Island, to bind out Apprentices, and for other purposes." In witness
whereof I have hereunto set my hand and seal, this   day of
in the year of our Lord

and shall be valid and effectual, 7 G. 4, c. 26, s. 2.

The Corporation and Justices and Vestrymen shall lay and allot the **Lay out towns,**
lands in the formation and establishment of Towns, villages or farms, and in **&c**
such other way as to afford useful employment for Paupers either in agriculture or manufactures, 7 G. 4, c. 26, s. 3.

And shall also make such rules and regulations as to the allotting and **Make regulations**
laying out of such lands, and the employment or settlement of Paupers there- **as to allotments**
on, as are best calculated to promote habits of industry amongst them, and
afford them the means of maintenance, not repugnant to the prerogative or
laws, 7 G. 4, c. 26, s. 4

And may by deed, demise, lease or grant, all or any part of the lands **Leases, &c**
to any person for such term of years, and under such reservations, conditions
and restrictions, as shall seem meet, and calculated to promote the objects of
the act, 7 G. 4, c. 26, s. 5.

Incorporated as "The Corporation of the City and Parish of Kingston" **Incorporation**
and "The Justices and Vestry of the parish of   7 G. 4, c. 26, s. 6.

All deeds &c., shall be exempted from Stamp Duty, 7 G. 4, c. 26, s. 7. **Exemption from Stamps**

Pawnbrokers.

All persons using and exercising the trade or business of a Pawnbroker **Limitation of**
may demand and take from all persons applying to redeem any goods **rates of profit on**
pawned, a profit at the following rates beyond the principal lent, before **pledges**
being obliged to re-deliver the same :—

For every pledge on which there is lent, not exceeding 4s.: 3d. for
any time not exceeding 1 calendar month, and the same for every
calendar month afterwards including the current month, although
not expired;
Above 4s. and not exceeding 10s.: 3d. and 1d. additional for every 2s.
above 4s;
Above 10s. and not exceeding 20s.: 6d. and ½d. additional for every
2s. above 10;
Above 20s. and not exceeding 40s.: 8½d. and ½d. additional for every
3s. above 20s :
Exceeding 40s. and not exceeding £10 . 1s. 2d. and ½d, additional for
every 5s. above 40;

to be in full for all interest due, and charges for Warehouse-room, 11 V.
c. 36, s. 1.

Where the party applies to redeem within 7 days after the first calen- **Computation of**
dar month, he may redeem without paying any thing by way of profit for **month and parts**
the 7 days, or part elapsed. After the first 17 days, and before the expiration of the first 14 days of the second month, he may redeem on paying
the profit for one calendar month, and the half of another, but after the expiration of the first 14 days, and before the expiration of the second
calendar month, the Pawnbroker may demand the profit of the whole
second month, and the like regulation and restriction shall take place
in every subsequent calendar month, wherein application is made to re- **Abatement of**
deem. Where payment cannot be made in the current coin, the Pawn- **excess over cur-**
broker shall wholly abate the excess from the sum to be received, 11 V., **rent coin**
c. 36, s. 2.

Particulars of pledges to be entered in book

Persons taking goods by way of pawn, shall, before lending any money thereon, enter or cause, &c., in a fair and regular manner, in a book to be kept for the purpose, a description of the goods received in pawn, pledge, or exchange, the money to be advanced, with the day of the month and year, and the name of the person by whom pawned, the name of the street and number of the house, if numbered, where such person abides, and the name and place of abode of the owner of the goods, according to the information of the person pawning, into all which circumstances the Pawnbroker is required to enquire of the party pawning before any money is lent. In all cases the entry shall be made within 4 hours after the goods are pawned, and the entry of the pledge shall be numbered progressively, as received, viz:

Within 4 hours
And numbered

The first Pledge received in pawn in the first month after the Act comes into operation, shall be numbered No. 1; the second, No. 2; and so on progressively until the end of the month. The first Pledge received in the next month shall be numbered No. 1; the second, No. 2; and so on progressively until the end of the month.

And the like regulation shall be observed in every succeeding month.

Number to be written or printed on note
Note and particulars

Upon every note or memorandum respecting any such Pledge, shall be fairly and legibly written or printed, the number of the entry, and every such person shall, at the time of taking the pawn, give to the person pawning a note or memorandum, fairly and legibly written or printed, or in part written and in part printed, containing in like manner a description of the goods received in pawn, the money advanced, with the day of the month and year, and the name and place of abode, and number of the house, if said to be numbered, of the person by whom the goods are pawned, and also the name and place of abode of the owner, according to the information aforesaid, and upon which, or the back, shall be fairly written or printed the name and place of abode of the Pawnbroker, which note the party pawning shall accept in all cases, and the Pawnbroker shall not receive and retain the pledge unless he do so. The note shall be delivered gratis, and produced to the Pawnbroker before he is obliged to re-deliver the goods, except as after excepted, 11 V., c. 36, s. 3.

To be delivered to pawner in all cases gratis, and produced at time of redemption

Profit received to be endorsed on duplicate which is to be kept for a year

Where any goods are redeemed, the Pawnbroker shall at the time fairly write or endorse, or cause &c., upon every duplicate, the amount of the profit taken, and keep the duplicate for one year, 11 V., c. 36, s. 4.

Pawning goods without authority
Penalty summarily recoverable and application

Any person knowingly and designedly, pawning, pledging or exchanging, or unlawfully disposing of the goods of any other person, not being employed or authorised by the owner, may be apprehended by warrant of a Justice, and on conviction before any Justice, shall forfeit not exceeding £5 nor less than 20s, and the full value of the goods to be ascertained by the Justice, and if not forthwith paid, shall be committed to hard labour not exceeding 3 calendar months unless sooner paid. The forfeiture when recovered shall be applied towards making satisfaction to the party injured and defraying the costs of the prosecution as adjudged reasonable by the Justice; but if the party injured decline to accept satisfaction and costs, or there is any overplus they shall be applied for the use of the poor, 11 V., c. 36 s. 5

Forging or selling counterfeit notes
Apprehension without warrant

Commitment

If any person counterfeit, forge or alter, or cause, &c., or utter, vend or sell any note or memorandum knowing it to be counterfeit, &c. with intent to defraud any person, his servants or agents to whom it is uttered or produced, shewn or offered, which he has reason to suspect is counterfeit, &c., may seize and detain and deliver him, as soon as conveniently may be, into the custody of a Constable, to be conveyed as soon as conveniently may be to a justice; and if upon examination it appears that he is guilty, the Justice may commit him for not exceeding 3 calendar months, 11 V., c. 36, s. 6.

Apprehension without warrant of persons offering to pawn or redeem goods under suspicous circumstances

If any person who offers by way of pawn, &c. any goods, is not able, or refuses to give a satisfactory account of himself, or of the means by which he became possessed, or wilfully gives any false information to the Pawnbroker, or his servants, as to whether they are his own property or not, of his name, or place of abode, or of the name and place of abode of the owner, or if there is any other reason to suspect that the goods are stolen, or otherwise illegally or clandestinely obtained, or if any person not entitled, nor having any color of title by law to redeem goods in pawn, attempt, or endeavour to redeem the same, any person, his servants or agents to whom the goods are offered, or with whom they are in pledge, may

seize and detain the person and goods, and deliver the person immediateTo be taken be-
ly into the custody of a Constable, who shall, as soon as may be, con-fore a Justice for
vey him and the goods before a Justice, and if the Justice, upon ex-examination
amination and enquiry, has cause to suspect that the goods were stolen,
or illegally or clandestinely obtained, or that the person offering and
endeavouring to redeem them has not any pretence or color of right so
to do, he may commit the person into safe custody for a reasonableCommitment for
time (as to power to bail, see Justices 13 V., c. 24, s. 14; 13 V., c. 35, safe custody
s. 16) to obtain proper information on the subject, in order to be further
examined, and if upon either of the examinations it appears to the sa-Commitment
tisfaction of the Justice that the goods were stolen, &c., he may commit the offender to be dealt with according to law, where the nature of
the offence authorizes such commitment, by any other law, or where not,
the commitment shall be for not exceeding 3 calendar months, 11 V., c. 36,
s. 7.

Any person, knowingly buying, or taking in as a pledge, &c., anyKnowingly buy-
goods of any manufacture, or part or branch of any manufacture, either ing or taking in
mixed or separate, or any materials plainly intended for the composing or pledge unfinish
manufacturing of any goods after they are put into a state or course of ed goods or ap-
manufacture, or into a state for any process or operation to be thereupon parel intrusted to
or therewith performed, and before they are completed or finished be washed, &c.,
for the purposes of wear or consumption, or any linen or apparel entrusted or made up
to any person to wash, scour, iron, mend, manufacture, work up, finish or
make up, on conviction before a Justice, shall forfeit double the sum given
for, or lent on the same, to be paid to the poor, and recovered as other forfeitures under this Act, and shall be obliged to restore the goods and materials to the owner in the presence of the Justice, 11 V., c. 36, s 8.

If the owner of any goods of any manufacture, &c., or any linen, &c.,Search warrant
as in the previous section, unlawfully pawned, makes out by oath, or solemn for any such
affirmation of a Quaker, before any Justice, that there is just cause to sus-goods
pect that any person within his jurisdiction has taken to pawn, &c., any such
goods or materials, linen or apparel so entrusted of such owner, and without his privity or authority, and make appear to the Justice probable
grounds for the suspicion, he may issue his warrant for searching within
the hours of business the house, warehouse or other place of the person
charged as suspected, and if the occupier, on request by any constable authorized to search by warrant, refuses to open and permit the house, &c.
to be searched, any constable may break open the same within the hours of
business and search, as he thinks fit, for the goods, materials, linen or
apparel suspected to be there, doing no wilful damage ; and no Pawnbroker
or other person shall oppose the search ; and if any of the goods are found,And restoration
and the property of the owner made out to the satisfaction of any such Justice, by oath or solemn affirmation or confession, any Justice may thereupon
cause them to be forthwith restored to the owner, 11 V., c. 36, s. 9.

If the owner of any goods unlawfully pawned, pledged, or exchanged,Search warrant
makes either on his oath or by the oath of a credible witness, or solemn affirma-where other goods
tion of a Quaker, before a Justice, that such owner has his goods unlaw-are pawned
fully obtained or taken from him, and there is just cause to suspect that
any person has taken to pawn, or by way of pledge, or in exchange, any
goods of such owner, and without his privity or authority, and make appear to the satisfaction of such Justice probable grounds for the owner's suspicion, any Justice may issue his warrant for searching, within the hours
of business, the house, warehouse, or other place of any person so charged
or suspected to have received or taken in pawn, or by way of pledge, or
in exchange, any such goods, without the privity of or authority from the
owner, and if the occupier refuse to open the house, &c. any constable may
break it open and search, as he thinks fit, for the goods suspected to be
there, doing no wilful damage ; and no Pawnbroker or other person shall
oppose or hinder any such search, and if upon the search, any of the goods
which have been so pawned, &c. are found, and the property of the owners
from whom they have been unlawfully obtained or taken is made out to his
satisfaction, by oath, affirmation or confession, any such Justice may causeProceedings to
the goods to be restored, 11 V., c. 36, s. 10.recover goods

If any goods are pawned, &c., for securing moneys lent thereon,pawned for not exceeding £10 or
not exceeding in the whole £10, and the profit thereof, and if within one their value on
year after [proof being made on oath or affirmation by a credible witness, payment or ten-
and by producing the note or memorandum directed by this Act (s. 3.) der of principal
and profits

the pawning within one year, or one year and 3 months as the case may be, (s. 14, 15) any pawner who was the real owner at the time of pawning, his executors, administrators or assigns, tender to the lender, on the security of the goods pawned, his executors, &c. the principal money borrowed and profit, according to the table of rates (s. 1, 2) and the person who took the goods in pawn, his executors &c., without reasonable cause, neglect or refuse to deliver back the goods pawned for any sum not exceeding the principal sum of £10, to the person who borrowed the money, his executors, &c., in any, such case, on oath or affirmation as aforesaid by the pawner, his executors &c., or other credible person, any justice of the parish where the person who took the pawn, his executors &c., dwell, on application of the borrower, his executors, &c., shall cause the person who took the pawn, his executors, &c., within the jurisdiction, to come before him, and examine on oath &c., the parties and witnesses, and if tender of the principal and profits is proved to have been made (the principal not exceeding £10) to the tender, &c., by the borrower, his executors, &c.; within the space of one year, or one year and three months, as the case may be, on payment of the principal money and profits due thereon to the tender &c., and in case of refusal to accept same before the justice he shall thereupon by order under his hand direct the goods pawned forthwith to be delivered up to the pawner, his executors, and assigns, and on neglect or refusal to deliver up or make satisfaction for the goods as the justice shall order, he may commit the party refusing, until he deliver up the goods or make such satisfaction or compensation as he adjudges reasonable for the value, to the party entitled to the redemption. (see s. 20.) 11 V., c. 36, s. 11.

Person producing note to be deemed owner

Any person who at any time produces any note, or memorandum to the person with whom the goods were pawned, as the owner, or as authorized by him to redeem, and requiring a delivery, shall be deemed so far as respects the person having the goods in pledge, the real owner or proprietor; and the Pawnbroker after receiving satisfaction of principal and profit, shall deliver the goods to him, and be indemnified, unless previous notice has been given to him, from the real owner, not to deliver

Unless notice is given not to deliver them or that the goods have been fraudulently, &c., obtained or the note lost, &c., by owner

them to the person producing such note, or unless notice has been given that the goods have been, or are suspected to have been fraudulently, or feloniously taken or obtained, and unless the real owner proceeds, as after directed for redeeming the goods where the note has been lost, mislaid, destroyed or fraudulently obtained from him, 11 V., c. 36, s. 12.

Proceedings in case of lost, note by owner, &c., to obtain goods

If any Pawnbroker has had previous notice, or any note or memorandum is lost, mislaid, destroyed, or fraudulently obtained from the owner, and the goods remain unredeemed, he shall, at the request of any person, who represents himself as owner, deliver to the person applying a copy of the note so lost, &c., with a declaration in the Form required by the Act substituting declarations in lieu of Oaths, (see Oaths, 6 V., c. 24) of the particular circumstances attending the case, printed or written, or in part printed and in part written, or the copy as stated to him by the party applying, for which the Pawnbroker shall receive 3d. from him, and such person shall thereupon prove his property in, or right to such goods, to the satisfaction of a Justice of the parish where they were pawned, &c., and shall make the declaration before the Justice, who shall authenticate it, whereupon the Pawnbroker shall suffer him, on leaving the copy of the note, and the declaration, to redeem them, 11 V., c. 36, s. 13.

Goods forfeited at the end of the year

Pledges above 20s to £10 to be sold by auction

All goods pawned shall be deemed forfeited, and may be sold at the expiration of one whole year exclusive of the day whereon they were pawned, and goods no forfeited, on which above 20s., and not exceeding £10, have been lent, shall be sold by public auction, and not otherwise, by order of the person having the same in pawn, after the expiration of the year; but the person employed to sell shall cause them to be ex-

Catalogues and

Advertisement

posed to public view, and catalogues to be published, containing the name and place of abode of the Pawnbroker, the month the goods were received in pawn, and the number of the pledge, as entered in his book, and an advertisement giving notice of such sale, and containing the Pawnbroker's name and place of abode, and the month the goods were received in pawn, to be inserted 2 days in some public newspapers, 2 days, at least, before the first day of sale, and the goods pledged with every Pawnbroker, shall be inserted apart from each other, on pain of forfeiting to the owner not exceeding £10, nor less than 40s., 11 V., c. 36, s. 14.

If any person entitled to redeem before or on the expiration of the year, give notice in writing, or in the presence of one witness, to the person having the goods in pledge, or leave the same at his place of abode, not to sell at the end of the year, they shall not be sold until after the expiration of 3 calendar months after the year, during which 3 months the owner may redeem upon the terms of this Act. 11 V., c. 36, s. 15.

All persons with whom any goods are pawned shall enter in a book to be kept, a true account of the sale of all such goods sold as aforesaid, expressing the day of the month when pledged, and the name of the person pledging, according to the entry made at the time of receipt; and where the sum pledged thereon does not exceed 20s, expressing also the day of sale, the price obtained, and the name and place of abode of the person to whom sold; where it is upwards of 20s, expressing also the day when, and the money for which the goods were sold, with the name and place of abode of the auctioneer according to the information from him; and in case any goods are sold for more than the principal money and profit due thereon at the time of sale, the overplus shall be paid on demand to the person by whom or on whose account they were pawned, his executors, &c.; in case demand is made within 3 years after sale, the necessary costs and charges being first deducted, and the persons who pawned the goods or for whom they were pawned, their executors, &c., shall, for their satisfaction, be permitted to inspect the entry of sale, paying 3d and no more. If any person refuse to permit any person who pawned the goods, or is entitled to such overplus money to inspect the entry as aforesaid, such person, if an executor, &c, or assignee, at such time producing his letters testamentary, or of administration or assignment, or certificate, (under 27 V., S. 1, c. 16,) or in case the goods were sold for more than the sum entered, or if any such person shall not make such entry, or shall not have bona fide, according to the directions, sold, or refuses to pay the overplus upon demand (executors, &c., producing their letters, &c., or assignment) he shall forfeit £10, and treble the sum the goods were originally pawned for, to the person by whom or on whose account they were pawned, his executors, &c., to be levied by distress and sale by warrant of 2 Justices, 11 V., c. 36, s. 16.

No person having any goods in pledge shall, under any pretence, by himself or any other for him, purchase any such goods during the time they remain in his custody as such pledge, except at public auction as aforesaid (s. 14), nor suffer them to be redeemed with a view or intention to purchase, nor shall any person taking or having any goods in pledge, make or cause &c., any contract or agreement with any person, offering to pledge or pledging with the owner, for the purchase, sale, or disposition of the goods before the expiration of one year from the time of pledging, nor shall any Pawnbroker purchase or receive, or take any goods in pledge from any person who appears under 12, or to be intoxicated with liquor, or purchase or take in pawn, or exchange the note or memorandum of any other Pawnbroker, or buy any goods in the course of his trade or business before 8 a.m. or after 6 p.m. throughout the year, or employ any servant, apprentice, or other person under 16 to take in pledges, nor receive or take in goods by way of pawn, pledge or exchange before 8 a.m. or after 6 p.m., 11 V., c. 36, s. 17.

All persons following the trade or business of a Pawnbroker, shall cause to be printed or painted in large legible characters, the rate of profit allowed to be taken by them, and of the expense of obtaining a second note or memorandum when the former one has been lost, mislaid, destroyed or fraudulently obtained, and place the same in a conspicuous part of the shop or place wherein he carries on such trade, so as to be visible to and legible by persons coming to pawn or redeem goods at such shop, 11 V., c. 36, s. 18.

And also cause to be painted or written in large legible characters over the door of each shop or other place of business, the first or Christian and Surname, or names of the person or persons carrying on the trade, and the word "Pawnbroker" or "Pawnbrokers" as the case may be, following: penalty £10, for every shop or place so made use of, for the space of one week, without having the name or names and words so painted or written, to be recovered by distress and sale, by warrant of 2 Justices; and in case sufficient distress is not found, or the penalty is not forthwith paid, the Justices may commit the offender for not exceeding 3 calendar months, or less than 14 days, unless the penalties and charges are sooner paid, 11 V., c. 36, s. 19.

If in the course of any proceedings before a Justice under this Act, it appears or is proved that any goods pawned have been sold before the time allowed, or otherwise than according to the directions, or have been embezzled or lost, or have become or been rendered of less value than at the time of pawning, by the default, neglect or wilful misbehaviour of the person to whom they where pledged, his executors, &c., agents or servants, the Justice may allow and award a reasonable satisfaction to the owner, in respect thereof, or of the damage, and the sums so allowed, in case they do not amount to, the principal and profit due, shall be deducted thereout, and the Pawner, his executors, &c. may pay or tender the balance due after such deduction, and upon so doing, the Justice shall proceed as if the pawner, his executors, &c., had paid or tendered the whole money due for principal and profit; If the satisfaction awarded equals or exceeds the principal and profit, the person to whom the same were pawned, his executors, &c., shall deliver the goods to the owner, without being paid anything for principal or profit, and shall also pay such excess to the person entitled: Penalty, £10, 11 V., c. 36, s. 20.

Damages may be allowed by Justice for goods lost or injured in the hands of Pownbrokers in deduction of principal and profits, or if in excess Pawnbroker may be ordered to pay the excess; see s. 11

Upon complaint on oath, or information of a witness, wherein an information is laid against any Pawnbroker for having offended against this Act, or respecting any dispute between any Pawnbroker and person having pawned goods, or the owner of goods pawned, or respecting any Felony or other matter, or on any other occasion, which, in the judgment of any Justice, makes the production of any book, note, voucher, memorandum, duplicate or other paper necessary, which is or ought to be in the hands, custody or power of any Pawnbroker, such Justice may summon him to attend with all or any book, &c., which is or ought to be in his custody or power, relating to the same, and which he is required to produce in the state they were at the time the pawn was received, without any alteration, erasement or obliteration. In case of neglect or refusal to attend or produce the same in its true and perfect state, the Pawnbroker, unless he shews good cause for such neglect or refusal, shall forfeit not exceeding £10, nor less than £5. 11 V., c. 36, s. 21.

Pawnbroker to produce books, &c., when required by Justice

In case any Pawnbroker in any wise offend, he shall for every offence in neglecting to make, or cause, &c., in a fair and regular manner in his books any such entry as is required, forfeit not exceeding £10, and for every other offence where no forfeiture or penalty is provided or imposed on any particular or specific offence, not less than £10 or more than £2 (sic.) 11 V., c. 36, s. 22.

Penalty for not making entries in book

For offences where no sum specified

All forfeitures shall be levied by distress and sale, and in default of goods, the offender may be committed for not exceeding 3 calendar months, unless sooner paid; one moiety to be awarded to the parties complaining, the other for the use of the poor, 11 V., c. 36, s. 23.

Recovery and application

No Pawnbroker shall be liable to prosecution unless information is given of the offence within 12 calendar months after its commission, 11 V., c, 36, s. 24.

Prosecution to be within 12 months

Any Justice may direct any Pawnbroker to be indicted by the Clerk of the Peace as a public prosecution, 11 V., c. 36, s. 25.

Indictments ; see 19 V., c. 10, s. 17

No person who has been convicted of any fraud, or of obtaining money under false pretences, or of any Felony, shall be allowed to prosecute or inform against any person for any offence against this Act, 11 V., c. 36, s. 26.

Persons convicted of fraud, &c., or felony not to prosecute

Act not to extend to persons lending money upon pawn at the rate of £6 per cent. per annum, interest, without taking any further profit for the loan or forbearance on any pretence, 11 V., c. 36, s. 27.

Not to extend to pawners at £6 per cent. only

The Act shall extend to the executors and administrators, or assigns of deceased Pawnbrokers in the same manner as to the Pawnbroker when living, except that no executor or administrator shall be answerable for any penalty or forfeiture personally, or out of their own moneys or estates, unless incurred by their own act or neglect, 11 V., c. 36, s. 28.

Executors, &c., not personally liable, except for their own act or neglect

Any person sued, molested, or prosecuted for anything done in pursuance of this Act, may plead the general issue, and give the special matter in evidence, and if a verdict pass for the defendant, or the plaintiff becomes

Protection from actions

nonsuited, the defendant shall have full costs, as between Solicitor and Client, 11 V., c. 36, s, 29.

Form of conviction, 11 V., c. 36, s. 30.
Right of appeal, 11 V., c. 36, s. 31.

Payment of Money into Court.

The defendant in all personal actions [except for assault and battery, false imprisonment, libel, (see as to libel in newspapers or periodicals, 14 V., c. 34, s. 2,) slander, malicious arrest or prosecution, criminal conversation, or debauching the plaintiff's daughter or servant] by leave of the Court or a Judge, (in the case of one or more of several defendants, 28 V., c. 37 s. 18,) may pay into Court money by way of compensation or amends in such manner, and under such regulations as to costs, as the Judges shall by rules or orders from time to time direct, 8 V., c. 28, s. 10. *When allowed See Court Supreme pleadings, 28 V. c 37, s. 18-27*

Penal Servitude.

No person shall be sentenced to transportation after 1st January, 1858, 21 V., c. 14, s. 1. *Transportation abolished and penal servitude substituted*

Any person who, but for this Act, might have been sentenced to transportation, shall be liable, at the discretion of the Court, to be kept in Penal Servitude within this Island, 21 V., c. 14, s. 2.

Instead of transportation for 7 years, or not exceeding 7 years, Penal Servitude shall be awarded for 4 years. Instead of transportation exceeding 7 years and not exceeding 10 years' Penal Servitude for not less than 4, and not exceeding 6 years. Instead of transportation exceeding 10 year and not exceeding 15 years, Penal Servitude for not less than 6 and not exceeding 8 years. Instead of transportation exceeding 15 years, Penal Servitude not less than 6, and not exceeding 10 years. Instead of transportation for life, Penal Servitude for life, 21 V., c. 14, s. 3.

When at the discretion of the Court, one of any two or more terms of transportation might have been awarded, the Court shall have the like discretion to award one of the two or more terms of Penal Servitude in relation to such terms of transportation, 21 V., c. 14, s. 4.

This Act shall not affect the authority or discretion of any Court in respect of any punishment they may now award other than transportation; but when such other punishment may be awarded instead of or in addition to transportation, the same may be awarded instead of or in addition to the substituted punishment under this Act, 21 V., c. 14, s. 5. *Not to affect the award of any other punishment*

When the Governor extends mercy to any offender convicted of any offence liable to death, on condition of his being kept to Penal Servitude for any term of years, or for life, the intention of mercy shall have the same effect and may be signified in the same manner, and all Courts, Justices and others shall give the like effect thereto, and to the condition of the pardon, as in cases where the Governor now extends mercy, upon condition of transportation beyond seas, the order for the execution of such punishment being substituted for the order of transportation, 21 V., c. 14.'s. 6. *In substitution of sentence of death*

Every person except as after mentioned, who is kept in Penal Servitude shall be employed on the public roads, or other public works, or otherwise kept to hard labor in such part of the Island as the Governor shall direct, and either in irons or under such other restraint, and subject to such correction as may be necessary for his safe custody and strict discipline; and for the purpose of being so employed, may be removed from place to place by sea or land, and confined in such public gaol at such penal station, or in such place of confinement, or be otherwise kept in custody as the Governor shall direct from time to time, and until such direction, shall be imprisoned in the General Penitentiary, and there kept to hard labor. Every person convicted of any capital offence, whose punishment shall be commuted for Penal Servitude for life, shall be confined in some public prison in close custody, and kept to hard labor in separate confinement for the remainder of his life, 21 V., c. 14, s. 7. *Employment of convicts sentenced to. See prisons, 24 V., c. 22 s. 8*

Confinement of prisoners sentenced to death and punishment commuted

Solitary confinement

The Governor may make regulations for the employment, safe custody, management and discipline of the convicts under sentence of Penal Servitude, and enforce their observance by solitary confinement not exceeding 14 days at any time, and not to be repeated at a less interval than 42 days, by placing in irons, and by such other prison discipline as may be prescribed in that behalf; but no regulation awarding any such punishment shall come into operation until published in the "Jamaica Gazette", 21 V., c. 14, s. 8.

Punishment for being at large while under sentence

If any person sentenced to Penal Servitude for any term other than for life, is afterwards at large without some lawful cause before the expiration of the term, he may, on conviction, be kept in Penal Servitude for not exceeding 5 years from the expiration of the original sentence, 21 V., c. 14, s. 9.

Where sentenced for life

If under sentence to be kept in Penal Servitude for life, every such offender on conviction, shall be kept in solitary confinement during such periods not exceeding 14 days at a time, or three months in the space of one year, as the Court shall direct, 21 V., c. 14, s. 10.

Rewards for discovery, &c

Whoever discovers and prosecutes to conviction, or gives such information as shall lead to the conviction of any offender being at large contrary to this Act, shall be entitled to a reward from the Treasury not exceeding £20 at the discretion of the Judge, 21 V., c. 14, s. 11.

Rescue, &c.

Rescuing or attempting to rescue, or assisting in rescueing, or attempting, &c., any convict under sentence of Penal Servitude, from the lawful custody of any Gaoler, Overseer or other person conveying, removing, transporting or re-conveying such convict, or aiding or assisting any convict under sentence of Penal Servitude, to escape from the lawful custody of any Gaoler Overseer, or other person: Penal Servitude for not exceeding 3 years, 21 V., c. 14, s. 12.

Indictment

In any indictment against any offender for being found at large, or against any person who shall rescue, &c., or aid or assist, &c., it shall be sufficient to charge and allege the sentence or order made for the Penal Servitude of such offender, without charging or alleging any indictment, trial or conviction of such offender; and such last-mentioned offender may be tried either **Trial** in the parish where he has been apprehended, or in that wherein sentence of Penal Servitude was passed against him, 21 V., c. 14, s. 13.

Certificate of sentence

The certificate, in writing, under the hand of the clerk or other officer having the custody of the records of the Court, where such sentence or order of Penal Servitude has been made or recorded, containing the subtance thereof, shall be sufficient, and received in evidence of such sentence or order, upon (sic)   f of the signature and official character of the person signing, 21 V., c. 14 prod 4.

Convicts within, 18 V., c. 23

Every person sentenced to Penal Servitude shall also be deemed sentenced to imprisonment in the General Penitentiary within the meaning and for the purposes of the Penal Servitude Act, 1855, (18 V., c. 22;) and his labor deemed convict labor within the Convict Labor Payment Act, 1855, (18 V., c. 23), 21 V., c. 14, s. 15.

Pardon

Not to affect the prerogative of mercy, or any delegated authority to pardon vested in the Governor, 21 V., c. 14, s. 17.

Short title

The Secondary Punishment Act, 1857, 21 V., c. 14, s. 18.

Perjury and Subornation of Perjury.

Punishment

Besides the punishment already to be inflicted according to the laws now in force, any person convicted of wilful and corrupt Perjury or Subornation of Perjury may be sent to some house of correction within the county, not exceeding 3 years, to be kept to hard labor or Penal Servitude for 4 years; but **See prisons Not to be adjudged to stand in the pillory** no person shall be adjudged to stand in the pillory, 4 V., c. 22, s. 1; 21 V., c. 14, s. 3.

Indictment for perjury

It shall be sufficient to set forth in any information or indictment for Perjury the substance of the offence charged, and by what Court or before whom the oath was taken (averring such Court or person to have a competent authority to administer the same) with proper averments to falsify the matter wherein the Perjury is assigned without setting forth the bill, answer, information, indictment, declaration, or any part of any record or proceedings in law or equity other than as aforesaid, and without setting forth the commission or authority of the court, or person before whom the Perjury was committed, 4 V., c. 22, s. 2.

In every indictment, &c., for Subornation of Perjury, or for corrupt bargaining or contracting with others to commit Perjury it shall be sufficient to set forth the substance of the offence charged upon the defendant, without setting forth the bill &c., or the commission or authority of the Court or person before whom the Perjury was committed, or agreed or promised to be committed, 4 V., c. 22, s. 3. *For subornation*

The Judges of the Supreme Courts of Common Law or Equity, Justices of Assize, or Justices of the Peace in Special or Petty Sessions if it appear to them that any person has been guilty of Perjury in any evidence given, or in any affidavit, deposition, examination, answer or other proceeding before them, may direct him to be prosecuted for such Perjury in case there shall appear a reasonable cause for the prosecution, and commit him until the next Session of Oyer and Terminer or Gaol Delivery for the County (Circuit Court of the parish, 19 Vic. c. 10) within which the Perjury was committed, unless he enter into recognizance with one or more sureties for his appearance and to surrender and take his trial, and not depart the Court without leave, and bind over the witnesses for the prosecution, and give the party bound to prosecute a certificate without fee, which shall be proof of the prosecution having been directed, and upon production thereof, the Court before whom the trial takes place, shall allow the costs, unless it otherwise specially direct, but no such direction or certificate shall be given in evidence upon the trial against any person, 16 V., c. 15, s. 20. (superseding 4 V., c. 22, s. 4). *Directions to prosecute for perjury, proceedings thereon at public expense*

In every indictment for Perjury, or for unlawfully, wilfully, falsely, fraudulently, deceitfully, maliciously or corruptly taking, making, signing, or subscribing any oath, affirmation, declaration, affidavit, deposition, bill, answer, notice, certificate or other writing, it shall be sufficient to set-forth the substance of the offence charged upon the defendant, and by what Court, or before whom the oath &c. was taken, made, signed, or subscribed, without setting forth the bill, answer, information, indictment, declaration, or any part of any proceeding either in law or in equity, and without setting forth the commission or authority of the Court or person before whom such offence was committed, 16 V., c. 15, s. 21. *Indictments for perjury-*

In every indictment for Subornation of Perjury, or for corrupt bargaining or contracting with any person to commit wilful or corrupt Perjury, or for inciting, causing or procuring any person unlawfully &c., to take &c., any oath, &c., it shall be sufficient wherever such Perjury or other offence has been committed, to allege the offence of the person who actually committed such Perjury or other offence in the manner before mentioned, and then to allege that the defendant unlawfully, wilfully and corruptly did cause and procure the said person the said offence in manner and form aforesaid to do and commit. Where such Perjury or other offence has not been actually committed, it shall be sufficient to set forth the substance of the offence charged upon the defendant without setting forth or averring any matter before rendered unnecessary to be averred in the case of Perjury. 16 V., c. 15, s. 22. *For subornation*

Permanent Revenue Fund.

Established out of the Revenue from the Land Tax, fines, forfeitures, and escheats, and certain Customs Duties on Imports (unless other full provision is made by the Legislature) to meet the civil list (schedules A and B,) of £25,000 and £30,000 to meet the interest and sinking fund to redeem the Government Guaranteed Loan of £500,000, 17 V., c. 29, s. 36-42, 45 46. *Established*

Subject to which charges the revenue shall be appropriated by the Legislature for the public service as they think proper, and all bills for appropriating such surplus, or for imposing any new tax or impost shall originate in the Assembly, but subject to all the conditions of the appropriation of any tax or impost as herein provided, 17 V., c. 29, s. 47.

The salaries to the holders of offices enumerated in Schedule B., shall, on the persons now filling the offices ceasing to be holders thereof, cease, and the several offices, except of Chief Justice and Clerk of the Crown, determine, 17 V., c. 29, s. 48.

The debts and liabilities of the public, in Schedule F., shall be discharged out of the £500,000 Loan, 17 V., c. 29, s. 50.

No orders for payment of money under this Act shall be liable to Stamps, 17 V., c. 29, s. 52.

3 U

6d per gallon on rum in lieu of land tax A duty of 6d. per gallon on Rum and other Spriits distilled and consumed in the Island, substituted for the Land Tax revenue transferred to the Main Road Fund, 21 V., c. 34, s. 28.

SCHEDULE, 17 V., c. 29.

A., s. 11, 45 To the Governor's Secretary (see 18 V., c. 30) £1200 0 0

Towards payment, as far as as may be necessary, of judicial salaries, to be appropriated, *pro rata*, according to the amount of salaries given under any Act of the Legislature of this Island, the sum of 9800 0 0

> The residue of the salaries of the present holders of these offices, to be paid otherwise as by law provided.

To the order of the Governor to defray the following salaries and expenses, No. 1 to No. 6, inclusive:

No. 1. To the Captain-General	....	£1500	0 0
No. 2. President of the Legislative Council	....	600	0 0
No. 3. Chaplain of the Legislative Council	....	60	0 0
No. 4. Clerk to the Legislative Council	....	414	0 0
No. 5. Librarian to the Legislative Council	....	60	0 0
No. 6. Usher of the Black Rod	....	270	0 0
To the Attorney-General	....	240	0 0
To the present holder of the office of Assistant Clerk to the Council, so long as he continues to hold the office		300	0 0
To each Member of the Executive Committee, at the rate of		800	0 0
To the Secretary of the Executive Committee		400	0 0
To the Members of the Executive Committee, in full discharge of all contingencies of office	....	200	0 0
To the Speaker of the Assembly	....	600	0 0
To the Clerk of the Assembly	....	600	0 0
To the Sergeant-at-Arms	....	300	0 0
To the Chaplain of the Assembly	....	50	0 0
To the Librarian of the House of Assembly	....	100	0 0
To the Receiver-General	....	1,000	0 0
To the Auditor-General	....	600	0 0
For Clerks and other contingencies of Receiver-General and Audit Offices , ...	....	2000	0 0
To the Governor and Privy Council, for extraordinary and unforeseen expenses, not exceeding		1000	0 0
To the pay of the Officers of Fort Charles, and towards the repairs of the Forts and Fortifications of Fort Charles (see 26 V., c. 2)	....	750	0 0

(per annum.)

B., s. 45-48

To the Captain of the Train in Spanish Town	....	27 12 0
To the Auditor-General, under Council Fund	....	150 0 0
Public Messenger	....	300 0 0
Chief Justice	....	72 0 0
The Clerk of the Crown...	....	150 0 0

C., n. 38

				£	s.	d.	
Ale				3	0	0	per tun
Asses				0	4	0	per head
Bacon				0	4	0	per cwt
Barley				0	0	3	per bushel
Beef, dried				0	4	0	per cwt.
Beef, salted or cured, per barrel of 200lbs			0	6	0	" "
Beans				0	0	3	per bushel
Beer				3	0	0	per tun
Bread or Biscuits				0	2	0	per cwt.
Bricks				0	2	0	per 1000
Butter				0	3	0	per cwt
Calavances				0	0	3	per bushel
Candles, composition, per box, of 56lbs...		0	2	0	
" Tallow, per box, of 56lbs.			0	1	0	
" Wax or Spermacitty, per box of 56lbs.		0	4	0	
Cattle, neat....				0	10	0	per head

	£	s.	d.	
Carriages, not used for agricultural purposes, for every £100 ...	5	0	0	
Cheese	0	4	0	per cwt
Cider	3	0	0	per tun
Cocoa	0	5	0	per cwt
Coffee, the produce of, and imported from a British possession	0	10	0	per cwt
Corn, Indian ..	0	0	3	per bushel
Fish, dried or salted h	0	1	0	per cwt
" smoked, not oterwise enumerated or described	0	1	0	" "
" Alewives, pickled....	0	1	0	per barrel
" Herrings, pickled	0	1	0	" "
" Ditto smoked	0	0	3	per box
" Mackerel, pickled....	0	1	0	per barrel
" Pickled, not otherwise enumerated or described	0	2	0	" "
" Salmon, smoked	0	5	0	per cwt
" " wet or salted..	0	5	0	per barrel
Flour, Rye....	0	1	0	" "
" Wheat	0	2	0	per "
Goats	0	2	0	per head
Hams	0	4	0	per cwt
Horses, Mares, and Geldings	1	0	0	per head
Indigo	0	0	3	per lb.
Lard	0	2	0	per cwt
Meat, salted or cured, per barrel of 200lbs	0	6	0	" "
Meal or Flour, not wheat...	0	1	0	per barrel
Molasses, produce of, and imported from a British possession	0	2	0	per cwt
Mules	0	10	0	per head
Oats	0	0	3	per bushel
Peas	0	0	3	" "
Perry	3	0	0	per tun
Pork, salted or cured, per barrel of 200lbs	0	6	0	
Porter	3	0	0	per tun
Rice	0	1	0	per cwt
" undressed	0	0	6	per bushel
Salt	0	0	1	per cwt
Sausages	0 . 5	0		" "
Sheep	0	2	0	per head
Soap, per box of 56lbs......	0	1	0	per box
Spirits, Brandy..	0	3	0	per gallon
" Gin....	0	2	0	" "
" Rum, proof, and imported from British possession ..	0	3	0	" "
" Whiskey	0	2	0	" "
" all other Spirits, cordials, or compounds	0	3	0	" "
Sugar, refined	0	0	1	per lb
" unrefined, produce of, and imported from a British possession	0	5	0	per cwt
Swine	0	2	0	per head
Tea	0	1	0	per lb
Tobacco, manufactured, including Cavendish, for every pound weight	0	0	1	per "
" manufactured, for every pound weight	0	0	1	per "
" Segars, for every pound weight	0	0	8	per "
Tongues	0	4	0	per cwt
" salted or cured, per barrel of 200lbs	0	6	0	
Wheat	0	0	1	per bushel
Wines, whether in bulk or bottled	7	10	0	per tun
Wood, for one thousand feet of Pitch Pine Lumber, by superficial measure of one inch thick	0	6	0	
" for every one thousand feet of white pine lumber, or other lumber, by superficial measurement of one inch thick	0	4	0	
" shingles, cypress, more than 12 inches in length, per 1000	0	3	0	
" Boston chips, and all shingles not otherwise enumerated or described	0	2	0	per 1000

	£	s.	d.
Wood, wood hoops	0	1	0 per 1000
" staves and heading, red or white oak, or ash...	0	4	0 per 1000

And after these rates, for any greater or less quantity
of such goods respectively.

On all other goods, wares and merchandize, plantation
supplies, and effects of every description, not
previously enumerated, for every £100 value   2   0   0

D., s. 40		
Birds, singing	Free.
Books, printed, and printed paper	"
Bullion	"
Clothing, Army and Navy	"
Coals	"
Coin	"
Coke	"
Cotton, wool	"
Diamonds	"
Dogs	"
Dyewoods	"
Fish, fresh	"
Flax	..
Fruit, fresh	"
Guano, being manure	'
Gums	"
Hay and straw	"
Hemp	"
Hides, raw	"
Ice	"
Leeches	"
Malt, dust	"
Manures	"
Meat, fresh	"
Necessaries, Regimental and Navy, (cattle excepted)	"
Oil cakes, whole, or in powder	"
Plants, growing	'
Poultry	"
Resins	"
Salt Rock	"
Sarsaparilla	"
Slates	"
Soda, Ash	"
Specimens illustrative of natural history	"
Tallow, grease, tallow grease, or grease and slush	"
Tortoise Shell	"
Tow	"
Turtle	"
Vegetables, fresh	"
Wax, bees	"

E., s. 40	
Coffee, foreign	Prohibited
Molasses, foreign (repealed, 24 V., c. 13)	"
Rum, foreign	"
Sugar, refined, and sugar candy, except refined in bond, in the United Kingdom	
Sugar unrefined, foreign	"

(These articles are all now admitted. Imports, 28 V., v. 10.)

F., s. 50		£	s.	d.
Jamaica Life Assurance Company	25,500	0	0
Island Cheques in circulation	52,337	0	0
Court of Chancery Deposits..	19,798	10	4
Insolvent Act Deposit Account (see 19 V., c. 5)	5583	4	9
Island loan	212,312	13	4
Trustees of marriage settlement of Duke and Dutchess of Buckingham	821	1	8
John Auvray	100	0	0
Heir at law of St. Denton, exor of John Tait, et al	70	0	9

	£	s.	d.
Heir at law of John Eardly Wilmot	203	6	8
Exchequer bills, 13 V., c. 25, [£24,000 due, and £12,000 due July, 1854]	36,000	0	0
Exchequer bills, 14 V., c. 30, [£8,060 due, and £7500 due August, 1854	15,560	0	0
Jamaica orphan asylum	1000	0	0
Proposed issue of Island cheques and certificates to meet outstanding public liabilities to 5th January, 1854	100,000	0	0
	£469,285	17	6
Rest to be applied to the payment of deposits, &c.	30,714	2	6
	£500,000	0	0

Petty Debts.

The Petty Debt Act, 1856, 19 V., c. 37, s. 1.

All claims and demands in the nature of Debts, or of liquidated damages, not exceeding £10, and all claims or suits for unliquidated damages, or arising out of torts in which the damages claimed do not exceed 40s., may be recovered before 2 Justices of the parish where the Debts were contracted or arose, or in which the wrong occurred, or wherein the Debtor or person sought to be charged resides, 19 V., c. 37 s. 2.

Short title

Debts or liquidated damages not exceeding £10, unliquidated damages or torts not exceeding 40s to be recovered before two Justices of the parish where contracted or occurred or defendant resides

Executors or Administrators may sue or be sued, but Judgement when given against any defendant sued as such shall be enforced against the goods of the Testator or Intestate, and in the warrant of distress, the Collector shall be directed to execute the same upon the goods of the Testator or Intestate, 19 V., c. 37, s. 3.

Executors, &c

The jurisdiction under this Act shall extend to the recovery of any demand not exceeding £10, being the whole or part of the unliquidated balance of a partnership account, or of a legacy or distributive share of an Intestates assets, 19 V., c. 37, s. 4.

Partnership, accounts, legacies, distributive share

£6 per cent interest shall be recoverable when the debt is overdue after the expiration of the credit; such principal and interest not to exceed £10, 19 V., c. 37, s. 5.

Interest

No sum shall be recovered as and for rent of houses, lands or hereditaments, other than at the rate fixed upon at the commencement of the tenancy, or during the tenancy by the express agreement of the landlord and tenant, 19 V., c. 37, s. 6.

Rent

No debt or demand of a larger amount than £10, then actually due, and payable or claimable shall be split to bring it within the jurisdiction, but any plaintiff being a creditor to a larger amount than £10, or entitled in a suit for unliquadated damages, or for a tort, to recover more than 40s damages, may sue for and restrict himself to a less amount, and recover judgment for the reduced sum in full of his debt or claim; and where he so elects, the election shall be stated in the body of the process or noted in the Judgment, 19 V., c. 37, s. 7.

Demand not to be split to bring it within jurisdiction, but plaintiff may restrict himself to a less amount in full

A plaintiff may conjoin as many distinct causes of complaint as he pleases within the limits aforesaid, but no cause of action on contract which may by law be conjoined, and which may then be enforceable shall be split for the purpose of bringing separate actions, and a recovery in one suit or contract shall debar the plaintiff from enforcing any other contracts which might have been enforced at the time of the institution of the former suit; and a defendent subsequently sued for any such claims of the same class may plead the former recovery as a defence, and establish the same by evidence, although the former record does not disclose the fact as before provided, 19 V., c. 37, s. 8.

Conjunction of distinct causes of complaint
All causes of action on contracts then enforceable to be conjoined or plaintiff debarred from enforcing the others

Two or more promissory notes or bills of exchange, or other securities for money upon which the defendant may be liable, and held by the same plaintiff, shall be considered one cause of action; and if the holder elect to resort to the jurisdiction of the Justices for the recovery of any one or more, he shall be held to have made his election irrespective to the aggregate amount of such notes, bills and securities actually due at the time of issuing process at his instance, 19 V., c. 37, s. 9.

Two or more notes, bills or securities in plaintiffs hands actually due at time of issuing process

Claims against several jointly liable may be recovered against one or more

Where a plaintiff has any demand against two or more persons jointly answerable, it shall be sufficient if any or either of such persons, or their duly constituted representative be served with process, and Judgment may be obtained and enforced against the defendant or defendants, or either of them so served, or their goods, notwithstanding the others jointly liable may not

Who after satisfaction may sue for contribution

have been served or sued, or may not be within the jurisdiction of the Justices; and every such person or either of them against whom Judgment has been obtained, and who shall have satisfied the same, shall be entitled to recover under this Act contribution from any other person jointly liable, 19 V., c. 37, s. 10.

Notice to be served of defence of set off. Statute of limitations, insolvency, coverture or infancy

No defendant shall be allowed to set off any debt or demand claimed to be due to him from the plaintiff, or to set up, by way of defence thereto, the benefit of the statute of limitations, or a discharge as an Insolvent Debtor or coverture or infancy, unless a notice, in writing, (Form) setting forth the set-off or defence, and the particulars thereof have been given to the plaintiff, or if more than one, to one of them, by delivery of a copy to him, or to a servant or inmate of his known residence or place of business, 2 clear days at least previous to the hearing or adjudication, 19 V., c. 37, s. 11.

Evidence of insolvency

In proof of the defence of a discharge under the Insolvent Debtors' Act, it shall be sufficient to produce the copy of the order, or discharge, attested by the Clerk of the Supreme Court, with his certificate subscribed or endorsed or annexed thereto, setting forth an extract of the passage or entry in the Insolvent's schedule, shewing the debt claimed as inserted therein. Clerk of the Court's fee, 1s 6d; and no proof of the signature shall be necessary but the production of the attested copy order and certificate shall be prima facie evidence of the facts stated. The form of certificate shall be to the effect following :—

I certify that the schedule, as filed in my office, of A. B., of the parish
of the Insolvent named in the above order of discharge,
contains the following entry
Debts due by the Insolvent
Here set out verbatim the extract required.

Given under my hand this day of 18
C. D. Clerk of the Supreme Court, 19 V., c. 37, s. 12.

Summons and particulars

On application by or on behalf of any plaintiff, a summons, with the plaintiff's particulars of demand annexed (to be furnished by the plaintiff to the Clerk of the Peace in duplicate) shall issue (signed by the Clerk of the Peace without the signature of a Justice, 23 V., c. 35, s. 1), requiring the defendant (or defendants in case process is prayed against 2 or more) to appear and answer the claim on a day to be named in the summons, which

Service

shall be served by delivery of a copy to the defendant, with a copy of the particulars of demand annexed, or by delivering the same and explaining the meaning and nature thereof to a servant or inmate of his known residence or place of business, or in case of his absence from the Island, to his

5 days if in parish 12 days if not

duly constituted representative, at least 5 clear days before that mentioned for the hearing, if the defendant reside in the parish, or if out of it, 12 clear days' notice shall be given, 19 V., c. 37, s. 13.

Notice of hearing at any succeeding court

If any summons is not disposed of on the day named, from any cause, it may be heard and determined at the next, or any succeeding Court upon notice, (Form Schedule) served on the defendant free of charge to him, 19 V., c. 37, s. 14.

3 days before

Of which 3 days notice at least shall be given, 20 V., c. 20, s. 6.

Proof of service

Upon the day fixed for hearing, the Justices in Court shall have authority to establish the service, and upon service being duly proved and established, if the defendant being publicly called does not appear, but allows the

Default Adjudication

same to pass by default, the summons shall be marked default, and the Justices before whom service is established, or those at any succeeding Court,

No further notice necessary for 3 succeeding Courts

shall have power to adjudicate thereon, proof of the debt or claim being duly given and established on oath. It shall not be necessary to serve any further notice for any of the next 3 succeeding Courts, at which the summons may be brought on for adjudication, 19 V., c. 37, s. 15.

Adjudication by single Justice by consent

If the defendant appears, and both parties consent, a single Justice may adjudicate, 19 V., c. 37, s. 16.

If adjudication by single Justice declined, he may adjourn case and make a minute on summons, on each adjournment

If upon the appearance of a defendant, and either party refuse to submit to an adjudication by a single Justice, he may adjourn the hearing until the succeeding Court-day, and upon a minute of such adjournment being made on the summons, it shall stand adjourned to the next succeeding

Court-day, and so from time to time until final adjudication can be had; and it shall not be necessary to serve any notice on the defendant of the adjournment, but the minute on the summons and the notification thereof publicly in Court shall be sufficient, 19 V., c. 37, s. 17.

Not then necessary to serve further notice

The service of all summons shall be proved on oath, setting forth the time, place, and mode of service; and judgment shall not be awarded in any case until the plaintiff has duly proved his demand, 19 V., c. 37, s. 18.

Service of summons to be proved on oath, as also plaintiff's demand see s. 26

On the hearing, the parties, their wives or husbands, and all other persons may be examined on behalf of the plaintiff of defendant, upon oath or affirmation, in cases where persons are allowed to affirm, 19 V., c. 37, s. 19.

Parties, wives or husbands may be examined

Any Justice, on the application of a plaintiff or defendant, may issue a notice, (Form Schedule), requiring the attendance of any person required to give evidence, or to produce any books, papers or writings directed by the summons, touching the matter at issue, and after service and payment, or tender of reasonable travelling expenses, such persons shall be bound to appear on the day fixed for the hearing for the purpose indicated in the notice or summons; and on refusal so to do, or after appearance to be examined and give evidence, or to produce such books, &c., if shewn to be in his possession or under his control, such person shall be liable to a penalty not exceeding £6, after conviction on complaint, and to be recovered by levy and sale of his goods under the hands of 2 Justices, unless in case of non-attendance satisfactory reasons be adduced for his non-attedance; the fine to be paid to the Collector of Taxes for the use of the poor; and in failure of goods whereon to levy, the Justices may sentence the offender to the Common Gaol for not exceeding 30 days; but no such conviction shall prejudice the right of, or preclude the party damnified from maintaining a civil suit for recovery of damages sustained, by reason of the witnesses' neglect to attend, or refusal to be examined, 19 V., c. 37, s. 20.

Witness documents, enforcement of attendance and production

Penalty

Not to prejudice right of action

The Justices may award costs in their discretion to the party in whose favor judgment is pronounced, and in any case where a party is by summons directed to him induced to travel a distance of not less than one mile to the place appointed for disposing of such summons, and attends to defend the summons, and the plaintiff does not appear, or fails to prosecute his claim, or is non-suited, or has judgment awarded against him, or the summons dismissed, the plaintiff shall, independently of and in addition to the costs of the defence, be adjudged to pay the travelling expenses of the party summoned, such last mentioned costs not to exceed in the whole 10s., to be recovered, if payment be not forthwith made, by warrant of distress under this Act; and where any plaintiff by means of notice of set off or defence served on him by any defendant, attends to dispute the same and establish his claim, and the defendant appears after service of such notice, but suffers judgment to pass against him by default, or, having appeared, fails to prove such set off or defence, and judgment is obtained against him, the defendant shall be adjudged to pay his travelling expenses not exceeding 10s, to be recovered as aforesaid, 19 V., c. 37, s. 21.

Costs
Travelling expenses of defendant

Of plaintiff

In awarding costs, the Justices may include the costs of perfecting the judgment, and obtaining execution and payment, 20 V., c. 20, s. 2.

Costs of perfecting judgment, &c., may be included in the costs awarded

On every Court-day and before proceeding with the business, the Collector shall lay a return before the Justices in writing, and on Oath, (Form Schedule), of all process issued to him, distinguishing such as have been served from such as remain unserved, and the reasons for non-service, and on the first Monday in each month, file a return (Form Schedule), of all warrants of distress in his hands, and shewing the receipt and appropriation of all moneys received by him up to that day, the amount remaining in his hands, and the reason why not paid over to the party entitled, and the cause of non-execution of such process as has not been fully executed in the Clerk of the Peace's Office for the reference and inspection of the public (see s. 38), and the Collector shall be in attendance at his office every Friday to pay over any moneys in his hands to the parties entitled, but if any Friday happens to be a holiday, then on the next succeeding day of that or the following week which happens not to be a holiday. No such return shall stay the execution of any writ, but every warrant not fully executed and satisfied shall remain in the hands of such collector and continue in force until final execution, 19 V., c. 37, s. 22.

Collector's returns of process issued

Monthly returns of receipts and appropriations

Weekly payments

Warrants to remain in Collector's hands until satisfied

See S. 38; 23 V., c. 35, s. 2

Any Justice may issue summonses and other process for service and execution on defendants or witnesses in parishes other than that from which the process issues, 19 V., c. 37, s. 23.

Process may be executed out of parish of justice issuing

Any summons or process required to be served or executed out of the parish, shall be served or executed by the Collector of the parish into which it is sent, 19 V., c. 37, s. 24.

Service, &c., out of the parish may be proved by affidavit

The service or execution of any summons or process effected out of the parish from which it issued, may be proved by affidavit, purporting to be sworn before any Justice of the parish in which it was effected, and shall explicitly state the number of miles, if any, at which service was effected, from the nearest District Court of the parish in which service was effected; and mile money shall only be awarded according to the number of miles at which it was effected, from the District Court of the parish nearest to the place of service; and if the distance is not stated, the ordinary service money of 1s only shall be allowed to, or be presumed to be charged by the Collector effecting service, 19 V., c. 37, s. 25.

Mile money

Payment by instalments

At the time of adjudication, the Justices may grant the defendant time not exceeding 2 calendar months, for paying the debt and costs by instalments, specifying the amount and time of payment of each, upon his procuring some person to be bound as his surety for payment, (Form Schedule); and in case of non-payment of any instalment, the plaintiff may enforce payment of the debt and costs against the surety, under this Act, without detriment to his right to enforce such judgment against the defendant, 19 V., c. 37, s. 26.

Surety

In proportion to defendants earnings

The Justices shall examine the defendant on oath, as to his means of payment, in respect to his earnings, and fix the amount and pei of instalments, in due proportion to his earnings, 19 V., c. 37, s. 27. rod

Enlargement of time

If it shall at any time appear to the Justices by whom any order for payment by instalments is made, either by oath or affirmation of any person or otherwise, that any defendant is unable from sickness or other sufficient cause to pay any instalment at the time limited, they may enlarge the time to a future day, upon such terms as they think fit, and so from time to time, until it appears by the like proof that the temporary cause of disability has ceased. No such order shall release the surety, 19 V., c. 37, s. 28.

Not to release surety

Revocation at instance of plaintiff

If at any time after adjudication and grant of time, before it expires, it appears necessary to revoke it, any two Justices, upon application of any plaintiff, may alter any order previously made for the payment by instalments or otherwise, and make further order for payment of the whole or the balance of the debt and costs forthwith, or in any other manner, and thereupon the surety shall be discharged from his liability; and the Justices may require further security or otherwise; and the plaintiff shall be restored to his original position, and right of distress, unless further time be granted and further security given, 19 V., c. 37, s. 29.

Further order

Discharge of surety

Judgments to be recorded by Clerk of the Peace

All judgments to be awarded shall be entered up and recorded by the Clerk of the Peace, and the originals filed, and a fee of 1s 6d for recording each shall be paid at the time of entering up such judgment by the person in whose favor it is pronounced, and it shall not be compulsory to the Clerk of the parish to do so, or to issue any process thereon, until the fee for recording is paid or tendered, 19 V., c. 37, s. 31.

Fee

Minutes of evidence

The Magistrates' Clerk shall take minutes of the evidence given in all defended or contested causes, to be kept with the orignal summons and proceedings; his fee to be paid by the party succeeding, 1s 6d for taking such minutes, to be taxed as part of his costs, and received as the evidence in the cause on an appeal; and the Clerk of the Peace shall furnish copies of the evidence and proceedings to parties requiring same, on being paid at the rate in Schedule, 19 V., c. 37, s. 32.

Fee

Evidence on appeal

Copies

See appeal, 21 V., c. 22, s. 29

Fees of Clerks of the Peace and Collectors

The fees of Clerks of the Peace and Collectors shall be as in Schedule, 19 V., c. 37, s. 33; as amended by 20 V., c. 20, s. 7, and 23 V., c. 35, s. 4.

Cross judgments

The Justices may order cross judgments between the parties to be set off, and award execution for the difference to the party having the larger judgment, and satisfaction shall by the Clerk of the Peace be entered on both judgments for the sums so satisfied on each, 19 V., c. 37, s. 35.

Warrant of distress

Any one Justice may, on demand of the plantiff, issue a warrant, (Form Schedule), directing the Collector forthwith to levy the debt and costs and charges of the levy upon the goods of the defendant (except his necessary wearing apparel and tools of trade), and to sell the same at the usual place of sales of levies within one week after the levy, returning any overplus to the defendant on demand, after satisfying the debt and costs and charges, and further directing the Collector in default of goods, to imprison the defendant in the nearest prison for 10 days, unless the debt and costs be sooner paid, 19 V., c. 37, s. 36.

Or in default commitment for 10 days unless sooner paid

Any person so arrested in default of payment shall be conveyed to the nearest debtor's gaol in any adjoining parish, if that in which he is arrested is not provided with one; and the Collector making the arrest may convey him thither, although out of his parish; and any person obstructing him, or rescuing or attempting to rescue the defendant, or any defendant resisting or refusing to accompany the Collector whilst in custody, and being convicted, shall forfeit not exceeding £10 nor less than £5, and in default of payment, shall be committed to any prison for not exceeding 10 days, 23 V., c. 35, s. 6.

When in an adjoining parish

Obstruction rescue or refusal to accompany Collector

As soon as a levy is made, the Collector shall furnish the defendant with, or leave at his residence with some inmate, or affix at the outer door of his residence, a true list of the goods levied on, describing their nature and quality, signed by the Collector or his deputy, 19 V., s. 37.

Notice of levies to be given defendants

If a levy when sold is insufficient, after deducting all lawful expenses, to satisfy the full amount directed to be levied, the Collector may, notwithstanding the first levy, and notwithstanding the imprisonment of the defendant, levy under the same warrant for the whole or balance remaining due from time to time until the whole amount is satisfied. A monthly return shall be made to every warrant which has remained in the Collector's hands until satisfied (see s. 22). No defendant shall be liable to be imprisoned more than once on each judgment. and if it becomes necessary at any time to issue a further warrant on any judgment on which a defendant has been imprisoned, the party applying for such subsequent warrant of distress shall notify the fact of such previous imprisonment to the Clerk of the Peace, who shall thereupon expunge from the subsequent warrant the direction to take and imprison the defendant's body, 19 V., c. 37. s. 38.

Further levies may be made notwithstanding insufficient previous levy and imprisonment of defendant
Monthly returns

Defendant not to be imprisoned more than once
If afterwards a further warrant issue the direction to take defendants body to be expunged

A distress warrant may, from time to time as occason requires, issue for enforcement of any judgment until complete satisfaction; and a plaintiff in any judgment in any Petty Court of the precinct of St. Catherine may issue a warrant directed to the Collector of any one of the parishes comprising such precinct in which the defendant resides or where it is to be executed, 23 V., c. 35, s. 2.

Warrants to issue from time to time
On judgments in precinct of St. Catherine

Any Justice, on production to him of a warrant, duly signed and issued, shall, at the request of the party p   ng it, endorse thereon an authority to any Collector within his jurisdiction to execute it according to the exigency, and thereupon the Collector to whom it is endorsed shall proceed to execute it within the parish or precinct for which he is Collector, and forthwith, on execution or the earlier request of the plaintiff, return the warrant, with his return thereto into the Court from which it issued, and pay the proceeds of any levy to the plaintiff or his agent, and the plaintiff may proceed to issue further process as occasion may require into other parishes until full satisfaction, 20 V., c. 20, s. 1.

Endorsment by a Justice for execution by a Collector of another parish in his jurisdiction
Such Collector's duty

Further process

The plaintiff on satisfaction of a judgment by warrant in writing, shall direct the Clerk of the Peace to enter up satisfaction on the margin of the record, 23 V., c. 35, s. 5.

Satisfaction

The plaintiff or any assignee of his, may assign a judgment, which shall be recorded in the Clerk of the Peace's Office, on payment of 1s fee, and shall be in the words, or to the effect following :—

Assignment

I   have this   day of   18   assigned
under a judgment obtained by me or by   against
for the sum of £   for damages, and the sum of £
for costs in the Petty Debt Court of the Parish of   on the
day of   18   and there is now due thereon the
sum of £   for damages £   for costs, and I have
received the sum of £   in full consideration thereof, 23 V., c. 35, s. 7.

None but plaintiffs or defendants in person, or by their counsel or attorney or other person duly authorized in writing, shall appear to prosecute or defend suits, 19 V., c. 37, s. 51.

Who may appear to prosecute or defend

But no Collector shall be permitted to act as advocate or agent, 20 V., c. 20, s. 3.

No Collector permitted

Collectors Their appointment

Elections and appointments of Collector of Petty Debts shall be made, as a vacancy occurs or occasion requires, by the Justices in Special Sessions, for the purpose assembled, 20 V., c. 20, s. 2.

Continuance in office Security at his expense

Who shall continue to act in such offices until death, resignation or dismissal. No summons, warrant or other proceeding shall be directed to or executed or served by any Collector, until he has given security in a bond at his expense to the Crown, with one or more surety, to be approved of by the Justices in Special Session at the time of appointment, or within such other period as may be fixed : penalty, in not less than £200 in other parishes, and not less than £500 in Kingston, for the due execution by the Collector and his Deputies of the duties of the office, and for accounting for and paying over all moneys collected by or paid to him or them, or which shall otherwise come to his or their hands in the execution, or by color of

Bond cautionary Without detriment to proceedings by summons as for moneys had and received by any party damnified

Bond to be approved by Solicitor of the Parish at their expense

the office, which bond shall stand cautionary for all sums to be received and collected by such Collector, without detriment to the right of the party damnified of proceeding in a summary manner by a summons, (Form Schedule); and as for moneys had and received to the use of the plaintiff for the recovery of the amount so received by the Collector or his Deputies, by virtue of any process under this Act, such bond when prepared to be submitted for perusal and approval of the Solicitor of the parish, at the expense of the parish, 19 V., c. 37, s. 41.

Process to be served only by Collector or his deputies

Except summons to witnesses or notices

All process shall be executed by the Collector, or his duly authorized Deputies, and service of summons, or execution of warrants or other process otherwise effected shall be void ; but any party may effect service by himself or agent of any summons to witnesses, or notices, 19 V., c. 37, s. 42.

Collector's to appoint deputies and notify same, and discharges to Clerk of the Peace to be notified in his office

Penalty for acting as deputy without authority or notification

Any Collector may appoint as many Deputies as he deems necessary, and immediately upon each appointment give notice in writing to the Clerk of the Peace, who shall record, in a sheet to be hung up conspicuously in his office, a list of the names of such Deputies ; and the discharge and revocation of each appointment shall, in like manner, be notified and recorded. Any person who acts as Deputy without sufficient authority, or whose appointment is not so notified or recorded, may be tried and punished summarily before 2 Justices, and be subjected to a fine of not exceeding £10, and in default of payment, to imprisonment for not more than 3 calendar months, with or without hard labor ; and every Deputy so appointed shall be liable to the penalties imposed upon his principal; and be subject to the summary jurisdiction of the Justices in like manner as his principal. The Collector and his sureties shall be liable for all the acts of his Deputies, 19 V., c. 37, s. 43.

Penalty on Collector for neglect in above or other cases not provided for

In every case of neglect or omission to make such return, or in the performance of any duty on the part of any Collector not otherwise provided for, the offending Collector shall be liable to a penalty not exceeding £10, to be recovered before 2 Justices, and in default of payment, to be imprisoned in the nearest prison for not exceeding 30 days, 19 V., c. 37, s. 44.

Extortion not paying or accounting for moneys received

Conviction to operate a discharge and disqualification to hold the office in any parish, until reversed

If any Collector be charged with extortion, or with not duly paying or accounting for any money levied or received by him, 2 Justices shall enquire into the charge, and upon being satisfied of the truth thereof, shall order the re-payment of any money extorted, or the payment of any money levied or received, with all reasonable costs. And in addition, they may impose a penalty not exceeding £20 on such Collector, and in default of immediate payment, may sentence him to be imprisoned in the nearest prison for not exceeding 3 months ; and every such conviction, unless and until reversed, shall operate to discharge him from his office, and to disqualify him from holding the office for any parish for the future, 19 V., c. 37, s. 45.

Justices in special Session may remove Collectors

And summon and examine witnesses on oath

The Justices in Special Sessions assembled for the purpose, shall have power to remove and dismiss such Collector to be appointed, or any Collector now holding office, upon complaint, on oath, established to their satisfaction : to which end they may summon and examine, on oath, all persons they deem necessary, 19 V., c. 37, s. 46.

Liability of Collector for negligent, &c. execution of process or omission

If any Collector, by wilful default or connivance, or by neglect or omission lose the opportunity of serving, levying or executing any process issued to him for service or execution, any 2 Justices, upon complaint and proof, may adjudge him to pay to the complainant the sum sought to be recovered by the warrant or process, or so much as they think proper, and may in addition impose a fine on the Collector not exceeding £5, and enforce the fine if any, and the sums so awarded with costs, by warrant of distress ; and for want of sufficient distress, commit him to the nearest prison for not exceeding 30 days; the fine to be paid to the Collector of Taxes to the use of the poor. But not to exonerate the sureties from the penalty of their bond in such default, 19 V., c. 37, s. 47.

Sureties not exonerated

On the removal, resignation or dismissal of a Collector, he shall deliver over to his successor all summonses, warrants or proceedings in his hands unserved or unexecuted, and such successor shall act upon and enforce the same as if they had been originally directed to him, and the sureties of the removed, &c., Collector shall not be discharged from their bond in respect of any breach of duty previously to the transfer to his successor, nor until such summonses and warrants and proceedings have been delivered over, and the provisions of this Act complied with, 19 V., c. 37, s 48.

On removal, &c., sureties liable for previous breaches and also until process transferred to the successor

All summonses, warrants, process or other proceedings against any Collector, shall be directed to and served and executed by any Policeman or Constable of the parish in which they shall issue, or are to be served or executed, but they shall not in any other respect be employed or engaged in carrying this Act into execution, 19 V., c. 37, s. 49.

Proceedings against Collectors to be executed by police, &c., but no other

If any Collector or his authorized Deputy is assaulted in the execution of his duty, or if any rescue is made or attempted to be made of any goods levied upon, or of the body of any defendant under caption under process, the offender shall be liable to a fine not exceeding £5, and in default of payment, to be imprisoned in the nearest prison, for not exceeding 30 days, but the party aggrieved may institute any other legal proceedings civilly against the offenders for redress, 19 V., c. 37, s. 50.

Assaulting Collector or deputy Rescue of goods or defendant

Party aggrieved may proceed civilly for redress

None but the plaintiffs or defendants, in person or by their counsel, attorney or other person duly authorized in writing, shall appear to prosecute or defend suits before any Justices, 19 V., c. 37, s. 51.

Persons to act before Justices

No Collector of Petty Debts shall be permitted to act as the advocate or agent of any person before any Justice under 19 V., c. 37 or this Act, 20 V., c. 20, s. 4.

Not a Collector

The Forms in Schedule may be adapted and varied to meet the requirements of each particular case, 19 V., c. 37, s. 52.

Forms

Where a distress is made or caption effected for debt or costs, or for fine or penalty, the distress and imprisonment, or either, shall not be deemed unlawful, nor the party a trespasser, on account of any defect or want of form in the information, summons, conviction, suit, warrant of distress or other proceeding relating thereto, nor the party a trespasser ab initio, on account of any irregularity afterwards done by the party distraining or imprisoning, but the person aggrieved by the irregularity, may receive satisfaction for the special damages on an action upon the case, 19 V., c. 37, s. 53.

Distress or caption not to be deemed unlawful or the party a trespasser for defects in form or a trespasser ab initio for subsequent irregularities, but may recover special damages in action on the case

In any action against a Justice, Collector or other officer for anything done in pursuance of this Act, or in fulfilment of the duties hereby imposed, the pa sued may plead the general issue and give the special matter in evidence, 19 V., c. 37, s. 54.

Justices, &c., may plead general issue and give special matter in evidence

False swearing, declaring or affirming, declared wilful and corrupt Perjury, 19 V., c. 37, s. 55.

False swearing, &c.

Assigning, transferring, delivering or making over any goods to any other person, in trust for, or to the use, benefit or advantage of the person making the assignment or transfer, or of any other persons, or purchasing any goods in the name of another, but covertly to his own use, in order, or with intent to defeat any execution under this Act, unless proved to have been made bona fide and for valuable consideration, shall be deemed fraudulent and void as against any debt subsisting at the time of the transfer, assignment or purchase, 19 V., c. 37, s. 56.

Fraudulent transfers to defeat creditors void

All penalties and fines shall, unless otherwise directed, be recovered summarily before 2 Justices, and applied, one moiety to the party suing, the other to the Collector of Taxes for the use of the poor, and in failure of goods, they may sentence the offender to the nearest prison for not exceeding 3 calendar months; and such alternative sentence may be awarded in the first instance, and be directed in the original warrant of distress, or after a return thereto in the discretion of the Justices, 19 V., c. 37, s. 57.

Recovery and application of penalties

On application by or on behalf of any Collector, being a defendant, sued in an action at law for any act done in execution of his office (the application being made before plea by affidavit, shewing that the defendant

Proceedings by Collector to obtain order for plaintiff in action against him to interplead with 3rd party claiming right to the property in question

does not claim any interest in the subject matter of the suit, but that the right is claimed or supposed to belong to some third party), the Court may make an order, calling on the the third party to appear and state the nature of his claim; and if the Court thereafter think fit, to order such third party to make himself defendant in the action instead of the Collector, and to proceed to trial in the action, and to make such other rules and orders as to costs or other matters as may appear just and reasonable, 19 V., c. 37, s. 58.

Proceedings by way of interpleader before the Justices

If any adverse claim be set up by any person, to property levied upon by the Collector, the adverse claimant intending to assert his right thereto, shall forthwith issue a summons to the Collector, (Form Schedule), requiring him to suspend the sale of the property levied upon, until the title is determined by 2 Justices in Petty Sessions, and they shall be empowered to determine the right and title to the disputed property, and award either that the property be delivered up to the claimant or be retained by the Collector, and by him disposed of in satisfaction of the writ or writs under

Subject to appeal

which it was levied; and the judgment shall be subject to appeal as in other cases of summary adjudication, 23 V., c. 35, s. 3.

SCHEDULE to 19 V., c. 37.

	s.	d.
Collector's fees		
For serving each summons to appear and answer	1	0
" " copy summons to appear and give evidence, when required	1	0
And in addition to such service money (and on all process served and executed by him or his deputy), he shall be entitled to mile-money, at the rate of 6d. per mile, to be reckoned and estimated from the Court-House of the parochial town, 23 V., c. 35, s. 4.		
For executing each warrant of distress	2	0
And in addition, 1s. in the £ on the amount of debts and costs, when levied or collected, to be deducted in the first instance, after sale of goods, or receipt of such collections, and to be a charge on, and be levied for, from the defendant.		
Clerk of the Peace		
For each original summons to appear and answer, including form, and filling up	0	9
Each copy	0	3
Recording each judgment	1	6
Each warrant of distress or other such process, including form, filling up, and attendance on Magistrates to have it signed	0	9
For each original summons, to include not more than six witnesses, including form, filling up, and attendance on Magistrate to have it signed ...,.	0	9
For each copy	0	3
For copies of evidence, when required, taken in contested causes	1	6

Summons to appear and answer

Name of parish or precinct

To , of the parish of
You are hereby required to appear before the Justices, at
on the day of next at
o'clock, then and there to answer the claim of
touching a certain debt or claim, as the case may be (set forth the nature of the debt or claim), otherwise that judgment shall pass against you by default.

Given under my hand this day of in
the year of our Lord, 18

Notice to appear when case not heard in the first instance

JAMAICA, ss.
Parish

A. B. vs. C. D.

Take notice, That this cause will be heard on the day
of next.
Dated this day of 18

A. B. plaintiff.

To C. D., defendant.

Name of parish or precinct. . . . .

To , Collector of Petty Debts for the parish of
You are hereby required on sight hereof, forthwith to levy ' the sum
of being the amount of a certain claim adjudged
against in favor of together with
the sum of pounds, for costs upon the goods (except the
necessary wearing apparel and tools of trade) of the said
and you are also required to sell the goods so distrained within the
space of one week from and after such levy, and out of the proceeds
thereof to satisfy the amount of the said claim of the said
together with the costs aforesaid, and to return any overplus to the
said and you are hereby further required in default
of finding sufficient goods whereon to levy the whole of the said
debt and costs, to arrest the said by the body, and
imprison him for the space of ten days in the nearest gaol, unless
such debt and costs, or so much thereof as thou canst not levy, be
sooner paid ; and for so doing, this shall be your sufficient warrant.

Given under our hands, this day of in
the year of our Lord, 18

JAMAICA, ss.

Name of parish or precinct.
To of the parish of
Take notice, That I (or we) will at the hearing of this case set up the
following grounds of special defence (here state the nature of the
defence.)
Given under my hand (or our hands) this day of
18

JAMAICA, ss.

Parish or precinct.
To (Witness's name and description.)
These are to require you to appear and give evidence at
in the parish of at o'clock,
on the day of one thousand eight hundred and in a matter of complaint, in which is
the plaintiff, and the defendant, on the part and behalf of the said plaintiff, (or defendant). Therefore fail not at your
peril.
Given under my hand, this day of in
the year of our Lord, 18

JAMAICA, ss.Security for payment when time
given

Parish.

A. vs. B.

Judgment recovered the day of 18
Debt £
Costs £
In consideration of the forbearance conceded to B. the defendant, in the
liquidation of the Judgment by the following instalments, namely,
the sum of £ on the day of
and the sum of £ on the day of &c., &c.
I hereby become bound for the due and punctual payment thereof in
the manner aforesaid, and in default of payment of any one instalment, I engage to pay you forthwith thereafter the amount which
shall remain due to you.
Dated this day of 18
To Mr. A., the plaintiff.

JAMAICA, ss.

Parish.
A Return of all summonses issued and served by Collector of Petty Debts for the parish of , from the
day of , to the day of 186

Plaintiff.	Defendant.	How and when served.	Reasons why Summons not served.

JAMAICA, SS.
Parish.

A. B., collector of Petty Debts for the parish of
being duly sworn, maketh oath and saith, that the above Return exhi
bits a true, faithful and correct statement of all summonses issued
and served by him during the above period.

A. B., Collector.

Sworn to before me at   in the parish of   this
day of   in the year of our Lord, 18

Warrant for amount of debt against Collector

Name of parish.

To   Policeman and Constable of the parish of
You are hereby required at sight hereof forthwith to levy the sum
of   being the amount of a certain claim in which
is the plaintiff, and   is defendant, adjudged in favour of
the said   against   the Collector of Petty
Debts, for wilful negligence and omission in his duty in that behalf,
together with the sum of   for charges upon the goods
(except the necessary wearing apparel and tools of trade) of the
said   , and you are also required to sell the goods so distrained within the space of one week from and after such levy, and out
of the proceeds thereof, to satisfy the claim of the said   together with the charges aforesaid, and to return any overplus to the
said   and for want of such distress or of a sufficient distress,
you are hereby required to arrest the said   by his body, and
convey him to the nearest gaol, there to remain for the space of
days, or till he shall have satisfied the said sum, and all charges
aforesaid, or be otherwise discharged by due course of law: and for
so doing, this shall be your sufficient warrant.
Given under my hand this   day of   18

Warrant for penalty against Collector

Name of parish or precinct.

To   Policeman and Constable of the parish of
You are hereby required, on sight hereof, forthwith to levy the sum
of   being the amount of a certain fine adjudged
against   being a Collector of Petty Debts of the
said parish, for that he the said   did receive a
certain summons for service, (or warrant for execution), at the suit of
against   and wilfully neg-
lected, and omitted to serve, (or execute) the same, (or if the default
be non-payment of money then), and having received the money due

due thereon, wilfully neglected and omitted to pay over the same to the plaintiff therein according to law, (or if the charge be for not making a return) did receive certain summonses and warrants for service and execution, and wilfully neglected and omitted to make the return required by law, upon the goods and chattels, (except the necessary wearing apparel and tools of trade), of the said and you are also required to sell the goods so distrained within the space of one week from and after such levy, and out of the proceeds thereof, after payment of the sum of the costs and charges on the warrant, to pay the said fine to the Collector of taxes of the said parish; and, for want of such distress, or for a sufficient distress, you are to convey him to the nearest gaol, there to remain for the space of days, or till he shall have satisfied the said sum, and all charges, or be otherwise discharged by due course of law; and for so doing this shall be your sufficient warrant.

Given under my hand, this   day of   18

JAMAICA, s.s.

   Parish

Return of warrants of distress

A Return of all Warrants of Distress in the hands of A. B., Collector of Petty Debts for the Parish of   from the 1st day of to the 31st (or as the case may be).

WARRANTS UNEXECUTED AS PER LAST RETURN IN HANDS OF COLLECTOR.

Plaintiff.	Defendant.	Amount of Damages and Costs.	Return thereto.	Reason why the same has not been executed, to be stated at full length.

WARRANTS ISSUED SINCE LAST RETURN.

Plaintiff.	Defendant.	Amount of Damages and Costs.	Return thereto.	Reason why the same has not been executed, to be stated at full length.

JAMAICA, ss.

Parish

             Collector of Petty Debts in the parish of being duly sworn, maketh oath and saith, that the foregoing return exhibits a true, faithful and correct account of all warrants of distress which were unexecuted and remaining in his hands at the period of his last return, and also a true, faithful and correct account of all warrants of distress issued to and received by him since his last return during the above mentioned period, and that the return set opposite to such respective amount, and the reasons also assigned for the non-execution thereof, as above set forth, are true and correct in every particular.

    Sworn, &c.

SCHEDULE.—23 V., c. 35.

Summons adverse claim 23 V., c. 35, s. 3.

JAMAICA, ss.

To the Collector of Petty Debts of the Parish of

    Take Notice, that you are hereby required to suspend the sale of certain property, levied on by you under a Distress Warrant, A. vs. B., until the title thereto be determined : and for that purpose you are required to appear before the Court of Petty Sessions to be held at
    in the parish of   on   the
day of   next (or instant), to shew cause why the said property, that is to say (enumerate them) should not be delivered up to L. M., of, &c., &c., who claims to be entitled thereto as owner thereof (stating how the title thereto was acquired).

Given under my hand this   day of .   18

        C. P., Clerk of the Peace of the parish of

Pilots.

No one to act as Master Pilots, without commission, certificate and license

    No person shall act as a Master Pilot who shall not produce when required by any one with whom he may be concerned, in such capacity, a regular warrant or appointment as a Pilot, under the hand and seal of the Governor, and a certificate conformably to this Act, (Form Schedule), or the Act in force at the date of his appointment, and a license under this Act, (Form Schedule) ; Penalty, £100 for every time he acts without such warrant and license, 19, V., c. 15, s. 2.

Nor as Pilot of 2nd class without certificate and license

    Nor as a Pilot of the second class, without production as above of a certificate and license ; Penalty, £50, 19 V., c. 15, s. 3.

Pilots to be examined

Board of examination

    Before any person is appointed a Master Pilot or Pilot of the second class, the Custos, Mayor or Senior Magistrate of Kingston, or Custos or Senior Magistrate of the parish in which he resides shall, on a written application for the purpose, nominate at least two experienced commanders of merchant vessels who have entered such port not less than five times, two experienced commanders of coasting vessels, and two Master Pilots having a competent knowledge of the harbours, coasts, shoals, quays, and channels of and about the Island, who shall meet together at some convenient time and place to be fixed by the Custos, Mayor or Senior Magistrate, and form themselves into a board, and examine the person touching his skill in the navigation of vessels, and his knowledge of such harbours, &c., or of such of them as he within the limits of which he applies to be appointed ; and if the Board find him duly qualified and proper to be appointed Master Pilot or Pilot of the second class, they shall grant him a certificate under their hands, (Form Schedule).

Certificate Master Pilot to obtain Governor's Warrant Declaration to be endorsed

No person to whom a certificate is granted shall act as a Master Pilot, until he has obtained a warrant under the Governor's hand and seal, and subscribed the following declaration, to be endorsed thereon before any Magistrate :—

    I, A. B., do declare, that I will faithfully, diligently and truly Pilot all ships or vessels entrusted to my care, to the best of my skill and knowledge, and that I will not undertake to conduct any vessel into or out of any harbour, port, creek or bay of this Island, with which, or with the channels, shoals and quays of which I am not well acquainted.

No Pilot of the second class shall be entitled to have a certificate granted to him before he takes the following declaration before any Magistrate :—

I, A. B., do declare that I will faithfully, diligently and truly Pilot all vessels entrusted to my care to the best of my skill and knowledge, and that I will not take charge of any vessel of a draught of water exceeding 12 feet at the time of taking charge of such vessel save and except in cases where no Master Pilot can be had, nor undertake to conduct any vessel which I may be entitled to Pilot into or out of any harbour, port, creek or bay of this Island, with which, or with the channels, shoals and quays of which I am not well acquainted, 19 V., c. 15, s. 4.

For Kingston Harbour Master to be of Board
For the port of Kingston, the Harbour-Master shall be a constituent member of the board for examination, 19 V., c. 15, s. 5.

3 Members a quorum
Any 3 members of the board shall be a quorum, 19 V., c. 15, s. 6.

Penalty for non-attendance
If any commander of any merchant vessel, coasting vessel, or Master Pilot nominated to examine any person, or the Harbour-master of Kingston, neglect or refuse to act, except upon sufficient cause to be shewn to the satisfaction of such Custos, &c., he shall forfeit £10, 19 V., c. 15, s. 7.

Appointment of an officer of the Navy who shall preside
When any person applies to be examined, the Custos, &c., shall send a request, in writing, to the senior Naval Officer in command of H. M.'s vessels of war in any port, to appoint a commissioned officer of the Navy to attend to examine, and who if he attend shall preside and exercise the same power as is given to the other members, and also sign the certificate of qualification of the person declared competent, 19 V., c. 15, s. 8.

Clerk of the Peace to register certificate. Fee
The Clerk of the Peace nearest to the port where such Pilot resides, shall register at length the certificate of every Master Pilot, or Pilot of the 2nd class in a book in his office, and thereafter return the original to the Master-Pilot or Pilot of the 2nd class. His fee 5s, 19 V., c. 15, s. 9.

Within one month after appointment
Security bond
Every Master Pilot and Pilot of the 2nd class shall, within one calendar month after his appointment, cause the certificate of his qualification to be registered, and within the same period enter into bond to the Queen, with one or more sureties, each Master Pilot in £200, with one surety in £200 or two in £100 each, and each Pilot of the 2nd class in £100, with one surety in £100, or two sureties each in £50, to be approved of by the Custos, &c., to answer any damages or expenses to arise or be occasioned by his unskilfulness or negligence, which bond shall be kept by the Clerk of the Peace. To be kept by the Clerk of the Peace Fee His fee 7s 6d, besides Stamp duty, for preparing and witnessing the execution, which it shall be his duty to do. Such sureties at any time upon giving 28 days' notice of their desire or intention of surrendering such suretyship, Surety may give notice of surrender may call upon such Pilot to procure other sureties to be approved of as aforesaid, to enter into bond, and upon the new surety having executed such bond, the original surety shall be forthwith discharged from further liability. Such Pilot shall be disqualified from acting after the expiration of Pilot disqualified to act after notice expires the notice, until the new surety is given, under penalty of £10; but no But surety not relieved until new Bond executed surety shall be relieved from his liabilities until the new bond is executed, 19 V., c. 15, s. 10.

Annual Licenses
Every Pilot shall take out an annual license in the form provided, or as near as circumstances permit, on or before 1st January, to be granted by the Clerk of the Peace nearest the port where he resides, on presentation of his certificate, and which shall extend to the 31st December in each current or succeeding year : Penalty, £20. Fee Clerk of the Peace's fee for issuing and recording license in a book, 5s, besides Stamp, 19 V., c. 15, s. 11.

Stamp
Stamp on Master Pilot's License, 20s : Pilot of second class, 10s. 19 V., c. 15, s. 12.

Previous license to be delivered up
No license shall be granted to any Pilot who does not deliver up to the Clerk of the Peace his license for the previous year to be cancelled, 19 V., c. 15, s. 13.

In case of a suspension of license new license for the remainder of current year may be given after suspension ended
When a license has been suspended for a time which will expire after 1st January in any year, the Clerk of the Peace may, afterwards, on the expiration of the term of suspension, grant the Pilot a license for the remainder of the then current year, 19 V., c. 15, s. 14.

No Pilot to be surety of another. Proceedings on bond to be commenced within 6 months after damage
No Pilot shall be permitted to be surety of another. Proceedings under the security bond shall be commenced within 6 months after any damages are incurred, 10 V., c. 15, s. 15.

Lists of pilots, &c
to be furnished to
Custom's Officers
The Clerks of the Peace were required to furnish the Collector and
Controller of Kingston and Sub-Collectors or other principal officers at every
port within the limits of the certificate registered by them, lists of the
names of all Pilots whose certificates were registered in their office, with the
dates and registration, and the names of the ports for which each Pilot has
qualified, with the names and residences of the sureties in, and the date of
the Bond. made out and signed by them, 19 V., c. 15, s. 16.

And upon every subsequent registration, shall cause the names and
residences of the party and his sureties, with all other particulars before
required, to be furnished to them, 19 V., c. 15, s. 17.

Penalty for acting
without registra-
tion or bond
Limits of liability
for damages
Every Pilot who acts without such registration of his certificate, and
without entering into a Bond, shall, for every time he acts, forfeit £5. No duly
qualified Pilot who has executed the bond, and shall be piloting or conducting within the limits of his certificate any vessel which he is duly qualified
to pilot, shall be liable to any action for damages at the suit of the party aggrieved, in any greater sum than the amount of the penalty of the bond, and
the pilotage payable to him in respect to the voyage in which the vessel is
for any loss or damage from or by reason of his neglect, or want of skill
whilst acting as Pilot on board, 19 V., c. 15, s. 18.

Merchant vessels
to accept services of
the first qualified
pilot who offers
Yachts, droghers;
and ships' boats ex
empted
The master of every merchant vessel bound to any port, &c., of this
Island shall receive the first Pilot qualified to take charge who first offers his
services as Pilot on board, or in case of refusal he, or the owner or consignee shall pay to such Pilot the pilotage fee. Not to oblige any pleasure
yacht, drogher actually engaged in the coasting trade, or any ships' boat
employed in transporting produce or other goods from one port to another in
this Island, or further, to take a Pilot or subject the same to any charge for
pilotage, 19 V., c. 15, s. 19.

When signal is
hoisted for a pilot
in harbour the first
who offers his ser-
vices to be accepted
or paid the piloting
fee
When a signal for a Pilot is hoisted on board a vessel in any harbor,
&c., the master shall be bound to take the first qualified Pilot who offers his
services on board, and on refusal to receive him, shall be obliged to pay
him the rate allowed for pilotage equally as if he had been taken on
board, 19 V., c. 15, s. 20.

Penalty for refus-
ing or delaying to
take charge of ves-
sel
If any Pilot when not actually engaged, refuses or declines, or wilfully
delays to go off to. or on board of, or to take charge of any vessel wanting
a Pilot, and within the limits specified in his certificate, and of which he
is qualified to take charge, upon the usual signal for a Pilot being displayed
from the vessel, or upon being required so to do by the Captain, or by any
commissioned or warrant officer of any vessel in H. M's service, or by the
master or any other person having the command of the vessel, or interested therein as principal or agent, and unless it be unsafe for such Pilot to
obey the signal, or comply with the requisition, or he is prevented by
illness or other sufficient cause to be shown by him, or if any Pilot who
Or refusing to
pilot, &c., after en-
gagement
has been engaged to pilot the same, or after going alongside before the
service has been performed for which he was hired, and without leave
of the Captain if in Her Majesty's service, or of the master or commander, if not, quits or refuses to perform such service, he shall forfeit
not exceeding £50, nor less than £10, and be liable to be dismissed
from being a Pilot, or suspended from acting as such, on conviction before
2 Justices. 19 V., c. 15, s. 21.

Pilot boats to be
painted black with
a white streak, and
to carry a Blue
Peter
The sides of every Pilot boat shall be painted black, and the upper
streak next the gunwale white, and shall, while afloat, carry a flag at the
the mast head, or on a sprit or staff, or in some equally conspicuous
situation, of large dimensions, proportioned to the size of the boat, which
shall be a blue flag with a white centre, commonly called "The Blue
Peter," and shall be kept in a clean condition so as to be easily discerned
at a sufficient distance, and the boat shall also have the name of the mas-
Pilot's name and
number to be paint-
ed on mainsail
tor Pilot, or Pilot of the 2nd class for the time being painted in broad black
letters, at least 6 inches in length on the main or principal sail, and number
expressed in his license: penalty not exceeding £5, 19 V., c. 15, s. 22.

Penalty for dis
playing flag when
no pilot on board
If any boat, not having a qualified Pilot on board, carry such distinguishing flag, the owner, or master in charge displaying or carrying same shall
forfeit not exceeding £50, 19 V., c. 15, s. 23.

Pilot not to be
taken to sea without
consent
No Pilot shall be taken to sea beyond the limits of his district by the
Commanding Officers of any of Her Majesty's Ships, or by the master, or
other person having the command of any other vessel, without his free
consent, except under circumstances of unavoidable necessity, and then

over and above his Pilotage, he shall receive '10s. per diem, inclusive of the day on which the vessel passed the limit, and until he be returned to the port where he was taken on board, or until he has been discharged from the ship for a sufficient time to have enabled him to return there, 19 V., c. 15, s. 24.

In case of necessity to be paid 10s a day exclusive of pilotage

If any Pilot taking charge of a vessel, arriving inwards, or bound to any port in this Island, quits before her arrival at the place to which she is bound without the consent of the Captain, &c., unless some other duly qualified Pilot with such consent come on board and take the charge and conduct of the ship for the residue of the voyage, he shall forfeit all pay or reward to which he might be entitled, and be also subject to a penalty of £10, 19 V., c. 15, s. 25.

Pilot quitting vessel without leave during voyage inwards

The consignees or agents of any vessel from whom any money due to a qualified Pilot for pilotage has been recovered or is recoverable, or by whom any such money has been paid, may retain out of any money received or to be received on account of the vessel or owner, sufficient to discharge the pilotage, and any expenses attending the same, 19 V., c. 15, s. 26.

Consignees may retain out of moneys received for the ship, the fees for pilotage and expences

A particular description of the person of every Pilot shall be written in or endorsed on his license, by the person granting it, and any Captain. &c., on receiving a Pilot on board, shall inspect his license, and if he has reason to believe he is not the person to whom the license was granted, shall forthwith transmit a copy to the Clerk of the Peace by whom it was granted, stating the date, with such account and description of the person producing the license as may lead to the discovery of the offender, 19 V., c. 15, s, 27.

Description of the Pilot to be written on his license Captain to inspect same; his duty if he suspects the party not to be the person to whom the license was granted

Any duly qualified Pilot within the limits of his certificate may supersede in the charge of any vessel any person not qualified to act for such ship, or not authorized so to act within such limits, or acting beyond the extent of his qualification ; and every person assuming or continuing in the charge or conduct without being a duly qualified Pilot, or without being qualified to act as a Pilot within the limits in which the ship actually is, or beyond the extent of his qualification, as expressed in his certificate, after any Pilot duly qualified to act has offered to take charge, shall forfeit not exceeding £30, nor less than £10. But any person may lawfully, and without being subject to any penalty, assume or continue in charge as a Pilot, where and so long as a Pilot duly qualified has not offered to take charge or made a sign for that purpose, or where and so long as the ship is in distress, or under circumstances which render it necessary for the Master to avail himself of the best assistance at the time to be procured, 19 V., c. 15, s. 28.

Qualified pilots to supersede such as are not qualified Penalty on the latter assuming or continuing in charge after duly qualified pilot has offered When unqualified persons may act

The fees payable to the Master Pilot, or Pilot of the 2nd class for Pilotage, shall be at the rates in Schedule, 19 V., c 15, s. 29.

Rates of Pilotage

All complaints against Master or 2nd class Pilots for any misconduct or neglect in the performance of their duty, shall be heard by 2 Justices, who, upon conviction, may fine the offender not exceeding £10, or imprison him in the nearest prison for not exceeding one calendar month, and may, if they see fit, in addition, adjudge his license to be forfeited, or may suspend him from acting for such time as they deem proper. The enforcing any penalty or punishment, shall not be a bar to any recovery for damages by the party aggrieved against the Pilot, 19 V., c. 15, s. 30.

Complaints to be heard before two Justices Penalty Besides forfeiture of license or suspension Not to affect right to damages

All Differences between any Pilot and any Master, Commander, Supercargo, Owner or Consignee, of any vessel, British or Foreign, or between any Pilots respecting the pilotage of any vessels received by the Gunner of Fort Charles as after provided, shall be heard before 2 Justices who may call before them all parties, and examine them on oath, and make such award as they see just, and for enforcing their attendance, may issue their warrants under their hands and seals, authorizing any Policeman to apprehend and bring such parties before them : and for better enforcing the payment of fees due to Pilots, the Gunner of Fort Charles on affidavit of any Pilot stating the amount of fees due to him for the Pilotage of any vessel, British or Foreign, may demand from the person having charge the amount stated to be due, and on refusal or omission to pay, the vessel shall not be allowed to pass the Fort. The Gunner may deduct 6d. in the £ out of the money he receives for his trouble, paying over the remainder to the Pilot entitled to the fees; and in respect to

Differences respecting pilots' fees Two Justices may determine them Enforcement through Gunner of Fort Charles Gunner's fees Gunner may demand beforehand

fees for pilotage outwards of foreign vessels if required by pilot

Foreign vessels, the Gunner may demand, before hand, the fees of any Pilot taken on board, for the Pilotage outwards, if the Pilot requires it, 19 V., c. 15, s 31.

In Kingston Harbour Master may determine complaints with consent of parties

In cases brought for adjudication in Kingston, the Harbour Master may determine any complaints or matters in difference, where the parties are willing to leave the matter to his adjudication, and shall have the same powers as are given to 2 Justices of Kingston. 19 V., c. 15, s. 32.

Second class pilots may pilot vessels of not. exceeding 12 feet draught

Pilots of the 2nd class, under 15 V., c. 26, or to be appointed, upon the registration of their certificates, and upon entering into bond and obtaining a license, may act in that capacity in piloting vessels of a draught not exceeding 12 feet at the time of taking charge, 19 V., c. 15, s. 33.

Penalty for acting during suspension or after forfeiture of certificate

If any person suspended or adjudged to have forfeited his certificate and license, during the time of suspension, or after such adjudication takes upon himself to conduct any ship as a Pilot, he shall be liable to all the penalties, to be recovered and applied as provided against any person who pilots and conducts a ship without being qualified as a Pilot, 19 V., c. 15, s. 34.

No persons to be appointed Master Pilot until he has served as second class for 12 months at least and certified to be competent

No person shall be apppointed a Master Pilot until he has served as a 2nd class Pilot for at least 12 calendar months, and thereupon, after undergoing a further examination, and being certified to be fit and competent to assume the duties of Master Pilot, he shall be entitled to obtain a warrant or appointment for such purpose, 19 V., c. 15, s. 35.

On complaint Pilot to deliver to Clerk of the Peace his certificate and license which if forfeited or the pilot suspended are to be endorsed and delivered to the Clerk of the Peace to be cancelled or held during suspension

Previous to entering into any complaint against any Pilot, the Justices shall require him to deliver the license to the Clerk of the Peace or other Officer officiating, and if they adjudge the certificate and license to be forfeited, or the Pilot is suspended on conviction, they may endorse thereon the judgment of forfeiture or suspension, and deliver them to the Clerk of the Peace to be cancelled, if forfeited, or held by him during the period of the suspension, 19 V., c. 15, s. 36.

Recovery and application of penalties

All penalties where not otherwise declared, shall be recovered before 2 Justices, and applied one half to the Crown, the other to the informer with full costs, 19 V., c. 15, s. 37.

Service to Militia or other public or parochial duty

Pilots while acting as such shall be exempted from serving in the Militia, or in any other public or parochial duty, or office, except during Martial law, when they may be compelled to serve in any Fort nearest to their place of abode, or convenient to them in the discharge of their duty as Pilots, 19 V., c. 15, s. 38,

False evidence

False evidence punishable as perjury, 19 V., c. 15, s. 39.

H. M. S. ships not compellible to take Pilots

Not to extend to Her Majesty's vessels, as to their being compelled to take Pilots on board, 19 V., c. 15, s. 40.

SCHEDULE.

Pilots certificate

JAMAICA SS.

This is to certify that in pursuance of an Act, passed in the 19th year of Her Majesty Queen Victoria, entitled " An Act to consolidate and amend the several Acts of this Island, relating to Pilots, we whose names are hereunto subscribed, having been appointed according to the provisions of the said Act, have formed ourselves into a Board, and examined. A. B., of
touching his skill and ability in the navigation of vessels, and his knowledge of the harbours, coasts, shoals and channels, of this Island (or in and about the ports of   as the case may be) and find him duly qualified and proper to be appointed a " Master Pilot," or " Pilot of the 2nd class" for the said Island (or ports of as the case may be)

Given under our hands at   the   day of

Here follow the signatures and description of the Members of the Board.

No,   Parish of

JAMAICA, ss.

        DESCRIPTION.

Master Pilots
license

Age	
Height	
Hair	
Forehead	
Eyes	
Nose	
Mouth	
Beard	
Face	
Color	
Any other particular	

The bearer hereof, of the parish of
in the Island of Ja-
maica, whose description appears
in the margin of these Presents, is
duly qualified as a Master Pilot, to
take charge of, and conduct all Vessels bound to or sailing from the
port hereinafter mentioned (specify
them), and has on the day hereof
taken out his annual license, enabling him to act from the 1st day of
January, to the 31st day of December, 18   as required by the Act
(here set out the title of this Act).

    Given under my hand and seal,
this   day of   18

         A. B.
      Clerk of the Peace.

Second class pilots No.   Parish of
license

JAMAICA, ss.

DESCRIPTION.

Age	
Height	
Hair	
Forehead	
Eyes	
Nose	
Mouth	
Beard	
Face	
Color	
Any other particular	

The bearer hereof, of the parish of
in the Island of Ja-
maica, whose description appears
in the margin of these presents, is
duly qualified as a Pilot of the second class, to take charge of and
conduct all vessels of a draught, at
the time of taking charge of any
such vessel, not exceeding 12 feet,
and other vessels where no Master
Pilot can be had, bound to, or sailing from the port hereinafter mentioned (specify them), and has on
the day hereof taken out his annual
license, enabling him to act, from
the 1st day of January, to the 31st
day of December, 18   as required by this Act (here set out
the title of this Act).

Given under my hand and seal,
this   day of   18

A. B.
Clerk of the Peace.

FEES.

CLASSIFICATION of PORTS.	PILOTAGE.	BRITISH TONNAGE.						
		800 Tons and upwards.	500 Tons and under. 800.	350 Tons and under. 500.	250 Tons and under. 350.	200 Tons and under. 250.	150 Tons and under. 200.	Under 150 Tons.
		£ s.	£ s.	£ s.	£ s.	£ s.	£ s.	£ s.
FIRST CLASS.								
Kingston, Manchioneal }	Inwards from Sea	6 0	5 8	4 16	4 4	3 12	3 0	2 8
St. Ann's Bay & Falmouth }	Outwards to Sea	4 0	3 12	3 4	2 16	2 8	2 0	1 12
SECOND CLASS.								
All Ports not enumerated	Inwards from Sea	4 16	4 4	3 12	3 0	2 8	1 16	1 10
Above, except Port Royal	Outwards to Sea	3 4	2 16	2 8	2 0	1 12	1 4	1 0
THIRD CLASS.								
Port Royal	Inwards from Sea	4 10	3 12	3 0	2 14	2 2	1 16	1 10
	Outwards to Sea	2 16	2 8	2 0	1 16	1 8	1 4	1 0

There shall be paid for Pilotage into Old Harbour, for every Ship or Barque, £5 8s; and every Brig or Brigantine or Snow £2 14: and every Schooner or Sloop, £1 7s; A like sum also for Pilotage, out clear of the quays, or shoals, of all such Vessels.

Porters and Carriers.

To be registered

All persons who seek employment as Porters or Carriers, or other transient job work by the day or portions of a day, in Kingston or any other town, shall give in their names and places of abode to the Clerk of the Common Council, if resident in Kingston, or if in any other town to the Clerk of the Vestry, or if such persons reside out of any town, but usually seek employment in Kingston or any other town, they shall be registered in the town where they seek employment, and in the registry the true place of abode shall be described; and in addition, it shall be stated that he usually seeks employment in the city of Kingston, or other town, **Distinguishing number** as the case may be, and every registration shall be distinguished by a separate number; and whenever any person so seeking employment changes **Change of residence** his place of residence, he shall give notice thereof, and the new place of residence to the Clerk of the Common Council or the Vestry, within 14 days after such change, and they shall immediately insert such change of residence in the registry, 1 V., c. 38, s. 1.

Certificate

Whenever any such person applies to be registered, the Clerk of the Common Council or Vestry shall grant him a certificate that he has been duly registered in the registry book of the city or town, and therein also express the number of the register, and at the time of the first registration de- **Badge** liver to him a distinguishing badge, to be determined upon by the Common Council or Justices and Vestry, containing the initial letter or letters of the town, and the distinguishing number of the registration; and upon **Endorsment of change of residence** every registration of the change of residence, shall endorse upon such cer- **Fee for badge for the parish** tificate a memorandum thereof. No fee or reward shall be taken for the registration, certificate, endorsement, &c., but for every distinguishing badge the Clerk of the Common Council or Vestry shall demand and be paid for the use of the parish 5s. (3s. stg.), 1 V., c. 38, s. 2.

Copies of registration, &c., to be furnished to Police Officer or Chief

The Clerk of the Common Council shall, within 14 days after the registration of any person, or of his change of residence, furnish the Police Officer of the City, and the Clerk of the Vestry of any other parish shall, within the like period, after any such registration, furnish to the Chief or Head Constable of the town, a true copy of the entry; and such Police Officer or Chief Constable shall thereupon immediately enter every such original registration. in a book to kept by him, in alphabetical order, and shall also immediately after he is furnished with a copy of the entry of the change of residence of every such person, also enter such change of residence in such books, 1 V., c. 38, s. 3.

Fresh annual certificates

Between 1st and 15th January in every year, there shall be a new registration of all persons so seeking employment, which shall be considered as an original registration, and entail upon all persons so seeking employment, and upon the Clerk of the Common Council and Police Officer of Kingston, and Clerk of the Vestry and Chief Constable of the other towns the same duties as are required to be performed in respect of the original registrations; and no registration or certificate shall be of any force after the 15th January next ensuing its date, 1 V., c. 38, s. 4.

Stations for persons seeking employment

The Common Council and Justices, and Vestry shall appoint and set apart particular places or stations in each town for the resort of persons so registered, and desirous of seeking employment while unemployed, 1 V., c. 38, s. 5.

Badge to be worn

Every person so registered shall, while employed or seeking employment, constantly wear exposed on his left arm, the badge furnished to him **And certificate ready to be produced** at the time of registration, and shall also have ready to be produced, if required, his certificate of registration, and actually produce it to any person **Registered persons to be preferred for employment** offering to hire or employ him. It shall not be lawful for any person to hire or employ as a Porter or Carrier, or for any transient job, for which persons are usually hired by the day, or portions thereof, any other than some person so registered, if, at the time the services of any unregistered person are engaged, there was any registered person at the station waiting for and desirous of employment; and in case of complaint of any infraction of this Act, in the last mentioned respect, the burthen of proving that there was no registered person waiting for and desirous of employment, shall be **Servants** thrown upon the party complained of. Not to extend to the hiring or employment of servants or domestics, 1 V., c. 38, s. 6.

No person so registered shall lend out or transfer his certificate or badge to any other person, on any pretence, and in case of any such loan or transfer both the owner and the borrower or transferree, shall be punished, 1 V., c. 38, s. 7.

Certificate or badge not to be transferred

If any person so registered lose or destroy his certificate or badge, or it become worn out, torn or defaced by wear or accident, or otherwise, and he makes satisfactory proof, (by declaration, 6 V., c. 24,) before a Justice of the parish in which he is registered, of his identity as the individual named in the original registration, the Clerk of the Common Council or Vestry shall, from time to time, renew such certificate or badge, similarly numbered as the original registration, on payment to him of 2s. 6d. (1s. 6d. sterling) for his own use. Before any certificate or badge is renewed, the party applying shall make (a declaration, 6 V., c. 24,) before a Justice to that effect, and that it has not been transferred or delivered by him, or with his knowledge or privity to any other person whomsoever ; or if it has not been lost or destroyed, he shall deliver it up to the Clerk, 1 V., c. 38, s. 8.

Renewal of certificate or badge Declaration, 6 V., c. 24

Fee

Whenever any Clerk of the Common Council or Vestry renews any certificate, he shall on the face thereof express that it is a renewed certificate and the date of renewal, and insert a memorandum thereof in the original book of registration, and give immediate notice in writing to the Police Officer or Chief Constable, who shall also insert a similar memorandum in the book to be kept by him; and no other than the lastly renewed certificate shall be of any effect. Any person having in his possession a certificate prior in date to that lastly renewed, as also the person who has been registered, shall be liable to be apprehended and punished, unless they give satisfactory proof that the possession had not been parted with, or obtained contrary to the spirit and intention of this Act, 1 V., c. 38, s. 9.

Renewal to be expressed on certificate
Noted on the register and communicated to Police Officer, &c., and entered by them
No other effectual
Having prior certificate in possession

The Common Council and Justices, and Vestry may grant remuneration by way of salary, to be paid out of the parochial funds to the Clerk of the Common Council and Police Officer or Clerks of the Vestries, and Chief Constables for the duties imposed upon them, 1 V., c. 38, s. 10.

Salaries to Clerks &c.

If any person whatsoever shall, in any respect, offend against the provisions of this Act, the Sitting Magistrates of Kingston, or any 2 Justices in the other parishes, may punish the offender by fine not exceeding £5, (£3 stg.) to be levied by distress and sale, and in default of payment by committal, with or without hard labor, not exceeding 14 days, 1 V., c. 38, s. 11.

Penalties

Possessory Title after 7 Years.

All persons who hold or shall hold any Lands or Hereditaments under any Deed, Will or Conveyance, or under any patent, for which Quit Rent has or shall be paid for 20 years at least from the date, though the same or any assignment be lost, or who hold or shall hold under any order, and have paid or shall pay Quit Rent for the time aforesaid, and have been or shall be in the actual peaceable and quiet possession and occupation of such Lands and Hereditaments for 7 years, from their first possessing the same, either by themselves or those under whom they claim, (or who by mistake have fallen. cleared, improved by building, cultivated, or fenced such Lands, whether belonging to H. M. or any other person, added 14 G. 3, c. 5,) shall hold and enjoy the same against H. M., and all other persons, 4 G. 2, c. 4, s. I, explained by 14 G. 3, c. 5.

Persons holding lands under deed, will, or conveyance or under patent or order on which quit rents have been paid for 20 years
In actual quiet possession and occupation for 7 years
By themselves or those under whom they claim or who by mistake have fallen and cultivated the lands
To hold the same against the Crown and all persons

The right and title of any person under 21, woman under coverture and persons of unsound memory excepted, provided they respectively bring their actions for such estate within 3 years after the person under age attains 21, or woman under coverture becomes sole, or persons of unsound memory become compos mentis. Act not to confirm or give title to any person seized or possessed of any Lands conveyed or devised to any charitable use, mortgagee or lessee of any Lands mortgaged or in lease, or to any other person, to any Lands possessed as attorney or guardian, or otherwise, in right of another, or to any particular use, trust, curtesy, dower, estate for

Except infants, women under coverture and persons of unsound mind, who bring

3 Y

years, or for life or entail, or to any person claiming under any mortgagee or lessee, attorney or guardian, or other person seized or possessed, to the use of, or in trust for another, or under such tenants by the curtesy in dower for years or for life, but the same shall remain and be to all intents and purposes as before this Act, 4 G. 2, c. 4, s. 1.

Sidenote: actions within 3 years after removal of disabilities

Sidenote: Not to confirm titles of persons seized to charitable uses, Mortgagees, Lessees, Attorneys, Guardians, Trustees, Tenants, by curtesy, dower, tenants for years or life or in tail

---

Pounds.

The Justices and Vestry of each parish shall erect one or more Pounds at an expense not exceeding in each parish in the whole £100, 15 V., c. 11, s. 2.

Sidenote: Justices and Vestry to erect pounds

And shall repair and keep them in good condition at an expense not exceeding in any parish in any one year £50, 15 V., c. 11, s. 3.

Sidenote: And keep them in repair

And shall select the most central and convenient places as the sites for erecting the Pounds, attention being paid to the convenience of the parishioners and the proper supervision and examination of the Pounds; and shall appoint committees for the purpose, whose duty it shall be to visit each Pound once at least every quarter, and report the state and condition to each quarterly Vestry, with such recommendations as they deem necessary for their good government, 15 V., c. 11, s., 4.

Sidenote: To be erected in central places

Sidenote: Committees of Vestry to visit And report thereon quarterly

And shall appoint to each Pound a proper person to be keeper, residing on or in the immediate neighborhood; the salary of each keeper not to exceed £60 per annum, payable quarterly; with power to remove or dismiss any who misbehave or are guilty of impropriety or neglect of duty and appoint others. In case of the death of any Pound-keeper, the Custos or resident senior officer may appoint a person to take charge of the Pound, until the appointment of a new Pound-keeper by the Justices and Vestry, 15 V., c. 11, s. 5.

Sidenote: Appointment of poundkeepers

Sidenote: Salary

Sidenote: Removal

Sidenote: In case of death Custos to appoint a person to take charge until appointment

The owner or occupier, or his agent, of any plantation, pen, or other premises who finds any horned cattle, or any horse, mare, gelding, colt, mule, ass or sheep trespassing upon any land belonging to or in his possession, may, if he thinks proper, take and convey, or cause, &c. to the nearest Pound, the stock so found trespassing, and the keeper of the Pound shall receive them, and pay to the party bringing them the sums in Schedule A, as remuneration for his trouble. Where persons take up any description of stock, and instead of sending the whole at once to the Pound, detain and send them singly, or one by one, or in portions, thereby unnecessarily increasing the expense to the owner, they shall, on conviction before 2 Justices, forfeit equal to double the amount paid by the Pound-keeper upon stock so sent in, and in default of payment and costs, the Justices shall issue their warrant, directing any lawful constable to levy the amount on the offender's goods, and in the absence of sufficient goods whereon to levy or recover the forfeiture and costs, shall commit the offender for not exceeding 10 days, 15 V., c. 11, s. 6.

Sidenote: Stock trespassing may be sent to the nearest pound

Sidenote: And receive from poundkeeper the sums in Schedule The whole to be sent at once

Sidenote: Penalty

No person when taking any horned cattle, &c., to the Pound shall ride or suffer any to be ridden. Any person transgressing in these respects, or violently striking, beating, bruising, or otherwise ill-using or injuring any stock, when taking them to the Pound, or at any other time whilst in his possession, shall, on conviction before 2 Justices, forfeit not exceeding £5, 15 V., c. 11, s. 7.

Sidenote: Strays not to be ridden or illused on the way to the pound or while in party's possession

No person taking up stock found trespassing on land belonging to or in his possession, shall detain or keep them in his possession, without sending them to the Pound, longer than 24 hours, except when Sunday intervenes. Penalty not exceeding £5 for every stray so detained, 15 V., c. 11, s. 8.

Sidenote: Stock not to be detained longer than 24 hours except when Sunday intervenes

Before any Pound-keeper receives any stock into the Pound, he shall require the party bringing them, to state his name and place of abode, and the name and place of abode of the person who sent them, and the name of the place, and the day and time where and when found, all which he shall enter in a book for the purpose. Any person wilfully making any false statement, or giving any false answers to any questions put to him to elicit the above information shall, on conviction, forfeit not exceeding 20s.; and in such book the Pound-keeper shall also enter the date and hour

Sidenote: Questions to be put and entries made by pound keeper in his books before receiving stock Penalty for falsely answering

when the stock is received, the color, mark if any, and description, and the amount paid as remuneration to the pa   bringing the same; such book to be open to public inspection from 10 a.m. to 4 p. m., Sunday excepted, without fee or reward. Any Pound-keeper guilty of any neglect or refusal in making the necessary entries, or shewing the book when required to do so, or wilfully making any false or incorrect entries, shall forfeit not exceeding £20, and be liable, besides, to dismissal, 15 V. c. 11, s. 9. *Book open to inspection*

Every Pound-keeper shall demand and receive for every head of horned cattle, horse, mare, gelding and mule, on delivery, 3s.; for every ass, 2s.; for every sheep, 1s. for poundage; for the feed and care of every horse, mare, gelding or mule, 1s. 6d.; every head of horned stock, and for every ass, 1s.; for every sheep, 6d. for every day the stock are impounded, with the charge for advertising, if paid. All advertisements shall be published in the "Jamaica Gazette," and no other newspaper while it continues to be published. Where stock have been in the Pound longer than a day, no charge shall be made for feed for the day on which they are taken out, if by or before 10 a. m.; after that hour, and before 6 p. m., half a-day's feed, and no more, shall be charged on that day. Any Pound-keeper demanding or receiving any higher amount for poundage or feed, shall forfeit 20s. for every offence, 15 V., c. 11, s. 10. *Rates to be paid for poundage, feeding, and advertising* *Penalty*

He shall not charge or receive any payment for the feed of any stock taken out of the Pound within 2 hours after being brought, nor more than at the rate of half a-day's feed, if taken out during the same day. Penalty, 20s. No charge shall be made for poundage or feed of the follower of any mare, cow, or ass less than 6 months old. No stock shall be delivered until the amount paid for bringing the same to the Pound, and the poundage, feed and advertising are paid, 15 V., c. 11, s. 11. *Rates for feed when taken out same day* *No charge for followers under 6 Months* *No stock to be delivered until all charges including bringing in stock are paid*

The Pound-keeper shall keep all entire horses, mules, asses, bulls and rams separate and apart from each other, and from the other animals, and see that each stray is supplied daily with good wholesome fodder and water, viz. 3 bundles of grass of 28lbs. each to every horse, mare, gelding or mule, and 2 bundles of the same weight to each head of horned stock and ass, and shall enter each day in the Pound book of strays the quantity of grass delivered into the Pound, and weekly declare to the truth thereof before a Justice; and upon proof of his neglect or inattention to this part of his duty to the Justices and Vestry in Quarterly or Special Vestry assembled, they shall dismiss him, and appoint another; but if he can shew that a sufficient quantity of fodder and water was not supplied by the Justices and Vestry, he shall not be dismissed, but the persons whose stock was kept without a sufficient quantity of fodder and water, may proceed against them, 15 V., c. 11, s. 12. *Entire stock to be kept apart* *Fodder and water* *Entries in books thereof* *Penalty for neglect, dismissal* *Unless the insufficiency is the fault of the Vestry*

Every Pound-keeper shall publish once a-week in the "Jamaica Gazette," during its existence, and thereafter in any paper to be named by the Justices and Vestry, a correct list of all the strays in the pound under his charge, describing them as fully and particularly as possible, which shall appear for 4 weeks consecutively. Sheep shall not be advertised for more than 2 weeks. Penalty for omission, not exceeding £5. No stray shall be advertised, until it has been 24 hours in the pound, 15 V., c. 11, s. 13. *Advertisements of strays* *For 4 weeks* *Sheep 2 weeks* *After 24 hours in pound*

No Pound-keeper shall hire out, let, use or employ for his own benefit, or permit, or suffer any other person to do so for his benefit, any stock in the pound under his charge. Penalty, £5, and liability to immediate dismissal. 15 V., c. 11, s. 14. *No stock sent to the pound to be used, &c*

Every Pound-keeper shall, on the 1st day of every month, make out a return of the number of strays received into the Pound, the money paid to the parties bringing them, and of the quantity of fodder and water received for their use during the past month (Form Schedule B) Also a return of the number of strays claimed and delivered up, the moneys received for bringing them to the Pound, and for the poundage, feed and advertising, and for strays sold, and of all moneys paid to the Parochial Treasurer (Collector of Dues) during the past month (Form Schedule C), and deliver up such returns to the Clerk of the Vestry, on or before the 7th of *Monthly returns* *To Clerk of the Vestry* the month, to be filed in his office for the use of the Justices and Vestrymen, and such other persons as may desire to refer to them. Wilfully making a false or incorrect return, or neglecting or omitting to make any return: Penalty not exceeding £5, 15 V., c. 11, s. 15.

Penalty

Stocks suffering under infectious disease not to be received, if afterwards, &c., to be destroyed and buried or burnt by order of a Justice at parish expense

No Pound-keeper shall receive any horse, mare, gelding, mule, ass or horned stock into the Pound, suffering from any infectious disease or distemper, or any usually considered so. If any stock afterwards become so, the Keeper shall apply immediately to a Justice, who, upon proof by competent judges that the stock is diseased or distempered, and ought not to be kept in the pound, shall authorize him to destroy it, and bury or burn the carcase, or cause it to be done, as also to pay such sum for burying or burning as he deems reasonable, and to charge the same in his account with the parish. The authority to destroy the stray, as well as to pay for burying or burning the carcase, shall be in writing signed by the Justice, and left with the Poundkeeper, 15 V., c. 11, s. 16.

Stock to be advertised for sale

Sale

Payment of proceeds

Poundkeeper not to purchase

Every Pound-keeper shall, with the consent of a Justice, cause all stock remaining in the Pound, that have been advertised, (s. 13) to be advertised for public sale at the nearest public place, or such as the Justices and Vestry direct; and on a given day and hour to be named in the advertisement, and at such place, day and hour put to sale, and sell or cause, &c., all such strays to the highest and best bidder, and for the most money to be had, and pay over the amount of sales to the persons the Justices and Vestry appoint to receive same (Collector of Dues) without deduction. The Pound-keeper shall not be directly or indirectly concerned in the purchase of any stray sold by him. Penalty, £10, besides relinquishing the purchase, 15 V., c. 11, s. 17.

Owner entitled to any surplus on proof of property within 3 months after sale

The owner of any stray sold, who, within 3 months of such sale, proves to the satisfaction of the Justices and Vestry that it was his property, shall be entitled to the nett proceeds of the sale, after deducting the poundage, feed, advertisement if paid, and other expenses, if there be any surplus remaining, 15 V., c. 11, s. 18.

Justices and Vestry to contract for the supply daily of fodder & water to pounds

Penalty

Excuse

Inhabitants, witnesses

The Justices and Vestry shall at convenient periods enter into contract or agreement with persons willing to engage with them to furnish such quantities of good wholesome grass, hay, or other fodder, and water, as may be daily required for the use of the stock, in each Pound, and pay for the same out of the parochial funds. Every Justice and Vestryman of a parish, the Justices and Vestry of which omit or neglect, or refuse to engage for and secure the regular supply of fodder and water, shall forfeit and pay £20, to be recovered in any Court of Record, one moiety of which to go to the person who sues, and the other to the poor. Upon proof by any Justice or Vestryman, that he voted for and was desirous that fodder and water should be supplied agreeably to this Act, be shall not be liable to the penalty. Any inhabitant may be a witness, 15 V., c. 11, s. 19.

On failure by Justices and Vestry the committee or a member may procure them

But not through the Poundkeeper

When the Justices and Vestry fail to procure contracts for the supply of any Pound with fodder or water, the Committee under s. 4, or any Member may purchase or make arrangements for the supply, but in no case shall the Pound-keeper be permitted himself to supply, or procure fodder or water from others: penalty on Pound-keeper offending 20s besides being liable to dismissal by the Justices and Vestry, 15 V., c. 11, s. 20.

Driving of stock or making gaps in fences, &c., to impound strays

Penalty

Any person who leads or drives any horned or other stock from any Plantation, Penn or other Property, not belonging to him or in his possession, or belonging to or in his employer's possession, on the public Highway, or any adjoining Property, for the purpose of impounding them as strays or stock trespassing, or who cuts, breaks or removes any fence or enclosure, or makes gaps therein or in any division wall or fence to enable stock to stray or trespass, with intent to impound them, shall, on conviction before 2 Justices, forfeit, not exceeding £5 or be imprisoned with or without hard labor, not exceeding 60 days, 15 V., c. 11, s. 21.

The **Keeper** of any Pound shall, on the 7th of every month, pay, or cause, &c., to the person appointed by the Vestry to receive same (Collector of Dues) the balance of all sums he has received during the previous month, as such Pound-keeper, for the poundage, feed and advertising stock, and for the sale of all such as remain unclaimed and are sold in consequence, after deducting the amounts paid to parties bringing stock to the Pound, In default of payment for more than 10 days, he shall be liable to a penalty not exceeding £20, and to be dismissed at the discretion of the Justices and Vestry. The money so paid over shall form part of the parochial funds, and be applied in payment of the expenses of the Pounds in the first instance, 15 V., c. 11, s. 22. *Monthly payments over of balances in Pound keeper's hands*

Penalty

Moneys parochial funds applicable in first instance to expenses of pounds

Rescuing or taking away by force any Stock from the custody of the person by whom the same was taken up or is being taken to the Pound: penalty for every head of Stock rescued, &c. not exceeding £5, 15 V., c. 11, s. 23. *Rescuing, &c., Stock taken up on being taken to the pound*

If any person who has been duly called upon according to Law to make, renew, or repair a line fence, refuses or neglects to do so after having been called upon, he shall be debarred from claiming damage for trespass, and from impounding the Stock of the person who made the requisition. Penalty, 20s, recoverable before 2 Magistrates, 15 V., c. 11, s. 24. *After call to repair line fences, persons debarred from damages for trespass or impounding stock*

All penalties, the recovery of which is not pointed out, shall be recovered before 2 Justices, and levied on the offender's goods; and in default of goods whereon to levy, the Justices shall sentence the parties to be imprisoned for not exceeding 60 days, 15 V., c. 11, s. 25.

SCHEDULE.

	£	s.	d.	
For every Cow, Calf, Bull, Heifer, Steer, Horse, Mare, Gelding, Colt, Mule or Ass, if brought in singly	0	1	6	*Charges to be paid to Persons taking stock to the pound*
If 3 brought in together, at the rate each of	0	1	0	
Above 3 brought in together, at the rate each of	0	0	6	
For 5 or less number of Sheep	0	1	6	
Every additional Sheep, where the number exceeds 5	0	0	3	

RETURN

A Return of the Number of Strays received into the Pound under my Charge, of the Sums of Money paid to Parties bringing them to it, and of the Quantity of Fodder and Water received for their use, between the   day of   and the   day of   18

Date when Received.	Number of Horses and Mares.	Number of Mules.	Number of Asses.	Number of Horned Stock.	Number of Sheep.	Amount paid to Parties bringing them.	No. of bundles of Fodder of 28lbs. received Daily.	No. of Imperial Gallons of Water received Daily.	From whom the Fodder and Water were received.
1									
2									
3									
4									
5									
6									
7									
8									
9									
10									
11									
12									
13									
14									
15									
16									
17									
18									
19									
20									
21									
22									
23									
24									
25									
26									
27									
28									
29									
30									
31									

B. s. 15]

I, _____ do hereby certify that the foregoing is a correct Return of Strays received into the Pound under my charge, of the Sums of Money paid by me to Parties bringing them to the same, and of the quantity of Fodder and Water received by me for their use, daily, during the Month of _____ 18 .

A. B.

A Return of the Number of Strays Delivered up, and of the Sums of Money Received and Paid by Order of the Justices and Vestry by me, as Pound Keeper, between the ___ day of ___ and the ___ day of ___ 18

Date when Delivered.	No. of Horses and Mares Delivered.	No. of Mules Delivered.	No. of Asses Delivered.	No. of Horned Stock Delivered.	No. of Sheep Delivered.	Amount Paid for bringing same to Pound.	Amount Received for Poundage.	Amount Received for Feed.	Amount Received for Advertising.	Amount Received for Strays Sold.	Total Received.	Amount Paid by the Order of the Justices and Vestry.
1												
2												
3												
4												
5												
6												
7												
8												
9												
10												
11												
12												
13												
14												
15												
16												
17												
18												
19												
20												
21												
22												
23												
24												
25												
26												
27												
28												
29												
30												
31												

[C., s. 15]

I, ___ do hereby certify that the foregoing is a correct Return of the number of Strays delivered up, and the Sums of Money received and paid by me, as Pound-Keeper, between the ___ day of ___ and the ___ day of ___ 18

A. B.

Prisons.

County Goal Surry

A Goal shall be built in Kingston for the County of Surry, 32 G. 2, c. 3, s. 1.

Cornwall

That of Montego Bay shall be the County Goal of Cornwall, 56 G. 3, c. 20.

Parochial Gaols

The Justices and Vestries of parishes remote from County Goals were empowered to purchase land and build Goals or places of confinement for offenders within their respective districts, 14 G. 3, c. 6.

To be maintained at the public expense

Prisoners sentenced by the Supreme or Assize Courts to Houses of Correction, or whose sentence shall be commuted to hard labor in such Prisons shall be maintained at the public expense 1 V., c. 28, s. 7.

Gaolers to deliver lists of prisoners to Judges of Circuit Courts

Goalers shall deliver to the presiding Judge, Attorney-General and Clerk of the Court on the 1st day of each Circuit Court, a list of the prisoners in the County Goal, or prison of such Court, 19 V., c. 31, s. 3.

Prisons abolished

The prisons of Vere, St. John, Port-Royal, St. David, and Manchioneal in St. Thomas in the East, shall cease to be acknowledged or used as Prisons after 28th March, 1843, 6 V., c. 52, s. 1.

Those of St. George, St. Mary (since re-established, 28 V., c. 22, s. 1,) St. Ann, Westmoreland, St. Elizabeth and Clarendon, upon the removal of the Prisoners, 6 V., c. 52, s. 2.

These maintained

The following Prisons shall be maintained, viz; Portland, St. Thomas in the Vale, Trelawny, the Female Prison of St. James, Hanover, Manchester, St. Catherine, St. Thomas in the East, 6 V., c. 52, s. 3.

Lock up houses

The discontinued Prisons shall be used only as lock up houses, for keeping persons charged with offences before summary trial, or committal by the Magistrates for trial, and as Police Stations, and shall be under the superintendence of the parochial authorities, 6 V., c. 52, s. 7.

Female Penitentiary

A portion of the General Penitentiary Kingston, shall be appropriated to the reception and confinement of females sentenced to imprisonment in the Penitentiary, and shall be the Female Penitentiary of the Island for the reception of convicted female Felons and other female offenders subject thereto, 16 V., c. 23.

Short title

The Penal Servitude Act, 1855, 18 V., c. 22, s. 1.

Licenses to prisoners to be at large

The Governor may grant a license to any convict sentenced to imprisonment in the Penitentiary, to be at large in the Island, or such part thereof as shall be expressed in the license during such portion of his term of imprisonment, and upon such conditions as to him shall seem fit, with power at pleasure to revoke or alter it, 18 V., c. 22, s. 2.

During which period he shall not be liable to be imprisoned by reason of his sentence, but may go at large according to the terms of the license, 18 V., c. 22, s. 3.

After undergoing half the sentence

No such license shall be granted before the Convict has undergone one half of the sentence under which he has been imprisoned, 18 V., c. 22, s. 4.

On revocation of license convict to be recommitted

If any license is revoked, the Governor may signify the same by his Secretary to the nearest Justice, and require him to issue his warrant, under his hand and seal, for the apprehension of the convict to whom it was granted; and the Justice shall issue his warrant accordingly, which may be executed by any Policeman or Constable to whom it is delivered, or transferred in any part of the Island without endorsement, and the convict shall be brought as soon as conveniently may be before such or some other Justice, who shall thereupon make out his warrant, under his hand and seal, for the recommitment of the convict to the General Penitentiary, and who shall be so recommitted, and thereupon be remitted to, and undergo the residue of his original sentence as if no license had been granted, (Forms of Warrant of apprehension and commitment, Schedule) 18 V., c. 22, s. 5.

Conditions of license Service in agricultural labour for 3-4ths of the period 1-4 to be remitted in the event of good behaviour

Conditions to be contained in every license, in addition to or independently of others; 1st.—That the convict shall be bound to serve as an agricultural labourer such person as the Governor shall from time to time appoint, for 3-4ths of the period for which the license shall be granted. 2nd.—In the event of good behaviour, the remaining fourth shall be given up to the convict, and the production of the license shall in such case be equivalent to evidence of a full pardon. 3rd.—He shall be bound to serve as such as a labourer

To serve 6 days a week

6 consecutive days (except Sunday, Good Friday and Christmas day)

in each week, and 9 hours a day, unless prevented by sickness or excused by his employer. 4th.—The employer shall pay him at the rate of 9d for every day of labour, and provide him wholesome lodging, medical attendance, when sick, by a qualified practitioner, and medicines and medical comforts as may be ordered by the medical attendant; and on the first entrance into service, he shall be supplied by his employer with a decent new suit of clothes of oznaburgh of a pattern usual amongst agricultural labourers, 18 V., c. 22, s. 6.

To be paid 9d a day, lodging, medicine, &c., a suit of clothes

In case of neglect of work, absence without leave of employer or his agent, absconding, or any misconduct, on the complaint on oath of the employer or agent, any Justice may issue his warrant to bring the convict before two Justices, who, if the complaint is established, may re-commit the convict to the Penitentiary by warrant, and he shall undergo the residue of his original sentence, and be incapable of receiving any further license, 18 V., c. 22, s. 7.

In case of misconduct to be re-committed

In case of the breach by any employer or his agent of any condition before contained, or any other condition in the license, any Justice, on complaint of the convict on oath, may cause the employer or agent to be summoned before two Justices, who shall hear the matter, and adjudicate and enforce their judgment in the like manner, and by the like process as complaints and judgments under the Masters and Servants' Act, 5 V., c. 43, and the proceedings shall be by them certified to the Governor, who may determine the service, and assign the services of the convict to another employer for the residue of the period, 18 V., c. 22, s. 8.

Breach of contract by employer

Act not to affect the prerogative of mercy, 18 V., c. 22, s. 9.

SCHEDULE, 18 V., c. 22.

To the Constable of   and to all other Peace Officers
in the Parish of

Warrant to apprehend; s. 7

Whereas it hath been duly certified by direction of His Excellency the Governor, that (&c., stating the certificate). These are therefore to command you in Her Majesty's name, forthwith to apprehend the said A. B., and to bring him before (me) or some other Justice or Justices of the Peace in and for the parish in which he shall be apprehended, to be dealt with according to law.

Given under my hand this   day of   in the
year of our Lord   at   in
the parish aforesaid.

L. S.

To the Constable of   and to the Keeper of the Common
Gaol or other Prison at   in the parish of

Warrant of commitment, s. 7

Whereas by warrant under my hand (or under the hand of
) dated the   day of   after
reciting that it had been certified by the direction of His Excellency the Governor (&c., as in the certificate) it is commanded to the Constable of   and all other Peace Officers of the said parish, in Her Majesty's name, forthwith to apprehend the said A. B., and to bring him before (me) or some other Justice or Justices of the Peace in and for the parish in which he shall be apprehended, to be dealt with according to law : And whereas the said A. B. hath been apprehended under and by virtue of the said warrant, and being now brought before (me) it is hereupon duly proved to me upon oath, that the said A. B. is the same person who is named and charged in and by the said recited warrant, These are therefore to command you the said Constable, in Her Majesty's name, forthwith to take and safely convey the said A. B. to the General Penitentiary in Kingston, and there to deliver him to the Keeper thereof, together with this precept, to be there safely kept under his original sentence, or until he shall be thence delivered by due course of law.

Given under my hand, this   day of
one thousand eight hundred and

3 z

The Convict Labor Payment Act, 1855, 18 V., c. 23, s. 1.

Short title

Payment by the public and parishes for convict labor

8d. for every day of labor shall be paid to the Receiver-General for every Convict employed or worked upon the public roads or thoroughfares, or upon any undertaking of a public or parochial nature, under any Act authorizing such employment or working, 18 V., c. 23, s. 2.

Contracts with Inspector of Prisons

Or according to the terms of any contract, for any particular work which the Inspector of Prisons is authorized to enter into with the sanction of the Governor and Executive Committee, 24 V., c. 19, s. 2.

How payments are to be made

Such payments in respect of the accounts for labor on roads or thoroughfares, to be secured and made to the Receiver-General out of the funds paid for the purposes, and to be charged to the respective parishes in which such labor is employed. Where such labor is employed upon any other undertaking of a public or parochial nature, payment at the rate aforesaid shall be made out of the funds granted for public works, or the moneys raised and paid to the Receiver-General on account of the parishes, according as the undertaking is of a public or parochial nature, 18 V., c. 23, s. 3.

Quarterly returns to Receiver-General from Inspector

County Surveyors, Clerk Vestry, Clerk Commissioners of Highways, Clerk Common Council

To enable him to charge the respective accounts

The Inspector of Prisons shall make, on oath, a return to the Receiver-General within 10 days after 28th March, 30th June, 30th September, and 31st December, of the labor performed by convicts in each parish during the preceding quarter, specifying the respective nature of the works or undertakings upon which such labor has been employed. Each Surveyor of public works for the county, the Clerk of each Vestry, and Clerk of each Board of Commissioners of Highways and Bridges and the Clerk of the Common Council of Kingston, shall make a like return at the like periods to the Receiver-General, who shall, by means of the several returns, ascertain the sums chargeable for convict labor, and the funds out of or against which they are chargeable, and pay or charge the same accordingly, and make entries thereof in the respective accounts, 18 V., c. 23, s. 4.

Extension of powers to employ convict labor

For the more extended and useful employment of Prison labor, the Governor and Executive Committee may sanction the employment of any male convict in the General Penitentiary or any Prison, in or upon any public or parochial work or undertaking, or under any contract agreeably to 24 V., c. 19, s. 2, (sup.) or under any contract with any person, but with such limit only, as to distance from the Penitentiary or Prison to which the convict may be committed, as the Governor and Executive Committee may at any time and in any case direct, 28 V., c. 22, s. 8.

Buildings and tents for convicts so employed

The Governor with such advice may sanction the hiring of any suitable buildings, or the purchase of the materials for, and the erection of suitable moveable buildings, or the purchase of tents as in any case they approve of, for the convenient location and secure custody, and healthy lodgment of convicts so employed, 28 V., c. 22, s. 9.

Short title

The Prisons' Consolidation Act, 1856, 20 V., c. 11, s. 1.

Interpretation
Prison

Superintendent Officer

Prisoner

Hard labour

Labour

"Prison" shall mean the General or Female Penitentiary, District Prison, House of Correction, County or other Gaol, and any Convict or Prison Ship; "Superintendent," the Jailor, keeper, or person in charge of a Prison; "Officer," any person holding any office in or connected with any Prison, and any Boatswain, Under-keeper, Turnkey, Assistant or Guard, or person employed in any Prison (other than as a domestic servant) under any Superintendent to do duty by day or night, or to keep watch; "Prisoner," any person sentenced to or confined in any Prison under any sentence of a Court or warrant of a Justice, or for want of bail or sureties, or otherwise detained by legal authority; "Hard Labor," labor on roads and streets, at the Quarry and in the Brick-yard, and in breaking and crushing stones and bones, (also labor on the tread-wheel, at the crank, and at shot-drill respectively, 28 V., c. 22, s. 10); "Labor," any other description of labor, 20 V., c. 11, s.2.

General and Female Penitentiaries Brickyard and Stone Quarry at Rock Fort

The County Gaols, Kingston, St Jago de la Vega and Montego Bay

Prisons in Portland, St Thomas in the Vale, Trelawny, St James, Hano-

The lands and buildings comprising or belonging or attached to the General and Female Penitentiaries, and the lands and buildings of the Brick yard and Stone Quarry at Rock Fort, attached thereto and connected therewith in the parish of Kingston, and the lands and buildings composing or belonging to the County Gaols in Kingston, St. Jago de la Vega and Montego Bay, and the lands and buildings respectively composing or belonging, or attached to the Prisons in Portland, St. Thomas in the Vale, Trelawny, St. James, Hanover, Manchester, St. Catherine and St. Thomas in the East shall continue subject to the superintendence of the Executive

Committee, performing the functions of the Commissioners for superintending the buildings belonging to the public, 20 V., c. 11, s. 4.

ver, Manchester, St. Catherine, and St. Thomas in the East continued under the Superintendence of the Executive Committee as Board of works

The Governor, if he thinks fit and Executive Committee, may re-establish, and for that purpose cause to be re-occupied the buildings, lands, and premises formerly occupied as a Prison at Stennett's Town, St. Mary to be designated "The St. Mary's District Prison," (for Prisoners from St. Ann, St. Mary, Metcalfe and St. George), 28 V., c. 22, s. 1.

St. Mary's District Prisons

To be used as a District Prison for the custody of convicted felons and other offenders, or in part to any convenient extent as a lock up, and for cases of commitment before trial, as the Governor and Executive Committee direct, and the buildings and premises may be altered, fitted or arranged by the like direction as shall be necessary, and in all respects the Prison shall be regulated and managed, and all the Prisoners or persons committed, and the commitments thereto, and the officers, servants and attendants shall be governed by 20 V., c. 11, and other Acts relating to Prisons, 28 V., c. 22, s. 2.

Uses

The Governor and Executive Committee may direct that any Prison may be altered, fitted or arranged, or any public buildings converted into Prisons as may seem necessary or advisable for the reception and custody of prisoners, when it may, for greater economy or better discipline or management, be advisable to remove from any other Prison; and may allow, by way of compensation to the officers, servants or attendants of any Prison from which prisoners may be so removed, and which in consequence may cease to be used as a Prison, such amount of salary, pay or wages, as the Governor, with the advice aforesaid, deems reasonable, 28 V., c. 22, s. 6.

Alteration, &c,, of other Prisons

Compensation to officers, &c., of Prisons which cease to be used

The expense of altering, fitting or arranging the buildings at Stennett's Town, or any Prison shall not exceed in the case of the Stennett's Town Prison, £100, and of any other public buildings or Prisons, £500, and shall be paid on the Governor's warrant, with the advice of the Executive Committee, out of the funds applicable for Prison expenditure, 28 V., c. 22, s. 7.

Expenses of alterations, &c

The Executive Committe, if it be found necessary for extending the boundaries of any Prison, or rendering it more secure, or for the purpose of brick making, or otherwise profitably or usefully employing the prisoners, may contract for the purchase in fee simple of any lands not under cultivation, and on which are no substantial and valuable buildings, and which are bounded by or join upon any such Prison, or are adapted for brick-making or other profitable or useful employment, to be conveyed to H. M. for the use of the public, and to be applied to the purposes aforesaid, 20 V., c. 11, s. 5

Powers of Executive Committee to purchase additional land for prisons

In case the owner or person interested in the land neglects or refuses to treat, or does not agree for the sale, or by reason of absence, incapacity or other impediment is prevented from treating or agreeing, or refuses to accept of the money offered for the purchase, the Executive Committee may give or cause, &c., to the person interested, or leave or cause, &c., at the house of the tenant or person in possession, notice in writing, signed by one of them, describing the land intended to be purchased, and purporting that the value will be adjusted and settled by a Jury, to be warned to attend at the time and place therein to be mentioned, not earlier than 30 days after such notice has been given or left, and any Justice, upon application by the Executive Committee, or any person authorized by them, and proof that notice has been so given or left, shall issue his warrant to the Provost Marshal to summon and return a Jury of 14, to meet at a time and place to be mentioned in the warrant, being that mentioned in the notice, out of whom a Jury of 7 shall be drawn by ballot, and the Justices shall summon such witnesses on both sides as are required, and if Jurors or witnesses do not attend, shall adjourn as he thinks fit, and shall require the Jury on their oath, and the Jury shall be sworn well and truly to enquire of and find the value of the land mentioned in the notice, and the respective estate and interest of every person seized and possessed thereof, or interested therein or in any part thereof, and shall assess and award the sum or sums of money to be paid for the absolute purchase in fee simple of the land and their finding shall be conclusive against all persons claiming any estate, right or interest in the land, which inquisition and proceedings of the Justice and Jury, under the hands and seals of the Provost Marshal or his Deputy, and of the Jury, shall be returned into the Secretary's Office, and recorded and kept among the records, and deemed a record, and it or a copy shall be evidence in any Court. The Justice shall administer the oath to the Jury and witnesses. If the Justice cannot attend

In case of refusal or incapacity to treat

The Executive Committee may serve notice of their intention to purchase

At a valuation by a Jury

30 days after service

A Justice to direct Provost Marshal to summon a Jury of 14

7 to be balloted

Witnesses to be summoned

Oath of Jurors

Their award final

Inquisition to be final

And recorded

Evidence, Justices to swear jury and Witnesses

Any other Justice may attend and act	on the day fixed in the notice, or on any day to which the meeting is adjourned, any other Justice shall attend, carry on and conclude the proceedings, and if they be interrupted, or do not take place at the appointed time, another warrant shall issue for instituting new proceedings from time to time until they be perfected. No person shall be sworn upon the Jury who has any interest in, or is in any way concerned for the land, 20 V., c. 11, s. 6.

Any other Justice may attend and act
Fresh proceedings

No interested person to be upon Jury

on the day fixed in the notice, or on any day to which the meeting is adjourned, any other Justice shall attend, carry on and conclude the proceedings, and if they be interrupted, or do not take place at the appointed time, another warrant shall issue for instituting new proceedings from time to time until they be perfected. No person shall be sworn upon the Jury who has any interest in, or is in any way concerned for the land, 20 V., c. 11, s. 6.

Penalty on Provost Marshal or Deputy Jurors

If the Provost Marshal or Deputy make default in any matter required to be done by him, he shall forfeit £20, to be recoverable by the Executive Committee, by action of debt at the suit of the Attorney-General on behalf of her Majesty. If any person summoned and returned upon a Jury does not appear, or refuses to be sworn, or if a Quaker to affirm, or in any manner neglects his duty, he shall, unless he shews reasonable excuse to the Presiding Justice, forfeit not exceeding £5, nor less than 40s ; the penalties to be paid to the Receiver-General in aid of the costs of the enquiry, and in addition, every Juryman shall be subject to the same regulations and penalties as if they had been returned for the trial of an issue in a Circuit Court, and had been therein guilty of the like offence, 20 V., c. 11, s. 7.

Parties summoned to give evidence

If any person summoned to give evidence, and to whom a tender of his reasonable expenses have been made, fail to appear without sufficient excuse, to be adjudged of by the Justice, or if any person (whether summoned or not) who appears, shall refuse to be examined on oath or affirmation touching the subject matter in question, he shall forfeit to the party aggrieved not exceeding £10, nor less than 40s, 20 V., c. 11, s. 8.

Jurors to be paid 1 guinea each
Provost Marshal, 3 guineas
Witnesses

Each of the Jurors warned to attend any enquiry, shall be entitled to one guinea for each case in which he attends and is sworn, and the Provost Marshal or his Deputy three guineas for each Jury warned. The witnesses who attend and give evidence shall be paid at the same rates as for attendance at Circuit Courts, by order of the Executive Committee, out of the moneys to be granted for the purposes of this Act, 20 V., c. 11, s. 9.

Money awarded to go as the land would

The money awarded by a Jury for the purchase of any land, shall be of the same nature as the land, and subject to the like uses, trusts and limitations, and rules of descent, as such lands and the rents and profits, 20 V., c. 11, s. 10.

Payment of money awarded not exceeding £20 to party entitled to rents and profits

Where the money awarded does not exceed £20, the Executive Committee may order it to be pa   to the party entitled to the rents and profits, or in case of coverture, infancy, lunacy, idiotcy or other incapacity, such money shall be paid to their husbands, guardians, committees or trustees for their use ; but if the parties so entitled, refuse to accept, the money may be invested by the Receiver-General as after directed, 20 V., c. 11, s. 11.

Exceeding £20 to be invested by Receiver General

If any money exceeding £20, which shall belong wholly or in part to any Corporate Body, Ecclesiastical or Civil, or to any trustee, executor or administrator, tenant for life or in tail, or married woman seized in her own right, or entitled to dower, or infant or issue unborn, or lunatic, or idiot, or any person under any other disability or incapacity, or not having the absolute interest in the land, or if the land is limited in strict or other settlement, or if the owner or other person having the absolute interest, refuses to accept the money awarded, or is absent from the Island, or cannot after diligent enquiry be found, or is not known or discovered, the Receiver-General shall invest, or have invested, all such money in the names jointly of the Receiver-General and Registrar in Chancery, in the Public Funds, or Parliamentary Securities of Great Britain, as may be di-

Or the Executive Committee may direct it to remain in his hands without interest

rected by the Executive Committee, in one entire sum, or in parcels ; and if it be shewn to their satisfaction to be right to delay the investment, the money may be directed to remain in the hands of the Receiver-General, but without interest, 20 V., c. 11, s. 12.

Investments subject to Chancery Deposit Acts

Every sum of money invested shall be subject to the provisions of the Chancery Deposits Acts, 18 V., c. 33, and 19 V., c. 5, so far as they apply, except 18 V., c. 33, s. 6 7 repealed, 20 V., c. 11, s. 13.

Lands Vested in the Crown upon payment

Upon payment or investment of the moneys awarded, the lands shall vest in H.M. for the use of the public, free from incumbrances, and the Executive Committee shall be entitled to, and shall have immediate possession, 20 V., c. 11, s. 14.

Maintenance of suits

The Executive Committee may maintain in the name of the Crown any actions of ejectment or other proceedings at law or in equity to recover or obtain possession, as also for any trespass or encroachment, or damage or injury committed or done thereon. 20 V., c. 11, s. 15.

The Governor may do the following acts :—

Powers of Governor

1. As vacancies occur he may appoint an Inspector of Prisons, with power to remove him and appoint another.

Appointment of Inspector

2. Also a Superintendent, Chaplain, Surgeon, Matron and such other Officers and Attendants for the General and Female Penitentiaries as he judges necessary, and a Superintendent, Surgeon, Matron, and such other Officers as he considers necessary for the Prison in Trelawny, with power to remove them. There shall be only one Chaplain and one Surgeon, (see s. 33) to the General and Female Penitentiaries. 20 V., c. 11, s. 16.

Officers of Penitentiaries and Trelawny Prison

The Governor with advice of the Executive Committee, may make any alteration which appears advisable, and calculated to effect an improved organization and system in the general management and in the staff of Officers and Attendants (except only the Surgeon and Chaplain of the General and Female Penitentiary) and thereupon appoint the necessary Officers and Attendants, and remove persons so appointed. The expenditure for salaries or wages shall in no case exceed the amount of the salaries or wages of the Officers or Attendants now employed. 24 V., c. 19, s. 1.

Governor and Executive Committee may make alterations for improvement of Penitentiaries and in staff of Officers and attendants
Not exceeding present costs

The powers of appoinment and removal of Superintendents, Surgeons, Matrons, Keepers and other Officers to any Prison, vested in the Justices of any precinct or parish, are transferred, and shall be exercised by the Governor, 28 V., c. 22, s. 5.

The Governor may appoint and remove, and fill up the places of the Officers, Servants, and Attendants of the St. Mary's District Prison, with salaries at the rates per annum : Superintendent, £120 ; Surgeon, £60 ; First Officer, £25 ; Second ditto, £20 ; Third ditto, £20 ; Matron and Nurse, £25, 28 V., c. 22, s. 3.

3. He may also visit and inspect any Prison at any time and examine the Officers and Prisoners or any of them as he thinks proper.

Inspect Prisons, &c.

4. Make rules and regulations with the advice of the Privy Council, from time to time for the government of the several Prisons, for the guidance and direction of the Officers, for the management of the prisoners, for a different classification of prisoners of each sex in any Prison, for the individual separation of all or any of the prisoners confined in such Prison, (due regard being had to the proper supervision, religious and other instruction and employment of the prisoners, and to the internal economy of the Prison) and with the advice of the Privy Council, to alter and amend any rules and regulations by this Act provided or at any time existing. Such rules and regulations and alterations or amendments, to be certified by the Clerk of the Privy Council to the Inspector of Prisons, and also to the Justices of the parish where any Prison is situate ; and at the expiration of 10 days after they have been so certified, such rules shall supersede those in this Act provided or existing at the time ; and the Inspector and Justices shall forthwith communicate all such new or altered or amended rules to the Superintendent of the Prison in which they are to have effect, and they shall be binding upon the Superintendents and all other persons, as effectually to all intents and purposes as if they had been hereby enacted.

Make and alter Rules and Regulations with advice of the Privy Council

Notifications thereof

Validity of such rules

5. Suspend or dismiss any Officers of any Prison, whose conduct appears to him to warrant it. No person so dismissed shall be eligible to any office in any Prison without the Governor's approval in writing.

Suspend or dismiss officers

6. Direct, in writing, by his Secretary as occasion may require, any prisoner confined under sentence for Felony or Misdemeanor of the 2nd class as herein defined, to be removed to some other Prison, to be imprisoned, kept and dealt with in the manner, and for the time directed by his original sentence, 20 V., c. 11, s. 16.

Removal of felons and misdemeanants of 2d class to other Prisons

Extended to the removal of any Prisoner committed for trial for Felony, subject to the terms of the warrant of original commitment, but to no other than a County Gaol, 25 V., c. 31.

Also of prisoners committed for trial for felony to a County Gaol

7. Appoint to each Prison, where there are generally confined 100 Prisoners or upwards, a Chaplain, who shall be a Clergyman of the Established Church, duly licensed by the Bishop, and to dismiss him upon his being found incompetent or negligent in the performance of his duties. Every Chaplain shall reside within one mile of the Prison to which he is appointed.

Chaplain to each prison where 100 prisoners are usually confined. Dismissal for cause
Residence

Employment of
Convicts sentenced
to hard labor on
Roads, &c.
See 18 V., c. 23,
s. 2.
24 V., c. 19, s, 2.
28 V., c. 22, s. 8, 9
8. Authorize the employment, or the working of any Convict or person sentenced to hard labor in any Prison upon the public roads or thorouhgfares, or upon any undertaking of a public or parochial nature, subject to such rules, orders, regulations and directions as to the number, class and description of Convicts, &c., who shall be ordered to work thereon, and the hours of labor, description of work, supervision and general arrangement and management, as the Governor, with the advice of the Privy Council, may frame and issue from time to time for the guidance and direction of the Superintendent of any Prison.

Appointment of
Salesman
S. 61, 64
9. Appoint a salesman in or for any Prison, to sell and dispose of all articles made in the Prison, and of any lime stone or sand ; and dismiss him, 20 V., c. 11, s. 16.

Powers of Executive Committee
Powers of the Executive Committee :—

To make contracts for Clothing, Diet, and necessaries, &c.
1. To make contracts or authorize the Inspector or Superintendents to make contracts for clothing, diet, and other necessaries, for the maintenance and support of the Prisoners, and for implements and materials to be used by them, as shall be found necessary.

Direct payment of
Accounts, &c.
When audited
See 21 V., c. 1, s.
15
Signature of orders
2. To direct payment by the Receiver-General, upon the audit by the Commissioner of the Board of Audit of the accounts for clothing, diet and other necessaries, and implements and materials, monthly, of the sums required to discharge such accounts, and to pay the salaries and hire of the Officers and other charges authorized, such orders to be signed by one of the Members, or such person as the Governor may name, and countersigned (by the Commissioner of the Board of Audit.)

Direct sales of
condemned stores,
&c.
3. To direct the salesman to sell periodically, all old and unserviceable building materials and condemned stores, 20 V., c. 11, s. 17.

Powers of Justices
of certain parishes
where prisons are
The Justices for the precinct of St. Catherine and the parishes of Kingston, St Thomas in the East, Portland, St. Thomas in the Vale, Manchester, Hanover and St. James, (as also those of Trelawny, in respect of the Prison at Falmouth, 24 V., c. 19, s. 3, and also St. Mary, 28 V., c. 22, s. 4) in Special Sessions assembled, shall do the following acts :—

Visiting Justices
2. From time to time as necessary to nominate 2 or more Justices who consent to be Visitors of each Prison within their jurisdiction, or arrange if they see fit among themselves to do the duties in turn.

Copies of rules to
be exhibited to be
accessible to every
prisoner
3. To cause copies of so much of the Rules of each Prison as from time to time relate to the treatment and conduct of prisoners, and the duties of the Officers, to be printed in legible characters, and fixed up in some conspicuous part of every Prison, so that every prisoner may have access thereto.

Returns
4. To make a return of the state of each Prison, and the condition of the prisoners, in such form as the Governor, with the advice of the Privy Council shall direct, with a statement of the number and description of Officers and servants employed, the salaries of each, and the authorities by whom they are appointed, 20 V., c. 11, s. 18.

Their powers (sub-section 1) to appoint Officers are transferred to the Governor, 28 V., c. 22, s. 5.

A visiting Justice
&c., to visit prison
daily
Examine Prisons,
&c

And redress abuses
One at least of the Visiting Justices so appointed, or who have con sented to act, shall personally visit and inspect each Prison once every day if practicable and expedient, and examine into the state of the buildings so far as to form a judgment as to the repairs, additions or alterations which appear necessary, strict regard being had to the classification, inspection, instruction, employment or hard labor required, and enquire into the behaviour and condition of the prisoners, and the means of setting them to work, and into all abuses in the Prison; and in matters of pressing necessity, and, within the power of his commission as a Justice, take cognizance of and redress any abuse, 20 V., c. 11, s. 19.

Powers and duties
of Justices although
not visitors with re-
spect to abuses, and
redress
Any Justice, without being appointed a Visitor, may enter into and examine every Prison of his parish as he sees fit, and if he discover any abuse, he is required to take it into immediate consideration, and report his opinion, in writing to the Custos, who shall thereupon summon a Special Session for the consideration of the same ; and the Justices shall adopt the most effectual measures for enquiring into and rectifying all abuses in the Prisons of their parishes which come to their knowledge as soon as the nature of the circumstances permit, 20 V., c. 11, s. 20.

The Officers to be appointed by the Governor shall be paid the salaries now attached to their offices, or which may be fixed by the Legislature, 20 V., c. 11, s. 21. Salaries of officers to he appointed by the Governor

The then Officers continued in office, at the salaries attached thereto, subject to removal by the Governor, 20 V., c. 11, s. 22. Then officers continued

The Inspector of Prisons may visit and inspect the several Prisons, examine any person holding any office, or receiving any salary or emolument, or any prisoner in any Prison ; call for and examine all books and papers relating to any Prison ; enquire into all matters touching any prisoner or person employed in any Prison, either alone or in the presence of any other person he may select, 20 V., c. 11, s. 23. Powers of Inspector

The Inspector is declared to be a Justice for every parish, but shall act only in the preservation of the peace, the prevention of crime, the detection and committal of offenders, and other matters connected with the discharge of his duties as such Inspector, 20 V., c. 11, s. 24. Inspector to be a Justice for every parish, but to act only in matters connected with his duties as such

He may recommend to the Governor such regulations in respect to dietary, clothing, and the employment of the prisoners in the several Prisons as he deems best calculated to ensure uniformity in the management of the Prisons, and promote the health of the prisoners, which recommendations when approved of by the Governor, with advice of the Privy Council, shall be certified by the Clerk of the Privy Council, to the Inspector, and to the Justices of any parish where a Prison is situate ; and 10 days after the same have been certified, they shall be binding upon the Superintendents and other Officers, and be carried out and enforced by them, 20 V., c. 11, s. 25. To recommend to the Governor regulations for dietary, clothing, employment and promotion of health of prisoners
Enforcement of recommendations

He shall, under the direction of the Executive Committee, cause provision to be made for supplying at the public expense, to all persons confined in the 3 County Gaols (except persons willing to maintain themselves) such wholesome and necessary food of the kind, quantity and quality , and such diet, in case of sickness, as shall be directed and authorized by the Physicians to the County Gaols, and approved of by the Governor, under any Acts in force for supplying prisoners in the Prisons with food and other necessaries, 20 V., c. 11, s. 26. And provide food under direction of the Executive Committee for prisoners in County Gaols [not willing to maintain themselves]

Wilfully obstructing the Inspector in the execution of any duty or power entrusted to him, a misdemeanor ; on conviction, to be punished by fine not exceeding £6, or imprisonment not exceeding 30 days, 20 V., c. 11, s. 27. Obstructing Inspector

The Superintendents of Prisons shall do the following acts :— Duties of Superintendent

1. Upon any prisoner being ordered to be removed, he shall forthwith, on receipt of the order permit and cause him to be removed to that which he is ordered. Removal of Prisoners

2. Make a report in writing, of the actual state and condition of the Prison under his charge, and of the number and description of prisoners or inmates confined therein, in Spanish Town to the Grand Court at every sitting, and in other parishes to the Circuit Courts at every sitting. In the case of the Penitentiaries, the report shall be made once a quarter to the Governor, in such form as he may direct. To report upon the Prison and prisoners in Spanish Town, to every Grand Court ; in other prisons to every Circuit Court
From Penitentiaries to the Governor quarterly

3. Hear all complaints touching disobedience of any rule of the Prison, assault by one prisoner upon another, when no dangerous wound or bruise is given, profane cursing and swearing, indecent behaviour, any irreverent behaviour at prayers, or when the Chaplain or other person appointed as directed by this Act is performing service, absence from prayers or when the minister is performing service, idleness or negligence in work, or wilful mismanagement of it, which are declared to be offences if committed by any prisoner. He may examine any person touching any such offence and determine thereon and punish the offence by ordering the offender to close confinement in the refractory or solitary cells, and by keeping him upon bread and water only for not exceeding 3 days, or for such time, not exceeding 6 days, as the Visiting Justice shall, by a written order, determine. Examination into and punishment of offences specified
Extent of punishment

4. The Superintendent of the Prison to which any prisoner is moved, shall receive him, and have the same powers over him, as if he had been originally sentenced thereto, 20 V., c. 11, s. 28. Power over removed prisoners

Superintendent to visit prisoners working on roads, &c

When the Governor directs or sanctions the employment of any convicts or persons sentenced to hard labor upon any road or thoroughfare, or upon any undertaking of a public or parochial nature, the Superintendent of the Prison (not the Penitentiary) from which they were sent, shall visit the road or place where they are at work, once in each day at least, if not more than 3 miles from the Prison, and direct, inspect and superintend the

And see that the officers are correctly performing their duties and not permitting intercourse with convicts

performance of the work, and see that the inferior officers or persons in charge of the convicts or persons so employed, are correctly performing their duties, and are not permitting any intercourse between the convicts and any other persons, except those appointed to superintend and direct their labor, or allowing them to receive any articles of food, drink, or other-

Penalty dismissal

wise, except such as are furnished by the Officers. Any Superintendent neglecting or refusing to perform the duties required, shall on the complaint of the Inspector, or any Visiting or other Justice, to the Governor, be liable to dismissal, 20 V., c 11, s. 29.

Penalty on superintendents and Officers contravening rules or act

If any Superintendent or other officer shall contravene any of the rules herein, or any existing rule or regulation, or do, omit or commit any act or thing contrary to this Act, in any Prison, he shall, on conviction before 2 Justices, forfeit not exceeding £10, and in default of immediate payment be committed not exceeding 30 days (unless sooner paid) to the Prison nearest to that of which he is or was Superintendent. The fine to be paid to the Receiver-General, and in addition such Superintendent or other

Dismissal

officer may be dismissed, 20 V., c. 11, s. 30.

Duties of Surgeon
Quarterly reports to Inspector
Journal

Every Surgeon shall attend at the Prison as required by this Act, and shall report every 3 months to the Inspector the condition of the Prison, and the state of the health of the prisoners and inmates under his care; he shall keep a journal in which he shall enter the date of every attendance in the performance of his duty, with any observations which may occur to him in the execution thereof, to be kept in the Prison, and be open

To be open to visiting Justices, and signed by them quarterly

to the inspection of the Visiting Justices, who shall every 3 months sign the same in proof of its having been produced to them, 20 V., c. 11, s. 31.

Hospital and Nurses

One or more apartments properly ventilated shall be set apart in each Prison as a Hospital or sick ward for diseased or sick prisoners, so arranged as to keep the sexes separate; and necessary nurses shall be provided to attend such prisoners in Hospital, 20 V., c. 11, s. 32.

Calling in a 2nd Medical Practitioner for consultation

Upon the appearance of any severe sickness among the inmates of the General and Female Penitentiaries, or either, the Inspector, as occasion requires, may call in the assistance of a second Medical Practitioner for consultation only, and the Executive Committee shall direct him to be paid such remuneration as according to the number of his visits is considered adequate, 20 V., c. 11, s. 33.

Prisoners not to be removed until reported on by Surgeon as fit

No order shall be made for the removal of any prisoner, until he has been examined by the Surgeon of the Prison in which he is confined, who shall report the state of his health; and he shall not be removed unless reported to be free from acute, dangerous or infectious diseases, and fit to be removed to another Prison, 20 V., c. 11, s. 34.

Chaplains duties

Every Chaplain shall, on every Sunday, Christmas day and Good Friday perform the appointed morning and evening services of the Church of England, and catechise or instruct such prisoners as are willing to receive instruction; he shall visit the Prison on such other days, and read such other prayers and portions of Scripture, and perform such other duties as are required by the rules and regulations; administer the holy Sacrament of the Lord's Supper to such prisoners as desire, and he deems in a proper frame of mind to receive it; frequently visit every room and cell occupied by prisoners, and direct such books to be distributed and read, and such lessons to be taught in the Prison as he deems proper for the religious and moral instruction of the prisoners; visit prisoners in solitary confinement, and afford spiritual assistance to persons under warrant or order for execution; have free access to all persons on whom sentence of death has been passed, except persons of a different persuasion who have requested that a minister of their own persuasion should be allowed to visit them; keep

Journal

a Journal in which to enter the times of his attendance on duty, with any observations which occur to him in the execution thereof, to be left in the Prison open to the inspection of the Visiting Justices, to whom he shall communicate from time to time any abuse or impropriety which comes to his knowledge, 20 V., c. 11, s. 35.

The Island Curates shall attend at the Prisons in their parishes to which no Chaplains are appointed, and perform Divine Service, and afford religious instruction to the prisoners, at such times and in such manner as the Governor shall direct, so as not to neglect their other parochial duties, 20 V., c. 11, s. 36.

Island Curates where no Chaplain

The Commissioner of the Board of Audit shall be Secretary to the Prison department generally by receiving, examining and auditing the whole of the Prison expenditure accounts before they are paid; he shall keep a separate account of the expense of each Prison, and the average number of prisoners in such Prison, for each year, and point out to the Executive Committee and Inspector any cases of apparent extravagance which comes under his notice, that it may be forthwith checked, and due economy enforced throughout the whole of the Prison establishments; and as such Secretary shall have all the powers of 18 V., c. 37 (repealed by 21 V., c. 1) in demanding books, papers, and vouchers, and examining them, and all persons connected with the Prisons, in the discharge of his duty as such Secretary, 20 V., c. 11, s. 37.

Secretary to prison department, his duties and powers; see 21 V., c. 1, s. 15 under which the duties are vested in the first Commissioner the second Commissioner having resigned

No female, except the wife or a member of the family, or a domestic servant of the Superintendent, or the officer appointed to act as his deputy, shall be allowed to reside or sleep in any Prison appropriated to the confinement of male Prisoners; nor shall any male, except the husband of the Matron, be allowed to reside or sleep in any Prison appropriated to the confinement of female Prisoners, 20 V., c. 11, s. 38.

No female to sleep in Prisons for males nor male in those for females, except, &c

Every person convicted of any misdemeanor connected with felony, or a felonious intent, or who shall be lawfully convicted and sentenced to hard labor in any Prison, shall be deemed a misdemeanant of the 2nd class; and every person convicted of any other misdemeanor, a misdemeanant of the 1st class, 20 V., c. 11, s. 39.

Misdemeanants of first and second classes

The rules in Schedule A shall be those of the General and Female Penitentiaries. The rules in Schedule B, those of the several other Prisons so far as applicable to all such prisoners as are not misdemeanants of the 1st class, as defined, or persons sentenced to imprisonment without hard labor, subject to the conditional alternative of release on payment of a fine. The rules in Schedule C, those for the governance of misdemeanants of the 1st class, and persons sentenced as aforesaid. Such last mentioned misdemeanants and persons shall be subject to such other rules and regulations in force in the Prison where they are confined as are not repugnant to those in Schedule C; and the rules in Schedule D shall be those for the governance of prisoners employed or worked upon the public roads, or in any undertaking of a public or parochial nature, and of the officers under whom they are placed, 20 V., c. 11, s. 40.

Rules.

Notwithstanding the 2nd clause in Schedule D, the Superintendent of any District Prison where there are lands belonging or appurtenant thereto, without the walls but adjoining, may employ within the limit of such lands any female prisoner under sentence of hard labour, under the same regulations as other prisoners under like sentences of hard labour. But no female prisoner shall be employed on the public roads or thoroughfares, or upon any undertaking of a public or parochial nature. 26 V., s. 2, c. 18.

When females in District Prisons may be worked without the walls

No person shall be imprisoned in any Prison which the Governor certifies, by writing under his hand to the Justices or other persons having authority over it, to be unfit to be used as a Prison. 20 V., c. 11, s. 41.

Prisons certified by the Governor to be unfit, not to be used

The Judges may sentence any person convicted of any felony or misdemeanor of the 2nd class to the nearest Prison appropriated for the reception of the particular class of convicts to which the Prisoner belongs. Justices may sentence and commit all offenders duly tried and convicted before them to the nearest Prison, notwithstanding it is out of the jurisdiction of the Court in which the prisoner is tried, 20 V., c. 11, s. 42.

Prisons for felons and misdemeanants of second class Prisons to which Justices may commit

Where any person is lawfully convicted of any felony or offence for which he shall by law now or to be in force be liable to imprisonment in the house of correction, the Court may order and adjudge him to be imprisoned and kept to hard labour in either of the penitentiaries for such term as the Court directs according to law. 20 V., c. 11, s. 43.

Other convicts who may be sentenced to a Penitentiary

No misdemeanant of the 1st class, nor any person sentenced to imprisonment subject to the conditional alternative of release on payment of a fine, shall be sentenced to or admitted into either of the Penitentiaries, except

Persons not to be sentenced to the Penitentiaries put to labor on roads, &c

4 A

as next after provided, nor shall be required, or put to labour upon any street, lane, or road or other public or parochial work in any parish, 20 V., c. 11, s. 45.

To prevent contamination arising from the association of prisoners in any Prison in which rules for the individual separation of prisoners shall be provided, any prisoner may be separately confined during the whole or any part of the period of his imprisonment, 20 V., c. 11, s. 46.

Separate confinement as aforesaid shall not be deemed Solitary Confinement within this or any other Act forbidding the continuance of Solitary confinement for more than a limited period, 20 V., c. 11, s. 47.

No cell to be used for the separate confinement of any prisoner which is not of such a size, and lighted, ventilated, and fitted up in such manner as may be required by a due regard to health, and furnished with the means of enabling the prisoner to communicate at any time with an officer; nor

Not to be used un-
til approved by the
Governor

shall be used for the purpose until its fitness in the several particulars has been certified, by the Inspector, to and approved by the Governor. Every prisoner so separately confined shall have the means of taking air and exercise at such times as shall be deemed necessary by the Surgeon, and shall be furnished with the means of religious and other instruction, also with the means of labour or employment, unless it is deemed advisable by the Governor to order otherwise, for a period not exceeding one calendar month, at any one time, 20 V., c. 11, s. 48.

A section of the
Penitentiary to be
set apart for Sol-
diers and Marines
convicted by Court
Martial

One section of the General Penitentiary shall be appropriated with the approbation of the Governor, and be deemed a prison, within any Act now or to be enforced for punishing mutiny and desertion; and any soldier or marine convicted by a Court martial may be sent to the Penitentiary and confined in such section, there to undergo the punishment awarded, and during the time specified in the sentence, or until discharged by an order made by competent authority, 20 V., c. 11, s. 49.

Portions of the
Male and Female
Penitentiaries to be
set apart as houses
of correction

The Inspector may set apart and appropriate such portions as may be necessary of the General and Female Penitentiary to be used as Houses of Correction for the purposes after mentioned. The portions so set apart shall remain under the care and management of the Superintendent and officers of the respective Penitentiaries, 20 V., c. 11, s. 50.

Justices of King-
ston, St. Andrews,
and Port Royal
may commit male
offenders to the
General Penitentia-
ry
And the Justices
of St. Catherine
precinct may com-
mit female offen-
ders to the Female
Penitentiary
Convict ship

The Justices in Petty Session, and the several Justices for Kingston, St. Andrew and Port-Royal, to whom authority is or shall be given, on conviction, to commit offenders to the House of Correction or Goal, may commit any such offender, if a male, to the General Penitentiary, and they, as also the Justices for the precinct of St. Catherine, to whom like authority is or shall be given, may commit and sentence female offenders to the Female Penitentiary, 20 V., c. 11 s. 51.

When a Convict or Prison ship is stationed at Kingston, or any other harbour, the Governor may direct the removal of any prisoner thereto, and the Judges may sentence convicted Felons thereto; and the Governor, in his discretion, may make all necessary rules relating to the working, and government of the prisoners so removed or sentenced, 20 V., c. 11, s. 52.

Punishment of
offences against pri-
son discipline and
regulations beyond
superintendants ju-
risdiction

If any prisoner is guilty of riotous conduct or continued resistance to the authorities, or of any repeated offence against any existing rule, or attempts to escape, or is discovered to be or have been aiding or endeavouring to aid any prisoner in escaping when no actual escape has taken place, or is guilty of any greater offence than the Superintendent is empowered to punish (see s. 28) he shall report the same to the Visiting Justices, or one of them; and any two of such, or any other two Justices may enquire into,

upon oath, and determine concerning any matter so reported, and order the offender to be punished by close confinement for not exceeding one mouth,

With close con-
finement
Or whipping with
Governor's confirm-
ation

or by whipping not exceeding 39 lashes, in the case of prisoners convicted of Felony or sentenced to hard labor. Such last mentioned punishment shall not be carried into execution until the evidence taken in the case has been certified by the Justices and submitted to the Governor, and the sentence has been confirmed by him; but the offender on being so sentenced, shall be put in close confinement until the Governor's pleasure is known. No such

Whipping in no
case to extend to
females
Prison breach or
escape, or escape
during conveyance

last punishment shall in any case extend to female prisoners, 20 V., c. 11, s. 53.

If any prisoner at any time during the term for which he has been sentenced to be imprisoned, break Prison, or escape either from the place of his original confinement, or from the Prison to which he has been ordered to be removed, or on his conveyance either to the place in which he has it the first instance been sentenced to be confined, or to the Prison to which he has been ordered to be removed, or from the officer or person having the lawful custody of his person or of the Prison from which he breaks or escapes, he shall be guilty of a misdemeanor, and punished by such further imprisonment not exceeding 3 years, as the Court before which he is tried shall adjudge, 20 V., c. 11, s. 54.

Escape from person having lawful custody
Misdemeanor
3 years further imprisonment

If any prisoner ordered to be employed upon any road or thoroughfare or upon any undertaking of a public or parochial nature, escapes or attempts to escape from the custody of any officer or person to whose care he was committed whilst so employed, he shall be liable to the same punishment as a prisoner escaping from any Prison in which he is confined, 20 V., c. 11, s. 55.

Escapes while employed on roads, &c., or attempt

Same punishment

If any person rescue any prisoner during any period of his confinement, either in the place of his original imprisonment, or in the Prison to which he is ordered to be removed, or during the time of his conveyance to the place in which he was in the first instance sentenced to be confined, or on his removal to the Prison to which he has been ordered to be removed, or whilst in the custody of any person in whose charge he shall be, or if any person be aiding or assisting in any such rescue, or in any breach of Prison, or any escape of any prisoner, or if any person having the custody of any such prisoner, or being employed as an officer by the person having such custody, voluntarily or negligently permits him to escape, or if any person shall, by supplying arms, tools, instruments, or disguise, or otherwise be in any manner aiding or assisting to any such prisoner in any escape, or attempt to escape, though no escape be actually made, or shall attempt to rescue any such prisoner, or be aiding or assisting in any such attempt, though no rescue be actually made, such person shall be guilty of a misdemeanor, and liable to fine or imprisonment, with or without hard labor, at the discretion of the Court, 20 V., c. 11, s. 56.

Rescuing prisoners from Prison or during conveyance

Or aiding or assisting

Voluntarily or negligently permitting escape
Supplying arms, &c., or otherwise aiding a prisoner to escape or attempting a rescue

Misdemeanor

Such fine not to exceed £100, nor imprisonment 12 months, 21 V., c. 16, s. 1.

If any person not being an officer or prisoner, carry or bring, or attempt or endeavour, by throwing over the walls, or by any other means, to introduce into any Prison any letters, tobacco, spirits, liquors or other articles not allowed by the rules, or shall do or commit any act in contravention of the rules herein provided, or of any existing rules, or contrary to this Act, any two Justices may hear and determine any complaint, and on conviction the person shall pay a fine not exceeding £3, and in default of immediate payment, be committed to the nearest Prison for not exceeding 20 days, unless sooner paid, the same to be paid to the Receiver-General, 20 V., c. 11, s. 57.

Supplying, &c., prohibited articles

Punishable before 2 Justices

Every person confined in any Prison (misdemeanants of the 1st class and persons sentenced to imprisonment without hard labour, subject to the conditional alternative of release on payment of a fine, and persons committed for trial excepted) shall be employed in work every day in the year (Sundays, Good Friday, Christmas Day, and those days during which ill health prevents him from working, excepted) and the hours of labor, and the quantity and quality of food and clothing shall be appointed and directed by the Governor, 20 V., c. 11, s. 58.

Hard labour

Hours of labor, food, and clothing to be directed by the Governor

When the sentence of imprisonment of any prisoner terminates on a Sunday, the person in charge of the Prison shall liberate him on the day previous, 20 V., c. 11, s. 59.

When imprisonment terminates on Sunday prisoner to be discharged on the day previous

Previous to the liberation of every prisoner, who has been settled in or committed from another parish, any visiting Justice may, if he sees cause, give an order, in writing, to put the prisoner in charge of the Police to be conveyed to the parish he belonged to, so arranging the time that his liberation at such parish, shall be on the day the sentence determines. The Policeman in every case shall give notice to the Inspector or one of the sergeants, that he has been set at large, with a description of his person. The Superintendent shall pay to the Policeman, in whose custody he is placed, for the prisoner's maintenance, not exceeding 9d. for every 20 miles the prisoner is to be conveyed, 20 V., c. 11, s. 60.

Prisoners may be returned in custody to be discharged in their parishes on the day the sentence ends

Maintenance

On the discharge from any Prison of any person who has been twice or oftener convicted, the Superintendent shall communicate to each Inspector of Police a description of such person, and the place of residence,

Superintendent's reports to police of the discharge of persons more than once committed

or locality, so far as may be ascertained, to which he is supposed to have gone, with any other circumstances within the Superintendent's knowledge or information, serving to identify him, which description and other information each Inspector shall communicate to the sergeants and privates

Duties of Police of his division, and it shall be their duty to keep watch for and over such person, his locations, haunts, associates and conduct ; and on any such person coming within, or departing from his district, being lost sight of, each Inspector of Police shall report to the Inspector of Prisons, and the Superintendent of the Prison from whom information was in the first instance received, the respective facts as they occur relating to his coming or departure, or being lost sight of, and all circumstances observations or remarks respecting his location, haunts, associates and conduct, from time to time, with any other particulars relating to him, which it may seem to the

Reports to Inspector of Prisons Inspector of Police advisable to communicate, and the Superintendent receiving such report, shall forthwith communicate the same to the Inspector of Prisons, who shall thereupon, as also whenever he himself receives from

And Governor any Inspector of Police a report respecting such person, submit the same with remarks or observations from himself, from time to time, for the information of the Governor, and for any instructions the case may require, 28 V., c. 22, s. 11.

Salesman, his remuneration The Executive Committee may renumerate the salesman for his trouble in selling articles made in any Penitentiary or other Prison, and keeping accounts of the articles sold, the person to whom sold, and of all moneys received by him in payment of the same, or which he may collect or, gather in, or sue for, or recover from parties owing the same. The remuneration to be by salary or commission, or partly by salary and partly by commission, on the amount of sales effected, 20 V., c. 11, s. 61.

To pay receipts to the Receiver-General The salesman shall pay to the Receiver-General all moneys he receives for bricks, lime and other articles sold, or work done by the prisoners, whenever they amount to £30, or upwards, and the Receiver-General's receipt shall be a discharge, and entitle him to credit for the amount in his accounts, 20 V., c. 11, s. 62.

The moneys to be carried to prison expenditure account The Receiver-General shall carry to the credit of the Prison expenditure Account all sums paid by the salesman ; the moneys to belong to the public and to be applied as the Executive Committee direct, towards the

And applied as Executive Committee direct erection or completion of the Penitentiaries, and the purchase of such machinery as may be useful or necessary in the production of articles for building purposes, or otherwise as they shall direct, 20 V., c. 11, s. 63.

Salesman to sue for and enforce payments The salesman may sue for and recover in his own name in any Court of Record, or under any Act for the recovery of Petty Debts, any moneys due for any article or work done, and issue writs and distress warrants on Judgments, and the moneys recovered and received shall be paid to the Receiver-General and carried to the credit of the Prison Expenditure Account

With consent of the Executive Committee but the salesman shall not institute legal proceedings against any person, or issue any writ or distress warrant without having first obtained the con-

Expenses sent or direction of the Executive Committee who may pay or allow the salesman to take credit in his accounts for the expense of suing and recovering any demand, 20 V., c. 11, s. 64.

Executive Committee may permit stones or marl to be taken from Rock Fort Quarry or Penitentiary or Prisons, for repair of roads or public or parochial purposes The Executive Committee may grant permission to any person to take any quantity of stone or marl from the Quarry at Rock Fort or the General Penitentiary or any District Prison, for the repair of any streets or roads, or for any other parochial or public purpose, subject to such regulations as they deem necessary ; but not to interfere with nor interrupt the labours of the Convicts at the Quarry or Penitentiary, or diminish the quantity of stones required for the use of the latter, 20 V., c. 11, s. 65.

Not to interfere with convicts **Allowances for parishes where there are no prisons for maintenance and medical attendance on prisoners and Crown witnesses** **Rates** In respect to parishes where there is no Prison, the Executive Committee may authorize payment by the Receiver-General out of the Prison expenditure moneys, of such sums as are required to pay the expenses of maintenance and medical attendance on all prisoners committed before summary trial, or before being examined and committed for trial at the Circuit Courts, or upon their removal from one Prison to another, also Crown witnesses unable to give security for their appearance, and all persons convicted and sentenced to imprisonment in any District Prison or the Penitentiary during their necessary detention in any such parish. The sum for maintenance not to exceed on an average 8d. per head per diem ; and the scale of charges for medical attendance not to exceed that for attendance on the Police, 20 V., c. 11, s. 66.

The Justices may cause convictions to be drawn up as follows, or to such effect :—

Be it remembered, that on the   day of   in the year of our Lord   A. B. is convicted before us, C. D. and E. F., two of Her Majesty's Justices of the Peace for the Parish of   for that the said A. B. (specifying the offence, and the time and place when and where the same was committed, as the case shall be), and the said A. B. is for his said offence adjudged by us the said Justices to forfeit and pay the sum of   and if such sum he no not paid immediately, we order that the same be levied by distress and sale of the goods and chattels of the said A. B., and in default of sufficient distress, we adjudge the said A. B. to be imprisoned in   for the space of unless the fine be sooner paid.

Given under our hands the day and year first above mentioned, 20 V., c. 11, s. 67.

Form of conviction

No order or conviction shall be quashed for want of form. No distress shall be deemed unlawful, nor the party making it a trespasser on account of any defect or want of form in the summons, conviction, warrant or distress or other proceedings relating thereto, nor the party a trespasser on account of any after irregularity ; but the party aggrieved may recover satisfaction for the special damage in an action for the irregularity, if tender of sufficient damages be made before action, 20 V., c. 1ˢᵗ, s. 68.

Proceedings not to be quashed for irregularity nor party a trespasser
Special damages
Tender

To any action the party may plead the general issue and give the special matter in evidence. If a verdict pass for the defendant, or the plaintiff become nonsuit, or discontinue after issue joined, or if, upon demurrer or otherwise, judgement is given against the plaintiff, the defendant shall recover costs, and have the like remedy as in other cases, and though a verdict is given for the plaintiff he shall not have costs out of purse unless the Judge certify his approbation of the action and verdict, 20 V., c. 11, s. 69.

Protection from actions

Penalties not otherwise declared shall be recovered before two Justices and enforced by warrant of distress ; and upon no sufficient distress returned any Justice may by warrant commit the defendant to the nearest Prison with or without hard labour, not exceeding 3 months, if not sooner paid, 20 V., c. 11, s. 70.

Recovery and enforcement of penalties

This Act shall be read as incorporated with 20 V., c. 11 and other Acts relating to Prisons, 28 V., c. 22, s. 12.

Incorporation of 28 V., c. 22, with other Acts

SCHEDULE A. to 20 V. c. 11.—PENITENTIARIES.
VISITING JUSTICES.

1. The Governor shall nominate 2 or more to be Official Visitors.
2. Who shall make arrangements among themselves for the performance of their duty.
3. To meet at the Prison once at least in each quarter.
4. To fix a scale of fines to be levied on the Subordinate Officers for negligence in the performance of their duties, (to form a fund for their relief in sickness.)
5. From time to time to cause the rules relating to the treatment and conduct of prisoners to be printed in legible characters and fixed up in conspicuous parts of the Prison, so that every prisoner may have access thereto.
6. At every meeting, to examine into the state of the buildings, the behaviour and conduct of the Officers, the general behaviour of the prisoners, and all abuses in the Prison, suggesting any practicable improvement.
7. A Visiting Justice may see any prisoner committed in close confinement, and may hear or receive any representation from him as to his treatment, and enquire into it.
8. To keep " The Visiting Justices Minute Book" in which are to be entered all visits and observations made by them either individually or collectively, the minutes of each meeting to contain the names of the Justices present, to be signed by the chairman and kept in the Prison.

THE SUPERINTENDENT.

1. Shall not directly or indirectly have any interest in any contract or agreement for the supply of the prison.

2. One of the Chief Officers best acquainted with the daily routine of prison duties, to be selected by the Superintendent and approved of by the Inspector, shall be appointed by the Governor, the deputy of the Superintendent, and shall fill his place whenever he is sick and unable to attend to his duties, or has occasion to be absent on leave. Such deputy whilst acting shall have all the power and be subject to all the duties of the Superintendent, and shall enter into the Superintendent's Journal the period when he took charge and delivered up the same on every occasion of the absence of the latter.

3. In case of absence for a night from unavoidable necessity he shall state the absence and cause in his Journal.

4. In case of misconduct he may suspend any Subordinate Officer, but shall record the particulars in his Journal, and the Officer shall continue suspended until the case is decided by the Visiting Justices or Inspector.

5. He is expected to exercise his authority with firmness, temper and humanity, to abstain from all irritating language, and not to strike a prisoner. He must enforce similar conduct on the Subordinate Officers.

6. In his Journal he shall record all punishments inflicted by his authority or that of a visiting Justice, the day on which punishment was inflicted and the cause; also all occurrences of importance within the Prison, particularly such as relate to the health, discipline or employment of the prisoners, or the infringement, from whatever cause, of any of the Prison rules.

7. To acquaint himself with the laws relating to the Prison and Prison rules, and strictly adhere to them, and be responsible for every infringement or relaxation.

8. To visit and inspect every ward, cell, yard and division of the Prison, and see every Prisoner once at least in every 24 hours, and in default of such daily visit and inspection, he shall state in his Journal how far he has omitted, and the cause; he shall, at least once during the week, go through the Prison at an uncertain hour of the night, which visit, with the hour and the state of the Prison at the time, he shall record in his Journal.

9. At all times to be ready to receive the complaint of any prisoner, and if well founded, immediately to redress or report it to the visiting Justices at their next meeting.

10. To take every precaution to prevent escape, and give orders for the daily examination of the cells, bars, bolts, locks, &c.; to order an examination of all parcels, letters and articles brought into Prison, and such an examination of Visitors to prisoners as he may deem requisite; adopt proper precautions against fire.

11. To direct an officer to search every prisoner on his admission, and after he has been examined and passed by the Surgeon, he shall dispose of him according to the appointed rule of separation or classification.

12. On admission of a prisoner, to see that the Storekeeper enters in the Prison register his name, probable age, height, features, religious persuasion, address of nearest relatives, and customary trade or employment; also see entered in the Prisoners' Property Book an inventory of all money, clothes, and other effects taken from any prisoner.

13. To read or cause, &c., to every prisoner on his admission, such of the rules as relate to the conduct and treatment of prisoners, and once in every three months repeat the same.

14. He, or in his absence, his deputy shall attend Divine Service in the Prison Chapel whenever it is performed; see that the prisoners attend, unless prevented by illness or excused by Prison regulation. A sufficient number of subordinate officers shall also attend in appointed rotation. The Superintendent or his deputy shall strictly observe the conduct of the officers, and take special care that the behaviour of the prisoners in Chapel is proper and orderly.

15. To attend, or take care that his deputy attends, at each distribution of food to the prisoners, and cause any article of food to be weighed or measured, if required by a prisoner.

16. To see that breakfast is served out to the prisoners as nearly as possible at 9 o'clock throughout the year, ¾ths of an hour being allowed for the meal; dinner to be served from 1st October to 31st March at ½ past 4, and the rest of the year at 5 o'clock.

17. To see the bedding is removed from the sleeping rooms, and aired every dry day.

18. To take care that the prisoners sentenced to hard labor are regularly so employed. When any are excused by the Surgeon, the Superintendent shall provide other employment for them.

19. Before the discharge of any juvenile prisoner, he is to inform his relatives or friends (if there be any whose name and residence can be ascertained) what day and hour he will be discharged. that they may attend to receive him.

20. To put no description of iron on a prisoner, unless in cases of absolute necessity; and to enter in his Journal full particulars of every such case, and give notice thereof forthwith to a Visiting Justice. Not to continue any iron on a prisoner longer than 24 hours, without an order in writing from a Visiting Justice, specifying the cause and the time during which the prisoner is to be ironed.

21. Once at least, each day, to visit every cell in which a prisoner is confined in solitary and separate confinement, and see they are kept clean well aired, and wholesome.

22. Daily to deliver, or cause, &c. to the Chaplain and Surgeon, lists of prisoners placed in solitary or separate confinement, and of those under punishment; and to the Surgeon a list of such as complain of illness, or are removed to the Hospital, or confined to their cells by illness, and notify to him the illness otherwise of every prisoner.

23. To attend to the written directions of the Surgeon for the supply of any additional bedding, clothing, or particular diet, or other article the Surgeon deems necessary for any sick prisoner; the order to specify the prisoner's name, and the quantities of the articles ordered.

24. To call the Surgeon's attention to any prisoner whose state of mind or body appears to require it. And if it appears injuriously affected by discipline or treatment to make such change, under the directions of the Surgeon as he thinks necessary, and report same in writing to a Visiting Justice for directions, entering the report in his Journal.

25. To carry into effect the written directions of the Surgeon for separating prisoners labouring under infectious diseases, or suspected thereof, and for cleaning, disinfecting and lime-washing any apartments occupied by such prisoners, and for washing, disinfecting, fumigating or destroying any apparel.

26. Upon the death of any prisoner, to give immediate notice to a Visiting Justice, the Coroner, and when practicable, to the nearest relative of the deceased.

27. To see the Clerk duly keeps and makes the proper entries in the several books to be kept by him.

28. To be responsible for the safe custody of the Journals, Registers, Account Books, Commitments, and all other Documents confided to his care, and see they are preserved unmutilated and unaltered.

29. The outer gate of the Prison shall be locked for the night not later than 9 o'clock, and the keys delivered to him, and a report made to him whether the officers who are to remain in the Prison are all present; the keys to be kept by him until the hour of unlocking in the morning, and no ingress or egress allowed between the hours of locking at night and unlocking in the morning, unless on special cases, to be entered in his Journal.

30. He, or in his absence his deputy, shall inspect every letter and parcel to and from a prisoner, and where he deems it expedient to withhold a letter or parcel to or from a prisoner, he shall lay it before a Visiting Justice for his decision.

31. He may demand the name and address of any visitor, and when he has any grounds of suspicion, search or cause, &c., male visitors, and under the like circumstances direct the matron to search female visitors, or in case of their refusal, deny them admission ; and if he know any cause why a visitor should not see a prisoner, he shall prevent any intercourse between them, and state his reasons in his Journal.

THE SURGEON.

1. To visit the Prison every morning and see every sick prisoner, and twice at least, in every week and oftener if necessary, every prisoner.

2. To keep a Journal, and enter the date of every attendance on duty, with any observations that occur to him in the performance, such Journal to remain in the Prison.

3. Once a quarter to report in writing to the Governor, the general state of health, of the prisoners, the disorders which have been most prevalent, and whether any connection may be traced between the diseases and the locality or state of the building, or the diet, employment, or other circumstances, also the number of deaths and hospital cases, and if any cases of insanity have occurred.

4. To examine every newly admitted prisoner before he is passed into the proper ward, and enter in his Journal, the name, number, probable age, and state of health of each on his admission.

5. To examine every prisoner about to be discharged or removed, making in his Journal a similar entry. No prisoner shall be discharged or removed if laboring under any acute or dangerous disease, until in his opinion the discharge is safe or unless the prisoner require to be discharged.

6. To see daily such prisoners as complain of illness or appear out of health, and either supply them with medicines in their wards or cells, or direct them to be removed to the hospital.

7. Prisoners in hospital shall be allowed such diet as he directs in writing. To report to the Superintendent any case for varying the diet or treatment of sick prisoners not removed to the hospital.

8. In all cases not unfavorable to health, to attend the sick in their rooms or cells, and not order their removal to the hospital unless he consider it necessary.

9. On receiving notice of the separate or solitary confinement of any prisoner, he shall pay particular attention to the case, and see the prisoner once a day whilst it continues.

10. Whenever he has reason to believe that either the mind or body of a prisoner is likely to be injuriously affected by the discipline or treatment, he shall report the case in writing to the Superintendent, with such directions as he thinks proper, and enter it in his Journal. The Superintendent shall thereupon alter or suspend the discipline accordingly, until a visiting Justice attend, who shall enquire into the case, and make such order as appears necessary.

11. To call the Chaplain's attention to any prisoner whose state of mind appears to require his special care.

12. To give directions in writing for separating prisoners having infectious complaints, or suspected thereof ; for cleansing, disinfecting and lime-washing any apartment occupied by such prisoners, and for washing disinfecting or destroying any apparel.

13. To remark in his Journal any neglect of cleanliness, want of drainage, or ventilation ; any bad quality of provisions or other cause affecting the general health of the Prison.

14. To enter in his Journal an account of all medicines or medical treatment ordered at each visit, with such observations as appear necessary.

15. According to a form to be supplied, to record the names of all who are receiving medicines or other articles appropriated for the sick, the date of every removal to and discharge from hospital, also the daily number of such patients, and the number under treatment in their wards or cells.

16. After the death of any prisoner, to insert in his Journal at what time he was taken ill; when it was first communicated to him; when the complaint assumed a dangerous character; when the prisoner died; his opinion before the Coroner, and the verdict.

17. When he is of opinion the life of a prisoner is endangered by his continuance in prison, to state in writing his opinion and the grounds, for the Governor's information.

18. To report in writing to the Superintendent any irregularity in the hospital which comes to his knowledge, or any difficulty or obstruction in the performance of his duty.

19. In case of sickness, necessary engagement, or leave of absence, he shall appoint a substitute, to be approved of by two visiting Justices, and his name and residence shall be specified in his Journal.

THE DISPENSER.

1. To reside in the Prison, and devote his entire time to the duties of his office.

2. To make up all prescriptions ordered by the Surgeon, and see that the medicines and nourishment are regularly administered by the nurses to the sick in the hospital.

3. At morning muster, to make out a list of prisoners who complain, and detain such as appear to him to be ill, until seen by the Surgeon.

4. To attend to every case of illness during the night, and when necessary send for the Surgeon.

5. Frequently to visit the hospital during the day, and forthwith report to the Superintendent any case in his opinion requiring the attendance of the Surgeon.

6. To take care that the diet ordered for each patient is punctually delivered, and of proper quality and quantity, and report to the Superintendent any irregularities in the supply.

7. To see that strict order and cleanliness are observed in the hospital department, and report to the Superintendent any neglect or misconduct on the part of the nurses or patients.

8. Not to leave the Prison without permission from the Medical Officer, or Superintendent.

THE CHAPLAIN.

1. On every Sunday, Christmas day and Good Friday, and on public Fast and Thanksgiving days, he is to perform the appointed morning and evening services of the Church of England, and preach a sermon. Divine service on these days to be at stated hours between 9, a. m. and 5, p. m.

2. He is daily to read prayers selected from the Liturgy, with a portion of Scripture, in the Chapel. In case of his unavoidable absence, (to be entered in his Journal) the daily Prayers to be read by the School-master. Portions of Scripture shall be read to the prisoners on other occasions when assembled for instruction.

3. To see and admonish every prisoner on admission and discharge, for which purpose proper arrangements shall be made by the Superintendent.

4. Once a month, at least, to see every prisoner separate from all other prisoners.

5. To visit the hospital and sick daily; frequently visit every room and cell occupied by prisoners, and attend at all reasonable times any prisoner who requires his spiritual advice and assistance.

6. To pay especial attention to the juvenile offenders, to prisoners in solitary or separate confinement, each of whom he is to visit daily.

7. To select proper books to be read by the prisoners, and superintends their distribution and preservation.

8. To have a room in the Prison for his own use.

9. To superintend the schools, and direct the course of instruction by the School-master. Prisoners may have one hour's instruction in class twice in the week, as the Chaplain or School-master find it practicable, care being taken that the privilege be made as far as possible an incentive to diligent labor. When a class is assembled for instruction, they should

4 B

be attended by a subordinate officer, and all communication between the prisoners prevented. The Chaplain will frequently attend the school and examine the Prisoners as to their progress.

10. To pay particular attention to the state of mind of every prisoner and if he think it likely to be injuriously affected by the discipline, or treatment, he shall report the same in writing to the Superintendent and Surgeon, entering the report in his Journal.

11. To keep a Journal for entering the times of his attendance in the performance of his duty, with any observation that occurs to him in its execution, together with all occurrences of importance.

12. Not to hold any Benefice with cure of souls, or any Curacy, nor any professional duties unconnected with the Prison, whilst holding the office of Chaplain.

13. In case of his absence on leave, to appoint a substitute to be approved by the Governor, inserting his name and residence in his Journal. He may at any time accept the service of a Clergyman of the Church of England, in the performance of a part of the Divine service in the Chapel, inserting his name in his Journal.

THE SCHOOLMASTER.

1. To instruct the prisoners in the schools and in their cells, under the direction of the Chaplain.

2. To make reports in writing to the Chaplain, as to the conduct and progress of the prisoners, which are to be filed, and a minute of them made in the Chaplain's Journal.

3. To take strict care that there is no communication between prisoners during instruction.

4. To distribute to the prisoners the books and other school materials, under the Chaplain's direction, keeping an account of their application.

5. To assist the Chaplain (if required) in making entries in the prisoners' character book.

6. To act as Clerk in the Chapel, attend on the Chaplain in his room before and after Divine Service, and see the chapel and books are kept in a proper state.

7. In the unavoidable absence of the Chaplain, to read the daily prayers.

THE STOREKEEPER.

1. To receive into his custody and be responsible for all provisions and other stores for dieting the prisoners, all materials for manufacture in the prison, and all articles when manufactured.

2. To have charge of and be responsible for implements for labor, and generally all the moveable Prison property, except such as is under the care of the Master Tailor, of which a strict account is to be kept; to give out nothing without a voucher from the superintendent or clerk.

3. The money and effects of the prisoners taken from them on admission, are to be under his charge, an entry of particulars being made in a book for the purpose, which he is to carry forthwith to the Superintendent to read over the items to the prisoner for his satisfaction and the prevention of errors.

4. To be further employed in searching for the best samples, &c. of articles, required in the Prison, as it may not be possible to procure by contract.

THE PRISON CLERK.

4. A Book-keeper to write up, from day to day, the series of books connected with the classification of the Prison ; to draw by requisition from the storekeeper all articles required for the diet and use of the prisoners, or for sale, and to assist the Superintendent in the returns and reports he is required to furnish. The Auditor will direct him in the best mode of keeping these numerous but necessary records, and see that they are not suffered to fall into arrear.

MASTER TAILOR.

To have charge of and be responsible for the Prison clothing, bedding and materials confided to his care, and not give out or deliver any without a voucher from the Superintendent or Clerk.

THE GATE KEEPER.

1. To allow the subordinate officers or servants to pass in and out at the times appointed by the Superintendent.

2. To take charge of all letters, parcels or articles sent in for any prisoner, and deliver them to the Superintendent.

3. To lock the gate at the appointed hour at night, and deliver the keys to the Superintendent, and receive them again at the hour of unlocking in the morning.

4. Carefully to examine the orders for admission of prisoners' friends. If he has grounds to suspect or believe the persons presenting them have obtained them under false pretences, he shall not admit them until he obtains directions from the Superintendent, to whom he shall immediately apply.

5. To endeavour by every means in his power to prevent the emblezzlement of any Prison property, or the admission of improper or prohibited articles, for which purpose he may examine all articles carried in or out.

6. To stop any person suspected of bringing in spirits or other articles for the prisoners, or carrying out any Prison property, giving immediate notice to the Superintendent, who may direct the suspected person to be searched.

SUBORDINATE OFFICERS.

1. Strictly to conform to the rules laid down for their conduct, obey the lawful orders of the Superintendent and assist him in maintaining discipline and order.

2. Absenting himself without leave or disobeying any lawful order of the Superintendent, or wilfully committing any breach of the rules, or in any other manner neglecting his duty shall, for every such offence, be subject to a fine not exceeding 3 days' wages, to be judged of by a Visiting Justice.

3. Forthwith to report to the Superintendent every instance which comes to his knowledge, of injury or damage to the Prison or property therein, and every instance of irregularity or misconduct of any prisoner under his charge.

4. Not to strike, lay hands on, or use threatening gestures towards any prisoner, except in self defence. Not to speak to any prisoner except in the performance of his duty, nor use indecent, irreligious, threatening or abusive language to any prisoner or other person.

5. To report to the Superintendent the names of prisoners who desire to see the Surgeon, or appear not to be in health.

6. Not to compel any prisoner to labour, who complains of illness or failing strength, until the Surgeon has seen him and given directions. He is to report all such cases to the Superintendent.

7. Not to be absent without leave in writing from the Superintendent. On going out with permission or on duty, he shall leave his keys, instruction book and report book in the Superintendent's office.

8. Not to be permitted to receive any visitors in the interior of the Prison without the Superintendent's permission.

9. To count the prisoners of his class at locking and unlocking time, and regularly report to the Superintendent the number present.

10. Fines are to be levied for negligence of duty, according to a scale to be regulated by the Visiting Justices, to form a fund for the relief of the officers when sick.

11. Not to read or otherwise employ himself while on duty, during which time he shall wear some badge of office to be determined upon by the Inspector.

12. To let no prisoner out of his yard on any pretence without the the direction of the Superintendent, or in his absence his deputy. Penalty 1st offence, to forfeit 3 days' wages. 2nd to be suspended. 3rd Dimissed.

13. Not to part with his keys but to the Superintendent, or in his absence

his deputy, nor go alone with the keys in his possession into a room or yard in which there is more than one prisoner.

14. To be supplied with a printed copy of the rules relating to his duty, which are to be read to each by the Superintendent or his deputy on the first Monday in every month.

15. Eight at least, exclusive of those who keep watch, must alternately remain each night in the Prison.

VISITORS.

1. Not to be admitted on Sunday, Christmas day or Good Friday, or during Divine service on other days, or at the hour of locking up or unlocking, or during the time of meals.

2. No prostitute or person of known bad character shall be permitted to visit any prisoner. The Superintendent shall prevent to the utmost of his power any prisoner from having access to, or communication with any of his former companions in crime.

3. All interviews between prisoners and their friends to take place in the room provided for that purpose, and in the presence of an officer.

4. The Superintendent, with the concurrence of the Surgeon may, in case of serious illness of any prisoner, admit a father, mother, wife, child, brother or sister to visit him, but not more than one at a time, except in cases of great emergency. The clothes of any visitor thus admitted to the interior of the Prison shall be examined by an officer at the outer lodge, so far as necessary to guard against the introduction of any article to the prisoner by such means. Females must be examined by the matron.

5. Not to be allowed to see more than one prisoner at a time, nor shall any visit extend beyond 20 minutes.

6. May inspect the Prison, accompanied by a Magistrate, but unless they sustain some official character, are to hold no communication with any prisoner.

7. The day for admission shall be Saturday, between 11 and 3 o'clock, but under special circumstances (to be entered in his journal) the Superintendent may admit a visitor at any other time.

8. Any visitor who misconducts himself or breaks the rules shall be immediately turned out by an officer, and the Superintendent may either refuse to admit him again, or place such restraints on his admission as he considers necessary.

PRISONERS.

1. Not to be received before the time of unlocking in the morning, nor after 7 at night. except under extraordinary circumstances.

2. To be discharged before 10, a.m.

3. To be searched before their discharge, to prevent them taking out letters or other articles.

4. Convicted of Felonies, or of Misdemeanors connected with Felony, not to receive more than one letter, or be visited by more than one friend once in every 3 months, such visit to be made on the last Saturday in the month.

5 Not to conceal under his clothes or elsewhere, or have in his possession any thing which may aid in an escape, nor any tobacco, snuff, pipe, flint and steel, or any other means of producing fire.

6. No male not separately confined shall be confined with less than 2 other prisoners.

7. Not to destroy, waste or damage any clothes or other articles belonging to the institution.

8. Not to use abusive, irreligious or threatening language, or be guilty of fraud or theft, or use any insulting gesture, or behave with rudeness towards any person.

9. To treat the Prison authorities with respect, and obey their lawful commands.

10. To behave decently and reverently in the Chapel, and not laugh or converse, or make signs to each other, or move from their places till directed by the Superintendent or other officer.

11. At the expiration of the time allowed for breakfast, and immediately before locking up in the evening, all remaining food shall be taken from them by their officers.

12. Prisoners who consider themselves ill-treated by any officer, may complain to the Superintendent, who shall enquire into the circumstances, and do what appear to him lawful and right. If prisoners continue dissatisfied, they shall have full liberty to represent the case to the Visiting Justices, but when making any complaint, they are required to speak one at a time, and quietly.

13. To be turned out of their rooms half an hour before sunrise, and to be locked in for the night, at sunset throughout the year.

14. Young prisoners shall on no account be placed with those who, either from age, or the offences of which they have been convicted, are more matured in crime.

15. Not to sell, exchange, or give away his food or clothing. All bargaining between prisoners is strictly prohibited.

16. None under punishment for offences committed in Prison or in solitary confinement under sentence of any Court, shall be permitted to receive any visit from friends, without an express order in writing from a Visiting Justice, stating the grounds on which it is given.

17. No Jew shall be compelled to labour on his Sabbath.

18. No prisoner shall be employed in the discipline of the Prison, or in the service of any officer, or in the personal service or instruction of any other prisoner.

19. If any prisoner is of a religious persuasion differing from that of the Established Church, a Minister of that persuasion, at his request, shall be allowed to visit him at reasonable times, under such regulations as may guard against the introduction of improper persons, or the supply of improper books. The names of prisoners so visited, and the names and addresses of Ministers so visiting, shall be communicated by the Superintendent to the Chaplain.

20. Prisoners under punishment for Felony, shall wear a party-colored dress; misdemeanants of the 2nd class, the usual Prison dress.

21. The hair of all prisoners, not misdemenants of the 1st class, shall be cut so often, and in such degree, as is necessary for the purposes of personal cleanliness.

Miscellaneous Rules.

1. No spirits, wine, beer, or other fermented liquor, shall be admitted for the use of any prisoner, nor furnished without a written order of the Surgeon, specifying the quantity, and for whose use.

2. Gaming of every kind is prohibited; and the Superintendent is to seize and destroy all dice, cards, and other instruments of gaming.

3. No dogs, poultry, pigeons, pigs or rabbits shall be kept in the Prison.

4. An abstract of such of the rules as relate to the conduct and treatment of prisoners shall be printed, and a copy suspended in the Superintendent's office.

5. No prisoner or officer shall be a Juror on any Inquest on the body of a prisoner.

6. A sufficient stock of such medicines as the Surgeon considers necessary, shall be constantly kept in the Prison.

7. Care shall be taken that all the provisions supplied to the prisoners be of proper quality and weight. Scales, and legal weights and measures shall be provided; and any prisoner may require to have any food served out to him weighed or measured before him by an officer.

Matron of the Female Penitentiary.

To reside in the Prison and do all acts which in the General Penitentiary would be done in analogous cases by the Superintendent, for which purpose she shall have in the Female Penitentiary all the power conferred upon the Superintendent, except in cases of prisoners misbehaving or being guilty of any breach of the rules, which are, immediately as they occur, to be reported by her to the Superintendent, to enquire into, hear, and dispose of them as in the case of male prisoners.

SCHEDULE B.

OTHER PRISONS

Applicable to prisoners not misdemeanants of 1st Class.

1. The Superintendent of every Prison to reside therein and occnpy such rooms and apartments as the Visiting Justices direct. Not to be concerned directly or indirectly in any other occupation or trade. He shall not, nor any other officer by himself, or by any person in trust for, or employed by him, sell, let, barter, or have any benefit from the sale, loan, or letting of any article, or any dealing to or with any prisoner or from the bireing of officers, directly or indirectly in any contract, or agreement for the supply of the Prison, nor receive any money, fee, reward, or gratuity on or for the admission of any visitor to the Prison or to the prisoners at the time of such visit, or at any other time.

2. A matron to be appointed in every prison where females are confined, who shall reside in the Prison, and constantly superintend the female prisoners. The wards, cells, and yards allotted to female prisoners shall be secured by locks different from those which secure the wards, &c. allotted to male prisoners, the keys to be kept by the matron. Female prisoners in all cases to be attended by female officers.

3. The Superintendent shall, except in case of sickness or absence (by leave of the Provost-Marshal in the case of the County Gaols), visit every ward, see every prisoner, and inspect every cell once at least in every 24 hours, or in the event of his omitting to do so, he shall insert in his Journal the extent and cause of his omission. When the Superintendent or other officer visits the female prisoners, he shall be accompanied by the matron, or in her absence, by a female officer.

4. The Superintendent shall keep a Journal, and insert his name daily, and state the hours he visited and inspected the cells and wards. The other officers shall also daily insert their names. The Superintendent shall record therein all punishments inflicted by his authority, and in case of the County Gaols, by the authority of the Provost Marshal or by that of the Visiting Justices, the day when inflicted, with every other circumstance of importance occurring in the Prison; the Journal to be laid before the Judge at every sitting of the Circuit Court, and signed by him in proof of its having been produced, as also to be produced whenever the Visiting Justices visit the Prison.

Due provision shall be made in every Prison for enforcing hard labor in the cases of prisoners sentenced thereto; and the means and materials requisite for their employment shall be provided; and when the work is of a nature to require previous instruction, it shall be afforded by the employment of proper persons.

6 The male and female prisoners shall be confined in separate buildings or parts of the Prison, so as to prevent them from seeing, conversing or holding any intercourse with each other. The prisoners of each sex shall be divided into distinct classes, care being taken that those of the following classes do not intermix.

IN GAOLS.

1. Debtors and prisoners confined for contempt of Court in civil process.
2. Prisoners convicted of Felony.
3. Ditto   ditto   Misdemeanor.
4. Ditto   committed on charge of suspicion of Felony.
5. Ditto   on charge of suspicion of Misdemeanor, or for want of sureties.

IN OTHER PRISONS.

1. Prisoners convicted of Felony.
2. Ditto   of Misdemeanors
3. Ditto   committed on charge or suspicion of Felony.
4. Ditto   Misdemeanor.
5. Vagrants. Crown witnesses also shall be kept separate.
6. The Visiting Justices shall at their discretion direct the employment of of any prisoner who is not exempted from the performance of

labor, in the performance of any menial office in the Prison, but no
prisoner shall be employed in the discipline of the Prison or in the
service of any officer, or in the service or instruction of any other
prisoner.

7. If the Superintendent at any time deem it improper or inexpedient for
a prisoner to associate with the others of the class to which he belongs, he may place him in any other class, or other part of the Prison, until he can receive the direction of a Visiting Justice, to whom
he shall apply with as iittle delay as possible, who shall ascertain
whether the reasons assigned warrant the deviation from the established rules, and give such orders in wiiting as he thinks fit under
the circumstances of each case; but no prisoner shall be placed before
trial with any convicted prisoner, nor shall a prisoner be removed from
the criminal to the debtor side.

8. Every prisoner sentenced to hard labor shall, unless prevented by sickness, be employed so many hours a day, not exceeding 10, as the Visiting Justices direct, exclusive of the time allowed for meals (Sundays, Good Friday, and Christmas day excepted). All prisouers (debtors and witnesses excepted) shall be locked up at 7 o'clock. The greatest
order and strictest decorum shall be observed by all prisoners when at
work.

9. The appointed Service of the Church of England shall be read by the
Chaplain, the Curate or other qualified person on every Sunday, Christmas day and Good Friday, and prayers selected from the Liturgy read at
least every morning by the Chaplain or Curate, and in case of una · id-
able absence by the Superintendent or other person approved by the Visiting Justices, and portions of the Scriptures shall be read to the prisoners
when assembled for instruction, by the Chaplain, or such person as he
appoints or authorizes; but no prisoner shall be required or obliged to
attend such prayers unless he be a member of the Church of England.
The Superintendents shall allow Dissenting Ministers or Catholic
Priests on every Sunday to read prayers or preach for such as are
members of their Churches, or congregations, and to teach such prisoners to read. No work is to be done on the Sabbath day except
cooking meals, and for ensuring the general and personal cleanliness of
the Prison and prisoners.

10. When the Superintendent is under the necessity of putting a prisoner
in irons or solitary confinement for misbehaviour, the particulars of the
case shall forthwith be reported to a Visiting Justice who shall hear
and determine the same; but no prisoner shall be kept in irons for
more than 24 hours without an order in writing from the Visiting
Justice, specifying the cause, and the time he is to be kept in irons.

11. The Justices in Special Sessions assembled shall prepare a Dietary of
plain and wholesome food for the prisoners, to be submitted to the Governor for approval previous to its being acted upon; regard being had so
far as relates to convicted prisoners, to the nature of the labor required or
performed, so that the allowance of food may be duly apportioned thereto.
Prisoners under the care of the Surgeon shall be allowed such diet as
he directs in writing, and care shall be taken that the provisions are
of proper quality and weight. The supply of ordinary food shall cease
on a prisoner going into hospital, when such diet only shall be allowed
as is directed by the Surgeons. Scales and legal weights and measures
shall be provided, and may, on application of any prisoner to the Superintendent, be used by such prisoner to ascertain the weight of any food
supplied him.

12. Prisoners not in the receipt of Prison allowance, whether confined for debt
or before trial for any supposed crime or offence, shall be allowed to
procure for themselves, and receive at proper hours any food, bedding,
clothing or other necessaries, subject to as strict an examination as may be
reasonable and expedient to prevent extravagance and luxury, within
the walls. All articles of clothing and bedding shall be examined to ascertain they are not likely to communicate filth or infection or facilitate escape.

13. No prisoner confined under sentence of any Court, or in pursuance of
any conviction before a Justice, shall receive any food, clothing or necessaries other than the Prison allowance, except such

as may appear expedient, with reference to the several classes of prisoners, or under special circumstances to be adjudged by one or more Visiting Justices.

14. The gates are not to be opened before 5, a.m., nor kept open after 7, p.m., (except in cases of fire or other urgent necessity), at which hours all persons employed in the Prisons must be within the walls. The Superintendents are expected to see this rule strictly adhered to, on pain of dismissal, and to report forthwith to the Visiting Justice any infringement of it.

15. No person to be allowed to visit for the purpose of communicating with a prisoner before 10 ,a.m., nor after 4, p.m., unless by an order in writing of a Visiting Justice; and persons visiting prisoners must leave at 4 o'clock, unless so permitted.

16. Every prisoner shall be provided with suitable bedding.

17. The Surgeon shall examine every prisoner before he is passed into the proper ward. None shall be discharged if laboring under any acute or dangerous disease, until in the opinion of the Surgeon it is safe, unless he require to be discharged ; his wearing apparel shall be cleansed and disinfected before it is returned to him. When insufficient for the purposes of health and deceney, other clothing shall be furnished to him.

18. No prisoners before trial shall be compelled to wear a prison dress, unless his own clothes are deemed insufficient or improper or necessary to be preserved for the purposes of Justice ; and no prisoner who has not been convicted of Felony, shall be clothed in a party colored dress.

19. The wards and ceilings of the wards, cells, rooms and passages used by the prisoners, shall be cleansed or scraped and lime-washed at least once every 4 months; the rooms, passages and sleeping cells, washed or cleansed every day, or oftener when requisite; and convenient places for the prisoners to wash themselves shall be provided. with an adequate allowance of water, soap, towels and combs.

20. All prisoners shall be allowed as much air and exercise as may be deemed proper for the preservation of health.

21. No wine, malt, or spirituous liquors of any kind shall be sold or admitted in any Prison for any prisoner, except as provided in Schedule C, or by an order from the Surgeon in writing, specifying the quantity, and for whose use it is required.

22. No gaming shall be permitted. The officers shall seize and destroy all dice, cards and other instruments of gaming found therein.

23. No money, perquisite or gratuity, under the name of garnish or any other term, or under any pretence, shall be taken or received from any prisoner on his entrance, or at any other time, or from any person on his account.

24. The Superintendent shall take charge of the moneys and effects brought in by every prisoner, or sent in for his use, for safe custody only, and to be restored to him, or to such person on his behalf as the Visiting Justices direct.

25. Upon the death of a prisoner, notice shall be given by the Superintendent forthwith to a visiting Justice and the Coroner. If the Coroner holds an inquest on the body, no officer or prisoner shall be a juror.

26. No Superintendent shall absent himself, unless compelled by law or on business connected with his office, without special leave from the Visiting Justices; and in case of the County Gaols, from the Provost Marshal, on pain of dismissal. He is strictly enjoined to see all the rules duly carried into effect, and particularly directed to adopt the utmost regularity and cleanliness in every department, and by a firm, yet kind mode of treatment, ensure to himself the respect and obedience of the prisoners. To see every prisoner in solitary confinement, morning and evening, at which time he is to see the food and allowance of water for each duly delivered.

27. The Visiting Justices shall appoint one of the officers (the County Gaols excepted) to act as Keeper, whenever the Superintendent is sick, or

necessarily absent, who shall, whilst performing his duties, have all his powers and be subject to his responsibilities.

28. The Officers shall keep watch every night, within the walls, one from 8 to 11, p.m., one from 11 to 2, a.m., and one from 2 to 5, a.m.

29. Repealed.—The Surgeon shall visit the Prison every morning, and see every sick and newly admitted prisoner, and prisoner under punishment imposed by a Visiting Justice or Superintendent, and twice at least in every week and oftener, if necessary, every prisoner confined, whether criminal or debtor. This rule shall be subject to alteration or amendment by the Governor, and be printed and fixed as other rules, and be observed in like manner as any other rule in Schedule B, 21 V., c. 16, s. 2.

SCHEDULE C,

MISDEMEANANTS OF 1ST CLASS, &c.

1. No Misdemeanant of the 1st Class shall be placed in the common reception cell, nor required to bathe in the common bath, or have his hair cut.

2. To be searched on admission by an officer, who shall take from him any dangerous weapon or articles calculated to facilitate escape. He may retain any money and effects brought into the Prison with him, and receive subsequently any money and other effects (subject to examination) not of an inconvenient, improper or dangerous kind.

3. To be lodged in any convenient and suitable apartment that can be provided consistent with his safe custody.

4. To be permitted to wear his own clothing.

5. Also to maintain himself, and receive at convenient hours any food, clothing, bedding or other necessaries, subject to examination and under such limitation, to be judged of by one or more visiting Justices, as may be requisite for preventing extravagance and excess.

6. Also to see his friends in his apartment between 10, a. m. and 4, p. m.

7. Also to write, send or receive letters or other papers.

8. Also at his own expense to be permitted the use of any books or newspapers, not of an objectionable kind, to be judged of by one or more visiting Justices.

9. Also to procure for himself wine, not exceeding one pint, or malt liquor not exceeding one quart, in 24 hours.

10. To be allowed such air and exercise as the arrangement of the Prison will permit.

11. Not to be required to perform any work or labor, clean his apartment, or make his bed, or perform any other manual office, but at his own request he may be supplied with or may procure any employment and materials and tools which the keeper deems safe and convenient.

12. His apartment shall be cleaned, his bed made, and his meals brought in by an officer.

13. If unable to maintain himself, he shall be provided with the Prison diet or allowance.

14. Any prisoner of his class who disobeys, evades, or abuses any rule applicable to this division of prisoners, shall be tried and dealt with under this Act.

SCHEDULE D.

PRISONERS EMPLOYED ON ROADS, &c.

1. No prisoner to be employed without the walls, who is not under sentence of hard labor.

2. In lieu of this, see 26 V., S. 2, c. 18, Employment of females.

3. No Juvenile prisoner shall be so employed.

4. In determining the number to be sent upon the roads or to other public work, regard shall be always had to the necessary duties to be performed within the Prison.

5. Prisoners not to be employed at a greater distance than 3 miles from their Prison, except under very special circumstances to be judged of by the Governor, and then only with his express sanction and direction.

6. Prisoners employed without the walls to leave at day break.

7. To be attended on the road and at their work by an adequate guard of Officers or Police.

8. The time for breakfast and a short rest, to be limited to three fourths of an hour.

9. To be drawn off their work at such time in the afternoon as will give them, at a reasonable rate of walking, a full hour before dusk for dinner, changing clothes, &c., preparatory to being locked up for the night.

See 28 V., c. 22, s. 9   10. To be always lodged in the Prisons to which they have been sentenced or transferred, except under very special circumstances to be judged of by the Governor, and then only with his express sanction and direction, and on no pretence whatever to be kept out after sunset.

11. Not to be intermingled, or directly associated, at their work, with hired laborers.

12. Only Officers or the Police appointed for the purpose, and who will be responsible for the manner they discharge their duty, shall exercise authority over them.

13. When their labour is required for any work of a public or parochial nature, other than what is under the authority of the Boards of Roads and Bridges, report shall be made to the Governor, of the nature and extent of such work, and his authority obtained before it is entered upon.

14. Prisoners must not be left together, at any time, without the proper supervision of an officer.

15. Subordinate officers never to leave the post assigned to them without a substitute and the Superintendents' permission.

16. To suffer no observations from prisoners to themselves, but such as the strictest necessity requires.

17. When on duty, to hold no communication with any person, except in relation to that duty.

18. As greater facilities are afforded to prisoners, by employment in public, for obtaining prohibited articles, there must be a corresponding vigilance on the part of the officers over them.

19. The Superintendent of each Prison shall report monthly to the Inspector, for the information of the Governor, the nature and the locality of the public or parochial works in which the prisoners have been engaged, stating the average number so employed.

20. The prisoners employed without the walls, and the officers who superintend them, are still amenable to all the rules of the existing Prison Law, as far as they are applicable to the circumstances in which they are placed.

Private Bills and Petitions.

Salaries in lieu of fees on   The fees of the officers of the Legislative Council and Assembly, on Private Bills and Petitions, were abolished, and salaries in lieu of fees were granted to the President of the Legislative Council, Clerk and Usher of the Black rod, and also to the Speaker of the Assembly, Clerk and Serjeant at Arms, in lieu of fees, 21 V., c. 17, s. 14.

Private bills   All Bills the object of which is not of public utility or improvement, but solely for the interest or benefit of private individuals, trading Corporations, Companies, or Societies, shall be considered as Private Bills, and upon each a Stamp Duty of £80, shall be levied and taken for the

Stamp on   use of the public; and no such Bill shall take rise in the House except upon Petition from the parties desiring the same, and after report from a select Committee to be appointed to enquire into the allegations of the Petition, 21 V., c. 26, s. 1.

To be impressed on 1st sheet of the draft bill and cancelled by the Clerk   Such Stamp Duty shall be impressed by the Receiver-General on payment to him of £80 (without allowing any discount) on the first sheet of the draft Bill, previous to its introduction, and the Stamp shall be cancelled by the Clerk of the House. On the presentation of the Bill, a receipt from the Receiver-General for the Stamp shall be produced to the Clerk of the Assembly, shewing the payment without discount, 21 V., c. 26, s. 2.

21 V., c. 26, s. 3, imposing a 10s. Stamp on certain Petitions presented to the Assembly, repealed, 28 V., c. 1.

Stamps on petitions repealed

Privy Council.

The functions and privileges of the present Council, (all of whom by name were declared to be Members of the Legislative Council, s. 2) whether exercised as a Privy Council, a Legislative or an Administrative Council, or as a Judicial Body, or otherwise, howsoever, were determined, 17 V., c. 29, s. 12.

Powers of late Council determined

Her Majesty may appoint such number of persons as she sees fit, to be the Privy or Advising Council of the Governor, who shall exercise and enjoy the like powers and authorities, as are now holden by the Members of the present Council when sitting, or acting as a Privy Council. Not to defeat or limit the power of Her Majesty to select, appoint or remove the Privy Councillors, 17 V., c. 29, s. 13.

Appointments and powers of the present Privy Council

The Secretary of the Executive Committee shall be the Clerk and execute the duties performed by the present Clerk, 17 V., c. 29, s. 14.

Their Clerk

£1,000 per annum appropriated out of the civil list, to the Governor, and Privy Council for extraordinary and unforeseen expenses, 17 V., c. 29, Schedule A.

£1000 per annum appropriated to

Produce, Protection of.

If any person have in his possession any quantity of sugar, pimento, or coffee exceeding 50lbs, any person who suspects it to be stolen may give information on oath before 2 Magistrates, stating a probable cause for believing it to be stolen, who shall summon the person in possession before them, and call on him to account for the means by which the same came into his possession, and if he cannot satisfactorily account for the same, it shall be forfeited to the parish for the good of the poor. Not to affect the claim of the rightful owner, or exempt the party from the penalties of the laws for stealing or receiving stolen goods, 10 G. 4, c. 15.

Forfeiture of When not satisfactorily accounted for

Provost Marshal.

In case of the death or removal of any Provost Marshal, so as he may be rendered incapable to make return of writs, the succeeding Provost Marshal is empowered to make return of the same, and in every thing else to act as effectually as the preceding Provost Marshal could have done, first giving security to the preceding Provost Marshal or his security, to indemnify them, and taking the same himself of the respective Marshals, and in all other respects qualified himself as by law required, 10 Ann, c. 4, s. 6.

Returns to writs by his successor

If any Provost Marshal dies, on or immediately before the return day of such process as has been duly lodged in his office, the several Deputy Marshals appointed by him shall continue in their office, and execute the same, and all things belonging thereto, in the name of the deceased, until another Provost Marshal is appointed and duly qualified. The Deputies shall be answerable for the execution of the office in all things, and to all intents and purposes during such interval, as the deceased Provost Marshal would have been, if living; and the securities given to the deceased by the Deputies, and their sureties, shall remain securities to the King, and to all persons for the due performance of the office, by the Deputies during such interval, 5 G. 4, c. 13, s. 1.

Until the appointment of a successor the deputies shall execute process

The returns to all such process, and to all inquisitions, and other proceedings which are required to be returned in the name of the Provost Marshal, shall during such interval be made in the name of the deceased Provost Marshal, and shall, except as to writs of venire facias, be signed by the several Deputy Marshals, by whom they were or might have been executed, and writs of venire facias, shall be signed by the person who was duly authorized by the deceased to issue precepts and sign his

Returns to such process

name thereto. Such Deputy Marshal, or Chief Clerk, shall not, by reason of his so signing the name of the deceased Provost Marshal, be entitled to any additional right, interest or emolument. Not to limit, extend, or alter the security held by any Patentee of the Office of Provost Marshal, or the responsibility of such Patentee in any manner, 5 G. 4, c. 13, s. 2.

Security

The Provost Marshal shall enter into recognizance with 2 sureties, before the Chief Justice, for the faithful and due discharge of his office, to be entered up and recorded in the office of the Clerk of the Crown, and signed by the Provost Marshal and his securities before the Chief Justice at the time, 15 G. 3, c. 7, s. 1.

Penalty for acting before

He shall not presume to enter upon or execute his office before he has entered into such recognizance, under the penalty of £1,000 (£600 sterling) and be rendered incapable of holding such office, 15 G. 3, c. 7, s. 2.

Notice of entering into security

He shall leave with the Clerk of the Crown, and Attorney-General, notice in writing of his intention of entering into such recognizance, with the names and additions of his intended securities, 4 days at least before, that the Attorney-General may, if he thinks fit, attend, 15 G. 3, c. 7, s. 3.

Amount of recognizance

The Provost Marshal's recognizance shall be himself in £20,000 (£12,000 t i g) and 2 sureties in £5,000 (£3,000 sterling) each, 15 G. 3, c. 7, s. 4 erl n

Fresh security

He shall be compelled to give fresh securities upon the death or insufficiency of his former sureties, upon being required by the Attorney-General, within one month after he has been so required, first giving to the Clerk of the Crown 4 days notice in writing of his intention of giving such fresh sureties, with the names and additions of the intended sureties, that the Attorney-General may, if he thinks fit, attend, to be taken as directed by 15 G. 3, c. 7 ; 4 G. 4, c. 12.

Deputies

He shall keep in each precinct a sufficient person to act as Deputy Marshal, who shall reside in the most convenient place of the precinct, in order to receive all such prisoners as shall be committed to him within the precinct, and also to execute all such writs and precepts as shall be directed to him by any Judge, or Justice of such precinct, 8 G. 2, c. 5, s. 12.

To attend courts

He or some person in his stead, lawfully deputed by him, shall attend the Justices during the whole time of their holding their Courts, 31 G. 2, c. 4, s. 21.

Alphabetical book of actions, warrants & writs

The Provost Marshal shall keep a book or register of all actions delivered in his office for service, and of all bench warrants, and other warrants from any Judge of the Supreme Court, or of the Attorney-General, and of all writs mesne or Judicial, in which the names of the defendants shall be first entered in an alphabetical manner, and then the names of the plaintiffs, together with the day when each action or summons, warrant or writ was lodged, and which shall be free and open for the inspection of all persons, 19 V., c. 31, s. 2.

Duties of deputies with respect to execution of process

Every Deputy Marshal shall be diligent in effecting the service and execution of all actions, warrants, precepts and process delivered or sent to him by the Provost Marshal, and in case of any neglect of duty, default, corruption or connivance in or concerning the non-service or non-

Penalty

execution of any process delivered or sent as aforesaid, the Supreme Court may, upon complaint, impose a fine upon the offending Deputy not exceeding £100 for each offence, or dismiss him, which shall render him incapable of again serving as a Deputy Marshal, unless by permission of the Court, entered of record in the office of the Clerk of the Court 19 V., c. 31, s. 5

Fees on service of action demandable in advance

The Provost Marshal shall, before service of any process for the commencement of any action, be entitled to demand and have from the plaintiff or person issuing it, the fees now payable for such service. If service be not effected before the next Session of the Supreme Court, he shall on demand of such plaintiff or person, or his Attorney at-Law, return the amount of service money so advanced, with interest at £10 per cent per annum, 19 V., c. 10, s 55.

Deputy Marshal's returns of summons to Provost Marshal

Every Deputy Marshal, shall before the first day of every Supreme Court, make his returns to the Provost Marshal of and concerning all writs of summons, returnable at such Court, whereon precepts shall come to his hands in convenient time for enabling the Provost Marshal to return them into the office of the Clerk of the Court as after required ; and in every case where a copy declaration has not been served, shall, together with his return of process, assign, in writing upon oath, the particular causes of non-service. In every case where he shall not make his return, or in case of non-service, assign the particular causes, the Court shall for every default impose a fine upon him, not exceeding £50 (£30 sterling) unless sufficient cause is shewn in writing upon oath , and also if required by the party interested, upon examination upon oath, viva voce in open Court, or upon interrogatories why such return, or such assignation of the causes of non-service was not made, and under an order of Court, to be made in every case of default without sufficient cause, shall pay all costs of the party complaining ; to be taxed, 43 G. 3, c. 20, s. 1.

The Provost Marshal shall, by the sitting of the Court on the first day thereof, return into the office of the Clerk of the Court all writs of summons returnable thereat, in case of non-service, with the causes assigned by the Deputy, endorsed upon the writs so non-executed. In every case of default, the Court shall set a fine upon him, not exceeding £50, and under an order of Court, in every such case to be made, shall pay all the costs of the party complaining ; to be taxed, 43 G. 3, c. 20, s. 2. *Provost Marshal's returns*

Every Deputy Marshal shall, on the first day of the Supreme Court, make his returns to the Provost Marshal of all writs of venditioni returnable, whereon precepts have come to his hands ; and in every case when a writ has not been fully executed shall, together with his return, either of nulla bona, or of any levy not to the full amount, assign, in writing and upon oath, the particular causes of non-execution, or short execution ; and where any levy is returned in custody, shall, with such return, set forth, in writing and upon oath, when the precept came to his hands, when the levy was made, and the cause why it has not been sold, or he shall be subject to penalties, examination costs, &c., as in s. 1, 43 G. 3, c. 20, s. 3. *Deputy Marshal's returns of venditioni to Provost Marshal*

The Provost Marshal shall, on or before 10 o'clock of the morning of Thursday of the first week of the Supreme Court, return into the office of the Clerk of the Supreme Court all writs of venditioni exponas returnable, and in case of non-execution or short execution with the causes assigned as aforesaid, and in case of a levy returned in custody with such declaration as aforesaid concerning the return endorsed upon the writ, not executed in whole or in part, or with such return of a levy in custody under penalty, &c., as in s. 2, 43 G. 3, c. 20, s. 4 ; 7 V., c. 43. *Provost Marshal's returns*

In every case of a levy returned by the Provost Marshal, as applicable in a course of priority, he shall (such return being made into the office of the Clerk of the Court as aforesaid) be allowed time for ascertaining the proportions wherein the levy is applicable, until the second Tuesday of the Court, 43 G. 3, c. 20, s. 5 ; 7 V., c. 43. *Apportionment of levies to priority*

In every case of refusal or failure by the Provost Marshal to pay over any moneys in his hands, demand of payment being first made by the person entitled to receive the same, or any person authorized by his order, the Supreme Court shall impose upon him a fine not exceeding £100 (£60 sterling) and he shall under an order of Court pay as compensation to the party aggrieved, over and above the sum withheld, a further sum at the rate of £10 per cent per annum, on the amount withheld, and shall also under such order pay the costs of the party aggrieved ; to be taxed, 43 G. 3. c. 20, s. 6. *Penalty for refusal to pay orders and any moneys in his hands*

In every other case of default of any Provost Marshal or Deputy, by any other Act incumbent on them, where any suitor complains (such default appearing to it) the Supreme Court may impose a fine upon the Provost or Deputy Marshal at its discretion, not exceeding £100 (£60 sterling) and who shall under an order of Court, in every such case to be made, pay the costs of the party aggrieved ; to be taxed. Nothing in the Act shall exempt any Provost or Deputy Marshal from any higher penalty under any other Act, nor affect any right of any suitor attaching by law upon any misfeasance, non-feasance or default, 43 G. 3, c. 20, s. 7. *In other cases of default by the Provost Marshal or Deputy* *Other liabilities preserved*

The Provost Marshal within 4 weeks after the Supreme Court shall make a perfect Schedule, subscribed by him, of all levies returned therein, shewing the manner and p   in which all levies are applicable and applied, and another Schedule of moneys remaining from levies of former Courts, shewing how they are applicable, to be made in alphabetical order according to the names of defendants and of the testators or intestates of *Schedules of levies, and their application to Clerk of the Court*

Fee

defendants as representatives of persons deceased, such Schedules to be verified upon oath of himself or his principal Clerk before a Judge, and delivered to the Clerk of the Court, to be recorded in a book for the purpose, and the original Schedule to be carefully kept (Provost Marshal's fee to be paid by Receiver-General £15) (£9 sterling) under penalty of £400 (£240 sterling) to be recovered by action of debt, one moiety to the Crown the other to the Informer with costs ; to be taxed, 43 G. 3, c. 20, s. 8.

Liability to costs of persons failing in application

If on motion or prosecution against any Provost Marshal or Deputy, the party fail, and it appear to the Court to have been made without just and probable cause, the party failing shall, under order to be made, pay the costs of the Provost Marshal or his Deputy ; to be taxed, 43 G. 3, c. 20, s. 9.

Enforcement of fees
See 19 V., c. 10, s. 55.

The Provost Marshal shall receive his fees immediately after the duty is performed, and if payment is refused or delayed, on proof of demand shall, under an order of Court, recover his legal fees from the Attorney who issued the process, with £6 per cent per annum from the day of demand, and costs ; to be taxed. But not to preclude the Provost Marshal from an e i lect on to enforce payment by any other remedy, 43 G. 3, c. 20, s. 10.

FEES OF PROVOST MARSHAL.

	Currency. £ s. d.	Sterling £ s. d.
10 Ann, c. 4, s. 8		
Every Commitment and Releasement at Common Law or in Chancery, each	0 2 6	0 1 6
Executing any Writ in St. Jago de la Vega	0 2 6	0 1 6
Executing a Writ of Possession, Seisin, Escheat, Cessavit or Assignment of Dower or Partition, besides mile-money, at 6d per mile	0 10 0	0 6 0
Summoning a Jury to execute a Writ of Possession, Escheat, Cessavit, or Assignment of Dower or Partition in St. Jago de la Vega, Kingston or Port Royal, or within 5 miles of any of the said towns	3 0 0	1 16 0
If above 5 miles	5 0 0	3 0 0
Return of a Habeas Corpus cum causa, if in St. Jago de la Vega	0 2 6	0 1 6
For his attendance on the prisoner to any other place, per day	0 4 4½	0 2 7½
For summoning a Special Jury	0 6 3	0 3 9
Return of a Venire Facias	0 1 3	0 0 9
Every Bond with sureties for appearance, to be paid by the defendant	0 0 7½	0 0 4½
Allowance of a Supersedeas	0 1 3	0 0 9
Copy of a Warrant	0 0 7½	0 0 4½
Executing all Writs of Enquiry, Partition, Proprietate Probanda, Forcible Entry, and Writs of Possession, each, besides mile money, at 6d. per mile	0 10 0	0 6 0
Serving every Summons at Common Law or Foreign attachment, besides mile money	0 2	0 1
Fees upon each Verdict	0 2 6	0 1 6
Serving all Summons and other Writs at Common Law, and all other Writs issuing out of the Court of Chancery, besides mile money	0 2 6	0 1 6
Every search in his Books	0 1 3	0 0 9
Each License to sell Drink	0 16 3	0 9 9
Levying a Debt by execution, for the first £100 and under, per pound		0 1 0
For all Sums over £100, per pound		0 0 6
And no more, nor more than is really due, without any pretence of mile money or other charge. When two or more Writs are lodged against the principal or his sureties, or any others, for the same debt, no more poundage fees shall be demanded or received than for the real debt and costs then due, 8 G. 2, c. 5, s. 10.		
Assignment of a Bail Bond	0 2 6	0 1 6
For executing every person	5 0 0	3 0 0

	Currency			Sterling·		
	£	s.	d.	£	s.	d·

To the Bailiff that keeps the Jury, for every action tried 0 1 3   0 0 9

Serving all process out cf the Supreme Court, (subpœnas and venditionis only excepted) per mile, 3d.

No Provost Marshal shall demand or take for the service of writs of summons, scire faciás, replevin or other process, more than 3d. per mile, which is allowed by 10 Anu, c. 4, unless where the Act has otherwise ordered, 8 G. 2, c. 5, s. 1. # G. 2, c. 5, s. 1

In order to ascertain the same and the respective distances of the several parishes from St. Jago de la Vega, the Provost Marshal shall be allowed for mile money at the rates following, for all writs of summons, scire facias. replevin, or other process in the several parishes : 8 G. 2. c. 5, s. 2

Parish	£	s.	d.	£	s.	d.
St. Catherine	0	0	9	0	0	5½
St. Dorothy	0	2	9	0	1	8½
Clarendon	0	7	9	0	4	8
Vere	0	7	0	0	4	2½
St. Elizabeth	0	17	6	0	10	6
Westmoreland	1	11	3	0	18	9
Hanover	1	11	6	0	18	10½
St, John	0	3	0	0	1	10
St. Thomas in the Vale	0	4	0	0	2	5
St. Ann	0	11	6	0	6	11
St. James	1	0	0	0	12	0
St. Mary	0	8	9	0	5	3
Port Royal	0	3	0	0	1	10
Kingston	0	4	6	0	2	5
St. David	0	9	3	0	5	?
St. Thomas in the East	0	16	0	0	9	8
St. Andrew	0	4	0	0	2	5
St. George	0	11	9	0	7	1
Portland	0	15	3	0	9	2

Besides 2s. 6d. (1s. 6d. stg.) for serving each writ, allowed by 10 Anu, c. 4, 8 G. 2, c. 5, s. 2.

For a Bail Bond on any writ of arrest, attachment, or other process of contempt out of the Supreme Court or Court of Chancery, or for a replevin bond .... 0 5 0   0 3 0 8 G. 2, c. 5, s. 3

For executing a writ of ne exeat insula, and mile money 0 10 0   0 6 0

For a Bond taken thereon 0 5 0   0 3 0

For every Warrant granted by a Justice, besides mile money, at 12d currency 0 10 0   0 6 0

For entering in his Books, the Clerk of the Courts Return of satisfaction of each Judgment, on payment by the defendant, his Attornies, Executors, &c. for each satisfaction 0 2 6   0 1 6 14 G. 3, c. 28, s. 16

Afterwards, every person was required at the first time of lodging a Writ of Execution to pay the Provost Marshal, 2s 6d (1s 6d stg.) in full for entering satisfaction upon such execution in his books, whenever it sho'ld appear by any means to be satisfied, and the Provost Marshal subjected to a penalty of £500 (£300 stg.) for every neglect or refusal : recoverable by action of debt, &c. one moiety to the informer, which sum the Clerk of the Court was directed to tax as part of the plaintiff's costs in every original execution, 21 G. 3, c. 23, s. 2, 3, 7.

The Writ of Execution is now abolished, 19 V., c. 10, s. 39.

His Fees for the execution of Writs of Emblements shall be the same as he is entitled to re- 15 G. 3, c. 1, s. 3

	Currency.	Sterling.
	£ s. d.	£ s. d.

ceive for the return of other inquests, 25 G. 3, c. 1, s.

For each Schedule of the application of Levies returned to the Supreme Court, to be paid by the Receiver-General 15 0 0   9 0 0

For executing a Bench Warrant or Warrant of any Judge, or of the Attorney-General, with mile-money at the rate of 8d per mile, for the first 20 miles, and 4d per mile for every mile above 20 :   0 12 0

Every Special Precept 0 7 6

For warning a Special Jury, to be paid by the party obtaining it.... ....   2 2 0

For warning Jury under Prisons Act 3 3 0

For executing a Writ of Attachment, a poundage of 5 per cent. on the amount for which the party is arrested, to be paid in the first instance by the plaintiff, and in addition

On the execution of the Writ. 0 5 0

For mile-money from his office in Spanish Town, to the parochial town of the Deputy, to whom the precept is directed, 1d per mile, if issued through the Clerk of the Court's Office. For mile-money for each mile, from the parochial town to the place to which the officer has to travel for the apprehension of the debtor, per mile 1s.

Mile-money in Kingston 0 3 0

On Forfeited Recognizances and Fines the usual fees and commissions

For each Election at which one Member of Assembly or a Coroner is returned, whether contested or not 3 0 0

Where two or more members are returned   5 0 0

(marginal references, left column)
43 G 3, c. 20, s. 8
19 V, c. 31, s. 4
19 V., c. 31, s. 6
20 V., c. 14, s. 7
20 V., c. 11, s. 9
21 V., c. 13, s. 12 13
21 V. c. 23, s. 11
22 V., c. 5, s. 8

Table of fees
A fair written table of his Fees allowed by this Act to be taken, shall be constantly and publicly kept up in his office, under penalty of £100, (£60 stg.) to be recovered by action of debt; one moiety to the informer.

Penalties
If he or any person for him asks, takes, demands or receives any greater or other fees or sums, or other reward, such officer or person shall forfeit £100 (£60 stg.) recoverable as above, and be further incapacitated to bear such office, 10 Ann, c. 4, s. 34.

For offences by the Provost Marshal or his deputies against this Act a penalty is imposed of £20 (£12 stg.), beyond those in 10 Ann, c. 4, one moiety to the informer, recoverable by action of debt, &c. 8 G. 2, c. 5, s. 17.

Public Buildings.

Assembly and public records
Commissioners were appointed to build an edifice for the use of the Council and Assembly, and for the conservation of the public records, and an Armory for keeping small arms; and the materials were vested in the Commissioners, 17 G. 2, c. 9, s. 1, 4-9.

Rodney's Statue
The Buildings erected or begun under the repealed Act, 30 G. 3, c. 21, on the North side of the Parade, St. Jago de la Vega, whereon to fix Lord Rodney's Statue, and erect Offices and Buildings for the public records, were placed under the jurisdiction of the Board of Works, and to be deemed public Buildings, 38 G. 3, c. 21, s. 1, 2.

Arsenal and Guardhouse
The Board of Works were empowered to purchase land to erect a new Arsenal and Guard House, on the West wing of the Temple, over Lord Rodney's Statue, 44 G. 3, c. 21.

Committee Rooms, Grand Jury Room and Parochial Offices St. Catherine
The Board of Works were empowered to erect a Building on the South side of the Square, in front of the King's House, for additional Committee Rooms for the Assembly, an apartment for the use of the Grand Jury of Middlesex, and offices for the parish and precinct of St. Catherine, and to let and hire such apartments as may not interfere with such purposes, 58 G. 3, c. 17, s. 1-7, 10.

The Court House in St. Jago de la Vega, (part of the above) shall be under the control and under the supervision of the Custos, 27 V., S. 1, c. 7, s. 29.

The Board of Works were also empowered to erect Buildings upon a piece of land adjoining the King's House ; for the use of the Negroes attached, 58 G. 3, c. 26. Land adjoining King's House

The powers of the Board of Works were transferred to the Governor, and Executive Committee. 17 V., c. 29. s. 22, 27. Executive Committee

Public and Parochial Buildings repairs.

The Governor and Executive Committee may, if they approve of the reason for the delay, when required by the Justices and Vestry, draw the sums set down for repairs of Churches and Chapels in the annual Schedule of Ways and Means, or any part thereof, and invest the same at interest if it can be obtained, to be ultimately applied to the purpose for which it was raised, when the Justices and Vestry signify their readiness to expend the same, provided they approve of the proposed ultimate expenditure, 23 V., S. 1, c. 37. Moneys for repairs may be drawn and invested at interest until required,

£17,890 9s. 3d. of the Loan of £40,000 under 24 V., c. 26, were appropriated to the repairs of Churches, Chapels, Rectories, School-houses and other parochial Buildings. 25 V., c. 16. Recent appropriations out of moneys raised on loans

£6,996 appropriated to the repairs of Court Houses, Police Stations, Lock-ups and other Buildings, used for public purposes in the several parishes, 25 V., c. 17.

The Committees under 25 V., c. 16 and 17, in each parish named in the Schedule hereto, shall apply the moneys under those enactments, and the £15,000 Loan under this Act, for repairing, enlarging, or newly building the Buildings stated in the Schedule, and may procure repairs to be done without tender in the absence of eligible tenders. Appointments of Committees of whom the Members of parishes shall form part. The repairs to the new Lunatic Asylum, St. Michael's School-house, Kingston, Bishop's Lodge, and Buildings at Maroon Town Barracks, to be made by the Board of Works. 26 V. S. 2, c. 20, s. 1-6.

Further provisions for repairs of public and parochial Buildings, and Streets of Kingston, by means of £17,500 additional Loan, 27 V., c. 37.

Public Hospital.

Masters of vessels trading to the Northward of the Tropic of Cancer, arriving at any port, shall pay 6d. (currency) per ton registered burden ; of those trading between the Tropics at the rate of 3d. (currency) per ton.— Sugar droghers and coasting vessels, at the rate of 2s. (currency) per ton, once a year, 46 G. 3, c. 28, s. 1. Tonnage dues appropriated for. To be collected by the Collector, &c. of Kingston, 23 V., c. 12, s. 11-14 ; see Tonnage Duties

For the use of sick or disabled seamen, and transient poor, 46 G. 3, c. 28, s. 3.

The Commissioners of the Public Hospital were empowered to purchase adjoining lands, and to enclose a part of Upper West Street, running through the centre of the Hospital lands, for its enlargment, 9 V.. c. 18, s. 4-7. Enlargement

The Hospital shall be under the superintendence of a Board of visitors, consisting of the Mayor, the Custos, and Members of Assembly for Kingston for the time, the Agent-General of Immigration, the Rector of Kingston, the Principal Medical Officers of the Army and Navy, stationed in the Island, severally for the time, and 6 other persons resident in or near to Kingston, to be nominated by the Governor, and removable at his pleasure, of whom two shall be Merchants, and 2 others qualified Medical men.— No Member shall have or receive any pecuniary interest direct or indirect in any contract entered into for or any supplies furnished to the institution, but any Member who shall be in any way so interested, shall ipso facto cease to be a Member of the Board. 5 members shall be sufficient to form a Board for the transaction of business, 26 V. S. 1, c. 4, s. 1. Board of Visitors 5 a quorum

4 D

Quarterly or other meetings—powers and duties

The Board shall meet once a quarter, or oftener if requisite, at the Hospital, and inspect and examine the books and accounts, inspect the wards, cells, stores and every other place, and the liquors and provisions, and medicines in store, if they think fit; receive and investigate any complaints by, or against any officer, servant, patient or inmate, and if they think necessary, report thereon to the Governor, and draw up and transmit to him such other reports and returns as they deem necessary, or which the Governor may call for, in respect of any matter relating to the Institution. Any member may call at, and inspect the Hospital, or any portion, at any hour, and see and examine any officer, servant, nurse or inmate. The Board of Visitors shall, as soon as practicable, draw up rules for their own guidance, to be submitted to the Governor in Executive Committee for their approval, and shall have power to suggest alterations, amendments and additions to such, as also to all other rules of the Institution as they may from time to time think necessary, for presentation by the Inspector for the consideration of the Governor in Executive Committee, 26 V., S. 1, c. 4, s. 2.

Chairman

The Board shall, at a general meeting to be held annually, on a day to be appointed by them, elect a Chairman to preside over all meetings at which he is present; but in case of his absence, the members present may appoint a Chairman pro tempore, 26 V., S. 1, c. 4, s. 3.

Visitors' Book

A Visitor's book shall be kept at the Institution, in which every member who visits the Institution shall enter the day and hour he visited, with any remarks respecting any matters connected with the management or regulation; a copy of all which entries shall be forwarded weekly

Copies of entries to be forwarded to Governor

to the Governor, by the Clerk, 26 V., S. 1, c. 4, s. 4.

Board may administer oaths, &c.

The Board may administer an oath or affirmation to any officer or inmate, when they think fit to institute enquiry on oath, &c., into any complaint. Wilfully giving false evidence, shall be deemed perjury; and procuring or instigating false evidence, subornation of perjury, and be punishable as such, 26 V., S. 1, c. 4, s. 5.

Inspector and Director
Salary—Duties

The Governor may appoint, and at pleasure remove, an Inspector and Director, (who shall also be Inspector and Director of the New Lunatic Asylum) at a salary not exceeding £400, whose duty it shall be particularly to receive, examine and certify the accounts, and direct and superintend the financial and general management of both Institutions. He shall also be charged with such further duties and functions, and subject to the rules instituted and approved of by the Governor in Executive Committee, and shall, in conjunction with the Consulting Physician or Surgeon, and the Ordinary Medical Officers, draw up, alter or amend rules, (subject to the approval of the Governor in Executive Committee) for the government and guidance of the patients, officers, servants and inmates, and for enforcing cleanliness, temperance, and decent and orderly behaviour throughout the Institution, and among the attendants and persons visiting

Rules to be exhibited and read, &c.

it. All rules so approved, shall be printed and hung up in a conspicuous part of each ward, and be read aloud publicly by the Clerk, in the presence of the Inspector, officers, attendants and servants once a month, and copies thereof shall be subscribed by the officers, attendants and servants,

Publication

or such as may be required to do so. Such as it may be deemed expedient to give general publicity to, may also be published in the "Gazette" or other newspaper, under the direction of the Governor in Executive Committee, 26 V., S. 1, c. 4, s. 6.

Annual reports for Legislature

The Inspector shall annually prepare and make up, and forward in triplicate, a report to the Governor, to be laid before the Legislature, of the state of the Institution to 30th September, as also of the expenditure and contract prices for the past year, the original of which before being copied, shall be submitted to the Board of Visitors, with the draft reports of the Medical Officers and Chaplain, as after provided, both of which the Inspector shall have copied in triplicate, to be forwarded for presentation, 26 V., S. 1, c. 4, s. 7.

Chaplain
Salary

The Governor may appoint, and at pleasure remove, a Clergyman of the Church of England, duly ordained, to be the Chaplain, at a salary not exceeding £60; but not to prejudice the rights of Ministers of other religious denominations from visiting under such rules as shall be made. It

Duties

shall be his duty to solemnize Divine Service at the Institution every Sunday, and on other convenient days of the week, and to visit the sick, admiulster the Sacrament, and afford religious consolation to the inmates. He shall annually, as soon after 30th September as possible, furnish the Inspect. or with a draft report as to the condition of the inmates during the past year, which after being laid before the Visitors, shall, when copied in tri. plicate, be forwarded by the Inspector to the Governor, 26 V.. S. l, c. 4, s. 8. *Annual report*

The Governor may also, when he thinks fit, a point and at plea. sure revoke the appoinment of one or more consultingPhysicians, or con. sulting Physicians or Surgeons, the appointment to be honorary merely, and without emolument, and they shall be ex officio Members of the Board, 26 V. S. 1, c. 4, s. 9. *Consulting physicians or surgeons*

Also to appoint, and at pleasure remove not exceeding 3 ordinary Medi. cal Officers, at salaries, not exceeding in the whole £360, among whom the wards and patients shall be divided as equally as practicable, one of whom shall retire annually from office, or as may be arranged by rules to be made, 26 V. S. 1, c. 4, s. 10. *3 ordinary Medi cal Officers* *Retirement*

They shall visit the Institution daily, or as often as they think needful and proper, and be responsible for the Medical or Surgical or Medical and Surgical care and treatment of the patients in their respective wards, but shall not be debarred from engaging in private practice ; they shall superintend and direct the resident Medical Officers to prepare the usual scales of dietary for the Institution, and see that the various registers, tables, and the Medical Journals and Case books of their wards are faithfully kept, and regularly written up, and the annual report prepared, (s. 7-13,) 26 V. S. J, c. 4, s. 11. *Their Duties* *May engage in private practice*

The Governor may. also appoint from among duly qualified Medical Practitioners, and at pleasure remove 2 or more resident Medical or Surgi. cal Officers at such salaries as the Governor, with the advice of the Executive Committee apportions, so that the whole cost does not exceed £600 per annum, to include Board, washing and servants. One to retire after 2 years service, or as the rules shall determine. During their continuance in office, they shall not engage in private practice, but shall devote their entire time and attention to the interest of the Institution. 2 at least, shall reside within the Institution, and implicitly observe the rules for their guidance and the directions of the ordinary Medical attendants in their wards, 26 V. S. 1, c. 4, s, 12. *Resident Medical Officers* *Not to engage in private practice*

One of the resident Medical Officers shall, in addition to his general duties, be also the Medical registrar, and he shall draw up and keep such statistical and other notes and tables as may be determined on by the ordinary Medical Officers, and shall under their direction prepare a draft report annually, to 30th September, which, as soon after as possible, shall be submitted to the Board, and then being prepared in triplicate, forwarded by the Inspector to the Governor, (s. 7, 11,) 26 V. S. 1, c. 4, s. 13. *One to be Medical Registrar*

The resident Medical Officers shall write up with the least possible delay all registers, tables and books, which shall be open to the inspection of the consulting and ordinary Medical or Surgical attendants, and the Inspecr, and shall be produced at the regular meetings of the Board, 26 V. S. 1, to 4, s. 14. *To write up re gisters, books, &c.*

In case of the death of any patient in the Institution, a notice and statement (Form Schedule) of the death and cause, and the name of any persons present at the death shall be drawn up and signed by the Clerk and Medical Officer under whose particular care the a m was, and a copy transmitted by the Clerk to the registrar of deaths for the district, 26 V. S. I, c. 4, s. 15. *Reports of deaths*

Persons intending to qualify themselves for the Medical profession, on producing satisfactory testimonials of character and education, and on the recommendation of 2 Medical Practitioners of this Island, shall be permitted to attend and witness the Medical and Surgical practice, as also the dispensing, subject to the rules for their government and guidance, on payment of such fees as may be determined on and sanctioned by the Governor in Executive Committee, 26 V. S. 1, c. 4, s. 16. *Medical Students may attend*

Any duly qualified Member of the Medical profession shall have free access to attend the Medical and Surgical practice at the ordinary hours of visiting and operating, as also to the postmortem examinations, and the use of the dead room under the rules, 26 V. S. 1, c. 4, s. 17. *As also Practi tioners*

The Governor may appoint and at pleasure remove the following officers who (the Clerk excepted) shall reside on the premises ; *Officers*

Apothecary

A qualified and competent Apothecary and Dispenser at a salary, not exceeding £150;

Steward

A Steward and Purveyor: salary £150.

Matron

A Matron; salary £80.

Clerk

A Clerk; salary £160,

Who for the same salary shall act as Clerk to the Lunatic Asylum, and to the visitors of both Institutions, and perform all such other duties as may be determined on, but shall not be required to reside on the premises.— Each of the above officers shall implicitly obey the rules for their guidance, and, with the exception of the Clerk, shall, in addition to their salaries, receive board, washing, and servants attendance, 26 V. S. 1, c. 4, s.18.

The Clerk shall be subject to all the provisions and requirements of this Act, and 25 V., c. 9, (Lunatic Asylum) relating to the Clerk of each Institution, 26 V. S. 1, c. 4, s. 19.

Other officers, nurses and servants to be appointed by the Inspector

All other officers, nurses, attendants and servants, shall be appointed and be removable by the Inspector, subject to the Governor's approval, and shall receive salaries and wages not exceeding such sums as the Governor in Executive Committee shall sanction. The selection and removal of nurses shall be with the concurrence of the Medical Officers. All nurses and attendants on the sick shall be under the immediate control and supervision of the Medical Staff, and where practicable preference shall be given to a trained nurse. The Inspector shall make rules for regulating the attendance and training of such nurses in the wards of the Hospital, subject to the approval of the Governor in Executive Committee, 26 V., S. 1, c. 4, s. 20.

Subordinate Resident officers, &c. rations

The subordinate resident officers, nurses and others, shall, in the discretion of the Board, and subject to the Governor's approval, receive rations or be dicted from and at the Institution daily, in addition to, or in lieu of salary, subject to the rules, 26 V., S. 1, c. 4, s. 21.

Governor in Executive Committee make alterations in Staff, &c.

The Governor in Executive Committee may make such alterations in . the staff of Medical and other officers and attendants as may appear advisable, and calculated to effect an improved organization in the management of the Institution and system, and thereupon appoint and remove any officers and attendants. The expenditure for salaries or wages of the officers, nurses, attendants or servants to be employed, shall in no case exceed in the aggregate the amount of salaries and wages by this Act authorized, 26 V, S. 1, c. 4, s. 22.

But not at an increased expenditure

Stores, &c. (except Medical and clothing) to be contracted for after advertisement by tender

No stores, provisions, wines or other necessaries (except Medical stores and materials for domestic or personal clothing which may be imported from the United Kingdom or elsewhere, with the sanction of the Governor in Executive Committee, without previous competition) shall be contracted for or purchased for the Institution, until after advertisements for the supply have been duly published in the "Gazette" or other newspaper, by order of the Governor in Executive Committee calling for tenders and who shall accept the most advantageous All contracts and securities for the performance thereof, shall be entered into with the Executive Committee on behalf of the public, and no contract shall endure longer than one year. In cases, of emergency, but not otherwise, the Inspector may make contracts for, or order supplies immediately required, not exceeding £20 at any one time, 26 V., S. 1, c. 4, s. 23.

Contracts and securities to be with Executive Committee for no more than one year In emergency

Hospital to be fitted for 200 beds at least & apportioned between the sexes A separate portion for seamen

The Hospital shall be fitted to contain 200 beds at least, subject at all times to the discretion of the Medical Staff, and the wards shall be apportioned between the two sexes as they recommend. A separate portion of the building, and separate wards, shall be set apart and appropriated for the reception of seamen, 26 V., S. 1, c. 4, s. 24.

Patients—In door and out door

The patients shall be divided into two classes. In-door patients to be admitted within the wards, and out-door patients receiving advice and medicines on application, at such times and on such conditions as are after mentioned, and subject to the rules, 26 V., S. 1, c. 4, s. 25.

Applicants as in patients

. Applicants for admission as in-patients will be received daily by the Ordinary Medical Officers at such hours as may be decided on; but all cases of accident or emergency, at any time of the day or night, by the resident Medical Officer on duty, 26 V., S. 1, c. 4, s. 26.

The resident Medical Officer shall daily at the hours fixed on, examine and prescribe for, if necessary, which prescriptions the Dispenser shall make up and dispense to all such poor and destitute persons as apply, and bring a ticket of recommendation from the Mayor or Custos of Kingston, or such other persons as the Governor in Executive Committee may nominate and appoint to grant such tickets, provid'd they be confined to persons unable from poverty to obtain Medical aid ; such officer keeping a record of all such cases, to be included in the annual report. The Governor in Executive Committee may employ the Parochial Medical Officers of Kingston to attend at their homes all such sick and destitute persons as are unab le to attend personally at the Hospital for advice, who shall obtain a written recommendation to this effect, addressed to the Parochial Medical Officer of the district, from any Ordinary or resident Medical Officer of the Hospital. Such recommendation only to be given to persons on the Pauper list, or to be accompanied by a certificate by the party recommending that the individual is bona fide incapable of procuring and paying for such Medical attendance. The persons recommending, shall do so according to rules to be issued to them under direction of the Governor and Executive Committee ; and the Parochial Medical Officers may forward all their prescriptions for the poor to be dispensed at the Hospital, and shall keep an account of all cases treated by them, and make a quarterly return to the Inspector, stating the particulars and result of treatment in each case, 26 V., S. 1, c. 4, s. 27.

No seaman, hired, articled or apprenticed to any vessel, and no person indentured or apprenticed to any estate or person, immigrant or person whatever, shall be admitted, except on occasion of serious accident or other extreme emergency, until the owner or consignee of the vessel, the proprietor or agent of the estate, or master or employer have given a letter of guarantee to the Inspector, undertaking to the extent of £20 for payment of the Hospital dues at the rate of 1s. 6d. per diem for Medical attendance, medicines and maintenance, and for payment also of his funeral expenses in case of his death, (except in case of immigrants, when the charge per diem to the employer shall not exceed 1s., and no employer of immigrants shall be subject to any dues, unless the immigrant is sent or taken by his direction or assent, 27 V., S. 3, c. 5, s. 13.] The owner or consignee of any vessel may limit his liability, under the letter of guarantee, to the period of her sailing, on giving two days notice in writing to the Inspector, prior to her departure ; and in case of notice, and the sick seaman being left in the Hospital after the vessel's departure, the Inspector shall ascertain from the Shipping Master (being an Officer of the Customs) whether any of the seaman's effects have been deposited in his charge, and if so, arrange with him for payment of the balance of dues and expenses incurred, 26 V., S. 1, c. 4, s. 28 ; 27 V., S. 2, c. 5, s. 13.

But not to prevent the admission of a sick seaman without employment, or other sick person in destitute circumstances, and unable otherwise to obtain Medical or Surgical aid and support. But in case any seaman was put on shore, and did not desert, or any other person admitted was indentured or apprenticed to any plantation or person, and did not discharge himself or abscond, and where it appears that the master of a vessel, or the master or employer of any seaman or other person so admitted, sought to evade payment of the Hospital dues and funeral expenses, or either, the owner or consignee, or employer or master, or his agent shall be liable for the dues and expenses, as fully as if the seaman, or indentured or apprenticed person had been sent under direct guarantee, 26 V., S. 1, c. 4, s. 29.

When policemen are sent, suffering from accident or disease, as in-patients, the Inspector on admission of the patient, may enter into an arrangement with the Inspector of Police of the parish for payment of one half of his daily pay, while he continues a patient, in full for Hospital dues; but not to include any expense for bringing or sending back the patient, or for burial, 26 V., S. 1, c. 4, s. 30.

To prevent persons coming up to Kingston, who are inadmissible, the Inspector in conjunction with the Consulting Physician, or Surgeon and Ordinary Medical men, shall draw up, or alter, or add such rules as are approved by the Governor as aforesaid, regulating the admission of in-patients from the distant parishes, and which shall be published and proclaimed as

---

Medical advice and prescriptions for the poor and destitute

On recommendation

To be included in annual report

When parochial Medical Officers are to attend such patients if unable to apply at Hospital

The prescriptions to be dispensed at the Hospital

Quarterly returns to the Inspector

No seaman or other person to be admitted except on emergency, without a letter of guarantee

Immigrants

Limitation of guarantee in case of seaman left in Hospital

Not to prevent admission of seamen out of employ, or destitute persons

When in such cases owners or consignees or employers are liable for dues and funeral expenses

Police admitted as in patients

Rules for admission of in-patients

To be published

widely as possible, in each parish as the Governor in Executive Committee may determine, 26 V., S. 1, c. 4, s. 31.

Patients may be sent to Bath or Milk River

Whenever it appears to the Ordinary Medical Officer, that patients laboring under severe rheumatic and other chronic diseases, would be benefitted by the use of the baths of St. Thomas the Apostle, or of Milk River, and any inmate is a fit subject for either establishment, he shall certify the same to the Inspector, who shall thereupon have power to direct the removal of the patient thereto, and defray all necessary expenses attendant on his removal and maintenance thereto and return if necessary. The Inspector shall satisfy himself that the patient is unable either in part, or in whole to defray such expenses himself, or with the assistance of his relations or friends, 26 V., S. 1, c. 4, s. 32.

To assist, if able, to defray expenses

Aid to destitute patients to return home

The Inspector upon the discharge of any destitute patient, may furnish him with means to support himself until he can return to his home or friends, not exceeding 1s. per diem, or 10s. in the whole, 26 V., S. 1, c. 4, s. 33.

Purveyor to take charge of property of patients, and enter same to be attested by a resident Medical Officer

To be liable for dues and expenses

If any patient at the time of admission is possessed of any property, it shall be taken charge of by the Purveyor or Steward, and full particulars entered in a book, the entry to be attested by a Resident Medical Officer. Such property, or a sufficient portion shall be liable for the medical attendance, medicine and support, at 1s. 6d. per day, of the patient and his funeral expenses, and may be sold by the Inspector to defray the same. Any remaining property and surplus sale moneys shall be delivered up and paid over to the patient on his discharge, or in case of his death to the parties legally entitled thereto upon application, 26 V. S. 1, c. 4, s. 34.

Enforcement of payment of dues or expenses out of estate of patient

If it appears to two Justices that any patient has any estate applicable to his maintenance, and more than sufficient to maintain his family, they may, on application of the Inspector, make an order in writing under their hands and seals to his nearest known relative or friend for payment of the Hospital dues and funeral expenses, or either, incurred by, or on his account, and if not paid within one month after a copy of the order has been left with, or at the residence or last place of residence of such relative or friend, they or any other Justices may, by an order under their hands and seals, direct any Collector of Petty Debts, or other person to seize so much of the money, and to seize and sell so much of the goods and chattels, and take and receive so much of the rents and profits of the lands and tenements of the patient, and of any other income of such patient as are necessary to pay the dues and expenses, or either, accounting for the same to the same or any other Justices, such dues and expenses, or either having been first proved to their satisfaction by the certificate of the Inspector or otherwise, as they may require, and the amount set forth in the order; and if any trustee or other person having the possession, custody, or charge of any property of such patient, or if any company or body, or person having any stock, interest, dividend, or annuity belonging or due to him, pay the whole or any part to defray the amount set forth in such order, the receipt of the Collector or person directed to receive same, shall be a good discharge 26 V., S. 1, c. 4, s. 35.

Payments over by persons, &c. having property, discharges

Recovery of moneys due in Petty Debt Courts

All Moneys owing by, or on account of patients or for their funeral expenses, may be recoverable by the Inspector in the Petty Debt Court of Kingston, or of the parish where the defendant resides or last resided, at his option without limitation as to the amount, 26 V., S. 1, c. 4, s. 36.

To be paid to the Receiver General

And when received for the Institution, shall be paid over to the Receiver-General to its credit, and be held applicable to its expenses, under warrant of the Governor, 26 V., S. 1, c. 4, s. 37.

Short Title

The Public Hospital Act, 1862, 26 V., S. 1, c. 4, s. 38.

SCHEDULE.

Notice of death of patients, s. 15

I hereby give you notice that   pauper (or a private) patient, admitted in this Hospital on the   day of (or out-door patient as the case may be, under treatment at this Hospital, and residing at   ) died therein (or at   ) in the presence of   on the   day of
                                                Clerk of the Public Hospital.

Dated the   day of   18

I hereby certify that the apparent cause of death of the said
as ascertained by post mortem examination (if so) was

Resident Medical Officer of the Public Hospital.

Public Officers' Sureties.

No Member of the Council or Assembly, or officer accountable to the Public, shall be accepted as Surety of any other Public Officer, 2 W. 4, c. 31.

See European Assurance Society, 27 V., s. 1, c. 35

Quarantine.

All vessels coming from, or having touched at any place from whence the Governor, with the advice of the Privy Council, has adjudged and declared it probable that any infectious disease or distemper highly dangerous to the health of Her Majesty's subjects may be brought, and all vessels and boats receiving any persons, goods, packets, packages, baggage, wearing apparel, books, letters or other article from any vessel coming from, or having touched at such infected place, whether they have come or been brought in such vessels, or have gone or been put on board the same, either before or after the arrival of such vessels, and whether they were or were not bound to any place in this Island, and all persons, goods and other articles on board of any such vessels so coming, &c., or on board any such receiving vessels or boats shall be liable to Quarantine within this Act; and any orders of the Governor and Privy Council concerning Quarantine and the prevention of infection from the time of the departure of the vessel from such infected place, or from the time when such persons, goods or other articles have been received on board; and all such vessels and boats, and all persons, as well pilots as others, goods and other articles on board such receiving vessel or boat shall, upon their arrival, be obliged to perform Quarantine in such place, time and manner as shall from time to time be directed by the Governor and Privy Council; and until they have performed and are duly discharged from Quarantine, no person, goods or other articles shall, either before or after the arrival of such vessels or boats, come or be brought on shore, or go or be put on board any other vessel or boat, in order to come or be brought on shore, although the vessels so coming from such infected place may not be bound to any port here, unless as shall be directed or permitted by the orders of the Governor and Privy Council; and all vessels and boats, whether coming from such infected place, or being otherwise liable to Quarantine, and all persons as well pilots as others, goods and articles whether coming or brought in such vessels or boats, or going or being put on board either before or after arrival, and although not bound to any port here, and all commanders, masters or others having the charge or command of any vessels or boats coming from any infected place, or otherwise liable to Quarantine, shall be subject to all provisions, rules, regulations and restrictions in this Act, or on any order of the Governor and Privy Council concerning Quarantine, and the prevention of infection, and to all penalties and punishments for breach or disobedience thereof, or of any order, 4 V., c. 32, s. 2.

Vessels, boats, persons, goods, &c. liable to quarantine

Pilots included

And subject to the provisions, &c. of the Act and quarantine orders

All goods and merchandize particularly specified in any orders brought or imported from any other country or place, in any vessel, and the vessels in which they are brought, and all vessels arriving from any place under any alarming or suspicious circumstances as to infection, shall be subject to such regulations and restrictions as shall be made by the orders of the Governor and Privy Council, 4 V., c., 32, s. 3.

Goods particularly specified, and vessels arriving under suspicious circumstances

The Governor, of his sole authority, may make such orders as he sees expedient upon any unforeseen emergency, or in any particular case, with respect to any vessels arriving, having any infectious disease or distemper on board, or on board of which any may have appeared in the course of the voyage, or arriving under any other alarming or suspicious circumstances as to infection, although they have not come from any place from which the Governor, &c. have adjudged and declared it probable any infectious disease, &c. may be brought, and also with respect of the persons goods and articles on board; and in case of any infectious disease or distemper appearing or breaking out in this Island, may make orders and give directions, in order to cut off all communications between any persons infected, and the rest of H. M's. subjects, as appear to the Governor expedient; likewise to make orders for shortening the time of Quarantine to be performed by par-

The Governor may make orders alone on emergency although the vessel has not arrived from an infected place

Also in cases of infectious diseases on land to cut off communication

ticular vessels, or persons, goods or articles, or for absolutely or conditionally releasing them from Quarantine ; which shall be as valid and effectual
as well with respect to the master, &c. and all other persons on board as
with respect to any having any intercourse or communication with them,
and to penalties, as any made with the advice of the Privy Council, 4 V.,
c. 32, s. 4.

Also shorten or release from quarantine.

The Governor with advice, &c. may, make rules and orders requiring masters, &c. of vessels, liable to Quarantine or on board whereof any
infectious disease, &c. actually is, to hoist such signals of such description,
and while within such distance from the coasts as therein directed, and
under such penalties and punishments as therein specified. Any commander
&c. having charge of any vessel, and knowing it is not liable to Quarantine, hoisting any such signal, shall forfeit £50 stg., 4 V., c. 32, s. 5.

Signals to be hoisted by vessels with infectious diseases, &c.

When any country or place is known or suspected to be infected, or
when any order is made concerning Quarantine or the prevention of infection, as often as any vessel attempts to enter any port, &c., whether appointed
for performance of Quarantine or not, the Health Officer or his assistant or
person authorized or appointed by the Governor, or if not, the principal
officer of the Customs, or other such officer authorized to act, shall go off to
the vessel, and at a convenient distance demand of the commander, &c.,
and he shall give a true answer, in writing or otherwise, and upon oath or
not as he shall be, by the Health Officer, &c., required, to all questions put
to him by virtue of the regulations of the Governor, &c. If the master, &c.
upon such demand refuse to make a true discovery in any of the particulars
concerning which he is interrogated, or if not required to answer upon oath,
gives a false answer to any question or interrogatory, he shall forfeit £100
sterling, 4 V., c. 32, s. 6.

Masters to give true answers to questions of Health Officer, his Assistant or Custom House Officer.

Penalty for refusing or giving false answers.

If it appears upon such examination or otherwise, that the vessel is
under such circumstances as render it liable to perform Quarantine, and the
port where it is arrived or attempts to enter, is not one where it ought
to perform Quarantine, the officers of any of H. M's. vessels or forts and all
other H. M's. officers, upon notice to them and any others they call to
their assistance, shall oblige the vessel to repair to the place appointed for
Quarantine, and use all necessary means for that purpose, by firing
guns or any other force. In case the vessel comes from or has touched at
any infected place, and the commander, &c. knowing so, or that some person
on board is actually infected, refuses or omits to disclose the same upon examination, or wilfully omits to hoist the signal to denote that his vessel is
liable to Quarantine, he shall forfeit £200 sterling, 4 V., c. 32, s. 7.

Vessel liable to quarantine may be obliged to repair to quarantine ground

Master not disclosing liability or hoisting signal liable to penalty

Every master, &c., of any vessel ordered to perform Quarantine, shall
forthwith, after arrival at the appointed place, deliver to the Health Officer,
&c., and who is required to demand his bill of health and manifest, with
his log book and journal : Penalty, £100 sterling, 4 V., c. 32, s. 8.

To deliver to Health Officer, &c. his bill of health, manifest, Logbook and Journal

If any master, &c., of any vessel liable to perform Quarantine, on
board of which any infectious disease, &c., has not then appeared, himself
quit or knowingly permit or suffer any seaman or passenger coming in the
vessel to quit by going on shore, or on board any other vessel or boat, before Quarantine is fully performed unless by license under any order to be
made, or shall not, within a convenient time, after due notice given for the
purpose, cause the vessel and lading to be conveyed into the place appointed to perform Quarantine, he shall forfeit £300 sterling. If any person
coming in any vessel liable to Quarantine, or pilot or other person going on
board, either before or after her arrival, shall, either before or after arrival,
quit the vessel, unless by license, by going on shore, or on board any
other vessel or boat, with intent to go on shore before the vessel is regularly discharged, any person may, by any kind of necessary force, compel
him to return on board, and he shall suffer imprisonment not exceeding 6
months, and forfeit £200, 4 V., c. 32, s. 9.

Penalty on master permitting seamen or passengers to quit ship

Or pilot or others quitting it

All persons liable to perform Quarantine, and others having had any intercourse or communication with them, whether in vessels, in a lazaret or
elsewhere, shall be subject, during the Quarantine or during the time
they are liable to Quarantine, to such orders as they receive from the
Health Officer, &c., who are empowered and required to enforce all necessary obedience, and in case of necessity, to call in others to their assistance, and the persons called in shall assist accordingly ; and such officers
or persons shall compel all persons liable to perform Quarantine, and persons

Such persons subject to orders of quarantine officer

Powers to enforce obedience

having had intercourse, &c. with them, to repair to such lazaret, vessel or place, and to cause all goods and articles comprised within any orders respecting Quarantine, to be conveyed to such lazaret, vessel, or place duly appointed in the manner and according to the directions made by any order. Persons wilfully refusing or neglecting to repair forthwith to the lazaret, &c., or escaping or attempting to escape thereout before Quarantine duly performed, may be compelled by the Quarantine Officers and watchmen, and other persons appointed to see Quarantine performed, by such necessary force as the case requires, to repair or return thereto; and the person refusing or neglecting, or actually escaping, shall forfeit £100 stg. 4 V., c. 32, s. 10. *Penalties of disobedience*

Any peace officer or other person may seize and apprehend any person who, contrary to this Act, has quitted or comes on shore from any vessel liable to Quarantine, or has escaped from or quitted any vessel under Quarantine, or lazaret, &c., for the purpose of carrying him before a Justice, and any Justice may grant his warrant for the apprehending and conveying any such person to the vessel from which he came on shore, or to any vessel performing Quarantine, or lazaret from which he escaped, or for confining him in any such place of safe custody, (not being a public goal) and under such restrictions as to having communication with others as in the discretion of a Justice, (calling to his aid, if he see fit, any medical person) appears proper, until he can be safely conveyed to a place appointed for the performance of Quarantine, or directions can be obtained from the Governor as to his disposal, and to make any further order, or grant any further warrant that may be necessary, 4 V., c. 32, s. 11. *Peace Officers or any other persons may seize offenders* *And carry them before a Justice* *Powers of Justices*

The Governor, with advice, &c., may issue his order, prohibiting all persons, vessels and boats from going, under any pretence, within the limits of any station assigned for the performance of Quarantine: Penalty for going with any vessel or boat within the limits, £100 stg. 4 V., c. 32, s. 12. *Prohibition from going within limits of quarantine station*

If any officer or person to whom it appertains to execute any order concerning Quarantine or the prevention of infection, or to see the same put in execution, knowingly and wilfully embezzle any goods or articles performing Quarantine, he shall forfeit his office, and become incapable to hold same, or take a new grant thereof, and forfeit £100 sterling. If any such officer or person desert from his duty when employed, or knowingly or willingly permit any person, vessels, goods or merchandize to depart, or be conveyed out of the lazaret, vessel or other place, unless by permission under an order of the Governor, or if any person authorized and directed to give a certificate of a vessel having duly performed Quarantine or airing, knowingly give a false certificate, he shall be guilty of a misdemeanor. If he wilfully or knowingly damage any goods performing any Quarantine under his direction, he shall be liable to pay £100 sterling damages and full costs to the owner, over and above the value of the goods damaged, 4 V., c. 32, s. 13. *Embezzlement by officers, &c., of goods performing quarantine* *Officers &c., permitting persons or goods to depart, or be taken away* *Giving false certificate of performance of quarantine* *Damaging goods,*

After Quarantine has been duly performed, and upon proof, on the oath of the master, &c., of the vessel, and of 3 or more persons belonging thereto, before the Collector, &c., of the port where Quarantine is performed or nearest thereto, or before the Health Officer or his assistant, or a Justice living near, that the vessel and persons have duly performed Quarantine, and the vessel and all persons are free of infection; and after producing a certificate to that purpose, signed by the Health Officer or person acting for him, such Collector or principal officer of Customs, or the Health Officer or his assistant, or Justice shall give a certificate thereof, and the vessel and persons shall be liable to no further restraint or detention on that account, 4 V., c. 32, s. 14. *Discharge from quarantine*

All goods and articles liable to Quarantine shall be opened and aired in the places, time and manner directed by the Governor with advice, &c., and after they are complied with, proof shall be made by the oaths of the master of the lazaret or vessel in which they have been opened and aired, and one of the guardians, or if there be one, then one of the officers authorized by the Customs to act in the service of Quarantine in the lazaret or vessel, or if there be no such officer, then of 2 or more witnesses serving there before the Health Officer or his assistant, in case the opening or airing is had at a place where he is established; or otherwise, before the Officer of Customs authorized to act, which oath they are authorized to administer, and to grant a certificate of such proof having been made, upon production of which to the proper Officer of Customs, the goods, and *Discharge of goods &c.*

4 E

other articles shall be liable to no further restraint or detention, 4 V., c. 32, s. 15.

Forging certificate &c, misdemeanor

Knowingly or wilfully forging or counterfeiting, interlining, erasing or altering, or procuring, &c., any certificate directed or required to be granted by any order touching Quarantine, or publishing any such forged &c., certificate, knowing it to be forged, &c., or knowingly or wilfully uttering and publishing any such certificate, with the intent to obtain the effect of a true certificate to be given thereto, knowing the contents to be false ; Misdemeanor, 4 V., c. 32, s. 16.

Landing goods or receiving them

Landing or unshipping, or moving in order to the landing or unshipping thereof, any goods, packets, packages, baggage, wearing apparel, books, letters, or other articles from on board any vessel liable to Quarantine, or knowingly receiving them after they have been so landed or unshipped : penalty £300 sterling. Clandestinely conveying or secreting or concealing, for the purpose of conveying any letter, goods, or other articles from any vessel performing Quarantine, or from the lazaret or place where they are performing Quarantine : penalty £100 sterling, 4 V., c. 32, s. 17.

Secreting letters goods, &c.

False swearing, &c.

Where any examination or answer shall be taken or made upon oath, the person authorized to take the same, may administer such oaths. Any person wilfully swearing falsely, or procuring another to do so, shall be guilty of perjury, or subornation of perjury, and be liable to the penalties thereof, 4 V., c. 32, s. 18.

Appointments of officers

Health Officers and their assistants, or other persons the Governor is empowered to appoint, may be appointed by any instrument signed by him ; and every thing required to be done by them, may in case of their absence or sickness be performed by the principal officer of the Customs ; to be authorized to act, 4 V., c. 32, s. 19.

Published orders and proclamations evidence

The publication in any newspaper (see Jamaica Gazette, 8 V., c. 46,) of any order of the Governor with or without the advice of the Privy Council, or of any proclamation, shall be sufficient notice to all persons and received as evidence of the making date, and contents, 4 V., c. 32, s. 20.

Recovery and application of penalties

All forfeitures and penalties shall be recovered in the Supreme Court, and be given two thirds to the informer, and one third to the Crown, for the benefit of the public of this Island, 4 V., c. 32, s. 21.

Action to be in name of the Attorney-General or of a person empowered by the Governor

But no action or prosecution shall be commenced unless in the name of the Attorney-General, or under the direction of the Governor, and in the name of a person by him empowered, 4 V., s. 32, s. 22.

Attorney-General may stay proceedings

And the Attorney General may stop proceedings as well with respect to the share of any person, as to that of the Crown, if upon consideration of the circumstances it appears to him fit, 4 V., c. 32, s. 23.

Offences for which no specific penalty provided to be tried before three Justices

Offences for which no specific penalty, forfeiture or punishment is provided, may be tried before 3 Justices : penalty on conviction, not exceeding £100 sterling or imprisonment not exceeding 3 months ; such forfeiture, to be paid two thirds to the party suing, and the remainder to the Crown, to be applied as the proceeds of other forfeitures are before directed, 4 V., c. 32, s. 24.

Answers of commander to questions to what extent evidence in suits
Direction to perform quarantine
Presumptive evidence of what

In any prosecution, suit or proceeding, the answers of the Commander &c., of any vessel to any question or interrogatory, shall be received as evidence so far as relate to the place from which the vessel came, or those at which she touched in the course of the voyage ; and when a vessel has been directed to perform Quarantine by any person authorized, they having been so directed, shall be received as evidence that the vessel was liable to quarantine, unless satisfactory proof is produced by the defendant, that the vessel did not come from, or touch at any such place as stated in the answers, or that the vessel although directed was not liable to perform quarantine.—

Also actual performance to be evidence of liability to quarantine

And where a vessel has in fact been put under Quarantine by any person authorized to act, and shall actually be performing same, the vessel shall be deemed liable to Quarantine without proving in what manner, or under what circumstances she became so, 4 V. c. 32 s. 25.

Protection from actions

The defendant to any action for any thing done under this Act, or any order may plead the general issue, and give the special matter in evidence, and if it appears to have been so done, the Jury shall find for the defendant. If the plaintiff be nonsuited or discontinue after appearance, or judgment is given upon any verdict, or upon demurrer against the plaintiff, the defendant shall recover [treble] costs, [see costs 8 V. c. 28 s. 21.], 4 V. c. 32 s. 26.

The then Health Officers continued in office, 4 V. c. 32 s. 27. Health Officers salaries

Salaries of Health Officers. (Schedule) to be paid quarterly by the Receiver-General, 4 V. c. 32 s. 28.

Masters of vessels before entry shall pay to the Collector and Controller in Kingston, and Sub-Collectors at other ports, to be paid over in the same manner as the Import Duties, to the Receiver General, for every ship or barque 20s. currency, (12s. sterling); Brig, snow or brigantine, 15s. (9s sterling); Schooner or sloop (Droghing vessels excepted) 10s. (6s. sterling) in aid of the expenses of this Act, 4 V., c. 32, s. 29. *Tax on shipping in aid of act*

The powers given to the Governor may be exercised by the person administering the Government, 4 V. c. 32 s 37. *Powers to be exercised by person administering the Government*

Actions to be brought within 6 months, 4 V. c. 32, s. 38. *Limitation of actions*

SCHEDULE.

Kingston	....	....	£500
Montego Bay	....		100
Falmouth	....	....	100
Morant Bay and Port Morant			60
Annotto Bay		....	50
Savanna-la-Mar			30
St. Ann's Bay		....	30
Port Antonio	....		20
Port Maria and Oracabessa	....	....	50
Rio Bueno	....		20
Lucea		....	30
Old Harbour and Salt River			50
Alligator Pond		....	20
Black River			20
Dry Harbour		....	20
Green Island	....		20

Health Officers salaries.

Railways.

CONVEYANCE OF MAILS.

In all cases of Railways already or to be made, by which passengers or goods are conveyed, the Postmaster General or the deputy Postmaster General for this Island may, by notice in writing under his hand, delivered to the Company of Proprietors, require the mails or post letter bags, after a day to be named in the notice, not less than 28 days from delivery, to be conveyed and forwarded by the Company on their Railway, either by the ordinary or special trains, at such hours or times in the day or night as he may direct, with the guards appointed by him in charge, and any other officer of the Post Office; and thereupon the Company shall, after the day to be named, at their own costs, provide sufficient carriages and engines on such Railways for the conveyance thereof to his satisfaction, and receive, take up, carry and convey by such ordinary or special trains, or otherwise as need may be, all such mails or post letter bags as shall be tendered to them or any of their officers, servants or agents, by any officer of the Post Office, and also receive and convey the guards in charge, and any other officers, and receive, take up, deliver and leave such mails or post letter bags, guards and officers at such places in the line of such Railway on such days and hours in the day or night, and subject to all such reasonable regulations and restrictions as to speed of travelling, places, times and duration of stoppages, and times of arrival, as the Postmaster General or deputy for this Island shall from time to time order. The rate of speed shall in no case exceed the maximum rate prescribed by the Directors for the conveyance of passengers by their first-class trains; but no alteration in the rate of speed of any train by which the mails are conveyed, shall be made without 6 calendar months' notice to the Postmaster General, &c., 9 V., c. 22, s. 1.

After notice any Company shall provide carriages and convey and deliver mails, guards and officers of the Post Office, subject to the regulations of the Post Master General

Rate of speed

If required the whole carriage shall be appropriated.

The Postmaster-General, &c., may if he sees fit, require the whole of the inside of any carriage to be exclusively appropriated for the purpose of carrying the mails, 9 V., c. 22, s. 2.

Or the Post Master General may send Her Majesty's carriages to be conveyed by the usual trucks or frames

If he is at any time desirous of sending any of Her Majesty's mail carriages or carts with the mails, guards and officers, instead of sending them by carriages provided by the Company, they shall at his request, signified by notice as aforesaid, cause such mail carriages &c. to be conveyed by the usual trucks or frames, subject to such regulations or restrictions as before mentioned, 9 V. c. 22, s. 3.

The Company and their officers to comply with the Post Office regulations.

For the greater security of the mails, the Company and their officers, servants and agents shall obey and perform all such reasonable regulations, respecting the conveyance, delivering and leaving of such mails, guards and officers of the Post Office mail carriages, &c., on any such Railways, or on the line thereof, as the Postmaster-General, &c., or such officer as he

But no person in charge of the engine to be interfered with

shall nominate in that behalf, shall in his discretion give or make ; but no officer or servant of the Post Office shall interfere with, or give orders to the Engineer or person having the charge of any engine upon any Railway; but if any cause of complaint arises, it shall be stated to the conductor or other officer having the charge of the train, or to the chief officer at any station, and in case of any default or neglect on the part of any officers or servants of the Company to comply with any regulations, the Company shall be wholly responsible, 9 V., c. 22, s. 4.

Remuneration

The Company shall be entitled to such reasonable remuneration, to be paid by the Postmaster-General, &c., as shall either prior to, or after the commencement of such service be agreed upon, or in case of difference of opinion between them, then as shall be determined by arbitration as after provided, but so that the services be not suspended, postponed or deferred by reason of such remuneration not having been fixed or agreed upon, or of the award not having been then made, 9 V., c. 22, s. 5.

Increase or diminution of remuneration and damages upon alteration of the service required

Notwithstanding any agreement or award fixing the amount of remuneration, the Postmaster-General, &c., may, by notice in writing, require, after a day to be named, not less than 28 days from the delivery, any addition to be made to the services in respect of which such agreement was entered into or award made.   In any such case, and also in case of a discontinuance of any part of such services as after provided, a fresh agreement shall be entered into, regulating the future amount of remuneration to be paid for such increased or diminished services as the case may be, or if the parties cannot agree upon the amount, it shall be referred to arbitration ; and such arbitrators may award any compensation they consider reasonable to be paid to any Company for any loss that may be occasioned to them by the discontinuance or alteration of the services previously agreed to be performed, but so that the increased or diminished services shall not be suspended, &c., by reason of the amount of the increased or diminished remuneration not having been fixed or agreed upon or award made, 9 V., c. 22, s. 6.

Determination of services on notice

The Postmaster-General, &c., may at any time give to any Company, by writing under his hand, 6 calendar months' notice that their services, or any part thereof, shall cease and determine; and at the expiration of the notice, the services or such part thereof, and the remuneration for the same shall determine, 9 V., c. 22, s. 7.

Determination without notice

Compensation

The Postmaster-General, &c., may at any time, by notice in writing, under his hand, absolutely determine the services or any part thereof, without previous notice, or on giving any notice less than 6 calendar months, and thereupon they shall cease accordingly.   In case he shall, without giving 6 calendar months' notice, determine the services or any part without any cause, or for any cause other than the default by the Company in the performance of any of the services to be required of them, or the breach by them of any of their engagements, the Postmaster-General, &c., shall make them a full and fair compensation for all loss thereby occasioned, the amount whereof, in case the parties differ, shall be ascertained by arbitration, 9 V., c. 22, s. 8.

Royal Arms to be painted on such carriages

On all carriages to be provided for the service of the Post-Office, there shall on the outside be painted the Royal Arms, in lieu of the name of the owner, and of the number of the carriage, and of all other requisites, if any, prescribed by law in respect of carriages passing on any such Railway, but the want of of the Royal Arms thereon shall not form an objection to its running, 9 V., c. 22, s. 9.

No Company shall make any bye-laws or regulations which militate against, or are contrary or repugnant to any of the enactments herein; and any made, so far as they militate against them, &c., shall be absolutely void, 9 V., c. 22, s. 10.

No bye-laws, &c. to be repugnant hereto

If the Company or any of their officers, servants or agents refuse or neglect to carry or convey any mails or post letter-bags when tendered to them by the Postmaster-General, &c., or any officer of the Post Office, or refuse to carry on their Railway, any mail carriages or carts, or to receive, take up, deliver and leave any such mails, mail guards, or other officers of the Post Office, mail carriages or mail carts, at such places at such times, on such days and subject to such regulations and restrictions as to speed of travelling, places, times and duration of stoppages as the Postmaster-General, &c. shall from time to time reasonably direct or appoint as before provided, or shall not obey and perform all such regulations respecting the conveyance of the mails, and post letter bags, mail carriages or carts on any such Railways as the Postmaster-General, &c., or such officer of the Post Office as he shall nominate shall make for the purposes aforesaid, the Company who, or whose officer, &c., shall so offend, shall forfeit not exceeding £20, the pa m   of or liability to which penalty shall not lesson or affect the liability of the Company under any bond, 9 V., c. 22, s. 11.

Refusal to convey mails, &c.

Not to affect the Company's liability under bond

The Postmaster-General, &c., if he thinks fit, may require the Company to give security by bond to Her Majesty, conditioned to be void if the Company shall from time to time carry or convey or cause, &c., all such mails or post letter bags, mail guards and other officers of the Post Office, mail carriages or mail carts in manner before mentioned, when required by the Postmaster-General, &c., or any officer of the Post Office duly authorized, and shall receive, take up, deliver and leave all such mails, &c., at such places, at such times, on such days, and subject to such regulations and restrictions as to speed of travelling, places, times and duration of stoppages as before mentioned, and shall obey, observe and perform all such regulations respecting the same as the Postmaster-General, &c., shall reasonably make, and shall well and truly do and perform and cause, &c., all such other acts, matters and things as by this Act are required or directed to be done or performed by or on behalf of such Company, their officers, servants and agents. Such bond to be taken in such sum and form as the Postmaster General, &c., shall think proper, and to be renewed whenever forfeited, and also whenever the Post Master General, &c., requires the same to be renewed; and if any Company, when so required, refuse or neglect for one calendar month after delivery of a notice from the Post Master General, &c., to execute to Her Majesty such bond to the effect and in manner aforesaid, or refuses or neglects to renew such bond whenever required, the Company shall forfeit £100 for every day during the period for which there shall be any refusal, &c., after the expiration of the month, 9 V., c. 22, s. 12.

Security by bond

Renewals

All notices by or on behalf of the Post Master General, &c., shall be considered as duly served on any Company, if given or delivered to any Director, or to the Secretary or Clerk of the Company, or left at any station 9 V., c. 22, s. 13

Notices]

When the Postmaster General, &c., and any Company are not able to agree on the amount of remuneration or compensation for services, it shall be referred to the award of 2 persons, one to be named by the Postmaster-General, &c., and the other by the Company, and if such 2 persons cannot agree, then to the umpirage of some third person, to be appointed by them previously to their entering upon the enquiry, and the award or umpirage shall be conclusive, 9 V., c. 22, s. 14.

Appointment of arbitrators

After any contract or award has continued in operation 3 years, any Company who consider themselves agrieved by the terms of remuneration fixed, may, by notice under their common seal, require it to be referred to arbitrators, to determine whether any and what alteration ought to be made therein, and thereupon the arbitrators or umpire to be appointed as above, shall proceed to enquire into the circumstances, and make their award therein as in the case of an original agreement, but the services performed shall not be interrupted or impeded, 9 V., c. 22, s. 15.

Reference after 3 years, upon notice from Company

Nomination of arbitrator for party making default,—time within which award to be made

In all references the Postmaster-General, &c., or Company as the case may be, shall nominate his or their arbitrator within 14 days after notice from the other party, or in default, the arbitrator appointed by the party giving notice, may name the arbitrator, and such arbitrators shall proceed forthwith in the reference, and make their award within 28 days after their appointment, otherwise the matter shall be left to be determined by the umpire. If he refuse or neglect to proceed and make his award for 28 days after the matter has been referred to him, a new umpire shall be appointed by the 2 first named arbitrators, who shall, in like manner, proceed, and make his award within 28 days. or in default be superseded, and so toties quoties, 9 V., c. 22, s. 16.

Recovery of penalties

The penalties shall be recovered before 2 Justices, with such costs as they think fit, and be levied by distress and sale of the Company's goods, 9 V., c. 22, s. 17.

Appropriation

And disposed of, one moiety to the prosecutor, 9 V., c. 22, s. 18.

Complaint within the month

And the complaint must be made within one month after the commission of the offence, 9 V., c. 22, s. 19.

Conviction

The conviction shall be according to the annexed Form, 9 V., c. 22, s. 20.

Want of form, &c.

The proceedings shall not be quashed for want of Form, nor be removed by Certiorari, or otherwise, 9 V., c. 22, s. 21.

Overplus of sales

Any overplus, after satisfying the sum distrained for, and the expenses of distress and sale, shall be returned on demand to the Company, 9 V., c. 22, s. 22.

Appeal

The Company may appeal, 9 V., c. 22, s. 23.

———

Form of conviction

Be it remembered that on the   day of
in the year of our Lord   A. B. was convicted before
us   of Her Majesty's Justices of the Peace for
the   (here describe the offence, and the time and
place when and where committed) contrary to an Act passed in
the 9th year of the reign of Her Majesty Queen Victoria, entitled an
Act to provide for the conveyance of Mails by Railways now or
hereafter to be constructed in this Island.

Given under our hands and seals the day and year first above written.

———

CONVEYANCE OF H. M's. FORCES, MILITIA AND POLICE.

Penalty on Company neglecting to convey them to the extent of its means

Whenever it is necessary to move any of the officers or soldiers of Her Majesty's Forces of the line, Ordnance Corps, Marines, Militia or the Police Force by any Railway, the Directors shall, under a penalty of £20 for each neglect or omission, permit such Forces respectively, with their baggage, stores, arms, ammunition and other necessaries and things, to be conveyed at the usual hour of starting, to the extent of the means of conveyance at the disposal of the Company, at the prices and on the conditions after provided, on the production of a rowe or order for their conveyance, signed by the proper authorities, 9 V., c. 23, s. 1.

Fares

All Railway Companies now or to be incorporated, or obtaining any extension or amendment of their powers, shall be bound to provide such conveyance at fares not exceeding 3d. per mile for each Commissioned Officer proceeding on duty, and also for each wife, widow or child above 12 years of any such officer, they being entitled to conveyance in a first class carriage, and not exceeding 1d. per mile for each soldier, marine or private of the Militia or Police Force; and also for each wife, widow or child above 12, of any such soldier entitled by any Act of this Island (see Troops, 45 G. 3, c. 10) or authorized by competent authority, to be sent to their destination at the public expense : (children under 3 so entitled, being taken free of charge ; those of that age or upwards, but under 12, so entitled, being taken at half the price of an adult) ; and such soldiers, marines and privates of the Militia or Police Force, and their wives, widows and children so entitled, being conveyed in carriages provided with seats, with sufficient space for their reasonable accommodation.

Luggage

Every officer, wife or widow, or child as aforesaid above 12, shall be entitled to take 1 cwt. of personal luggage, without extra charges ; and every soldier, marine, private, wife or widow, half cwt. of personal luggage. All excess of the above weights of personal luggage, and all public baggage, stores, arms, ammunition, provisions and other necessaries and things (except gunpowder and other combustible matters, which the Company shall only be bound to convey at such prices, and on such conditions as may be contracted for between the officer in charge of the Commissariat Department, or other officer duly authorized by the Governor, or the officer commanding the Forces in the case of the Army, Militia, and Police respectively, and the Company) shall be conveyed at charges not exceeding 1s. per ton per mile, the assistance of the military or other Forces being given in loading and unloading such goods, 9 V., c. 23, s. 2. *Public baggage, &c.*

Gunpowder, &c,

The penalty shall be recovered before 2 Justices, with such costs as they think fit, and be levied by distress and sale of the Company's goods, 9 V., c. 23, s. 3. *Recovery of penalty*

And disposed of one moiety to the prosecutor, 9 V., c. 23, s. 4. And the complaint must be made within one month after the offence, 9 V., c. 23, s. 5. *Appropriation. Complaint within one month*

The conviction shall be according to the annexed form, 9 V., c 23, s. 6. *Conviction want of form, &c.*

The proceedings shall not be quashed for want of form, nor be removed by Certiorari, or otherwise, 9 V., c. 23, s. 7.

Any overplus, after satisfying the sum distrained for, and the expenses of distress and sale, shall be returned on demand to the Company, 9 V., c. 23, s. 8. *Surplus of sales*

The Company may appeal, 9 V., c. 23, s. 9. *Appeal*

Be it remembered that on the   day of   in the year of our Lord   A.B. was convicted before us   of Her Majesty's Justices of the Peace for the   (here describe the offence, and the time and place when and where committed), contrary to an Act, passed in the ninth year of the reign of Her Majesty Queen Victoria, entituled "An Act for the conveyance of Troops and Police by Railways now or hereafter to be constructed in this Island." *Form of conviction*

Given under our hands and seals the day and year first above written.

Receiver-General.

His fees on Escheats Bonds, 10s. (6s. stg.), 31 G. 2, c. 18. *Fees*

On receipts for moneys paid into the Court of Chancery to the credit of any cause, besides Stamp, 5s. (3s. stg.), and on paying out any money under an order, 5s. (3s. stg.), 4 G. 4, c. 21, s. 2.

From the Island Secretary quarterly, for each Deed relating to land recorded, 3s., 21 V., c. 34, s. 23, superseding 8 V. c. 16, s. 8.

For Certificate on transfers of land of redemption of land tax, 3s., 21 V. c. 3, s. 24.

The fees under this Act, so long as his services are paid by a salary, and the contingencies of his office defrayed at the expense of the Island, shall be carried to the credit of the Man Road Fund Account, 21 V., c. 34, s. 36.

Provision for Receiver-General's salary, £1000 per annum ; for clerks and contingencies of Receiver-General's and Audit offices, £2000, out of the permanent revenue, 17 V., c. 29, Schd. A. *Salary and contingencies. Salary £1000, 21 Vic, 4, s. 4*

The Receiver-General shall perform the following duties :— *His duties*

1. Superintend the collection of the revenue, enforce the regular and punctual payment thereof, and of all other public taxes, duties and moneys it may be the duty of any officer or person to receive or get in.

2. Receive all moneys payable to the Public, and pay all demands against them.

3. Report to the Executive Committee all defaults and delinquencies of officers and Collectors of the Revenue, and by their direction, give instructions for the prosecution of the officers, &c., and Collectors of the Revenue.

4. Conduct in his own name all correspondence with public officers, or others respecting any matter connected with the gathering in of the public revenue, or the adjustment and settlement of any public account.

5. To superintend and manage the affairs generally of the office, 21 V., c. 4, s. 1.

Reports to Executive Committe

Also to report to the Executive Committee, in person or in writing, (as may be required) respecting all matters referred to him by them, or which appertain to his office, and generally to perform all services relative to the finances directed by them, 21 V., c. 4, s. 2.

To make no payment without warrant or order of the Governor, or Executive, and voucher certified

Not to pay any money out of the Treasury, except upon the warrant or order of the Governor or Executive Committee, or unless the voucher for payment, or the account to be paid (except for prison, police or hospital purposes) is certified by the first or sole Commissioner of the Board of Audit ; in the case of Prisons and the Public Hospital, by the [2nd Commissioner, now transferred under 21 V., c. 1, s. 15 to the] sole Commissioner of that Board ; and of the Police, by the Secretary of the Police department, as correct, 21 V., c. 4, s. 3.

Salary

Residence

In lieu of fees, &c.

Except under 18 V., c. 33

He shall be entitled to receive out of the Treasury an annual salary of £1200, payable quarterly on 31st March, 30th June, 30th Sept., and 31st December, but shall not be entitled thereto, unless residing and actually doing his duties in this Island, (unless absent on leave from competent authority) in lieu of all fees, commissions and charges, except only the commissions under 18 V, c. 33 (Chancery Deposits), 21 V., c. 4, s. 4.

To be collected as public moneys

Penalty

He shall continue to collect all fees he has been accustomed to receive, and commissions he is entitled to upon moneys come to his hands under any Act to be held and applied as public moneys, (except the commissions under 18 V, c. 33 for his own use.) Penalty, on conviction, to be deprived of his office, and to be incapable of being again appointed, 21 V., c. 4, s. 5.

Appoint Clerks and servants

He shall appoint and employ, with power to dismiss the Clerks and servants in his office without reference to the Executive Committee, and shall regulate and fix the hours of daily attendance of the Bookkeeper, Cashier and other Clerks and servants, subject to the approval of the Executive Committee, 21 V., c. 4, s. 6.

Cashier

Security

He shall appoint one of his Clerks to act as Cashier, and to have the custody of such sums of money as the Receiver General thinks proper to confide to his care for the payment of demands against the public, and may remove him, and demand and take such security for the faithful discharge of his duty, and duly accounting to him for any money confided to his care as shall seem sufficient for his own protection, not exceeding £2000, with one or more sureties to be approved of by him in the like sum, and to be taken in his name, 21 V., c. 4, s. 7.

Not to increase salaries

He shall not pay any increased salary to any Clerk without the sanction of the Executive Committee, 21 V., c. 4, s. 8.

Monthly statements of contingencies to be submitted to Executive Committee to direct payment

He shall lay before the Executive Committee monthly, a statement of the contingent expenses for Clerks salaries, office rent, taxes, postages, stationery or otherwise, who shall upon examination and approval, direct the payment, 21 V., c. 4, s. 9.

Office hours Supersedes 5W, & M. c. 3 s. 3.

The office shall be kept in Kingston, and opened for the transaction of public business every day (except Sundays, and holidays, (see 8 V, c. 30) from 9, a. m. to 3, p. m., 21 V., c. 4, s. 10.

Whenever the Receiver-General or any Clerk in his office is discharged by an Insolvent Debtor's Court, they shall be deemed to have vacated their offices, 21 V., c. 4, s. 11.

Daily cash book

He shall keep a cash-book to be constantly open to the examination of the Chief or sole Commissioner for examining the public accounts, in which to enter every sum received or paid each day at the time, the name of the person from whom received or to whom paid, and on what account or purpose, as well as the sums taken out of the chest to meet the demands of the day. The Receiver-General and Bookkeeper at the close of the business of each day, in the presence of each other, shall add up, and adjust the cash receipts and payments, and count the balance as it appears by the cash book, and lock it up in the public chest before leaving the office,

To be balanced

And signed. See Receiver General's moneys transfer

and each shall affix his signature to the daily cash balance so ascertained, counted and deposited, 21 V., c. 4, s. 12.

Such cash book shall belong to the public, and be deemed a book of record, and open to the inspection of the Executive Committee, or any Committee appointed by them to examine the book or count the public chest, or both, 21 V., c. 4, s. 13.

To belong to the public and open to the Executive Committee

He shall also keep or cause to be kept in a separate book, one general account of all the public cash received and paid by him, such account to be balanced once a week at least; Penalty £50, (£30 sterling), to be recovered in the Supreme Court, by action of debt, &c., 15 G. 3, c. 4, s. 2.

General cash account to be balanced weekly

The Book-keeper shall keep the public books in the manner directed by the Executive Committee, and use due diligence in punctually and, correctly posting the same, 21 V., c. 4, s. 14.

Book-keepers duty

He shall receive out of the Public Treasury an annual salary of £400 payable quarterly, on the same days, and subject to the same conditions as to residence and personal discharge of the duties of his office and absence from the Island on leave as before provided in respect to the Receiver-General, (s. 4,) 21 V., c. 4, s. 15.

His salary

The Governor may remove any Book-keeper, and when a vacancy occurs, fill up the same, 21 V., c. 4, s. 16.

Governor to fill up vacancies

All moneys belonging to or received on account of the public or parishes, shall continue immediately upon the receipt, to be lodged, in a chest, with two locks of different construction, the key of one of which shall be under the care and custody of the Receiver General, and the key of the other of the Book-keeper, and they shall take out of such chest on the morning of each day of business, any sum not exceeding £2000, which may be deemed requisite to meet the demands of the day, and if found insufficient, and after its expenditure, such further sum as may be necessary, and so on from time to time as the necessity arises, 21 V., c. 4, s. 17.

Moneys [to be lodged in a chest with 2 keys, one key to be kept by the Receiver General, the other by the Book-keeper

Moneys to be taken out for daily wants

See Receiver General's moneys transfer

On the death, resignation, removal or departure from the Island of the Receiver-General or Book-keeper, the key of the chest in his possession shall be delivered to the Governor by him, his executor or person in possession at his death. Every omission or refusal to deliver such respective key shall be an indictable offence, prosecuted as a public prosecution, and punished by fine or imprisonment in the discretion of the Court, 21 V., c. 4, s. 18.

On the death, &c. of either, his key to be delivered to the Governor

The Receiver-General and Book-keeper, or either, shall not use, lend or knowingly pay or apply the public moneys which come to their or either of their hands, or any part, otherwise than as by law required, nor act as a factor or attorney for any other person, or directly or indirectly carry on business as a factor or merchant, or engage in or transact any banking or commercial business, or hold any other office or appointment, under penalty of being deprived of his said office, nor shall either during his continuance in such office be elected or appointed or sit as a member of either branch of the Legislature, 21 V., c. 4, s. 19.

Receiver-General or Bookkeeper not to use, &c. public money, nor be engaged in business

Or be a Member of the Legislature

The Receiver-General and Book-keeper shall lay before the Executive Committee monthly statements or returns, to be signed by them, of all moneys in the Public Treasury at the end of each month, distinguishing the amounts in the notes of each Bank and in specie, according to $F_{or}m_s$ A and B in Schedule, or as may be directed by the Executive Committee, 21 V., c. 4, s. 20.

Monthly returns to the Executive Committee

The Receiver-General shall, within 30 days after the expiration of each quarter, send in to the Executive Committee a quarterly statement of the receipts of each quarter, with a statement of the receipts of the several quarters of the preceding year, in Form C in Schedule, or as may be directed by the Executive Committee, which shall be published in the "Jamaica Gazette," 21 V., c. 4, s 21.

Receiver-General's quarterly statements

The Receiver-General and Book-keeper shall make an annual return to the Legislature of the receipt and expenditure of the Public Revenue, and of the amount of cash in hand at the commencement, and the balance of cash at the end of the year ending 30th September; and also a return of the sums paid, and remaining due and unpaid at the end of each financial year, appertaining to the expenditure of such year, and such other returns relating to the finances as may be called for by the Executive Committee, 21 V., c. 4, s. 22.

Annual returns to Legislature

The Receiver-General shall, within 10 days after 20th March, June, September and December in each year, prepare and forward to the Clerks of the Boards of Highways and Bridges, and prepare and forward to the

Quarterly accounts to the Boards of Highways, and Clerks of the Vestry

4 F

Clerks of the Vestry, accounts either by statement or pass-book, showing payments and receipts during each quarter, such accounts merely to state the names of parties in whose favor any orders are drawn, and the amount, 21 V., c. 4, s. 23.

Previous bonds

Previous bonds of Receiver-General and Book-keeper continued in force, 21 V., c. 4, s. 24.

Security bond of Receiver-General and Book-keeper

Every Receiver-General and Book-keeper before entering upon their duties shall, at their own expense, enter into bonds to the Queen, the Receiver-General in (£5000 in lieu of £10,000, 28 V., c. 20, s. 1) and the Book-keeper in £500, with sureties to be approved of by the Executive Committee in such proportions as they shall be able and willing to be bound, so that the parts and shares so taken by the several sureties shall together amount to such sums of (£5000) and £500, 21 V, c. 4, s. 25.

Previous bonds entered into under 21 V., c. 4, s. 24, not to be affected by 28 V., c. 20, s. 1.

Duration and conditions

Bonds to be recorded

Evidence

Such bonds shall be in force for such number of years, and be made subject to such conditions as the Executive Committee shall direct and approve; and they shall cause the bonds to be recorded in the Secretary's Office, and the record or a certified copy shall be evidence, 21 V., c. 4, s. 26.

May be sued for further breaches

Limitation of sureties

Notwithstanding any recovery upon any bond, they may be again sued for any further breaches of condition from time to time; but the damages shall not, exclusive of costs, exceed the penalties; and each surety shall only be liable for, and satisfy so much of any loss or defalcation as the amount entered into by him shall bear to the whole sums, 21 V., c. 4, s. 27.

Departure from the Island of a surety

When any such bond expires, or any surety dies, or becomes insolvent, the Receiver-General (if his bond or surety), or the Book-keeper (if his) shall forthwith give notice thereof to the Executive Committee, and shall forthwith procure another or other sureties to be approved of in a bond or bonds of such amount as shall restore the security to the amount of (£5000, 28 V., c. 20, s. 1) or £500, and the Receiver-General and Book-keeper shall respectively, on any of their sureties departing from this Island, give notice thereof to the Executive Committee, and they may then, or at any other time, require them to give further security in the room of or in addition to the securities on any bond already given, in such sums, and within and for such time as the Executive Committee direct, and such further security shall be given accordingly, 21 V., c. 4, s. 28.

Sureties justifying false swearing

The Executive Committee may cause the sureties to justify on oath, which they or any Justice may administer. Any surety wilfully and corruptly taking a false oath shall be guilty of perjury, and punishable accordingly, 21 V., c. 4, s. 29.

Security of acting Receiver-General or Bookkeeper

When any person is appointed to perform the duties of the Receiver-General or Book-keeper during their absence on leave, he shall, before entering upon the duties, at his own expense enter into security by bond to Her Majesty, in the case of the Receiver-General in (£5000, 28 V., c. 20, s. 1) of the Book-keeper £500, with sufficient sureties to be approved of as aforesaid in bonds in such proportions of those sums for which they are able and willing to be bound, so that the parts or shares taken by the several sureties, shall together amount to the said sums of (£5000) and £500, and the bonds shall be subject to such conditions as the Executive Committee approve, and shall be recorded, and office copies shall be evidence. It shall be sufficient if the existing sureties of the Receiver-General or Book-keeper testify their consent in writing to the Executive Committee to continue liable on their bonds for the person appointed to act, 21 V., c. 4, s. 30.

Short Title

Receiver-General's Office Regulation Act, 1857, 21 V., c. 4, s. 33.

FORMS—21 Ý., v. 4.

Monthly return.
Moneys in Trea-
sury not paro-
chial. A, s. 20

Statement of all Moneys, other than Parochial Moneys, in the Treasury, on the   day of   18   , agreeably to the 21st Victoria, chapter 4, section 20.

In Treasury Certificates	......	....				
" Exchequer Bills	......	....				
" Island Treasury Notes	......	....				
" Colonial Bank Notes	......	....				
" Jamaica Bank Notes	......	....				
" Gold	......	....				
" Silver	......	....				
" Copper	......	....				
		....				
		....				
		....				
Total		....				

Particulars of the foregoing amount :

Customs' Deposits Accounts	......	....
Immigration Act, 15 Vic., ch. 39	......	....
Immigration Guaranteed Loan under ditto		....
Immigration Fund (under any other Act)		....
Ferry Road	......	....
Highways and Bridges	......	....
Cart Licenses	......	....
Penitentiary Building Account	......	....
Savings' Banks Deposits	......	....
Curates' Fund	......	....
Rectors' Fund	......	....
Court of Chancery	......	....
Insolvents' Deposits	......	....
Vere District Schools	......	....
Manchester ditto	......	....
Morant Point Light House	......	....
Plumb Point Light House	......	....
Copyright Act	......	....

Annotto Bay Junction Road Loan :

Loan ...	....	....
Tollage	....	....
Tax to repay...	....	....
Valuation of Lands		....

Island Cheques	....	....	....
Exchequer Bills....	....	....	....
Police Reward Funds	....	....	....

General Public Revenue as under :

Import Duty Act...	....	....	....
Customs' Tonnage Act	....	....	....
Transient Poor Law Tax	....	....	....
Health Officers	....	....	....
Public Taxes	....	....	....
1851, and previous years..		....	....
1852	....	....	....
1853	....	....	....
1854	....	....	....
1855	....	....	....
1856	....	....	....
1857	....	....	....

(and any further year from time to time)

Rum Duty Act :

Ditto Collecting Constables' Arrears	....
Stamp Duty Act....	....
The Governor's proportion of seizures	....
The Ordinary's Fees	....
Quit Rent Docket Fees	....
Fees to the Chief Justice	....
Fees of Registrar of Court of Chancery...	....
Fines, Forfeited Recognizances, &c.	....
Fees on Private Bills—Assembly	....

Metal Licenses		
Quit Rent Tax		
Still Licenses		
Less Duties Refunded		
Net (carry out)		

Total

NOTE.—If any new head of revenue or receipt should arise, it must be stated in a separate and particular item from time to time.

—

Monthly return of Parochial Moneys in Treasury, B, s. 20 Statement of all Parochial Moneys in the Treasury on the day of   18   , agreeably to the 21st Victoria, chap. 4, section 20.

In Colonial Bank Notes	....	....	
" Jamaica Bank Notes	....	....	
" Gold	....	....	
" Silver	....	....	
" Copper	....	....	
Total	....	....	

Particulars of the foregoing amount of £

Loan, 18 Victoria, chap. 60....	....	....	
Spirit License Act..	....	....	
Fines paid to Magistrates' Clerks	....	....	
Gunpowder Licenses	....	....	
Poundages	....	....	
Parish Tax on the rolls	....	....	
Parish Lands, &c.	....	....	

£

Proportion of the foregoing amount at credit of each undermentioned parish :

Kingston	.....	....	....			
Port Royal	....	....	....			
Saint Andrew	....	....	....			
Saint Thomas in the East.		....	....			
Saint David	....	....	....			
Portland	....	....	....			
Saint George	....	....	....			
Metcalfe	....	....	....			
Saint Catherine	....	....	....			
Saint John	....	....	....			
Saint Dorothy	....	....	....			
Saint Thomas in the Vale		....	....			
Clarendon	....	....	....			
Vere	....	....	....			
Manchester	....	....	....			
Saint Mary	....	....	....			
Saint Ann	....	....	....			
Saint Elizabeth	....	....	....			
Westmoreland	....	....	....			
Hanover	....	....	....			
Saint James	....	....	....			
Trelawny	....	....	....			
Total	....	....	....	....		

Note—If any new head of revenue or receipt should arise, it must be stated in a separate and particular item from time to time.

QUARTERLY RETURN

A Return of Revenue paid into the Public Treasury of Jamaica for the undermentioned periods ended 18

	FOR QUARTERS ENDED							
	18 (a)				18 (b)			
	31st Decer., 18 (a)	31st March, 30th 18 (a)	June, 30th Sept., 18 (a)	30th Sept., 18 (a)	31st Decer., 18 (b)	31st March, 18 (b)	30th 18 (b)	June, 30th Sept., 18 (b)
Import Duty Act.								
Customs' Tonnage Act.								
Transcient Poor Tax.								
Health								
Public Taxes.								
1851, and previous.								
1852.								
1853.								
'54.								
1855.								
1856.								
1857.								
(and any further year from time to time)								
Rum Duty Act.								
Ditto collecting his arrears.								
Stamp Duty Act.								
The Governor's proportion of seizures.								
The Ordinary's fees.								
Quit Rent Docket fees.								
Fees to the Chief Justice.								
Fees of Registrar Court of Chancery.								
Fines, Forfeited Recognizances, &c.								
Fees on Private Bills—Assembly.								
Metal Licenses.								
Quit Rent Tax.								
Still Licenses.								
	£							
Less duties refunded.								
Nett.	£							

Dated this   day of   18

Note (a).—These will always be the four several quarters' revenue of the preceding year for the time being, all of which are to be included in
every return. (b).—These columns will contain the revenue of the respective quarter and quarters of the current year, as the same advances up to
and inclusive of the last quarter's revenue, when ascertained.

Receiver General.

Receiver-General's Moneys Transfer.

The Governor may enter into arrangements with the Colonial Bank and Bank of Jamaica (both or either to the exclusion of the other, 24 V., c. 7), for lodging in those Banks all public, parochial and other moneys collected and gathered in or deposited with the Receiver-General, but such arrangements shall not entail any expense on the public, 21 V., c. 39, s. 1.

Arrangements for lodging in the banks all public, parochial, and deposit moneys of Receiver-General's Office

The Bank or Banks with whom any such arrangement may be made, shall be required to pay interest of not less that £3 per cent. per annum upon the daily cash balances at the credit of the accounts in their books, the accounts of which interest shall be made up and settled half-yearly, 24 V., c. 7.

Interest thereon

When such arrangements are entered into, all moneys, bills, notes and drafts required or authorized to be paid into the office of the Receiver-General shall from time to time be paid into the hands of the Colonial Bank and Bank of Jamaica (both or either, in accordance with such arrangements during the continuance thereof, 24 V., c. 7), and placed to the credit of an account to be opened in the books of the Bank, entitled "The Account of the public moneys of the Receiver-General" inserting the name in full of the Receiver-General for the time being, 21 V., c. 39, s. 2.

Moneys to be paid to banks in accordance with arrangements when entered into
Accounts to be opened, A

The public and other moneys heretofore kept in the Receiver-General's office having been transferred to the Colonial Bank instead of the above account, there shall be two accounts kept by the Bank or Banks, one to be marked A and entitled as above, and the other to be marked B, and entitled "The Account of the reserved Public Moneys of the Governor and Executive Committee," inserting the names in full of the Governor and the Executive Committee for the time being, 28 V., c. 20, s. 2.

B

Not to affect the accounts heretofore kept under 21 V., c. 39, s. 2, 28 V., c. 20, s. 3.

All moneys, bills, notes and drafts from time to time paid, deposited or carried to account by or in the names of the Governor and Executive Committe for the time being, shall be held by or for them, or in their names, in respect of their offices for the purpose of this Act; and upon the death, removal or resignation of them or either of them, shall vest in and be held by or for them, or their or his successors, or successor in office, and without any act or deed to be done by them or either of them, from time to time resigning or removed, their executors or administrators, or by any person, 28 V., c. 20, s. 4.

Moneys, &c. carried to account B to vest in those officers for the time being

Whenever at the hour of closing the Bank for business on any day, the amount at the credit of account A exceeds £5000, the Manager of the Bank shall transfer the excess to the credit of account B; and upon every occasion on which such excess occurs, he shall make such transfer, and so keep the two accounts as that the amount at the credit of account A shall not on the closing of the Bank on any day, exceed £5000, 28 V., c. 20, s. 5.

Account A to be so kept that the sum at credit shall not at the close of any day exceed £5000

Whenever the amount at the credit of account A is likely to prove insufficient to meet the demands on the Receiver-General, he shall apply to the Governor and Executive Committee, who, upon being satisfied of the necessity for doing so, shall direct the Bank to transfer from account B to account A. such an amount of money as appears necessary to meet such demands, and they shall give such directions as often as is shewn to be necessary, 28 V. c. 20, s. 6.

When necessary the Governor and Executive Committee may direct transfer from account B to account A to meet demands

The Governor and Executive Committee shall establish such rules and regulations as they think necessary for keeping the accounts of the Receiver General with the Banking Companies, and of such companies in relation thereto; and also for payment and appropriation of the moneys paid into the Banks, and alter and revoke them, and make others in lieu; and may also, if in their opinion it becomes necessary, suspend or discontinue the payment of the moneys into the Banks; and the Receiver-General observing the regulations, shall not be answerable for all moneys, bills, notes or drafts, paid or caused to be paid into the Banks, and the Banks shall be answerable for all moneys, &c., actually received by them, 21 V., c. 39, s. 3.

Governor and Executive Committee may establish regulations for keeping accounts and payment and appropriation of moneys
May suspend, &c. payments to banks

The Banks or some person authorized, shall daily, on receiving any money, &c., from or on account of the Receiver-General, deliver to the person paying in the same a receipt, which he shall lodge with the Receiver-General, who shall deliver to such person in lieu of the Bank receipt, a receipt signed by him, which, when countersigned by the Commissioner of the Board of Audit, who is required to countersign the same, shall be a sufficient discharge for the amount mentioned therein, 21 V, c. 39, s. 4.

Receipts for money paid

Payments, &c. to be made in accordance with rules
The banks shall not pay, apply or dispose of any part of the money, &c., paid in and placed to the account of the Receiver-General, or transfer the same or any portion from such account, except in accordance with the regulations, unless any such notes, bills or drafts are required by the Solicitor of the Crown for the purpose of instituting legal proceedings thereon, in which case they or any of them shall be delivered to the Solicitor or his clerk on the order of the Executive Committee, 21 V., c. 39, s. 5.

Delivery of notes &c for legal purposes

Receiver-General's payments to be made by cheques on the bank—form
Every sum due upon any debenture, bond, certificate or other instrument for payment of any money out of the Receiver-General's office, or directed to be paid by any Act, and all warrants issued by the Governor, or the Governor and Executive Committee, shall be paid by the Receiver General out of any money paid as aforesaid into either of the Banks on his account, in accordance with the regulations, by a cheque or draft signed by the Receiver General, and countersigned by the Book-keeper, or such other person as the Governor in his absence shall appoint, in which the name of the party in whose favor, and the number of the account or voucher in payment whereof the cheque is drawn, shall be inserted, 21 V., c. 39, s. 6.

Transfer of balance upon death, &c. of Receiver-General to his successor's account
Upon the death, resignation or removal of any Receiver-General, the balance of cash for which he at the time has credit with the Banks, shall as soon as a successor is appointed, vest in him, and until then in the person or persons for the time being authorized to execute the duties of the office in trust for the service of the public, and be forthwith transferred to the account of such successor or other person, to be applied to the service accordingly, 21 V., c. 39, s. 7.

Forgery
Knowingly and wilfully forging or counterfeiting, or causing or procuring, &c., or knowingly or wilfully acting or assisting in forging or counterfeiting the name of the Receiver-General, or of any Commissioner for examining the public accounts, or of any person acting for either of them, to any draft, instrument or writing, for or in order to the receiving or obtaining any of the money in the hands or custody of either of the Banks on account of the Receiver-General, or forging or counterfeiting, or causing or procuring, &c., or knowingly or wilfully acting, or assisting in forging or counterfeiting any draft, instrument or writing in form of a draft made by such Receiver-General or person as aforesaid, or uttering or publishing any such, knowing it to be forged and counterfeited, with an intention to defraud any person : Felony, punishable as is or was by law provided against any similar offence in respect of Island certificates and Receiver-General's checks, or Island Treasury notes, 21 V., c. 39, s. 8.

Punishment
Punishment, imprisonment not exceeding 3 years, with or without hard labor, or solitary confinement not exceeding one month at any one time, nor three months in any one year, 4 V., c. 46, s. 2, 12, or penal servitude not less than 4, and not exceeding 8 years, 21 V., c.14, s. 3.

Short title
The Receiver-General's Moneys Transfer Act, 1857. 21 V., c. 39, s. 9.

Quarterly statements of accounts with Banks to be published
The Receiver-General shall publish in the "Jamaica Gazette" a quarterly statement of the moneys paid into the Colonial and Jamaica Banks, the amounts drawn out, and the balance appearing to the credit of the Island Treasury in each Bank, 21 V., c. 39, s. 10.

Records, Public.

Presses for books &c
The respective officers of each public office shall provide convenient presses for all the books and papers belonging to their offices, having good doors, with locks and keys. The records shall be entered or transcribed into books bound with substantial leather covers, and a double cover for better preservation, 11 Ann, c. 4, s. 5.

Books to be substantially bound

Rectors' Fund.

Quarterly deductions from Rector's stipends whether lapsed or not
The Receiver-General shall retain £6 6s quarterly from each Rector's stipend to be appropriated as after directed, 9 V., c. 39, s. 2.

Whether there be any lapse of stipend or not, 9 V., c. 39, s. 6.

Rector's Fund and Trustees
All moneys of the fund already accumulated, and all sums herein directed to be retained, and all interest to accrue due on the Fund, as the same

becomes due, are vested under the name of the "Rectors' Fund" in the President of the Council, the Chief Justice, the Bishop, the Speaker of the Assembly, the Attorney-General, the Vice Chancellor, the Members for St. Catherine, Kingston, Port Royal, St. Andrew, St. Thomas in the Vale, St. George, St. Mary and Vere, and the several Rectors for the time being, and they or any five of them (two to be laymen) are appointed Trustees to hold the Fund; and the Receiver-General shall pay to their order, according to Form annexed, the interest now and to grow due upon the Fund, and also three-fourths of the sums already deducted and retained, payable to the Trustees of the Fund under repealed Acts (s. 1) and also ⅔ths of the sums before directed to be deducted and retained by him from the Rector's stipends, to be applied by the Trustees for the purposes of this Act; and the Receiver-General shall add the remaining ¼th of the sums to be deducted and retained by him to the capital of the Fund; and the Trustees with the assistance of an actuary (s. 11) when they require his services shall manage the Fund to the best advantage for the benefit of the persons interested, 9, V., c. 39, s. 3.

Rector's fund and Trustees

Quorum

Except under the circumstances after mentioned, every person who shall hereafter be appointed a Rector shall be examined by the Medical Officer of the Fund (s. 8,) and if it appear by a report under his hand that the life of such newly appointed Rector is bona fide and apart from all technical objections not a fair average life, and one which would be rejected according to the ordinary rules by which Insurance Offices are governed, the Trustees may give notice by their Secretary to such Rector that his family cannot participate in the benefits of the Fund in the ordinary manner, but that at his decease all his payments with their accumulated interest shall be restored to his family, in case he leave any within the degrees of relationship; and under the circumstances wherein a pension is granted by the Trust, and the notice shall be binding on the Rector, unless he survive 10 years, and continue to contribute to the Fund, when his family shall be entitled to all the benefits, 15 V., c. 30, s. 2.

Rectors to be examined by Medical Officer to ascertain if life insurable

Their claims on the fund

Every Rector to be hereafter appointed, shall appear before the Medical Officer to be examined, or in case of his refusal or neglect to submit to such medical examination, his family shall forfeit all interest in the Fund, 15 V. 30, s. 4.

Not appearing, to forfeit interest in fund

It shall not be necessary for any such Rector to submit to examination or appear before the Medical Officer, if, at and previous to his institution to the living, he has been in Holy Orders, and actually licensed and employed as a Clergyman in the Island for the full space of 5 years. It shall be discretionary with the Trustees, in case of a forfeiture in consequence of the Rector's failure to submit to the medical examination, to restore the family to their interest in the Fund, subject to such regulations or conditions as they think fit to impose, 15 V., c. 30, s. 5.

Examination dispensed with if 5 years in orders in the island

Restoration of interest in the fund

A list or registry of all the Rectors whose families are entitled to claim the benefit of the Fund, shall be made up and recorded in the Bishop's Registry Office, and no Rector to be appointed to any living, and subject to the medical examination, shall be included in the list, until a certificate has been given by the Trustees or their Secretary that he has been examined, 15 V. c. 30, s. 6.

Register of Rectors beneficially interested

On or before 31st March in each year, a return shall be made by every Rector to the Secretary, stating such information as to the ages of their wives, and the ages or marriages of their children, and such other particulars as the Trustees, under the advice of the Actuary or otherwise shall require, in the form prepared by the Trustees, and a copy shall be sent by the Secretary by the post to each member of the Fund on or before the 31st January. Penalty for omission to make such return, after three successive applications, to be made in writing by the Secretary, in the three several months, after 31st March, of 40s to the Fund, to be deducted by the Receiver-General from the next quarterly payment to be made to the Rector omitting to make such return, after the Receiver General's receipt of a notice from the Trustees to make such deduction, 9 V., c. 39, s. 14.

Annual returns of family

The interest now and to grow due on the capital of the Fund, with the ¾ths of the sums already retained, and also ⅔ths of the sums to be deducted from the annual stipends of the Rectors, or so much as shall be necessary, shall be appropriable and applied by the Trustees for the maintenance of the widows and orphan children of the Rectors who have died or shall die in the

Portion of fund to be appropriated for widows and children

4 G

possession of their benefices, or who under this Act shall be entitled to the same, in such manner and proportions as to the Trustees shall seem most charitable and proper, subject to the provisions after contained, 9 V., c. 39, s. 4.

Capital loaned to the public at interest

The present capital of the Fund, with the ¼th of the sums to be deducted from the stipends, shall remain in the hands of the Receiver-General as a loan to the public, for which he shall allow the Trustees interest quarterly, at the rate of £1 10 per cent. per quarter 9, V., c. 39, s. 7.

Reserved Fund

So much of the interest already pa a e and to grow due upon the capital of the Fund, and of the ⅜ths of the sums already and to be deducted, as shall not be drawn for and appropriated by the Trustees, shall remain in the Receiver-General's hands to their credit as a Reserved Appropriable Fund, on which interest at the rate of £1 10s per cent. per quarter shall be allowed ; and at the end of every quarter, the interest shall be added to the capital of the Reserved Appropriable Fund, 9 V., c. 39, s. 8.

Change in allowance of interest of Fund

The seventh section and so much of the eighth section of 9 V., c. 39, as relates to interest were repealed, and the Receiver-General was directed to allow interest annually at the rate of £6 per cent. on the capital of both Funds, as of the quarter-day next succeeding the passing of this Act (8th February, 1855,) and thereafter in respect of all further capital at £4 per cent. per annum only, 18 V., c. 19.

Interest now allowed

But afterwards interest was allowed at the rate of £6 per cent. per annum, from the 1st January, 1862, on the principal sums then at the credit of the Trustees, and on all further capital ; such part of the interest as should be unappropriated at the end of any year to be added to the capital, and bear the like interest, 25 V., c. 34.

Secretary

The Trustees were directed to appoint a competent person to be their Secretary, at such a salary, to be paid out of the Fund, as they should think proper, 9 V., c. 39, s. 10.

Actuary

The Secretary was directed to convene a general meeting of the Trustees by public advertisement in such newspapers as should be directed at the meeting, for the purpose of electing an Actuary of the Fund, if they thought proper ; the day appointed for such general meeting to be at least one month after the first publication of such advertisement. The Actuary to be appointed shall be an Actuary of one of the Life Assurance Societies in Great Britain, and shall be paid for his services out of the Fund, 9 V., c. 39, s. 11.

Removal of Secretary or Actuary

The Actuary or Secretary shall be only removable at a general meeting to be convened for the purpose, in pursuance of a resolution of a quarterly meeting, and in the manner pointed out for the election of the first Actuary (s. 11) ; and upon the removal of any Actuary or Secretary, the Trustees shall at such general meeting, and upon their death or resignation, at the first quarterly meeting afterwards, appoint another, 9 V., c. 39, s. 12.

Medical adviser

The Trustees were also directed to appoint as the medical adviser of their institution some one of the Resident Medical Practitioners already employed by any of the Insurance Offices in Jamaica, who shall, for every case examined, be remunerated out of the funds of the Trust, at the rate granted by the Insurance Office for which he is engaged for the examination of the health of an applicant for a policy from such office. In case of the death, absence, or inability to act of the regular medical officer of the Fund, or under any other special circumstances, the Trustees may call in the aid, and appoint for the occasion the medical officer of the Island Curates' Fund, or any Resident Medical Practitioner of Kingston or Spanish Town, and remunerate him for his services in the same manner as the medical officer of the Fund, 15 V., c. 30, s. 8.

Quarterly Meetings

The Trustees shall hold at least four meetings in each year, on the 2nd Tuesday in February and August in Kingston, and on the 2nd Tuesday in May and November in St. Jago de la Vega, for the purpose of transacting business. All orders on the Receiver-General for payments out of the Fund shall be in the form aforesaid (s. 3), and drawn and signed at each quarterly meeting by at least three of the Trustees, whereof two shall be laymen, and also by the Secretary. The trustees or any two of them may direct special or additional meetings to be convened and held either in Kingston or St. Jago de la Vega whenever necessary. Notice of any special or additional meeting, and of the purpose for which it is called shall be given in the " Jamaica Gazette" or any other newspapers, as directed by the Trustees ; and no other

Special meetings

business shall be transacted but such as is stated in the notice. If the object of calling the special meeting is the signing of orders for payment of annuities, the attendance of three Trustees with the clerk, shall constitute a legal meeting for such purpose, 9 V. c. 39, s 13.

The Receiver-General shall furnish the Trustees, at least fourteen days before each quarterly meeting, with a statement of the accounts of the immediately preceding quarter, 9 V., c. 39, s. 15. *Receiver-General to furnish quarter's accounts*

The Members and Rector of Kingston shall be Auditors of the accounts, and shall audit and attest the annual accounts to be laid before the Assembly, 9 V., c. 39, s. 16. *Auditors*

No child of any Rector to be hereafter appointed, born before their father became a licensed Clergyman in this Diocese, shall be entitled to claim any part or share, or participate in any of the advantages of the Fund, unless their father at his decease had been a contributing member for 10 years, in which case they shall be fully entitled, 15 V., c. 30 s. 1. *Children of Rectors born before their father became a licensed clergyman*

Nor any widow or children of any Rector, unless his name has been duly registered in the Bishop's Registry Office 15 V., c. 30. (s. 6.) *Widows and children of unregistered Rectors*
The names of all the present Rectors shall be forthwith inserted in the Registry, 15 V. c. 30, s. 7.

To entitle the widow and orphan children of any deceased Rector to a share of the benefit of the Fund, they must produce to the Trustees a certificate from the Justices and Vestry, in Vestry assembled, certifying the number, ages and other circumstances affecting their claims, 9 V., c. 39, s. 4. *Widows and children to produce certificate from the Vestry*

In case of the family of any deceased Rector becoming entitled to have his contributions restored to them with interest, the Trustees shall draw an order, according to the usual Form (9 V., c. 39, Sch.) on the Receiver-General, requiring him to pay out of the Funds of the Trust whatever amount shall appear to be due to the family, or they may, if they see fit, divide and apportion the sum among the several persons entitled to receive the same, as nearly as possible according to the scale by which the pensions are adjusted; and in the case of all or any of the children being minors, invest or otherwise appropriate the shares of such infant children in such way as shall appear to the Trustees most beneficial, 15 V., c. 30, s. 3. *Return and apportionment of contributions to widows and children not participating in Fund*

Upon the decease of any Rector who has resigned his living, or has been deposed, having previously contributed to the Fund for 10 years, the Trustees may apply towards the maintenance of his widow and orphans a sum equal to one half of the allowance which shall at the time be given to the widow and orphans of a Rector who has died in the possession of his benefice, or if he has contributed for 15 years, his widow and orphans shall be entitled to a full participation of the benefits of the Fund, but no widow shall be entitled to any benefit under this section, unless she was his wife at the time of his resignation or deposition, nor any orphan children, if born subsequently thereto, 9 V., c. 39, s. 5 *Claims of widows and children of Rectors not beneficed at death*

Annual allowances to widows and children from 1st January, 1846; widows, £52; first class orphans, £26; second class, £17 6s. 8d. No increase in the scale shall take place until the Reserved Appropriable Fund shall have accumulated and amount to £1500, whereupon the scheme of distribution shall be submitted by the Trustees to the Actuary for the time for re-adjustment, and also at the expiration of such other periods as shall be considered proper and necessary: and if the scheme in the opinion of the Actuary require any variation, it shall be made by a certificate in writing of the Actuary, to be presented and confirmed at the next quarterly meeting of the Trustees after receipt. The variation shall be framed upon the most correct calculations the circumstances will admit, and so that the interest of all persons having claims upon the Fund, whether in possession or expectancy, may be secured, 9 V., c. 39, s. 9. *Annual allowances*
Re-adjustment of Scheme

The Trustees shall at the quarterly meeting in November prepare and sign a report to be laid forthwith before the Assembly if in Session, or if not, within a fortnight after its next Session, setting forth and explaining the state of the Fund for the preceding 12 months, the names and ages of the parties having allowances therefrom, and the amounts and the particulars connected with parties who have ceased to have al- *Annual Report to the Legislature* lowances since the date of the last report, and the purport and effect of the opinion and advice given by the Actuary on the several points submitted to him, and the annual account of the Fund audited and attested by the Auditors, 9 V., c. 39, s. 17.

Rights of families of deprived Rectors, see Clergy, 22 V., c. 9, s. 33 34.

' Form of Order on the Receiver Gen e ral 9 V., c. 39, c. 3

To the Receiver-General,

Pay to the order of   the sum of
    being for (here state the purpose of the order).

Dated this   day of   **18**

A B ⎫ Trustees
C D ⎬ of the
E F ⎭ Rectors' Fund.

G H, Secretary.

Religious Worship (Dissenters.)

St 52, G. 3, c. 155, in force

Stat. 52 G. 3, c. 155 relating to religious worship and assemblies, and persons teaching and preaching therein is declared to be in force in this Island. Any two or more Justices holding special commissions under Statute 3 and 4 W. 4, c. 73, shall exercise all the jurisdiction and powers which under the above Act are exercised in England by Justices and by the General and Quarter Sessions therein mentioned, 4 W. 4, c. 41, s. 70.

Replevins.

Service

May be served at any time, 33 C. 2, c. 23, s. 10.

Costs of producing Stock, &c. when trial is put off

Whenever any horses, mules, asses or neat cattle, or other goods or chattels shall be produced by the plaintiff or defendant in obedience to any writ of replevin or subsequent process grounded thereon, or rule of Court made thereon, or shall be in the custody of the Provost Marshal by virtue of such process or orders, and the trial shall be put off on the motion of the parties not having the custody thereof, the Supreme Court may at their discretion award a reasonable recompense to be made to the party injured by the party putting off the trial, for the expenses of bringing, maintaining and carrying them back to the place from whence they were brought, and all charges and expenses attending the producing any goods or chattels at the Court, and compel payment by attachment or any other summary method, 30 G. 3, c. 2, s. 1.

When produced after return of eloinment, &c.

When produced after an eloinment on the writ of replevin or a nulla bona on a writ of withernam, or non est inventus, and writ of capias in withernam shall be returned, the party producing them shall not be entitled to the benefit of the recompense in the Court wherein either of the returns shall be made, in case the plaintiffs shall not go to trial in the subsequent Assize Court. When any plaintiff or defendant not having the custody gives notice in writing to the party having custody six days before the Assizes that he intends to come to trial in the same Court of Assize, then if the party having the custody produce them at the Court of Assize immediately ensuing such notice, such plaintiff or defendant shall not be entitled to any recompense, 30 G. 3, c. 2, s. 2.

When the property is in custody of the Provost Marshal, &c

When the property is in the custody of the Provost Marshal, and the trial is put off, the fees for detention shall be paid by the party on whose motion the trial is put off, 30 G. 3, c. 2, s. 3.

Costs of defendant when he succeeds

When Judgment passes for the defendant, or the plaintiff is nonsuit, the Supreme Court may award a reasonable recompense at their discretion to the defendant beyond the usual costs, for his charges, expenses and losses, by reason of bringing and producing, maintaining and carrying back the property, and compel payment by attachment, execution or other process, or by any summary method the Supreme Court thinks proper, 30 G. 3 c. 2. s. 4.

Maintainable for wrong detention

The action shall be maintainable in cases as well of wrongful detention of property as of the unlawful taking of property, 27 V., S. 1, c. 28, s. 1.

No writ of replevin shall be issued, unless in addition to the affidavits now required by the practice of the Court, an affidavit is filed by the party applying for the writ, or his lawful attorney, stating the names of the sureties, their residences, the amount of their property available as security with reference to the value of the property in dispute, and also stating that notice has been given to the party against whom the writ is sought to be issued, 27 V., S. 1, c, 28, s. 2. *Affidavit to ground writ*

No such writ shall be issued unless the affidavits are first filed, and the Judge before whom any application is made has first issued a summons, requiring the party against whom such replevin is sought, by himself or attorney, to appear and shew cause why it should not be issued. The Judge shall not be called upon to decide any questions properly triable before a Jury, 27 V., S. 1, c. 28, s. 3. *Summons to shew cause why it should not issue*

Before a writ issues in respect of any goods or chattels distrained on for taxes, the claimant shall file an affidavit, shewing how they were not so liable, and the grounds on which the adverse claim is founded, and shall procure an order of a Judge, authorizing the issue of such writ, an attested copy of which shall be served with the copy declaration in replevin. The Provost Marshal or his deputy, before executing the writ, shall require the bond of the plaintiff and of two sureties, to be approved of by the Provost Marshal or his Deputy, and the Collector of Dues, in a penalty to the Collector of Dues, sufficient to cover the value of the goods to be replevied, and £50 to cover the probable costs, and to be conditioned for payment of the sum distrained for, and of the costs of distress, and of the defence, or for a return of the goods, and payment of the defendant's costs in case of judgment against the plaintiff, or of a non suit or discontinuance; and unless such attested copy order is served with the copy declaration, or such bond is delivered, the Provost Marshal or his deputy shall abstain from executing such writ, 27 V., S. 1, c. 28, s. 4. *In case of replevin for taxes*

No writ of replevin shall be issued unless by fiat of a Judge, 27 V., S. 1, c. 28, s. 5. *No writ to issue without Judge's fiat*

In case of injury where the property is in danger of being wasted or made away with before the fiat of a Judge can be obtained for such replevin, a Justice may act substitutionally and issue such writ, 27 V., S. 1, c. 28, s. 6. *Or in case of urgency that of a Justice*

A Judge in Chambers may, on cause shewn, quash such writ issued as last beforesaid, and order the property so replevined to be restored, 27 V., S. 1, c. 28, s. 7. *Which may be quashed by a Judge in Chambers*

The action of replevin shall be maintainable for the recovery of timber wood and other trees severed and taken away from the land on which they were growing, although there be no proof that they were when severed or taken away from the land, ever as goods and chattels of any kind in the possession of the party claiming such land, 27 V., S. 1, c. 29. *Action maintainable for timber &c. severed*

Retired Judges and Chairmen of Quarter Sessions.

Upon the passing of the Judicial Amendment Act, 1855, (19 V., c. 10. the following annuities to the retiring Judges and Chairmen came into operation, payable out of the sum of £9800, appropriated by 17 V., c. 29, Sch. A., towards payment of Judicial salaries, by quarterly payments, and a proportionable part of the last quarter to the day of death: *Their Annuities*

The Chief Justice	....	....	£750
Senior Assistant Judge	....	....	600
Junior Assistant Judge	....	....	500
Each of the 4 Senior Chairmen of Quarter Sessions			450
Each of the Junior Chairmen	....	....	300

(19 V., c. 11

Rewards for Meritorious Conduct.

The Receiver-General, on warrant of the Governor, shall pay any sum directed to be paid to any policeman, constable, or other person as a reward for meritorious service rendered for the public benefit, 27 V., s. 1, c. 30, s. 38. *To be paid by the Receiver General*

Riots.

Riotously assembling to the number of 12, and not dispersing for an hour or more Felony

If any persons to the number of 12, or more, being unlawfully, riotously and tumultuously assembled together to the disturbance of the public peace, and being required or commanded, by any Justice, or if in Kingston by the Mayor, or senior Alderman, or other head Officer or Justice of the parish, precinct, or place where such assembly is, by proclamation to be made in the Queen's name, in the form after directed, to disperse themselves and peaceably to depart to their habitations, or to their lawful business shall to the number of 12 or more, notwithstanding such proclamation made, unlawfully, &c., remain or continue together for one hour after, such continuing together, to the number of 12 or more after such command and request made by proclamation, shall be Felony, and punishable by penal servitude from 4 years to term of life, or imprisonment not exceeding 3 years, 21 V., c. 11, s. 1, 21 V., c. 14, s. 3.

Order and form of Proclamation

FORM OF PROCLAMATION.—" The Justice or other person authorized to make proclamation, shall, among the Rioters, or as near to them as he can safely come, with a loud voice command or cause to be commanded silence to be, while proclamation is making, and after that shall openly and with loud voice, make or cause to be made proclamation in these words, or like in effect :—" Our Sovereign Lady the Queen, chargeth and commandeth all persons being assembled, immediately to disperse themselves, and peaceably to depart to their habitations or to their lawful business upon the pains contained in an Act made in the twenty-first year of Queen Victoria, for preventing tumults and riotous assemblies, God save the Queen." And every such Justice, Mayor, &c. within the limits of their jurisdictions, on notice of any such assembly, shall resort to the place, and there make or cause to be made proclamation, 21 V., c. 11, s. 2.

Apprehension

If such persons so unlawfully, &c. assembled, or, 12 or more of them, after proclamation made in manner aforesaid, shall continue together and not disperse themselves within one hour, they may be seized and apprehended by any Justice, Mayor, &c. Constable, Inspector, Sergeant and Private of Police or such other persons of age or ability as they shall command to be assisting, and forthwith carried before a Justice to be proceeded against for such their offences according to Law ; and if any persons so assembled shall happen to be killed, maimed or hurt by reason of their resisting the persons so dispersing, seizing or apprehending, or endeavouring, &c. then every such Justice, &c. shall be free, indemnified and discharged as well against the Crown as against all other persons, of, for, or concerning the killing, &c. of such person so assembled, that happens to be so killed, maimed or hurt, 21 V., c. 11, s. 3.

Opposing, &c. the making Proclamation

Not dispersing where Proclamation is prevented

If any persons oppose with force and arms wilfully, and knowingly obstruct, let, hinder or hurt any person beginning to proclaim or going to proclaim according to the proclamation hereby directed to be made, whereby such proclamation shall not be made, then every such opposing, &c., such person so beginning or going to make such proclamation, shall be Felony, punishable as in s. 1, and every such person so unlawfully, &c., assembled to the number of 12 or more, to whom proclamation should or ought to have been made, if it had not been hindered as aforesaid, shall likewise, in case they or any of them to the number of 12 or more shall continue together and not disperse themselves within one hour after such let or hindrances made, having knowledge thereof, shall be adjudged felons : punishment same as in s. 1. 21 V., s. 11, c. 4.

Compensation for property destroyed by rioters

Action for

If any church or chapel [or any building for religious worship, certified and registered according to the English statute, 1 W. & M., (c. 18, s. 19) for exempting their Majesties Protestant subjects dissenting from the Church of England, from the penalties of certain laws, (see repealed, s. 5)] or any dwelling house, mill, mill houses, boiling house, curing house, still house, trash house, warehouse, coffee mill, store, or other building, merchandize or steam engine, shall be demolished or pulled down wholly or in part by such persons so assembled, the inhabitants of the parish, or if in Kingston the inhabitants of the city and parish in which such damage is done, shall be liable to yield damages to the persons injured and damnified by such demolishing or pulling down wholly or in part; such damages to be recovered by action in the Supreme Court, and tried in the Circuit Court by the persons damnified, against two justices of the parish (the action for damages to any Church or Chapel to be brought in the name of the rector, minister, curate, or trustee in trust for applying the damages to be recovered in rebuilding or repairing the same) and on judgment being given in any such action for the plaintiff, the damages shall, at his, or his executor's or administrator's request, be estimated and stated as a separate item in the estimate of expenditure of the parish for that or the succeeding year, and shall be allowed and provided for as part of the parochial expenditure for such year, 21 V., c. 11, s. 6.

When any riot amounts to rebellion, or such combined resistance against the law (as) exceeds the authority of the magistracy and the power they can bring into action to suppress the same, the provisions for making compensation for damages shall be void, 21 V., c. 11, s. 7.

Not where the resistance exceeds the power of the magistracy to suppress it

No action shall be maintainable unless the persons damnified, or such as shall have knowledge of the circumstances of the offence, or the servants who had the care of the property damaged, shall, within 7 days after the offence, go before a Justice residing near and having jurisdiction over the place where the offence was committed, and state upon oath the names of the offenders, if known, and submit to the examination of the Justice, touching the circumstances of the offence, and become bound by recognizance to prosecute the offenders when apprehended; and no person shall be enabled to bring any such action unless he commence it within 3 calendar months after the commission of the offence, 21 V., c. 11, s. 8.

Proceedings to entitle parties to compensation

No inhabitant shall, by reason of inhabitancy, be exempted or precluded from giving evidence either for the plaintiff or for the defendant, 21 V., c. 11, s. 9.

Inhabitants competent witnesses

Where the plaintiff recovers judgment, whether after verdict or by default or otherwise, no writ of execution shall be executed upon either of the defendants or any inhabitant, but on receipt of the writ of execution the provost marshal shall make his warrant to the Receiver-General to pay the plaintiff the sum directed to be levied, which he shall do out of any moneys then in his hands or to come into his hands, 21 V., c. 11, s. 10.

Execution of writ by Provost Marshal

If the Justices who are sued, produce and prove before the Executive Committee an account of the just and necessary expenses incurred in consequence of any such action, if defended with their sanction, such expenses shall be paid on their order by the Receiver-General, and if judgment is given against the plaintiff when it has been defended with the sanction of the Executive Committee, the just and necessary expenses incurred in consequence of such action shall be paid in like manner over and above the taxed costs to be paid by the plaintiff; and if it be proved to them that the plaintiff is insolvent, so that the defendants can have no relief as to such taxed costs, the Executive Committee shall, if they think fit, order the same to be paid by the Receiver-General, 21 V., c. 11, s. 11.

Justices Costs

The Act shall be openly read at every Circuit (19 V., c. 10, s. 17) and Supreme Court. No person shall be prosecuted, unless the prosecution is commenced within 6 months, 21 V., c. 11, s. 12.

Act to be read in Courts. Prosecutions to be within 6 months

The Riot Act, 1857, 21 V., c. 11, s. 13.

Short Title

Robertson's Maps.

The extent and boundaries of the several counties and parishes as laid down and delineated in the 3 maps of the counties, and the General Map of the Island, made and published by James Robertson, surveyor in 1804, and approved of by the Assembly, shall be deemed to be the bounds, and conclusive to all intents, 50 G. 3, c. 15, s. 1.

Evidence of the boundaries of Counties and parishes

The originals presented to the Assembly shall be recorded in the Secretary's Office, and the records or copies duly proved or attested by the Secretary, or the printed copies of the published Maps shall all be received in evidence in all Courts, of the boundaries of the several counties and parishes in all cases, civil and criminal, and in all matters of litigation, 50 G. 3, c. 15. s. 2. *

---

* The subsequent establishment of the parishes of Manchester (55 G. 3, c. 23) and Metcalfe (5 V., c. 44), has somewhat altered the boundary lines of each of the counties, as also of the parishes of St. Elizabeth and Vere, St. Mary and St. George.

Rogues and Vagabonds.

Idle and disorderly persons
Prostitutes
Begging alms, &c.

Every common prostitute wandering in the public streets or highways, or in any place of public resort, and behaving in a riotous and indecent manner, every person who is able to labour or who is receiving parochial aid and shall be found wandering abroad or placing himself or herself in any public place street, wharf, highway, lane, court, piazza, or passago to beg or gather alms, or causing or procuring, or encouraging any child so to do, shall be deemed idle and disorderly persons, and on conviction before a Justice may be committed to the house of correction there (or on the public streets or highways?) to be

Excuse for begging

kept to hard labour not exceeding one calendar month; but no person shall be deemed to be an offender by reason of any such begging or gathering alms, or causing or procuring, or encouraging any child so to do, unless it shall be made to appear that he could by his own labour or other means, or by parochial funds appropriated for the purpose have been provided with the necessaries of life, 3 V., c. 18, s. 1.

Rogues and Vagabonds, persons convicted under, 3 V., c. 18, s. 1
Dealers in obeah
Fortunetellers
Wandering abroad &c.
Obscene prints, &c.
Exposing the person

Every person committing any of the offences mentioned in 3 V., c. 18, s. 1, after having been convicted as an idle and disorderly person; every person pretending to be a dealer in obeah or myalism; every person pretending or professing to tell fortunes, or using or pretending to use any subtle craft or device by palmestry or any such like superstitious means to deceive or impose upon any of H. M. Subjects; every person wandering abroad and lodging in any outhouse, or shed, or in any deserted or unoccupied building, or in any mill, sugar, or coffee works, watchhouse, trashhouse or other buildings, or within any cane, coffee, provision piece, pasture or enclosure, not having any visible means of subsistence, and not giving any account of himself or herself; every person wilfully exposing to view in any street,

Exposing wounds or deformities

road, highway, or public place any obscene print, picture, or other indecent exhibition; every person wilfully, openly, lewdly, and obscenely exposing his or her person in any street, public place or highway, or in the view thereof, or in any place of public resort; every person wandering abroad and endeavouring by the exposure of wounds or deformities to obtain or

Obtaining charity under false pretences
Gaming, &c, in the Streets
Having Housebreaking implements, or offensive instruments with intent to commit felony

gather alms; every person endeavouring to procure charitable contributions of any nature or kind under any false or fraudulent pretence; every person playing or betting in any street, road, highway, or other open and public place or with any table or instrument of gaming at any game or pretended game of chance; every person having in his or her possession or custody any picklock, key, crow jack, bit, or other implements with intent feloniously to break into any dwelling house, warehouse, store, shop, coach house, stable, or out-building, or being armed with any gun, pistol, hanger cutlass, bludgeon or other offensive weapon, or having upon him or her any instrument with intent to commit any felonious act; every person be-

Persons found in any house, &c. for an unlawful purpose

ing found in or upon any dwelling house, warehouse, store, shop, coach-house, stable, out-house or lock-up place in which goods are kept, or in any enclosed yard, pen, garden or crane, for any unlawful purpose; every sus-

Suspected thieves

pected person or reputed theif frequenting any wharf, or warehouse, near or adjoining thereto, or any street, highway, or avenue leading thereto, or adjacent thereto, with intent to commit felony; every person apprehended

Idle and disorderly persons resisting apprehension

as an idle and disorderly person and violently resisting any constable or other peace officer so apprehending him or her, and being subsequently convicted of the offence for which he was apprehended, shall be deemed a rogue and vagabond, and on conviction before a Justice may be committed to the house of correction to hard labour not exceeding 28 days; and every such

Forfeiture of implements and instruments

pick lock, key, crow jack, bit, and other implement, gun, pistol, hanger, cutlass, bludgeon, or other offensive weapon, and every such instrument shall by the conviction become forfeited, and may be destroyed or sold by order of the Justice, and if sold, the proceeds applied to the use of the parish, 4 V., c. 42, s. 2.

Abandoning wife and children

Every person who by work or other means is able to maintain himself and his wife and children, and who refuses or neglects so to do; every person who wilfully abandons his wife or children, whereby in either case such wife or children shall be left destitute or dependent for support upon public or private charity, shall be deemed to be a rogue and vagabond, and shall, on conviction before 2 Justices of the parish where the offence is committed, be for the first offence imprisoned, with or without hard labor, at the discretion of the Justices, for not exceeding 30 days, and for a second or any subsequent offence for not exceeding 3 months, 28 V., c. 5, s. 2.

In any prosecution under this Act, the wife or husband may give evidence for or against each other, 28 V., c. 5, s. 3.

Husband or wife may give evidence

Every person breaking or escaping out of any place of legal confinement before the expiration of the term for which he shall be committed, or ordered to be confined under this Act, and every person committing any offence which shall subject him to be dealt with as a rogue and vagabond, having been at some former time adjudged so to be, and duly convicted thereof, and every person apprehended as a rogue and vagabond, and violently resisting any Constable so apprehending him, shall be deemed an incorrigible rogue and may be committed by 2 Justices to the House of Correction until the next Quarter Sessions, (Circuit Court, 19 V., c. 10, s. 17,) for trial there, 3 V., c. 18, s. 3.

Incorrigible rogues breaking or escaping from place of confinement
Persons subsequently convicted as rogues and vagabonds, &c.
Violently resisting apprehension as a rogue, &c.

Any Constable, &c., may apprehend any person found offending, or in case none be within a reasonable distance, any person whosoever may apprehend him, and forthwith carry him before a Justice, or deliver him to a Constable for the purpose. If any Constable, or other peace officer refuse or wilfully neglect to take such offender into his custody and to take and convey him before a Justice, or shall not use his best endeavors to apprehend and convey before a Justice any person he finds offending, it shall be deemed a neglect of duty and punished as after directed 3 V., c. 18, s. 4.

Apprehension of offenders

Any Justice, upon oath being made before him that any person has committed or is suspected to have committed any offence against this Act, may issue his warrant to apprehend and bring before him, or some other Justice, the person so charged to be dealt with, 3 V., c. 18, s. 5.

Warrant for apprehension

When any incorrigible rogue has been committed for trial, the Court shall examine into the circumstances, and on conviction may order the offender to be imprisoned with hard labor, not exceeding 6 calendar months from the time of making such order, 3 V., c. 18, s. 7.

Punishment of incorrigible rogues

In case any Constable neglects his duty, or in case any person disturbs, hinders or obstructs him, or is aiding or assisting therein, he shall, on conviction before a Justice, forfeit not exceeding £20 (£12 sterling); and in case the offender shall not pay such sum, the same shall be levied by distress by warrant, and if sufficient distress cannot be found, he may be committed for not exceeding 30 days or until the fine be paid, such fine to be for the use of the parish, 3 V., c. 18, s. 8.

Constables neglecting duty—Obstructing them

Any Justice, upon information on oath that any person described to be an idle and disorderly person or a rogue and vagabond or an incorrigible rogue, is reasonably suspected to be harboured or concealed in any house or place, may by warrant authorize any Constable, or other person to enter at any time into such house or place, to apprehend and bring before him, or any other Justice every such idle and disorderly person, &c., then and there found, to be dealt with as before directed, 3 V., c. 18, s. 9.

Apprehension of idle, &c. persons' &c. harboured in any house

The Justice before whom any conviction of any offender, as an idle or disorderly person, &c., takes place, shall transmit the conviction to the next (Circuit Court, 19 V., c. 10, s. 17,) to be filed and kept of record, and a copy duly certified by the Clerk of the Peace, shall be evidence in any Court, or before any Justice, 3 V., c. 18, s. 10.

Conviction to be transmitted to Circuit Court
Certified copy evidence

The conviction of any offender as an idle and disorderly person, &c., shall be in the Form following or as near thereto as circumstances will permit:

Form of conviction

JAMAICA ss.

In the Parish of

Be it remembered that on the   day of   in the year of our Lord   at   in the County of   is convicted before me,   for that he the said   did (specify the offence, time and place, when and where the same was committed, as the case may be,) and I the said   adjudge the said for the said offence to be imprisoned, or to solitary confinement in the House of Correction, and there or on the streets and highways,

4 H

kept to hard labor for the space of   days, ensuing, from the
date hereof, this day to be accounted one.

Given under my hand and seal the day and year first above men-
tioned,   A. B., Justice of the Peace, 3 V., c. 18, s. 11.

Persons aggrieved may appeal, 3 V., c. 18 s. 12.

Roman Catholics.

Any person professing the Roman Catholic religion, appointed a member of the Council, or returned as a Member of Assembly, may sit and
vote, being in other respects duly qualified, upon taking and subscribing the oath, (Form), instead of those of allegiance, supremacy and abjuration, 10 G. 4, c. 12, s. 1.

The name of the Sovereign for the time being shall be substituted
from time to time for that expressed with proper words of reference. But
no Roman Catholic shall be capable of sitting or voting either in the
Council or Assembly, unless he first take and subscribe such oath before
the same persons, and at the times and places, and in the same manner as
the oaths and declarations now required by law are taken, made and subscribed. Any person professing the Roman Catholic religion, who shall
sit or vote without having first so taken and subscribed the oath, shall be
liable to the same penalties and disabilities, and the offence of so sitting or
voting shall be followed by the same consequences as are by law enacted,
in the case of persons sitting or voting in either House of Parliament, without taking, making and subscribing the oaths and declarations now required
by law, 10 G. 4, c. 12, s. 2.

Any Roman Catholic subject, otherwise duly qualified, may vote at elections of Members of Assembly, Coroners, Vestrymen, Aldermen or Common
Councilmen, upon taking and subscribing, if required the oath prescribed
instead of those of allegiance, supremacy and abjuration, and instead of any
declaration or oath required of them, and also on taking, if required, such
other oaths as may be lawfully tendered to voters, 10 G. 4, c. 12, s. 3.

The oath shall be administered in the same manner, at the same time,
and by the same persons as those for which it is substituted, and the certificate of the taking and subscribing the oath shall be of the like force
as a certificate of the taking and subscribing those for which it is substituted, and shall be given by the same person, and in the same manner as that now required, 10 G. 4, c. 12. s. 4.

They may hold all civil and military offices, and places of trust and profit under the Crown, and exercise any other franchise or civil right except
as after excepted (s. 8), upon taking and subscribing at the times and in the
manner after-mentioned the oath before appointed, instead of the oaths of allegiance, &c., and others now required to be taken by Roman Catholics,
10 G. 4, c. 12, s. 5.

They shall not be exempted from the necessity of taking any oaths or
making any declaration, not before-mentioned, required to be taken or sub
scribed by any person on his admission into any such office, or place of trust
or profit, 10 G. 4, c. 12, s. 6.

They may be members of any lay body corporate, and hold any civil office, or place of trust or profit therein, and do any corporate act, or vote in
any corporate election or other proceedings, upon taking the oath appointed,
instead of those of allegiance, &c., and on taking all the other oaths required of members of such lay corporations on admission to office or place,
10 G. 4, c. 12, s. 7.

But not to enable any person otherwise than they are now by law enabled, to hold any office, place or dignity of or belonging to the United
Church of England and Ireland, or the Church of Scotland, or any office or
place belonging to any public school, 10 G. 4, c. 12, s. 8.

Every Roman Catholic appointed to any office or place of trust or profit
under the Crown shall, within 3 calendar months next before such appointment, or otherwise before presuming to exercise or enjoy, or in any manner
act therein, take and subscribe the oath before the Grand Court or Circuit
Court (9 V., c. 10, s. 17) or any Judge; and the person administering the oath
shall make, sign and deliver a certificate, of the oath having been duly
taken and subscribed as often as demanded of him, which shall e sufficient

evidence of the person named having duly taken and subscribed such oath, 10 G. 4, c. 12, s. 9.

Otherwise such Roman Catholic shall forfeit to the Crown for the support of the government of this Island £200 (£120 sterling), and his appointment shall be altogether void, and the office vacant. The oath shall be taken by officers of Militia of the Roman Catholic religion at the same time and in the same manner as the oaths, &c., now required, 10 G. 4, c. 12, s 10.

No oath shall be tendered to or required of them to enable them to hold real or personal property, other than may be tendered to and required to be taken by other subjects, and the oath before appointed being taken and subscribed, shall be of the same force, and stand in the place of all oaths and declarations required by any law for their relief, 10 G. 4, c. 12, s 11.

All penalties shall be recovered by information on debt in the name of the Attorney-General as a debt to the Crown, for the use of the Island Government, 10 G. 4, c. 12, s. 12.

I A. B., do sincerely promise and swear that I will be faithful and bear true allegiance to His Majesty King George, the Fourth, and will defend him to the utmost of my power against all conspiracies, and attempts whatever which shall be made against his person, crown or dignity, and I will do my utmost endeavor to disclose and make known to His Majesty, his heirs and successors, all treasons and traitorous conspiracies, which may be found against him or them, and I do faithfully promise to maintain, support, defend, and to the utmost of my power, the succession of the Crown which succession by an Act entitled, an Act for the further limitation of the Crown, and better securing the rights and liberties of the subject, is and stands limited to the Princess Sophia, Electress of Hanover, and the heirs of her body, being Protestants, hereby utterly renouncing and abjuring any obedience or allegiance unto any other   claiming or pretending a right to the Crown of this realm, and I do further declare that it is not an article of my faith, and that I do renounce, reject and abjure the opinion, that Princes excommunicated or deprived by the Pope or any other authority of the see of Rome, may be deposed or murdered by their subjects or by any person whatever, and I do declare that I do not believe that the Pope of Rome, or any other foreign Prince, Prelate or person, State or Potentate, hath or ought to have any temporal or civil jurisdiction, power, superiority, or preeminence, directly or indirectly within this realm. I do swear that I will defend to the utmost of my power the settlement of property within this realm, as established by the laws, and I do hereby disclaim, disavow and solemnly abjure any intention to subvert the present Church establishment as settled by law within this realm, and I do solemnly swear that I never will exercise any privilege to which I am or may become entitled to disturb or weaken the Protestant religion, or Protestant Government in the United Kingdom, and I do solemnly, in the presence of God, profess, testify and declare, that I do make this declaration, and every part thereof, in the plain and ordinary sense of the words of this oath, without any evasion, equivocation or mental reservation whatsoever. So help me God.

Royal Mail Steam Packet Company.

The copy of their Charter of Incorporation enrolled in the Secretary's Office, and the record and copies thereof declared evidence, 6 V., c. 22.

Rum and Spirits.

Any maker of Rum may by himself, servants or others, vend and sell the same pure and unmixed, 33 C. 2, c. 5, s. 4.

No person, except a retailer, shall sell Rum in less quantity than 40 gallons, 22 V., c. 13, s. 65.

No license shall be granted to keep a Tavern on the same premises where any shop shall be kept to sell and retail goods of any description, 18 V., c. 55, s. 2.

RUM DUTIES.

Duty of 2s 6d per gallon

There shall be raised, levied, collected and paid to and for the use of Her Majesty, for the support of the Government of this Island, a duty of 2s. 6d. upon every Imperial gallon of Rum and other spirits distilled or made in this Island, until 31st March, 1869, 27 V., S. 1, c. 5, s. 1.

Collection and appropriation

To be recovered and collected under any Act now or to be in force for the collection of the duties on Rum and other Spirits distilled or made in this Island, the proceeds to be paid and applied by the Receiver-General towards the contingent charges and expenses of the Government, 27 V.., S. 1, c. 5, s. 3.

Additional duty of 3d per gallon

And in addition to the previous duty, a duty of 3d. upon every Imperial gallon of Rum and other Spirits on hand on any estate or place of manufacture, or in any warehouse for warehousing Rum, sold or to be sold for consumption, and of all Rum and other Spirits distilled and consumed in this Island on and after 9th December, 1864; to be ascertained, collected and appropriated as any other duty on Rum and other distilled Spirits, 28 V., c. 12.

Drawback on compounds

Every person exporting any quantity not less than 90 gallons of any cordial, liqueur or compound manufactured in this Island, and of which any Spirit distilled in this Island forms a component part, shall be entitled to receive by way of drawback, and be paid by the Receiver-General, on the Governor's warrant, the proportion of Spirit duty at the rate of 6d. for every gallon of any such cordial, liqueur or compounds exported, on its being certified by the Collector and Controller of Customs at Kingston, or the Sub-Collector at any other port of export, accordingly to the port from which the export has been made, that it has been satisfactorily shewn to them or him as the case may be, that the cordial, &c., exported was manufactured in this Island, and that not less than 20 gallons of Rum distilled in this Island were used as a component part in every 90 gallons of such compound, and that the full duty at not less than the rate of duty by this Act imposed on Rum distilled in this Island, was paid on the whole of the Spirit so used, which shall be in the annexed Form, 27 V., S. 1, c. 5, s. 4.

Certificate

These are to certify that   of the parish of has exported from the port of   in the ship or vessel called   ,   puncheons, containing   gallons of a cordial, liqueur, or compound called   and that the same was manufactured in this Island, and that*   gallons of rum or other spirits distilled in this Island have been used in the manufacture thereof and form a component part thereof, and that the full duty of   per gallon has been paid on such   gallons of rum or other spirit.

Given under our hands (or my hand) this   day of at the port of

                       Collector.
                       Controller.
                       Sub-Collector.

* The quantity must not be less than 20 gallons of Rum in 90 gallons of compound.

RUM METHYLATED.

Regulations for methylation in warehouse

The Executive Committee may permit any owner or factor of Rum, of not less degree of strength than 20 per cent overproof by Sykes' Hydrometer, or 21 proof by the glass bubble in general use, to mix Rum in a bending warehouse, in quantity not less than 50 gallons, with not less than one-ninth of its bulk measure of wood naphtha or methylic alcohol, or such other article or substance as they shall appoint, to render it unfit for use as a beverage, and incapable of being converted to that purpose, and thereupon the Rum and mixture shall be exempt from any duty, and be cleared from warehouse free of duty, 27 V., S. 1, c, 2, s. 1.

To be called Methylated Spirit

The mixture with wood naphtha or methylic alcohol shall be denominated "Methylated Spirit," with any other substance by such term as the Executive Committee may direct, 27 V., S. 1, c. 2. s. 2.

All wood naphtha or methylic acid or other article to be mixed with Rum shall be provided by the Executive Committee, and not liable to any duty on importation, and supplied to parties at the cost, including all charges of importation, 27 V., S. 1, c. 2, s. 3.

Article to be mixed to be provided by Executive Committee

Any Methylated Spirit may be exported free of duty, 27 V. S. 1, c. 2 s. 4.

Exportation free

DUTY COLLECTION.

Every person in charge of an Estate on which Rum is made, shall give in quarterly returns on oath, to the Receiver-General, on 31st December, 31st March, 30th June and 30th September, or within 14 days after, of all Rum on hand, at the last return, and of all Rum since made with an account of its disposal (Form Schedule A.,) 22 V., c. 13, s. 2.

Quarterly returns of rum made on estates

Accompanied by a declaration on oath (Form B.,) of the person usually in charge of the distillery (which any Justice may administer) that it is a true and faithful summary of the entries in the distillery book, and is correct in every particular, and that no Rum other than mentioned therein has been given away or consumed on the Estate, or sent away from it to any person or place during the period embraced in the return, 22 V., c. 13 s. 3.

Declaration to be annexed

In order to provide for the more effectual examination of the returns prescribed by 22 V., c. 13, s. 2, 29, and 23 V., c. 4, s. 19, (License Act) except in Kingston, the several returns, with the documents by which they are directed to be accompanied, instead of being transmitted to the Receiver-General, shall be transmitted to the sub-Collector of Customs if there be one, or if not to the Collector of Rum Duties in each parish, in all respects in the like Form, verified in the same manner, and containing the like particulars, and under the like recoverable as other penalties thereby directed; and the sub-Collector of Customs or Collector of Rum Duties, shall compare each Estate's return transmitted to him, with those sent in by the wholesale and annual retailers, 28 V., c. 27, s. 8.

To be sent to Collector

For examination

The sub-Collector or Collector of Rum Duties, as the case may be, shall carefully examine the returns transmitted to him, and from the best information he can obtain, shall endeavor to ascertain whether or not the returns are correct, and on each return shall certify that he has examined the same, and whether he finds it correct or otherwise, and in the latter case shall also state his reasons for believing the returns to be untruthful, 28 V., c. 27, s. 9.

And to be certified by him to the Receiver-General

The returns so certified shall be forwarded by them to the Receiver-General within 14 days after the 14th January, April, July and October, under a penalty of £1 for each return omitted to be duly forwarded, recoverable as any penalty under 22 V., c. 13, and 23 V., c. 4. Such returns shall be dealt with or proceeded upon in like manner, and with the like power, and subject to the like provisions of those Acts, as the returns thereby directed to be sent to the Receiver-General, 28 V., c. 27 s. 10.

Registered and forwarded

The sub-Collector, &c., shall to each person lodging his return give an acknowledgment of the receipt, 28 V., c. 27, s. 11.

To give receipt to persons lodging

A Book shall be kept on every estate, by the person in charge of the same, or of the distillery thereon (Form Schedule C), in which shall be entered weekly the quantity and strength of all Rum distilled during every week, and the disposal, shewing the quantity sold on the estate for consumption, the duty on which has been received by the person in charge, or authorized by the Proprietor or his Attorney, or the lessee or tenant, to receive the same, the quantity sent to a barquadier for exportation, the quantity so sent for sale or exportation as may afterwards be determined on, and the quantity sent to a factor or any other person for sale; and the person in charge shall, at the end of every quarter certify in the book, and sign the certificate that the entries therein are correct, and were made weekly, as the law directs, 22 V., c. 13, s. 4.

Still House Book

Whenever the Receiver-General, or Collector of Rum Duties, has cause to suspect the incorrectness of any return furnished, he shall by himself, or by a person he directs in writing, inspect the Still-house book, and take an account of all Rum on hand on the estate, 22 V., c. 13. s. 5.

To be open to inspection

Incorrect entries are not to be erased by scratching out or otherwise but the pen shall be drawn through them, and the correct entry made 22 V., c. 13, s. 6.

Correction of entries in

False entries—erasures

Any person in charge of an estate or distillery wilfully making a false entry or erasure, or removing a leaf from, or injuring or destroying the distillery book, to defeat the intention of the Act, shall be subject to a penalty not exceeding £ 20, or imprisonment other than in a County Gaol, not exceeding 3 calendar months, 22 V., c. 13, s. 7.

Refusal to produce book for inspection

Any person in charge of an estate or distillery, or any other person refusing admittance to the person authorized by the Receiver-General to visit any estate or distillery, to such estate or distillery, or hindering or preventing him from entering upon any estate or into any distillery, or refusing or declining to produce for inspection the book, or to shew any Rum returned as being or appearing by such book to be on hand, or in any way obstructing or causing him to be obstructed or hindered in the performance of any duty, shall be subject to a fine not exceeding £40, or imprisonment other than in a County Gaol, not exceeding 6 calendar months, 22 V., c. 13, s. 8.

Differences between rum made and accounted for

If upon examination of any such book, and comparison therewith of any return made to the Receiver-General, and upon ascertaining the quantity of Rum on hand at any given period on any estate, it appears there is a difference in the quantity and strength of the Rum made and accounted for, which cannot be explained to the satisfaction of the Receiver-General, the duty on the quantity unaccounted for shall, within ten days after the decision of the Receiver-General, be levied for and recovered, 22 V., c. 13, s. 9.

Allowance for consumption free of duty

The person in charge of any estate, where not less than 2000 gallons of Rum are annually made, or estimated to be made, may claim, and be allowed in each quarterly in-giving, not exceeding 25 gallons of Rum ; and where not less than 1000 gallons of Rum are made annually, 10 gallons per quarter, free of duty, upon making a declaration o be annexed to the quarterly in-givings, that the whole of that quantity has been actually used by himself, or for the purposes of the estate, or both, on the estate. All Rum consumed upon the estate, beyond the allowed quantity, shall be charged with the duty, 22 V., c. 13, s. 10.

Excess liable to duty

No duty on Rum exported or lost by leakage, &c.

No person in charge, shall be charged with the duty on any quantity of Rum shown on the returns to have been exported, and for which the export certificates have been delivered to the Receiver-General, nor on any quantity lost by leakage or evaporation, or during its transit from one part of the island to another, whether carried by land or by water, or from the place where the Rum was shipped to the vessel on board of which it was intended to be laden for exportation, or which has been stolen from any stillhouse; but the party or estate shall be exempt from the payment of duty upon so much Rum as is shewn to have been lost or stolen, by the production of a certificate on oath, and of such other evidence as shall be required by the Executive Committee, to shew the extent of the loss incurred, 22 V., c. 13, s. 11.

Certificates of export or warehousing to be transmitted with returns

The person making the returns shall transmit therewith all certificates of export and warehousing or other certificates granted on the exportation, warehousing, or transfer of any Rum to any warehouse during the time embraced in the returns, and which several documents shall be referred to in his returns, 22 V., c. 13, s. 12.

Rum for exportation to be shipped direct or warehoused

The person in charge of each Estate from which Rum has been sold for consumption in this Island shall, at the time at which quarterly returns are required to be made, transmit to the Receiver-General all duty paid permits which during the preceeding quarter had been delivered to him by the persons to whom Rum had been sold from the Estate during such quarter, which shall be an acquittance to the person or the Estate for the duties chargeable on the number of gallons of Rum mentioned in them, 28 V., c. 27 s. 12.

Also duty paid permits

All Rum sold from an Estate for exportation and sent to a barquadier, shall be carried direct from the barquadier to the vessel ; but should any circumstance render it necessary to land such Rum, it must in every such case be placed and kept in a duly appointed warehouse until it is cleared for exportation, 22 V., c. 13 s. 13.

Particulars of intended export by others than the person in charge to be made

When Rum is intended to be exported by any other than the person in charge of the Estate upon which it was made, the exporter, or his Agent, shall before the shipment deliver to the Receiver-General in Kingston, or the sub-Collector at any other port, a memorandum in writing on oath of the number of casks with the marks and numbers, name of the Estate on which made, the parish, number of gallons, strength, and such other particulars as the Receiver-General or sub-Collector shall require, 22 V., c. 13, s. 14.

The master of every vessel about to sail on his outward voyage, having Rum on board, shall, at the time of clearing, produce to the Receiver-General in Kingston or sub-Collector, a manifest (Form Schedule D.,) containing a full account of the Rum on board, with the marks of casks, name of Estate on which made, and of shippers, signed and declared to as correct, 22 V., c. 13, s. 15.

Manifests of rum on board to be produced at times of clearance

Every person in charge of an Estate exporting Rum shall, previous to clearance outwards of the vessel, produce to the Receiver-General in Kingston or sub-Collector, a declaration on oath (Form Schedule E.,) of the number of casks shipped, the marks and numbers, their contents in gallons, the strength of the Rum, and name of Estate and parish where made, and obtain a certificate of export, (Form F.,) 22 V., c. 13, s. 16.

Declaration and certificate of export

The Collector of Customs at Kingston shall not clear any vessel having Rum on board, until the master produces to him a certificate from the Receiver-General that the declaration and Rum manifest have been duly lodged with him; nor the sub-Collector at any outport until the manifest and declaration have been actually lodged with him, 22 V., c. 13, s. 17,

No vessel to be cleared without production of a certificate of lodgment of declaration and manifest

If any Rum cleared for exportation is not duly shipped on board the vessel on which it was cleared, or is not duly exported, or is unshipped or re-landed without the permission of the officers of Customs, it shall be forfeited, seized and sold by the officers of the Customs, and the proceeds, after payment of costs and charges, shall be paid to the Receiver-General, and the parties concerned, their aiders and assistants shall be liable to be indicted in the Circuit Court, and imprisoned with hard labor in the Penitentiary for not less than 3 nor more than 12 months, 22 V., c. 13, s. 18.

Omission to ship

All Rum purchased for export shall, where it has been deposited in a bonded warehouse, be gauged and proved previous to shipment, and when shipped from a place or port where there is no bonded warehouse shall be gauged and proved on board the vessel by the sub-Collector, or any other officer of Customs at the port, who shall keep an account of the strength and contents, marks and numbers of each cask, and transmit a copy to the Receiver-General, 22 V., c. 15, s. 19.

Rum purchased for export, and warehoused to be gauged &c.

When Rum which has been sent to a barquadier where there is a warehouse, is sold for exportation, it shall immediately be placed in a duly appointed warehouse, and there kept until cleared for exportation, 22 V., c. 13, s. 20.

To be warehoused as also when sent to a Barquadier for sale if there is a warehouse

As also Rum sent from an Estate for sale to a port or place where there is a warehouse, until sold and the duty paid, 22 V., c. 13, s. 21.

In every case in which Rum is intended to be removed from an Estate for exportation, or upon its being sold for consumption in the Island or for shipment direct from the barquadier to which it is sent from the Estate to the vessel in which it is to be exported, the quantity and strength shall be ascertained, previous to its being sent from the Estate, by the person in charge thereof, or of the distillery, and which shall be considered the correct quantity and strength, 22 V., c. 13, s. 22.

In all cases the quantity and strength must be ascertained before removal from the estate

Upon any Rum being sold for consumption in the Island, the purchaser shall obtain from the seller a bill of parcels stating the number of gallons and the strength of the rum, and before removal pay to the Receiver-General in Kingston, the sub-Collector at any other port, or Collector of Rum dues where there is no sub-Collector, the duty, and procure a duty paid permit for the same, (Form Schedule A.,) which he shall deliver to the person selling as his authority for delivering it, and no person shall deliver any Rum sold for consumption in this Island until the purchaser produces to and leaves with him a duty paid permit, 28 V., c. 27, s. 1.

Bill of Parcels for rum sold for consumption to be produced to Collector duty paid and a duty paid Form obtained before delivery

Previous to sending Rum from an Estate, the person in charge shall see that each cask is marked or branded with the Estate's mark and numbered consecutively from one upwards; commencing in each year with No. 1; and before removal of any duty paid Rum from the place of manufacture, the purchaser shall obtain from the Receiver-General, sub-Collector of Customs, or Collector of Rum Duties a delivery permit (Form Schedule B.,)

Casks to be marked and numbered before leaving the estate

Delivery permit

and containing the several particulars thereby required, and shall retain the delivery permit, 28 V., c. 27, s. 2.

Reward for giving information of offences

Every person who gives information to the Receiver-General, or any sub-Collector or Collector of Rum Duties, of any offence against this Act, shall be paid one fourth of the fine, penalty or forfeiture, (after payment of all costs, charges and expenses), which shall be proceeded for and recovered by reason of such information, and shall be a competent witness nowithstanding, 28 V., c. 27, s. 3.

Penalties

One half of the nett proceeds of all penalties recovered after payment of costs, &c., and the one fourth aforesaid, shall be paid to the officer who detains, seizes, or sues for the same, and the other half to the Receiver-General, and every officer and person who detains, &c., shall be a competent witness, 28 V., c. 27, s. 4.

Rum delivered without a duty paid permit, to be forfeited to the purchaser

If any Rum is delivered from an Estate for consumption in this Island, for which a duty paid permit has not been delivered by the purchaser to the seller, it shall be forfeited to the purchaser, and the seller shall not recover such Rum or its value or price in any Court of Justice, 28 V., c. 27, s. 5.

No action to lie on any bond, &c., of which the price of such Rum forms a portion

In any action on any bond, bill, note or other security, contract, agreement promise or undertaking, where the whole or any part of the consideration shall be for the value or price of any Rum, which has been removed or delivered without the proper duty paid and delivery permits, or either, having been procured and delivered, the defendant may plead and give evidence that such Rum was delivered without the duty paid and delivery permits having been obtained for the same, and if the Jury find it was delivered without the permits, or without either of them having been obtained and delivered as required, they shall find a verdict for the defendant, 28 V., c. 27, s. 6.

Receiver-General to supply forms of permit for distribution

The Receiver-General shall keep printed forms of duty paid and delivery permits in his office, and supply such permits bound in books, as they are required, to the Sub-Collectors and Collectors of Rum Duty, which shall be numbered consecutively from one upwards, and they shall, on receiving payment of the duty, fill up, sign and cut out progressively, and deliver to the person paying the duty a printed form of each such permits, making entry on the duplicate and counterfoil of all the particulars stated in such permits, 28 V., c. 27, s. 7.

Factors to be registered

And Gazetted

Before any person receives or disposes of Rum as a factor, he shall register his name, or that of his firm, place of residence and of business, with the Receiver-General, who shall keep a register of all such factors, and cause their names to be from time to time published in the "Gazette," 22 V., c. 13, s. 23.

To warehouse rum sent to them

Every factor to whom Rum is sent for sale or shipment, shall immediately upon its arrival, place and keep it in a warehouse until sold, transferred to some other person or warehouse, shipped to some other port, or exported, 22 V., c. 13, s. 25.

Quarterly returns

Every factor to whom Rum is entrusted for sale, shall on 31st December, 31st March, 30th June, and 30th September, or within 14 days after, give to the Receiver-General in Kingston an account on oath of the receipt and disposal of all Rum which has passed through his hands during the preceding quarter, accounting for what remained on hand from the previous return, (Form G), 22 V., c. 13, s. 26.

Rum sent from an estate for sale to be warehoused

Every owner, attorney, agent, lessee or tenant of an estate, and every other person to whom Rum shall be sent from an estate for sale, shall deposit the same immediately upon its receipt, in a warehouse duly appointed, until transferred, removed to some other warehouse, cleared for consumption on payment of duty, or exported, 22 V., c. 13, s. 27.

Duties, a charge on the estate

The duties on Rum, now or to be imposed, shall be a charge upon the lands of the estate whereon it is manufactured, and may be enforced against the same and all personal property found thereon at any time, and all goods and chattels belonging to, or in the possession of any person liable for such duties, until they are paid and satisfied, or otherwise discharged and accounted for, notwithstanding proceedings have been taken for any penalty in respect to such duties, 22 V., c. 13, s. 28.

And not to be affected until the duties are satisfied

Nor shall the charge or lien be lost, waived or affected by reason of any distress, action or other proceeding for the enforcement or recovery of the duties, until they are satisfied, discharged, or accounted for, 22 V., c. 13, s. 29.

The duties shall be charged by the Receiver-General agreeably to the returns. Persons who have caused Rum to be warehoused, shall be also charged and be liable for such duties, until full payment shall have been made, or the Rum exported, or a transfer made (the Rum being at the time in warehouse), in which case the person to whom the Rum has been transferred shall be liable, and charged, 22 V., c. 13, s. 30.

To be charged agreeably to returns—Charge in respect of rum warehoused

The duty on Rum warehoused, shall be calculated and paid on the quantity taken out for consumption, 22 V., c. 13, s. 31.

Duty to be on quantity taken out of warehouse for consumption

The Receiver-General shall cause proper entries to be made in books to be kept by him for the purpose, under the head of each parish, of all the Rum liable to duty, made in each year in each parish, as shall appear by the several returns made to him by the persons in charge, Sub-Collectors and Collectors of Rum Duty, or accounted for to himself as Receiver-General in Kingston, and shall procure all such returns to be examined and compared, and ascertain with all possible correctness the total quantity manufactured in each parish, the quantity exported, the quantity on which duty has been paid, that on which no duty has been paid, the quantity of the latter in warehouse, and the amount received for duty in each year, 22 V., c. 13, s. 32.

Rum duties accounts to be kept under the head of each parish

Returns to be examined to ascertain their accuracy

The Receiver-General shall, as soon as can be after each quarter, make up duplicate statements, (Form H) one to be delivered to the Executive Committee, and the other published in the Jamaica Gazette, 22 V., c. 13, s. 33.

Quarterly statements for Executive Committee and Gazette

And shall also, as soon as can be after 30th September, furnish annual returns to the Governor, for the Assembly, of the duties for the financial year, as far as he is then able to ascertain them, distinguishing the number of gallons made in each parish on which duty has been paid, the number remaining in warehouse, the number exported, the number consumed on estates, the number lost by leakage or evaporation and the number remaining on hand, and to be accounted for, whether at the barquadier or at the place of manufacture or deposit, 22 V., c. 13, s. 34.

Annual return for the Legislature

He shall remit the duties on all Rum purchased for the use of the army and navy, on proof that they have been paid, and that the whole of the Rum in respect of which remission of duty is claimed has been exclusively used by the army or navy, 22 V., c. 13, s. 35.

Remission of duties in favor of the army and navy

The Receiver-General may appoint a Clerk in his office, who shall also be the warehouse-keeper in Kingston, at a salary not exceeding £300 per annum out of the duties, with power to remove him, 22 V., c 13, s. 36.

Clerk and Warehouse keeper Kingston

When the In-givings shew, or it comes to the knowledge of the Receiver-General, Sub-Collector or Collector of Rum Duty, that the manufacture of Rum has ceased on any estate, the duty on all Rum remaining on hand, shall, after the demand by the Collector, be forthwith payable and be proceeded for, unless the person in charge immediately pay the duty or warehouse the Rum, 22 V., c. 13, s. 37.

Duties to be paid on rum warehoused when manufacture ceases on an estate

The Receiver-General, or any Sub-Collector or other Officer of Customs, Collector of Rum duty, Locker or Gauger, Justice, Inspector, Sergeant, Policeman or Constable are required, on view or information that any Rum which having been sent to a place where there is a warehouse for sale, or been shipped from a barquadier to be carried direct on board the vessel for exportation, has been landed or been sold for exportation, whilst at a barquadier has not been warehoused, or has been or is being removed from an estate in quantities less than 40 gallons and more than one gallon, without a written permit from the person in charge, to seize and carry away the Rum, and for that purpose to break open any outer door or enclosure in the day time, and call any peace officer to their assistance, who is required to give his aid without the necessity of any warrant, under a penalty of £5 for every refusal and neglect; and the Rum so seized shall be sold under the directions of the Receiver-General, Sub-Collector or Collector of Dues, and the proceeds, after paying costs and charges, shall be paid to the use of the Government. Every person in whose p   i   , or on premises in the occupation of whom any Rum is seized, one all forfeit equal to treble the amount of the duty, or £100, at the option of the Receiver-General, 22 V., c. 13, s. 38.

Power to seize rum improperly removed or disposed of

Rum to be sold

Besides treble duty, &c.

Relief in case of error

The Governor in Executive Committee may grant relief to any person shewing, within 12 months of the date of the in-giving, that an error has been made in any return, by the production of a copy, certified by the Receiver-General, and such other evidence as they require, accompanied in the case of export by a certificate of the Receiver-General in Kingston, or Sub-Collector, with the bills of lading and a declaration of identity, and the Receiver-General shall allow the amount of the relief, 22 V., c. 13, s. 39.

And they may also remit any penalty or a portion, 22 V., c. 13, s. 40.

Oaths of Collectors

Every Sub-Collector and Collector of Rum duty, before he proceeds to perform any duties, shall take and subscribe the following oath before a Justice of the parish for which he is appointed, and who shall transmit it to the Receiver-General to be kept by him :

I,   , Sub-Collector or Collector of Rum duty for the parish of   do swear that I will well and faithfully execute and perform the duties required of me as Collector of Rum duty. under the Act entitled the Rum Duty Collection Act, 1858, and without fear, favor or affection, use my utmost endeavors to discover and give information against every person who shall make a false return, or in any manner seek to evade the duty imposed upon Rum by any Act of the Legislature of this Island, or who shall be concerned as the factor of any estate, without being registered as by the above cited Act is required, or shall sell Rum as a dealer or retailer without being licensed within the parish for which I am appointed. So help me God, 22 V., c. 13, s. 41.

Fortnightly returns of Receipts of money, &c.

Each Sub-Collector and Collector of Rum duty shall, once in every fortnight, (see 3 V., c. 27, s. 13 infra) transmit to the Receiver-General the counterpart of every duty paid permit delivered by him, with a true and particular return of all moneys received for duty upon Rum, specifying the number of gallons of Rum upon which duty has been paid, the proof or strength, the amount of duty paid in respect thereof for each particular estate or person on which or by whom any such Rum has been sold, signed and certified as follows :

I, A. B., Sub-Collector or Collector of Rum duty for the parish of   do certify that the above is a just and true account of the quantity and strength of Rum, with the names of the estates from whence, or persons by whom sold, for which duty paid permits have been granted by me from the   day of   to the   day of   inclusive, and of the moneys which I have received for duty under any Act of the Legislature of this Island.   A. B.

and shall at the same time pay to the Receiver-General the amount of the moneys received by him for duty, deducting a commission of £2 10s. per centum by way of compensation for his trouble, 22 V., c. 13, s. 42.

Also of Locker and Gauger's returns

And shall once in every fortnight after the receipt of the returns to be made by the Locker and Gauger under any Rum warehousing Act, transmit the same to the Receiver-General with the counterparts or duplicates of all warehousing certificates granted by them on the warehousing of Rum 22 V., c. 13, s. 43.

Weekly transmission of duty paid and delivery permits and of receipts for duties

He shall once in every week transmit to the Receiver-General the duplicate of every duty paid permit, and every delivery permit delivered by him, with a true and particular return of all amounts received for Rum duties, according to such Form as the Receiver-General shall direct, and at the same time remit the amount of duties received by him to the Colonial Bank (see Receiver-General moneys transfer) or otherwise as by law directed, 28 V, c. 27, s. 13.

Distress warrant for duties on Receiver General's certificate

On production of a certificate of the Receiver-General, that Rum duties are due by or in respect of any Estate, or by any person on account of any Rum, any 2 Justices, on the request of the Sub-Collector or a Colleter of Rum duties, shall issue their warrant, authorizing the Sub-Collector or Collector to distrain for such duties on any goods found on such Estate, or in the possession of such person whereon a landlord might distrain for rent in arrear ; and such Sub-Collector or Collector, or his Deputy may break open any outer door or enclosure in the day time, and call any Peace officer to his assistance, who is required to give his aid without the necessity of any warrant under penalty not exceeding £5, 22 V., c. 13, s. 44.

Every Sub-Collector,&c., after keeping any distress for 14 days, unless redeemed, may sell same or a sufficient portion to satisfy any unpaid duties and expenses, including £5 per cent. commissions on the duties, and re turn the overplus on demand to the party distrained upon. Perishable goods may be sold earlier, allowing such reasonable time as the nature or state of the goods will permit to redeem. No distress shall be redeemable without payment of the duties and charges including commissions to the the date of tender, 22 V., c. 13, s. 45. Sale after 14 days unless redeemed Perishable goods

Before sale the Sub-Collector, &c., shall give 5 days notice in writing, affixed at the Court House, of the day and hour of the commencement of the sale, (between 10 and 12 o'clock) the articles levied upon, and the name of the person or property; or may, by consent of the party distrained on, or for sufficient cause adjourn any sale, giving a like notice, 22 V., c. 13, s. 46. 5 Days' notice of sale Adjourned Sale

Live stock levied upon may be allowed to remain on the Estate, &c., in the custody of the proprietor, on his request, and entering into bond (Form I) with 2 sureties (exempt from Stamps) in a penalty double the amount of the duties conditioned for their delivery at the time and place appointed for the sale, or adjourned sale, or payment at such time and place of the duties and commission; but not to release the Sub-Collector, &c., from his liability, to collect the duties 22 V., c. 13, s. 47. Live Stock, bond to produce at sale

Property in receivership may be distrained on without previous application to the Court of Chancery for permission, 22 V., c. 13, s. 48, Receivership property

Any Sub-Collector, &c., may proceed by action, or in the proper Court for debts not exceeding £10, when the duties do not exceed that sum to which the party is answerable, for the recovery of any duties in arrear, in his name, describing himself as Sub-Collector, &c., for the parish in which the duty is charged, and shall not be abated by death or removal, but the same and all subsequent process to enforce payment shall notwithstanding be continued in his name, under the direction of the Sub-Collector, &c., for the time being, until the duties and costs are paid, 22 V., c. 13, s. 49. Action and petty debt proceedings for duties

Upon the insolvency of any person charged with payment of Rum duties, the sum charged, whether it has become due or not, shall, to the extent to which the duties remain unpaid at the time of the insolvency, be the prior charge and lien upon his Estate and effects in the hands of the official or other Assignee, and be by them paid thereout, and the insolvent relieved and discharged from payment, 22 V., c. 13, s. 50. Duties, a prior charge on assets of insolvents in hand of Assignee Insolvent dis charged

When the goods of any person charged with duties or any instalment thereof, whether due or not due, shall be levied by the Provost Marshal under any process, or any Collector of Petty Debts, the Sub-Collector or Collector of Rum duties, may make solemn declaration in writing before a Justice in his parish that the person is indebted for unpaid Rum duties in such parish, and the amount, and that he is unable to find other sufficient goods whereon to distrain thereof, and the Provost Marshal or his Deputy or Collector of Petty Debts, or his Deputy, or both, shall pay over to such Collector, &c., the nett proceeds, or a sufficient portion thereof inor towards satisfaction of the Rum duties or instalment so declared to be due, upon being demanded, and the declaration or duplicate being delivered to the Provost Marshal, &c., to be returned to the Court as the authority for such payment, 22 V., c. 13, s. 51. Duties to be satisfied out of proceeds of levies by Provost Marshal, &c.

Every officer or person acting in the execution of any duty under this Act, shall be vested with all the powers and protections of Collectors of Taxes or Collectors of Dues, and they shall have the like power of entry to make a distress as Collectors of taxes or dues, 22 V., c. 13, s. 52. Officers, &c. vested with the powers and protection of Collectors of Dues

If the Receiver-General shall, by affidavit of himself or some other person, shew to a Judge that any person is indebted or accountable for Rum duties not less than £50, and neglects or refuses to pay the same and has not paid or accounted for the same as required by law, the Judge may issue an attachment, bearing date the day it issues, to the Provost Marshal or his deputy, to arrest the body and seize and secure the goods, chatels and personal property of any such person, or such goods as belong to him, or shall have come into the hands or possession of himself or of his executors, administrators or assigns wherever the same can be found; and in case the money due for such duties or the account of such person shall not be paid or rendered or satisfied or settled to or with the Receiver-General Attachments for duties against the person and property within 14 days after seizure, or a sale shall not be stayed by order of a Judge, the Provost Marshal or his Deputy shall sell and dispose of all such goods or any part thereof, and satisfy to the Receiver-General the sum not accounted for or paid over, with costs and charges, and restore the overplus to the person entitled, 22 V., c. 13, s. 53.

Bail and stay of sale

The party may apply to a Judge by affidavit to be admited to bail, and to stay the sale to enable him to a ly to the Court at its next sitting to discharge the attachment, which the Judge may grant on sufficient cause shewn, 22 V., c. 13, s. 54.

Forms of duty paid permits for distribution ; see 28 V., c. 27, s. 7, sup.

Printed Forms of duty paid permits bound up in a book, shall be supplied by the Receiver-General to the several Sub-Collectors and Collectors of Rum duty, and similar duty paid permits shall be kept in his office. Such permits in every book to be numbered consecutively from one upwards, and the numbers to be stamped or printed upon them. The Receiver-General, &c., on receipt of the duty upon any Rum, shall fill up and cut out progressively the printed form in the duty paid permit book, and deliver to the person paying the duty a signed duty paid permit, making a corresponding entry on the counterpart of all the particulars stated in such permit, which duty paid permit must be delivered to and left with the warehouse keeper before removing the Rum from his custody, 22 V., c. 13, s. 55.

Forms warehousing certificates

Similar provision for the supply of books of warehousing certificates to be delivered to the person warehousing Rum. On the deposit of Rum in the warehouse, and upon the production of the Locker and Ganger's certificate the Receiver-General, Sub-Collector, &c., shall fill up and cut out progressively from the printed forms in the book, and deliver to the person warehousing, a warehousing certificate signed by him, setting out the date, the number of casks and gallons, and strength of the Rum warehoused, the Estate and parish, the name of the factor, if warehoused by one. and of the person by whom warehoused, with the number and situation of the warehouse, making a corresponding entry in such counterpart and on the counterfoil of the particulars stated in such certificate, 22 V., c. 13, s. 56.

Penalties for selling, &c. contrary to regulations

If any person having any Rum in his care, custody or possession, cr under his control, sell or remove, or permit such Rum to be sold or removed, except as and under the regulations of this Act permitted, before duty paid, he shall forfeit not exceeding £100, nor less than £20 besides being liable for all the duties payable, 22 V., c. 13, s. 57.

Penalty for receiving rum contrary to regulations

If any person receive any Rum from any person or place (except in the cases and manner, and under the regulations,) before the duty has been paid, he shall forfeit not exceeding £100, nor less than £20, and shall be further liable for all duties payable thereon, 22 V., c. 13, s. 58.

Warrant of distress against party in charge and estate on Receiver-General's certificate

When any person in charge of any estate is convicted of having sold, disposed of, or removed any Rum, any 2 Justices of the parish in which the estate is, at the time of the conviction, or afterwards, upon requisition of the Receiver-General, Sub-Collector, &c., and on production of the conviction, or of a copy certified by the Clerk of the Peace, and on a certificate of the Receiver General, or other proof that the duties are due and unpaid, shall issue to the Sub-Collector or Collector of Rum Duty for the parish, a warrant under their hands and seals, authorizing him to distrain upon all and every the goods and chattels and personal property of the party so previously convicted ; and in addition, upon all and every the goods, chattels and personal property found upon the said estate, and all such goods, chattels and personal property so taken, to sell and dispose of, to satisfy and pay the said duties and the expenses of such distress and sale, including a commission of 6d. in the pound to the Collector of Rum Duty thereon, and to restore the overplus, if any, in the former case, to the party distrained on, and in the latter, to the owner or person representing the owner of the estate ; and it shall not be necessary to obtain any conviction for selling or disposing of Rum contrary to this Act, before enforcing any of the powers gi   by any other sections for the recovery of duties, 22 V., c. 13, s. 59. ven

Forgery, &c. of document under 22 V., c. 13

Every person who counterfeits or forges, or causes or procures to be, &c., or assists in counterfeiting or forging any permit, certificate or document by this Act required to be given by the Receiver-General, Sub-Collector, Collector of Rum Duty, or other person authorized to give the same in the stead of any such officer, or any part of any such permit, &c., or counterfeits any impression, mark or stamp provided or ap pointed by the Receiver-General to be put on such permit, &c., or who utters, gives or makes use of any counterfeited or forged permit, &c., knowing the same or any part thereof to be, &c., or any permit, &c., with any such counterfeited impression, &c., knowing the same to be counterfeited, and every p who knowingly or wilfully accepts or receives any counterfeited and forged permit, &c., or any certificate or document with such counterfeited impression, &c., knowing it to be counterfeited, shall be guilty of the like offence, and shall suffer such punishment as is, or was, by the laws of this Island, provided in the case of persons guilty of a similar offence in respect of Island Certificates and Receiver-General's Cheques, 22 V., c. 13, s. 60.

Felony ; punishable by imprisonment not exceeding 3 years, with or without hard labor or solitary confinement not exceeding one month at any one time, nor three months in any one year, 4 V., c. 46, s. 2, 12. Punishment

Or penal servitude not less than 4, nor exceeding 8 years, 21 V., c. 14, s. 3.

If any person shall counterfeit or falsify, or wilfully use when counter-feited or falsified, any duty paid permit, or delivery permit or document required by this Act, or shall by any false statement procure any writing or document to be made for such purpose, or utter, put off or publish any forged or counterfeited permit or document, knowing the same to be forged or counterfeited, he shall upon conviction be deemed guilty of a misdemeanor, and suffer imprisonment with or without hard labor, not exceeding 3 years, 28 V., c. 27, s. 15. Forgery, &c under 28 V., c. 27

On requisition by and receipt of a certificate signed by the Receiver-General, in the case of a factor, that no return has been made by him as required, and in the case of the person in charge of an estate, that it appears, by some previous return or by some certificate forwarded to him, which he shall specify, that certain Rum, specifying the quantity, remained on hand to be accounted for, or was manufactured on, or disposed of from the estate (naming it), in the charge of such person at some time during the quarter or other period of time elapsed since the last return, and the Rum remaining on hand has not been accounted for, and no return has been made to him in respect of the Rum manufactured upon the estate, or that, although a return has been made of the Rum manufactured on or disposed of from the estate during the period, the certificates, in respect of certain quantities of Rum mentioned in, and which ought to have been transmitted with the return, have not been sent to the Receiver-General, the Clerk of the Peace shall apply to a Justice, who, on production of the requisition from the Receiver-General, shall issue a summons to the factor, or person in charge of the estate, to appear and shew cause why, on referring to the certificate, he should not be convicted of the offence charged in the summons, and on his appearance, or in case of non-appearance on proof of service, any two Justices, may proceed to hear the case, and the Receiver-General's certificate produced before them, shall be sufficient evidence of the offence charged, and the Justices shall convict him, unless the party shew that the return or document had been duly transmitted, to the Receiver-General, [See 28 V., c. 27, s. 8, 12 sup.] previous to the date of the certificate, 22 V., c. 13, s. 61. Warrants against factor on Receiver-General's certificate

If any Sub-Collector, Collector of Rum Duties, Locker and Gauger, or other person acting in the execution of this Act, shall fail to make any returns, or transmit any document, or fail in the performance of any duty, or shall not comply with any written request of the Receiver General to report, or make a return to him on any matter within his duty, he shall forfeit not exceeding £10 nor less than £5, 22 V. c, 13, s. 62. Penalties on Collectors for neglect of duty

If any person neglect or refuse to make any return, or to transmit with any return, the certificates required to be transmitted within the times, or to perform any duty, or offend in any manner against the Act, he shall forfeit not exceeding £100 nor less than £20, and £6 for every week the return is neglected to be sent, or any of the documents transmitted, 22 V., c. 13, s. 63. On other persons

If any person neglect or refuse to transmit any duty paid permit, or any return required by this Act, on the days, or within the times mentioned, or to perform any duty or thing required to be done, or offend in any manner contrary hereto, he shall forfeit not less than £5 nor more than £20. 28 V., c. 27, s. 14. For neglect of duty under 28 V., c. 27

To be recovered, enforced and applied under, 22 V., c. 13; 28 V., c. 27, s. 17.

False swearing Falsely swearing or affirming in any particular in any return, or making a false or untrue statement, declaration or return with a view to evade the duty punishable as perjury, and further to pay by way of fine treble the amount of the duty so evaded or sought to be evaded, and the prosecution to be a matter of public prosecution, 22 V., c. 13, s. 64.

None but retailers shall sell Rum in less quantity than 40 gallons, 22 V., c. 13, s. 65.

No rum to be sold on retail on an estate No proprietor, lessee, or person in charge shall, by himself or agent sell Rum by retail on any Estate where Rum is manufactured penalty : £5 and on a second conviction imprisonment in any Prison, not a County Gaol, not exceeding 3 calendar months, 22 V., c. 13, s. 66.

Permits in writing on removal of rum in quantities less than 40 gallons for consumption When Rum sold on an Estate for consumption in this Island, is removed from such Estate in quantities less than 40 gallons, either at one or various times, the person in charge of the Estate or distillery shall give to the person taking it away, a permit in writing, stating the number of packages delivered to him, the number of gallons contained in them, and that the Rum had been purchased, and the date when granted, 22 V., c. 13, s. 67.

Rum not to be retailed under 28 proof No person keeping a shop in which Rum is retailed, shall retail the same at a weaker bubble proof than 28, by the correct Glasgow bubble : penalty 40s. recoverable before 2 Justices. The correctness of the bubble to be ascertained by comparison with Syke's Hydrometer, under the supervision of the Collector of Rum Duties of the district, 22 V., c. 13, s. 68.

Mixing liquor with other than pure water Every retailer discovered to have mixed any liquor sold by him with anything else than pure water, shall be liable, on conviction before two Magistrates, to a penalty not exceeding £5, 22, V., c. 13, s. 69.

Any person may be an agent to ship rum Any person may act as the agent of any other shipping Rum as before mentioned, without being licensed as a dealer, or registered as a factor, 22 V., c. 13, s. 70.

Recovery of penalties Penalties shall be recovered before 2 Justices, and the offender committed until paid, 22 V., c. 13, s. 71.

One moiety to be paid to the sub-Collector or Collector of Rum Duties for payment over to the Receiver-General, the other to the informer who is competent to give evidence, 22 V., c. 13, s. 72.

Penalties, 28 V. c. 27 Penalties imposed by this Act, the recovery of which is not otherwise directed, shall be recovered and applied under 22 V., c. 13; 28 V., c. 27, s. 17.

Interpretation "Rum" shall mean and include Distilled Spirits of every kind, and Cordials, Liqueurs or other compounds, whether distilled or not, of which Spirits manufactured in the Island form a component part. "Collector of Rum Duties," persons appointed to collect the duty where there are no Sub-Collectors of Customs ; "Officer," any person acting under this Act, 22 V., c. 13, s. 73.

The same meaning assigned to them in 28 V., c. 27, s. 16.

Short Title The Rum Duty Collection Act, 1858, 22 V., c. 13, s. 76.

Incorporation of 22 V., c. 13 The 22 V., c. 13, except so far as repealed, altered, or modified, or inconsistent with, or repugnant, incorporated with, 28 V., c. 27, s. 20.

SCHEDULE—22 V., c. 13.

Return of all Rum on hand, and made on or disposed of from
Estate in the Parish of   in the possession of
from the*   day of   18   to the   day of   18
    * The Quarter Days as in the Act mentioned.

	Puncheons.	Gallons.	Proof.
Remaining on hand on the day of 18 to be accounted for			
Made from the* day of 18 to the day of 18			
Total to be accounted for			
DISPOSAL.			
Exported as per accompanying export certificates			
Sold for consumption in the Island			
Sold for exportation as per export certificate			
Loss by leakage and evaporation			
Consumed on the estate duty free			
Consumed on the estate liable to duty			
Remaining to be accounted for next Givings-in, viz :— On the Estate .... At the Barquadier In the hands of Factor (naming him or them)			
Total accounted for			

I   do swear that the above is a just and true return
of all Rum made, consumed on, or disposed of from
Estate where such spirits are distilled, between the*   day of
    18   and the*   day of   18
and that the return is made out in the standard measure of this Island,
and that nothing in the said return is intended to evade the said duty,
or is contrary to the true intent and meaning of the Act, entitled " The
Rum Duty Collection Act, 1858."
Sworn before me, this   day of   18

I, A.B., the person in charge of the distillery on
Estate, in the Parish of   do swear that the return
hereunto annexed is a true and faithful summary of the entries in the
book kept in the distillery on this Estate as directed by "The Rum
Duty Collection Act, 1858," and is also a correct return of all Rum on
hand on the   day of   last past, and of all
Rum made from the   day of   to the
day of   18   and of the disposal of the same ; and
further, that no Rum other than the Rum mentioned therein has been
given away or consumed on the Estate, or sent from it to any person
or place during the period embraced in such return.

A.B.
Sworn before me, this   day of   18
    C.D., J.P.

* The Quarter Day as in Act mentioned

[Still House Book, C., s. 4.]

Still House Book on Estate in the Parish of

Year and Month.	Day.	Gallons of Rum Made.	Total weekly No. of Gallons Made.	Quantity Exported.	Quantity Sold for Consumption in the Island.	Quantity Sold for Exportation.	Loss by Leakage and Evaporation.	Quantity consumed on the Estate Duty free.	Quantity consumed on the Estate liable to Duty.	Remaining on the Estate to be accounted for.	At the Barque-dier.	In the hands of the Factor, naming him or them.

RUM MADE.

DISPOSAL

PORT OF

Mnsters of ves.
sels declaration, D.
s 15

An Account of all Rum made in this Island, and received on board the
Master, for

Shipping Marks, and Numbers.	No. of Casks.	No. of Gallons.	Proof.	By whom Shipped.	Estate on which Made.	Parish in which Made.	Date of Shipment.	Whither Bound.

I,   master of the   about to
sail from this port for   do declare that the foregoing
quantity of Rum, made in this Island, amounting in all to
casks, containing to the best of my knowledge and belief,
gallons, proof   is actually and bona fide on board of the said
ship   whereof I am master, for exportation, and that
I will not land, or deliver, or suffer to be landed or delivered out of
the ship, such Rum, or any part thereof, in any part of this Island,
without permission first obtained from the Receiver-General or Sub-
Collector of Customs.

Declared before me at the port of   this   day of
18

———

JAMAICA, ss.

Export Declaration
by person in charge,
E, s. 16

I, (1)   do declare that   puncheons or casks (2)
marked and numbered as per margin, and containing
gallons of Rum, proof   are of the produce or manufacture of (3)   in the parish of   in
the Island of Jamaica, and in possession of   for

(1) Proprietor of estate, or his known agent.

(2) Specify the description of spirits, if other than Rum.

(3) Name the Estate.

4 K

whom I am   and that such Rum hath been shipped on
board the   master for   for
exportation from this Island.

Declared before me
   this   day of   18   }

———

I   do declare that   puncheons or casks
marked and numbered as per margin, containing   gallons
of Rum, proof   shipped on board the
master for   for exportation from this Island, (1) is
the same Rum, and the whole of it purchased from
on the   day of   last, and manufactured on
             estate, in the parish of   (2) and
that such quantity is made up of, and includes the whole of
gallons of Rum, proof   manufactured on
estate, in the parish of   in this Island in the possession of   from whom I purchased the same on the
          day of   last, through
his factor or agent (if purchased from a factor or agent), and
gallons of water added thereto by me.

Declared before me this
             day of   18   }

———

Port of   day of   18

I hereby certify that   puncheons   hogsheads
quarter casks, marked and numbered as in the margin, and containing
             gallons Rum, proof   were cleared outwards
as shipped from this port on the   day of   18
on board the   master for   as the produce
of   estate in the parish of

Given under my hand this   day of   18

A. B, Receiver-General or C. D, Sub-Collector.

———

(1) When Rum has been reduced previous to shipment, leave out the words
"is the same Rum," down to " in the parish of   ."

(2) When the Rum has been shipped as p   a e , leave out the words
from the words "and that" down to the end.urch s d

[Factor's Return—G., s. 26.]

Return of the Receipt and Disposal of all Rum made in this Island that have passed through my or our hands as Factors, from the*
day of   to the   day of
18   18

(*The Quarter Days in the Act mentioned.)

R E C E I P T S.

Date of Receipt.	Estate on which Made.	Parish in which Made.	From whence, and from whom Received.	Casks.	Gallons.	Proof.
		Total.....	.....			

D I S P O S A L.

Date of Shipment.	Estate on which Made.	Parish in which Made.	Vessel by which Exported.	Whither Bound.	Person in whose Name Exported.	Person to whom Sold, if not Exported.	Casks.	Gallons.	Proof.

Casks.	Gallons.	Casks.	Gallons.	Proof.

Remaining on hand on the*   day of   18   to be accounted for
Total received as by above return...........
Total to be accounted for...........
Loss by leakage and evaporation...........
Total disposed of as by above return...........
Remaining on hand to be accounted for the next Giving-in...........

Total accounted for...........

I, A. B., do swear that the above is a just and true account of all Rum made in this Island, received by me (or by my firm of) and disposed of by me (or us) between the* day of 18 and the* day of 18 and that the return is made out in the standard measure of this Island, and that there is nothing in the above Giving-in contrary to the true intent and meaning of the Act, entitled ("The Rum Duty Collection Act,") day of 18
Sworn before me this day of ("The Quarter Days as in the Act mentioned.)

[Parish Rum Return, s. 33.]

PARISH OF ·
Copy of the Rum In-Givings for the Parish of
Hundred and _____ on the _____ day of _____ One Thousand Eight

NAMES OF THE ESTATES.	MADE.					DISPOSAL.					
	Remaining on hand per last Return of Proprietor, &c.	Made since last Return.	Total to be accounted for.	Sold for Consumption in the Island.	Exported as per Certificates.	Loss by Leakage and Evaporation on Estate.	Consumed on the Estate.	Remaining in Warehouse.	Loss by Leakage and Evaporation in Warehouse	Remaining on hand to be accounted for in last Return.	Total to be accounted for.

Receiver-General.

A True Copy,

JAMAICA, ss.

Know all men by these presents, that we, A. B., of the parish of
in the county of   and Island aforesaid, and C. D. and E. F., of the same parish, are held and firmly
bound to G. H., of the parish of   Esquire, Sub-
Collector of Customs, (or Collector of Rum Duty) of the said parish,
in the sum of   of lawful money of Jamaica,
to be paid to the said G. H., his executors, administrators or assigns,
for which payment, to be well and truly made, we bind ourselves
and each of us, and any two of us, and the heirs, executors, and
administrators of us, and each of us, and of any two of us jointly,
severally and respectively firmly by these presents.

Sealed with our Seals, dated this   day of   in
the year of our Lord one thousand eight hundred and

Whereas the said G. H., as Sub-Collector of Customs (or Collector of
Rum Duty) as aforesaid, has levied upon (state number and description of Stock) for the sum of   for Rum Duties
due to the public by the above bounden A. B., (or by
of   &c., as the case may be) for the year
and whereas the said A. B., as the owner or person in charge of
                    estate   has requested the said
Sub-Collector (or Collector of Rum Duty) to permit the said Stock to
remain on the said   until the day of sale,
and the above bounden C. D. and E. F. have consented to join the
said A. B. in this obligation,

Now the condition of this obligation is such, that if the said A. B., his
executors or administrators do and shall produce and deliver to the said
G. H., Sub-Collector of Customs (or Collector of Rum Duty) as aforesaid, his executors or administrators, the several hereinbefore mentioned Stock, at the time and place which shall be appointed for
the sale thereof, or in case of the postponement of the said sale,
then at the time and place fixed by such postponement and adjournment, or otherwise do and shall at the time and place of such sale,
or postponed or adjourned sale, well and truly pay to the said G,
H., as Sub-Collector of Customs (or Collector of Rum Duty) as aforesaid, his executors or administrators, the aforesaid sum of
                    being the amount of Rum Duties for which such levy
was made as aforesaid, together with the amount of the commissions of the said collector of taxes on the said sum of money, at and
after the rate of five pounds per centum, then this obligation to be
void and of no effect, otherwise to be and remain in full force and
virtue.

Signed, sealed and delivered in the presence of

                                                C. P.

[Duty Paid Permit A., s. 1.]

SCHEDULE—28 V., c. 27.

(Duplicate.)

(Original.)

DUTY-PAID PERMIT.

No. 186   No.   in the parish

No. 186   No.   in the parish

Sold from

being the produce of

estate, in the parish

Puncheons or Casks

containing   gallons

Proof, at 2s. 9d.

£

Paid by   to whom the

Rum has been sold.

* Marked and numbered as on the back.

Receiver-General,

Sub-Collector of Customs,

or

Collector of Rum Duties.

Sold from

being the produce of

estate in the parish

Puncheons or Casks

containing   gallons of

Proof, at 2s. 9d.

£

Paid by   to whom

the Rum has been sold.

* Marked and numbered as on the back.

Receiver-General,

Sub-Collector of Customs,

or

Collector of Rum Duties.

No
Date
Place where made
Parish
Place from which sold
Parish
Puncheons
    or
Casks
Gallons
Proof of
Amount of Duty Paid
Paid by
To whom the Rum has been sold
Marks of Casks
Numbers of ditto
    Receiver-General,
    Sub-Collector of Customs,
        or
    Collector of Rum Duties.

* N. B.—The Marks and Numbers of the Casks are to be stated on the Back.

[Delivery Permit B., s. 2.]

No.
Date
Place where made
Parish
Place where sold
Parish
Puncheons or Casks
Gallons
Proof
Amount of Duty Paid
By Whom
To whom to be delivered
Place whither to be conveyed
Marks of Casks
Numbers of Casks

Receiver-General,
Sub-Collector,
or
Collector of Rum Duties.

* N. B.—The Marks and Numbers of the Casks are to be stated on the Back.

SCHEDULE.

(Duplicate.)

DELIVERY PERMIT.

No. 186 No.

Permit puncheons or casks, containing gallons of proof, the produce of in the parish of and sold in the parish of

from { upon which duty has been paid by to be delivered to } and conveyed to

* Marked and numbered as on the back.

Receiver-General,
Sub-Collector,
or
Collector of Rum Duties.

(Original.)

DELIVERY PERMIT.

No. 186 No.

Permit Puncheons or Casks, containing gallons of proof, the produce of in the parish of and sold in the parish of

from { upon which duty has been paid by to be delivered to } and conveyed to

*Marked and numbered as on the back-

Receiver-General,
Sub-Collector,
or
Collector of Rum Duties.

WAREHOUSES.

The Governor in Executive Committee may authorize the warehousing of Rum in any warehouse in any port in which imported spirits may be warehoused, under 17 V., c. 2, which is extended and made applicable so far as it will apply, and also under the provisions of this or any other Act, regulating the warehousing of such spirits, and may appoint such number of places in addition as warehouses for Rum (or such number of other places for such purpose, but not exceeding 2 warehouses in Kingston, as they consider necessary, in which Rum shall be deposited without payment of duties, under such security, by bond from the proprietor or tenant with one or more sureties for the payment of the duties on all Rum deposited therein in such penal sum as they shall fix, and subject to the regulations of 17 V,, c. 2, and such others as they may make respecting the warehousing of Rum, and may revoke their approval of any warehouse, appoint others, and direct the removal of Rum therefrom, and its disuse as a warehouse for Rum, 22 V., c. 14, s. 1. *[To be appointed by the Governor and Executive Committee under regulations of 17 V., c. 2; see Customs]*

And may appoint in each place where there is a warehouse approved of, a proper person to execute the duties of Locker and Gauger under the control of the Collector and Controller of the Customs in Kingston, the Sub-Collectors at the other ports, and the Collectors of Rum duty at places where there are no Sub-Collectors at a salary, not exceeding, in case of a new appointment, £125 per annum, and where an officer of the Customs is appointed, not exceeding £40 per annum, in addition to his present salary, and require of him security for his good conduct as such as they deem reasonable, 22 V., c. 14, s. 2. *[Lockers and Gaugers] [Salary—Security]*

They may increase the salary of the head Locker and Gauger in Kingston to £250 per annum, 28 V., c. 27, s. 19. *[Head Locker, &c Kingston]*

Any person desirous of warehousing Rum shall make an entry with the Receiver-General, in Kingston or the Sub-Collector or Collector of Rum duty in any other place, containing such particulars and arranged in such form as the Receiver-General shall require, and the Receiver-General, &c., shall grant an order to the Locker and Gauger to receive the Rum corresponding with the particulars of entry, and shall authorize him to receive, warehouse, and gauge such Rum, and the person making the entry to whom the order is to be delivered shall be responsible for, and shall deposit such Rum in such warehouse (immediately upon its receipt if brought by land, and upon its being landed if waterborne, 28 V., c. 27, s. 18,) Penalty, treble the duties, or £100 at the Receiver-General's election, 22 V., c. 14, s. 3; 28 V., c. 27, s. 18, *[Warehousing entry in Kingston Receiving and gauging order]*

When in any place other than Kingston it is necessary to send Rum to a warehouse previously to making the entry, the Locker and Gauger may receive such Rum into the warehouse, and immediately report the receipt to the Sub-Collector or Collector of Rum duties, but the person sending the Rum must as soon after as convenient make the entry and obtain the order 22 V., c. 14, s. 4. *[Elsewhere]*

The Locker and Gauger shall retain the order as his warrant, gauge the Rum, and deliver to the person warehousing a certificate that the Rum has been duly warehoused, specifying the number of casks, the quantity of gallons in each, and the strength, 22 V., c. 14, s. 5. *[Lockers, &c. certificate]*

Upon the production of such certificate to the Receiver-General, &c., he shall give to the person who warehoused the Rum, a warehousing certificate, Form Schedule A., 22 V., c. 14, s. 6. *[Warehousing certificate]*

The holder of any Rum warehoused and entered in his name, may sell or transfer same, on giving notice in writing of such sale or transfer to the Receiver-General, &c., 22 V., c. 14, s. 7. *[Sale in warehouse]*

The Locker and Gauger in charge shall gauge the Rum if required, and transfer and enter it to the name of the purchaser in his book, and communicate the particulars of transfer with the names of the parties to the Receiver-General, &c., when the seller shall be released from all claim for duties, penalties or forfeitures to which the purchaser is liable, 22 V. c. 14, s. 8. *[Rum to be gauged if required, and transfer entered and reported to the Receiver General]*

Any person having Rum in a warehouse may examine and repair the casks, and fill up ullaged casks from others of the same Rum, draw off such Rum into their casks, and take samples under regulations to be made by the Customs without entry or payment of duty, 22 V., s. 14, s. 9. *[Examination, repairs, samples &c.]*

4 L

Removal, duty paid permit

Before any Rum is removed for consumption in the Island, the party intending to remove it must cause an entry to be made with the Receiver-General, &c., containing such particulars and in such form as the Receiver-General directs, and the Receiver-General, &c., shall grant an order corresponding with the particulars of the entry to the Locker and Gauger to gauge the Rum, who shall on receipt thereof gauge the Rum, and certify by endorsement thereon the contents in gallons, and strength of the several casks mentioned therein, and upon presentation of the orders so endorsed and payment of duties, the Receiver-General, &c., shall give to the person paying the duties a duty paid permit, which shall be the authority to the Locker and Gauger to deliver the Rum, 22 V., c. 14, s. 10.

Removal for exportation or to another warehouse

Before removal for exportation or deposit in another warehouse, the Receiver-General, &c., shall give an order on the Locker and Gauger for delivery without the payment of duty, subject to such regulations as he considers necessary, 22 V., c. 14, s. 11.

To be cleared within 2 years unless further time granted

All Rum warehoused must be cleared for exportation or Island consumption within 2 years from the first entry, unless further time be granted by the Governor in Executive Committee or the Receiver-General may cause it to be sold for payment of duties and charges, and the overplus to be paid to the proprietor, 22 V., c. 14, s. 12.

Lockers, &c books of deliveries and transfers

Books shall be kept by the Locker and Gauger in each place, containing full particulars of all deliveries into and out of warehouse, and transfers in warehouse, to be made in such form as the Receiver-General directs; and whenever Rum is ganged, the quantity and strength, ascertained by gauge and trial, shall be written against the entry of the Rum in such of the books as the Receiver-General directs, 22 V., c. 14, s. 13.

Fortnightly and Quarterly returns

Every Locker and Gauger shall, once in every fortnight in Kingston and St. Jago de la Vega, render to the Receiver-General, and in other places to the Sub-Collector, or Collector of Rum duty, a correct return containing such particulars, and arranged in such form as the Receiver-General directs, of all deliveries into or out of the warehouse under his charge and transfer, in warehouse during that time, and further, on 31st December, 31st March, 30th June and 30th September, or within 14 days after, make up a general return for the past quarter, shewing the quantities received and delivered out during, and the stock in warehouse, at the commencement, and expiration of each quarter, with a column, shewing the loss by leakage or otherwise in the warehouse, and such other particulars as the Receiver-General may require, such return to be signed by the Locker and Gauger, and delivered, 22 V., c. 14, s. 14.

Marks and numbers of casks and stowage

All Rum entered shall be warehoused with distinctive marks and numbers on each cask, and stowed so that easy access may be had to every cask, 22 V., c. 14, s. 15.

Penalty for omission on occupier

Every occupier of a warehouse omitting to mark, number or stow all Rum as directed shall forfeit £5, 22 V., c. 14, s. 16.

On receipt or delivery of rum not entered with Receiver-General, &c.

Or receiving into, delivering from, or taking out of warehouse any Rum, which has not been entered with the Receiver-General, &c., shall forfeit not exceeding £100, nor less than £20; and where Rum is delivered from or taken out of the warehouse contrary to this Act, shall be liable besides to the payment of treble the duties, 22 V., c. 14, s. 17.

Occupier to produce all rum deposited on demand

The occupier shall, on request of the Locker and Gauger or the Receiver-General, immediately produce to the officer making such request, any Rum deposited or received and not delivered out, under any of the provisions of this Act: Penalty £100 over and above the value and duties on every parcel not so produced, the value when received to be paid to the owner by direction of the Governor in Executive Committtee, on shewing that he was in no way implicated in, and had no knowledge of the making away with or removal of the Rum, 22 V., c. 14, s. 18.

Fraudulently opening warehouse

If any proprietor of Rum warehoused, or any person in their employ, with his knowledge, privity or consent, shall by any contrivance fraudulently open the warehouse, or gain access to the Rum, except in the presence of the Locker and Gauger acting in the execution of his duty, he shall forfeit £100, 22 V., c. 14, s. 19.

Concealing or removing rum

Concealing or removing, or being concerned in the concealment or removal of any Rum from the warehouse, harboring or concealing, or permitting, or suffering any such Rum to be harbored, kept or concealed

Penalty, treble the duty, or £100 at the Receiver-General's election, 22 V., c. 14, s. 20.

When any embezzlement or waste of any Rum takes place in any warehouse, through the wilful misconduct of any Locker or Gauger, he shall be guilty of a misdemeanor, and punished accordingly, 22 V., c. 14, s. 21.

Embezzlement or waste

When the proprietor prosecutes the Locker and Gauger to conviction, no duty shall be payable on the Rum so embezzled or wasted, and the damage shall be repaid by the Receiver-General under the Governor's warrant and directions in Executive Committee, 22 V., c. 14, s. 22.

Prosecutor prosecuting to conviction relieved of duties and damages to be repaid

The Governor in Executive Committee may remit or return duties on Rum lost by unavoidable accident on Rum while receivable into, remaining in, or on delivery from warehouse, 22 V., c. 14, s. 23.

Remission or return of duties on rum lost

Rum, &c., shall bear the same meaning as in 22 V., c. 13, s. 73 ; 22 V. c. 14, s. 24.

Interpretation

If any Locker and Gauger fail to make any return, or transmit any document required by this Act, or any Act for the collection of Rum duty, or fail in the performance of any duty under this or any other Act, or shall not comply with any written request of the Receiver-General to report or make a return to him on any matter within his duty, he shall forfeit not exceeding £10, nor less than £5, 22 V., c. 14, s. 25.

Omission to make returns &c. To same effect, 22 V., c. 13, s. 62

Penalties shall be recoverable before 2 Justices, and offenders committed until paid, 22 V., c. 14, s. 26.

Penalties

22 V., c. 14, except so far as repealed, altered or modified by, or inconsistent with or repugnant to this Act, is incorporated therewith, 28 V., c. 27, s. 20.

22 V., c. 14, incorporated into 28 V., c. 27

(Warehousing Certificate, s. 6.)

SCHEDULE—22 V., c. 14.

KINGSTON, or

No.

Date

Estate and

Parish

Casks

Gallons

Proof

Warehouse, No.

Street or place.

Name of party warehousing

Receiver-General,

or

Sub-Collector,

or

Collector of Rum Duties

KINGSTON, or

Duplicate.   18

No.

Produce of   estate

in the parish of

Casks containing

Gallons proof

Warehoused in bonding

Store No.   in

Street or place

by

Receiver-General,

or

Sub-Collector,

or

Collector of Rum Duties

KINGSTON, or

Original.   18

No.   No.

Produce of   estate

in the parish of

Casks containing

Gallons proof

Warehoused in bonding

Store No.   in

Street or place

by

Receiver-General,

or

Sub-Collector,

or

Collector of Rum Duties

LICENCES.

No licence shall be granted to retail Rum or other spirituous liquors, on any place whereon or on any part whereof Rum or other spirituous liquors are manufactured, 18 V., c, 26, s. 8, revived by 22 V., c. 13, s. 74.

Not to be granted on any place where Spirits are manufactured

No person shall, either himself, or by any one on his behalf, deal in, or sell spirits by wholesale or retail, or permit spirits to be sold in any house in his occupation without a license. (Form 1). Penalty not exceeding £100 nor less than £10, 23 V., S. 1, c. 4, s. 1.

No Spirits to be sold wholesale or retail without license

Every sale of spirits without a license, either wholesale or by retail, shall be taken to be a sale for profit, and evidence of any sale shall be evidence prima facia and conclusive, unless contradicted, of a sale for profit; and it shall be upon the defendant in any proceeding for a penalty or offence, to shew that the sale was not for profit, and every act of selling spirits without such license at any place, whether in any house or building, or covered or enclosed place, or in the open air, or in any quantity exceeding, or less than the quantity authorized by the license, shall constitute an offence against this Act by the person selling, 23 V., S. 1, c. 4, s. 2.

Sales for profit

No person shall hawk, or sell, or expose to sale any spirits in or about any street, lane, road, highway or other place, or in or from any boat or vessel upon the water or shore, or in any other manner or place except as is licensed or allowed under this Act : Penalty, forfeiture of all such spirits, and £10, or some mitigated amount not less than one half, 23 V., S. 1. c. 4, s. 3.

Hawking Spirits

Any person may seize and detain any spirits hawked or sold, or exposed to sale in any manner prohibited, and call on any Policeman or Constable, whose duty it is, either when called on or when he of his own view sees any person in the act of hawking, selling, or exposing to sale in any manner prohibited any spirits, to apprehend and detain the party, and seize the spirits, or to receive them when seized by any other person, and carry the spirits and person apprehended before two Justices, to be dealt with for the offence, 23 V. S. 1, c. 4, s. 4.

Spirits may be seized and hawker apprehended

Not to prevent any person in charge of any place whereon spirits are manufactured from selling, according to any Act for the collection of Rum Duty, or the personal representative of any person licensed who dies, or the Assignee of any Insolvent Debtor before the expiration of his license in respect of spirits coming to them in those capacities, from selling any such spirits in the house licensed, or the personal representative of any person not licensed, who shall die leaving a private stock of spirits, or any person from selling his private stock not exceeding 50 gallons at any sale, on departing from this Island, or any licensed retailer from selling any spirits upon the absolute and bona fide transfer of any business, and the whole stock in trade thereof, consisting of or comprising spirits, or any interest therein to any person either solely or as a partner with him on any change in the partnership for the transfer or release of his interest, or the Provost Marshal or any officer or person from selling any spirits under any process of law, or any Official Assignee from selling the unexpired term of any license of an insolvent as part of the assets, 23 V., S. 1, c. 4, s. 5.

Circumstances under which sales may be made

The Justices in Special Sessions shall annually grant licenses to deal in Spirits by wholesale or retail to such applicants as they consider proper to be licensed, 23 V., S. 1, c. 4, s. 6.

Justices to grant licenses

The Custos shall summon a Special Session to be holden on or before 31st March in each year, for the purpose of receiving applications from persons desirous of obtaining wholesale and retail licenses, to be summoned by public advertisement at least 7 days in the "Jamaica Gazette," or any newspaper usually published or in circulation in the parish, and such Session may be adjourned from day to day, or from one day to another, until the whole of the applications are disposed of; but if there are not 3 Justices present, any Justice may adjourn from day to day until 3 attend, 23 V., S. 1, c. 4, s. 7.

Special Sessions to be summoned

Adjournment

Any Custos thereunto required by the Clerk of the Peace, who refuses or neglects to summon such Special Session, shall forfeit not exceeding £30 ; and any Clerk of the Peace who refuses or omits to require the Custos to summon such Special Session within the time, shall forfeit not exceeding £30, nor less than £10, 23 V., S. 1, c. 4, s. 8.

Neglect to summon Session—Custos

Licenses may be granted at any time See 23 V., c. 25, s. 3, inf.

The Justices in Special Session, to be summoned in like manner as above, may grant licenses at any time during the year to applicants approved of; but they shall pa   the full amount fixed for every such license, 23 V., S. 1, c. 4, s. 9. y

Applications

All applications shall be made in writing, and lodged with the Clerk of the Peace of the parish in which the applicant intends to carry on business, at least 2 days previous to the day fixed for holding the Special Session;

Payment to Collector of Dues

and every person applying for a license, shall pay to the Collector of Dues the amount of the license, and three pounds on each license as a commutation in lieu of Stamp Duty (except in case of retail

Retail licenses

licenses in parishes other than Kingston and St. Catherine one moiety of which, and of the commutation Stamp Duties, shall be lodged at the same time with the application for every such license, 28 V., c. 25, s. 2;) and every application shall be accompanied by the receipt from the Collector of Dues (Form A) for the amount paid to him, and no application shall be entertained, which is not accompanied by such receipt; but if the application is refused or rejected, the Collector of Dues shall, on demand, repay the amount paid without deduction, 23 V., S. 1, c. 4, s. 10.

Sums payable for licenses

For each license to deal in or sell Spirits by wholesale, there shall be paid—

In Kingston	£10
In every other parish	5

For each license to retail Spirits, and for each Tavern license—

In Kingston and St. Catherine, for a retail license	£25
In Kingston for a tavern license	25
In each other parish for a retail license (28 V., c. 25, s. 1)....	20
For a tavern license	5

23 V., S. 1, c. 4, s. 11.

Separate whole sale, retail and tavern licenses

A license to sell Spirits by wholesale, shall not authorize the person to whom it is g te   to retail Spirits or to keep a tavern, nor shall a license to retail Spirits or to keep a tavern, authorize the person to whom it is granted, to sell Rum in quantities exceeding 100 gallons, or other Spirits in quantities exceeding 25 gallons; but no person who is approved shall be prevented from taking out a license to sell Spirits by wholesale, and also by retail, and as a tavern keeper, 23 V., S. 1, c. 4, s. 12.

Payment of 2nd moiety of retail licenses elsewhere than in Kingston and in St. Catherine

The other moiety of the retail license and commutation Stamp Duty therefore shall be paid to the Collector of Dues on or before 10th August, in default of which payment, any Justice shall, on application of the Collector of Dues, through the Clerk of the Peace, issue his warrant directing the recovery or enforcement of the second moiety and costs, and £50 as a penalty for the default, by distress and sale of the goods of the person to whom the license was granted or may have been transferred, and any goods found on the premises in respect of which the license is held, 28 V., c. 25, s. 2.

After 10th August proportional part of £20 license to be paid

Any such retail license applied for after 10th August, shall be chargeable with a proportional part only of the sums of £20 and £3, to be calculated for the fractional part of 12 months to elapse from the date of application until the 4th April ensuing, and the Collector of Dues receipt for such proportionate amount shall be lodged with the Clerk of the Peace, together with such application; 28 V., c. 25, s. 3.

Payments over by Collector of Dues to Receiver General

The Collectors of Dues shall pay over the moneys received for licenses, and stamps, (less 5 per cent commissions) to the Receiver-General, within 14 days after receipt, to be carried to the credit of the public for Spirit Licenses, and Stamp Duties respectively. Penalty on defaulting Collector, £20, 23 V., S. 1, c. 4, s. 13.

Clerk of the Peace's returns to Reciver General and Collector of Dues of licenses

The Clerks of the Peace shall transmit to the Receiver-General and Collector of Dues within 10 days after each Special Session, a return of the number of licenses granted thereat, and the names of the persons, distinguishing the wholesale, retail and tavern licenses: Penalty £20. And transmit a copy for publication in the Gazette within the same period under a like penalty, 23 V., S. 1, c, 4, s. 14.

Every Clerk of the Peace shall, under a penalty not exceeding £30 nor less than £10, keep a book to be provided by the Executive Committee, and enter and record therein all receipts and licenses within 10 days, and un der the like penalty cause a list of the names of all persons who obtain li censes to be fairly transcribed, and set up in the most public part of his of fice, 23 V., S. 1, c. 4, s. 15. *Records and lists of licenses by Clerk the Peace*

For every license there shall be paid to the Clerk of the Peace 10s. by the party for performing all his duties, and no other charge or demand shall be made under penalty of £20, 23 V., S. 1, c. 4, s. 16. *His fees*

Licenses shall be taken out within 14 days, or the right to take out the same or any other license of the same kind during the current year shall be forfeited, 23 V., S. 1, c. 4, s. 17. *Period within which to be taken out*

Licenses shall unless forfeited, continue in force until 5th April, in the succeeding year, 23 V. S. 1, c. 4, s. 18. *Duration*

Every wholesale vendor shall, on the 30th June, 30th Septr., 31st December and 31st March, or within 14 days after, so long as he continues to sell spirits by wholesale, make quarterly returns (declared to before a Justice) to the Receiver-General (Form B.,) of all spirits disposed of by him to any retailer or other person during the quarter, setting out their names in full. the date, quantity sold, name of the vessel in which, and the time when Brandy, Gin or other Spirits or Spirituous liquors were imported, if imported by himself, if not of the persons from whom, and the time when purchased. Every retailer and tavern keeper shall also make quarterly returns (declared to before a Justice at the above periods) of all Rum, Brandy, Gin, Whiskey and other Spirits or Spiritous liquors, imported by him or purchased in the Island, from an Estate or dealer in such Spirituous liquors during the quarter (Form C.,) mentioning the names in full of the vessel and master in which such Spirits were imported, and the date of importation, and the names in full of all persons, or of the firm or estate from whom and when purchased : Penalty 40s. for every day of neglect or imprisonment with or without hard labor not exceeding 10 days, 23 V. S. 1, c. 4, s. 19. *Returns of whole sale vendors* *Retailers and Tavern keepers*

No person shall sell Spirits by retail, or as a tavern keeper at more than one place under one license, penalty £50, 23 V. S. 1, c. 4, s. 21. *Tavern keepers*

Any person duly licensed may carry on his trade or business in booths, tents or other places at the time and place, and within the limits of holding any lawful or accustomed amusement or exhibition, or at any public races in the parish for which he has a license, at any time during which the sale of Spirits is not prohibited by law, 23 V. S. 1, c. 4, s. 22. *Places of amuse ment*

Retailers in Kingston and St. Andrews may, under the preceeding section, retail Spirits on the Kingston Race Course during the races, 23 V, S. 1, c. 4, s. 23. *Kingston Race Course*

The Custos may sanction the removal of the place of business of a retailer from one part to another in the same town, or parish, or the transfer of a license from one person to another by order (form D.) to be entered in a book by the Clerk of the Peace : His fee 1s. 6d., 23 V., S. 1, c. 4, s. 24. *Removal of place of business, trans fer of license*

No person licensed to sell by wholesale, who is not also licensed to retail spirits, shall sell Rum in quantities less than 100 gallons, or any Brandy Gin, or Whiskey in quantities less than 25 gallons, or any Brandy, whiskey, Cordials or Liqueurs imported in bottles in quantities less than 1 dozen reputed quart and two dozen reputed pint bottles: Penalty, £10, 23 V., S. 1, c. 4, s. 25· *Minimum quanti ties to be sold by wholesale dealers*

Every licensed retailer shall cause a board to be affixed in the front of the house in which he retails Spirits, over the door towards the public street, lane, or road with his name, and the words "Licensed to retail Brandy, Gin, Rum and other Distilled Spirits," painted in white letters on a black ground: Penalty not exceeding £3, 23 V., S. 1, c. 4, s. 26. *License bond*

Persons not duly licensed, selling or delivering Spirits to any one under pretence of his paying for eating only, without any charge for the Spirits shall be deemed to have sold Spirits without a license, and be liable to the penalties, 23 V., S. 1, c. 4, s. 27. *Evasions of license*

No person obtaining a tavern license shall sell Spirits, to be taken away for consumption in any other place: Penalty, not exceeding, £10 nor less than £2, 23 V., S. 1, c. 4, s. 28. *Spirits not to be sold for consump tion out of tavern*

Requisites for tavern licenses

No Tavern license shall be granted without proof by the evidence of persons of good repute, which evidence the Justices shall in no case dispense with, that the premises intended to be used as a tavern, possess sufficient and proper sleeping, and other apartments for the accommodation of travellers, and fit and proper stabling for horses, 23, V., S. 1, c. 4, s. 29.

Not to be granted where a shop is kept

Nor where a shop is [kept to sell goods of any description, 18 V., c. 55, s. 2.

Hours during which spirits may be retailed

No house in which Spirits are retailed shall be opened before daylight, nor kept open after 9 o'clock at night, and licensed retailers selling, or causing to be sold any Spirits, or opening, or causing to be opened. or keeping open their houses, or causing, &c., except between the hours aforesaid, shall forfeit not exceeding £10, nor less than £2, 23 V., S. 1, c. 4, s. 30.

Disorderly conduct in any retail shops and taverns

Any retailer or tavern keeper permitting or suffering, or not using his best endeavors to prevent and put an end to any disorderly or improper conduct in the house, or in pa   of the premises attached thereto, or not in all things conforming himself to law, and every person guilty of disorderly or improper conduct in the house or upon the premises, shall forfeit not exceeding £5 nor less than 10s., or be imprisoned, with or without hard labor, not less than 10 nor more than 30 days, 23 V., S. 1, c. 4, s. 31.

Prostitutes gambling

Upon information on oath that any house licensed as a tavern or for retailing Spirits, is permitted to be the resort of prostitutes or gamblers, or other dissolute or idle   rs   , or is allowed to be the scene of loose, disorderly or improper conduct,ous dancing or drumming, any Justice may summon the party licensed to appear before any two Justices to answer the premises, and summon and compel the attendance of witnesses, and examine them on oath, and on sufficient proof, the Justices shall certify the finding on the complaint to the Custos, with the evidence, and the Custos shall summon a Special Session of the Peace, to take into consideration the evidence and certificate, and the Justices in session may cancel the license, and direct proceedings to be taken against the person for recovery of the penalty imposed by this or any other Act, 23 V., S. 1, c. 4, s. 32.

Cancelling licenses

Recovery of penalties

Penalties shall be recovered by information before 2 Justices, and recoverable by distress, or, on failure of goods whereon to levy, by committment with or without hard labour, not exceeding 3 calendar months, 23 V., S. 1, c. 4, s. 33.

One moiety to be paid to the Receiver-General and the other to the informer, 23 V., S. 1, c. 4, s. 34.

False declarations

Falsely declaring : a misdemeanor to be prosecuted as a matter of public prosecution, 23 V., S. 1, c. 4, s. 35.

No witness or informer shall be disqualified from residence in the parish, 23 V., S. 1, c. 4, s. 36.

Interpretations

"House" shall mean a house built entirely or partially of brick or stone, and include any shop, tavern, yard, or place in, at, or adjoining, or appurtenant to which Spirits are sold or retailed, unless otherwise specially provided, or there is something in the subject or context rep$_n$g$_n$a$_n$t to such construction ; "Estate", the place whereon any Spirit is distilled or manufactured, "deal in, sell or retail," shall mean dispose of by barter or otherwise ; "Spirits", Rum, Brandy, Gin, Whiskey and other distilled Spirits and Spirituous Liquors ; "Occupation" shall mean possession, 23 V., S. 1, c. 4, s. 37.

Short Title

Spirit License Act, 1859, 23 V., S. 1, c. 4, s. 38.

In force until 31st March, 1867, 23 V., S. 1, c. 4, s. 40.

23 V., S-1, c. 4 incorporated with 23 V, c. 25

This Act shall be read as incorporated with 23 V., S. 1, c. 4 ; and applications for licenses made, granted, and disposed of, and licenses transferred and held or cancelled, subject to the conditions, penalties, or enactments thereof, except as altered, modified, or repealed, and all penalties by this Act recovered and appropriated as under the former, 23 V., c. 25., s. 4.

FORMS, &c.—23 V., c. 4.

JAMAICA, SS.

Wholesale License, s. 1

At a Special Session of the Peace, held in and for the parish of
         on the   day of   in the year
of our Lord, 186 for that purpose, A. B. of the said parish, having
been approved of as a vendor of Spirits by wholesale in such parish, and paid the tax required by law : These are to license the said
              to sell Spirits wholesale, or in quantities not
less than are mentioned in the "Spirit License Act, 1859," from the
      day of   186   to the 5th day of April,
in the year of our Lord, 186

Dated this   day of   186

JAMAICA, SS.

Retail License, s. 1

At a Special Session of the Peace, held in and for the parish of
        on the   day of   in the year
of our Lord, 186   for that purpose, A. B. of
having been approved of as a retailer of Spirits, to be consumed
in, or conveyed from a certain house at present occupied by him
situate at   (in a town, state street, and number)
in the said parish, and paid the tax required by law : These are
to license the said   to sell and dispose of
Spirits by retail, to be drank and consumed on the premises abovementioned, or to be taken therefrom, at the option of the purchaser, in quantities not exceeding the quantities mentioned in
"The Spirit License Act, 1859 ;" and provided that he do not wilfully or knowingly permit drunkenness or other disorderly conduct on his said premises, but do maintain good order and rule
therein : This license to be in force until the fifth day of April, in
the year of our Lord, one thousand eight hundred and

Dated this   day of   in the
year of our Lord, one thousand eight hundred and

JAMAICA, SS.

Tavern Licenses, s. 1

At a Special Session of the Peace, held in and for the parish of
        on the   day of
in the year of our Lord, 186   for that purpose, A. B. of
      having been approved of as a retailer of Spirits, to be
drank or consumed in a certain tavern for the accommodation of
travellers, situate at   (in a town, state street
and number) in the said parish, and paid the tax required by law :
These are therefore to license the said   to sell
and dispose of Spirits, to be drank and consumed on the abovementioned premises, and provided the said
does not permit drunkenness or other disorderly conduct in his said
tavern and premises, nor permit or suffer any Spirits to be conveyed from or out of his said premises, and maintains good order
and rule therein : This license to continue in force until the fifth
day of April, one thousand eight hundred and

Dated this   day of   one thousand eight
       hundred and sixty

Received   day of   186   from
        of the Parish of   the sum
pounds, for a   License, for the Parish of
and the further sum of three pounds, in lieu of Stamp Duty thereon.

Collector of Dues
receipt, s. 10, As to
receipts for moieties
of £30 license and
stamp, see 28 V., c.
26, s. 2, 3

Collector of Dues for the Parish of

4 M

[Wholesale Vendors Return, B. s. 19.]

A Return of all Rum, Brandy, Gin, Whiskey, Liqueurs, Cordials, and other Strong Waters sold by me, (1) of the Parish of (2), Wholesale Vendor of Spirits, from the (3) day of (4) to the (5) day of (6) 186 of (7)

Year, Month and day of the Month when each sale was effected.	Names in full of the persons or of the Firms to whom sold.	Number of gallons of Rum, and strength of same sold.	Number of gallons of Brandy, and strength of same sold.	Number of gallons of Gin, & strength sold	Number of gallons of Whiskey, & strength.	Number of bottles of Brandy (imported in bottles,) sold.	Number of bottles of Liqueurs and Cordials (imported in bottles) sold.	Number of gallons of other Distilled Spirits and strength.	Name of the Vessel in which the Brandy, &c. sold was imported.	Year and Quarter of the Year in which the importation took place	Name of the Person or Firm from whom the Rum or Brandy was purchased, in case of its having been purchased.	Year and Quarter of the Year in which the purchase was made.	State whether the quantity sold is a part, or the whole of the quantity purchased; and if a part, then mention the entire quantity purchased.

1.—Name of Wholesale Vendor.
2.—Name of the Parish in which he carries on business.
3. 4.—Day of January or March, or otherwise, as the case may be.
5. 6.—31st day of March, 30th June, or otherwise, as the case may be.
7.—1860 or otherwise, as the case may be.

I, (A. A.) do declare, that the above is a just, true, and correct Return of all the Distilled Spirits and Spirituous Liquors sold by me during the Quarter of the Year ended the day of A. B. 186 last.

Declared before me, this day of

C. D., Justice of the Peace.

[Retailers and Tavern Keepers' Return, C. s. 19.]

A Return of all Rum, Brandy, Gin, Whiskey, Liqueurs, Cordials, and other Strong Waters, Purchased and Imported by me (1) of the Parish of (2) Retailer of Spirituous Liquors (or Tavern Keeper as the case may be, from the (3) to the (5) day of (4) day of (6) 186 186 (7)

Year, Month, & Day of the Month when each Purchase was Made.	Name of the Estate, Person or Firm from whom each Purchase was Made.	Number of Gallons of Rum (& the strength) Purchased.	Number of Gallons of Brandy (and the strength) Purchased.	Number of Gallons of Gin Purchased, and Strength.	Number of Gallons of Whiskey Purchased and Strength.	Number of Bottles of Brandy (Imported) Purchased in Bottles.	Number of Bottles of Liqueurs and Cordials (Imported in Bottles) Purchased.	Year, Month and Day of the Month when each Importation took place.	Name of the Ship or Vessel, and of the Master in which Imported.	No. of Galls. of Brandy (and the strength) Imported.	Number of Gallons of Gin Imported, and Strength.	Number of Gallons of Whiskey Imported, and Strength.	Number of Bottles of Brandy Imported in Bottles.	Number of Bottles of Liqueurs and Cordials Imported in Bottles.

I, (A. B.) do declare, that the above is a just, true, and correct Return of all the distilled Spirits and Spirituous Liquors purchased and imported by me during the quarter of the year ended the day of 186
A. B.

Declared before me, this day of 186

C. D., Justice of the Peace.

1.—Name of the Retailer or Tavern Keeper.
2.—Name of the Parish in which he carries on Business.
3, 4.—Days of January or March, or otherwise (as the case may be.)
5, 6.—Days of March or June, or otherwise (as the case may be.)
7.—1860 or otherwise, (as the case may be.)

Transfer of License, D, s. 94   Jamaica, ss.

Parish of

Ordered,   day of   186

That   carrying on business as a retailer, or tavern keeper, in the   of   have permission to transfer his license from the house for which it was originally granted to the house now in his possession, at
(state street, and number of house, if in a town, or situation, otherwise), or to   of the said
of   for the sale of Spirits by retail (or as tavernkeeper, as the case may be.)

                 A. B.
           Custos or Senior Magistrate

St. Domingo or Hayti.

Removal of obstructions to trade and intercourse   For the removal of all obstructions to a trading and free intercourse between this Island and St. Domingo or Hayti, by the repeal of such laws as tend to hinder or prevent such intercourse, 39 G. 3, c. 29 and 41 G. 3, c. 17 are repealed, 6 V., c. 13.

Salvage.

Summoning persons to assist in preservation of vessel and cargo in distress   The Custos and Justices and Collector and Controller of the Customs of every parish, upon application by, or on behalf of any Commander of any Vessel in danger of being stranded or run on shore, may command the Constables nearest to the sea coast where the vessel is in danger, to summon and employ so many persons as shall by them be thought necessary, to the assistance and preservation of the vessel and cargo, and may also demand assistance from the superior Officer of any Vessel of War or Merchant Ship, riding at anchor near the place, of their boats, and such hands as they can conveniently spare ; such officer in case of refusal or neglect shall forfeit £200 (£120 stg.), to be recovered by the superior Officer of the Vessel in distress with full costs by action of debt, &c., 53 G. 3, c. 25, s. 1.

Officers of other vessels

Payment of Salvage   The Officers of the Customs and Master of any Vessel, and all others acting or employed in the preserving of any Vessel or Cargo, shall, within 30 days after the service, be paid a reasonable reward by the Commander or Owners of the Vessel in distress, or Merchant whose Vessel or Goods shall be saved, and in default the Vessel or Goods saved shall remain in the custody of the Collector or Controller until all charges are paid, and such Officer and Master, of the Vessel and all others employed, shall be reasonably recompensed for the assistance and trouble or security given, to the satisfaction of the parties to receive the same ; and in case the Commander or Owners of the Vessel saved, or Merchant whose Goods are saved, shall disagree with such Officer touching the moneys deserved by any of the parties employed, the Custos or Chief Magistrate, on application for the purpose, may give public notice for a meeting to be held, as soon as possible, of any three or more Justices to examine persons on oath, touching the Salvage of the Ship or Goods, and to adjust the quantum of Salvage, and allot the same among the persons concerned in such Salvage, which shall be binding upon all parties and recoverable by action by the respective parties to whom it is allotted, 53 G. 3, c. 25, s. 2.

Ascertainment & recovery

Salvage in the case of Persons not employed   If any person not employed by the Master or Owners or others lawfully authorized in their absence, save any Ship or Goods, and cause the same to be carried for the benefit of the owners or proprietors into a port or to any adjoining Custom House or place of safe custody, immediately giving notice to a Justice or Custom House Officer, or discovering to any such Magistrate or Officer where any such Goods are wrongfully bought, sold or concealed, he shall be entitled to a reasonable reward for such services to be paid by the Master or owners of the Vessel or Goods, and to be adjusted, in case of disagreement about the quantum, as before directed to be adjusted and paid, 53 G. 3, c. 25, s. 3.

Ascertainment of vessel cargo, master and owners whence and where   The Officer of Customs or other person acting, shall procure all persons belonging to the Vessel and others who can give any account thereof, or of the cargo, to be examined on oath before a Justice, as to the name or descrip tion of the Vessel, the Master and Owners, and owners of the Cargo, of the ports from or to which the Vessel was bound, and the occasions of her distress, which examinations the Justices are to take down in writing, and deliver a copy, with a copy of the account of the goods, to the Collector or Controller, who shall forthwith transmit a copy to the Receiver-Generel to be published in the London Gazette and in this Island for 2 months successively or so much as shall be necessary for the information of the persons concerned, 53 G. 3, c. 25, s. 4. *bound and cause of distress. Account of goods to be sent Receiver-General & advertised*

If no person appears to claim the Goods saved, the Chief Officer of Customs of the nearest port shall apply to 3 of the nearest Justices, who shall put him or some other responsible person in possession of the goods, they taking an account to be signed by the officer, and if not legally claimed within 12 calendar months by, or on behalf of the owner, then public sale shall be made, and if perishable goods, they shall be forthwith sold under the direction of 3 magistrates, and after all charges deducted, the residue with an account of the whole moneys shall be transmitted to the Receiver-General to be applied in aid of the public funds, 53 G. 3, c. 25, s. 5 *Custody of goods in the absence of claimants Sale and disposal*

Upon the rightful owner appearing and shewing, by affidavit or other proof, his right to the money, to the satisfaction of the Judges of the Supreme Court at any sitting of the Court, the Commissioners of public accounts shall direct the Receiver-General to pay the amount, deducting the charges he may have incurred, 53 G. 3, c. 25, s. 6. *Proceeds to be paid to the owner on proof of claim*

If any person besides those empowered by the Custos or Justices, Officer of Customs or Constables enters, or endeavours to enter on board any Vessel in distress without the leave of the Commander, or of the Officer of Customs, or Constables, or molests them in the saving of the Vessel or Goods, or endeavours to impede or hinder the saving of any Vessel or Goods, or when any Vessel or Goods are saved, takes out or defaces the marks of any Goods before they are taken down in a book for the purpose provided by the Commanding Officer and the Officer of the Customs, he shall within 28 days make double satisfaction to the party grieved, at the discretion of three or more of the next Justices, and in default shall be committed to the county goal for 6 calendar months ; and the Commander of the Vessel, Officer of the Customs or Constables on board may repel by force any such person, 53 G. 3, c. 25, s. 7. *Obstructing persons engaged in salvage, defacing marks, &c.*

Force to repel such persons

In case any goods are found upon any person, that were stolen or carried off from any vessel in distress, he shall, immediately on demand, deliver the same to the owner or person by the owner authorized to receive the same, or in default shall be liable to pay treble the value of the goods, to be recovered by the owner on an action, 53 G. 3, c. 25, s. 8. *Goods stolen or carried away*

In any action against any person for any thing done or caused to be done under this Act, and in executing any of the powers, orders or directions, he may plead the general issue, and give the special matter in evidence, and if the plaintiff become nonsuit, or discontinues, or a verdict pa es against him, or judgment is given against him on demurrer, the defendant shall recover full costs. If any Officer of the Customs by fraud or wilful neglect abuses the trust hereby reposed in him, he shall forfeit treble damages to the party grieved and be incapable of the same or any other employment relating to the office, 53 G. 3, c. 25, s. 14. *Protection from Actions*

No writ shall be sued out or copy of any process, at the suit of a subject, served on any Justice or Officer of the Customs, or any acting under his orders or directions, until notice in writing thereof has been delivered to him or left at his place of abode, by the Attorney or agent of the party intending to sue, at least one calendar month before, in which shall be clearly and explicitly contained the cause of action, and on the back shall be endorsed the name and place of abode of such Attorney or Agent, who shall be entitled to a fee of 26s 8d (16s stg.), for preparing and serving the notice and no more ; and no plaintiff shall recover a verdict unless it is proved upon the trial that such notice was given, but in default, the defendant shall recover a verdict and costs, and no evidence shall be given by the plaintiff on the trial of any cause of action except such as is contained in the notice, 53 G. 3, c. 25. s. 15. *Notice of Action, &c.*

Savings' Banks.

Persons entitled to the benefit of the Act on filing rules

.Any number of persons forming a Society for establishing and maintaining any Institution in the nature of a Bank to receive deposits of money for the benefit of the depositors to accumulate the produce of so much as shall not be required by them, their executors or administrators at compound interest, and to return the whole or any part of the deposit, and the produce thereof, deducting the necessary expenses of management, but deriving no benefit from such deposit or the produce, and desirous of having the benefit of this Act shall cause the rules and regulations for the management of the Institution to be entered, deposited and filed as after directed, and thereupon shall be entitled to the benefit of this Act. The privilege of paying and receiving money under the Act shall be extended to such Institutions as may form their rules and regulations accordingly, and the Trustees may receive Funds and grant receipts as hereby authorized. But no Institution shall be so entitled unless sanctioned and approved of by the (Circuit Court, of the parish, 19 V., c. 10, s. 17) or some one authorized and appointed by them, 7 W. 4, c. 14, s. 1.

Rules to be entered, Transcripts deposited with Clerk of the Peace and certified

Amendment, &c. of rules.

No Institution shall have the benefit of the Act unless the rules and regulations are entered in a book to be kept by an Officer, and open for the inspection of the depositors, and a transcript deposited with the Clerk of the Peace and filed by him, and a certificate of filing signed by him on a duplicate returned to the Institution within 10 days ; his fee 10s (6s stg.). Rules may be altered and amended or repealed, but such new rules shall not be of force until entered, and transcripts filed and certified, fee 5s (3s stg.), 7 W. 4, c. 14, s. 2.

To be submitted to a Barrister

And laid before Judge of Circuit Court for rejection or confirmation

Before depositing any transcript or amendment with the Clerk of the Peace, the Trustees must submit the transcript, at the expense of the Institution, to a Barrister to be appointed by the Government to ascertain whether they are in conformity to law, and who shall give a certificate thereof, or point out in what parts they are repugnant ; his fee not to exceed £2 13 4 (£1 14 0.) The transcript, signed by two Trustees, and Barrister's certificates, shall be laid before the (Judges of the next Circuit Court, 19 V., c. 10, s. 17,) for rejection or confirmation. The rejection of any rule shall be signified by the word " rejected" or " disapproved" written opposite the rule and signed by the Judge, and notice given by the Clerk of the Peace within 10 days to the two Justices (trustees) who signed the transcript. No rule making alterations in the hour of attendance need be laid before such Barrister previous to enrolment, 7 W. 4, c. 14, s. 3.

Rules to be binding

All Rules duly entered shall be binding. The entry in the book or transcript shall be binding on the members, officers and depositors all of whom shall be deemed to have full notice by the entry and deposit ; and the entry or transcript, or an examined copy shall be received as evidence. No Certiorari shall be allowed to remove the rules into any Court. Fee for copy which is to be exempt from stamp duty 2s 6d (1s 6d) stg. per legal sheet, 7 W. 4, c. 14, s. 4.

Treasurer &c. to derive no benefit except salary &c. Trustees or Managers to receive none ; see 24 V., c. 10, s. 4

The Rules shall provide expressly that no Treasurer, Trustee, or Manager shall derive any benefit from any deposit, save only such salaries, allowances, or other necessary expenses as shall, according to the rules, be provided for the charges of management and for remuneration to officers exclusive of the Trustees or Managers who shall not have any salary or allowance beyond their actual expenses, 7 W. 4, c. 14, s. 5.

Security of Officers

Any Treasurer, Actuary, or Cashier entrusted with the receipt or custody of money, and every officer receiving any salary or allowance for his services shall give security by bond to the Clerk of the Peace. Fee 26s 9d, (16s stg). The bond, in case of forfeiture shall be sued in the name of the Clerk of the Peace, for the use of the institution, they indemnifying him, and to be exempt from stamp duty, 7 W. 4, c. 14, s. 6.

Effects vested in the Trustee, who may sue or be sued

All moneys, effects and securities shall be vested in the Trustees and their successors without any assignment whatever, and who may sue or be sued in their proper names in respect thereof and the same shall be alleged to be their property in criminal and civil suits, 7 W. 4, c. 14, s. 7.

Liable only for wilful neglect ; see 9 V., c. 41, s. 1, 3

No Trustee or Manager shall be personally liable except for his own acts, and then only for wilful neglect or default, 7 W. 4, c. 14, s. 8.

Account and payment and delivery over of moneys and effects

Persons having any moneys, effects, or funds, or entrusted with the disposition, management, or custody thereof, or of any securities, books, or papers, or property relating thereto, their executors or administrators shall on demand of two Trustees and two Managers, or by their order or authority, or at any general meeting of the Trustees or Managers give in their accounts, to such Trustees and Managers, or general meeting or to the institution or to such persons who may be nominated to receive the same for examination and allowance or disallowance, and shall on the like demand pay over all moneys in their hands, and assign and transfer or deliver all securities and effects, books, papers, and property in their handes or custody to such person as the Trustees and Managers shall appoint, and in case of neglect or refusal the trustees may exhibit a petition to the (Circuit Court) who may proceed thereon in a summary way, and make such order thereon upon hearing all parties as to such Court, in their discretion shall seem just, which shall be final; and all assignments, sales, and transfers in pursuance of any such order shall be effectual, 7 W. 4, c. 14, s. 9.

The Trustees and Managers, or a majority, at a meeting publicly convened, and amounting to no less than 7, may make arrangements with the Commissioners of Accounts (Executive Committee, 25 V., c. 37, s. 1) for investing moneys deposited in the Savings' Bank in the Public Chest, or with the Directors or Managers of any public Bank established in this Island under any Act of the Legislature, or of Great B.itain for the investment of deposits upon such rate of interest, terms and conditions as to them may seem eligible ; but no moneys shall be invested in any other manner, except such sums as may necessarily remain from time to time in the hands of any Treasurer, 7 W. 4, c. 14, s. 10. Investment in the public chest or public banks

The Commissioners of Public Accounts may receive for the use and to the credit of the Island, deposits, and repay the same upon such terms to such amount, and at such interest, and under such regulations as may appear proper to them. 7 W. 4, c, 14, s. 11. Interest on deposits with the public

The interest payable to depositors by the Trustees or Managers shall not exceed £4½ per cent per annum, 7 W. 4, c. 14, s. 12. Interest to depositors

The receipts of minors shall be sufficient discharges in respect of deposits from them, or for their benefit, 7 W. 4, c 14, s. 13. Receipts of Minors

As also of married women, unless the husband or his representatives give the Trustees notice of the marriage, and require payment to be made to him or them, 7 W. 4, c. 14, s. 14. Or married women

No sums shall be paid into any Savings' Bank by any person by ticket or number or otherwise, without disclosing his name, profession, business occupation, and calling and residence, which are to be entered in the books, 7 W. 4, c. 14, s. 16. No sum to be received without name calling and residence of party.

Trustees on behalf of other persons may make deposits, and their or their executors or administrators' receipts shall be valid discharges, 7 W. 4, c. 14, s. 17. Deposits by Trustees

The Trustees shall not receive from any one depositor more than £200 in the whole in any one year, ending 1st May, nor receive or hold from any one depositor any sum which with principal and interest exceeds in the whole £400. Whenever the sum standing in the name of any one depositor exceeds £400, all interest thereon shall cease, 10 V., c. 18, s. 2. Limits of deposits

Upon the death of a depositor, if his deposit exceeds £50 it shall only be paid to his representatives, on probate or letters of administration. If not exceeding £50, and it satisfactorily appears to the Trustees and Managers that no will was left, and no letters of administration are likely to be taken out, they may pay the same according to the rules, or divide it among the persons appearing to them to be entitled according to the statute of distributions, which payment as well as those to the representatives shall be valid discharges. Persons claiming a superior right to the moneys, shall have legal remedy against the persons who receive, 10 V., c. 18, s. 3. Payment in case of death where deposit exceeds £50 When not exceeding £50
Remedies against person receiving

No power of attorney or instrument of any kind required by this Act, Administration Bond or Letters Testamentary of any depositor, where the whole of the estate and effects of any depositor shall not exceed £50 (£30 sterling) shall be liable to Stamp Duty, 7 W. 4, c. 14, s. 20. ... Instruments exempt from stamps where estate does not exceed £30 stg.

Disputes concerning any deposits shall be referred to 2 arbitrators, one to be chosen by the Trustees or Managers, and the other by the party with whom the difference may be, and if they shall not agree, the matter in difference shall be referred in writing to the Barrister appointed by the Governor, and the award by the arbitrators or a Barrister shall be conclusive Reference to arbitration without appeal, and shall declare by whom the Barrister's fee shall be paid. The proceedings are exempted from Stamp Duty, 7 W. 4, c. 14, s. 21.

Exempt from stamps

Deposits may be rejected or returned

The Trustees and Managers may accept or reject moneys offered for investment, or return moneys invested to any depositor, 7 W. 4, c. 14, s. 23

Branch Banks

Branch Banks may be established to facilitate the business, but nothing in their formation or rules shall be inconsistent with this Act, 7 W. 4, c. 14, s. 24.

Misfeasance, &c. proceedings how enforced

If any Trustee, Manager, Treasurer, Secretary or other officer is guilty of any misfeasance, or wilful non-feasance or other breach of duty, whereby any loss of the funds or property of the Bank accrues, not amounting to a fraudulent taking or misapplication to his own use, and the majority of the Board of Managers refuse or neglect to direct the institution of proceedings to enforce the rights of the Bank, the Trustees shall, of their own authority institute the necessary proceedings, 22 V., c. 41, s. 1.

Application to Supreme Court

Or if they refuse, any depositor may apply to the Supreme Court for a rule to compel the Trustees to proceed to enforce the rights of the Bank, or to punish the offending officers, 22 V., c 41, s. 2.

Surplus Fund not to make good until failure to recover from the officers

The surplus fund to the credit of each Bank shall not be applied to redeem such losses, until after failure to recover them from the officers occasioning or implicated in the same, 22 V., c. 41, s. 3.

Retirement of Trustees

One-third in rotation of the Trustees and Managers shall in each year retire from office, and an election shall take place annually in June to supply vacancies, 22 V., c. 41, s. 4.

Annual election of President, &c.

The President, Vice President, Secretary, Treasurer and Auditor shall be elected annually in June, or as soon as practicable thereafter, and after the election of Trustees and Managers for the current year, 22 V., c. 41, s. 5.

Time and place of elections

The President, or in his absence any Vice President shall fix the time and place for holding the elections of the officers, 22 V., c. 41, s. 6.

President &c. ineligible to be Secretary, &c.

The President, Vice President, or any Trustee or Manager shall be ineligible to be Secretary, Treasurer or Auditor while holding such office, 22 V., c. 41, s. 7.

Secretary and Treasurers books of account

The Secretary and Treasurer shall each deposit with the President their books of accounts and transactions, made up to the termination of the financial year, one month before the election in June. The financial year to be considered as terminating on 30th April, 22 V., c. 41, s. 8.

Quarterly and Special Meetings

The President, Trustees and Managers shall meet quarterly to receive the accounts of the Secretary, Treasurer and Auditor, and as often intermediately as the business of the Bank shall render special meetings necessary, 22 V., c. 41, s. 11.

Payments to depositors

No money shall be paid out to any depositor save by the Treasurer, on production of an order, drawn by the Secretary and countersigned by a Manager, who shall respectively sign or initial the depositor's book in respect to the draft, and on presentation of the order on the Treasurer, the deposit book shall also be presented to and initialed by the Treasurer, 22 V., c. 41, s. 12.

Orders on Treasurer to be compared with depositors book before payment

Before any order is drawn on the Treasurer, the depositor's book shall be compared by the Manager in attendance, with the account open in the books of the institution, to ascertain if they correspond, 22 V., c. 41, s. 13.

Drafts from Treasury

Provision shall be made in concurrence with the Executive Committee for drawing moneys from the public treasury, 22 V., c. 41, s. 14.

Rules to be amended in conformity with Act

The rules and regulations of the Banks shall be amended in conformity with this Act, 22 V., c. 41, s. 15.

Annual Statement to be hung up in place of business

The Trustees and Managers shall yearly, within one month from the annual statement and settlement of the accounts cause a clear and complete general statement of the transactions, accounts and situation of the affairs of the Institution, to be signed by two Trustees and two Managers, and countersigned by the Secretary or Treasurer, to be hung up in the place of business, specifyng the balance due from the Institution to the depositors for principal and interest, setting out the number of depositors, and the balance claimed from the Treasury, and cause a copy to be published in one of the weekly papers of the County, 24 V., c. 10, s. 2.

The interest or dividends due to each depositor shall be computed half yearly to 1st May and 1st November, and at no other periods, 24 V., c. 10, s. 3, *Interest to be computed half yearly*

The Treasurers and Secretaries shall be paid salaries to be fixed at the annual meeting in June, but not to exceed in the aggregate the annual surplus balance arising from the transactions of the year to the credit of the Bank, and on no account shall the surplus fund to the credit of the Bank be interfered with, 24 V., c. 10, s. 4. *Treasurers' and Secretary's salaries*

Seamen.

Persons receiving or entertaining seamen belonging to any trading ship in harbour, after the ship's bell ringing to set watch at 8 o'clock at night, shall forfeit for each 40s. (24s. stg.,) one half to the poor, the other half to the master prosecuting, to be recovered by warrant from a Justice, 33 C. 2, c. 17, s. 7. *Entertaining them after 8 p. m*

No seaman belonging to any vessel shall be trusted for anything; those trusting or retaining them in their houses, shall lose the money they trusted them withal. Victuallers or retailers of strong liquors trusting any seafaring man not generally residing upon, or belonging to this Island, above 40s, (24s. stg.) though he have bond or bill for the same, shall lose the money they trusted him withal. If any commander of a vessel entice away any seaman belonging to any other ship, before he is lawfully discharged, he shall forfeit £15 sterling, half to the King, and half to him that shall sue in any Court of Record, 35 C. 2, c. 4, s. 6. *Not to be trusted* *Enticing away seamen*

Complaints and disputes between owners, consignees or masters of ships arriving in any port of this Island, or trading to or about the coasts thereof, and the Seamen or seafaring persons employed, shall be heard by two Justices, whose decision shall be final and not subject to appeal, and who are to grant a summons or warrant against the person complained of, and in case of appearance or non-appearance, shall examine the parties and witnesses on oath, and make order for the delivery of the chest, tools, clothes and effects, and payment of the wages demanded and proved, or such part as to them shall seem just; provided the sum sought to be recovered do not exceed £20 (£12 stg.) for any one seaman, and the application be not delayed beyond 2 days after the refusal of the owner, &c., to deliver the seaman's chest, &c., or pay the wages demanded; and in case of non-delivery or non-payment beyond 24 hours after such determination, the Justices shall forthwith thereafter issue their warrant to levy the sum they award by distress and sale, rendering the surplus, if any, to the defendant, after payment of costs (not exceeding 50s. (30s. stg.) on any one proceeding) and charges to be apportioned by the Justices as they think proper; and for want of distress, may commit the defendant to Gaol, until he satisfy the damages, costs and charges, for 30 days, 2 W. 4, c. 32, s. 1. *Complaints between owners, &c. of vessels and seamen to be summarily heard* *Without appeal* *Not exceeding £12, nor to be delayed beyond 2 days* *Enforcement of orders*

The Justices may receive evidence of the misconduct or misfeasance of such seamen, and make abatement in the wages demanded, or if they deem the complaint frivolous or vexatious, they may dismiss it with costs not exceeding 50s. (30s. stg.), and in case of non-payment, commit the complainant to Gaol not exceeding 10 days. Act not to bar any seaman from proceeding otherwise for recovery of his wages, or to interfere with any regular articled and indented seaman when the owner or master, entering into such articles for any specific voyage, is ready to comply with the stipulations therein, and produces the agreement, for want of which the seaman shall not be delayed in any of his remedies, 2 W. 4, c. 32, s. 2. *Evidence of misconduct* *Abatement of wages* *Frivolous complaints—Costs* *Not to bar other remedies* *Articles for specific voyage* *Production of agreement*

Act in force till 31st December, 1833, 2 W. 4, c. 32, s. 3. *Continuance of Act*

But continued by 4 W . 4, c. 19.

Secretary, Island.

His office shall be kept at St. Jago de la Vega, 33 C. 2, c, 12, s. 1. *Office*

He shall provide two distinct books, and in each of them keep an alphabet of the names of the several persons parties to the records in his office in one, the name of each grantor, feoffor, donor, &c., in the other, the name of each grantee, feoffee, donee, &c., leaving a discre- *Fore and back alphabets* tionary room between each letter for inserting such a number of names as will make it of use for some time, 11 Ann, c. 4, s. 5.

Separate book and index to bonds to the Crown

He shall keep a separate book for recording bonds to the Crown, as also an index thereto, 27 V., S. 1, c. 31, s. 15.

Inventories on leaving office

Secretaries or persons acting as such, on delivering possession or leaving office, shall deliver Inventories of books of record to the new Secretary, to be signed by both, and entered in a book to be kept for the purpose in the office, and a copy sent, signed as aforesaid, to the Clerk of the Supreme Court's office, which Inventories or copies shall be good evidence against the Secretaries, in case of embezzlement of any books. Penalty, £1000 (£600 stg.) 11 G. 2. c. 4, s. 4.

Recoverable in the Supreme Court by action of debt, one moiety to the informer, 11 G. 2, c, 4, s. 5.

Papers 20 years in office

He shall destroy Deeds and other papers (except Wills) recorded in his office, and remaining there for 20 years. 21 G. 3, c. 23, s. 5.

Fees

56 G, 3, c. 19, s. 1

His fees shall be—

	Currency. £ s. d.	Sterling. £ s. d.
For recording every Deed or instrument lodged or brought into his office not after mentioned, per sheet of 160 words [60 G. 3, c. 23, s. 5]	0 2 6	0 1 6
Recording every plat [for each division, 60 G. 3, c. 23, s. 5]	0 2 6	0 1 6
Receipts for Deeds and other writings	0 0 5	0 0 3
Dockets furnished Receiver-General—for Conveyance of Land [21 V., c. 34, s. 23]	0 0 0	0 1 6
Receiver-General's fee on Conveyances and Patents of Land [21 V., c. 34, s, 23]	0 5 0	0 3 0
Marriage License and Bond, including drawing out affidavit, filing same and bond, and all incidental expenses	0 17 6	0 10 6
Affixing the Island Seal	0 10 0	0 6 0
Entering satisfaction on Mortgage, including search	0 3 4	0 2 0
Citations, one name	0 3 4	0 2 0
" more than one, each additional name	0 1 8	0 1 0
Sending book into Court per order	0 3 4	0 2 0
Entering Caveat and publishing same	0 1 8	0 1 0
Publishing Proclamations	0 6 8	0 4 0
Recording Crop account	0 3 4	0 2 0
Moving for a Writ of Error	0 13 4	0 8 0
Filing Writ of Error	0 0 10	0 0 6
Moving to have the Return opened, and furnishing copies	0 13 4	0 8 0
Copy of the Writ, Return and Transcripts	2 0 0	1 4 0
Filing same	0 0 10	0 0 6
Writ of Certiorari and Return	0 6 8	0 4 0
Filing same	0 0 10	0 6 0
Copy Certiorari and Return	0 6 8	0 4 0
Filing Joinder in Error	0 10 0	0 6 0
Copy of Rejoinder	0 6 8	0 4 0
King's Bond on Appeal	0 5 0	0 3 0
Making out Testamentary or Administration Bond, where the sum sworn to does not exceed £50 (£30 sterling)	0 5 0	0 3 0
Making out in the like case a Dedimus to swear Executors or Administrators or Appraisers, and to return an Inventory, including the recording, each	0 6 8	0 4 0
Making out in the like case a Probate of a Will, or a Will and Codicils, a Warrant of Appraisement, Letters Testamentary and Letters of Administration, including the recording, each (exempt from Stamp tax)	0 3 4	0 2 0
Making out Letters of Administration, Warrant of Appraisement, Dedimus to return Inventory, and Dedimus to swear Appraisers, above £50 (£30 sterling)	1 13 4	1 0 0
Filling up Bond to return Inventory (so that the whole exceed not £2 6s. 6d. (£1 8s. sterling)	0 6 8	0 4 0

	£	s.	d.	£	s.	d.
Making out Letters Testamentary, Warrant of Appraisement, Dedimus to return Inventory, and Dedimus to swear Executors	1	13	4	1	0	0
Filling up Bond to return Inventory	0	6	8	0	4	0
Making out Dedimus to swear witnesses and Probate, each	0	6	8	0	4	0
Recording Will, long or otherwise, and Dedimus	1	0	0	0	12	0
Filing Petition for further time to return Inventory	0	6	8	0	4	0
Moving for an order for commission to prove a Will in solemn form	0	3	4	0	2	0
Commission	0	16	8	0	10	0
Filing Interrogatories	0	0	10	0	0	6
Filing Commission	0	0	10	0	0	6
Order to pass Publication	0	1	8	0	1	0
For all copies of the Laws, or of any Deed or Instrument of writing, lodged or recorded in his office, to be paid by the person demanding such copies, per sheet of 160 words [60 G. 3, c. 23, s. 5]	0	2	6	0	1	6
For entering each Protest	0	16	8	0	10	0
For taking out each Protest	0	8	4	0	5	0
For Searches and Extracts, every 3 hours	0	1	8	0	1	0
For attesting each copy of the Laws	0	1	3	0	0	9
For filing authority to withdraw, and withdrawing Caveat	0	1	8	0	1	0
Filing affidavits of Service of Citation, each	0	1	3	0	0	9
For lists of Registered Medical Men, to be paid under Governor's Warrant	0	0	0	2	0	0
For inserting higher degree or qualification on Register	0	0	0	0	10	0
For attending meeting of Examiners on Governor's Warrant	0	0	0	1	1	0
Counting duplicate Registers of Dissenters' Marriages, per legal sheet of 160 words	0	0	0	0	0	3

To be paid monthly, as also the Recording Fee by the Public.

56 G. 3, c. 19, s. 11
60 G. 3, c. 23, s. 6

23 V., S. 1, c. 17, s. 7, 11. 24

26 V., S. 2, c. 10, s 2

Each figure in any deed or writing recorded, shall, for the purpose of calculating and charging fees, be considered as a word. Penalty on the Secretary, his agent, deputy or clerk for demanding or receiving greater or other fees than prescribed, £50 (£30 stg.) 56 G. 3, c. 19, s 2. *Figures to be counted as words*

He shall record in books to be provided at his own cost, all the laws and all deeds, and other writings lodged in his office, or delivered to him or his clerk, in a fair legible hand, within (90 days, 60 G. 3, c. 23, s. 1). Penalty, £50 (£30 stg.) 56 G. 3, c. 19, s. 3. *Time for recording*

He shall make an entry immediately of the lodgment of every deed, &c., in the File Book to be kept in his office. Penalty, £50 (£30 stg.) 56 G. 3, c. 19, s. 4. *File book*

The Secretary, or a confidential clerk, shall examine all the records with the originals, and within one month after filling each book, cause to be written on the last page of each book, an affidavit that all the deeds and other instruments recorded in the book have been carefully examined, and are true copies of their originals, to be sworn to before a Judge, and signed by the Secretary or Clerk, and Judge. Affidavit exempt from Stamp duty. Penalty, £50 (£30 stg.). False swearing, perjury, 56 G. 3, c. 19, s. 5. *Records to be examined and sworn to*

He shall furnish copies of all deeds, &c., within 14 days after an entry made of the copy wanted, in the copy book, in the rotation in which the entries are made. Penalty, £50, (£30 stg.) 56 G. 3, c. 19, s. 6. *Copies to be furnished within 14 days*

He shall deliver stamped receipts for every deed, &c., lodged or delivered to the party at the time, and also deliver bonds, warrants, dedimuses, and other testamentary and administration papers so soon as demanded. Penalty, £50, (£30 stg.) 56 G. 3, c. 19, s. 7. *Stamped receipts Instruments to be delivered on demand*

He shall by himself, or a confidential clerk, for whom he is responsible, keep the custody of all deeds, &c. and records, and not permit any of them to be carried out of office, unless under order of a competent Court. Penalty, £50, (£30 stg.) 56 G. 3, c. 19, s. 8. *No record to be carried out of office without an order*

Delivery of original deeds

     • If required, he shall deliver all original deeds, &c., 90 (60 G. 3, c. 23, s. 1) days after lodging, to any party producing the receipt, or to the grantee, lessee or party deriving a beneficial interest under it, or his **See 21 G. 3, c. 23, s. 8** torney or Solicitor, upon their giving a receipt for the original on the margin of the record, and making oath that the receipt had unintentionally been lost or destroyed. Penalty, £50 (£30 stg.) 56 G. 3, c. 19, s. 9.

After 2 years recorded

     After any deed or paper has been recorded 2 years, and the person to whom it belongs not having the receipt to produce, but the same is lost or mislaid, the Secretary shall deliver the deed or paper to the person applying, and making it appear to the Secretary that it is his property, and giving a receipt therefor, 21 G. 3. c. 23, s. 6.

Office hours

     His office shall be kept open from 7 a. m. to 3 p. m. every day except Sundays and Holidays. Penalty, £50, (£30 stg.) 56 G. 3, c. 19, s. 10.

Searches and extracts

     All persons shall have access to the office during the time it is kept open, and make searches, and take extracts or dockets, on paying at the rate of 1s. 8d. (1s. stg.) for every 3 hours employed. Penalty on the Secretary or his deputy, or clerks for impeding or disturbing any such person, £50, (£30 stg.) 56 G. 3, c. 19, s. 11.

Table of fees

     He shall constantly keep up a Table of Fees in his office in Spanish-Town and Kingston. Penalty on Secretary and Deputy Secretary for each day's neglect or delay, £50, (£30 stg.) 56 G. 3, c. 19, s 12.

Recovery of penalties

     Penalties not exceeding £50 (£30 stg.) shall be recovered in a summary manner before two Justices, who are empowered to commit offenders until payment, 56 G. 3, c. 19, s. 13.

Oath of office

     No person shall enter upon or execute the office, until he has taken an oath before the Governor for the faithful discharge of his duty, and enter**Securtly** ed into recognizance, himself in £10,000 (£6000 stg.) and 2 or more sureties in £5000 (£3000 stg). Penalty, £1000 (£600 stg.) recoverable in the Supreme Court, half to the informer, 56 G. 3, c. 19, s. 14.

Justification of sureties

     No person shall be accepted as a security until he makes oath before the Chief Justice that he is, at the time of entering into the same, worth £2500 (£1500 stg.) after payment of all his just and lawful debts. False swearing declared perjury, 56 G. 3, c. 19, s. 15.

Notice of entering into recognizances

     All future Secretaries shall leave with the Clerk of the Crown and Attorney-General respectively, notice in writing of his intention of entering into recognizance, with the names and additions of his intended sureties, 4 days at least previously, that the Attorney General may, if he thinks fit, attend at the time; which security shall be signed by the Secretary and his sureties before the Chief Justice, and be recorded in the office of the Clerk of the Crown, 56 G. 3, c. 19, s. 16.

Convicted in a penalty in the Supreme Court incapable of holding office

     If any Secretary at any time incur any penalty in this Act mentioned, which is recoverable in the Supreme Court, he shall, from the time he incurs the penalty and is convicted, be rendered incapable of holding the office, 56 G. 3, c. 19, s. 17

Recognizance to keep records, &c. in good order; see 27 V., s. 2, c, i expires 31st Decr. 1865

     He shall, under penalty of £5000 (£3000 sterling) before his entrance upon the office, enter into recognizance himself in £5000 (£3000 sterling) and 2 securities in £2,500 (£1,500 sterling) each, that he will from time to time, at his own cost and charge, keep in good order and repair the deeds, records and alphabets of his office, and have copies fairly transcribed of such as shall in any wise require transcribing, 60 G. 3, c. 23, s. 3.

Recovery of penalty

     The penalty shall be recoverable in the Supreme Court, half to the informer, 60 G. 3, c. 23, s. 6.

     The recognizance of the Secretary was reduced to himself £1,000, and 2 or more sureties in a sum amounting in the aggregate to £2,000, to be approved of by the Governor and Executive Committee, and taken before any Judge, but not to prevent the Secretary from giving security to the amount of £2,000 under 27 V. S. 1, c. 35 (European Assurance Society.) The person taking office and giving security under this Act, to be subject to any reforms of any nature which may hereafter be found necessary for the public benefit. In force to 31st December, 1865, 27 V. S. 2, c. 1.

Fresh security

     He shall give fresh securities upon the death or insufficiency of former sureties, on being required by the Attorney-General within one month, giving to the Clerk of the Crown 4 day's notice, with the names and additions of his sureties, that the Attorney-General may attend if he thinks fit, 4 G. 4, c. 12.

Every Deed and Record transcribed, shall be carefully examined by the Secretary or the Examiner, in his office, and verified as prescribed by 56 G. 3, c. 19, s. 5, and shall be deemed authentic, valid and effectual, 60 G 3, c. 23, s. 4. *Transcript to be examined and sworn to*

Any person taking down any book of Record from its shelf or place, and not returning it to its right place, shall forfeit 40s. (24s. sterling) recoverable before a Justice of St. Catherine, to go to the informer, unless he is a witness, in which case it shall go to the poor, 11 G. 4, c. 12, s. 1. *Taking down books and not replacing them*

The Secretary or any person deputed by him, shall not receive any Deed or writing to be recorded without an affidavit, (declaration, 6 V., c. 24,) exempt from Stamp duty, of the number of legal sheets of 160 words counting figures as such. Penalty £10 (£6 sterling) recoverable as before mentioned, 11 G. 4, c. 12, s. 2. *Affidavits quarterly of writings to be recorded*

Attorneys-at-Law, shall be allowed 4d. (currency) per sheet, for counting, unless he drew the instrument, and 3s. 4d. (2s. sterling) for the affidavit, 11 G. 4, c. 12, s. 3. *Fee for counting*

The Secretary shall charge for recording for the number of sheets sworn to, and no more. Penalty £10 (£6 sterling) recoverable as before mentioned, unless he satisfy the Magistrate that the person was mistaken, and that the (declaration) states a less number of sheets than the Deed or instrument contains, 11 G. 4, c. 12, s. 4. *Charges for recording to be regulated accordingly, unless shewn to be errneious*

He shall record Duplicate Registers of Dissenter's marriages, 4 V., c. 44, s. 9 ; 14 15 18 26 V. S. 2, c. 10. *Registers of Dissenters marriages*

His authority to appoint Deputies, at the several ports under 31 G. 2, c. 19, 51 G. 3, c. 17, and 5 W. 4, c. 19 was repealed, and the right to fees on vessels and droghers ceased upon the death of the then Patentee, 5 V., c. 15. *Powers to appoint deputies at outports repealed — Cesser of fees on vessels*

Servants.

When any insolvent is indebted at the time of becoming insolvent to any Overseer, book-keeper, Clerk or servant, in his employ, for salary or wages, any Judge of the Insolvent Court may order, not exceeding 6 month's salary or wages, and not exceeding £60 to be paid to him and he shall be at liberty to prove as a creditor for any excess, 25 V., c. 29, s. 1. *Payments from Insolvent's estate of Salary of Overseer, Bookkeeper, Clerk or Servant not exceeding 6 months or £60—Proof of excess*

When indebted to any laborer or workman for wages or labor, any Judge of the Insolvent Court may order not exceeding £10 to be paid to such laborer or workman out of the Estate, and he may prove as a creditor for any excess, 25 V., c. 29, s. 2. *Not exceeding £10 to laborers or workmen—Proof of excess*

Complaints and disputes between Masters and Servants hired, contracted, or indented, (Overseers and other Servants receiving wages exceeding £100 (£60 stg.) per annuum excepted) shall be heard by 2 Justices, who may examine on oath the parties and witnesses, and make order for payment of such wages as shall seem just, provided the sum sought to be recovered do not exceed £100 (£60 stg.) nor the application delayed in the Master's life time beyond 12 months after the sum became due, nor beyond 3 months after the estate becomes represented. In case of non-payment for 14 days after such determination, a distress warrant may issue against the goods of the Master, 55 G. 3, c. 19, s. 1. *Complaints to be heard summarily Parties may be examined Sum not to exceed £60, nor application delayed beyond 12 months or 3 months after estate represented Distress warrant*

The Justices may hear any complaint, although the Master is dead, notice of the complaint being given to the representative, and enforce payment by distress and sale of the deceased's goods, 55 G. 3, c. 10, s. 2. *Hearing notwithstanding Master's death*

The Justices may receive evidence of the misconduct or misfeasance of such Servant, and make abatement in the wages ; and upon complaint on oath by any Master against any such Servant of misconduct, neglect, or misdemeanor in his service, 2 Justices may hear the same and punish the offender, if a hired Servant, by commitment not exceeding one calendar month, by fine not exceeding £20 (£12 stg.) for the use of the poor of the parish, enforced by imprisonment, or by abating a part of the wages; if an indented Servant, by all, any, or either of those ways, or by canceling the indentures, and in case of imprisonment, the Servant shall serve all the time he has been imprisoned, in addition to the period fixed by his *Evidence of misconduct—abatement of wages Commitment of servant, abatement of wages, cancelling indentures, additional service for time of imprisonment*

Discharge from service in case of illtreatment

indentures. . Upon the complaint on oath by an indented Servant against his Master, of any misusage, refusal of necessary provisions, cruelty or other ill treatment, 2 Justices may summon the Master and examine into the complaint, whether he appear or not, upon proof of the service, and proof being made of the truth of the complaint, may discharge the Servant from his indentures under their hands and seals, 55 G. 3, c. 19, s. 3.

No Certiorari

No certiorari shall issue to remove proceedings into the Supreme Court, 55 G. 3, c. 19, s. 1.

Contracts of servants in husbandry, mechanics domestics. &c,
Summary Jurisdiction for breach of contract misconduct, &c, penalty

If any Servant in husbandry, or any mechanic, artificer, handicraftsman, field or other laborer, person employed in droghers, or other person, or any household or other domestic Servant, body Servant, or any other class of Servant shall contract with any other person to serve him for any time certain, or in any other manner, and shall not enter into or commence his service according to his contract, such contract being in writing and signed by the contracting parties, or having entered into such service (whether the same shall be in writing or not) shall absent himself from his service before the term is completed, (whether the contract is for a time service, or work certain, or under the provisions after contained, unless for some reasonable cause, or shall neglect or refuse to fulfil the same, or shall be guilty of any other misconduct, miscarriage misdemeanor, or ill behaviour in his service, or in the execution thereof, or otherwise respecting the same, the offender, on conviction before 2 Justices of the parish where the offence was committed or the Servant found, shall pay not exceeding £3, or may be imprisoned, with or without hard labour, not exceeding 30 days, 5 V., c. 43, s. 1

Abatement of wages

And the Justices may, in addition, abate the whole or any part of the wages due, to be retained by and to the use of the employer, and no wages shall accrue during imprisonment, 5 V., c. 43, s. 2.

Misusage, cruelty, &c,

Two Justices may, on complaint on oath by or on behalf of any Servant against any employer for any misusage or refusal of necessary provision (where the contract includes maintenance and support), or for cruelty or illtreatment, upon conviction, impose a fine not exceeding £20 and costs, and in default of payment, commit him for not exceeding 30 days, unless sooner paid, 5 V., c. 43, s. 3.

Duration of contract, notice to determine

In the absence of any express agreement to the contrary, every contract for service shall be taken to be a contract for a month certain from the time of entering thereon, and to be terminated only by mutual consent, or by 15 days notice at any time in writing, or in the presence of a witness, or for good cause, 5 V., c. 43, s. 4.

Improper determination

If otherwise terminated by the employer, he shall forfeit to the Servant equal to one month's wages, or if the rate of wages was not fixed, such sum as the Justices may consider fair for a month's hire according to the class of the servant and the nature of the duties contracted to perform, beyond the wages due at the time, 5 V., c. 43, s. 5.

When for a time certain performance of a particular act

If any employer, after he has retained any Servant for a service for a time certain, or the performance of any particular act, puts away, dismisses or discharges any such Servant or other person before the termination or completion of his contract, unless there for some reasonable and sufficient cause, the offender, unless he is able to prove by a witness such reasonable and sufficient cause for putting away the Servant, shall forfeit to the Servant not exceeding £5, as 2 Justices shall consider a reasonable remuneration, and if not paid at such period as they may direct, to be recovered as after directed, 5 V., c. 43, s. 6.

Discharge for misconduct

But any employer may discharge any Servant who is guilty of any misconduct, misdemeanor, or wilful omission or neglect of duty, without notice, or payment of any beyond the wages due at the time of discharge, and on any complaint to a Justice by the Servant in respect of such discharge, such misconduct, &c. shall be a sufficient answer, 5 V., c. 43, s. 7.

Terminating contract for illusage. or other good cause

On any complaint by an employer against his Servant for terminating the contract without notice as aforesaid, where it was for a time uncertain, or before its expiration, the Servant may shew by evidence that he did so in consequence of ill-usage or for some other good cause, as a sufficient answer, 5 V., c. 43, s 8.

Discharge of servant-award of wages by Justices

Upon any complaint by any employer or Servant, the Justices may discharge the Servant from the contract or service, in addition to any other order, and at the time of the discharge shall award to the Servant such propor tion of the wages appearing due as they think reasonable, and give the employer or Servant, as the case may require, such discharge and award of wages under their hands, to be enforced as after directed, 5 V., c. 43, s. 9.

In cases of contracts by laborers to work by the day, week or month, and in such specified time to perform a certain quantity of work by the measure, heap, weight or tale, if any person contracting to cut, heap, pack, chip, or clean any canes, grass, bundle wood or cord wood, logwood, fustic or other dyewood, or other description of wood, or break, blast or cut any stones, or pick any coffee or pimento, shall stack or pack, cord, heap, pile, weigh or measure, or count out by the tale or otherwise, any cordwood, bundlewood, logwood, fustic, or other dyewood, or other description of wood, or canes, grass or other commodity, or any coffee, pimento or stones, in any false or fraudulent manner, with intent to deceive or defraud his employer, or if any person shall take and remove, or convey away any such canes, wood, grass, coffee, pimento or other commodity or stones from one heap or parcel to another, with intent to deceive or defraud his employer, he shall, on conviction, forfeit not exceeding £5, or be committed not exceeding 3 months, 5 V., c. 43, s. 11.

Frauds by laborers contracting to perform work by measure, heap, weight or tale

All contracts entered into in writing or verbally in presence of two witnesses between employers and laborers for a time certain, or for the performance of any work by contract, job or task, shall be dealt with under this Act in compelling on the part of the laborers the proper performance of such contract, job or task within the stipulated time, and on the part of the employer the fulfilment of his engagement, 5 V., c. 43, s. 12.

Contracts in writing, or before 2 witnesses for a time certain, o r by job, or task may be enforced

If any person shall entrust to or with any other person (although he has not entered into any express contract of service) any goods not exceeding £10 in value, for sale or for carriage and delivery to another, or in any other manner to dispose of the same, and any such person shall make default in accounting for any of the proceeds of any such, or for any of such articles so entrusted to him, or shall not duly deliver or dispose of the same. such person, on conviction before 2 Justices, may be committed, with or without hard labor not exceeding 30 days, or shall forfeit over and above the value of the goods, a fine not exceeding £3, and in default of payment and costs if ordered, shall be committed not exceeding 30 days. unless payment of the value, fine and costs be sooner made, 5 V., c. 43, s. 13.

Persons entrusted with goods not exceeding £10 for sale, carriage or disposal otherwise, and n o t accounting for the proceeds, or value

All complaints, differences or disputes between any employer or Servant touching any wages or allowances due to the Servant, shall be heard by 2 Justices of the parish where the Servant is employed, who may make such order for payment of so much wages, clothing and allowance as shall appear to them according to the terms of the contract to be due, provided the wages or allowance do not exceed the sum or value of £50, and the application is made within 6 months after the same became due, or in the event of the Master's death, within 3 months after the estate is represented. 5 V., c. 43, s. 14.

Complaints t o be heard by 2 Justices of the parish, where t h e servant is employed, if the wages or allowance exceed not £50, and the application is made within 6 months after due or 3 months after estate represented

If not paid or made within such period as the Justices direct, they shall enforce the order by distress and sale, 5 V., c. 43, s 15.

Enforcement by distress & sale

Where any employer resides at a distance from the parish, or is absent from the Island or parish, where his business is carried on, or where his Servant is employed. and entrusts his business to the management and superintendance of Attorneys, Agents, or Managers, the Justices may, on complaint of any such Servant for non-payment of wages, summon the Attorney, Agent or Manager, to appear before 2 Justices of the parish, at a reasonable time, and who shall hear the complaint and make an order directing payment by him of the wages due not exceeding £50, and in case of refusal or non-payment within such period as the Justices direct, the same and costs may be enforced by warrant of distress and sale of the goods of the owner or of the Attorney, &c., rendering the overplus to the owner or Attorney, &c., for his use, after payment of charges, 5 V., c. 43, s. 16.

Enforcement of payment against agents when the employer is absent from the island or parish, and entrusts h i s business t o a n Agent not exceeding £50.

No person shall be liable to be convicted of any offence by his co-partner in trade without his privity or consent: but when any penalty for wages or other sum is ordered to be paid, and the party neglects or refuses. the same may be levied by distress and sale of the copartnership goods or the separate property of any one or more copartners, and no preceedings for wages shall be set aside, on account of the omission of any copartners in the proceedings, and the Justices may make order upon any one or more

No person liable for the offences of his co-partner

Proceedings for wages against Partners

copartners for payment; and service of a copy of any summons, process or order upon any one shall be sufficient service upon all, 5 V., c. 43, s. 17.

Enticing away servants

Any person knowingly enticing or inveigling away any Servant, who accordingly quits the service of any other person, before the expiration of his contract, or, having employed such Servant without a previous knowledge of his retainer, receiving and continuing to employ him after notice, shall be liable, on conviction on the oath of one or more witnesses, before 2 Justices of the parish in which the enticing or inveigling, or that in which the employment took place, to a fine, not exceeding £20, nor less than 40s with costs to be paid forthwith or within such period as the Justices direct, 5 V., c, 43, s. 18.

Payment of sums awarded and forfeited and penalties

All sums awarded for wages or forfeited for discharging a servant without notice, shall be paid to the Servant. Sums forfeited by any employer for ill usage of a servant, may in the discretion of the Justices be paid to the Servant as compensation, or to the use of the poor; Sums forfeited for the amount of any wrong or injury done to the party aggrieved if known notwithstanding the employer, servant or party aggrieved may have given evidence; where not known, in the same manner as a penalty; Penalties, whether in addition to the amount awarded for any injury or otherwise, to the use of the poor. Where several persons join in the commission of the same offence, and shall on conviction each be adjudged to forfeit a sum equivalent to the amount of the injury done, no further sum shall be paid to the party aggrieved, than shall be forfeited by one of the offenders only, and the corresponding sums forfeited by the other offenders shall be applied in the same manner as a penalty, 5 V., c. 43, s. 19.

In case of several forfeitures for same offence.

Enforcement by distress and sale or imprisonment

Awards of wages, fines, penalties, forfeitures and costs, if not paid at the time of conviction, or such time as the Justices appoint shall be enforced by warrant of distress and sale. Any overplus, after deduction of the amount of wages, &c. and costs, as also the costs of distress and sale, to the defendant on demand; and in default, the Justices may direct an employer, for non-payment of wages, to be imprisoned in any Gaol, without hard labor, or any other defendant or offender, in the Gaol or House of Correction, with or without hard labor, not exceeding 3 calendar months, unless sooner paid, 5 V., c. 43, s. 20.

Summons or warrant; hearing exparte

Upon complaint on oath before a Justice, a summons may issue for the appearance of the party, and if he do not appear, upon proof of the service at least 4 days before the time appointed, by delivery to him personally, or by leaving the same at his place of abode, with an adult member or inmate of his family, the Justices may proceed to hear the case ex parte, or issue a warrant for his apprehension, or a warrant may issue in the first instance (unless where otherwise specially directed) 5 V., c. 43, s. 21.

Where recovery by distress and sale, would be injurious the defaulter may be committed

Where the recovery by distress and sale would be ruinous or injurious to the defaulter and his family, or it appears by confession, or by the oath of a witness, that he has not sufficient goods, whereon to levy, the Justices may withhold the warrant, and commit the defaulter as if a warrant had issued and a return of nulla bona made thereon, 5, V., c. 43, s. 22.

Prosecution to be within 3 calendar months and employers or servants may be examined

Prosecutions shall be commenced within 3 calendar months, and employers or servants may be examined on oath as well as any witnesses, including inhabitants of the parish, 5 V., c. 43, s. 23.

Summons to witnesses

Any Justice may, at the request of any party to a complaint, issue a summons to any witness, and if he neglect or refuse to appear or to offer a reasonable excuse for his non-attendance, or after appearing refuse to be examined and give his evidence, the Justice or Justices may (proof on oath in case of any person not appearing, being first made of the service of the summons, by delivering it personally, or by leaving it at his usual place of abode with some adult member or inmate of his family at least 24 hours before the time appointed for the trial) by warrant commit him to some prison within their jurisdiction for not exceeding 30 days, or until he submit to be examined and give evidence, 5 V., c. 43, s. 24.

Want of form irregularities in proceedings

No Order, Award or Conviction shall be quashed for want of form, nor distress deemed unlawful, or the party a trespasser on account of any defect in the proceedings or subsequent irregularity, but the person aggrieved by the irregularity, may recover for special damage in an action on the case unless after tender of sufficient amends, 5 V., c. 43, s. 25.

Right of Appeal, 5 V., c. 43, s. 26. *Appeal*

Masters, Mistresses, Foremen, Attorneys, Agents, Managers, Clerks and *Interpretation,* other persons engaged in the hiring, employing or superintending the labor *Employer* or service of every and all of the descriptions of Servants or other persons enumerated and comprised in this Act shall be deemed "Employers." Any *Wages* money or other thing had or contracted to be paid, delivered or given as a recompense or remuneration for any labor or other service done or to be done, whether within a certain time or to a certain amount, or for a time or an amount uncertain, shall be deemed "Wages." Any agreement, under- *Contract* standing, device, contrivance or arrangement on the subject of wages, whether written or oral, direct or indirect, to which any employer and any description of Servants or other persons enumerated in this Act are parties, or are assenting, or by which they are mutually bound, or whereby either has endeavored to impose an obligation on the other "a Contract." All *Servant* Servants in husbandry, mechanics, artificers, handicraftsmen, laborers, persons employed in droghers, or other persons, all household or other domestic Servants, body Servants, laundresses or other Servants "Servant," 5 V., c. 43, s. 27.

Any person falsely personating any Master or Mistress, or the execu- *Personating* tor, administrator, wife, relation, steward, agent or servant of any such *master &c.—false* Master or Mistress, and either personally or in writing giving any false, *character* forged or counterfeit character to any person offering to be hired as a servant into the service of any person, 3 V., c. 48, s. 1.

Any person knowingly and wilfully pretending, or falsely asserting in *Pretending to* writing that any Servant has been hired or retained for any period of time or *have been hired* in any station or capacity other than that for, or in which he hired or re- *at any time or in* tained the Servant in his service, or for the service of any other person, *any station as a* 3 V., c. 48, s. 2. *servant*

Any person knowingly and wilfully, pretending, or falsely asserting *Falsley assert-* in writing that any Servant was discharged or left his service at any other *ing in writing* time than that at which he was discharged or actually left such service, or *that a servant* that any such Servant had not been hired or employed in any previous ser- *was discharged or* vice contrary to truth, 3 V., c. 48, s. 3. *left service, or* *that he had not* *been hired or em-* *ployed*

Any person offering himself as a Servant, asserting or pretending that *Offering one-* he has served in any service in which he has not actually served, or with *self as a servant,* a false, forged, or counterfeit certificate of character, or in anywise adding *and pretending* to or altering, effacing or erasing any word, date, matter, or thing con- *to have served* tained in or referred to any certificate given to him by his last or any for- *any where, or* mer actual Master or Mistress, or by the attorney, overseer, retainer or *with a false or al-* superintendent, or other person duly authorized by such Master or Mistress *tered certificate* to give the same, 3 V., c. 48, s. 4. *of character*

Any person before in service, when offering to hire himself as a Servant *Falsely pretend-* in any service whatsoever, falsely and wilfully pretending not to have been *ing not to have* hired or retained in any previous service as a Servant, 3 V., c. 48, s. 5. *been hired in any* *previous service*

On conviction of any or either of the above offences before two Jus- *Penalties on* tices of the parish where the offence was committed, shall forfeit not ex- *conviction before* ceeding £5 stg., one moiety to the informer and the other to the Church- *2 Justices* wardens, for the use of the parish, to be enforced by distress and sale; failing which the offender shall be committed for not exceeding 3 calendar months nor less than one calendar month, unless the penalty is sooner paid with costs, 3 V., c. 48, s. 6.

The informer shall be a competent witness, but in that case the penalty *Informer a com-* shall be paid to the Churchwardens, 3 V., c. 48, s. 7. *petent witness*

Form of conviction, 3 V., c. 48, s. 8. *Form of convic-* *tion*

Right of Appeal, 3 V., c. 48, s. 9. *Right of appeal*

Sligo Water Company.

Incorporation, establishment and regulation of, 5 W. 4, c. 38; 1 V., c. 9; *Incorporation,* 19 V., c. 41. *&c.*

Such of the inhabitants of the Town of St. Jago de la Vega as are de- *Inhabitants of* sirous of having water laid into their own houses or out-offices may, at their *St. Jago de la* own expense (having obtained the consent of the Corporation under their *Vega may lay* common seal) open the ground between the Company's pipes and their *down pipes f* *supply of water*

Agreement with company for payment houses or out-offices, and lay leaden or other pipes (the bore to be ascertained by the Corporation) in any road, street, &c., in the town and places adjacent, paying the Company yearly, quarterly or monthly such sum for the water as shall be agreed upon. **In default of payment, the company may cut off the communication with the main** In case of default in payment, the Company may cause the person's pipes communicating with their main p p to be cut off. Moneys in arrear shall be recoverable by distress and sale of the goods of the persons liable, in the same manner as in cases of rent in arrear. **Recovery of arrears by distress** Persons laying or causing to be laid any pipe to communicate with a Company's pipe without their consent shall forfeit to the Cempany 20s. [12s. sterling] **Inhabitants may remove their pipes** a day. Inhabitants may remove their pipes, 5 W. 4, c. 3, s. 16.

Petty debt process or action The Company may also sue for and recover by petty debt process, or action or suit at law or in equity, any demand for overdue water rates, 19 V., c, 41, s. 11.

Destroying or damaging works Demolishing, destroying, damaging, &c. any acqueduct, pipe, reservoir, erection, engine, pipe, plug, &c., or any part thereof: Felony, within benefit of Clergy, 5 W. 4, c. 38, s. 20.

Hindering the corporation or servants, &c. in the performance of works, &c. Hindering or interrupting the Corporation, their agents, workmen or servants in the performance of any of the works, or in the exercise of any of their authorities, or procuring the same to be done: Penalty, not exceed £10, (£6 sterling), and the amount of damage to be recovered in the same manner as the penalty, 5 W. 4, c. 38, s. 21.

Using water without license or diverting same No person other than those chargable with and paying duties shall take to his use any part of the water, or shall without license from the corporation divert the water or any part in any way from its place or course. Penalty £50 (£30 sterling), to be recovered by action of debt by the Corporation to its own use, with full costs, besides being liable to answer in damages, 5 W. 4, c. 38, s. 22.

Bathing, washing or polluting water Bathing in the cut or trench or any reservoir or pond, washing any dog or animal therein, or putting, placing, throwing or casting or causing to be put, &c., into any of the aqueducts, canals, &c , pipes, reservoirs or other means of containing or carrying water, any earth, stones, dirt, rubbish, dust, ashes. or filth or washing or cleansing any thing in the reservoirs or ponds whereby the water may be polluted, injured or affected as to its use or quality, or doing any other act by means of which the free passage or course of the water may be in anywise obstructed or hindered, or any other nuisance or annoyance may be occasioned or happen to the water, or doing any other mischief, injury or damage to any of the aqueducts, &c.: Penalty £100 (£60 sterling) recoverable by action of debt by the Corporation, with full costs, besides liability in damages, 5 W. 4, c. 38, s. 23.

Using water to extinguish fire Any person may use the water in extinguishing any fire happening to any house in the town without compensation to the Company, 5 W. 4, c. 38, s. 24.

Supplying others with water Persons supplied with water by virtue of this Act, supplying any other person with any part, shall forfeit not exceeding £5 (£3 sterling) to the Company, 5 W. 4, c. 38, s. 26.

Who may cut off the supply of water in addition to, or in lieu of the penalty, 19 V., c. 41, s. 14.

Except to persons supplied by the Company But not for supplying any other person, also supplied, during the time his pipes or cocks are out of repair, the same being repaired as soon as possible, 5 W. 4, c. 38, s. 27.

Recoveries, &c., of penalties All penalties (concerning the recovery of which no particular direction is given), if not paid on demand, shall be recoverable by warrant of distress and sale, of a Justice, not a Member of the Corporation, and when recovered shall be paid to such person as the Corporation shall appoint, for its use, and the warrant shall contain a clause, directing the commitment of the offender, in case a sufficient distress cannot be found for not exceeding 28 days, unless the penalty and charges are sooner paid, 5 W. 4, c. 38, s. 28.

Damages under £12 **See 19 V., c. 41, s. 11, sup.** Damages where the Corporation does not seek to recover more than £20 (£12 sterling), shall be recoverable before a Justice, not a Member, who on complaint on oath shall issue his warrant to the Constables to empanel and return at a time and place (within 10 days from the application,) 12 good and lawful men, of whom 3 shall try the complaint, and assess the damages, and give their verdict under their hands to such Justice, and another warrant to take and bring the person complained of before him;

and on receiving the verdict shall commit the party until he pays the damages and costs, 5 W. 4, c. 38, s. 30.

No proceedings before any Justice shall be quashed for want of form only (the rest of the clause relating to the removal of proceedings by Certiorari into the Supreme Court appears to be repealed by the Appeal Act, 21 V. c. 22), 5 W. 4, c. 38, s. 31. *Want of form*

No action shall be commenced against any person for anything done in pursuance of this Act until after 30 days notice thereof, nor after a sufficient satisfaction or tender to the party aggrieved, nor after 9 months after the fact committed. The defendant may plead the general issue, and give the special matter in evidence, and that it was done in pursuance or by the authority of this Act; and if it appear to be so done, or that the action has been commenced after the time limited, or in any other manner than directed, the jury shall find for the defendant; and upon a verdict for the defendant, or if the plaintiff is non-suit or discontinues after appearance, or if upon demurrer judgment is given against the plaintiff, the defendant shall recover his full costs out of purse, to be taxed, 5 W. 4, c. 38, s. 32. *Protection from actions*

In all cases of recovery of any penalty or damages the plaintiff shall have judgment for his full costs out of purse, to be taxed, 5 W. 4, c. 38, s. 33 *Costs*

In case of any action of replevin for any distress, the defendant may plead the general issue, and if successful, shall be entitled to a verdict, &c. and costs as in s. 32, 5 W. 4, c. 38, s. 34. *Replevin*

Any Provost-Marshal or deputy, Justice or Vestryman making default shall forfeit £50 (£30 sterling), to be recovered by action of debt by the Corporation to its own use, with full costs out of purse, to be taxed. Constables shall forfeit £20 (£12 stg.). Persons returned upon any inquest, and neglecting their duty without a reasonable cause shewn, in writing upon oath, and allowed by a Justice in writing under his hand, shall forfeit £10 (£6 stg.). Such penalties to be recovered, levied and applied to the use of the Corporation, 5 W. 4, c. 38, s. 35. *Penalties on Provost, Marshal or Deputy Justices, Constables, Jurors*

No reservoir shall be made within 300 yards of the King's House, without the Governor's consent, 5 W. 4, c. 38, s. 39. *No Reservoir within 300 yards Kings House*

Where pipes are laid into any yard, house, land or other premises, and the parties or owners have discontinued taking or paying for the use of the water, or have forfeited their right thereto, the agents of the Company, under a written authority from the President of the Board of Directors, may enter into any such house, &c., and remove any pipe or other property of the Company; and on any resistance being made to such agent, the parties so resisting, or causing resistance, shall forfeit three times the value of the pipes, and the expenses of laying them, to be recovered as herein provided for, 19 V., c. 41, s. 15. *Right of entry to remove pipe or other property of the Company*

The Manager or Engineer, or other persons, acting under the authority of the Company or Directors, may at all reasonable times in the day enter into any yard, &c., supplied with water, by the Company to inspect and examine if there be any waste, undue diversion, or illegal appropriation of the water supplied; and if refused entrance or admittance, the Company may cut and turn off the water, 19 V., c. 41, s. 16. *To examine into waste, &c., of Water. On refusal they may cut off the water*

The reservoirs, and other works lands, and premises of the Company in use, and the Company in respect thereof shall not be rated, charged, or assessed, for the payment of any public or parochial charges, or other impositions, 19 V., c. 41, s. 29. *Recovery of penalties*

Penalties under this Act, shall be recovered in the manner mentioned in 5 W. 4, c. 38, s. 28. Damages not exceeding £20 as mentioned in s. 30, and subject to the provisions of s. 31, and actions and proceedings against the Company, or any person for any thing done in pursuance of this Act, shall be subject to the provisions of 5 W. 4, c. 38, s. 32, 33, and 34; 19 V., c. 41, s. 21.

Small Pox and Infectious Diseases.

Whenever Small Pox, or any infectious Disease or distemper, dangerous to health, breaks out or appears in any place, the Governor may make orders, rules and regulations, for the prevention as far as possible of its spreading in the Island, or any district, parish, town or port, or for the relief of sufferers, and the speedy interment of persons dying of any such disease or distemper, 4 V., c. 32, s. 30. *Governors orders to prevent spread of diseases. Relief of sufferers and speedy interment. See also Quarantine, 1 V., c. 63, s. 4.*

Publication of order—notice, evidence

The publication of any order in any newspaper shall be notice to all persons, and evidence of the date and contents of such order, 4 V., c. 32, s. 31.

Infringement of or preventing execution of orders

Any wilful infringement of any such order, or refusal or neglect to obey, resistance to, or obstructing the execution, declared to be a misdemeanor, and the party shall also incur, and be liable to a penalty, not exceeding £5, nor less than £1. No person against whom any penalty is recovered or who has suffered imprisonment for non-payment shall be liable to be indicted, 4 V., c. 32, s. 32.

Recovery of penalties
Enforcement

Such penalties shall be recoverable before 2 Justices 4 V., c. 32, s. 33, To be levied, in default of payment, by warrant of distress and sale, or if it appear that the offender has no sufficient goods, within their jurisdiction, whereon to levy any penalty, costs and charges, they may, without issuing a warrant of distress, commit the offender for not exceeding 14 days, unless sooner paid, as if a warrant had been issued, and a return of nulla bona made thereon, in which case also they may commit the offender for 14 days or such shorter period, 4 V., c. 32, s. 34.

Such penalties shall be paid to the Treasurer for the use of the parish, 4 V., c. 32, s. 35.

Expenses

The expenses of this Act shall be paid by the Receiver-General, 4 V., c, 32, s. 36.

Protection from actions

For protection from actions see Quarantine, 4 V-, c. 32, s. 26, 38.

Special Cases.

May be stated for the opinion of the Court by consent

After issue joined the parties may by consent and order of a Judge state the facts in the form of a Special Case for the opinion of the Court, and agree that a judgment be entered up for the plaintiff or defendant by confession or nullo prosequi immediately after the decision, or otherwise as the Court may think fit, 8 V., c. 28, s. 13.

Stamps.

Short title

The Stamp Duty Act, 1865, 28 V., c. 9, s. 1.

Stamp Duties

There shall be raised on the several instruments mentioned in the Schedule, the duties therein specified, 28 V., c. 9, s. 2.

Adhesive Stamps dies—servant

The Receiver-General shall provide at the public expense, such quantity of adhesive Stamps as may be necessary, and sufficient Stamps or Dies for denoting and impressing the duties; and employ a servant at a salary not exceeding £30 per annum, to work the stamping presses, and perform such other duties as may be required of him in the Stamp office, 28 V., c. 9, s. 3.

Chest for deposit and custody of Adhesive Stamps and dies

All adhesive Stamps shall be made up into packets or parcels, and properly labelled by the Commissioner of Stamps, with the denomination and amount of Stamps contained therein; and such adhesive Stamps, and the Stamps or Dies when not in use, shall be deposited, and kept locked up in the Stamp office chest, which shall have 2 locks of different construction, one of the keys of which shall always be kept by the Receiver-General, and the other by the Commissioner of Stamps. The adhesive Stamps shall be taken out of such chest at such times, and in such quantities as may be necessary for the supply of persons applying to purchase, by the Commissioner in the presence of the Receiver-General or his recognized Clerk, and the Stamps or Dies shall also, in every case be taken out of such chest for use when required, and again deposited therein in the presence of the Receiver-General or his Clerk, 28 V., c. 9, s. 4.

Commissioner of Stamps
Office and attendance

Oath

The Governor may appoint under his hand and seal, a Commissioner of Stamps, who shall hold office, except as herein provided, during the existence of this Act, and attend daily at the Receiver-General's office in Kingston (Sundays and Holidays excepted) from 9 a. m. till 3 p, m., and shall record his appointment in the Secretary's office, and make out in writing the following oath, which he shall subscribe and take before a Judge, and lodge with the Secretary of the Executive Committee; and in case he acts before he has recorded his appointment, and taken the oath, he shall forfeit £500 :—

I A. B. do swear, truly and faithfully to execute and perform the duties of Commissioner of Stamps, under an Act entitled " The Stamp Duty Act, 1865," and that I will, without fear, favor or affection, inform against any person who shall evade or attempt to evade any part of the said Act, contrary to the true meaning and intent thereof. So help me God.

Not necessary to issue a new appointment to the present Commissioner, nor for him again to take the oath, 28 V., c. 9, s. 5.

The Governor may remove him for any misconduct or neglect of duty, **Removal** and when a vacancy occurs, may fill up the same, 28 V., c. 9, s. 6.

The Commissioner shall be paid a salary of £300, by quarterly or **Salary** monthly payments, in full of all contingencies of office not specifically provided for, 28 V., c. 9, s. 7

In case of sickness or other incapacity, he may, by writing under his **Deputy** hand, with the consent of the Receiver-General, appoint a deputy, for whose acts and defaults he shall be responsible, 28 V., s. 8.

He shall pay every day, by or before 3 p. m. into one of the Banks **To make daily** with which arrangements have been made by the Governor and Executive **payments into the** Committee, under 21 V., c. 39, and 27 V., c. 7, as the Governor shall di- **Bank** rect, all moneys received by him for Stamps, whether impressed or adhesive, during the day, and all other moneys he received on the previous day, after payment into the Bank, 28 V., c. 9, s. 9.

He shall enter into a joint and several bond, with 2 or more sureties, to **Security bond** be approved of by the Governor and Executive Committee, to the Queen in £200, conditioned for the due performance of his duties and payment over of moneys, and compliance with the other requirements and conditions of this Act, in such form as the Governor and Executive Committee approve, and so as that the sureties become bound in such proportions of the £200 as they are able and willing to undertake, and as shall together amount to £200, 28 V., c. 9, s. 10.

He shall render to the Executive Committee on the last day of each **Quarterly Ac-** quarter, or within 10 days after, or whenever required, an account on oath **counts to Executive** of the value of the Stamps delivered and impressed by him, or under his di- **Committee** rection or superintendence, on each day during the period embraced in such account. Penalty, £100, 28 V., c. 9, s. 11.

He shall produce to the Receiver-General, or the Clerk appointed by **Daily Accounts** him, at or after 3 o'clock each day, all requisitions for Stamps, impressed **with the Receiver-** and adhesive, made to him, and the receipt of the bank for all moneys **General** lodged by him during such day, and the Receiver-General or Clerk shall compare such requisitions and receipts with the entries in the book kept by him, (s. 40) and if found correct, certify such entries at the foot, 28 V., c. 9, s. 12

The Receiver-General shall be liable for all moneys paid by the Com- **Liability of Re-** missioner into the bank to the credit of the account of the public moneys of **ceiver General** the Receiver-General, 28 V., c. 9, s. 13.

A discount of £10 per cent. shall be allowed to all persons purchasing **Discount** at the Stamp Office in Kingston Stamps to the value of £5 or upwards, unless otherwise provided, 28 V., c. 9, s. 14.

Each Collector of Dues shall be a distributor of Stamps, and be styled **Distributors** " Collector of Dues and Stamp Duties," to whom the Receiver-General shall issue such quantity of Adhesive Stamps, and stamped paper, and printed forms of the respective denominations or values necessary to meet the demands of the public ; and every Collector in office, who may not have given security under any previous Stamp Duty Act, before being entrusted with Stamps for distribution, shall give additional security; and every Collector **Security bond** of Dues and Stamp Duties shall give further or new security according to the provisions of the Tax Collection Act, (27 V., S. 1, c. 31) or any other or future Act regulating the security to be given by Collectors of Dues ; and any person to be hereafter appointed, shall enter into security as aforesaid, to account for all Stamps, and stamped paper, and printed forms, which shall from time to time be delivered to him, and shall from time to time be sold or remain on hand, and also to account for and pay over all moneys received by him for the sale of such Stamps, and paper, and printed forms, as fixed by this Act or the Schedule ; and shall render such account to the Re- **Account and pay-** **ment**

Liability of Re-
ceiver General for
his default.

Collectors' com-
mission

Charge for paper

Penalty for de-
manding higher
rates

Certificates of ad-
mission of Barris-
ters and solicitors

Preparing deeds,
&c. for reward, not
being a barrister,
&c.

Compensation for
Stamp Duties on
Bank Notes

ceiver-General as that officer shall direct, and pay over the moneys received by him at the periods fixed for the payment of other moneys received by him as Collector of Dues, 28 V., c. 9, s. 15.

In case the Receiver-General omits to get in and compel such periodical account and payment by the Collector of Dues and Stamp Duties, he shall be charged with whatever moneys in consequence fall due and in arrear from any defaulting Collector on these accounts, 28 V., c. 9, s. 16.

The Collector shall, as a remuneration for his trouble and services, be allowed to retain from the proceeds of sales of such Stamps, paper and printed forms, £5 per cent. commission, 28 V., c. 9, s. 17.

Collectors and dealers in the sale of stamped paper, may demand over and above the amount of the Stamps according to the following scale :—

On every Slip with a stamp or stamps of the value of 1s. 6d.,

2s., 2s. 6d. or 3s.	......	......	......	0	0	1
Above 3s.	......	......	......	0	0	2
Sheet or half-sheet of Foolscap or Folio Post.		......	0	0	1¼
Medium Paper	......	......	......	0	0	3
Royal ...	......	......	......	0	0	6
Imperial	......	......	......	0	0	9
On each Sheet or half-sheet of Printed Forms		......	0	0	3

which shall include and satisfy the charge for paper, 28 V., c. 9, s. 18.

If any Collector or dealer in Stamps demand any amount for any Stamp beyond its value, or for paper, or for any form beyond the rate fixed, he shall forfeit not exceeding £10, 28 V., c. 9, s. 19.

Every certificate of the admission of a Barrister and a Solicitor, Attorney or Proctor to practice in the Courts of this Island, shall be stamped, and signed by the Clerk of the Court and Crown, or his deputy. Any Barrister or Solicitor who shall not, upon his admission, take out a certificate of admission is declared incapable of acting. practicing or officiating in any Court or otherwise in such capacity ; but one certificate so stamped and signed, shall entitle a Barrister, Solicitor, &c. to admission in every Court, and none who has taken out his certificate shall be required to produce it, 28 V., c. 9, s. 20.

Any person who, for or in expectation of any fee, gain or reward, directly or indirectly draws or prepares any conveyance, deed, will or instrument relating to any real or personal estate, or any proceedings in law or in equity (such person not being a Barrister, Solicitor, Attorney or Proctor, or person employed solely to engross any Deed, Instrument or proceeding not drawn or prepared by himself, or a person drawing or engrossing the same for his own account, or a public officer drawing or preparing official instruments applicable to his office and in the course of such duty) shall forfeit for each offence £20, 28 V., c. 9, s. 21.

Any Banking Corporation or copartnership may issue and re-issue notes payable to bearer on demand, without being stamped, upon giving security, by bond to Her Majesty, of two of the Directors, Members or partners, together with the Manager, Secretary, Cashier or Accountant, as the Executive Committee shall require, in such penalty as the duties may be computed to amount to during the period of any year, with condition to deliver to the Commissioner of Stamps, within 12 days after the last day of each of the months of March, June, September and December in every year during the existence of this Act, a just and true account, verified upon the declaration of any Director, Manager, Secretary, Cashier or Accountant, to be made before any Justice, of the amount or value of all their promissory notes in circulation on some given day in every week, for the space of one quarter of a year, prior to the quarter-day immediately preceding the delivery of such account, together with the average amount or value according to such account, and pay or cause to be paid to the Receiver-General as a composition for the duties which would otherwise have been payable for such promissory notes issued within the space of one year, 20s. for every £100, and also for the fractional part of £100 of such average amount or value of such notes in circulation. And the Executive Committee may fix the time of making such payment, and specify the same in the condition; which bond may be required to be renewed at their discretion as often as it is forfeited, or any party dies, becomes insolvent, or resides beyond the seas, 28 V., c. 9, s. 22.

No Banker shall issue any unstamped Promissory Note for money paya. ble to the bearer on demand, without taking out a license yearly for the purpose, to be granted by the Commissioner of Stamps, on payment of the full duty without any allowance of discount, and which shall specify the name and place of abode of the person, or name and description of any body corporate to whom it is granted, and the name of the town or place where, and of the Bank, as well as the partnership or other name, style or firm under which the notes are to be issued; and where g a t to persons in partnership, shall specify the names and places of abode of all the persons concerned in the partnership, whether all their names appear in the Promissory Notes or not, and in default the license shall be absolutely void. It shall be dated on the day on which it is granted, and have effect and continue until the 31st December following, both inclusive. Any license since 31st December last shall inure until 31st December next, 28 V., c. 9, s. 23.

License to issue unstamped Notes

Any such license shall continue in force notwithstanding any alteration in the partnership, 28 V., c. 9, s. 24.

To continue notwithstanding change in partnership

Some one Director, or the Manager, Secretary, Cashier or Accountant shall, within each period for rendering the quarterly account, also make, subscribe and deliver to the Commissioner a declaration in writing before a Justice, of the amount or value of all shares in the capital stock, funds, estates, business, or profits of the Bank transferred or assigned during the quarter last expired, and that each instrument of transfer or assignment has been duly and fully impressed with the Stamp duty the same is required to bear. And for every neglect or omission, every Director and the Manager, &c., of the defaulting Corporation or Copartnership, shall forfeit £10. 28 V., c 9, s. 25.

Quarterly returns of transfers of shares in Banks

The Commissioner shall not stamp any Foreign Bill of Exchange, or any Bill of Lading, unless offered in a set of three parts or bills; and every set shall have the word first, second, or third written or printed on the face of each part, previous to its being stamped, 28 V., c. 9, s. 26.

Foreign Bills of Exchange, bills of Lading to be stamped in sets

No Foreign Bill of Exchange, or Foreign Bill of Lading, shall be drawn, accepted or endorsed, or subscribed or written, negociated or made use of, except in sets of at least 3 parts, and stamped as herein provided, otherwise they shall not be admissible in evidence in any Court or proceeding, 28 V., c. 9, s. 27.

And so drawn &c., and negotiated

The master of any vessel clearing with goods for exportation, shall not sign any bill of lading, unless presented to him in a set of three parts at least, and unless duly stamped. £5 penalty, 28 V., c. 9, s. 28.

Masters not to sign Bills of Lading except on stamped sets

The Secretary of the Island shall give a separate receipt for each instrument to be recorded, and shall not enter or record any instrument, without delivering a stamped receipt. Penalty, £30, 28 V., c. 9, s. 29.

Island Secretarys receipts

The Receiver-General shall furnish printed forms of foreign Bills of Exchange and foreign Bills of Lading duly stamped, and in sets, to the several Collectors, 28 V., c. 9, s. 30.

Foreign Bills and Bills of Lading to be supplied Collectors in sets

Instruments or documents subjected to Stamp duty, shall only operate for one purpose, unless stamped in addition for each other object or purpose embraced therein or affected thereby, according to the rates fixed for such other object or purpose respectively, 28 V., c. 9, s. 31,

Instruments to be stamped for each object

Duties may be made up by several Stamps, and Stamps of greater value than hereby required, may be used on any instrument, 28 V., c. 9, s. 32.

Several stamps or of greater value

Adhesive Stamps not exceeding 2s. in amount, may be used upon any instrument, except foreign Bills of Exchange, or foreign Bills of Lading, 28 V., c. 9, s. 33,

Adhesive Stamps 2s.

So long as adhesive Stamps of 5s. and 10s. denominations remain on hand, they may be used to any amount on Supreme Court writs, and on such documents in the Courts of Chancery and Ordinary as when once returned and filed remain in the custody of the Registrar, or Clerks of the Courts. The Registrar and Clerk of each of such Courts shall cancel the adhesive Stamps, by writing his signature so that, as nearly as may be, one half appears on the writ or document, and the other half on the cancelled Stamp, and shall mark on each cancelled Stamp the day, month and year of such filing and cancellation. Penalty, £2; 28 V., c. 9, s. 34.

5s, 10s

By others

Every person who uses an adhesive Stamp, or into whose hands any instrument bearing an uncancelled adhesive Stamp comes, and every person before whom any affidavit or other instrument bearing an adhesive Stamp is deposed to, shall, before he delivers it out of his hands, custody or power, cancel or obliterate the Stamps, by writing his name on the instrument, and across the Stamp affixed, so that a part of the name or signature shall be written on the instrument, and the remaining part on the Stamp; and the date of the instrument shall also be written on the cancelled Stamp. If any person write or deliver any instrument with any adhesive Stamp thereon, without bona fide in manner aforesaid effectually cancelling or obliterating such Stamp, he shall forfeit not less than 20s., nor more than £10, 28 V., c. 9, s. 35.

Instruments not duly stamped under previous Acts

All instruments liable under any former Stamp Act, and not impressed with any, or the proper Stamps may at any time, upon production of an affidavit to the effect after provided, be impressed with the full amount of Stamps required by this Act for instruments of a similar nature, and may thereafter be used and given in evidence as if they had been originally duly stamped, 28 V·, c. 9, s. 36.

Stamps exceeding 2s, to be impressed previously to writing, &c.

Every instrument required to be stamped to an amount exceeding 2s, except as aforesaid, shall be written on paper, parchment or vellum, which has been first impressed with the Stamps prescribed, nor shall any instrument, written, printed or executed contrary to this Act be admissible in evidence, 28 V., c. 9, s. 37.

To be impressed in presence of Receiver-General, or Clerk

All Stamps shall be impressed by the Commissioner or by his direction in the presence of the Receiver-General or his Clerk, 28 V., c. 9, s. 38.

Instruments which may be stamped after writing, &c. Printed forms Accounts Current Instruments executed out of the Island, &c. escrows On payment of additional stamps by way of penalty

The Commissioner shall not impress any Stamp on any instrument after writing, printing, preparing or executing the same, except as after-mentioned: printed forms not filled up or used, accounts current not signed, instruments executed or shewn to the satisfaction of the Commissioner to have been prepared out of the Island, or lodged in escrow prior to this Act. Any instrument not stamped, or not fully stamped, may be stamped upon payment of the following penalties in the shape of additional Stamps, viz:—If brought to be stamped within 12 months after the first signing or executing, on payment by way of penalty of equal to one half of the duty or deficiency; after that period, of a sum equal to the whole duty or deficiency; where brought to be stamped within 3 months after the first signing or executing, and it appears to the Commissioner on oath or otherwise to his satisfaction that it was not duly stamped by reason of accident, mistake or inadvertency or necessity, and without any wilful design or intention to evade the payment of the duty, the Commissioner may cause the instrument to be duly stamped on payment of the whole, or the deficiency of the duty required without any penalty; but not any inland or foreign bill of cxehange, or

Bills and Promissory Notes

promisory note after the lapse of 14 days from the date of execution, 28 V., c. 9, s. 39.

Commissioner upon payment of duties and requisition for stamps not less than £5, to grant receipt and stamps less discount

The Commissioner shall, under penalty of £30, upon being paid the duties for any quantity of Stamps required by and specified in the written requisition of any person, not less in amount than £5, in which shall be specified the date, name of the person paying the duties, the number, denomination, and value of the Stamps required, the amount of discount allowed, and of the duties then paid, grant a receipt for the duties in which the date, name and amount less the discount shall be stated; and under a like penalty deliver such amount of adhesive Stamps, and impress on all such papers as are brought for the purpose, such amount of Stamps as are prescribed, and for which duty has been paid, and forthwith return the same to the owner; and shall duly enter into proper books of account (s. 12), kept for the purpose, a true account of the Stamps delivered and impressed, 28 V., c. 9, s. 40.

And enter an account thereof

Issue of Stamps to Governor's Secretary for Commissions, &c.

The Receiver-General and Commissioner shall, on application in writing of the Governor's Secretary, supply him with Stamps for Commissions and other documents issuing from his office, and shall once in every month account to the Receiver-General for all Stamps so received without any deduction for discount; and no Commission or document shall be issued except on duly Stamped paper, vellum, or parchment, the Stamps whereon have been so furnished, 28 V·,c. 9, s. 41.

No discount allowed

Any instrument liable to be and not duly stamped, shall not be pleaded or admitted in evidence in any proceeding in any Court of Equity, 28 V., c. 9, s. 42.

If with intent to evade this Act, a consideration or sum of money is expressed to be paid in any instrument less than the amount actually paid or agreed to be paid, the instrument shall be void, 28 V., c. 9, s. 43.

No instrument made, executed, taken, or acknowledged out of this Island, and liable to duty, shall be admitted in any Court, or entered of record in any office until it has been duly stamped, 28 V., c. 9, s. 44.

Upon the tender in evidence of any instrument other than Inland and foreign Bills of Exchange and Promissory Notes, the Officer of the Court before reading it, shall call the Judges attention to any omission or insufficiency of the Stamp, and it shall not be received in evidence until the whole or the deficiency of the Stamp Duty, to be determined by the Judge, and the penalty (s. 39), with an additional penalty of £1 has been paid, 28 V., c. 9, s. 45.

The officer, upon payment to him of the duty and penalties, shall give a receipt therefor, and the instrument shall be admissible, saving all just exceptions on other grounds, and an entry of the payment and amount shall be made in a book kept by the officer, who shall, at the end of each sitting, make a return of, and pay over the moneys to the Receiver-General, distinguishing the amounts for duty and penalties, and stating the name of the cause and parties paying, and the date, if any, and description of the instrument to identify it. In case of neglect in either of the respects aforesaid. the offending officer shall be subject to an attachment out of the Supreme Court to enforce payment of the moneys, with the costs of all proceedings, on application to a Judge by or on behalf of the Receiver-General, 28 V., c. 9, s. 46.

The Commissioner shall, upon the production of the receipt, impress upon the instrument the proper Stamps in conformity with such receipt, 28 V., c. 9, s. 47.

The Stamps and penalties so received in the Circuit Court shall be noted under a separate head, in the return of forfeited recognizances and fines ; those in the Magistrates' Courts in the monthly return of fines, under a separate head, and the amounts shall be paid by the respective officers in the manner and at the times directed by any Act in force for the payment over of moneys received by them, 28 V., c. 9, s. 48.

Every public officer required to supply any Stamp may demand the amount from the person requiring it, and every Solicitor, Attorney and Proctor may demand from his client all sums he has expended for Stamps on his behalf, 28 V., c. 9, s. 49.

Every Solicitor, Attorney or other person, bespeaking a copy of any instrument from any public office chargeable with a Stamp duty shall, under a penalty of £10 for each wilful neglect, take out and pay for such copy within 14 days after he is informed that it is ready for delivery, 28 V., c. 9, s. 50.

Any public officer who wilfully or fraudulently enters or records any instrument chargeable with duty and not duly stamped shall forfeit not exceeding £50, and if he issues any office copy, or any copy of any instrument without the Stamps imposed, or commits or connives at any fraud or practice whereby the duties are lessened, impaired or lost, he shall upon conviction forfeit not exceeding £50 and his office, and if any Attorney, Solicitor or Proctor is guilty of, or of pa t at g in any fraud or practice in any of the respects aforesaid, and is convicted, he shall be disqualified from practising in any Court, 28 V., c. 9, s. 51.

Giving or accepting with intent to evade this Act, any receipt or acquittance in which a less sum is expressed than that actually paid and received, or separating or dividing the sum actually paid or received, lent or advanced, into divers receipts, bills of exchange, drafts or orders, or other instruments or writings, or being guilty of, or concerned in any other contrivance or device with such intent : Penalty, £10, 28 V., c. 9, s. 52.

Evading or attempting to evade this Act by giving, receiving, or negotiating any instrument charged with a duty, not impressed with or not otherwise bearing the proper amount of Stamps prescribed : Penalty not exceeding £5, 28 V., c. 9, s. 53.

The Receiver-General and Commissioner may exchange for others all Stamps on instruments inadvertently or undesignedly spoilt, obliterated or otherwise rendered unfit for use, upon production to them of the entire sheet

Affidavit

or piece of paper, or instrument upon which the Stamp is impressed, and of an affidavit, taken before a Justice or Commissioner, to the effect following :

> I do swear that the several sheets or pieces of paper or instruments hereunto annexed, and hereunder specified, were inadvertently or undesignedly spoilt, and that no consideration has been received for the same by any person. viz: (here set forth a description of the documents.)

And if satisfied that it has not been executed by the parties, or has not been used for the purpose expressed, the Receiver-General and Commissioner shall exchange it for a Stamp or Stamps of equal value, to be impressed upon such paper or instrument as the party requiring the same shall produce, free of charge, but if of opinion that it is not really and bona fide a spoilt Stamp, they may refuse to exchange it. All such spoilt Stamps must be tendered within 6 months from the time they were spoilt, 28 V., c. 9, s. 54.

To be destroyed

All spoilt Stamps shall be destroyed in the Stamp Office in the presence of the Commissioner and Receiver-General, 28 V., c. 9, s. 55.

Forgery

If any person shall forge or counterfeit, or cause or procure, &c., any adhesive or other Stamp, or any die, or any part of any Stamp or any die provided, made, issued or used in pursuance of this or any former Act relating to any Stamp Duties, or shall forge, counterfeit or imitate, or cause or procure, &c., the impression or any part of the impression of any such Stamp or die upon any vellum, parchment or paper, or shall stamp or mark, or cause or procure, &c., any vellum, &c., with any such forged or counterfeited Stamp or die, or part, &c., with intent to defraud the revenue of

Uttering, selling or exposing for sale forged stamps

any of the duties hereby granted, or any part thereof ; or if any person shall utter or sell, or expose to sale any vellum, &c., having thereupon the impression of any such forged or counterfeited Stamp or die, or part, &c., or any such forged, counterfeited or imitated impression, or part of impression, knowing the same respectively to be forged, counterfeited or imitated ; or if any person shall surreptitiously or privately and secretly

Surreptitious use of stamps

use any Stamp or die which has been so provided, made or used, or shall by any false pretence, or crafty or subtle deceit, device or means, obtain or procure to be impressed upon, or affixed to any vellum, &c., any such Stamp or die, or any part thereof, or the resemblance of any such Stamp or die, or

Fraudulent removal of stamps to other instruments

part thereof, with intent to defraud the revenue of any of the duties or any part thereof ; or if any person shall fraudulently take, cut or tear off, or cause or procure, &c., the impression of any Stamp or die which has been provided, made, issued or used in pursuance of this or any former Act, for expressing or denoting any duty, or any part of such duty, from any vellum, &c., with intent to use the same for or upon any other vellum, &c., or any instrument charged or chargeable with any of the duties

Aiders and abettors

hereby granted, the offender and every person knowingly and wilfully aiding, abetting or assisting any person in committing any such offence,

Felony—Punishment

on conviction, shall be adjudged guilty of felony, and shall suffer punishment by imprisonment for such term of years as the Court directs, 28 V., c. 9, s. 56.

Suits may be in name of Her Majesty or Attorney General

Any suit, prosecution or proceeding against any person for taking or retaining, or for losing, damaging or destroying any adhesive Stamp, or any vellum, &c., upon which any Stamp denoting any duty has been impressed or put, or for any other cause of action or proceeding, may be com-

Allegations of property or value

menced, instituted and proceeded with in the name of Her Majesty or of the Attorney-General on her behalf, in which the property in such adhesive Stamps or in such vellum, &c., so stamped, shall be described to be and be taken to be in her Majesty, and the value, the amount denoted by the Stamp ; and in any prosecution for embezzling or stealing such adhesive Stamps, vellum, &c., so stamped, marked or impressed, or for any other offence, it shall be sufficient in the indictment or information to state and describe the property in the same to be in her Majesty, 28 V., c. 9, s. 57.

Removing adhesive stamps

Fraudulently getting off or removing, or causing or procuring, &c., from any instrument, any adhesive Stamp which had been affixed thereto and used, or affixing or using, or knowingly receiving such removed Stamp: Penalty not exceeding £10, 28 V., c. 9, s. 58.

Other fraudulent acts

Doing or practising, or being concerned in any fraudulent act, contrivance or device, not specially provided for, with intent to defraud her Majesty or the government or public of this Island, of any duty imposed by this Act: Penalty not exceeding £20, 28 V., c. 9, s. 59.

All penalties exceeding £50 shall be recovered by action of debt, &c., those not exceeding £50 before 2 Justices, with such costs as they think fit : and unless forthwith paid, shall be levied by distress and sale, or in default, the offender shall be committed to the nearest Prison for not exceeding 3 months, 28 V., c. 9, s. 60. Recovery of penalties

And applied one moiety to the person who sues or prosecutes, 28 V., c. 9, s. 61. Application

Eve ry prosecution shall be commenced within 6 months, 28 V., c. 9, s. 62. Commencement of prosecution

The Executive Committee, whenever satisfied that any mistake has been made in the imposition of duties, may direct the restoration of any overpaid duties, or otherwise rectify any mistake, and allow to the Receiver-General any deduction they consider him fairly entitled to on his account for Stamps, 28 V., c. 9, s. 63. Refund of duties rectification of mistakes

In force until 31st December, 1867, and notwithstanding its expiry or repeal, any offence, penalty or liability, may be prosecuted and punished as might have been done during its continuance, 28 V., c. 9, s. 65. Continuation—

"Instrument" shall include every deed, writing, printed form, document, paper, matter or thing charged with or made liable to any Stamp duty, 28 V., c. 9, s. 66. Interpretation "Instrument"

SCHEDULE.
Part the First.

	£	s.	d.
Agreement—			
On every agreement, or any minute or memorandum of an agreement under hand only (and not otherwise charged in this Schedule. nor expressly exempted from all stamp duty) where the matter is of the value of £20 or upwards, whether it be only evidence of a contract, or obligatory upon the parties from its being a written instrument	0	4	0
Where divers letters are offered in evidence to prove any agreement between the parties who have written them, it is sufficient if any one is stamped with a duty of 4s. at any time before it is given in evidence.			

EXEMPTIONS FROM THE PRECEDING, AND ALL OTHER STAMP DUTIES.

	£	s.	d.
Memorandum, or agreement for the hire of any laborer, artificer, tradesman, manufacturer, or menial Servant			
Memorandum, letter, or agreement made for, or relating to any goods, wares and merchandize			
But any memorandum or agreement, intended as preparatory to a more formal instrument, and so stated on the face of it, may be stamped with the duty hereby imposed, if made within this Island at any time within ninety days after date, and if made out of the Island, within six months after			
Annuity, Re-purchase of—			
Any release or assignment of an annuity, or rent charge, made subject in, and by the original grant thereof, to be redeemed or re-purchased shall, on the re-purchase, be exempted from the duty on a conveyance or transfer of land, and be charged only with the duty imposed upon a deed not otherwise charged			
Appointments—			
On every original appointment of Island or Stipendiary Curate	6	13	3
On every appointment by her Majesty's Letters Patent, to any public office of this Island	40	0	0
On every appointment in execution of a power of land or other property, real or personal, or of any use or interest therein, where made by any writing, not being a deed or will	0	13	3

On every appointment to an office of emolument, payable by the public, a sum equal to two per cent. upon the salary (for one year) affixed to such office, in addition to any other stamp. (See Commission.)

EXEMPTIONS FROM THE PRECEDING, AND ALL OTHER STAMP DUTIES.

                                              £ s. d.

All appointments to any public office, where the party is to officiate for another during his absence from his duties, by leave of the Governor

Articles of Clerkship—

On every article of clerkship or contract, whereby any person shall first become bound to serve as a clerk, in order to his admission as a Solicitor, Attorney and Proctor in the Courts of this Island....   ....   26 13 3

On every article of clerkship or contract, whereby any person shall become bound to serve as a clerk, in order to any such admission, for the residue of the term for which he was originally bound, in consequence of the death of his former master, or of the contract between them being vacated by consent, or by rule of Court, or in any other event 0 13 3

Award—

On every award   ....   ·0 8 0

Bankers' Cheques—

On every cheque to be drawn on any Banker, Bank, or Banking Firm or Company in this Island on, from and after the first day of February, one thousand eight hundred and sixty-five 0 0 1

Bills, or Cheques for Money—

On every Cheque, Draft or Order for the payment of any sum of money, not less than forty shillings, to, or in favor of any person at sight, or on demand, on any person or firm, other than a Banker or Banking Firm or Company, at sight, or on demand 0 0 1

And, until dies or adhesive stamps of one-penny denomination are received for the purposes of this Act, it shall be lawful to make use of Post Office Stamps or labels of the like denomination, until the first day of March, one thousand eight hundred and sixty-five; and the Receiver-General shall keep a separate account of all Post Office Stamps or labels so made use of

Bills of Exchange, (Inland)—

Draft or Order, or Acceptance for the payment to the bearer, or to order, at any time otherwise than on demand, of any sum of money amounting to ten pounds, and not exceeding thirty pounds...   ....   0 0 3

Above thirty pounds, and not exceeding fifty pounds 0 0 9

Above fifty pounds, and not exceeding one hundred pounds   0 1 3

Above one hundred pounds, and not exceeding two hundred pounds 0 2

Above two hundred pounds, and not exceeding three hundred pounds..   ....   0 3 0

Above three hundred pounds, and not exceeding four hundred pounds 0 4

Above four hundred pounds, and not exceeding five hundred pounds 0 5

Above five hundred pounds, and not exceeding one thousand pounds 0 6

Above one thousand pounds, and not exceeding two thousand pounds 0 13 0

Above two thousand pounds, and not exceeding three thousand pounds 1 6 9

And where it shall exceed three thousand pounds 2 0 0

Inland bill, draft or order for the payment of any sum of money weekly, monthly or at any other stated period, if made payable to the bearer, or to order, or if delivered to the payee, or some person on his or her behalf, when the total amount of the money thereby made payable shall be specified therein, or can be ascertained therefrom — *The same duty as on a bill payable to bearer, or order, at any time otherwise than on demand, for a sum equal to such total amount.*

EXEMPTIONS FROM THE PRECEDING, AND ALL OTHER STAMP DUTIES.

	£.	s.	d.
All drafts or orders drawn on the Receiver-General; but they shall, notwithstanding, be liable, at the time of payment, to the duty imposed on receipts.			

Bills of Exchange (Foreign)—

	£	s.	d.
Drawn in sets, according to the custom of merchants, for every part or bill of each set, where the sum made payable thereby shall be for ten pounds, and not exceeding fifty pounds	0	0	3
Above fifty pounds, and not exceeding one hundred pounds	0	0	9
Above one hundred pounds, and not exceeding two hundred pounds	0	1	3
Above two hundred pounds, and not exceeding five hundred pounds	0	2	0
Above five hundred pounds, and not exceeding one thousand pounds	0	4	0
Above one thousand pounds, and not exceeding two thousand pounds	0	8	0
Above two thousand pounds, and not exceeding three thousand pounds	0	13	3
And where it shall exceed three thousand pounds	1	6	9
But all foreign Bills of Exchange shall be stamped at and after the rates hereinbefore mentioned, notwithstanding that the sums for which such bills shall be drawn shall be expressed in dollars, francs, or any other description of money of account.			

Bills of Lading—

	£	s.	d.
Drawn in sets of three for goods, wares or merchandize, to be exported from this Island, on each part or bill	0	0	9
On each receipt for goods, wares or merchandize carried coastwise	0	0	3

Bonds—

	£	s.	d.
Bond given as a security for the payment of any definite and certain sum of money, amounting to thirty pounds and under fifty p	0	2	0
Fifty pounds and under one hundred pounds	0	3	3
One hundred pounds, and under two hundred pounds	0	6	9
Two hundred pounds, and under three hundred pounds	0	10	0
Three hundred pounds, and under five hundred pounds	0	13	3
Five hundred pounds and under one thousand pounds	0	16	9
One thousand pounds, and under two thousand pounds	1	0	0
Two thousand pounds, and under three thousand pounds	1	3	3
Three thousand pounds, and under four thousand pounds	1	6	9
Four thousand pounds, and under five thousand pounds	1	13	3
And for all sums amounting to, or exceeding five thousand pounds	2	0	0

Bond—

When the money secured, or to be ultimately recoverable thereon, shall be limited not to exceed a given sum, the same duty as on a bond for such limited sum.

And when the total amount of the money secured, or to be ultimately recoverable thereon, shall be uncertain, and

£   s.   d

without limit, the same duty as on bond for a sum equal
to the amount of the penalty of such bond.

And where there shall be no penalty of the bond in such
last-mentioned case, such bond shall be available for
such an amount only as the ad valorem duty denoted by
any Stamp or Stamps thereon shall extend to cover.

Bond given as a security for the payment of any sum of
money which shall be in part secured by a mortgage, or
other instrument, or writing, hereinafter charged with
the same duty as on a mortgage bearing even date with
such bond, or for the performance of covenants contained in such mortgage, or other instrument, in writing, or for both those purposes 0 13 6

Bond given a sa collateral or auxiliary security for the payment of any annuity, upon the original.creation and sale
thereof, where the same shall be granted, or conveyed,
or secured by any other deed, or instrument, liable to
and charged with the ad valorem duty hereinafter imposed on conveyances, upon the sale of any property   ..   0 13 6

Bond given as a security for the payment of any annuity
(except upon the original creation and sale thereof), or
of any sum or sums of money, at stated periods (not
being interest for any principal sum, nor rent reserved, or
payable upon any lease), for any definite and certain
term, so that the total amount of the money to be paid
can be previously ascertained, the same duty as on a
bond of the like nature for the payment of a sum of
money equal to such total amount.

Bond given as a security for the payment of any annui-
ity (except as aforesaid), or [of any sum or sums of
money at stated periods (not being interest for any principal sum, nor rent reserved, or payable upon any lease),
for the term of life, or any other indefinite period, so that
the whole money to be paid cannot be previously ascertained.

Where the annuity, or sum secured, shall not amount to
ten pounds per annum   0   4   0
To ten pounds and under fifty pounds per annum   0   8   0
To fifty pounds, and under one hundred pounds per an-
num 0 12   0
One hundred pounds, and under two hundred pounds per
annum 0 16   0
Two hundred pounds, and under three hundred pounds
per annum   1   0   0
Three hundred pounds, and under four hundred pounds
per annum   1   6   6
Four hundred pounds, and under five hundred pounds per
annum 1 13   6
Five hundred pounds, and under seven hundred and fifty
pounds per annum   2   0   0
Seven hundred and fifty pounds, and under one thousand
pounds per annum   2   6   6
One thousand pounds per annum, or upwards 2 13   6
Bond, commonly called counter bond, for indemnifying
any person who becomes bound or engaged as surety
for the payment of any sum of money, or annuity 0 13   6
Bond for the due execution of an office, and to account
for money received by virtue thereof 0 13   6
Bond of any kind whatever, not otherwise charged in this
Schedule, nor expressly exempted from all Stamp
duty 0 13   6

Bond—

Any transfer or assignment of any such bond as aforesaid, and which shall have paid the proper ad valorem
duty on bonds.

Where the principal money secured by the bond shall not

£ s. d.

exceed five hundred pounds, the same duty as on a
bond for the total amount of such principal money.
And in every other case, such transfer or assignment
shall be chargeable with the duty of 0 13 6

EXEMPTIONS FROM THE PRECEDING AND ALL OTHER STAMP DUTIES.

£ s. d

All security or penal bonds to Her Majesty, her heirs
and successors.
Bonds given by Collectors of Dues and Stamps, Collectors of Rum Duties, and their sureties, for the due
payment of money collected by them, or otherwise relating to their offices.
Bail bonds and replevin bonds.

Certificates—

On every Certificate of the admission of a Barrister, to
practice in the Courts of this Island 13 6 6
On every Certificate of the admission of a Solicitor, Attorney, Conveyancer, or Proctor, to practice in the Courts
of this Island, where the person had entered into articles of clerkship or contract, dated after the passing of
the "STAMP DUTY ACT, 1855," or of this Act, and duly
stamped, according to the provisions of such Act, or of
this Act 80 0 0
And on every other certificate of the admission of a Solicitor, Attorney, Conveyancer, or Proctor, to practice
in the Courts of this Island 106 13 6
But no one person is to be obliged to take out more than
one certificate, although he may act in more than one of
the capacities aforesaid, or in several of the Courts
aforesaid

Charter Party—

On every Charter party 1 6 6

Circular Notes—Bankers or others—

The like amount, and progressive rates of ad valorem
duties shall be paid thereon respectively, as are by this
Act or Schedule charged on Foreign Bills of Exchange
of corresponding amount

Commissions—

On every grant, letters patent, or commission of Chief
Justice and Vice Chancellor, so long as the same offices
shall be held conjointly 133 6 6
On every grant, letters patent, or commission of Chief
Justice, if the office be held separately 100 0 0
Vice-Chancellor, if the office be held separately 75 0 0
Assistant Judge of the Supreme Court 95 0 0
On every commission of Custos Rotulorum for any Pre-
cinct or Parish within this Island 13 6 6
On every commission or writ of association for Magis-
trates, and each nomination therein 2 0 0
On every commission of Master in Ordinary in the Court
of Chancery (no new Commission is to be granted, 28
V., c. 36, s. 11) 26 13 6
On every commission of Master Extraordinary in the
Court of Chancery 0 13 6
On every commission or appointment of Attorney-General   26 13 6
Advocate-General 13 6 6
On every commission of General Officer of the Militia of
this Island 26 13 6
Field Officer in a Regiment of Militia 4 0 0
On every commission or appointment conferring the rank
of Field Officer, otherwise than herein set forth 40 0 0
On every commission of Captain of a Troop, or Compa-
ny in any Regiment 3 6 6

	£	s.	d.
On every commission or appointment conferring the rank of Captain, otherwise than above set forth	133	6	6
On every commission of Lieutenant or Cornet of a Troop, or Lieutenant or Ensign of a Company of any Regiment of Militia	1	13	6
On every commission or appointment conferring the rank of Subaltern, otherwise than above set forth	66	13	6
On every commission of Adjutant or Quarter-Master in the Militia	1	13	6
On every commission or appointment of Surgeon in the Militia	4	0	0
Assistant Surgeon in the Militia	1	13	6
Lieutenant of a Fort on the Island establishment	16	0	0
Staff or Brevet Officer not herein specified, conferring rank above that of Captain	80	0	0
Physician-General, Surgeon-General, or Apothecary-General of the Militia, and their respective deputies	80	0	0
Adjutant-General in the Militia	26	13	6
Quarter-Master General	80	0	0
Muster Master-General	80	0	0
Barrack-Master-General of Militia	80	0	0
Deputy to any of the four last-mentioned Officers	80	0	0
Aide-de-Camp to the Commander-in-Chief	40	0	0
On every commission or warrant of Aide-de-Camp and Major of Brigade to a General Officer	16	0	0
On every commission of Judge Advocate-General	40	0	0
Deputy Judge Advocate-General	80	0	0
Deputy Judge Advocate to a Regiment of Infantry, or Troop of Horse	4	0	0
On every commission in the Militia, not herein specified	80	0	0
On every commission, grant, warrant or appointment from the governor of any office or employment, of the annual value of £100, not otherwise charged in this Schedule, nor expressly exempted from all Stamp duty	2	0	0
And when the same shall exceed one hundred pounds, for every additional one hundred pounds (see Appointment)	4	0	0

EXEMPTIONS FROM THE PRECEDING, AND ALL OTHER STAMP DUTIES.

All commissions, when the party is to officiate for another during his absence from his duties, by leave of the Governor.

Conveyances—

Conveyance, whether grant, bargain and sale, assignment, transfer, release, or any other kind or description whatever, or order or decree of the High Court of Chancery of England, or this Island, or other competent jurisdiction or authority, operating as a conveyance upon the sale of any land, tenements, rents, annuities or other property, real or personal, or of any right, title, interest, or claim into, out of, or upon any lands, tenements, rents, annuities, or other property ; that is to say, for or in respect of the principal or only deed, instrument, order, decree or writing, whereby the lands or other things sold shall be granted, or otherwise conveyed to, or vested in, the purchaser or purchasers, or any other person or persons by his or their direction.

	£	s.	d.
Where the purchase or consideration money therein, or thereupon expressed, shall not exceed ten pounds	0	6	6
Exceeding ten pounds, and not exceeding twenty pounds	0	13	6
Exceeding twenty pounds, and not exceeding fifty pounds	1	6	6
Exceeding fifty pounds, and not exceeding one hundred pounds	2	0	0
Exceeding one hundred pounds, and not exceeding two hundred pounds	2	13	6

	£	s.	d
Exceeding two hundred pounds, and not exceeding three hundred pounds	3	6	6
Exceeding three hundred pounds, and not exceeding four hundred pounds	4	0	0
Exceeding four hundred pounds, and not exceeding five hundred pounds	4	13	6
Exceeding five hundred pounds, and not exceeding six hundred pounds	5	6	6
Exceeding six hundred pounds, and not exceeding seven hundred pounds	6	0	0
Exceeding seven hundred pounds, and not exceeding eight hundred pounds	6	13	6
Exceeding eight hundred pounds, and not exceeding nine hundred pounds	7	6	6
Exceeding nine hundred pounds, and not exceeding one thousand pounds	8	0	0
Exceeding one thousand pounds, and not exceeding one thousand five hundred pounds	10	6	6
Exceeding one thousand five hundred pounds, and not exceeding two thousand pounds	13	6	6
Exceeding two thousand pounds, and not exceeding two thousand five hundred pounds	16	13	6
Exceeding two thousand five hundred pounds, and not exceeding three thousand pounds	20	0	0
Exceeding three thousand pounds, and not exceeding three thousand five hundred pounds	23	6	6
Exceeding three thousand five hundred pounds, and not exceeding four thousand pounds	26	13	6
Exceeding four thousand pounds, and not exceeding four thousand five hundred pounds	30	0	0
Exceeding four thousand five hundred pounds, and not exceeding five thousand pounds	33	6	6
Exceeding five thousand pounds, and not exceeding five thousand five hundred pounds	36	13	6
Exceeding five thousand five hundred pounds, and not exceeding six thousand pounds	40	0	0
Exceeding six thousand pounds, and not exceeding six thousand five hundred pounds	43	6	6
Exceeding six thousand five hundred pounds, and not exceeding seven thousand pounds	46	13	6
Exceeding seven thousand pounds, and not exceeding seven thousand five hundred pounds	50	0	0
Exceeding seven thousand five hundred pounds, and not exceeding eight thousand pounds	53	6	6
Exceeding eight thousand pounds, and not exceeding eight thousand five hundred pounds	56	13	6
Exceeding eight thousand five hundred pounds, and not exceeding nine thousand pounds	60	0	0
Exceeding nine thousand pounds, and not exceeding ten thousand pounds	63	6	6
And for every additional one hundred pounds, and also for any fractional part of one hudnred pounds	0	13	6

NOTE.—The purchase, or consideration money, is to be truly expressed and set forth, in words at length, in or upon every such principal or only deed, order, decree, or instrument of conveyance.

And where any lands, or other property, held under different titles, contracted to be sold at one entire price for the whole, shall be conveyed to the purchaser in separate parts or parcels by different deeds, orders, decrees, or instruments, the purchase, or consideration shall be divided and apportioned as the parties think fit, so that a distinct price or consideration for each separate part or parcel may be set forth in or upon the principal or only deed, order, decree, or instrument of conveyance relating thereto, which shall be charged with the ad valorem

duty in respect of the price or consideration money   £ s. d.
therein set forth.

And where any lands, or other property, contracted to be
purchased by two or more persons jointly, or by any
person for himself and others, or wholly for others, at
one entire price for the whole, shall be conveyed in
parts or parcels by separate deeds, orders, decrees, or instruments to the persons for whom the same shall be purchased for distinct parts or shares of the purchase-money,
the principal or only deed, order, decree, or instrument
of conveyance of each separate part or parcel shall be
charged with the ad valorem duty in respect of the
sum of money therein specified as the consideration for
the same.

But if separate parts or parcels of such land, or other property is conveyed to, or to the use of, or in trust for different persons, in and by one and the same deed, order,
decree, or instrument, then such deed, order, decree, or
instrument shall be charged with the ad valorem duty
in respect of the aggregate amount of the purchase or
consideration moneys therein mentioned to be paid, or
agreed to be paid for the lands or property thereby conveyed.

And where any person, having contracted for the purchase
of any lands, or other property, but not having obtained a
conveyance thereof, contracts to sell to any other person,
and the same in consequence is conveyed immediately to
the sub-purchaser, the principal or only deed, order, decree, or instrument of conveyance shall be charged with
the ad valorem duty in respect of the purchase or consideration money therein mentioned to be paid, or agreed
to be paid by the sub-purchaser.

And where any person, having contracted for the purchase of any lands, or other property, but not having obtained a conveyance thereof, contracts to sell the whole
or any part or parts thereof, to any person or persons,
and the same in consequence is conveyed by the original seller to different persons in parts or parcels, the principal or only deed, order, decree, or instrument of conveyance of each part or parcel thereof, shall be charged
with the ad valorem duty in respect only of the purchase or consideration money therein mentioned to be
paid, or agreed to be paid for the same by the person or
persons to whom, or to whose use, or in trust for whom the
conveyance is made, without regard to the amount of the
original purchase-money.

But where any sub-purchaser takes an actual conveyance
of the interest of the person immediately selling to him,
which shall be chargeable with the ad valorem duty, in
respect of the purchase or consideration money paid, or
agreed to be paid by him, and shall be duly stamped accordingly, any deed, order, decree, or instrument of
conveyance to be afterwards made to him of the property
in question, by the original seller, shall be exempted from
the ad valorem duty, and be charged only with the ordinary duty on deeds, orders, decree, or instruments of
the same kind, not upon a sale.

And where any lands, or other property, separately contracted to be purchased of different persons, at separate
and distinct prices, are conveyed to the purchaser, or as
he shall direct, in and by one and the same deed, order,
decree, or instrument, such deed order, decree, or instrument shall be charged with the ad valorem duty in respect of the aggregate amount of purchase or considera-
tion-moneys therein mentioned to be paid, or agreed to
be paid for the same.

And where any lands or other property are sold and conveyed in consideration wholly, or in part, of any sum of

money charged thereon, by way of mortgage or otherwise, and then due and owing to the purchaser, or are sold and conveyed, subject to any mortgage, bond, or other debt, or to any gross or entire sum of money to be afterwards paid by the purchaser, such sum of money or debt shall be deemed the purchase or consideration money, or part of the purchase or consideration money, as the case may be, in respect whereof the ad valorem duty is to be paid : Provided, where the mortgagee or other person in the situation of mortgagee, shall become the purchaser of the equity of redemption, the duty shall be charged upon the true and real value of the property, as if it stood unmortgaged, to be calculated and ascertained as if (is) after directed in this Schedule, under the head of settlement.

And where, upon the sale of any annuity or other right, not before in existence, the same shall not be created by actual grant or conveyance, but shall only be secured by bond, warrant of attorney, covenant, contract or otherwise, the bond or other instrument by which it is secured, or some one of such instruments, if more than one, shall be deemed and taken to be liable to the same duty as an actual grant or conveyance.

And where there are several deeds, orders, decrees, instruments or writings for completing the title to the property sold, such of them as are not liable to the ad valorem duty, to which the same may be liable, and which shall upon the face thereof, refer to the principal deed, order, decree or instrument bearing the ad valorem stamp, shall be charged with the duty to which the same may be liable, under any general or particular description of such deeds, orders, decrees, instruments or writings contained in. this Schedule : Provided, That when any deed, order, decree, instrument or writing, not liable to such ad valorem stamp, is tendered to the Secretary of this Island for the purpose of being recorded, the principal deed, order, decree or instrument, bearing the ad valorem stamp, shall also be produced, and the fact of such production, and the amount of such ad valorem stamp shall be certified by the Secretary on such other deed, order, decree or instrument, and such certificate shall be deemed sufficient evidence of the ad valorem duty having been impressed on the principal deed, order, decree or instrument, without its being necessary to produce the same in evidence

And where in any case not hereby expressly provided for, of several deeds, orders, decrees, instruments, or writings, a doubt shall arise which is the principal, it shall be lawful for the parties to determine for themselves which shall be so deemed, and to pay the ad valorem duty thereon accordingly ; and the other deeds, orders, decrees, instruments or writings on which the doubt arises shall, upon the face of each of them, refer to the principal deed as bearing the ad valorem duty.

And where there are duplicates of any deed, order, decree or instrument chargeable with the ad valorem duty, exceeding two pounds, one of them only shall be charged therewith, and the other or others shall be charged with the ordinary duty on deeds, orders, decrees or instruments of the same kind, not upon a sale.

And where any deed, order, decree or instrument operating as a conveyance on the sale of any property, operates also as a conveyance of any other than the property sold by way of settlement, or for any other purpose, or also contains any other matter or thing besides what shall be incident to the sale and conveyance of the property sold, or relate to the title thereto, every such deed, order, decree or instrument shall be charged, in addition to the duty to which it is liable, as a conveyance on the sale of property, with such further stamp duty, as any separate deed, order or decree containing the other matter would have been chargeable with.

EXEMPTION FROM ANY STAMP DUTY UNDER THE PRECEDING HEAD "CONVEYANCE."

	£	s	d.

Any deed, order, decree or instrument, whereby any policy of assurance on the life of any person, or for the insurance of any property, shall be assigned or transferred by the insurer to any person, the original policy having been duly stamped.

EXEMPTION FROM ALL STAMP DUTIES WHATEVER.

Conveyance of land as a site for any Church or Chapel of any religious denomination.

Copartnership—

	£	s	d.
On all articles of copartnership or other agreement to that effect	1	6	6

Customs' Warrants—

	£	s	d.
On and from the first day of January, one thousand eight hundred and sixty-five on Customs' Warrants, inwards and outwards, per set	0	0	3

Deeds—

On every deed, order, decree or other instrument executed wholly out of this Island, and not bearing the British ad valorem Stamp, the same duty as is hereby imposed on deeds or instruments of a like nature executed in this Island,

On every deed, order, decree or instrument, executed partly out of this Island and partly in this Island, and on which the British ad valorem duty has been impressed, one half the duty imposed on deeds or instruments of a like nature, executed wholly in this Island.

	£	s	d.
And on every deed, order, decree, or instrument, wholly executed out of this Island, and bearing the British ad valorem Stamp, the like ad valorem duty as on deeds executed in this Island, or in the option of the parties, a duty of	3	6	6

Duplicate or counterpart of any deed, order, decree, or instrument whatsoever, chargeable with any Stamp duty or duties under this Schedule, where the Stamp duty or duties chargeable as aforesaid shall not amount to the sum of thirteen shillings and six pence, the same duty or duties as shall be chargeable upon the original deed, order, decree, or instrument.

	£	s	d.
And when the Stamp duty or duties shall amount to the sum of thirteen shillings and six pence or upwards	0	13	6
On every deed of any kind whatever, not otherwise charged in this Schedule, nor expressly exempted from all Stamp duty	0	13	6

Escheats—

	£	s	d.
On every patent of Escheat, if, by the judgment in Escheat, the premises appear to be of or under the value of two hundred pounds	6	13	6
And if the same exceed two hundred pounds, then for every additional one hundred pounds, and also for any fractional part of one hundred pounds	3	6	6
On every letter of preference for Escheat	1	6	6

Kettubah—

On every Kettubah, or Jewish contract of marriage, the same Stamps as on settlements.

£ s. d.

Lease—

Lease of any lands or hereditaments, granted in consideration of a sum of money by way of fine, premium, or other gross sum paid for the same, without any yearly rent, or with any yearly, under twenty pounds ⎫ The same duty as for the conveyance on the sale of lands for a sum of money of the same amount.

Lease of any lands or hereditaments at a yearly rent, without any sum of money, by way of fine, premium, or other gross sum paid for the same :

Where the yearly rent shall not amount to one hundred pounds 0 13 6

Where it amounts to one hundred pounds, and not to two hundred pounds 1 0 0

To two hundred pounds and not to three hundred pounds   1 6 6

To three hundred pounds and not to five hundred pounds   2 0 0

To five hundred pounds, and not to one thousand pounds   2 13 6

And where the same amounts to one thousand pounds or upwards 4 0 0

And where such rent progressively increases then the amount of duty, payable upon the highest rent reserved.

Lease of any lands or hereditaments, granted in consideration of a sum of money, by way of fine, premium or other gross sum, and also of a yearly rent, amounting to twenty pounds or upwards. ⎫ Both the ad valorem duties payable for a lease, in consideration of a fine only, and for a lease according to the amount of rent reserved thereon.

Lease not otherwise charged in this Schedule, and for the counterpart or duplicate of any lease whatsoever ..   0 13 6

And where any lease is granted for a consideration, by way of fine, p em m, or other gross sum, payable in produce, or the yearly rent is so payable, then and in such case, such produce shall be estimated for the purpose of reducing the same to a pecuniary value, at and after the rates following :

For each hogshead of sugar :....   ....   12 0 0

For each puncheon of rum 10 0 0

For each tierce of coffee 12 0 0

And the duty shall be charged on the amount arising on such estimate, as if the fine, premium, or other gross sum or yearly rent had been expressed in money.

EXEMPTION FROM ANY STAMP DUTY UNDER THE PRECEDING HEAD "LEASE."

Leases of waste or uncultivated land to any person, for any term not exceeding three lives, or ninety nine years, where the fine shall not exceed five shillings, nor the reserved rent one pound one shilling per annum, and the counterparts or duplicates of all such leases.

Legacies—

On every receipt or other discharge for any legacy given by any will or testamentary instrument, or for the clear residue (when devolving to one person) and for every share of the clear residue (when devolving to two or more persons) of the personal estate of any person (after deducting debts, funeral expenses, legacies, and other charges first payable thereout) whether the title to such residue, or any share thereof, accrues by virtue of any testamentary disposition, or upon a partial or total intestacy :

Where such legacy, residue, or share of residue amounts to fifty pounds, and is under one hundred pounds 2 13 6

	£	s.	d.
One hundred pounds, and under two hundred pounds	4	0	0
Two hundred pounds, [and under three hundred pounds	5	6	6
Three hundred pounds, and under four hundred pounds	8	0	0
Four hundred pounds, and under five hundred pounds	10	13	6
Five hundred pounds, and under six hundred pounds	13	6	6
Six hundred p un , and under seven hundred pounds	16	0	0
Seven hundred pounds, and under eight hundred pounds	18	13	6
Eight hundred pounds, and under nine hundred pounds	21	6	6
Nine hundred pounds, and under one thousand pounds	24	0	0
And for every additional one hundred pounds, or fractional part thereof, the further sum of	2	13	6

And the person or persons receiving any such legacy, residue or share of residue, is and are hereby declared to be charged and chargeable with the payment of the stamp duties hereby imposed, and not the heir, executor or administrator of the deceased, unless when otherwise directed by the will.

EXEMPTIONS FROM ANY STAMP DUTY UNDER THE PRECEDING HEAD " LEGACIES."

Legacies and residues, or shares of residue of any such estate or effects as aforesaid, given or devolving to, or for the benefit of the husband or wife, children or grand children of the deceased.

Letters—

	£	s.	d.
On every letter of marque	26	13	6

On every letter or power of attorney, and every decree or order of the Court of Chancery of England or of this Island, or other competent jurisdiction or authority, operating as a power for the recovery of debts in this Island, or for the sale of o e **1 6 6**

On every letter or power of attorney, and every decree or order of the Court of Chancery of England or of this Island, or other competent jurisdiction or authority, operating as a power for managing any Pen, Plantation, or Sugar Estate or Estates, and whether the same shall or shall not include a power for the recovery of debts or other purposes. **4 0**

On every letter or power of attorney, and every decree or order of the Court of Chancery of England or of this Island, or other competent jurisdiction or authority operating as a power for managing premises mentioned in any such power, which consist of only a place of residence, habitation, or woodlands not opened, or common pasture, and whether the same shall or shall not include a power for the sale of such property, or for the recovery of debts **1 6 6**

On every letter or power of attorney, and every decree or order of the Court of Chancery of England or of this Island, or other competent jurisdiction or authority, operating as a power authorizing a party to acknowledge payment and satisfaction of a mortgage demand **0 4 0**

On every other letter or power of attorney, or decree or order as aforesaid, not herein charged with a stamp duty, or exempted from all stamp duty, and upon every substitution under a letter or power of attorney, or any decree or order as aforesaid **1 6 6**

But in case any letter or power of attorney, or decree or order shall not disclose what art a real estate is to be managed, it shall be lawful for the Secretary of the Island, or the person officiating for him, to require the production of a declaration, to be taken before a Justice of the Peace, stating the nature of the real estate, in order that the said officer may be satisfied that the proper stamp is impressed on such letter, power or decree or order.

	£	s.	d.

Licenses—

On every annual license to retail Fire-arms	4	0	0
On every annual license to Hawkers and Pedlars	1	6	6
On every annual license for selling gunpowder	4	0	0
On every license, to be taken out yearly by any banker or bankers, banking company or corporation, or other person or persons who shall issue any promissory notes for money, payable to the bearer on demand, and allowed to be re-issued	66	13	6
On every marriage license	0	13	6

Mortgage—

Mortgage, further charge in security of, or affecting any lands, estate or property, real or personal, whatsoever.

Also any conveyance, order, decree or instrument, disposing of any lands, Estate or property whatsoever, in trust to be sold, or otherwise converted into money, which shall be intended only as a security, and shall be redeemable before the sale or other disposal thereof, either by express stipulation or otherwise, except where such conveyance, order, decree or instrument shall be made for the benefit of creditors generally, or for the benefit of creditors specified, who shall accept the provision made for payment of their debts, or who shall exceed five in number.

Also any defeazance, declaration or other deed, order or decree of the Court of Chancery of England, or of this Island, or writing for defeating or making redeemable, or explaining or qualifying any conveyance of any lands, estate, or property whatsoever, which shall be apparently absolute, but intended only as a security.

Also any agreement, contract, or bond, accompanied with a deposit of title deeds for making mortgage, or such other security, or conveyance, or instrument as aforesaid of any lands, estate, or property, comprised in such title deeds, or for pledging or charging the same as a security.

When the same respectively shall be made as a security for the payment of any definite and certain sum of money advanced or lent at the time, or previously due and owing, or forborne to be paid, being payable:

Not exceeding one hundred pounds	0	13	6
Exceeding one hundred pounds, and not exceeding two hundred pounds	1	0	0
Exceeding two hundred pounds, and not exceeding three hundred pounds	1	6	6
Exceeding three hundred pounds, and not exceeding four hundred pounds	1	13	6
Exceeding four hundred pounds, and not exceeding five hundred pounds	2	0	0
Exceeding five hundred pounds, and not exceeding six hundred pounds	2	6	6
Exceeding six hundred pounds, and not exceeding seven hundred pounds	2	13	6
Exceeding seven hundred pounds, and not exceeding eight hundred pounds	3	0	0
Exceeding eight hundred pounds, and not exceeding nine hundred pounds	3	6	6
Exceeding nine hundred pounds, and not exceeding one thousand pounds	3	13	6
Exceeding one thousand pounds, and not exceeding one thousand five hundred pounds	5	6	6
Exceeding one thousand five hundred pounds, and not exceeding two thousand pounds	7	0	0
Exceeding two thousand pounds, and not exceeding two thousand five hundred pounds	8	13	6
Exceeding two thousand five hundred pounds, and not exceeding three thousand pounds	10	6	6

	£	s.	d.

Exceeding three thousand pounds, and not exceeding three thousand five hundred pounds   **12 0 0**

Exceeding three thousand five hundred pounds, and not exceeding four thousand pounds   **13 13 6**

Exceeding four thousand pounds, and not exceeding four thousand five hundred pounds   **15 6 6**

Exceeding four thousand five hundred pounds, and not exceeding five thousand pounds   **17 0 0**

Above five thousand pounds   **20 0 0**

And where the same respectively shall be made as a security for the repayment of money, to be the thereafter lent advanced, or paid, or which may become due upon an account current, together with any sum already advanced, or due, or without, as the case may be, other than and except any sum or sums of money to be advanced for the insurance of any property comprised in such mortgage or security against damage by fire, or to be advanced for the insurance of any life or lives, pursuant to any agreement in any deed, whereby any annuity shall be granted or secured for such life or lives:

If the total amount of the money secured, or to be ultimately recoverable thereupon, shall be limited, not to exceed a given sum, the same duty as on a mortgage for such limited sum.

And if the total amount of the money secured, or to be ultimately recoverable thereon, shall be uncertain, and without any limit, then the same shall be available as a security or charge for such an amount only of money or stock intended to be thereby secured as the ad valorem duty denoted by any stamp or stamps thereon will extend to cover.

Any transfer or assignment of any such other security as aforesaid, or of the benefit thereof, or of the money thereby secured.

When no further sum of money shall be added to the principal money already secured   **0 13 6**

But no such deed, order, decree, or instrument as aforesaid shall, in any of the said several cases be chargeable with any further or other sum than is hereby expressly provided, by reason of its containing any further or additional security for the payment of such money, or any interest thereon, or any new covenant, proviso, power, stipulation, or agreement, or other matter whatever in relation to such money, or the interest thereon, or by reason of its containing all or any of such matters.

Any deed, order, decree, or instrument made for the further assurance only of any estate or property, which has been already mortgaged, pledged, or charged as a security by any deed, order, decree, or instrument, which shall have paid the ad valorem duty on mortgages or bonds, under any act or acts in force at the time of making such last-mentioned deed, order, decree, or instrument.

Also, any deed, order, decree, or instrument made as an additional or further security for any sum or sums of money already secured by any deed or instrument, which has paid the ad valorem duty on mortgage or bond chargeable as aforesaid   **0 13 6**

If any further sum of money is added to the principal money already secured, such deed, order, decree, or instrument for further assurance, or additional or further security, either by the mortgagor, or by any person entitled to the property by descent, devise, or bequest from such mortgagor, shall be chargeable only with the ad valorem duty on mortgages under this Act, in respect of such further sum of money, in lieu of the duty aforesaid, not-

£ s. d.

withstanding the same deed, order, decree, or instrument may contain any covenant either by the mortgagor, or by any person entitled us aforesaid, proviso, power, stipulation, or agreement whatsover, in relation to the money already secured, or the interest thereon.

Where several distinct deeds, orders, decrees, or instruments, falling within the description of any of the'instruments, hereby charged with the ad valorem duty on mortgages, shall be made at the same time for securing the payment or transfer of one and the same sum of money the ad valorem duty, if exceeding two pounds, shall be charged only on one of such deeds, orders, decrees, or instruments, and all the rest shall be charged with the duty to which the same may be liable under any more general description of the same, contained in this schedule.

EXEMPTIONS FROM THE SAID AD VALOREM DUTY ON MORTGAGES, ETCETERA, BUT NOT FROM ANY OTHER DUTY TO WHICH THE SAME MAY BE LIABLE.

Any deed, order, decree or other instrument, made in pursuance of, and in conformity to any agreement, contract, or bond charged with, and which shall actually have paid the ad valorem duty.

Any deed, order, decree, or other instrument, made for the further assurance only of any estate or property already mortgaged, pledged, or charged as security by any deed, order, decree, or instrument which has paid the ad valorem duty hereby charged.

Any deed, order, decree, or other instrument made as an additional or further security for any sum or sums of money already secured by any deed, order, decree or instrument, which has paid the ad valorem duty hereby charged, to be exempt from the ad valorem duty hereby charged, so far as regards such sum or sums of money, in case such additional or further security is made by the same person or persons who made the original security; but if any further sum of money is added to the principal money already secured, or is thereby secured, to any other person, the ad valorem duty shall be charged in respect of such further sum of money.

Any deed, order, decree, or instrument, whereby any policy of assurance on the life of any person, or for the insurance of any property, is assigned or transferred by the insurer to any person as a security for money lent or advanced, the original policy having been duly stamped, as by this act required.

And the deeds, orders, decrees, and instruments, hereby exempted from the ad valorem duty shall, on the face of them, refer to the deed, order, decree, or instrument bearing the ad valorem duty : Provided, That when any deed, order, decree, instrument, or writing, not liable to such ad valorem duty is tendered to the Secretary of this Island for the purpose of being recorded, the principal instrument bearing the ad valorem stamp shall also be produced ; and the fact of such production, and the amount of such ad valorem stamp shall be certified by the Secretary on such other instrument ; and such certificate shall be deemed sufficient evidence of the ad valosem duty having been impressed on the principal one, without its being necessary to produce the same in evidence.

Mortgages, et cetera, with a conveyance of the equity or right of redemption or reversion, or other matter in the same instrument.

Where any instrument operates as a mortgage, or other

£ s. d.

instrument hereby charged with the ad valorem duty on mortgages, and also as a conveyance of the equity or right of redemption, or reversion of any lands, estate or property therein comprised to, or in trust for, or according to the direction of a purchaser, such instrument shall be charged, not only with the ad valorem duty on mortgages, but also with the ad valorem duty before charged on a conveyance upon the sale of any property; but where the equity or right of redemption or reverston is thereby conveyed or limited in any other manner, such instrument shall be charged only as a mortgage.

And in all other cases where a mortgage or other instrument hereby charged with the ad valorem duty on mortgages is contained in one and the same deed, order, decree or writing, with any other matter or thing (except what shall be incident to such mortgage or other instrument) such deed, order, decree or writing shall be charged with the same duties as such mortgage or other instrument, and such other matter or thing would have been separately charged with, if contained in separate deeds or writings.

Orders—

On every order to a Minister to publish in his Church the intention of a party to apply to the Legislature for a private Bill 4 0 0

On every order for land or an other beneficial order under the sign manual, or sealyat arms of the Governor, for any sum exceeding twenty pounds 1 6 6

Order of the Court of Chancery of England or of this Island, or other competent jurisdiction or authority, relating to the sale, mortgage or management of land, &c. (See Conveyance—Letters of Attorney—Mortgage.)

Patents—

On every patent not otherwise charged in this Schedule, nor expressly exempted from all stamp duty 1 6 6

EXEMPTION FROM ALL STAMP DUTY.

Patents of pardon.

Plats—

On every plat, survey, or other Surveyor's return returned into any Court or office, or annexed to any deed or other instrument. 0 2 0

On every copy of a plat, survey, or other Surveyor's return issued from any public office 0 2 0

Policies—

On every policy of assurance or insurance, or other instrument, by whatsoever name the same is called, whereby any assurance shall be made of, or upon any building, plantation, goods, wares, merchandize or other property, from loss or damage by fire only :

Where the sum insured shall not exceed one hundred pounds 0 5 6

And for every additional one hundred pounds, or fractional part thereof, up to five hundred pounds 0 5 6

And where it exceeds five hundred pounds, and not exceed one thousand pounds 2 0 0

And where it exceeds one thousand pounds, and not two thousand pounds 2 13 6

And where it exceeds two thousand pounds, and not five thousand pounds 4 0 0

And where it exceeds five thousand pounds 6 13 6

On every policy of assurance or insurance, or other instrument, by whatever name the same is called,

£ s. d.

whereby any assurance shall be made upon any ship or vessel, or upon any goods, merchandize, or other property on board of any ship or vessel, or upon the freight of any ship or vessel, or upon any other interest in or relating to any ship or vessel which may lawfully be insured :

Where the sum insured shall lnotexceed two hundred pounds   0 4 0

Where the sum insured exceeds two hundred pounds, and not five hundred pounds 0 6 6

And if the whole sum insured shall exceed five hundred pounds, then for every five hundred pounds, and also for any fractional part of five hundred pounds, whereof the same consists....   ....   0 3 6

On every policy of assurance, or insurance, or other instrument, by whatever name called, whereby any insurance is made upon any life or lives, or upon any event or contingency relating to, or depending upon, any life or lives :

Where the sum insured amounts to one hundred pounds   0 2 6

And upon every additional one hundred pounds, up to one thousand pounds, the further sum of 0 2 6

And if the sum insured exceed one thousand pounds, then, for every five hundred pounds, and also for any fractional part of five hundred pounds, whereof the same shall consist 0 6 6

But any insurances effected for periods less than twelve months shall be charged proportionately at the rates aforesaid, according to the fractional parts of a year for which they may be respectively effected

Presentations—

On every presentation to a benefice, or church living 13 6 6

EXEMPTIONS.

Every case of simple and bona fide exchange of benefices between Rectors, or between Island Curates, or Stipendiry Curates, allowed and taking place at the instance of the respective incumbents.

Promissory Note for the payment to the bearer on demand—

Of any sum of money. not exceding one pound 0 0 3
Exceeding one pound, and not exceeding two pounds 0 0 6
Exceeding two pounds, and not exceeding five pounds 0 1 0
Exceeding five pounds, and not exceeding ten pounds 0 2 0
Exceeding ten pounds, and not exceeding twenty pounds..   0 3 0
Exceeding twenty pounds, and not exceeding thirty pounds   0 4 0
Exceeding thirty pounds, and not exceeding fifty pounds   0 5 0
Exceeding fifty pounds, and not exceeding one hundred pounds 0 10 0
Which said notes may be be re-issued after payment thereof as often as shall be thought fit.

Promissory Note for the payment to the bearer, or to order, at any time after date or sight thereof for the principal sum—

Exceeding ten pounds, and not exceeding thirty pounds   0 0 3
Exceeding thirty pounds, and not exceeding fifty pounds   0 0 6
Exceeding fifty pounds, and not exceeding one hundred pounds 0 1 6
Exceeding one hundred pounds, and not exceeding two hundred pounds 0 2 0
Exceeding two hundred pounds, and not exceeding five hundred pounds 0 4 0
Exceeding five hundred pounds, and not exceeding one thousand pounds 0 6 6
Exceeding one thousand pounds, and not exceeding two thousand [pounds]   ....   ,,,, ...   0 13 6
Exceeding two thousand [pounds] 1 6 6

£ s. d

Promissory note for the payment of any sum of money by instalments, or for the payment of several sums of money at different days or times, so that the whole of the money to be paid shall be definite and certain.

The same duty as on a promissory note, payable to bearer, or to order at any time after date or sight thereof.

And the following-Instruments shall be deemed and taken to be Promissory Notes, within the intent and meaning of this schedule, viz :

I owe you, or engagement, in writing, to pay money.

EXEMPTIONS FROM THE FOREGOING AND ALL OTHER STAMP DUTIES

All promissory Notes for the [payment to the bearer, or to order, at any time after date or sight thereof, of sums under ten pounds.

Protests—

On every protest, or other Notarial Act, under the hand of a Notary Public, or Deputy Notary Public, done in this Island   0   4   0

Receipt, or Discharge given for or upon the payment of Money (the Duties whereon shall be paid by the party receiving the Money).—

Amounting to ten pounds, and not amounting to fifty pounds   0   0   1½
Amounting to fifty pounds and upwards   0   0   3
And where any sum of money is therein expressed or acknowledged to be received in full of all demands   0   1   6

And any Note, Memorandum, or writing whatsoever, given to any person for or upon the payment of money, whereby any sum of money, debt, or demand, or any part of anydebt or demand therein expressed, is expressed or acknowledged to have been paid, settled, balanced, or otherwise discharged or satisfied, or which imports or signifies any such acknowledgment : And whether the same shall or shall not be signed with the name of any person, shall be deemed and taken to be a receipt for a sum of money of equal amount with the sum, debt, or demand so expressed or acknowledged to have been paid, settled, balanced, or otherwise discharged and satisfied, within the intent and meaning of this schedule, and shall be charged with a duty accordingly.

And any receipt or discharge, note, memorandum, or writing whatsoever, given to any person for or upon the payment of money, which contains, imports, or signifies any general acknowledgement of any debt, account, claim, or demand, debts, accounts, claims, or demands, whereof the amount is therein specified, having been paid, balanced, settled, or otherwise discharged or satisfied, or whereby any sum of money therein mentioned is acknowledged to be received in full, or in discharge, or satisfaction of any such debt, claim, account, or demand, debts, accounts, claims, or demands, and whether the same shall or shall not be signed with the name of any person, shall be deemed and taken to be a receipt in full, within the intent and meaning of this schedule, and shall be charged with the duty of one shilling and six pence accordingly.

Provided : That any letter, or one of divers letters, importing or signifying any receipt or acknowledgement, within the meaning of this schedule, may be stamped at any time before being tendered in evidence ; and, where there are divers such letters, it shall suffice to stamp one of such letters, in relation to one transaction or claim.

£ s. d.

And all receipts, discharges and acknowledgments of the description aforesaid, which shall be given for, or upon payment made by or with any Bills of Exchange, Drafts, Promissory Notes, or other securities for money, shall be deemed and taken to be receipts given upon the payment of money within the intent and meaning of this schedule.

Receipts—

And all receipts or discharges given or granted to the Receiver-General for or in respect of any moneys payable by him out of the Public Treasury (except moneys payable as drafts on Island certificates and exchequer bills), other than as after excepted, shall be chargeable after the like scale of duty.

EXEMPTIONS FROM THE PRECEDING DUTIES ON RECEIPTS.

Receipts or discharges written upon promissory notes, bills of exchange, drafts, or orders for the payment of money, duly stamped, according to the laws in force at the date thereof.

Letters by the general post, acknowledging the safe arrival of any bills of exchange, promissory notes, or other securities for money.

Receipts for any moneys paid into any Savings' Bank of this Island.

Receipts or discharges endorsed, or otherwise written upon, or contained in any bond, mortgage, or other security, or any conveyance, deed, or instrument whatever, duly stamped, according to the laws in force at the date thereof, acknowledging the receipt of the consideration-money therein expressed, or the receipt of any principal money, interest, or annuity thereby secured.

Releases or discharges for money by deeds duly stamped according to the laws in force at the date thereof.

Receipts or discharges for the return of any duties of Customs upon certificates of over entry.

Receipts given or granted by the Receiver-General, or any of his deputies, or by any Collector of Dues, for or in respect of any public or parochial or other taxes or duties, or given or granted by the Justices and Vestry of any parish, or the Common Council of Kingston.

Receipts or acknowledgments on the records of the Secretary's Office, of the payment of a mortgage debt.

Receipts.—

On every receipt granted by the Island Secretary, for deeds or papers recorded in his office. 0 2 0

On every receipt granted by the Island Secretary, for recording annual returns of Attorneys, or Trustees, commonly called "Crop Accounts" 0 4 0

Settlements—

Any deed, or any order or decree of the Court of Chancery of England, or of this Island, or other jurisdiction or authority, or instrument whatever whether voluntary or gratuitous, or upon any good or valuable consideration other than a bona fide pecuniary consideration, whereby any certain and definite sum or sums of money (whether chargeable on lands or other hereditaments or not, or to be laid out in the purchase of lands or other hereditaments or not, and, if charged or chargeable on lands or other hereditaments, whether to be raised at all events or not, or whereby any lands, tenements, rents, annuities, or other property real or personal, or any right, title, interest, or claim in-

£   s.   d.

to, out of, or upon any lands, tenements, rents, annuities, or other property is settled, or agreed to be settled
upon, or for the benefit of any person or persons, either
in possession or reversion, either absolutely, or conditionally, or contingently, or for life, or other partial interest,
or in any other manner whatsoever.)

If such sum or sums of money, or the value of such property, shall not amount to one thousand pounds   1   6   6

And if the same amount to one thousand pounds, and not
to two thousand pounds 2 13 6

Two thousand pounds, and not to three thousand pounds   4   0   0

To three thousand pounds, and not to four thousand
pounds   5   6   6

Four thousand pounds, and not to five thousand pounds .. 6 13   6

Five thousand pounds and not to six thousand pounds   .. 8   0   0

Six thousand pounds, and not to seven thousand pounds .. 10   0   0

Seven thousand pounds, or upwards   13   6   6

NOTE —The value of such property, if real estate, to be ascertained from the roll, or last corrected roll of the assessment of property if there inserted, if not, or if property
of any other nature, by a declaration of the true and real
value of the same.

EXEMPTIONS FROM STAMP DUTIES UNDER THE PRECEDING HEAD " SETTLE-
MENTS."

Bonds, Mortgages, and other securities operating as settlements, if chargeable with the ad valorem duties on
bonds and mortgages hereinbefore granted.

Deeds, or instruments of appointment, apportionments in
execution of powers given by any previous settlement,
deed, or will to, or in favor of, persons specially named
or described as the object of such powers.

Deeds, or instruments merely declaring the trusts of any
money, pursuant to any previous settlement, deed or
will, or for securing any gifts or dispositions made by
any previous settlement, deed or will.

Wills, testaments and testamentary instruments, and dispositions, mortis causa, of every description.

Schedule—

Inventory or catalogue of any lands or hereditaments, or
of any furniture, fixtures, or other goods or effects,
or containing the terms and conditions of any proposed
sale or lease, or the conditions and regulations for the cultivation and management of any estate, plantation, pen
or other property leased or agreed to be leased, or containing any other matter or matters of contract or stipulation whatsoever, which shall be referred to, in, or
by, and be intended to be used or given in evidence as
part of, or as material to, any agreement, lease, bond,
deed, order, decree or other instrument charged with
any duty, but which shall be separate and distinct from,
and not endorsed on, or annexed to such agreement,
lease, bond, deed, order, decree or other instrument.

Where any such inventory, schedule, or catalogue, shall
be so referred to, in, or by any such agreement, lease,
bond, deed, order, decree, or such other instrument as
aforesaid, chargeable with any Stamp Duty, not exceeding ten shillings, the same duty as shall be so chargeable
on such agreement, lease, bond, deed, order, decree, or
other instrument.

And where any such schedule, inventory, or catalogue
shall be referred to, in, or by any lease, bond, deed, order, decree, or such other instrument as aforesaid, chargeable with a Stamp Duty exceeding ten shillings, then for
every additional pound of the amount of the last-mentioned duty, a further progressive duty of   0   1   6

	£	s.	d.

Warrants—

	£	s.	d.
On every pilot's warrant for one port	8	0	0
And for more than one port	13	6	6
On every warrant and appointment of interpreter of foreign languages	2	0	0
Health-officer in Kingston	20	0	0
Health-officer at Montego-Bay or Falmouth	10	0	0
Health-officer for any other port	6	13	6
Quarter-gunner of a fort on the island establishment	24	0	0

GENERAL EXEMPTIONS FROM ALL STAMP DUTIES.

All Acts of the Legislative Council and Assembly, Proclamations, Acts of State, Votes, or matters printed by order of either branch of the Legislature, or of any Vestry in the Island, inquisitions, and other proceedings taken before any Coroner or Magistrate : all proceedings for enforcing Militia duties.

All probates, or acknowledgments of any deed, or instrument in writing, written in anypart thereof, or annexed thereto.

All accounts of produce, commonly called crop accounts.

All bonds, and other official documents whatsover, relating to the service of Her Majesty's Customs in this Island, Her Majesty's Commissariat or Ordnance Department : or any Military or Naval board in this Island, or relating to the public service in this Island.

All leaves of absence to persons holding honorary appointments.

(Part the Second)
CONTAINING THE DUTIES ON LAW AND OTHER PROCEEDINGS.

Affidavits—

	£	s.	d.
On every Affidavit, whether joint or several, in one suit or matter, to be filed, read, or used in the Court of Chancery	0	4	0
For each additional suit or matter	0	4	0
In any other Court in this Island	0	2	0

Answer.—

	£	s.	d.
In the Court of Chancery. { To any Bill or information	2	0	0
On Affidavit in answer by a respondent to any cause petition	2	0	0

Appearance—

	£	s.	d.
On every appearance of a defendant or respondent in Chancery	0	2	0

Appointment—

	£	s.	d.
On every appointment of bailiff of the crown, guardianship, or committee of a lunatic	3	6	6

Attachment—

	£	s.	d.
On every Attachment issuing out of the Court of Chancery	0	8	0

Attestations—

	£	s.	d.
On every public Attestation to an appeal from the Court of Chancery	3	6	6
From any other Court	2	13	6
On every Attestation or exemplification that shall pass the seal of this Island, or of any Court thereof	1	6	6

Bill—

	£	s.	d.
On every Bill in Chancery	3	6	6
On every information in Chancery	3	6	6

	£	s.	d.

Cause Petition—

On every original Cause Petition 3 6 6
Supplemental ditto 1 0 0

Certificates—

On every Certificate of an officer of any Court of Judicature, or public office in this Island, or from any Clerk of
the Peace in this Island 0 2 0

Citation—

On every Citation out ot the Court of Chancery 0 8 0
Out of any other Court 0 2 0

Claim—

On every claim, or proof of debt, filed or lodged in the Master's Office 0 6 6

Commission—

On every Commission out of the Court of Chancery, Supreme Court, or any other Court of Judicature in this
Island 0 13 6

Court of Ordinary—

On every will bond, or on the dedimus to prove the will,
at the option of the Island Secretary, and on every administration bond, where the personal property is under
twenty pounds 0 13 6
Amounting to twenty pounds, and under fifty pounds 1 6 6
Amounting to fifty pounds, and under eighty pounds 2 0 0
Amounting to eighty pounds, and under one hundred
pounds 2 13 6
Amounting to one hundred pounds, and under one hundred
and fifty pounds 4 0 0
Where the personal property amounts to one hundred and
fifty pounds, and is under two hundred pounds 5 6 6
Amounts to two hundred pounds, and under two hundred
and fifty pounds 6 13 6
Amounts to two hundred and fifty pounds, and under three
hundred pounds 8 0 0
Amounts to three hundred pounds, and under three hundred and fifty pounds 9 6 6
Amounts to three hundred and fifty pounds, and under four
hundred pounds 10 13 6
Amounts to four hundred pounds, and under four hundred
and fifty pounds 12 0 0
Amounts to four hundred and fifty pounds, and under five
hundred pounds.... .... 13 6 6
And for every additional one hundred pounds or fractional
part, the further sum of 2 13 6

And no will bond, or administration bond shall issue out of
the Court of Ordinary of this Island until a declaration by
the executor, p   g the will, or the person to whom
the grant of administration has been made, of the probable value of the deceased's estate has been produced to
the Island Secretary by the party requiring the probate
of a will or grant of administration ; and should the inventory upon being presented to be recorded, exceed the
amount declared to, the additional duty, to make up such
difference, shall be paid (less the discount allowed by the
foregoing act, if such difference shall amount to five
pounds), to the Receiver-General, and the inventory shall
be impressed with a stamp or stamps of the value or
amount of such additional duty, and no such inventory
shall be received until the production to the Island Secretary of a receipt by the Receiver General, stating
that such difference of duty (less discount, where allow-
able as aforesaid), has been paid into the Stamp Office ;

£ s. d.

and thereupon the Island Secretary shall notify the fact
on the original inventory, and on the record thereof respectively.
And in all cases, where probate or administration has been
commenced before the coming into operation of this Act,
and in which the aforesaid ad valorem duty shall not
have attached, there shall be impressed upon each of the
following instruments remaining to be taken out, videli-
cet :

The letters testamentary, or letters of administration, and
on every dedimus potestatem, and warrant of appraise-
ment, a Stamp duty of 0 13 6
On all articles, or any libel exhibited for the probate in
solemn form of a will or codicil   3   6 6
Answer to such articles or libel   2   0 0

EXEMPTION FROM THE PRECEDING AND ALL OTHER STAMP DUTIES.

All will bonds, and administration bonds, relating to the
estate of any common soldier or sailor who shall be slain,
or shall die in Her Majesty's service (the same so appearing
by a certificate under the hand of the officer under whom
he served).

Dedimus.—
On every Dedimus issuing out of the Court of Chancery   0 13 6

Demurrers—
On every Demurrer in the Court of Chancery 0 13 6
In any other Court   0   2 0

Depositions—
On every engrossment of Depositions or answers to interrogatories in any Court of law or equity 0 13 6

Disclaimer—
On every Disclaimer in the Court of Chancery 0 13 6

Enrolment—
On every Enrolment of a final decree   3   6 6

Examinations—
(See Depositions.)

Exceptions —
On every Exception, or set of Exceptions in a cause in
Chancery 0 13 6

Executions—
On every writ of execution out of the Court of Chancery   0 13 6

EXEMPLIFICATIONS OF WILLS AND OF JUDICIAL AND OTHER PROCEEDINGS.

(Vide paper stamps)

Guardianship—
On every letter or appointment of guardianship issuing out
of the Court of Chancery   3   6 6

Informations—
(See bills in Chancery).

Interrogatories—
In every court of law or equity, or Court of Ordinary   0 13 6

Inquisitions—
On every Inquisition in extent, the subject of one writ   0   6 6
And for every additional writ included in such Inquisition   0   4 0
On every other Inquisition, the subject of writs issued from
the Supreme Court   0   6 6

4 S

	£	s	d.

Judgments—

On every authority for entering satisfaction on a Judgment	0	1	6
On every assignment of a Judgment	0	4	0
On every authority for entering satisfaction on a Judgment obtained in any Court of Common Pleas	0	1	6
On every distress warrant under twenty shillings in the petit debt court in any parish	0	0	3
On every distress warrant under forty shillings, ditto	0	0	6
On every distress warrant above forty shillings, ditto	0	0	9

Manucaption—

On every Manucaption	0	4	0

Notice—

Of filing cause petition	0	4	0

Office Copies—

(See Paper Stamps).

Orders—

On every attested copy order in any court of this Island	0	2	0

Petitions—

On every Petition in any suit or matter in any court of this Island, except in the Court of Chancery	0	2	0

In the Court of Chancery—

On every Petition for a receiver, for a commission de lunatico inquirendo, or for a grant or gift from the crown	2	0	0
On every other Petition (save cause Petition)	0	6	6

Pleas—

On special Pleas n the Court of Chancery	0	13	6
In any other court	0	2	0

Recognizances—

On every Recognizance in the Court of Chancery	2	0	0
On every other Recognizance, except in criminal cases, and in appeals from the summary jurisdiction of Magistrates	0	4	0
On every Recognizance in appeal from the summary jurisdiction of Magistrates	0	2	0

Rejoinders—

On one or more Rejoinders in the Court of Chancery	0	6	6
In any other court	0	2	0

Replications—

On one or more Replications in the Court of Chancery	0	6	6
In any other court	0	2	0

Subpœnas—

On every Subpœna issuing out of the Court of Chancery	0	8	0
On every Subpœna issuing out of the Supreme Court of Judicature in this Island	0	0	6

Summons—

On every original Summons issued by Justices of the Peace on the private prosecution of any party, or on the information to ground same, at the option of the party	0	1	6
On each warrant issued by Justices of the Peace on the private prosecution of any party, or on the information to ground same, at the option of the party	0	1	6

Suggestions.—

On every Suggestion in the Court of Chancery	0	13	6
In any other Court	0	2	0

Warrant.—

(See next after Summons.)

	£	s.	d.

Writs.—

	£	s.	d.
On every Writ of error	1	13	6
On every Writ of certiorari	0	13	6
On every Writ of partition :....	0	6	6.
On every Writ of Emblements	0	6	6
On every Writ of dower	0	6	6
On every Writ of possession	0	6	6
On every Writ, and on each process for contempt, issuing out of the Court of Chancery (except the Writ of execution ante)	0	8	0
On every other Writ issuing out of the Supreme Court ..	0	2	0

EXEMPTIONS FROM THE PRECEDING AND ALL OTHER STAMP DUTIES.

All Writs of habeas corpus, and all Writs of summons or arrest, filed or lodged with declarations.

All motion papers in the Supreme Court of Judicature, and the Court of Chancery of this Island.

All side-bar rules entered up in the office of the Clerk of the Supreme Court.

All rules and orders to compel the making up of issues in causes pending in the superior Courts of law.

All notices in Chancery, Supreme, and Circuit Courts of this Island.

All pleas of the general issue, all imparlances and similiters.

All affidavits and declarations, made pursuant to any Act of this Island.

All process and proceedings for, or on the behalf of any person legally admitted to sue or defend in forma pauperis, and all proceedings in criminal suits and prosecutions whatsoever.

(Part Third.)

Paper Stamps.—

All exemplifications of wills, and every other exemplification, all proceedings and copies sent to this Island to be recorded, used, or given in evidence in any Court, which are not charged with any specific duty under this Act, shall be subject to, and be impressed with Paper Stamps hereinafter respectively specified.

All masters' reports in Chancery; all accounts of guardians, trustees, mortgagees in possession, required to be recorded in the Secretary's Office of this Island; Inventories; all office copies, authenticated by the Island Secretary, Clerk of the Court, Clerk of the Crown, Registrar in Chancery, Clerk of the Patents, and Registrar of the Diocese, shall be written, transcribed, engrossed, or printed upon paper, vellum, or pa m of the descriptions hereinafter mentioned; and such paper vellum, or parchment, and each sheet thereof, shall be stamped with the duties, and the same shall contain the number of lines hereinafter mentioned; and, for the p of this Act each side of the paper, vellum, and parchment shall be deemed a separate sheet.

	£	s.	d.
Imperial and royal paper, or any paper, vellum, or parchment of the same size, and containing not more than forty lines of writing	0	4	0
And for every additional forty lines of writing, and also for any fractional part of forty lines of writing on the same sheet	0	4	0
Demy or medium paper, or any paper, vellum, or parchment of the same size, containing not more than thirty lines of writing	0	2	0
And for every additional thirty lines, and also for any fractional part of thirty lines of writing on the same sheet ..	0	2	0
Post paper, or any paper, vellum, or parchment of the same or smaller size, containing not more than twenty-four lines	0	1	6

	£ s. d.
And for every additional twenty-four lines, and also for any fractional part of twenty-four lines of writing on the same sheet .... , ...	0 1 6

In respect to Master's reports in Chancery, and accounts current, any person may write the same upon both sides of a sheet of paper, without being liable to pay any further Stamp Duty than is hereby imposed upon one side of such paper.

Sunday, Good Friday, Christmas Day.

Opening place of business

Police Constables direction to close

Lodging Houses and Taverns—sales of bread or ice

Every person who, on the Lord's Day, Good Friday or Christmas Day, opens any place of business except Druggists Shops and Dispensaries, shall be liable to a penalty not exceeding £10. Any Police Constable may require and direct any person so offending, to close such place of business, and every refusal to comply with such directions, shall be considered a separate offence. Not to apply or extend to Lodging Houses and licensed Taverns, nor to the establishments for the sale of bread or ice, provided they are closed from 10 to 5 o'clock, 7 V., c. 14, s. 21.

The above clause shall not prevent any Lodging House or licensed Tavern from being kept open at any time, provided they are designed for the accommodation of travellers and lodgers, 11 V., c. 14, s. 4.

Offering or exposing goods for sale

Any person who, on the Lord's Day, Christmas Day or Good Friday, offers or exposes for sale any goods, wares or merchandize, shall be liable to a penalty not exceeding 40s. for each offence of selling : but not to prevent the sale of milk, bread, ice or greens, or the delivery of grass before 10 a. m., and after 5 p. m., 7 V., c. 14, s. 22.

Christmas Day

The provisions of 7 V., c. 14, s. 21-22, so far as they prevent or prohibit the opening of any place of business, or the offering or exposing for sale any goods on Christmas Day, shall only extend during the hours of Divine Service, 7 V., c. 35.

Subpœna, Writ of

Names of 3 witnesses in one writ

The names of 3 witnesses only shall be inserted in one writ in civil cases, 20 V., c. 22, sch.

Surveyors.

To be indentured for 5 years, examined and commissioned.

Except as after-mentioned, no person shall be qualified as a Surveyor unless he has been bound by indenture to serve some legally admitted Surveyor for 5 years, and during the term has continued in the active service of his employer, and been examined and commissioned as after mentioned. Penalty not less than £10, and not exceeding £50, to be recovered summarily. Not to prevent any apprentice so bound, from performing the duties and office of a Surveyor for his employer, with his sanction, 22 V., c. 40, s. 2.

Not to be apprenticed under 16—stamp—to be recorded in Clerk of the Courts Office

No commissioned Surveyor shall take any person as his apprentice, under 16. The indenture shall be impressed with a £30 stamp, and shall within 6 months of its execution be lodged in the Clerk of the Supreme Court's office, who shall record it : and in default of its being lodged and recorded within that period, it shall be void, 22 V., c. 40, s. 3.

Order to be examined

Affidavit

Any person who has served an apprenticeship, may apply to the Supreme Court for an order to be examined, admitted and sworn as a Surveyor of Land, and the Court shall, on its appearing to them on affidavit that he has served 5 years under articles duly executed, and has complied with this Act, make an order directing any two or more duly qualified Surveyors to examine him as to his qualification, 22 V., c. 40, s. 4,

One of the Examiners to be a Crown Surveyor

False certificates

One of whom shall be a Crown Surveyor ; and any Surveyor so appointed, who gives a false certificate to any candidate for examination, shall be liable to a penalty of £100, to be recovered summarily ; and any commission obtained under such fabricated certificate, shall be void, 25 V., c. 27, s. 1.

On an attested copy of the order being served on the Surveyors, they shall appoint a day and place for proceeding with such examination, which shall be public, and shall embrace a knowledge of Mathematics, theoretical and practical Land Surveying, including Trigonometrical Surveying and Railway Surveying, Drafting, Platting. Protracting and Isometrical and Topographical Drawing; and if the examination appear satisfactory to the Surveyors, they shall certify to the Court or a Judge in Chambers, if it is not sitting, that such person has been found qualified, which shall be sworn to by them before a Justice or Commissioner of the Grand Court, and upon its being produced to the Court or a Judge, the Court or Judge shall cause an order to be entered up in Clerk of the Court's office, authorizing and empowering such person to act as a Surveyor of Land, on his taking out the necessary commission, 22 V., c. 40, s. 5.

Day and place of examination, which is to be public
Subjects to be embraced
Certificate
To be sworn to
Order authorizing party to act on taking out Commission

The examination shall be held in the Court House of the most convenient town of the County in which the candidate resides; and the Surveyors to examine, shall publish in the "Gazette" a notification of the time and place, and if they do not meet, a fresh notice shall be given, 25 V., c. 27, s. 2.

Examination to be in a Court House of the County
And notice advertized

The Surveyors appointed to examine any apprentice or other person applying for a commission, shall be pa, by him a fee of 2 guineas for each Surveyor not exceeding two, 22 V., c. 40, s. 3.

Examiner's fees

On presentation to the Governor of an attested copy of the order, such person shall be entitled to receive a commission as a Land Surveyor, which shall be impressed with a stamp duty of £60, in lieu of all other stamps and fees, and shall be signed by the Governor. And no person shall act or take upon himself the office or duties of a Surveyor until he has taken out such commission, and been duly gazetted. If the stamp duty of £30 on the indenture of apprenticeship has been already paid, the commission shall bear a stamp of £30 only, 22 V., c. 40, s. 6.

Commission
Stamp
No person to act until the Commission is Gazetted
Reduced Stamp

Any person legally qualified to act as a Surveyor in Great Britain, or Ireland or in the Colonies, shall be qualified to act as a Surveyor of, and in this Island, if he makes it appear on application to the Court, that he was so duly qualified; in which case the Court may make an order for his obtaining, in like manner and subject to the Stamp Duty and publication in the Gazette, a commission before provided, 22 V., c. 40, s. 7.

Persons legally qualified in Great Britain, Ireland, or the Colonies

No Surveyor shall p m his name to be used by any person other than his lawful indented apprentice. Penalty £50, to be recovered summarily, 22 V., c. 40, s. 8.

Not to permit their names to be used except by their apprentices

Persons heretofore duly commissioned shall be qualified, 22 V., c. 40, s. 9.

Persons previously commissioned

No Surveyor shall deliver any plat whereby any parcel of land shall pass the Broad Seal, before he has surveyed and measured the land, on every side where accessible, and has seen the lines fairly made, and the corner trees marked X, and the plat shall truly represent the respective parcels of land, with their bounds and bearings, and describe the sort of wood every corner tree is of, with the alphabetical marks, and also contain a scale of distances, and measurments. Penalty, £100, 22 V., c. 40, s. 10

Requisites of plats to pass the Broad Seal

On all writs of view, or orders of Court, the Surveyors concerned, shall in every diagram, or scheme of the lands in question, or those adjacent, which they shall return with such writs, or orders, or lay before the Court and Jury, faithfully lay down and describe all old marked trees and lines, and fixed, or known, and reputed boundaries, on oath, and lines fixed under former orders, or patents and writs of view on the lands comprized within the schemes or diagrams. Penalty, £50, 22 V., c. 40, s. 11.

Diagrams on writs of view or orders of Court

When any Surveyor intends to survey, or re-survey lands under writs of view, orders of Court, or by the employment of any person, he shall give 10 days notice, in writing, at least, of his intention, and express in the notice what particular run of land of the neighbouring proprietor, or person in possession he intends to run upon, by what authority, and by whom employed, and which of the lines of the run, the particular corner, the course intended, the day and hour he purposes to begin to run the lines,

Notices of Survey

from which corner, and on which course only he shall proceed. Penalty, £100 for every wilful omission, 22 V., c. 40, s. 12.

Defacing, &c. lines or marked trees, &c.

Any Surveyor or other person who defaces, destroys, or removes any lines upon earth, or any land marks, or marked tree, post or pillar shall be liable to a penalty of £100 recoverable summarily, 25 V., c. 27, s. 3.

Returning plats by virtue of orders under the Broad Seal covered by a prior plat

If any Surveyor wilfully returns any plat or diagram, surveyed by him, by virtue of any order under the broad seal, which is afterwards found to be covered by any prior plat or plats, he shall be subject to a penalty of £100, besides being liable to make good all such damages, as any person shall suffer by him, or on account thereof.

Where the person for whom the land has been returned points it out

If the person for whom the land has been returned as belonging to the Crown shall have pointed it out to the Surveyor, as Crown land, and have required the return to be made, knowing it or any part to be covered by any prior plat, he shall also in like manner, over and above damages to persons aggrieved, forfeit as after provided, £100, 22 V., c. 40, s. 14.

Fresh notices to be given in case of sickness, &c,

When any Surveyor, after giving notice of survey, is in consequence of sickness or other inability, unable to attend on the day appointed, he shall give information thereof, and before proceeding with the survey, issue fresh notices, but shall not be entitled to charge therefor, 22 V., c. 40, s. 15.

Notice of resumption

If after commencing a survey, he is by illness or unavoidable necessity unable to complete it, he must give further notice of resumption of the survey, at the line or boundary where he had left off; such notice, shall not be subject to stamp duty, 22 V., c. 40, s. 16.

Appointment by the Court of Surveyors on ejectments

In any ejectment wherein a Surveyor has not been appointed, or dies, or is removed, the Court on application may appoint one or more Surveyors to make surveys, 22 V., c. 40, s. 17

Oath to be administered by them

The Surveyor so appointed and having accepted such appointment, shall in open Court take and subscribe the following oath, to be administered by the Court, the title of the cause being superscribed :—

> I, A. B., do swear that I will well and truly and faithfully make the necessary traverses of the land in dispute in the present ejectment, and that I will make a just and impartial representation thereof in the diagram by me to be signed, without favor or affection to either party So help me God, 22 V., c. 40, s. 18.

Oath previous to taxation of bill

No Judge shall order the taxation of the bill of any Surveyor for any work done, on any writ of view or order of Court, unless the Surveyor performing the same first take and subscribe the following oath :—

> I, A. B., do swear that all and every the traverses, protractions, reducing, extending and slipping of plats, and other work charged in the above account, have been by me truly and faithfully made, done and performed in the above cause, and the same and every part thereof was proper and necessary to be done to determine the boundaries of the land in dispute in the above cause, and that there are no charges in the said account but what are allowed in "The Land Surveyor's Act, 1858." So help me God.

Order for payment of taxed bill

Which may be administered by any Justice, and shall be inserted at the foot of the account, otherwise the taxation shall not be taken and received. Such taxation shall be sufficient authority for the Supreme Court to order payment to such Surveyor, and enforce same by attachment or otherwise

Notice of taxation to the person liable

against the person deemed by the Court liable; and before any Judge orders any bill to be taxed, notice shall be given of the day, time and place of taxation, to the person liable to pay the amount, 22 V., c. 40, s. 19.

Notices to Surveyors in ejectment suits, both to proceed to make survey

In ejectment suits, the Surveyor of the plaintiff or defendant shall give 10 days' notice in writing to the other, of his intention to traverse the line in dispute, and thereupon they shall both proceed to make the necessary surveys and traverses, and mutually communicate to each other their respective field notes, or other information, 22 V., c. 40, s. 20.

Diagram and copies to be furnished when only one Surveyor

If there be but one Surveyor, the diagram to be exhibited to the Court and Jury shall be signed by him, and 4 copies made and signed, one for the Court another for the Jury, another for the plaintiff's Attorney, and the fourth for the defendant's attorney.

Where there are 2

In case there be two Surveyors, the diagram shall be made out by the plaintiff's Surveyor from the field notes taken by himself and the defendant's Surveyor in the presence of each other, and mutually communicated, and shall be signed by the two. The defendant's Surveyor shall make two copies, one for the Court and the other for the defendant's attorney, and shall in due time deliver the latter to the defendant's attorney. The plaintiff's Surveyor shall also make two copies, one for the Jury, the other for the plaintiff's attorney, and in due time deliver the latter to the plaintiff's attorney. In both cases the diagrams shall be delivered to the parties by the Surveyor solely appointed, or appointed by the plaintiff, and he or they shall deliver a copy to both parties, at least 10 days before the trial, 22 V., c. 40, s. 21 To be delivered 10 days before the trial

No Surveyor other than such as were appointed by, and have executed the order of the Court, shall be admitted to give evidence touching the fixing of any plat, or otherwise in explanation of the diagram returned into Court, 22 V., c. 40, s. 22 None but the Surveyors appointed to be admitted to give evidence in explanation of the diagram

The bill of such Surveyor, or of both Surveyors, to be taxed, shall be paid by the party against whom judgment is given, or who discontinues or is nonsuited; and in case of a new trial being granted by the party applying therefor, the adverse party giving security, to be approved of by the Court, to refund the money if the verdict is given for the party applying. If on the trial of any ejectment wherein the plaintiff has obtained an order for running the lines, a verdict is found for the plaintiff, if it appear to the Court before whom the ejectment is tried, that the defendant had been for 5 years in quiet possession of the land recovered, and the Court so certifies, and that the verdict was in their opinion obtained principally on the evidence of fixing of plats, the plaintiff shall pay the Surveyor or Surveyors appointed by the Court the amount of his taxed bill, and the defendant shall not be liable to pay the same, 22 V., c. 40, s. 23. By whom the Surveyor's bills shall be paid In case of new trial

No Surveyor shall wilfully demand or receive greater fees than the undermentioned, under the penalty of £10, and disqualification from office, 22 V., c. 40, s. 24. Fees

—

SCALE OF CHARGES, No. 1.

	£	s.	d.
Traversing road, per chain	0	0	2
" gullies, per chain	0	0	4
" river-courses, per chain	0	0	6
" or running lines, per chain	0	1	6
" Jury road, per mile, inclusive of plan	6	0	0
Attending Juries, per day, for the purpose of pointing out new road	2	0	0
Laying out Railways, per mile	7	0	0
Making levels for any purpose, per mile	2	0	0
Laying out Tramroads, per mile	6	0	0
Every single lot of foot land	0	16	0
Every additional lot, if the whole do not exceed 10 lots, for each lot, and diagram, exclusive of stamp	0	5	0
Every additional lot, if total does not exceed 20 lots	0	4	0
For every lot exceeding 20 lots	0	3	0
Laying out lots of ¼ an acre, and not exceeding 5 acres	1	0	0
5 acres, and not exceeding 10	2	0	0
10 acres, and not exceeding 20 (25 V., c. 27, s. 4)	2	10	0
20, and not exceeding 30	3	0	0
For every diagram of the above, exclusive of stamp	0	6	0
For every additional 10 acres, above 30 acres, and not exceeding 100	0	12	0
For every diagram of the above, exclusive of stamps	0	16	0
All surveys above 100 acres to be charged for by the chain as above.			
Making search in the Secretary's Office, per day	1	0	0
Writing out original notice of survey, exclusive of stamp....	0	2	6
Writing out each copy of notice....	0	1	0
Attending by appointment to survey any land when the person employing such Surveyor does not attend at the time and place appointed	2	2	0
And in addition, mile money at 1s 6d per mile, from the Surveyor's residence.			
Attending by appointment to meet another Surveyor, or to run a line when such Surveyor does not attend, or the run-			

ning of the line is interrupted, 25 V., c. 27, s. 4] 2 2 0

For every plain plan of any property over 100 acres, the same having been previously surveyed, according to agreement.

For embellished plans, drawings, &c., as agreed on.

Copies of old plans as agreed on.

General plans of any number of properties or districts, as agreed on.

SCALE No. 2.

Where an entire property is surveyed—

For every subdivision on any property, Penn or Estate of any description of cultivation, common ruinate or woodlands, when such subdivisions are fenced, or have known boundaries and the survey is intended entirely for Plantation use, and the subdivisions do not average more than 2½ acres for each subdivision 0 4 0

For every subdivision not exceeding or averaging more than 5 acres 0 8 0

More than 10 acres each 1 0 0

" 20 " 2 0 0

" 30 " 2 5 0

For every additional 10 acres over 30 .... 0 5 0

When the lines are run at the same time, the Surveyor may charge for running them, according to Scale No. 1, notwithstanding they form a part of the boundary of such subdivisions, and they are contiguous to each other.

SCALE No. 3.

For visiting a Pen, Sugar Estate, Coffee Plantation, or other property, for the purpose of surveying any part of the cultivation, when the whole property is not surveyed.

For any number of subdivisions not exceeding 5, and when they average not more than 2½ acres each for each subdivision.... .... 0 6 0

For each subdivision not exceeding 10 and not averaging more than 5 acres 0 10 0

Not exceeding 20, and not averaging more than 10 acres 1 0 0

Exceeding 20 subdivisions, and not averaging more than 20 acres each 1 10 0

Exceeding 20 and averaging more than 20 acres, but not more than 30, each subdivision 2 0 0

For every additional 10 acres in each subdivision 0 5 0

22 V., c. 40, s. 24.

Penalty of £100 for any of the following offences :—

Penalties for

Forging certificate of qualification

Knowingly forging or counterfeiting, or causing, &c., any certificate of qualification.

Knowingly having a forged certificate

Knowingly and without lawful excuse, having or being possessed of such forged or counterfeited certificate, knowing it to be forged.

Borrowing or lending or using a certificate

Borrowing or lending, or making use of, or allowing any one to make use of any certificate of qualification for any unlawful purpose.

Representing oneself to have obtained a Commission

Untruly representing oneself to have obtained a commission for the purpose of acting as a Surveyor, 22 V., c. 40, s. 25.

Recoverable summarily

Such penalties shall be recoverable summarily, for the benefit of the informer, 22 V., c. 40, s. 26.

Within 12 months

But complaint must be made within 12 calendar months, 22 V., c. 40, s. 27.

Summoning witnesses

The Justices may summon witnesses in like manner, and with the same powers as in other cases, 22 V., c. 40, s. 28.

Overplus distrained on to be returned

Where money is directed to be levied by distress, any overplus after payment of the amount and expenses, shall be returned on demand to the party distrained upon, 22 V., c. 40, s. 29.

Want of Form—Irregularities

No distress shall be deemed unlawful, nor the party a trespasser, on account of any defect or want of form in the summons, conviction, award of distress or other proceeding relating thereto, nor the party a trespasser ab initio, on account of any irregularity afterwards committed ; but all persons aggrieved by an defect or irregularity, may recover satisfaction for the special damage inyan action on the case, 22 V., c. 40. s. 30.

Provision enabling the then agents for Surveyors who had acted as such for 5 years previously, to obtain commissions, 22 V., c. 40, s. 31.

. Oath shall include the affirmation, in case of Quakers, or other declarations or solemnity lawfully substituted for an oath in the case of other persons exempted by law from the necessity of taking an oath, 22 V., c. 40, s. 33. Interpretation Oath

The Land Surveyor's Act, 1858, 22 V., c. 40, s. 34. Short Title

Form of notice, s. 12

Sir (or Madam, as the case requires.)

I hereby give you notice, that I am employed by   to survey and run out a certain (here describe nature of survey), situate and being in the parish of   and known by the name of   and which adjoins lands said to be in your possession or belonging to you, and that I shall commence to run the same on   the . day of   18   at   of the clock of the   noon of that day, beginning at the corner of or road, and proceed (here state the course of chains), at which time and place you are requested to attend, by yourself, or a duly qualified Surveyor as you may think fit, and in the mean time, I will make such traverses as I may deem requisite.

Dated this   day of   18

To

                                                                Signature.

Time, Computation of

After the first day of the next Session of the Legislature, [16 October 1856] in all acts, the word "month" shall mean calendar month, unless words be added shewing Lunar month to be intended. In all cases in which any particular number of days is prescribed by any Act, or mentioned in any rule or order of Court, made in pursuance of any such Act for the doing of any act or for any other purpose, the same shall be reckoned, in the absence of any expression to the contrary, exclusive of the first and inclusive of the last day, unless the last day falls on a Sunday, Christmas-day, Good-Friday Monday or Tuesday in Easter, or a day apppointed for a public Fast, or Thanksgiving, in which case the time shall be reckoned exclusive of that day also, 18 V, c. 31, s. 6. Month

Reckoning days

Sunday, &c.

Titles of Congregations, Religious, Educational and Charitable Societies.

Whenever freehold, leasehold or other landed property has been or shall be acquired by any Congregation of persons associated or Society for religious purposes, for the promotion of education, or for any eleemosynary or charitable purposes, as a Chapel, Meeting-house or other place of Religious worship, burial ground or cemetery, Hospital, Poor-house, Asylum, or other Institution for eleemosynary or charitable purpose, or as a dwelling-house and Glebe for the Minister of such congregation, or as a School-house, and School-master's house and grounds, College, Academy or Seminary; and grounds, hall or rooms for the meeting or transaction of the business of such congregation or Society, or for the furtherance of its objects, when the conveyance, assignment or other assurance has been or may be taken to or in favor of Trustees to be from time to time appointed, or of any party named therein, or subject to any Trust for the congregation or Society, or the individuals composing the same. such conveyance, &c., shall not only vest the freehold, leasehold or other property in- the parties named therein, but also in their successors in office for the time being, and the old continuing Trustees, if any, jointly, or if none. then wholly in such successors for the time being, who may be chosen and appointed in the manner provided or referred to in the conveyance, &c., or in any separate deed or instrument declaring the Trusts thereof; or if no mode of appointment is prescribed or referred to, or the power be lapsed, then as shall be agreed upon by the Congregation or Society upon such or the like Trusts, and subject to the same powers and provisions as are contained or referred Vesting of property in Trustees from time to time without actual transfer

4 T

to in such conveyance, &c., or separate deed or instrument, or upon which the property is held, without the necessity of any transfer, assignment, conveyance or other assurance ; and whether such formality has or has not been prescribed in the original conveyance, &c., or any such separate deed **Not to invalidate actual transfer** or instrument. But not to invalidate the appointment of a new Trustee or Trustees, or the conveyance of the legal estate in any such   r which may hereafter be made as heretofore as by law required, 16 V. c. 44, s. 1.

Evidence of appointments
For the purpose of preserving evidence thereof, every choice and appointment of new Trustees shall be made to appear by some deed, under the hand and seal of the Chairman of the meeting at which the appointment is made, executed in the presence of the meeting, and attested by two witnesses in the form or to the effect hereunder stated, or as near thereto as the circumstances will allow, and shall be received as evidence in all Courts, and proceedings in the same manner, and on the like proof of other deeds and conveyances, and shall be evidence of the truth of the contents, 16 V., c. 44, s. 2

Proof and Record Stamp
Every such appointment shall be impressed previously to, or within 30 days of execution, with a Stamp of 10s. during the present Stamp Act, (9 V., c. 12, by the necessity of a Stamp, under 28 V., c. 9), and may be proved and recorded as other deeds, and the record shall enjoy all the privileges attached to the record of deeds of conveyances, 16 V., c. 44, s. 3.

Form of appointment of new Trustees
Memorandum of the choice and appointment of new Trustees of the
(describe the Chapel or other property) situate at   in
the parish of   in the county of
at a meeting duly convened and held for that purpose (in the Vestry of the said Chapel) on the   day of   18

A. B. of, &c., Chairman.

Names and descriptions of all the Trustees on the (original Constitution or last appointment) of Trustees, made on the
day of   18

A. B. of, &c.
C. D. of, &c.
E. F. of, &c.
G. H. of, &c.

Names and descriptions of all the Trustees in whom the said (Chapel) and premises now become legally vested—

First   Old continuing Trustees.

E. F. now of &c.

Second   New Trustees now chosen and appointed.

B. A. of, &c.
B. B. of, &c.

Dated this   day of   A. D. 18
W. S. Seal.

Signed, sealed and delivered by the said W. S. as Chairman of the said Meeting, at and in the presence of the said Meeting, on the day and year aforesaid, in the presence of

C. D.
E. F.

Tonnage Duties.

Public Hospital ; see 24 V., c. 3, s. 2
Public Hospital. —On vessels trading to the northward of the Tropic of Cancer, 6d per ton. On vessels trading within the Tropics, 3d per ton; On Sugar Drogbers and Coasting Vessels, 2s. per ton once a year. (Old Currency,) 46 G., 3, c. 28 s. 1

Marine Hospital, Savanna la Mar
Savanna-la-Mar Marine Hospital.—On vessels arriving at Savanna-la-Mar trading to the northward of the Tropic of Cancer, 1s. per ton. Those trading between the Tropics, 6d. (Old Currency,) Vessels of War, Droghers and Coasting Vessels exempted, with power to the Justices and Vestrymen to regulate the tax, not exceeding such rates, 53, G., 3, c. 22, s. 4.

Montego Bay Marine Hospital.—On vessels arriving and loading at Montego Bay from Europe, 1s. 6d. per ton. On vessels trading between the Tropics, or owned by persons resident in St. James, trading to the British Colonies in America, or the United States, 4d. a ton. Vessels trading from the British Colonies, or United States, 8d. a ton, (Old Currency,) with power to the Corporation to lessen rates, Droghers excepted, but to pay not exceeding £3 (Old Currency) for every such man they send to the Hospital; and in case of contagious sickness, the Corporation, at the instance of the Health Officer, shall compel them, 60 G., 3, c. 16, s. 4. Montego Bay

St. Mary's Marine Hospital.—On vessels arriving at either of the ports of Port Maria, Oracabessa and Rio Nova Bay, trading to the Northward of the Tropic of Cancer, 1s. 6d. per ton ; on those trading between the Tropics, 9d. a ton (Old Currency) ; but the Justices and Vestry may regulate the tax, not exceeding those sums. Ships of War, Droghers and Coasting Vessels excepted, 1 G. 4, c. 16, s. 2. St. Mary's

Annotto Bay Marine Hospital.—On vessels arriving at Annotto Bay trading to the Northward of the Tropic of Cancer, 1s. 6d. per ton. On those trading between the Tropics, 9d. per ton (Old Currency). Vessels of War, Droghers and Coasting Vessels excepted; but the Justices and Vestry may regulate the tax not exceeding those sums, 1 G., 4, c. 20, s. 4. Annotto Bay

Falmouth Marine Hospital.—On vessels arriving at Falmouth trading to the Northward of the Tropic of Cancer, 10d. per ton. On vessels trading between the Tropics, 5d. per ton (Sterling,) 23 V., c. 20, s. 4 Falmouth

Morant Point Light House.—On all vessels which enter and clear out of this Island, 6d. (Old Currency,) per ton every voyage, 3 V., c. 66; s. 5. Morant Point Light House

Plumb Point Light House.—On vessels entering either of the harbours of Port Royal and Kingston ; Vessels navigated wholly or in part by steam, 2d. per ton. not oftener than once in 3 Calendar months. Other vessels 6d. per ton. Droghers and other Ships, Sloops and vessels (other than steam vessels) engaged in the coasting trade, or trading within the Tropic of Cancer, once within 12 calendar months, other vessels on every entry, 15 V., c. 17, s. 9. Plumb Point

Vessels arriving at Port-Royal to land passengers, receive orders, or calling off the port to take Pilots on board, shall not be liable to Dues under 15 V., c. 17, s. 9 ; 26 V. S. 2, c. 9, s. 2.

Customs salaries—During the continuance of this Act, (until 31st March, 1867,) there shall be paid a duty of 2s. per ton, on all vessels of more than 40 tons burthen, not being droghers, arriving at any of the ports of this Island, in addition to any other duty or Tonnage imposed by any other Act, 23 V., c. 12, s. 10. Customs Salaries Rates and Vessels liable to ; see 24 V., c. 3, s. 8

Payable at the time of entry to the Collector and Controller at Kingston, and the Sub-Collector at every other port, by the master, who shall, at the same time state in writing the Tonnage of his vessel, 23 V., c. 12, s. 11. Collection

At the time of entry, the register, or if there is none, the sea-letter shall be deposited with the Collector and Controller, or Sub-Collector, until the Duties are actually paid. Masters making fraudulent entry or exhibiting false register or sea-letter, with intent to evade payment of Duty, shall forfeit not exceeding £60, nor less than £20, to be recovered before 2 Justices, and in default of payment, the offender shall be committed to Gaol, not exceeding 3 months, nor less than 3 weeks, unless sooner paid, 23 V., c. 12, s. 11, 12. Frauds

The Tonnage of foreign vessels shall be ascertained by the same mode of measurement as British vessels, and the Duty paid accordingly, 23 V., c. 12, s. 13. Foreign Vessels

A duty of 2s. per ton shall be levied once a year upon droghers employed in the coasting trade, in addition to any other Duty on Tonnage imposed by any other Act, 23 V., c. 12, s. 14. Droghers

All steam vessels shall be permitted to enter the ports of this Island, and depart therefrom free from all Tonnage Dues, whether they import or export cargo, 14 V., c. 56, s. 2. Steam Vessels

All vessels importing coals for the use of such steam vessels, shall be exempt from all Tonnage Dues, provided they import no other cargo, and take no cargo from the Island other than fruit, vegetables, ground provisions or preparations thereof, the growth of this Island, and proof be Coal Vessels given to the satisfaction of the Receiver-General and officers of Customs, that the coals have been imported solely for the use of steam vessels and are deposited in a depot to be appropriated exclusively to that purpose, 14 V., c. 56, s. 3.

Not receiving or discharging cargo

No vessel shall be subject to the payment of any Tonnage Dues, except Light-House Dues, when they neither discharge nor receive cargo, but only land passengers and their baggage, or receive passengers, their luggage and stores, 16 V., c. 27, s. 1.

Vessels in distress

When any vessel in distress puts into port for the purpose of repairs, no Tonnage Dues whatsoever shall be levied or paid, nor any Stamp Duty exigible on the Governor's warrant for the sale of cargo on board for defraying the cost of repairs, 16 V., c. 27, s. 2.

Steam Vessels conveying passengers and mails
Ice Vessels
Vessels partially laden

Until 31st March, 1867, all steam vessels engaged in the conveyance of passengers and mails shall be exempted from all Tonnage Duty (the Plumb Point Light-House duty excepted), as also all vessels laden exclusively with ice, or with ice, fruit, poultry, fresh fish and fresh butter. All vessels partly so laden and partly with other goods, shall pay duty only on the tonnage of the other goods as computed by the officers of the Customs, 23 V., c. 12, s. 15.

Vessels laden partly with coals for the use of steam vessels, and partly with other goods, shall pay Tonnage Dues only on the Tonnage of the goods so imported. Vessels laden exclusively with coals, for the use of steam vessels shall continue exempted under 14 V., c. 56 ; 23 V., c. 12, s. 16.

Exporting fruit, &c. only

Vessels arriving laden partly with coals, and partly with other goods which shall have paid Duty upon the Tonnage of such goods, may take away fruit, vegetables, ground provisions and preparations thereof, the growth and produce of this Island, without being subject to any further Tonnage Dues, 23 V., c. 12, s. 17.

Vessels entering inwards or outward partially laden

Whenever any sailing vessel now wholly or partly exempt from the payment of Tonnage duties on arrival, shall enter or clear outwards with cargo, in lieu of the paying of Tonnage Duties of 2s. under 23 V., c. 12, and 4d. under 46 G. 3, c. 28, on her whole Tonnage, there shall be paid the Tonnage Duties of 2s. and 4d. for every ton of measurement or space occupied by the produce or goods of which the outward cargo consists, 23 V., c. 3, s. 2.

Duties on cargo actually landed only

Entering outward with partial cargo

Vessels entering inwards with cargo covering less than the Tonnage of the vessel according to the register or measurement, shall in lieu of duties on her whole Tonnage, pay duties on the amount of Tonnage from which cargo shall be actually landed, to be calculated on every registered ton of space occupied by goods entered inwards to be landed at any of the ports of this Island : provided that on entering outwards with cargo, there shall be paid Tonnage Dues under the above Acts, on every registered ton of space occupied by produce, or merchandize, in excess over the amount of registered tons, on which duties were paid at the period of entry, the total amount of duties in no case to exceed the whole tonnage of the vessel as per register or measurement, 24 V., c. 3, s. 3.

Ascertainment of tonnage

Consignees, Owners, or Masters entering or clearing inwards or outwards, and claiming to pay on the proportion of registered Tonnage occupied by goods actually to be landed, shall notify such claim to the Customs Officers at Kingston, or any other port, who shall cause the amount of registered Tonnage so represented to be ascertained as after provided, 24 V., c. 3, s. 4.

Payment where to be made

Payment of duties according to the provisions of this Act, shall be made at the port where cargo is first entered, or at the final port of clearance whence outward cargo is exported, and the duties shall be levied, enforced and paid over in the same manner as the duties of Customs under other Acts, and carried to the same accounts as the duties under 23 V., c. 12, and 46 G., 3, c. 28 ; 24 V., c. 3, s. 5.

Rule for ascertaining duty

The Collector and Controller at Kingston, or the Sub-Collector at every other port shall decide the rate of space occupied by goods so landed, or shipped on the same principle, or by the same rule as freight is now admeasured in the case of vessels bringing a portion of other cargo than Ice for importation, and the duties shall be paid thereon accordingly, 24 V., c. 3, s. 6.

Lighthouse Dues

This Act shall not lessen the liability of every vessel to the payment of Light House duties, 24 V., c. 3, s. 7.

Nor shall apply to Droghers or vessels arriving from ports within the Tropic of Cancer. In respect to vessels from such last mentioned ports, a duty of 2s. per ton on the whole Tonnage, shall be levied once a year in addition to any other duty on tonnage imposed by any other Act, in like manner as it was levied previously to 23 V., c. 12; 24 V., c. 3, s. 8

Droghers vessels trading within the Tropic of Cancer

When it shall appear to the Officers of the Customs by the Manifest or otherwise, that the inward cargo of any vessel consisted wholly of Coal or Ice, or that she had no inward cargo, but arrived wholly in ballast, and has cleared out with a cargo wholly of dye or other woods the growth and produce of this Island, save only two tons and no more of other general cargo which shall be allowed to each such ship, they may remit unto, and release the vessel from payment of one half the amount of Tonnage Dues which would have been demandable had she arrived and cleared out with a full general cargo, and collect the other half, to be applied for the use of the government of the Island, 26 V., S. 2, c. 22.

Vessels laden with dye or other woods

Vessels resorting to the port of Kingston for the sole purpose of repairs, or being hauled up on the Slip Dock, are also exempted from Tonnage Dues; and in case any such vessel enters or clears outwards with cargo, or having brought cargo, enters inwards the same or any part, such vessel shall be charged with Tonnage or other Dues under 23 V., c. 12, and 46 G. 3, c. 28, on her whole Tonnage, or under 24 V., c. 3, on the measurement of Tonnage occupied by such outward cargo, or from which cargo shall be actually landed, under and subject to the provisions of such Acts, or either of them as the case requires, 28 V., c. 39, s. 20.

Vessels using Kingston Slip Dock

Towns and Communities, Offences in

Offences punishable by penalty not exceeding 40s. :—

1. In any thoroughfare in any town, or on any highway feeding or foddering any horse or other animal, or shewing any caravan containing any animal, or any other show or public entertainment, or shoeing, bleeding, or farriering any horse or animal, except in cases of accident, or exercising, training or breaking any horse or animal, or cleaning, making or repairing any part of any cart or carriage, except in cases of accident, where repair on the spot is necessary.

Feeding horses, &c. in thoroughfares

Breaking, &c. horses

2. In any thoroughfare in any town turning loose any horse or cattle, or suffering to be at large any unmuzzled ferocious dog, or in any place wilfully setting on or urging any dog or other animal to attack, worry or put in fear any person, horse, or other animal.

Horses, &c. at large. Unmuzzled dogs. Urging dogs &c. to attack persons, &c.

3. By negligence or ill usage in driving cattle or any other animal causing any mischief to be done by them to any person or property, or in the driving, care or management of such cattle or other animal, wantonly or unnecessarily impeding or obstructing the free passage of any person along any thoroughfare or highway, or not being hired or employed to drive such cattle or other animal, wantonly and unlawfully pelting, driving or hunting, or injuring or hurting any such cattle or other animal.

Negligently driving cattle, &c.

Wanton injury to animals

4. Having the care of any cart or carriage and riding on any part thereof, or on the shaft, or on any horse or animal drawing it, without having and holding the reins, or being at such a distance from such cart or carriage as not to have the complete control over every horse or other animal drawing the same.

Riding on carts, &c. without holding reins or having control over horses

5. In any thoroughfare in any town riding or driving furiously, or on any thoroughfare or highway riding or driving so as to endanger the life or limb of any person, or to the common danger of the passengers.

Furious riding or driving

On a repetition of the offence after a first conviction and proof thereof, penalty not exceeding 60s., or without a pecuniary penalty, commitment with or without hard labor, not exceeding 30 days, 11 V., c. 14, s. 1.

6. In any thoroughfare causing any carriage with or without horses or other animals to stand longer than may be necessary for loading or unloading, or for taking up or setting down passengers, except carriages standing for hire in any place allowed by a competent authority; or by means of any carriage, or any horse or other animal wilfully interrupting any public crossing, or wilfully causing any obstruction in any thoroughfare or highway.

Obstructing thoroughfares unnecessarily

Riding, &c. on footway

7. Leading or driving any horse or other animal, or drawing or driving any carriage upon any footway, or fastening any horse or other animal so that it may stand across or upon, or impede any footway ; carrying or conveying along any thoroughfare or highway in or on any carriage, any timber, lumber, iron, or thing made of any materials so that the same or any part shall extend across the carriage two feet beyond the wheels.

Carrying timber, &c. extending beyond wheels

8. Rolling or carrying any cask, tub, hoop, or wheel, or any ladder, plank, pole, or placard upon any footway, except for loading or unloading any cart or carriage, or of crossing the footway, or for the performance of any immediate or indispensable work, or for the repair of any building under the regulations after mentioned.

Carrying casks, &c. on footway

9. After being made acquainted with the regulations, or directions made by competent authority for regulating the route of horses, carriages and persons during the time of Divine Service, or at any other time through any town, wilfully disregarding or not conforming thereto.   (See s. 5.)

Not conforming to regulations for route of carriages, &c.

10. Without the consent of the owner or occupier, affixing any bill or paper against or upon any building, wall or fence, or pale ; or writing upon, soiling, defacing, or marking any such building, &c.

Affixing bills to or defacing walls, &c.

11. In any thoroughfare or public place, indecently exposing the person.

Exposing the person

On a repetition of the offence after a first conviction and proof, penalty not exceeding 60s., or without penalty, commitment, with or without hard labor not exceeding 30 days, 11 V., c. 14, s. 1

12. Selling or distributing, or offering for sale or distribution, or marking on any fence, wall or building any obscene figure, drawing, painting or representation ; or singing any profane, indecent or obscene song or ballad ; or writing or drawing any indecent or obscene word, figure or representation, or using any profane, indecent or obscene language.

Obscene drawings, songs or language

On a repetition, similar increased punishment as above, 11 V., c. 14, s. 1

13. Using any threatening or abusive and calumnious language to any other person publicly as shall tend to provoke a breach of the peace, or using such language, accompanied by such behaviour to any person publicly as shall tend to a breach of the peace.

Threatening or abusive language

14. Except in the performance of a duty legally imposed, or for giving an alarm of fire, or as a warning to passengers in dangerous or narrow roads, blowing any horn or shell, or using any other noisy instrument, or beating any drum in any public square, streets or lanes of any town.

Blowing horns, &c.

15. In the streets, lanes or squares of any town, or in any thoroughfare or highway, wantonly discharging any fire arms, or making any bonfire, or throwing or setting fire to any firework, or to the danger or annoyance of any passenger or inhabitant, throwing or discharging any stone or other missile, or flying any kite, or playing at any game.

Discharging Fire-arms, Bonfires, Fire works, Throwing Stones, Flying Kites, &c

16. Wilfully and wantonly disturbing any inhabitant by pulling or ringing any door bell or knocking at any door without lawful excuse, or wilfully and unlawfully extinguishing the light of any lamp, or unlawfully entering into any dwelling-house, building or premises to the annoyance of any person therein.

Ringing door bells, knocking at doors, extinguishing lights, entering dwellings

17. In any thoroughfare in any town or in any highway, tyring any wheel, or burning, dressing or cleansing any hoop, or cleansing, firing, washing or scalding any cask or tub, or wilfully making any fire on or in any prohibited place.

Tyring wheels, firing casks, making fires

18. Burning any wood, shavings, rubbbish or sweepings, or throwing any dirt, litter, ashes, or any carrion, fish, offal, rubbish, or broken bottles in any street, lane or road, 7 V., c. 14, s, 1.

Burning wood, &c., throwing dirt, &c. in streets

Any constable may take into custody, without warrant, any person committing any of the before-mentioned offences within his view, and in like manner when the offender is unknown, any such offender charged by any other credible person with recently committing any of such offences, though not committed within his view, but within view of the person making the charge, 7 V., c. 14, s. 2.

Apprehension of above offenders

The following offences punishable by fine not exceeding 40s :—

1. Exposing for sale or show in any highway or thoroughfare in any town to the annoyance of the inhabitants or passengers, except in a market or place lawfully appointed for that purpose, any goods or animal, or cleaning or dressing any animal, or hewing, sawing, boring or cutting any timber or stone, or slacking, sifting, or screening any lime, or making or dressing up or painting any article or material, or washing or cleansing any utensil whatever, or washing or hanging up or spreading any clothes or linen, provided a complaint be made by any inhabitant residing near the place where the offence is committed.

Exposing goods, cleaning animals, cutting timber, &c., slacking lime, making up, &c. articles, washing or hanging up clothes in thoroughfare

2. Throwing or laying in any thoroughfare any coals, stones, slates, shells, lime, bricks, timber, iron or other materials (except building materials or rubbish thereby occasioned, which shall be placed or enclosed so as to prevent any mischief happening to passengers).

Throwing rubbish, &c.

3. Beating or shaking in any thoroughfare, any carpet, rug, or mat, (except door-mats before 8 a.m.) or causing any offensive matter to run from any manufactory, slaughter-house, butchers' yard or dung hill into any thoroughfare or any uncovered place, whether or not surrounded by a wall or fence ; but it shall not be deemed an offence to lay sand, litter, or other materials in any thoroughfare in case of sickness to prevent noise, if removed as soon as the occasion ceases.

Beating mats Offensive matter

4. Emptying or beginning to empty any privy between 4 a.m. and 10 p.m. or removing along any thoroughfare any night soil or other offensive matter between 4 a.m. and 10 p.m., or wilfully or carelessly slopping or spilling any such offensive matter in the removal, or not carefully sweeping and cleaning every place in which any such offensive matter has been placed, slopped or spilled, or discharging or allowing to run from his premises any putrid or noxious water or other offensive matter into any street, lane, or thoroughfare, or into any other place or premises in the occupation of any other person.

Emptying privies Night soil, &c.

5. Keeping any pigstye to the front of any thoroughfare within any town, not being shut out from such thoroughfare by a sufficient wall or fence, or keeping any swine in or near any street or in any dwelling so as to be a common nuisance.

Pig Styes

6. Exposing any thing for sale in any private piazza or public place, unless with the consent of the owner or other person authorized to give such consent, or upon or so as to hang over any carriage-way or foot-way, or on the outside of any house or shop, or setting up or continuing any pole, blind, awning, line or other projection from any window, parapet, or other part of any house, shop or other building, so as to cause any annoyance or obstruction to the inhabitants or passengers in any thoroughfare, except in case of sickness, to prevent noise or accident or in repairing any building, provided the same be removed as soon as the occasion ceases.

Exposing goods in piazzas, &c. projections from windows, &c.

7. By the negligent use or management of fire in improper places, damaging any property or injuring any person.

Improper fire places

8. Wilfully disturbing any meeting or assembly or any congregation, assembled for religious worship, or for any religious service, or rite in any burial ground, or disturbing or molesting any person thereat, 7 V., c. 14, s. 3.

Disturbing religious meetings

No person other than those acting in obedience to lawful authority shall discharge any cannon or other firearm of greater calibre than a common fowling-piece within 500 yards of any dwelling house in any town, to the annoyance of any inhabitant thereof ; persons after being warned of the annoyance by any inhabitant, discharging any such firearms shall be liable to a penalty not exceeding £5, 7 V., c, 14, s. 4.

Discharging firearms

The Magistrates may from time to time as occasion shall require, make regulations for the route to be observed by all persons in charge of carriages, horses or other animals, for preventing obstruction of the streets and thoroughfares within any town, and give directions to the constables for keeping order, and preventing any obstruction of the thoroughfares in any case when they may be thronged or liable to be obstructed, 7 V., c. 14, s. 5.

Magistrates may make regulations for route of carriages, &c.

Any Householder, personally or by his servant, or a police constable may require any street-musician, juggler, dancer, actor or showman to depart from the neighborhood of his house : and every person sounding or playing upon any musical instrument, or making any other noise or disturb-

Street musicians

ance in any thoroughfare near any house, after being so required to depart, shall be liable to a penalty not exceeding 40s, 7 V., c. 14, s. 6.

Destroying dogs

Any Constable may destroy any dog or other animal reasonably suspected to be in a rabid state, or which has been bitten by a dog or animal in a rabid state ; and the owner permitting any dog or animal to go at large, after having information or reasonable ground for believing it to be in a rabid state, or to have been bitten by a dog, &c. in a rabid state, shall be liable to a penalty not exceeding £5, 7 V., c. 14, s. 7.

Drunkenness and riotous or indecent behavior

Being guilty in any thoroughfare, while drunk, of any riotous or indecent behavior in any public place : Penalty not exceeding 60s, or committal instead, not exceeding 10 days, 7. V., c. 14, s. 8.

Drunken persons lying about streets, &c.

Being found drunk in any town, lying about the streets or other public places or on any piazza, opened or enclosed : Penalty not exceeding 40s, and in default of payment at such time as the Magistrates shall appoint, commitment for not more than 10 days, 7 V., c. 14, s. 10

On a repetition of either of the offences against s. 3 and 10, after a first conviction and proof thereof, penalty not exceeding 60s, or without penalty, commitment with or without hard labor not exceeding 30 days, 11 V., c. 14, s. 1.

Apprehension of disturbers of the peace, persons loitering in highway, &c. between 9 p.m. and 6 a. m.

Any Constable may take into custody without a warrant, all drunken, loose, idle and disorderly persons he finds disturbing the public peace, or any inhabitant or passenger and all persons he shall find between 9 p. m and 6 a. m. lying or loitering in any highway, piazza, or other open place, and not giving a satisfactory account of themselves, 7 V., c. 14, s. 9.

Loose and disorderly persons, &c.

Persons in any town conducting themselves in a loose, idle, noisy and disorderly manner, thereby disturbing the peace and good order of the community or to the annoyance, discomfort or obstruction of the inhabitants or passengers, shall be deemed violaters of the public peace, and liable to a penalty of not more than 40s, and in default of payment at the time appointed, commitment with or without hard labor not exceeding 10 days, or imprisonment in the first instance, 7 V., c. 14, s. 11.

Apprehension of offenders

Any Constable and all persons he calls to his assistance, may take into custody without a warrant, any person who within the Constable's view offends in any manner against this Act, whose name and residence shall be unknown to the Constable, and cannot by enquiry be ascertained by him, but not otherwise except as to offences mentioned in the first class of offences (s. 1), 7 V., c. 14, s. 15.

To be taken before a magistrate or after 6 p. m., to police station

Every person taken into custody in the day time without warrant shall be forthwith taken before a Magistrate, or, if after 6 p. m., delivered to the custody of the sergeant or police constable in charge of the nearest police station, to be secured until he can be brought before a Magistrate to be dealt with according to law, or gives bail for his appearance before a Magistrate, 7. V., c. 14, s. 16.

Recognizance by person giving in charge

When any person charged by any other person, is, without warrant, in custody, at any station house, after 6 p.m., the sergeant or constable in charge may require the party making the charge to enter into recognizance, without sureties conditioned as after mentioned, and on his refusal may detain him until he comply or can be brought before a Magistrate, and if he deems it prudent may discharge from custody the person so charged upon his entering into recognizance with or without sureties, conditioned as aftermentioned, 7 V., c. 14, s. 17.

Of party charged

Recognizances to be without fee

Every such recognizance shall be taken without fee or reward, and conditioned for the appearance of the person bound before a Magistrate at the next Court, the time and place of appearance to be specified in the recognizance ; and the sergeant or police constable, shall enter in a book, the name, residence and occupation of the party and his sureties, if any, with the condition and the sum thereby acknowledged, and shall return every such recognizance to the Magistrates present at the time and place when and where the party is bound to appear, or to some other Magistrates, within 24 hours after taking the recognizance, and in the event of a Sunday intervening within 48 hours, 7 V., c. 14, s. 18.

Non-appearance

If the party do not appear at the time and place or before the termination of the sitting, the Magistrates shall certify on the back of the recognizance that the party has not complied with the obligation, and the Clerk of the Peace shall make the like estreat, as in other cases, and the

Magistrates shall immediately issue a warrant for the apprehension of the offender to answer the charge, or g   evidence as the case may be, or the Magistrates may, on application of any person on behalf of the party, postpone the hearing, and with consent of the sureties enlarge the recognizance, and when the matter is determined the recognizance shall be discharged without fee or reward, 7 V., c. 14, s. 19. *Postponing hearing*

Any Constable may take charge of any carriage, horse or other animal or goods in the charge of persons taken into custody, and deposit them in a place of safe custody until application is made for the same by the owners or agent, or the offender is discharged from custody to be delivered to the par   entitled on payment of all expenses incurred by the keep, 7 V., c. 14, s. 20. *Property in charge of persons taken into custody*

Every p   who by committing any offence herein forbidden has caused any harbour damage to any person or property, and does not make amends to the satisfaction of the person aggrieved shall, on conviction, pay not exceeding £10 as to the Magistrates appears to be reasonable amends besides the penalty, and the evidence of the person aggrieved shall be admitted, but if he is the only witness examined in proof of the offence, the sum ordered for amends shall be applied as the penalty, 7 V., c. 14, s. 23. *Amends for hurt or damage*

For every Misdemeanor or offence for which no special penalty is appointed, the offender shall be liable to a penalty not exceeding £5, or imprisonment not exceeding one calendar month. Not to prevent persons from being indicted for indictable offences made summarily punishable or liable to penalties or punishment under any other Acts, but so as not to be twice punished, 7 V., c. 14, s. 24. *Penalty to offences not specially provided for Where otherwise punishable*

On information upon oath the Magistrate may summon the person charged to appear before two Magistrates to answer who may proceed ex parte on failure to appear, or grant their warrant for the apprehension of the offender, or the Magistrate may, in the first instance, issue a warrant without any previous summons, 7 V., c 14, s. 25. *Proceedings on complaints*

The Justices may on non-payment of a penalty or amends, either forthwith or within such time as they may allow, not exceeding 30 days (on defendant giving security in double the amount of penalty or amends, and costs for his appearance at the time and place the Magistrates hold their Court to abide the further judgment of the law or non-payment by recognizance which, if forfeited, shall be estreated) commit the offender to hard labor, or otherwise for a term not exceeding 10 days, or if the sentence be hard labor, not exceeding, (30 days, 25 V., c. 11), where the sum shall not exceed 40s, and not more than 30 days ; where the sum exceeds that amount. The imprisonment to cease on payment of the sum due, and the costs shall be paid to the party entitled ; the amount of amends to the party aggrieved, or where the amount cannot be so appropriated, the same and all penalties shall be paid to the Treasurer for the use of the parish ; or the Magistrates may adjudge such part of any penalty as they deem proper, not exceeding one-half, to the use of such persons who have contributed to the conviction, in such proportions as they think fit, 7 V., c. 14, s. 26. *Security for payment of penalty or amends* *Commitment* *Application of penalty and amends*

Inhabitants may be witnesses, 7 V., c. 14, s. 27. *Witnesses*

The Magistrates may allow costs, and enforce payment in the same manner as penalties, 7 V., c. 14, s. 28. *Costs*

If the Magistrates find any misdemeanor to have been accompanied by a felonious intent, or that it ought to be prosecuted by indictment, they shall abstain from any adjudication thereon, and deal with the case as if this Act had not been passed, 7 V., c. 14, s. 30. *Abstaining from adjudication*

Prosecutions shall be commenced within 3 Calendar months, 7 V., c. 14, s. 31. *Prosecutions within 3 months*

The Justices, after signing the same, shall cause to be transmitted, convictions under 7 V., c. 14, by the Clerk of the Magistrates, to the Circuit Court (19 V., c 10. s. 17), and on any information for a subsequent offence the conviction, or an examined copy, certified by the Clerk of the Peace shall be sufficient evidence, and the conviction shall be presumed to be unappealed against until the contrary be shewn, 11 V., c. 14, s. 3. *Evidence of conviction*

Powers of Appeal, 7 V., c. 14, s. 32 ; 11 V., c. 14, s. 5. *Appeal*

4 U

Interpretation
Carriage, Town
"Carriage" shall mean any waggon, wain, sledge, truck, cart, dray carriage, chaise, or other wheel carriage, whether drawn by horses, cattle, &c., or without animals. "Towns" shall comprehend Cities and Villages, 7 V., c. 14, s. 34.

Traction Engines.

May be used upon any public road, highway, or thorourghfare, 26 V., S. 2, c. 19, s. 1.

May be used on roads

Regulations res-pecting their use The Main Road Commissioners may make rules and regulations with regard to their running, and for the protection of property adjacent to, and of passengers, and of the general traffic on such roads; and for the infraction of any such regulation, the owners of Traction Engines shall be liable to a penalty not exceeding £50, nor less than' 40s, to be recovered before 2 Justices under 13 V., c. 35, and any Acts amending same, 26 V., S. 2, c. 19, s. 2.

Exemption from Import Duties No duty shall be charged on any Traction Engines imported within 5 years, 26 V., S. 2, c. 19, s. 3.

Tradesmen, Breaches of Trust.

Not repaying ad-vances or neglect to perform contract If any Tradesman contract to perform any work for reward (whether the amount at the time be fixed or not), and in pursuance and on the faith of the contract receives by way of advance, or in anticipation of such reward any sum not exceeding in the whole £10, or if any moneys not exceeding in the whole £10 shall be paid to the Tradesman for the purchase of materials for the work, or for any other purpose in relation thereto, and shall with-out any lawful excuse neglect, or refuse to perform such contract within the time specified, or, in the absence of any agreement as to time, within such time as the Justices deem reasonable, and shall neglect or refuse when so required to repay to the person with whom he contracted or his agent law-fully authorized the moneys so received, he shall, on conviction before two Justices of the parish where the contract was made, or the Tradesman at the time of the complaint is resident, be adjudged to pay, over and above the amount so received, a penalty not exceeding £5, 24 V., c. 12, s. 3.

Not returning ma-terials delivered If any Tradesman having contracted as aforesaid, receives any mate-rials not exceeding in value £5, for the purpose of being wrought up or used in the work agreed to be performed, and without any lawful excuse neg-lects or refuses to perform his contract within such specified or reasona-ble time, and neglects or refuses, when required, to return to the person or his agent the materials or any part thereof so delivered, he shall on convic-tion pay, over and above the value of the materials, not exceeding £5, 24 V., c. 12, s. 4.

If any goods or chattels of any description or value whatever are de-livered to a Tradesman or other person to be repaired, fashioned, altered or cleansed for reward (whether the amount be specified or not) and he without lawful excuse, neglects or refuses to repair, &c., the same, and after the expiration of such specified or reasonable time neglects or refuses when so required to return the same, or any part thereof, such Tradesman or other person shall on conviction forfeit over and above the value of the goods, &c., detained, not exceeding £5, 24 V., c. 12, s. 5.

Selling, pawning or misappropriat-ing materials If it appear upon proof that the Tradesman or other person has sold, pawned, converted to his own use, or otherwise misappropriated any mate-rials, goods or chattels delivered to him for the purposes stated, the Justices may abstain from the infliction of any penalty, and in lieu thereof adjudge the offender to be imprisoned in any Jail, House of Correction, or Peniten-tiary with or without hard labor for not exceeding 90 days, 24 V., c. 12, s. 6.

Imprisonment If any fine or penalty, with costs, if adjudged, be not paid forthwith, or within such time, not exceeding 30 days, as the Justices shall appoint, they may adjudge the offender to be imprisoned with or without hard labor, for not exceeding 90 days, 24 V., c. 12, s. 7.

Compensation to party aggrieved The party aggrieved, shall, on conviction, be entitled to receive out of any fine or penalty imposed and paid, such sums as shall in the opinion of the Justices be adequate compensation for the injury he proves to have been sustained by him, 24 V., c. 12, s. 8.

Act not to prejudice or effect the right of lien of any Tradesman as at present existing, 24 V., c. 12, s. 9. **Right of lien**

All proceedings shall be in conformity with 13 V., c. 35, except so far as any thing in this Act may be repugnant thereto, 24 V., c. 12, s. 10. **Proceedings to be under 13 V., c. 35**

Any breach of contract, where the amount or of the contract or of the materials furnished, or money advanced exceeds the limit of £10, and is beyond the jurisdiction of the Justices, unless the informant and defendant consent to submit to such inferior jurisdiction, shall be prosecuted as a fraud, and be punishable on indictment by fine alone or by fine and imprisonment with or without hard labor for not exceeding one year, 24V., c. 12, s. 11. **Where amount exceeds £10**

"Tradesman" shall include handicraftsman, artificer, manufacturer, laundress, and workman, or person following any trade, business, or mystery whatever; "Materials" goods, wares, articles, chattels and things of any kind; "Work," any work in any trade, handicraft, manufactory or business, and any repairing, fashioning, altering or cleansing whatsoever, 24 V., c. 12, s. 12. **Interpretation— Tradesman, Materials, Work**

Tramroads.

When any person or persons shall be desirous, at their own expense, of making a Tramroad in any district, they may form themselves into a Company for the purpose, by the name of "The Proposed   Tramroad Company," and apply to the Main Road Commissioners by petition in writing, to be signed by them, their attorneys or agents, specifying the local situation, and length, and name of the proposed Tramroad, and the points from and to which it is proposed to lay down the same. and the estimated cost, the names of the plantations and lands from, through or along which it will pass, the roads along, over or across which it is intended to carry the same, and stating that it is proposed to lay down and complete it on the terms and conditions of this Act, 25 V., c. 44, s. 3 **Petition to form Company**

To be accompanied by a plan or section made by a Civil Engineer or sworn Surveyor, on a horizontal scale of 400 feet to one inch, and a vertical scale of 50 feet to an inch, and on no other scale, shewing the direction and gradients of the Tramroad, the plantations or lands through which it will pass, its relative bearing to any public road, and the points at which it is proposed it shall traverse or meet any such public road. Such petition and plan to be delivered to the Secretary of the Main Road Commissioners, and open to inspection at his office. The petitioners shall cause a copy of the petition to be published in the "Jamaica Gazette," 25 V., c. 44, s. 4. **Plan** / **Petition to be Gazetted**

Any person interested in any lands through or along which such Tramroad is intended to pass, and the Engineers or Commissioners of any roads, upon, along, over, under or across which it is intended to be carried, may within 3 calendar months from the first publication of the petition, leave with the Secretary, objections in writing to the granting of the petition, of which he is to give notice to the petitioners, 25 V., c. 44, s. 5. **Objections to petition—Notice**

All such petitions and objections thereto shall be signed by the petitioner, his Solicitor, or other agent; and notice of any matter shall be given to such Solicitor or agent, and be sufficient, 25 V., c. 44, s. 6.

Such petition and any objections thereto, shall be considered and heard by the Main Road Commissioners not earlier than 4 calendar months after the first publication of the petition, who may call for and require the production by the petitioners of any sections or plans of the proposed Tramroad or any other information, and may grant, reject or modify the petition, with such variations and conditions as they think proper as to the extent, line or direction, and as to both or either of the termini; but no such variation to be allowed, until notice has been given by the Company in the "Gazette," at least 4 calendar months before the order allowing same; and whenever any petition is granted with any variation, an amended plan of the Tramroad, in accordance therewith, shall be deposited with the Secretary, 25 V., c. 44, s. 7. **To be considered by Main Road Commissioners, variations to be Gazetted Amended plans**

Final order

On the granting of the Petition in whole or in part, the commissioners shall make a final order under their seal and signed by their secretary, and shall authorise the formation of the Tramroad, specifying the points from and to which, and the plantations and lands, or the names of their owners, through and, the roads upon, along, over, under and across which the Tramroad may be carried, and the times within which the same shall be commenced and completed, and may on cause shewn extend or vary the time for commencement and completion ; and a plan certified by the secretary shall be annexed to the final order, 25 V., c. 44, s. 8.

Incorporation of Company

On the final order being made and the construction approved of, the Company shall be a body corporate by the name of " The Tramroad Company," and shall have a common seal, power to contract, sue, and be sued, and purchase and hold lands for the use of the undertaking, and shall by virtue of such final order be authorised to construct and manage such Tramroad accordingly, and subject to the supervision or direction of the Main road Commissioners, who may direct an inspection, and report thereon at any time, to be made by the Chief Engineer of roads and bridges or any sworn surveyor, 25 V., c. 44, s. 9.

Powers to establish

Powers to establish the Company, 25 V., c. 4, s. 10-24.

Plans and estimates to be furnished by Chief or County Engineer His remuneration

The Main road Commissioners may direct the Chief Engineer of roads and bridges, or Engineer of the county in which any Tramroad is or is intended to be laid down, to prepare and furnish plans, specifications, and estimates, and give supervision and examination, and in all respects to render such services and perform such duties on and in respect of any such Tramroad or intended Tramroad as the Commissioners in their own judgment or on the application of any Tramroad Company think proper to direct, and he shall be paid such remuneration as the Governor and Executive Committee award to be paid, and included as a charge in the cost of constructing or maintaining such Tramway, 25 V., c. 44, s. 25.

Crossing, &c. roads

The Main road Commissioners may order and permit the Company to carry the Tramroad upon and along, or over, under, or across any main or other public road or highway upon such terms, &c., as they think proper, 25 V., c. 44, s. 26.

Powers of Company

The Company may, with or without workmen and other servants, enter upon and take possession of any lands not more than 100 yards from the line laid down in the plan annexed to the final order as the line of the proposed Tramroad, and take and set out for the Tramroad any part of the land not more than 20 feet in breadth, and cut drains and dig and carry away any gravel, stone, sand, or other materials out of the grounds or enclosures of any persons (not being the ground whereon any house stands, garden or yard planted, walk or avenue to any house, or any parcel of provision ground) wherein such drain may be necessary for keeping the road in good order or whereon any such materials are or may be found, and from time to time to carry away so much as the Company or any person employed by them shall judge requisite for making, draining or keeping in repair or amending such road or drain, paying such rates for such materials and for the damage done to the owners or occupiers of the grounds as the Main road Commissioners shall judge reasonable. Persons molesting, hindering, or obstructing the Company or the persons employed by them in cutting or covering any drains or in digging and carrying away any gravel, &c., shall forfeit not exceeding £10, 25 V., c. 44, s. 27.

Taking away materials

Persons without the consent of the Company taking away any materials purchased or gathered for the repair or use of any such road, bridge, or drain, or any materials out of any quarry or pit made, dug or opened for the purpose of getting materials for any such road, bridge or drain, without the permission of the Company, shall forfeit not exceeding £10. But not to prevent the person in possession of the land on which the quarry or pit is situate from digging and removing materials for his own use, 25 V., c. 44, s. 28.

Advances by Governor and Executive Committee for construction of 3-4ths of cost

If, after any final order has been made for the construction of any. Tramroad, the Company so desire, the Governor, in Executive Committee, shall, on the recommendation of the Main Road Commissioners, cause to be advanced, from time to time, any sums of money in and towards its construction, not exceeding ¾ths of the estimated costs of such construction, 25 V., c. 44, s. 29.

Before such advance is in any case made, the Company shall shew to the satisfaction of the Commissioners that the amount which has been expended in the necessary prosecution of the undertaking, is not less than one-fourth of the estimated cost, 25 V., c. 44, s. 30.

On proof of an expenditure of 1 4th by company

Where it is found the actual cost exceeds the estimated cost, further calls shall be made on the shareholders for the sum, or at least ¼th of the sum required to complete it, and the Governor in Executive Committee shall advance to the Company on application, and on due proof of the sums so raised having been expended in the necessary prosecution of the undertaking, a further sum not exceeding ⅜ths of the sum required for its completion, 25 V., c. 44, s. 31.

Further calls on Shareholders where the cost exceeds the estimates

No money shall be advanced for the purpose aforesaid unless and until an estimate of the cost and expense of making the Tramroad has been furnished and delivered to the Main Road Commissioners, and an estimate of the probable returns to be derived from the Tramroad, and from what sources, has also been stated and rendered to them, 25 V., c. 44, s. 32.

Estimates of costs and returns to be delivered to the Commissioners before advance is made

Such advances and interest at £6 per cent. per annum, and a sinking fund thereon, to redeem the principal, shall be the first lien on the Tramroad and the fines and tolls, 25 V., c. 44, s. 33.

Advances, interest and sinking fund to be the first lien

The Main Road Commissioners may appoint and remove a Commissioner or Director for the supervision and management of the Tramway, and the outlay and expenditure of the advances, 25 V., c. 44, s. 34.

Commissioner to supervise outlay and expenditure of advances

While any moneys are due for advances and interest, the Company must make quarterly accounts of the receipts and expenditure of the Tramroad to the Main Road Commissioners; to be audited yearly by the sole Commissioner of Audit; and a copy when audited shall be laid before the Main Road Commissioners, and published under their direction in the " Jamaica Gazette," 25 V., c. 44, s. 35.

Accounts of receipts and expenditure; audit to be Gazetted

The accounts of all moneys to be expended or received on account of any Tramway for tolls, rates, commutation, or otherwise on hand on account thereof, shall be audited by the Commissioner or Director appointed by the Main road Commissioners at the end of every month, and the balance paid to the Receiver-General to the credit of the Tramway; and the Governor in Executive Committee shall retain so much as, on the report of the Receiver General is necessary to defray the interest of the moneys advanced at £6 per cent. per annum, as shall become due each half-year, and such further sum by way of sinking fund as shall be fixed to pay the principal to be advanced in not less than 21 years, 25 V., c. 44, s. 36.

Monthly audit of receipts on hand; payment to the Receiver-General to the credit of the Tramway Return of half yearly interest and sinking fund

If after providing at the end of each year for interest and sinking fund, and for interest at £6 per cent. on the shares held by any Company, there is any surplus, the same to be applied to the redemption of debentures, 25 V., c. 44, s. 38.

Surplus after providing £6 per cent on Shares, to be applied to redemption of debentures

After any lands have been taken and set out for any Tramway, all bodies politic or corporate, tenants for life, or in tail, or for any other partial, or qualified estates, or interest on behalf of themselves, their heirs, executors and administrators, and also all persons seized and entitled in remainder, or reversion for their respective estates and interests, and for the husbands, guardians, trustees, committees or attorneys of such of the owners, or proprietors, or persons interested as shall be femes covertes, infants, lunatics, idiots, or absent from the island, or otherwise incapable of acting for themselves, and for all other persons seized, or possessed of, or interested in such lands, may contract for, sell and convey the lands to the Tramway Company, at the expense of the Company, as far as circumstances permit in the following form :—

Conveyances of land to the Company

I A. B. of   in consideration of the sum of   to me paid by the   Tramroad Company pursuant to an Act passed in the twenty-fifth year of the reign of Her Majesty Queen Victoria, entitled an Act to amend and in aid of the twenty-second Victoria, chapter ten, for the formation of Tramroads, do hereby grant and alien to the said Company and their successors and assigns all that   together with all ways, rights and appurtenances thereto belonging, and all such estate, right, title and interest in and to the same, and any part thereof as I am, or shall become seized, or possessed of, or as I am by the said Act authorized, or empowered to convey, to hold the premises to the said Company their

Form

successors and assigns for ever according to the true intent and meaning of the said Act. In witness, &c., 25 V., c. 44, s. 39.

Compensation for injuries

The Company may pay to the owner of any land so entered upon, or set out under this Act, and to any other person having any estate or interest, or charge upon such land or any part, such sum as the Main Road Commissioners deem reasonable by way of compensation for the injury done to any land so entered upon, or for the value of any land taken for the purposes of such Tramroad, 25 V., c. 44, s. 40

Or in lieu a right to the use of the Tramroad may be agreed for

The Company, in lieu of compensation in money, may grant to the owner of any plantation, or lands, who is willing to accept same, the right to use the Tramroad within the limits of such plantation or lands without any charge, or at a reduced charge upon such terms as may be agreed upon, 25 V., c. 44, s. 41

Proceedings to acquire lands, &c. where compensation is refused or not offered

If the compensation offered is refused by the owner, or any persons having any estate or interest in, or charge upon such lands, or if no compensation is offered to such owner or other person, the like proceedings shall be taken under this Act in respect to the formation of any Tramroad, or alteration, as are provided under 21 V., c. 32, or any subsequent Act now or to be in force in respect to the alteration of any Main Road, or the laying out of any new road; and such Main Road Act from s. 10, to s. 22, inclusive, (See that title,) and any such subsequent or other Act as far as applicable shall be incorporated with this ; and the County Engineer shall be the Engineer to act under this Act, 25 V., c. 44, s. 42.

Deposit of compensaton with Receiver-General

If any question arise as to the title of the owner or other person having estate or interest in, or charge upon any lands taken, the Company may deposit the compensation with the Receiver General to be placed to the credit of the parties interested (describing them as far as the Company can) subject to the control and disposition of the Supreme Court, 25 V., c. 44, s. 43.

Applications to the Supreme Court to order distribution

Upon the application of any party making claim to the money so deposited, or any portion, or the lands by any interest therein, the Supreme Court in a summary way, and after such notice as it deems fit, and to such persons as it directs, shall order distribution according to the respective estates, titles or interests of the claimants, and make such further order as it deems fit, 25 V., c. 44, s. 44.

Parties in possessl sion as owners, &c. to be deemed entitled until the contrary is shewn

If any question arise respecting the title, the parties in possession as owners, or in receipt of the rents, as being entitled at the time of the lands being taken, shall be deemed lawfully entitled until the contrary is shewn to the satisfaction of the Court, and they and all claimants under them, or consistently with their possession, entitled to the money deposited, which shall be paid and applied accordingly, 25 V., c. 44, s. 45.

Rates for carriage of passengers and goods

With consent of the Commissioners Table of Tolls

Commutation

The Company may carry and convey upon the Tramway or other road, all such passengers, produce and goods as shall be offered to them, and levy and take for their use and benefit for such carriage and conveyance, such fares and tolls as they from time to time fix, with the consent of the Main Road Commissioners, who shall have power to alter or amend same. A Table of the tolls shall be kept in some open and conspicuous place, on or near the Tramroad; and they may receive from year to year sums by way of commutation of the Tolls from any person using the Tramroad as agreed, 25 V., c. 44, s. 46.

Company's regulations

The Company may from time to time make regulations for the using and working the Tramroad, and loading or unloading carriages thereon, the carriage and payment of the fares of passengers, and the times of arrival and departure of carriages, and for the preventing or abatement, or removal of trespassers upon, or obstructions or injuries, or destructions to the Tramroad, 25 V., c. 44, s. 47.

Bye laws to enforce regulations To be approved by Commissioners Penalties for infringements Summary prevention

And for better enforcing such regulations, may from time to time make and alter bye-laws not repugnant to the laws or the provisions of this Act, and to be approved and confirmed by the Main Road Commissioners. Any person offending against any bye-law, shall forfeit not exceeding £10, to be imposed by the Company in any bye-law as a penalty, and if the infraction or non-observance of any such bye-law or other regulation be attended with danger or annoyance to the persons using the Tramroad, or hindrance to the Company in the lawful use, they may summarily interfere to obviate or remove the danger, annoyance or hindrance, without prejudice to any penalty incurred by the infraction of any such bye-law, 25 V., c. 44, s. 48.

Such bye-laws shall be painted on boards, or printed on paper, and pasted on boards, and hung up, or affixed and continued on the front or other conspicuous part of every station, so as to give public notice thereof, and be renewed when obliterated or destroyed ; and no penalty imposed by any bye-law shall be recoverable unless so kept published, 25 V., c. 44, s. 49.

Bye-laws to be exhibited

Such bye-laws when so approved and confirmed, published and affixed, shall be binding upon all parties, and sufficient to justify all persons acting under them, and in proof of their approval, confirmation and publication it shall be sufficient to prove that a printed paper or painted board containing a copy purporting to have been approved and confirmed by the Main Road Commissioners, was affixed and continued in the manner directed ; and if afterwards displaced or damaged, then that it was replaced as soon as conveniently might be. 25 V., c. 44, s. 50.

Proof of

All penalties imposed by the bye-laws, or this act, shall be payable to the Company and recoverable in a summary manner before two Justices, and may be enforced under 13 V. c. 35 or any other act now or in force relating to summary convictions or orders, and carried to the credit of the Tramroad, 25 V., c. 44. s. 51.

Payment and enforcement of penalties

If for 5 consecutive years after the completion of any Tramway the net profits shall not be found adequate to reimburse the interest upon any advances, and the Company shall for 6 months, after demand of payment, in writing and signed by the secretary of the Executive Committee, has been served at their office, fail to pay to the Receiver-General all arrears of interest, the Governor in Executive Committee may appoint a bailiff to take possession of the Tramway and all carts, trucks, carriages, engines, machinery, animals, buildings, lands and chattels belonging or appertaining thereto, and lease for the highest and best rent that can be obtained the right to use and work the same upon such terms as seem proper to the Governor in Executive Committee : provided it be conditioned that all fares and tolls be first applied towards the maintenance in proper order and repair as shall be approved of by them, and until payment of all arrears of interest and of the whole or such part as they shall direct of the principal money advanced, all the rights and privileges of the Company shall cease, and all the rents and profits applied in liquidation of the interest and principal money, 25 V., c. 44, s. 52.

Powers of Governor in Executive Committee to lease tramroad if the net proceeds are insufficient to reimburse the interest on advances and the company fail to pay the arrears
Conditions of lease

If at any time during the 21 years, the Company refund all advances and interest the powers of superintendence and control shall cease, 25 V., c. 44, s. 53.

Cesser of powers of superintendance on payment of advances

All materials imported for the construction, maintenance or use of any Tramroad shall be admitted free of all import duties or impost, and all instruments and documents under this act shall be exempted from Stamp duty, 25 V., c. 44, s. 54.

Materials to be imported free of import duty
Exemption from Stamp

" Owner" shall mean the person having the ostensible possession or enjoyment of the rents and profits of any land, 25 V., c. 44, s. 55.

Owner

22 V., c. 10, and this Act may be cited as " The Jamaica Tramroad Acts, 1858—1862."

Short Title

Tramroad, Kingston.

The Board of Works were authorized to construct and lay down a Tramroad from the Brickyard attached to the General Penitentiary, along Thames Street and Potters Row, to the New Lunatic Asylum, at the East end of that Street in Kingston, and employ so many of the convicts, officers and servants, in the Penitentiary, as the Governor shall permit, in assisting to lay it down, 27 V. S. 1, c. 12, s. 1.

From Penitentiary, Brickyard, to New, Lunatic Asylum

Upon, over, under or across the said streets, and the streets and lanes intersecting the same from the Brickyard on the West to the boundary line of the New Lunatic Asylum on the East, where the streets terminate, 27 V. S. 1. c. 12, s. 2.

Over Streets and Lanes

The Board of Works by the persons employed or directed by them may take and use the portion of Thames Street and Potters Row last mentioned for the purposes of the Tramroad, and survey and take levels thereof for the purpose of making such Tramway, and employ workmen and servants to superintend and perform such work ; but the Tramroad shall not occupy more than 4 feet in breadth of such streets, and shall if practicable be laid down on one side thereof, 27 V. S. 1, c. 12, s. 3.

May occupy 4 feet in breadth of streets, and to be laid on one side

For carriage of bricks, &c.
From 6 a.m, to 5 p.m.

The Tramroad when completed may be used for the carriage of bricks lime, clay, and other materials to and from the brickyard, and New Lunatic Asylum, but shall not be used before 6 a. m. or after 5 p.m·, 27 V. S. 1, c. 12, s. 4.

Motive power speed

The bricks to be used may be drawn by convicts, or by horses or mules. They shall not proceed at a greater speed than 4 miles per hour, or be used without a properly adjusted break attached to one of them, and the superintendence of a careful person, 27 V. S. 1, c. 12, s. 5.

Rails not to project more than 1 inch,

The iron rails shall not be permitted at any time to be more than 1 inch above the surface of such portions of the streets as are immediately in connection therewith, 27 V. S, 1, c. 12, s. 6.

Levelling bridge &c.

The Board of Works may cause the portion of the streets before mentioned to be leveled and repaired, and construct any bridge, culvert or drain necessary for the purposes of the Tramroad, 27 V. S· 1, c. 12. s. 7.

Board of works to keep the Tramroad and streets in repair

So long as the Tramroad remains on the streets, the Board of Works shall maintain the streets from the Western boundary of the new Lunatic Asylum lands, and the entire breadth, in thorough repair at all times, and should the Tramroad be taken up or renewed, they shall restore the streets and leave them in good order, 27 V., S. 1, c. 12, s. 8

Transient Traders.

Repeal of Acts

7 V., c. 46 and all Acts thereby repealed, relating to, repealed, 19 V., c. 26,

---

Treasonable and Seditious Meetings, Unlawful Oaths.

Exciting insurrection to compel the Governor, Council, and Assembly to change the Constitution or to intimidate them or moving strangers to invade the island, evidenced by writing, &c. or overt act.

Compassing, imagining, inventing, devising or intending to levy war, or excite insurrection against the Government of this Island, as by law established, in order by force or constraint to compel the Governor, Council or Assembly, or either of them to consent to alter or change the constitution as by law established, or to put any force or constraint upon or to intimidate or over awe them or either of them, or to move or stir any foreigner or stranger with force to invade this Island; and such compassing &c. expressing, uttering or declaring by publishing any printing or writing, or by any overt act or deed; treason: punishment death, 4 G. 4, c. 13, s. 1. See criminal punishment, 19 V.c. 22, s. 2.

Administering or taking oath or engagement to engage in any rebellious or seditious purposes or to be of any associations, &c., for such purpose or not to reveal any confederacy,, &c., or oath or engagement.

In any manner or form, administering or causing to be administered, or being aiding or assisting at, or present at and consenting to the administering or taking of any oath or engagement purporting or intended to bind the person taking the same to engage in any rebellious or seditious purpose, or to disturb the public peace, or to be of any association, society, or confederacy formed for any such purpose, or to obey the order or command of any committee or body of men not lawfully constituted, or of any leader or commander or other person not having authority by law for that purpose, or not to inform or give evidence against any associate, confederate or other person, or not to reveal or discover any unlawful combination, conspiracy or confederacy, or not to reveal or discover any illegal act done or to be done, or not to reveal or discover any illegal oath or engagement which may have been administered to or tendered to or taken by such or any person, or the import thereof : felony [punishment, Penal Servitude for 4 years, 21 V. c. 14, s. 1.] Taking any such oath or engagement, not being compelled thereto : Felony, [Penal Servitude for 4 years, 21 V. c. 14, s. 1.]

Compulsion not to excuse unless revealed to a Justice.

Compulsion shall not justify or excuse any person taking such oath &c., unless he shall within 4 days, if not prevented by actual force or sickness, and then within 4 days after the hindrance ceases, declare the same with the whole of what he knows touching the same, and the persons by whom and in whose presence, and when and where such oath or engagement was administered or taken, by information on oath before a Justice, 4 G. 4, c. 13, s. 3.

Accessories

Persons aiding and assisting at or present at, and consenting to the administering or taking of any such oath or engagement, and persons causing the same to be administered or taking though not present, shall be deemed and tried as principals, although the persons who actually administered the oath or engagement, have not been tried, 4 G. 4, c. 13, s. 4.

It shall not be necessary to set forth in the indictment for administering or causing &c., or taking any oath &c., or aiding &c., the words of such oath or engagement, but it shall be sufficient to set forth the purport or some material part thereof. Any engagement or obligation in the nature of an oath, shall be deemed one in whatever form or manner administered or taken, and whether actually administered by any person to another, or taken without administration by another, 4 G. 4, c. 13, s. 5.

Sufficient to state the purport of the oath, &c., in indictment
What t o b e deemed an oath

Every person indicted shall have delivered to him free of expense, a true copy of the whole indictment, 5 days at least before trial, 4 G. 4, c. 13, s. 7.

Copy of indictment to be delivered

When any Justice or Police Officer receives information on oath, or has reasonable cause to suspect that any meeting or assembly is held for the purpose of exciting or stirring up any person to commit any act of insurrection or insubordination, or to obtain, otherwise than by lawful means, any alteration or change in the Constitution or Government of this Island, as by law established, or to commit any of the crimes and offences mentioned in 4 G. 4, c. 13, or for any seditious purpose, he shall forthwith proceed to the meeting and require and take the assistance of any number of Constables or officers, within the place where the meeting is holden, or any other persons, within aid and assistance, and order and direct, in Her Majesty's name, all persons he finds there assembled peaceably to disperse, and if any persons, notwithstanding they have been ordered to disperse, continue together for half an hour, the persons so continuing, on proof that the meeting was of a seditous or treasonable nature, shall be guilty of felony, [4 years, Penal Servitude, 21 V. c. 14, s. 1,] 7 W. 4, c. 12 s. 1.

Dispersion o f meetings

Persons continuing together after order to disperse

If any person with force and arms, wilfully and knowingly oppose, obstruct or wilfully let, hinder, or hurt any such Justice or Police Officer, or any person acting in aid or assistance of any Justice or Police Officer, who shall attend, or be going to attend to disperse any such meeting, and if any person so being at any such meeting, shall with force and arms, wilfully &c., oppose, &c. any Justice, Police Officer or other persons acting in their aid or assistance in the arresting, apprehending or taking into custody or detaining in execution of any person offending against this act, or endeavouring so to do, he shall be guilty of felony, [4 years, Penal Servitude, 21 V. c. 11, s. 1.] 7 W. 4, c. 12, s. 2.

Obstru c t i n g, &c., Justice, police Officer or persons acting in their aid

If any person is sued for anything done in pursuance of this act, the action or prosecution shall be commenced within 6 months, and he may plead the general issue, and give the special matter in evidence, and if, on the trial, a verdict pass for the defendant, or the plaintiff is non-suited or discontinues, or judgment is given for the defendant upon demurrer or otherwise, he shall have full costs, and if it appear to the commissioners of public accounts, [Executive Committee] that the plaintiff has not the means of paying costs, sufficient to reimburse the defendant, they may order the Receiver-General to defray the costs, out of purse, 4 G. 4, c. 13, s. 11.

Actions for things done in pursuance of Act, commence m e n t of, General issue, costs

No writ shall be sued out against, nor any copy of any process, at the suit of a subject. served on any Justice, Police Officer, or any person acting in their aid or under their orders, until notice in writing of the intended writ or process has been delivered to him, or left at his usual place of abode, by the attorney or agent for the party who intends to sue, at least one calendar month before, in which shall be clearly and explicitly contained the cause of action the party has, or claims to have, on the back of which shall be endorsed the name and place of abode of such attorney or agent; and no plaintiff shall recover any verdict unless it is proved upon the trial, that such notice was given, but in default the defendant shalt recover a verdict and costs as aforesaid. And no evidence shall be permitted to be given by the plaintiff on the trial of any cause of action, except such as is contained in the notice, 4 G. 4, c. 13, s. 12.

Notice of action

To be proved on trial
And evidence confined to causes expressed therein

Trespasses.

Trespassing with fire arms, cutlasses or dogs, by entering upon the premises of any private residence, or upon any land without leave of the proprietor, tenant or occupier, for the purpose of hunting, shooting or otherwise, on conviction before two Justices, penalty not exceeding £5, (£3 sterling) with costs, or commitment, not exceeding 14 days, 3 V. c. 43, s. 13.

Trespassing. with firearms, &c

Trespassers resisting, &c., occupier or his servants

If any person being in the act of committing a trespass, resist by violence or assault any persons occupying private premises or land, or the servant or any person authorized by either of them, he shall, on conviction forfeit not exceeding £10 (£6 sterling) over and above any penalty he may have incurred by contravening this act, and in default of payment at such time as the Justices may seem fit, imprisonment with or without hard labour, not exceeding 20 days, 3 V. c. 43, s. 14.

Trespasses on private residence enclosed or cultivated land

Committing a trespass by entering, not having lawful business on the premises of any private residence, or upon land belonging to any proprietor or occupier, which is enclosed, or in any manner cultivated: Penalty on conviction before two Justices, not exceeding 40s and costs, in default of immediate payment, or within such time as they appoint to be recovered as after provided, 14 V. c. 46, s. 2.

Trespassing after notice to quit. Giving false account or continuing upon or returning to the land. Apprehension

The proprietor or occupier or his servants may require the person so trespassing, forthwith to quit the premises or land, and tell his christian and surname, and place of abode; and if he refuses to do so, or gives a false or illusory account of himself, or wilfully continues upon or returns to the premises or land or any part thereof, the proprietor or occupier and his servants may apprehend him and cause him forthwith to be taken before a Justice, who may bind him over to appear and be summarily tried before 2 Justices, and on conviction, he shall forfeit 40s and costs; in default of immediate or other payment to be recovered as after provided, 14 V. c. 46, s. 3.

Entering upon unenclosed land to damage, &c., any tree, cut wood, or steal any fruit or root, or to cut grass

Any person charged with entering on any unenclosed land for the purpose of trespassing to damage or destroy any tree, or to cut wood, or to steal and take and carry away any fruit or root used for food of man or beast, or to cut grass, on conviction before 2 Justices, shall forfeit not exceeding 20s and costs, to be recovered as after provided if default is made in immediate payment, or at such time, as they appoint, 14 V. c. 46, s. 4.

Trespassing with a gun or lighted torch during the night

If any person is found passing along any private road, through any lands or premises of any proprietor or occupier, with a gun or lighted torch, during the night, without the consent of the proprietor or occupant, he shall, on conviction before 2 Justices, forfeit not exceeding £3 and costs, in default of immediate or other payment, as they direct, to be recovered as after provided, 14 V. c. 46, s. 5.

Persons entering upon and occupying land without just claim or apparent title may be removed and punished

If any person enter upon and occupy any lands belonging to, or in the possession of any person, without the leave of the proprietor or person in lawful possession, any justice may by warrant, which he is required to grant upon oath, charging any such trespasser with having without any just claim or apparent title entered upon, and occupied or taken possession of any such lands, cause him to be brought before two justices, who on conviction may cause the trespasser to be removed from the possession, and inflict a penalty, not exceeding £3 and Cost, in default of immediate or other payment, as they direct, to be recovered as after mentioned, 14 V. c. 46, s. 6.

No person to be removed after one year's possession or having just claim or apparent title

No Justice shall convict any person or inflict a fine upon, or give any order to dispossess such occupier, if it appear that he has by himself, or those under whom he claims title, been in quiet possession of the land for one year, or has any just claim or apparent title to the lands, or the occupation thereof, 14 V., c. 46, s. 7.

Appeal

Power of Appeal 14 V. c. 46, s. 8.

Application of penalty

Penalties shall be paid to the Churchwardens to the use of the Poor 14 V. c. 46, s. 9.

Proceedings

On information on oath, a Justice may summon the party to appear before two Justices, who on failure to do so, may proceed exparte, or they or either of them, may issue a warrant for his apprehension; or the Justice before whom the complaint is made, may issue his warrant in the 1st instance, 14 V. c. 46, s. 10.

Enforcement of penalties

All penalties and costs shall be recovered by distress and sale, and in default of goods, the party may be committed for not exceeding 30 days, or until paid, 14 V. c. 46, s. 11.

Convictions, warrants and orders shall be according to Forms to 13 V. c. 35. No objection to be allowed for any defect in or want of form or substance, or for any variance between such information, summons or warrant, and the evidence at the hearing, 14 V. c. 46, s. 12.

The words "proprietor or occupier," shall include tenants, lessees, procuration attorneys and agents, 14 V. c. 46, s. 13.

"Proprietor or Occupant"

Troops.

Rations to Her Majesty's Troops stationed in this Island, 30 G. 3, c. 9, 2 G. 4, c. 21.

Rations

Provision for the carriage of army baggage on a march, and allowances to Officers as subsistence money, 45 G. 3, c. 10·

Carriage of baggage, &c,

Supply of water to Up Park Camp, 6 G. 4, c. 16.

Up Park Camp, water

Unlawfully having in possession, or keeping or knowingly detaining, buying, exchanging or receiving from any soldier, deserter, or other person, on any pretence, or soliciting or enticing any soldier, knowing him to be such, to sell any arms, ammunition, clothes or military furniture, or any provisions, or any sheet, or other articles used in Barracks, provided under Barrack regulations, or any Regimental necessaries, or any article of forage provided for any horses belonging to Her Majesty's service, or changing the article of forage, or changing the color of any clothes, on conviction before 2 Justices, forfeiture of not exceeding £5, (£3 sterling) and treble the value of the articles of which the offender becomes possessed, and in default, commitment to hard labor, not exceeding 2 calendar months, 1 V., c. 22, s. 2.

Purchasing Soldiers' necessaries. &c

On proof on oath of a reasonable cause to suspect that any pe   n has in his possession, or on his premises any property of the above description, on or with respect to which any such offence has been committed, a Justice may grant a warrant to seach for the property, as in the case of stolen goods, 1 V., c. 22, s. 3.

Search Warrant

The Officers of the ordinance empowered to make a carriage road from the Botanic Garden to the military station at Newcastle, 8 V. c. 43.

Road from Botanic Garden to New Castle

Trustees

When any person seized or possessed of any real or personal property, or any estate or interest therein by way of mortgage, or upon any description of Trust, is out of the jurisdiction, or not amenable to the process of the Court of Chancery, or not duly represented by Attorney, or it is unknown or uncertain whether they are living or dead, or they unlawfully refuse to convey or assure the property, estate or interest, the Court may appoint any other person to do so in his name, and as the Court may direct, 4 W. 4, c. 33, s. 1.

Court of Chancery may appoint trustees to act for others out of the jurisdiction not amenable to its process, unrepresented, unknown if living or dead, or refusing to convey

Every such direction or appointment shall be signified by an order made on the petition of any person beneficially entitled to the property, estate or interest sought to be conveyed or assured, and if such person be an infant, upon the petition of his guardians ; if idiots, lunatic ; or of unsound mind, of their Committees, 4 W. 4, c. 33, s. 2.

By order on petition

This Act shall extend to cases in which the person seized or possessed may have some beneficial interest, or any Trust property, or any estate or interest therein has devolved on any executor, or administrator in his representative capacity, 4 W, 4, c. 33, s. 3.

To apply where the party has a beneficial interest or the trust has devolved upon an executor &c.

The appointments may be applied for, and made whether a suit is pending or not ; if made in the course of any suit, no bill of revivor, supplemental bill, or other like proceeding shall be required to ground any application for such appointments or to revive or continue the suit afterwards, 4 W.4, c. 33, s. 4.

Appointment may be made whether a suit is pending or not ; no bill of revivor, &c

No application for any appointment shall be made, unless public notice has been given 4 weeks consecutively in the several County papers, of the intention to make such application, which shall state at what sitting of the Court the application is intended to be made, and shall also be published 6 calendar months at least before the sitting mentioned therein, 4 W. 4, c. 33, s. 5.

Notice of application to be advertised

The bona fide payments and the receipt of any person to whom any money is payable upon any express or implied Trust, or for any limited purpose, or of the survivors or survivor of two or more mortgagees or holders, or the executors or administrators of such survivor,

Bona fide payments to

or their or his assigns, shall effectually discharge the person pay-ing from seeing to the application, or being answerable for the mis-application thereof, unless the contrary is expressly declared by the in-strument creating the trust or security, 8 V., c. 19, s. 8.

May pay moneys into Receiver Gene ral's Office to at- tend orders of the Court of Chancery

All Trustees, executors, administrators or others having in their hands any moneys belonging to any Trust, or the major part of them, may on filing an affidavit, shortly describing the interest creating the Trust, ac-cording to the best of their knowledge and belief, pay the same into the Receiver-General's office to the account of the Receiver-General, in the matter of the particular Trust (describing the same by the names of the parties as accurately as may be, for the purpose of distinguishing it) in trust, to attend the orders of the Court of Chancery; and his receipt shall be a sufficient discharge for the money paid, 11 V., c. 13, s. 1.

Orders of the Court on petition for investment and payment of moneys and interest and ad- ministration of the trust

Such orders as shall seem fit shall be from time to time made by the Court of Chancery in respect of the Trust moneys so paid in and deposit-ed, and for the investment and payment thereof, or of any interest, and for the administration of any such Trusts generally, upon a petition to be pre-sented in a summary way to the Chancellor, without bill, by such party or parties as to the Court shall appear to be competent and necessary; and service of the petition shall be made upon such persons as the Court sees fit and directs; and every order shall have the same authority and effect, and shall be in force, and subject to rehearing and appeal, as if made in a suit regularly instituted; and if it appears that any such Trust Funds cannot be otherwise safely distributed, the Chancellor may direct any suit or suits to be instituted, 11 V., c, 13, s. 2.

Vice Chancellor may make rules

The Vice-Chancellor shall have power to make such orders as from time to time shall seem necessary for better carrying the provisions of this Act into effect, 11 V., c. 13, s. 4.

United Royal Agricultural Society and Society of Arts, Ma-nufactures and Commerce.

Incorporation.

Incorporation of "The Royal Agricultural Society of Jamaica," 7 V., c. 49.

Afterwards incorporated with "The Royal Society of Arts," under the title of "The United Royal Agricultural Society and Society of Arts, Manu factures and Commerce," 27 V., S. 1, c. 22.

United States Ships' Registers.

Deposit with con- sul or accredited agent

The Registers of all vessels belonging to the United States arriving in this Island, shall be deposited with the Consul or Agent resident here, and duly accredited. No such vessel shall be permitted to quit any port before all duties payable by the vessel or cargo, have been paid or secured. Act not to be in force unless there is an accredited Agent resident. At ports where there is no Vice-Consul or Agent, the Deputy Receiver-General shall continue to hold the Registers until one is appointed, and the appoint-ment notified to the Governor, 2 W. 4, c. 47.

United States Steam Mail Communication.

Agreement for conveyance of a mail between New York and Kingston once a month

The Governor may name any two members of the Executive Com-mittee, on behalf of the public, to enter into agreement from year to year, for not exceeding five years, or for a term not exceeding [five years, 27 V., S. 1, c. 1, s. 1]. with any company or individual in this Island or else-where, or the Agent of any company or individual out of this Island, for the conveyance of a Mail in a steam vessel to and from New York, in the United States and Kingston once in every month [27 V., s. 1, c. 1, s. 1], and within such number of days as shall be agreed upon. Every mail shall consist of as many bags or packages to be provided by the company or person with whom the contract is entered into as shall be requisite, suffi-cient to protect the contents from damage by water or other liquid sub-stances, and to contain letters, newspapers, periodicals, books, and such other articles as by the laws or regulations for the government of the Post Office Department in the United States, or this Island, may be sent through either of such Post Offices, and of such weight, as shall be fixed by the agreement; such Mails to be made up, or got ready at the Post Offices for transmission on the days agreed upon for the departure of the vessels to carry them, 23 V., c. 11, s. 2.

Upon proof to the Governor's satisfaction that the agreement has faithfully been carried out, he shall, by warrant to the Receiver-General, direct payment of the sum monthly, or quarterly, agreed to be paid by the public, not exceeding £500 a-month, or £6000 a-year, which the Receiver-General shall pay in full satisfaction for such service, 22 V., c. 48, s. 2. *Payment for service*

Whenever an agreement is entered into for a term of years, it may be terminated by the Executive Committee on behalf of the public, and the company or party, by giving 12 months' notice of the desire to do so, 22 V., c. 48, s. 3. *Termination of contract*

Upon any failure of the company to perform faithfully and punctually the service, or any portion, the Governor may withhold payment of the whole, or such part as he thinks proper, of the money payable for the month or other period for which the failure takes place, 22 V., c. 48, s. 4. *Withholding payment on failure to perform contract*

From the day of the commencement of the service under any agreement, to be notified by the Governor in the "Jamaica Gazette," the duties in the schedule shall be collected by the Customs Officers, under statute 16 and 17 V., c. 107, relating to the British Possessions, 22 V., c. 48, s 5. *Customs duties to be collected*

And to be by them paid weekly to the Receiver-General, to be by him applied as after directed, and to the purposes of this Act, and any residue to the public use, 22 V., c. 48, s. 6.

Out of which, £1800 a-year shall be reserved and applied to the purposes mentioned in the Kingston Town Dues' Act, 11 V., c. 10, the duties under which Act shall cease to be collected, 22 V., c. 48, s. 7 ; 23 V., c. 11, s. 3–5. *Application of duties £1800 per annum for Kingston Town dues*

The duties under 22 V., c. 48, shall continue to be levied and collected and paid over and applied, so long as any contract shall exist, or endure, for the conveyance of a Mail as aforesaid, and no longer, 27 V., S. 1, c. 1, s. 2. *The duties to be collected during the continuance of any contract only*

SCHEDULE to 22 V., c. 48.

	s.	d.
Ale, Beer, Cider, Perry, per ton	2	0
Alewives, per barrel	0	3
Asses, each	1	0
Bread and Biscuts, per cwt.	0	3
Barley, per bushel	0	1
Beef, per barrel	0	3
Butter, per firkin	0	2
Brandy, per gallon	0	2
Bricks, per 1000	0	8
Candles, per box	0	1
Corn, per bushel	0	1
Codfish, dried, per cwt.	0	2
Cheese, per cwt.	0	3
Coals, per ton	0	8
Cattle, neat, each	1	0
Flour, free of duty under this Act	0	0
Goats, each	0	6
Gin, per gallon	0	2
Horses, each	4	0
Hoops (wood), per one thousand	1	0
Herrings, per barrel	0	3
Lard, per firkin	0	2
Lumber, per one thousand feet	1	0
Meal, per barrel	0	3
Mackerel, per barrel	0	3
Mules, each	4	0
Oils, per gallon	0	3
Oats, per bushel	0	1
Pork, per barrel	0	3
Peas and Beans, per bushel	0	1
Rice, per cwt.	0	2
Salmon, per barrel	0	3
Smoked Salmon, per cwt	0	3

					s.	d.
Soap, per box	....	....	....	....	0	2
Salt, per cwt.	....	....	....	....	0	7
Sugar, refined, per one hundred pounds			....	....	0	4
Sheep, each	....	....	....	....	0	6
Swine, each	....	....	....	....	0	6
Staves, red and white, per one thousand				....	1	0
Shooks, hogsheads and puncheons, each				....	0	1
Shingles, per one thousand	....	....	....		0	·8
Tea, per one hundred pounds		....	....	....	4	0
Tobacco, per one hundred pounds		....	....	....	4	0
Tongues, wet, per barrel	....	....	....	....	0	3
„ dry, per cwt.	....	....	....		0	3
Wheat, per bushel	....	....	....	....	0	1
Wine in bulk and bottles, per tun		....	....	....	4	0
On all other goods, wares, and merchandise, and effects of every description, not previously enumerated, for every one hundred pounds value					2	0

Vaccination.

Vestry to appoint — The Vestry of each parish shall at the meeting for the election of parochial officers in each year, elect one or more p r duly qualified as after enacted to be Parish Vaccinators, 28 V., c. 41, sohs

One parish. or district vaccinators — They may either appoint one Vaccinator for the whole parish, or divide it into districts, and appoint one for each, 28 V., c. 41, s. 2.

Qualification — The qualification for office shall be either that the candidate is a registered Medical Practitioner, or that he presents a certificate, signed by 2 qualified Medical Practitioners, that he is competent to perform the operation, and to judge of and record its results, (Form A.) 28 V., c. 41, s. 3.

Vaccinators to appoint days and places, and perform vaccination personally — Each parish Vaccinator shall immediately after his appointment, arrange with such Ministers of Religion of all Denominations, and Schoolmasters or other persons appointed by the Vestry as are willing to act within the parish or district, and appoint certain days to attend at their Churches, Chapels, schools or stations, to vaccinate such persons or children as present themselves, or are brought to him for Vaccination, and shall perform the Vaccination himself, and not by deputy or agent, 28 V. c. 41, s. 4.

Returns of Stations &c. to Clerk of the Vestry — And as soon as he has determined on and arranged his stations, shall, make a return thereof, and of the names and occupations of the persons to countersign his returns, and the probable date of his attendances, to the Clerk of the Vestry, (Form B.) 28 V., c. 41, s. 5.

Clerk of the Vestry's return to the Executive Committee — The Clerk of the Vestry, as soon as possible after the election of Vaccinators, shall make a return to the Executive Committee, (Form C.) giving the name of each Vaccinator appointed, his qualification, and if not a regularly qualified Medical Practitioner, the names of the 2 Practitioners who signed the certificate, the district, names of the stations, and name and occupation of the person, and the station, to countersign his returns, 28 V., c. 41, s. 6.

Duties of vaccinator to make 3 visits to vaccinate, observe results and revaccinate when needed — Each Vaccinator shall visit each station on three separate occasions at intervals not shorter than 7 days, nor longer than 9 days.

On the first occasion, he shall vaccinate such persons or children as present themselves, or are brought to him to be vaccinated; on the second, he shall observe and record on a list to be kept in duplicate (Form D), the result of the vaccination performed the previous week, re-vaccinate such cases as failed on the previous occasion, and vaccinate any others who come, or are brought to him for the purpose; on the third, he shall observe and record the result of his vaccinations and re-vaccinations on the second visit, 28 V., c. 41, s. 7.

Return to be countersigned — The Minister, Schoolmaster or person appointed, shall countersign the record (Form D), 28 V., c. 41, s. 8.

Upon, or immediately after the successful Vaccination, the Vaccinator shall deliver to the person, or the father, mother, or the person who has the care, nurture or custody of the child, a certificate under his hand, (Form E) that he has been successfully vaccinated, and the number to be inserted in such certificate shall be the same under which he is registered in Form D, 28 V., c. 41, s, 9. Certificate of successful vaccination

Every Vaccinator shall make out in duplicate the returns, (Form D,) and forward them to the Clerk of the Vestry, 28 V., c. 41, s. 10. Return D. to be forwarded in duplicate to the Clerk of the Vestry

Who shall present them to the Vestry at their next Quarterly meeting, for examination and attestation by the Board, who shall do so, subject to any note or observation that appears to them to be proper, and which they shall subjoin to, or endorse upon the same in writing, by the Clerk, who shall note thereon the date of the meeting, and subscribe and state it to have been done by order of the Board, and shall forward one copy so examined and attested, with any such note or observation to the Secretary of the Executive Committee, with the application for the payment, 28 V., c. 41, s. 11. To be submitted to the Vestry A copy to be sent to Executive Committee with application for payment

And shall file and preserve the other copy so examined and attested, with any such note or observation by the Vestry thereon, as a parish record, 28 V., c. 41, s. 12. The other to be filed

In the event of any Practitioner or Vaccinator being of opinion, after 3 successive Vaccinations, that any person or child is insusceptible of the Vaccine disease, he shall deliver to such person, or the father, &c., of such child a certificate under his hand, (Form F.) that such person or child is insusceptible of Vaccine disease, 28 V., c. 41, s. 13. Certificate of insusceptibility

The salary or remuneration of the Vaccinator shall be at a rate not exceeding 1s. for each case certified to have been successful, to be paid on the Governor's warrant, to be issued after reception and examination by the Executive Committee of the attested Vaccination returns from the Vestry, 28 V., c. 41, s. 14. Remuneration

Each parish Vaccinator shall be supplied with Vaccine lymph in glass tubes, at the public expense, and the Chief Medical officer at the Public Hospital shall import, when necessary, from some Vaccine establishment in Great Britain, a sufficient quantity of the lymph in tubes, along with a supply of spare tubes for preserving the lymph, 28 V., c. 41, s. 15. Supply of lymph

He shall not register the name of any person who has been already vaccinated, or who bears the mark of previous successful Vaccination, 28 V., c. 41, s. 16. Persons already vaccinated not to be registered

The Executive Committee shall cause to be provided all such books, certificates, schedules, notices, regulations, and other forms as they deem requisite, and transmit them when necessary to the Clerk of the Vestry for delivery to the Vaccinators, 28 V., c. 41, s. 17. Forms to be provided by the Executive Committee

On the location on any estate, plantation, or settlement of any liberated Africans, or East Indian, Chinese or other Coolie Immigrants, the person in charge shall send information to the Vaccinator of the parish or district, who shall, not exceeding three months after receipt of such information, visit and vaccinate such of the Africans, or Coolies and children, as he considers in a fit state to be successfully vaccinated; and shall record the results, and issue certificates in cases which prove successful, and forward in duplicate the returns to the Clerk of the Vestry, which shall be brought before the Vestry, and be examined and attested, subject to any note or observation by the board, and one copy forwarded to the Executive Committee, and the other preserved as a parish record as other Vaccination returns, 28 V., c. 41, s. 18. Vaccination of liberated Africans, Chinese, and Coolies

The person in charge may, if he prefers it, have the operation performed by any qualified Medical Practitioner, under contract to attend the immigrants of the estate, but the Medical Practitioner shall not receive remuneration from any Government fund provided for Vaccination purposes, 28 V., c. 41, s. 19. Or they may be vaccinated by the Medical attendant on the immigrants upon the estate

Each Sub-Agent of Immigration, at his periodical visits, shall ascertain that the requirements have been complied with. If any person in charge has neglected or refused, the Sub-Agent shall procure it to be forthwith carried out, by requiring and authorizing the Vaccinator of the parish or district, as occasion may require, at any hour between 8, a.m. and 4, p.m., to enter on any such estate and vaccinate the immigrants and their children, or such as are fit for Vaccination, giving seven days' notice to the person in charge, of Sub-agents to ascertain that the act has been complied with. If not to require the vaccinators to do so

At the expence of the person in charge.
Enforcement

his intention ; and for such services the Vaccinator shall, on completion thereof, be paid by the person in charge 1s. for every immigrant or child successfully vaccinated according to the return. In case of any default the amount shall be recovered by warrant (Form L), to be issued by the Agent-General, 28 V., c. 41, s. 20.

Obstructing vaccination

Any person preventing any such authorized Vaccinator, from entering on any such estate, or preventing or obstructing him from carrying out the Act, shall, on conviction before two Justices, pay a fine not exceeding £5, 28 V., c. 41, s. 21.

Enforcement of vaccination

Right to vaccination on paying 1s

Costs where vaccinated before trial

Parents or guardians of any child or family of children under 12, shall cause them, if not previously vaccinated, to be vaccinated within 12 months after the passing of this Act, (21st February, 1865; came into operation 1st May), by the Medical or other officer, or person appointed and paid by the public ; penalty not exceeding 20s., or in default of payment, imprisonment not exceeding 30 days. Any person above 12, on pa ing not exceeding 1s. to the Medical officer or other person, shall be entitled to be vaccinated. No conviction shall take place where it is proved that the parents or guardians have taken the child or children to be vaccinated previous to the day of trial ; but they shall be liable to pay the costs, 28 V., c. 41, s. 22.

Failing to register a successful, or registering an unsuccessful case

Every vaccinator who fails to register any person or child successfully vaccinated by him, or who registers the Vaccination of any person or child not successfuly vaccinated, shall forfeit not exceeding 20s. for each such case, 28 V., c. 41, s. 23.

Forging, &c. certificate

Forging or counterfeiting any certificate, or knowingly uttering or using any forged or counterfeited certificate, a misdemeanor, and to be punished accordingly, 28 V., c. 41, s. 24.

Receiving unauthorized remuneration

Any pa Vaccinator who demands or receives any remuneration, fee or reward from any person, or in any manner otherwise than is provided for any services rendered in that capacity, shall pay a penalty not exceeding 20s., 28 V., c. 41, s. 25.

Personating parish vaccinator, &c

Any person who pretends to be, or acts as a parish Vaccinator, without having been duly appointed, or pretending to be such, demands or receives any remuneration from, or reward for vaccinating any person, or falsely and deceitfully personates any parish Vaccinator, with intent to induce any person to be vaccinated by him, or fraudulently to obtain any remuneration, fee, or reward, or to defraud any Board of Vestry, Clerk of the Vestry, or other officer or person whomsoever, shall pay a penalty not exceeding £5, 28 V., c. 41, s. 26.

Vaccination out of district not to be paid from funds

No parish Vaccinator shall be paid from the funds to be appropriated for the Vaccination of any person or child beyond the limits of his district, 28 V., c. 41, s. 27.

Inoculation—penalty

Producing, or attempting to produce in any person, by inoculation with variolus matter, or by wilful exposure to variolus matter, or to any article, matter or thing impregnated with variolus matter, or wilfully by any other means producing the disease of Small-pox within this Island. Penalty not ceeding £5, 28 V., c. 41, s. 28.

No pupil to be admitted into a free School without a certificate

Removal of such as may gain admission

No person or child shall be admitted as a pupil into Smith's Charity School, St. Jago de la Vega, Jamaica, Manning's, Wolmer's, Rusea's Free Schools, Manchester District Schools, Vere District School, and Munro and Dickenson's School without producing a certificate according to one or other of the Forms. Should any child or person have gained admission into any such school without complying with this Act, he shall cease to be received as a pupil; nor shall any one so disqualified be again admitted as a pupil until after the lapse of six months, and on having complied with the Act, 28 V., c, 41, s. 29.

Registers to be kept by masters

The masters of the above schools shall ascertain that the requirements are complied with, and enter on a register (Form I) the particulars of the certificate presented by each pupil, and the Government Inspector of Schools, in addition to all other duties, shall examine such register and satisfy himself it is duly kept, and the entries are according to fact, 23 V., c. 41, s. 30.

Inspector of Schools to satisfy himself they are kept

And shall report the result of his inspection to the Governor, and where the requirements are not properly complied with, shall make a special report thereon, 28 V., c. 41, s. 31.

If it appear that any master of any such school has wilfully or knowing-ly permitted any pupil to enter his school without having fully complied with the requirements, he shall forfeit and pay such sum, to be deducted from his salary, as the Governor may think fit, 28 V., c. 41, s. 32. Masters knowing-ly receiving pupils contrary to act

Act not to prevent any qualified Medical Practitioner, whether or not appointed as a parish vaccinator, or from performing Vaccination in any part of the Island, or issuing the certificate E, so long as he does so either gratuitous-ly or by private contract, but none except a regularly appointed parish vacci-nator shall be entitled to remuneration from the funds to be appropriated by the Government for the purpose of this Act, 28 V., c. 41, s. 33, Vaccination by Qualified Practition-ers

Qualified Medical Practitioners shall, on application to the Clerk of the Vestry, be supplied with such forms as they require, 28 V., c. 41, s. 34. Medical practition-ers to be supplied with forms

The forms E and F may be signed by any qualified Medical Practitioner or parish Vaccinator, but the forms G and H shall be valid only when sign-ed by a qualified Practitioner, 28 V., c. 41, s. 35. Persons to sign Forms, E. F. G. H.

Penalties shall be recovered according to any Act at the time in force relating to summary convictions, and appropriated to the credit of " the Fur-ther Immigration Fund, 1861," 28 V., c. 41, s. 36. Recovery and ap-propriation of pen-alties

The Justices, or any 2, at their first Petty Session Court in April, July, and October in the first year after the passing of this Act, or at any Pet-ty Session Court at any other time, shall direct the Sergeant or some police-man in any city, town, village or parish to give public notice (Form K) by printed bills, posted on the entrance doors of the Court-house, Churches, Chapels, School-houses, market houses and Police Stations, and in such other manner as they think fit, requiring all parents and guardians to cause their children to be vaccinated : such forms to be furnished by the Justices and Vestries, 28 V., c. 41, s. 37. Public notices calling upon pa-rents and guardi-ans to have children vaccinated

All returns by Vaccinators shall be declared to before a Justice; and a false statement shall subject the party to the penalties of perjury, 28. V., c., 41, s. 38. Returns to be de-clared to
False statements

The Vaccination Act, 1865, 28, V., c. 41, s. 39. Short Title

FORMS.

Certificate of vac-cinators competen-cy, A, s. 3

JAMAICA, SS.
Parish of
We the undersigned regularly registered Medical Practitioners do here-by certify that we consider   of the parish of   is competent to perform the operation of Vaccination, to recognize and judge of its results, and to record the same, and that he has suffi-cient acquaintance with the general forms of [the] disease to be able to select proper subjects both for obtaining lymph and for undergoing Vaccination.
Dated this   day of   18

JAMAICA, SS.
Parish of
District of
} Return of Stations at which
   Parish Vaccinator has appointed
   to hold Vaccinations. Return of Sta-tions, B, s. 5.

No. of Stations.	Names of Sta-tions.	Name and Occupation of Person who will Countersign Returns.	Probable Dates of Visiting Stations.

[Return of Vaccinators, C. 36.]

Jamaica, ss.—Parish of

Return of Vaccinators appointed, their respective Districts, and the Vaccination Stations in each District.

Name of each Vaccinator appointed.	Qualification.	If not Medical Practitioner, names of those who signed his Certificate.	Name of District to which each has been appointed.	Names of Stations appointed by each Vaccinator for meeting the people, to be given opposite the respective District.	Name and Occupation of Person who is to sign the Returns at each Station.	Observations.

[Vaccination Return, D., s. 7-10, 18.]

Jamaica, ss.—Vaccination Return for the Parish of ———————— ————— Station.

N.B. It is particularly requested that successful cases be marked simply with a large "S." Unsuccessful with a large "U," under the head "Results."

*No.	Name.	Vaccinated on.	Seen on.	Result.	Re-Vaccinated on.	Seen on.	Result.	Observations.
								Synopsis of this Sheet.
								Successful No.
								Unsuccessful No.
								Parish Vaccinator.

Certified correct, to the best of my judgment and belief.

Curate of

Master of   School,

* The number herein entered must correspond with those of certificates issued, according to Form E.

Certificate of suc-
cessful vaccination,
E, s. 9, 33, 35

JAMAICA, ss.

   Parish of

*No.

   I certiy that on the   day of   186
   I vaccinated   of the parish of   and that I again
   saw the said   on the   day of
   and that the Vaccination was successful.

A. B. Qualified Practioner, or C. D.
Vaccinator appointed by Vestry.

   *N.B. The No. in this certificate must correspond with the number on
the return, Form D.

————

JAMAICA, ss.

Certificate of in-
susceptibility, F s.
13, 35

   Parish of

   I, the undersigned, hereby certifiy, that I am of opinion that
   of the parish of   is insusceptible of the Vaccine
   disease.
      Dated this   day of   186

(State qualification)

————

JAMAICA, ss.

Certificate of
marks of successful
vaccination, G, s.
35

   Parish of

   I certify that   of the parish of   bears
   marks of a successful Vaccination.
      Dated this   day of   186

(State Medical qualification.)

   N.B. This form can be signed only by a regularly qualified Medical
Practitioner.

————

JAMAICA, ss.

Certificate of hav-
ing had small pox,
H, s. 35

   Parish of

   I certify, that I have carefully exaimined   of
   the parish of   and I am satisfied, and hereby certify
   accordingly, that the   has passed through a regular
   attack of Small-pox.
      Dated this   day of   186

(State Medical qualification.)

   N.B. This form can be signed only by a regular qualified Medical Practioner.

[School Register Return, I., s. 30.]

Register of Vaccination Certificates kept at _____ School.

Name of Bearer.	Date of Admission.	Form of Certificate.	Date of Certificate.	Certificate Signed by	Qualification of Signer of Certificate.	Observations.

NOTICE.

To all parents and guardians.

You are hereby required, immediately after this notice, to cause any child or children under your protection or charge, to be vaccinated according to the provisions of the "Vaccination Act, one thousand eight hundred and sixty-five ;" and, in default of your so doing, you will be subjected to a penalty of twenty shillings, or imprisonment for thirty days, for each offence.

Dated this   day of   186

FORM OF WARRANT.

Warrant to levy
vaccinator's ac-
count for Immi-
grants, L, s. 20

Whereas default hath been made in payment of the sum of due for Vaccination of immigrants located on estate, in the parish of   according the provisions of " The Vaccination Act, 1865 :"

These are therefore to command you to levy the said sum of by distress of any goods or chattels to be found upon the said estate, in the said parish, upon which a landlord might distrain for rent in arrear ; and if, within fourteen days next after such distress by you taken, with or without previous apprisement, the said sum, and the charges of distraining and keeping the same, shall not be paid according to the scale fixed by the Act of the first Victoria, chapter twenty-five, then that you do sell the said goods and chattels, so by you distrained, and, out of the money arising by such sale, that you do pay the said sum of   to   parish vaccinator of the said parish, under the provisions of "The Vaccination Act, 1865," returning the overplus, if any, on demand, to the proprietor, overseer or manager of the said estate, after retaining the charges on the scale aforesaid of distraining and keeping such distress.

Given under my hand, this   day of   18

Agent General of Immigration.

To any policeman of the parish of

Variances between Pleadings and Evidence.

Amendment of
pleadings in civil
cases of indictment
for misdemeanor
where there is a
variance between
the written or print-
ed matter in evi-
dence, and the reci-
tal in the pleadings.
Costs

The Supreme and Assize Courts may, if they see fit, cause the declaration, information, indictment, and other pleadings on which any trial may be pending for a civil action, or for any misdemeanor where any Variance appears between any matter, in writing, or print produced in evidence, and the recital or setting forth thereof upon the declaration, &c. whereon the trial is pending, to be forthwith amended in such particulars by an officer of the court, on payment of such costs, if any, as the court thinks reasonable ; and thereupon the trial shall proceed as if no Variance had appeared ; and the order for amendment shall be endorsed on such declaration, &c., and recorded with the judgment in the office of the Clerk of the Court or Crown as the case may be, 2 W. 4, c. 10.

For any offence
whatever
See Indictment,
16 V., c. 15, s. 1-3

Any Court of Oyer and Terminer and General Gaol Delivery may, if it sees fit, cause the indictment or information for any offence whatever, when any Variance appears between any matter, in writing, or print produced in evidence, and the recital or setting forth in the indictment, &c., to be forthwith amended in such particulars by an officer ; and after such amendment, the trial shall proceed in the same manner, in all respects, both with regard to the liability of witnesses to be indicted for perjury, or otherwise, as if no such Variance had appeared, 13 V., c. 7, s. 4.

Amendments
generally in civil
actions quo war-
ranto informations
or mandamus
where they are not
material to the me-
rits or cannot pre-
judice the action or
defence

Any Court of Record holding plea in civil actions, and any Judge sitting in a Court of Assize, if they see fit, may cause the record, writ, or document, on which any trial may be pending in any civil action, or in any information in the nature of a Quo Warranto, or proceedings on a Mandamus when any Variance appears upon the proof, and the recital or setting forth on the record, writ or judgment of any contract, name or other matter, or circumstance, in any particular in the judgment of the Court or Judge, not material to the merits of the case, and by which the opposite party cannot have been prejudiced in the conduct of his action, prosecution or defence, to be forthwith amended by an officer of the Court, or otherwise, both in the part of the pleadings where the Variance occurs, and in every other part it may become necessary to amend, on such terms as to payment of costs or postponing the trial to be had before the same or another jury, or both payment of costs and postponement, as such Court or Judge thinks reasonable. In case the Variance is in some particulars in the judgment of the Court or Judge not material to the merits, but that the party may have been prejudiced in the conduct of his action, prosecution or defence, they may cause it to be amended upon payment of costs, and withdrawing the record or postponing the trial as they think reasonable ; and after the amendment, the trial shall proceed, if to be proceeded with, in the same manner, both with respect to the liability of witnesses to be indicted for perjury and otherwise, as if no such Variance had appeared, and the order for amendment shall be endorsed upon the record, writ or document. Any party who is dissatisfied with the decision of such Judge, sitting in a Court of Assize, respecting the allowance of any such amendment, may apply to the Supreme Court for a new trial upon that ground, and if they think the amendment improper, a new trial shall be granted upon such terms as the Court thinks fit, or may make such other order as to them seems meet, 8 V., c. 28, s. 11.

Costs postponing trial, withdrawing record

Order to be endorsed on document Review by Supreme Court

The Court or Judge, instead of causing the record or document to be amended, may direct the jury to find the facts according to the evidence, and thereupon the finding shall be stated on the record or document; and notwithstanding the finding on the issue joined, the Supreme Court shall, if they think the Variance immaterial to the merits, and the mis-statement such as could not have prejudiced the opposite party in the conduct of the action or defence, give judgment according to the very right and justice of the case, 8 V., c. 28, s. 12.

Instead of amendment the facts may be found specially for Judgment of the Supreme Court

Venditioni Exponas, Writ of.

Immediately upon Judgment being entered up in the Supreme Court, the party in whose favor Judgment has passed, may issue his writ thereupon to the Provost Marshal, who shall immediately proceed to execute the same according to its exigency ; and upon the sale of any levy made thereunder, pay over the proceeds, deducting his legal commission to the party issuing it. Henceforth, the writ of execution upon a Judgment as heretofore used, shall no longer be of any force or effect ; and all proceedings shall be of the same effect, though no such writ has been issued, as if it had been so issued, proceeded on, and returned according to the present practice of the Provost-Marshal's office, 19 V., c. 10, s. 39.

May issue immediately after judgment

Levy thereunder to be paid to the party issuing Writ of Execution abolished

The Writ shall henceforth be in the following terms or effect, and be endorsed with the direction to levy, and the further costs of delay of execution according to the present practice :

Form of writ Endorsement

The Queen to the Provost Marshal greeting: We command thee that of the goods and chattels, real and personal of A. B., thou shalt levy and cause to be levied (for debt or damages) as also costs of suit which C. D. hath recovered against him, and the amount thereof thou immediately render to the said C. D., but if thou canst not find sufficient goods or chattels by which the whole amount aforesaid may be satisfied, that then thou take the body of the said A. B., and him safely keep, so that thou have his body before us at our next Court, to satisfy the said C. D. of the said amount recovered as aforesaid, or so much thereof as by thee cannot be levied, and have thou then and there this Writ. Witness, &c., 19 V., c. 10, s. 40.

Together with the debt, damages and costs, or other moneys directed to be levied under any Writ of execution, the Provost Marshal, shall be empowered by virtue of the Writ to levy from the defendant, the poundage fees now by law allowed to him on the execution of Writs of Venditioni, 19 V., c. 10, s. 41.

Poundage Fees

All Writs of Venditioni shall be marked and endorsed by the plaintiff, or his assignee or attorney, whose power is recorded in the Secretary's Office, or the executor, administrator or other legal representative of the plain

Endorsement and signature of levy

tiff, or assignee, or the Attorney-at-Law, by warrant or order in writing of the parties. If marked or endorsed with an intent to distress the defendant for more than is really due, the offender shall forfeit £100 (£60 sterling) and if an Attorney-at-Law, shall, besides the penalty, be further liable to be discharged from practising in any Court, if the Judges before whom he is convicted, from the circumstances, think proper, 24 G. 2, c. 16, s. 1.

Not to be lodged or executed without endorsement

The Provost Marshal shall not execute, or suffer to be lodged in his office any such Writ, unless first marked and endorsed. Penalty, £100, (£60 sterling, one moiety of the penalties to be to the party injured, to be recovered by action of debt, &c., 24 G. 2, c. 16, s. 2.

When property bound by writ

Time of receipt to be endorsed on writ

No Writ of Venditioni shall bind the property of the goods of the debtor against whom it is sued forth, except from the time it was delivered to the officer to whom it is directed, with the full and faithful intent on the part of the person causing it to be issued, that it should be faithfully executed, and the exigency complied with; and for the better manifestation of the time, the officer to whom it is directed shall, upon receipt thereof, without fee, endorse the hour, day, month and year when he first received it, 19 V., c. 10, s. 42.

Stay of execution, &c.

If the plaintiff, assignee or other person legally holding any Judgment on which a writ of Venditioni has been lodged, gives notice in writing to the Provost Marshal and to his deputy, to stay the execution for the ensuing Court, or for any other period, or that the same be returned tarde or nulla bona, the Provost Marshal after receiving such notice, shall not issue the writ from his office, nor include the same in any precept to his deputy, nor shall any deputy after receiving such notice, execute the same, or pretend to exact or levy fees by virtue of such writ. Penalty, £300, besides being liable to an action for damages by the person aggrieved by such illegal execution or exaction. If the plaintiff &c. lodges

Special precept

a writ of Venditioni, and desires to take out a special precept thereon, it shall forthwith be granted by the Provost Marshal, on payment of 7s. 6d therefor. And the deputy to whom it is delivered shall, on receiving the writ and precept, proceed to execute it in the manner directed by the plaintiff, &c., or his Attorney-at-Law. And for want of such direction, he shall use his utmost diligence to execute the writ. And when a special precept is taken out, the Provost Marshal shall not include the writ in any other, nor shall he or any deputy pretend to levy or exact fees on such writ, unless a legal levy is made. Penalty, £300, besides being liable to

To be directed to a lawful deputy

an action for damages by the person aggrieved by such illegal execution. Every special precept shall be directed to a lawful deputy, 19 V., c. 31, s. 6.

Moneys, notes, bills, &c. to be taken

By virtue of any such writ, the Provost Marshal or other officer having the exution thereof, may and shall seize and take any money, Receiver-General's cheques or Bank notes, and any other Cheques, Bills of Exchange, Promissory Notes, Bonds, Specialties or other securities for

Moneys, bank notes, &c. to be paid the party suing out the writ

money belonging to the person against whom the writ issued, and shall pay or deliver to the Party suing out such execution any money, Receiver-General's Cheques or Bank Notes so seized, or a sufficient part in satisfaction, and proceed, after due notice, to put up to public sale, and sell all such other Cheques, Bills of Exchange, Promissory Notes, Bonds, Specialties, or other securities for money, and pay over to the party issuing

Bills of Exchange &c. to be sold and proceeds paid over

the writ, the proceeds or a sufficient part to discharge the amount; and if after satisfaction, with the usual poundage and expenses, any surplus remains in the Provost Marshal's or other officer's hands, it shall be paid

Assignment, endorsement

to the party against whom the writ issues. If any specialty or security requires any assignment or endorsement, for the purpose of vesting it in a purchaser, the officer shall assign or endorse it, without rendering himself personally liable; and it shall be as valid as if it had been made by the party previously entitled, 8 V., c. 48, s. 9.

Plantation horses or utensils not to be taken where other goods are offered

No horses or utensils belonging to a plantation, brick, or pot-work, shall be taken in execution, where the party offers goods for satisfaction of the debt and costs, 33 C., 2, c. 23, s. 10.

After the defendant's body is taken his effects may be levied on under another execution

Where the defendant's body is taken in execution, if any effects afterwards appear, the plaintiff may take out another execution, and levy the same on the effects for satisfaction of the debt, 33 C., 2, c. 23, s. 16.

No notice against warranting title to be inserted in advertisements for sale

The Provost-Marshal or his Deputies shall not insert a nota bene against his warranting the title, or anything to that affect in his advertisements for the sale of cattle and other things, 8 G., 2, c. 5, s. 4.

Upon writs, no more effects of the defendant shall be sold than will really and bona fide satisfy the respective debts, costs and fees due on the writs; and if it be found necessary to sell effects exceeding the amount of the debt and costs, the Provost-Marshal or his deputy shall return the overplus to the owner within 10 days after the sale, if demanded, 8 G. 2, c. 5, s. 7.

No more effects to be sold than will satisfy writ, or where necessary overplus to be returned

On all returns to executions, the particulars on which any levy is made, shall be described, 8 G. 2, c. 5, s. 8.

Particulars of levy to be described in returns

Whenever two or more Venditionis are lodged against the principal and his sureties, or any others for one and the same debt, no more poundage fees shall be demanded or received than for the real debt and costs due, 8 G. 2, c. 5, s. 10.

Several writs for one debt

All Marshals shall, upon all seizures, give the defendants, or any person demanding the same on account of any defendant, a receipt, containing a particular, full and exact account of the goods, chattels, or other things they seize or take into their custody under any Venditioni or other writ or process, 8 G. 2, c. 5, s. 14.

Receipts with full particulars of seizures to be given if demanded

All levies made by Deputy-Marshals under writs of Venditioni, shall be sold within 21 days after they have been taken under such writs, notice of the time and place of sale being first given for 2 consecutive weeks in such newspaper as the notices of Insolvent Debtors may be by law required to be inserted, 19 V., c. 31, s. 7.

Levies to be sold within 21 days after being advertised 2 consecutive weeks

Every Deputy-Marshal shall return and pay to the Provost-Marshal, the net proceeds of the sales of all levies made by him within 10 days after the sale, and deliver therewith the accounts sales of such levy, 19 V., c. 31, s 8.

Net proceeds and account sales to be returned to the Provost Marshals within 10 days after sale

Whether the proceeds of any levy under any writ have been paid over or not, or whether the writ has been executed or not, or only partly executed, the Provost Marshal shall return the writ on or before the first day of the then next meeting of the Court, and in such return, shall specify how and in what manner every levy that has been made upon every such writ that has come to his hands has been disposed of; and in case no levy, or an insufficient levy has been made, he shall state the reason, 19 V., c. 10, s. 39.

Returns of writs to be made on or before the first day of the next Court by the Provost Marshal

Every Deputy Marshal shall, on the first day of every Supreme Court make his returns to the Provost Marshal of all Writs of Venditioni returnable at such Court, whereon precepts have come to his hands; and when a writ has not been fully executed, shall, with his return of "nulla bona," or of any levy not to the full amount, assign, in writing, and upon oath, the particular causes of such non-execution or short execution; and where a levy is returned in custody shall, with the return, set forth, in writing and upon oath, when the precept came to his hands, when the levy was made, and the particular causes why it has not been sold. Penalty for every default: fine not exceeding £50 (£30 stg.), unless cause is shewn to the Court, in writing upon oath, and also, if required by the parties interested, upon examination on oath, viva voce in open Court, or upon interrogatories to be exhibited, why such return, or such assignation of the causes of non-execution or short execution, or such declaration touching a levy returned in custody, was not made. And in every case of default, without good cause shewn, the Deputy Marshal shall, under an order of Court, which in every such case shall be made, pay the costs of the party complaining, to be taxed, 43 G, 3, c 20, s. 3.

Deputy Marshals' returns to the Provost Marshal of writs

See for additional particulars, 19 V., c. 31, s. 10

Examination on oath in Court or upon interrogatories

The Provost Marshal shall, on or before (10, a,m., of the 1st Thursday, 7 V., c. 43), of the Supreme Court, return into the Clerk of the Courts' office all writs of Venditioni returnable at such Court, and in cases of non-execution or short execution, with the causes assigned as aforesaid, and in every case of a levy returned in custody, with such declaration concerning such return endorsed upon the writ. In case of default, fine not exceeding £50 (£30 stg.], and under an order of Court, wh.ch in every such case shall be made, the costs of the party complaining, to be taxed, 43 G. 3. c. 20, s. 4; 7 V., c. 43.

Provost Marshals' return to the Court, see 19 V, c. 10 s. 39

In every case of a levy returned as applicable in a course of priority, the Provost Marshal shall, (the return being made as aforesaid), be allowed time for ascertaining the proportions whereon it is applicable, 43 G. 3, c. 20, s. 5.

Levies applicable to priority

Until the 2nd Tuesday of the Court, 7 V., c. 43.

4 Y

Penalty on Provost Marshal failing to pay over moneys

On refusal or failure by the Provost Marshal to pay over any moneys in his hands, demand being first made by the person entitled, or his authorized agent : fine not exceeding £100 (£60 stg.), and also as a compensation to the party aggrieved, over and above the sum withheld, £10 per cent. per annum on the amount, under an order of the Court in every such case to be made, with costs, to be taxed, 43 G. 3, c. 20, s. 6.

Schedules of levies and their application

The Provost Marshal shall, within four weeks after every Supreme Court, make a fair and perfect schedule subscribed by him of all levies returned in such Court, shewing fully and particularly how they are respectively applicable and applied, as also another schedule of all moneys remaining in his hands from levies of former Courts, shewing in like manner how they are applicable. Such schedule to be made in alphabetical order according to the names of the defendants in the writs, and of the testators or intestates of defendants as representatives of persons deceased, and ve-

To be sworn to
And delivered to the Clerk to be recorded and kept

rified upon oath by the Provost Marshal or his principal clerk before a Judge, and delivered to the Clerk of the Court to be recorded in a book to be kept for the purpose, and the original carefully kept by the Clerk of the Court, (with the date of the filing endorsed thereon, 20 V., c.22, s. 25.)

Provost Marshals' fee
Penalty on Provost Marshal

The Provost Marshal's fee for every schedule shall be £15 (£9 stg.), to be paid by the Receiver-General. For every default or neglect the Provost Marshal offending shall forfeit £400 (£240 stg.), to be recovered by action of debt, one moiety to the Crown, the other moiety to the informer, with full costs out of purse, to be taxed, 43 G. 3, c. 20, s. 8.

Clerk of the Court

Penalty on the Clerk of the Court £50, recoverable by attachment on the application of the Attorney-General, 20 V., c. 22, s. 25, 39 ; 27 V. S. 1, c. 4.

Payment in vacation of proceeds of levies returned as not sold

Where the returns now by law required to be made by the Provost Marshal and Deputy Marshal, to the Supreme Court, shew that a levy has not been sold, the Provost Marshal shall, immediately upon the payment into his office of the net proceeds by the Deputy Marshal, proceed in the vacation after the court to apply such net proceeds in a due course of law, without delaying the payment until the ensuing court, and shall be allowed time for ascertaining the proportions wherein the levy is applicable, until the ex-

14 days after receipt

piration of 14 days after receipt of such money, 19 V., c. 31, s. 9.

Not to dispense with the returns required by law
Particulars to be returned by deputies to the Provost Marshal in addition to the requirements of 43 G. 3, c, 20, s. 3

Nothing herein shall dispense with the returns by law required to be made by the Provost Marshal and Deputy Marshals at the Supreme Court concerning Venditionis ; and every Deputy Marshal in respect of writs on which levies have been made, where the amount has not paid the writ in full, shall shew in the return, and in addition to the particulars now by law required, the days on which the sale took place, and when the moneys were returned, and paid by him to the Provost Marshal ; and the Provost Marshal

And by him delivered with the writs to the Clerk of the Court

shall deliver with the writs into the clerk of the Court's office the returns made by the Deputy Marshal in like manner as he is now required to deliver in returns, 19 V., c. 31, s. 10.

Provost Marshals' returns of the proceeds of such levies and of the accounts sales ; advertisements of levies their appropriation, and the parties to whom payable

Upon payment into his office of any moneys the proceeds of any levy returned as not sold under any writ the Provost Marshal shall make a return thereof, and of the particulars of the accounts sales delivered by the Deputy Marshal to the Clerk of the Court, within 7 days thereafter, and also at the expiration of the time before allowed him for ascertaining the proportion wherein the levy shall be applicable, advertize in such newspaper as aforesaid (s. 7), the amount in his hands received, the proportions in which the same are applicable, and the parties to whom payable ; and shall also, at the expiration of seven days from the termination of each Supreme Courts advertize in such newspaper the moneys in his hands received under all writs of Venditioni lodged in his office returnable for such Court, the proportions in which they are applicable, and the parties to whom payable, 19 V., c. 31, s. 11.

Liability of Provost Martial and Deputies

In case of any default or neglect by the Provost Marshal or any deputy in any matter in this or any other Act required in the execution and return of any Venditioni, they shall be amenable to the Supreme Court, and punishable under 43 G. 3, c. 20 ; 19 V., c. 31, s. 12.

Purchases by or on behalf of Deputy Marshals of levies

If any Deputy Marshal purchase in his own or any other person's name on his account any levies exposed by him to sale, the purchase and sale shall be void, and on application to the Supreme Court the levies shall be ordered to be forthwith re-sold, and the costs of the application paid by the Deputy Marshal, and for a second offence he shall be incompetent to hold the situation for ever thereafter, 19 V., c. 31, s. 13.

Whoever shall not do his duty and comply with the direction of this Act, or offend against its meaning, shall, for every offence on which a penalty is not already imposed, forfeit £30, which penalty, and all other penalties in this Act mentioned and not declared how the same are recoverable, shall be recovered by action of debt, &c., one half to the Crown, 19 V., c. 31, s. 16.

. The Provost Marshal shall provide and keep books, back alphabets of priorities. in which to enter the names of the defendants in every writ of execution, with all levies made upon writs of venditioni or other writs lodged against such defendants, and the levies made each Court liable thereto, in so fair and clear a manner that every plaintiff or defendant may at one view discover how much money has been paid, or returned into office, subject to the writ of execution. Penalty £500 (£300 stg). Which books shall remain in the office subject to the inspection of any person upon payment of 1s 3d (9d sterling) for every search. Any Provost Marshal upon leaving office taking away, or by any means destroying any such book shall incur a penalty of £10000 (£6000 sterling), 21 G. 3, c. 23, s. 4.

Such penalites shall be recoverable by action of debt, &c., one moiety to the informer, 21 G. 3, c. 23, s. 7.

The Clerk of the Supreme Court shall keep books, in which shall be regularly entered, upon the returns of all writs from the Provost Marshal's Office into his, the names and additions of every plaintiff and defendant in such writs, the amount of the debt and damages, with the costs of suit and delay, and the levy marked, or endorsed on the writ, with the names of the persons who signed the direction to levy, and each entry shall specify the Court each writ is returnable, with the Provost Marshal's return, which books shall be received as books of record; and the same, or a transcript therefrom of any writ duly authenticated by the Clerk of the Court, shall be received as evidence in any Court, as also of the original judgment when it has been lost or mislaid, 20 V., c. 22, s. 22.

Vendryes Henry.

Act authorizing his admission to practice as an Attorney, Solicitor and Proctor, 24 V., c, 25.

Vestries and Churchwardens, Clerks of the Vestry.

The Custos shall, on or before 10th of July, issue his warrant to the Inspector, or in his absence, Serjeant, or any Policeman or Constable, forthwith to summon the persons qualified to vote for Members of Assembly and by an advertisement in the 'Jamaica Gazette,' and written notice posted upon the door of the Court House, and some other building used for parochial purposes, for not less than 7 days, require such persons to meet at the Court House, some day to be fixed by him in July, to elect 10 Vestrymen and 2 Churchwardens for the year; and should a sufficient number not be elected on the day, issue his warrant for another election on another day, the notice before provided being given, and so from time to time, until the number is completed, 27 V., S. 1, c. 7, s. 1.

Should any circumstance prevent the Custos from issuing his warrant, or voters from meeting at the above periods, the Custos shall issue the warrant, and the voters meet and proceed to the election at any other time, and as soon after as convenient, 27 V., S. 1, c, 7, s. 2.

To render the election of a Vestryman or Churchwarden valid, the votes of at least 6 voters must be recorded in his favor, 27 V., S. 1, c. 7, s. 3.

The persons elected at any time during the year shall, subject to vacation of office, as by this Act provided, continue to hold such offices, until others have been elected for the following year, 27 V., S. 1, c. 7, s. 4.

The Clerk of the Vestry (Kingston excepted) shall take the poll, or, in his absence, the Custos shall appoint a person, 27 V., S. 1, c. 7, s. 5.

Marginal notes:

Second offence

Penalties and recovery where not otherwise provided

Back alphabets of priorities

Alphabetical books of dockets of writs to be kept by the Clerk of the Court

To be received as records; evidence

Admission as an Attorney, &c

Advertisement and notices for the election of Vestrymen and Churchwardens in July

Further notices, &c

Where warrant not issued or election proceeded with

6 votes at least be recorded

Person selected to continue in office until others are elected for the following year

Clerk of the Vestry to hold poll, ab sence

Adjournment of poll in case of riot, &c

When the proceedings are interrupted by riot or open violence, the Clerk of the Vestry, or other person appointed, shall adjourn the poll from time to time, and if necessary, from day to day. Should Sunday or a Holiday intervene, until the day after, and until the interruption has ceased, upon which he shall proceed with the election at the same place, 27 V., S. 1, c. 7, s. 6.

Hours of holding

The poll shall be opened between 9 and 10 a. m., and closed at 4 p. m. Where there is no contest, or the contending parties agree, and 6 votes have been polled, the poll may be closed at any time previously, 27 V., S. 1, c. 7, s. 7.

Qualifications

No person shall be eligible as a Vestryman or Churchwarden, unless he is a freeholder or taxpayer, and qualified to vote for Members of Assembly, nor eligible as a Churchwarden unless he is also a communicant of the Church of England, nor any person eligible as a Vestryman or Churchwarden who cannot read and write, 27 V., S. 1, c. 7, s. 8.

Nomination not to be received unless on the list of voters

The person taking the poll shall not receive the nomination of any candidate, or record any vote in his favor, if his name is not on the list of voters for the year, 27 V., S. 1, c. 7, s. 9.

Justices may sit and vote and be elected if qualified

Any Justice may sit and vote in the Vestry, and shall not be prevented from being elected a Vestryman or Churchwarden, if qualified, 27 V., S. 1, c. 7, s. 10.

Quarterly list of Justices to attend Vestry

Notices to them

None prevented

The Custos, after 1st July, and before the holding of the Vestry for the quarter ending 30th September, shall make a list of resident Justices, and fix the quarters in the next 12 months, in which they will be required to attend the Quarterly and other meetings of Vestry. The Magistrates' Clerk shall thereupon furnish the Clerk of the Vestry with a copy of such list, and give notice in writing to each Justice named therein, within 5 days after the list is made, of the Vestries he will be required to attend. Not to prevent any Justice from attending out of his turn, if he think fit, 27 V., S. 1, c. 7, s. 11-

Disqualifications to sit or vote

No person shall be permitted to sit or vote in Vestry as a Justice, Vestryman or Churchwarden, who has, or shall be convicted of fraud before any Insolvent or other Court, or upon whom Judgment has or shall pass for any felony or infamous crime, or who shall, within 2 years next preceding his election, have availed himself of the benefit of the Insolvent Debtors' Act, or being a Vestryman or Churchwarden, shall cease to be an elector of the parish, and qualified to vote for Members of Assembly, or who shall not, on being required by any member of the Vestry, write out the words in Schedule C, and sign his name thereto in legible characters, 27 V., S. 1, c. 7, s. 12.

Officers ineligible

No Collector of Dues or his deputy, Deputy Marshal or his deputy, Crier of the Court, Collector of Petty Debts or his deputy, Clerk of the Church or a Chapel, Organist, Organ Regulator, Parochial Schoolmaster, Clerk of the Market, Poundkeeper, Almoner, Sexton or Beadle of the parish shall be eligible as Vestryman or Churchwarden, 27 V., S. 1, c. 7, s. 13.

Elections of disqualified persons void

Seats of disqualified persons vacated

New election

The election of any disqualified person shall be ipso facto void. If any Vestryman or Churchwarden already elected, is disqualified in any of the above ways, his seat shall become vacated thereby, and the Custos shall issue his warrant for the election of some other person in his room, 27 V., S. 1, c. 7, s. 14.

Not to vote on any question in which they are interested

No Justice, Vestryman or Churchwarden shall vote on any question in which he has any personal interest, under penalty of £20; nor shall the Custos or Chairman receive his vote on any such question, 27 V., S. 1, c. 7, s. 15.

Quorum—Supersedes, 22 V., c. 47, s. 1

No Vestry shall be formed or complete, unless 2 Justices and 3 Vestrymen be present, 27 V., S. 1, c. 7, s. 16.

Absence from Vestry

If any Vestry duly summoned, be not formed by want of sufficient attendance, every Justice whose quarter it is to attend, absent without a reasonable excuse, to be approved of by a majority of members present; and every Vestryman absent without excuse, to be in like manner approved of, shall forfeit not exceeding £5, nor less than £2, 27 V., S. 1, c. 7, s. 17.

Notice of meeting to same effect, 22 V., c. 47, s. 2

Notice in the "Jamaica Gazette, by authority," signed by the Clerk of the Vestry, by order of the Custos or senior Magistrate, of the time and place of holding any meeting, shall be a sufficient summoning, 27 V., S. 1, c. 7, s. 18.

Any person duly elected, who refuses or neglects to serve, shall forfeit £5, to be recovered as after-mentioned ; his seat shall be taken to be vacated, and himself not eligible to be re-elected for the same year; and no person shall be compelled to serve for more than 2 consecutive years, 27 V., S. 1, c. 7, s. 19.

Refusal to serve

Not compatible beyond 2 years

Upon the death, departure from the Island without leave, or permanent inability of any Vestryman or Churchwarden, his seat shall be vacated. In any case declared to be a cause of vacancy, the Custos shall, upon its occurring, issue his warrant, as in the case of an original election, to fill up the vacancy ; and the same notice shall be given, and time allowed between the warrant and the day fixed for the election, and the same qualifications required as in cases of original election, 27 V., S. 1, c. 7, s. 20.

Filling up vacancies

The proceedings of any Vestry held during any vacancy, shall not be thereby invalidated, and whenever less than 10 Vestrymen, or less than 2 Churchwardens are elected at the annual election, those elected shall proceed to the discharge of the duties of the Vestry, as if the full complement had been elected, 27 V., S. 1, c. 7, s. 21.

Vacancies not to invalidate proceedings

In case of a double return, the Custos shall issue his warrant for a new election, as in case of a vacancy, 27 V., S. 1, c. 7, s. 22.

Double return

The Rector and Churchwardens shall be entitled to sit and vote in the Vestry, but their presence shall not be necessary to constitute a legal Vestry, 27 V., S. 1, c. 7, s. 23.

Rector and Churchwardens

No Vestry shall make any order without having first given timely notice to the Minister as he there, 32 C. 2, c. 7, s. 1.

Rector to be warned

Any Justice, Vestryman or Churchwarden guilty at any meeting of any rude, insulting or contumacious behaviour to any member present, or to any officer of the Board, or person in attendance, or by his conduct obstructing or preventing the business of the Vestry from proceeding, or departing from the Vestry without permission of the Chairman, whereby their proceedings shall be interrupted or impeded, shall forfeit not exceeding £5, nor less than 40s. ; the business to proceed, notwithstanding the departure of any Justice, &c., so long as there are remaining 3 members of the Vestry Board, unless the Custos or Chairman consider it necessary, in consequence of such obstruction, to adjourn the Vestry for such period as he thinks proper, or to another day, which he is authorized to do, 27 V., S. 1, c. 7, s. 24.

Rude behaviour, &c. at Vestry

Business may be proceeded with before 3 members or may be adjourned

The Justices, Vestrymen, Churchwardens, and Clerk of the Vestry during their attendance on, and for 24 hours previous to, and after the holding of any Vestry, shall be protected against all mesne and judicial process in civil causes, 27 V., S. 1, c. 7, s. 25.

Protection from civil process

The Custos shall summon the Vestry in July, and prepare in detail, according to Schedule A, an estimate of the expenditure of the parish for the ensuing financial year; and also, in Form B, or as may at any time be by law directed or be required by any change in the objects of taxation, or alteration, or addition of any source of parochial revenue, an account of all parochial revenue receivable by the Collector of Dues ; and the Clerk of the Vestry shall, as soon as the estimate and account have been passed by the Vestry, transmit 3 copies of each to the Secretary of the Executive Committee for their approval, who may reduce the amount of any of the items in such estimate, which, when approved, and endorsed as approved by the Secretary and returned, shall be taken as the estimate for the year mentioned therein, and shall not be changed or varied in any respect by the Vestry, 27 V., S. 1, c. 7, s. 26.

Estimates of expenditure and taxation

To be approved by Executive Committee

And returned

It shall be the duty of the Vestry to make provision for the maintenance of the poor and indigent inhabitants, and particularly such as are sick and diseased, either by means of out-door allowance or the establishment of an Alms House for their reception, or both. The Vestries of two or more adjoining parishes may join in forming an union for the relief of their poor, in which case the expense of the Union Alms House or houses shall be borne rateably according to the number of poor each parish shall send to the Alms House, but not to authorize or empower the Vestry of any parish to expend any sum for the poor larger in amount than is provided in the estimate of

Provision for the poor

Union Alms House

Admission

expenditure for the year, or to incur any debt or liability, for payment of which no provision is made. No person shall be admitted into any Alms House without an order to the Superintendent, signed by one Church-warden or by two Justices, or one Justice and Vestryman, 27 V., S. 1, c. 7, s. 27.

Appropriation of portions of the sums in estimates to other purposes with assent of Executive Committee

The Vestry, when it appears that the whole or any portion of any sum provided in the estimates for the current financial year, for any particular purpose, will not be required, may apply, upon obtaining the assent of the Executive Committee to such expenditure, such sum or portion as remains unexpended to any other purpose in their opinion required to be performed, during the financial year, for the benefit of the parish, 27 V., S. 1, c. 7, s. 28.

St. Jago de la Vega Court House

The Court House, in St. Jago de la Vega, shall be under the control and subject to the supervision of the Custos of the precinct of St. Catherine, 27 V., S. 1, c. 7, s. 29.

Quarterly and other Vestries

The Custos on 28 September, 28 December, 28 March, and 28 June, or within 10 days thereafter, and at such other times as may be necessary, shall summon the Vestry to meet for the disposal of any business to be

Quarterly accounts and orders for payment

brought before it; and at each of the meetings to be held on or after any of the days last mentioned, all accounts against the parish for the quarter then expired shall be examined, and, if found correct, passed. And the Custos or Chairman shall, during its sitting, draw orders on the Receiver-General in payment of the accounts passed by the Vestry, and salaries of parochial officers, to be countersigned by the Clerk of the Vestry, and contain the name in full of the party in whose favor it is drawn, the amount in words,

Schedule to be forwarded to the Commissioner to audit accounts

and the purpose or account for which it is to be paid. The Clerk of the Vestry shall, immediately after the Vestry, forward to the Commissioner for examining the public accounts a schedule signed by him, in which shall be cor-

Amounts exceeding one-fourth of estimate

rectly stated the particulars of the drafts. And whenever a larger amount than 1-4th of that allowed in the estimate for any item of expenditure which could not be accurately ascertained at the period of making up the estimates

Or in excess of estimate

is required, at the end of any quarter, or the amount is larger than is provided in the estimate, the Custos or Chairman may draw for a sum larger than 1-4th of that provided in the estimate for such particular item, and so on until the amount is exhausted; and thereafter for the excess against

Against funds for unforeseen expenses

the amount provided for unforseen expenses. And should this latter amount have been fully drawn, or the balance not be sufficient to meet the excess,

Against unexpended amount

then against any amount to remain unexpended on the estimate for the year;

Total of drafts not to exceed total of estimate

but in no case shall the total amount drawn for any year exceed the total allowed on the estimate, nor any amount be drawn for unless it has been ac-

To be only for bona fide expenditure

tually and bona fide expended and is due at the time, or is accruing due for any estimate not completed. Where sums are included in the estimates, not

Subjects of gross expenditure

the subject of quarterly or other periodical payments, but are in gross for one expenditure, the full amount may be drawn for at one time in payment of the particular expenditure, upon the due performance of the service for which the amount was provided, 27 V., S. 1, c. 7, s. 30.

Certificate at foot of schedule

The Clerk of the Vestry shall certify at the foot of the schedule that all the accounts or items therein mentioned are due and bona fide due, or are accruing due for any estimate not completed, and that no sum has been introduced for which goods or services or goods have not been received by or for the use of the parish, 27 V., S. 1, c. 7, s. 31.

No item to be allowed in estimate unless mentioned in schedule

No item of expenditure shall be included in the estimate which is not mentioned in schedule A, or when introduced shall be struck out and disallowed by the Executive Committee, 27 V., S. 1, c. 7, s. 32.

Custos, &c., to preside.

The Custos when present shall preside at each meeting, and may, with consent of the Vestry, adjourn from day to day or from one period to another for the despatch of business, and the Chairman presiding in his ab-

Casting vote

sence shall have the same power, and when there is an equality of votes they shall give the casting vote, but shall not be entitled to a double vote, or to vote and give the casting vote besides, 27 V, S. 1, c. 7, s. 33.

Clerk of the Vestry to be sworn

The Clerk of the Vestry, before he acts, shall be sworn in open Vestry, under penalty of £100, faithfully and diligently to perform the duties of his office, in the manner directed by the laws, to the best of his knowledge, skill, and ability; to be administered by the Chairman, 27 V., S. 1, c. 7 s. 34.

The Vestry may grant leave of absence to its Clerk for not exceeding 6 months, 27 V., S. 1, c. 7, s. 35.

Leave of absence to

In case of his sickness or absence with leave, the Justices and Vestry may appoint a deputy nominated by him and approved of by them, who shall perform the duties and be subject to the penalties imposed on Clerks of Vestries. In the event of the Clerk not nominating a deputy, the Justices and Vestry shall appoint one, 27 V., S. 1, c. 7, s. 36.

Deputy

The Clerk of the Vestry of St. John may keep an office and transact parochial business as such in St. Jago de la Vega ; the Clerk of the Vestry of Port Royal in Kingston, 27 V., S. 1, c. 7, s. 37.

Clerk of the Vestry St John Port Royal

All moneys provided on the estimates for the repairs of any Church, Chapels, or other buildings shall be applied and paid on tenders, and contracts to be taken agreeably to 26 V., c. 20, by the committee or quorum of the Vestry or Common Council appointed as thereby directed, and on the certificate of a quorum of such committee that the work the subject of certificate has been properly completed or progressed with, to a value equal to the sum recommended to be paid ; and all such repairs shall be executed under the supervision and direction of a quorum of such committee, or some person appointed by them for the purpose, 27 V., S. 1, c. 7, s. 38.

Repairs of Churches and other buildings

The Building Committee shall submit for approval to the Vestry Board all contracts for work before they are certified, and upon the partial performance or completion of such contracts, they shall be referred to the Vestry before any advances or payments are made, 27 V. S. 1, c. 7, s. 39.

Contracts and payments to be referred to Vestry

When the Clerk of the Vestry is not the Collector of Dues, the latter shall on application of the Clerk of the Vestry, furnish the information required for making up Schedule B, 27 V. S. 1, c. 7, s. 40.

Collector of dues to furnish information to make up Schedule B.

The Mayor or Senior Alderman in Kingston shall perform the acts required to be done by the Custos of any other parish ; the Court of Common Council the acts to be done by the Vestry ; and the Clerk of the Common Council, those to be done by the Clerk of the Vestry, and shall each be liable to the penalties imposed upon the Custos, Justices and Members of the Vestry or Clerk of the Vestry for neglect or violation of any of the provisions of this act, 27 V. S. 1, c. 7, s. 41.

Duties, &c, of Mayor, &c., Common Council and Clerk of the Common Council of Kingston

The Churchwardens of each parish shall be incorporated as " The Churchwardens of the parish of   " to sue and be sued, and do all acts for or in respect of all parochial matters, that other persons may or ought to do, suffer or be subject to, but shall not incur any liability for the parish without having first obtained the sanction of the Vestry, 27 V. S. 1, c. 7, s. 42.

Churchwardens incorporated

No Churchwarden shall be entitled to any Commission for any parochial moneys paid into his hands, 39 G. 3, c. 22, s. 22.

The Vestry of each parish except Kingston, shall at a meeting to be convened after 10th July, elect their usual parochial officers, and the persons so elected shall continue in office, unless removed, or it is otherwise provided by law, until 30th June, in the succeeding year, and further until an election take place, 27 V , S. 1, c. 7, s. 43.

Election of Parochial Officers

The supply of all goods and performance of services, and work of every kind required for the use of, or to be done or performed for any parish, shall be the subject of public competition, and the Vestry shall yearly, and from time to time, as any contract for the supply of any article, or performance of any work expires or determines, require tenders to be sent in, and accept the lowest or most advantageous tender, as they think proper, 27 V., S. 1, c. 7, s. 44.

The supply of goods and performance of services to be the subject of tender

The Vestry shall, on requisition from the Justices in Special Sessions, hire and keep in repair commodious buildings, or rooms for holding district Courts, the situation to be determined by the Justices in Special Sessions, 27 V. S. 1, c. 7, s. 45.

Hire of District Court Houses

The Justices and Vestry or Corporation of Kingston shall not become plaintiffs or commence any proceeding, or incur any expense on account of any proceeding at law or in equity, without first obtaining the sanction of the Executive Committee to the particular suit or expenditure ; and if any action &c., is brought or threatened against them, no defence shall be entered or expense incurred therein, unless the sanction of the Executive Committee has been first had, 27 V. S. 1, c. 7, s. 46.

No action to be brought or expence incurred in defence without the sanction of the Executive Committee

Penalty for neglect of duty

Persons omitting, neglecting, or refusing to perform any act &c., at the particular time mentioned, for which no penalty is prescribed, shall forfeit not less than £5, nor more than £30, 27 V., S. 1, c. 7, s. 47.

Not to extend to such as vote for performance of the duty

But not to extend to any Justice, Vestryman or Churchwarden present at any Vestry, who votes for the performance, 27 V, S. 1, c. 7, s. 48.

Clerk of the Magistrates to take proceedings

The Clerk of the Magistrates shall, on payment of the usual fees, institute all necessary proceedings on information of any member of the Vestry or person aggrieved, for the recovery of any penalty; and on neglect or refusal, the Executive Committee, on complaint of any person aggrieved, may upon enquiry, and the complaint proving well founded, direct the Receiver-General to deduct the maximum penalty, which might have been recovered, from any salary or emolument to be payable to him, to be carried to the credit of the public, 27 V. S. 1, c. 7, s. 49.

Recovery of penalties for the use of the public

Penalties shall be recovered summarily before 2 Justices not named or appointed in the list to attend the Vestries of the quarter, and in default of payment or goods whereon to levy, the offender may be imprisoned in the nearest gaol not exceeding 30 days; the penalties to be paid or remitted to the Receiver-General, and carried to the credit of the public, 27 V. S. 1, c. 7, s. 50.

False declartions

Falsely declaring to any matter, indictable as a misdemeanor, 27 V. S. 1, c. 7, s. 51.

Short title

Short Title "The Vestry Election and Regulation Act, 1863," 27 V S. 1, c. 7, s. 53.

Duration

Duration of Act from 1st January, 1864, to 31st March, 1870, 27 V.. S. 1, c. 7, s. 54.

Vestry dinners

The Justices and Vestry shall not charge their parishes with any expense for dinner, except at one meeting in each quarter, nor more than £10 (£6 sterling) for the expense. No such charge shall be made or allowed in St. Catherine and Kingston, 39 G. 3, c. 22, s. 24.

Leave of absence
Kingston, 18 V., c. 61, s. 18, 26
Clerk of the Vestry: 27 V., S. 1, c. 7, s. 35, 36

The Justices and Vestrymen may grant leave of absence to Vestrymen, and to the holders of any public or parochial office in their gift, not exceeding 2 calendar months, and their places shall not be deemed vacated. No more than 2 Vestrymen shall be absent on leave at the same time. In the case of any office of emolument or profit the person obtaining leave of absence, shall provide a sufficient deputy to perform the duties during his absence, who shall be approved of by the Justices and Vestry, 10 V. c. 34.

Clerks of the Common Council and Vestry

The present Clerks of the Common Council and Vestry continued in their offices. They shall not be removable, except for just cause of complaint, to be heard and decided by the (Circuit Court, 19 V., c. 10, s- 17) who shall have full power to investigate such complaint, summon witnesses, and remove the Clerk, 16 V., c. 43, s. 1.

The Common Council, and Justices and Vestry shall appoint others where vacancies arise upon death, removal or resignation, and the person appointed, shall not be removable, except for just cause of complaint, to be made and decided as aforesaid, 16 V., c. 43, s. 2.

Residence

Every Clerk of the Vestry shall reside permanently in the parish, and if absent for 4 consecutive weeks without the consent in writing of 3 Magistrates in Special Sessions, on satisfactory cause shewn, he shall be deemed to have resigned his office, 16 V., c. 43, s. 3.

Incapacities

No Clerk of the Vestry shall be capable, while holding the office, of being elected, or sitting or voting as a Member of Assembly, or of any Vestry, Public or Parochial, or other Board or Commission, either for the parish for which he is Clerk of the Vestry, or any other, 16 V. c. 43, s. 4

And every such election &c., is declared ipso facto, null and void, 16 V. c. 43, s. 5, 6.

Each Clerk of the Vestry shall make up a statement in detail of the various returns required to be made by him in each quarter, under the several existing laws, and of the various returns required to be made by him under orders of either branch of the Legislature, to 28th March, June, September and December, to be verified on solemn affirmation before any Justice of the island, and lodged in the office of the Clerk of the Assembly, within 20 days after such quarter day, 16 V. c. 43, s. 7.

The Receiver-General shall not pay him any salary under the authority of any Act except he produce a certificate from the Clerk of the Assembly, that the returns up to the quarter preceding the application for payment have been lodged, 16 V., c. 43, s. 8.

Salary of Clerk of the Common Council to 31st March, 1867, £460; of each Clerk of the Vestry for Manchester, St. Ann, St. Thomas in the East, St. Elizabeth, Westmoreland, Hanover, St. James and Trelawny, £260; St. Catherine, Clarendon, St. Mary, £250, St. Thomas in the Vale, St. Andrew, Metcalfe, £210; St. John, St. Dorothy, Vere, Port Royal and St. George, £160, payable monthly or quarterly, 23 V., c. 19, s. 1, Sch. **Salaries**

SCHEDULE to 27 V. S. 1, c. 7.

PURPOSES FOR WHICH PROVISION MAY BE MADE BY THE VESTRY OF EACH PARISH. A.; s. 26, 32

Church :—

Provision for Sacramental purposes.
Repairs to Parish Church and Chapels.
Salary of Parish Clerk, of Clerks of Chapels, Sextons, Beadles, Organist, Organ Regulators, and Bellows Blowers.
Cleaning Church and Chapels.
Lighting same, including Lamps.
Ringing Bells.
Regulating and repairing Clocks.
Cleaning Church and Chapel yards, and burial grounds, and repairing fences to the same.
Duty and Registry Books.

Administration of Justice :—

Repairs of Court-House, and rent and repairs of District Court-Houses.
Allowances to Keepers of the same.
Expenses of Lock-up Houses, including repairs.
Medical evidence.
Solicitor of the Parish, or law expenses.
Stationery, Lights, Candlesticks, Water.

Imposition and Collection of Dues :—

Books, Forms and Stationery.
Remuneration for making returns of persons possessing taxable property, and for aiding to discover and proceed against persons in default, or in arrear for taxes, and otherwise assisting in the Collection of Taxes.

Protection of Property :—

Purchase and Repairs of Fire-Engines, Pumps, and Hose.
Pay to Captains of Fire-Engines and laborers to work same, when necessary.
Pay to Keeper of Fire-Engines and Pumps.
Salary of Clerk and Surveyor to Firewardens.
Reward to persons who have assisted in extinguishing Fires.

Markets :—

Commutation to Clerks of Markets.
Building and repairs of Market-Houses, Wharves and Stalls.
Pay to keepers of Markets.
Copies of Standard Weights and Measures, Beams, Scales, and Rings.

Pounds :—

Rent and Repair of Pounds.
Salary of Pound Keepers.
Fodder and Water for Stock.

Paupers :—

Rent and Repair of Alms-House and Asylum.
Salary of Surgeon, Superintendent, and Matron to same, and of Surgeon to out-door poor.
Hire of Nurses, and maintenance of Paupers, sick and well, medicines, coffins, and interments, and for transient poor.
Salary of Almoners.

4 Z

Miscellaneous:—

Schoolmasters to Parochial Schools.
Rent of School Houses.
Salary of Recorder (in Kingston.)
Ditto of Keeper of the town Clock, and repair of same.
Ditto of Harbour Masters.
Law charges, taking polls at Elections in Kingston.
Printing and Advertising.
Expense of a night watch.
Supply of Water.
Unforeseen and extraordinary expenses.
Any other expenditure sanctioned or required by any Act of the Legislature.

Account of the Property, Real and Personal, in the Parish of
in the year 186   liable to Taxation.

B, s. 25

No.			
	Total number of Houses, &c. liable under the "License and Registration Duties' Act," and amount payable thereon		
	Total number of wheels of Wagons, Wains, and Trucks, (Railway and Tramway Trucks excepted), carts and drays, water carts, and spring carts liable under ditto, and amount payable thereon		
	Total number of hackney carriages liable under ditto, and amount payable thereon		
	Total number of wheels of gigs, chaises, and carriages liable under ditto, and amount payable thereon		
	Ditto ditto used solely for livery stable purposes, and amount payable thereon.		
	Total number of horsekind used on main or parochial roads, and liable under ditto, and amount payable thereon		
	Ditto ditto used solely for livery stable purposes, and amount payable thereon.		
	Total number of asses liable under ditto, and amount payable thereon		
	Total number of horsekind, asses, and horned stock liable under ditto, and amount payable thereon		
	Total number of working cattle liable under ditto, and amount payable thereon		
	Total number of sheep liable under ditto, and amount payable thereon		
	Total number of boats liable under ditto, and amount payable thereon		
	Total number of fire-arms, licensed to be used on the premises of the owner, liable under ditto, and amount payable thereon		
	Total number of fire-arms, licensed to be kept and used otherwise, liable under ditto, and amount payable thereon		
	Total number of acres of land liable under ditto, and amount payable thereon		
	Total number of feet of foot land liable under ditto, and amount payable thereon		
	Probable revenue from undermentioned sources, viz:		
	Licenses to retail spirits, at............................		
	Ditto to keep taverns, at................................		
	Ditto to hawk and peddle, at............................		
	Ditto to sell gunpowder, at.............................		
	The pounds..........................		
	The parish lands, and houses, and pumps......		
	The markets............................		
	The fines............................		
	(Add any other item, or source of parochial revenue not above enumerated or given, and the amount thereof respectively.)		

I do hereby claim to sit and vote in this Vestry, being qualified according to law.

Words to be writ. ten and signed by claimants to vote, C. s. 59

Waste.

No action to be for No action of waste shall be permitted to be brought or allowed to lie in any Court, 33 C. 2, c. 23, s. 6, 19, V., c. 46, s. 3.

Weights and Measures.

Measures of length—the yard the standard The yard hitherto in use, and which when compared with a pendulum, vibrating seconds of time in the latitude of London, in a vacuum at the level of the sea, is in the proportion of 36 inches to 39.1393 inches, shall be the genuine standard of that measure of length or lineal extension called a yard and shall be the unit or only standard measure of extension, wherefrom or whereby all other measures of extension, whether lineal, superficial, or solid, shall be derived, computed and ascertained, and all measures of length, shall be taken in parts or multiples or certain proportions of the standard yard. One-third of the standard a   shall be a foot, one-twelfth of the **Parts or mutiples** foot an inch, the pole or perch in length shall contain five and-a-half such yards ; the furlong two hundred and twenty such yards and the mile, one thousand seven hundred and sixty such yards, 6 V., c. 28, s. 2.

Superficial measures
Multiples of yard All superficial measures shall be computed by the standard yard, or certain parts, multiples or p   t   . The rod of land shall contain one thousand two hundred and ten square ya ds ; the acre 4840 square yards, being 160 square perches, poles or rods, 6 V. c. 28, s. 3.

1 lb, Troy weight the standard of weight Parts The standard brass weight of 1lb troy weight, shall be the unit or only standard measure of weight from which all other weights shall be derived computed and ascertained. One-twelfth part of the troy pound shall be an ounce ; one twentieth part of the ounce, a penny weight ; one-twenty-fourth part of the penny weight, a grain ; so that five thousand seven hundred and sixty such grains shall be a troy pound, and seven thousand such grains, a pound avoirdupois, one-sixteenth part of the pound, avoirdupois, an ounce avoirdupois, one sixteenth part of such ounce, a dram ; and the grains shall be in proportion to a cubic inch of distilled water, weighed in air by brass weights at the temperature of sixty-two degrees of Farenheit's thermometer, the barometer, being at 30 inches, which is equal to 252.458 grains, and the pound troy shall consist of 5760 such grains, 6 V. c. 28, s. 4.

Multiples The stone weight shall be deemed to contain 14 standard pounds of avoirdupois ; an hundred weight eight such stones, and a ton twenty such hundred weight, 6 V. c. 28, s. 5.

Measures of capacity
Gallon the standard The standard measure of capacity as well for liquids, as for dry goods shall be the gallon containg 10 lbs. avoirdupois weight of distilled water weighed in air at the temperature of sixty-two degrees of Fahrenheit's thermometer, the barometer being at thirty inches, and the measure of the capacity now used in England shall be the unit and only standard measure of capacity from which all other measures of capacity to be used as well for **Parts and multiples** wine, beer, ale, spirits and all sorts of liquids as for dry goods, shall be derived &c., computed and ascertained, and all measures shall be taken, in parts or multiples or certain proportions of the imperial standard gallon ; the quart shall be the one-fourth part of such standard gallon, and the pint the one-eighth part ; two such gallons shall be a peck, and eight a bushel, and eight bushels a quarter of corn or other dry goods, 6 V. c. 28, s. 6.

For goods sold by the bushel The standard measure of capacity for corn, lime, potatoes, salt, fruit or other goods usually sold by the bushel, shall be the aforesaid bushel containing 80lbs avoirdupois weight as aforesaid, the same being made round with a plain and even bottom, and being nineteen and a half inches from outside to outside, and shall be stricken, when used, with a round stick or roller, straight and of the same diameter from side to side, 6 V, c. 28, s. 7.

Contracts to be according to the standard weights and measures and no other All contracts, bargains, sales and dealings in this Island, for any work to be done, or for any goods or other thing to be sold, delivered, done or agreed for by weight or measure, shall be construed to be made, and had according to the standard weights and measures, ascertained by this Act, and by none other, 6 V., c. 28, s. 8.

Articles sold by weight to be by avoirdupois weight Exceptions All articles sold by weight, shall be sold by avoirdupois weight, except gold, silver, platina, diamond or other precious stones ; and drugs when sold by retail, and such excepted articles, and none others, may be sold by troy weight, 6 V., c. 28, s. 9.

The Receiver-General shall import for the use of Metcalfe, a copy or model of each of the standard yard, pound, gallon, and bushel, and each part and multiple thereof, as now used in England, to be deposited in the Clerk of the Peace's office, and there kept that reference may be had to them when necessary, and the copies or models of the standard weights and measures which have been deposited, and are now in the office of the Clerks of the Peace for the several parishes, shall remain in such parishes for the purpose aforesaid. [These were imported under the repealed act, 5 W. 4, c. 23, s. 8.] In the case of a new parish, copies or models shall be imported for it, and lodged in the Clerk of the Peace's office, for the purpose aforesaid, 6 V. c. 28, s. 10.

Copies or models

To be kept in the Clerk of the Peace's Office

The Justices and Vestry were also required to order and procure for the use of the Inspectors, duplicates of the models of the weights and measures, the duplicate weights of brass or iron, and the measures of pewter or tin, to be compared with the copies of the standards once at least in every three months by the Inspector in the presence of the Clerk of the Peace, and if found short, deficient or untrue, shall be destroyed, and the Inspector omitting to compare the duplicates with the standards quarterly, is declared liable to be dismissed from his office, 6 V., c. 28, s. 10.

Duplicates for Inspectors of Weights and Measures
Comparison with standards

The Justices and Vestry were also required to procure two triangles, and two true beams, and two pairs of scales for the use of the parish ; one triangle, one beam and one pair of scales to be kept in the Clerk of the Peace's office for the purpose of verifying any weights brought to such office for the purpose, and the others to be delivered to the Inspector to enable him to try the weights in his parish, 6 V., c. 28, s. 10.

Triangles, beams, Scales

6 Vic., c. 28, (s. 10, pt. 11, pt. 13 pt.) was repealed so far as it extends to charge or affect any parish with the payment of any money for salary to Inspectors of Weights and Measures, or to procure duplicates or copies or models of the weights, measures, or other implements in the Act mentioned, or to authorize the appointment of any such Inspector in any parish, except Kingston, St. Catherine, Trelawny, and St. James, 10 V., c. 46, s. 1.

Partial repeal of 6 V., c. 28, s. 10, pt. 11, 13 pt.

In these parishes the Act shall continue, except so far as it authorizes and requires them to raise a tax for carrying on the same, in which respect it is repealed, 10 V., c. 46, s. 2.

The salaries of the present Inspectors for the above parishes until 31st March, 1867, are, St. Catherine, St, James and Trelawny, £30 each ; Kingston, £60, 23 V., c. 19, s, 1, Sch.

Salaries of Inspectors

Upon any vacancy occurring in the situation of Inspector in any of these parishes, no new appointment shall take place, but the duties shall be performed by the Inspector of Police, or any one of the Sergeants, without any salary or remuneration beyond that attached to his office as such Inspector or Sergeant, 23 V., c. 19, s. 4.

Upon vacancies duties to be performed by police

The Inspectors may enter any shop, store, wharf, warehouse, stall, yard or place wherein goods or anything shall be kept or exposed for sale, or weighed for the purpose of shipping, conveyance or carriage, and weigh all weights, and try all measures, beams, or scales or other weighing machines, and compare and try the same with weights and measures equal to the copies of the standards required to be kept in the offices of the Clerks of the Peace, and if any are found deficient, light, unjust or untrue they shall be seized by the Inspector and taken before two Justices, who, on its being so shewn, shall declare them forfeited, and order them to be destroyed, and the persons in whose possession they were found shall forfeit not exceeding £10 for each weight, measure, beam, scale or machine forfeited and ordered to be destroyed. When the difference between any weights and the copies of the standards is not considerable, and shall not in their opinion have been occasioned by any improper means or with any fraudulent intent, but by the usual wear and tear and loss of weight by rust occasioned by exposure to damp air, the Inspector may refrain from seizing any such weights, and proceed to adjust them and make them equal to the copies of the standards, by attaching and firmly fastening to them one or more iron rings. No such rings to be attached to any weight under 14lbs. avoirdupois. It shall not be lawful for any person to use any weight of lead or tin, and all such weights may be seized and destroyed by the Inspector, and seized and taken before two Justices by any other person, which Justices shall order them to be immediately destroyed, 6 V., c. 28, s 19.

Power to enter shops, &c
To compare and seize false weights, &c

Forfeiture and destruction and penalty

Repair and adjustment

No fees, Inspec tions to be once in 3 months

The Inspector shall not be entitled to any fee from the parties in pos-session of any weights and measures he may adjust. He shall inspect the weights and measures in each place of public business once at least in every three months, 6 V., c. 28, s. 13.

Stamps to weights and measures

The Justices and Vestry and Corporation may, if they see fit, cause a stamp to be put on all weights and measures used in their parishes, and any person refusing to permit the stamp to be put on any weight or measure by the person appointed for that purpose shall forfeit not ex-ceeding £10, 6 V., c. 28, s. 14.

Forging, &c., Stamps

Persons making, forging or counterfeiting, or causing, &c., or acting, or knowingly acting, or assisting in making, &c. any stamp or mark adopted and used by the authority of the Justices and Vestry or Corpora-tion for stamping or marking any weights or measures to denote that they have been compared, adjusted and approved, shall forfeit not exceeding £20. Selling, uttering or disposing of, or exposing to sale any such ille-gal weight or measure with or without such forged or counterfeit stamp or mark, penalty not exceeding £10, and the illegal weights and measures shall be forfeited and destroyed, 6 V., c. 28, s. 15.

Seizure, &c., by persons on whom imposition is at-tempted
Penalty for vexa-tious seizure

Any person on whom any imposition shall be attempted by the use of any illegal weights or measures, or to whom they may be offered for sale, may seize and carry them before two Justices, who shall hear and determine the complaint, but if it appears that the persons who seized them did so wrongfully or vexatiously he shall be liable to a penalty not exceeding £10, 6 V., c. 28, s. 16.

Copies not to be removed from Clerk of the Peace's of-fice

The copies of the weights and measures and multiples shall not be re-moved from the Clerk of the Peace's office, but shall be kept therein for the purpose of comparison and verification. Penalty for taking or at-tempting to remove any of them, or triangle, beam or scales, not exceeding £50. It shall be the duty of the Clerk of the Peace to see that proper care is taken of the weights and measures, and triangle, beam and scales, and that they are not injured but are in good order, clean and ready to be used in comparing or verifying any weights or measures brought to his office for the purpose. Penalty £10. For his trouble he may demand remune-

His remuneration

ration from the Justices and Vestry not exceeding £6 per annum, 6 V., c. 28, s. 17.

Suspension, &c., of Inspector—deliv-erey up of copies of weights, &c

The Justices and Vestry, if they find it necessary to suspend or dismiss the Inspector, may direct him to bring to and leave in the Clerk of the Peace's office all copies of weights and measures, and the triangle, beam and scales provided to be given to him. Penalty for neglect or refusal to comply with such direction £10, over and above the value of the articles he refuses or neglects to deliver up, 6 V., c. 28, s. 18.

Penalties and en-forcement

For every offence for which no penalty is provided the offender shall in the discretion of two Justices before whom the conviction takes place, either be liable to a penalty not exceeding £20, or imprisonment not ex-ceeding 30 days, 6 V., c. 28, s. 19.

Two Justices may convict any person charged with any offence and award the penalty, and in default of payment sentence the offender to be imprisoned not exceeding three calendar months, 6 V., c. 28, s. 20.

Application

Penalties when recovered shall be paid to the Treasurer for the use of the poor, 6 V., c. 28, s. 21

Costs

The Justices may allow costs and enforce payment in the same manner as penalties, 6 V., c. 28, s. 22.

Commencement of prosecution

Prosecutions shall be commenced within three calendar months, 6 V., c. 28, s. 24.

Appeal

Power to appeal, 6 V., c. 28, s. 26, 27.

West Indian Incumbered Estates.

Commissioners, 3 Judges

The Commissioners to be appointed in this Colony in pursuance of the Acts of Parliament " The West Indian Incumbered Estates' Acts, 1854-1858," shall be any three of the Judges of the Supreme Court for the time being who, or any two of whom to be so appointed, shall, whenever sitting at such times and places as they or any two of them shall appoint for the holding of sittings for the purposes of those Acts, have jurisdiction over all matters to be brought before them in the Court to be established, as provided by the Acts of Parliament and this Island, 25 V., c. 1, s. 2.

The Clerk of the Supreme Court or his deput shall be the Secretary to the Commissioners under the Acts, 1854-58, and the Provost Marshal or his deputy the sole Executive officer of the Judges as Commissioners for the service of all process to be issued by the said Commissioners, and they shall be entitled to such fees as shall be settled by the Commissioners under the powers in the Act, 1854, contained, subject to such disallowance or alteration by the Legislature of this Colony as is in the 13th section mentioned, 24 V., c. 4, s. 2. *Secretary Clerk of the Court Executive officer, Provost Marshal Fees*

There shall be paid by the several suitors under this and the recited Acts, before all proceedings, such fees in respect of the business and duties to be by the Judges performed, as shall be fixed by the Commissioners in England under the Act, 1854, s. 13, subject to such disallowance or alteration by the Legislature of this Colony, 24 V., c. 4, s. 3. *To be paid by suitors in respect of the Judges*

Such fees shall be paid by means of stamps impressed on the proceedings, procurable from the Receiver-General on the distribution, and no discount shall be allowed, 24 V., c. 4, s. 4. *By means of stamps*

The Commissioners shall be paid, on the warrant of the Governor, by means of the fund from stamp duties for their services, such salary or remuneration as shall be ascertained and fixed in proportion to the number of days each shall sit, 21 V., c. 4, s. 5. *Judges remuneration thereout*

The fees, when settled and approved, shall be demandable by and payable to the Secretary and Provost Marshal or deputy, to whom they shall be awarded as remuneration by the suitors in the Court to be established, and payment may be demanded before performance out of the duty. Demanding or taking greater or other fees shall be deemed a petty misdemeanor and extortion. Penalty on conviction before two Justices not exceeding £20, nor less than £5, and amends to the party aggrieved in treble the amount demanded, such penalty and amends to be enforced according to the provisions of any Act to be in force relating to summary proceedings before Justices, in a consolidated form in one summons, and conjoined in all the other process therefor, 24 V., c. 4, s. 6. *The fees to Clerk of the Court and Provost Marshal to be demandable before performance of services Extortion*

The Secretary and Provost Marshal, shall cause a list or Schedule of all fees payable to be publicly exhibited at all times in their offices. Penalty £5, by each, to be recovered as last aforesaid. The Judges shall cause a list of all fees to be published at the public expense in the "Jamaica Gazette" before any proceedings are had in the Court, or any fee shall be demanded or become payable, 24 V. c. 4, s. 7. *Lists to be exhibited in their offices Fees to be gazetted*

Wharves, Public.

If any owner of any Wharf, or any person acting under him, receives payment for any goods landed on or delivered at his Wharf, or for any vessel lying and delivering or landing thereat, or on the adjacent beach, the wharf shall be deemed a public wharf, 7 V., c. 57, s. 2. *Where payment is received to be Public Wharves*

All persons keeping public Wharves shall keep a book, wherein they shall fairly enter the marks and numbers of all goods landed on or delivered at their Wharves ; as also the names of the persons or estates by or to whom landed or delivered, and of the vessels out of which taken or shipped, and shall give receipts for all goods so delivered or landed at or upon their wharves, to which books all persons shall have free access during the working hours of the day at such Wharf. Any owner or wharfinger neglecting to keep such book, make such entries, or give such receipts, or refusing access to such books if demanded, shall forfeit £10, 7 V., c. 57, s. 3. *Books of entries To be open to inspection*

All keepers of public Wharves shall receive, ship, and put into proper and good stores, or other safe and dry places, such goods and other articles which are liable to damage by getting wet, at the rates and prices set forth in the Schedules, and also to weigh and gauge, if required, the sundry produce of this Island, or any other articles when received, landed, delivered or shipped at their Wharves or put under their care and custody. Penalty on Wharfinger or owner, £5, 7 V., c. 57, s. 4. *Goods to be received, stored, &c., rates Weighing and Gauging*

. Every Owner, Wharfinger or person acting by, for or under them, refusing to deliver goods received (if demanded during the working *Refusal to deliver goods on tender of wharfage rates* hours) to the persons to whom they stand entered in the books of such Wharf, or their order, the owner or Wharfinger shall forfeit £5; Provided payment is tendered for the wharfage and storage at the rates annexed, 7 V., c. 57, s. 5.

Cranes and sheds removal of goods from exposure Wharfingers shall erect a proper crane for landing, and sheds or other places of security for preserving from the inclemency of the weather, or influence of the sun, all goods and produce landed at, or brought to their Wharves; and no produce or other articles shall be allowed to remain exposed at the sea beach longer than the necessary time for removing them from the Wharf to the shed. Every description of goods or produce shall be placed on skids of the height of 4 inches at least from the ground, or properly secured. Penalty, £5; and further liability to an action at law for whatever goods shall be damaged for want of such precaution, or lost and stolen therefrom, 7 V., c 57, s. 6.

Books to be declared to quarterly. Every Wharfinger shall, under the penalty of £10, on 31st March, 30th June, 30th September, and 31st December in every year, make a declaration before a Justice not interested in the Wharf, that the accounts entered in his Wharf book from the   day of January preceding, are true and just, which declaration shall be subscribed by the Wharfinger, and acknowledged by the Magistrate taking the same, and entered in the Wharf book on the day it is taken.

——

I A. B., Wharfinger of   do declare that all the accounts of wharfage, storage, weighing, prices, shipping, receival and delivery of all goods, and of all produce of this Island, brought to this Wharf, and entered in this book, from the   day of   to this day, are just and true, and entered to the best of my knowledge, pursuant to the directions of an Act entitled " An Act to regulate Wharves and the rates of wharfage and storage throughout the Island."

Evidence Which entries so declared, shall be received and taken as valid evidence in all Courts, 7 V., c. 57, s. 7.

Alphabetical lists of rates to be exhibited All Wharfingers shall affix, and constantly keep up in view in some public place, under cover from the weather, at or near the weigh house or place of weighing goods on their wharves, an exact list of the rates of wharfage and storage as appointed by this Act, properly digested in an alphabetical manner. Penalty, £2; 7 V., c. 57, s. 8.

Neglect of duty, demanding higher rates than allowed Any Wharfinger or person acting for or under him, neglecting or refusing to do or perform their duty as before set forth, or asking, demanding, receiving or taking any greater or larger prices or rates than are mentioned in the Schedules for shipping, receiving, storing, shedding, weighing, skidding, gauging and properly securing the goods delivered at his Wharf shall forfeit £5; 7 V., c. 57, s. 9.

Packages to be removed within 3 months in Kingston or 4 elsewhere or 1-4th additional rates paid All packages of dry goods, provisions, bottled and all cask liquors (rum excepted) landed on any wharf, and not taken away by the owner in 3 months in Kingston and 4 months in all other parts of the Island after landing, the Wharfinger may demand and receive for all such g   so lying over for every 3 months, ¼th of the original wharfage, provided they have been stored or housed and delivered when sent for, and 10 days notice be given to the parties concerned, 7 V., c. 57, s. 10.

Lending or using goods on wharves Wharfingers giving, lending or using, or consenting, or being in any way privy to any person in their employment giving, lending or using any goods landed on their wharves, without the consent of the owners or persons entitled, the Wharfinger shall, on conviction before 2 Justices, be liable to a fine not exceeding £20, or imprisonment not exceeding 30 days, without prejudice to any other remedy at law the party suffering such loss may be entitled to, 7 V., c. 57, s. 11.

Dyewoods to be weighed, lumber, &c., measured, placed in separate lots and initialed Wharfingers receiving logwood, fustic or other dyewoods, or lumber, staves and shingles, shall weigh the dyewoods, take an account of the measurement of such lumber, and count such staves or shingles, and place them respectively in separate lots, marking the initials of the names of the parties to whom they belong on each lot. Penalty, on conviction before 2 Justices, not exceeding £20, or imprisonment not exceeding 30 days, 7 V., c, 57, s. 12.

In case there shall be any goods which have remained on any public Wharf for 2 years or upwards unclaimed, or in case the consignee or owner refuses or neglects to pay to the owner or Wharfinger, or person in possession, or his agent, the usual and legal rates of wharfage, shipping and bonding, they may, by themselves or agents, sell, or cause to be sold by public outcry the same, and the moneys arising from such sales shall be applied by the owner, Wharfinger, or person in possession, or his agents, in defraying the amount due for wharfage, shipping, storing and bonding, and the expenses of advertising the sale as after directed, and the usual commissions to the agent, factor or auctioneer for selling, and the residue, if any, shall be paid by the owner, &c., to the Receiver-General, to be kept in the public chest without interest, until claimed by the person entitled, and on due proof to his satisfaction, 7 V., c. 57, s 13. *Goods unclaimed for 2 years or upwards*

If any goods or chattels shipped and landed on any public wharf after this Act, shall remain thereon two years unclaimed, and the person to whom they were consigned or belong refuses or neglects to pay to the owner, wharfinger or person in possession of such wharf or his agent, the usual and legal rates for wharfage, shipping, storing and bonding, they may sell and dispose of the same as lastly provided, the monies to be applied in like manner; but in neither of the events aforesaid, until they have advertized the goods consecutively for at least one calendar month in three of the county papers, giving full and specific particulars and descriptions of the goods, the dates of landing, by what vessel, the port from whence shipped, and the name of the shipper, if within their knowledge, 7 V., c. 57, s. 14. *To be advertised before sale*

Any owner, Wharfinger or person in possession, or his agent, omitting neglecting or refusing, or purposely withholding 14 days after sale, the surplus, by not paying it in to the Receiver-General, shall forfeit £50, to be recovered by action at the suit of the Attorney-General for the use of the Government of this Island, 7 V., c. 57, s. 15. *Surplus to be paid to the Receiver General within 14 days after sale*

Every Wharfinger or person acting under him shall give notice to any party having goods at his wharf, should any loss thereof from any cause be apprehended of such loss being likely to ensue, and in the event of such loss without such notice having been given, the wharfinger shall, on summary conviction before two Justices, forfeit not exceeding £10, to be paid to the Treasurer of the parish, which shall not prevent the party suffering such loss seeking his remedy for the value by action or otherwise, 7 V., c. 57. s. 16. *Notice to be given to owners where loss is apprehended*

Working hours shall be from sunrise until sunset, except in Kingston, where they shall be from 7, a.m., until 4, p.m., 7 V., c. 57, s. 17. *Working hours*

All books referred to in section 3, shall be kept by the proprietor or person in possession as occupier, lessee or tenant, on the premises accessible to all parties, in a proper state of preservation, for six years. Penalty £20, or in default imprisonment of 30 days, 7 V., c. 57, s. 18. *Books to be preserved for 6 years*

Penalties not exceeding £10 shall be recovered in a summary manner before two Justices, who may commit the offender to Gaol in default of payment, not exceeding three months, until the fine be paid; and all penalties shall be paid to the Churchwardens for the support of the poor, 7 V., c. 57, s. 19. *Recovery and application of penalties*

SCHEDULE.—7 V., c. 57.

KINGSTON, PORT-ROYAL, SAINT DAVID'S, SAINT THOMAS IN THE EAST, PORTLAND, SAINT GEORGE'S, METCALFE, SAINT CATHERINE'S, SAINT DOROTHY'S, VERE, MANCHESTER, CLARENDON. *A., s. 4*

	£.	s.	d.
Bales, bundles, boxes, cases, chests, and trunks, not exceeding eight feet, except as hereinafter specified, per cubit foot	0	0	4½
Above eight feet	0	0	3
Bolts of canvass, oznaburgh, and crocus, loose, each	0	0	3
Cordage, per one hundred and twelve pounds	0	0	7½
Mahogany, cedar, and other hard timber, per one thousand feet	0	12	0
Nicaragua and cam wood, per ton	0	10	0
Logwood, fustic, lignumvitæ, ebony, and other dye, and hardwoods, per ton	0	7	6
American scantling, plank, boards, staves, and heading, per one thousand	0	9	0

	£	s.	d.
Shingles packed, two shillings ; loose, per one thousand, three shillings.			
Oars and handspikes, per dozen	0	1	6
Vats and butts of malt liquor, &c., per one hundred gallons	0	3	0
Butts of wine and spirits	0	6	0
Pipes of wine, brandy, and gin	0	4	6
Hogsheads of sugar	0	3	0
Tierces of sugar	0	2	0
Barrels of sugar	0	0	9
Puncheons of rum	0	2	0
Hogsheads of salt, lime, coals, and slates, each....	0	3	0
Hogsheads of salt fish....	0	3	0
Hogsheads tobacco, per one hundred and twelve pounds	0	0	4½
Hogsheads of oats, earthen and glassware, and others of a similar description, each	0	2	3
Hogsheads of porter, beer, and cider, each	0	1	6
Tierces of coffee	0	2	0
Puncheons of hams, &c-	0	2	0
Tierces of ginger, pimento, rice, cornmeal, bottled liquor, earthen and glassware, &c., each	0	1	6
Barrels of flour, and other dry provisions. each	0	0	6
Barrels of tar, pitch, turpentine, wet provisions, sugar, salt, coffee, pimento, or others of a similar description, each	0	0	9
Drips and pots for sugar refiners, two for	0	0	4½
Grind stones and tombstones, per one hundred and twelve pounds	0	0	9
Shooks, empty hogsheads, or puncheons, each	0	0	6
Wood hoops, per one thousand	0	0	6
Ox bows, per dozen	0	0	6
Hides	0	0	3
Bags of all descriptions, per one hundred and twelve pounds	0	0	9
Puncheons of temper lime	0	2	3
Corn, salt, &c., per bushel, one penny half-penny ; if stored, per bushel, three pence			
Coach or chariot, including wheels, each	1	10	0
Chaise or cart, each	0	12	0
Chairs, tables, jointers, piano-forte, desks, side-boards, &c., per cubit foot	0	0	6
Ploughs, each, and harrows	0	3	0
Hams, cheese, loaf sugar (loose), each	0	0	1
Triangles, each	0	3	0
Jack screws, each	0	0	9
Chests of tea	0	1	6
Crates of earthen and glassware, one shilling and six pence, three shillings and four shillings and six pence.			
Hampers and baskets of cheese and potatoes, per one hundred and twelve pounds	0	0	9
Jugs and jars of all descriptions, per gallon	0	0	1½
Firkins of butter, beef, tongues, herrings, &c , each	0	0	4½
Kegs of paint, at the rate of fifty-six pounds for	0	0	3
Kegs of vinegar, peas, gruts, biscuits, currants, &c. each	0	0	3
Boxes of soap and candles, per one hundred and twelve pounds	0	0	9
Boxes of pickles, British compounds and preserves, from three pence to	0	1	6
Ironware, also pewter, copper, lead, tin and brass of all descriptions, per one hundred and twelve pounds	0	0	6
Bricks, tiles and slates, per one thousand	0	9	0
Paving stones, each	0	0	4½
Drip stones, nine pence to	0	1	6
Puncheons and tierces of corn	0	1	3
Hogsheads of corn	0	2	0
Chests of arms	0	6	0
Truss hoops, per sett	0	0	9
Smiths' bellows, each	0	3	0
Butt and pipe staves and heading, per one thousand	0	15	0
Spades and shovels, per dozen	0	0	6
Horses, mules, asses and horned cattle, each	0	2	3

	£	s.	d.
Sheep, hogs and goats, each	0	0	4½
Bags of coffee, receiving, weighing, tiercing and shipping, four pence half-penny (27 V. S. 1, c. 21, s. 13) per one hundred and twelve pounds	0	0	4½
Bags of pimento, per bag of 120lbs. (27 V. S. 1, c. 21, s. 1)	0	0	4½
Barrels and half-barrels gunpowder	0	6	0
Kegs of gunpowder	0	1	6

And all goods, wares and merchandize not herein particularly enumerated and set forth shall be paid for in proportion to the foregoing rates.

TRELAWNY, SAINT JAMES, HANOVER, WESTMORELAND, SAINT ANN'S, SAINT MARY'S AND SAINT ELIZABETH'S.   B., s. 4

	£	s.	d.
Worms for stills, per one hundred and twelve pounds	0	0	7½
Window glass, cheese, cordage (including cables), sheets of lead, lead or pewter pipes in cases or bundles, per one hundred and twelve pounds	0	0	6
Boxes of soap and candles, bar iron, sheet iron, tin, iron hoops, grapnels, anchors, loose iron work, mill cases, mouth pieces, and plates, grating bars, dampers, wain tyre, gudgeons, axles, carriage guns (including their carriages), shot, standard weights, pig and bar lead, grindstones, paints (dry and ground in oil), per one hundred and twelve pounds	0	0	4½
Nails, dry salt-fish and bacon, per one hundred and twelve pounds	0	0	3

BY MEASURE.

	£	s.	d.
Every thousand feet of boards, plank, scantling or American lumber	0	7	6
Paving stones, per square yard	0	0	9
Boxes or cases of flint glass, ironware, earthenware, and all dry goods, in bales, trusses, cases, crates, trunks, boxes, &c. per cubic foot	0	0	3
Coals and slack lime when loose, per bushel	0	0	1½
Corn and salt when loose, per bushel	0	0	1½

BY TALE.

	£	s.	d.
Bricks, tiles, creese and very large slates, per thousand	0	6	0
Shingles, when packed, per thousand, three shillings, unpacked	0	4	6
Staves and puncheon heading, per thousand	0	7	6
Wood hoops, per thousand, if stored, six shillings; not stored, three shillings	0	3	0
Bottled liquor in casks, cases or hampers, per dozen	0	0	2

BY THE GALLON.

	£	s.	d.
Oil and vinegar	0	0	1½
Empty butts, per hundred gallons	0	0	7½
Butts, hogsheads, puncheons, and barrels of porter, beer, cider, &c. in bulk, per ton of two hundred and fifty-two gallons	0	3	0
Taches, coppers and boilers, per hundred gallons	0	1	0
Stills with head, per ditto	0	1	6

BY PACKAGE.

	£	s.	d.
Barrels of pitch, tar, turpentine, and rosin, barrels of beef, pork heads, cheeks, and other Irish or American cured provisions, also boxes or cases of pipes	0	0	6
Barrels of flour, corn, cornmeal, peas, beans, onions, potatoes, barrels of herrings, or other cured fish, hampers of onions or potatoes, hogsheads, puncheon, and tierce packs, with heading for each	0	0	4½
Hogsheads, puncheon, and tierce packs or shooks, without heading, for each	0	0	3
Cases of pickles, hampers of tin, earthenware, copperware, or loaf sugar, empty puncheons, and sets of truss hoops, for each	0	0	4½
Every tierce of rice, one shilling and six pence, half tierce	0	0	9
Triangles, beaufets, or corner cupboards, if small, one shilling and six pence, if large	0	2	3

	£	s.	d.
Chests of tea, one shilling, half chests, for each....	0	0	6
Cases of chests of medicines, also dining tables, if small, nine pence, if large	0	1	6
Coach, chariot, post-chaise, and landau, including the carriage and wheels	0	19	6
Phæton, ditto)	0	12	0
Chaise or kittereen, ditto ...., ...	0	9	0
Barrels and half barrels of gunpowder, for each	0	6	0
Kegs of ditto for each	0	1	6
Hogsheads of corn, peas, and beans	0	1	6
Tierces and puncheons of ditto	0	1	0
Hogsheads of coals, salt, slates, and slacked lime .	0	2	0
Tierces of ditto	0	1	3
Puncheons of temper lime, also if cased in hogsheads	0	2	3
Hogsheads of dry goods, two shillings, puncheons of ditto, one shilling and six pence, tierces of ditto, one shilling, barrels of ditto	0	0	6
Puncheons of loaf sugar	0	1	6
Pipes of wine, brandy, gin, &c. three shillings, butts	0	4	6
Kegs and jugs of pulse, also boxes of tobacco, each	0	0	3
Firkins of butter, tallow, lard, tongues, &c.	0	0	3
Chairs in bundles, every two	0	0	4½
Kegs and jars of tripe, for every two	0	0	4½

Loose.

	£	s.	d.
Each anvil, and each plough, complete	0	1	6
Each piece of oznaburghs, canvass, or crocus	0	0	3
Each coopers' jointer, and each roll or bundle of leather	0	0	4½
Each smiths' bellows, if small, one shilling and six pence, if large	0	2	0
Each dripstone, nine pence, if with a frame	0	1	6
Hoes, bills, axes, and oxbows, per dozen	0	0	6
Shovels and spades, per dozen	0	0	9
Iron pots, large and small, per dozen	0	1	0

Colonial Produce.

	£	s.	d.
For each hogshead of sugar	0	2	3
For each tierce of ditto	0	1	6
For each puncheon of rum	0	2	0
For each hogshead of ditto	0	1	0
For each puncheon or tierce of coffee or cocoa	0	1	6
For coffee or cocoa in other packages, except bags, per one hundred and twelve pounds	0	0	3
For each bag of coffee, cocoa, ginger, and pimento	0	0	4½
For each bag of cotton, one shilling and six pence ; each pocket of ditto	0	0	9
For every one thousand feet of cedar, mahogany, or other hardwood	0	9	0
For each ton of dyewood, lignumvitæ, and ebony .. .	0	7	6
Lancewood spars, per dozen	0	1	0
Sarsaparilla, per one hundred and twelve pounds	0	1	0
Tortoiseshell, arrowroot, tamarinds, and indigo, per one hundred and twelve pounds	0	0	6
For hides, wet, per dozen one shilling ; dry, per ditto ..	0	0	6
For castor oil, per gallon	0	0	1½

And all goods, wares, and merchandize, not herein particularly enumerated and set forth, shall be paid for in proportion to the foregoing rates.

Whipping.

<table>
<tr><td>Abolished</td><td>It shall not be lawful for any Court to [direct that any offender, shall be whipped in any case whatsoever, and the punishment of whipping is abolished accordingly, 4 V., c. 52, s. 7</td></tr>
<tr><td>Revived Obeah, &c</td><td>It may be inflicted on convictions of obeah and myalism, (see that title) 19 V., c. 30, s. 2.</td></tr>
</table>

Also in some offences against Prison discipline under sentence of Visiting Justices confirmed by the Governor, (see title Prisons) 20 V., c. 11, s. 35. *Prison discipline*

The Judge of any Circuit Court, may, in his discretion, after this Act comes into operation, in lieu of, or in addition to the punishment already authorized by law, sentence any male, convicted before him of any of the illegal acts or offences next described, to be whipped, viz : *Other cases*

Every 2nd or subsequent conviction for stealing, destroying, or damaging with intent to steal any cultivated plant, root, fruit, or other vegetable production used for the food of man or beast, or for medicine, or for distillation or dyeing, or for or in the course of any manufacture, growing in any garden, orchard or provision ground whether enclosed or not, or in any cane, coffee or pimento field. Stealing any horse, mare, gelding, or colt, filly, mule or ass, or any bull, cow, ox, heifer or calf, or any ram, ewe, sheep or lamb, pig, or goat, or wilfully killing any of such animals with intent to steal the carcass, skin or any part, or wilfully maiming any of the said animals, and for any second or subsequent consequent conviction for stealing any domesticated animal or any animal ordinarily used for human food, or feloniously receiving any such property or animals, knowing them to have been stolen, 28 V., c. 18, s. 2.

When awarded, the number of stripes shall be specified in the sentence ; but no sentence under the Act shall direct or authorize more than 25 stripes to be administered to a convict under 16, nor more than 50 stripes to a convict above or of that age, 28 V., c. 18, s. 3. *Number of stripes*

The place of punishment shall be appointed by the Governor, 28 V., c. 18, s. 4. *Places of punishment*

The punishment shall never be inflicted, except in the presence of the Surgeon of the Prison, who is required to attend, or in his absence some other duly qualified Medical Practitioner, who is empowered to interpose after partial execution of the sentence, and to direct the postponement of the remainder until the convict is able to undergo it, 28 V., c. 18, s. 5. *Punishment in presence of the Surgeon, &c* *Who may interpose*

There shall be also present at the infliction of every such Whipping, or any part thereof, whenever the punishment is inflicted in the district where the offence was committed, 2 Constables appointed under 27 V. S. 1, c. 30, who shall be summoned by any Visiting Justice of the prison in which the convict is imprisoned from the district or neighbourhood in which the offence was committed, 28 V., c. 18, s. 6. *2 of Constabulary force to be present*

The Surgeon or Medical Practitioner present shall within 7 days after every infliction, or any part thereof, furnish a report to the Governor of the condition of the convict, and whether the punishment has been fully or partially and to what extent inflicted, 28 V., c. 18, s. 7. *Surgeons report to the Governor*

The Governor may under the circumstances of any case direct a further postponement, or altogether remit the remainder of such punishment by order to the Superintendent or Jailor, who and all others are to be governed thereby, 28 V., c. 18, s. 8. *Governor may postpone or remit the remainder of the punishment*

Act not to come into operation until the Royal assent has been received and notified in the Jamaica Gazette, 28 V. c. 18, s. 9. *Royal assent*

Wills.

The following words which in their ordinary signification have a more confined, or a different meaning, shall in this Act, except where the nature of the provision, or the context exclude such construction, be interpreted as follows :—" Will," shall extend to a Testament, a codicil, an appointment by Will or by writing in the nature of a Will, in exercise of a power, and also to a disposition by Will and Testament, or devise of the custody and tuition of any child, and to any other testamentary disposition. " Real Estate" shall extend to messuages, lands, rents, tenements and hereditaments, whether freehold or of any other tenure, and whether corporeal, incorporeal, or personal ; and to any undivided share thereof, and to any estate, right, or interest (other than a chattel interest) therein : " Personal Estate," shall extend to leasehold estates and other chattels real also, to moneys, shares of Government and other funds, securities for money (not being real estates), debts, choses in action, rights, credits, goods, and all other property whatsoever which by law devolves upon the executor or administrator, and to any share or interest therein, 3 V., c. 51, s. 1. *Interpretation* *Will* *Real estate* *Personal estate*

Property devisable

Every person may devise, bequeath, or dispose of by his Will, executed as after required, all real and personal estate which he shall be entitled to, either at law or in equity at the time of his death, and which, if not so devised, bequeathed, or disposed of, would devolve upon the heir-at-law of him as if he became entitled by descent of his ancestor or upon his executor or administrator; and the power given shall extend to estates pur autre vie, whether there shall or shall not be any special occupant thereof, and whether the same shall be freehold or of any other tenure, and whether a corporeal or incorporeal hereditament; and also, to all contingent executory or other future interests in any real or personal estate, whether the testator may or may not be ascertained as the person, or one of the persons in whom the same may become vested, and whether he may be entitled thereto under the instrument by which the same were created, or under any disposition thereof by deed or will, and also to all rights of entry for conditions broken, and other rights of entry; and also to such of the same estates, interests, and rights respectively, and other real and personal estate as the testator may be entitled to at the time of his death, notwithstanding he may become entitled to the same subsequently to the execution of his will, 3 V., c. 51, s. 3.

Estates pur autre vie

If no disposition by Will is made of any estate pur autre vie of a freehold nature, the same shall be chargeable in the hands of the heir if it comes to him by reason of special occupancy as assets by descent, as in the case of freehold land in fee simple. If there be no special occupant of any estate pur autre vie, whether freehold or of any other tenure, and whether a corporeal or incorporeal hereditament, it shall go to the executor or administrator of the party that had the estate thereof by virtue of the grant; and if it comes to the executor or administrator, either by reason of a special occupancy or by virtue of this Act, it shall be assets in his hands, and shall go and be applied and distributed in the same manner as the personal estate of the testator or intestate, 3 V., c. 51, s. 4.

Minors married women

No Will made by any person under 21 shall be valid, nor a Will made by any married woman, except a Will as might have been made by her before this Act, 3 V., c. 51, s. 5.

Signature and attestation

No Will shall be valid unless it be in writing and executed as after mentioned, viz., it shall be signed at the foot or end thereof by the testator, or by some other person in his presence and by his direction, and such signature shall be made or acknowledged by the testator in the presence of two or more witnesses present at the same time; and such witnesses shall attest and shall subscribe the Will in the presence of the testator, but no form of attestation shall be necessary, 3 V., c. 51, s. 6.

Position of signature

Every Will shall, so far only as regards the position of the testator's signature, or of the person signing for him, be deemed valid if the signature be so a at or after, or following, or under or beside or opposite to the end of the Will, that it shall be apparent on the face of the Will that the testator intended to give effect by such his signature to the writing signed as his Will; and no such Will shall be affected by the circumstance that the signature shall not follow or be immediately after the foot or end of the Will, or by the circumstance that a blank space intervenes between the concluding word of the Will, and the signature, or that it is placed among the words of the testimonium clause, or of the clause of attestation, or shall follow or be after or under it, either with or without a blank space intervening, or shall follow or be after or under or beside the names or one of the names of the subscribing witnesses, or by the circumstance that the signature shall be on a side or page or other portion of the paper or papers containing the Will, whereon no clause or paragraph, or disposing part of the Will is written above the signature, or that there appears to be sufficient space, on or at the bottom of the preceding side or page, or other portion of the same paper on which the Will is written, to contain the signature; and the enumeration of the above circumstances shall not restrict the generality of the enactment, but no signature shall be operative to give effect to any disposition or direction which is underneath, or follows it, nor to any disposition or direction inserted after the signature is made, 25 V., c. 26, s. 1.

Effect of Action wills already made

This Act shall apply to every Will already made, where administration or probate has not already been granted or ordered by a Court of competent jurisdiction, in consequence of the defective execution of such Will, or where the property, not being within the jurisdiction of the Court of Ordinary of this Island, has not been possessed or enjoyed by some person claiming to be entitled thereto in consequence of the defective execution, or the right has not been decided to be in some other person than those claiming under the Will, by a Court of competent jurisdiction in consequence of its defective execution, 25 V., c. 26, s. 2.

The word "Will" shall be interpreted as directed in 3 V., c. 51, s. 1; 25 V., c. 26, s. 3.

"Will"

The Will's Act amendment Act, 1861, 25 V., c. 26, s. 4.

Short title

No appointment made by Will in exercise of any power shall be valid unless executed in manner before required. Every Will so executed, shall so far as respects the execution and attestation, be a valid execution of a power of app ntment by Will, notwithstanding it is expressly required that a Will made in exercise of such power should be executed with some additional or other form of execution or solemnity. Any soldier in actual military service, or any mariner or seaman being at sea may dispose of his personal estate as before this Act, 3 V., c. 51, s. 7.

Appointments by Will in execution of powers

Wills of soldiers and seamen

Every Will executed as hereinbefore required shall be valid without any other publication, 3 V., c. 51, s. 8.

Publication unnecessary

If any person attesting the execution, be at the time or afterwards incompetent to be admitted a witness to prove the execution, the Will shall not on that account be invalid, 3 V., c. 51, s. 9.

Attesting witness afterwards incompetent

If any person attests the execution of any Will to whom or to whose wife or husband, any beneficial devise, legacy, estate, interest, gift or appointment of or affecting any real or personal estate (other than, and except charges and directions for the payment of any debts) shall be thereby given or made, such devise, &c., shall, so far only as concerns the person attesting, or the wife or husband of such person, or any person claiming under such person or wife or husband, and such person so attesting shall be admitted a witness to p e the execution of such Will, or its validity or invalidity notwithstanding such devise, &c., 3 V., c. 51, s. 10.

Witnesses taking benefit under Will.

In case by any Will any real or personal estate is charged with any debt, and any creditor or the wife or husband of any creditor whose debt is so charged attests to the execution, the creditor, notwithstanding such charge, shall be admitted a witness to prove the execution of such Will, or the validity or invalidity thereof, 3 V., c. 51, s. 11.

Creditors witnesses

No person shall on account of his being an executor of a Will be incompetent to be admitted a witness to prove the execution, or the validity or invalidity of the Will, 3 V., c. 51 s. 12.

Executors witnesses

Every Will made by a man or woman, shall be revoked by his or her marriage, except a Will made in exercise of a power of appointment when the real or personal estate thereby appointed would not in default of such appointment pass to his or her heir, executor, or administrator, or the person entitled as his or her next of kin under the statute of distributions, 3 V., c. 51, s. 13.

Revocation by marriage

No Will shall be revoked by any presumption of an intention on the ground of an alteration in circumstances, 3 V., c. 51, s. 14.

Not by presumption

No Will or codicil or any part thereof shall be revoked otherwise than as aforesaid, or by another Will or codicil executed as before required, or by some writing declaring an intention to revoke the same and executed in the manner a Will is required to be executed, or by the burning, tearing or otherwise destroying the same by the Testator, or by some person in his presence, and by his direction with the intention of revoking the same, 3 V., c. 51, s. 15.

How to be effected

No obliteration, interlineation or other alteration made in any Will after the execution shall be valid or have any effect, except so far as the words or effect of the Will before such alteration shall not be apparent, unless such alteration is executed in the like manner as is required for the execution of the Will; but the Will with such alterations as part thereof, shall be deemed to be duly executed if the signature of the Testator and the subscription of witnesses be made in the margin or on some other part of the Will opposite or near to such alteration, or at the foot or end of, or opposite to a memorandum referring to such alteration, and written at the end or some other part of the Will, 3 V., c. 51, s. 16.

Obliterations, interlineations alterations inoperative unless duly executed

Will revived only by re-execution or codicil

No Will or codicil or any part thereof which shall be in any manner revoked shall be revived otherwise than by the re-execution thereof, or by a codicil executed as before required, and shewing an intention to revive the same ; and when any Will or codicil which shall be partly revoked and afterwards wholly revoked is revived, the revival shall not extend to so much as was revoked before the revocation of the whole, unless an intention to the contrary is shewn, 3 V., c. 51, s. 17.

Subsequent conveyance not to affect Will of real or personal estate, of which testator can dispose at the time of death

No conveyance or other act made or done subsequently to the execution of a Will of or relating to any real or personal estate therein comprised, except an act by which the Will is revoked as aforesaid, shall prevent the operation of the Will with respect to such estate or interest in such real or personal estate, as the testator shall have power to dispose of by Will at the time of his death, 3 V., c. 51, s. 18.

Will to take effect as if executed immediately before death

Every Will shall be construed with reference to the real and personal estate comprised in it, to speak and take effect as if it had been executed immediately before the testator's death, unless a contrary intention appears by the Will, 3 V., c. 51, s. 19.

Lapsed real estate to pass under residuary devise

Unless a contrary intention appears by the Will, such real estate or interest therein as shall be comprised or intended to be comprised in any devise therein, which shall fail or be void by reason of the death of the devisee in the lifetime of the testator, or of the devise being contrary to law, or otherwise incapable of taking effect, shall be included in the residuary devise, if any contained in such Will, 3 V., c. 51, s. 20.

When leasehold estate passes with freehold under a devise of land

A devise of the land of the testator, or of the land of the testator in any place, or in the occupation of any person mentioned in his Will, or otherwise described in a general manner, and any other general devise which would describe a leasehold estate, if the testator had no freehold estate which could be described by it, shall be construed to include the leasehold estates of the testator, or his leasehold estates or any of them, to which the description shall extend as the case may be, as well as freehold estates, unless a contrary intent appears by the Will, 3 V., c. 51, s. 21.

Real property comprised in a general devise of land.

A general devise of the real estate of the testator, or of his real estate in any place, or in the occupation of any person mentioned in his Will, or otherwise described in a general manner, shall be construed to include any real estate, or any real estate to which the description extends (as the case may be) which he may have power to appoint in any manner he may think proper, and shall operate as an execution of such power, unless a contrary intention appears by the Will; and in like manner a bequest of the personal estate of the testator, or any bequest of personal property described in a general manner, shall be construed to include any personal estate, or any personal estate to which the description extends (as the case may be) which he may have power to appoint in any manner he may think proper, and shall operate as an execution of such power, unless a contrary intention appear by the Will, 3 V., c. 51, s. 22.

Bequests of personal property described in a general manner.

Devise of real estate, without words of limitation.

Where any real estate is devised to any person without words of limitation, the devise shall be construed to pass the fee simple, or other the whole estate or interest which the testator had power to dispose of by Will in such real estate, unless a contrary intention appear by the Will, 3 V., c. 51, s. 23.

Restrictive import of "die without issue" &c.

In any devise or bequest of real or personal estate, the words " die without issue" or " die without leaving issue," or " have no issue," or any other words which may import either a want or failure of issue of any person in his lifetime, or at the time of his death, or an indefinite failure of his issue, shall be construed to mean a want or failure of issue in the lifetime, or at the time of the death of such person, and not an indefinite failure of his issue, unless a contrary intention appear by the Will, by reason of such person having a prior estate tail, or of a preceding gift being without any implication arising from such words a limitation of an estate to such person or issue or otherwise. But not to extend to cases where such words import if no issue described in a preceding gift shall be born, or if there shall be no issue who shall live to attain the age, or otherwise answer the description required for obtaining a vested estate by a preceding gift to such issue, 3 V., c. 51, s. 24.

Devise of real estate to a trustee or executor to pass a fee simple, except &c.

Where any real estate (other than or not being a presentation to a Church) is devised to any trustee or executor, such devise shall be construed to pass the fee simple, or other the whole estate or interest the testator had power to dispose of by Will in such real estate, unless a definite term of years, absolute or determinable, or an estate of freehold, shall thereby be given to him expressly or by implication, 3 V., c. 51, s. 25.

Where any real estate is devised to a trustee without any express limitation of the estate to be taken by him, and the beneficial interest in such real estate or in the surplus rents and profits is not given to any person for life, or such beneficial interest is given to any person for life, but the purposes of the trust may continue beyond his life, the devise shall be construed to vest in such trustee the fee-simple or other the whole legal estate the testator had power to dispose of by Will in such real estate, and not an estate determinable when the purposes of the trust shall be satisfied, 3 V., c. 51, s. 26.

Where any person to whom any real estate is devised for an estate tail, or an estate in quasi entail, dies in the lifetime of the testator leaving issue who would be inheritable under such entail, and any such issue shall be living at the time of the death of the testator, such devise shall not lapse but shall take effect as if the death of such person had happened immediately after the death of the testator, unless a contrary intention appears by the Will, 3 V., c. 51, s. 27.

> Devise of estate tail where the devisee dies in testator's lifetime leaving issue.

Where any person being a child of the testator, to whom any real or personal estate is devised or bequeathed for any estate or interest not determinable at or before the death of such person, shall die in the lifetime of the testator leaving issue, and any such issue shall be living at the time of the testator's death, such devise or bequest shall not lapse but shall take effect as if the death of such person had happened immediately after the death of the testator, unless a contrary intention appears by the Will, 3 V., c. 41, s. 28.

> Devise or bequest to a child of the testator. who dies leaving issue living at the testator's death.

This Act shall not extend to any Will made before 1st January, 1841. Every Will re-executed, re-published, or revived by any codicil shall, for the purposes of this Act, be deemed to have been made at the time of its re-execution, &c., nor shall this Act extend to any estate pur autre vie of persons dying before 1st January, 1841, 8 V., c. 51, s. 29.

> Act not applicable to Wills made before Jan. 1841, unless republished or revived.

Witnesses, &c., Expenses, Criminal Prosecutions.

The Court before which any person is prosecuted, indicted, or tried for any felony or aggravated misdemeanor, may, when it sees proper and at the request of the prosecutor, order payment to him of the costs and expenses he may incur in the prosecution, together with any expense he may incur in attending any trial, 20 V., c. 13, s. 2.

> Prosecutor's costs

As also, if it sees proper, and at the request of any person who has appeared before any Grand Jury, or at any trial on recognizance or subpoena to give evidence before any Grand Jury, or at the trial of any such felony or aggravated misdemeanor, or as an interpreter of foreign languages (where his services are deemed necessary), may order payment to such person of such sums as shall seem reasonable to re-imburse him the expenses he has incurred in attending before the Grand Jury, or at such trial as such witness or interpreter, 20 V., c. 13, s. 3.

> Costs of witnesses who appear before the Grand Jury, or at the trial, and recognizance or sub poena, or Interpreters.

The order for payment to any prosecutor or other person shall be forthwith made out and drawn on the Receiver-General, and delivered by the Clerk of the Court to such prosecutor or other person, on being paid for the same 3s. 4d. (2s. stg.) for the prosecutor, and 1s. 8d. (1s. stg.) for each other person, which the Receiver-General shall, upon sight, forthwith pay to the person named therein, or to any one authorized to receive the same on his behalf, 1 V., c. 28, s. 19.

> Order for payment.

When on any trial for felony or aggravated misdemeanor, any person appears to the Court to have been active in or towards the apprehension of any person charged with any of such offences, the Court may order the Receiver-General to pay to such person such sum as to the Court shall seem reasonable under all the circumstances of the case, which he is to pay on sight to the person named therein, or to any one authorized by him, 1 V., c. 28, s. 20.

> Rewards to persons active in the apprehension of persons charged with offences.

In case of felony or aggravated misdemeanor, the Executive Committee may direct payment by the Receiver-General of any sum which to them may appear reasonable for keeping in this island from going abroad any person who appears to be a material witness, or is bound

> Costs of keeping witnesses in the Island, bringing witnesses from other pa

rishes, whose de-
positions are re-
quired to be
taken in presence
of the accused. or
for making ana-
lyses
under recognizance as such to give evidence, or for the necessary travelling and maintenance expenses of any material witness whose deposition
it may be proper to take in the presence of any accused person, but who
may reside in some other parish than where the accused is; or for remuneration to any person who shall make any analysis required in any prosecution for felony or otherwise, 20 V., c. 13, s. 4.

Written Acknowledgments, &c.

Acknowledg-
ments to take case
out of the Statute
of Limitations,
must be in wri-
ting, and signed
by the party to
be charged
Joint contract
ors, &c.

Part payment.

Actions against
joint contractors,
where some are
barred, and oth-
ers bound by ac-
knowledgment.
In actions of debt, or on the case, grounded upon any simple contract,
no acknowledgment or promise by words only, shall be deemed sufficient
evidence of a new or continuing contract, whereby to take any case out of
the operation of the Statute of Limitations, 21 Jas. 1, c. 16, or to deprive
any party of the benefit thereof, unless it is made or contained by or in some
writing to be signed by the party chargeable. Where there are 2 or more joint
contractors, executors or administrators of a contractor, none shall lose the
benefit of the enactment so as to be chargeable by reason only of any written
acknowledgment or promise made and signed by any others. Not to alter or to
take away, or lessen the effect of any payment of any principal or interest made
by any person whatever. In actions against 2 or more joint contractors or
executors, or administrators, if it appears at the trial or otherwise that the
plaintiff though barred as to one or more, is, nevertheless, entitled to recover
against any other of the defendants by virtue of a new acknowledgment,
or promise or otherwise, judgment may be given and costs allowed for the
plaintiff, as to the defendants from whom he recovers, and for the other
defendants against the plaintiff, 9 G. 4, c. 20, s. 1.

Endorsement of
part payment,
No endorsement or memorandum of any payment written or made upon
any promissory note, bill of exchange, or other writing by or on behalf of
the party to whom such payment is made, shall be deemed sufficient proof
of such payment, to take the case out of the operation of the Statute of Limitations, 9 G. 4, c. 20, s. 3.

Set off.
The recited Act (21 Jas. 1 c. 16) and this Act shall apply to the case of
any debt or simple contract alleged by way of set off on the part of any
defendant either by plea, notice, or otherwise, 9 G. 4, c. 20, s. 4.

Ratification of
contracts made
during infancy,
No action shall be maintained whereby to charge any person upon any
promise made after full age to pay any debt contracted during infancy, or
upon any ratification after full age of any promise or simple contract made
during infancy, unless the promise or ratification is made by some writing,
signed by the party to be charged therewith, 9 G. 4. c. 20, s. 5.

Representa-
tions respecting
others. to enable
them to obtain
credit, &c.
Nor whereby to charge any person upon or by reason of any representation or assurance made or given concerning or relating to the character,
conduct, credit, ability, trade or dealings of any other person, to the intent
or purpose that he may obtain credit, money or goods upon, unless such representation or assurance be made in writing, signed by the party to be
charged therewith, 9 G. 4, c. 20, s. 6.

Stamps.
No memorandum or other writing made necessary by this Act shall be
deemed an agreement within the meaning of the Stamp Acts, 9 G. 4, c 20,
s. 7.

ADDENDA.

FREE SCHOOLS, TITCHFIELD.
Page 209, after 19 V., c. 49, s. 1.

Five of whom to be a quorum to do business, 26 G. 3, c. 7, s. 1.

JAMAICA RAILWAY COMPANY.
Page 309, after 7 V., c. 25.

And. Branches, 9 V., c. 30.

INDEX.

INDEX.

CIVIL PROCEDURE.
See Amendments.

CLAIMS FOR GOODS SEIZED.
See Customs, 17 V., c. 2, s. 24-28.

CLERGY. Page 64
7;1V., c. 61, s. 3 ; 5 V., c. 25, s. 2 ; 19 V.,
c. 35, s. 4 ; 19 V., c. 6, s. 1, 3, 4 ; 25 V.,
c. 36, s. 2-4 ; 22 V., c. 9, s. 1-11 ; 28 V.,
c. 43, s. 2·; 22 V., c. 9, s. 12-28 ; 23 V.,
c. 9, s. 2 ; 22 V., c. 9, s. 29 ; 23 V., c. 9,
s. 1 ; 28 V., c. 43, s. 3 ; 22 V., c. 9,
s. 30-41 ;|22 V., c. 23, s. 1-13 ; 28 V., c. 43,
s. 1 ; 22 V., c. 23, s. 15-58 ; 25 V., c. 21,
s. 2, 3 ; 22 V., c. 23, s. 59 64, 66-68.
See Forgery, 4 V., c. 46, s. 8-10 ; 21 V.,
c. 14, s. 3.

CLERK OF THE COMMON COUNCIL,
KINGSTON.
See Kingston Corporation. Vestries.

CLERKS, PARISH.
See Clergy, 22 V., c. 23, s, 35, 36.

CLERKS OF THE PEACE AND MAGIS-
TRATES. Page 80
3 V., c. 65, s. 46 ; 19 V., c. 10, s. 32 ; 23 V.,
c. 18, s. 1-8, 10-13.
See Administrations, Petty, 27 V., S. 1,
c. 16. Appeals, 21 V., c. 22 ; 27 V., S. 1,
c. 15. Apprentices, Parish, 7 G. 4,
c. 26, s. 16-20. Billiard Tables, 39 G 3,
c. 7, s. 6, 8, 9. Circuit Courts, 25 V.,
c. 33, s. 3 ; 19 V., c. 10, s. 28-31 ; 28 V.,
c. 33, s. 7 ; 20 V., c. 22' s. 18 ; 19 V.,
c. 10, s. 48. Clergy, 22 V., c. 9, s. 21.
Collectors of Dues, 27 V., S. 1, c. 31,
s. 5. Constabulary Force, 27 V., S. 1,
c. 30, s. 3, 9, 12, 14, 15. Constables, Special, 4 W. 4., c. 29, s. 2, 3
Ejectments, &c., 25 V., c. 46, s. 1-
5, 14. Fines, &, 21 V., c. 23, s. 1-4,
8, 10-12. Friendly Societies, 6 V., c. 27,
s. 3, 8, 11, 12. Gunpowder, &c., 19 V.,
c. 14, s. 2-6, 9-13. Hackney Carriages, 10 V., c. 29, s. 2; 19. Highways, 25 V., c. 18, s. 6, 12, 23, 25,
28, 39, 41, 43. Holidays, 8 V., c.
30. Immigrants, 22 V., c. 1, s. 54,
58. Juries, 19 V., c. 23, s. 6,
Justices. Indictable Offences, 13 V.,
c. 24, s. 14. Convictions, 13 V., c. 35,
s. 13 ; 18 V., c. 57, s. 4-10. License,
&c. Duties, 28 V., c. 28, s. 2, 16, 19,
20, 22-24, 29, 31-33,-37, 41, 44. Lumber Measurers, 9 V., c. 20, s. 2. Main
Roads, 21 V., c. 32, s. 11, 14, 16. 18, 21.
Medical Practitioners, 13 V., c. 21, s. 2,
19 V., c. 32, s. 4, 5, 13. Militia Volunteers, 28 V., c. 39, s. 19, 65, 66.
Petty Debts, 19 V., c. 37, s. 13 ; 23 V.,
c. 35, s. 1 ; 19 V., c. 37, s. 31-33, 35,
38 ; 23 V., c. 35, s. 5, 7. Pilots, 19 V.,
c. 15, s. 9-14, 16, 17, 27, 36. Rum

Duties, Collection, 22 V., c. 13, s. 59,
61. Licenses, 23 V., S. 1, c. 4, s. 8, 10-
11 ; 28 V., c. 25, s. 2, 3 ; 23 V., S. 1,
c. 4, s. 14-17, 24. Savings' Banks,
7 W. 4, c. 14, s. 2'4, 6. Vestries, &c.,
27 V., S. 1, c. 7, s. 49. Weights and
Measures, 6 V., c. 28, s. 10-12, 17-18.

CLERK OF THE SUPREME COURT
AND CROWN. Page 83
20 V., c. 22, s. 1-10, 12, 14 ; 27 V., S. 1, c. 4'
s. 3 ; 20 V., c. 22, s. 15-17, 19-29, 31-
34, 36-39, 42 ; 27 V. S. 1, c. 4, s. 1
See Circuit Court, 20 V., c. 22, s. 18.
Collectors of Dues, 27 V., S. 1, c. 31,
s. 17. Commissions, Special, Court
Supreme, 8 V., c. 28, s. 20; 19 V.,
c. 10, s. 24, 35. Fines, &c, 1 G. 3, c. 13,
s. 1, 3-5 ; 20 V., c. 22, s. 30, 39. Friend.
ly Societies, 6 V., c. 27, s. 3, 8, 12.
Holidays, 8 V., c. 30. Judgments,
&c. 14 G. 3, c. 28, s. 6 ; 20 V., c. 22,
s. 23, 24. 3 9; 3 V., c. 65, s. 18; 27 V.,
S. 1, c. 27, s. 2, 3 ; 11 G. 3, c, 20, s. 2
20 V., c. 22, s. 28, 31; 14 G. 3, c. 28;
s. 15. Juries, 19 V., c. 23, s. 8 ; 21 V.,
c. 25, s. 2; 23 V., c. 33, s. 2 Juries
Special, 20 V., c. 14, s. 4-8. Land Tax,
&c. 21 V., c. 34, s. 29-34. Records,
Public. 11 Ann, c. 4, s. 5. Venditioni,
43 G. 3, c. 20, s. 8 ; 20 V., c. 22, s. 25,
39, 22. West Indian Incumbered Estates, 24 V., c. 4, s. 2-7.

CLERK OF THE VESTRY
See Assembly, 22 V., c. 18 ; 28 V., c. 2 ;
27 V., S. 1, c. 9. Vestries, &c.

CLERK, OF THE WARRANTS. Page 85
10 Ann, c. 4, s. 32.

CLERKS AND SERVANTS.
See Larceny, 27V., S. 1, c. 33, s. 53, 54

CLOTH FALSELY MARKED, SELLING
See Criminal Punishment, 1 V., c. 28, s. 4.

CLIPPINGS OF COIN.
See Coin, 14 G. 3, c. 18, s. 2, 3.

COALS, CHARCOAL.
See Malicious Injuries, &c. 27 V., S. 1.
c. 34, s. 17, 18.

COASTING VESSELS.
See Droghers.

COCKFIGHTING.
See Cruelty to Animals, 25 V., c. 10, s. 3.

COIN. Page 85
24 G. 2, c. 19, s. 9 ; 3 V., c. 39, s. 10 ; 5
V., c. 28 ; 7 V., c. 51 ; 1 V., c. 21, s. 3 ; 6
V., c. 40 ; 14 G. 3, c. 18, s. 1-4 ; 19 V., c.
29, s. 1 ; 21 V., c. 14, s. 3 ; 14 G. 3, c. 18,
s. 9 ; 1 V., c. 28, s. 4.

CONCEALING THE BIRTH O F A CHILD.
See Offences against the Person, 27 V. S. 1, c· 32, s. 51.

CONDITIONS PRECEDENT.
See Court Supreme Pleadings, 28 V, c. 37, s. 7.

CONSOLIDATING PROCEEDINGS IN CHANCERY.
See Court of Chancery, 15 V. c. 16, s 15.

CONSPIRACY TO MURDER.
See Offences against the Person, 27 V. S. 1, c. 23, s. 3.

CONSPIRACIES.
See Criminal Punishment, 16 V., c. 15, s. 29. Offences against the Person, 27 V. S· 1, c. 32, s. 3. Treasonable, &c. Meetings, 4 G. 4, c. 13, s. 3.

CONSTABLES.   Page 106
35 C. 2, c. 4, s. 7 ; 10 Ann, s. 4, s. 17.
See Police.

CONSTABULARY FORCE.   Page 106
27 V., S. 1, c. 30.
See Whipping, 28 V. c. 18, s. 6,

CONSTABLES, SPECIAL.   Page 109.
4 W. 4, c. 29.
See Jamaica Railway Co., 7 V. c. 25, s. 115, 116.

CONTINGENT DEBTS.
See Companies Winding up, 28 V., c. 42, s. 48.

CONTINGENT AND EXECUTORY INTERESTS, RIGHTS OF ENTRY.
                                      Page 110
3 V., c. 51, s. 3 ; 8 V., c. 19, s. 4, 6.
See Court of Chancery, 18 V., c. 58, s. 3.

CONTINUANCES, &c.
See Court Supreme Pleadings, 28 V., c. 37, s. 38.

CONTROVERTED ELECTIONS.
See Assembly, 41 G. 3, c. 18 ; 22 V., c. 5, s. 20, 22, 24–27 ; 24 V., c. 8.

CONVEYANCES TO QUALIFY VOTERS.
See Assembiy, 22 V., c. 5, s. 32.

CONVICT LABOR PAYMENT.
See Prisons, 18 V., c. 23 ; 24 V., c. 19, s. 2 ; 20 V., c. 11, s. 16

CONVICT SHIP.
See Prisons, 20 V., c. 11, s. 52.

CONVICTIONS AND ORDERS.
See Justices, 21 V., c. 9, s. 1 ; 13 V., c. 35, s. 17, 18.

CQPIES OR FAC SIMILIES.
See Indictment, 16 V., c. 15, s. 67.

COPPER COIN.
See Coin, 6 V., c. 40.

COPYRIGHT.   Page 111
22 V. c. 21, s. 2–10, 12, 13.

CORONERS   Page 112
11 G. 3, c. 15 ; 41 G. 3, c. 13, s. 2-4 ; 58 G. 3, c. 23, s. 1-3, 8, 9 ; 8 G. 4, c. 22, s. 4, 5 ; 10 V., c. 12, s. 2, ; 17 V., c. 23 ; 17 V., c. 38 ; 19 V., c. 17 ; 20 V., c. 9 ; 23 V., c. 19, s. 1-3, 5
See Assembly, 22 V., c. 5, s. 6, 16. Martial Law, 11 V., c. 7, s. 2. Medical Practitioners, 13 V., c. 21, s. 3.

CORROSIVE FLUIDS, &c.
See Offences against the Person, 27 V., S. 1, c. 32, s. 26.

COSTS.   Page 113
24 G. 2, c. 19, s. 1-3 ; 1 G 3, c. 21 ; 29 G. 3, c. 13, s. 2 ; 5 V., c. 50 ; 8 V., c. 28, s. 21-22 ; 19 V., c. 10, s. 36-37 ; 22 V., c. 28 ; 25 V., c. 46, s. 13 ; 26 V., S. 2, c. 15 ; 28 V., c. 35 ; 28 V., c. 37, s. 1.
See Abatement, 8 V., c. 28 s. 4, 5. Amendments, 27 V., S. 1, c. 14. Appeal, 21 V. c. 22, s. 31 ; 27 V., S. 1, c. 15, s. 3, 6. Assembly 22 V., c. 5, s. 27. 8 V., c. 28, s 23. Commissions de bene esse and Foreign, Companies incorporated, 27 V., S. 2, c. 4, s. 50. Companies Winding up, 28 V., c. 42, s. 3, 5. Court of Chancery, 11 V., c. 34, s. 1, 4, 15 V., c. 16, s. 3, 27 V., S. 2, c. 3, s. 5 ; 28 V., c. 36, s. 3, 13. Court of Ordinary, 6 V., c. 55, s. 3, Court Supreme Pleadings, 28 V., c. 37. s. 4. Customs, 17 V., c. 2, s. 27-28. Defamation, 14 V., c. 34, s. 8 ; 18 V., c. 44. Ejectments, &c., 25 V., c. 46, s. 7, 13. Executors &c., 8 V., c. 28, s. 14. Interpleader, 7 V., c. 32, s. 3, 7. Juries, Special, 20 V., c. 14, s. 11. Justices, 21 V., c. 9, s. 23. Justices Convictions, 13 V., c. 35, s. 18 ; 24, 26, 28. Landlord and Tenant, 1 V., c. 26, s. 3, 17-19. Offences against the Person, 27 V., S. 1, c. 32, s. 61-62. Partition, 8 G. 1, c. 5, 8 V., c. 28, s. 22. Patents for Inventions, 21 V., c. 30, s. 18, 21, 30. · Pawnbrokers, 11 V., c. 36, s. 29. Petty Debts, 19 V., c. 37, s. 21 ; 20 V., c. 20, s. 2. Provost Marshall, 43 G. 3, c. 20, s. 1-4, 6, 7, 9, 10. Replevin, 30 G. 3, c. 2. Sligo Water Co., 5 W. 4, c. 38, s. 33-34,

25 V. c. 12, s. 41 ; 21 V. c. 32, s. 30-34 ; 25 V. c. 12, s. 28 ; 27 V. S. 1, c. 36. s. 8 ; 21 V. c. 32, s. 35 ; 27 V. S. 1, c. 36, s. 9 ; 25 V. c. 12, s. 13-17, 19-22, 27 V. S. 1, c. 36, s. 10 ; 25 V. c. 12, s. 30, 43 ; 21 V. c. 32, s. 59-63 ; 25 V. c. 12, s. 26-28, 46, 47, 49, 50 ; 27 V. S. 1, c. 36, s. 13 ; 26 V. S. 2, c. 8.
See Import Duties, 28 V. c. 10, s. 17. Traction Engines, 26 V. S. 2, c. 19, s. 2. Tramroads, 25 V. c. 44, s. 3-9, 25, 26, 29-32, 34-36, 40, 48.

MAIN ROAD FUND. Page 450
21 V. c. 34, s. 1, 2, 36, 40.

MALICIOUS INJURIES TO PROPERTY. Page 450
27 V. S. 1, c. 24, s. 1-65.
See Companies winding up, 28 V. c. 42, s. 55.

MALICE.
See Malicious Injuries, 27 V. S. 1, c. 34, s. 47.

MANDAMUS, PROHIBITION, &c. Page 458
7 V. c. 32, s. 8.

MANIFESTS.
See Customs, 17 V. c. 33, s. 32

MANSLAUGHTER.
See Coroner 8 G. 4, c. 22, s. 4-5. Offences against the Person, 27 V. S. I c., 32, s. 4, 5, 8

MANUFACTURE, GOODS &c.. IN PRO-CESS, &c.
See Larceny, 27 V. S. 1, c. 33, s. 47, 48. Malicious Injuries &c., 27 V. S. 1, c. 34, s. 3, 14

MARKETS Page 459
9 V. c. 38, s. 1-11 ; 10-V. c. 30 ; 21 V. c. 12 ; 27 V. S. 1, c. 10.
See Offences Against the Person, 27 V., S. 1, c. 32, s. 33

MAROONS Page 461
36 G. 3, c. 33 ; 25 V. c. 4 ; 19 V. c. 25

MARRIAGE. Page 462
3 V. c. 51, s. 13 ; 4 V. c. 44, s. 8
See Clergy, 2 V. c. 23, s. 22, 24' 38-50. Dissenter's Marriages; Wills, 3 V. c. 51, s. 13.

MARRIAGE, BREACH OF PROMISE OF
See Evidence, 22 V. c. 16, s. 4

MARRIAGES DE FACTO Page 462
4 V. c. 44, s. 20-22

MARTIAL LAW. Page 462
11 V. c. 7 ; 21 V. c. 20
See Militia, 9 V. c. 35, s. 96, 97 ; 22 V. c. 43, s. 13, 14 ; 9 V. c. 35, s. 98-109. Militia Volunteers, 28 V. c. 38, s. 43-46.

MASTERS IN CHANCERY. Page 463
27 V. S. 2, c. 3, s. 6 ; 28 V. c. 36, s. 8-12.

MEDICAL PRACTITIONERS. Page 463
13 V. c. 21, s. 1-3, 19 V. c. 17 ; 23 V. S. 1, c. 17, s. 1-6 ; 26 V. S. 2, c. 23, s. 1, 2, 4 ; 23 V. S. 1, c. 17, s. 7-11 ; 23 V. S. 2, c. 1, s. 2-4 ; 23 V. S. 1, c. 17. s. 14-19 ; 23 V. S. 2, c. 1, s. 5, 6 ; 23 V. S. 1, c. 17, s. 21-24 ; 23 V. S. 2, c. 1, s. 8 ; 23 V. S. 1, c. 17, s. 25, 26 ; 23 V. S. 2, c. 1, s. 7.
See Coroners, 19 V. c. 17. Immigrants, 27 V. S. 2, c. 5, s. 10-13. Public Hospital, 26 V. S. 1, c. 4. s. 16, 17. Vaccination, 28 V. c. 41, s. 3, 13, 33, 34. Whipping, 28 V. c. 18, s. 5, 7.

MENACES.
See Threats, &c.

MERCHANTS BREACH OF TRUST.
See Larceny, 27 V. S. 1, c. 33, s. 60-62

MERCHANT SHIP NG Page 468
27 V. S. 1, c. 18. PI

MERRICK'S CHARITY.
See Charities Perpetual Annuities, 28 V. c. 23.

METALS, OLD. Page 469
19 V. c. 32.

METHYLATED SPIRITS.
See Rum and Spirits, 27 V. S. 1, c. 2.

MILITARY DEFENCES. Page 471
12 G. 1, c. 11, s. 3 ; 6 V. c. 34 ; 19 V. c. 44, s. 45 ; 26 V. S. 2, c. 2 ; 6 G. 2, c. 10 ; 10 G. 2, c. 6 ; 22 G. 2, c. 19 ; 12 G. 3. c. 12 ; 23 G. 3, c. 9 ; 32 G. 3, c. 25 ; 34 G. 3, c. 20 ; 42 G. 3, c. 27 ; 47 G. 3, c. 27 ; 36 G. 3, c. 33, s. 3 ; 32 G. 3, c. 31 ; 35 G. 3, c. 42 ; 36 G. 3, c. 20 ; 40 G. 3, c. 35 ; 40 G. 3. c. 36 ; 44 G. 3, c. 25 ; 46 G. 3, c. 24 ; 47 G. 3, c. 17 ; 48 G. 3, c. 22 ; 57 G. 3, c. 23.

MILITIA. Page 473
9 V. c. 35, s. 3-5, 2, 6 ; 22 V. c. 43, s. 1 ; 9 V. c. 35, s. 7, 115, 22 V. c. 43, s. 2-7 ; 9 V. c. 35, s. 18 ; 22 V. c. 43, s. 8-11, 17 ; 9 V. c. 35, s. 29, 30 ; 22 V. c. 43, s. 18-50 ; 28 V. c. 38, s. 76 ; 22 V. c. 43, s. 12 ; 9 V. c. 35, s. 35, 114, 36-40, 42-67, 71-82, 88 ;

PAROL DEMURRER.
See Infants, 18 V. c. 58, s. 1.

PARSONAGE HOUSES, GLEBE LAND,
&c.
See Clergy, 22 V. c. 23, s. 11.

PARTIES TO RECORD.
See Evidence, 22 V. c. 16, s. 2, 4.

PARTITION.   Page 518
8 G. 1, c. 5; 8 V. c. 28, s. 22; 19 V. c. 31,
s. 15; 43 G. 3, c. 28, 8 V. c. 19, s. 2.
See Jurors warned on Writs, &c. 43 G. 3,
c. 28.

PARTNERSHIPS, LIMITED.   Page 518
16 V. c. 21.

PATENTS.   Page 518
33 C. 2, c. 12, s. 7; 35 C. 2, c. 12, s. 1; 2
Ann, c. 7, s. 1-3; 4 G. 2, c. 4, s. 7.
See Escheats. Evidence, 4 G. 2, c. 5, s. 2.
Land Tax, &c. 21 V. c. 34, s. 35. Sur-
veyors, 22 V. c. 40, s. 10, 14.

PATENTED IMPROVEMENTS. Page 519
16 V. c. 32, c. 34; 16 V. c. 33.

PATENTS FOR INVENTIONS. Page 519
21 V. c. 30.

PAUPERS.   Page 528
7 G. 4, c. 26, s. 1-7.
See Vestries, &c. 27 V. S. 1, c. 7, s. 27.

PAWNBROKERS.   Page 529
11 V. c. 36.

PAYMENT OF MONEY INTO COURT.
Page 535
8 V. c. 28, s. 10.
See Court Supreme Pleadings, 28 V. c.
37, s. 18-20. Defamation, 14 V. c. 34,
s. 2.

PENAL SERVITUDE.   Page 535
21 V. c. 14.
See Prisons, 18 V. c. 22.

PENITENTIARY.
See Chancery Deposits, 19 V. c. 5, s. 23.
Prisons, 16 V. c. 23; 20 V. c. 11.

PERJURY AND SUBORNATION.
Page 536
4 V. c. 22, s. 1; 21 V. c. 14, s. 3; 4 V. c. 22,
s. 2, 3; 16 V. c. 15, s. 20-22.
See Companies Winding Up, 28 V. c. 42,
s. 56. Evidence, 7 V. c. 5, s. 2; 7 V.
c. 31, s. 1.

PERMANENT REVENUE FUND.
Page 537
17 V. c. 29, s. 36-42, 45-48, 50, 53; 21 V. c.
34, s. 28.

PERPETUAL ANNUITY.
See Loan, Government

PERSONATING BAIL.
See Forgery, 4 V. c. 46; s. 6; 21 V. c. 14,
s. 3.

PERSONATING MASTERS, &c.
See Servants, 3 V. c. 48.

PETITIONS OF COURSE.
See Court of Chancery, 28 V. c. 36, s. 1, 2.

ST. DOMINGO, OR HAYTI. Page 668
6 V. c. 13.

SACRILEGE.
See Larceny, 27 V. S. 1, c. 33, s. 35.

SALVAGE Page 668
53 G. 3, c. 25, s. 1-8, 14, 15.
See Larceny, 27 V. S. 1, c. 33, s. 50-52.

SATISFACTION.
See Judgments, 27 V. S. 1, c. 27, s. 2, 3;
11 G. 3, c. 20, s. 2; 20 V. c. 22, s. 28, 31;
14 G. 3, c. 28, s. 15, 16. Mortgages, 33
C. 2, c. 12, s. 4; 8 V. c. 19, s. 7, 8. Petty
Debts, 19 V. c. 37, s. 35; 23 V. c. 35, s.
5.

SAVINGS' BANKS. Page 670
7 W. 4, c. 14, s. 1-14, 16, 17; 10 V. c. 18, s.
2. 3; 7 W. 4, c. 14, s. 20, 21, 23, 24; 22 V.
c. 41, s. 1-8, 11-15; 24 V. c. 10' s. 2-4.

SCIENTIFIC WITNESSES.
See Court of Chancery, 27 V. S. 2, c. 3
s. 3, 4.

SEAMEN. Page 673
33 C. 2, c. 17, s. 7; 35 C. 2, c. 4, s. 6; 2 W.
4, c. 32; 4 W. 4, c. 19.
See Offences against the Person, 27 V. S.
1, c. 32, s. 32. Public Hospital, 26 V.
S. 1, c. 4, s. 28, 29.

SECONDARY PUNISHMENTS
See Penal Servitude.

SECRETARY, ISLAND. Page 673
33 C. 2, c. 12, s. 1; 11 Ann, c. 4, s. 5; 11 G.
4, c. 4, s. 4, 5; 21 G. 3, c. 23, s. 5; 56 G.
3, c. 19, s. 1, 11; 60 G. 3, c. 23, ss. 5, 6; 21
V. c. 34, s. 23; 23 V. s. 1, c. 17, s. 7, 11,
24; 26 V. S. 2, c. 10, s. 2; 56 G. 3, c. 19,
s. 2-9; 21 G. 3, c. 23, s. 6; 56 G. 3, c. 19,
s. 10-17; 60 G. 3, c. 23, s. 3, 6; 27 V. S. 2,
c. 1; 4 G. 4, c. 12; 60 G. 3, c. 23, s. 4; 11
G. 4, c. 12; 4 V. c. 44, s. 9, 14, 15, 18; 26
V. S. 2, c. 10; 5 V. c. 15.
See Companies Incorporated, 27 V. S. 2,
c. 4, s. 11, 12, 17. 41. , 10
c. 4, s. 2. Governor, 18 Deeds, 7, s. Ann
Holidays, 8 V. c. 30. Land Tax, &c,
26 V. S 2, c. 21, s. 2, 3; 21 V. c. 34, s.
23. Laws of the Island, 33 C. 2, c.
24, s. 1; 10 Ann, c. 4, s. 3. Medical
Practitioners, 23 V. S. 1, c. 17, s. 1, 2, 4,
5; 26 V. S. 2, c. 23, s. 1. 2, 4; 23 V. S.
1, c. 17, s. 7-11, 18, 24. Patents, 33 C.
2, c. 12, s. 7. Patents for Inventions,
21 V. c. 30, s. 16, 20, 22-26. Records,
Public, 11 Ann, c. 4. s. 5. Stamps, 28
V. c. 9, s. 29.

SEDITIOUS MEETINGS.
See Treasonable Meetings,' &c.

SEIZURES.
See Customs. 17 V. c. 2, s. 19-22, 24-27.

SELF-DEFENCE.
See Offences against the Person, 27 V.
S. 1, c. 32, s. 6.

SEPARATE CONFINEMENT.
See Prisons, 20 V. c. 11, s. 46-48.

SERVANTS. Page 677
25 V. c. 29; 55 G. 3, c. 19; 5 V. c. 43, s. 1-9,
11; 3 V. c. 48.
See Larceny, 27 V. S. 1, c. 33, s. 53-54.

SERVICE OF PROCESS OUT OF JU-
RISDICTION.
See Court of Chancery, 6 V. c. 56, s. 1-3.

SET OFF.
See Mutual Debts.

SETTING FIRE TO PROPERTY.
See Malicious Injuries, 27 V. S. 1, c. 34,
s. 1-8, 16-18, 33-35. Offences against
the Person, 27 V. S. 1, c. 32, s. 11.

SEXTONS.
See Clergy, 22 V. c. 23, s. 36. Kingston
Corporation, 18 V. c. 61, s. 18.

SHEEP.
See Larceny, 27 V. S. 1. c. 33, s. 9, 10.

SHIP'S STORES.
See Customs, 17 V. c. 33, s. 26, 30.

SHOAL WATER.
See Patents, 35 C. 2, c. 12, s. 1.

SHOOTING, CUTTING, WOUNDING,
&c.
See Offences against the Person, 27 V. S.
1, c. 32, s. 12, 16-18.

SIGNALS, FALSE.
See Malicious Injuries, 27 V. S. 1, c. 34,
s. 38.

SLANDEROUS WORDS TO MAGIS-
TRATES.
See Criminal Punishment, 1 V. c. 28, s. 4.

SLIGO WATER COMPANY. Page 681
5 W. 4, c. 38, s. 16; 19 V. c. 41, s. 11; 5 W
4, c. 38, s. 20-24, 26; 19 V. c. 41, s. 14; 5
W. 4, c. 38, s. 27, 28, 30-35, 39; 19 V. c.
41, s. 15, 16, 29, 21.

SMALL POX AND INFECTIOUS DIS-
EASES. Page 683
4 V. c. 32, s. 30-32, 34-36, 38;

Lightning Source UK Ltd.
Milton Keynes UK
UKHW020410090119

334943UK00009B/1403/P